The Cultures of the West

A History

Clifford R. Backman
Boston University

New York   Oxford
OXFORD UNIVERSITY PRESS

Oxford University Press is a department of the University of Oxford.
It furthers the University's objective of excellence in research,
scholarship, and education by publishing worldwide.

Oxford   New York
Auckland   Cape Town   Dares Salaam   Hong Kong   Karachi
Kuala Lumpur   Madrid   Melbourne   Mexico City   Nairobi
New Delhi   Shanghai   Taipei   Toronto

With offices in
Argentina   Austria   Brazil   Chile   Czech Republic   France   Greece
Guatemala   Hungary   Italy   Japan   Poland   Portugal   Singapore
South   Korea   Switzerland   Thailand   Turkey   Ukraine   Vietnam

For titles covered by Section 112 of the US Higher Education Opportunity Act,
please visit www.oup.com/us/he for the latest information about
pricing and alternate formats.

Published by Oxford University Press
198 Madison Avenue, New York, New York 10016
http://www.oup.com

Library of Congress Cataloging-in-Publication Data
Backman, Clifford R.
  The cultures of the West : a history / Clifford R. Backman.
    p. cm.
  ISBN 978-0-19-538889-3 – ISBN 978-0-19-538890-9 – ISBN 978-0-19-538891-6
  1. Civilization, Western.   2. Religion and civilization.   3. Science and civilization.
  4. Philosophy and civilization. I. Title.
   CB245.B324 2013
   909'.09821--dc23
                    2012033151

9 8 7 6 5 4 3 2

Printed in the United States of America on acid-free paper

This book is for
Graham Charles Backman
Puero praeclaro, Scourge of Nations;

and for my mother
Mary Lou Betker,
with my best love;

and in memory of my brother
Neil Howard Backman, USN (ret.)
(1956–2011)
who found his happiness just in time.

BRIEF CONTENTS

1. Water and Soil, Stone
   and Metal 3
   10,000 BCE–2100 BCE

2. Law Givers, Evil Emperors, and
   Dangerous Gods 33
   2100 BCE–486 BCE

3. The Chosen People 69
   1200 BCE–538 BCE

4. Greeks and Persians 97
   2000 BCE–479 BCE

5. Hellenism and Second
   Temple Judaism 131
   499 BCE–142 BCE

6. The Empire of the Sea: Rome 171
   753 BCE–180 CE

7. Paganisms and Christianities 205
   40 BCE–305 CE

8. The Early Middle Ages 237
   306–750 CE

9. Reform and Renewal 283
   750–1258

10. Worlds Brought Down 327
    1258–1453

11. Renaissances and
    Reformations 373
    1350–1550

12. The Last Crusades 415
    1492–1648

13. Science Breaks Out
    and Breaks Through 465
    1500–1700

14. From Westphalia to Paris:
    Regimes Old and New 503
    1648–1750

15. The Enlightened 553
    1690–1789

16. The War against Absolutism 591
    1789–1815

17. Industrialization and Its
    Discontents 625
    1750–1850

18. The Birth of Modern Politics 665
    1815–1848

19. Nationalism and Identity 705
    1801–1903

20. The God Problem 745
    1799–1907

21. The Modern Woman 783
    1860–1914

22. The Great Land Grab 815
    1880–1914

23. From Nihilism to Modernism 849
    1880–1939

24. The World at War (Part I) 887
    1914–1918

25. Radical Realignments 931
    1919–1939

26. The World at War (Part II) 977
    1937–1945

27. The Theater of the Absurd 1017
    1945–1968

28. Something to Believe In 1057
    1945–1988

29. Global Warmings 1091
    1989–2001

30. Hearts and Minds
    Going Forward 1125
    2001–Present

CONTENTS

List of Maps xvi
Introduction: Why History? xix
About the Author xxix
A Note to the Reader xxx

1. Water and Soil, Stone and Metal 3
10,000 BCE–2100 BCE
The Tigris and the Euphrates 3
Early Sumer: Kings and Warriors, Priests
    and Scribes 6
The Idea of Empire 9
Mesopotamian Life: Cities and Slaves,
    Letters and Numbers 12
Religion and Myth: The Great Above and
    Great Below 16
Ancient Egypt 20
Social Strata in Egypt 24
The Kingdom of the Dead 27

**2. Law Givers, Evil Emperors,
and Dangerous Gods** 33
2100 BCE–486 BCE
Old Babylon 34
Middle Kingdom Egypt 40
The New Kingdom Empire 45
The Indo-European Assault 50
The Age of Iron Begins, ca. 1200 BCE 56
Persia and the Religion of Fire 60

3. The Chosen People 69
1200 BCE–538 BCE
A Great Nation 69
The Bible and History 72
The Land of Canaan 77
Dreams of a Golden Age 80
Women and the Law 83
Prophets and Prophecy 87

By recognizing the Fertile Crescent's connective role—that is, its nature as a commercial center or meeting-point for the central Asian and eastern Mediterranean economies—Sargon highlighted what was to become perhaps the dominant trait of Middle Eastern history, its strategic significance as the connection-point between East and West.

Priests and Rabbis 89

A Genius for Reinvention. 91

4. **Greeks and Persians** 97

   2000 BCE–479 BCE

   From Chaos to Tragedy 97

   The Mycenaean World: Heroes and Kings 99

   The End of an Age and Mythic Ancestors 104

   Colonists, Hoplites, and Tyrants. 110

   A Cult of Masculinity 115

   Sparta: The Militarization of the Citizenry. 118

   Miletus: A Merchant Oligarchy and
       the First Philosophers. 121

   Athenian Democracy 124

   The Persian Wars 125

5. **Hellenism and Second Temple Judaism** 131

   499 BCE–142 BCE

   The Classical Age. 132

   Women, Children, and Slaves. 134

   The Polis: Ritual and Restraint 135

   Civilized Pursuits: Epic and Lyric Poetry 138

   The Birth of Tragedy 139

   The Peloponnesian Disaster 143

   Medicine as Natural Law: Hippocrates. 147

   Mathematical Ordering and Sophistry 148

   Socrates and the Meaningful Life 150

   Plato and Ideal Forms 152

   Aristotle and the Pursuit of Happiness 155

   Alexander the Great. 158

   A Mongrel but Magnificent World 160

   Second Temple Jews and Judaism 163

   The Maccabean Revolt. 166

6. **The Empire of the Sea: Rome** 171

   753 BCE–180 CE

   Links to a Heroic Age 172

   Republic, Property, and Family 176

   The Republic of Virtue 178

   Size Matters 180

The Greeks themselves, and especially the Athenians, came to regard the mid-5th century BCE with a determined awe, recalling it as a lost halcyon era that outshone anything that came before it or since. Through the centuries, much of Western culture has continued the love affair and has extolled "the glory that was Greece" as one of the two or three pinnacles of human achievement.

Can the Republic Be Saved? 185

The Golden Age: The Augustan Era 187

The Sea, The Sea. 190

Roman Lives and Values. 194

The "Five Good Emperors". 200

7.   **Paganisms and Christianities**. 205

      40 BCE–305 CE

      The Jesus Mystery 206

      A Crisis in Tradition 210

      Ministry and Movement 214

      What Happened to His Disciples? 216

      Christianities Everywhere. 218

      Romans in Pursuit 221

      Pagan Vitality. 225

      Stoicism and Neoplatonism 229

8.   **The Early Middle Ages** 237

      306–750 CE

      The Imperial Crisis 238

      Imperial Decline: Rome's Overreach. 239

      Martyrdom and Empire 242

      A Christian Emperor and a Christian Church 244

      The Rise of "New Rome". 247

      A Splendid, Beleaguered Capital. 249

      "The Age of Ignorance" 253

      The Islamic Revelation. 256

      From Preacher to Conqueror 258

      Compulsion or Conversion?. 261

      Sunnis and Shi'a 265

      Classical Traditions and Western Expansion 266

      Barbarian Kings and Scholar-Monks. 268

      Divided Estates and Kingdoms 271

      The Body as Money and Women as Property 273

      Christian Paganism 275

      Pockets of Intellectual Life 277

9.   **Reform and Renewal** 283

      750–1258

      Two Palace Coups 284

The western world had never seen a military juggernaut like this: in 622 Muhammad and his small group of followers had been forced from their home in Mecca, yet within a hundred years those followers had conquered an empire that stretched from Spain to India, an area twice the size of that conquered by Alexander the Great.

The Carolingian Ascent 286
Charlemagne 288
Imperial Coronation 292
Carolingian Collapse 294
The Islamic Empire 296
Sunnis and Shi'a 297
The Qur'an and the Philosophers .298
The Splintering of the Caliphate 303
The Reinvention of Western Europe 304
Mediterranean Cities 307
The Reinvention of the Church 310
The Crusades 313
But Not a War against Islam 316
Parliaments and the Mamluk Empire 318
Judaism Reformed, Renewed, and Reviled 319

10.   **Worlds Brought Down** 327
1258–1453
Late Medieval Europe 329
Scholasticism 331
Mysticism 334
The Guild System 337
The Mendicant Orders 338
Early Representative Government .340
Chivalry 342
The Hundred Years' War 346
The Plague 348
Conquest of the Islamic World 352
In the Wake of the Mongols 356
A New Center for Islam 360
Conservatism and Reaction 362
The Ottoman Turks 364
Persia under the Il-Khans 368

11.   **Renaissances and Reformations** 373
1350–1550
"I Fixed upon Antiquity" 374
Classicism, Humanism, and Statecraft 375
The Political and Economic Matrix 380
The Renaissance Achievement 384

Like the humanists who sought to restore ancient morals, Luther sought to re-create what he believed to be Christian belief and practice as they had existed in the apostolic Church. He saw himself as a restorer, not a revolutionary, a liberator rather than an insurrectionist.

The Protestant Renaissance 388
Erasmus: Satirist and Itinerant Scholar. 390
Martin Luther: The Gift of Salvation 392
Rebellion against the Church: "Ninety-Five Theses" 395
The Reformation Goes International 400
Scholars and Activists. 401
Protestantism without Luther 402
Calvin: Protestantism as Theology 405
The Rebirth of Satire. 408
Utopias and Book Burnings 408
Rabelais: The In-House Catholic Attack 410

12. **The Last Crusades** 415
1492–1648
The New World. 416
New Continents and Profits 419
Conquest and Epidemics 424
New Crops and the Enclosure Movement 426
The Patriarchal Family. 428
Sexual Morality. 431
Enemies Within: Witches and Jews 434
The Jews of the East and West 436
Wars of Religion 441
The Peace of Augsburg and the Edict of Nantes 442
The Church of England 446
The Thirty Years' War 449
Wars of Religion: The Eastern Front 452
The Waning of the Sultanate 454
New Centers of Intellectual Life .456
The Ottomans: From Strife to Warfare. 459

13. **Science Breaks Out
and Breaks Through** 465
1500–1700
The Copernican Drama. 467
Galileo and the Truth of Numbers 471
The Other Scientific Revolution. .474
The Council of Trent, 1546–1563 474
The Society of Jesus. 476
Inquisition and Inquiry 479

When Western science revived in the 16th century, it did so once again hand in hand with Christian faith. It is a modern conceit that science advanced only when it divorced itself from religion; that divorce became finalized only in the 19th century. The Scientific Revolution therefore needs to be understood as an offshoot of religious history.

The Revolution Broadens 484
The Ethical Costs of Science 487
The Islamic Retreat from Science 490
Thinking about Truth 491
Descartes and the Quest for Truth 494
Newton's Mathematical Principles 496
The Choices for Western Society 498

14. **From Westphalia to Paris:**
Regimes Old and New 503
1648–1750

The whole of society became obsessed with rule-making and breaking. Rules of etiquette, standards of spelling and usage, norms for musical composition and visual art, academic curricula, domestic architecture, even the subtle social demands of fashion—all these felt the pressure to conform.

The Peace of Westphalia: 1648 505
The Argument for Tyranny 508
The Social Contract 510
Absolute Politics 513
Police States 515
Self-Indulgence with a Purpose .518
Mercantilism and Absolutism 521
Mercantilism and Poverty 524
Domesticating Dynamism:
    Regulating Culture 526
Decency and Modesty 528
The Birth of Private Life 531
The English Exception 533
Civil War and Restoration 536
Ottoman Might and Islamic Absolutism 538
Safavid Pleasures 540
The End of Order 542
The Slave Trade and Domestic Subjugation 544
The Return of Uncertainty 548

15. **The Enlightened** 553
1690–1789

The Origins of the Enlightenment 554
Learning from Our Worst Mistakes 557
Locke and the Administration of
    the Commonwealth 559
Bayle and Religious Toleration .561
Free Markets and Rational Punishment 562

Diderot and the Circulation of
   the Enlightenment.................................565
Voltaire and the Limits of Optimism.................567
Rousseau: "Mankind Is Born Free" 570
Jewish Enlightenment..............................573
Haskalah and Hasidism 575
The Jews and Europe's Ambivalence 576
The Unenlightened 578
Assessing the Enlightenment 582

16. **The War against Absolutism**....................591
     1789–1815
A Revolution in Western History? 591
Revolutionary Road................................595
The Revolution Turns Radical.......................599
Napoleon and the War against Absolutism 601
The Rush to Empire................................605
The Continental System 607
How to Judge a Revolution 610
Downfall..615
Leaving the East Behind...........................620

17. **Industrialization and Its Discontents**..........625
     1750–1850
England's Head Start..............................626
Innovation and Infrastructure.....................630
Trying to Catch Up to England 633
Trying to Catch Up to Europe 639
"The Sick Man of Europe"..........................642
Life in the Industrial Age 645
Riots and Reform 650
Women and Children Last...........................652
The Romantic Generation...........................655

18. **The Birth of Modern Politics** 665
     1815–1848
Conservatism in Power.............................666
Royalism and Nationalism 669
The Moral Component of Conservatism...............673

To analyze human nature scientifically, the new generation felt, was to cheapen it by reducing people to machines. The human heart, in a clinical sense, can be studied as a matter of medical science— but the passions it houses are mysterious, darkly powerful, beyond reason.

The Challenge of Liberalism 677

Industrial Capitalism and Its Critics 680

The Real Revolution of 1848 685

Karl Marx and Revolution 687

The Collapse of the "Concert of Europe" 691

Women and the Cult of Domesticity 693

Popular Magazines and the Novel. 696

19.   **Nationalism and Identity** 705

1801–1903

Nationalism in Theory 706

Nationalism in Practice: Germany and Italy 711

Frustrated Nationalism: Hungary

and Ireland 721

Assimilation and Zionism 729

Islamic Nationalisms 735

Reforming Islam 737

However it is defined, nationalism was and remains a potent force. It may in fact be the most vital element in modern political history.

20.   **The God Problem** 745

1799–1907

Nietzsche: A Cosmos without God. .745

Who Killed God? 749

The Theory of Creation 752

Evolution by Natural Selection 755

The Bible and History 759

The Protestant Churches' Response 763

The Catholic Counterattack 769

The War on Modernism 772

Modernism, Secularism, and the Jews. 774

The Islamic Exception 777

21.   **The Modern Woman** 783

1860–1914

The Appetite for Reform 783

Whose Rights Come First? 788

Suffragists and Suffragettes. 792

Love and the "Modern Woman" 796

School, Work, and the New Woman. 803

Women, Islam, and Nationalism 807

Honor Killing and Genital Cutting 810

22. The Great Land Grab 815
1880–1914
"The White Man's Burden" 816
The Second Industrial Revolution 819
Looking Overseas 826
Missionary Europe 833
A Gilded Age 836
Western Ways: Emulation and Resistance 842

23. From Nihilism to Modernism 849
1880–1939
Sickness unto Death 850
A Wave or a Particle? 854
Relativity and Space-time 856
The Will to Power 860
Logic and Language 864
From Phenomenology to Existentialism 866
The Illness of Western Society 869
Sexuality and Psychoanalysis 872
Beyond the Pleasure Principle 875
Modernism and Irony 877
The Artistic Truth Within 880

24. The World at War (Part I) 887
1914–1918
The Run-Up to War 888
The Balance of Power 892
A New Map of Hell 896
The War in the Trenches 901
The Home Front 905
Officers and Gentlemen 909
Russia's Revolution 912
Bolshevism and the Laws of History 915
Exporting Revolution 918
How Not to End a War 921
Young Turks 925

25. Radical Realignments 931
1919–1939
History for Beginners 932

What people took away from the new physics was the broader idea of relativity— no fixed points, no absolute time, no absolute space. And the more we learned about the universe, the more immense, confusing, unexpected, and for some more frightening it seemed to be.

Parceling Out Nations 936
New Rights and New Economies 939
The Great Depression............................941
The Search for Someone to Blame 945
Modernism, Experiment, and Trauma 948
The Rise of Fascism: Italy and Spain............955
Nazism in Germany...............................960
Oppression and Terror in Russia.................964
A New Deal?.....................................966
Appeasement and Pacifism 969

26. The World at War (Part II)....................977
1937–1945
A Place in Memory...............................978
The War in Europe...............................979
Wars in the Pacific 983
Atrocities and Holocaust 987
Making Amends 993
The United Nations and Human Rights.............996
Atomic Fissures................................ 1000
Women in, and against, Fascism 1004
World War II and the Middle East 1009
Arab Nationalism and Growing Zionism...........1011

27. The Theater of the Absurd 1017
1945–1968
Setting to Work 1019
Alienation and the Absurd......................1021
The Cold War and Decolonization................ 1023
Decolonization 1026
The Welfare Society and the Economic Boom....... 1029
Social Conservatism, Economic Liberalism,
    and the Postwar Boom 1033
A Generation of Rebellion......................1035
Turning Point: 1967–1968.......................1040
The Female Factor 1044
Women, Islam, and the State....................1046
The Structures of Thought 1051

From the introduction of gunpowder weapons and the creation of mass armies, the frequency and scale of massacres in wartime have increased dramatically. The mere pressing of a button or the pulling of a trigger can produce carnage to equal that at Thermopylae or Actium, Hastings or Hattin, Breda or Lepanto.

28.   Something to Believe In 1057

1945–1988

Religious Observance and "Spiritual Anxiety" 1058

Science and Secularism 1060

The Catholic Reformation 1064

Postwar Protestantism 1069

The Fundamentals of Protestantism 1071

Jewish Revival—And Conflict 1074

International Judaism and the Myth of Israel 1078

Islamic Revolutions 1082

Ba'athism and Brotherhood. 1086

29.   Global Warmings 1091

1989–2001

One Year, Four Crises 1093

The United States of Europe. 1104

Feminism's Third Wave 1109

Women and the Global World 1111

Islam and Its Discontents. 1113

But Why Terrorism? 1115

Economic Globalization. 1119

30.   Hearts and Minds Going Forward 1125

2001–Present

"Why Do They Hate Us?" 1126

War and Peace, from the Balkans to Palestine 1130

Israel, Palestine, and the Arab Spring 1135

Veiled Threats 1138

Debt, Taxes, and Liberty 1142

Free Market? What Free Market? .1147

What Is the Greater West Now?. 1151

Reference Maps A-1

Glossary. G-1

Credits C-1

Index. I-1

The West has entered the 21st century in full-throttle disputes over the purpose and limits of government and the responsibilities of individuals in society.

List of Maps

Map 1.1	Early Agricultural Sites
Map 1.2	Sumer and the Ancient Near East
Map 1.3	Sargon's Empire
Map 1.4	Ancient Egypt, ca. 2686–2181 BCE
Map 2.1	The Babylonian Empire under Hammurabi
Map 2.2	Middle and New Kingdom Egypt
Map 2.3	The Middle East and the Mediterranean, ca. 1400 BCE
Map 2.4	The Sea Peoples
Map 2.5	The Assyrian Empire
Map 2.6	The Persian Empire
Map 3.1	The Land of Canaan
Map 3.2	Israelite Kingdom under David
Map 4.1	Minoan and Mycenaean Greece, ca. 1500 BCE
Map 4.2	Greek and Phoenician Colonies
Map 4.3	The Persian Wars
Map 5.1	Athens, Sparta, and their Allies during the Peloponnesian War
Map 5.2	Campaigns of Alexander the Great
Map 5.3	The Hellenistic World, ca. 200 BCE
Map 6.1	Archaic Italy
Map 6.2	The Western Mediterranean in the 3rd Century BCE
Map 6.3	Rome and Its Neighbors in 120 BCE
Map 6.4	The Roman World at the Death of Augustus
Map 6.5a,b	The Mediterranean: Greek and Roman Perspectives Compared
Map 6.6	Trade in the Roman Empire
Map 7.1	Judea in the Time of Jesus
Map 7.2	Early Christian Communities, ca. 350 CE
Map 8.1	The Roman Empire, ca. 300 CE
Map 8.2	The Byzantine Empire in the Time of Justinian
Map 8.3	Constantinople in the 6th Century CE
Map 8.4	Arabia in the 6th Century CE
Map 8.5	Muslim Conquests to 750 CE
Map 8.6	The Economy of Europe in the Dar k Ages
Map 8.7	The Frankish Kingdom, ca. 500
Map 8.8	Monasteries in Western Europe, ca. 800 CE
Map 9.1	The Conversion of the Germans to Christianity
Map 9.2	Charlemagne's Empire

Map 9.3   The Islamic World in 1022 CE
Map 9.4   The Mediterranean World, ca. 1100
Map 9.5   The First Crusade and the Crusader States
Map 9.6   The Muslim World, c. 1308 CE
Map 9.7   Principal Centers of Jewish Settlement in the Mediterranean, ca. 1300 CE
Map 10.1   Europe in 1300
Map 10.2   Medieval Universities
Map 10.3   Medieval Heresies, ca. 1200–1350
Map 10.4   The Hundred Years' War
Map 10.5   The Black Death
Map 10.6a,b   Mongol Conquests and Successor States
Map 10.7   Mamluks and Ottomans, ca. 1490
Map 10.8   From Greek to Turkish: Changes in Place Names in Anatolia, 1000–1500
Map 11.1   Renaissance Italy
Map 11.2   The Domains of Charles V
Map 11.3   The Protestant Reformation, ca. 1580
Map 12.1   Africa and the Mediterranean, 1497
Map 12.2   The Portuguese in Asia, 1536-1580
Map 12.3   European Exploration of the Americas, 1519–1542
Map 12.4   The Transfer of Crops and Diseases after 1500
Map 12.5   Expulsions and Migrations of Jews, 1492–1650
Map 12.6   Wars and Revolts in Europe, 1525–1660
Map 12.7   Ottoman-Safavid Conflict
Map 13.1   Centers of Learning in Europe, 1500–1770
Map 14.1   Europe in 1648
Map 14.2   Three Islamic Empires: the Ottomans, the Safavids, and the Mughals
Map 14.3   World Trade Networks, ca. 1750
Map 14.4   The Atlantic Slave Trade, 1501–1867
Map 15.1   Jewish Communities in Poland-Lithuania
Map 15.2   Subscriptions to the *Encyclopédie*
Map 15.3   Urban Population of Europe in 1800
Map 16.1   Napleonic Europe, 1799-1815
Map 16.2   Ottoman Losses in the Balkans and Crimea, 1699–1774
Map 17.1   Industrializing Britain by 1850
Map 17.2   Industrializing Europe by 1870
Map 17.3   The Shrinking Ottoman Empire
Map 17.4   Europe's Largest Cities in 1850
Map 18.1   Europe in 1815
Map 18.2   Centers of Revolution, 1848
Map 19.1   The Peoples of Europe, ca. 1850

Map 19.2   The Unification of Germany
Map 19.3   The Unification of Italy
Map 19.4   Paris in 1890
Map 19.5   The Great Famine, 1841–1851
Map 19.6   The Pale of Settlement, 1835–1917
Map 19.7   Wahhabi Expansion, 1765–1818
Map 20.1   Jewish Emigration from Russia, 1880–1914
Map 21.1   Wining the Vote: Women's suffrage in the Greater West, 1906–1971
Map 22.1   Industrialization and Manufacturing, 1870-1914
Map 22.2   The Scramble for Africa
Map 22.3   The Carving Up of Southeast Asia
Map 22.4   European Immigration, 1880–1914
Map 24.1   European International Investment, 1914
Map 24.2   European Alliances, 1878-1914
Map 24.3   World War I, 1914–1918
Map 24.4   The Russian Revolution
Map 24.5   Europe and the Middle East in 1914 and 1922
Map 25.1   Ethnic Minorities in East-Central Europe, 1930
Map 25.2   Countries on the Gold Standard, 1929 and 1934
Map 25.3   Expansion of the Italian Empire, 1922-1939
Map 25.4   Right-Wing Dictatorships in the Greater West, 1919–1939
Map 26.1   World War II in Europe, 1939–1945
Map 26.2   The Japanese in China, 1931–1941
Map 26.3   World War II in the Pacific, 1937–1945
Map 26.4   The Death Camps, 1941–1945
Map 27.1   Displaced Peoples in East and Central Europe, 1942–1952
Map 27.2   Military Blocs in Europe, 1948-1955
Map 27.3   Decolonization Since 1945
Map 27.4   The Six-Day War
Map 27.5   The Vietnam War
Map 28.1   Jewish Immigration to Israel Since 1948
Map 29.1   The Fall of Communism in Eastern Europe and the Soviet Union
Map 29.2   Water Pollution and Carbon Monoxide Emissions Worldwide
Map 29.3   The European Union
Map 29.4   Terrorist Attacks within the Greater West, 1990–2001
Map 29.5   The World Trade Organization
Map 30.1   Wars and Conflicts in the Greater West, 1990–2012
Map 30.2   The Arab Spring
Map 30.3   European Muslim Population, 2012
Map 30.4   Population Growth in the Greater West, 2012

Introduction:
Why History?

Through most of my school years I hated history; it seemed a dull exercise in memorization, a slightly sophisticated version of the game of trivial pursuit. Names and dates, followed by more names and dates. *The Battle of Actium was fought in what year? 31 BCE. Name the three ships that sailed to the New World with Christopher Columbus in 1492. The Niña, the Pinta, and the Santa María. Who fought in the Battle of Lepanto? The Holy League (Spain, Venice, the Papal State) and the Ottoman Turks, in 1571. Who delivered the sermon entitled "Sinners in the Hands of an Angry God"? Jonathan Edwards, in 1741. When was the Interstate Commerce Commission established? 1887. Whose assassination in 1914 triggered the start of World War I? Archduke Ferdinand of Austria.* And so on. Important facts all, but deadly boring when treated, as they invariably were, merely as data points to be learned by rote and recited on demand. Occasionally my teachers assigned map quizzes, usually pertaining to battles, which pleased the part of me that enjoyed pretending to be a field commander drawing up my forces to launch brilliant attacks on incompetent enemies. But then all pleasure disappeared when we were subsequently given photos of paintings and sculptures that "illustrated what life was like" in whatever time period was then under discussion. My failure was total. Try as I might, I never could find much to say, or think, or feel, or care about in 17th-century Dutch still lifes ("Oh, look! A loaf of bread!") or 18th-century French rococo landscapes filled, to my jaded eye, with prissy aristocrats in fake settings. No, history bored me, but I was good at it and so kept at it. (Good grades mattered.) My breakthrough moment came in college, when, with the help of my then-girlfriend, I realized that what I hated was not history itself but most of my history teachers—those dry, pinched souls who crushed everything that was vital, interesting, and important out of the great drama of human life. Out of my life, at any rate. History, after all, is the story of people, and anyone who finds people interesting ought therefore to find history interesting. If a person finds history boring, the problem lies either with him, as an unimaginative lout, or with the way in which the history is presented. Rejecting immediately, of course, the former as impossible in my case, I decided firmly on the latter. Blame the messengers, in other words, not the message. Over the years, I have become increasingly convinced of the correctness of this view. In their desire to present all the facts, most of my teachers—and most of the historians they had us read—simply drained all the life out of the subject.

Part of the problem lay in method. Teaching and writing history is difficult, in large part because of the sheer scope of the enterprise. Should one barrage a student or a reader with facts, clearly and objectively stated, and expect her to see the meaningful patterns in them, or should one discuss the patterns, the Big Ideas, and the deeper questions of human life confronted by any particular society in the past, and then allow her to teach herself enough factual details to corroborate and illumine those larger themes? Both approaches have value, and each has its own weaknesses. Most large-scale history books tend to choose the first option and make a fetish of their factual comprehensiveness and strict objectivity of tone. The problem with this approach is that it too often works only for those few who are already true believers in history's importance and leaves most students and readers yawning in their wake. I knew a fellow in college who was one of these true believers; he could recite the names and dates, in order, of every king of England and every archbishop of Canterbury from 1066 to the present. Impressive, in a nerdy way. But he had no idea at all how to explain the causes of England's civil war in the 17th century, or why the British voted their national hero, Sir Winston Churchill, out of office immediately after the end of World War II. Probably for both good and ill, I choose the latter option—to teach and write history by emphasizing ideas and trends, and the values behind them; to engage in the debates of each age rather than to narrate who won them. Once people are genuinely interested in a topic and can see the reasons to care about it, it seems to me, they can pick up the essential facts by themselves. Moreover, experience has taught me that they will do so.

Four years ago, when Oxford University Press invited me to write a general history of the Western world, I warned them that my approach to the topic would be a bit out of the ordinary. I wanted to write a book that would irritate people, inspire them, confuse them, make them question themselves, and sometimes enlighten them, but certainly always engage them. There are enough books already published to make bored readers fall asleep over. My first eccentricity, if that is what it is, is that I wanted to write a book that had opinions and argued with readers. No one falls asleep in an argument, I figured. My second eccentricity, I warned, is that I do not believe in Western civilization as it is usually defined. I believe instead in what I call—and what nearly became the title of this book—the Greater West. It's time to explain.

There are as many histories of any society as there are historians willing to write them. The shape, themes, and degrees of detail in each result from whatever each author considers of greatest importance—politics, social development, technology and science, economics, gender relations. A focus on any particular theme produces a different understanding of who we have been and therefore who we are. Like the changing patterns in a child's kaleidoscope, the smallest shift of attention or emphasis reveals new configurations of ideas and insights into the way we see ourselves. No single vantage point can claim primacy; as Albert Einstein (1879–1955) theorized and subsequent scientists affirmed, the truths revealed by every perspective in the cosmos are equally true to each observer. But that does not mean one cannot be wrong. "Facts are stubborn things," wrote the American statesman John Adams (1736–1826), in a very different context, "and whatever may be our wishes, our inclinations, or the dictates of our passion, they cannot alter the state of facts and evidence." Historians can disagree, for example, about the specific causes of an event like the Franco-Prussian War (1870–1871), or about its consequences for subsequent generations; but the factual realities of those specific people in those specific places, performing those specific actions, cannot be tampered with. The challenge of writing history, but also its deepest value and most enduring purpose, is in the selection and assemblage of those facts, and the conclusions one draws from them.

To follow a single theme, or a clutch of them, is one way to mediate between comprehensive factuality and meaningful interpretation, and hence the preference by most writers of large-scale histories to select discrete vantage points, to trim the material in such a way that emphasizes, for example, political events. Seen this way, the history of the Greater West emerges as a centuries-long march toward the development of the modern democratic nation-state. A focus on social themes traces the evolution of social classes, the family, interethnic relations, and dominant moral codes. An economic approach emphasizes the everyday common struggle to survive in the world—the production of food, developments in manufacture and commerce, the passing on of property—and culminates not only in modern prosperity but in the belief in a fixed set of economic laws that govern human life. The unspoken corollary of this approach is that it is the recognition of this set of laws to which modern prosperity owes thanks; capitalism thus appears not as a customary practice or an ideology but as a subdiscipline of natural science.

This book too adopts a thematic approach, but a theme seldom utilized in contemporary histories. While paying due attention to other aspects of Western development, it focuses on what might be called the history of values—that is, on the assumptions that lie behind political and economic developments, behind intellectual and artistic ventures, and behind social trends and countertrends. Consider for example, the achievements of the Scientific Revolution (1500–1750). The advances made in fields like astronomy (Nicolaus Copernicus, Johannes Kepler, Galileo Galilei), chemistry (Robert Boyle), and medicine (William

Harvey) did not occur simply because individuals smart enough to figure out new truths happened to come along. Harvey's discovery of the circulatory system was possible only because the culture in which he lived had begun, albeit hesitantly, to allow the dissection of human corpses for scientific research. For many centuries, even millennia, before Harvey's time, cultural and religious taboos had forbidden the desecration of bodies. But the era of the Scientific Revolution was also the era of political absolutism in Europe, a time when prevailing sentiment held that the king was all that stood between mankind and barbarism. Any enemy of the king—for example, anyone convicted of a felony—therefore deserved the ultimate penalty of execution and dissection. No king worship, no discovery of the circulation of the blood. At least not at that time.

Similarly, the search for underlying value assumptions illuminates the effort to explain the gloomy outlook, bordering on nihilism, of the modernist movement of the early 20th century. For the preceding hundred years Europe's traditional Christianity had wavered and withdrawn in the face of industrialism, migration, economic despair, and the intellectual assaults of Darwinian evolution, the so-called higher criticism of the Bible, and the radically new physics of quantum theory and relativity. The trauma of World War I simply was a bloody culmination of the longer trend of the loss of religious belief. A godless universe might still have an underlying order and purpose, but quantum theory and relativity demolished any hope of finding them. For the most stubborn holdouts determined to retain a belief in a meaningfully ordered cosmos, though, World War I crushed any last shreds of hope. If nothing is permanent, true, and purposeful, the modernists thought, then human life is a wasteland of pointless impressions, blind desires, and empty hopes.

> What are the roots that clutch, what branches grow
> Out of this stony rubbish? Son of man,
> You cannot say, or guess, for you only know
> A heap of broken images, where the sun beats,
> And the dead tree gives no shelter, the cricket no relief,
> And the dry stone no sound of water. Only
> There is shadow under this red rock,
> (Come in under the shadow of this red rock),
> And I will show you something different from either
> Your shadow at morning striding behind you
> Or your shadow at evening rising to meet you;
> I will show you fear in a handful of dust.
> (T. S. Eliot, The Waste Land, 1922)

On the other hand, the collapse of order was liberating to some. Just as modernist poets like Eliot freed themselves from rhyme and meter, so too did modernist music (Arnold Schoenberg, Paul Hindemith, Igor Stravinsky, Alban Berg) discard traditional compositional structure and tonality. In painting, movements like Dadaism and cubism explored nonrepresentational forms and played with the very idea of visual sense.

A history that emphasizes the development of values inevitably distorts the record to some extent, for obviously not every person living at a given time held those values. Medieval Christians did not uniformly hate Jews and Muslims, believe the world was about to end, support the Inquisition, and blindly follow the dictates of the pope. Not every learned man and woman in the 18th century was "enlightened" or even wanted to be. The young generation of the 1960s was not composed solely of war resisters, hippies, drug aficionados, feminists, and rock-music lovers who celebrated free love in the muddy fields at Woodstock (although many people now of a certain age like to pretend that they were then). With this caveat in mind, however, it remains possible to offer general observations about the ideas and values that predominated in any era. This book privileges those ideas and sensibilities and views the events of each era in relation to them.

And it does so with a certain amount of opinion. To discuss value judgments without ever judging some of those values seems cowardly and is probably impossible anyway. Most large-scale histories mask their subjectivity simply by deciding which topics to discuss and which ones to pass over; I prefer to argue my positions explicitly, in the belief that to have a point of view is not the same thing as to be unfair. Does this risk confusing the reader who might mistake my opinion for accepted fact? Possibly, I admit. But education is as much about teaching students to evaluate arguments as it is about passing on knowledge to them, and students cannot learn to evaluate arguments if they are never presented with any. Or if they are asleep.

In a second departure from tradition (which in this case is really just habit), this book interprets Western history on a broader geographic scale than other historians do. All full-scale histories of Western civilization begin in the Fertile Crescent, the ancient region made up of Mesopotamia (in modern-day Iraq), Palestine (modern-day Syria, Lebanon, and Israel), and Egypt—but after making a quick nod to the origins of Islam in the 7th century they focus almost exclusively on western Europe. Attention moves like the sun ever westward, through ancient Greece to Rome, thence to Britain, France, and Germany (with a bit of Italy and Spain thrown in when unavoidable), and finally embraces America once it emerges from its international isolation in the 20th century. The Muslim world thereafter enters the discussion only when it impinges on European actions. This book overtly rejects that view and insists on including the region of the Middle East in the general narrative, as a permanently constitutive element of the Greater West. For all its current global appeal, Islam is essentially a Western religion, after all, one that has its spiritual roots in the Jewish and Christian traditions and the bulk of whose intellectual foundations are in the classical Greco-Roman canon. To treat the Muslim world as an occasional sideshow on the long march to western European and American world leadership is to falsify the record and to get the history wrong. Most textbooks touch repeatedly on the Islamic world, of course, but do so only in episodic fashion—and those episodes are invariably whenever Europe and the Middle East are in conflict.

A simple analogy shows the poverty of this approach. Consider any long intimate relationship you have had—perhaps a romantic tie, a family connection, a work colleague, or a long friendship. If someone were to write the history of that relationship but in the process examined only the arguments you had, it could not possibly (no matter how detailed and "objective") be an accurate history of the relationship. It could not possibly be even an accurate history of the arguments, since it would view them entirely out of context. That is the situation with the Greater West. The "European world" and the "Middle Eastern world" have been in a continuous relationship for millennia, buying and selling goods, sharing technologies, studying each other's political ideas, influencing each other's religious beliefs, learning from one another's medicine, facing the same challenges from scientific advances and changing economies. We cannot explain who we are if we limit ourselves to the traditional scope of Western history; we need a Greater Western perspective, one that includes and incorporates the whole of the monotheistic world. Nearly every one of the fundamental turning points in European history (the developments of agriculture, literacy, urban life, monotheistic religion, religious heresy; debates over tolerance, over intellectual freedom, over the rights of women; the Black Death; the invention of gunpowder; the discovery of the larger global world; the challenge of secularism, the debate over reason, the Enlightenment (called *al-Nahda* in Arabic); the catastrophic conquests of Napoleon Bonaparte; the changes brought by rapid industrialization; the First and Second World Wars, the Cold War; and the rise of modern feminism, liberalism, and conservatism) have been experienced jointly by the European and Middle Eastern societies. And not only have we confronted the same challenges, we have interacted with each other intimately in our responses to each new development. Only by broadening our focus can we do justice to each other and to the reality of how our histories have played out. This expanded view introduces a rafter of new difficulties, for apart from the unfamiliar nature of much of the new material, it forces the additional compression and selection of more traditionally mainstream matters.

I am very much aware of the risks involved by this approach. In order to discuss, for example, the campaigns to reform and modernize Islamic understandings of women's roles in society in the early 20th century, this book gives less attention to many of the most significant activists for women in Europe and the United States. A woman like Aletta Jacobs (1854–1929), the first university-trained female physician in the Netherlands, a champion of women's health and the right to suffrage, deserves more space than she receives here (although I point out that she is discussed at greater length here than in any other book of this sort). I wanted to make room, however, for women like Huda'i Sha'arawi (1879–1947), the pioneering Egyptian feminist. The payoff seems worth it, if the end result is a broader recognition that the Islamic world's development has closer parallels with the European and American society than has generally been thought or acknowledged.

Since religious belief has traditionally shaped so much of Greater Western culture—whether for good or ill is every reader's responsibility to determine—I have placed it at the center of my narrative. Even for the most unshakeable of modern agnostics and atheists, the values upheld by the three great monotheisms have had, and continue to have, a profound effect on the development of our social mores, intellectual pursuits, and artistic endeavors. The history of religion does not explain all of Greater Western history, but it is as useful a handle as any to grasp the whole, as are politics, economics, society, and intellectual life. It seems to me to be worth trying, especially since religious misunderstanding and friction dominate so much of our current attention.

In another break with convention, the book incorporates an abundance of primary sources into the narrative. I have always disliked the boxed and highlighted source snippets that pockmark so many of today's textbooks. Any teacher who is honest knows that most students do not read them. It seems to me that any passage worth quoting is worth working into the text itself—and I have done so, with some brio. But a word about them is necessary. For the first three chapters I have needed considerable help. I am ignorant of the ancient Middle Eastern languages and have relied on the current version of a respected and well-loved anthology from my own undergraduate days.[1] When discussing the sacred texts of Judaism, Christianity, and Islam I have used their own authorized translations. Simple courtesy, it seems to me, calls for quoting a Jewish translation of the Bible when discussing Judaism; a Catholic, Orthodox, or Protestant Bible whenever discussing those main branches of Christianity; and the English version of the Qur'an prepared by the

---

[1] Nels M. Bailkey and Richard Lim, *Readings in Ancient History: Thought and Experience from Gilgamesh to St. Augustine*, 7th ed. (Wadsworth, 2011).

royal publishing house in Saudi Arabia when discussing Islam.[2] Last, some of the political records I cite (for example, the Cairo Declaration of Human Rights) are quoted from their official English versions. But apart from these special cases—all duly noted—every translation in this book, from chapter 4 onward, is my own.

SUPPORT MATERIALS FOR *THE CULTURES OF THE WEST*

The Cultures of the West comes with an extensive package of support materials for both instructors and students.

- **Companion Web Site (www.oup.com/us/backman)**: For students, the site includes quizzes, flashcards, documents, interactive maps, and links to YouTube videos. Access to the student site is unrestricted. For instructors, the site includes an instructor's resource manual that provides for each chapter, a detailed chapter outline, suggested lecture topics, learning objectives, suggested Web resources and digital media files. It also includes, for each chapter, approximately 30 multiple-choice, short-answer, true-or-false, and fill-in-the-blank questions as well as approximately 10 essay questions.
- **Instructor's Resource DVD:** Includes PowerPoint slides and JPEG and PDF files for all the maps and photos in the text; an additional four hundred map files, in PowerPoint format, from *The Oxford Atlas of World History*; and approximately 250 additional PowerPoint-based slides organized by theme and topic. The DVD also includes the Instructor's Resource Manual, and the test questions can be customized by the instructor.
- **Sourcebook for *The Cultures of the West,* Volume One: To 1750:** Edited by Clifford R. Backman and Christine Axen, it includes approximately two hundred text sources in Western civilization, organized to match the chapter organization of *The Cultures of the West*. Each source is accompanied by a head-note and reading questions. Free when bundled with the text.
- **Sourcebook for *The Cultures of the West,* Volume Two: Since 1350:** Edited by Clifford R. Backman and Christine Axen, it

---

2   *Tanakh: The Holy Scriptures,* by the Jewish Publication Society; *New American Bible,* published by the U.S. Conference of Catholic Bishops; *New Revised Standard Version,* published by Oxford University Press; and *The Orthodox Study Bible.* For the Qur'an I have used *The Holy Qur'an: English Translations of the Meanings, with Commentary,* published by the King Fahd Holy Qur'an Printing Complex (A.H 1410).

includes approximately two hundred text sources in Western civilization, organized to match the chapter organization of *The Cultures of the West*. Each source is accompanied by a head-note and reading questions. Free when bundled with the text.

- **Mapping the Cultures of the West, Volume One: To 1750:** Includes approximately forty full-color maps, each accompanied by a brief headnote. Free when bundled with the text.
- **Mapping the Cultures of the West, Volume Two: Since 1350:** Includes approximately forty full-color maps, each accompanied by a brief headnote. Free when bundled with the text.
- **Now Playing: Studying Western Civilization Through Film:**(available in both student and instructor editions) is a concise print supplement that provides synopses, recommended scenes, and discussion questions for thirty of the most commonly assigned films in Western Civilization classes. Qualified adopters can receive a Netflix subscription with their adoption. *Now Playing* can be bundled with *The Cultures of the West* at no additional cost.
- **E-book for *The Cultures of the West* (both volumes):** An e-book is available for purchase at **http://www.coursesmart.com.**

BUNDLING OPTIONS

The Cultures of the West can be bundled at a significant discount with any of the titles in the popular Very Short Introductions or Oxford World's Classics series, as well as other titles from the Higher Education division world history catalog (**http://www.oup.com/us/catalog/he**). Please contact your OUP representative for details.

ACKNOWLEDGMENTS

Working with Oxford University Press has been a delight. Brian Wheel is the person who talked me into attempting a new history of the Greater West. I am grateful for the confidence he showed in me and for all the encouragement he offered. Charles Cavaliere, Brian's successor, served as point man, guiding me through the entire project with grace and kindness. His cheery enthusiasm kept me going through many a difficult hour. If the prose in this book has any merit, please direct your compliments to John Haber, prince of editors. I shall miss working with him. Lauren Aylward, Theresa Stockton, Lisa Grzan, Eden Kram, Meg Botteon, Kim Howie, and the rest of the staff shepherded me through the marketing and production phase and deserve all the credit for the wonderful physical design of the book—images, captions, layout, and font.

Some two dozen external reviewers, anonymous to me, read various chapters of this book as they emerged from my printer. Those who did not wish to remain anonymous include Robert Brennan, Cape Fear Community College; Gregory S. Brown, University of Nevada–Las Vegas; Scott G. Bruce, University of Colorado–Boulder; William Caraher, University of North Dakota; John Cox, University of North Carolina–Charlotte; Jason Coy, College of Charleston; Lynda Pinney Domino, Simpson College; Steven Fanning, University of Illinois at Chicago; Irina Gigova, College of Charleston; Laura Hutchings, University of Utah; Andrew Jenks, California State University–Long Beach; Erik N. Jensen, Miami University; Andrew Keitt, University of Alabama–Birmingham; Thomas A. Mason, Indiana University–Purdue University Indianapolis; David Matz, St. Bonaventure University; Charles A. Maxfield, DeSales University; Martin Menke, Rivier College; David A. Messenger, University of Wyoming; Peter J. Myers, Palo Alto College; Stephen Norris, Miami University; Devin Pendas, Boston College; Michael Redman, University of Louisville; Pete Rottier, Kent State University; Mark Edward Ruff, Saint Louis University; Wendy Sarti, Oakton Community College; Thomas J. Schaeper, St. Bonaventure University; Linda Bregstein Scherr, Mercer County Community College; Stuart Smyth, University at Albany–SUNY; Laurie Sprankle, the Community College of Allegheny County; Jane Strother, Campbell University; Victoria Thompson, Arizona State University; Hans P. Vought, SUNY–Ulster County Community College; Janet M. C. Walmsley, George Mason University; David White, McHenry County College; and Matthew Donald Zarzeczny, the Ohio State University. Reading their criticisms felt at times like falling face-first into a threshing machine. (You know who you are, reader no. 6!) I am grateful nonetheless for every comment they offered; our profession depends on people offering honest criticism of one another's work. If I have not accepted every one of their suggestions, they should still feel proud of the work they did. This is a better book, and I hope that I am a better teacher, because of their unsung efforts.

My doctoral student at Boston University, Christine Axen, has been a support from the start. She has taught with me, and occasionally for me, through the last three years, and I appreciate the time she took away from her own dissertation research to assist me on this project—pulling books from the library, running down citations, suggesting ideas. Now that Oxford has asked me to prepare a companion volume of primary texts for this book, Christine has proved such an immense help that she will share the title page with me when that volume appears.

To my wife, Nelina, and our sons, Scott and Graham, this book has been an uninvited house guest at times, pulling me away from too many family hours. They have put up with it, and with me, with patience and generosity that I shall always be thankful for. Their love defines them and sustains me.

With so many good people supporting me, I should have finished sooner. I'll do better next time.

About the Author

Clifford R. Backman is Associate Professor of History at Boston University, where he has taught since 1989. He is author of *The Decline and Fall of Medieval Sicily: Politics, Economy, and Religion in the Reign of Frederick III, 1296–1327* (1995) and *The Worlds of Medieval Europe* (Oxford University Press, 2003). His current projects are a biography of King James II of the medieval Crown of Aragon and a study of Arnau de Vilanova, the infamous heretic who was the personal physician to four successive popes.

A Note to the Reader

I follow a few basic conventions. Instead of the old BC (Before Christ) and AD (Anno Domini) designations for centuries, I use the new norms of BCE (Before the Common Era) and CE (Common Era). Dates are given, whenever possible, for every figure mentioned in the book. Political leaders are identified by the years they were in power—hence (r. 0000–0000) means that he or she *ruled* during those years, and, in the modern era, (g. 0000–0000) means that he or she *governed* during them. All other dates, unless otherwise noted, are life- and death-dates.

One of the chief difficulties of the "Greater Western" approach is the sheer number of unfamiliar names. The history of the Islamic Middle East, this book argues, has to take into account national or ethnic differences, as much as the more familiar distinction between Sunni and Shia Muslims. To help with this, I have indicated wherever possible the ethnicity of an individual. [A] denotes an Arab. [K] indicates an ethnic Kurd. [P] identifies a Persian (Iranian). [T] signals that the person is a Turk. The reasons for these designations will be clear as the chapters unfold.

The Cultures of the West

A History

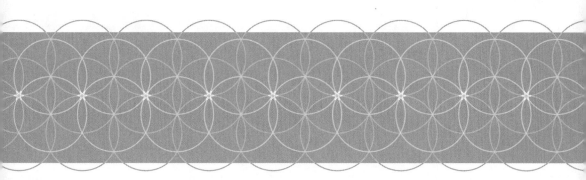

CHAPTER 1

Water and Soil, Stone and Metal

10,000 BCE—2100 BCE

The origins of Western civilization lie in southern Iraq. The region was called Sumer five thousand years ago, and it was the site of the first consistent use of agriculture, the domestication of animals that made farming possible, the construction of cities, and the invention of writing. At first glance it seems an unlikely place for civilization to begin: the soil is sandy, summertime temperatures regularly surpass 110°F (43°C), and the dull flatland receives a scant eight inches of annual rainfall. (By comparison, most of the Mediterranean basin receives nearly four times as much.) There was no stone to quarry, no metal ores to mine, and little timber with which to build. Bordered by the relatively low-lying Zagros Mountains of Iran to the east, it nevertheless lay exposed to raiding groups from the Iranian steppe.

THE ANCIENT NEAR EAST

But it was first in Sumer that true civilization began. It brought early agriculture, trade, and an empire. It brought writing, ancient songs, and ancient deities. When Egypt became a second cradle of civilization, its firm social hierarchy extended even to the kingdom of the dead.

THE TIGRIS AND THE EUPHRATES

Sumer lay in the narrowing plain between the lower reaches of the Tigris and Euphrates rivers. The Sumerians had access to the Persian Gulf, whose headlands reached about one hundred miles further inland in ancient times than they do today. Yet they never developed a maritime tradition and remained resolutely bound to

◀ **Sumer** Sumerian noblewoman wearing a shawl, possibly denoting preparation for a wedding. ca. 2100 BCE.

- The Tigris and the Euphrates
- Early Sumer: Kings and Warriors, Priests and Scribes
- The Idea of Empire
- Mesopotamian Life: Cities and Slaves, Letters and Numbers
- Religion and Myth: The Great Above and Great Below
- Ancient Egypt
- Social Strata in Egypt
- The Kingdom of the Dead

CHAPTER OUTLINE

the soil. Sandy though that soil was, it was made fertile by the flooding of the two great rivers, as the winter rains of Syria and the spring thaws of the snows of the Taurus Mountains to the far north brought layer upon layer of silt to fertilize the land. Twisting slowly eastward through narrow defiles until they reached the high plains of Syria and Kurdistan, the rivers plunged dramatically southward, picking up speed as they approached the site of today's city of Baghdad. The Tigris River, with its deep bed, flooded less broadly but with a strong current. The Euphrates, on the other hand, was broad and shallow, overran its banks easily, and scattered highland silt over a wide expanse. The faster-flowing Tigris usually reached its high-water mark in April, while the Euphrates generally reached full flood about a month later. By managing this water via an elaborate network of levees, reservoirs, and irrigation canals, the Sumerians were able to produce abundant yields of summer grains for themselves and prairie grasses for their herds. Crop yields may have reached ratios as high as 30:1—that is, thirty bushels of grain harvested for every bushel of seeds planted, a ratio comparable to that produced by American farms in the first half of the 20th century.

Archeological evidence suggests that the Ubaids—the first identifiable group to settle in the region—began farming in Sumer perhaps as early as 7000 BCE. Remnants of irrigation tunnels, built of stone, date at least to 5900 BCE and possibly earlier. Archeologists in the last hundred years have discovered even older settlements involving agriculture in other sites throughout the Middle East. At Jericho in Palestine, for example, evidence of grain storage—though not necessarily of grain production—reaches back to 9000 BCE. Agriculture also developed in northern Mesopotamia only two hundred years later, then on the south-central Anatolian plateau around 7500 BCE, and finally in southern Russia and along the banks of the Black Sea ca. 7000 BCE, after the geological shifting of continental plates opened the Dardanelles and let the saltwater of the Mediterranean pour in, to create the Black Sea out of what used to be a freshwater lake. But only Sumer gives evidence of continuous settlement, systematic agriculture, developed urban

CHAPTER TIMELINE

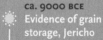

ca. 9000 BCE
Evidence of grain
storage, Jericho

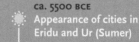

ca. 5500 BCE
Appearance of cities in
Eridu and Ur (Sumer)

ca. 7000 BCE
Earliest evidence of
farming in Sumer

ca. 4000 BCE
Beginning of
Bronze Age

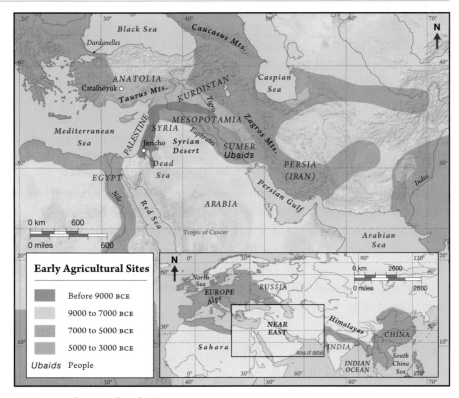

MAP 1.1 Early Agricultural Sites

life, and the use of writing. From there the technique of farming spread eastward into India, westward to the coastal plains of the eastern Mediterranean, and even as far as western Europe (see Map 1.1).

Archeology and guesswork are our only guides to these developments. Early agriculture depended on collective labor, and lots of it: until native animals such as oxen were domesticated, the brutal work of cutting open the soil, planting seeds, weeding, pruning vines, cutting stalks, and grinding grains had to be done by hand. Skeletal remains of early agriculturalists—chiefly women—display agonizingly

ca. 3500 BCE
Earliest evidence
of writing (Sumer)

ca. 2350 BCE
Reign of Akkadian
King Sargon I

ca. 3150 BCE
Egypt united under
a single ruler

ca. 1500 BCE
First appearance of
wheeled vehicles in Egypt

curved spines. Men, on the other hand, hunted, gathered, and ruled. Villages began to appear, some of them rather large; for safety, the people at most sites constructed stone or earthen walls to protect them from attack. The early settlement at Jericho had a population of roughly two thousand people by 7000 BCE and a fortification wall that may have reached thirty feet in height. In west-central Anatolia, at about the time Jericho was completing its wall, cattle breeders settled at Çatalhöyük, where their population swelled to between eight and ten thousand. They built a village of closely placed mud-brick homes that, interestingly, were entered via holes in their roofs.

Primitive metal tools appeared around 7000 BCE as well, when small bits of raw copper were hammered into shape with stones. By 5000 BCE early settlers had learned how to smelt copper ore into the pure metal, which they then either cast into molds or, by 4000 BCE, mixed with tin in order to produce bronze. Bronze was significantly stronger than its component parts, and its use in weaponry and farm implements spread throughout the Near East quickly—inaugurating the **Bronze Age** (4000–1500 BCE).

EARLY SUMER: KINGS AND WARRIORS, PRIESTS AND SCRIBES

Rich in potential for grain-producing but lacking the stone and metal needed to bring it about, the Sumerians had to develop trade relations. These reached to the ore-rich but grain-poor settlements along the upper Tigris River and westward into Palestine and lower Anatolia. Sumerian grain traveled well in the arid atmosphere of the Near East, and the masses of heavy stone and metal they needed to produce it were easily transported down the strong current of the Tigris. But maintaining these important commercial ties over such long distances compelled the Sumerians to develop writing. With it they could keep records of orders, shipments, revenues, and obligations.

The origins of the Sumerians are unknown since their language is unrelated to any other known tongue, whether ancient or later. It is likely that they entered the Tigris-Euphrates plain, as did most of their subsequent invaders, from the Zagros Mountains in Iran.[1] Sumerians were not the only inhabitants of Mesopotamia, of course, but they were the dominant group until their conquest by the Akkadians around 2500 BCE. Their founding myths identify Eridu and Ur as their first cities; archeological evidence confirms that these appeared as early as

---

[1]   This region is also known as Mesopotamia, which derives from the ancient Greek name for the area. It means "between the rivers."

5500 BCE and contained as many as fifty thousand inhabitants at their peak, and were followed soon by settlements at Uruk, Lagash, Nippur, and Kish; Sumerian cities were considerably larger and more complex than the rural villages in Palestine, Syria, and Anatolia.[2]

While most people worked the land, economic specialization developed quickly. Stonemasons, merchants, rivermen, weavers, dyers, civil and hydraulic engineers, metalworkers, potters, and scribes—all emerged as distinct occupations. In the first centuries, these cities were governed by clan elders, who perhaps worked in concert as a primitive form of municipal council. They could not, however, defend the Sumerians against invaders or satisfy the whims of the deities who controlled the natural forces of heat, wind, and water. These constant needs resulted in the rise of new twin nodes of power—militarily backed monarchies and divinely appointed priesthoods.

Kingship and priesthood commonly emerge together in Western societies, sometimes in contest with one another and sometimes elided into each other. Military action was most efficiently directed by a single commander to whom everyone owed obedience—the king, whose formal title was **lugal**. Protection against the gods, especially the unpredictable deities that the Sumerians believed in, required the priests. This large and permanent caste was charged with anticipating the gods' desires, interpreting their actions, and above all propitiating their wrath through prayer and sacrifice. Given their joint responsibility for protecting the people from harm, kings and priests have traditionally worked together: kings stand as bulwarks and standard-bearers of the priests' institutionalized religion, while priests serve to consecrate kings and bless their actions. In the ancient Near East, and well into Europe's own history, the worst crises frequently occurred when the secular and religious powers were at cross-purposes.

> Given their joint responsibility for protecting the people from harm, kings and priests have traditionally worked together: kings stand as bulwarks and standard-bearers of the priests' institutionalized religion, while priests serve to consecrate kings and bless their actions.

The Sumerians' own king list, written around 2100 BCE but reflecting a much older oral tradition, fancifully boasted that an unbroken string of monarchs had governed Sumer for well over two hundred thousand years. This tradition reached back even before the worst crisis of all: a mythical Great Flood sent by capricious gods that covered the entire earth and all but annihilated mankind. Much like the Biblical tale of Noah and the Ark, for which it served as a model, the Great Flood

---

2   Settlements were also heavily fortified. Uruk had a full six miles of battlements surrounding it.

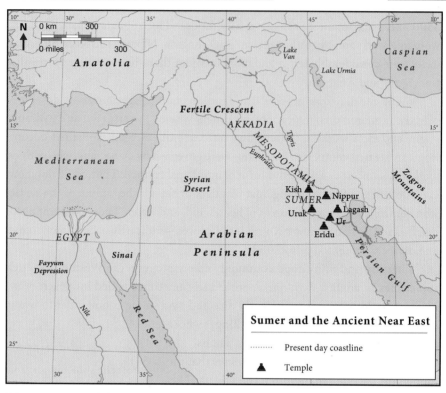

MAP 1.2 **Sumer and the Ancient Near East**

never happened but retained its mythic power because of the peoples' genuine fear of actual flooding. The Tigris and Euphrates occasionally swelled to unusual size and covered farms, fields, and flocks.[3] This legend, told in the great Sumerian poem the *Epic of Gilgamesh*, served to remind the people of the unpredictability of the gods while creating a reference point for the start of their own history.

Sumer consisted of a sprawl of independent city-states, each governed by a lugal, a priestly caste, or an uneasy combination of the two (see Map 1.2). The earliest king we can identify with any certainty was En-Mebaragesi, who ruled over Kish, near the site of the later city of Babylon, around 2600 BCE. His most significant achievement was the construction of the temple in Nippur, the home of the great sky god Enlil. En-Mebaragesi ruled during the so-called Early Dynastic Period, which lasted from 2900 to 2350 BCE. The king list relates that political dominance in Sumer temporarily passed from Eridu and Shuruppak, in the south, to Kish, in the north, and that after Kish's brief ascendance, southern Sumer once again took the lead (though with power then centered on Ur, Uruk, and Lagash). Some enthusiasts take this assertion literally

---

[3] It seems likely that the legend of the Great Flood, if it had any basis in historical fact at all, originated with the creation of the Black Sea.

and suggest that the Great Flood legend refers to an actual event. They try to synchronize it with the unusually large layer of silt deposits that settled over part of lower Sumer at some point between 3000 and 2900 BCE. But the chronologies of the king list and the archeological record disagree with one another by many centuries.

The Sumerians invented writing during this age, starting with primitive early pictograms, or drawn representations of objects. These gave way to a sophisticated system of ideograms, which represent concepts, and phonograms, or marks indicating syllabic phonetic values. The latter are similar to the shortcuts used by today's text messengers. Sumerian writing used nearly two thousand symbols, which meant that literacy remained a tightly held monopoly of professional scribes, who consequently enjoyed positions of great significance in society. Without them, kings and priests could not compile records, issue decrees, or establish legal or liturgical canons. By far the most famous of the Early Dynasts was Gilgamesh, who ruled Uruk around 2600 BCE. Tradition credits him with building the battlements surrounding that city and claims that after his death the grateful people of Uruk gave him a magnificent burial: they diverted the Euphrates River, buried his body in the exposed riverbed, and then released the waters once again into their original channel so their ruler would lie forever beneath the great river.[4] But Gilgamesh is best known as a literary figure, the hero of the later Babylonian epic that bears his name.

A Semitic people called the Akkadians overwhelmed the Sumerian city-states around 2350 BCE and established the Akkadian Period, which lasted until about 2100. They had lived for several centuries along the upper Tigris, trading with the Sumerians and the peoples of Syria. Although they were foreigners, the Akkadians respected Sumerian culture and adopted its language, institutions, and religion. The most successful of the Akkadian kings was Sargon I (ca. 2350 BCE), who conquered everything from lower Sumer to northern Syria, all the way to the Mediterranean (see Map 1.3). This fierce conqueror boasted constantly of his cruelty as a matter of policy, making him perhaps the first ruler who found that simply maintaining a reputation for savagery can hold a large population in check as effectively as actual savagery can.

THE IDEA OF EMPIRE

Sargon placed family members in control of the territories he conquered, thereby governing a knitted-together empire.[5] This was a surprisingly new idea. The Sumerians had fought plenty of wars over the centuries, but their custom had always been to

---

[4] In 2003 a team of German archeologists discovered what they believe to be the ancient city of Uruk. The excavation is still underway; Gilgamesh's grave has yet to be located.

[5] Sargon installed one of his daughters as high priestess of the temples to the Sumerian moon goddess. Her name was En-Heduanna, and she is history's first known female author. Several of the hymns she wrote have survived.

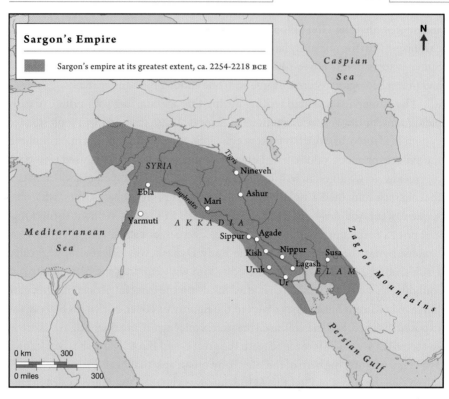

MAP 1.3 Sargon's Empire

defeat a neighbor and then to withdraw and receive annual tribute from the conquered. The notion of actually governing the lands they conquered seems never to have occurred to them. Sargon, however, saw that a hitherto unimagined level of wealth and power could result not only from controlling grain-rich Sumer but also from commanding the trade routes of upper Mesopotamia. Through this region Sumerian grain traveled northward, while textiles, metalwork, and animal products of the northern portions of the **Fertile Crescent** moved south. His empire far exceeded any earlier kingdom in its magnificence, but its real significance lay in the model of strategic authority that it established. By recognizing the Fertile Crescent's connective role—that is, its status as a commercial center or meeting point for the central Asian and eastern Mediterranean economies—he highlighted what was to become perhaps the dominant trait of Middle Eastern history, its strategic significance as the connection point between East and West.

> By recognizing the Fertile Crescent's connective role—that is, its status as a commercial center or meeting point for the central Asian and eastern Mediterranean economies—he highlighted what was to become perhaps the dominant trait of Middle Eastern history: its strategic significance as the connection point between East and West.

The Sumerians had commonly referred to their rulers as shepherds of the people. The Akkadians, however, would have none of that. An inscription from the reign of one of Sargon's successors—his grandson Naram-Sin—describes him as "the Strong, the Ruler of Akkad":[6]

> Even when the four corners of the earth were united in opposition to him, [he] emerged victorious . . . and took captive all the kings who had united against him. Because he had saved Akkad in time of crisis, all the people of the city begged of the gods—of Ishtar, in Eanna; of Enlil, in Nippur; of Dagan, in Tuttel; of Ninhursaga, in Kesh; of Enki, in Eridu; of Sin, in Ur; of Shamash, in Sippur; and of Nergal, in Kutha—that Naram-Sin might be worshipped as a god in Akkad. Accordingly, they built a temple for him in the center of the city.

Sargon's empire collapsed roughly one hundred years after his death, and control of the region was restored to a series of native kings known collectively as the Third Dynasty of Ur (ca. 2100–2000 BCE). This was the last period of Sumerian history, since the Ur dynasts were ultimately displaced by new waves of invaders who poured over Mesopotamia (or simply through it en route to Palestine) after 2000 BCE: the Semitic Amorites from southern Iran (2000–1600), the Hittites, an Indo-European group from central Anatolia (1600–1400), the Mitanni (1500–1300, also Indo-Europeans), and the Assyrians (1500–600, a Semitic-speaking group) from the northernmost reaches of the Tigris River. There were others, too. But these groups generally disdained Sumerian culture and did their best to suppress or supplant it. Their interests lay more in the northern and western reaches of the Fertile Crescent, from Syria and Anatolia down through Palestine and approaching Egypt. As Sumer declined, the priestly caste went into elegiac mode, writing and preserving sad hymns to their gods and laments for the lost glories of the early city-states.

There is some evidence that economic decline contributed to the invaders' disdain for the Sumerian way of life. Centuries of flooding and irrigation had left high quotients of mineral salts in the farm fields. Since these salts rose to the surface as the water was absorbed into the land, the quality of the soil deteriorated, reducing productivity. Local farmers attempted to stop the decline by introducing new grains, but it seems clear that the gradual corrosion of the alluvial plain, which worsened the further south one went toward the confluence of the two great rivers, brought an end of Sumerian life. It was no coincidence that the Amorites, the group to succeed the Akkadians, built a new capital for themselves

---

[6]   The Akkadians thus appear to have introduced the cult of king worship.

considerably further to the north, a city that remained the dominant Mesopotamian city for many centuries thereafter: Babylon.

MESOPOTAMIAN LIFE: CITIES AND SLAVES, LETTERS AND NUMBERS

So much for the political framework. But what do we know about how people in early Mesopotamia lived, what they believed, and how they understood the world?

Since agriculture is what brought them there in the first place, it is right to start with their working of the land. Farming occupied probably 90 percent of the population, who used wooden plows, bronze-tipped seed drills, and stone-bladed hoes. Mesopotamia comprised roughly eight thousand square miles (twenty thousand square kilometers) of land fed by a network of major stone canalways and an elaborate sprawl of subsidiary smaller channels, which divided the land into relatively regularly spaced and equally sized plots. While the largest estates belonged to the kings and temple priests, most farmland was held privately. Whole clans, rather than individuals, owned each plot of land, and they worked out for themselves the distribution of tasks and profits. In most cases the consent of the whole clan was needed before any parcel of land could be sold. Yet it remains unclear how that consent was achieved—whether by all the adults equally, solely by the men, under the leadership of the clan elders, or by some other means. Clans who wanted to relinquish their landownership, perhaps to migrate northward into Syria or into Palestine (as did the Hebrew patriarch Abraham around 1800 BCE), resorted to adopting would-be buyers into their clan in order to facilitate the sale of their property. Inheritance practices were **patrilinear**, through male heirs, although, in the absence of one, women could own property and give evidence in courts.

A barter economy predominated, with farmers giving grain portions to the various craftsmen—carpenters, smiths, potters, and weavers—who produced the tools they needed to work the land. Payments in kind were likewise made to the priests in the local temples. Commoners also owed a certain amount of labor to their communities, usually for the all-important tasks of maintaining the irrigation canals and urban fortifications. All adult men fought to defend the city-state from attack and were responsible for supplying their own weapons and equipment. Law allowed for divorce and remarriage, although women were not considered equal partners of their husbands.

The cities that dominated Sumer were built of sun-baked brick and surrounded by deep moats and fortified battlements. The major streets within each city ran from the gates to the market squares and then to the temples and the royal palace. These streets could accommodate two-way traffic of chariots and ass-drawn wagons and carts; branching off these were tangles of narrow byways and alleys where the bulk of the people lived in cramped, low-roofed huts. Open space came at a premium; the wealthy displayed their status and good fortune by building interior courtyards in their palaces. Larger towns like Ur, Uruk, Lagash, Kish, and Nippur held populations as large as forty or fifty thousand, but five to ten thousand was more common. Rank and filthy, these towns had no sewers; human waste was simply dumped into the unpaved streets, where it was foraged (and added to) by crowds of swine, goats, oxen, and dogs. Clean water to drink was a luxury, which accounts for the Sumerians' early invention of beer—the alcohol in it forestalled the proliferation of pathogens.

Temples dotted the cityscape. Sumerians believed in and sacrificed to hosts of deities, but each city observed the formal recognition of a particular patron god, for whom they erected vast terraced pyramid-like mounds called **ziggurats**, atop which stood lavishly decorated temples that served as the earthly home of the god or goddess. Sumerian religion maintained that the gods had invented humans in order to serve them and perform the labor that they would otherwise have to do for themselves; hence temple worship involved prayer, the singing of hymns, and offering the deities an array of gifts. Priests received a percentage of every farmer's produce and of every manufacturer's wares. In return, they presided over the temples' rites and kept the gods appeased. Human life was subject to the whims of the gods. The Sumerians believed that their deities commanded the forces of nature; and while the deities were generally benevolent (hence Sumerian prosperity), they could nevertheless act capriciously and were easily roused to anger.

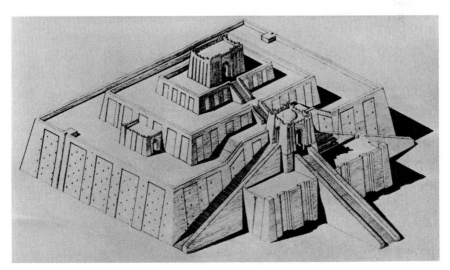

Artist's Reconstruction of the Ziggurat of Ur, ca. 2500 BCE   Worshippers ascended the long stairs to the first platform, where there stood a gatehouse through which they gained admittance to the upper levels. At the top of the ziggurat was the shrine, in which the priests conducted their rituals.

Priests often worked alongside the king to govern the city-state, creating a de facto theocracy. To aid in that work, and to keep a careful tally of payments made or yet owed to the deities, the priestly caste invented writing—Mesopotamia's greatest single contribution to the world. The earliest surviving documents (records of payments received from votaries, primarily) come from Uruk and Kish around 3500 BCE. Sumerian scribes wrote by pressing figures into mud or clay tablets that were then either sun-dried or baked until hardened; the script they developed is called **cuneiform**.[7] Cuneiform markings represented ideograms and groupings of letters in syllables, rather than individual letters. The first alphabet developed two thousand years later, in Palestine, among the Canaanites and the Phoenicians.

Once the syllabary code had become established, Sumerian scribes set to work recording economic transactions, astronomical charts, religious poems and prayers, medical regimens, legal decrees, arithmetical calculations—all manner of things. Among the most interesting are early word lists. These lists were not dictionaries, but rather groups of related nouns—four-legged animals, birds of various sizes, types of flowers and other plants, species of fish, and varieties of precious stones and metals. Such lists probably originated as study guides for learning the cuneiform script.

Yet they also represent mankind's first documented efforts to make sense of the world, by classifying its components and seeking order among its bewildering variety.

A second set of markings depicted numbers. Sumerian mathematics used place-value numerals, with both base-ten and base-sixty notations. (The latter survives in our division of time into sixty-minute hours and sixty-second minutes.) By 2300 BCE they had either invented or imported the abacus. They used arithmetic to keep financial accounts and for studying the constellations and the movement of the planets in the night sky. Since their survival depended on knowing when to expect the spring floods, they paid close attention to measuring time. They

Early Writing   A clay receipt, ca. 2300 BCE, tallying the number of sheep and goats in a particular herd; perhaps part of a bill of sale, but also perhaps a record for taxation purposes.

---

[7]   Cuneiform literally means "wedge-shaped" in Latin, after the indentation made into the clay by a reed stylus.

followed a solar calendar but divided it into twelve lunar months, which necessitated the insertion of a thirteenth month every third year. The flooding of the rivers eroded the Sumerians' mud-brick buildings and boundary markers, so they quickly became adept at basic geometry in order to re-create their washed-away property lines.

Slavery appeared early in Sumer. Two principle sources of slaves existed: debt bondage and the taking of captives in war. People who owed money to landlords or merchants seldom sold themselves into slavery; instead, they sold their family members. The practice may have begun as the offering of a child as collateral for a loan or as a ransom against a promise to repay a debt. Failure to pay resulted in the child's permanent loss of freedom. War captives and their descendants, however, probably represented the larger portion of the slave population. The Sumerians generally avoided using slave labor in the fields, since the opportunities for escape were too great. Instead, slaves remained in the cities, working as domestic servants, laborers in workshops, and concubines. The frequent warring between the city-states, and between the Sumerians and their invaders, resulted in a steady supply of new slaves—which was a necessity in ancient times, since the harshness of slave life meant that slave populations were seldom self-sustaining. Their mortality rates almost always exceeded their birth rates. Given the vulnerability of this population, therefore, the Sumerians kept their slaves from the backbreaking work of tilling the land and maintaining the irrigation canals. Slaves were used instead to help around the house and the work yard.

Oral custom and written law structured Sumerian life, and as early as 2300 BCE at least one ruler, Ur-Ukagina of Lagash, had brought these laws into a single, published code that articulated the pursuit of justice, not the preservation of inherited right, as the aim of government. Economic specialization in the cities had created a degree of social stratification that ancient custom could neither address nor restrain, leaving thousands vulnerable to exploitation in every city. Written law emerged from this as an effort to reform society by restricting the rights of the powerful. Ur-Ukagina's law code survives only in fragments and in references found in later texts. The portions that survive limit the rights of the priestly caste and wealthy landowners to evict tenants and seize their property, exempt widows and orphans from paying taxes, and oblige the government to meet the funeral expenses of the poor. One inscription reads: "[Ur-Ukagina] freed the people of Lagash from usury, burdensome controls, hunger, theft, murder, and seizure of their property. He established freedom. Widows and orphans were no longer at the mercy of powerful individuals."[8] This effort to relieve oppression did not last long, however: the Akkadians conquered Sumer shortly after Ur-Ukagina's reign. Subsequent rulers,

---

8   This inscription contains the first known use of the word for "freedom" in any Western language: *ama-gi*.

however, continued to produce reformist codes, the most famous of all being that instituted by the Babylonian ruler Hammurabi (ca. 1700 BCE).

RELIGION AND MYTH:
THE GREAT ABOVE AND GREAT BELOW

Sumerian religion, as reconstructed from myths and ritual prayers written in Babylonian times, consisted of a complex web of relations. It encompassed at least three strata of existence: Heaven, the Great Above, and the Great Below.

The Sumerians regarded the day and night sky as the high overarching bowl of Heaven, a fixed semisphere where dwelt Anu (meaning "sky," literally, but representing the divine force itself) and a group of spirits known as the Igigi. The Great Above consisted of the space from the dome of the sky down to the surface of the Earth; this was the dwelling of the Annunaki—the assemblage of gods and goddesses to whom the people of Sumer sacrificed and offered prayers, and whose aid they invoked. Enlil, the god of the air, reigned supreme here; the other chief gods were Utu, the sun god (called Shamash by the Akkadians), Nanna Suen, the moon god (Sin to the Akkadians), Nin-Khursaga, the Earth goddess (Akkadian Ishtar), and Enki, the god of waters (later identified with the Babylonian god Ea); but the names of at least fifty other Annunaki survive. Mankind was the creation of Enki, who had made humans specifically to provide food and comfort for the gods. People, in other words, were the servants of the gods in the most literal sense. Interestingly, the deities in the Annunaki did not create the world but were in fact created by it.

The world itself came about through the movement of two primordial forces—the male and female principles (Abzu and Tiamat, respectively)—which resulted in the creation of the physical world and then of the gods themselves. But the Annunaki feared the creation of even more gods, who presumably might have supplanted them, and so Enlil killed their mother, Tiamat, and Enki slew Abzu. The murdered parents thus descended into the Great Below, the world beneath the surface of the Earth. Also beneath the Earth was Kur (Ersetu to the Akkadians), which was the Land of No Return, the place to which all humans went after death. The Sumerians believed there were two separate entrances to the world of the dead, one in the caves of the Zagros Mountains and another in a secret staircase hidden in the city of Uruk. After dying, all Sumerians entered Kur by one of these portals, whereupon they received judgment from a council of six hundred gods. It is hard to say what the purpose of such judgment was, however, since all the dead were consigned equally to spending eternity wandering naked and exposed through an endless expanse of darkness, dust, and heat.

Each city-state possessed its own unique patron deities, and it was the joint responsibility of the lugal and his corps of priests to lead their societies in ritual

The Standard of Ur, ca. 2500 BCE   This plaque, made of lapis lazuli embedded in wood, portrays farmers, carters, scribes, merchants, and priests en route to offer their sacrifices to the deities.

worship. Sumerian gods numbered more than three thousand, but most of them remained unknown outside their local cult centers. Only the major deities like Enlil, Enki, and Ishtar enjoyed wide recognition, through the stories that made up Sumerian mythology. Each deity represented a force of nature and was anthropomorphic in form and all too human-like in behavior. But the gods stood well beyond human understanding. A crude barter characterized human-divine relations: the Sumerians courted favor from the gods by offering them prayers and appeasing them with gifts, while the gods blessed the people (when it suited them) by sending favorable conditions for the growing of abundant food.

The gods were capricious, though, and could lash out in anger by sending a burning drought, a devastating flood, a plague of crop-eating insects, or a wave of foreign invaders. Sumerian priests guarded against such divine fickleness by reading omens in the organs of animals sacrificed in the temple, by interpreting dreams, or by seeing coded messages in the flight patterns of birds. Religious life in Sumer thus consisted largely of maintaining favorable but distant relations with the gods and goddesses. Heavenly interaction with humans spelled doom as often as it brought delight.

> Religious life in Sumer thus consisted largely of maintaining favorable but distant relations with the gods and goddesses. Heavenly interaction with humans spelled doom as often as it brought delight.

Sumerian mythology consisted of an intricate web of tales. Their gods, it turns out, were energetically incestuous, making it all but impossible to work out their genealogy. To illustrate with just the first generations: Anu, the great god principle in Heaven, fathered Tiamat and Abzu, who then consorted with one another and produced two mud deities named Lahmt and Lahamu. These siblings then paired off to produce Kishar, a fertility goddess, and her brother Anshar, the god of the North Star, and these two then somewhat predictably came together—but unpredictably they somehow gave birth to Anu, their own great-grandfather. From this point on, the family tree becomes impossibly tangled.

In earliest times the tales lacked a strong moral element; the gods exhibited the same self-interest that humans did and pursued their pleasures and whims accordingly. By the start of the second millennium, however, many myths bear witness to a heightened interest in justice and a sense of rational moral order. A hymn to the goddess Nanshe of Lagash, for example, lauds her as the deity who "sees the oppression of man over man, who is the guardian of orphans, . . . the caregiver of widows, who seeks justice for the poor, . . . who comforts the homeless and shelters the weak."

The best-known of the moralized Sumerian hymns comes from the Babylonian period. Known as the Shamash Hymn after the Babylonian name for the sun god Utu worshipped in the city-state of Sippur, it offers praise for the god's relentless protection of the weak and troubled:

> You care for all the peoples of the lands,
> And everything that Enlil/Ea . . . has created is entrusted to you.
> All that draws breath you shepherd without exception. . . .
> The whole of mankind bows to you,
> Shamash, the universe longs for your light. . . .
> You stand by the traveler whose road is difficult,
> To the seafarer in dread of the waves you give [comfort]. . . .
> You save from the storm the merchant carrying his capital;
> The [boatman] who sinks in the ocean you equip with wings;
> You point out settling places to refugees and fugitives, and
> To the captive you point out [escape] routes known only to you.

The hymn goes on to praise Utu/Shamash for punishing corrupt judges and dishonest merchants, for granting long life to those who work for justice, and for rewarding the honest and kindly. The lugals, too, came to be valued as much for the extent to which they provided justice, since their temple duties of leading sacrifices and observing the chief festivals of the religious year gained in significance.

A contrary tradition in Sumerian myth laments the unpredictability of the gods' affections and care to protect the righteous. "The Poem of the Righteous Sufferer" expresses the agonies of an unnamed Sumerian who despite his strict ritual observance has nevertheless suffered the loss of his wealth and social position:

> I gave my attention to supplication and prayer:
> To me prayer was discretion, sacrifice my rule.

The day for reverencing the god was a joy to my heart;
The day of the goddess's procession was profit and gain to me.
The king's prayer—that was my joy,
And the accompanying music became a delight for me. . . .
Who knows the will of the gods in heaven?
Who understands the plans of the underworld gods?
Where have mortals learnt the way of a god?
He who was alive yesterday is dead today.
For a minute he was dejected, suddenly he is exuberant.
One moment people are singing in exaltation,
Another they groan like professional mourners.
Their condition changes like the opening and shutting of the legs,
When starving they become like corpses,
When replete they vie with the gods.
In prosperity they speak of scaling heaven,
Under adversity they complain of going down to hell.
I am appalled at these things; I do not understand their significance.

A later Babylonian writer reworked the myth and turned this poem into a song of praise for the god Marduk. This patron deity of Babylon comes to the sufferer's aid and restores him to happiness, ending with a paean to traditional teaching and ritual.[9] In the original tale, however, the dominant tone is despair. The narrator seeks not an end to human suffering but merely an explanation for it. Why do the wicked prosper? Why are the lives of the righteous filled with want, fear, violence, and confusion? Why will the gods not spare humans from the pain of life?

To judge from their literary remains, the people of Mesopotamia thought deeply, almost obsessively, about these matters. The parlous nature of life almost demanded it. After all, the land they inhabited had many natural blessings but was vulnerable to invasion by raiders seeking to snatch away the very blessings the Sumerians worked so hard to procure. Moreover, the rivers that gave such abundant life to the region also destroyed it by unpredictable and uncontrollable flash flooding. The more the Sumerians prospered, the more likely they were to be attacked. These were ironies of a most soul-searching kind. If the gods could alternately bless and batter humans so capriciously, is it vain to regard the world as being in any way ethically ordered? And if life lacks moral sense, is it worth the agony of living it? Can we have trust in heaven? Attitudes shifted with time and fortune, but the Sumerians, while not unremittingly gloomy, recognized

---

[9]   The Babylonian tale may have provided a model for the Hebrew author of the biblical Book of Job.

that life is serious business. They had deep souls, gave thanks for small blessings, but kept a wary eye open for all manner of the world's senseless agony. Among their many extraordinary contributions to Western culture was the invention of the conscious search for meaning in life. And that may be their most important contribution of all.

ANCIENT EGYPT

Southwest of the Fertile Crescent, along the banks of the Nile River in Africa, lay the second cradle of Western civilization. The Nile originates in two sub-Saharan tributaries—one in northern Ethiopia, fed by Lake Tana, and the other stretching all the way south to Lake Victoria in Uganda. They meet near today's Sudanese capital city of Khartoum. From there the Nile flows northward, dropping through a series of dramatic cataracts, or waterfalls, before reaching the gentle sloping plane of Egypt itself.

For six hundred miles it meanders slowly northward, cutting a green swath of fertile land on either side of the riverbed, until about a hundred miles shy of the Mediterranean it branches out in a delta with no fewer than seven major openings to the sea, spread over nearly two hundred fifty miles of coastline. This delta region forms "Lower Egypt," and the six-hundred-mile-long river valley directly south of it comprises "Upper Egypt." Together, the two regions made up approximately twelve thousand square miles (thirty-one thousand square kilometers) of arable land, and they were home to human communities dating back to 5000 BCE.

Egypt thus consisted of two extremely long strips of land on either side of the Nile, between four and twelve miles across, and a vast triangular delta. The waters of the Nile swelled annually, beginning in August. At their peak in September, they reached nearly twenty feet above their low ebb in April and May, bringing more than one hundred million tons of rich sediment to replenish the banks. Spring planting thus began when the greatest amount of land was exposed, and the harvest was brought in just before the next replenishing flood began. People lived in small communities along the river's edge as early as 5000 BCE but did not begin to farm the land until approximately 3500. Until then, they tended their flocks, living off the plants and trees that grew naturally along the shores.

Away from the cultivated shores of the Nile, the rest of Egypt was all but uninhabitable, with nothing but arid desert to the east, west, and south. The relatively small land bridge of the Sinai Peninsula, the only point of contact between the African and Asian continents, narrowed to a span of only forty miles as it approached Egypt proper. Controlling the movement of peoples through so small an area posed little trouble through most of Egypt's history. Nature thus blessed Egypt with a concentrated abundance of fertile soil, an easy means of communication and transport, and a protective surrounding that kept invaders out for nearly fifteen hundred years. The marshy delta's port cities comprised Egypt's only exposure to other peoples, and hence the fortification of the harbors represented the only significant military expense of her rulers. Soldiers were well paid by the affluent government, and with no enemies to contend with they could devote all their energies to policing their own people. Moreover, and unlike Sumer, Egypt had abundant resources in stone and metal ores and hence could engage in impressive building projects, like palaces and pyramids. Timber was the only vital natural resource unavailable, but this was easily procured via trade through the delta cities and then shipped upriver. By such natural advantages Egypt unified early, developed a strong central government, and enjoyed more lasting peace and prosperity than any other early culture.

Human settlements based on agriculture appeared as early as 5000 BCE. The first languages used in the region belonged to the Hamitic and Semitic families. These suggest that the earliest settlers arrived from the northern coast of Africa to the west and from Palestine and Syria to the northeast. By 4000 BCE the construction of rafts made of papyrus reeds, which grew abundantly in the marshlands, enabled the groups stretched along the river to be in continuous contact. Technologies of tool making, copper mining, irrigation, swamp drainage, and stone carving spread accordingly (see Map 1.4).

Given the ubiquity of arable land along the river, the earliest Egyptians did not congregate in cities but instead spread out more or less evenly in hundreds of small villages; hence the first organized states emerged as regional groupings, called **nomes**, along segments of the river. These nomes eventually coalesced into larger units, until finally, around 3150 BCE, the entire kingdom was unified under a single ruler. Tradition credits a man named Menes with the feat; after him Egyptian kings wore a crown that joined the characteristics of crowns of the earlier rulers of Lower Egypt and Upper Egypt.[10] (Many scholars have replaced the semilegendary Menes with Narmer, whose position as first ruler of a united Egypt is corroborated by an engraved palette that illustrates the combined kingship.) The division of Egypt's history into thirty dynasties was the invention of a native historian of the Hellenistic era named Manetho, after Alexander the Great had conquered the kingdom in 332 BCE. Scholars have since tinkered with the details but have kept Manetho's general scheme.

---

[10] The word pharaoh, which means "palace" or "great house," did not come into general use until 1500 BCE or so. Since the Egyptians believed their ruler to be a god, to speak his name aloud was blasphemy.

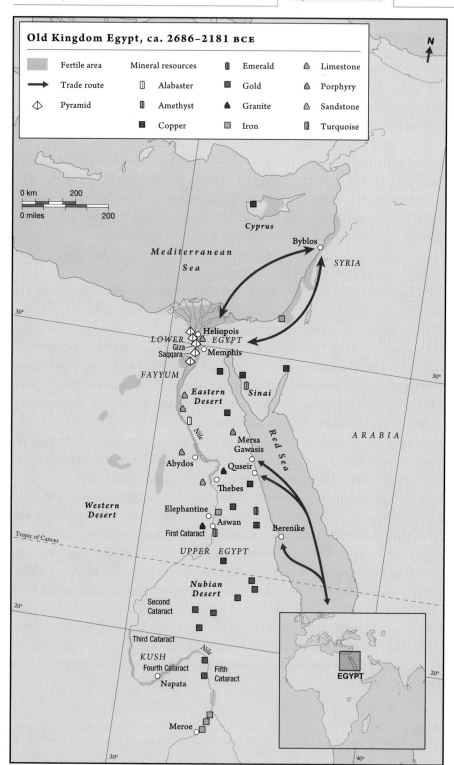

MAP 1.4   Ancient Egypt, ca. 2686–2181 BCE

Narmer Palette   This plaque commemorates King Narmer (a.k.a. Menes—Old Kingdom pharaohs had as many as five names each), the first ruler to unite Lower and Upper Egypt. The front image *(left)* portrays Narmer as he prepares to smash the skull of a rival with a mace. To the right the god Horus, in the shape of a falcon, brings him captives. Narmer wears a kilt, with the tail of a bull (symbolic of strength) attached to his backside. The reverse side of the plaque *(right)* shows another bull, at the bottom, breaking through the fortifications of a city and trampling a victim, while above, servants attend to two great beasts whose long necks are entwined, a scene that presumably represents the union of the Lower and Upper Kingdoms. On top, a ruler with his servants carries banners and the spoils of war.

An identifiable Egyptian civilization thus took shape at roughly the same time that organized Sumerian society began—around the start of the third millennium BCE. This corresponds with the appearance of writing in both societies. The Egyptians—who had established trade relations with the Sumerians by that early time—may have acquired the idea of writing from Mesopotamia. Unlike the Sumerian cuneiform, however, the Egyptians developed a system of **hieroglyphs** (literally, "sacred carving"), based on a combination of pictograms and phonetic

Ancient Egypt
Archaic Period: 3150–2686 BCE (Dynasties 1–2)
Old Kingdom: 2686–2134 BCE (Dynasties 3–6)
First Intermediate Period: 2134–2035 BCE (Dynasties 7–10)
Middle Kingdom: 2035–1640 BCE (Dynasties 11–12)
Second Intermediate Period: 1640–1570 BCE (Dynasties 13–17)
New Kingdom: 1570–1070 BCE (Dynasties 18–20)
Third Intermediate Period: 1070–664 BCE (Dynasties 21–26)
Late Period: 664–332 BCE (Dynasties 27–30)

signs. The Egyptians wrote on a kind of paper made of woven strips of papyrus reed that was much easier to use than the Sumerians' clay tablets, and which made it possible for Egyptian scribes to devise two cursive scripts (known as demotic and hieratic scripts) that made record keeping considerably easier. As a result, the written records of Egypt vastly exceed those of Mesopotamia in both number and variety, and the arid condition of the local environment enabled them to survive the long centuries more or less intact. For the first four dynasties, in fact, more of their writings survive than the buildings they lived in, for the latter were made of baked mud brick, which erodes rapidly even in Egypt's dry climate. They reserved expensive stone for the palaces and tombs of the wealthy and for the temples presided over by the influential priestly caste.

SOCIAL STRATA IN EGYPT

Society was strictly stratified, and social distinctions were expressed by dress codes. Most Egyptians worked the land. Slavery existed but was not as widespread as in Mesopotamia. Egypt's relative insulation from outsiders deprived it of the main source of slaves: prisoners of war. Besides, the pharaoh had an unquestioned right to force his subjects to join labor crews for public-works projects. Slightly above the farmers in social status were the simple artisans: brewers, weavers, stonemasons, bricklayers; even higher were the makers of luxury items for the elites: goldsmiths, jewelry makers, perfumers. A smaller corps of professionals stood above these: physicians, scribes, architects, priests, and civic officials. In theory, all Egyptians were equal under the law regardless of class or sex, and even the lowliest farmer could hope to petition the vizier for redress of a legal complaint; but that was theory, not reality.

Monogamous marriage was the norm for Egyptians, although it was not required by law, and men of all classes frequently took additional wives or concubines. Women, however, were subject to harsh legal punishment and social ostracism for engaging in sex outside of marriage to a single husband. Both sexes, though, could own property, enter contracts, and settle disputes in court.

The basic Egyptian diet consisted of varieties of grain—whether as bread, gruel, or beer—supplemented with a few vegetables (leeks, garlic, squash, and lettuce, especially), along with figs, dates, and fish. Meat was a rare treat for commoners, as was wine. Two other food practices date back to the Old Kingdom: the keeping of bee colonies, for honey and wax, and the netting of wild geese as they followed their own food trail along the river's edges.[11] June to September was the

---

[11]   The Egyptians learned early the trick of fattening the geese by feeding them large quantities of raw bread dough.

flooding season, October to February saw the growing of the grain fields, and March to May was the harvest. Given the brutal heat, most Egyptians wore little clothing. Children, in fact, generally went naked until they entered puberty, and it was common for men to shave and oil their entire bodies. Most peoples' homes, too, were designed to offset the heat: simple mud brick, often painted white, remained relatively cool throughout the day, and all cooking was done in small open-air patios. They covered their homes' packed-earth floors with reed mats. Egyptians followed a solar calendar but never developed the technological tools or scientific expertise of the Sumerians. Even wheeled vehicles did not appear until the New Kingdom, ca. 1500 BCE.

Ruler worship dominated Old Egyptian life—or at least it was the dominant characteristic of the regimes that produced the evidentiary record. The pharaoh was a living god, the source of justice and stability, the munificent owner of the whole of Egypt and its people, and the embodiment of the people's hopes and love. This official adoration was ubiquitous, endless, and drearily constant for nearly two thousand years. Officials who wanted to remain in the pharaoh's good graces had to adopt a fawning, obsequious tone that makes a modern reader squirm:

> To the great King, my Lord, the Sun-God from Heaven, thus I, Prince Zatatna of Acre, Your servant, the most humble servant of the Great King—indeed, the very dirt beneath Your feet, the ground upon which You tread—sends greeting. Seven times, O Great King, seven times, O Sun-God from Heaven, I fall, prostrate and helpless, at Your feet.

So began a typical piece of provincial administration. The unremitting glorification given to the pharaoh in the third and second millennia BCE, much of it on a colossal scale, would have brought an envious tear to the eye of many a 20th-century fascist dictator. The great pyramids and the monumental sculptures in the Valley of Kings tell only part of the tale. In the New Kingdom era the priests wrested power from the pharaoh and tried to govern independently. Consequently—or possibly not, depending on how one reads the evidence—Egyptian wealth and power diminished considerably. For now, though, statues of the pharaohs adorned every temple; inscriptions praising their magnificence appeared in every city; hymns in their honor rang out in every religious service.

From their palace at the capital city of Memphis, strategically and symbolically located at the point where the Delta joined the long river valley of Upper Egypt, the pharaohs controlled every aspect of public life through cults of personality backed up by armies of bureaucratic and military officials. Each nome was administered by a nomarch appointed by the king, and they all reported to a central official called a vizier. The nomarchs oversaw all public works projects, coordinated food distribution, heard appeals, and dispensed justice. Assisting all these was an army of scribes who kept census records, tallied tax revenues, noted expenditures, and issued the government's decrees. Members of the royal family held many of these posts.

Few states in Western history have experienced such completely centralized rule. Despite its invention and wide use of writing, however, Egypt never bothered to write down the laws of the land. Since the pharaoh, a living god, walked the earth, whatever he said at any moment was, in effect, the law. When he, in a carefully calculated moment, summoned the Nile to begin its annual rise, the river duly responded; the sun shone at his command; the earth produced its bounty because he willed it. And a ruler mighty enough to command the very Earth's obedience did not hesitate to demand the submission of its inhabitants. Slavery was thus regular but not widespread, for the common people were in fact expected to obey the pharaoh's every expressed whim without hesitation or complaint. The pharaoh was understood to be the god Horus. When he died he became an even greater deity by being absorbed into Osiris, an amalgam of all pharaohs merged into one, the ruler of the underworld where his absolutist authority never ended. Royal officials received estates from the pharaoh in return for their service, rather than salaries. The pharaohs likewise endowed mortuary cults and temples in order to promote the worship of themselves after their deaths on earth.

> Few states in Western history have experienced such completely centralized rule. Despite its invention and wide use of writing, however, Egypt never bothered to write down the laws of the land. Since the pharaoh, a living god, walked the earth, whatever he said at any moment was, in effect, the law.

It was an efficient way to govern, to be sure, and under benevolent rulers and judicious officials ancient Egypt enjoyed a material standard of living that vastly exceeded that of any contemporary society, until the end of the Old Kingdom (ca. 2100 BCE). By then, the pharaohs had alienated so much of their land that they began to have trouble meeting their vast administrative costs, prompting the nomarchs to challenge royal power for the first time and thereby inaugurating the First Intermediate Period. Old Kingdom glories should not be overstated, though. In the early centuries, contentment among the population often consisted simply of the absence of famine and the presence of peace, with little more to enrich daily life. By those standards pharaonic Egypt succeeded beyond expectations, but the achievement was nature's rather than the Egyptians'. Safe from foreign aggression because of the surrounding deserts, easily unified by the quiet-flowing Nile, and fed by the abundance of grain and fruit sprouting along its banks, Egypt had only not to disturb nature's rhythms in order to reap its rewards.

Accordingly, the supreme virtue of Egyptian culture was **ma'at**—a recognition of the world's ordering and a commitment not to upset it. Scholars commonly translate ma'at as "justice," which is too generous. Ma'at, in practice, was a kind of moral stasis, an acceptance of the world as it is, a reluctance to change anything for fear that the result might be worse than the reality already experienced. Early Egypt thus embodied a conservative principle that may be its most significant legacy to Western culture.

The contrast between it and the tumultuous but dynamic societies of Mesopotamia is striking. In Sumer, a messy congeries of cultures was in perennial conflict—challenging, experimenting, wondering, often failing, but always adapting to new circumstances and incessantly searching for meaning in the apparent jumble of it all. In archaic Egypt, the theocracy held power for two thousand years by feeding its subjects' stomachs while starving their minds by turning passivity into the supreme civic virtue.

THE KINGDOM OF THE DEAD

Old Kingdom Egypt lacked much of the variety and sophistication of the Middle and New periods; its life revolved obsessively, and monotonously, around the pharaoh. Even its religious life proved to be another aspect of pharaoh worship. Egyptian religion was a mix of local myths and traditions that defies easy description. Each nome revered a specific local deity, most of them animal-shaped, and a statue of whom stood in the local temple, and whose cults formed the center of village religious life. The temple statue was believed to be the god or goddess, not merely to represent him or her; individual homes often would have small statuettes to the deity in a corner, to whom the people offered small gifts of grain, oil, or wine at mealtimes.

A company of major deities ruled over the local gods, and probably served to create a sense of a shared culture among the peoples of Lower and Upper Egypt. One of these major gods, named Ptah, was credited with creating the world, but beyond this he played little role in Egyptian mythology. The most important deities by far were the incestuous brother and sister Osiris and Isis, whose love for each other set the whole cosmology in motion. Osiris became the first god-king of the earth that Ptah had created; but his brother Seth, jealous of Osiris's kingship and possibly of his relations with Isis, killed Osiris, chopped him up, and scattered bits of his body all the length of the Nile. Distraught, Isis searched out every piece and with the help of Anubis, the god of mummification, reassembled Osiris's body, bringing it miraculously back to life just long enough for Isis to enjoy one last sexual union with her brother, who promptly died again after completing the deed. But the job was done: Isis became pregnant and in time gave birth to the

A Section from a Book of the Dead Scroll   The scroll was prepared for—and possibly even by—a royal scribe named Hunefer. Thebes, ca. 1275 BCE. The god Anubis brings Hunefer (*far left*) into the judging chamber, watched over by Isis and Osiris (*far right*). In the middle scene Hunefer's heart is weighed in the scales against the feather that symbolizes ma'at. The weighing is successful, and Hunefer then approaches the enthroned Osiris to receive his reward. Isis stands behind the throne. The Hunefer Scroll is among the best known of surviving Book of the Dead texts. Since the outcome of the judgments was seldom in doubt, it was not unusual or blasphemous for a well-placed scribe like Hunefer to prepare his own scroll and depict his own salvation after death.

god Horus—who eventually grew to manhood, avenged his father by killing Seth, and took over the rulership of the world. Every pharaoh was thus believed to be a new incarnation of Horus, the god himself walking the earth. And upon his death every pharaoh transformed into Osiris, who ruled over the realm of the dead for eternity.

The Isis-Osiris myth remained central to Egyptian culture for thousands of years, until it was supplanted by Christianity in the early centuries CE—which was itself replaced by Islam in the 7th and 8th centuries CE. As a tale of resurrection, of life defeating death, it leaves something to be desired. Osiris, after all, was revived only briefly. He came and he went. Nevertheless, his tale expressed at least the notion of life's renewal, a cycle of generation, death, and regeneration that paralleled the rhythm of flood, planting, and harvest along the great Nile's banks. Temples and statues to Isis and Osiris were erected all throughout the kingdom and reminded people everywhere of the universality of the pharaoh's authority. In the afterworld Osiris judged the souls of the dead pharaohs before admitting them to his realm—a realm that was remarkably similar to life along the Nile. Not a better life but simply *more* life, which the Egyptians seem to have regarded as blessing enough. Common people in the Old Kingdom received vastly simpler burials, the arable land on the bank being too precious to use for commoners' graves. Buried well away from the great pyramid valleys and far from the Nile Itself, they were assumed to move easily into the afterworld—where they continued to farm, mine, and manufacture, in service to the redeemed pharaohs forever.

Admission to the afterworld was not automatic for a pharaoh, yet neither was it tied closely to ethical behavior in his lifetime. Their religion held that the soul of the deceased wandered through a dim wasteland, beset by various demon-spirits, in search of the House of Judgment where Osiris, along with forty-two other judges, would decide whether or not the dead soul could enter. One could in theory remain lost in the wasteland for eternity, but the ancient Egyptians fortunately possessed a canon of helpful texts that led one to paradise. These incantations, magic spells, proclamations, and hymns were inscribed on the walls of the royal tombs—hence their collective name of Pyramid Texts. These texts guided the dead through the wasteland and provided sets of prayers and incantations that could be used against the demons. Moreover, they supplied the answers needed to satisfy the questions posed by Osiris and the other judges. With such scripted clues, the pharaoh's eternal reward was assured. After passing the examination, the dead ruler then made a final solemn declaration:

> I have not done evil to mankind.
> I have not oppressed the members of my family. . . .
> I have not brought forward my name for exaltation to honors.
> I have not ill-treated servants.
> I have not belittled a god.
> I have not defrauded the oppressed of their property.
> I have not done that which is an abomination to the gods. . . .
> I have made no man to suffer hunger.
> I have made no one to weep.
> I have done no murder.
> I have not given an order for murder to be done for me.
> I have not inflicted pain. . . .
> I have not committed fornication. . . .
> I have not encroached on the fields of others. . . .
> I have not cut into a canal of running water. . . .
> I have not obstructed a god in his procession
> *I am pure! I am pure! I am pure! I am pure!*

After which the god Anubis weighed the dead pharaoh's heart on a scale, and if the purified heart weighed no more than a feather, the soul was admitted to the eternal presence of Osiris.

Religion thus had little, perhaps nothing, to do with ethics. Whether one received reward or torment in Osiris's realm depended not on the quality of one's life but simply on whether or not the pharaoh received the proper send-off; hence the obscene expense on pyramids, tomb-temples, and burial gifts. The departed pharaoh's confession before Osiris lacks any positive spirit of morality; virtue consists of not performing evil rather than actively doing good. Just as ma'at did not equal justice, so too did the spiritual purity that entitled one to enter paradise imply nothing more than formulaic correctness. In the earliest centuries only members of the royal family could receive the supreme reward, but the privilege of salvation was extended to the nobles in the Middle Kingdom period, and to all Egyptians generally—although only in the New Kingdom many centuries later.

While it lacked the emotional complexity of Sumerian religion, Egyptian religion possessed an attractively hopeful belief in the unstoppable resilience of life. Death, while not exactly a thing to be yearned for, did not need to be feared. It represented only a rite of passage—not into an Eden but back to the shores of the Nile, where time would run as endlessly as the great river itself.

WHO, WHAT, WHERE

Bronze Age
cuneiform
Fertile Crescent
hieroglyphs
lugal

ma'at
nomes
patrilinear
ziggurats

SUGGESTED READINGS

Primary Sources

The text of Ur-Ukagina's law code on pages 15–16 is adapted from Nels M. Bailkey and Richard Lim, *Readings in Ancient History: Thought and Experience from Gilgamesh to St. Augustine*, 6th ed. (Boston, 2002), p. 20. The Shamash Hymn is found in Bailkey and Lim, p. 22.

"The Poem of the Righteous Sufferer" is found in W. G. Lambert, *Babylonian Wisdom Literature* (Oxford, 1960), pp. 31–35. The Book of the Dead and The Pyramid Texts can be found in *Ancient Egyptian Literature* (Berkeley, 2006) by Miriam Lichtheim.

Anthologies

Bailkey, Nels, and Richard Lim, eds. *Readings in Ancient History: Thought and Experience from Gilgamesh to St. Augustine* (2002).

Bryce, Trevor. *Letters of the Great Kings of the Ancient Near East: The Royal Correspondence of the Late Bronze Age* (2003).

Foster, John L., trans. *Ancient Egyptian Literature: An Anthology* (2001).

Glassner, Jean-Jacques. *Mesopotamian Chronicles* (2004).

Lichtheim, Miriam. *Ancient Egyptian Literature: A Book of Readings* (2006).

Vanstiphout, Herman. *Epics of the Sumerian Kings: The Matter of Aratta* (2004).

Studies

Anthony, David W. *The Horse, the Wheel, and Language: How Bronze-Age Riders from the Eurasian Steppes Shaped the Modern World* (2010).

Aruz, Joan. *Art of the First Cities: The Third Millennium BC from the Mediterranean to the Indus* (2003).

Assmann, Jan. *The Mind of Egypt: History and Meaning in the Time of the Pharaohs* (2003).

———. *The Search for God in Ancient Egypt* (2001).

Bottéro, Jean. *Everyday Life in Ancient Mesopotamia* (2001).

———. *Religion in Ancient Mesopotamia* (2004).

Brewer, Douglas J., and Emily Teeter. *Egypt and the Egyptians* (2007).

Charvát, Petr. *Mesopotamia before History* (2002).

Crawford, Harriet. *Sumer and Sumerians* (2004).

Foster, Benjamin R., and Karen Polinger Foster. *Civilizations of Ancient Iraq* (2010).

Glassner, Jean-Jacques. *The Invention of Cuneiform: Writing in Sumer* (2003).

Harris, David R. *Origins of Agriculture in West Central Asia: An Environmental-Archaeological Study* (2010).

Hodder, Ian. *The Leopard's Tale: Revealing the Mysteries of Çatalhöyük* (2006).

Kemp, Barry J. *Ancient Egypt: Anatomy of a Civilization* (2006).

Leick, Gwendolyn. *Mesopotamia: The Invention of the City* (2003).

———. *Sex and Eroticism in Mesopotamian Literature* (2003).

Liverani, Mario. *Uruk: The First City* (2006).

Robins, Gay. *The Art of Ancient Egypt* (2008).

Silverman, David P., ed. *Ancient Egypt* (2003).

For additional resources, including maps, primary sources, visuals, web links, and quizzes, please go to **www.oup.com/us/backman**.

CHAPTER 2

Law Givers, Evil Emperors, and Dangerous Gods

2100 BCE–486 BCE

NEAR EAST AND EASTERN MEDITERRANEAN

The second millennium BCE can hardly be topped for drama. Droughts, famines, civil wars, foreign invasions, frightful new weapons, and brutal empires—all these characterized the age and marked its major turning points. Four empires dominated the era: Egypt's Middle and New Kingdoms, the Babylonian (and later Persian) Empire in southern Mesopotamia, the Assyrian Empire of northern Mesopotamia, and the Hittite Empire in Asia Minor. Between these powerful kingdoms lay a sprawl of smaller states along the eastern Mediterranean coastline and skirting the southern edges of the Anatolian mountains. Once established, this patchwork of big and small states lived in relative harmony, in a dense web of commercial, cultural, and diplomatic connections that inspired some remarkable advances in each society.

Around 1200 BCE, however, newcomers appeared—outsiders loosely related by their dialects of a new language family known as Indo-European. Their waves of invasion set off a chain reaction of political collapse and economic ruin that wiped out nearly every state in the Near East. It left the peoples adrift and unsure, vulnerable to new regimes, and exposed to new ideas about human fate, man's relationship with the divine, the purpose of government, and the essence of morality. By 1000 BCE, or thereabouts, Western history had taken on a radical realignment that would have been unthinkable only two hundred years earlier. This realignment led to the birth of Western culture's first two great religions, Judaism and Zoroastrianism.

Moreover, the interaction of the Indo-European groups and the primarily Semitic

◀ **Imperial Warrior** A Persian archer, part of a procession, in glazed brick. From the palace of Darius the Great in Susa (550–486 BCE). These elite soldiers served as the king's personal bodyguards.

- Old Babylon
- Middle Kingdom Egypt
- The New Kingdom Empire
- The Indo-European Assault
- The Age of Iron Begins, ca. 1200 BCE
- Persia and the Religion of Fire

CHAPTER OUTLINE

peoples of the Fertile Crescent opened the way for the development of the **Greater West**—a world that bridged Europe and western Asia. This Greater West was composed not of a single hybrid culture but rather of the sense of a shared destiny in a large matrix of individual cultures. Europe and the Middle East have remained bound into and with one another ever since, by bonds of trade, intellectual cross-fertilization, cultural overlap, and religious rivalry.

OLD BABYLON

The city of Babylon was founded around 1950 BCE by the Semitic-speaking Amorites, who seized control of Sumer soon after the turn of the second millennium. Its location at the nexus of several trade routes through the northern Mesopotamian plain made it a strategic base for extending power out of Sumer itself and northward toward Syria, from which the Amorites themselves had come. The most famous of the early Babylonian rulers was Hammurabi (r. 1792–1750 BCE), the first great lawgiver and liar in Western history. A large archive of his diplomatic records survive, which document his crafty rise to power. At the start of his reign Babylon was simply one among many Amorite kingdoms and was by no means the largest or strongest. Unable or unwilling to challenge his neighbors on the battlefield, he instead managed to persuade all of them of the existence of numerous conspiracies against their crowns. He passed endless false rumors, usually of his own making and reiterated in person by his many ambassadors. They warned each city-state of a plot supposedly being hatched in another. Believing the lies, the other Amorite kings continually attacked one another for nearly twenty years and exhausted themselves in the process. Hammurabi then went on the offensive and in less than a decade conquered them all. He emerged as the sole ruler of virtually the entire Tigris-Euphrates region; thus was built the great Babylonian Empire (see Map 2.1).

Shortly thereafter, he issued a set of laws known as the Code of Hammurabi, texts of which presumably were distributed throughout the empire. He likewise

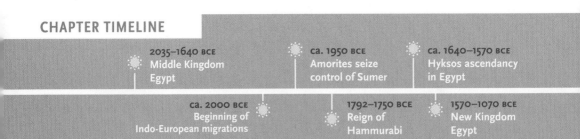

CHAPTER TIMELINE

2035–1640 BCE Middle Kingdom Egypt	**ca. 1950 BCE** Amorites seize control of Sumer	**ca. 1640–1570 BCE** Hyksos ascendancy in Egypt
ca. 2000 BCE Beginning of Indo-European migrations	**1792–1750 BCE** Reign of Hammurabi	**1570–1070 BCE** New Kingdom Egypt

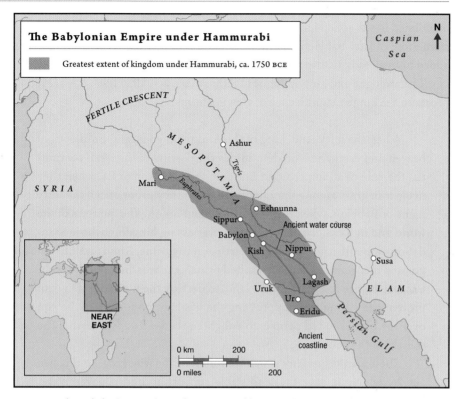

MAP 2.1   The Babylonian Empire under Hammurabi

had the entire Code engraved upon an eight-foot column of basalt, as a permanent record of his greatness as a ruler. As propaganda, the Code could hardly have been more successful, since scholars have credited Hammurabi as the first great lawgiver in Western history ever since. Ironically, though, the Code is not in fact a true law code: it contains only 282 clauses, addressing issues like property rights, water rights, marriage, violent crime, and wage regulations. It neglects to mention many equally vital aspects of Babylonian life, such as the commercial marketplace that formed the lifeblood of the economy. More significantly, the Code is never

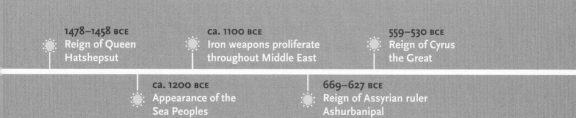

1478–1458 BCE
Reign of Queen
Hatshepsut

ca. 1100 BCE
Iron weapons proliferate
throughout Middle East

559–530 BCE
Reign of Cyrus
the Great

ca. 1200 BCE
Appearance of the
Sea Peoples

669–627 BCE
Reign of Assyrian ruler
Ashurbanipal

mentioned in the actual judicial records that survive from Hammurabi's reign or from those of later Babylonian kings. Its statutes may simply represent new laws added to an already-existing body of legislation.[1]

The prologue and long epilogue together make up half of the Code's text and proclaim the king's magnificence in glowing terms:

> When the lofty Anu, king of the Anunnaki gods, and Enlil, lord of heaven and earth, he who determines the destiny of the land, committed the rule of all mankind to Marduk, the chief son of Ea; when they made him great among the Igigi gods; when they pronounced the lofty name of Babylon; when they made it famous among the quarters of the world and in its midst established an everlasting kingdom whose foundations were firm as heaven and earth—at that time, Anu and Enlil appointed me, Hammurabi, the exalted prince, the worshiper of the gods, to cause justice to prevail in the land, to destroy the wicked and evil, to prevent the strong from oppressing the weak, to go forth like the sun over the black-headed people, to enlighten the land and to further the welfare of the people. . . .
>
> These are the just laws which Hammurabi, the wise king, established and by which he gave the land stable support and good government. Hammurabi, the perfect king, am I. . . . The great gods called me, and I am the guardian shepherd whose scepter is just and whose beneficent shadow is spread over my city. In my bosom I carried the people of the land of Sumer and Addad; under my protection they prospered; I governed them in peace; in my wisdom I sheltered them. . . . The king who is pre-eminent among kings am I. My words are precious, my wisdom is unrivaled. By the command of Shamash, the great judge of heaven and earth, I make justice to shine forth on the land. By the order of Marduk, my lord, no one may scorn my statutes, and my name shall be remembered with favor in Esagila forever. . . . In the days that are yet to come, for all future time, may the king who is in the land observe the words of justice which I have written upon my monument! May he not alter the judgments of the land which I have pronounced, or the decisions of the country which I have rendered! May he not scorn my statutes! If that man have wisdom, if he wish to give his land good government, let him give attention to the words which I have written upon my monument! And may this monument enlighten him as to procedure and administration, the judgments which

---

[1]   Could Hammurabi have created the Code primarily as a monument to himself?

I have pronounced, and the decisions I have rendered for the land! And let him rightly rule his black-headed people; let him pronounce judgments for them and render for them decisions! Let him root out the wicked and the evil from his land! Let him promote the welfare of his people! Hammurabi, the king of justice, to whom Shamash has committed truth, am I. My words are weighty; my deeds are unrivalled; only to the fool are they vain; to the wise they are worthy of every praise.

The actual statutes of the Code seem an afterthought in comparison.

Despite its cultic bluster, the Code tells us much about how Babylonian society differed from the Sumerian one it supplanted; in fact, the bluster itself tells much of the tale. As we saw in chapter 1, the Sumerian chief military executive (or lugal), assisted by scribes and priests, had supervised a battery of local officials—with a complex web of traders, craftsmen, and farmers. The Babylonians replaced this norm with a top-heavy and decidedly heavy-handed plutocracy. Hammurabi's conquests had resulted in the monopolization of wealth by his royal court and armed supporters. Vast estates and commercial concerns controlled by the Babylonian elites took the place of the more diverse economy of the Sumerians. Most of Babylonia's inhabitants remained legally free but were nevertheless land tenants or commercial dependents of the nobles who dominated the palaces and temples. The Babylonians also expanded the use of slave labor on their estates and began to buy and sell slaves on the international market.

Social stratification was more rigid as well, and the penalties for offenses against one's superiors were severe. Women of all classes, except for slaves, had the right to divorce abusive husbands and to receive financial support from husbands who divorced them without good cause. Capital punishment was meted out unhesitatingly for any number

Propaganda Device   The top portion of the stele on which is inscribed the Law Code of Hammurabi, ca. 1700 BCE.

of crimes—murder, assault, rape, theft, and adultery (applicable to women only) were the most common—but the means varied according to sex: men were killed by the blade, women by drowning.

Hammurabi also introduced a form of religious imperialism that both paralleled and legitimated his political oppression. The worship of Marduk, the patron god of the city of Babylon, became required throughout the empire; Hammurabi's subjects could continue to worship their old gods only if they accepted Marduk as the supreme Babylonian deity. Interpreting his military conquests as the worldly enactment of Marduk's spiritual victory over all other gods and goddesses, Hammurabi stands at the beginning of a long Western tradition of justifying warfare as a religious duty. If the Divine Authority demands that His followers engage in warfare—and indeed if He in some sense needs them to do it in order to fulfill His own cosmic aims—then what else can pious followers do? Such warfare is not only morally justifiable, because divinely sanctioned, but is in fact an act of religious devotion itself.

> Interpreting his military conquests as the worldly enactment of Marduk's spiritual victory over all other gods and goddesses, Hammurabi stands at the beginning of a long Western tradition of justifying warfare as a religious duty.

It is striking how frequently religious warfare, like Hammurabi's conquests, occurs throughout Greater Western history. We shall see it again and again in later chapters: the milhemet mitzvah ("war of religious obligation") that inspired the Hebrews to seize their Promised Land from the Canaanites, Philistines, and Amalikites; the jihad-stoked conquests of the medieval Muslims and the Crusades of medieval Christians; the Wars of Religion of 16th-17th century Europe; the efforts to tame the "Godless heathen" of the New World or "to bring Christianity to the savages" of Africa in the 18th and 19th centuries; the fight for "God and country" in World War I; and the struggle against "Godless communism" in the second half of the 20th century. In each case, when it comes to war and religion, each justifies and inspires the other. Western culture is not unique in this regard, of course, and wars without an explicitly religious motive have been equally numerous, but religiously based conflict is a notably recurring element in Western history. Hammurabi is our first religious zealot, and the society he created, though it lasted only two centuries after his death, left a bitter legacy of lies, greed, and smug brutality. Few people mourned the passing of the Old Babylonian Empire.

It did produce a literary masterpiece, however. An anonymous Babylonian scribe gathered a number of folktales about the semimythical Sumerian king Gilgamesh—ruler of Uruk some eight hundred years before the Babylonian conquest—and wove them together into an epic of remarkable sophistication. The *Epic of Gilgamesh* relates the adventures of a powerful but egotistical king whose arrogance leads him to offend the gods. Unexpectedly, the gods' subsequent plot to kill him fails when Gilgamesh tames the savage half-man half-beast Enkidu, whom they had sent to destroy him, and the two become friends and pursue a series of heroic adventures. When the gods strike again by slaying his beloved new friend, Gilgamesh is filled with panic at the inevitability of death. He spends the rest of the epic on a doomed quest for enlightenment and the secret to eternal life.

The poem notably credits women for their civilizing influence on men. Enkidu, for example, is tamed by an encounter with a temple priestess:

> The lass beheld him, the savage man,
> The barbarous fellow from the depths of the steppe. . . .
> [She] freed her breasts, bared her bosom,
> and he possessed her ripeness.
> She was not bashful as she welcomed his ardor.

They spend six days and seven nights in nonstop passion; then Enkidu undergoes a transformation that estranges him from the other animals of the steppe:

> After he had had his fill of her charms,
> He set his face toward his wild beasts.
> On seeing him, the gazelles ran off,
> The wild beasts of the steppe drew away from [him]. . . .
> His [legs] became motionless. . . . Things were not as they were before.
> Now he had wisdom, broader understanding.
> Returning he sat at the feet of the harlot. . . . She says to him,
> "Thou art wise now, Enkidu; thou art become like a god."

Gilgamesh himself, seeking to drown his sorrows after Enkidu's death, receives some sensible advice from a kindly barmaid who is actually the grain goddess Sippur in human form:

> Gilgamesh, . . . the life thou pursueth, thou shalt not find.
> When the gods created mankind,
> Death for mankind they set aside,
> Life in their own hands retaining.
> Thou, Gilgamesh, let full be thy belly,
> Make thou merry by day and by night.
> Of each day make thou a feast of rejoicing,
> Day and night dance thou and play!

> Let thy garments be sparkling fresh,
> Thy head be washed; bathe thou in water.
> Pay heed to the little one that holds on to thy hand,
> Let thy spouse delight in thy bosom!
> For this is the task of mankind!

Gilgamesh, however, obsessively continues his quest and learns of a magic plant growing on the floor of the sea. Whoever pulls the plant from its root and eats it will in fact gain eternal life. Eventually Gilgamesh locates the plant by tying heavy stones to his feet and walking the ocean floor. When he arrives back on shore and is about to eat the plant, however, a giant serpent emerges from the sea, snatches the plant from his hand, and pulls it back to the depths. Gilgamesh is left alone and hopeless on the shore, doomed to the death he could not avoid.

The poem depicts old Sumerian culture but was written down, in the full version in which it survives, in Babylonian times and in the Babylonian tongue. Little seems added to the original Sumerian folktales. The Babylonian compiler merely changed the names of several of the characters and of the gods into Babylonian ones. Thus the figure who tells Gilgamesh about the Plant of Life is named Ziusudra in the Sumerian fragments that survive but is called Utnapishtim, a Babylonian name, in the full compiled version. Was the compiler merely trying to make the text more appealing to a Babylonian audience?[2]

A more subversive aim is possible too: perhaps the poet or compiler hoped the epic could inspire the Babylonians to strive after something more than the wealth and power they hoarded so single-mindedly. Gilgamesh at the beginning of the poem is arrogant, self-centered, and boastful. He sounds more than a bit like Hammurabi in the bombastic claims of the Code. At the end he is broken, fearful, and sad beyond expression, but he has grown into spiritual maturity. He has become deserving of pity and even forgiveness.

MIDDLE KINGDOM EGYPT

The erosion of royal authority, beginning in the Fifth Dynasty of the Old Kingdom, brought about the First Intermediate Period in Egypt (2135–2034 BCE). In this relatively brief but turbulent period, the local nomarchs usurped royal power, plundered farmers' property, and engaged in widespread lawlessness. Mentuhotep II, the first pharaoh of the Eleventh Dynasty, however, was able to subdue the nomarchs and restore central authority from Thebes. It was the start of several

---

[2]   Was the compiler of *Gilgamesh* trying to depict Babylonians as something more than greedy, venal, boorish oppressors?

periods of empire, including reigns of the most active and powerful pharaohs and the origins of a new religious tradition, monotheism.

Mentuhotep II's reign ushered in the Middle Kingdom (2035–1640). Thebes lay in Upper Egypt, roughly three hundred miles south of the traditional capital at Memphis. Moving the capital there allowed for closer oversight of the nomarchs. It also provided a base for launching new military expeditions southward, up the great river, into Nubia, in order to secure control of the strategic cataracts and to acquire the vast stone quarries and gold deposits found there.

With restored fortunes, the pharaohs of the Middle Kingdom were able to renew public building programs—such as land reclamation in the delta and the extension of irrigation networks and reservoirs along the river. They could even pursue military expansion beyond Egypt's natural borders, into Sinai and along the Syrian coast. These projects required more laborers than the local population could provide, however, which led the pharaohs to recruit groups of foreigners (hyksos in Egyptian) to work in the mines and fields. As the number of foreigners grew, especially in the delta, where they were concentrated, and as resistance to their presence grew among the native population, tension arose. This tension eventually resulted in an overthrow of the government by the foreigners, an uprising that inaugurated the Second Intermediate Period (1640–1570 BCE), which is sometimes referred to as the **Hyksos ascendancy**.

Egyptian religion continued to be a myriad of local cults rather than a single organized faith. The cults remained *henotheistic*: while they recognized the existence of other deities, each locale proclaimed allegiance to a particular god or goddess as their special protector. In the case of the pharaoh's court, new prominence was won by Amon-Ra, the patron deity of the city of Thebes. The most significant development in religion, however, was the extension of salvation (that is, entry to the House of Judgment) to the nomarchs, other nobles, and wealthy commoners. The heavenly reward was no longer a monopoly of the pharaohs. The cause of this development is unknown, but the means of it is clear: the contents of the Pyramid Texts began to circulate among the well-to-do. They were also inscribed onto papyrus books, or coffin texts, placed alongside the bodies in their tombs.

By the end of this period, the various coffin texts had been consolidated into the **Book of the Dead**, the only full-length text of any sort that Egypt contributed to Western literature until the 19th century. This book, when placed in a casket, theoretically opened the gates of paradise, such as it was, to anyone who died with it in his or her possession. The Book of the Dead, though, is not a work of literary art; it is an anthology of incantations, magical spells, boilerplate praise poems, and cribbed solutions to the riddles put to one by Osiris at the entrance to the House of Judgment. Although of great historical interest, these writings are negligible as poetry or prose musings. Ma'at, acceptance of the world's right ordering, remains the dominant

Voyage to the Next World   This wonderfully preserved wooden coffin held the remains of a Middle Kingdom priest named Nekhtankh. The hieroglyphs invoke the gods Osiris, Isis, Nephthys, and others to provide Nekhtankh with all the food and comforts he will need in the afterlife. The vivid eyes represent the priest's soul looking expectantly to the voyage into the next world.

focus and the supreme virtue. To the extent that Osiris and his council truly judged anyone's ethical behavior in life, they did so according to the dead soul's record of sustaining ma'at, which in most cases meant not performing injustice.

The Middle Kingdom did produce an exceptionally large body of writing—mythological stories, folktales, handbooks of practical advice, medical regimens, travelogues, some earnest love poetry, personal letters, and professional treatises (on being a successful merchant, civil administrator, estate manager, or whatever). Few of them interest anyone other than specialists, however. The mix suggests that the intellectual tenor of the age was above all else pragmatic and hardworking—no nonsense about theoretical or abstract notions, no deep introspection, no intellectual playfulness or even curiosity. Egypt never produced anything remotely like the *Epic of Gilgamesh* or the works of the ancient Hebrew psalmists and prophets. It never matched the philosophers, tragedians, or epic and lyric poets of ancient Greece. The popular father-to-son advice handbooks—usually called "Instructions"—display a genuine if somewhat formulaic concern for ethical behavior. They urge the recipient to work hard at his trade, to obey his

superiors, and to cultivate a modest demeanor; they praise charitable acts and denounce corruption and exploitation of the poor.[3] Should one fall short of the moral standard, the Book of the Dead was there to help.

The Instructions left behind by several Middle Kingdom pharaohs have an altogether different tenor, one that reflects the less elevated general position they held in comparison to their godlike Old Kingdom predecessors. In his Instruction to his son, Amenemhet I, for example, urges "hold yourself apart from those subordinate to you . . . and be on guard even when you are asleep." Trust no one, neither family nor friend, and be especially watchful of the treacherous nomarchs, he warns. The advice, in this case, was sound: Amenemhet left his Instruction unfinished, and a later scribe completed it with a wry note that the great king had been assassinated by one of the officials in the royal court before he could finish the memo.

Middle Egypt's great arts were architecture and sculpture—practical arts both, since most of the works produced served the purpose of promoting or

---

[3]   The Instructions were not intended for general audiences, which may account for their vaguely memo-like quality.

Ushabti   Funerary figures who accompanied the new dead on their journey were called *ushabtis*. They were the servants of the dead, charged with providing food and water, performing physical labor, and in some cases providing sexual amusement. The hieroglyphs found most frequently on ushabtis quote a passage from the sixth chapter of the Book of the Dead: "Hail, ushabti! If [the deceased] be decreed to do any work in the afterlife, let every task that stands in his way be removed—whether plowing fields, tending the water channels, or carrying sand."

extending the might of the pharaoh. Painting and sculpture followed stylistic and iconographic norms that dated to the Old Kingdom with simple lines, flat surfaces, and a modest palette of colors. Funerary figurines made of clay or wood were exceedingly common. Though simple in design, these figures (called **ushabti**, or "those who respond") represented the servants who continued to work for one in the afterlife. Science and technology mattered little, since Egypt's technological needs were simple and were amply met by the might of the river and the availability of the virtual slave labor of the masses. Mathematical knowledge was not widespread. Government officials probably understood and used all four computational operations—addition, subtraction, multiplication, and division. They employed fractions to a limited extent and were able to estimate the area of a circle by measuring the diameter, subtracting one-ninth of its value, and squaring the result. (Since the area of a circle is in fact πr^2, they in effect approximated p to about 3.16.)[4] Egypt also did not develop wheeled vehicles until the New Kingdom and relied on oxen and donkeys (for plowing and carting, respectively) long after the Babylonians had already domesticated horses for farming and for pulling wheeled chariots.

---

[4]   Only a handful of engineers could handle simple geometry or algebra.

The modest stability of the Middle Kingdom collapsed quickly when the Semitic-speaking foreigners admitted to the realm suddenly rose in revolt and took control of most of the delta region around 1700 BCE. The precise identity of this group is still debated, and Egyptian sources refer to them only as the Hyksos ("foreigners"). Whoever they were, they were aided by the arrival of thousands of their countrymen who had raced across Sinai on light, horse-drawn chariots. Armed with simple bows, long lances, and swords made of bronze, the Hyksos quickly seized control of the Nile delta and forced the rulers in far-southern Thebes to recognize their overlordship. The Hyksos style of warfare unnerved the Egyptians, who used neither cavalry nor archers (since trees to make bows were relatively rare) and had traditionally relied on swarms of infantrymen armed with copper-tipped spears and stone-headed clubs.

For seventy years, from 1640 to 1570 BCE, the Hyksos dominated Egypt while building extensive commercial and diplomatic links with Palestine, Syria, and the islands of the Aegean Sea. During that time the Nubians to the far south broke away from the rulers in Thebes and established an independent kingdom called Kush. The Theban rulers thus found themselves trapped between foreigners at each end of the Nile, but they capitalized on the direness of the situation by inspiring their soldiers to pursue the noble cause of national liberation—which they promptly did, after quickly studying the new techniques of war. With their modernized army, they drove the Hyksos from Egypt around 1570 BCE and pursued them all the way to Palestine, a campaign that inaugurated Egypt's golden age—that of the New Kingdom (1570–1070 BCE).

THE NEW KINGDOM EMPIRE

The embarrassment of the Hyksos conquest proved to the Egyptians that the defense provided by their surrounding deserts no longer sufficed. Realizing that Egypt's relative isolation was at an end, the pharaohs of the New Kingdom decided to seize the initiative by extending their might to other lands. They subdued the Nubians to the south, which guaranteed Egypt's access to the gold mines of the region—a necessity now that gold had been established as the international standard for commerce throughout the Near East. From this vantage point they opened new trade routes down the western shores of the Red Sea and as far away as present day Sudan and Somalia (see Map 2.2).

Militarily, the reinvigorated army—now led on the battlefield by the pharaoh himself—conquered all of Palestine and advanced into Syria as far north

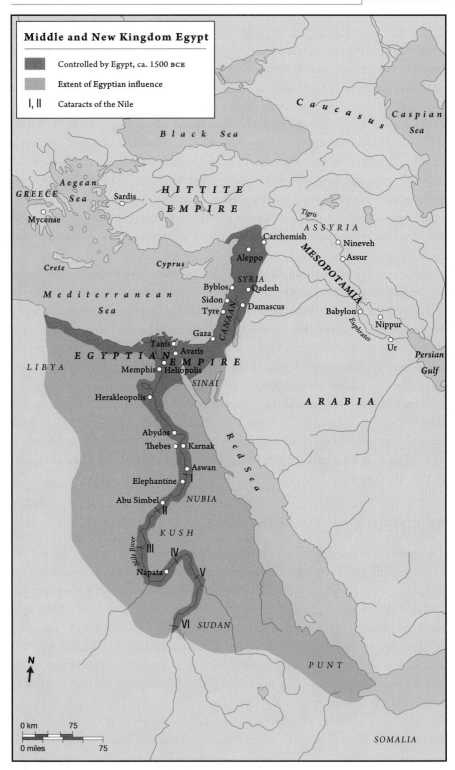

Middle and New Kingdom Egypt

- Controlled by Egypt, ca. 1500 BCE
- Extent of Egyptian influence
- I, II   Cataracts of the Nile

MAP 2.2   Middle and New Kingdom Egypt

as the city of Aleppo. The most aggressive of the new Eighteenth Dynasty rulers was Thutmose I (r. 1504–1492 BCE), who was also the first pharaoh to be entombed in the new necropolis of the Valley of the Kings. Thutmose led his army into Syria until he reached the banks of the upper Euphrates, where he erected a victory plaque and proclaimed himself the greatest of Egypt's rulers. He had "surpassed the achievements of all the kings who lived before me. . . . The gods have delighted in my reign, and their temples have been filled with celebration. . . . I have pushed the boundaries of Egypt as far as the sun shines, . . . and I have made her triumphant over every land." His victories consisted more of looting raids than true conquests; nevertheless, his reign marked Egypt's transition into a fully militarized society in which army officers replaced civil officials as the backbone of the administration. Booty and tribute poured into the royal coffers, as did the gold from the recaptured Nubian mines, and the increased wealth allowed him to construct scores of luxurious palaces for the high military caste and a network of new temples to gods both old and new. The god of military victory, named Amen, predictably rose in religious prominence during this period. His main temple at Karnak, just across the river from Thebes, received a series of massive additions and embellishments until it became a vast complex of halls, temples, administrative buildings, and storehouses, making it by far the largest religious compound in the ancient world.

Valley of the Kings   Though grander than most, the temple complex of Queen Hatshepsut is characteristic of the Middle Kingdom period. Instead of remote pyramids, notable Egyptians constructed elaborate malls with administrative offices, altar rooms, libraries, treasuries, and living quarters.

The reign of Queen Hatshepsut (r. 1478–1458 BCE) was notable for its prosperity and peace, but is best remembered for the spectacular mortuary temple she had constructed at Deir el-Bahri—a series of terraced gardens and broad colonnades carved into the high cliffs of the river valley. All the pharaohs of the New Kingdom after Thutmose I chose to be buried in this Valley of the Kings. The burial sites were separate from the mortuary temples themselves. They hoped that this manner of entombment—in deep caves whose entrances were then concealed—would foil grave robbers.

The royal family practiced traditional brother-sister marriage, the idea behind it being that only the daughter of a pharaoh was sufficiently exalted to be the queen of another pharaoh. These marriages were usually but not always asexual. Every pharaoh, however, had dozens if not hundreds of wives in his harem, by whom he produced his heirs. Hatshepsut was the daughter of Thutmose I, the queen of Thutmose II (r. 1492–1478), and the bane of her stepson Thutmose III (r. 1458–1425). He was thus the half sister of Thutmose II and the stepmother of Thutmose III.[5]

Although Thutmose III officially began his reign upon his father's death in 1478, he was a child and lived for twenty tense years under the firm control of his stepmother. Once he took control for himself, he ordered his stonemasons to deface Hatshepsut's images and erase her name from all monuments. He dedicated his reign to extending Egypt's might even further into Palestine and Syria, personally leading as many as sixteen campaigns. He left a network of client kings to do the actual work of governing the empire, taking their sons with him back to Thebes in order to be indoctrinated in Egyptian law and custom. In this way, when these children grew to maturity, they could govern their lands in an increasingly Egyptian context. Diplomatic marriages between the daughters of the client kings and the Egyptian royal sons were also common; but no Egyptian princess was ever wedded to a foreign king.

The goal of "Egyptifying" the broader Near East had less to do with aiding the development of civilization than with simply bringing more people, whether slave or free, into the service of the pharaoh. If Egypt could no longer retain its splendid isolation, then the rest of the world should at least recognize the need to sustain the ma'at that only passive acceptance of pharaonic rule could effect. Driving the point home were the huge reliefs of Egyptian armies and their victorious generals that bedecked palace and temple walls everywhere they went. Additions to the temple complexes at Karnak and Luxor further attest to the grandeur of imperial Egypt at its height.

---

[5]   Egyptian law allowed for a woman to rule in her own right, although the occurrence was rare enough that royal monuments portrayed her with a fake beard.

The reigns of Amenhotep III (r. 1390–1352 BCE) and his son Amenhotep IV (r. 1352–1338 BCE) mark both the pinnacle of the New Kingdom and the point at which it began a downturn. The priests who presided over the temples now controlled roughly a quarter of the empire's land. Concerned about their growing power—especially about the priests at Karnak, home of the sun god Amon-Ra—Amenhotep IV instituted a radical change: renaming himself Akhenaten, he elevated a minor solar deity called Aten to supreme status among the gods. Egyptian mythology in fact maintained separate cults for different phases and aspects of the sun. The god of the sunrise was different from the god of the sun at noontime, for example, and the god of sunset was yet another distinct entity. Amon-Ra was thought of principally as the heat energy of the sun.[6] Akhenaten closed the temples to Amon-Ra, violently suppressed their cults, and promoted Aten as the sole true and universal deity.[7] (He even had Amon-Ra's name chiseled out of royal inscriptions.) He hoped to forestall popular reaction by emphasizing that it was the royal family's obligation to worship Aten, while the obligation of the Egyptian people was to continue worshipping the pharaoh as always.[8] He abandoned the palace at Thebes and erected a new capital some three hundred miles to the north at a place called Akhetaten, now known as el-Amarna.

The belief in a single, supreme deity—or **monotheism**—was a novelty, and it did not go over easily with the people. They still craved the consolation of their all but certain eternal blessedness in the old faith. Akhenaten and Nefertiti, though, while undoubtedly motivated in part by a desire to break the power of the priests, were genuine enthusiasts for the new religion. Tradition credits the pharaoh with composing the heartfelt Hymn to Aten:

> The belief in a single, supreme deity—or monotheism—was a novelty, and it did not go over easily with the people. They still craved the consolation of their all but certain eternal blessedness in the old faith.

> Thou appearest beautifully on the horizon of heaven,
> Thou living Aten, the beginning of life!
> When thou art arisen on the eastern horizon,
> Thou hast filled every land with thy beauty.

Whatever its limitations as poetry, it conveys genuine passion, a devotion quite unlike the tired formulaic chants of the Book of the Dead.

---

[6]   The new god Aten was originally the physical sphere comprising the sun. Under Akhnaten's imposed monotheism, though, Aten incorporated all the many aspects of the sun.

[7]   The pharaoh's new name meant, literally, "the one dedicated to Aten."

[8]   Akhenaten's queen was Nefertiti, the famous beauty.

Family Hour at the Pharaoh's   Bas relief, ca. 1350 BCE, portraying Akhenaten and Nefertiti along with three of their six daughters. Akhenaten is best remembered for his effort to replace traditional Egyptian religion with a new cult devoted to a single god called Aten. In this scene, the royal family offers prayers to this sun deity. The image continues a little-understood artistic tradition that portrays Akhenaten in androgynous fashion. Note that his body is more curvy than that of his queen, a famous beauty.

Akhenaten's plans went awry, however, for he underestimated both the popularity of Amon-Ra and the priests' determination to hold onto their lofty position. Akhenaten gradually became something of a religious recluse, isolated at el-Amarna and ignoring the needs of the empire. His successors on the throne—Tutankhamen, Ay, and Horemheb—quickly suppressed the new cult and restored the old faith. Eventually, a new pharaoh arose from the ranks of the military and restored the empire's fortunes. Ramses II (r. 1279–1212 BCE), Egypt's only ruler known as "the Great," repulsed the Hittite advance on the Syrian territories and built temples, palaces, and statues on a colossal scale. Perhaps one-half of all the Egyptian monuments that survive today belong to Ramses II's reign.[9] Tradition associates him with the evil pharaoh in the story of the Biblical book of Exodus, but Hebrew enslavement in Egypt and a subsequent release under the messianic leadership of Moses is not supported by any surviving Egyptian documentary or archeological evidence. Nevertheless, the reign of Ramses II was a last gasp of glory before Egypt once again fell to outsiders. Peoples from far away swept through the Aegean Sea, over Egypt, and rampaged through the rest of the Near East around 1200 BCE.

THE INDO-EUROPEAN ASSAULT

The newcomers were a motley crew, related to one another by language: each spoke one of a family of languages known today as **Indo-European**. In 1786 an Englishman named Sir William Jones (1746–1794), then serving as a judge in colonial India, delivered a paper to the Asiatic Society in which he observed that

---

[9]   Statues and temple-pillars were not the only erections of Ramses II. He reportedly fathered nearly two hundred children by his various wives and concubines.

Great Temple of Ramses II   Ramses ordered the construction of this massive temple to hold his remains, ca. 1250 BCE. The colossal statues on the façade are all representations of Ramses himself (whom no one ever accused of subtlety). Statues and paintings of the pharaoh, often showing him receiving the worship of various gods and goddesses, are situated throughout the temple.

ancient Sanskrit (the ancestor from which the major languages spoken in northern India are derived) shared an exceptional number of word roots and grammatical forms with ancient European tongues like Greek, Latin, Gothic, and the Celtic languages; from this he argued that they must therefore be related. This common ancestor soon came to be called Proto-Indo-European and is now believed to have originated somewhere north of the Black Sea.[10] The idea had been put forth in a more general way a hundred years earlier by a Dutch philologist, but Jones (who spoke thirteen languages fluently and could read another fifteen) produced enough data to make the theory rightly his own.

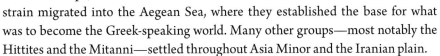

The Indo-European peoples, an extremely numerous horde of nomadic shepherding nations, began to radiate from their homeland near the Black Sea as early as 2000 BCE. Several groups moved into western Europe, the forerunners of the Celts and the Goths. One strain migrated into the Aegean Sea, where they established the base for what was to become the Greek-speaking world. Many other groups—most notably the Hittites and the Mitanni—settled throughout Asia Minor and the Iranian plain.

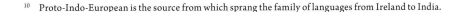

[10]   Proto-Indo-European is the source from which sprang the family of languages from Ireland to India.

The **Hittites** initially settled in north-central Anatolia in a sprawl of small states, but by 1700 BCE they had united into a single kingdom (see Map 2.3). From the time they appeared on the scene, they were an aggressive, war-loving society. Although they raided Mesopotamia regularly (they even sacked Babylon in 1595 BCE), the Hittites focused their military efforts on the Egyptian-held portions of Syria and Palestine. They advanced slowly. Though superior in arms, the Hittites could not put as many soldiers on the field as the Egyptian army could. The turning point came in 1286–1285 BCE, when Egypt, under Ramses II, and the Hittites, under their king Hattusilis III, declared a truce after an inconclusive battle at Qadesh and established the first written peace treaty in Western history:

> Behold: Hattusilis, the great chief [of the Hittites], has made a treaty with [Ramses], the great ruler of Egypt, beginning this day, to establish good peace and brotherhood between us forever. . . . And the children of the children of the great ruler of the Hittites shall live in brotherhood and peace with the children of the children of Ramses, . . . and hostilities between them shall cease forever.

The peace did not last long. The Hittites, it turned out, had a gift for conquest but none for government, and their unified kingdom faced continual challenges from regional warlords who preferred their own local despotism to the national brand. When yet another wave of Indo-European invaders swept through the area, the Hittite kingdom collapsed.

Called the **Sea Peoples** by the Egyptians, this new group attacked swiftly throughout the Aegean and eastern Mediterranean seas, setting off shockwaves of dispossessed war refugees much farther inland than the Sea Peoples themselves ever advanced. The Sea Peoples appeared in the Nile delta in 1207 and within twenty years had gained control of most of it. They effectively ended the Egyptian empire in Palestine, since the pharaohs no longer had access to the sea and hence could not engage in trade or diplomacy.

The Sea Peoples fought on land as an infantry, bearing double-edged swords made of bronze and javelins; they also had an innovation: plate armor. Bronze was easily shaped into close-fitting armor that protected their soldiers far more reliably than any earlier type of protective covering. The Hittites and the Egyptians who slowly learned from them had relied on lightly clad archers who rode lightweight chariots; their greater speed and agility could wreak havoc on most ancient infantries, armed as they mostly were with clubs and spears. But the bronze armor of the Sea Peoples gave them enough protection against archers that they could hold their formations and defeat the Egyptian and Hittite forces.

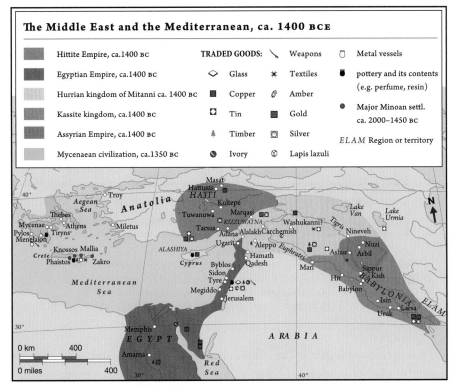

MAP 2.3   **The Middle East and the Mediterranean, ca. 1400 BCE**

No one knows who the Sea Peoples were. Obviously they arrived by sea and most likely spoke an Indo-European language, or group of languages, but these facts suggest only that they came from the northern shores of the eastern or central Mediterranean. Theories abound. Were they the Philistines described in the Hebrew Bible? Were they a rival tribe of the Mycenaean Greeks, or the Trojans, or the Hebrews, or the Siculi (the indigenous people of Sicily)? Egyptian records occasionally identify specific subsets among the Sea Peoples, which suggests that they used the name as a catchall for a whole swarm of different ethnic groups.[11] Whoever they were, and wherever they came from, they left behind a trail of annihilation so great that virtually no records survive to describe their wreckage until they reached Egypt. In Greece alone, 90 percent of the population was obliterated.

In Egypt, our first written and pictorial evidence of the Sea Peoples comes from an inscription set up by Ramses III in 1176 BCE to commemorate a rare victory over the intruders. The carved relief shows attackers of many varieties, wearing distinctive clothing and headdresses and carrying an assortment of weapons. The text of

---

[11]   Among the specific peoples named by the Egyptians were the Habiru, whom some believe to have been the Hebrews.

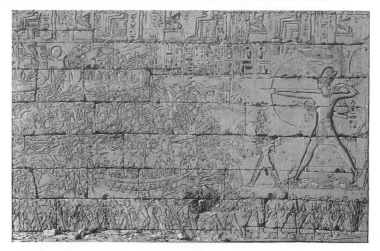

The Sea Peoples Defeated   This wall engraving from the mortuary temple of Ramses III, ca. 1180 BCE, at Medinet Habu, shows the pharaoh, at right, leading an ambush of the Sea Peoples. Ramses had blocked the channels of the Nile Delta, which prevented the Sea Peoples' advance, and then unleashed an archery assault on the ships as they struggled to turn course and escape to the sea.

the inscription—it is part of the temple complex at Medinet Habu in the western district of Thebes—clearly was intended to revive flagging hopes. One portion depicts Ramses III in his war chariot, leading his brave troops to battle; its caption reads in part:

> The king, rich in strength as he rides forth, filling the hearts of the [Sea Peoples] with fear and awe; sole lord, whose hand is capable, conscious of his strength, like a valiant lion lying in wait for wild cattle, freely going forward, his heart confident, smashing thousands into heaps in the space of a moment. His power in the fray is like a fire, making all who assail him to collapse in ashes.

Another wall depicts Ramses in the midst of the battle, scattering an army of terrified Sea Peoples:

> Behold him, as when Set rages, overthrowing the enemy, . . . trampling down the plains and hill-countries; the enemy lies prostrate, beaten from head to tail before his horse. His heat burns up their bodies like a flame. Hacked to pieces are their bodies, throughout eternity.[12]

---

[12]   Set (also spelled Seth) was the wrathful god of the desert.

The destruction caused by the Sea Peoples was vast. In southern and southeastern Europe, they annihilated whole cities. Few Near Eastern or Egyptian cities disappeared altogether, by contrast, but the invaders smashed old trade routes and splintered the diplomatic connections that had kept the region relatively stable from 1500 to 1200 BCE. The three major states of the era—New Kingdom Egypt, Hittite Anatolia, and Babylonian Mesopotamia—had generally managed to keep the wider region peaceful and had kept commerce moving. Even the smaller states that provided a sort of buffer zone between the major empires had thrived for those three centuries. But the destruction caused by the Sea Peoples sent shockwaves of displacement and despair through all three empires (see Map 2.4).

The disappearance of the Sea Peoples is as much a mystery as is their origin. Despite Ramses III's fanciful inscriptions, no evidence exists of an annihilating defeat of them or of their continued horrific progress through the Near East to afflict other nations elsewhere. Hence it is likely that they were absorbed into the indigenous populations. This assumption helps to explain the unusual degree of cultural innovation, economic realignment, political reconfiguration, and religious change that occurred in the Sea Peoples' wake. And an important part of that change was the perfecting of an old technology: the refining of iron.

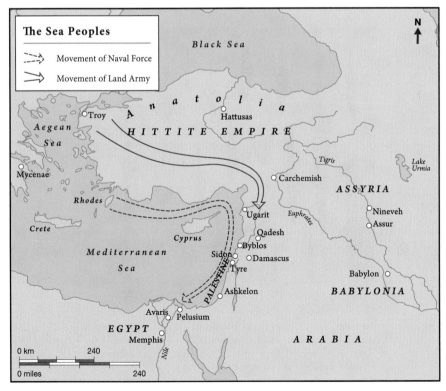

MAP 2.4   The Sea Peoples

THE AGE OF IRON BEGINS, ca. 1200 BCE

Iron ore is plentiful in the Near East, and people had been mining it for a long time. Objects made of iron have been dated as early at 5000 BCE. By 1200 BCE, metalworkers had begun to perfect their methods. By repeating the process of heating, quenching, hammering, they also could produce iron objects of ever greater strength. With new weapons and new trading goods, power shifted again and again. The changes culminated in a new model of statecraft under the Persians and a new religion of fire, Zoroastrianism.

Iron ore was not an obvious choice. It is brittle and will produce a usable metal only after it is melted and its impurities burned away. The process, while simple to describe, is difficult to master. Iron melts at a much higher temperature than copper (the main constituent element in bronze) and must remain in its melted state for a considerably longer time. The constant temperature needed is difficult to achieve with primitive wood fires. Moreover, iron, ironically, is a weaker metal than bronze and is more susceptible to deterioration by moisture. Even in the dry climate of the Near East, iron can easily oxidize (that is, rust). A clash between an iron sword and a bronze sword would invariably end with the iron sword shattered.

Iron Weapons   Armies in the ancient Near East fought primarily with spears, arrows, and knives, rather than swords. Limited metal-ore resources were the reason. Swords did not become common until the arrival of the Indo-European peoples.

Given these disadvantages, what was gained by producing iron weapons and tools? Simply put, mass production. Iron ore is abundant throughout the region, and, consequently, once the production process was perfected, people of all walks of life could afford iron implements.[13] By 1100 BCE iron weapons began to proliferate; by 800 BCE most common homes were well supplied with iron pots, tools, and utensils. The problem with bronze was that its two constituent parts—copper and tin—are both considerably rarer and are seldom found in the same region. In order to maintain a constant supply of bronze, the Near East had to maintain steady commercial relations; any disruption in the long-distance movement of these metals and the available supply of bronze disappeared. This is precisely what happened with the invasions of the Sea Peoples and the mass waves of refugees they set in motion. Trade networks that had proliferated during the years from 1600 to 1200 BCE simply disintegrated. The abrupt decline in the availability of bronze gave the advantage to the iron-brandishing Sea Peoples (whoever they were).

With the Hittite empire destroyed, Assyria and Babylon set reeling, and Egypt sent into yet another Intermediate Period (the Third, 1070–664 BCE), the political map of the ancient Near East changed dramatically. New peoples and states arose, some of them of old provenance, others of newcomers. The ethnic jumble of the turn of the millennium exacerbates the problem of identifying the Sea Peoples and tracing their movements. The region resembled a busy intersection whose traffic lights have gone out at rush hour. Groups like the Phoenicians, the Canaanites, the Philistines, the Amalikites, the Kassites, the Amorites, the Aramaeans, the Mitanni, the Moabites, and the Hurrians—to name only the best known—appeared on the scene in a bewildering tangle.

The **Phoenicians**, to pick just one, were particularly successful, since they took to the sea and established a network of trading colonies that stretched across the major Mediterranean islands (Cyprus, Sicily, Sardinia, the Balearics) and along the northern coast of Africa. Their name, which the ancient Greeks picked up from a West Semitic dialect, meant "the purple people"—a reference to their expertise in dyeing.[14] Later writers like the Greek historian Herodotus reported that Phoenician sailors claimed to have circumnavigated Africa, although this is doubtful. The Phoenicians' most important contribution to Western history was the dissemination of its alphabet, which simplified the task of writing. Theirs was among the first alphabets in Western history, but since it

---

[13] Iron is actually the sixth most abundant element in the universe. It makes up roughly 5 percent of the earth's crust.

[14] The waters off the shore of ancient Phoenicia (roughly, today's nation of Lebanon) had large populations of murex snails, from whose shells a distinctive reddish-purple dye was made.

provided the model for the alphabet later adopted by the Greeks, it led directly to the development of the alphabet used in the Western world today. The most famous of Phoenician cities was Carthage, which they founded sometime in the 9th century BCE, in present-day Tunisia, and which later challenged Rome for mastery of the entire Mediterranean.

The **Philistines**, by contrast, settled in the territory just south of Phoenicia. They are best known as the villains in the Hebrew conquest of the Promised Land, the barbarous people whose champion was the giant Goliath. Possibly an offshoot of the Peleset (one of the groups singled out by the Egyptians as being among the Sea Peoples), they in fact were an urban, commercial people who practiced little agriculture—just enough to put them at odds with pastoralist groups like the Hebrews.[15] Their origins likely lay in Mycenaean Greece. Little is known of their language, but archaeological remains link them with ancient Greek culture. The Philistines introduced grape and olive vines to the Holy Land, which are indigenous to the Greek archipelago, for example. Their architectural styles—as exemplified by the great citadels at Ashdod, Ashkelon, and Gaza—likewise resemble the fortified palaces of the Mycenaeans. The Philistines lived in the cities but controlled the agricultural hinterland and the regional trade routes. Most important, the Philistines occupied the region of Palestine that provided much of the copper and tin needed to produce bronze. Their control of such strategic sites and their access to superior weaponry, while making it impossible for their foes to forge similar weapons of their own, is what made the Philistines so substantial a foe to the advancing Hebrews.

> Phoenicians' most important contribution to Western history was the dissemination of its alphabet, which simplified the task of writing. Theirs was not the first alphabet in Western history, but since it provided the model for the alphabet later adopted by the Greeks, it led directly to the development of the alphabet used in the Western world today.

The disruptions caused by the Sea Peoples inspired a radical militarization of the **Assyrians**, who lived along the upper reaches of the Tigris. Terrified of attack from the strangers to the west, and unsure of the Hittites and Babylonians to their north and south, respectively, Assyrian culture turned militant and relied overtly on the use of violence and terror to maintain order. Their political fortunes rose and fell, depending on the relative ruthlessness of subsequent rulers, but from the mid-12th century BCE Assyria earned a well-deserved reputation for savagery that lasted for at least six centuries. From their imposing capital at Nineveh, the Assyrians maintained a large standing army of more than one hundred thousand soldiers

---

[15]   Traditionally, societies based on permanent settlement do not get along well with nomadic groups. Think of the conflicts between the cattle ranchers and farmers of the American West in the 19th century.

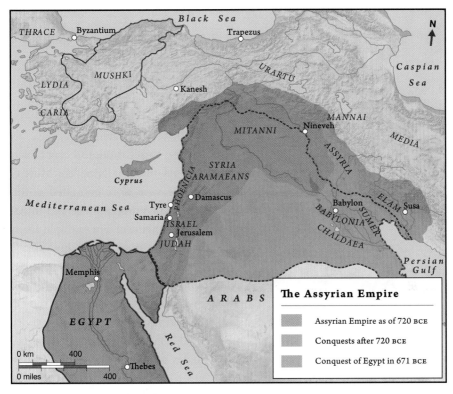

MAP 2.5 **The Assyrian Empire**

divided into specialized units (infantry, cavalry, archers, engineers, and so on) that, uniquely among ancient armies, trained to work in concert (see Map 2.5).

The Assyrians were the first army to use iron weapons extensively and may also have pioneered another technological advance: they added carbon and nickel to refined iron, to produce steel. Steel blades were significantly stronger than both iron and bronze blades and resisted decomposition. Producing it was expensive, however, which meant that many centuries would pass before steel production became widespread. The Assyrians knew the value of broadcasting their fearsome strength at arms, though. The victory monuments they erected depicted brutal scenes of slaughter, decapitation, rape, and torture, often in chilling detail. Their goal was to frighten people into submission, and it usually worked. When warnings failed, the army did its dirty work with gusto—going so far on occasion as to annihilate entire populations. This was the fate of the "ten lost tribes of Israel," who fell to the Assyrians in 722 BCE. Assyrian law dictated corporal

> The Assyrians knew the value of broadcasting their fearsome strength at arms, though. The victory monuments they erected depicted brutal scenes of slaughter, decapitation, rape, and torture, often in chilling detail.

Assyrian Cruelty   The Assyrians were among the most feared of ancient peoples. Through most of the 8th century BCE they were ruled by a series of bloody-minded and ruthless kings who employed sadistic violence as a means of commanding obedience, and they commemorated their worst atrocities with sculptures, engravings, and paintings of all sorts, to remind people of what could happen to them if they opposed the king. This relief, from the palace at Nineveh of the ruler Sennacherib (r. 705–681), shows the torture and slaughter of Jews after the battle of Lachish.

punishments for hosts of crimes, resulting in thousands of publicly performed mutilations a year. On the other hand, at least one Assyrian ruler (Ashurbanipal, r. 669–627 BCE) built the first known library in Western history. Archeologists have recovered thirty thousand clay tablets from its ruins in Nineveh. Most of this treasure store consisted of foreign literary works preserved in Assyrian cuneiform. For example, many modern editions of the *Epic of Gilgamesh* are based on Assyrian redactions unearthed at Nineveh.

Assyria's cruelty had earned it the furious hatred of its neighbors. In 612 BCE an alliance led by the Medes and the Chaldeans stormed into Nineveh and reduced it to ashes and dust. Within another decade all vestiges of Assyrian might were destroyed. The new victors did not introduce an era of good feeling, however. The Medes, an Indo-European people, were happy to return to Iran, knowing that the Assyrians were gone once and for all. That left the Chaldeans, the Semitic-speaking residents of southern Babylonia (known also as neo-Babylonians), in control of all of Mesopotamia and much of the Levant, where they adopted Assyrian methods and ruled by brute force. One of the neo-Babylonian kings, Nebuchadnezzar II (r. 605–562 BCE), led his army into Jerusalem, destroyed the Hebrew Temple, and carried tens of thousands of Hebrews into slavery back east, in Babylon.

PERSIA AND THE RELIGION OF FIRE

Still another group arose in the middle of the 6th century BCE, a people who toppled the neo-Babylonians and brought some stability to this near-hopeless situation that had continued, off and on, since 1200 BCE. These were the Persians, an Indo-European nation whose origins are unknown. Led by an energetic and charismatic ruler named Cyrus (r. 559–530 BCE), they lived near the midpoint of the eastern shore of the Persian Gulf. Suddenly and unexpectedly, the Persians united their various tribes, freed themselves from the overlordship of the Medes, and defeated their next neighbor, the Lydians. They then invaded Mesopotamia so quickly that Babylon surrendered without a fight.

Cyrus was the undisputed master of the east, the largest empire the Western world had yet seen. He freed the Hebrews and allowed them to return to Jerusalem, where they quickly established a semiautonomous vassal state. Such largess was typical of Persian rule, but it resulted from strategic, not altruistic, thinking. The Persian Empire was simply too large for a central government to administer effectively. It was a land empire that, in contrast to Egypt, did not have a grand reliable waterway running through its center to allow easy unification. Cyrus thus portioned out his empire with care and forethought. Why govern a group like the Hebrews, when they could do so themselves? So long as they recognized Persian overlordship, caused no trouble, and sent payments of tax and tribute on time, Cyrus was wisely content to let them go their own way. The Hebrews were not the only people treated in this manner.

Cyrus' son and heir, Cambyses (r. 530–522 BCE), conquered Egypt herself and advanced far into Anatolia, uniting the entire Near East for the first time. The great Persian Empire ultimately stretched from the Hellespont in the west to the Indus River in the east, from the upper Nile in the south to the middle reaches of the Black, Caspian, and Aral Seas in the north. It covered well over two thousand miles on an east-west axis and more than a thousand miles from north to south. The ancient world had seen nothing like it (see Map 2.6). The Persians instituted a single

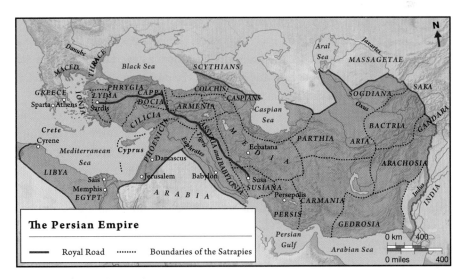

MAP 2.6   **The Persian Empire**

currency and a standardized system of weights and measures, but otherwise allowed their subject peoples to govern themselves according to their own traditions. After centuries of Egyptian, Hittite, Assyrian, and Babylonian brutality and imperialism, the light-handed approach of the Persians was a welcome relief—which explains the relative absence of rebellion against the new rulers. The conquered could consider, and perhaps even admire, Persian culture, science, and religion.

The death of Cambyses triggered a dynastic crisis, since he died young and without an heir. Eventually a cousin named Darius carried the day. His reign lasted from 521 to 486 BCE, during which time he reformed the administration and undertook an extensive campaign to improve the empire's infrastructure. His projects included the famed Royal Road, a 1,600-mile roadway from Sardis (near the Aegean coast, in Anatolia) to Susa (near the Persian Gulf, in modern-day Iran) that became the main artery for moving goods, capital, services, information, and soldiers through the heart of the empire. Darius also cut a canal that connected the Nile with the Red Sea, to facilitate trade with Egypt, and brought systematic irrigation to the Iranian plateau for the first time, which dramatically increased the agricultural production of the land. Last, he built a vast new capital in Persepolis, two hundred miles east of Babylon. The move calmed people's concerns about having an emperor breathing down their necks and brought the eastern half of his empire, which extended to India, within his gaze. With a calm and peaceful interior at last, with a single currency, and with physical barriers to efficient interaction removed, the economy of the Near East roared to new life. The material standard of life improved for most people, and for most of those it improved dramatically. The Persians had created not just a new state but a new model of statecraft: imperialism via accommodation and tolerance.

The stunning political and social success of the Persians paved the way for a revolution in religious life, for they brought with them a new religion that spread rapidly throughout the Near East and remained the dominant faith of that part of the world until the rise of Islam in the 7th century CE.

The Persians originally had a polytheistic religion not unlike the ancient Sumerian faith, with deities of various types representing natural elements and forces. In what may have been a self-conscious effort at reform, a man named Zoroaster began to preach the supremacy of a single god and the requirement of an ethical basis of life as the proper way of worshipping him. It was the beginning of **Zoroastrianism**, the first transnational Western religion.

We know little of Zoroaster (which is the Greek version of his Persian name, Zarathustra); he lived sometime around 1300 BCE and claimed to have received a vision of this "Wise Lord," **Ahura Mazda**. Ahura Mazda, he preached, was the one true and eternal God, altogether wise, just, and good; significantly, though, Ahura Mazda was not all-powerful—for he had an adversary named Angra

Persepolis   Persian nobles on their way to the imperial court.

Mainyu, later known as Ahriman. "Truly there are two primal spirits, twins renowned to be in conflict. In thought, word, and act they are two: the Good and
the Bad" (Yasna 30.3). It was in order to defeat Ahriman, Zoroaster taught, that
Ahura Mazda created the world and all living things, to provide a battleground
for the cosmic struggle.

Zoroaster composed a sequence of hymns to Ahura Mazda. These seventeen
poems—known as the Gathas—were passed on orally for many centuries until
the Persians acquired writing. By the time the Gathas were finally written down
in the 3rd century CE, a great number of other holy texts had been produced by
other Zoroastrian priests. These were combined with the original Gathas, and
the result was the **Avesta**—the holy book of the Zoroastrians.[16]

The creation myth of this new faith maintained that Ahura Mazda disseminated his spirit in seven unique forms called spentas, or "Holy Immortals," who
created the seven principal elements: Sky, Water, Earth, Plants, Cattle, Man, and
Fire. Ahriman brought death into the world, but Ahura Mazda so ordained that

---

[16]   The Avesta consisted of twenty-one books, but only fragments remain, since the Muslim conquerors of
the Middle Ages searched out every copy they could and destroyed them.

the first five elements are self-regenerating, always bringing more life and therefore more good into the world. Man alone bears the responsibility of choice. The ethical quality of our lives determines not only our own fates but the fate of the world.

Zoroaster wanted to emphasize the unity of mankind, the fact that all peoples regardless of ethnicity are linked by moral necessity and that all lives have value. Indeed, our lives have a vast purpose—not merely, as in the Sumerian and Egyptian religions, an obligation to serve—that ennobles us and gives meaning to our suffering. God's final element, Fire, exists to inspire and assist us. It represents God's righteousness and truth, his purifying strength, and our hope. Living righteously meant regular prayer (five times daily) always in the presence of fire, performing various temple rituals, and following a high ethical standard of honesty, charity, cleanliness, and respect for nature. In this way, Zoroastrians had every hope of personal salvation, which meant joyous reunion with Ahura Mazda in paradise and the satisfaction of playing a role in God's ultimate victory over Evil. The Gathas enjoined believers to love all peoples, to aid the poor, to practice generous hospitality. They showed respect for nature by not eating animals before the animals had attained maturity and could reproduce. Persian temples drew freely on Sumerian, Akkadian, Babylonian, Assyrian, and Egyptian architectural styles to emphasize that Ahura Mazda was the god of all nations and tribes.

> Zoroaster wanted to emphasize the unity of mankind, the fact that all peoples regardless of ethnicity are linked by moral necessity and that all lives have value. Indeed, our lives have a vast purpose—not merely, as in the Sumerian and Egyptian religions, an obligation to serve—that ennobles us and gives meaning to our suffering.

Zoroastrian priests were called **magi**. Their primary responsibility was to tend the sacred fires in the temples, where various rituals central to Zoroastrian life were conducted: marriage, initiation rites, burial rites. Special study was required to become a magus, mostly involving study of the fast-multiplying Avesta texts and memorization of liturgical prayers, but the magi, while highly respected, were not regarded as possessing supernatural powers. Priests and laity remained distinct, but they interacted socially and even intermarried. Priests wore white garments that represented purity; initiated laity were identified primarily by wearing a lengthy cord called a kusti. Zoroastrianism recognized differences between the sexes. It had special temple rites, for example, to help women conceive and to purify them after childbirth. But it allowed all men and women, boys and girls, equal access to the temples and performed the same initiation rites for them all. Away from the temple, women believers could lead the family in prayers and even perform certain rituals. Women wore saris but not veils.

Zoroastrian belief spread rapidly. The state did not forbid other religions or attempt to suppress them, which may have been the key to Zoroastrianism's success. For many subjects of the empire, Ahura Mazda became a kind of benevolent overlord, while their traditional deities were left as immortal spirits in service to the great God. But the ethical element of the faith needs emphasizing. Before Zoroaster, early religions posited no connection between religion and morality. The Sumerian gods, for example, cared only how people treated them, not how they treated each other. The Egyptians were required to obey the divine pharaoh and never upset the order of ma'at—but the only moral expectation placed on them by their religion was not to do harm. Zoroastrian faith gave people

Keeping the Flame Alive　A ring of Zoroastrian priests celebrate their New Year festival with a ritual dance around the sacred flame. Once the most widespread religion in the ancient world, Zoroastrianism today has only two hundred thousand followers worldwide. Low birth rates and high rates of conversion to more mainstream religions are contributing to their rapid decline.

the luxury of feeling that their actions mattered: the way they treated each other helped to create a better world. It appealed to the millions who wanted meaning in life. It assured them that they were good, that their deeds and strivings had purpose, and that a higher ethical standard made life more tolerable for everyone.

WHO, WHAT, WHERE

Ahura Mazda	Indo-European
Assyrians	magi
Avesta	monotheism
Book of the Dead	Philistines
Epic of Gilgamesh	Phoenicians
Greater West	Sea Peoples
Hittites	ushabti
Hyksos ascendancy	Zoroastrianism

SUGGESTED READINGS

Primary Sources

The best translation of *The Epic of Gilgamesh*, quoted on pages 39–40, is found in *Myths from Mesopotamia* by Stephanie Dalley.

The Instruction of Amenemhet I is found in Parkinson, R. B., ed. and trans. *The Tale of Sinuhe and Other Ancient Egyptian Poems, 1940–1640 BC* (2009), pp. 206–208.

The text of the inscription at Medinet Habu is adapted from Bailkey and Lim, *Readings in Ancient History: Thought and Experience from Gilgamesh to St. Augustine*, 6th ed. (2002), p. 54.

Source Anthologies

Hoffner, Harry A., Jr., trans. *Letters from the Hittite Kingdom* (2009).

Black, Jeremy, trans. *The Literature of Ancient Sumer* (2004).

Chavalas, Mark W, ed. *The Ancient Near East: Historical Sources in Translation* (2006).

Luckenbill, Daniel David, ed. *Annals of Sennacherib* (2005).

Moran, William L., ed. and trans. *The Amarna Letters* (2000).

Studies

Akkermans, Peter M. M. G., and Glenn Martin Schwartz. *The Archaeology of Syria: From Complex Hunter-Gatherers to Early Urban Societies, ca. 16,000–300 BC* (2003).

Aubet, Maria Eugenia. *The Phoenicians and the West: Politics, Colonies, and Trade* (2001).

Boardman, John. *Persia and the West: An Archaeological Investigation of the Genesis of Achaemenid Persian Art* (2000).

Briant, Pierre. *From Cyrus to Alexander: A History of the Persian Empire* (2006).

Brosius, Maria, ed. *Ancient Archives and Archival Traditions: Concepts of Record-Keeping in the Ancient World* (2003).

Bryce, Trevor. *The Kingdom of the Hittites* (2005).

———. *Life and Society in the Hittite World* (2004).

Day, John V. *Indo-European Origins: The Anthropological Evidence* (2001).

Fleming, Daniel E. *Democracy's Ancient Ancestors: Mari and Early Collective Governance* (2004).

Galil, Gershon. *The Lower Stratum Families in the Neo-Assyrian Period* (2007).

Grajetzki, Wolfram. *The Middle Kingdom of Ancient Egypt: History, Archaeology, and Society* (2006).

Holloway, Steven W. *Aššur Is King! Aššur Is King!: Religion in the Exercise of Power in the Neo-Assyrian Empire* (2002).

Joannès, Francis. *The Age of Empires: Mesopotamia in the First Millennium BC* (2005).

Leick, Gwendolyn. *The Babylonians: An Introduction* (2002).

Meskell, Lynn. *Private Life in New Kingdom Egypt* (2004).

Morris, Ian, and Walter Scheidel, eds. *The Dynamics of Ancient Empires: State Power from Assyria to Byzantium* (2009).

Oates, Joan, and David Oates. *Nimrud: An Assyrian Imperial City Revealed* (2001).

Oren, Eliezer D. *The Sea Peoples and Their World: A Reassessment* (2000).

Ray, John. *Reflections of Osiris: Lives from Ancient Egypt* (2001).

Roehrig, Catharine H., ed. *Hatshepsut: From Queen to Pharaoh* (2005).

Silverman, David P., Josef W. Wegner, and Jennifer Houser Wegner. *Akhenaten and Tutankhamun: Revolution and Restoration* (2006).

Tyldesley, Joyce A. *Ramesses: Egypt's Greatest Pharaoh* (2001).

Van de Mieroop, Marc. *King Hammurabi of Babylon: A Biography* (2005).

Wiesehöfer, Josef. *Ancient Persia from 550 BC to 650 AD* (2001).

Yasur-Landau, Assaf. *The Philistines and Aegean Migration at the End of the Late Bronze Age* (2010).

For additional resources, including maps, primary sources, visuals, web links, and quizzes, please go to **www.oup.com/us/backman.**

א אֱלֹהִים אֵת הַשָּׁמַיִם וְאֵת הָאָרֶץ: וְהָאָרֶץ הָיְתָה תֹהוּ וָבֹ

שֶׁךְ עַל־פְּנֵי תְהוֹם וְרוּחַ אֱלֹהִים מְרַחֶפֶת עַל־פְּנֵי הַמָּיִם: וַיֹּאמֶ

הִים יְהִי אוֹר וַיְהִי־אוֹר: וַיַּרְא אֱלֹהִים אֶת־הָאוֹר כִּי־טוֹב וַיַּבְדֵּ

הִים בֵּין הָאוֹר וּבֵין הַחֹשֶׁךְ: וַיִּקְרָא אֱלֹהִים ׀ לָאוֹר יוֹם וְלַחֹשֶׁ

א לַיְלָה וַיְהִי־עֶרֶב וַיְהִי־בֹקֶר יוֹם אֶחָד: פ וַיֹּאמֶר אֱלֹהִ

רָקִיעַ בְּתוֹךְ הַמָּיִם וִיהִי מַבְדִּיל בֵּין מַיִם לָמָיִם: וַיַּעַשׂ אֱלֹהִ

הָרָקִיעַ וַיַּבְדֵּל בֵּין הַמַּיִם אֲשֶׁר מִתַּחַת לָרָקִיעַ וּבֵין הַמַּיִם אֲשֶׁ

ל לָרָקִיעַ וַיְהִי־כֵן: וַיִּקְרָא אֱלֹהִים לָרָקִיעַ שָׁמָיִם וַיְהִי־עֶרֶב וַיְהִ

ל יוֹם שֵׁנִי: פ וַיֹּאמֶר אֱלֹהִים יִקָּווּ הַמַּיִם מִתַּחַת הַשָּׁמַיִם אֶ

ד אֶחָד וְתֵרָאֶה הַיַּבָּשָׁה וַיְהִי־כֵן: וַיִּקְרָא אֱלֹהִים ׀ לַיַּבָּשָׁ אֶ

CHAPTER 3

The Chosen People

1200 BCE–538 BCE

Sometime between 1800 and 1700 BCE, a tired old man in the city of Ur, near the confluence of the Tigris and Euphrates rivers, began to hear a voice in his head.[1] His name was Abram, and according to the stories passed on about him he was then seventy-five years old, poor, and childless. The voice came from heaven, and it told Abram to take his family—which consisted of his wife, Sarai, his nephew Lot, and their servants—and to leave Ur and go where God would lead him. "The LORD said to Abram, 'Go forth from your native land and from your father's house to the land that I will show you. I will make you a great nation, and I will bless you; I will make your name great, and you shall be a blessing. I will bless those who bless you and curse him that curses you; and all the families of the earth shall bless themselves by you'" (Genesis 12.1–3).

It is a tale filled with complex meanings and the promise of a great nation. It is a part of the library of books now called the Hebrew Bible, but also a tale of the unwitting founding of two great nations and three religions.

◀ **In the Beginning**   This beautiful page of the opening of the book of Genesis—here showing its Hebrew name "Bereshit" ("in the beginning") in enlarged letters—comes from a multivolume edition of the Bible planned for publication in Germany in the 1930s. This first volume appeared just before Hitler's rise to power in 1933; the rest of the project was never completed. By long-standing Jewish tradition the text of the Scriptures is never adorned with representational imagery, in order not to distract attention from the holy word. Decorative elements consist almost entirely of the beautiful presentation of the script itself.

A GREAT NATION

Being a pious man, Abram and his family obeyed without hesitation. Their trek followed the course of the Fertile Crescent. God led them

- A Great Nation
- The Bible and History
- The Land of Canaan
- Dreams of a Golden Age
- Women and the Law
- Prophets and Prophecy
- Priests and Rabbis
- A Genius for Reinvention

CHAPTER OUTLINE

northward through the Mesopotamian plain, westward across Syria, then southward into the land of the Canaanites in Palestine. At Shechem, which was roughly in the center of Canaan, the Lord actually appeared to Abram and promised to give all the surrounding land to his offspring. That promise is only the beginning of the tale's complex relationship to history.

Abram built the Lord an altar as a way of giving thanks, but he may have wondered whether the gift was such a blessing. The land was then suffering from a horrific famine, which forced Abram and his family to continue travelling southward in search of food, past the Negev desert, then westward across Sinai and into Egypt. This was a dangerous move, because Abram's wife was an exceptionally beautiful woman, and he believed the Egyptians to be so lecherous that someone might kill him in order to get to her. Pleading his self-concern, he persuaded Sarai to pose as his (presumably unmarried) sister. Pharaoh's agents saw her beauty and sent her to the royal palace as a new addition to his harem. "And because of her, it went well with Abram; he acquired sheep, oxen, asses, male and female slaves, she-asses, and camels" (Genesis 12.16). But the Lord sent a plague upon the pharaoh because of the wrong done to Sarai, and so the pharaoh sent her and Abram packing. They returned to Palestine, where the Lord repeated his promise of dominion over the land and descendants as numberless as the stars in the night sky.

A decade passed without either promise being fulfilled. When Abram was eighty-six, Sarai sent her own servant, an Egyptian maiden named Hagar, into his bed in order that he might produce a child by her. Hagar became pregnant, and Sarai, embarrassed at the ease with which Hagar had achieved what she herself had never been able to accomplish, beat her harshly. Hagar eventually gave birth to a son to whom Abram gave the name Ishmael. Another dozen years passed. The Lord appeared to Abram again and repeated his promises, but this

---

[1]   According to the Bible, Abram came from "Ur of the Chaldeans." But by the time the Chaldeans appeared in Mesopotamia (around 700 BCE) the city of Ur had long since ceased to exist.

CHAPTER TIMELINE

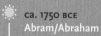
ca. 1750 BCE
Abram/Abraham

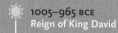
1005–965 BCE
Reign of King David

ca. 1200 BCE
Hebrews begin to
move into Palestine

965–928 BCE
Reign of King
Solomon

time he told Abram to change his name to Abraham, while Sarai was henceforth to be called Sarah. Moreover, God ordered Abraham to circumcise himself and Ishmael and to promise to circumcise all their male offspring on the eighth day after their birth. Abraham did indeed cut off his own foreskin, and some short time later, remarkably, the ninety-nine-year-old Abraham and the ninety-year-old Sarah did conceive a child—a son. They named him Isaac and duly circumcised him on the eighth day. Sarah was joyful to have a child at last but could not help resenting the continued presence of Ishmael and his mother, Hagar, so she ordered them to leave the household. The story takes a bittersweet turn when the Lord speaks to Hagar for the first time and assures her that he has a plan for Ishmael as well: "I will make a great nation of him" (Genesis 21.18).

Whether or not it accords with historical truth, the story reflects a tradition that this one man, Abram/Abraham, was the patriarch of two great nations. Through Sarai/Sarah he fathered the nation of the Hebrews, out of which developed the religion of Judaism, while with his Egyptian concubine Hagar he produced the line that resulted in the Arab nation and their faith of Islam.

The tale bristles with difficulties: why was Abram/Abraham chosen? Why was his family led to the land promised to them at a time of famine, when they could not live there? How did Abram/Abraham justify handing his beloved wife over to the pharaoh's lust? After their release from Egypt, why did God repeat his promise to Abram/Abraham's family, only to let another ten years go by before fulfilling it? After Hagar produced Ishmael, why did he let another twelve years pass before allowing Isaac to be born? And why he did make Hagar endure twelve years of Sarai/Sarah's bullying before extending any consoling promise to her?

But even this is only the beginning of the complexities that dog the effort to know the origins of the children of Abraham. Political and religious ideologies play an important role in this problem, of course, but even more fundamental is the vexing question of the Bible itself and its usefulness as a historical source. The debate is as old as the Bible itself.

950 BCE
Composition of first
biblical texts

ca. 587 BCE
Fall of Jerusalem to the
Chaldeans; beginning
of Babylonian Captivity

ca. 721 BCE
Assyrians conquer Israel

ca. 538 BCE
Persian emperor Cyrus
the Great allows Jews
to return to Jerusalem

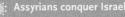
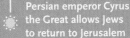

THE BIBLE AND HISTORY

To begin, it is not a book but a library. The Hebrew Bible consists of twenty-four books written over a period of nearly one thousand years. According to Jewish tradition, the entire set of books was finally established, ordered, and canonized around 450 BCE by a group remembered as the "Men of the Great Assembly" (Anshei Knesset ha-Gedolah). Most scholars, however, would regard that as too early a date and prefer something around 250 or 200 BCE—and they place the composition of the first biblical texts as early as 1100 BCE.

Many Christians will be surprised by a first look at the Hebrew Bible, since it organizes the books in a way unfamiliar to Christian tradition. The Hebrew Bible is commonly known as the **Tanakh**—an acronym based on the letters *T* (for **Torah**, meaning "Instructions"), *N* (for Nevi'im, or "Prophets"), and *K* (for Ketuvim, or "Writings")—and it groups its books accordingly. It has the five books attributed to Moses under the first heading, the prophets from Joshua to Malachi under the second, and all the remaining writings under the third. Moreover, there are two distinct versions of the Jewish Bible: the Masoretic text compiled in Hebrew in the 2nd century CE, and the Greek text, the **Septuagint**, compiled around 200 BCE for the Greek-speaking Jews of the Hellenistic era. Jewish tradition, supported by textual criticism, regards the Masoretic text as a definitive re-creation of the lost version put together by the Men of the Great Council. It thus has priority over the Greek version, which is actually five hundred years older.

The Dead Sea Scrolls   The scrolls are a collection of 972 ancient texts found in a dozen caves near Qumran, by the Dead Sea. The scrolls consist largely of Hebrew biblical texts (roughly 40 percent of the total), with a somewhat smaller number of apocryphal biblical writings. The rest of the collection consists of legal and devotional texts. Most of the scrolls are on parchment and are written in Hebrew, Aramaic, Greek, and Nabataean.

TABLE 3.1 **Comparing the Canons of the Jewish Bible**

	HEBREW VERSION	SEPTUAGINT [GREEK]	
Torah	Genesis	Genesis	**Pentateuch**
	Exodus	Exodus	
	Leviticus	Leviticus	
	Numbers	Numbers	
	Deuteronomy	Deuteronomy	
Nevi'im	Joshua	Joshua	
	Judges	Judges	
	1 Samuel	Ruth	
	2 Samuel	1 Samuel (called 1 Kingdoms)	
	1 Kings	2 Samuel (called 2 Kingdoms)	
	2 Kings	1 Kings (called 3 Kingdoms)	
	Isaiah	2 Kings (called 4 Kingdoms)	
	Jeremiah	1 Chronicles	
	Ezekiel	2 Chronicles	
	12 Minor Prophets[1]	1 Esdras	
		2 Esdras	
		Job	
Ketuvim	Psalms	Psalms	
	Proverbs	Proverbs	
	Job	Ecclesiastes	
	The Scrolls[2]	Song of Solomon	
	Daniel	Isaiah	
	Ezra	Jeremiah	
	Nehemiah	Lamentations	
	1 Chronicles	Ezekiel	
	2 Chronicles	Daniel (includes material not in the Tanakh)	
		12 Minor Prophets	
		Tobit	
		Judith	
		Wisdom of Solomon	
		Ecclesiasticus	
		Baruch	
		1–2 Maccabees	
		3 Maccabees	
		Prayer of Manasseh[3]	
		4 Maccabees (appendix)	

Notes:

[1]The Minor Prophets are Hosea, Joel, Amos, Obadiah, Jonah, Micah, Nahum, Habakkuk, Zephaniah, Haggai, Zechariah, and Malachi. The Tanakh regards these as a single book; the Septuagint prints them as individual books.

[2]The Scrolls (also regarded as a single book) consist of The Song of Songs (called the Song of Solomon in the Septuagint), Ruth, Lamentations, Ecclesiastes, and Esther.

[3]The last seven texts are not part of the Hebrew canon.

The Septuagint text varies from the Masoretic in some significant ways, most especially in its acceptance of certain additional books that do not appear in the Hebrew tradition.[2]

The variations in the canon are important: the Hebrew scriptures evolved over time rather than emerging fully formed and perfect at a single moment in history.[3]

The problems are obvious. For one, they ascribe impossibly long lives to the early leaders of the Hebrews. Abraham, we are assured, died in his 175th year, and his son Isaac died aged 180. We are told that Isaac's son Jacob died when he was very old, although a precise age is never given, but Jacob's son Joseph reportedly lived to be 110. A second problem is that the Scriptures coopt stories from other ancient Near Eastern cultures as if they had occurred uniquely to the Hebrews. The legend of Noah and the Ark clearly derives from the Sumerian tale of the Great Flood, to pick the most obvious example. Even the single most important episode in defining the Hebrews as a people presents a problem. Here, Moses leads them out of Egyptian bondage, receives the Torah on Mount Sinai, and guides them to the Promised Land. The story establishes the Hebrews' special **covenant** with God, and yet there is virtually no archeological or documentary evidence for it outside of the Bible itself.

> These difficulties hardly negate the Bible's value as a historical source. Rather, we must read the texts on their own terms: they portray not an earthly history in the usual sense but the development of a relationship—the growth of a people's understanding of their connection to a transcendent deity.

These difficulties hardly negate the Bible's value as a historical source. Rather, we must read the texts on their own terms: they portray not an earthly history in the usual sense but the development of a relationship—the growth of a people's understanding of their connection to a transcendent deity.

Whatever the Bible may lack in exact historical accuracy, it makes up with a searing depiction of a difficult, demanding, and inscrutable God. He places extraordinary obligations on a small, persecuted minority from whom he expects the highest degree of ethical behavior. And their failures to live up to that standard are narrated again and again. The Hebrews are depicted as the **Chosen People**—but that status confers more obligations than rewards. They are Chosen, but not in the sense of favored. Rather, they are held responsible for maintaining a standard of moral behavior and pursuing justice on earth. How else can one interpret the travails of Abraham? Along with the repeated promises and the constant requirement of waiting for fulfillment, he must undergo tension and division within his own household. God tests Abraham far more frequently than he rewards him, and those tests are severe.

---

[2]   The Roman Catholic and the Orthodox churches regard the Septuagint version as normative. Protestant churches usually print the Septuagint's extra books (which they call the Apocrypha) as a type of appendix.

[3]   As historical sources, the Hebrew scriptures are both uniquely valuable and uniquely problematic.

Most cruelly of all, God tells Abraham to take his son Isaac to the top of a hill outside Moriah, pin him on a rock slab that serves as a crude altar, and sacrifice him. Abraham brings him there, ties him up, draws his knife, and begins to plunge it toward his own son, who is old enough to speak and hence to understand what his father is doing. Only when the knife is about to slit Isaac's throat does God intervene and stay Abraham's hand. The Lord then says to Abraham:

> Because you have done this and have not withheld your son, your favored one, I will bestow My blessing upon you and make your descendants as numerous as the stars of heaven and the sands on the seashore; and your descendants shall seize the gates of their foes. All the nations of the earth shall bless themselves by your descendants, because you obeyed My command. *(Genesis 22.16–18)*

We are never told Isaac's reaction to the episode, but we can infer it. He comes across as a passive, almost doddering, figure throughout his own brief part of the Genesis narrative.

The origins of the Bible remain subject to debate even after three thousand years of intense study. The first books to be composed, scholars agree, were the five books of the Torah, which began to appear, in various forms, around 950 BCE and perhaps a bit later than that. What makes dating the texts so challenging is that several authors and editors had a hand in the process. Most Biblical scholars hold to the so-called **Documentary Hypothesis**, which holds that the texts as they survive result from the intertwining of several writers' work, writers known by the initials J, E, D, and P. These indicate, respectively, the Yahwist author (ca. 950 BCE), the Elohist Author (ca. 750 BCE), the Deuteronomist author (ca. 650 BCE), and the Priestly author (ca. 550 BCE). Some scholars add a still later figure known as R, for the Redactor.

The Yahwist (J) is believed to have been the first, and his writings can be identified by his use of the term **YHWH** to stand for God. J is presumed to have written most of Genesis, and certainly those parts of it that relate the stories of Abraham and his descendants. J's God is always YHWH in Hebrew (which English-language Bibles represent by the all-capitals word LORD), and as we have seen, YHWH frequently intervenes directly in his human characters' lives.

The Elohist (E), by contrast, uses a different word[4] but never depicts any direct human encounters with him. In Genesis, the long final section telling the tale of Joseph and his brothers comes from E. (Joseph is the first human being in the Bible who never sees or hears God personally, yet still believes.) E's handiwork is the patchiest, with few long passages apart from the Joseph story, which suggests that it reflects an oral as opposed to written tradition, something interwoven

---

4   Elohim, meaning simply "god" or "deity."

TABLE 3.2 **Chronology of Composition of Hebrew Bible**

DATE	THE TORAH	THE PROPHETS	THE WRITINGS	DEUTEROCANONICAL
1300s				
1200s				
1100s				
1000s				
900s	The Yahwist "J" author			
800s	The Elohist "E" author	Amos Hosea Isaiah Micah		
700s		Zephaniah Nahum Habbakuk Jeremiah	Joshua Judges 1–2 Samuel 1–2 Kings	
600s	Middle portion (ch. 12–29) of Deuteronomy. Priestly "P" author.	Obadiah Ezechiel Isaiah, I–II Haggai Zechariah		
500s	Later portions of Deuteronomy	Isaiah, III	Job Ruth	
400s		Malachi Obadiah Joel Jonah Ezra-Nehemiah	Proverbs Esther Ecclesiastes 1–2 Chronicles Lamentations	
300s				
200s			Daniel	Sirach Ecclesiastes
100s				Tobit Wisdom 2 Maccabees
1				1 Maccabees

All dates are approximate and BCE

here and there throughout the J narrative. Around 750 BCE, the argument goes, as the Assyrian armies marched toward the Hebrew lands, E set to work, trying to preserve the tales handed down among those who settled in the northern part of Palestine as a counterbalance to J's heavy emphasis on the Hebrews in southern Palestine. This desire to preserve the traditions of the northern Hebrews may explain why E so frequently tells stories of sibling rivalry, such as that between Jacob and Esau (Isaac's sons) and between Joseph and his brothers.

The Deuteronomist (D) is the most controversial of the authors. Some scholars consider him to be the author of the book of Deuteronomy but of little else, whereas others regard him as the most critical figure in Biblical transmission. The latter see evidence of his influence throughout the whole of Torah and throughout the historical narratives from Joshua to 2 Kings. In 621 BCE, during repair work on the Temple in Jerusalem, laborers uncovered a long-lost manuscript that consisted of Deuteronomy and (presumably) the rest of the Torah, plus new historical material. D insists on the absolute centrality of allegiance to Torah and worship in the Jerusalem Temple, but also relentlessly describes the crisis of the Assyrian conquest and the approach of the Babylonians as the result of a national failure of morals and observance.

Finally, the Priestly Author (P), or more likely authors, set to work after the fall of Jerusalem to the Babylonians in 587 BCE, inserting a vast body of priestly ordinances from the time of the First Temple into the traditional material of Torah. P's handiwork is woven throughout the first books of the Bible but is especially evident in the book of Leviticus and in the first ten chapters of Numbers. P is also responsible for the first chapter of Genesis (J's version of Creation had begun with chapter 2), for a priestly version of Abraham's covenant with God (Genesis 17), and the story of Moses's death (Deuteronomy 34).

Not all Biblical scholars adhere to the Documentary Hypothesis. Many prefer other explanations for the Bible's abrupt shifts, inordinate repetitions, and frequent contradictions. Everyone agrees, however, that the Bible is a patchwork of many writers' hands—as well as the product of considerable revision, expansion, editing, and rearrangement. It is above all a testament to the Jews' perseverance, their faithful determination to make sense of their experience, and their longing for God. As we shall see, much of that experience consisted of repeated persecution and oppression.[5]

> Everyone agrees, however, that the Bible is a patchwork of many writers' hands—as well as the product of considerable revision, expansion, editing, and rearrangement. It is above all a testament to the Jews' perseverance, their faithful determination to make sense of their experience, and their longing for God.

THE LAND OF CANAAN

Whatever their legendary origins, the Hebrews began to move into Palestine sometime around 1200 BCE. This is a long time after their supposed arrival under Abraham in 1800 BCE. The Bible tells of four hundred years of enslavement in Egypt, followed by a heroic march of liberation and the conquest of Canaan.

In the Bible the march of liberation was led by Moses, to whom was given the first elements of the Torah. As mentioned before, however, no non-Biblical evidence exists for a large Hebrew presence in Egypt at any time during the New Kingdom. Nor is there evidence for a dramatic Hebrew rebellion and subsequent release from bondage. It seems unlikely that events of such magnitude would

---

[5]   The Jews' experience makes the Bible above all else a map of human pain.

go utterly unmentioned in the hundreds of thousands of Egyptian records that survive from the New Kingdom era. Yet it seems equally unlikely that a nation would invent a legend of their own humiliating enslavement if it had no basis in fact. All that can be said with certainty is that when the Hebrews moved into Palestine, around 1200 BCE, they brought with them an unshakeable conviction: God, they believed, had vouchsafed the land to them. In return, they felt a special obligation to live according to an exacting ethical and ritual code, to care for the poor and downtrodden, and to serve the cause of justice.

They were not necessarily a single people and may instead have been a loose assemblage of speakers of related dialect groups. The Bible describes the Hebrews' division into twelve tribes. Figures known as **judges** held a combination of religious and political authority over each tribe, together with military leadership in times of war. The Hebrews could communicate with the other Semitic groups who had already settled the land—the Amalekites, Amorites, Aramaeans, Canaanites, and the Phoenicians—but the Hebrews were overwhelmingly a pastoral people. Their movement over the land with their herds put them at odds with the other Semites who were chiefly farmers and town dwellers. While they remained seminomadic, the Hebrew tribes had carved out certain zones for themselves by 1000 BCE. Those in the hilly south called themselves the people of **Judah**, while the northern-based tribes took the name of **Israel** (see Map 3.1).

Religious life centered on the family, with daily prayers and rituals to observe the emerging body of Torah. The judges and a caste of priests drawn from the tribe of the Levites led communal services that frequently involved some form of animal sacrifice (the "burnt offerings" referred to in the Bible). The Hebrews did not proselytize to non-Hebrews and focused instead on broadening the acceptance of YHWH among their own. Indeed, the Bible tells repeatedly of the people returning to the worship of Golden Calves and other idols.[6]

The Hebrews maintained the political autonomy of each tribe for as long as they could, but when the Philistines conquered the southern coastal plain of the Levant, they were forced to mount a united defense against annihilation. They entered the alliance thinking it would be temporary, and internal bickering made concerted action difficult. In 1050 BCE, or thereabouts, the Philistines demolished the main Hebrew sanctuary at Shiloh and carted off the **Ark of the Covenant** as a war trophy. After that military catastrophe, the bulk of the people called out for the creation of a Hebrew monarchy. Only a clear central command under a charismatic figure with military skill, they argued, could hold the confederation together and destroy the Philistines.

---

[6]   Many Hebrews still felt pulled to the polytheism of their Semitic neighbors—which suggests that the strict monotheistic faith in YHWH was of relatively recent origin. Indeed, many scholars suggest that the development of Jewish monotheism owed something to the westward conquests of the Zoroastrian Persians.

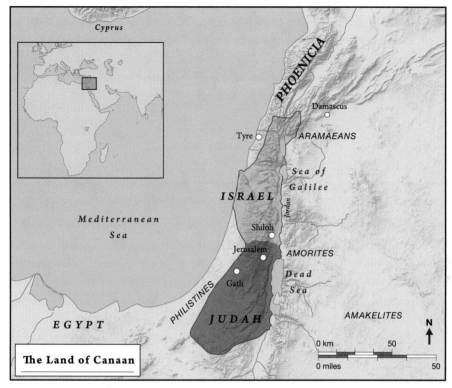

Cyprus

PHOENICIA

Damascus

Tyre   ARAMAEANS

Sea of
Galilee

I S R A E L

Jordan

Mediterranean
Sea

Shiloh

Jerusalem

AMORITES

Dead
Sea

PHILISTINES   Gath

E G Y P T   J U D A H   AMAKELITES

N

0 km   50

0 miles   50

The Land of Canaan

MAP 3.1   **The Land of Canaan**

One of the tribal Judges, named Samuel, advised against it but in the end he agreed, and he selected a military officer named Saul to be the first king of all the Hebrews. Samuel acquiesced after getting this message from YHWH:

> Heed the demand of the people in everything they say to you. For it is not you they have rejected; it is Me they have rejected as king. Like everything else they have done ever since I brought them out of Egypt to this day—forsaking Me and worshiping other gods—so they are doing to you. Heed their demand; but warn them solemnly, and tell them about the practices of any king who will rule over them. (*1 Samuel 8.7–9*)

Saul stopped the Philistine advance into the hills but was unable to push them back to the coast. The stalling of the war effort, coupled perhaps with Saul's personal shortcomings, led Samuel to withdraw his already tepid support and to promote a new leader to take his place. This was David, an ambitious member of Saul's court. David launched a campaign of his own against the Philistines, paralleling that of Saul, and scored a series of quick victories that won him the popular support of the Hebrews. Saul, jealous of David's success and envious of his popularity, banished him from his court. David became an outlaw, trapped between the Philistine coast and the Hebrew hill country, where he began to plot his takeover of Saul's throne. He did so by becoming a mercenary, fighting for the Philistines in the final battle that killed Saul. Shortly afterwards—by tradition, in 1005 BCE—David took the throne for himself.

DREAMS OF A GOLDEN AGE

David's reign (1005–965 BCE) is noted for three achievements. He pushed the borders of the Israelite kingdom to their greatest expanse, from the Gulf of Aqaba in the south to fifty miles north of the Sea of Galilee; he established Jerusalem as the capital city; and he composed psalms (see Map 3.2).

Politically, the Israelites were now among the most powerful nations in the Near East. The choice of Jerusalem for the capital of his kingdom showed David's shrewdness, for its central location made it well placed to watch over both the northern and southern tribes. Even more important, the city, which had been founded centuries earlier by the Canaanites, had no prior religious significance for the Hebrews. Hence it was unlikely to fuel tribal competition for privilege. David brought the Ark of

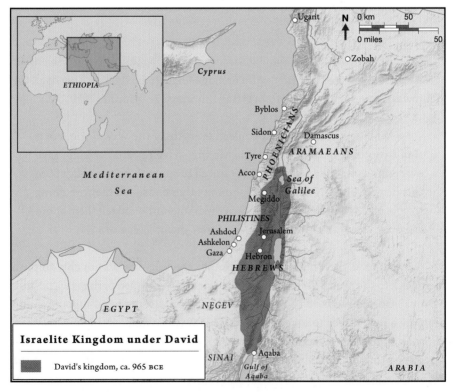

MAP 3.2   Israelite Kingdom under David

the Covenant into the city and began to construct a magnificent palace for himself (which he financed with a combination of heavy taxation, forced loans, and slave labor). As for the psalms, 1 Samuel 16.23 describes David as a musician of talent. Yet if David indeed wrote any of them, they are only Psalms 1 through 41.

David's son Solomon (r. 965–928 BCE) succeeded him and threw his considerable energy into enlarging his father's palace complex. He also began construction of a temple to house the Ark of the Covenant. The Bible devotes three entire chapters to describing the Temple (1 Kings 6–8). Everything about it deserved mentioning, starting with its size—thirty feet wide, ninety feet deep, with three stories. It had latticed windows, inlaid wood paneling, carved cherubim, chains that secured double doors leading into the inner sanctuary where the Ark was placed, and statuary embossed with gold leaf. This was, the Bible assures us, a house fit for the Lord. Solomon also expanded the royal palace until it formed a vast complex with the Temple.

Moreover, he built the Israelites' first commercial fleet, which sailed out of the Gulf of Aqaba at the kingdom's far southern tip on the Red Sea. It put Israel in direct contact with Upper Egypt, Ethiopia, and the coastal peoples of the Arabian peninsula. The Israelites sold the copper that they (or their slaves, actually) mined from the rich veins found in the southern Negev. The trade was highly lucrative and helped to finance the palace and Temple projects.

The Bible portrays Solomon, like his father, as a wise and great ruler who championed the causes of justice and piety.[7] Solomon wrote psalms, too, and is credited with writing the books of Proverbs and the Song of Songs. Both men, however, could be selfish and despotic, and despite their genuine positive traits were nowhere near as popular in their lifetimes as in later centuries. Their sexual appetites were tireless: David pursued married women as well as servant girls, and Solomon, we are told, had seven hundred wives and three hundred concubines, including "the daughter of Pharaoh, women of the Moabites, Ammonites, Edomites, Zidonians, and Hittites" (1 Kings 11.1). They had cruel streaks, too. In the story of the beautiful Bathsheba, David intentionally ordered her husband into battle so that he could then claim the widow for himself. After a victory over the people of Zobah, David took over twenty thousand Canaanite soldiers captive as slaves and had all their horses hamstrung. Solomon's consorts were of an exceptionally large number, but his bed-hopping was not intrinsically wrong. Polygamy was common among the early Israelites, especially among the elites.

Most likely, the overwhelmingly flattering nature of the Bible's portrayal of these men resulted from the role they played in strengthening the cult of YHWH. All their conquests, their building projects, their artistic endeavors, their efforts to provide justice for the people—everything was done in service to the God whose great Temple

---

7   "King Solomon excelled all the kings on earth in wealth and in wisdom. All the world came to pay homage to Solomon and to listen to the wisdom with which God had endowed him" (1 Kings 10.23–24).

The Temple of Solomon Artist's reconstruction of Solomon's palace and the Temple in Jerusalem, built in the middle of the 10th century BCE.

they had raised in Jerusalem. Compared to this, what did some sexual peccadilloes matter? The Bible's compilers gladly held up the David-Solomon era as the Golden Age of ancient Israel, and the tales of these two kings entered Jewish folklore.

The romanticization of David and Solomon introduced an entirely new element into Western culture, or at least one for which no earlier evidence survives—namely, the popular belief in a past paradise, a lost era of former glory, when humanity had attained a perfection of happiness. This is more than mere nostalgia, and it has been a hallmark of Western life ever since. Throughout the centuries Western societies have attempted to evoke or re-create a golden age—a past from which we have declined and to which we hope to return. Our reformations therefore tend to be *reformations*, efforts to restore past glories rather than to create new ones. It might be the Jews' struggle to reestablish themselves in the Promised Land. It might be American mythmaking about the Founding Fathers, the old West, or a pristine game of baseball before Astroturf and the designated hitter. In each case, Western culture has sought to return to a perfection we have lost.

According to the Bible, the northern tribes refused to accept Solomon's son Rehoboam as their king and broke away to form a separate realm. Hence from 937 to 721 BCE there were *two* Hebrew kingdoms—the kingdom of Israel in the north, with its capital at Shechem, and the kingdom of Judah in the south, still centered on Jerusalem. Judah, though smaller, had the advantage of its relatively isolated

> Throughout the centuries Western societies have attempted to evoke or recreate a golden age—a past from which we have declined and to which we hope to return. Our reformations therefore tend to be *reformations*, efforts to restore past glories rather than to create new ones.

TABLE 3.3   **More Dreams of a Golden Age**

We encounter many romanticized ideals of past greatness in history, including these:

The Jews	A Greater Israel
Greece	Periclean Athens
Imperial Rome	The glories of the Republic
Feudal Europe	An Arthurian Camelot
Renaissance Italy	The perspective, harmony, and virtue of classical Rome
Protestant Reformation	The spiritual and communal perfection of the first Christians
Islam	The fabled tolerance and high culture of the medieval caliphate
Ottoman Empire	The magnificence of Suleiman the Magnificent
France	The First, Second, or Third Republics; the First, Second, or Third Empires
England and America	The reign of Queen Victoria
America	The Founding Fathers The cowboy gunmen of the Old West The common man (e.g., Frank Capra films, Norman Rockwell paintings) Slain leaders (Abraham Lincoln, John F. Kennedy)

position in the hills. As a state and, more importantly, as a people, Israel disappeared with the arrival of the Assyrians in 732 BCE. These brutal conquerors annihilated tens of thousands and sent the rest off into slavery throughout the Assyrian Empire, where they vanished—the famous Ten Lost Tribes of Israel. The people of Judah, henceforth known as Jews, held out until they were overwhelmed by the Chaldeans, or Neo-Babylonians, under their ruler Nebuchadnezzar, in 587 BCE. This began the **Diaspora** ("exile" or "scattering"). The Chaldeans destroyed the Temple at Jerusalem and took the Jews eastward into the **Babylonian Captivity**.

WOMEN AND THE LAW

Fixing the status of women in ancient Jewish society is no easy task, but not, as with other Near Eastern peoples, because of a dearth of evidence. The Bible devotes hundreds of pages to describing, praising, criticizing, legislating, berating, lamenting, and expressing gratitude for the women of the Hebrew world. The image that emerges from it is complex and sometimes self-contradictory, and yet it is clear that Jewish society gave its women more social autonomy, legal rights, education, and respect than any other ancient group, with the possible exception of the Persian Zoroastrians—whose treatment of women remains far less understood because of the paucity of sources. (Most of the archives and libraries of the Zoroastrians were destroyed, often intentionally, during the Islamic conquests of the 7th and 8th centuries CE.)[8]

---

[8]   No other ancient people has left such varied and detailed records about how they regarded their mothers, wives, sisters, and daughters.

Ten Lost Tribes of Israel   The Assyrians invaded the northern Hebrew kingdom of Israel in 732 BCE and completed its conquest of the land by 720. Campaigns against towns along the former border with the Kingdom of Judah continued for another quarter century. This relief depicts Israelite captives loading provisions onto a cart, in preparation for their long trek into enslavement in the east. An Assyrian soldier stands guard in the center. One entire room in the Assyrian palace at Nineveh was devoted to depicting this particular campaign of the ruler Sennacherib (r. 705–681) against the Israelite city of Lachish. This relief forms just one small component of the larger pictorial narrative. The biblical version of the campaign appears in II Chronicles, ch. 32.

The legendary and narrative passages depicting the pre-Mosaic era invariably describe women as having been created in order to help, if not to serve, men. From Sarai/Sarah on, Hebrew women appear overwhelmingly in the roles of dutiful daughters, obedient wives, and loving mothers. Enough exceptions to the pattern exist, however, to suggest that many women did carve out different paths for themselves. Moses's own sister, the prophetess Miriam, helped to guide the Hebrews across the Red Sea and led their celebration of thanksgiving once they had reached the other side. Another prophetess, Deborah, actually governed one of the twelve tribes during the era of the Judges. And a married woman named Huldah was so respected for her knowledge of Jewish Law that King Josiah of Judah (r. 641–609 BCE) entrusted her with validating a newly discovered Torah-scroll fragment found in Jerusalem. Two other women, whether historical or not, were deemed significant enough to deserve entire Biblical books devoted to their stories: Esther, a young Jewish girl who becomes queen of Persia and uses her position to forestall a plot to annihilate the Jews within the empire, and Ruth, the main character (and a convert to Judaism) in a charming story about long-suffering love, faithful friendship, and fulfillment.[9]

The Torah established the framework for women's roles in Jewish society. As usual, the discrepancies between male and female prerogatives are first to draw one's attention. The Law strictly demands virginity of girls before marriage but lays no comparable burden on boys; women cannot give testimony in civil or criminal cases; a husband can divorce his wife for cause, but not vice versa unless the husband agrees to the split. On the other hand, tradition gave girls the right to a basic education (usually enough to allow them to read the Scriptures and guide their own children's early religious education), guaranteed their entitlement to inherit property, allowed them limited economic autonomy, and accorded protection to widows. The bans on women entering the Temple or performing other liturgical rites during menstruation or immediately after giving birth, times when they are labeled "impure" or "unclean" (Hebrew *tumeh*), may seem misogynistic but appear less so when one considers the more numerous conditions that rendered a man tumeh—such as touching the carcasses of proscribed animals, experiencing nocturnal emissions, developing a rash or sore on his skin, or even just acquiring a bald patch in his beard. To be tumeh did not denote sinfulness or a loss of self-worth; it meant only that one was not ceremonially fit for certain religious rites and needed to undergo a ritual purification or cleansing. Nevertheless, women of all ages were generally regarded as individuals needing higher degrees of protection and guidance.

The fifth commandment given to Moses on Mount Sinai enjoined all Hebrews to honor their mothers and fathers equally, and a later rabbinical judgment declared—rhetorically, not juridically—"Death to him who strikes or curses his own mother." But the tenth commandment forbade men from coveting their neighbors' wives, houses, work animals, "or any other thing belonging to your neighbor," a command that would seem to regard wives as possessions rather than people. Within marriage, the Law required husbands to honor, support, and work on behalf of their wives at least to an extent that matched the value of the property a woman brought into the marriage by her dowry. Wives who brought no domestic servants into their marriage were expected to perform six specific household tasks for their husbands: grinding grain, cooking, cleaning, spinning and weaving, bed preparation, and child nursing. A Jewish wife was entitled to relinquish one of these essential labors for every servant provided by her dowry.[10] Wives were exempt from an obligation to perform fieldwork. The Law expected women as well as men to make annual visits to the Temple in Jerusalem, especially

---

[9]   To this day, Jews in Iran are referred to colloquially as Esther's children.

[10]   Mothers led the prayers that preceded the main daily meal, and in pre-Temple times they participated in performing ritual sacrifices.

at Passover, and provided special bathing spaces for women to prepare themselves for entering the House of the Lord.

Among the most popular of Biblical books is the **Song of Songs**, also known as the Song of Solomon, which consists of a poetic dialogue between a bride and bridegroom that celebrates married love in all its emotional and physical intimacy. Centuries of religious commentary have interpreted the text as an allegory of the covenant between God and his people, but a simpler reading sees in it a hymn to the joy that married union brings in equal measure to man and wife. The bride speaks first:

> Oh, give me the kisses of your mouth,
> For your love is more delightful than wine.
> Your ointments yield a sweet fragrance,
> Your name is like finest oil—
> Therefore do maidens love you.
> Draw me after you, let us run!
> The king has brought me to his chambers.
> Let us delight and rejoice in your love,
> Savoring it more than wine.   *(Song of Songs 1.2–4)*

To which the bridegroom sings in reply:

> You have captured my heart,
> My own, my bride,
> You have captured my heart
> With one glance of your eyes,
> With one coil of your necklace.
> How sweet is your love,
> My own, my bride!
> How much more delightful your love than wine,
> Your ointments more fragrant
> Than any spice!
> Sweetness drops
> From your lips, O bride;
> Honey and milk
> Are under your tongue;
> And the scent of your robes
> Is like the scent of Lebanon.   *(4.9–11)*

Sexual delight is an intrinsic element of married love, and the Law recognizes the woman's full enjoyment of it. But pleasure is not the only reason for marriage. God's first instruction to Adam and Eve in the Garden of Eden was to reproduce: "Be fertile and increase, fill the earth and master it." Every Jewish man therefore was expected to marry as early as possible, which most priests and rabbis interpreted to mean the onset of puberty. The Torah not only declines to praise celibacy, it never even mentions it.[11] A girl could not be forced into marriage before puberty and retained a limited right to refuse a marriage partner proposed by her father after she had reached it. The Law does not demand marriage of all females as it does of males, but rabbinical tradition advises women not to remain single, lest they come under suspicion by their neighbors as sexual adventuresses.

Women in ancient Israel and Judah, on the whole, were better off than most of their contemporaries: they could own and inherit property, received at least a basic education, enjoyed legal rights in marriage, participated actively in the religious life of the community, and received the respect of their peers and the veneration of their families so long as they obeyed the Law.

> Women in ancient Israel and Judah, on the whole, were better off than most of their contemporaries: they could own and inherit property, received at least a basic education, enjoyed legal rights in marriage, participated actively in the religious life of the community, and received the respect of their peers and the veneration of their families so long as they obeyed the Law.

PROPHETS AND PROPHECY

The splitting of the Hebrew kingdom and the subsequent disappearance of the successor states prompted the arrival of the age of the great prophets. Samuel, last of the Judges, was the first of the great prophets. After him came Elijah and Elisha (both mid- to late 9th century BCE), Amos and Hosea (mid-8th century), Isaiah and Micah (late 8th century), Jeremiah (late 7th to early 6th centuries), and Ezekiel (early 6th century). The Minor Prophets—so called for the length, not the significance, of their prophetic books—came too. Allowing for differences between them as individuals, the prophets as a group shared a calling to warn the Hebrews of the approaching Assyrian and Babylonian dangers and to interpret those dangers as signs of YHWH's growing displeasure. By failing to uphold standards of justice, decency, and observance of the Torah, they warned, the people had placed themselves in both mortal and spiritual peril; as Jeremiah put it in his Temple sermon:

> Thus said the LORD of Hosts, the God of Israel: "Mend your ways and your actions, and I will let you dwell in this place. Don't put your trust

---

[11] The prophet Jeremiah is the only Jewish figure in the Hebrew Bible known to have been celibate (see Jeremiah 16.2).

in illusions and say, 'The Temple of the LORD, the Temple of the LORD, the Temple of the LORD are the [buildings].' No, if you really mend your ways and your actions; if you execute justice between one man and another; if you do not oppress the stranger, the orphan, and the widow; if you do not shed the blood of the innocent in this place; if you do not follow other gods, to your own hurt—then only will I let you dwell in this place, in this land that I gave to your fathers for all time." *(Jeremiah 7.3–7)*

In casting the blame for their misfortunes upon themselves, the Jews introduced the essential notions of self-criticism and moral responsibility into Western culture. It hardly seems possible to imagine a Sumerian interpreting a calamity like the Hittite invasion as anything other than divine whim, or to picture an Egyptian interpreting the Hyksos catastrophe as the consequence of a moral failing on Egypt's part. Earlier societies had senses of morality, but those morals had little to do with their religions. The Jews, however, went even further and conflated faith and morals to a degree that they could not be separated or distinguished.[12] **She'ol** was the Biblical underworld, and yet the ancient Hebrews did not believe in separate places of reward and punishment in the afterlife. A good life of devotion to YHWH, ethical behavior, and commitment to justice was desirable for its own sake, not as a means to a heavenly end. Ethic and action were necessary components of each other, intrinsic and inextricable.

This was a revolutionary development in Western life, but one that hardly made the Jews any happier a people. Joy and agony are both present on every page of the Bible, and indeed the Scriptures are often at their greatest expressive power when crying out in pain. Among the psalms attributed to David, one that has entered Jewish liturgy as a daily prayer for supplication is the following:

> O LORD, do not punish me in anger,
>> do not chastise me in fury.
>> Have mercy on me, O LORD, for I languish;
>> heal me, O LORD, for my bones shake with terror.
>> My whole being is stricken with terror,
>> while You, LORD—O, how long!

---

12 Among ancient Near Eastern cultures, only the Zoroastrianism of the late-coming Persians connected ethics with religious observance.

O LORD, turn! Rescue me!
>   Deliver me as befits Your faithfulness.
>   For there is no praise of You among the dead;
>   in Sheol, who can acclaim You?
>   I am weary with groaning;
>   every night I drench my bed.
>   I melt my couch in tears.
>   My eyes are wasted by vexation,
>   worn out because of all my foes.
>   Away from me, all you evildoers,
>   for the LORD heeds the sound of my weeping.
>   The LORD heeds my plea,
>   the LORD accepts my prayer.
>   All my enemies will be frustrated and stricken with terror;
>   they will turn back in an instant, frustrated.   (Psalm 6)

Few ancient texts expressed comparable sentiments; only the Sumerian "Song of the Righteous Sufferer" comes close to such power.

PRIESTS AND RABBIS

The loss of Jerusalem, the Temple, and the land of their fathers, and the Jews' captivity in Babylon represented crises of the highest order. Had YHWH abandoned the Jews, turned his back on them, and revoked the promises he had made to Abraham and Moses? These concerns motivated the prophets to call the Jews to stricter observance of Torah, to stamp out immoral behavior, and to turn their hearts and minds to YHWH. But how was stricter observance of Torah possible when the Jews no longer lived in a Jewish society? The question prompted a shift in authority from the priestly caste to rabbis and the Bible itself. When the Persian emperor finally allowed the Jews to return from captivity, the same questions divided Jewish society.

For nearly five hundred years Jewish religious life had centered on the home and the Temple. To live an observant Jewish life, while ethically challenging, was logistically simpler in a mostly Jewish realm: the distances involved were, after all, not so great. The daily disciplines of prayer, charity, fair dealing, and hospitality were practiced in the home. The ritual demands of communal worship could be observed by intermittent journeys to the Temple in Jerusalem. The high priests controlled Temple life, performed the rituals, resolved disputes, and represented the community of the Chosen. The king administered the realm, defended the people, and worked to keep the economy afloat.

Now the Jews were shorn of centuries of tradition—exiled from their beloved Temple, the ritual prayers, ceremonies, and sacrifices that provided spiritual sustenance and communal identity. They were in captivity and in the minority, facing day-to-day situations that had never occurred in their own kingdom. In these times, established law no longer clearly applied. Does the prohibition of a Jew eating under the roof of a non-Jew apply to a Jewish slave of a Babylonian master? May a Jew indentured to a Persian employer obey his boss's commands on the Sabbath? Under what conditions may a Jew enter a business partnership with a non-Jew? If no Jewish physician is available, may an ill or wounded Jew seek care from a Gentile physician? Such problems had been addressed to some extent in the past, but usually in the abstract. These questions, and others like them, were now urgent.

Compounding the difficulties, the priestly caste had been largely eradicated or marginalized. To whom, then, could the Jews turn for answers? During the fifty years of their Babylonian Captivity, they turned increasingly to their rabbis. The status of **rabbi** had a long lineage going back centuries. Originally an honorific term, the word meant something like "master," in the sense of a person of skill: a man who learned a craft from an expert might call that expert his rabbi, just as a person might honor a special tutor. By the 6th century BCE, however, a rabbi was specifically a teacher of Jewish law. Shorn of their Temple lives, the Jews turned to the rabbis, who became the de facto leaders of the Jews in exile. Rabbis continued to teach Torah but also increasingly became religious judges. Their role was to extrapolate from the principles of Torah, so as to redefine an authentic Jewish life in radically changed circumstances. The incremental growth of a body of rabbinical law—analogous to the tort law of modern societies—came to heavily influence Jewish life and identity, even to the point where legal scholars started to refer to rabbinical judgments as the expression of an Oral Torah that supplemented the written Law. In response, groups of exiled priests began to revise the codified Torah, inserting laws and rituals associated with the P author and reemphasizing the centrality of priestly worship in Jewish life.

In 538 BCE the Persian emperor Cyrus the Great (r. 576–530 BCE) released the Jews and allowed them to return to Jerusalem. His decision triggered a predictable conflict. Must the new generations of Jews, who never knew Temple worship or the authority of the priests, relinquish rabbinical teaching and leadership? Was rabbinical Judaism merely a temporary measure in an emergency, or was it a new and authentic way of being a Jew? Moreover, who would decide—the priests? The rabbis? The people themselves?

The prophets Haggai and Zechariah, whose books appeared at just this time, urged the rebuilding of the Temple and reestablishment of priestly authority. Did the construction of a Second Temple on the ruins of the First mean the restoration of the old order, or could rabbinical tradition somehow embrace and even subsume the traditions of the past? This conflict motivated much of the compiling, editing, and rewriting of the Bible described earlier in this chapter. The territory of Judah remained under Persian control for another two hundred years, until Alexander the Great began his conquest of the entire Near East around 330 BCE, but the situation remained in flux.

As late as 458 BCE, the prophet Ezra came to Jerusalem from Babylon with his own edition of the Torah, promoting reform along rabbinical lines. Ezra, indeed, is the essential source for rabbinical Judaism, a second Moses in his authority. While the book emphasizes Ezra's charisma to establish his authority, it relies even more on a decree by the Persian emperor Artaxerxes I (r. 465–424 BCE):

> Artaxerxes king of kings, to Ezra the priest, scholar in the law of the God of heaven, and so forth. And now, I hereby issue an order that anyone in my kingdom who is of the people of Israel and its priests and Levites who feels impelled to go to Jerusalem may go with you. For you are commissioned by the king and his seven advisers to regulate Judah and Jerusalem according to the law of your God, which is in your care, and to bring the freewill offering of silver and gold, which the king and his advisers made to the God of Israel, whose dwelling is in Jerusalem. . . . And you, Ezra, by the divine wisdom you possess, appoint magistrates and judges to judge all the people in the province of Beyond the River who know the laws of your God, and to teach those who do not know them. Let anyone who does not obey the law of your God and the laws of the king be punished with dispatch, whether by death, corporal punishment, confiscation of possessions, or imprisonment. *(Ezra 7.12–15, 25–26)*

A GENIUS FOR REINVENTION

Judaism's genius for reinvention helped it to survive tumultuous changes in its social and political fortunes. Whatever their earliest origins, the Hebrews entered Palestine with a developing understanding of their uniqueness. Rare monotheists in an overwhelmingly polytheistic world, they sustained a faith in their responsibility to God and in their exclusive rights to a particular homeland. Its dissolution and loss was only the first of many catastrophes that prompted them to reengage with tradition, to reinterpret their past and present lives, and to chart new paths for their development.

The result of this reinvention is the Bible itself, as it took shape after shape. Where tradition before had been primarily oral, the Hebrew Scriptures gradually emerged as a canon. It and the centuries of commentary that followed represent a uniquely fascinating archive of a people's dreams and disappointments.

Factions of Jews debated not only the proper ways of worshipping YHWH and adhering to his laws but even the fundamental issue of who exactly was a Jew.

The Babylonians, after all, did not forcibly relocate every single Jew to the east. A rigid social group, or caste, may make religious, social, or economic distinctions. The Babylonians had carted off primarily the higher-caste Jews in *all* those senses, in an effort to decapitate Jewish society and render it more pliant.[13]

The numbers involved are small. The population of Judah before the Exile had been perhaps as low as thirty thousand, one-quarter of whom were sent into captivity. Certainly that was enough to end Judean life as it had existed. The economy of the fifty-year Persian era declined to mere subsistence level; effective government ended and was replaced by Persian overseers whose chief interest was the collection of tribute. The biblical book of Lamentations vividly depicts the despair felt by the people who interpreted Judah's fall as a sign of God's rejection of them:

> The Lord has laid waste without pity
> All the habitations of Jacob;
> He has razed in His anger
> Fair Judah's strongholds.
> He has brought low in dishonor
> The kingdom and its leaders.
> In blazing anger He has cut down
> All the might of Israel;
> He has withdrawn His right hand
> In the presence of the foe;
> He has ravaged Jacob like flaming fire,
> Consuming on all sides. *(Lamentations 2.2–3)*

Adding to the misery, many Jews had decided to reject the YHWH cult altogether and had assimilated into the culture and religion of their captors. Jeremiah, who was among the Jews who went to Egypt, prophesied YHWH's further wrath upon the apostates who gave themselves over to foreign gods:

> And now, thus said the LORD, the God of hosts, the God of Israel: 'Why are you doing such great harm to yourselves, so that every man and woman, child and infant of yours shall be cut off from the midst of Judah, and no remnant shall be left of you? For you vex me by your deeds, making offerings to other gods in the land of Egypt where you have come to sojourn, so that you shall be cut off and become a curse and a mockery among all the nations of earth. . . . I am going to set my face against you for punishment, to cut off all of Judah. I will take the remnant of Judah

---

[13]   Except for professionals and artisans, the majority of the population in the Persian era remained behind.

The Second Temple   Reconstruction model of the Second Temple, built after the return of the Hebrews from the Babylonian Captivity, after 547 BCE.

who turned their faces toward the land of Egypt, to go and sojourn there, and they shall be utterly consumed in the land of Egypt. They shall fall by the sword, they shall be consumed by famine; great and small alike shall die by the sword and by famine, and they shall become an execration and a desolation, a curse and a mockery. I will punish those who live in the land of Egypt as I punished Jerusalem, with the sword, with famine, and with pestilence. Of the remnant of Judah who came to sojourn here in the land of Egypt, no survivor or fugitive shall be left to return to the land of Judah. Though they all long to return and dwell there, none shall return except [a few] survivors.' *(Jeremiah 44.7–8, 11–14)*

The Temple, then nothing but ruins, remained at least a site of symbolic significance. It is possible that some sort of communal religious life had taken place there during the Exile, but the records are unclear. But when the emperor Cyrus decreed that the Jews were free to return to Judah and to rebuild their Temple, surprisingly few chose to do so. Life in Babylonia and Egypt had been better than the captives had expected. The general tolerance with which they were treated, together with the Jews' own adaptive skills, brought them a level of material prosperity that they had not been able to achieve in remote Judah. The small minority of exiles who returned to Jerusalem consisted primarily of those associated in one way or another with the Temple and palace. Their efforts to reestablish their old authority in Jerusalem left the

The "Wailing Wall"   All that remains of
the Second Temple today.

Diaspora communities free to develop their rabbinical traditions without resistance.

Few of the Jews who had remained behind in Judah welcomed the idea of re-installing the old hierarchy, so relations between the population and the return-ees remained tense. The elites, widely suspected of collusion with the Persian overlords, made matters worse by refer-ring to themselves as "the children of the Exile" while dismissing the rest of the population as "the people of the land." Intentionally or not, the Temple faction implied that they alone were the true bearers of Jewish tradition. Ezra and Nehe-miah, the two most prominent prophets of the mid-5th century BCE and ardent champions of the Temple party, railed against Jews who had married outside the faith and those who undeservingly claimed the traditional self-identification of "children of Israel" and "children of Abraham."

Economic factors played a role in this conflict too. Many of the returnees had put up their old properties as collateral for loans: they needed cash to recapitalize their business concerns. When some of those concerns failed, their property was often seized.

With so much at stake, it hardly comes as a surprise that so much effort at recording, revising, expanding, editing, and reinterpreting the Scriptures took place in this era. The Jews of the 6th and 5th centuries BCE were in a crucible of intense political and economic heat that compounded and aggravated the painful struggle to define Jewish identity. YHWH was proving to be a harsh taskmaster, and his people were learning that to be chosen was not necessarily to win.

WHO, WHAT, WHERE

Ark of the Covenant	Israel
Babylonian Captivity	rabbi
Chosen People	Septuagint
covenant	She'ol
Diaspora	Song of Songs
Documentary Hypothesis	Tanakh
Judah	Torah
judges	YHWH

SUGGESTED READINGS

Primary Source

Berlin, Adele, and Marc Zvi Brettler, eds. *The Jewish Study Bible: Jewish Publication Society Tanakh Translation* (2004).

Anthologies

Arnold, Bill T., and Bryan E. Beyer, eds. *Readings from the Ancient Near East: Primary Sources for Old Testament Study* (2002).

Hallo, William W., ed. *The Context of Scripture* (2002).

Studies

Bartor, Assnat. *Reading Law as Narrative: A Study in the Casuistic Laws of the Pentateuch* (2010).

Esler, Philip F. *Ancient Israel: The Old Testament in Its Social Context* (2006).

Finkelstein, Israel, and Neil Asher Silberman. *The Bible Unearthed: Archaeology's New Vision of Ancient Israel and the Origin of Its Sacred Texts* (2002).

——. *David and Solomon: In Search of the Bible's Sacred Kings and the Roots of the Western Tradition* (2007).

Flusser, David. *Judaism of the Second Temple Period.* Vol. 1, *Qumran and Apocalypticism* (2007).

——. *Judaism of the Second Temple Period.* Vol. 2, *The Jewish Sages and Their Literature* (2009).

Halpern, Baruch. *The First Historians: The Hebrew Bible and History* (2003).

Hays, J. Daniel, and Tremper Longman. *The Message of the Prophets: A Survey of the Prophetic and Apocalyptic Books of the Old Testament* (2010).

Hendel, Ronald. *Remembering Abraham: Culture, Memory, and History in the Hebrew Bible* (2004).

King, Philip J., and Lawrence E. Stager. *Life in Biblical Israel* (2002).

Liverani, Mario. *Israel's History and the History of Israel* (2007).

Pardes, Ilana. *The Biography of Ancient Israel: National Narratives in the Bible* (2000).

Person, Raymond F., Jr. *The Deuteronomic History and the Book of Chronicles: Scribal Works in an Oral World* (2010).

Schiffman, Lawrence H. *Qumran and Jerusalem: Studies in the Dead Sea Scrolls and the History of Judaism* (2010).

——. *Understanding Second Temple and Rabbinic Judaism* (2003).

Smith, Mark S. *The Memoirs of God: History, Memory, and the Experience of the Divine in Ancient Israel* (2004).

Stavrakopoulou, Francesca, and John Barton. *Religious Diversity in Ancient Israel and Judah* (2010).

Van der Toorn, Karel. *Scribal Culture and the Making of the Hebrew Bible* (2009).

Weinfeld, Moshe. *Normative and Sectarian Judaism in the Second Temple Period* (2010).

——. *The Place of the Law in the Religion of Ancient Israel* (2004).

For additional resources, including maps, primary sources, visuals, web links, and quizzes, please go to **www.oup.com/us/backman.**

CHAPTER 4

Greeks and Persians

2000 BCE–479 BCE

G reek history begins around 2000 BCE, when the first Indo-European settlers appeared around the Aegean rim. In the Mycenaean age, those on the mainland grew wealthy— and in the epic poetry of Homer, the Greeks took them for their ancestors. The Greeks themselves drew up armies, established colonies, and developed the first philosophers. They founded the city-states of Miletus, Sparta, and Athens, and they came into collision with a great empire in Persia. But their origins lie in legends.

GREECE AND PERSIA

Aegean Sea · Black Sea · Caucasus · GREECE · Asia Minor · Sicily · Crete · Mediterranean Sea · PHOENICIA · MESOPOTAMIA · PERSIA · Nile · EGYPT · Red Sea

◄ **Koure** Starting in the Archaic Age, Greek sculptors popularized the use of figures called *kouros* ("youth") and *koure* ("maiden"), in worship of Apollo. The purpose of the statues is still debated. Male *kouroi* are usually nude, beardless, and standing erect in a posture reminiscent of Egyptian statuary. This statue of a *koure* was produced in the mid-6th century BCE and was used to mark the grave of the woman who modeled for it. The artist's inscription at the base gives her name, Phrasikleia. It reads: "The grave marker of Phrasikleia. I shall be called a maiden *[koure]* forever, since the gods allotted me this identity instead of a marriage. Aristion of Paros carved me."

FROM CHAOS TO TRAGEDY

The legends are not always pretty: the cosmos began with primordial Chaos, out of which emerged the elemental forces of Gaia (Earth), Eros (Love), Tartarus (Abyss), and Erebus (Darkness). Earth brought forth, through self-gestation, Uranus (Sky)—which is when the trouble began. Uranus took his own mother, Gaia, as his wife, and they produced the twelve Titans. One of them, Kronos castrated his father, overthrew his mother, and took up lordship of the heavens, subjecting his Titanic brothers and

- From Chaos to Tragedy
- The Mycenaean World: Heroes and Kings
- The End of an Age and Mythic Ancestors
- Colonists, Hoplites, and Tyrants
- A Cult of Masculinity
- Sparta: The Militarization of the Citizenry
- Miletus: A Merchant Oligarchy and the First Philosophers
- Athenian Democracy
- The Persian Wars

CHAPTER OUTLINE

sisters to his rule, except for his sister Rhea (Fertility), whom he took as his queen. Fearing that one of his children might do to him what he had done to his own father, Cronos took each child that Rhea produced and ate it. Rhea, we are told, disliked this; so she took the next child that came along (Zeus, the god of Thunder) and hid it and gave Cronos a stone wrapped in a blanket to eat instead. When Zeus grew to manhood, he drugged Cronos with a potion that made him vomit all his children. Zeus then rallied his revived siblings to join him in killing Cronos and seizing control of heaven.

The Birth of Athena   The patron goddess of Athens, Athena was said to have been born, fully grown, from the head of her father, Zeus. In this image from ca. 500 BCE, Athena springs from Zeus's skull. Hephaistos, the forger god who had cracked Zeus's head open with his axe, to speed up the delivery, has apparently fled the scene. Apollo and Hermes appear on the left; Ares and Aphrodite on the right.

All this was just the beginning of the story. Greek mythology consists of hundreds of tales regarding the great **Olympian deities** (Zeus and his siblings, who lived on the mythical Mount Olympus), demigods, and heroes, whose adventures display astonishing creative power and vitality. Themes of incest, patricide, and rebellion occur with unnerving frequency. Like some of their Near Eastern peers, Greek gods and goddesses can be petulant, vain, and full of self-importance, but they also embody virtues of honor, justice, and love. They do not always act admirably, but they do not act without reason. If anything, the myths portray life as an intricate web of passionate feeling and reaction. Each myth leads into and influences the next. A spurned wife here emerges as a wrathful harridan there. A proud king in one story becomes the humbled fallen in another. Greek mythology presents a

CHAPTER TIMELINE

2500 BCE	1375 BCE	776 BCE
Beginning of Minoan Culture on island of Crete	Mycenaeans seize Knossos	First Olympic Games held

1600 BCE	1450 BCE	1200 BCE
Appearance of Mycenaeans in Greece; use of Linear B script	Mycenaeans destroy and/or take over most cities in Crete, with exception of Knossos	Dark Age begins; Mycenaean Greece destroyed

universe of emotion, ambition, and a search for justice—but it also portrays, often with horrifying effect, the unexpected consequences of every action. Life began with Chaos, as the Greeks saw it, and it usually ends in tragedy.

THE MYCENAEAN WORLD: HEROES AND KINGS

Although the first settlers may have been of diverse origins, they quickly developed a sense of a cultural unity and began to refer to themselves as a single people—the Hellenes.[1] They inhabited a larger territory than the Greek mainland itself. In ancient times, the term Greece meant the rough circle of land consisting of the Greek peninsula to the west, the coasts of Macedonia and Thrace to the north, coastal Asia Minor to the east, and the island of Crete to the south, plus the scores of smaller islands throughout the Aegean Sea. The climate is magnificent, with year-round sun and modest rainfall, but the land itself is harsh. Greece proper has a wild, jagged coastline with few harbors broad and deep enough for mooring large vessels. Inland the countryside is mountainous and irregular: less than 20 percent of the land is arable. The land was covered with forests in the Neolithic Age, but by the time the Hellenes arrived most of the trees had long since disappeared. Making matters worse, mineral ores were scarce, rivers even scarcer, and the waters of the Aegean Sea were not particularly well-stocked with fish.

What made the Aegean rim so attractive was the sea: sailing through the calm waters was easy at any time of the year. Distances were short, and the sheer abundance of islands meant that one never risked getting lost. (Ancient mariners navigated by landmarks rather than by the stars.) Hundreds of coastal communities could thus be in constant contact with one another. The Hellenes may have settled in a vast sprawl of isolated sites, but by devoting themselves to trade they could prosper. Although they were generally able to feed and clothe themselves, the

---

[1]   The English words Greece and Greek derive from the Latin names for the region and its people: Graeca and Graeci, respectively.

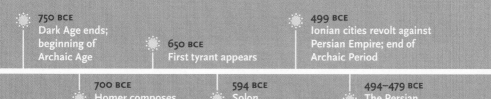

750 BCE
Dark Age ends;
beginning of
Archaic Age

650 BCE
First tyrant appears

499 BCE
Ionian cities revolt against
Persian Empire; end of
Archaic Period

700 BCE
Homer composes
the *Iliad* and
Odyssey

594 BCE
Solon
established as
leader in Athens

494–479 BCE
The Persian
Wars

ancient Greeks never developed much of a manufacturing base; they shipped goods from one site to another rather than producing goods of their own. Transport, not industry, made their fortunes. Their high degree of contact with other cultures meant more than a strong economy as well; it also exposed them to ideas, technologies, value systems, political institutions, artistic styles, and religious practices. The result was an exhilarating cultural adaptivity—a willingness to criticize old ideas and to experiment with new ones. The physical chaos of the Aegean rim gave birth to a brilliant civilization that lived passionately, sought order and justice, and questioned the meaning of life, of time, and of death. And like many of the plays for which it is renowned, ancient Greek culture ended tragically.

> The physical chaos of the Aegean rim gave birth to a brilliant civilization that lived passionately, sought order and justice, and questioned the meaning of life, of time, and of death. And like the most renowned of the plays it produced, ancient Greek culture ended tragically.

The first signs of Aegean prosperity and creative energy emerged in Crete. In 1899 a British archaeologist, Sir Arthur Evans (1851–1941), unearthed a magnificent palace complex at Knossos—with three stories and nearly thirteen hundred rooms. Evans mistakenly identified it as the

Knossos   Artist's reconstruction of the Minoan palace at Knossos. A massive, labyrinthine complex, the palace was built and rebuilt throughout the years 1700–1400 BCE. It had nearly 1,300 separate living spaces, work rooms, storage areas, galleries, and halls. There was, however, only one toilet connected to a drain, although an efficient sewer system carried off waste water poured into it at various collection sites. The one working toilet was in the queen's bedroom.

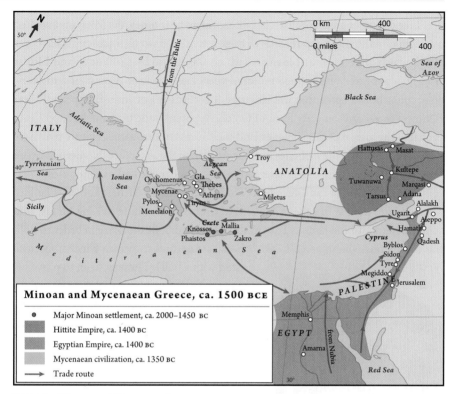

MAP 4.1   **Minoan and Mycenean Greece, ca. 1500 BCE**

palace of the Greeks' legendary ancient king Minos and gave the name **Minoan** to a culture that had its heyday from 2000 to 1500 BCE (see Map 4.1). The palace actually belonged to an exceptionally wealthy trader and shipping magnate, who ruled over Knossos itself but not the entire island. Subsequent excavations have found numerous other palaces, though none quite so splendid. Vibrant decoration—murals, statuary, frescos, tiling, pottery, textiles, and metalwork—characterized them all, which suggests that Minoan wealth was widely spread. Moreover, none of the palaces had fortifications of any kind, which likely means that naval defenses were sufficient to keep marauders away. Homes of town dwellers have been found, too—more modest, but still more attractive and comfortable than common urban homes in Middle Kingdom Egypt or Hittite Anatolia.[2] Minoan ships carried tons of Egyptian wheat, Greek olive oil and wine, Palestinian metalwork, Anatolian textiles, and Babylonian spices.

---

[2]   Rural peasants constituted the bulk of the Minoan population, but few traces of their lives have been found.

Like the other great commercial cultures of ancient times, the Minoans invented a system of writing to keep records of their activities. Two distinct scripts have survived, which are known as **Linear A** (which was in use by 1800 BCE) and **Linear B** (which appeared about three hundred years later). Linear A remains a mystery, although scholars agree that the language it records is not Indo-European. Linear B, however, records an early form of Greek. Apparently the trader culture on Crete predated the arrival of the Hellenes, and the success of that earlier culture may have been what attracted the Hellenes into the Aegean in the first place. Numerous Greek legends, after all, describe their fascination with Minoan life and magnificence.

The stories about the Greek hero Theseus are among the best known. Theseus, a prince from the city of Athens, traveled to Crete to pay tribute to King Minos, who sent the hero into the famous Labyrinth. Minos had built the maze in order to hold the monstrous Minotaur (a freakish beast created when Minos's lecherous wife mated with a bull). Theseus, keen to prove his heroism, finds the Minotaur, slays it, and retraces his path out of the Labyrinth and into the arms of Minos's daughter.[3] The Greek fascination with Crete thus seems well documented; their arrival on the island around 1500 BCE coincides with the transition from Linear A to Linear B. Minoan Crete taught the Greeks seafaring, commerce, writing, and the rudiments of government. By 1400 BCE, though, disaster struck. Whether it was an invasion or a natural calamity like an earthquake, the island of Crete was devastated, and their social and commercial empire—now in the hands of the Hellenes—began to fade.

The Phaistos Disk This disk was found in 1908 by archeologists working at the Minoan palace of Phaistos, which is on the island of Crete. Nearly six inches (15 cm) in diameter, it has a spiral of various symbols stamped into the clay on each side. All efforts to decipher the code have failed, leading some individuals to suggest, predictably, that the disk is a hoax. Other interpretations argue that it is a calendar, an astronomical chart, or even a game board. Take your pick.

The Hellenes living on the Greek mainland then began to dominate the Aegean. The years from roughly 1600 to 1200 BCE are known as the age of **Mycenaean Greece**, after the city of Mycenae, which according to tradition was the city ruled by the legendary king Agamemnon. Like their mythical king, the Mycenaeans were haughty, cocksure, and militaristic. What kept them from becoming a powerful empire was their internal division. The Greek mainland consists of hundreds of highland valleys and plains separated by irregular mountains and deep defiles; by controlling a handful of mountain passes, a tribal

---

3 Legend has it that the god Zeus, when hiding from his cannibalistic father, went to Crete and hid inside another labyrinth until he was ready to rebel against Cronos.

leader could effectively seal off an entire plateau area and create an autonomous, if isolated, miniature kingdom for himself. Once in control, these leaders governed through a tightly centralized royal court made up of military officers and bureaucrats, who lived and worked in the enormous citadel-palaces constructed from large stone blocks. Common peasants, nominally free but little better off because of it, and slave teams worked the land and tended the herds. Peasant women weaved fabric, minded children, and prepared food. Handfuls of artisans engaged in leatherwork, winemaking, and metalsmithing.

Virtually all of the surviving Linear B tablets consist of supply lists for the kings' armies. They detail grain rations, wine allowances, clothing, and armor allotments. Larger kingdoms engaged in mass manufacture. The palace at Pylos, on Crete, for example, maintained over four hundred bronzesmiths on site. Since that many workers would produce vastly more armor and weapons than their king needed, it seems clear that Mycenaean Pylos specialized as an arms manufacturer.

The intense competition for raw materials, markets, and control of trade routes kept the Mycenaeans in more or less constant conflict with one another—which, in turn, validated their militarism. A king kept his position of dominance by acquiring the things his people needed, which he did by trade when possible but by force

Mycenaean Warrior Vase   The "warrior vase" was named by Heinrich Schliemann, the 19th-century archeologist who discovered it. It is a mixing bowl (*krator* in Greek) used for mixing wine and water and dates to the 12th century BCE. The armor and weaponry are characteristic of the Mycenaean Age—nobleman warriors in short tunics with breastplates and greaves (leg armor). Helmets, shields, and spears complete the look.

when necessary. Conquest and gain were self-justifying. These are precisely the conditions and perhaps the only conditions that can turn figures like Agamemnon and Achilles into heroes. Royal tombs, shaped like inverted beehives, were veritable display-houses of weaponry and armor, to which were added miniatures of chariots and battleships, all surrounded by wall drawings of war scenes and the slaughtering of captives.

Little is known of Mycenaean religion. Various texts mention the names of several gods—most notably Zeus, Poseidon (the god of the sea), and Demeter (the goddess of grain). Since the Mycenaeans built no temples, which might have left some record of their activities, however, we know nothing about communal religious life, or indeed if any existed at all. Homes had individual shrines within them, either for the worship of ancestors or for petitioning the few gods whose names have survived. Yet no prayers or inscriptions survive to describe the content of their faith. The beehive tombs and their grim contents tell us more about Mycenaean life than any afterlife they might have believed in. In this way, at least, the first Greeks resemble the Old Kingdom Egyptians: states of great wealth and power, possessed of technological skill and access to other cultures, and with developed literacy, but with no intellectual or literary heritage of any note. Two hundred years, from 1400 to 1200 BCE, is a long time for a literate people to go without to producing anything worth remembering.

> The beehive tombs and their grim contents tell us more about Mycenaean life than about any afterlife they might have believed in. In this way, at least, the first Greeks resemble the Old Kingdom Egyptians: states of great wealth and power, possessed of technological skill and access to other cultures, and with developed literacy, but with no intellectual or literary heritage of any note.

THE END OF AN AGE AND MYTHIC ANCESTORS

The later Greeks insisted on claiming the Mycenaeans as their ancestors, though, and ascribed to them the epic adventures of their mythical heroes. When Homer composed the **Iliad**, sometime around 750 BCE, he chose a tale set in Mycenaean times—the events of the Trojan War. In reality, the war occurred as one of the many struggles by the newcomer Greeks to seize part of the Aegean rim; but in Homer's reimagining, the tale becomes one of Greek honor and military destiny.[4] The son of King Priam of Troy, named Paris, has been appointed the judge of a beauty contest between three goddesses. Each goddess bribes Paris, who ultimately selects the goddess (Aphrodite) who offered him the most beautiful mortal woman on earth.

---

[4]   Troy was an important trading city in northwestern Asia Minor.

That woman was Helen, the wife of King Menelaus of Sparta (and the brother of Agamemnon), who is promptly delivered to Troy as Paris's prize. The war then begins when all the Mycenaean kings join forces to avenge the injury done to Menelaus's honor. Homer assuredly based his epic on ancient oral traditions, but the *Iliad* can hardly be taken to represent Mycenaean culture accurately. If anything, it describes aspects of the Dark Age (1200–800 BCE) that separated Homer's world from Agamemnon's. But telling tales of Mycenaean heroes, powerful rulers, and their origins in a murky distant era of violently contending gods gave the Greeks a sense of rootedness. It tied them to their new Aegean home and tried to make sense out of the chaos of their lives.

The Mycenaean age ended abruptly with the invasion, around 1200 BCE, of the Dorians, one of the groups sometimes associated with the Sea Peoples who caused so much damage in Egypt and the Levant. The Dorians spoke a dialect of early Greek and may well have been present in the Aegean rim for some time. The Mycenaeans had thrown up a considerable number of new fortifications (and reinforced existing ones) around 1250 BCE, which suggests they saw trouble coming. But the Dorians, by themselves, could hardly have brought about the decline of the Mycenaeans and the start of the Dark Age, for the calamity that hit Greece proved so monumental that it must have resulted from other factors as well— whether plague, famine, civil strife, emigration, or a combination of them all.

> A single, astonishing fact drives the point home: between 1200 and 800 BCE Greece lost 90 percent of its population. This was perhaps the worst single scenario in the general upheaval caused by the Sea Peoples through the eastern Mediterranean and the Near East.

A single, astonishing fact drives the point home: between 1200 and 800 BCE Greece lost 90 percent of its population. This was perhaps the worst single scenario in the general upheaval caused by the Sea Peoples through the eastern Mediterranean and the Near East. The agrarian peasants in Greece were the least well-off farmers of the ancient Near East, given the harshness of their land, and were therefore least able to survive the catastrophe. The town dwellers of the Aegean cities were in a better position, but once the demographic hemorrhage interrupted the trade cycle, there was little they could do to compensate. Hence everyone presumably fled or was cut down by war, famine, or disease before they could flee. By the time the Dark Age ended, around 800 BCE, the Greeks had not only declined in dramatic numbers but had also shifted tenancy. A majority of those who survived had moved from the inland plateaus to the coastal towns, where they attempted to take up new trades. The days of isolated rural kingdoms were over.

And that is precisely what Homer laments in the *Iliad* and *Odyssey*. These epic poems, like all great art, work on many levels; on the political level, they are conservative, romanticized nostalgia, another instance of lament for a lost, idealized past. The *Iliad*'s heroes are all kings, and the conflicts dramatized by the poem all center on the issue of the honor due to them:

- The need to avenge Menelaus's honor starts the war.
- Achilles feels a seething rage when Agamemnon is awarded one of his maidservants, which Achilles regards as a shameful trammeling of his honor.
- Only one common soldier among the Greeks is given a speaking part in the epic: Thersites, who in Book 2 urges his comrades to give up the fight and return to Greece. Odysseus humiliates him for dishonoring his king and beats him with his staff in front of all the soldiers.
- Achilles brings dishonor to King Priam of Troy by desecrating the corpse of Priam's slain son.

The long, loving descriptions of each Greek king's noble mien, battlefield bravery, magnificent armor, and stately speech—everything, then, serves Homer's goal of lauding the halcyon past of Mycenaean monarchy. In an early scene in the *Iliad*, as the Greeks take the field to prepare for yet another battle, Priam leads Helen to the ramparts that surround Troy so that she can identify the Greek leaders for him.

> "Come, Helen," said Priam, "and tell me who is that great and powerful man over there? Others are taller than he, but never have I seen a warrior more finely formed, more noble in bearing; surely he is a king."
> Beautiful Helen replied, . . . "That is Agamemnon, the son of Atreus, the lord
> of the Argos plain, a noble ruler and dread warrior." . . .
> Then old Priam looked out again, and this time he beheld Odysseus, and asked,
> "And who is that one? He is a head shorter than Atreus's son, but has broader shoulders and a more powerful chest. He has laid his armor and
> weapons on the ground, and strides commandingly up and down the ranks
> like a burly ram keeping a flock of silver-fleeced sheep in line."
> And Helen, the heavenly beauty, answered him, "That is Odysseus, the son

of Laertes, the skillful mastermind, Ithaca-born (that raw, stony
  island!),
who knows every trick and stratagem of war." *(Iliad 3.150–220)*

Homer laments the passing of the heroic age of landed kings and dreads the coming
of the new, diminished Greece of coastal cities with their petty concerns.

Another famous passage, toward the end of the poem, describes the impossibly ornate new armor made for Achilles by the forge god Hephaestus when
Achilles finally gets over his anger at Agamemnon and decides to reenter the fighting. Hephaestus finishes the suit of armor with a splendid new shield, on which he
casts fantastically precise scenes—including an image of two cities, contrasting the
effete mundane present with the manly heroic past:

[Hephaestus] forged two cities also, fair and bustling: in one there were
wedding scenes and feasts, crowds with torches leading brides
from their chambers and escorting them through the streets.
Loud wedding songs broke out and young men danced
while flutes and lyres played; women stood in their doorways and
  watched.
A crowd stood in a market, for there was a quarrel over the
  compensation
one man owed another for a murder he had done. The first man
swore to the crowd that he had paid all, and the other denied it. . . .
The town elders sat on chairs of stone set in a circle, holding staves
put into their hands by heralds; with the help of a staff
each elder rose in turn to voice his judgment. Two talents of gold
lay at the circle's center, a payment for the one whose judgment
  would be
the most straightforward and true.

Around the other city, however, two besieging armies in shining
  armor,
Divided on what to do: whether to sack the city or to spare it in
  return for
half the citadel's treasure. The townsfolk would not concede to either
  plan,
and secretly armed themselves to break the siege. . . .
They filed out, led by Ares and Pallas Athena, who were clad in golden
  robes. . . .

When the besieging armies, meeting in council, heard [the citizen-
soldiers, lying in ambush]
They mounted their horses and sped towards where the sound was
coming from.
The armies drew up in battle lines by the riverbanks and hurled
their bronze-tipped javelins. Then Strife and Riot joined the fray,
and dreadful Fate too—who dragged a wounded man, an unwounded
one,
and a dead one as well behind Her. [Fate's] tunic was soaked with
blood,
and She, Strife, and Riot joined the battle and fought like living men,
and dragged their dead away.   *(Iliad, 18.490–500, 509–512, 516–518, 530–540)*

The contrast is clear: a society of shallow merrymakers, pettiness, decrepit officials,
and justice for sale, and a society of manliness, resolve, and bold action. Greece,
Homer wails, once the home of heroes, has become a nation of whiners.

The Trojan Horse   This is one of the earliest representations (ca. 670 BCE)
of the stratagem that supposedly ended the Trojan War. Greek soldiers hid
inside the wooden sculpture that was given as a parting gift to the victorious
Trojans and emerged from it at night and opened the city gates to the entire
Greek army. The story does not appear in the Iliad but is mentioned in the
Odyssey. In this image, taken from an amphora (a large storage vessel for
wine, oil, or water) found at Mykonos, the Greeks are shown as though
peering through windows.

The *Odyssey* treats the same theme. With the end of the Trojan War, wily Odysseus, the king of Ithaca, spends ten years struggling to get home to his devoted wife, Penelope, and his loving son, Telemachus.[5] In the meantime, his royal palace has been taken over by "suitors"—young upstarts from the town who try to persuade Penelope that Odysseus is dead and to get her to choose one of them as a new husband. Hence we have the noble king's adventure, in which he proves his superiority to every challenge, and a society, Ithaca, paralyzed with self-doubt. The suitors represent the "new" society of Homer's own time—brash, pushy, self-interested, and ignoble. The poem is a lament: *When, oh when, will our king come back? Oh, if only our king were here, we would then see justice and right order restored!*

But if Homer romanticizes the long past, he mistakenly attributes to it many of the qualities of his own time. The Mycenaean kings were vastly wealthier than any of the royals on display in the epics—not through any particular merit of their own, but simply because they hoarded their societies' money more brutally than those of Homer's own time did. Moreover, the ancient kings did not necessarily stand in the thick of the fray the way Agamemnon, Ajax, Menelaus, Odysseus, and others do in the poems; they directed the fighting from a safe distance instead. And much of the armor, weaponry, and tactics described in the poem differed profoundly from those used by the Mycenaeans.

The Dark Age obviously had its share of calamities. Still, once the demographic collapse had occurred and the migration of the survivors to the coasts had taken place, Greece was not a place of unrelenting misery. The decreased population meant that the amount of food needed to maintain it also declined, to the point where the mainland was able to feed itself unaided by imports from Egypt and Asia Minor. Since the foodstuffs produced in Greece—grain, oil, wine, and meat—were difficult to preserve in the bright heat, the rulers of Homer's time tended to distribute surpluses among the people, thus ensuring at least an absence of famine. The upland villages and coastal towns were small enough to be self-governing, which inspired a sense of independence among the people; identifying themselves as the sustainers of their own communal lives, they gradually coined a new word—**polis** (plural poleis)—for their communities. The polis referred to the physical town, the people who resided in it, and the group identity they shared. To belong to a polis meant more than happening to reside in a particular locale; it meant being a constituent element of something larger than oneself, participating in a web of mutual obligations, responsibilities, and rights.

---

[5] Odysseus battles giant beasts, survives shipwrecks, is seduced by a goddess, visits the underworld, taunts the sea god Poseidon, encounters witches, and outwits one foe after another.

COLONISTS, HOPLITES, AND TYRANTS

As the Homeric era gave way to the **Archaic period** (750–500 BCE), the poleis of Greece began to extend their reach by establishing networks of colonies. These networks extended around the Aegean rim, then into the Black Sea, and ultimately westward into the Mediterranean. With the expanded reach of the poleis came other changes as well—including a society built for war. This brought with it highly trained armies, periods of political reform under tyrants, a cult of masculinity, more constraints on women, and ritualized homosexual contact among the aristocracy.

The colonies were not military expansions. The Greeks generally searched out uninhabited harbors, established small coastal settlements around them, and then opened trade relations with the populations further inland (see Map 4.2). Inheritance practices lay behind this growth. Greek custom dictated that a man's estate was divided by his legitimate heirs—an easy enough matter when it comes to cash, flocks and herds, and portable property. But what about a man's farmland? A farm may be large enough to survive subdivision among a man's sons, but what happens to those subdivisions when the next generation comes along? At a certain point (and usually an early one), the portions of land received by individual heirs cannot support a family. This forced many heirs to sell their land, usually to a sibling but in theory to anyone with available funds. With the money, they would then relocate to a colony and set up anew.

The colonists, in other words, were neither military adventurers nor impoverished exiles but landholders—specifically, landholders who had cashed out their equity and were looking for new investments. An entrepreneurial spirit, not an exploitative one, drove Greek colonization. Given that fact, it is not surprising that groups of these entrepreneurs from a single polis would set out together in search of new settlement. Personal connections and a sense of shared identity also caused them to establish commercial ties with the polis from which they had come. In this way, the Greek colonies established were not just dependencies of the home city-state, to be exploited for domestic gain. Rather, they took on the character of smaller reproductions of the home city. They were independent and self-governing, yet united in identity with the original polis.

Between 750 and 500 BCE, the Greeks established hundreds of colonies around the Aegean rim, the Black Sea, and the entire perimeter of Asia Minor, across southern Italy and Sicily, and along the southern coast of France and the eastern coast of Spain (see Map 4.2). A handful of colonies appeared along the North African coast as well.[6] This explosive growth coincided almost exactly with the collapse of

---

[6] There were two types of colonies: apoidikiai and empora, the first self-governing, the second governed from the mainland as trading outposts.

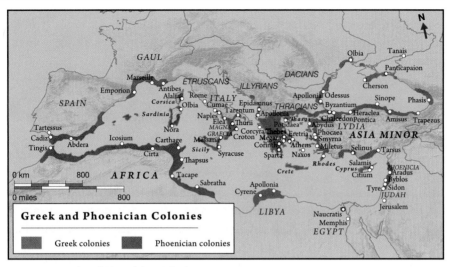

MAP 4.2   Greek and Phoenician Colonies

Israel under the Assyrians (722 BCE) and the conquest of Judah by the Babylonians (587 BCE). The coincidence was not entirely coincidental, for the turmoil in the Holy Land interrupted the commercial activity of the Phoenicians, who had previously been the main actors on the sea-lanes. The Greeks thus had few competitors for control of the sea-lanes, and certainly none with the geographical advantages they had. Because of the opportunities abroad, most Greek cities maintained fairly stable population levels in the Archaic period, and many colonies outstripped their home cities in size.

Steady home population levels contributed to two contradictory developments: the involvement of individuals in the public life of their communities and the concentration of wealth (and consequently of power) in a small coterie of families. Greek democracy was never fully democratic in the modern sense of the term. However, it did encourage, and result from, the active involvement of skilled workers, merchants, shippers, and financiers in the life of their poleis and corresponding colonies. As for the colonists themselves, they actively sought out contact with their neighboring or host populations, but were careful not to assimilate. Ethnic pride forbade that—for the Greeks, like many other ancient cultures, regarded themselves as superior to other nations. Moreover, the ease and speed of contact with the mainland kept the colonists' cultural identity as Greeks strong. Panhellenic religious festivals and celebrations like the Olympic Games (the first of which took place in 776 BCE) helped to keep the scattered Greek colonists in close contact with one another. But because the overseas Greeks encouraged contact with their non-Greek neighbors, a steady exposure to new ideas, technologies, and practices helped promote innovation. It is no accident that many of ancient Greece's greatest thinkers and artists came from the colonies rather than the mainland.

But because the overseas Greeks encouraged contact with their non-Greek neighbors, a steady exposure to new ideas, technologies, and practices helped promote innovation. It is no accident that many of ancient Greece's greatest thinkers and artists came from the colonies rather than the mainland.

One did not have to be a prominent merchant, civic official, or intellectual to serve one's polis. Every male between the ages of sixteen and sixty served in the polis's military force. The use of trained infantry did not originate with the Greeks, but with the Assyrians—although there is no clear evidence that the Greeks learned the technique from them. Earlier military strategy, if it can be called that, consisted of mass swarmings of foot soldiers under the leadership of chariot-riding kings or generals. Once the battle lines were drawn up, the fighting quickly devolved into a free-for-all. The Greeks, however, perfected fighting in trained units. They had to, since their depleted population meant that they could never count on having superior numbers on the field. What they came up with was the notion of groups of foot soldiers holding tight formation as a block, eight horizontal lines of ten to twenty men each, who stood shoulder to shoulder and moved as a single unit. Called a **phalanx**, such a unit rushed at the enemy and smashed through them, like a kind of foot-powered armored tank. Each soldier wore a breastplate and helmet, had a short sword at his belt, and carried a round shield (called a hoplos in Greek) and a thrusting spear. By combining their weight and momentum, they made up a powerful force.[7]

It required long hours of training to develop an effective phalanx, for each soldier had to overcome the instinct to fend for himself by swinging his sword at everything that moved. Instead, the soldiers had to hold formation and fight as a single group. This had two important consequences. First, since all men fought in their polis's army, all had to attain a degree of physical conditioning—and hence the Greek emphasis on exercise. Athletic games (such as the Olympics), public training facilities, sporting events, and the like all played important roles in Archaic Age culture, a fact we can see in the artwork of the time. Greek painting, sculpture, and poetry emphasize the beauty of a fit male physique more so than any other ancient culture. To be fit and strong, they believed, was more than to be beautiful: it was freedom itself. Second, the hoplite army underscored and confirmed the

---

[7]   The name for these soldiers, hoplites, derives from the shields they carried.

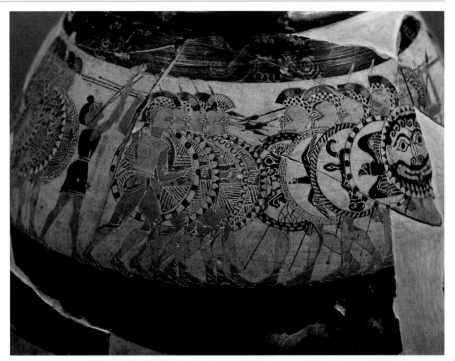

Hoplites   The circular shield of Greek infantry was called a *hoplon*, hence the soldiers'
name. Hoplites were literally "shield bearers," and even though their principal weapon
was a spear, it is fitting that they were named for their defensive gear. The circular
shields held by rows of footmen overlapped one another and presented thus a solid wall
of defense. The company, like the civil societies they represented, depended on group
action to survive. Their discipline and group-mindedness are evident here in the uniformly faceless soldiers, the perfect alignment of their marching feet, and the parallel
lines formed by their spears.

interdependence of the polis. It was the body politic, the community that literally
stood together as one or perished. A phalanx was living proof that people are stronger together than apart.

And this led to trouble. The more the Greek cities relied on the new armies,
the more important the commoners who made up their ranks became. These soldiers paid for their own equipment and took battlefield instructions from one another through a combination of verbal and manual signals. The aristocrats who
made up the charioted officer class declined in importance accordingly, which had
important repercussions for political life. A city that depends on its common men
for survival cannot deny them political power. This is why the Archaic Age was
filled with social strife—and why Homer's great epics are politically significant.
The stratified society ruled by noble kings and aristocratic heroes was giving way

to a primitive but encouraging egalitarianism, a world of merchants, craftsmen, teachers, colonists, and workers.

Powerful aristocracies, however, do not go away quietly. Popular demands for a greater voice in government usually inspired a conservative reaction of some sort, and the stridency of the debate intensified in boom-and-bust cycles. An early effort at social revolution occurred at Athens in 632 BCE, when a popular athlete named Cylon tried unsuccessfully to rouse the masses against the nobles and wealthy merchants who ran the polis as an oligarchy. A dozen years later the city council gave extraordinary authority to a fellow aristocrat named Solon, to institute reforms that might free the city from class strife. His efforts ultimately failed, which resulted in a more populist figure named Pisistratos seizing power around 560 BCE. He was Athens's first tyrant.

> A city that depends on its common men for survival cannot deny them political power. This is why the Archaic Age was filled with social strife—and why Homer's great epics are politically significant. The stratified society ruled by noble kings and aristocratic heroes was giving way to a primitive but encouraging egalitarianism, a world of merchants, craftsmen, teachers, colonists, and workers.

The word tyrant carries a pejorative meaning in English, but in ancient Greek a **tyrant** (*tyrannos*) was simply a person who seized power temporarily in order to bring about dramatic reform in a politically deadlocked state. In terms of social class, the tyrants were aristocrats but were allied with the masses. Some Marxist historians have seen them as the first "dictatorships of the proletariat," which is not entirely wrong. The difference between Solon and Pisistratos was that Solon had been the nobles' candidate for temporary dictatorship, while Pisistratos was the popular champion. The Archaic Age is peppered with occasional tyrannies, among the best known of which was the tyranny at Thebes of a semilegendary figure named Oedipus. (It ended badly.) Tyrannies seldom lasted longer than a decade or two, since the reasons for it had either been achieved by that time or else were deemed hopeless. In either case the tyrant lost the popular support of the hoplites, which put an end to his power.

Tyrants were installed in order to reform the state and were judged good or ill according to that standard alone. The methods they employed were of less significance. Pisistratos went so far as to wound himself with a spear, so that he could ride his chariot into the Athenian marketplace, blood dripping from his injury, and claim to have survived an assassination attempt from his rivals. All this was to whip the crowd of his supporters into a frenzy and quiet his rivals. Solon, it should be noted, became one of Pisistratos's closest advisors.

Here is how the historian Herodotus described the education of one tyrant, Periander of Corinth (r. 627–587 BCE), by another, Thrasyboulos of Miletus (d. 388 BCE):

> Periander was initially a kinder tyrant than his father [Cypselus] had been, but after he had absorbed the lessons of Thrasyboulos, the tyrant of Miletus, he became even more bloodthirsty than Cypselus had been. . . . [After Periander sent an ambassador to Miletus] Thrasyboulos led this messenger into a grain field outside the city. . . . Over and over again, whenever he saw a wheat stalk growing higher than its neighbors he cut it down and threw it away, until he had at last done away with all the strongest and most flowering of the wheat stalks. He spoke no words as he passed through the entire field, and then dismissed the messenger. After [the messenger] returned to Corinth, Periander asked him eagerly what Thrasyboulos had said. The messenger replied that Thrasyboulos had said nothing and that he thought Periander had sent him to deal with a madman who destroyed his own property. . . . But Periander, interpreting Thrasyboulos's actions well, understood right away that his [Thrasyboulos's] advice was to kill Corinth's leading citizens. From this point onward Periander inflicted every imaginable type of brutality on his people.

Not all tyrants were as vicious as Periander, but most Greeks were glad to see the days of the tyrants pass—even if they remained darkly fascinated by them in their histories and stage tragedies.

A CULT OF MASCULINITY

Archaic Greece developed a cult of masculinity that distinguished it from other ancient cultures. Theirs was a society built for war, in which every man sixteen to sixty was expected to serve in the hoplite army. Women, they were persuaded, were inferior creatures who contributed nothing to the public life of the community and hence did not deserve the social or political advantages of citizenship. Except for slave girls and women of the lowest working class, who might work as cleaners or seamstresses, women were essentially unseen in Greece. Girls received little or no education and were raised with the idea that their sole function in life was to marry, produce children, and care for their household. At marriage a young woman became the legal dependent of her husband, having the same rights as (and no more than) the children she would produce. Apart from going to the market or the public well, visiting family members, and attending funerals and a handful of religious ceremonies, women (that is, all females above the age of twelve) were never to appear alone in public. Doing so would bring shame upon the household and give the father or husband leave to punish her severely.[8] Most homes in fact were physically divided into male and female zones, often with the female rooms enclosed behind a locked door to which the husband kept the key.

Citizenship in a polis, like ownership of property, was hereditary and a right so precious as to inspire an obsession with legitimate birth. A woman's seclusion, the Greek male insisted, was an essential measure to protect her from harm but more especially to ensure that any child she bore was indeed his own. Maintaining a woman's invisibility was the best way, men determined, to maintain her chastity before marriage and fidelity within it. Female virginity was an absolute requirement for marriage, except for cases of a man wedding a widow. Before a wedding, young brides typically offered special prayers and presented gifts at a temple to the virgin goddess Artemis; these gifts often consisted of the toys enjoyed by the bride in her girlhood. As a sexually experienced wife, she would no longer have need of them.

> Except for slave girls and women of the lowest working class, who might work as cleaners or seamstresses, women were essentially unseen in Greece. Girls received little or no education and were raised with the idea that their sole function in life was to marry, produce children, and care for their household.

Since men in the Archaic period commonly did not marry until they were thirty years old, they thereby placed substantial sexual strains upon themselves.[9] Only three outlets for this pent-up energy existed: the use of female slaves as forced sexual partners, recourse to prostitutes, or sex with another man. The culture tolerated all three practices within certain limits. Slave girls had little hope of escaping sexual persecution. As the property of the man of the house, they had no choice but to submit to his attentions. In many cases, though, slave girls faced more violent treatment from the wives of their masters, particularly if the husband took a particular liking to a servant and favored her over sexual play with his wife.

Prostitutes were another option. Called *hetairai* in Greek ("companions," literally), these women were professional hostesses who offered meals and music in addition to sex; they received customers in their own residences, for the most part, but higher-priced hetairai also offered a kind of catering service, attending aristocratic symposia (drinking parties) and entertaining guests with music, dancing, and

---

[8]   A man who caught his wife committing adultery was legally entitled to kill her. A man who suspected his wife of adultery, but lacked proof, could beat her with impunity.

[9]   Girls were married soon after they reached the age of menstruation—somewhere around fifteen—in order to get maximum use of their fertile years.

Love for Sale   The Greeks enjoyed drinking cups with comic or bawdy scenes portrayed at the bottom—an ancient equivalent of today's thermally sensitive drinking glasses on which an image of a clothed beauty turns naked once the ice goes in—cheap frat-boy humor. Here an older man propositions a young "beautiful lad" (as the inscription *pais kalos* has it) with a sack of coins. Their robes, finely trimmed, mark them as members of the upper classes, for whom such homoerotic play was considered a unique privilege.

some practiced banter, in addition to the expected sexual couplings. These more expensive escorts were usually foreign-born, which added an element of exoticism to the otherwise tawdry business.

Homosexual contact was accepted, and even approved of, by society so long as certain norms were followed. First, it was a unique privilege of the aristocracy. Middle-class or working-class men who engaged in it received ridicule and hostility—ridicule because they were assumed to be too poor to afford a hetaira or not manly enough to rape a slave girl, and hostility because they were usurping an aristocratic right. Second, aristocratic homosexuality was regarded as an aspect of love, not merely as sexual release. Older men took noble youths, usually aged twelve to fifteen, under their protection, to guide them in the ways of society, government, and elite culture. Sexual relations were understood to be a part of this tutoring, with the young partner servicing the desires of the elder. To have intercourse with such a youth brought no shame. It was understood to be a right of high position in society. Call it "mentoring with privileges." But the vision of an enlightened Greek world in which mature and sophisticated men initiated compliant, elegant, noble youths into the joys of same-sex love without any shame on either part is a utopian fantasy. The culture simply gave its aristocrats free rein to penetrate anyone they wanted, except for other men's wives. There is no doubt that genuine love existed between many noble elders and their mentored youths; but there is no reason to regard all these arrangements as mutually and freely chosen.

What the Greeks despised was the inversion of sexual roles. For a grown man to receive intercourse, rather than to perform it, was a disgrace. Likewise, the exclusive enjoyment of sex with other males, whether one was in the active or passive role, they found repellent. The ancient Greek language has no words corresponding to the English word homosexual—either as a noun or an adjective. Having sex with another man was something that one did, a socially sanctioned rite of passage for the elites; but it did not define a human type.

SPARTA: THE MILITARIZATION OF THE CITIZENRY

Evidence (not all of it absolutely convincing) attests to roughly nine hundred poleis in the Archaic period, including the Black Sea, Aegean, and Mediterranean colonies. In order to appreciate the variety of forms "political" life could take, three examples should suffice. Sparta, Miletus, and Athens were the most powerful city-states of the age. And each was powerful in a different way.

Sparta boasted the most impressive military. It was a brutally efficient city—a large community in which an exceptionally large slave population (as much as three-quarters of the city's inhabitants) performed the labor of producing food, building homes, tending animals, weaving cloth, and doing basic craftwork. The slaves' labor freed the Spartan citizens to pursue the solitary goal of preparing for war. They did so neither to repel foreign invasion nor for overseas conquests of their own but simply to keep their enormous slave population in check. A revolt by the slaves, called **helots**, in the mid-7th century BCE had nearly toppled the Spartans and persuaded them to stay on their guard.

The militarization of the citizenry in the mid-7th century was nearly absolute and began at childbirth. City officials examined every infant born, to judge if it was healthy enough to keep; those who failed to pass muster were abandoned in the nearby mountains. Military training began at age seven for both boys and girls, with group exercise, marching drills, and athletic competitions, especially wrestling and javelin hurling. The sexes separated at age twelve, with girls taught elementary reading and writing and domestic economy, while boys were handed over to live in military barracks and instructed in fighting with weapons.

Diets were sharply restricted—not to combat obesity, but in order to inspire the boys to become effective thieves. Food thieves were punished harshly, not for the crime of theft but of getting caught. The food they stole was from their own farms. When training began at age seven, each boy was awarded a farm by the state. This farm was run for him by slaves. A hungry Spartan lad was expected to sneak from his barracks, dash to his own farm, steal his own food, and make it back without being caught or observed at either end. The idea was to acquire real-life experience of enduring the pains of hunger, of learning to move about without being seen, and of becoming self-reliant. Plutarch (d. 120 CE) describes an episode in which a young Spartan, having gone off in search of food, caught a fox. On the way back to his barracks, some older Spartans came upon him in the dark. Rather than face the humiliation of being caught, the young man hid the live fox under his cloak and never gave a hint of it to the elders, even as the fox bit and clawed its way into his entrails.

Boys were taught basic literacy, but the bulk of their training was military. At age twenty they began active service in the hoplite army. If they served ten straight years, they were granted full Spartan citizenship, which involved the right to speak in the assembly and to hold leadership positions in the polis. If a Spartan married while in his twenties, he still lived in his barracks—and had to sneak out at night to visit his wife. He was then punished, if he was caught, for the crime of being caught.

The superhuman rigor of Spartan training is obviously overstated, and one may wonder why so many historians take seriously this claim to severe self-denial and principled masochism. Disciplined people often boast of their self-denial, and often enough they amplify it in the boasting. Moreover, undisciplined people often exaggerate the discipline of others. It is significant that the only detailed contemporary description of Spartan life comes from Xenophon (427–354 BCE), an Athenian who witnessed the humiliating defeat of his city by the Spartans in the Peloponnesian War (431–404 BCE), as we will see in chapter 5. He dramatizes Spartan life in his book *Hellenica* ("Greek History"), in which he narrates the failure of Athenian democracy and his own disillusionment with his city. A later work, *The Constitution of the Lacedaemonians*, written in 388 BCE, provides the colorful detail. And the better known *Life of Lycurgus* by Plutarch draws heavily on Xenophon's treatise but adds considerable amounts of gossip and hearsay.[10]

Xenophon blamed Athens's defeat on its lack of order and discipline, the very traits he so admired in his adopted Sparta. All Spartan men, he insists, had the right to beat any Spartan youth for misbehavior; and the father of that youth, after learning of the beating, would beat the child again in order to show his solidarity with his peers. To discourage materialism and greed, he reports, Sparta forbade the use of gold and silver and instituted a new coinage made of iron—which was so valueless that it would require a wagonload of cash to make even

---

[10]   When the war ended, Xenophon went into voluntary exile and ultimately ended up in Sparta, where he lived for twenty years before finally returning to Athens in 366.

Spartan Youths   The popular cult of Sparta as the site of practical discipline, order, and commitment was largely a creation of the Enlightenment. In the 19th century the painter Edgar Degas (1834–1917) portrayed Spartan youths as happy, grounded, playful, and, above all, purposeful. Here he imagines a group of spirited girls challenging some boys to a wrestling match.

a modest purchase. A Spartan man who was too old to satisfy his wife's sexual longings and produce children, he says, was required by law to appoint a young stud to be his wife's lover—which the elder Spartan always did with equanimity, knowing that he was doing what was best for the polis. Xenophon's description of the relentless rigor of Spartan life can hardly be believed, but it is the beginning of a tradition—one that the Spartans were keen to propagate. It was also a tradition that the Athenians wished to elaborate, since it lessened the embarrassment of their defeat in the Peloponnesian War. Who could blame them for falling to such superhumans?

Despite such exaggerations, Sparta was a notably disciplined and austere place. The artwork and music that had characterized its earlier history all but disappeared. Spartan life aimed at a single goal—keeping its citizens strong and resolute enough to keep the helots in place. The deadening effect on the society of this frightened narrowness of vision might well have been the undoing of Sparta, had it not been for a slow-gathering threat—a Persian invasion of Greece. Military dangers justify military precautions and give their founders an aura of foresight. The enormity of the Persian danger enhanced the perceived wisdom of Sparta's military reformers and added to their reputation for superhuman fortitude.

MILETUS: A MERCHANT OLIGARCHY AND THE FIRST PHILOSOPHERS

Miletus offered a sharp contrast to Sparta. Located on the western coast of Asia Minor, it was a commercial and cultural hub, involved equally in mainland Greek and Anatolian affairs. Miletus (modern Milet) originated in the Mycenaean period, declined during the Dark Age, and then reemerged as one of the Archaic Age's most vibrant cities. It had as many as a hundred colonies, most of these in the Black Sea region, like Sinope and Trapezus, its two most important colonies and the Turkish cities of Sinop and Trabzon today.[11]

Located on a small but strategic peninsula, Miletus was one of the principal way stations for Greek goods entering Asia Minor. There was also a fair-sized harbor, although accumulating sediment from the Maeander river—Büyük Menderes today—has since filled it, and it now lies roughly three miles (five kilometers) from the sea. It was also close to the inland city of Sardis, the western terminus of the Royal Highway built by the Persians as the main thoroughfare running through the heart of their empire. This made it a natural distribution point for Persian goods throughout the eastern Mediterranean. In constant contact with the Greek, Hittite, Phoenician, and Egyptian worlds in addition to the Lydian and Persian ones, Miletus was among the most cosmopolitan of cities in the 7th and 6th centuries BCE. It acquired a reputation producing for high-quality ceramics and eccentric intellectuals—like the philosophers Thales (624–546 BCE), Anaximander (610–546 BCE), and Anaximenes (585–528 BCE), and the early historian Hecataeus (550–476 BCE).

MILETUS AND THE AEGEAN, ca. 550 BCE

Governed by a merchant oligarchy, the people of Miletus saw greater potential for growth in the Mediterranean than in the land trade with Persia, and so they organized the other coastal cities of Asia Minor into an alliance called the **Ionian League**. A reputation for rebelliousness reached far back in the city's history.[12] The Persians took control of Miletus when they conquered the whole of Asia Minor and set up a series of tyrants to govern the city in their stead. Herodotus relates that the first of these, Histiaeus (d. 494 BCE), joined in the Persian campaign against the Scythians in southern Russia (what is now Ukraine), using his city's service to the empire as a means of extracting the right to colonize throughout the Black Sea. Given the extraordinary number of Miletus's colonies in the area, Herodotus's tale may be true. Even so, doubts about the city's truest loyalties continued, whether eastward with Persia or westward with the Greeks.

---

[11] Miletus's colonies focused on shipping slaves, timber, and wheat from the region of southern Russia. All were in short supply in the Aegean.

[12] As early as 1320 BCE, in the first recorded reference to the city, Miletus was cited as a center of rebellion. The Hittite king Mursili II ordered it to be razed as a consequence.

When the Ionian League finally broke with Persia in 499 BCE, Miletus (and its new tyrant, Aristagoras) joined the revolt and became its leader. Persia exacted a terrible revenge, however, leveling the city shortly thereafter. The destruction of the city was so great that it inspired Phrynichus, one of the earliest Greek tragedians, to compose a play on the theme in 492 BCE. *The Capture of Miletus,* we are told, won first prize in the dramatic competition of that year but upset the audience so severely that the judges forbade any playwright in future to compose another tragedy on the theme. And, for good measure, they hit Phrynichus with a heavy fine. The play survives only in small fragments.

Miletus's greatest claim to fame, however, is as the birthplace of philosophy. The first three true philosophers in Western history—Thales, Anaximander, and Anaximenes—all appeared there. The city's essence as a cultural crossroads no doubt contributed much to this development, although evidence of a heightened appreciation for **rationalism** is present in Greek culture going back to Mycenaean times. What Thales and his followers began was the effort to systematize the observations one draws from everyday experience. Cause and effect surround us at all times, of course, and to notice that fact does not take genius. We observe the world's workings everyday: seeds buried in soil grow into plants; wood placed in fire is itself inflamed, whereas metal or stone is not; wine, when drunk, produces lightheadedness; the shadow produced by a stick placed vertically in the ground lengthens, shortens, and changes direction as the sun moves through the sky. To explain the relation of cause and effect, when discussing details of the natural word, is the realm of science. Thales and his followers, however, went further: they tried to ascertain whether all of nature followed a rational order. Was nature in fact a system? Was there, or is there, a set of universal truths that hold together the material world—and if so, how can we learn them? Does human life exist within an eternal code of truths larger than anything our cultural traditions or religions teach us? This is the realm of philosophy.

Thales, the first philosopher, never wrote a word. Philosophy, he believed, is best explored in conversation. The answer to every question, after all, raises another question (at least if the answer is at all interesting). A written text, however, is finite and fixed and therefore cannot possibly be completely right. Anaximander, his student, disagreed on that point and wrote reams. Their conclusions may seem unimpressive now but, if looked at correctly, seem remarkably insightful. Consciously or not, they and Anaximenes all began with an assumption that provides the foundation of all of modern physics—the conservation of matter. Everything came from somewhere, and since the complexity and variety of the world is obviously increasing as we move forward in time, then everything must be traceable to a single point, a single element, if we move backward through time.

What was this universal source? For Thales it was water, the primordial substance from which everything derives. Anaximander posited the existence of a single infinite ether, a malleable goo that took different forms when subjected to opposing forces of heat and cold, wetness and dryness. Anaximenes went even further and added the complicating factor of air, which affects the shape-shifting of the ether by its relative density or lightness. What is interesting about these speculations is the way they hint at a theory of evolution. If the entire physical cosmos has a common beginning, and if the world we observe is still constantly changing, then surely we ourselves came to be through a process of change in the past.[13]

Nothing like this had ever quite been attempted before. The mutability of the physical world has always been known. The Sumerians complained about it incessantly, and the Egyptians saw it as a deviation from the stability offered by obedience to the pharaoh. The Hebrews initially regarded it as the fulfillment of YHWH's design, then later feared that he had turned his back on them and his plan. The Ionian Greeks, however, were the first to approach the mutability of the physical world as a rational problem and to test their interpretations of it with logical arguments. This was to be one of the ancient world's greatest legacies for Greater Western culture—a sense of order, a search for meaning, and a tradition of submitting one's ideas to critical inspection.

> The Ionian Greeks, however, were the first to approach the mutability of the physical world as a rational problem and to test their interpretations of it with logical arguments. This was to be one of the ancient world's greatest legacies for Greater Western culture—a sense of order, a search for meaning, and a tradition of submitting one's ideas to critical inspection.

The Ionian thinkers even submitted religion to critical analysis. The boldest figure of all was Xenophanes of Colophon (570–480 BCE), who noted that deities in every culture tend to have the physical characteristics of the culture: thus Ethiopian gods and goddesses have black skin and curly hair, while Greek artists portray their divinities with olive skin and dark wavy hair, and the barbarians of Thrace (a region well to the north of Greece) worship deities with fair skin, reddish hair, and blue eyes. His conclusion? Humans make gods in their own image—not, as the Hebrew Bible says, the other way around. If cattle could speak, Xenophanes quips, they would pray to gods who look like cattle. His main concern was to turn people away from the Olympian-deity cults, which he regarded as poetic nonsense, and to examine life through critical reason.[14]

---

[13] Anaximenes even asserted that humans must have been, at one time, fish.

[14] Xenophanes held that reason can guide us toward the truth. It is impossible to know the truth with absolute certainty—but the point, he insists, is to make the effort.

Radical speculation like this declined in Ionia after the Persians conquered Lydia in 494 BCE and acquired control of Miletus. The philosophers either fled or joined the resistance. The mode of critical thinking begun in Miletus spread quickly to the Greek mainland, however, where it took root especially in the city of Athens.

ATHENIAN DEMOCRACY

Athens is older than Jerusalem, older than Nineveh, older than Thebes. Perhaps only Jericho, of all the cities of the Western world, has a longer history of continuous human settlement. As early as 3000 BCE, Neolithic tribesmen built a fort atop the Acropolis, and people have lived there ever since. Geography favors it: the hilltop provides a natural defensive position from which to control the nearby plains, which provide farmland and pasturage. The Eridanus river flowed through the center of the town (it has long since dried up), and the port of Piraeus lies only six miles (ten kilometers) away. Athens thus had ready access to natural resources and communication links but was also sufficiently isolated to enjoy natural protection. Athens was already a leading city in Mycenaean times and was able to hold out against the marauding Sea Peoples, although it then went into the same sharp decline as the other cities of the Dark Age. As the clouds cleared by 700 BCE, Athens stood ready to take advantage once again of its uniquely strong position, and under the leadership of the landholding aristocracy the city slowly seized control of the entire region of Attica.[15] By the mid-600s BCE, however, so many new people had been added to the roster of Athenians that they began to challenge the authority of the aristocrats. The clash between the privileges of the few and the demands of the many is what led to the tyrannies of Solon and Pisistratus mentioned before.

Like other Archaic Age cities, Athens experimented—at times against its will—with a variety of constitutions, some democratically created, some imposed by occasional autocrats. Legal distinctions between classes, tribes, and precincts (called demes in Greek) were redrawn, laws were drafted and redrafted, and both executive and judicial institutions were reorganized. The system as established in 510 BCE remained more or less in place until Alexander the Great conquered Athens in 338 BCE, and it provides the model for our understanding of Athenian democracy.

We should begin by understanding that democracy's limitations. Full participatory citizenship was restricted to somewhere between 5 and 10 percent of the population: slaves, women, the working poor, and most lesser craftsmen and artisans were denied the right to vote in the assembly and to hold municipal office. The

---

[15]   Athens grew by bringing smaller neighboring towns into its jurisdiction—what classical historians call *synoikismos* ("gathering together in a single home"). "Urban sprawl" works just fine.

numbers come from Thucydides, who reckoned the number of actual citizens as forty thousand. He put the number of slaves in Athens as high as four hundred thousand, and the number of noncitizen residents at seventy thousand. Called metics, they had no democratic rights and had to pay for the privilege of residing in the city.

Still, no other ancient society placed power in the hands of so many of its people. It may be more accurate, statistically speaking, to regard Athens as an unusually large oligarchy rather than as a true democracy, but the real accomplishment of the constitution lay not in the size of the electorate; it was in its strict definition and supervision of the powers of civic officials. Officeholders in Athens served the city and its constitution, unlike those in other ancient societies who served a king or regarded their own will as the constitution. An Athenian-style democracy today would not be admitted to the European Union and would even come under criticism by the Organization of African States, although it would probably get a favorable nod from Russia and China. But in the context of its time, Athens's experiment with government by (some of) the people was a rare and beautiful thing.[16]

The main body of the government was the citizens' Assembly (*ekklesia* in Greek), which met to consider new legislation, adjudicate trials, and set policies. As many as five to six thousand men comprised the assembly at any one time, which was obviously too cumbersome a group for any effective governance; hence most day-to-day government was performed by a smaller group called the council (*boule*). Chosen by lots, the members of the council selected the leading magistrates; these were not elections in the modern sense, but an actual lottery. Elections were reserved for the positions of *strategoi*—the military commanders in charge of the citizen army. Magistracies and command positions were for one-year terms, and while popular strategoi could serve an unlimited number of consecutive terms, all magistrates were removed from office after a single term.

THE PERSIAN WARS

By the 490s BCE Sparta, not Athens or Miletus, was the strongest polis in Greece. Most other cities of the time would have named it as their leader, if asked. As tensions rose with the advancing Persian Empire, more and more poleis turned to the Spartans for guidance; not only was their army the strongest in Greece, but Sparta—alone among Greek cities—did not have overseas colonies. This assured people that Sparta's leadership in a Panhellenic military force would play no favorites. Few people trusted the Athenians to be so selfless.

---

[16]   The bulk of the Athenian constitution was the work of a reformer named Cleisthenes, who established the new system in 508 BCE.

The Persian Wars (494–479 BCE) did not have to happen. Persia had been eager enough to conquer all of the Near East and to bring Zoroastrianism to the world, but the empire initially showed no signs of determination, or even desire, to add Greece to its dominion. Doing so, after all, would require the Persians to develop maritime skills that they neither had nor needed. The Greeks controlled the sea-lanes throughout the eastern Mediterranean and the Black Sea. Since the Persians controlled everything else, the Greeks had no one else with whom to trade. Conquering the people would have been a waste of resources.

Revolt by the Ionian Greeks changed all of that. The trouble started in Miletus, which had been governed by a brief series of Persian-affiliated tyrants. The Greek colonies along the Ionian coast (Ionia being the westernmost province of Asia Minor) tired of sending their taxes and tribute eastward and waited only for a leader to organize them into a full-scale rebellion. The rebels' chance came when the tyrant of Miletus, Aristagoras, gambled that the Greek mainland would come to the Ionians' assistance and that the Persians, lacking a navy, would let the Ionian colonies go. He was right and wrong in equal measure. The coastal colonies did unite in seceding from Persia, and the mainland Greeks did come to their aid; but Persia refused to let the challenge to their authority go unanswered.

When Sparta balked at sending its troops to Miletus, the Athenians, sensing an opportunity, leaped in. In 499 BCE they led a smallish force that sacked the Persians' provincial capital at Sardis (modern Sart). But then the Athenians declared victory and went home, leaving the Ionian cities to face the Persian emperor's wrath alone. That emperor was Darius (r. 521–486 BCE). He decided to teach the Athenians a lesson, and in 490 BCE he sent an army of twenty thousand elite troops across the Aegean with orders to land on the mainland and to march on Athens and destroy it. The armies met on the plain at Marathon, where the Athenian phalanx smashed through the Persian infantry line. The Greek writer Herodotus records that 6,400 Persians were killed, while the Athenians lost only 192. Darius, humiliated, withdrew. Athens rejoiced in its victory and its new standing as the champion of all of Greece (see Map 4.3).

One of the city's leading politicians, Themistocles (524–459 BCE), advised the polis that the Persians would undoubtedly come back and that the Athenians should therefore prepare. They did so by investing in a fleet of two hundred new warships called **triremes**, thereby turning Athens into a major naval power. Introduced, according to Thucydides, in the 8th century BCE, they were oared warships, with three tiers of rowers. Constructed of pine or fir, they were relatively light ships that, with a well-trained crew, could attain very high speed. With a bronze-tipped hardwood prow, they were extremely effective at ramming into the hulls of opposing ships.[17]

---

[17]   Another favorite tactic was to build up speed, approach alongside an enemy ship, withdraw the oars, and let the momentum of the trireme shear away the oars of the foe, leaving him helplessly adrift.

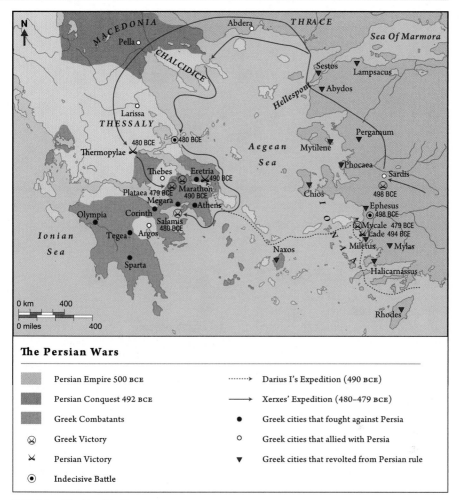

The Persian Wars

▨	Persian Empire 500 BCE	⋯⋯▸	Darius I's Expedition (490 BCE)	
▨	Persian Conquest 492 BCE	⟶	Xerxes' Expedition (480–479 BCE)	
▨	Greek Combatants	●	Greek cities that fought against Persia	
⊗	Greek Victory	○	Greek cities that allied with Persia	
⤫	Persian Victory	▼	Greek cities that revolted from Persian rule	
⊙	Indecisive Battle			

MAP 4.3   **The Persian Wars**

The empire did strike back, in 480 BCE. Darius's son Xerxes (r. 486–465 BCE) was then in charge, and he assembled the largest army in ancient history for a land assault. Herodotus reckoned it at 1.7 million soldiers, but most historians estimate the real figure was about one-tenth of that. The Persians marched north from Sardis, crossed the Hellespont, moved westward across Thrace and Macedonia, and prepared to invade Greece from the north. The Persian threat finally persuaded most of the Greeks to unite in defense. Sparta fought a heroic frontline action at the battle of Thermopylae (480 BCE), while the Athenians harried the Persians supply ships. Greek victories at Salamis (480 BCE)—a naval battle—and at Plataea (479 BCE) finally forced Xerxes to give up and return to Persia. Greece was poised to enter its golden age.

WHO, WHAT, WHERE

Archaic period	Mycenaean Greece
helots	Olympian deities
Iliad	phalanx
Ionian League	polis
Linear A	rationalism
Linear B	triremes
Minoan	tyrant

SUGGESTED READINGS

Primary Sources

Herodotus. *The Persian Wars.*

Hesiod. *Theogony.*

——. *Works and Days.*

Homer. *The Iliad.*

——. *The Odyssey.*

Thucydides. *The Peloponnesian War.*

Xenophon. *Hellenica.*

——. *Constitution of the Lacedaemonians.*

Anthologies

Buckley, Terry. *Aspects of Greek History, 750–323 BC: A Source-Based Approach* (2010).

Lefkowitz, Mary R., and Maureen B. Fant, comps. *Women's Life in Greece and Rome: A Source Book in Translation* (2005).

Nagle, D. Brendan, and Stanley M. Burstein. *Readings in Greek History: Sources and Interpretations* (2006).

Rice, David G., and John E. Stambaugh. *Sources for the Study of Greek Religion* (2000).

Studies

Bagnall, Nigel. *The Peloponnesian War: Athens, Sparta, and the Struggle for Greece* (2006).

Brunschwig, Jacques, and Geoffrey E. R. Lloyd, eds. *Greek Thought: A Guide to Classical Knowledge* (2000).

Camp, John M. *The Archaeology of Athens* (2002).

Cartledge, Paul A. *The Spartans: An Epic History* (2003).

De Souza, Philip. *The Greek and Persian Wars, 499–386 BC* (2003).

Dickinson, Oliver. *The Aegean from Bronze Age to Iron Age: Continuity and Change between the Twelfth and Eighth Centuries BC* (2007).

Ducat, Jean. *Spartan Education: Youth and Society in the Classical Period* (2006).

Gere, Cathy. *Knossos and the Prophets of Modernism* (2009).

Graham, Daniel W. *Explaining the Cosmos: The Ionian Tradition of Scientific Philosophy* (2006).

Hall, Jonathan M. *A History of the Archaic Greek World, ca. 1200–479 BCE* (2006).

Holland, Tom. *Persian Fire: The First World Empire and the Battle for the West* (2005).

Langdon, Susan. *Art and Identity in Dark Age Greece, 1100–700 BCE* (2010).

Pedley, John. *Sanctuaries and the Sacred in the Ancient Greek World* (2005).

Pomeroy, Sarah B. *Spartan Women* (2002).

Pomeroy, Sarah B., Stanley M. Burstein, Walter Donlan, Jennifer Tolbert Roberts, and David Tandy. *Ancient Greece: A Political, Social, and Cultural History Third Edition* (2012).

Schofield, Louise. *The Mycenaeans* (2007).

Snodgrass, Anthony M. *The Dark Age of Greece: An Archaeological Survey of the Eleventh to Eighth Centuries* BC (2000).

Thomas, Rosalind. *Herodotus in Context: Ethnography, Science, and the Art of Persuasion* (2002).

Waterfield, Robin. *The First Philosophers: The Presocratics and the Sophists* (2009).

For additional resources, including maps, primary sources, visuals, web links, and quizzes, please go to **www.oup.com/us/backman.**

CHAPTER 5

Hellenism and Second Temple Judaism

499 BCE–142 BCE

THE CLASSICAL AND HELLENISTIC WORLD

The Classical and Hellenistic Ages witnessed all the best and worst of ancient Greek life. The first, the Classical Age, ran from the defense of Greece against Persia to the conquest of Persia by the Greeks under Alexander the Great (479–323 BCE). The Hellenistic Age that followed ran from Alexander's death to the conquest of the East by the Romans (323–327 BCE). A sense of euphoria swept through the people after their victory over Xerxes, and the Athenians felt more euphoric than any. Their bravery at Marathon and their decision to build a fleet of triremes had led directly to the Persians' defeat. Now, with the exception of Sparta and a few outliers, every polis in Greece recognized Athens's new position of leadership.

Its leadership meant more than military achievements. Athens embodied a life of ritual and restraint, the birth of medicine, and the search for a meaningful life. Yet it seems only right that one of its greatest achievements, along with epic and lyric poetry, was tragedy, for its golden age ended with the disastrous war between Athens and Sparta. The Peloponnesian War lasted twenty-seven years and consumed much of the Greek peninsula. As it happened, of the period's greatest philosophers—Socrates, Plato, and

◀ **Medical Science** This sarcophagus from the 1st century BCE shows a physician—recognizable from the surgical implements hanging on the wall behind him—who perhaps moonlighted as a veterinarian (hence the horse).

- The Classical Age
- Women, Children, and Slaves
- The Polis; Ritual and Restraint
- Civilized Pursuits: Epic and Lyric Poetry
- The Birth of Tragedy
- The Peloponnesian Disaster
- Medicine as Natural Law: Hippocrates

- Mathematical Ordering and Sophistry
- Socrates and the Meaningful Life
- Plato and Ideal Forms
- Aristotle and the Pursuit of Happiness
- Alexander the Great
- A Mongrel but Magnificent World
- Second Temple Jews and Judaism
- The Maccabean Revolt

CHAPTER OUTLINE

Aristotle—the last taught the military heir to the disaster, Alexander the Great. The ensuing Hellenistic Age also coincided with a time of Jewish rebirth and Hellenization.

THE CLASSICAL AGE

Despite their celebrations, none of the Greeks believed they had seen the end of the Persian threat. Athens argued successfully for the creation of a military alliance among all the poleis, one dedicated to maintaining a strong defense and, if possible, even pressing the offensive into Persian territory. The alliance was called the **Delian League**, named for the Aegean island of Delos where the group's treasury was kept. By 470 BCE, in other words, Greece was victorious, independent, organized, self-confident, and quickly amassing wealth. The Greeks could be forgiven if they felt a bit of pride. They could be forgiven, too, if they did not foresee that the next great conquests, following their downfall, were to come from peoples they knew as little more than barbarians. They could have noticed even earlier the return of the Jews, freed by the Persians, to Jerusalem.

Golden ages seldom last very long, and the Greek one was no different. They also are seldom as golden as people believe them to have been. The start of the Persian Wars in 499 BCE and the end of the Peloponnesian War in 404 BCE mark the **Classical Age**, when Greece witnessed an impressive vitality in civic life, economic prosperity, artistic expression, and literary achievement. The Greeks themselves, and especially the Athenians, came to regard the mid-5th century BCE with a determined awe, recalling it as a lost halcyon era that

> The Greeks themselves, and especially the Athenians, came to regard the mid-5th century BCE with a determined awe, recalling it as a lost halcyon era that outshone anything that came before it or since. Through the centuries, much of Western culture has continued the love affair and has extolled "the glory that was Greece" as one of the two or three pinnacles of human achievement.

CHAPTER TIMELINE

499 BCE Start of the Persian Wars

490 BCE Darius of Persia invades Greece

479 BCE Persian Wars end

478 BCE Delian League established

outshone anything that came before it or since. Through the centuries, much of Western culture has continued the love affair and has extolled "the glory that was Greece" as one of the two or three pinnacles of human achievement. A more sober viewer can admire the brilliance of the time without overlooking its less praiseworthy elements.

Most of the great achievements of the age were connected in some fashion to Athens. That city, in the heady atmosphere of patriotic victory over Persia and its newfound prosperity, had ample material and spiritual resources to devote to education, urban development, artistic expression, and religious ritual. Moreover, Athenian ties to the Ionian cities understandably grew closer, which brought an injection of the vigorous intellectualism of Asia Minor into Athenian life. The stimulus was significant.

The greatest of Athenian leaders, Pericles (495–429 BCE), lavished money on building temples, theatres, schools, and public meeting houses. He held the office of strategos ("general") from 462 to 429 BCE. This was an elected office with a one-year term, but the Athenian constitution placed no limit on the number of terms a strategos could serve; Pericles won reelection thirty-two times. Although he himself had a high aristocratic lineage, he was an ardent populist who broadened the scope of Athenian democracy. Poor Athenians could not vote on legislation but could attend the assembly. He made it easier for them to participate in civic life by offering to reimburse their lost day wages if they wished to attend the municipal council meeting.[1] Athens's gain was the rest of Greece's loss—for no other city had anything like the cultural flowering of Periclean Greece. But even with all its advantages, the flowering of life in Athens was possible only because Athens controlled the treasury of the whole Delian League and appropriated its funds.

Though prosperous, Greek life in the Hellenic era was surprisingly modest. Most homes were comfortable but simple; no palaces were built, not even by those

---

[1]   Pericles' generosity attracted the best architects, sculptors, playwrights, scholars, scientists, and poets to Athens.

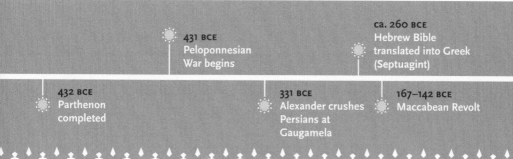

432 BCE
Parthenon
completed

431 BCE
Peloponnesian
War begins

331 BCE
Alexander crushes
Persians at
Gaugamela

ca. 260 BCE
Hebrew Bible
translated into Greek
(Septuagint)

167–142 BCE
Maccabean Revolt

Pericles   Bust of the statesman and general (strategos) "Pericles the Athenian, son of Xanthippos"—as the inscription reads. 5th century BCE.

few who did achieve great wealth. Personal luxuries were spurned. Instead, prosperous Greeks spent their money on commercial investment, public building projects, and supporting arts and education. Temples, public halls, amphitheaters, baths, and athletic fields all benefited from private largess.

WOMEN, CHILDREN, AND SLAVES

Women were strictly segregated from public life, and girls remained at home until the day of their marriage, when they moved into the home of their husbands. Apart from trips to the market and occasional attendance at religious ceremonies, Greek women lived utterly enclosed lives. Every home had a specially designated "woman's zone" (**gynaeceum**), in which women passed the time with their children and servants. A woman never entered the public area of her house, where visitors might appear, without the permission of her husband. Children started their education at home, learning their letters and numbers and some music from their mothers. Boys usually began attending schools at age seven. These were private institutions that included rigorous physical education, since at age eighteen all boys began military service in the hoplite infantry.

Girls began another kind of service even earlier. From the time of her first menstruation a girl was considered marriageable; this frequently happened as early as age fourteen, the idea being to take maximum advantage of her fertile years. "We have prostitutes for pleasure," wrote one Athenian, "concubines for company, and wives for producing heirs and maintaining the household." Affectionate marriages certainly existed, but few Greeks wed for love. Take two representative gravestone inscriptions:

> Here by this busy road lies Aspasia, a worthy wife now dead. Her husband Euopides put up this monument for her in memory of her good disposition; she was his consort. *(Chios, 5th century* BCE*)*

> The woman buried here cared neither for clothes nor money in her lifetime, but only for her husband and for maintaining an upright reputation. Dionysia, your husband Antiphilus inscribes your tomb in return for the youthful years you shared with him. *(Athens, 4th century* BCE*)*

From the time of her wedding, a woman all but disappeared into her husband's house, seldom going into public, and devoting her days to childrearing and weaving. Greek culture abhorred idleness, and since most households—even relatively poor ones—had slaves to do the bulk of domestic labor, married women traditionally kept busy at the loom.[2] A healthy wife might expect to have ten pregnancies in her lifetime, although it remains unclear how many miscarriages she might suffer or how many of her children might die in infancy.

Decorative Painting on a Case from the 5th Century BCE   In this scene a woman examines a sample of cloth being shown to her by a weaver.

Wives governed their households—watching over their children, planning menus, caring for household items—but slaves performed most of the domestic chores. Classical Greece lived off slave labor, but slave populations in the ancient world were not self-perpetuating. The conditions of their lives were so harsh that their mortality rates exceeded their birth rates. The Greeks thus constantly needed fresh supplies of slaves in order to continue their lives of democratic freedom. Apart from domestic work, most slaves were used in farm labor and menial shopwork. The least fortunate of the male slaves were put to work in mining or as oarsmen in Greek ships; the least fortunate of the females were the forced sexual partners of their male owners.

> Classical Greece lived off slave labor, but slave populations in the ancient world were not self-perpetuating. The conditions of their lives were so harsh that their mortality rates exceeded their birth rates.

THE POLIS: RITUAL AND RESTRAINT

Each polis administered its major religious celebrations, which naturally differed from one another depending on the particular deities associated with each city. In Athens itself, the two most significant festivals were the Panathenaia, a celebration held every May in honor of the goddess Athena, and the Great Dionysia, a festival honoring Dionysius. (The Panathenaia is the scene famously depicted on the frieze of the Parthenon, now in the British Museum.) Religion was ritualistic, and

---

2   Odysseus's wife, Penelope, who spent twenty years at her loom while patiently waiting for her husband to return from his wanderings, was an iconic image.

The Panathenaia   The Panathenaia was the great religious festival held every four years in Athens, in honor of the city's patron goddess. This scene depicts the preparations for the opening ceremony, the high point of which was the solemn procession of Athena's sacred robes to the Acropolis.

it neither asserted a creed nor promoted an ethical code.[3] People presented offerings, performed their prayers, and honored the gods in song. But apart from insisting on observing the required rituals, the religion taught little. No uniformity of opinion existed regarding the afterlife, although the great majority of Greeks believed in **Hades**, a shadowy afterworld to which all who received funeral rites went, regardless of the morality or immorality of their earthly lives. Those who did not receive a proper funeral were thought to wander the world as ghosts.

The Greeks disdained the luxurious diets of the Persians, which they considered a sign of their supposed decadence, and most ate simple meals. Herodotus (1.133) is bemused by Persian eating and drinking habits:

> The day they value most of all is a birthday; on one of those they think it right to set up a greater banquet than usual—for wealthier Persians will arrange to have an ox, horse, camel, or ass roasted whole and set out before them (the less well-to-do use smaller beasts). They eat only a little of their main course but an abundance of desserts; moreover, they never use salt. This is why the Persians say that we Greeks are still hungry when we finish eating, for there is nothing worth having after we finish our main course—but if some delicacies were given us, we would eat our fill. The Persians are very devoted to wine (but they never vomit or piss in front of one another). Such are their customs.

---

3   The ancient Greek language had no word corresponding to the English words "belief" or "beliefs" in their religious sense.

They will get drunk even when discussing the most important matters. The following day the host of the house they are in will ask them—now that they are sober—to reconsider their decisions of the night before. If they are still so inclined, the matter is settled; if not, not. If it happens that they deliberate an issue when sober, they reconsider it later when they are drunk.

For the Greeks, grains, olive oil, and wine formed the basis of all meals. Breakfast commonly consisted of barley bread dipped in wine. Lunch was usually a form of soup or stew (made chiefly of lentils, onions, and beans, since fresh vegetables were hard to come by in the cities), accompanied by cheese and honey. Dinner was eaten at nightfall and was the largest meal of the day. For most people this was the only meal at which meat was served. Pork was the cheapest meat, and each city had its own favorite preparation.[4] Fish was relatively rare inland; the coastal cities and the Aegean islanders had little success transporting it inland without spoiling. Men and women always ate separately; in a small house the men ate first, then the women, then the male servants, and finally the female servants. Most Greek houses did not have stone ovens; instead, women cooked by heaping red-hot coals on a flat stone and setting an inverted clay bowl over the pile. Once the stone was hot, they scraped away the coals, placed the food on the heated stone, covered it with the hot bowl, and surrounded the bowl with the coals again. Having such little regard for artful food preparation, however, the Greeks tended to devalue the role that women played in it. Food was fuel, not pleasure.

Drinking, however, was another matter. The Greeks developed the first vintage wines, and among the many civic officials in local government was the person responsible for affixing the municipal seal to wines for export. By reputation, the best wines came from three Aegean islands: Chios, Lesbos, and Thasos; the wine produced in Achaea, the mainland district surrounding Athens, was among the worst. Claudius Aelianus (d. 235 CE), a Roman historian who wrote in Greek, records that Achaean wine was reputed to induce miscarriages in pregnant women.

Wine was drunk throughout the day, always cut (diluted) with water. Drinking uncut wine was considered barbarous, as was the drinking of wine by women, except in Sparta, where moderate wine drinking was thought to increase a woman's fertility. Drinking to excess was also looked down upon, except at **symposia**, the all-male drinking parties where getting drunk was the whole point. Plato's dialogue

---

4   The Spartans' signature dish was melas zomos, a dark, thick stew made of pork, vinegar, and pigs' blood. In Aristophanes' play *Peace* (l.374), a small piglet is said to cost three days' wages for a civil servant.

Divine Wine   A drinking cup depicting the goddess Athena pouring wine for the famous hero Herakles, 5th century BCE.

The Symposium is the most famous depiction of one of these parties, although it is not characteristic. Few people can drink that much and still engage in such intelligent discussion. Still, some Greeks, like the philosopher Socrates, earned renown for their ability to imbibe.[5]

CIVILIZED PURSUITS: EPIC AND LYRIC POETRY

Others gained renown for more civilized pursuits like poetry, at which the ancient Greeks excelled. Epic poetry was still composed in the classical period, but shorter poetic forms like lyric and elegy—the first sung to accompaniment on a lyre, the second to the music of a flute—gained in popularity. The two greatest lyric poets were Pindar (522–443 BCE) and Sappho (ca. 620–570 BCE). Pindar made his name by composing odes for special occasions. Among his most popular verses were a series of odes in honor of victors in athletic contests like the Olympic Games. His poetry is notoriously difficult to translate since he delights in sophisticated meters and rhetorical flourishes.

---

[5]   Socrates never went drink-for-drink against Milo of Croton, a 6th-century BCE Olympic athlete who reportedly ate twenty pounds of meat daily—which he washed down with two gallons of wine.

Sappho, however, invites translation. Her poetry (or what survives of it, anyway) depends less on technical tricks, more on acute observation and emotional directness. According to tradition she wrote some nine volumes of poetry, although only one poem survives in its entirety, a hymn to Aphrodite. Many of the surviving fragments express homoerotic love, and Sappho's island home of Lesbos has given its name to lesbianism. Here she describes her envy of a man who is enjoying her beloved's company at table:

> That man seems to me equal to the gods,
> the one who sits opposite you
> and listens so closely
> to your sweet voice
>
> and your beguiling laughter—
> oh, how the heart in my chest is stirred!
> For whenever I look at you, even for a moment,
> to speak is beyond me—not one single word;
>
> my tongue freezes in silence;
> a lick of flame runs beneath my skin;
> my eyes can see nothing;
> my ears hear only a din;
>
> a cold sweat covers me;
> my body trembles—and I sigh
> and turn greener than grass
> and think I might die.

THE BIRTH OF TRAGEDY

It may seem ironic that the greatest artistic expression of the age was tragedy, but it is not. What epic and lyric poetry were to the Archaic Age, poetic stage tragedy was to the Classical—its characteristic and most powerful expression. Tragedy was more than an art form; it was a public rite and a civic obligation. Athens led the way, although the other major cities soon staged tragedy festivals as well.

The first tragedies we know of were staged in the time of Cleisthenes in the 6th century BCE—indeed, it is possible that the development of tragedy was one of the civic reforms he inaugurated—but the genre possibly dates even earlier.

The earliest complete plays that have come down to us are seven dramas by Aeschylus (525–456 BCE), who introduced nonchorus characters on the stage, which made dialogue possible. Tragedy's origins are uncertain, but it likely originated with the choral odes sung by crowds to the god Dionysius at the spring festival held in his honor in Athens. Dionysius was famously the god of wine, of passionate feeling, of life force. A latecomer to the Greek pantheon, he was a potent but disruptive force, one who promised his followers transformative experience, a sense of moving out of oneself (ecstasy—from Greek ek stasis, meaning "out of nonmovement").

This was an unnerving development. Greek religion had always been passionately adhered to without ever being essentially emotive. Gods and goddesses often had, and played, individual favorites among human beings. Athena's protection of Odysseus comes to mind, as does Hera's guardianship over women in childbirth. Yet they seldom felt or showed any actual emotion toward humans except for episodic wrath. People offered prayers and sacrifices to the Olympian deities, but the relationship between the faithful and the deities was more contractual than intimate. Wanting a good grain crop, they prayed to Demeter, who granted the wish or not depending on whether she liked their offerings. The cult of Dionysius was different. People turned to him not for favors but for spiritual elation and passionate release.

The German philosopher Friedrich Nietzsche (1844–1900) famously attributed tragedy to the Greek world's efforts to rein in the raw emotional power of the Dionysian cult. By subsuming these choral celebrations into a carefully managed public theatrical rite, he argued, the leaders of Athens created tragedy, a genre that provides a cathartic release of elemental passions within a strictly controlled setting. Nietzsche got many details wrong in his analysis, but his *Birth of Tragedy out of the Spirit of Music* (originally published in 1872 and revised in 1886) remains one of the most stimulating books ever written about ancient Greece.

Certain norms governed the practice, one of the most important being that tragic playwrights were expected not to compose original stories but to draw from the store of well-established popular legends and folktales. Sophocles (496–406 BCE) was not the only playwright to write a tragedy about Oedipus; his is simply the best-known version. To the Greeks, it simply required more artistry to captivate an audience with a story they already knew; to rely on an original plot was a cheap stunt—the ancient stage equivalent of a computer-generated special effect in today's movies. One can be startled by such a thing, even impressed, but not emotionally moved. The playwright Euripides (485–406 BCE) was often criticized for his use of innovations—original or little-known stories, unexpected plot twists, surprise endings—although most people granted his

The Amphitheater at Delphi   The amphitheater dates to the 4th century BCE and was renowned for its extraordinary acoustical design, which allowed (and still allows) a whisper to be heard by thousands of people, even in the upper rows.

brilliance with language and characterization. Every major polis staged tragedies as a ritual of religious observance. Athens was the center of theatrical culture with its annual festival called the Dionysia, for which playwrights submitted trilogies of new tragic plays (plus a burlesque piece called a satyr play that served to help the audience recover from the tragic gloom). A civic council selected the most promising plays and produced them for the festival, at which attendance was required of all adult male citizens. At the end of the festival, the audience selected the best trilogy of the year, and its author was granted awards and high honor.

The point of tragedy was to inspire fear and sympathy, which it accomplished by showing the relentless nature of fate and exploiting the paradox that people take pleasure in observing the suffering of others—a paradox made doubly ironic by the world's indifference to human pain. To the Greeks the cardinal sin was **hubris**—the excessive pride that leads people to think that they are in control of their own lives—for the hard reality is that our fates are fixed. Greek morality consisted of recognitions: of our obligations, our limitations, the futility of our aspirations, and our helplessness against the world's indifference. For the Greeks, we cannot alter what the world does to us, but we can control how we respond and adapt to our fates.

In the tales of the Theban ruler Oedipus, the hero begins the play believing he has escaped the fate decreed for him at birth—namely, that he would kill his father and marry his own mother. He discovers that he has done precisely that. Horrified by the revelation, he blinds himself and spends the rest of his life as a wandering beggar. In *Oedipus at Colonnus* the playwright Sophocles has the chorus sing a sorrowful ode as the blind beggar sits in despair:

> What foolishness it is to desire more life, after one has tasted
> A bit of it and seen the world; for each day, after each endless day,
> Piles up ever more misery into a mound. As for pleasures: once we
> Have passed youth they vanish away, never again to be seen.
>
> Death is the end of all.
> Never to be born is the best thing. To have seen the daylight
> And be swept instantly back into dark oblivion comes second.
> *(lines 1211–1238)*

Other plays tell equally disheartening stories and fill the stages with tears, blood, and crushing misery. The point of this was to drive home a crucial point: there is no reason to expect life to be happy. We are not owed comfort or contentment, and it is wrong to believe we have a right to either or both. To believe that such a right exists is in fact the surest way of achieving neither and ending tragically. Such misery is not a matter of life being fair or unfair; life is simply life, and we ought not to resist or bemoan it.[6] Life thus has no metaphysical meaning, is ennobled by no cosmic purpose—after all, we all spend eternity as mere shadows in a dark and dank afterworld, regardless of the moral quality of our earthly existence. Happiness in life is possible, but it is not a birthright, and the only control we can exert over our existence is to accept what comes. A gloomy outlook but a necessary one, to the Greeks: only by facing this hard reality can we truly have courage, and only thus can we accept both the good that happens and the evil that comes to us. Tragedy humbles us and reminds us to be thankful for small blessings.

> Happiness in life is possible, but it is not a birthright, and the only control we can exert over our existence is to accept what comes. A gloomy outlook but a necessary one, to the Greeks: only by facing this hard reality can we truly have courage, and only thus can we accept both the good that happens and the evil that comes to us.

---

[6]   "Let weeping cease, then," sings the chorus in *Oedipus at Colonnus*'s last lines, "and let there be no mourning. These things are in the hands of the gods."

THE PELOPONNESIAN DISASTER

Named for the Peloponnese, the peninsula on which Sparta and Corinth stood, the **Peloponnesian War** (431–404 BCE) lasted for twenty-seven years, although there were periods of truce. The result would be the ruin of Greece. Trying to make sense of it all, in turn, would motivate Athenian contributions to history, medicine, mathematics, and philosophy.

Athens had learned neither humility nor gratitude after the Persian War. Heady with pride and headstrong with determination to retain leadership in Greece, the Athenians spent most of the 5th century BCE bullying the city-states they had helped to defend against Darius and Xerxes. At first, no one dared to question them. When the Athenians began to withdraw funds from the Delian treasury to build up and beautify their own city, only Sparta (and its closest ally, Corinth) sniffed about Athenian hypocrisy. Through the 470s and 460s, however, several cities grumbled openly about Athens treating them like colonies—to which Athens responded by attacking and colonizing them outright (see Map 5.1).

Athenian garrisons were established across Greece, and corps of Athenian officials was set in charge of polis after polis. If they ever questioned their

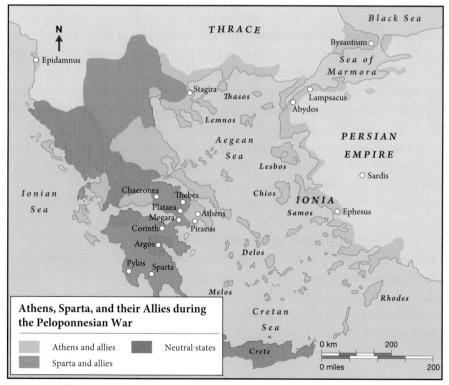

MAP 5.1   Athens, Sparta, and Their Allies during the Peloponnesian War

entitlement to an empire, no evidence of it survives. By 440 Pericles had established a peace treaty with Persia so that he could set his sights on Sparta and Corinth, the last barriers to Athenian control of all of Greece. After several more years of provocations and last-minute resolutions, open war between Athens and Sparta erupted in 431 BCE.

Sparta's army was superior to that of Athens, but the Athenian navy ruled the sea—so there were few pitched battles. Instead, the Spartans laid a protracted siege of Athens by land, while the Athenian ships established a blockade that kept food and goods from reaching Sparta by sea. The stalemate favored Athens, until an epidemic of typhus struck the city in 429 BCE and killed roughly one-third of the population, including Pericles. Factionalism then broke out, and Athens began to collapse.

Meanwhile the Spartans struck their own deal with the Persians, who agreed to provide them with a fleet of their own triremes. The Spartans themselves knew little of sailing, but there were enough enemies of Athens around by now to fit out a navy, and by 407 BCE the new naval force challenged Athenian invincibility, which effectively assured a Spartan victory. In 404 the Spartan army entered Athens itself, and the war was over. Corinth and Thebes both demanded the destruction of the city, but Sparta demurred. Instead, they pulled down Athens's fortifications, scuttled its fleet, installed a committee of thirty Athenians, the **Thirty Tyrants**, to govern the defeated city, and returned to Sparta as fast as they could.[7] The Spartan king Pausanias (r. 409–395 BCE) finally intervened and helped to restore democracy in 401 BCE.

Athens never recovered from its defeat, nor did Greece from the general ruin. A pallid democracy was restored in 401, but with its imperial revenues lost and most of its territories scorched, the Athenian economy remained constricted. Sparta shied away from playing any larger role in Greek affairs and focused on suppressing any helots who may have been encouraged by the disaster to attempt rebellion. This made Greece a tempting target for a resurgent Persia, which soon began to ponder another invasion. As it happened, someone else beat them to the punch.

Catastrophes can have beneficial effects. By their very completeness, catastrophes can sweep away cultural clutter, show the failure of institutions, expose social fault lines, and inspire a willingness to rethink old assumptions. The collapse of Greece in the Peloponnesian War led to at least a few positive developments. Politically, the poleis were too weakened to cause further trouble. They spent most of their time bickering internally, trying to find whom

---

[7]   The Thirty Tyrants murdered some fifteen hundred of their political rivals and confiscated their money and property.

or what to blame for the Hellenic downfall, but not all this search for explanations involved snide finger-pointing. A number of brave individuals made deep and serious inquiries into the nature of politics, the weakness of human will, the causes of greed, the quest for justice, and the desire to believe that the world makes sense. These issues had long been essential concerns of Greek cultural and intellectual life but had been examined and explored more in artistic genres such as poetry and tragedy. The intellectual life of post–Peloponnesian War Greece had a more analytical and scientific quality.

Herodotus (484–425 BCE), we saw earlier, had given an exciting new direction to this inquiry when he all but invented historical writing with his *History of the Persian Wars*. Previous historical writing—with the partial exception of the historical books in the Hebrew Bible—had consisted largely of propagandistic narratives, lists of deeds, blow-hard memorials, and the occasional funerary inscription. Herodotus was the first to gather information firsthand, to organize it systematically, and to present it critically—some say not critically enough, but that is for each reader to decide. His successor Thucydides (460–395 BCE) extended Herodotus's methods and created something entirely original.

His *History of the Peloponnesian War* is an astonishing achievement in many ways. Recognizing, as he writes in the book's stately preface, that "the war, when it began, would be great and important beyond any previous war," Thucydides dedicates himself to following it in detail. Before writing, he conducted interviews, reviewed documents, and checked contradictory accounts, paying attention to technological and logistical details with the thoroughness of a general preparing for battle. For Thucydides, the Peloponnesian War was the first ideological war in Western history—a conflict not merely between political states but between states of being. Athenian greed and hubris, and Spartan envy and suspicion, tell only part of the tale. Thucydides digs deeper and presents both sides acting out of different conceptions of freedom.

> For Thucydides, the Peloponnesian War was the first ideological war in Western history—a conflict not merely between political states but between states-of-being.

Freedom, of course, is a relative quality; one often defines freedom in terms of what one is free *from*. To militaristic Sparta, freedom meant freedom from chaos and unpredictability; to hyperambitious Athens it meant freedom from restraint in the pursuit of its desires and perceived rights. Thucydides sees a measure of truth in each point of view but is too committed to political realism to cast his vote entirely for one side or the other. In fact, the casting of votes is itself something Thucydides believes little in. Rather, he identifies as Athens's greatest weakness not its selfishness and hypocrisy but its commitment to democracy. Thucydides argues that democracy, despite its theoretical appeal, is doomed to fail because it is based upon a

TABLE 5.1   **Athens in the 5th Century**

DATE			
499	Ionian Revolt	430	Birth of Xenophon; Euripides, *Heracleidae*
496	Birth of Sophocles		
494	Phrynicus, *Capture of Miletus*	429	Death of Pericles
490	Darius invades Greece; Battle of Marathon	428	Birth of Plato; Euripides, *Hippolytus*
		427	Sophocles, *Oedipus Rex*
484	Birth of Herodotus	425	Death of Herodotus; Aristophanes, *Acharnians*; Euripides, *Andromache*
480	Birth of Euripides; Battle of Thermopylae		
		424	Aristophanes, *The Knights*; Euripides, *Hecuba*
479	Battles of Salamis, Plataea; Persian War ends		
		423	Aristophanes, *The Clouds* Euripides, *The Suppliants*
478	Delian League established		
477	Athens assumes control of Delian League	422	Aristophanes, *The Wasps*
		421	Aristophanes, *Peace*; Peace of Nicias
472	Aeschylus, *The Persians*	420	Euripides, *Electra*
470	Birth of Socrates; death of Xenophanes	416	Euripides, *Heracles*
468	Sophocles' first victory	415	Euripides, *The Trojan Women*; Sicilian Expedition; herms mutilated
463	Aeschylus, *The Suppliants*		
460	Birth of Thucydides and Hippocrates; Pericles rises to power in Athens	414	Aristophanes, *The Birds*; Euripides, *Ion*, *Iphigeneia in Tauris*
458	Aeschylus, *Oresteia*	412	Euripides, *Helen*
456	Death of Aeschylus; birth of Aristophanes	411	Aristophanes, *Lysistrata*, *Thesmophoriazusae*
455	Euripides, *Peliades*	410	Euripides, *Phoenician Women*
454	Athens confiscates Delian League treasury	409	Sophocles, *Philoctetes*
		408	Euripides, *Orestes*
451	Pericles' citizenship law enacted	407	Sophocles, *Oedipus at Colonus*
447	Construction of Parthenon begun	406	Death of Sophocles and Euripides; Euripides, *Bacchae, Iphigeneia in Aulis*
446	Death of Pindar		
442	Sophocles, *Antigone*	405	Aristophanes, *The Frogs*
438	Euripides, *Alcestis*	404	Peloponnesian War ends Regime of the Thirty Tyrants
432	Parthenon completed		
431	Euripides, *Medea*; Herodotus begins *Persian Wars*; Peloponnesian War begins	403	Democracy restored to Athens
		399	Death of Socrates

lie—namely, the notion of human equality. To drive his point home, Thucydides composes a handful of brilliant set pieces, either wholly fictitious events or highly imaginative reconstructions of speeches, dialogues, and debates. (The best known of these are "Pericles' Funeral Oration" of 429 [2:34–46], the "Mytilenian Debate" [3.37–50], and the "Melian Dialogue" [5.85–113].) They give Athens's commitment to its democratic ideal elaborate expression, but also subtly expose it as nearsighted, contradictory, and ultimately hopeless.

Thucydides' history breaks off suddenly, in Book 8, with the battle of Cynos-sema in 411 (a minor victory for Athens over the new Spartan naval force). He leaves the last seven years of the war untreated. The work is clearly unfinished, although historians disagree why the book was never completed. It seems certain that a ninth book was intended, to reflect the nine-book structure of Herodotus's *Persian Wars*; but Thucydides completed enough of his masterpiece to leave the Greek tragedy dissected and exposed with unmatched and gimlet-eyed skill. He leaves the reader with little to hope for in human nature, but wishing for more and more of his extraordinary and dispassionate insight.

MEDICINE AS NATURAL LAW: HIPPOCRATES

Just as Thucydides had given clear-eyed diagnoses of Greek political decline, Hippocrates of Kos (460–370 BCE) divorced illness and disease from superstitions and religious beliefs. In the process, he made human suffering—or, at least, one type of human suffering—a feature of the natural world. His separation of physical health from religious issues also makes him the founder of Western medicine.

Earlier traditions, as in Egypt and Babylon, had built up an understanding of how to treat various maladies, but knowledge of how the body works, how diseases function, and why any given remedy works (or does not) remained mysteries. Such things were attributed to astral influences, spells cast by demons, and the whims of the gods. Hippocrates was the first to study medicine systematically, in order to work out the processes by which herbs and treatments produced their effects. He and his successors compiled the *Hippocratic Corpus*, seventy volumes that discuss maladies (such as epilepsy, the "sacred disease") as natural phenomena rather than divine curses. He was the first to categorize diseases and therefore to produce a preliminary sketch of a natural structure. Acute, chronic, endemic, and epidemic were the first categories, followed by subcategories according to organs and bodily systems.

Hippocrates famously composed an oath to be sworn by all physicians, marking the official start of their careers. The original form of the Hippocratic oath goes as follows:

> I swear by Apollo, Asclepius, Hygeia, and Panacea, and do bear witness before all gods and goddesses that I will remain true to the following oath, to the best of my ability and judgment:

> that I will hold as dear to me as my own parents the man who taught me this art [of medicine], will live with him, and if necessary will share my possessions with him;

that I will regard his children as my own brothers, and will teach them this same art;

that I will prescribe health regimens for the good of my patients to the very best of my ability and will never intentionally do harm to anyone;

that I will give no poison to anyone, not even if asked to do so, nor will I advise anyone [to take poison]; neither will I give any woman a pessary to induce abortion;

that I will preserve the purity of my life and my practice;

that I will not perform surgery for gallstones, not even for patients suffering terribly, and that I will instead leave this for those who specialize in this task;

that I will enter homes only to serve the good of my patients, and avoid causing any kind of harm—especially any kind of seduction to engage in sex with any woman or man, free or enslaved, in the home;

and that I will always preserve the confidentiality of anything I learn about my patients and their households in the practice of my profession, not permitting anything to be spread about.

To the extent that I faithfully keep this oath, may I live my life and practice my art enjoying always the respect of all men; but if I fail to do so, and if I violate this oath, may the opposite be the case.

The Oath sworn by new physicians today is considerably different.

But the significance of Hippocrates' work lay not only in its contributions to medical science: he also regarded mankind as part of the natural landscape—capable of, and responsive to, rational analysis. He severed medicine from religion and allied it with philosophy.

MATHEMATICAL ORDERING AND SOPHISTRY

Philosophy, of course, was the area of the Greeks' greatest and most enduring achievement. Much had happened in this field since the Milesians. A group of philosophers known as the **Pythagoreans**—named after Pythagoras (570–495 BCE), who had developed the famous theorem about right triangles—had directed philosophy away from the Milesian focus on primal essences. The Pythagoreans sought instead to identify the rational ordering of those essences, the laws that governed their interaction; hence their focus on mathematics. Heraclitus of Ephesus (mid-5th century BCE), for example, tried to explain the world's obvious

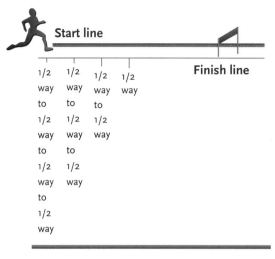

Start line

Finish line

1/2 way
1/2 way
1/2 way
1/2 way

1/2 way
1/2 way
1/2 way

1/2 way
1/2 way
to

1/2 way

FIGURE 5.1   **A Paradox of Zeno. Like the arrow, the runner will never reach his destination.**

diversity and changeability as a rational patterning and repatterning of opposing forces (hot/cold, light/dark, wet/dry, etc.). If closely observed, even the infinite progressions of a child's kaleidoscope follows a rational pattern. Hence the almost Daoist tone in some of his sayings: "We step and yet we do not step into the same river twice; we are and we are not." "A road goes uphill and downhill at once—it is the same road."[8]

Zeno of Elea (ca. 490–420 BCE) introduced a number of mathematical paradoxes that seem to presage Einstein's theories about time-space continuums. Imagine, for one, that an archer unleashes an arrow at a target. After a certain interval of time the arrow will traverse half the distance; after another, although briefer, interval of time the arrow will traverse half of the shorter distance that remains; after a third interval the arrow will reach the midpoint of the now even shorter remaining distance (see Figure 5.1). The paradox is that the arrow, in crossing an infinite number of midway points en route to the target, will in fact never reach the target. Another Pythagorean, Empedocles of Acragas (ca. 450–390 BCE), undercut Heraclitus's argument about the interplay of opposing forces. Empedocles observed that such coming into existence and passing from existence of new substances makes no sense, since it would necessarily mean the coming into existence and passing from existence of nonexistence itself. Empedocles committed suicide by hurling himself into a live volcano shortly thereafter, thus putting an end to his logical misery.

---

[8]   "No god or man made the world," wrote Heraclitus. "It is the same for all, always was, is, and will be, an eternal fire eternally kindled and extinguished in equal measures."

A second group of thinkers called the **Sophists** also had their day. Few of their names have come down to us, but in any case the Sophists specialized in packaging ideas rather than in producing anything original. Their emphasis lay in rhetorical skill rather than in genuine investigation: in the bustling economic scene of classical Athens, they aimed to help enterprising people to prosper. The Sophists' closest modern-day analog would be motivational speakers, investment gurus, self-help guides, and leadership coaches of cable-television specials and expensive weekend seminars. They traveled from city to city, offering tuition in everything from public speaking and career guidance to introductory surveys of exciting "useful knowledge" from around the world. These activities are easily mocked as derivative and shallow, and the Sophists have come in for more than their fair share of criticism over the centuries. But to audiences in Periclean Athens, stuffed like game hens with a comfortless religion and the crushing gloom of tragedy, lighter fare like this must have been a welcome respite.

SOCRATES AND THE MEANINGFUL LIFE

The Peloponnesian War crushed the optimism offered by the Sophists. In their place arose a trio of the most influential and impressive philosophers in history, whose lives, written works, and the schools they established changed Western intellectual culture forever. These three individuals—Socrates (469–399 BCE), Plato (427–347 BCE), and Aristotle (384–322 BCE)—permanently altered the direction and scope of philosophy. For the subsequent fifteen hundred years Western science, religion, and politics, as well as philosophy itself, followed the intellectual trajectories they established.

Socrates is the most enigmatic of the three. At least partially trained in the Sophist tradition, he pulled philosophical inspection away from the theoreti-

cal model making of the Milesians and Pythagoreans and insisted that it pursue questions that actually matter to any thinking individual who wants to live meaningfully. Geometrical schema are fine, Socrates felt—but what good are they for answering questions like *What is the right way to live? How can one know anything for certain? What is love?* or *What is justice?* Socrates' signal achievement was to make philosophy a practical urgency—"to pull philosophy back down from the sky," as the Roman writer Cicero put it.

Socrates He was reputedly the ugliest but wisest man in Greece during the Classical Age. 4th century BCE.

Ethics and politics (by which he meant communal ethics), not cosmology and natural science, were the essential concerns of philosophical enquiry, he insisted, or else why bother?

Since he left no writing of his own, we know little about his life. Reputedly the ugliest but most charming man in Athens, he married a woman named Xanthippe, had a family, worked as a stonemason, fought in the Athenian army, participated in municipal government, and had a variety of homosexual lovers. At the age of seventy he was arrested on charges of impiety and corrupting the youth of the city; after an eventful trial he was convicted and sentenced to death by poison—a fate he reportedly accepted with calmness and grace. The charges against him may well have been politically motivated, or at least partly so. Socrates criticized democracy as an irrational political system and had close friends among leading antidemocratic figures in Athens—most notoriously, a sexual relationship with Alcibiades. The charge of impiety rested on his claim to be inspired by a "divine spirit" (daimonion). The corruption charge asserted that he intentionally urged his pupils to question the values handed to them by society.

Socrates founded no formal school but inspired so many later thinkers that he may be the single most influential figure in Western philosophy. Certainly he set the terms of debate, for from his own time until the 19th century ethics and politics remained the central topics of inquiry. Only with the work of Karl Marx and Georg Friedrich Hegel—both mid-19th-century writers— did philosophy turn from these concerns toward the kind of philosophy dominant today. They helped make philosophy the study of the systems (economic, ideological, and linguistic) which restrain, shape, and perhaps control our thinking and lives.

Almost all that we know of Socrates' life and thought comes from four sources: the dialogues of his greatest pupil, Plato; the essays of another pupil, Xenophon; a few scraps of commentary by Aristotle (Plato's student); and a hilarious caricature of him in the comedy *The Clouds* by Aristophanes (446–386 BCE). Together, they present a coherent though not conclusive portrait—of the man whose misfortune was to reach his greatest fame when a sore and humiliated Athens was least inclined to tolerate criticism of its democratic greatness.

Socrates is associated more with a method than a set of ideas. That method consisted of patient and thorough questioning, rather than the assertion of observations or deductions. A consistent pattern emerges in all his appearances in his pupils' dialogues. When asked, for example, to describe the best political system, he begins by asking what we mean by Justice—the quality that all political life aims to supply. Only by understanding the terms we use, Socrates insists, can we begin a proper inquiry. Nothing can be assumed if we wish to seek true understanding. Usually his interlocutors, turned in every direction by his clever questioning, end up admitting that they have no idea how to define anything, and Socrates declares that true philosophical inquiry can therefore at last begin. What the prosecutors at his trial failed to grasp was that Socrates did not doubt that Justice (or Love, or Being, or Truth, or Goodness) exists. He was merely willing to entertain such a doubt as a stimulus to thinking about it.

Despite his charisma and brilliance, or perhaps because of them, he was a terribly annoying man. Think of a conversational bully who delightedly dismantles the ideas of others but never fully offers ideas of his own to replace them. In *The Republic*, Plato's longest and most intricate dialogue, Plato presents Socrates tearing to shreds the ideas of four different characters regarding the nature of Justice. Then, when asked to offer his own definition, Socrates spends the next six books of the dialogue discussing the ideal form of government—but without ever offering his own definition of what Justice actually is. In the end he wins by exhausting his opponents, not by defeating them. Nevertheless, by exposing so brilliantly the human capacity to speak without thinking, Socrates set philosophy on a new course, one pursued avidly by his most brilliant student, Plato.

PLATO AND IDEAL FORMS

Plato came from a wealthy, aristocratic family. Brothers, half-brothers, and cousins populate many of his dialogues—presumably an indication of his pride in his kin. He received an excellent education in mathematics, music, literature, gymnastics, and philosophy, all of which are discussed and cited extensively in his writings. He seems, unlike his teacher, never to have had a profession apart from teaching in the **Academy**, the school he founded when he reached the age of forty. He never married and was wholly homoerotic. As the Peloponnesian War drew to its close, he thought of taking an active role in politics, but he was enraged at the ham-fisted rule of the Thirty Tyrants. When the restored but nearly impotent democracy sentenced Socrates to death, he all but washed his hands of active public life. He took refuge at Megara for a while and possibly traveled to Sicily and southern Italy. Returning to Athens around 385 BCE, he established the Academy, took on pupils, and began to lecture and compose dialogues.

The period from 385 to 360 BCE were the years of his greatest productivity and originality. He peopled his dialogues with artists, politicians, poets, sophists, and orators from the Athenian scene. References to poets and playwrights, often including quotations, appear in almost every dialogue, as do many of the writers themselves. In the last dozen years of his life, 360–347 BCE, perhaps tiring after long labor, he began to outline and dictate in rough form his dialogues to his students, who then fleshed them out in a more turgid, "academic" style. The extraordinary literary polish of the middle years gradually disappeared, although his mind remained as sharp as ever. He became increasingly conservative as he

Plato's Academy   A Roman reimagining of a Greek scene. This mosaic (ca. 100 BCE) shows a half dozen philosophers gathered, presumably, around Plato. Unlike his student Aristotle, who famously paced constantly while lecturing, Plato, a high aristocrat, enjoyed his leisure. Here he rests against a tree while examining a scroll.

aged, though, and by the time he wrote *The Laws,* one of his last works, he was deeply embittered by the world's foolishness.

Most of the dialogues repeat a pattern. Socrates encounters a group somewhere in or near Athens and joins their conversation. It might be at an evening entertainment, along a road to a temple, sitting in a town square, or chatting in a portico. Picking up on an apparently offhand comment by one of the group, Socrates begins to probe his fellows' attitudes, language, convictions, and assumptions until they admit hopeless befuddlement and beg Socrates to set them aright. Socrates sometimes obliges but just as often demurs: the dialogue functions not as a means to a dogmatic conclusion but as an invitation to the reader to continue the discussion. Plato's earliest dialogues, most historians agree, present a historically accurate portrait of Socrates' own philosophy. As the years went on, though, he increasingly used Socrates as a literary device, a mouthpiece for his own ideas.

Plato begins with an observation: the world we observe with our senses is pale and imperfect—defective, jumbled, and filled with apparent contradictions.

And yet we intuit order within it. We see parts of things; we intuit whole things. We observe, for example, two chairs. They may be of different sizes and shapes, made of different materials, weigh different amounts, exhibit different colors, have different combustion points if we apply a flame to them, or even (for the brave) may smell and taste different. And yet we know that they are both indeed chairs. They possess some quality—"chairness"—that perhaps we cannot define, but, like the famous example of the U.S. Supreme Court judge discussing pornography: we know it when we see it.

Plato's philosophy argues that "chairness" really and truly exists; it is an example of what he terms the **Ideal Forms**. Where does it exist? Perhaps in a parallel universe, or as an idea in the mind of God. Who can say? The point is that it does exist, and that everything we perceive as a chair possesses it. Thus to Plato our world should be thought of as a pallid reflection of the world of Ideal Forms, a corrupt descendant filled with flawed and partial representations of the Forms. The Ideal Forms constitute ultimate reality, while our physical world is a cheap knockoff. Plato's dialogues can be thought of as a series of discussions, each about a particular abstract Form—Love, Beauty, Goodness, Art, or Justice—for we can only understand our world in relation to the Forms it so imperfectly represents.

> The Ideal Forms constitute ultimate reality, while our physical world is a cheap knockoff. Plato's dialogues can be thought of as a series of discussions, each about a particular abstract Form—love, beauty, goodness, art, or justice—for we can only understand our world in relation to the Forms it so imperfectly represents.

Plato insists that we can in fact understand the Ideal Forms because of the dual nature of human beings: we are not merely animated flesh but eternal souls temporarily housed in physical bodies. Each soul carries deep within itself an instinctive knowledge of the Ideal Forms, a memory of ultimate reality as yet lacking a clear shape. That is why we feel we know what "chairness" is even though we struggle to express it in words. Plato's philosophy is essentially romantic and mystical. It yearns for and aspires to an ineluctable perfect state of existence that seems as though it should be within our grasp. If only we can keep talking, if only we can remain willing to strip away untested assumptions, if only we can help one another along the way, we will eventually attain the true meaning of Love, Beauty, Goodness, Truth, and Happiness.

No other writer comes close to Plato's skill at portraying philosophy as a kind of pilgrimage, a journey toward a salvation that can be attained only with other people. There are no solitary revelers in Plato's world. Each of his dialogues ends differently, in terms of whether or not a true understanding of any particular Form is attained. Yet they all end with a warm feeling of community, of

Two 4th-Century BCE Busts, Portraying Plato and Aristotle   By tradition, Aristotle is always shown with a shorter beard than his teacher's.

something special having been shared. It is the process of philosophy as much as the ideas attained by it that Plato portrays so lovingly and unforgettably.

ARISTOTLE AND THE PURSUIT OF HAPPINESS

Aristotle was Plato's most distinguished pupil and has a good claim to be among the three or four most influential thinkers in Western history. A tireless worker, he threw himself into the study of everything from ethics and metaphysics to botany and poetics. Ancient sources credit him with as many as two hundred separate treatises, some of very great length. Roughly thirty treatises survive, perhaps more and perhaps fewer, depending on the debated authenticity of a handful of texts.

Despite their unflagging brilliance, though, most of the texts consist not of Aristotle's own writing but of lecture notes later collated and stitched together (according to tradition, by his son, Nicomachus). The books as we have them are leaden, cramped, repetitive, and graceless. If his lectures were in fact like these composite transcripts, Aristotle was a brilliant but dull teacher. The contrast with Plato could hardly be any stronger. Plato was an artist of the highest order; his dialogues have polish, wit, sharp characterization, and narrative drive. They manage the neat trick of expressing complex ideas with such clarity that anyone can grasp them. Aristotle, by contrast, comes across as an astonishing but long-winded polymath struggling to control a buggy Power-Point presentation.

The ideas that come through are vital, even though his range makes it difficult to present them in a systematic way. The key to Aristotle lay in his method: unlike his teacher (but very much like his own father, a physician) Aristotle began not with the theoretical examination of the Ideal Forms but with intense scrutiny of the tangible natural world. He accepted the notion of the Ideal Forms, or claimed to, but he believed that their essential elements appear physically within each object. Existence consists of the continual interplay of Ideal Form and earthly matter—rather like the way our genetic coding continues to affect our physical development throughout our lives. Aristotle, then, offers a compromise between Plato's Idealism and the rough materialism of the Milesians.

Moreover, Aristotle asserts that the continuous nature of the interplay of forces drives the universe forward toward a goal. Everything is in a state of be-coming. A seed is on its way to becoming a seedling, then a plant in full flower, then a withering husk, then a decayed nutrient for another seed. Each existing thing, whether animate or not, plays a role in the unstoppable push forward to new life. Since we ourselves are part of this impetus of birth, life, and decay, we can take solace in knowing that our existence is ennobled with purpose. Every existing thing, he says, has a **telos**—an intrinsic purpose, a necessary role in the cosmic drama. The telos of an animal embryo is to become that animal; that of teeth is chew food. For Aristotle's great teacher, the physical world is a flaw and a hindrance to our understanding. Aristotle instead sees the world as a process—a march forward into ever new being (and hopefully, but not necessarily, ever better being).

But do human beings have a telos? If so, is it a general telos applicable to the whole species, or is it unique to each nation or even each individual? I know of a philosophy professor (an Aristotelian, no less) who preyed on female students. When his university learned of it and fired him, he argued that sexual craving for young women was, however unfortunately, his telos and that he therefore had no choice but to pursue them. He consequently sued the university for discrimina-tion against a person with a handicap. He lost.

Aristotle wrestled with these questions over and over. If human life is teleo-logical, is that not the same as saying it is fated or even predetermined? Are we in control of our own destinies, and if not, then what sound basis can there be for morality? Aristotle's answer is characteristically complex. He begins with the observation that ethics is a practical science, not a theoretical one. The point of it is to learn how to act and live a well-ordered life, not to gain some abstract knowl-edge about the nature of Goodness for its own sake.

Most people, he says, would agree on most ethical propositions: that happiness is better than sadness, that pleasure is preferable to pain, or that courage is superior to fearfulness. We all might disagree on specifics regarding those virtues. Some, for example, might take greater pleasure in being renowned for beauty than for intelligence. But everyone would agree that to have a good reputation for something is a positive ethical value. What interests Aristotle is the relationship between these values. Is courage of greater or lesser value than loyalty? Is it more important to be temperate in one's desires or to be well-liked? Whatever their relative standings, he insists that happiness (*eudaimonia* in Greek—meaning "being in accordance with the spirits," literally, or "living well," colloquially) is the supreme virtue, toward which all other virtues point. To Aristotle happiness must entail something intrinsic to human beings as a species. It is something we possess or experience that no other creatures can; and this, he says, is our capacity for rational thought. If we follow the use of reason, if we cultivate it as a means of life, we can and will attain happiness. Whether or not we are happy has little to do with the contingency of world events and is the product of our own choices—choices in our actions and in how we react to the world. In this way, individual free will is preserved, as is the notion of a human telos. In other words, our telos is to pursue happiness; but whether or not we achieve it, or the way in which we achieve it, is up to us.

> To Aristotle happiness must entail something intrinsic to human beings as a species. It is something we possess or do that no other creatures can; and this, he says, is our capacity for rational thought. If we follow the use of reason, if we cultivate it as a means of life, we can and will attain happiness.

Plato and Aristotle were both interested in politics, though only at a distance. Two of Plato's last dialogues—*The Republic* and *The Laws*—describe a vision of an ideal society, one in which an oligarchy of philosopher-kings would oversee the day-to-day governance of society. A group of Guardians would in turn direct the education, training, and administration of everyday life. The bulk of common humanity is neither able to nor cares to govern its own affairs and is happy to leave the work of running the world to its superiors. It is not clear how Plato intends us to read this treatise. Socrates' arguments never appear so weak reasoned and faulty anywhere else in Plato's writings. He even interrupts the text with allegorical tales that highlight the futility of drawing clear conclusions about anything.

Aristotle, on the other hand, took a genuine interest in politics—even to the point of writing constitutions for various poleis—although he had no direct involvement in political life that we know of. After Plato's death in 347 BCE, Aristotle left Greece altogether and lived in Asia Minor for four years. In 343 BCE King Philip of Macedon (r. 359–336 BCE) invited Aristotle to come to Pella, the capital of Macedon, and tutor his teenage son. Aristotle took the job, in a kingdom to the north of Greece inhabited by a tribe that spoke a language of disputed relation to Greek. There he spent eight years teaching the lad, and then in 335 BCE he finally returned to Athens and established his own school, the **Lyceum**, where he spent the rest of his life giving his interminable lectures.

The lad he tutored in Pella, however, most definitely took an interest in politics. His name was Alexander.

ALEXANDER THE GREAT

Alexander the Great (r. 336–323 BCE) was the greatest conqueror of the ancient world. He took over from his father the realm of Macedon, a semi-Greek kingdom with an inferiority complex, and much of Greece proper, which his father had briefly subdued. By 334 BCE Alexander was firmly in control of all of Greece and had already determined to advance eastward against the Persian Empire. And that was just the start.

In its bloody, insurrection-filled past, Macedon also had suffered in the invasions by Darius and Xerxes. The Greeks themselves regarded the Macedonians as barbarians—or at the very best as poor backward cousins. While Greece prospered during the Periclean age, Macedon remained ignored and reviled. But the self-destruction of Greece during the Peloponnesian War gave Philip, and then his son, dreams of glory. With the discovery of vast gold mines in the southern Balkans, Philip became wealthier than the Delian League had been at its height.

Alexander succeeded to the Macedonian throne in 336 BCE, and within two years he had swooped down on all of Greece. No one could stand in his way, since all the poleis were in such weak condition. In turning his sights to Persia, his thinking was sound. The conflict between Greece and Persia had never been settled definitively. Internal discord and political strife had followed the defeat of Xerxes' forces in 479 BCE, but by the time of the Peloponnesian conflict Persia was already trying to manipulate the outcome in Greece in order to prepare the way for another attempt. Alexander simply recognized, correctly, that Greece would never be free of the Persian threat. He decided to settle the matter once and for all by reversing the scales and sending his Greek army to topple the throne in faraway Persepolis.

Alexander the Great   A Roman copy (1st century BCE) of a Greek original bust.

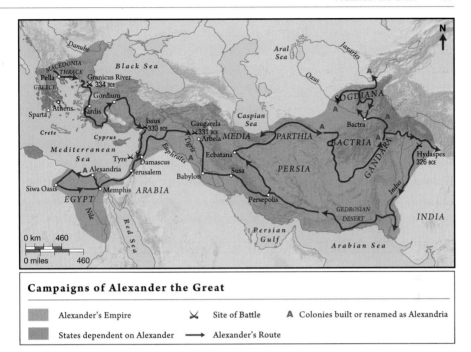

Campaigns of Alexander the Great

Alexander's Empire	⚔ Site of Battle	▲ Colonies built or renamed as Alexandria
States dependent on Alexander	→ Alexander's Route	

MAP 5.2   Campaigns of Alexander the Great

The narrative of Alexander's campaigns is well known. In 334 BCE he took Asia Minor; within two more years he had conquered the Holy Land and Egypt. By 331 BCE he had advanced through Syria and met the main Persian army at Gaugamela, not far from the ancient Assyrian city of Nineveh along the upper Tigris, and slaughtered it.[9] He then marched to Persepolis, deep into today's Iran, and in 330 BCE he destroyed the capital. Determined to press on until every last vestige of Persian power was defeated, Alexander spent five more years on campaign through the territories of Parthia and Bactria (today's eastern Iran and Afghanistan), then down the Indus River valley, where his astonished men encountered Indian war elephants. Alexander still wanted to press on and take India, but his exhausted men threatened to mutiny, and so in 325–324 BCE he reluctantly led his forces back west to the city of Babylon. It was the most stunning military adventure of the ancient world, an unparalleled feat (see Map 5.2).

But it is one thing to conquer vast territory, and quite another to create an empire. Alexander's long-term plans are unknown, for in 323 BCE he took ill and died, aged thirty-three. He had taken care to establish in his wake a sprawl of Greek-styled cities. Some were newly built from nothing (like Alexandria, in

---

9   After the battle of Gaugamela, the Persian emperor Darius III fled into the nearby hills, where he was murdered by a local tribal chieftain. This ended the Achaemenid dynasty.

Egypt), others refashioned with Greek institutions and laws. Within them he placed a loose network of libraries stocked with copies of the best of Greek literature, science, philosophy, and mathematics. He added to these the gathered manuscripts of Persian high culture too—many translated into Greek for the widest dissemination. He also arranged (in fact, ordered on penalty of death) for his leading officers to divorce their Greek wives and to take Persian ones instead. It is unclear whether Alexander intended by this to create a utopian postethnic society. Perhaps he intended simply to develop a new aristocracy, one that identified itself with a new race of his own manufacture. In either case, he was developing an amalgam.

A MONGREL BUT MAGNIFICENT WORLD

The eastern Mediterranean traditions had included the Greek, Egyptian, and Hebrew. The Persian and Babylonian traditions had included the Mesopotamian valley and the eastern lands that had absorbed and assimilated them. As Alexander's vast battlefield settled into relative peace, a single Hellenistic civilization embraced and absorbed both. This mongrel but magnificent world was the **Hellenistic Age** (327–30 BCE), and it lasted until the Romans finally came in the 1st century BCE and instigated a new era.

The political narrative of the time is not particularly interesting. Many wars and palace coups came and went, but none in service of a significant new idea. In general terms, Alexander's enormous war zone split quickly into a quartet of separate states, each governed originally by one of his leading generals: Ptolemaic Egypt, Seleucid Asia, Attalid Anatolia, and Antigonid Greece.[10] Because the new rulers and settlers came from throughout Greece, and not simply from a single city like Athens, the Hellenistic world had a broader degree of cultural cohesion. A single dialect of Greek developed and came into general usage throughout the territories—this was the "common" (*koine*) Greek in which, ultimately, most of the Christian New Testament was written. In all four kingdoms the governments were tightly centralized, and efficient tax collection led to the building up of vast treasuries (see Map 5.3).

Apart from supporting their armies, the main expenditure of the governments was the construction of more and more cities. Manufacturing and

> It is unclear whether Alexander intended to create a utopian postethnic society. Perhaps he intended simply to develop a new aristocracy, one that identified itself with a new race of his own manufacture. In either case, he was developing an amalgam.

---

[10]   Take the -ic and -id endings off the dynastic adjectives, add -us (or -os, if you're a Hellenic purist), and you'll have the names of the first succeeding generals.

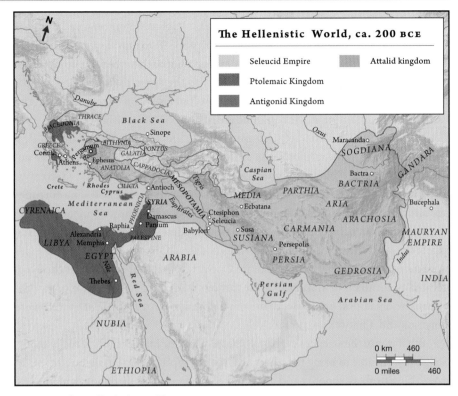

MAP 5.3   **The Hellenistic World, ca. 200 BCE**

commerce were the hallmarks of Hellenistic life, and these required a solid and expansive urban base. At least three hundred new cities were founded in this era, and hundreds more received huge injections of money to improve their infrastructures. Within a century of its construction, Alexandria had a half million inhabitants; Seleucia had a quarter million.[11] The Seleucids poured money into refurbishing their Mediterranean and Black Sea harbors and extended their roadways into India. The Ptolemies in Egypt hired geographers and cartographers to search out and map new overland trade routes into Arabia, Ethiopia, and Nubia. The Antigonids invested in canals and a vastly increased fleet of ships that was able to trade with Spain and Britain (important sources of silver and tin, respectively).

Not everyone prospered. Farming was still the occupation of the great bulk of the population, and farmers generally lived in poverty throughout the Hellenistic years. Poor crop yields were not the cause. Farmers steadily produced abundant quantities of foodstuffs, and the proliferation of cities meant the increased,

---

[11]   Pergamon, the cultural capital of the Attalid kingdom, had an amphitheater that could seat ten thousand and a library that contained two hundred thousand scrolls.

and increasingly easy, availability of markets. Rather, intentionally harsh tax policies in all the kingdoms kept small farmers poor. Two motives prompted such exploitation: a desire not to impede the development of the urban economies, and a perverse belief that abject poverty would keep the agrarian population incapable of rebellion. Hellenistic splendor thus resulted less from a general prosperity than from the intentionally inequitable redistribution of wealth.

Hellenistic literature, art, and intellectual life were generally not as dramatic, innovative, and profound as in the Classical period. Then again, the autocratic nature of Hellenistic government may not have permitted as creative a spirit to flourish. Cultural life seldom thrives in police states. The fortunes acquired by those in trade and industry, as well as in government, meant a widespread demand for decorative arts—statuary, jewelry, frescos and mosaics, tapestries—to adorn the homes and villas of the well-to-do. The preferred styles were more ornate, as with the elaborate Corinthian style of columns or the exaggerated naturalism of statues like the famous Laocoön. In literature, historical writing and pastoral poetry were the most popular genres (the best writers were Polybius and Theocritus, respectively).

But it was in the sciences especially that Hellenistic intellectual life really shone. Scholars were able to bring together the Greek, Egyptian, and Persian traditions in everything from astronomy and geometry to mathematics, medicine, and physics. The wide availability of libraries and laboratories—both of which were considered "must-have" accessories of the well-to-do—sparked many new abstract and practical advances, word of which spread rapidly. Aristarchus of Samos (310–230 BCE) and Eratosthenes of Cyrene (285–194 BCE) were the preeminent astronomers.

Three Examples of Hellenistic Sculpture, Showing a New Emphasis on Movement and Gesture   The first shows a gladiator or other competitive fighter (identifiable by his lack of armor—or of anything else). The second depicts the goddess Venus in a surprisingly modest pose. The third, which is a Roman copy of a lost Greek original, depicts the legendary figure of Laocoön as he is beset by sea-serpents.

Between them, they proved that the earth and other planets revolved around the sun and determined the circumference of the earth.

In geometry, Euclid (330–270 BCE) led the way. *The Elements of Geometry* became the basic textbook for teaching the subject for fifteen hundred years. In medicine, figures like Herophilus of Chalcedon (335–280 BCE) introduced (briefly, and on the sly) the practice of human dissection, from which he determined the role of the heart in transmitting blood through the arteries—a bit of knowledge quickly lost until it was rediscovered by the English physician William Harvey in the 17th century. Archimedes of Syracuse (287–212 BCE)—the physicist famous for shouting "eureka" ("I've got it!") and running naked through the street—determined the law of specific gravity, devised the first compound pulley, and invented the hydraulic screw propeller.

SECOND TEMPLE JEWS AND JUDAISM

Freed from Babylonian bondage by Cyrus the Great in 539 BCE, the exiled Jews returned to Jerusalem and set to rebuilding their Temple, which they completed roughly twenty years later. The delay resulted from and illustrates some of the tensions that roiled the Jewish world. The Jews who had gone into captivity (the "Children of the Exile") and those who had remained behind (the "People of the Land") regarded one another with deep suspicion and hostility, and their descendants continued the conflict for at least two generations. Who were the "true Jews"—those who had endured foreign enslavement or those who had stayed behind in the Holy Land at great risk to their own safety?

> Who were the "true Jews"—those who had endured foreign enslavement or those who had stayed behind in the Holy Land at great risk to their own safety?

To make matters even more complicated, both groups had developed new devotional and legal traditions. Both communities had turned for guidance to networks of rabbis, or legal scholars. For the "Children of the Exile," return to Jerusalem meant the restoration to power of the high priestly family, along with the primacy of Temple worship. The "People of the Land" dismissed the priestly family as mere pawns of the Persian Empire.[12] (The "People of the Land" faction has been edited out of the Jewish canon, for the most part, although it is possible that Isaiah 55–56 carries echoes of their position.) Accusations of treason, corruption, and apostasy flew back and forth. Moreover, many Jewish men in each camp had married non-Jewish women, given the relative shortage of females during the long years of hardship, and the resulting offspring became the

---

12   The prophet Ezra was a partisan of the "Children of the Exile."

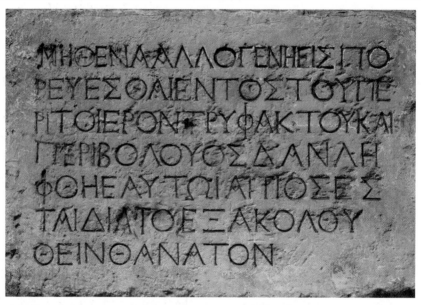

Plaster Cast of an Inscription from the Ruins of the Second Temple Written in Greek, the inscription stood outside the outermost wall of the Temple grounds; it states that only Jews may enter the Temple precinct itself. Non-Jews found within the walls potentially faced the penalty of death.

objects of much debate on the authenticity of their Jewishness. (Ezra casts the inter-Jewish conflict in economic terms.) Such conflicts continued for another two or three centuries, which resulted in the remarkable amount of legal and literary activity discussed earlier. Most notably, earlier religious texts were revised and new ones produced, down to the revisionist history of 1–2 Chronicles (with which the Jewish canon now ends), which was penned around 350 BCE.

Thus the Jews entered the Hellenistic period engaged in intense debate about their communal identity. The two principal factions soon divided into a multiplicity of sects, distinguished by doctrinal divisions, tribal and political loyalties, class distinctions, and linguistic identities. Opposing notions of political overlordship played a role, too. Both Ptolemaic Egypt and Seleucid Asia claimed jurisdiction over Judea until 198 BCE, forcing the multiple Jewish factions to perform a careful balancing act between the two foreign powers. Judea held no interest for either power, so long as the Jews paid the taxes levied upon them. Yet the rival imperial claims on the land led to the development of large Jewish communities within both Egypt and Asia Minor.

In Alexandria alone, as many as fifty thousand Jews resided, a figure that had quadrupled by the time the Romans replaced the Ptolemies. These Jews retained their religious identity but became so Hellenized that by around 260 BCE they needed to have the Bible translated into Greek, since they no longer understood Hebrew. According to a text known as the *Letter of Aristeas*, a group of seventy-two

Biblical scholars gathered in Alexandria and carried out the task, thus producing the version of Scripture called the **Septuagint** (that being the Latin word for "seventy"). The *Letter of Aristeas* further reports, delightfully, that the seventy-two translators miraculously *spoke as one throughout the entire project, agreeing on each and every word of the translation. Aristeas was a Greek-speaking Jewish historian who lived roughly one hundred years after the Septuagint was completed.*

The Jews in Seleucid Asia likewise Hellenized to a considerable extent, and many rose to positions of social and even political power.[13] Jewish Hellenization involved more than adoption of the Greek language. A partial religious **syncretism**, or union of doctrines, occurred as well, as Judaism made contact with and adopted certain characteristics of the dominant Zoroastrian faith. This is most apparent in the development of an apocalyptic tradition within mainstream Judaism (with its tenets regarding the approach of a messiah) and among some lesser strands such as the Gnostic sects. YHWH's justice shall come upon earth, scatter and destroy His enemies, and reward faithful Israel:

> Behold the LORD Himself
> Comes from afar
> In blazing wrath,
> With a heavy burden—
> His lips full of fury,
> His tongue like devouring fire,
> And His breath like a raging torrent
> Reaching halfway up the neck—
> To set a misguiding yoke upon nations
> And make a misleading bridle upon the jaws of peoples,
>
> For you, there shall be singing
> As on a night when a festival is hallowed;
> There shall be rejoicing as when they march
> With flute, with timbrels, and with lyres
> To the Rock of Israel on the Mount of the LORD.
>
> For the LORD will make His majestic voice heard
> And display the sweep of His arm
> In raging wrath,
> In a devouring blaze of fire,
> In tempest, and rainstorm, and hailstones. *(Isaiah 30.27–30)*

---

[13] The stories of Tobit, who gained high status in the old Assyrian Empire, and of Daniel, who became advisor to the king of Babylon, were written in the Seleucid era and depict that era's outlook.

The feverish moralism of Zoroastrianism can be detected in a passage like this, showing the two faiths as complementary. Still, apocalyptic belief among most Jews did not develop until after the defeat of the Maccabean Revolt.

THE MACCABEAN REVOLT

The Revolt of the Maccabees (167–142 BCE) originated with a contested succession to the Jerusalem high priesthood during the reign of the Seleucid king Antiochus IV Epiphanes (r. 175–164 BCE). Two main contestants emerged: Jason and Menelaus. Their very names suggest the degree of Hellenization that took place even in the Holy City. Neither was a paragon of virtue.

Jason paid Antiochus a large bribe to win the post, which left Menelaus with no choice but to offer an even larger one; but unfortunately Menelaus did not have enough cash on hand, so he broke into the Temple treasury and stole some golden vessels. The theft outraged the people, and the city erupted in riot. Antiochus invaded the city and established a garrison of his Syrian soldiers on the Temple Mount. These soldiers, consisting of followers of both the Greek and Zoroastrian religions, demanded some sort of accommodation for their religious rites—and Antiochus (with Menelaus's consent as high priest) allowed pagan altars to be set up within the Temple.

This profanation triggered a full-scale Jewish rebellion against Seleucid rule. The leaders of the rebellion were a family called the Hasmoneans—Mattathias and his five sons—but the rebellion itself took its name from that of the eldest Hasmonean son, Judas Maccabeus. The revolt is a great heroic episode in the history of the Jews and, ironically, their last military victory until the establishment of the modern state of Israel in 1948.

The odds were certainly against them, given the size and strength of the Seleucid forces, but the Jewish rebels showed remarkable tenacity. (A story from their retaking of the Temple itself, in 164 BCE, is the origin of the celebration of Hanukkah.) The surprised and exhausted Seleucids gave up the fight in 142 BCE and granted Judea independence. Their new dynasty, the Hasmoneans, would remain in power until they were ultimately brought down by the Romans in 70 CE.

Despite the heroic nature of the revolt, however, the main Jewish texts that record its history, the books known as 1–2 Maccabees, were not admitted into the Biblical canon. The ostensible reason for this—that they may have been written directly in Greek and hence lack a Hebrew source/counterpart—only partially explains their omission. The Septuagint Bible, including 1–2 Maccabees, remained in widespread use in the Jewish world for three hundred years; communities from North Africa to Mesopotamia used it, as did numerous communities within

Palestine itself. The great Jewish philosopher Philo of Alexandria (d. 50 CE) used it. Rabbinical scholars drew upon it in establishing new legislation. Syrian Jews used it to prepare their own translation of the Bible into vernacular Syriac (the Peshitta).[14] For the rest of the Hellenistic period, and for at least two hundred years beyond, the Greek Septuagint was widely accepted canon in the Jewish world. The spread of Christianity in the first two centuries CE, however, altered Jewish attitudes toward their Greek Bible. Because Christians also used the Septuagint, it became tainted in their eyes.

Returning to the Hebrew canon was a way of asserting their difference from the Christians, indeed their independence from them. Hence they began to reconstitute the Hebrew text. The process of producing this version—by compiling old manuscripts, collating excerpts from older liturgical material, and at times even reconstructing the text from memory—resulted in the Masoretic text, the definitive Hebrew-language canon still in use today. (It was codified in the middle of the 3rd century CE.) 1–2 Maccabees, while still revered as part of the Jewish literary tradition, lost its canonical status. In order to disassociate themselves from the upstart new sect, the Jews cut themselves off from the Biblical version that most of them used. In the process, they decanonized the books that record the last great triumph of their ancient era.

---

[14] The Peshitta presents a host of linguistic and interpretive difficulties. The Jewish Scriptures were translated into Syriac from the Septuagint by Jewish scholars (although many passages suggest that they were based on the Hebrew text), but later Christians seem to have rendered a separate Syriac version, which they supplemented with a Syriac version of the New Testament texts. An altogether separated textual tradition is the Targumin—which consists of an Aramaic version of the Scriptures. The Targumin reflect a closer reliance on the Hebrew Bible than on the Septuagint.

WHO, WHAT, WHERE

Academy	Peloponnesian War
Classical Age	Pythagoreans
Delian League	Septuagint
gynaeceum	Sophists
Hades	symposia
Hellenistic Age	syncretism
hubris	telos
Ideal Forms	Thirty Tyrants
Lyceum	

SUGGESTED READINGS

Primary Sources

Herodotus. *The Persian War.*

Thucydides. *The Peloponnesian War.*

Xenophon. *Hellenica.*

Anthologies

Cohen, S. Marc, Patricia Curd, and C. D. C. Reeve. *Readings in Greek Philosophy: From Thales to Aristotle* (2011).

Irby-Massie, Georgia, and Paul T. Keyser. *Greek Science of the Hellenistic Era: A Sourcebook* (2002).

Lefkowitz, Mary R., and Maureen B. Fant. *Women's Life in Greece and Rome: A Source Book in Translation* (2005).

Tracy, Stephen V. *Pericles: A Sourcebook and Reader* (2009).

Studies

Bagnall, Nigel. *The Peloponnesian War: Athens, Sparta, and the Struggle for Greece* (2006).

Bosworth, A. B. *The Legacy of Alexander: Politics, Warfare, and Propaganda under the Successors* (2005).

Briant, Pierre. *Alexander the Great and His Empire: A Short Introduction* (2010).

——. *From Cyrus to Alexander: A History of the Persian Empire* (2002).

Burn, Lucilla. *Hellenistic Art from Alexander the Great to Augustus* (2005).

Connelly, Joan Breton. *Portrait of a Priestess: Women and Ritual in Ancient Greece* (2009).

De Ste. Croix, G. E. M. *Athenian Democratic Origins, and Other Essays* (2005).

——. *The Origins of the Peloponnesian War* (2002).

Dillon, Matthew. *Girls and Women in Classical Greek Religion* (2002).

Grabbe, Lester L. *A History of the Jews and Judaism in the Second Temple Period* (2006–2008).

Hölbl, Günther. *A History of the Ptolemaic Empire* (2001).

Humphreys, S. C. *The Strangeness of Gods: Historical Perspectives on the Interpretation of Athenian Religion* (2004).

Jonker, Louis. *Historiography and Identity (Re) Formulation in Second Temple Historiographical Literature* (2010).

Kagan, Donald. *The Peloponnesian War* (2003).

Navia, Luis E. *Socrates: A Life Examined* (2007).

Neils, Jenifer, and John H. Oakley. *Coming of Age in Ancient Greece: Images of Childhood from the Classical Past* (2003).

Reeve, C. D. C. *Philosopher-Kings: The Argument of Plato's "Republic"* (2006).

Romm, James. *Ghost on the Throne: The Death of Alexander the Great and the War for Crown and Empire* (2011).

Roochnik, David. *Beautiful City: The Dialectical Character of Plato's "Republic"* (2008).

———. *Retrieving the Ancients: An Introduction to Greek Philosophy* (2004).

Saxonhouse, Arlene W. *Free Speech and Democracy in Ancient Athens* (2008).

Shanske, Darien. *Thucydides and the Philosophical Origins of History* (2009).

Sourvinou-Inwood, Christiane. *Tragedy and Athenian Religion* (2003).

Thomas, Carol G. *Alexander the Great in His World* (2007).

Warren, James. *Presocratics: Natural Philosophers before Socrates* (2007).

Weinfeld, Moshe. *Normative and Sectarian Judaism in the Second Temple Period* (2005).

———. *The Place of the Law in the Religion of Ancient Israel* (2004).

———. *Social Justice in Ancient Israel and in the Ancient Near East* (2000).

Zuckert, Catherine H. *Plato's Philosophers: The Coherence of the Dialogues* (2009).

For additional resources, including maps, primary sources, visuals, web links, and quizzes, please go to **www.oup.com/us/backman.**

CHAPTER 6

The Empire of the Sea: Rome

753 BCE–180 CE

ROME AND THE MEDITERRANEAN

The Romans believed themselves descended from the noble Trojans who had lost their city to Homer's Greeks. They may not have known their own true origin, or they may simply have desired a better one. According to their legend Aphrodite, the Greek goddess of love, fell head over heels for Anchises, a member of the younger branch of the Trojan royal family. Two things resulted from their tryst: a son named Aeneas and the infliction of blindness on Anchises when he was caught boasting of his sexual escapade to some other soldiers.[1] Aeneas played no very great role in the Trojan War, although he famously helped his father escape to safety. After the Greeks had set Troy ablaze, he carried the blind old man on his back through crumbling ruins of flaming timbers. His postwar travels took him into the central Mediterranean, where he learned of a prophecy that he would found a great new nation in central Italy, at a place called Latium.

After a series of adventures Aeneas did indeed reach Latium and brought the region under his control. But he did not found the city of Rome itself. That was the work of two much later descendants of Aeneas, the twin brothers Romulus and Remus, who, also according to the legend, laid the city's foundations in 753 BCE and established a dynasty. Its kings ruled until a rebellion in 509 BCE overthrew the monarchy and established a republic.

From this early date, level-headed pragmatism drove Roman political policies; but even pragmatists like to fantasize about noble ancestors and destined greatness. These spoke, too, to their image as a republic of virtue, even as internal struggles put in doubt the republic's very survival. And indeed Rome achieved its golden age under an emperor, Augustus, and as an empire linked by the Mediterranean Sea.

◀ **Roman Women** Wallpainting from Herculaneum, near Rome, 1st century CE, depicting a set of ladies being groomed by a servant hair-dresser.

- Links to a Heroic Age
- Republic, Property, and Family
- The Republic of Virtue
- Size Matters
- Can the Republic Be Saved?

- The Golden Age: The Augustan Era
- The Sea, The Sea
- Roman Lives and Values
- The "Five Good Emperors"

CHAPTER OUTLINE

LINKS TO A HEROIC AGE

Their imagined link with Greece's heroic age mattered much to the Romans. On the practical level, an illustrious genealogy and a prophetic fate helped to legitimate, in their own eyes at least, the Romans' lording it over the other tribal and ethnic groups of central Italy. Surrounded by aggressive societies (like the Etruscans and Sabines to the north and east and the Aurunces, Hernici, Marses, and Vosici to the south), the Romans sought safety by conquering those peoples but being careful to incorporate them into their body politic. Although a monarchy, early Rome nevertheless had a brace of advisory and legislative councils (called the Senate and the *comitia curiata*, respectively) that admitted representatives of the other tribes.

On a deeper level, the Romans craved a linkage with ancient heroes because it had none of its own. Mythical tradition told of seven monarchs who began Rome's rise in the world. These legendary kings, who supposedly ruled from the founding of the city to the founding of the republic (753–509 BCE), were for the most part a competent bunch, but none of them would have made a suitable hero in an epic poem. (The regnal dates given here and in Table 6.1 are traditional. Since the existence of the kings themselves is doubtful, the dates of their reigns should not be regarded as factual.)

Not exactly a rogues' gallery, especially when compared to some of the emperors who followed them half a millennium later, but nothing really to boast about, either.

The Romans wanted legitimacy and grandeur, and forging a link with the Homeric heroes provided both.[2] Moreover, by emphasizing their supposed Hellenic roots, the Romans hoped to position themselves as the natural successors to Alexander's empire. Since the Carthaginians had also targeted that particular role, the Romans' claim to Homeric lineage can be seen as a propaganda

---

[1]   Zeus, Aphrodite's father, blinded Anchises by hurling down a lightning bolt from Mount Olympus that struck him in the eyes.

[2]   Our knowledge of early Rome derives from archeological remains and sources centuries later. In 387 BCE a Gaulish army invaded and (unintentionally, one assumes) burned down the municipal archives.

CHAPTER TIMELINE

753 BCE
Legendary
foundation of Rome

ca. 450 BCE
First Roman law
code (Twelve Tables)

264 BCE
First Punic War

509 BCE
Establishment of
Roman Republic

367 BCE
Election of the first
plebian consul

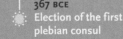

TABLE 6.1 **Rome's Kings**

Romulus (r. 753–715 BCE)	Formed the Roman army into its distinctive shape of individual legions, each composed of six thousand infantry and six hundred cavalry. But he is best remembered for the mass kidnapping of thousands of Sabine women to provide wives for his troops.
Numa Pompilius (r. 715–673 BCE)	Established the priesthood of the Vestal Virgins and abandoned the old lunar calendar for a solar one.
Tullius Hostilius (r. 673–642 BCE)	Was a bloodthirsty warrior who so neglected the gods that on his deathbed, when he cried out to be saved, Zeus blasted him with a thunderbolt that turned his palace and his body instantly to ashes.
Ancus Marcius (r. 640–616 BCE)	Built the first bridge across the Tiber river and founded the port at Ostia, thus connecting Rome to the sea. Otherwise he did nothing more noteworthy than establishing Rome first's saltworks.
Tarquinius Priscus (r. 616–579 BCE)	An Etruscan, doubled Rome's size by conquering the Etruscans, and used the booty he won to finance the construction of the Roman Forum and the Circus Maximus. He also built Rome's sewer system.[1]
Servius Tullius (r. 579–535 BCE)	Revised the constitution, made socioeconomic status the determinant for voting rights, built the great Temple to Diana, and was murdered by his daughter and her husband, Tarquinius Superbus.
Tarquinius Superbus (r. 539–509 BCE)	A violent, loutish, sensualist whose excesses led to his expulsion and the permanent overthrow of monarchy in 509 BCE.

[1] Showing their practical side, the Romans called their sewer the Cloaca Maxima—"the Giant Shithole."

ploy against their main Mediterranean rival. That state's ancestry led back not to Greece but to the Semitic-speaking Phoenicians.

The early Greeks had the stimulus of continual contact with the other peoples of the eastern Mediterranean, but the Romans were in a different situation altogether: Italy, geographically speaking, faces westward. The Apennine mountain chain runs down the eastern edge of the peninsula, forming an imperfect but still significant natural barrier to approach from the Adriatic Sea. Moreover, most of Italy's abundant and fertile agricultural plains, as well as most of her natural harbors, stretch down the western coast. And apart from the great Po River complex that runs eastward across the northernmost part of the peninsula, almost

31 BCE
Octavian defeats Marc Antony at Actium; beginning of Roman Empire

212 CE
Roman citizenship extended to all free peoples living in the empire

146 BCE
Rome undisputed master of the Mediterranean

96 CE–180 CE
Reign of the "Five Good Emperors"

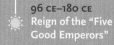

all of Italy's rivers flow westward. The only parts of Italy easily accessible to the Greeks were the southern third of the peninsula and the island of Sicily, where we find Greek settlements established as early as the mid-8th century BCE—the time of Homer. For these reasons the earliest **Latins** (the name given to the people who settled the region of Latium) had the greatest degree of commercial and cultural contact not with Greece but with the Etruscans, an advanced society to the north with whom they had close but uneasy relations (see Map 6.1).

The **Etruscans** were a literate people who left behind a considerable body of writing (especially inscriptions). However, since their language is poorly understood, all that we know of them derives from archeological remains plus whatever the Romans and others wrote about them. They were excellent metalsmiths and builders; the Romans appear to have learned the techniques of arch building from them. The Etruscans also introduced the Romans to the blood sport of gladiatorial contests. Such contests originated as an aspect of funeral observances, an offering made in honor of the deceased, and was extremely popular. The historian Livy (Titus Livius [59 BCE–17 CE]) describes a plethora of such games in 174 BCE:

> Many gladiatorial games were held in that year; most of them were unremarkable, but one really stood out from the rest—namely, the games

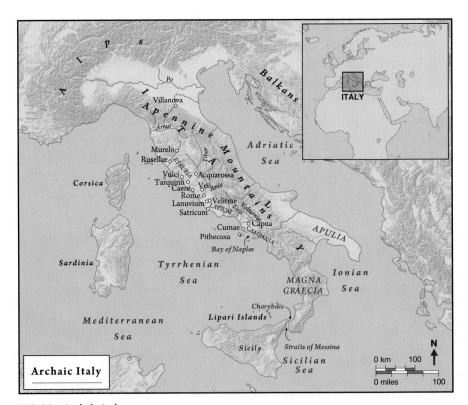

MAP 6.1   Archaic Italy

staged by Titus Flaminius to commemorate the death of his father. These
games lasted four days, including the public food distribution, the general
banquet, and the handful of theatrical performances that accompanied
them. The high point of the festivity, of course, was the three-day contest
in which seventy-four gladiators (a high number, in those times) fought.

Titus Flaminius here was a Roman general who later played a big role in the
conquest of Greece.

Apart from providing Rome with two of its seven kings, the Etruscans influenced the Latins in two profound ways: morals and religion. If we can credit the
stories told about them by the Romans and Greeks, the Etruscans were prosperous and enjoyed their prosperity to the hilt. They held sumptuous feasts twice
daily—with both male and female guests reclining on pillowed couches, richly
decorated homes, and flowing rivers of wine. Descriptions fill many disapproving
Latin and Greek pages—for the Romans, making a virtue of their own relative
want, largely disdained luxury as nothing more than self-indulgence. They never
aspired to Spartan levels of austerity, but they placed a high value on frugality and
self-discipline. Moral strength demanded sacrifice, as they saw it, and the placing
of the common good before individual desire. In this way, the Etruscans taught
the Romans by negative example.

In religion, however, their influence was direct and positive. The Etruscans practiced divination, or the reading of prophetic signs in certain natural phenomena—
the shape of a slaughtered animal's liver, the blood spatter of a beheaded chicken,

Wrestling Match   In this fresco from around 500 BCE from the "Tomb of the Augurs" at
Tarquinii, two men wrestle over three metal cauldrons, which are probably the prizes of their
contest. The cloaked figure to the left carries a curved staff known as a *lituus*, which was a
sign of kingship and, at Rome, a mark of the priests known as augurs, who had charge of the
"auspices." One of the chief ways to take the auspices was by defining a field of vision with
a *lituus*, and then observing within it the behavior of birds. Here, the cloaked figure seems
to be supervising the contest, while the *lituus* and the birds flying over the combatants may
indicate that he was seeking to foretell the result.

the rumbling sound of thunder or the groaning of a volcano, or the flight pattern of a group of birds. Divination was common throughout early Italy, but the Etruscan diviners were considered the best.[3] The Romans adopted their practice and remained dedicated believers in it for many centuries. The individuals trained to read signs were called haruspices (singular haruspex), and while the Roman religion never fully recognized them as priests, Roman society turned to them before any undertaking and took their warnings with the utmost seriousness.

REPUBLIC, PROPERTY, AND FAMILY

In place of the overthrown monarchy, the Senate in 509 BCE established a **res publica**, a republic, or commonwealth. Its constitution—mostly unwritten—changed numerous times over the centuries but remained based on the crucial idea of the separation of powers. An elaborate system of checks and balances prevented any individual or group from amassing too much power. The Senate was the dominant body, composed of members of Rome's leading noble families, but its work was complemented by a number of legislative assemblies and executive magistracies. Most magistrates served one-year terms, so campaigning and deal making were more or less constant. Since different social groups were involved in the different offices, prudence dictated that families and classes would form alliances that would compete for choice political positions and passing legislation.

In all, the Republic functioned very much in the spirit of Aristotle's ideal city-state, a smallish, organic society whose government involved all the leading figures of the city in a constantly changing network of mutually dependent relationships. Initially, the class of patricians held the upper hand, but within two generations the struggle between social orders had progressed to the extent that the Republic promulgated—sometime around 450 BCE—its first written law code. Known as the **Twelve Tables** (the name derives from the original dozen wooden slabs on which the code was written and set in public), it formed the basis for all subsequent Roman jurisprudence. It survives only in fragments, but the outline of its contents provides a good sense of its scope.

To judge from their remains, the Tables regarded property rights as the paramount concern of society. Indeed, the internal struggles of the first hundred years of the Republic centered on opening more avenues of government to the enterprising nonpatrician classes, whose strength came from their prosperity rather than noble lineage. In part, property issues featured so prominently in the laws because a debtor's creditor could legally sell him into slavery, if the circumstances warranted it. The Tables, therefore, defined those circumstances. Although the official census

---

3   Livy wrote: "When it came to signs and omens regarding public life, Roman custom was to consult nobody except Etruscan haruspices" (*History* 1.56).

TABLE 6.2 **The Twelve Tables**

Table 1	Laws Regarding Pretrial Preliminaries
Table 2	Laws Regarding Trials
Table 3	Laws Regarding the Execution of Judgments
Table 4	Laws Regarding *Patria Potestas*
Table 5	Laws Regarding Inheritances
Table 6	Laws Regarding Property
Table 7	Laws Regarding Real Property
Table 8	Laws Regarding Torts
Table 9	Laws Regarding the Rights of the Public
Table 10	Laws Regarding Religion
Table 11	Supplementary Laws
Table 12	Supplementary Laws

recognized a hierarchy of six classes, Roman social tradition divided the populace into two groups: patricians could trace their lineage to the members of the first Senate in 509 BCE, while everyone else was plebian. Since the census originated as a means of determining the army service owed by each citizen, military needs, not economic roles, determined social structure.

The essential social unit was the **familia**, a broader institution than "family." A familia consisted of an entire household and included the various aunts, uncles, nephews, nieces, cousins, close friends, clients, concubines, attendants, and house servants who lived under the same roof. It was firmly patriarchal, like the society as a whole. The head of the household (the **pater familias**) held complete authority over the entire familia and was, legally speaking, the sole possessor of its property. Moreover, the pater familias possessed a legal right known as *patria potestas* ("paternal power," the subject of the fourth of the Twelve Tables), which gave him the right of life and death over his family. Several passages in the Twelve Tables limn the extent of paternal power:

To any father is given the power of life and death over his children.... A father has the power to sell any child of his into slavery, but if a child is sold three times by his

Pater Familias An upper-class Roman, identifiable by the robe he wears, is shown holding the busts of his ancestors, probably his father and grandfather. Deceased parents became the household gods of Roman families, and processions with these busts were a common ritual at festivals.

father, he shall be free of his father after the third time. . . . In order to re-pudiate a wife, a husband shall simply say to her "Manage your [dowry] property for yourself," take away her keys to the house, and expel her.

The father's authority was absolute and not to be questioned. The Romans saw justice in this arrangement, since it was the father's responsibility, ultimately, to preserve the honor of the familia. Without it, a family could not hold its place in society.

THE REPUBLIC OF VIRTUE

Honor means different things to different people. Etymologically, it derives from the Latin word for burden (*onus, oneris*), reflecting the toil and struggle one must maintain to achieve it. To the Romans, honor consisted of playing one's appointed role in the familia and in the Republic. A father's honor lay in preserving his family's economic, social, and moral well-being. The Republic helped by implementing the office of **censor**, one that quickly became the most prestigious and feared of all the Roman magistracies.

From Plutarch's *Life of Cato the Elder* (ch. 16):

> The office of censor, one might say, towered above every other civic honor and was in fact a perfect climax to a political career. Its powers were many and widespread, and included the authority to inspect the lives and morals of the citizens. The people who created the censorship believed it right not to leave people free to act as they wished without others' seeing and judging them—not in marriage, the begetting of children, the workings of everyday life, or socializing with one's friends. In fact, they deemed these to be the very aspects of a man's life where he shows his truest character.

Plutarch then goes on to describe Cato's most famous exercise of censorial power. A prominent senator named Lucius Quintius had conducted an unseemly relationship with a handsome young lad. Once, when the two were reclining together after a dinner that included too much wine, the young lad declared that he loved Lucius so much that he had run to his house when summoned, even though he had been watching his first gladiatorial combat ever and had been looking forward to seeing a man slaughtered. Lucius, ever the attentive lover, then ordered a convicted criminal beheaded in front of his beloved, to make up for what the lad had missed. Cato, horrified, stripped Lucius of his senatorial rank.

The censor had three specific duties: to maintain the **census** (the official list of all citizens of Rome, their property, and legal class), to administer the finances of the state for all public works, and, most ominously, to preserve public morals.

The first two duties are self-explanatory, but the third deserves comment.[4] The censors could reward or punish an individual, and by extension his entire familia, by entering notations in the official census about the person's moral health. A black mark in the census imposed a moral stain called infamy (*infamia*), which meant the loss of the right to vote or participate in public life, the loss of admission into proper society, the ruin of any hopes to establish suitable marriages for one's children, and a permanent demotion in social status. Hence Romans considered it essential to observe, and to be seen to observe, the moral standards demanded by society.

What ethical crimes earned the censor's black mark? Most had to do with a failure to exercise proper leadership of the familia: living amid excessive luxury; neglecting one's crop fields; overindulgence of one's spouse and children; failure to observe norms regarding marriage, inheritance, or divorce; cruelty to slaves; failure to take care of one's clients; commercial fraud; or participating in disreputable trades like acting or prostitution.

The Romans valued simplicity. Clothing, though coded to distinguish social classes, was unelaborate. Diets consisted of bread, simple vegetable dishes, fruits, and roasted meat, plus wine, which they invariably cut with water. Education in the early Republic was minimal except for those of senatorial or equestrian rank, and it took place entirely in the home: boys received the basics of literacy and numeracy, were stuffed with moral tales of figures from Roman history, and began physical training as a preparation for military service; girls, on the other hand, were instructed in homecrafts like spinning, weaving, and sewing. Economic life centered on farming and local handcrafts, and much of the trade was by barter; in fact, the Republic did not even have a standard coinage until 289 BCE. Houses were simple low structures turned inward to face a central open courtyard; poorer families resided in multiunit apartments that were based on the same design. The images in modern popular culture of the egregious luxury, feasting, and sensual

Customers at a Breadmaker's Stall   Pompeii, 1st century CE.

---

4   To the Romans, certain moral duties were so significant that they deemed it necessary to certify a person's proper observance.

indulgence of the Roman elites are mostly exaggerations. Just as important, when excesses really did exist, most Romans disapproved.

Their religion was polytheistic and animistic, focusing on a multitude of gods and spirits. The well-known deities of Jupiter, Venus, Mars, and the rest bore close resemblance to the Olympian gods and goddesses of the Greeks, and in later centuries the Romans emphasized the union of their mythologies. But for most Romans the smaller local divinities took precedence, especially the family deities known as the "**household gods**" (*lares familiares*), the daily worship of whom was the responsibility of the pater familias. These spirits watched over the family farmland, the household, and possessions. Family ancestors continued to care for their descendants, and so prayers of dedication, thanksgiving, and respect were given to them always.

Religious life demanded constant, dutiful observance, following precise formulas of wording, gesture, and offering. Any mistake or omission rendered the ritual null and void. Since the Romans believed their well-being depended on the care of their spirit gods, observation of proper ritual was a matter of crucial significance. Religion was not a source of joy or spiritual exaltation but rather a moral responsibility. It is not accidental that the characteristic descriptor of Rome's legendary founder, Aeneas, was the Latin adjective *pius*—not pious, but dutiful.

> Since the Romans believed their well-being depended on the care of their spirit gods, observation of proper ritual was a matter of crucial significance. Religion was not a source of joy or spiritual exaltation but rather a moral responsibility.

SIZE MATTERS

The institutions, practices, and civic values established by the early Republic faced a dramatic challenge when the Republic began to expand. By 387 BCE the Roman Republic might had extended only through a sweep of territory roughly thirty miles (fifty kilometers) from the city. The increased area brought with it an increased population, which Rome incorporated under its constitution. Conquered landowners and shopkeepers kept their property and legal rights, but now, as Roman plebeians, they paid taxes to the Republic. The Republic in turn used the additional revenues to connect towns with networks of roads and to bring fresh water into them with systems of aqueducts.

The larger the Republic grew, however, the more concessions it had to make to the **plebeians** who made up the bulk of the population. As early as 400 BCE plebeians had won the right of eligibility to the lower magistracies, and in 367 BCE the Republic elected its first plebeian **consul**—the executive office in charge of the government.[5] Soon the plebeians demanded a voice of their own in government, and the Republic responded by creating a plebeian council (*concilium plebis*)

---

[5]   Two consuls served each year, sharing executive power.

that played an advisory role. After the next wave of conquests, however, which extended the Republic's power through all of central Italy, the decisions of the plebeian council were made binding even if disapproved by the Senate.

The rise in power of the lower orders appeared to increase the democratic nature of the Republic, but the aristocracy offset this by strengthening their ties with individual clients among the plebeian leaders. Moreover, the complex series of checks and balances between the various assemblies and magistracies prevented any single group from monopolizing power (see Figure 6.1). The Greek historian Polybius (200–117 BCE) was a great admirer of the Republic and was among the first to champion Rome as the natural successor to the Hellenistic world. He wrote: "The result of this ability the various classes have to help or hinder each other mutually is to create in effect a unified government that can respond to any emergency; it is impossible to find a constitution better than this" (*Histories* 6.18).

The conquest of territory gained momentum throughout the 3rd century BCE. It is not clear how much of this resulted from intentional expansionism and how much from successful defensive strategies. However it occurred, by 265 BCE the Romans were in control of nearly the whole of the Italian peninsula and with their command of the westward-facing harbors were poised to move out into the sea-lanes. But there was a problem, because most of the western Mediterranean then lay under the control of Carthage. This wealthy North African city had been founded as a Phoenician colony in the 9th century BCE and came to oversee a vast commercial empire. Carthage had more money, more military power, and more naval experience than the Romans. Carthage was also closer to the island of Sicily than Rome was, and Sicily mattered enormously: it was one of the three greatest grain-producing regions in the ancient world, the other two being Egypt and Asia

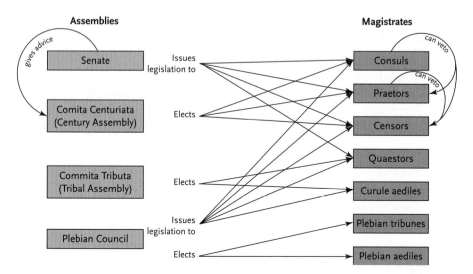

FIGURE 6.1   **Constitution of the Roman Republic**

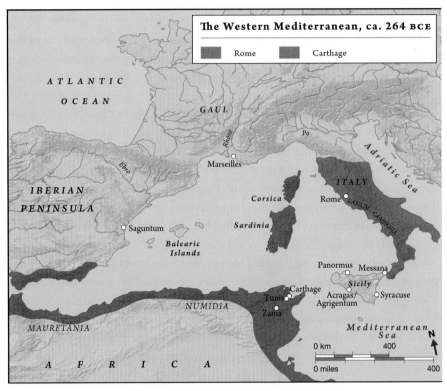

MAP 6.2   The Western Mediterranean in the 3rd Century BCE

Minor. If Sicily fell into Carthaginian hands, Roman Italy would be hard-pressed to feed itself (see Map 6.2).

Neither Rome nor Carthage saw any workable way for them to share control of the Mediterranean, and consequently they never really tried. Rome had two factors in its favor: the solid loyalty of the peoples they had incorporated into the Republic and its mastery of a new technique of naval warfare. By dropping a series of large spiked planks onto the deck of an opposing ship, they could affix it to the Roman vessel, which allowed their soldiers to cross over and fight an infantry battle on the high seas. Between 264 and 146 BCE Rome fought three bloody, ruinous wars with Carthage, won each time, and ended up as the master of the entire western Mediterranean basin. These became known as the **Punic Wars** (the name coming from the Latin word for the Carthaginians—Poeni—that is, Phoenicians), the first being a war for Sicily (264–241 BCE); the second being a war for control of Spain (218–201 BCE); and the last being an assault directly on north Africa (149–146 BCE), which ended with the complete destruction of Carthage and the sale into slavery of every Carthaginian who survived the carnage.[6]

---

[6]   The oft-told tale of the Romans' plowing the Carthaginian fields with salt to ruin the soil and prevent anyone from resurrecting the city is untrue.

But that hardly ended matters. Off in the east, King Philip V of Macedonia (r. 221–179 BCE) had supported Carthage in its second war with Rome, which prompted the Republic to declare war on him in 200 BCE. Philip surrendered in 197 BCE and Rome freed the Greek poleis that had been under Philip's control, then pulled back. But when the Seleucid emperor Antiochus III (r. 223–187 BCE) moved his army into newly liberated Greece, the Romans returned (191 BCE), drove him out, and pursued him across Asia Minor. Ironically, the Romans' decisive victory over Antiochus took place at Thermopylae, the site of the heroic stand of the Spartan forces against the army of Darius. According to the Greek historian Appian (95–165 CE), the Romans lost only two hundred men at Thermopylae, compared to the Seleucids, who lost ten thousand. (See his *Roman History* 4.20.) So began Rome's expansion into the eastern Mediterranean. By the end of the third Punic War Rome had seized all of Greece and most of Asia Minor. In 146 BCE Rome stood as the undisputed master of the whole sea (see Map 6.3).

The problem was that the Romans had not exactly planned for their success. Their political system, designed to govern a compact land-based republic, unexpectedly found itself in awkward possession of a vast, scattered, sea-based empire. What to do? In the absence of an imperial plan, the Republic simply handed over the

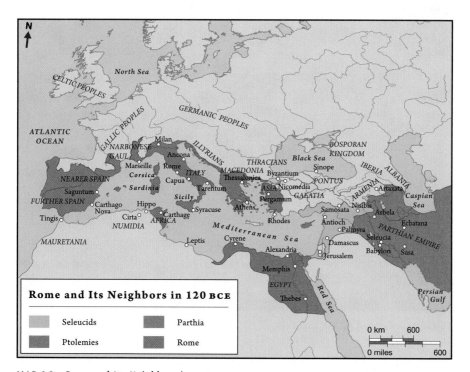

MAP 6.3   **Rome and Its Neighbors in 120 BCE**

conquered lands to the generals who had taken them, thus outsourcing the expense of maintaining the armies and running the provinces. These generals were thus able to amass vast personal fortunes, and they promptly used these to fund further campaigns and to buy influence with the various councils, assemblies, and magistrates back in Rome. To prevent civil servants from being corrupted by bribes, the Republic developed the tradition of assigning the leading magistrates, after their term of office was complete, to provincial governorships. This got them out of the city and away from the avenues of power, but it also gave them the means to raise fortunes of their own so that they could reenter Republican politics with full coffers.

In other words, the Republic tried to combat corruption by spreading the corruption around. This revolving-door movement from central government to provincial leadership and back again proved immensely profitable to the forty or fifty families who monopolized the process. It also caused terrible hardship and turmoil for the bulk of the people.

The 3rd century's wars had left many of Italy's farms physically and financially ruined, the victims of rampaging soldiers, neglect, or cheap imports of grain that knocked Italy's farmers out of the market. Many thousands of small landholders therefore sold their lands to the rich, who established vast plantations (called **latifundia** in Latin) that specialized in commercial crops like olives and grapes.

Roman Aqueduct   A Roman aqueduct, from Pont du Gard, near Nimes, in France. Built in 19 BCE. The water ran through a channel at the top.

With so many slaves available because of the wars, there were few employment opportunities for the displaced rural classes, who simply flooded into the cities instead, transforming these early manufacturing and commercial centers into centers of consumption.

The population of Rome itself increased to unheard-of levels: from somewhere around one hundred thousand before the First Punic War (264 BCE) to easily five times that figure a little over a century later. By the beginning of the Common Era, the city held well more than a million people within its borders. The government distributed "bread and circuses"—that is, food and entertainment—in order to keep the crowds quiet, but clearly something needed to be done. By the middle of the 2nd century BCE, voices in government were crying out for dramatic reform of the constitution as the only way to prevent the Republic from collapse. But what form would such reforms take?

CAN THE REPUBLIC BE SAVED?

From 133 to 27 BCE the Roman world suffered through a brutal series of internal wars and political struggles. While the names kept changing, the issues at stake and the remedies proposed for them did not. The fundamental issue was whether or not the Republic could, or even should, be saved. Did an empire require a different form of government altogether, and if so, then what form should that government take? Conservative politicians wanted to preserve the constitution at any cost; they believed that traditional Roman values and virtues, if earnestly retained, could make the republican framework work for the whole Mediterranean sprawl. Reformers, on the other hand, were convinced that the Republic was dead, or dying, and that hard-headed realism demanded sweeping change—although not increasing democracy. The battles were fought in stages: between the Gracchi brothers and the Senate (133–122 BCE), between Marius and Sulla (86–82 BCE), between Pompey and Julius Caesar (52–44 BCE), and finally between Marc Antony and Octavian (42–27 BCE).

With the Gracchi, the specific issue had been economic: what should be done about the displaced poor farmers? The Gracchi brothers, Tiberius and Gaius, championed a land redistribution plan that most in the Senate thought too radical; the brothers were assassinated (Tiberius in 133, Gaius in 122 BCE). Marius, a war hero who had served several terms as consul, altered a long-standing policy regarding military recruitment. Admission to the army had earlier required the ownership of land—the idea being that those with a vested interest in the Republic would make the most loyal and effective fighters. But Marius saw how the vast numbers of displaced farmers, and their replacement with large slave-driven latifundia, meant that there were fewer landholders from whom to draw the number of soldiers needed to defend the state. After all, Rome now controlled an empire three thousand miles from end to end. So he dropped the land-ownership requirement altogether. Those opposed to him, led by Sulla, feared that admitting the lowest orders in society would weaken the Republican spirit of the army. After Marius's death, Sulla spent three years undoing Marius's reforms and annihilating those who had supported him. The Republic lurched from one political extreme to another.

Julius Caesar and Pompey the Great (Gnaeus Pompeius Magnus) were both headstrong, powerful egoists, and each regarded himself as Rome's only hope for the future. Ostensibly, Caesar was the radical reformer, while Pompey was supported by the conservatives in the Senate. In reality they both probably wanted the same thing—namely, to run the empire as an empire. The centuries-old system of endless checks and balances between governmental assemblies and offices made efficient administration impossible. And Caesar and Pompey (whose backgrounds were as decidedly undemocratic military commanders) each wanted to institute a streamlined single-command administration. Caesar's power base was in the west; he had conquered Gaul. Pompey had made his name and fortune fighting in the east. Matters came to a head in 52 BCE when the Senate appointed Pompey as sole consul and declared Caesar an enemy of the state. War ensued.

In 49 BCE Caesar drove Pompey from Rome; Pompey fled east to raise more troops. Caesar caught up with him in Greece the following year and in a battle at Pharsalus defeated him. (Pompey escaped from the battle, but was later captured and assassinated.) Caesar returned to Rome and became sole ruler. In 46 BCE he took the title of *dictator*, a constitutional position that gave absolute executive power to a figure selected by the Senate for a set term in emergency situations. Two years later, after he had declared himself dictator for life, he was murdered by a group of nobles who feared that he was going to institute a monarchy.

Dreams of keeping a workable Republic died hard. When the civil struggle entered its final phase, between Marc Antony and Octavian, many still thought the old constitution could be restored. Antony soon left for Egypt to get support from the last ruler of the Ptolemaic dynasty, Cleopatra, with whom he was in love. When Octavian finally defeated Marc Antony at the battle of Actium in 31 BCE, Octavian not only put an end to the strife but added Egypt to the empire as well. Taking the title **Princeps Augustus** (meaning "first in honor"—his name being the first one on the list of Roman citizens kept by the censors), he instituted a new chapter in

> Augustus made a cult of playing by the old rules and upholding traditional values even while reinventing the political system. His reign was unusually successful. The Roman Empire had begun.

Rome's history and inadvertently gave himself a new name: Augustus. Recognizing the utility of maintaining a democratic image, Augustus ruled the empire as an emperor but steadfastly maintained the fiction of the Republic, portraying himself merely as the person who put into action the decrees made by the Senate. Augustus made a cult of playing by the old rules and upholding traditional values even while reinventing the political system. His reign was unusually successful. The Roman Empire had begun.

THE GOLDEN AGE: THE AUGUSTAN ERA

Augustus and all his successors as rulers of Rome held the title of **imperator**, usually translated as "emperor" but which in Republican times was the word for a victorious general, especially one granted the right to a triumph. This was an official recognition of exceptional military achievement, in which the triumphant general was allowed to parade his troops within the city limits amid songs, prayers, speeches, and festivities. At all other times the army was forbidden to cross the city limits (a line called the pomerium) and enter Rome itself. The only organized fighting force permitted within the pomerium was the imperator's personal bodyguard corps—the Praetorian Guards, who also functioned as a police force.

The emperors (the early ones, anyway) scrupulously avoided anything that smacked of monarchy: their homes were comfortable but not palatial; they wore simple dress; they walked the streets of Rome, took part in public debates, and attended religious services. Even their constitutional and honorific titles had Republican roots. The early emperors—not counting the aberrant moral monsters like Caligula (r. 37–41 CE) and Nero (r. 54–68 CE)—cultivated auras of humility, honoring Republican traditions even while exercising central command.[7] Caligula and Nero have been accused of nearly every imaginable vice: incest, theft, graft, torture, murder, prostitution. Nero famously allowed the Great Fire of Rome to blaze for days without doing anything about it, then blamed the Christians for it and staged a bloody persecution of them that resulted in thousands more deaths. After nearly two hundred years of civil strife, most Romans were willing to accept autocracy so long as the autocrats kept the peace, promoted prosperity, and did not flaunt their power.

To accomplish those goals the emperors needed to control the army, facilitate urban growth, and help to integrate the hundreds of ethnic groups that lived within the empire. First of all, the army needed to be professionalized. In Republic times, soldiers had been essentially the paid employees of the generals who commanded them. Caesar had conquered Gaul, for example, largely in

---

[7]   Caligula reportedly had his favorite horse ordained as a priest and tried to appoint it to a consulship.

order to acquire a fortune with which he could recruit even more soldiers, in preparation for his struggles with Pompey. Following custom, as many of Pompey's defeated soldiers as Caesar could afford to pay joined his army; and when Octavian/Augustus defeated Marc Antony at Actium, the same held true for him. Augustus's immediate concern upon starting his reign as imperator was to shrink the gargantuan army he had inherited. Hence he commandeered all of Egypt as his personal domain and used the money available through it to offer pensions and award estates to over a quarter million soldiers. This action reduced the army to a manageable twenty-eight legions. Soldiers henceforth received their pay, according to a set scale, directly from Rome itself instead of from the generals.

Given the size of the empire, most government had to be local—which meant that western Europe had to be urbanized. Municipal traditions in the east were widespread and strong, but the west (meaning North Africa, the Spanish peninsula, and virtually all of Europe north of the Alps) remained overwhelmingly rural. Most of Europe itself, moreover, consisted of a vast, dense forest in which the tribal inhabitants had established a sprawl of occasional clearings. To bring order to this world, the emperors began to build cities and a network of roads to connect them. Most inland cities began as military encampments that settlers refilled after the soldiers had moved on. The officials placed over these new settlements administered their surrounding districts, maintained the roads, and established all the public buildings needed to foster Roman civilization: temples, theaters, bathhouses, market squares, courts. So long as they maintained order, kept the population reasonably happy, and avoided blatant corruption, most municipal leaders, and later the provincial governors who represented the next higher stage of the imperial bureaucracy, enjoyed considerable freedom of action. In this way the empire operated more as a confederation of semi-independent city-states and provinces than as a monolithic empire taking orders from an absolutist central regime (see Map 6.4).

Many elements of Roman life contributed to social integration. The twin religious policies of toleration and syncretism played particularly important roles. Polytheisms, generally speaking, accommodate one another easily. My belief in one river god does not necessarily undermine or threaten your belief in another: two different rivers, two different deities—and hence no need for one religion to challenge or usurp the other. And of course it is even possible that the two are the same god manifested and understood differently in different places. When the Romans absorbed first Greece and then the rest of the Hellenistic lands, they recognized the similarities between their faiths. The Greek thunder god Zeus approximated the Roman sky god Jupiter; Aphrodite paired with Venus; Athena resembled Artemis. Such parallels were not coincidental. Polytheisms originate as attempts to explain natural phenomena: storms at sea happen because the sea god is angry about something, for example. And since Mediterranean societies confronted the same major phenomena, the divine powers they used to explain them bore certain

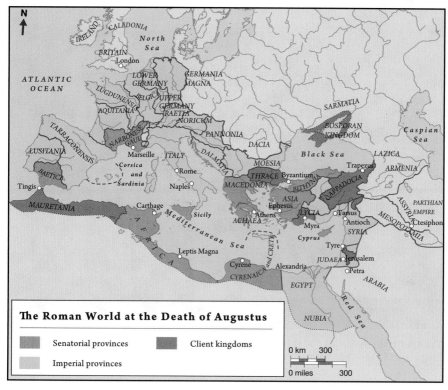

MAP 6.4   The Roman World at the Death of Augustus

similarities. By encouraging the Mediterranean peoples to recognize the same gods and goddesses, the Romans fostered a single, multiethnic civilization.

However, only the higher divinities were merged in this way—the gods and goddesses of Mount Olympus. Daily religious observances for most people still focused on local deities and ancestral worship. This led the emperors to inaugurate communal ruler worship. The custom began as a civil recognition of the deification of late rulers; thus Augustus promoted the deification of the assassinated Julius Caesar, while Tiberius (r. 14–37 CE) championed the postmortem deification of Augustus. Late rulers were to be regarded as universal "household gods"—symbolically, a pater familias to the entire empire; only much later, beginning with the mad Caligula, did the notion arise of recognizing the divinity of the living emperor. By encouraging, and then by requiring, subjects to worship emperors (past or present) as divinities, the Romans tried to keep a degree of common religious practice among the people, so as to counteract the forces that pulled them apart. It did not matter whether or not anyone actually believed in the emperor-god. It mattered only that they were willing to participate in a public, communal ritual once a year in which thanks were given to the divine ruler for his guidance. Dutiful observance, not sincere conviction, was both the goal and the spirit of the requirement; a cohesive civil society, not spiritual enlightenment, was the aim.

The Ara Pacis   Procession of senators and high priests, from a sidewall of the Ara Pacis, the "Altar of Peace," completed in 9 CE.

THE SEA, THE SEA

The Mediterranean Sea—"Our Sea" (**Mare nostrum**) to the Romans—was the essential infrastructure holding the empire together. Geographically, the sea consists of two deep basins separated by an underwater ridge between Sicily and Tunisia, with narrow straits at either end. (The Strait of Gibraltar connects it with the Atlantic Ocean to the west, and the Dardanelles links it to the Sea of Marmara, the Bosporus, and the Black Sea to the northeast.) With a surface area of nearly a million square miles (2.5 million square kilometers), it stretches 2,200 miles from west to east and nearly 1,000 miles at its greatest north-south expanse. Water enters the sea through the two straits and from a handful of rivers—the Nile in Egypt, the Ebro in Spain, the Rhône in France, the Po in Italy. However, the warm climate causes faster than usual evaporation, which in turn causes the Mediterranean's higher than usual salinity—hence the proliferation of salt pans around the coastline.

Despite those million square miles of surface area, though, the Mediterranean is not large enough to have a significant tide. Ships can thus set sail at almost any hour of any day, a significant advantage for the trading cities that surround it. The dominant surface currents circle counterclockwise in both basins, with separate counterclockwise epicycles on either side of the Italian peninsula—that is, in the Tyrrhenian and Adriatic Seas. The Mediterranean's temperate climate results from its fortunate geography, and its smooth waters are a consequence of the relative narrowness of the Strait of Gibraltar: most north Atlantic storms cannot pass through the Strait and instead are diverted up the western coastline of Europe. (This is one reason why it rains so much in England.)

Given these inviting conditions, ancient sailors had an easy time crossing the Mediterranean. Moreover, the many islands and jutting promontories like the Italian and Greek peninsulas meant that sailors could ply the sea-lanes without ever losing sight of land, which made it easy to reach faraway ports without getting lost. The ancients steered by landmarks rather than by the stars. Peoples as far apart as eastern Spain and the Holy Land could be in regular and reliable contact with one another, buying and selling wares, sharing ideas, and establishing permanent relationships. And in fact they needed such contact, because none of the coastal societies were economically self-sufficient. Mountains ring most of the basin, while the Sahara Desert stretches along its southern expanse, which meant that most Mediterranean cities were cut off from their hinterland. In many places the mountains reach almost to the coast. Hence coastal societies could not produce all the foodstuffs and material goods they needed to survive, and therefore they needed to trade with one another in order to stay alive. The natural qualities of the sea made this trade possible virtually year-round—even for bulky, heavy commodities.

The Romans recognized that their central position in the Mediterranean was an ideal site from which to create a network of links between all the peoples of the sea. With Carthage in ruins, no rival stood in Rome's way. But lust for power was not the only motive behind Rome's expansion—and may not even have been the most prominent one. The Mediterranean linked hundreds of coastal societies; a ship sent out from Rome could reach Barcelona in only three days, Alexandria in ten. And these societies shared similar agricultural methods (terracing arid hinterlands, widespread use of irrigation systems), similar diets (grains, fish, olive oil, and wine), and similar social organizations (tradesmen and merchants playing the lead, rather than large landholders). If we think of the Mediterranean as a single entity, then the attractiveness of uniting them under a single administration becomes clear: with a single

> If we think of the Mediterranean as a single entity, then the attractiveness of uniting them under a single administration becomes clear: with a single currency, single law, single tariff code, and single system of weights and measures in place, goods, capital, and services will move with optimal efficiency, raising everyone's standard of living.

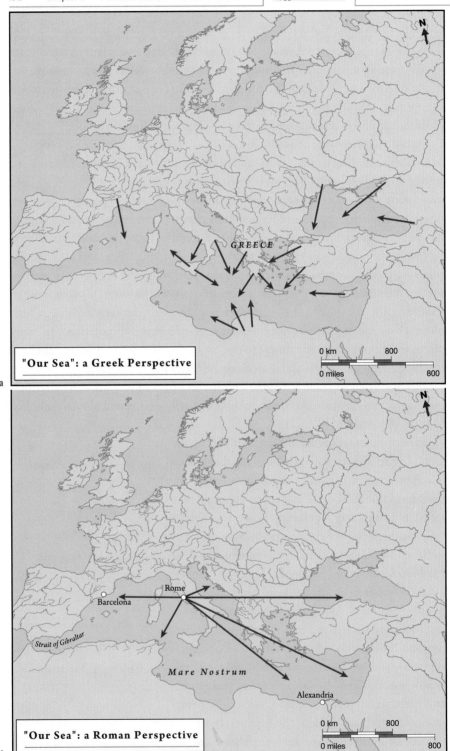

"Our Sea": a Greek Perspective

a

"Our Sea": a Roman Perspective

b

MAP 6.5a,b   The Mediterranean: Greek and Roman Perspectives Compared

*Adapted from Malkin, Irad. *A Small Greek World: Networks in the Ancient Mediterranean* (2011).

currency, single law, single tariff code, and single system of weights and measures in place, goods, capital, and services will move with optimal efficiency, raising everyone's standard of living (see Map 6.5a,b).

Experience within Italy had convinced the Romans that people will put up with the loss of political freedom if they can still prosper economically, while policies of inclusion of subjected peoples within the dominant society will go far to relieve civil unrest. When attempting to secure a new territory, the regime begun by Augustus therefore took care to "Romanize" its institutions and trade, reinstall local rulers as representatives of the empire, and then withdraw. Since travel by sea was so quick, the Romans seldom had to occupy the lands they conquered. Word of any rebellion would reach the imperial court quickly, and a fleet could be dispatched long before the rebellion had a chance to take root. In other words, a town or district newly added to the Roman Empire could conceivably never see a Roman soldier again, as long as the laws were obeyed, the taxes paid, and things kept quiet.

Rome's army added territories to the empire, of course, but also provided a tool for social engineering. Taking further Alexander the Great's policy of cultural integration, the Romans opened the army to recruits from every part of the empire—enrolling Celts, Dacians, Illyrians, Libyans, Phoenicians, and Syrians alike, plus many others. In turn, their combined military experience helped bring Roman culture to the provinces. Recruits received three meals a day and a regular salary, traveled from one end of the empire to another, and helped to keep the peace and serve the common cause. Along the way they learned Latin, acquired the basics of Roman law and morals, and practiced Roman civic religion. The goal was to break down each soldier's sense of particular ethnic nationality and replace it with a new identity, based on membership in a larger, interconnected

Loading Grain in a Transport Ship   A worker here pours grain into a barrel; once full, the barrel would be rolled into the cargo area below deck. The name of the ship—*Isis Giminiana*—is given at the far left. The ship's master (*magister*) is Faurales, and the merchant is Abscanius. Two other workers haul sacks of grain up the gangplank, at the right. This fresco comes from Ostia, a port city at the mouth of the Tiber, ca. 200 CE.

Tombstone of a Roman Soldier   Marcus Valerius Celerinus, a citizen of Agrippina in southern Spain and a veteran of the Tenth Legion, had this tombstone prepared "on his own behalf and for the sake of his wife, Marcia." The tomb is in Cologne, Germany, where the pair settled after his retirement from the military. ca. 100 CE. The carving presumably portrays Marcus Valerius at a meal (the Romans ate lying down) surrounded by friends.

society. After twenty years of service, each soldier received either a cash pension or the grant of an estate and could enjoy all the fruits of citizenship.[8] The estates awarded were large, prosperous, and never in the individual soldier's original homeland. Having created a "Roman"—that is, someone whose self-identity and personal allegiance went beyond mere ethnicity, someone who participated in an idea of human unity—the last thing the government wanted was to restore him to his place of birth. In this way, the army used to fullest effect the ability of the Mediterranean, Mare Nostrum, to integrate the peoples of the empire, redistribute them, and cement the idea of "Romanness."

The emperor was the commander in chief of all the legions. In practice, however, the regular command of each legion was given to an imperial representative known as a legate (**legatus**), whom the emperor selected from the members in the Senate. In smaller provinces that required the presence of only a single legion; the legate also served as the provincial governor. In larger provinces, two or more legions were assigned; a separate legate was assigned to each legion, but the autonomous provincial governor served as a superior commander to each legate. In this way, senators endorsed imperial power, while the throne made a point of recognizing senatorial privilege. Even more important, Rome placed senators in positions in which their status was publicly seen. The fiction of republicanism was thus given continual attention, even as true control of the army remained centralized in the emperor's hands.

ROMAN LIVES AND VALUES

The first two centuries CE are known as the era of the Roman Peace, or **Pax Romana**. Like all historical labels it represents only a partial truth, and while most of the empire experienced a sustained if sometimes strained tranquility,

---

[8]   Citizenship was a prerequisite for joining the army. But noncitizens could enlist in the auxiliary forces and earn citizenship after retirement—to be passed on to their sons.

there was more than enough discontent around to keep the soldiers busy. Consider the rebellion in England in 60 CE led by Boudicca, the widow of a Briton tribal king. Some Roman soldiers had plundered the dead king's home, tied up and flogged Boudicca, and made her watch as they raped her daughters. After the attack, Boudicca rallied the Britons to drive the Romans from England. As Tacitus (*Annals*, 14.32–35, 37) narrates it:

> Then a horde of Britons surrounded [the Roman garrison at Camulodunum—modern Colchester] and ransacked and set the town all ablaze, forcing the garrison to take refuge in the temple [to the divine emperor Claudius]; this temple was stormed after a two days' siege. Rome's ninth legion, under the command of Quintus Petulius Cerialis Caesius Rufus, tried to relieve the town but was first stopped, then routed, by the victorious Britons, who massacred the entire infantry.... [Boudicca's troops] delighted in plunder and scarcely gave a thought to anything else, for they continually passed right by Roman encampments and garrisons and headed straight for whatever targets had the most loot and the least protection. The Roman and provincial dead in those places is reckoned at seventy thousand, for the Britons had no interest in taking or ransoming prisoners or exchanging prisoners. All they wanted was to slit Roman throats or put nooses around them, to put Romans to the torch or to crucify them.... Boudicca circled her soldiers in a chariot in which her daughters rode with her, and cried out: "Britons! You are accustomed to female commanders in war time. I am the daughter of accomplished warriors, but I am not now fighting for wealth or for a realm. Rather, I fight simply as an ordinary woman who has lost her freedom; I fight for the wounds done to my body and for the outrage done to my daughters. Roman malice knows no bounds—they murder old men and rape young girls. May our gods grant us the revenge we deserve!'"

In a subsequent battle outside London, in 61 CE:

> The Roman regular troops, keeping near to a gorge that offered a measure of natural defense, held their ground and hurled their javelins with deadly effect at the approaching Briton army and then rushed suddenly forward in wedge formation together with the auxiliary troops. Then our cavalry units, lances in forward position, broke whatever was left of Briton resistance. Their fleeing soldiers could not escape, since their own circle of wagons blocked off any retreat. Our troops spared no one, not even the women or beasts of burden; all, pierced by our weapons, were added to the heaps of the dead. What a glorious victory this

was, one to be compared with our most legendary triumphs. By one report nearly eighty thousand Britons were killed, while we suffered only four hundred dead and slightly more wounded. As for Boudicca, she poisoned herself in the aftermath.

Even so, for all the signs of discontent, no ancient society experienced anything close to the prosperity and social stability of the empire during these two centuries. Cities multiplied and grew, rights of citizenship were continually extended to more and more people, and piracy in the Mediterranean came to an end. Literacy spread, and something close to a regular system of justice ordered everyone's lives, and in 212 CE every person in the empire who was not a slave was declared a citizen (see Map 6.6). The elaborate commercial networks allowed each region of the empire to specialize in producing what it did best.

Two significant economic weaknesses remained, however. First was reliance upon slave labor. Slaves comprised as many as 20 percent of the empire's population, which meant that certain labor-intensive activities—agriculture and mining in particular—were vulnerable to labor shortages. In the ancient world, the mortality rates of slave populations usually exceeded their birth rates, which meant that societies dependent on slave labor continually needed to add new

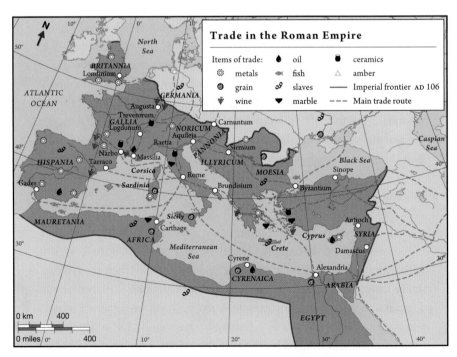

MAP 6.6   Trade in the Roman Empire

Thamagudi, Modern Timgad, Algeria   Founded by the emperor
Trajan in 100 CE, Thamagudi boasted a theater, a forum, and
paved streets aligned in a checkerboard pattern.

slaves to the mix just to stay even. As long as the empire kept conquering new
territories—and thus acquiring new slaves—the problem was held at bay, but
only temporarily. The second weakness was Roman fondness for Asian luxury
goods like silk and spices, which they purchased in large quantities. This passion
drained gold and silver reserves from the western economy. Until the end of the
2nd century CE, western mines were able to keep up, but productivity declined
quickly thereafter, which raised the danger of currency devaluation. But during
the Pax Romana years these were only potential weaknesses; for the time being,
abundance and comfort were the hallmarks of Roman economic life.

The Romans adopted many of the great Greek intellectual and artistic achievements, but popular prejudice of the time regarded Greek culture as effete. They
saw it as too inclined to luxury, idleness, and pleasure, especially when compared
to the manly self-discipline and pragmatism that they liked to think was the essence of Romanness. Some of this is simply the swagger of the victor, but it would
be a mistake to dismiss it outright. Roman culture valued a sense of duty—to the
familia, to the household gods, to one's city, and finally to the empire. A good
life was a life of virtue, of owed service duly performed. These were the values
the Romans brought with them into the eastern Mediterranean, where they

encountered the two dominant philosophies of the Hellenistic era: **Epicureanism** and **Stoicism**.

Of the two, Stoicism appealed more to the Romans. Among philosophers the most prominent Roman Stoics were the tragedian, essayist, and statesman Seneca (4 BCE–65 CE) and the former slave turned moralist and teacher Epictetus (55–135 CE). Seneca dedicated many years of his life to serving the empire, even taking on the thankless task of tutoring the teenaged Nero. Even so, he was reputedly epicurean in certain ways—including the bad habits of seducing married women and taking bribes—but these reports may be mere rumors put about by jealous rivals. In the year 65 CE Nero accused Seneca of complicity in an attempt to murder him and ordered his former teacher to commit suicide. Seneca complied by slitting his wrists, only his blood flowed so slowly that he never lost consciousness; he drank poison next, but it too failed to kill him. Finally Seneca immersed his slashed arms in a hot bath. The warmth opened his veins, the blood ran out, and he finally died. Amid reams of bad writing, he left a few pearls: "Act toward men as though God were always watching; speak to God as though men were always listening." "You can tell a man's character by how he receives praise" (*Epistles* 2.2 and 52.12, respectively).

Epictetus, by contrast, lived a life of poverty and austerity. Born lame and into slavery, he nevertheless learned some philosophy from a local teacher after his owner moved to Rome; after gaining his freedom, he went on to teach philosophy himself. In 93 CE he moved back to Greece and set up a school. He remained poor and lived alone until he took in a homeless boy whom he raised. He died in 135. His most memorable passage comes from his *Encheiridion* (*Handbook*):

> In life, you ought always to behave as you would at a formal banquet. A dish is being passed around and it comes to you—so reach out your hand politely and take a modest helping, and then pass the dish along without delay. If a dish does not come your way, don't act out your longing for it by stretching out your hand for it. Just wait until it comes to you. This is how you should act regarding everything in life—including children, wife, career, and wealth. (ch. 15)

Stoic ethics conformed to Roman morals in the broadest sense—with their emphasis on duty, forbearance, self-discipline, and concern for others.[9] Above all,

---

> Roman culture valued a sense of duty—to the familia, to the household gods, to one's city, and finally to the empire. A good life was a life of virtue, of owed service duly performed.

---

[9]   Stoics believed one should pursue virtue for its own sake, seek tranquility rather than renown, and value wisdom and calm over ambition and glory.

one ought to serve Rome, praise Rome, live for Rome—for only in the empire and its vision of the unification of all societies in a single working whole can the harmony of the world be attained. Here is how the first-century poet Virgil (70 BCE–19 CE) described the empire's destined mission:

> Others shall cast their bronze to breathe
> with softer features, I well know, and draw
> living lines from the marble, and plead
> better causes, and with pen shall better trace the paths
> of the heavens and proclaim the stars in their rising;
> but it shall be your charge, O Roman, to rule
> the nations in your empire. This shall be your art:
> to lay down the laws of peace, to show mercy
> to the conquered, and to beat the haughty down. *(Aeneid 6.1012–1028)*

For at least 150 years after Augustus, they did this rather well. Dividing society between **honestiores** ("the better people") and **humiliores** ("the lesser people"), they provided a reliable infrastructure for urban life and a consistent form of justice for each. The honestiores consisted of the senatorial and equestrian classes, municipal officials, and army veterans, and their status entitled them to immunity from torture, lesser criminal fines, and, in capital crimes, exemption from crucifixion. (Like Seneca, honestiores condemned to death were allowed to commit an honorable suicide rather than face the intentionally humiliating and agonizing death by crucifixion.) The humiliores consisted of everyone else in the empire apart from the slaves—who, in terms of the law, were counted as property rather than people. People were expected to obey the law, pay their taxes, participate in public religious rites, and hold to the ethical duties of family care and public service; if they did so, the empire largely left them alone. Even in the prosecution of crime, Roman tradition was to allow matters to be resolved with as little state involvement as possible.

Most civil cases were tried without any public officials whatsoever. A plaintiff filed a complaint with a local magistrate called an aedile who maintained a list of individuals in the vicinity who held Roman citizenship. Any citizen accepted by the plaintiff and defendant could serve as judge. The aedile's role was limited to making sure the temporary judge understood the basics of the law as it pertained to the type of case he was judging. The judge's decision was then entered in the municipal records, and the matter was closed.

Taxes were collected by a tax-farming system. The imperial court determined its budgetary needs for the year and then apportioned the revenues owed by each province, district, and city in order to meet that need. Local officials, who presumably understood the economic realities of their own territories better than administrators back in Rome did, then collected taxes accordingly as they thought most fair and effective given local conditions. If they gathered more than they were required to send to Rome, they kept the surplus (public officials did not receive salaries); if they failed to meet their tax obligation, they were expected to make up the deficit out of their personal funds. Personal profit from public taxation was not frowned upon. In fact, some profit was necessary if the official was to be held liable for years of deficit. What sounds like an invitation to abuse actually worked fairly well. If an official collected so much tax that the people began to grumble, Rome would hear of it quickly enough and deal with the overaggressive governor.

The system was sufficiently effective to survive even disastrous reigns like those of Caligula (r. 37–41 CE) and Nero (r. 54–68 CE), whose well-known personal licentiousness went down poorly with most Romans precisely because such indecency was so very un-Roman. Domitian (r. 81–96 CE), an obsessively controlling personality, left most of the Senate disaffected with his failure to maintain the Augustan fiction of Republican rule, but he did leave the treasury with a surplus in spite of an ambitious building campaign and several expensive military ventures.

THE "FIVE GOOD EMPERORS"

The high point of the Pax Romana came during the reigns of the so-called Five Good Emperors: Nerva (r. 96–98 CE), Trajan (r. 98–117 CE), Hadrian (r. 117–138 CE), Antoninus Pius (r. 138–161 CE), and Marcus Aurelius (r. 161–180 CE). This was the time of the empire's greatest physical expanse and its greatest prosperity, but what really made these emperors so "good" was that they returned to the Republican fiction, giving the Senate its due respect while exercising autocratic control. Moreover, each of the five had the decency not to have a surviving heir, which allowed the Senate to appear to be the deliberative body for the selection of the next emperor. In reality, each of the five adopted his most capable general, who then became his successor after carefully going through the motions of a supposed senatorial election.

The rulers appointed the provincial governors, district officials, and municipal chiefs who then administered the empire locally. Most came from the class of urban elites known as the **curiales**. Their chief duties were to provide justice, collect taxes, maintain roads and waterways, and keep the cities and harbors in good repair. Given the Roman means of tax gathering, these civil servants could acquire great wealth; but their sense of civic-mindedness obliged them to make up for public deficits personally. They were expected to use their own funds to provide public entertainments, food distributions, and religious ceremonies in honor of the emperors. That so many curiales did so provides an index of the strength of Roman public spirit.

During the Pax Romana, in sum, the Stoic and dutiful ethos cultivated by the Romans helped them to create a remarkably stable and proud society. They saw themselves as the heirs to the Greek and eastern worlds, and they eagerly absorbed whatever in those traditions had practical value. Yet they also regarded themselves as morally superior, less inclined to luxury and ease, and dedicated to strong virtues and a hardheaded sense of pragmatic living. Those given to other values were the objects of scorn. For example, the Jews, who refused to Romanize or to serve in the army, were reviled even though the Romans respected the antiquity of their traditions. Marcus Aurelius, author of the popular work known as the *Meditations*, described the secret of the Stoical Roman soul and its superiority to a weak, showy spirit that had appeared on the scene:

> A beautiful soul is one that is equally ready at any given moment to relinquish the body and give itself over to extinction and annihilation, or to continue living. Such preparedness must be the result of conscious judgment reached through reason and with dignity if it is to persuade anyone else; it must never result from obstinacy or with soul-killing display—as it does with the people called Christians. *[Meditations 11.3]*

Roman Public Spirit   Tombstone of the mid-second century from Gorsium, Pannonia (Hungary). This monolithic tombstone combines decoration in the Greco-Roman style—such as the grape-vine spiraled columnettes—with local elements. The two women portrayed are wearing "native" dress, with heavy turbans, prominent pendant necklaces, and large pins on their shoulders. At the foot of the stone, two servants are shown frontally under a curved border characteristic of art from the region. The beautifully cut Latin inscription translates, "To the spirits of the dead. Publius Aelius Respectus, city councilor of the municipality, while alive made this for himself and for Ulpia Amasia, his wife. Aelia Materio, their daughter aged ten, is placed here. The parents put up this monument for her memory." The names indicate that the family are all Roman citizens, and the father specifies that he is a city councilor in his community, although without naming it.

WHO, WHAT, WHERE

censor	Latins
census	legatus
consul	Mare nostrum
curiales	pater familias
Epicureanism	patria potestas
Etruscans	Pax Romana
familia	plebeians
honestiores	Princeps Augustus
household gods	Punic Wars
humiliores	res publica
imperator	Stoicism
latifundia	Twelve Tables

SUGGESTED READINGS

Primary Sources

Epictetus. *The Handbook.*

Livy. *History of Rome.*

Marcus Aurelius. *Meditations.*

Plutarch. *Parallel Lives.*

Polybius. *The Histories.*

Seneca. *Epistles.*

Suetonius. *The Twelve Caesars.*

Tacitus. *Annals.*

———. *The Histories.*

Source Anthologies

Beard, Mary, John North, and Simon Price. *Religions of Rome* (2005).

Cherry, David, ed. *The Roman World: A Sourcebook* (2001).

Kraemer, Ross Shepard, ed. *Women's Religions in the Greco-Roman World: A Sourcebook* (2004).

Lefkowitz, Mary R., and Maureen B. Fant, comps. *Women's Life in Greece and Rome: A Source Book in Translation* (2005).

Mellor, Ronald, ed. *The Historians of Ancient Rome: An Anthology of the Major Writings* (2004).

Warrior, Valerie M. *Roman Religion: A Sourcebook* (2001).

Studies

Beard, Mary. *The Roman Triumph* (2009).

Beard, Mary, John North, and Simon Price. *Religions of Rome* (2005).

Boatwright, Mary T. *Hadrian and the Cities of the Roman Empire* (2002).

Carcopino, Jérôme. *Daily Life in Ancient Rome: The People and the City at the Height of the Empire* (2008).

Eck, Werner. *The Age of Augustus* (2007).

Everitt, Anthony. *Augustus: The Life of Rome's First Emperor* (2007).

Fraschetti, Augusto. *The Foundation of Rome* (2005).

Goldsworthy, Adrian. *Caesar: Life of a Colossus* (2008).

———. *The Complete Roman Army* (2011).

———. *The Punic Wars* (2000).

Grubbs, Judith Evans. *Women and the Law in the Roman Empire: A Sourcebook on Marriage, Divorce, and Widowhood* (2002).

Haynes, Sybille. *Etruscan Civilization: A Cultural History* (2000).

Holland, Tom. *Rubicon: The Last Years of the Roman Republic* (2005).

Horden, Peregrine, and Nicholas Purcell. *The Corrupting Sea: A Study of Mediterranean History* (2000).

Lendon, J. E. *Empire of Honour: The Art of Government in the Roman World* (2001).

Milnor, Kristina. *Gender, Domesticity, and the Age of Augustus: Inventing Private Life* (2005).

Mouritsen, Henrik. *Plebs and Politics in the Late Roman Republic* (2001).

Reydams-Schils, Gretchen. *The Roman Stoics: Self, Responsibility, and Affection* (2005).

Rives, James B. *Religion in the Roman Empire* (2007).

Schultz, Celia E. *Women's Religious Activity in the Roman Republic* (2006).

Seager, Robin. *Pompey the Great: A Political Biography* (2002).

———. *Tiberius* (2005).

Southern, Pat. *The Roman Army: A Social and Institutional History* (2007).

Speller, Elizabeth. *Following Hadrian: A Second-Century Journey through the Roman Empire* (2004).

Williamson, Callie. *The Laws of the Roman People: Public Law in the Expansion and Decline of the Roman Republic* (2005).

For additional resources, including maps, primary sources, visuals, web links, and quizzes, please go to **www.oup.com/us/backman**.

CHAPTER 7

Paganisms and Christianities

40 BCE–305 CE

THE EARLY CHRISTIAN WORLD

The establishment and spread of Christianity may be the central fact of Western history. Few other phenomena have affected so many people in so many ways. Few have so shaped cultural values, have comforted or tormented so many individuals, have had such influence on intellectual life, or have so worked their way into the very fiber of Western identity. Without Christianity, there would be no cathedrals at Chartres, Ely, Milan, Notre Dame de Paris, or Seville. There would be no monasteries of Monte Cassino or Mont Saint-Michel; no Hagia Sophia in Istanbul; and no universities. There would also be no music of Johann Sebastian Bach, Giovanni Pierluigi da Palestrina, Henry Purcell, or Arvo Pärt; no poetry of Dante Alighieri, John Milton, Anna Akhmatova, Czeslaw Milosz, or Geoffrey Hill; no paintings by Michelangelo Buonarroti or Michelangelo Caravaggio; no novels by Fyodor Dostoevsky, James Joyce, François Mauriac, Flannery O'Connor, or Annie Dillard; no philosophy by Saint Augustine, Saint Thomas Aquinas, Immanuel Kant, Søren Kierkegaard, Bernard Lonergan, or Karl Barth. It is even arguable that without Christianity there would have been no Islam, and hence the historical success of Christianity would be the single most influential development in all of Greater Western history.

On the other hand, without Christianity there would have been no Crusades, no Inquisition, no blood libel against the Jews, no forced baptisms of the Native Americans or sub-Saharan Africans, no Wars of Religion in the 16th and 17th centuries, and no Holocaust

◀ **The Good Shepherd**
This wall painting, ca. 100–200 CE, depicts Jesus as the Good Shepherd. Note the heavily Romanized style: Jesus is beardless and wears a Roman tunic. The fresco is in the Catacombs of Saint Priscilla, under the city of Rome. Early Christians used these catacombs as a burial site and for worship. It was much more common among the early Christian generations to portray Jesus as the Good Shepherd than to depict a crucifixion scene.

- The Jesus Mystery
- A Crisis in Tradition
- Ministry and Movement
- What Happened to His Disciples?
- Christianities Everywhere
- Romans in Pursuit
- Pagan Vitality
- Stoicism and Neoplatonism

CHAPTER OUTLINE

in the 20th. No persecutions of Galileo Galilei or Charles Darwin. No agonized debates over abortion, contraception, or homosexuality—or at least, not the same debates that we currently have.

Both lists could be extended easily and infinitely. The history of Christianity in the Greater West is complex, as is its legacy. One would be hard put to identify another idea, invention, school of thought, technology, or value system that has penetrated so far into the DNA of Western culture—and shaped so much of what is both good and bad in it. In this chapter we will see how Christianity arose, how it became a Roman religion, and how it absorbed such intellectual currents of the classical world as Stoicism and Plato.

THE JESUS MYSTERY

The story fascinates, thrills, comforts, angers, and embarrasses at every turn, often all at once. It has touched everything from Western political ideas to sexual mores. Christianity began as an obscure reformist sect within Palestinian Judaism, at one time numbering no more than fifty or so believers. It went on, after three centuries of persecution by the Roman state, to become the dominant faith on our planet.

Approximately 2 billion people today identify themselves as Christian; given a current world population of roughly 5.6 billion, Christians therefore comprise 35 percent of the total. Islam comes in second place, with 1.2 billion faithful (21 percent). Hinduism, with nearly 800 million adherents, ranks third (14 percent). Judaism, by contrast, makes up only 0.27 percent of the world population, numbering a mere 15 million. Jews, indeed, are almost statistically insignificant—an irony, given the hate-filled perceptions of them by anti-Semites (see Figure 7.1).

That development was neither rapid nor assured, however. Instead, Christianity spread with almost painful slowness and suffered repeated and severe setbacks along the way.[1] As late as 300 CE, if one could have surveyed the whole of

---

[1]   As many as eight hundred years after the death of Jesus of Nazareth, the religion was still at risk of being wiped out.

CHAPTER TIMELINE

40 BCE
Beginning of Herodian dynasty in Judea

ca. 5 BCE
Birth of Jesus

25 CE
Jesus begins his ministry

64 CE
Christians persecuted under Nero; death of Peter

66–70 CE
Great Jewish Revolt

- ■ Christian, 1,965,993,000
- ■ Muslim, 1,179,326,000
- ■ Hindu, 767,424,000
- ■ Non-religious, 766,672,000
- ■ Buddhist, 356,875,000
- ■ Tribal religion, 244,164,000
- ■ Atheist, 146,406,000
- ■ New religions, 99,191,000
- ■ Sikh, 22,874,000
- ■ Daoist, 20,050,000
- ■ Jewish, 15,050,000
- ■ Baha'I, 6,251,000
- ■ Confucian, 5,067,000
- ■ Jain, 4,152,000
- ■ Shinto, 3,571,000
- ■ Parsi (Zoroastrian), 479,000

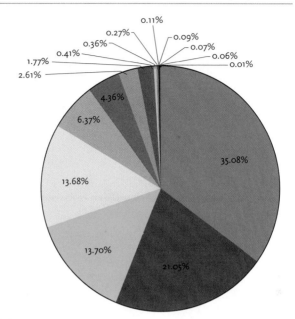

FIGURE 7.1   **The World's Religions**

the Roman Empire and then placed a bet on which religion in it was most likely to become the dominant religious force in the Western world, hardly anyone would have picked Christianity. By that date, even after three hundred years of ardent evangelizing, teaching, bearing witness, and, as Christian tradition asserts, the performing of countless miracles by missionaries, Christians made up no more than 2–3 percent of the empire's population and possibly as little as 1 percent.

Moreover, biology, not conversion, accounts for the lion's share of whatever growth did occur in those years. Christians married other Christians and raised their children in the faith. Conversions certainly did take place, and those who brought the gospel of Jesus to the pagans did so at the risk of their lives, a fact later Christians pointed to with pride. But conversions occurred in far smaller

ca. 126 CE
Pantheon built
in Rome

161–180 CE
Reign of Roman
emperor Marcus
Aurelius

355–430 CE
Life of Augustine of Hippo

ca. 140 CE
Last books of the
New Testament
composed

284–305 CE
Reign of Roman
emperor Diocletian

TABLE 7.1 **The Books of the New Testament in the Order of Their Composition**

YEAR (CE)	TEXT	AUTHOR
50	1 Thessalonians	Paul
54–55	Galatians	Paul
55	Philemon	Paul
56	Philippians	Paul
56	1 Corinthians	Paul
57	2 Corinthians	Paul
57–58	Romans	Paul
(66–73: Jewish Revolt and Rome's Subsequent Destruction of the Temple)		
68–73	Gospel of Mark	Mark
70–90	1 Peter	?
80–85	Gospel of Luke	Luke
80–85	Acts of the Apostles	Luke
80–90	Colossians	? (attributed to Paul)
80–100	James	? (attributed to James, brother of Jesus)
85–90	Gospel of Matthew	Matthew
85–90	Hebrews	? (attributed to Paul)
90–95	Gospel of John	? (attributed to the Beloved Disciple)
90–100	Ephesians	? (attributed to Paul)
90–100	2 Thessalonians	? (attributed to Paul)
90–100	1–2 Timothy, Titus	? (attributed to Paul)
90–100	Jude	? (attributed to Jude, brother of Jesus)
92–96	Revelation	John
95–100	1–2 John	?
120–130	3 John	?
130–140	2 Peter	?

Authors of the Gospels and the Book of Revelation

Matthew	Matthew, a tax collector, was one of the original twelve apostles. By textual evidence, the author was a Jewish Christian who spoke Greek, Hebrew, and Aramaic, who drew on Mark's Gospel and was also not an eyewitness to Jesus's life.
Mark	Mark is attributed by tradition. This is the "John Mark" mentioned in the Acts of the Apostles, who helped Paul on his first missionary tour. Textual evidence suggests the author was a Greek speaker, not an eyewitness to Jesus's ministry, and is addressing an audience that has already experienced persecution.
Luke	Luke was a physician and fellow missionary with Saint Paul. Textual evidence reveals a Greek speaker who knew the Jewish Bible only in its Greek (Septuagint) version and was also not an eyewitness to Jesus's career. Drew on Mark's Gospel. Author was not from Palestine and was almost certainly not born Jewish; hence possibly a Greek who converted to Judaism before subsequently converting to Christianity.
John	Tradition attributes this gospel to John, the son of Zebedee and one of the original twelve apostles. Textual evidence suggests the author was actually a redactor—a disciple of John who later gathered his teacher's sayings. It is possible that the redactor's work was itself later edited, ca. 100–110, by another disciple contemporaneous with the author of 3 John. And the author of Revelation is not the same John.

numbers than many like to think. Christians had a significantly higher profile in the cities of the eastern Mediterranean by the end of the 3rd century CE. Still, through vast stretches of the empire the very name of Jesus had yet to be heard, much less adored.

How a tiny sect thus grew to dominate Western culture is not easy to explain. Even after two thousand years, scholars are still as busy as ever trying to figure it out. Two problems stand in the way and probably always will. First, no one approaches the issue of historical Christianity with absolute objectivity. Try as they might to remain detached, scholars are influenced by their personal convictions—even if the conviction is an intentional denial of belief. Second, our principle source for the history of Jesus's life and the careers of his early followers is the **New Testament**, which is a compilation of notoriously difficult texts written over a period of nearly a century. Many other texts— gospels, epistles, miracle narratives, collections of sayings—written in the 2nd and 3rd centuries CE were considered "biblical" in their time but are largely unheard of today. Even as authoritative a figure in Christian teaching as Saint Augustine (354–430) used a New Testament that few people would now recognize.

The canon of the New Testament as the modern world knows it did not become settled until the late 4th century. And its specific wording—reconciling variant readings and filling gaps—was not set until the early 5th, a long time after the events it purports to relate. Twenty-seven texts comprise the New Testament:

- four gospels (Matthew, Mark, Luke, and John)
- a narrative of the apostles' activities immediately after Jesus's death
- seven authentic epistles by Saint Paul
- seven more epistles that tradition attributes to Paul but that he almost certainly did not write
- seven more epistles falsely accredited to four of the original twelve apostles
- a densely symbolic dream vision of the end of the world

None of these twenty-seven works were written in Jesus's lifetime. Jesus himself wrote nothing and is never reported to have ordered his followers to write his teachings down. Hence the lateness of our closest written evidence of Jesus and his ministry. This lateness, combined with the many flaws in the texts, leaves any effort to understand the rise of Christianity facing enormous challenges.

What are some of those flaws? Many are simple discrepancies in chronology. Matthew, Mark, and Luke, for example, all state that the Last Supper took place on Passover, while John records that it occurred sometime before it. Others are flat-out errors—such as Luke's famous setting of the scene in his Infancy narrative, at the start of his second chapter:

> In those days a decree went out from Emperor Augustus that all the world should be registered. This was the first registration and was taken while Quirinius was governor of Syria. All went to their own towns to be registered. *(Luke 2.1–2)*

There was no census of the entire empire under Augustus, however, only a handful of provincial censuses. Moreover, the only census of Judea that Luke could possibly refer to (when Quirinius was the governor of Syria) took place in either 6 or 7 CE, which is at least a decade too late for Jesus's birth. Jesus was actually born between the years 7 and 3 BCE. The modern calendar, based on the number of years since the birth of Jesus, was invented in the 6th century by a Syriac monk who worked backward from his own time, based on the reigns of Roman emperors. But in the process he made an arithmetical mistake—something easily done when working with Roman numerals—which explains how Jesus was actually born several years "before Christ."

Other flaws (if they are flaws) are occasional tensions between the portrayals of Jesus's character in the gospels. Luke's Jesus, for example, shows a particular sensitivity toward women, whereas Matthew depicts a Jesus who shows hardly any interest in them at all—not even in his own mother. Mark's Jesus is a terse miracle worker who, apart from calling people to repent their sins, speaks mostly in parables; John's Jesus, by contrast, is loquacious to an extreme and capable of both precise common-sense speech and sophisticated philosophical language. These aspects of the New Testament texts add to their fascination for the faithful, and to the frustration of nonbelieving readers.

A CRISIS IN TRADITION

The basic outlines of Christian growth are fairly well known, but the precise knowledge of how, when, and where the faith spread, what the specific mechanisms for development were, even the exact content of what people actually believed at any particular time, remain unclear and hotly debated. One rare point of agreement among scholars today is that the history of Jesus of Nazareth and the movement he founded must be understood in the context of Jewish tradition. Jesus was a Jew, as were all of his original followers, none of whom regarded their commitment to Jesus and his teachings as an abrogation of their Jewish identities.

Indeed, they saw Jesus rather as the fulfillment of Jewish prophecy. In his own words, as recorded by Matthew:

> Do not think that I have come to abolish the law or the prophets. I have come not to abolish but to fulfill. For truly I tell you, until heaven and earth pass away, not one letter, not one stroke of a letter, will pass from the law until all is accomplished. Therefore, whoever breaks one of the least of these commandments, and teaches others to do the same, will be called least in the kingdom of heaven; but whoever does them and teaches them will be called great in the kingdom of heaven. *(5.17–19)*

These assurances might have quieted more Jewish concerns, however, if Jesus himself had been more strictly observant of Torah. Instead, he provoked widespread ire by performing work on the Sabbath, allowing his followers to call him the **messiah**, speaking scornfully of the Temple, and, most boldly of all, referring to himself as the Son of God. By Jesus's lifetime several Jewish traditions were in existence and in uneasy dialogue with one another, but none of them was quite prepared for this.

One rare point of agreement among scholars today is that the history of Jesus of Nazareth and the movement he founded must be understood in the context of Jewish tradition.

The Hellenistic era had resulted in many Jewish factions, divided primarily by two factors: their relative commitments to Temple observance and the authority of the priests, on the one hand, and the new focus on rabbinical leadership and the "oral Torah," on the other. Added to this mix was a potent new element: the belief in a coming apocalypse. This moralism resulted from the rising trend of exogamous marriage (or marriage outside of Judaism) and the exiled Jews' close contact with Zoroastrianism. The political scene contributed a number of factors as well. After the Maccabean revolt against the Seleucids had succeeded, Judea was ruled by the Hasmonean dynasty for a century, the last independent Jewish state until the 20th century (see Map 7.1). While the era had helped foster a Jewish national spirit, however, the Jews were sharply divided toward the dynasty itself. By long tradition Jewish kingship belonged solely to the lineage of the ancient ruler David, which made the Hasmoneans usurpers in the eyes of many. Struggles within later generations of the dynasty only confirmed their critics' opinion of them as imposters. Thoroughly Hellenized, the Hasmonean kings even bore Greek names rather than Hebrew ones.

The kings tried to gain legitimacy by associating themselves closely with the Temple priests and their most important political allies, a party known as the **Sadducees**. These were one of three "philosophical sects" (hairesis) into which

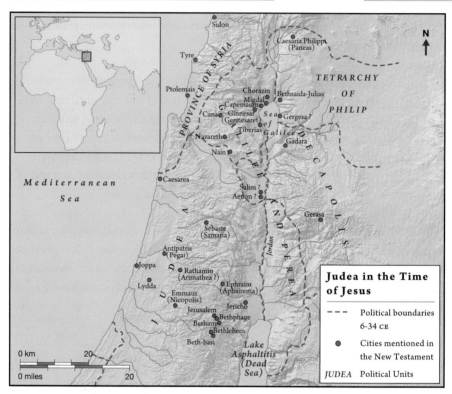

MAP 7.1   Judea in the Time of Jesus

Judea was divided, according to the Jewish historian Josephus (37–100 CE); the other two were called the **Pharisees** and the **Essenes**. The Sadducees were an aristocratic party, the ideological descendants of the "Children of the Exile." They were reputedly strict upholders of Temple ritual, dedicated to the literal reading of Scripture and the rejection of the Oral Torah—"reputedly" because much of what is known of the Sadducees' thought comes from the testimony of writers hostile to them—including the authors of the four Christian gospels, as well as Josephus.

Opposing them were the Pharisees, the party more closely associated with the "People of the Land" and the rabbinical tradition. The Pharisees generally came from the common stock (although, being urbanites, they regarded themselves as superior to the outlying rustics) and resisted Hellenization. They also held a number of religious beliefs that set them apart from other Jews—most notably, a belief in the immortality of the soul and the resurrection of the dead.[2] They took the lead in advocating the arrival of a messiah, a savior of the Jewish

---

[2]   The most renowned figure, believed to have been a Pharisee, was the Babylonian scholar Hillel (110 BCE– 10 CE, according to tradition), who is considered the central figure in establishing the core of the rabbinical law and its commentaries—the oral tradition that would later be codified in the Talmud.

people who would return them to freedom and safety. The Essenes, the third Palestinian sect mentioned by Josephus, are more difficult to identify. It is even possible that the word is a catchall term used by writers like Josephus to describe a host of minor Jewish sects that shared certain views. An ascetic community, they lived in isolated congregations and dedicated themselves to repentance and prayer in the hope of achieving mystical union with YHWH. The Essenes were the most eschatological sect within Judaism, meaning they were characterized by expectations of an imminent apocalyptic end of the world, although it is difficult to generalize how widely believed such ideas were.[3]

Jesus of Nazareth thus entered a Jewish world in high-voltage turmoil. When the Romans, led by Pompey the Great, conquered Judea in 63 BCE, they dismissed and jailed the Hasmonean king and ruled in his name for twenty-five years, while Pompey and then Marcus Crassus plundered the province mercilessly. In 40 BCE they installed a new dynasty, the Herodians. The Jews had mostly disdained the Hasmoneans, but they ardently hated the Herodians, and for good reason. Herod the Great, named "king of Judea" in 40 BCE but not actually in power until three years later, was a venal, dissolute, and brutal figure (r. 37–4 BCE). He murdered anyone who stood in the way of his authority—which included two high priests,

his brother-in-law, his mother-in-law, and even his wife. A lover of massive, soulless architecture, Herod built and rebuilt palaces, Roman temples, gardens, amphitheaters, hippodromes, baths, and fountains across Judea—including an ambitious restoration of the Jerusalem Temple itself. And he paid for it all with heavy taxation. Perversely, he ordered a golden imperial eagle to be installed over the gate into the restored Temple. When two rabbis complained of the blasphemy, Herod had them burned alive. Herod died in 4 BCE, after which the emperor Augustus divided Judea into three provinces, one of which was administered by a Roman procurator; the other two went to Herod's sons, Herod Antipas and Philip.[4] By the time Jesus

Jerusalem in the Time of King Herod A modern model of Jerusalem at the time of the Herodian Temple (ca. 50 BCE).

---

[3]   The Essenes were probably the group whose collected writings, the Dead Sea Scrolls, were discovered at Qumran in 1946.

[4]   Pontius Pilate was the most famous of the Roman procurators in Judea; he held the post for a decade (26–36 CE).

began his ministry, sometime around 25 or 26 CE, Judea was crackling with religious rivalries and social-political tensions.

MINISTRY AND MOVEMENT

The gospels of Matthew and Luke relate a handful of episodes from Jesus's childhood and youth, but only become detailed when Jesus begins his ministry, around the age of thirty. An early follower of John the Baptist, a Jewish revivalist preacher who prophesied the arrival of the messiah and urged his listeners to penance and passionate commitment to God, Jesus took up John's cause after his own baptism. The gospels then relate how Jesus traveled throughout Judea, performing miraculous healings, driving out demon spirits, calling people to a revivified faith and universal love, and especially teaching them about the approach of "the kingdom of God." What he meant by this last point is by no means clear. Some of his followers (and his critics) understood him to be talking about Heaven itself, God's own dwelling place; others regarded the "kingdom" as a state of spiritual grace, a soulful enlightenment. To still others the "kingdom" was this world, the world we inhabit, but made just and perfect by a heavenly appointed ruler, a new King David—earthly life as it should be, in other words.

The differences matter. If the kingdom Jesus spoke of was indeed a paradise and an afterlife, then he was speaking the language of the Pharisees. If he meant a spiritual state of utopian soulfulness, then he was appealing to the Essenes. If he intended an earthly kingdom marked by justice and order, then the Sadducees might have been the intended audience. And still other possibilities existed. As it happened, Jesus's oblique language could have appealed to everyone, which meant that it displeased and offended far more people than it attracted. In the life-and-death struggle of 1st-century Palestine, Jewish scholars on all sides were still fighting over the exact lettering of sacred texts, their meaning, and the purposes to which they were put. For them, Jesus's words often sounded so confusing as to be provocative:

> Then the disciples came and asked him, "Why do you speak to [the crowds] in parables?"
>
> He answered, "To you it has been given to know the secrets of the kingdom of heaven, but to them it has not been given. For to those who have, more will be given, and they will have an abundance; but from those who have nothing, even what they have will be taken away. The reason I speak to them in parables is that 'seeing they do not perceive, and hearing they do not listen, nor do they understand.'" *(Matthew 13.10–13)*

At the same time, he also taught:

> Blessed are the poor in spirit, for theirs is the kingdom of heaven
> *(Matthew 5.3)*

and:

> But many who are first will be last, and the last will be first *(Mark 10.31)*

which seemed to want it both ways. How can those with an abundance of spiritual enlightenment deserve an increase, while those without will lose what little they have? How can Jesus then turn around and promise that the spiritually poor will be the ones to enter the kingdom while the others will languish? Were these the teachings of a holy man or of a con man?

Jesus was not a solo act. His public ministry began with his joining a movement already in existence—the penitential and revivalist sect of John the Baptist:

> In those days John the Baptist appeared in the wilderness of Judea, proclaiming, "Repent, for the kingdom of heaven has come near!". . . Then the people of Jerusalem and all of Judea were going out to him, and all the region along the Jordan, and they were baptized by him in the river Jordan, confessing their sins. *(Matthew 3.1–2, 5–6)*

The word baptize comes from the Greek *baptizein*, a transitive verb meaning "to dunk" or "to plunge." Jewish tradition had long involved people giving themselves ritual baths of purification; John's innovation was to actively plunge the faithful into the water. He therefore could be referred to as "John the Plunger."

Jesus himself did not begin to preach and to baptize until after learning that Herod Agrippa had arrested John. Jesus thus assumed leadership of a preexisting popular movement, but he quickly put his own stamp on it by summoning a corps of personal disciples, the Twelve Apostles, who then broadcast the idea that Jesus himself was the long-promised messiah. John's more general revivalist movement thus became specifically a Jesus movement, a sect dedicated to his unique ministry. He traveled throughout Galilee, Samaria, and Judea proper—an area roughly forty miles from east to west and roughly eighty miles from north to south—and preached the primacy of a passionate love of God over a formal observance of rituals. The desire and intent behind our actions, he seemed to say, matter more than the actions themselves. When criticized for his inexact observance of Torah, he replied that YHWH cares more for the sincerity in our hearts than for the mechanical precision of our rites (Jesus here quotes two Torah verses: Deuteronomy 6.5 and Leviticus 19.18):

> When the Pharisees heard that [Jesus] had silenced the Sadducees, they gathered together, and one of them, a lawyer, asked him a question to test him.
>
> "Teacher, which commandment in the Law is the greatest?"
>
> [Jesus] said to him, "'You shall love the Lord your God with all your heart, and with all your soul, and with all your mind.' This is the greatest and first commandment. And a second is like it: 'You shall love your neighbor as yourself.' On these two commandments hang all the Law and the Prophets." *(Matthew 22.34–40)*

Jesus's own criticisms of the Pharisees and Sadducees display flashes of temper and a sharp tongue. It is small wonder that the leaders of the two groups grew irritated with him, locked as they were in a bitter struggle to lead the Jewish people and indeed to define the faith itself. They showed little patience for a quick-witted upstart who evinced little respect for either of them.

WHAT HAPPENED TO HIS DISCIPLES?

Jesus's popularity with the Jewish crowds is uncertain. Large numbers of people, perhaps even thousands at a time, regularly turned out to see him and listen to his teaching. However, many of those were undoubtedly mere curiosity seekers, wanting to see him perform one of his famous miracles, rather than true followers of his movement. To many Jews, and perhaps to most of them, he was an item in the short-term news cycle, the subject of gossip and debate, and nothing more; the evidence clearly suggests that he received only the passing attention of most Jews. Even his most loyal disciples had moments of confusion about his mission. After Jesus's arrest by the Romans, many of those followers melted away with extraordinary speed.

When the gospels describe Jesus's final entry into Jerusalem for the Passover holiday, the streets of the city are packed with crowds wanting to get a look at him. The texts present the episode, in fact, as a triumphal messianic march, which may well be how his truest followers perceived it. Yet it was probably the result of the high spirits of thousands of pilgrims visiting the Holy City. The gospels describe thousands of people waving palm fronds at Jesus and strewing them upon the path he took through the city. If this description is accurate, one can just as easily see a knowing playfulness or mock enthusiasm in their gestures, rather than evidence of mass ecstatic religious deliverance. The burden of proof is on those who assert the gospels' historical accuracy.

What tipped the scales against Jesus, ultimately, was the zeal of his disciples to have him recognized as the long-prophesied messiah. This, indeed, is the principal function of Matthew's gospel. Alone of the four gospel writers, Matthew aims specifically at a Jewish audience and focuses on describing those ideas and actions of Jesus that proved he was the long-promised savior. Echoes of the prophets can be heard everywhere. But there was a problem. Jewish tradition anticipated the arrival of an earthly savior, one who would create a safe, unified state for the Jews—in which justice will flourish and YHWH will be praised. Even as messiah, Jesus appeared otherwise; he was a savior of eternal souls, not the leader of a political revival. He did things no messiah was ever expected to do (such as to violate the Sabbath and speak disrespectfully of the Temple), and did *not* do the things that were expected of the savior.

> Jewish tradition anticipated the arrival of an earthly savior, one who would create a safe, unified state for the Jews—in which justice will flourish and YHWH will be praised. Even as messiah, Jesus appeared otherwise; he was a savior of eternal souls, not the leader of a political revival.

This combination made it all but impossible for most Jews to accept him in that role. And in fact the overwhelming majority of Jews did not accept him. The passion narratives in the New Testament are highly dramatic set pieces filled with betrayals, storm clouds, grim-faced soldiers, wailing crowds, moments of tender intimacy, fear and confusion, last-minute conversions, heart-rending questions, and finally stoic acceptance of God's merciful plan to save all mankind. But despite the extraordinary goings on, so compelling and moving to the faithful, the Jews as a whole rejected Jesus's claims to be the messiah.

It is unclear whether this simple claim sufficed to warrant an accusation of blasphemy—the official complaint levied at Jesus by the Jewish head council. Nonetheless, by the time of Jesus's arrest, he had sufficiently alienated enough members of the community to turn them against him. More important to the Roman prefect, Pontius Pilate, was the popular talk among Jesus's supporters that he was the "King of the Jews." This smacked of treason against the Roman state, for only the emperor had the right to designate a client king within the confines of the empire. When Pilate ordered Jesus to be crucified, a sign bearing the words "Jesus of Nazareth, King of the Jews" was placed on the cross above his head.[5] It was Roman practice, when crucifying criminals, to identify their crime in this way.

Pontius Pilate's career as a Roman official is well-known, and so was his taste for rough politics. Philo of Alexandria (20 BCE–50 CE) described him as a "rigid, stubborn, and cruel [administrator] who was known to execute lawbreakers even without a trial.... [He was] venal and violent, and he committed innumerable thefts, assaults, persecutions, and executions of the most extraordinary ferocity" (*Embassy of Gaius* 38.299–305). Josephus describes an incident when Pilate confiscated funds from the Temple and used them to fund the construction of an aqueduct; when the Jews predictably gathered outside his court to complain,

---

5   In Latin, the inscription on the cross reads Iesus Nazarenus Rex Iudaeorum—hence the acronym INRI that appears frequently in images of the crucifixion.

Pilate had secretly scattered dozens of armed soldiers, dressed as Jews, among the crowd. At his signal, the soldiers drew their swords and began attacking the Jews indiscriminately, killing several dozen protestors (*Antiquities* 18.3.2). One inscription survives that attests to him; it was discovered in 1962 in the ruins of a Roman theater at Caesarea Maritima and is now on view in the Israel Museum in Jerusalem. It is a dedicatory inscription, whose Latin reads: [DIS AUGUSTI]S TIBEREUM [PO]NTIUS PILATUS [PRAEF]ECTUS JUDAE [FECIT D] E[DICAVIT] ("Pontius Pilate, the prefect of Judea, had the Temple to Tiberius built and dedicated it to the august gods").

After Jesus's death, the small cohort of people still faithful ran immediately into hiding, since the Romans were determined to stamp the sect out. Soldiers searched for them from street to street. Then something extraordinary happened. Three days after Jesus was buried, groups of believers began to appear in the streets of Jerusalem proclaiming joyously that they had seen Jesus resurrected from the dead.

In three days they had transformed, apparently as a group, from terrified fugitives hoping to escape capture into a company of bold, confident witnesses. They not only acknowledged their belief in Jesus but broadcast it at every turn, even at the risk of death.

For the next few decades, until they themselves began to die in the 50s, 60s, and possibly 70s CE, those early disciples traversed the eastern half of the empire telling anyone who would listen about the transformative saving power of Jesus "the Christ" (the Anointed One, literally). Threats of popular violence or of state persecution posed no barrier to them. They faced execution with stoic calm, according to both Christian and pagan reports, happy to embrace the death that would reunite them with their savior. Faithful Christians then and now have no doubt what caused the extraordinary transformation of that small group of disciples during those three days of hiding in Jerusalem; nonbelievers can only wonder. But one thing is clear: something dramatic happened to those people.

> Faithful Christians then and now have no doubt what caused the extraordinary transformation of that small group of disciples during those three days of hiding in Jerusalem; nonbelievers can only wonder. But one thing is clear: something dramatic happened to those people.

CHRISTIANITIES EVERYWHERE

Whatever happened in Jerusalem to those first disciples, afterward they went out into the eastern Mediterranean determined to spread the message of Jesus. The problem, of course, was in agreeing upon what that message actually was—and for whom it was intended. Was the Christian message intended for the Jews? For the Jews alone? For all people everywhere? There were factions in the early Christian movement supporting each of those views, plus others. Since Jesus and his initial disciples were all Jews, could non-Jews become his followers? And if they did, did they have to observe Jewish teaching and tradition, as the apostles themselves continued to do? If a non-Jew wanted to become a Christian, in other words, did he or she have to convert to Judaism first?

Problems like these abounded, causing many rifts to break out in the Christian movement; and the problems were exacerbated by the fact that no one had the universally recognized authority to settle such disputes as they arose. Saint Peter undoubtedly was the leader of the original twelve, but who should lead the movement after Peter's death in Rome in 64 CE? Peter's line of successors as bishop ("overseer") of the Christian community in Rome insisted that they were the heirs of Peter's own spiritual authority and hence were to be accepted as the supreme leaders of all Christians everywhere. But hardly anyone agreed with them. Why shouldn't the bishop of Jerusalem, the site of Jesus's Passion, take precedence? Others argued for the primacy of Antioch, the home of the first major Christian community outside of Jerusalem. Some insisted that Jesus's brother James (one of Jesus's four siblings—three brothers and a sister—mentioned in the gospels) had a hereditary right to lead the community. Still others insisted that there should be no single leader at all and that guidance of the church should be left to a council of all the bishops together.

Until such matters could be resolved the early Christians had no way to reconcile the differences in their beliefs—of which there were many. The apostles and early missionaries, after all, preached their messages in synagogues and market squares throughout the eastern Mediterranean, hoping to win as many converts as possible as quickly as possible; but these were the centers of ancient cultures that reached back two thousand years and more (see Map 7.2).[6] The missionaries, predictably, faced flurries of questions. Even those whose hearts were inclined to accept the new faith may have required some intellectual satisfaction before they were willing to commit:

- How can the One True God, Jesus, and the Holy Spirit be three separate beings and one indivisible being at the same time?
- If Jesus was "coeternal" with God, why is there no mention of him in the two-thousand-year tradition of Hebrew writings?
- If Jesus was God in human form, wasn't the fact that he felt temptation, fear, and loneliness (things to which God is presumably immune) evidence that Jesus was at best a lesser version of God?
- How could Jesus's mother, Mary, still be a virgin after the conception and birth of a child?

---

[6] Literacy was high: most of the people who heard Christian testimonies were fairly well versed in Hellenistic traditions.

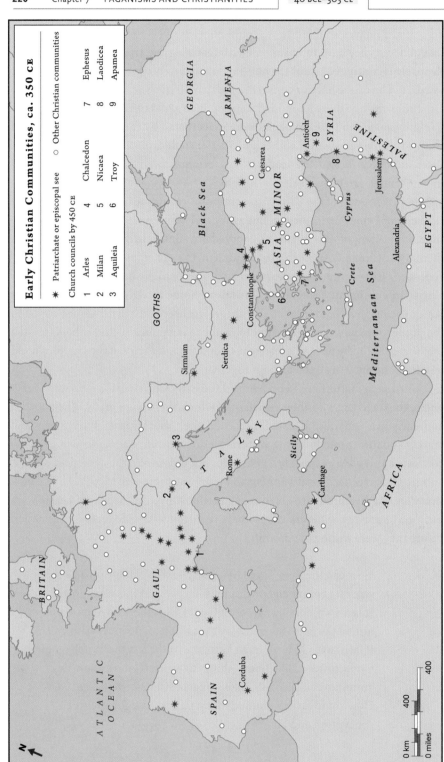

Early Christian Communities, ca. 350 CE

✳ Patriarchate or episcopal see   ○ Other Christian communities

Church councils by 450 CE

1 Arles	4 Chalcedon	7 Ephesus
2 Milan	5 Nicaea	8 Laodicea
3 Aquileia	6 Troy	9 Apamea

MAP 7.2   Early Christian Communities, ca. 350 CE

To crowds familiar with Greek philosophy and the Hebrew Scriptures, not to mention Greek, Persian, or Egyptian medicine, such questions were not easily dismissed.

Answers to such questions are possible; but the apostles and other missionaries were not in regular contact with one another, and they seldom agreed with one another when they were. The communities of converts they established therefore believed starkly different things. For the first three centuries after Jesus's death, in fact, it is inaccurate to speak of Christianity existing at all. What existed instead were many dozens of **christianities** (with a lower-case "c"), each with its own beliefs, liturgical traditions, and customs. There were communities of Christians that denied Jesus's divinity and believed good works were necessary for the salvation of some Christians but not for all. Others believed that Jesus had never in fact died at all but instead had gone into hiding. Some maintained that Jesus passed along some body of

The Gospel of Thomas Opening page of the Gospel of Thomas, one of many gospels that circulated among early Christians. Most of these apocryphal gospels date well into the 3rd century, but Thomas's is much closer in date to the four canonical Gospels of the New Testament. This papyrus manuscript is in the Coptic Museum in Cairo.

secret knowledge, given only to a few initiates, that gave them the key to understanding that reconciled Christian revelation with Greek philosophy. Still others insisted that baptism was all that was needed to achieve salvation—and that God, Jesus, and the Holy Spirit existed as three separate deities. Some communities believed in the immediate immanence of the Second Coming. They took Jesus at his literal word when he declared that "this present generation shall not pass before the kingdom of God appears." Others counseled a more patient attitude, thinking that the End might not come for a long time. Some believed in bodily resurrection; others found the idea horrifying and ridiculous. Some practiced strict sexual asceticism; others were widely accused of extremes of licentiousness that even included incest.

ROMANS IN PURSUIT

Most Christians practiced their faith in secret, gathering in homes, in remote spots outside the city, in caves, or in warehouses—wherever they might escape notice. They needed to do so because Roman authorities were still in active

Masada   Ruins of the Jewish fortress at Masada, where rebel Jews pursued by the Roman army made their last stand. The Dead Sea can be glimpsed in the background. Masada is today the site where Israeli recruits take their oaths of military service.

pursuit of them, for two good reasons. To the Romans religion was a public affair, a means of uniting society in the observance of shared rituals. In contrast, Christians largely withdrew from society and taught, as far as the Romans understood it, that the affairs of this world are meaningless, the only meaningful reality being one's existence in the heavenly kingdom yet to come. To the Romans, this notion was both insipid and criminally aberrant. Christians seldom served in the army and refused to perform sacrifices to the emperor, which called into question their political loyalty. To the stoic Roman mind, engagement in the affairs of the world was a duty and a sign of virtue; to devalue the affairs of the world seemed not ascetic but immoral. Moreover, Christians still spoke of their departed Jesus as a king, and as far as the Romans saw it, loyalty to a dead traitor was as bad as loyalty to a live one. Worse still, the Christians were said to practice ritual cannibalism. Indeed, the central purpose of their gathering together was to eat the physical remains of their god Jesus.[7]

The second thing that condemned Christians in Roman eyes was their relationship with Judaism. The Romans had no love for the Jews, who were arguably the most volatile and troublesome people in the empire, but grudgingly respected the antiquity of their religion. When the great Jewish Revolt of 66–70 CE erupted,

---

[7]   Even if the Christians ate the body of Jesus only symbolically, in bread and wine, the idea was repulsive to Roman sensibilities.

Rome responded with heavy force, crushed the rebels, destroyed the Temple, killed untold thousands of Jews, and dispersed the rest once and for all. The slaughter was memorably fierce, and was meant to be. In only a few years the Jews had passed from being, to Roman eyes, the denizens of a hard-to-handle province to a despised race of stiff-necked ingrates. As the troops marched through Palestine in search of more Jews to kill or exile, they inevitably encountered groups of Christians who were eager to disassociate themselves from the Jewish majority. It is not a coincidence that the Christian Gospels began to be written at this time, with large servings of anti-Jewish language.

By the 70s and 80s CE the number of Christians who were not ethnically Jewish finally overtook the number who were. That itself required some redefinition of the relationship between the two faiths; but when the Jews became the leading active enemy of the Pax Romana, there was additional reason for the Christians to emphasize that they were not Jewish. The gospels make the case with unnerving thoroughness.

> But when [John the Baptist] saw many Pharisees and Sadducees coming for baptism, he said to them, "You brood of vipers! Who warned you to flee from the wrath to come? Bear fruit worthy of repentance. Do not presume to say to yourselves, 'We have Abraham as our ancestor'; for I tell you, God is able from these stones to raise up children to Abraham." *(Matthew 3.7–9)*

> After this Jesus went about in Galilee. He did not wish to go about in Judea because the Jews were looking for an opportunity to kill him. Now the Jewish Festival of Booths was near. . . . The Jews were looking for him at the festival and saying, "Where is he?" And there was considerable complaining about him among the crowds. While some were saying, "He is a good man," others were saying, "No, he is deceiving the crowd." Yet no one would speak openly about him for fear of the Jews. *(John 7.1–2, 10–13)*

> Jesus said to [the Jewish leaders], "If God were your Father, you would love me, for I came from God and now I am here. I did not come on my own, but he sent me. Why do you not understand what I say? It is because you cannot accept my word. You are from your father the devil, and you choose to do your father's desires. He was a murderer from the beginning and does not stand in the truth, because there is no truth in him." *(John 8.42–44)*

Of course, to argue that one is not Jewish is not necessarily the same thing as to be an anti-Semite, but such an emphasis, made over a sufficiently long time span, certainly opens the door to the evolution of a type of Jew hatred. And as the christianities slowly spread around the Mediterranean, they continually had to repeat and refine their non-Jewishness: the diaspora of the Jews meant the side-by-side establishment of new Jewish communities in the cities as well. Wherever Christian communities took root, in other words, so too did new Jewish ones, and the efforts to explain themselves to the pagans began over and over again.

Persecution by the Romans was intermittent but brutal. Under certain emperors—Nero (r. 54–68 CE), Domitian (r. 81–96 CE), Maximinus (r. 235–238 CE), Decius (r. 249–251 CE), and Diocletian (r. 284–305 CE) being the most notorious—many tens of thousands of Christians were arrested and killed. The lucky ones were quickly executed; the others faced torture and humiliation before vast crowds in Roman forums. Popular resistance to Christians was ubiquitous and took many forms, from angry words to social ostracism to rough street violence, but persecution itself began in Rome as a deliberate policy before spreading, in the 2nd and 3rd centuries CE, into the provinces.

The first persecution occurred under Nero, during whose reign the first Christian communities were established in Rome under Saints Peter and Paul. When the city experienced a catastrophic fire in 64 CE, Nero found the newcomer Christians to be a convenient scapegoat and contrived for them a gruesome means of execution: he ordered hundreds of Christians to be covered in bloody animal skins, which made them the prey of packs of wild dogs; others were crucified; still others he had coated in paraffin and set alight as human torches. When the provincial governors took up the cause, they attempted to balance viciousness with some sense of fairness: Christians who relapsed into paganism were forgiven, while those who held Roman citizenship were remanded to imprisonment in the capital. Only noncitizens who remained obstinate in refusing to renounce their Christian faith received the death sentence.

The christianities deserved hateful treatment in Roman eyes for any number of reasons. The tendency of monotheisms to deny the reality of all other divinities is partially to blame, but the empire did not find any deviation from standard pagan practices absolutely unendurable. (They did not, after all, always crush the Jews.) Moreover, it was not at all clear to the Romans—or indeed even to many of the Christians themselves—that Christianity was a strictly monotheistic faith. Later, most Christians believed in the mystery of the **Trinity** (that is, the existence of a single God in a union of three separate and divine "Persons"). For the first three centuries CE, though, this was simply a high-intensity muddle that set Christians against Christians with much of the same ferocity that the Romans reserved for all of them.

More to the point was the secrecy with which Christians practiced their faith. Religion was a public activity in the Pax Romana period, a necessary means by which people developed a communal identity and a sense of shared destiny. Romanness was more than a matter of citizenship; it comprised an ethical vision of human unity, a vision whose living symbol was the emperor. To reject the imperial cult and the universal Olympian gods, in Roman eyes, was to reject this foundational vision and to sow discord. The refusal of most Christians to serve in the army—the principle instrument for constructing Romanness—

Catacombs   Early Christian burial niches in the catacomb of Saint Callisto, in Rome.

only added to their ignominy. And of course the common Christian teachings that the affairs of this world do not matter and that one ought to worry only about the life in the world to come struck most Romans as simply but profoundly weird. The christianities therefore tore at the social fabric, and their followers therefore richly deserved to be torn to shreds by yapping packs of wild dogs. The punishment was not cruel but fitting and even mimetic.

PAGAN VITALITY

The fact that Christianity ultimately rose to dominate Western culture can blind us to the residual strength of the pagan cults. Roman religions continued to thrive for centuries, attracting new adherents and shaping both civic and personal lives by the millions. If anything, the empire's portfolio of *religiones licitae* ("legally approved religions") grew faster and stirred hearts deeper than Christianity could even hope to do. Moreover, pagan religion did not remain static but rather continued to develop new ritual traditions, emotional resonances, and intellectual sophistication. Rome embraced new deities by the score (including, of course, the deified emperors themselves) and built thousands of new temples across the empire. Paganism must be seen, in other words, as a vital, thriving, expansive, and energetic network of cults, not as a dusty relic patiently awaiting Christian conversion and enlightenment.

The expanding cult of the emperors is the most visible development in religious life. From the moment that Augustus dedicated the first temple to the deified Julius Caesar in 29 BCE, the veneration of Rome's supreme leaders became one of the most important public rituals. The practice was intended to unite the people in an act of thanksgiving for the blessings of the Pax Romana.[8] Augustus's own deification followed immediately upon his death in 14 CE, and after this the pattern was set for the regular, though not absolutely consistent, elevation of emperors to divine status after their deaths. The political motive behind emperor worship is obvious, but that does not necessarily mean emperor worship was insincere. Most ancient pagan religions did not divide the physical world and the heavenly world as absolutely as the Jewish and Christian monotheisms did. Divine forces permeated the physical world and caused or affected most natural phenomena, and the gods themselves wandered through our world at will and spoke to people through signs and oracles. Pagan folklore and literature was full of tales of humans venturing into the afterworld, too: Odysseus, Orpheus, and Aeneas are the best-known examples. So the idea that a living human ruler could be imbued with divine qualities was not out of the question, no matter how transparently self-serving such a notion might be.

In the first three centuries CE, nearly half of all state temples erected were dedicated to deified emperors living or dead. Statues of them were frequently added throughout the empire to temples that were already dedicated to another god or goddess. Emperors also imported into the capital city gods from regions around the empire that were associated in some way with the personal history of the ruler. Septimius Severus (r. 193–211 CE), for example, built a massive new temple of 140,000 square feet (13,000 square meters) in the heart of Rome in honor of Bacchus and Hercules. Neither was unfamiliar, but their unique pairing was the cultic practice of Septimius's hometown in North Africa. It highlighted the emperor as the living embodiment of cultic and civic unity—the linchpin holding together the whole fabric of the Pax Romana.[9]

The **Pantheon**, built by the emperor Hadrian (r. 117–138 CE), was an all-purpose temple dedicated, as its name suggests, to the whole roster of major deities within the empire. Consisting of a portico (or porch) with a colonnade of three ranks of granite columns, behind which emerged a vast rotunda covered with a splendid

---

[8]   The temple, on the south side of the Forum, formed the most regularly used backdrop for public speeches by later emperors.

[9]   The Pantheon dome, which weighs five thousand tons (4,500 metric tons) is the largest unreinforced concrete dome ever constructed.

concrete dome, it was—and remains—a stunning site. Bright shafts of sunlight shoot through a circular opening at the top of the dome and move through the area of the temple as the sun courses through the sky. The Pantheon was consecrated as a Catholic church in the seventh century, named in honor of Santa Maria dei Martiri.

The state cult took great pains to absorb and authorize new cults in the provinces, so that religious life not only took on a unifying structure but grew more varied while doing so. New cults arrived with every generation and every territorial expansion of the empire. The best known were the cults of Cybele (or Magna Mater—the "Great Mother"), Isis, Mithras, and Sol Invictus (the "Unconquered Sun"), but there were countless others. These cults had diverse and often obscure origins. The Mithras cult, for example, originated in

The Pantheon   Interior of the Roman Pantheon, whose construction was finished around 126 CE. The dome consists of reinforced concrete and is by far the largest concrete dome ever constructed. A circular opening at the top lets in (apart from rain) a dazzling beam of light that moves around the walls, illuminating the shrines of the various Olympian deities.

Asia Minor but claimed descent from the ancient Persian religious figure of Zoroaster, whereas the cult of Isis—which had certainly begun in very ancient Egyptian times—took on its Roman shape in Hellenistic Greece. In other words, what many of the provincial cults had in common was a fictional ancient and eastern ancestry, and this convenient invention lent spiritual weight to the cult's claims.

Historians often refer to these new cults collectively as "Eastern mystery religions," but they shouldn't. The term implies a set of energetic new faiths sharing oriental origins and a common practice—ritually initiating worshippers into a set of secret mysteries. Such teachings are said to have imbued the new devotee with spiritual knowledge and direct contact with the divine. A Belgian historian, Franz Cumont (1868–1947), put forth this notion in 1906. The vast bulk of evidence discovered since then, however, refutes Cumont's chronology, his suggested provenance of the cults, and the interpretive role they play in explaining the rise of Christianity.

Were these new religions a reaction against the centralizing efforts of the emperors? If so, they failed. The embrace of the new practices by Rome revitalized pagan religion in the first three centuries CE. It encouraged believers to participate in civic rituals and filled their hearts and minds with hope and comfort. In 110 CE the governor of Bithynia wrote admiringly to the emperor Trajan (r. 98–117) about the resurgence in traditional religion:

> It is now indisputable that temples long abandoned are being used frequently and that sacred rituals long forgotten are being observed again. The meat of sacrificial animals can be purchased anywhere one goes, too, whereas so long ago buyers of it could hardly be found. Judge from this how many peoples' lives can be reformed; all they need is a chance at repentance. *(Pliny the Younger, Letters 10.96–97)*

Pliny's closing line suggests a new development in religious thought—the belief in, and the desire for, forgiveness of sins. The idea was not altogether new. Ancient paganism stressed community with others in the present world more than the attainment of another, better life in a world yet to come. It privileged the ideas of civic virtue and ritual exactitude over ethical improvement, and it emphasized *doing* good instead of *being* good. In other words, instead of earning forgiveness of one's sins and whatever reward such forgiveness would entail, it stressed acting to unite the community.

Some of the provincial cults, like those of Isis and Mithras, did posit an afterlife to which repentant believers went. (The afterlives of the unrepentant or the unbelievers were less clear.) Those who died in the cults' good graces could look forward to an eternal reward of some sort. A 3rd-century CE epitaph erected on the tomb of Aurelia Prosodos, an Isis worshipper, by her husband, Dioskourides, reads: "To the gods of the underworld, Dioskourides, husband of Aurelia Prosodos, the best and sweetest of companions, erects this memorial. Farewell my lady! May Osiris grant you a draught of cool water." In the Isis cult, Osiris revived the worthy deceased with a drink from an underworld spring, which began their enjoyment of eternal peace and pleasure.

Dead Man Walking   The 2nd-century BCE painting on linen depicts the goddess Isis as she leads the newly deceased, who carries the peacock feather that signifies his purification at the examination by Osiris, to the underworld god Anubis.

In another innovation, several of the new cults were text-oriented. Religious writings are as old as the dirt in Egypt, of course, but earlier examples (with the exception of the Jewish scriptures) were by and large mere collections of set prayers and ritual formulas. Influenced by the Hellenistic spread of philosophical and literary inquiry and the textual frenzy of Second Temple Judaism, however, the new religions of the first centuries CE produced a new type of religious literature. These speculative, interpretive texts explored ideas about the relationship between the mundane and divine worlds, the nature of human life, and the purpose of human suffering. The gods of the provincial cults were not simply divine potentates demanding rote prayers and well-practiced rituals. Instead, they were benevolent beings who understood human difficulties and desired that we live upright and ethical lives—in some cases (Isis, Mithras, the christianities) in order to attain an otherworldly salvation, but in others (some strains of Judaism, for instance) simply in order to pursue justice and morality for their own sakes. The new texts were not scriptures—that is, they did not have the canonical status of the Jewish and Christian writings; nor did they fill the same sort of liturgical function. Instead, they explored the intellectual ramifications of their central conceits.

Good examples are the "Attis" poem by the 1st-century CE poet Catullus (84–54 BCE), the long essay "On Isis and Osiris" by Plutarch (46–120 CE), and the philosophical verse treatise *On the Nature of Things* by Lucretius (99–55 BCE). Works like these dissociate philosophy from religion, a development that enriched both traditions. Philosophy received a new stimulus, by focusing less on the nature of the universe and more on the human lives within it. In turn, religion became increasingly a thing to think about and not simply to perform. As the ancient Greek thinker Epicurus (341–270 BCE) had famously put it: "Any philosopher's words that do not aim to relieve human suffering are meaningless." The new provincial cults increasingly sought more than universal order and the submission to fate or divine desire. Instead, their followers desired solace, forgiveness, and the promise of a personal contentment. The Greater Western world entered the Common Era with a new attitude of spiritual and intellectual questing—an attitude that would shape the civilization of the next thousand years.

> The Greater Western world entered the Common Era with a new attitude of spiritual and intellectual questing—an attitude that would shape the civilization of the next thousand years.

STOICISM AND NEOPLATONISM

Two philosophical schools offered alternatives to all the pagan and Christian faiths, even while contributing to their intellectual development: Stoicism and Neoplatonism. The first, Stoicism, in fact dated back to Hellenistic times, well into

Marcus Aurelius   Equestrian statue of the great emperor and Stoic philosopher. His reign, which ended in 180 CE, marks the highpoint of the Pax Romana.

the 3rd century BCE, but it received new life from Roman writers like Seneca and Cicero. They saw in it the perfect expression of Roman virtues such as self-discipline, service to community, and calm acceptance of divine law. Another burst of Stoic philosophy—a widespread and influential one, considering its source—came from Marcus Aurelius, who ruled the Roman Empire from 161 to 180 CE. His aphorisms, compiled in a book that he called "Notes to Myself" but is now known as the *Meditations*, appealed to many Imperial Age pagans and early Christians. (It helped that Aurelius wrote his book in Koine Greek, the same dialect used by the New Testament authors, which made his teachings more readily accessible to the adherent of the early christianities.) In line with earlier Stoic tradition, he believed the world is governed by an overarching sense of order and purpose, in service to which human lives play out. The only true happiness results from accepting one's limitations, keeping one's disappointments and frustrations in perspective, and performing one's duties to one's family, society, and the gods.

Aurelius's term for "order and purpose" is the Greek **Logos**, which resonated with anyone familiar with the Gospel of Saint John, where the word had much the same meaning.[10] The Logos, in the Stoic sense, gives not only a sense of the cosmos's purposefulness but also a measure of solace. It addresses the individual seeking both a place in the transient world and a permanent one in the divine world to come:

> The handiwork of the gods is replete with Providence, and the hand of Fate is not detached from nature. Rather, Fate spins and weaves the threads that Providence ordains. Everything flows from the home of the gods; more than that, a sense of needful purpose and well-being pervades the whole creation of which you are a part. Every part of the natural world contains and preserves an element of goodness that is given to it by the very nature of the world as a whole. . . . Take comfort in this thought, and live always by these doctrines. If you wish to face death with something other than mumbling confusion, give up your fascination with study, and let your heart be at rest and express simple gratitude to the gods for what they have done. *(Meditations 2.3)*

---

10   Meaning "word," literally, logos can also be seen in the suffix "-ology" that denotes so many English terms for science—like biology, geology, and meteorology.

Stoicism offered more than a set of rules to follow or a group of ideas to adhere to. Some examples: "No action is good if performing it causes you to violate a trust or behave shamelessly" (3.7). "Do not act as though you will live ten thousand years, for death is the fate that awaits you. Therefore, while you're alive and able, seek the Good" (4.17). "Do not hold life itself to be the only thing of value. Consider the infinite measures of time and space that lie behind you and before you; in the face of these eternities, what difference does it make whether you live for three days or three generations?" (4.50). "If a cucumber is bitter, throw it away; and if your path is full of briars, change direction. That is all you need to do. It is not for you to ask, 'Why do such things exist?'" (8.50). Stoicism cultivated the soul and urged people to perform spiritual exercises through daily reflection, prayer, and contemplation of the fact of mortality. The Stoics called these practices the discipline of **askesis**—meaning "peace of mind"—from which English word *asceticism* derives. Many early Christian leaders saw the compatibility between their religious beliefs and Stoic ethics and used the pagan notions to explain their faith.

The Platonic tradition also kept its appeal with pagans and, increasingly, Christians, in an amalgam known as **Neoplatonism**. A series of Plato's disciples continued teaching at the Academy long after his death in 347 BCE, most of them engaged in collecting, editing, codifying, and commenting Plato's vast writings. A loose network of Platonist schools also spread across the Hellenistic lands, which ensured that Plato's philosophy and his way of doing philosophy would have the most wide-reaching influence in the centuries following his death. Plato taught the existence of an Ideal Universe, from which our muddled and benighted cosmos derives. This harmonized with many of the new provincial cults and provided them with intellectual support. Most of the later Platonists were equally passionate in observing their pagan convictions. In Plato they thus found an intellectualized version of their cults.[11]

Plutarch (46–120 CE), a wealthy Greek who was an enthusiastic supporter of the empire, dedicated his life as a priest of the Oracle of Apollo at Delphi. He also composed a shelf of stylized biographies, moral essays, literary criticism, and Platonic commentaries. His best-known and best-loved work is the series of *Parallel Lives*, in which he pairs eminent statesmen from Greek and Roman history. In these lively, intimate portraits of their respective virtues (or lack thereof), his concern is not with the details of political history but with the moral character of his subjects.[12]

---

[11] Saint Ambrose of Milan (340–397) and Saint Augustine of Hippo (354–430) are among the Church Fathers. Boethius (480–524), the greatest Christian philosopher of the early Middle Ages, is another.

[12] William Shakespeare used North's Plutarch when composing *Julius Caesar, Antony and Cleopatra*, and *Coriolanus*.

As he himself put it, he was interested in "the offhand occasion, word, or anecdote . . . that brings to light men's true tempers more than the story of any of their great battles, even those in which ten thousand men may have died." Nevertheless, Plutarch knew how to tell a good story. His narratives of the disastrous Athenian campaign to Syracuse, of Pompey's defeat at Pharsalus and subsequent death, and of the suicide of emperor Otho, for example, are gripping set pieces. The *Parallel Lives* have been popular ever since Plutarch's own time. Roman society read them avidly, as did most Christian scholars at least until the 4th century. In the Renaissance, Sir Thomas North (1535–1604) produced the first version in English in 1597—although he cribbed it from a French translation since he knew no Greek.

Plutarch's essays, by contrast, which medieval commentators grouped under the catchall title of *Moralia* ("Ethical Matters"), have never been as popular but give an indication of the breadth of his interests. They move from "Consolation to My Wife," written after the death of their infant daughter, to the profound "On the Delay of Divine Justice," which tackles the problem of why evildoers prosper. Yet another, the speculative "On the Face of the Man in the Moon," attempts a cosmology—a system for explaining the origins and structure of the entire universe. In all, the *Moralia* unite a committed Neoplatonic philosophy with a commonsense search for the alleviation of suffering. Pagan religion received a jolt of intellectual rigor in the works of writers like Plutarch, which helps to account for its continued vitality even after Rome reached the peak of its power.

Many early Christians felt the attraction of that rigor as well. Saint Augustine of Hippo embraced Neoplatonic tenets in his attempt to explain the existence of evil in a universe created by a good and loving God. (The explanation: evil is a void, not a presence; it comprises simply an absence of good.) Another leading writer, the Alexandrian theologian and Biblical exegete Origen (185–254), used the Neoplatonic notion of *emanation*—the idea that the created world results from the outward-flowing essence of life from the eternal center of the Logos. In this way he explained the migration of souls from the Heavenly Divine and out into the created world. Origen supplemented this notion with the idea of spiritual return, a kind of undertow of purified souls flowing back toward the creating center. This idea did not originate with him; his younger contemporary Neoplatonic philosopher Plotinus (204–270; a pagan) had been elaborating the concepts of spiritual resurrection and return, as handed on to him by his own teachers, for years. But Origen was the first Christian thinker of note to explicate salvation in intellectual terms derived from a philosophical tradition.

Also Neoplatonic, but ultimately unorthodox from the Christian perspective, was Origen's denial of bodily resurrection. Origen is a unique figure in Christian history: he is regarded as one of the great church fathers, the first Christian philosopher of any note, yet most of his published ideas were formally condemned by later councils. He left behind an enormous body of writing; Saint Jerome credited him with nearly two thousand separate works. That is clearly an exaggeration, but nevertheless, the enormity of his production is one reason why there has never been a satisfying biography made of him.

A later writer (ca. 500), known as Pseudo-Dionysius the Areopagite, went even further. He distinguished between the return of all living creatures to their source (a pagan notion) and a uniquely Christianized version of the idea, in which souls were not subsumed into the Divine Identity but instead had the Likeness of God restored to them by divine grace. This may seem too subtle a distinction, but Pseudo-Dionysius deemed it necessary in order to avoid pantheism. His identity remains a mystery. Until the 12th century his works were believed to have been written by Dionysius the Areopagite—the Christian convert mentioned in Acts 13.17 and whom popular tradition long conflated with Saint Denis, the patron saint of France (d. 250). In the 12th century the scholar Peter Abelard proved the impossibility of Dionysius being the author, a discovery for which he was nearly killed by angry monks. Hence the awkward attribution to "Pseudo-Dionysius." Revered throughout the Christian world, Pseudo-Dionysius is a saint in the Orthodox Churches; his idea of theosis (the taking on of the Likeness of God by the saved soul) is a central aspect of the Orthodox theology of salvation.

Aspects of Neoplatonism can be found in many other early theologians, including Saint Jerome (ca. 347–420 CE), who produced the definitive Latin version of the Bible—called the Vulgate—for western Christianity. Still another, John Scotus Eriugena (815–877), was a 9th-century Irish scholar prominent in the court of Charles the Bald (r. 843–877) in France and of Alfred the Great (r. 871–899) in England.[13]

> Like the pagan cults, early Christianity received high-octane intellectual fuel injections from Stoicism and Neoplatonism. Both enriched it enormously by adding to its intrinsic emotional appeal a degree of sophistication that it had previously lacked.

Eriugena was the most brilliant scholar of his age. Most his works, being so heavily influenced by Neoplatonism, were later condemned by the church. One pope (Honorius III, r. 1216–1227) even described them as "crawling with worms of heretical perversion." Among those perversions was Eriugena's claim that hell does not exist as a place but only as a condition, and that its punishments were purifying rather than punitive.

Like the pagan cults, early Christianity received high-octane intellectual fuel injections from Stoicism and Neoplatonism. Both enriched it enormously by adding to its intrinsic emotional appeal a degree of sophistication that it had previously lacked. For the next fifteen hundred years Christian philosophers, scientists, mathematicians, and logicians were among the leading scholars in Western civilization

---

[13]   Eriugena was known to be a quick wit. When Charles the Bald, goading him, asked what was the difference between a drunkard and an Irishman, Eriugena replied, "Only a table."

and usually made up the majority of them. This was not necessarily because of the cultural hegemony of the Latin and Greek churches, but simply because the Christian faith itself invited, prompted, and demanded intense intellectual effort. It inspired the fascination of what is difficult, and required its followers to acknowledge complex ideas about the nature of world, human freedom, the meaning of suffering, and the purpose of existence.

Most notably, these early centuries of the Common Era introduced an emphasis on self-awareness, self-examination, and self-criticism. They urged the development of personal conscience and the constant striving for meaning and improvement, ideas that would mark Western culture indelibly. Such concerns had existed before, of course, but never with the same degree of emotional urgency and intellectual resolve. Western culture became marked by a kind of intellectual and spiritual restlessness, convinced that life has genuine meaning and purpose but never quite certain that it had discovered them. All the same, it was confident that the effort to find them was necessary and ennobling.

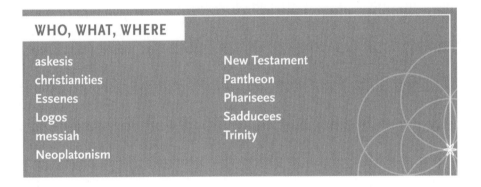

WHO, WHAT, WHERE

askesis
christianities
Essenes
Logos
messiah
Neoplatonism

New Testament
Pantheon
Pharisees
Sadducees
Trinity

SUGGESTED READINGS

Primary Sources
Eusebius of Caesarea. *The History of the Church.*
Josephus. *The Antiquities of the Jews.*
———. *The Jewish War.*
Marcus Aurelius. *Meditations.*
Philo of Alexandria.

The Dead Sea Scrolls.
The Gnostic Gospels.
The Nag Hammadi Library.
The New Jerusalem Bible.

Anthologies
Elliott, Neil, and Mark Reasoner, eds. *Documents and Images for the Study of Paul* (2010).
Ehrman, Bart D. *The New Testament and Other Early Christian Writings: A Reader* (2003).

Warrior, Valerie M. *Roman Religion: A Sourcebook* (2001).

Studies

Brakke, David. *The Gnostics: Myth, Ritual, and Diversity in Early Christianity* (2011).

Brennan, Tad. *The Stoic Life: Emotions, Duties, and Fate* (2005).

Brown, Peter. *The Body and Society: Men, Women, and Sexual Renunciation in Early Christianity* (2008).

———. *The Rise of Western Christendom: Triumph and Diversity, AD 200–1000* (2003).

Denzey, Nicola. *The Bone Gatherers: The Lost Worlds of Early Christian Women* (2008).

Ehrman, Bart D. *Lost Christianities: The Battles for Scripture and the Faiths We Never Knew* (2005).

Engberg-Pedersen, Troels. *Cosmology and the Self in the Apostle Paul: The Material Self* (2011).

Ferguson, Everett. *Backgrounds of Early Christianity* (2003).

Fredriksen, Paula. *Augustine and the Jews: A Christian Defense of Jews and Judaism* (2008).

———. *From Jesus to Christ: The Origins of the New Testament Images of Jesus* (2000).

———. *Jesus of Nazareth, King of the Jews: A Jewish Life and the Emergence of Christianity* (2000).

González, Justo L. *The Story of Christianity.* Vol. 1, *The Early Church to the Dawn of the Reformation* (2010).

Jacobs, Irving. *The Midrashic Process: Tradition and Interpretation in Rabbinic Judaism* (2008).

Johnson, Luke Timothy. *Among the Gentiles: Greco-Roman Religion and Christianity* (2010).

———. *The Writings of the New Testament: An Interpretation* (2010).

Lampe, Peter. *From Paul to Valentinus: Christians at Rome in the First Two Centuries* (2003).

Lieu, Judith M. *Christian Identity in the Jewish and Graeco-Roman World* (2004).

Luijendijk, AnneMarie. *Greetings in the Lord: Early Christians and the Oxyrhynchus Papyri* (2009).

MacMullen, Ramsay. *Romanization in the Time of Augustus* (2008).

Meier, John P. *The Vision of Matthew: Christ, Church, and Morality in the First Gospel* (2004).

Rasimus, Tuomas, Troels Engberg-Pedersen, and Ismo Dunderberg, eds. *Stoicism in Early Christianity* (2010).

Stark, Rodney. *Cities of God: The Real Story of How Christianity Became an Urban Movement and Conquered Rome* (2007).

Wilken, Robert Louis. *The Christians as the Romans Saw Them* (2003).

———. *The Spirit of Early Christian Thought: Seeking the Face of God* (2005).

For additional resources, including maps, primary sources, visuals, web links, and quizzes, please go to **www.oup.com/us/backman**.

CHAPTER 8

The Early Middle Ages

306–750 CE

THE EARLY MIDDLE AGES

T he Greater Western world underwent a series of shocks from
the 4th to the 8th centuries that gave a radically new direction to its development. Roman might had peaked in the late 2nd
century, after which imperial control entered a holding pattern
while internal squabbles dominated the political scene. Those
squabbles centered on a constitutional problem: the empire had
never established an orderly process for succession to the throne,
which meant that the death of each emperor triggered some sort
of contest for power. It led to a period of Roman decline, but also to the rise of a
"new Rome" in the east—in Byzantium. Christianity, too, met a new development in a new revelation, the rise of Islam. And Christianity, in turn, changed in
character, turning inward amid a Europe of warring rulers and scholar monks.

These four centuries are known as the **Dark Ages** in western Europe and as
the Age of Ignorance (*al-Jahiliyyah*, in Arabic—also translatable as the "Age of
Barbarism") in the Islamic world; for the Greek-
speaking lands of the eastern Mediterranean,
however, this was a heroic age when the achievements of the ancient world were fortified by the
rapid development of Christianity. From their
magnificent new capital city of Constantinople
on the Bosporus—the strait separating the Black

◀ **Crown of King Recesvinth**
The Visigoths were justly
famous for their metalwork, and
this crown (worn only in formal
ceremonies) is one of their
best-known pieces. It is made
of gold encrusted with
rock crystals, pearls, and
sapphires.

• The Imperial Crisis
• Imperial Decline: Rome's Overreach
• Martyrdom and Empire
• A Christian Emperor and
    a Christian Church
• The Rise of "New Rome"
• A Splendid, Beleaguered Capital
• "The Age of Ignorance"
• The Islamic Revelation
• From Preacher to Conqueror

• Compulsion or Conversion?
• Sunnis and Shi'a
• Classical Traditions and
    Western Expansion
• Barbarian Kings and Scholar-Monks
• Divided Estates and Kingdoms
• The Body as Money and
    Women as Property
• Christian Paganism
• Pockets of Intellectual Life

**CHAPTER
OUTLINE**

Commodus as Hercules
The emperor Commodus (r. 180–192) loved to portray himself as a manly man, and, rather like Vladimir Putin today, he regularly staged rigged athletic contests in which he always emerged victorious. Here he has had himself sculpted as Hercules.

Sea and the Mediterranean—the people of this new Byzantine Empire achieved a level of wealth, power, and cultural glory that were never seen again. They also witnessed the spread of a great new religion in Islam.

THE IMPERIAL CRISIS

Trouble emerged for the first time, in a major way, with the death of Marcus Aurelius in 180. Aurelius had designated his son Commodus (r. 180–192) to succeed him, but Commodus was a poor ruler, a snarky, ill-mannered lout who threw tantrums when he did not get his way. He thought of himself as a great athlete, dressed in lion skins, carried a club, and wanted everyone to call him Hercules. And in fact his petulance led more than once to his ordering the execution of senators and officials who had opposed his wishes. The political atmosphere grew rancid in a way it had not been in a hundred years. Commodus's death set off a civil war between a host of civil and military officials, and this became the unfortunate pattern for nearly every imperial succession throughout the 3rd century. The army accordingly grew in prominence as the sole bulwark against social decay, which meant that power passed almost exclusively to a series of generals; but since each successive general's claim to legitimacy came only from having seized power by brute force, ambitious rivals in the military in turn killed each one. In the sixty-seven years from 218 to 285 there were as many as eighty-three claimants to the throne—only a handful of whom died of natural causes.

CHAPTER TIMELINE

284–305 CE
Reign of Roman emperor Diocletian

313 CE
Edict of Milan

330 CE
Founding of Constantinople

480–547 CE
Life of Benedict of Nursia

312 CE
Battle of the Milvian Bridge

323–325 CE
Council of Nicea

391 CE
Christianity becomes official religion of Roman Empire

Nonstop war undermined the economy by disrupting farming and commerce, and the warmongering generals made matters worse by intermittently devaluing the currency so they would have more coinage on hand with which to pay their troops. But this triggered runaway inflation and drove hordes of laborers into the cities in search of employment or alms, causing the urban centers to become choked with homeless and desperately poor people. The smallpox virus then did the rest. By the end of the 3rd century the empire was reeling from disaster to disaster, the army was divided, decimated, and demoralized, and the economy sputtered and wheezed like a dying engine.

> By the end of the 3rd century the empire was reeling from disaster to disaster, the army was divided, decimated, and demoralized, and the economy sputtered and wheezed like a dying engine.

IMPERIAL DECLINE: ROME'S OVERREACH

By cruel coincidence, this was when the imperial borders suddenly faced their most severe challenge with the inrush of the Germanic peoples along the Rhine-Danube frontier and the renewed attack of the Persian Empire, which was then under the Sassanid dynasty, in the east. The earliest Germans to arrive in large numbers, the Ostrogoths and Visigoths, were bribed with money and promises of assistance. They were asked only to spare the cities of the eastern Mediterranean and move instead into the underpopulated rural west, but the Persians could not be so easily disposed of. The lure of controlling the Holy Land and the Hellespont—the linchpins between the European and Asian economies—proved too great, causing the Persians to determine on outright conquest.

The Romans fought back valiantly but with little luck. The low point for them came in 260, when the Persians captured the emperor Valerian (r. 253–260) in battle. They held him as a slave, forcing him to kneel on all fours as a stepping stool for the Sassanid ruler when he mounted his horse. The mad succession

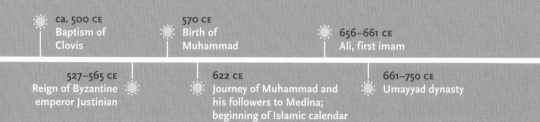

ca. 500 CE
Baptism of Clovis

570 CE
Birth of Muhammad

656–661 CE
Ali, first imam

527–565 CE
Reign of Byzantine emperor Justinian

622 CE
Journey of Muhammad and his followers to Medina; beginning of Islamic calendar

661–750 CE
Umayyad dynasty

of emperors continued unchecked, the western provinces of the empire became overrun with invading Germanic groups, and effective government from the center all but disappeared.

A respite appeared with the long reign of a stern, no-nonsense emperor named Diocletian (r. 284–305). He came from a long line of Dalmatian peasant farmers, had received only an elementary education but was raised with a deep belief in the rightness of the empire, and had sought a career in the army. A talented soldier, he rose quickly through the ranks and was popular with the soldiers he commanded. When the briefly serving emperors Carus (r. 282–283) and Numerianus (r. 283–284) died—according to several ancient sources, Carus being struck by lightning and Numerianus of a mysterious eye inflammation—the army overwhelmingly threw its support behind Diocletian, who faced enormous problems. They included a wrecked economy, a restive army, Germanic and Persian invasions, and a bloated, inefficient administration. His solutions were as blunt as his personality.

Persian Ascendancy   This is the most famous of the Sassanid rock reliefs, not only because of its workmanship but because of the scene it portrays: the great victory of Shapur I (r. 241–272) over the Roman emperors Valerian and Philip the Arab. Valerian was captured, executed, then stuffed and mounted on the wall at Shapur's palace.

The worthless currency that had triggered the inflation could hardly be helped: Europe's known gold and silver mines were largely tapped out by Diocletian's time, and without an influx of precious metals the fiscal crisis would continue. Diocletian addressed the problem by essentially withdrawing Rome's currency from circulation and returning the empire to a barter economy. Taxes were collected in kind (clothing, food, tools, manufactured goods, or whatever), and imperial soldiers were paid in the same. The debased coinage—once recaptured, melted, and recast—eventually regained some of its value in Mediterranean trade, but a true money economy would not return to continental Europe until the 10th century. He similarly recast the imperial army into separate civil and military divisions, with one force of "border troops" manning the Rhine-Danube frontier. This long line of fortified stations, together with a separate force of "palace troops," served as a roving field army that was under direct imperial command. Diocletian's border troops were essentially a form of civil militia made up of deputized residents, both Roman and German, of the frontier areas.

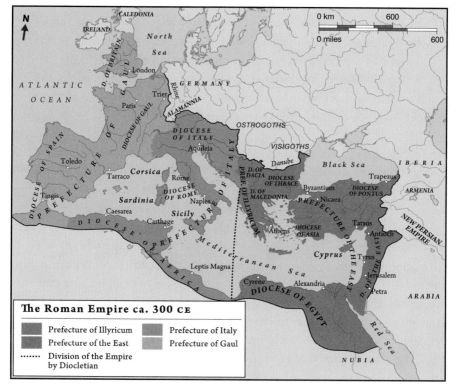

MAP 8.1   **The Roman Empire, ca. 300 CE**

The palace troops, the more professional fighting force, who were paid with real cash, were thus freed to concentrate on the struggle against the Persians to the east, with good results.

Last, Diocletian chose not to streamline the administration, but to cut it into separate units, instituting the **Tetrarchy**—a new system whereby the empire was formally divided into two halves, east and west, with a separate emperor (*augustus* in Latin) for each (see Map 8.1). Moreover, each augustus was assisted by a **caesar**, or junior emperor, who succeeded to the position of his augustus upon that person's death or retirement and who then appointed a new caesar to assist him. At a stroke, Diocletian eased the bureaucratic burden on the central administration and resolved the constitutional crisis by providing a regular means for the selection of new augusti.

MARTYRDOM AND EMPIRE

Diocletian is best remembered for instituting the longest and most vicious of the state attacks upon Christians.

> In the nineteenth year of Diocletian's reign…in the month of April…near the time when Christians celebrate the Passion of the Savior…[imperial decrees] were promulgated that demanded the flattening of all Christian churches, the burning of all Christian books, the humiliation of all Christian leaders, and the imprisonment of all servants of Christ who refused to denounce their faith,

wrote Eusebius of Caesarea (263–339), the most reliable chronicler of the Great Persecution, at the outset of his *History of the Church*. He then went on to describe, chapter by bloody chapter, the beating, flaying, decapitation, drowning, burning, rape, and mauling by animals of thousands of Christian martyrs.

Diocletian was less interested in wiping out the Christians than he was in persuading them to participate in civic celebrations of the imperial cult. After all, his own wife and daughter were reported to have been Christians. What mattered instead was the unraveling of social cohesion across the empire. For centuries Rome had been held together by a carefully cultivated public spirit, a sense of Romanness, and the commitment to an ideal greater than parochial ethnic or religious concerns. Diocletian promoted the cult of emperor worship as a unifying force, a living symbol of everyone's participation in a world larger than themselves. The Christians' refusal to endorse the official cult, or even to give it empty lip service, seemed to strike at the very heart of the empire, and he therefore concluded that they had to be crushed into submission.

But that is not what happened, at least not with the majority of them. Many of the thousands whom Diocletian sent to their death accepted their fate with quiet resolve and even, if we can trust our sources, with some measure of happiness. Martyrdom, they felt, was a prize to be embraced. Reunion after death with the Christ whom they had served in secret all their lives seemed too great a blessing to merit dreading the temporary unpleasantness that preceded it. Crowds eager for blood and tears certainly saw all the blood they could possibly want but, instead of tears and wailing, too often had to put up with hymns, prayers, and laughter.

Medallion of Saint Mamai   Saint Mamai, an early martyr popular with the Georgian people in the Caucasus, was thrown to the lions by the Romans in 275 CE. This 11th-century medallion depicts Mamai fearlessly astride a lion while brandishing a cross, symbolizing the victory over death won by Mamai and by all believers in Christ.

Martyrologies—the narrative records of martyrs' sufferings—can seldom be taken literally. Their whole purpose is to glorify God by testifying to both the unimaginable sufferings endured by his saints and the stoic calm and joyful spirit expressed by those saints even when caught in the lion's maw or pierced by the executioner's blade. The more gore, the better, and the more superhuman the acceptance of brutal death, the better still. Few writers could resist the implicit invitation to exercise their imaginative and descriptive powers, and fewer still even attempted to resist. Hence, when a Christian writer like Lactantius (240–320) penned his vivid chronicle *On the Deaths of Those Persecuted for Christ*, he found it easy to identify plenty of victims of Roman cruelty; the challenge lay in maintaining the fever pitch of his descriptions of the horrors they suffered. As with the history of Eusebius of Caesarea, after thirty pages of Lactantius's nonstop beheadings, eviscerations, poisonings, burnings, beatings, and beast manglings, one can sense the writer's rhetorical exhaustion—and there are still three hundred pages to go.

Nevertheless, even allowing for exaggeration in the sources, enough Christians accepted their martyrdom with such grace that the Romans who witnessed it were astonished and befuddled. What was it about this religion that could enable someone to accept death happily, even eagerly? Was this something to envy or was it simply insane? It is unclear how many Romans, if any, were sufficiently moved by the martyrs' behavior to convert to the faith. Yet it is certain that the Great Persecution got more people thinking about Christianity, and perhaps talking about it, than had been before. If Diocletian had intended to annihilate the faith, his plan backfired.

It is unclear how many Romans, if any, were sufficiently moved by the martyrs' behavior to convert to the faith. Yet it is certain that the Great Persecution got more people thinking about Christianity, and perhaps talking about it, than had been before. If Diocletian had intended to annihilate the faith, his plan backfired.

A CHRISTIAN EMPEROR AND A CHRISTIAN CHURCH

In 305, having done all that he could to save the empire, an exhausted Diocletian resigned from the imperial office (the only person to do so in Roman history) and returned to his homeland farm, dedicating his last years to his private passion: growing cabbages. His mechanism for the orderly transfer of power failed in its first attempt, however, and another civil war quickly engulfed the empire. When the smoke finally cleared a new emperor sat in the throne: Constantine the Great (r. 306–337), whose eventful reign changed everything—for he was the first Roman emperor to be a Christian.

According to the source most contemporary with the event, Constantine's conversion had occurred on the eve of the battle that would decide the civil war. A rival named Maxentius had also claimed the imperial title in 306; attempts to negotiate a power-sharing arrangement continually failed, and in 312 the two sides broke into open warfare. The conclusive battle took place a few miles north of Rome, at the Milvian Bridge. Reportedly, a heavenly voice spoke to Constantine in a dream and told him to embrace Christianity and to paint the cross on his soldiers' shields before the next day's battle. He did so, won the battle, became sole emperor, and committed himself to Christianity on the spot. The story seems too contrived to be true. It suggests, none too subtly, that the religion itself caused the military victory, even though the soldiers can hardly have been believers. From this point on, it implies, imperial success could only come so long as the empire served the Christian God.

However the conversion occurred, it did in fact occur. Constantine's conversion must have been sincere since there was no conceivable political advantage to gain from it. Christians, by the year 312, made up no more than 2 or 3 percent of the Roman population and may have constituted as little as 1 percent. Even if one considers only the urban population of the eastern half of the empire—that is, the geographic area and demographic group with the highest proportion of Christians—the new faith made up no more than 10 percent of the populace.

The impact of his conversion was immediate and dramatic. In 313 he issued the **Edict of Milan**, which legalized Christianity and guaranteed religious freedom for all faiths within the empire:

> It pleases us to remove altogether the legal restraints issued heretofore regarding the Christians, any one of whom may henceforth practice the Christian faith, if he wishes, freely, openly, without molestation . . . and in free and unrestricted liberty of religious worship. . . . And moreover, in order to promote peace in our time, we grant to all religions [within the Empire] the right of free and open observance of their faith.

Constantine did more than legalize Christianity, though; he opened the imperial coffers in support of it. He ordered that public funds be made available to compensate individuals whose property and cash deposits had been confiscated for religious reasons. He poured money into building churches, training priests,

Dear Prudence   Mosaic of Christ in his heavenly throne, surrounded by his apostles and Saints Prudence and Praxedis. From the 4th century on, the Good Shepherd iconography of Christ gave way to images of Jesus as the mighty king of heaven or the stern judge of the Last Day. The kinder, gentler Jesus did not become the norm again until the 12th century.

promoting evangelical missions, copying sacred writings, and setting up Christian charitable houses. He granted Christians special tax privileges and showed personal preference for selecting Christians to serve in government offices. Not surprisingly, Christianity began to spread among the people of the east at a rate never before experienced.

Paganism remained legal for several more decades but the momentum was now decidedly in Christianity's direction. The years of struggle and persecution were over. By the end of the 4th century the majority of the eastern Roman population had embraced the new faith, and it became the official religion of the Roman Empire in 391, thanks to the emperor Theodosius I (r. 379–395).

Freed from persecution and permitted at last to practice their faith openly, Christians now poured into the town squares to preach—and this is when the long-simmering problems of the "christianities" came into focus. To his horror, Constantine found that no two Christian groups believed the same things, embraced the same values, worshipped in the same way, read the same canon, or recognized the same authority. Most accepted Jesus of Nazareth as the biblical messiah and Son of God, but many did not. Most believed that he had died on the Cross and rose from the dead, but many did not. Most believed that he was physically present in the consecrated bread and wine of the Eucharist, but many did not. Most believed that he was in some way coeternal with God the Father and the Holy Spirit, but many did not. Constantine recognized that the christianities risked continued fracturing and internal fighting unless something was done. Accordingly, he summoned an ecumenical council to meet at the eastern city of Nicaea, ordering the leaders of every Christian community in the empire to come. With one notable exception, the bishops all came. The council lasted for two years (323–325), passed dozens of resolutions, and symbolically capped their activity by issuing the **Nicene Creed**, which has stood ever since as the universal standard, the statement *par excellence* of fundamental Christian belief.

Constantine regarded the newly standardized Christian Church as his own dominion. He had tradition behind him: in pagan Rome the emperor had held the title of **pontifex maximus** ("chief priest"), which made him the leader of the entire cult. The empire did not distinguish between political authority and religious authority, and Constantine saw no reason to alter the arrangement simply because the religion itself had changed. Taking the formal title of "thirteenth apostle," Constantine insisted that the emperor, so long as he himself was a Christian, was by that fact alone the supreme authority over the Christian church.

This brought him into conflict with the pope, Sylvester I (r. 314–335)—the one and only bishop who refused to attend the Council of Nicaea, since doing so would have implied a recognition of the emperor's authority over the church. (The pope did send a representative, though, to keep an eye on things.) Papal claims to power rested on Saint Peter. Since he had undeniably been the leader of the original group of Apostles, and since he had ended his days as the bishop of the Christian community of Rome, his successors as bishop of Rome therefore inherited the leadership of the church. The problem for those successors was that few Christians outside of Rome accepted their logic. Peter's original authority was beyond question, but after Peter's death (in 64 CE) the leadership of the community of bishops was an open question. Why should the bishop of Jerusalem not take precedence? Or the bishop of Antioch (the first city outside of Jerusalem to have a formally organized community)? Why should leadership not be left to a free election among all bishops? As it happened, most of the popes for the first thousand years of Christian history had little authority outside of their own city of Rome. Many were respected and even granted special honors, but few were obeyed. Starting with Constantine, the holders of the imperial title assumed their own supremacy over the church and exercised it.[1]

THE RISE OF "NEW ROME"

Constantine arrived at one additional epoch-making decision: in 324, in the midst of preparations for the Council of Nicaea, he decided to abandon Italy and build a new capital city in the east. He chose the site known to the ancient Greeks as *Byzantion* (in Latin, *Byzantium*), on the promontory between the Sea of Marmara and the Black Sea. This was where Europe and Asia met, the nexus of east-west trade, and the strategic node for overseeing the administration of the eastern empire. By the 4th century it seemed clear that the western half of the Roman Empire was in severe decline. And while most hoped for its survival, Constantine and his successors recognized that the eastern half of the empire was the more important half, being the virtual cradle of Western civilization. It was an urban, commercial, literate, and sophisticated world, newly given an additional sense of unity and purpose by

> Constantine and his successors recognized that the eastern half of the empire was the most important half, being the virtual cradle of Western civilization. It was an urban, commercial, literate, and sophisticated world, newly given an additional sense of unity and purpose by its now-rapid assumption of a Christian character.

---

[1] Pope Sylvester did the best he could, under the circumstances. He approved the legislation of the Council of Nicaea, including the Creed, and simply reissued it under his own name.

its now-rapid assumption of a Christian character. The western half of the empire, in contrast, was weaker, poorer, ruder, agrarian, and expendable.

From the new capital built on the site of Byzantium, now renamed Constantinople, the rulers of the **Byzantine Empire** kept their eyes trained eastward, vaguely acknowledging their links to the backward west but putting little effort into propping up the crumbling administration there. The Byzantines regarded their eastern empire as a "new Rome" purged of its pagan past and explicitly dedicated to creating a Christian realm. The new capital was formally dedicated on May 11, 330.

The Byzantine Empire of the 4th and 5th centuries wrapped around the eastern edges of the Mediterranean like a giant reversed letter C. It included all of today's countries of Libya, Egypt, Israel, Jordan, Lebanon, Syria, Turkey, and most of the Balkan states (see Map 8.2). Hundreds of ethnic groups resided within this zone, chiefly in the cities or within a day's journey of them. Since travel and communication were so easy, thanks to the long-familiar sea-lanes and coastal roads, the government in Constantinople was able to retain centralized rule. The heart of the empire was the great Asia Minor landmass, the center of grain production. Within a few generations, Byzantine society sloughed off its use of Latin and reverted to the Greek that had been the norm there until the arrival of the Romans.

The territory of Greece itself held a sentimental place in Byzantine hearts but was a relatively minor province in terms of economic and cultural life. The real nodes of energy apart from Constantinople itself were the coastal

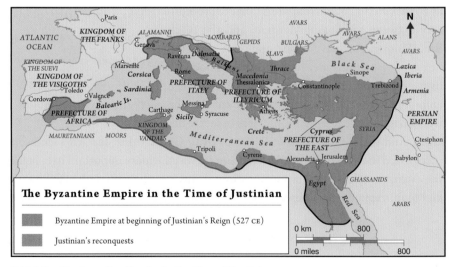

MAP 8.2   **The Byzantine Empire in the Time of Justinian**

cities—Thessalonika, Ephesus, Antioch, Caesarea, Tripoli, and Alexandria—and a handful of inland cities like Jerusalem, Damascus, and Chalcedon. Manufacturing, trade, shipping, and finance were their lifeblood, but they also maintained hundreds of schools, academies, libraries, salons, and theaters that kept alive the classical traditions of literature, philosophy, and to a lesser degree science. In addition, the 4th and 5th centuries saw a frenzy of church building as Christianity at last sank its roots deeply into the culture.

The Byzantines did not give up entirely on the west, but their readoption of the Greek language represented a practical, not merely a symbolic, turning away from the Latin-speaking west. Trade between east and west declined precipitously, since the west produced little that the east needed, apart from slaves. The western empire continued to hobble along with its own augustus (who was decidedly subordinate to the augustus in Constantinople). But in 476 a German general named Odoacer put an end to the sham: he deposed the weakling ruler and declared the western empire dead.

The Byzantine emperors occasionally showed some interest in influencing western matters by forming ties with several of the Germanic warlords who thenceforth dominated Europe. Justinian I (r. 527–565) actually reconquered much of southern Italy and the central part of the North African coast, in a quixotic effort to reconstitute the old empire. His efforts failed in the end, though, since the economic gains from the conquests never came close to offsetting the expense of the military effort. He scored more lasting achievements with his vast construction projects within the city of Constantinople, including his completion of the magnificent Church of Hagia Sophia, and his compilation of the *Corpus iuris civilis* ("Corpus of Civil Law"). The *Corpus* formed the basis of all jurisprudence in Byzantium until the 15th century and provided a model for the development of the canon law of the Catholic Church.

A SPLENDID, BELEAGUERED CAPITAL

The stalling out of Justinian's military efforts turned into actual losses of territory by his immediate successors. Under emperors Maurice (r. 582–602) and Phocas (r. 602–610) Byzantium lost Egypt, Palestine, Syria, and parts of Asia Minor itself to the Persians, who made another of their periodic efforts to control the western reaches of the Fertile Crescent. These were hard-fought campaigns that nearly brought Byzantium to its knees. Heraclius (r. 610–641) spent his entire reign in a life-or-death struggle to put the empire back on solid footing. But so much territory had been lost that he lacked the funds to pay his soldiers, a weakness that also allowed groups of Avars, Bulgars, and Slavs to encroach on imperial lands in the Balkan region.

Heraclius reorganized the army into a new system of **themes** (Greek *thema*, meaning "regiment" or "division"), which apportioned the lands of the empire to the military officers and gave them civil and economic jurisdiction over them. The commanders then subdivided their zones into individual landholdings for each soldier serving under them. In this way, Heraclius stripped away the bloated, centralized imperial administration and replaced it with the army itself—which now, instead of receiving salaries from Constantinople, derived its own revenue from its landholdings and the fees it collected in return for its civic functions. It was a radical move, but one that dramatically improved military morale and effectiveness, since the soldiers henceforth had reliable sources of income and a personal stake in defending the empire from further attack.

Thus restructured, the Byzantine world achieved high degrees of prosperity and stability. Constantinople acted as the economic hub of the empire: all commerce passed through it. The city fiercely guarded its monopolies on coinage, interest rates, weights and measures, and manufacturing standards, through which it exercised direct control of trade. In Justinian's time the Byzantines had learned how to cultivate silkworms and to spin the silk they produced, which allowed them to begin their own manufacturing of high-value silk cloth. The loss of market share felt by the silk traders from the Near East helped trigger a wave of wars against the Byzantines throughout the 7th and 8th centuries.

The splendor of the city was extraordinary, with hundreds of churches, fine palaces, theaters, baths, and bazaars (see Map 8.3). Most of the empire's cities suffered from Constantinople's dominance, since the capital drained commercial life from the provinces. Provincial cities continued, of course, but they became more political and religious administrative centers than sites of industry and trade. This change had important social and cultural consequences for the old class of urban elites. The descendants of the Roman curiales, they had previously formed the backbone of intellectual and cultural life, but they gradually disappeared from the 7th century on. Those curiales had been chiefly responsible for cultivating and preserving classical learning, everything from Homeric epics to Athenian stage tragedies and the works of the great philosophers. But the narrowing provincial character of the cities resulted in a narrowing of urban education as well. Primary schooling remained available in most cities, but beyond this level the only education consistently available was religious—devotional writings, hagiographies (or lives of the saints), ecclesiastical chronicles, and the like. In other words, what the provinces gained in piety they lost in general intellectual sophistication. High culture throve only in the capital.

The Persians unleashed a new campaign into the Holy Land in 612 and two years later took Jerusalem. A rebellion against the Persians by the city's Christian inhabitants led to a brutal crackdown. For three days the Persian

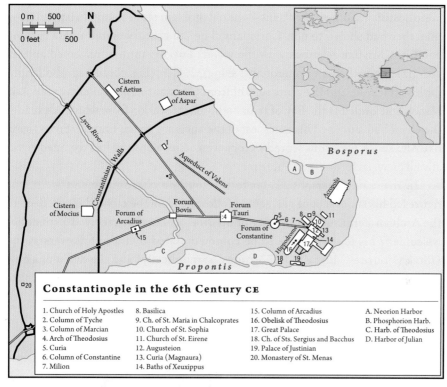

MAP 8.3   **Constantinople in the 6th Century** CE

soldiers smashed Christian shops, homes, and churches until hardly a single Christian building was left standing by 614. A late Byzantine chronicler named Theophanes described it:

> In this year, the Persians conquered all of Jordan and Palestine, in-cluding the Holy City, and with the help of the Jews they killed a multi-tude of Christians—some say as many as ninety thousand of them. The Jews [from the countryside], for their part, purchased many of the sur-viving Christians, whom the Persians were leading away as slaves, and put them to death too. The Persians moreover captured and led away not only the Patriarch of Jerusalem, Zechariah, and many prisoners, but also the most precious and life-giving Cross.

Theophanes' account is not entirely reliable in its specifics, but it seems clear that a bloodbath occurred, and it was a harbinger of things to come. From the 7th century onward, a new tone of open hostility toward non-Christians entered much Christian writing, and military conflicts in the east took on qualities of religious revenge seeking. Up to this time, Christians generally had shown much more hostility to other Christians—the old problem of the many christianities—than they had shown to non-Christians. The 7th century marks a dark turning point in Christian relations with the world. The Byzantines, reformed and re-energized, launched a counteroffensive in 622. Heraclius chose a symbolic spot for his attack: he and the army set sail from Constantinople, sailed around Asia Minor, and landed at the Bay of Issus—the exact location from which Alexander the Great had launched his conquest of the ancient Persian Empire. From there, like Alexander, Heraclius scored victory after victory until he had regained virtually all of Syria, Jordan, and Palestine.

In that same year of 622, far to the south, a charismatic and ambitious figure led his small sect of persecuted followers from the city of Mecca, deep in the Arabian Peninsula, to the city of Medina, where they received a friendlier welcome. This journey came to be commemorated by those followers as the *Hijrah* ("journey," literally, but "exodus" symbolically) and the dawn of a new age. They carried with them a sense of divine mission—to bring their new faith, Islam, to all the Arab peoples. Their leader was Muhammad, the Prophet of Allah (570–632).

Hagia Sophia   Three views of the Hagia Sophia, constructed during the reign of Justinian (527–541) in Constantinople: external view (the minarets were added under the Ottomans, who converted the church into a mosque); two internal views that give a sense of the massive interior and its brilliant play with sunlight.

"THE AGE OF IGNORANCE"

The Arabs had inhabited the peninsula that bears their name for many centuries. It is a forbidding place, roughly one million square miles (2.6 million square kilometers), consisting of an arid central plateau that slopes from west to east and is surrounded by several deserts. Most notable are the rocky Nefud (or Syrian) Desert in the north and the Great Arabian Desert (Arabic *Rub' al-Khali*, or "Empty Quarter"), which alone makes up a quarter of the entire peninsula.[2] Two mountain ranges exist, one running parallel to the Red Sea coast on the southwest and the other stretching along the peninsula's southeastern coast, the site of today's country of Oman. Some water is available: several stretches of marshland dot the Red Sea coastline, and large aquifers run beneath much of the peninsula, but usually at depths too great to reach. Where the levels of sand and rock are not too extreme, some natural oases and wadis—seasonal riverbeds—occur, and it is possible to dig wells (see Map 8.4).

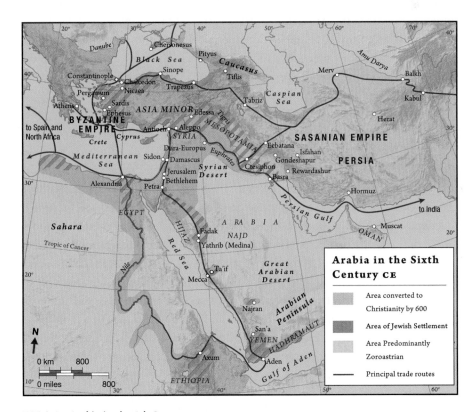

MAP 8.4   Arabia in the 6th Century CE

---

[2]   The sands of the Great Arabian Desert reach depths, in spots, of more than one thousand feet (three hundred meters). Daytime temperatures, moreover, can reach 130°F (55°C) in the summer.

But the essential geographical fact of premodern Arabia is that only 1 percent of the land could support agriculture and permanent human settlement. Division of the Arab peoples is thus a natural consequence of geography. The highland plateau accommodates grazing of sheep and goats and is the traditional home of the nomadic Bedouin tribes; the fertile southwestern coastal zone is the abode of the Yemeni Arabs. Between those extremes, pre-Islamic tradition claimed that most of the peninsula's people are descended from two legendary ancestors: Qahtan and Adnan. Qahtan, according to the tradition, was the progenitor of the "pure Arab" people (al-Arab al-aribah) in the southern part of the peninsula, while Adnan fathered the "Arabized Arabs" (al-Arab al-musta'ribah) of the north. By the start of Islam in the 7th century, Qahtan and Adnan were reinterpreted as the offspring of Ishmael, the son of the Biblical patriarch Abram/Abraham through his concubine Hagar.

Whatever their origins, many Arab tribes were united by their language, of which each group possessed its own distinct dialect. Arabic is a Semitic language, related to the tongues of the ancient Akkadians, Assyrians, Babylonians, and Hebrews; and indeed the Arabian Peninsula is thought by many to be the point of origin of all the Semitic peoples. Clan and tribal identities ran deep, and everything from the dialect one spoke to the head-dress one wore and to the lengthy chains of patronyms that comprised one's name marked one as the member of a particular group, with particular social standing.[3]

Such markers mattered, for the peoples of Arabia lived by trade, and long-established traditions existed that gave each group specific rights and privileges. Distributors rather than producers, the Arabs produced few commercial goods that interested the non-Arab world, but made their living largely by bringing luxury goods from China, India, and sub-Saharan Africa into the eastern Mediterranean. The silk route across Asia carried silks, spices, and perfumes overland from China, through India and Persia, and into Byzantium, and provided opportunity for the northern Bedouin tribes; but other routes existed as well. The Yemenite tribes of the southern peninsula brought goods by ship out of India, then up the Persian Gulf, where they were handed off to the tribes of the Najd plateau. Sabaean tribes along the Red Sea coastline carried gold and gemstones from Ethiopia northward to Syria and Palestine. The Arabs, acculturated to the harshness of the terrain and mounted on their camels, made ideal long-distance carriers. Their caravans stretched across the endless miles linking east and west, north and south.

Arab historians termed the period before the advent of Islam the "Age of Ignorance" or "Age of Barbarism" (al-Jahiliyya). The simple absence of Islam

---

3   The dialects spoken by many of the southern-most tribes have more elements in common with the Semitic languages in Ethiopia than with the Arabic dialects found elsewhere throughout the peninsula.

suffices to merit the name. Indeed, some writers used the term to embrace all of human history, but most Arabs defined **al-Jahiliyya** more precisely as the period from the death of Jesus to the birth of Muhammad in the year 570 CE. Many of those intervening years were in fact particularly chaotic. Clashes arose between the Roman and Persian Empires, between the Byzantines and the Persians, and between Christian sects, all to the north, and to the south between the Yemenites of Arabia and the Abyssinians of Ethiopia. These struggles caused occasional but severe disruptions of the Arab trading networks, disruptions that often boiled over into violence between tribes and clans.

Muhammad belonged to the Hashim clan within the Quraysh tribe, a group that had long been associated with administering the great pagan shrine in the commercial city of Mecca. This shrine, called the **Ka'ba**, was a kind of Arab pantheon, an ecumenical temple to all the pagan deities of all the Arab peoples. Pilgrims from all over the peninsula came to Mecca to pray at the shrine and

An Oasis in the Desert   This is the Khaybar oasis north of Medina. Khaybar was home to the largest Jewish community in Arabia. After the Prophet Muhammad led his community on the Hijrah from Mecca to Medina, in 622, he attempted to convert the Jews there, many of whom were members of a tribe known as the Banu Nadir. Jewish resistance to conversion led to tense relations with the Muslims, who were in possession of an army once Muhammad became the governor of the city. In 625 the Banu Nadir were expelled from Medina and made their way north to Khaybar. In 628 Muhammad attacked Khaybar and killed most of the Jewish population. The episode lives on in both Jewish and Islamic life. Palestinians today often shout "Khaybar! Khaybar!" when demonstrating against the Israelis. A rocket popular with Hezbollah terrorists has been dubbed Khaybar II.

present offerings to the gods. These pilgrims, together with the merchants who frequented the city, made Mecca a particularly vibrant city with more cross-cultural contact than most Arab sites. A sizeable Jewish community existed too, although there is no evidence of any meaningful Christian presence until the early 6th century. Abyssinian warlords in Ethiopia, who had recently converted to Christianity, then crossed the Red Sea and seized parts of the southern Arabian coast.

Such back-and-forth attacks were commonplace in ancient times, with Arab chieftains often in control of coastal Ethiopia and Ethiopian chieftains often in control of coastal Arabia. In the 6th century, however, with Byzantium and Persia at war to the north and with African tribesmen gaining power in the south, an urge to promote pan-Arab cohesion took root and fostered a militaristic streak in Arab society that regarded the entire non-Arab world as a threat to its existence. The problem was: What could unite so disparate a sprawl of tribes and clans? The answer came in the form of a divine mission and the identification of the Arabs as a new Chosen People.

THE ISLAMIC REVELATION

This was the context in which the Prophet Muhammad received his revelations and in which his followers received his teachings. Muhammad had been born into poverty and began his rise in the world when he went to work for a wealthy widow named Khadija and began to handle her commercial interests. After several years, he and Khadija married. Muhammad's trading activities brought him out of Arabia and as far north as Syria, long solitary journeys that suited his meditative temperament. At some point Muhammad made contact with Judaism and Christianity, although we do not know the specifics of what he learned or how.

In the year 610, at the age of forty, Muhammad received the first of a series of dazzling visions that continued for the rest of his life. They summoned him to a unique role—as the final prophet of the One True God—and they called upon the Arab people to unite and bring God's message, as delivered through Muhammad, to all the nations on earth. This message was the **Qur'an**, a divine text inscribed on a golden tablet in heaven by God Himself. In his mystical transports, Muhammad saw the heavenly text and read it aloud to his followers. (In Arabic, the book's title means "recital.")

The core message of the Qur'an is that all religions are false except for belief in the One True God, called Allah in Arabic, who created all things and has ennobled human life with a divine purpose, which is to serve and worship him through a regimen of daily prayers and adherence to his laws. To those who do so, the merciful and compassionate Allah will grant the reward of eternal bliss in a paradisiacal garden; the remainder of sinful mankind, by Allah's stern but just judgment, will enter eternal torment in a fiery hell.

> Praise be to Allah, Who hath sent His Servant the Book, and hath allowed therein no crookedness. (He hath made it) straight (and clear) in order that He may warn (the godless) of a terrible punishment from Him, and that He may give glad tidings to the believers who work righteous deeds, that they shall have a goodly reward, wherein they shall remain for ever; further that He may warn those (also) who say, "Allah hath begotten a son": No knowledge have they of such a thing, nor had their fathers. It is a grievous thing that issues from their mouths as a saying. What they say is nothing but falsehood! *(Qur'an 18.1–5)*

The Qur'an identifies Christians and Jews as the "People of the Book," who deserve a measure of respect but who also have a special obligation to recognize the completion of their revelational history in Allah's Prophet. Pagan polytheisms, however, deserve little patience:

> Those who disbelieve, among the People of the Book and among the polytheists, were not going to depart (from their ways) until there should come to them clear evidence—the Messenger from Allah, rehearsing scriptures kept pure and holy: wherein are books right and straight. Nor did the People of the Book make schisms, until after there came to them clear evidence. And they have been commanded no more than this: to worship Allah, offering Him sincere devotion, being true (in faith); to establish regular prayers; and to give zakat [a special tax for charity]; and that is the religion right and straight. Those who disbelieve, among the People of the Book and among the polytheists, will be in hell-fire, to dwell therein (for aye). They are the worst of creatures. Those who have faith and do righteous deeds—they are the best of creatures. Their reward is with Allah: Gardens of Eternity, beneath which rivers flow; they will dwell therein for ever; Allah well pleased with them, and they with Him: All this for such as fear their Lord and Cherisher. *(Qur'an 98.1–8)*

Mankind's chief responsibility is therefore submission (*islam* in Arabic) to Allah's absolute authority—and that duty gave its name to the religion, **Islam**. Among the virtues that Allah commands are modesty, charity, and sobriety. Moreover, He requires tolerance of Judaism and Christianity, Islam's revelational predecessors, but directs his faithful to eradicate stiff-necked pagans who reject Islam.

Muhammad preached to the crowds in Mecca soon after his first revelation, and as the revelations continued his message became more refined. He came to describe Islam as the final and perfect phase of the relationship established by God in his covenant with the patriarch Abram/Abraham. The Arabs themselves, he preached, are descended from Abraham's liaison with his concubine Hagar, which produced their son, Ismail. Islam thus stands in an evolutionary relationship with Judaism and Christianity. Jesus, the Qur'an proclaimed, was in the line of prophets that began with Moses. The role of the prophets was to elaborate a better understanding of God's desires, and as the Jews continued to disobey and misunderstand, God continued to send prophets—including Jesus. The Christians, though, had also failed—in failing to live up to what God expected of them and in their shocking mistake of thinking Jesus was actually God. All this had inspired Allah to make one last, full, and perfect revelation through Muhammad and the revealing of the Qur'an.

FROM PREACHER TO CONQUEROR

Muhammad preached that Allah had chosen the Arab people to bring this message to the world, and that this mission was therefore intended to bring an end to tribal strife. The people of Mecca, and especially the Quraysh leaders who owed their status to their role in Arab paganism, did not take kindly to Muhammad's call to end the pagan cults. In 622, after twelve years of tense conflict, the Meccans drove him and his small company of believers from the city.[4] Muhammad then journeyed northward to Medina. This journey (the Hijrah) is commemorated by Muslims as the beginning of Islam's expansion and marks year one of the Islamic calendar. Medina, a commercial and cultic rival of Mecca, proved more receptive to Muhammad's teaching, and within two years Muhammad was in fact in command of the city.

Success in Medina inaugurated a discernible tonal shift in the spreading of the Islamic message, since from 624 on the Prophet was in possession of an army. The Qur'anic passages revealed in Medina have a more activist and determined tone than the earlier Meccan revelations, and later Islamic texts depict the Prophet from this point on as a conqueror as much as a preacher. Ibn Ishaq (704–768), Muhammad's first biographer, proudly relates how the Prophet, after defeating the Jewish community at Medina, which had allegedly plotted against

---

[4]   The ninth surah (chapter) of the Qur'an expresses Allah's anger at the pagan leaders in Mecca who had sometimes befriended the Prophet and turned against him, as the local power struggle worked itself out.

him, beheaded between seven hundred and nine hundred of the Jewish leaders. Buoyed by his success, Muhammad then began a series of rapid military ventures to defeat the Meccans and seize control of the peninsula. In 629, after five years of fighting, Muhammad was victorious. Once both Mecca and Medina were in his hands, Muhammad was able to bring most of the Arabian Peninsula under his command before his death in 632. Given the sparse settlement of Arabia, the strategic key was to gain control of the handful of trade routes connecting the peninsula with the outer world. Muhammad understood this from his commercial travels. Once his Muslim forces were in a position to cut off the supply routes, the rest of the Arab tribes had no alternative but to surrender.

Before he died, Muhammad purified the Ka'ba of its pagan trappings and rededicated it to Allah with a newly revealed truth: the large Black Stone encased within the shrine had been sent to earth from heaven in order to show Adam and Eve where to build their first altar. Displaced by the Great Flood described in the Hebrew Bible, the long-forgotten stone was found by Abraham and his son Ishmael, who identified it and built a temple to house it, the very first temple to Allah. The Ka'ba is that temple—and although what stands there now is a later, rebuilt temple, it still occupies the original site established by Abraham. It is thus the holiest site on earth to Muslims, who pray five times daily while kneeling in

Completing the Hajj Pilgrimage (*hajj*) to Mecca is an obligation of every able-bodied Muslim. The endpoint of the pilgrimage is the sacred Ka'ba, the holiest site in Islam. Pilgrims perform a circular march (*tawaf* in Arabic) around the temple. Those who cannot enter the precinct may perform the tawaf on the roof.

the direction of it. Muslims who make the required ritual pilgrimage (hajj) to Mecca walk in procession seven times around the Ka'ba. Those lucky enough to get next to the "House of Allah" (*Bayt Allah*, as it is known) will kiss the stone, which has the wondrous ability to absorb the believer's sins and render him pure.[5] The mosques built for communal worship by Muslims contain an inset wall notch that points in the direction of the Ka'ba and provides the visual focal point for group prayers.

From the Prophet's death in 632, Muslim leaders also kept an eye on the international scene, to prepare for the military expansion of Islam; Muhammad himself had clearly intended to advance northward into Palestine and Syria and was making plans to do so when he caught a sudden fever and died. The long wars between Byzantium and Persia had exhausted both empires, and the time was right for the Arab advance. Muhammad had died without naming a successor, however. Most of the leading figures, known as the "Companions of the Prophet," threw their support around Muhammad's father-in-law Abu Bakr, who took the title of **caliph** (*khalifah al-rasul Allah*, meaning "deputy of the Prophet of God").

Abu Bakr (r. 632–634) spent two years completing the conquest of Arabia and subduing Muslim groups who had rejected his succession. Upon his death, the Companions chose Umar (r. 634–644), an early convert, to succeed Abu Bakr. Umar directed his army northward, and within two years the Arabs had conquered Jerusalem, Antioch, and Damascus. Only one year later, in 637, Muslim forces took the Persian capital of Ctesiphon. According to Persian sources, the Arab soldiers were dazzled by the opulence of the capital and went on a looting spree. Taking care to send the required one-fifth of the booty to caliph Umar, back in Medina, the army still netted enough for each soldier (reputedly eighteen thousand of them) to receive twelve thousand gold coins. Moreover, forty thousand Persian nobles were brought back to Medina as slaves.

The rest of the Persian Empire surrendered to the Muslims by 651. Egypt fell to the Arabs in 646—a crucial development that deprived Byzantium of a most important food source. It also triggered a quantum leap for the Muslims in developing as a naval power: when the Muslims took Alexandria, Egypt's major port, two-thirds of the Byzantine imperial fleet happened to be tied up in the harbor. For a desert-dwelling people, the Arabs took to the sea very quickly; this is why.

By 677 Muslim forces had reached the walls of Constantinople itself.[6] By 711 the Arabs had extended their conquests all along the coast of North Africa, had

---

[5] According to Qur'anic tradition, the stone was originally a brilliant white color but has absorbed so many sins over the centuries that it has turned black.

[6] The Byzantines drove the invaders off by using a weapon called Greek fire—a naphtha-based compound that burst into flame when it came in contact with water.

Dome of the Rock   Exterior view of the Dome of the Rock mosque in Jerusalem. Completed in 691, the mosque is built upon the site, according to tradition, from which the Prophet pushed off from Earth during his mystical Night Journey through the heavens. Apart from this tradition—which for Muslim faithful has Qur'anic authority behind it—there is no evidence that Muhammad ever visited Jerusalem.

taken Sicily and the Balearic Islands, and had crossed the Strait of Gibraltar and seized Visigothic Spain. The Western world had never seen a military juggernaut like this: in 622 Muhammad and his small group of followers had been forced from their home in Mecca, yet within a hundred years those followers had conquered an empire that stretched from Spain to India, an area twice the size of that conquered by Alexander the Great (see Map 8.5).

> The Western world had never seen a military juggernaut like this: in 622 Muhammad and his small group of followers had been forced from their home in Mecca, yet within a hundred years those followers had conquered an empire that stretched from Spain to India, an area twice the size of that conquered by Alexander the Great.

COMPULSION OR CONVERSION?

With their stunning victory over a much-weakened Persia and with their containment of a much-weakened Byzantium, there was no power on the scene capable of halting or even slowing the Arab advance. Moreover,

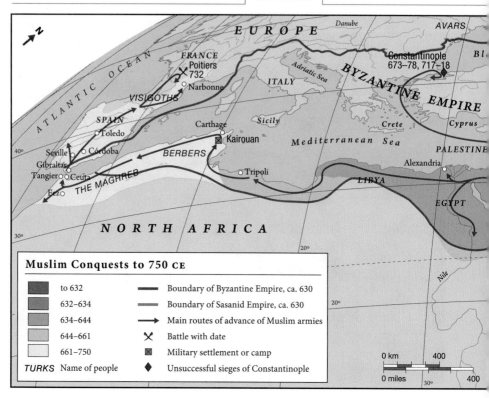

MAP 8.5   Muslim Conquests to 750 CE

many people welcomed the Muslims for the relief they brought from the ever-increasing taxes levied upon them by the Greeks and Persians to finance their wars with one another. Muslim attitudes to their new subjects took some time to work out. The fraternal and quasi-evolutionary relationship between Judaism, Christianity, and Islam prevented the Muslims from persecuting Jews and Christians. The Qur'an itself insists that "there is no compulsion in religion"—meaning that Jews and Christians cannot be forced to accept Islam—since Allah's desire is for genuine conversion, not a terrified acceptance of new faith to avoid execution. Caliph Umar, in return for the surrender of the inhabitants of Jerusalem, guaranteed the religious freedom of the Jews and Christians residing there and laid out the terms by which the communities would live. This text, known widely as the Pact of Umar, formed the model for the Muslim legal doctrine of the **dhimmi**, the "protected minorities" living under Islamic authority. The Jews and Christians, as People of the Book, deserved such treatment, in the hope that respectful handling by their Muslim rulers would help them to see the superiority of Islam and thereby win their conversion.

    The Persians fared less well. Though regarded by some early Muslim leaders as another People of the Book and therefore deserving of legal protection,

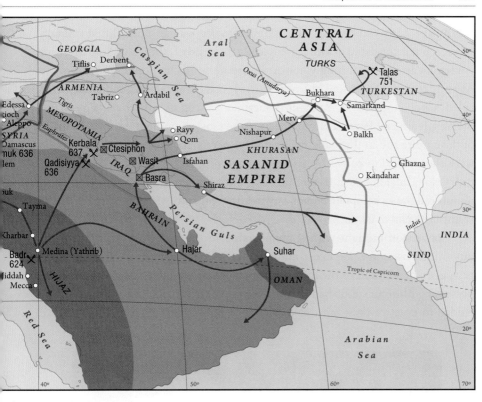

the Zoroastrian Persians were widely regarded as mere pagans. And most of the Arab soldiers and clerics, citing Qur'anic authority, claimed the right to compel the conversion of pagans, to destroy their temples and idolatrous art, and to set fire to their sacred writings after a four-month grace period:

> But when the forbidden months are past, then fight and slay the pagans wherever ye find them, and seize them, beleaguer them, and lie in wait for them in every stratagem (of war): but if they repent and establish regular prayers and pay zakat, then open the way for them, for Allah is Oft-Forgiving, Most Merciful. *(Qur'an 9.5)*

Arab chronicles assert that the victorious Muslims never faltered in observing the dhimmi status of law-abiding Persians; Persian sources, on the other hand, document widespread atrocities at the local level. Surviving legal records contain no reference to a single Muslim being prosecuted for violating the rights of a Zoroastrian. That may indeed mean that no such violations took place, but it is more likely that such violations were never prosecuted.

By the early 8th century the Islamic empire was an unqualified military success, but it consisted of a microscopically thin grid of ethnically Arab Muslims governing an overwhelmingly non-Arab and non-Muslim population. From the Atlantic coasts of Spain and Morocco to the Indus River valley in India, the Arabs ruled a polyglot mix of Romano-Hibernians, Visigoths, Berbers, Egyptians, Syrians, Jews, and Persians (to name only the most prominent groups). In much of the empire the Arabs made up less than 1 percent of the population. Subjects were encouraged to convert to Islam through positive appeals and by imposing restrictions on non-Muslim activities. The most important restriction, rigorously monitored, was a complete ban on any public expression of a non-Islamic faith or of any criticism of Islam.

Conversion brought with it membership in the governing society, immunity from most non-zakat taxes, military and political preferment, and economic privileges, in addition to the innate spiritual blessings of the faith. Non-Muslims possessing dhimmi status had to pay a heavy poll tax (*jizya*). They were also forbidden to practice their faith or discuss it in public, could not testify against a

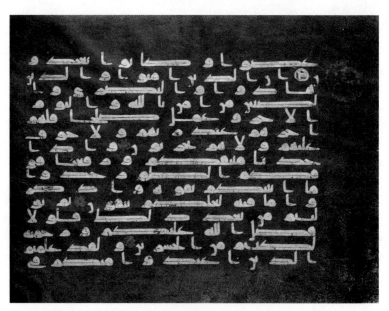

An Early Qur'an   The Qur'an is, to all Muslims, the Holy Book of God, written by him in heaven on tablets of gold. The text came to Earth by means of the Prophet's revelations. God allowed Muhammad to see the holy text and recite passages aloud to his followers. These passages were saved and memorized by the community, and after the Prophet's death in 632 they were compiled and transcribed. But there is no human agency in the production of the text itself, which makes the Qur'an unique among the scriptures of the three Greater Western monotheisms. Pictured here is a fragment from an early North African Qur'an, written in Kufic script.

Muslim in a court of law, and had to wear special items of clothing that identified their inferior status—usually a wide belt called a *zunnar*. Although Muslims could take dhimmi-status wives, their offspring were automatically regarded as Muslim. Islamic law forbade dhimmis to construct new houses of worship for themselves, and strict jurists denied them the right to fix older houses falling into disrepair, since such construction work would effectively constitute a public expression of their faith. As a result churches, synagogues, and Zoroastrian temples everywhere decayed until they were no longer safe for use, and the communities that had used them effectively ceased to worship as communities.

Given this combination of positive enticements to convert and restrictive discouragements to continue in their own faith, the subjects of the Arab empire gradually began to embrace Islam. Nevertheless, the process was slow, and it was not until the 10th century that Islam became the majority religion in the empire, a point at which Muslim popular attitudes toward their dhimmi neighbors changed dramatically for the worse.

SUNNIS AND SHI'A

Caliph Umar died in 644, stabbed by a Persian slave who resented the Arab take-over. When the Muslim leaders met to select the next caliph, two main contenders vied for the position: Uthman ibn Affar, an early convert from among the Quraysh tribe, and Ali ibn Abi Talib, the Prophet Muhammad's nephew and son-in-law (Ali had married Muhammad's daughter Fatima). Most of the community pre-ferred Uthman, who subsequently became the third caliph (r. 644–656). The disgruntled Ali did not have to wait long for his turn, however, since Uthman was murdered by a party of Egyptian rebels who saw no reason why Egypt's ac-ceptance of the Islamic faith had to entail the country's political subjection to the culturally inferior Arabs.

Ali was elected to succeed Uthman, becoming the fourth caliph (r. 656–661), and he quickly established his capital at the fortified eastern city of Kufa, on the banks of the Euphrates River about one hundred miles south of Bagh-dad. The move disappointed many Arab leaders, who felt it as an insult to their homeland and therefore transferred their allegiance to a kinsman of the slain Uthman, a figure named Mu'awiya who had served as the provincial governor of Syria and resided in Damascus, a heavily Arabized city. Tensions between Mu'awiya and Ali rose with each passing year and could well have broken out into full-scale civil war, except that Ali was murdered in Kufa in the year 661 by a local rebel.

This series of elections, rebellions, and murders triggered the fundamen-tal schism of the Muslim world into the Sunnis and Shi'a. (In Arabic *Shi'a* is the plural noun, *Shi'i* is the plural adjective.) The rift is both political and religious. **Sunni** Muslims regarded selection by the community as the sole legitimate means to leadership of the Islamic world. The **Shi'a**, on the other hand, insisted that political and religious legitimacy could pass only to members of the Prophet's hereditary line. For them, Ali and his descendants via Fatima were thus forever the true successors to Muhammad. The Sunnis take their name from the *sunan* ("principles" in Arabic), the written and oral legacy of the Prophet's teachings and personal actions. The Shi'a (whose name derives from *shi'at Ali*, "the party of Ali") stress the divine appointment of the **imams**, the heavenly appointed heirs of Muhammad, whose words and judgments they regard as infallible. The Shi'a regard Ali as the first imam and the first true caliph, and consequently they reject most of the religious customs established under caliphs Abu Bakr, Umar, and Uthman.[7]

The antagonism between Sunnis and Shi'a grew sharper as their traditions developed. The Shi'a comprised roughly a tenth of the Islamic world, and while Shi'i dynasties rose to power in Egypt and parts of North Africa, Persia quickly became and remained the heartland of Shi'ism.

CLASSICAL TRADITIONS AND WESTERN EXPANSION

The Arabs' conquests exposed them to the Greater West's centuries-long intellectual, scientific, and artistic traditions, but they disdained any aspect of Zoroastrian learning and resented the Persians' embrace of Shi'ism. This made the Arabs much more open to the Greco-Roman and Judeo-Christian intellectual legacy. But the Arabs were new to literacy and could not access the texts available to them. Starting in the 8th century, groups of Syrian Christians—mostly scholar-monks—began to translate the writings of the ancient Greeks and Romans into Arabic for the benefit of their new rulers. Their activity was prodigious: within two or three generations the whole corpus of Western thought lay available for Arab scholars to read. It included the mathematical and geometrical works of Euclid and Archimedes, the medical knowledge of Hippocrates and Galen, the historical texts of Herodotus and Thucydides, the books of the Hebrew Bible and the New Testament, and works of geography, astronomy, poetry, and law. Roman histories, legal texts, Stoic meditations, and technical treatises were available too. The leading Muslim scholars absorbed most of this knowledge eagerly, finding in it much that was of immediate practical value.

---

[7] Several denominations of Shi'ism developed in the early centuries, differing from one another primarily in the individuals each recognized as a true imam.

As a rule, any text or genre of inquiry that could be reconciled with Islamic doctrine received a warm welcome. It made the Muslim world for several centuries considerably more knowledgeable about the classical tradition than Latin Europe. But the Greek philosophical tradition was another matter. Under the first caliphs, and then under the Umayyad dynasty, which ruled the empire from 661 to 750, however, the study of Greek philosophy was regarded as dangerous and possibly blasphemous. Why would anyone look to pagans like Plato and Aristotle for answers to questions about the purpose of human life, the nature of truth, the definition of justice, or the understanding of morality? After all, all those answers were available in the Qur'an and the sunnah.

Starting in the 8th century, groups of Syrian Christians—mostly scholar-monks—began to translate the writings of the ancient Greeks and Romans into Arabic for the benefit of their new rulers. Their activity was prodigious: within two or three generations the whole corpus of Western thought lay available for Arab scholars to read.

Numerous Islamic philosophers did indeed read Greek philosophy (especially Aristotle). Al-Kindi (d. 870), al-Farabi (d. 951), Ibn Sina (d. 1037), al-Ghazali (d. 1111), and Ibn Rushd (d. 1198) all wrote brilliant commentaries upon it. But in the medieval era most of these figures were despised by other Muslims and had to live in nearly perpetual exile, traveling from city to city and court to court, offering their skills in medicine to Arab nobles in return for temporary safe haven. To the great bulk of Islamic society, philosophy was not necessarily evil but merely irrelevant, a brain-churning waste of time when one could be pondering the Qur'an and the judgments of Islamic legal scholars. Greek tragedy also fell on deaf ears among the Muslims, for the idea of an inexorable fate other than the determination of the all-knowing Allah was anathema to them. Consequently, the great plays were neglected absolutely—never performed, never recopied, never commented upon.

The Umayyad dynasty moved the empire's capital from Mecca to Damascus, a more central location for overseeing such a vast empire and for pursuing the ultimate goal of conquering Constantinople. The dynasty was not at all popular and even today is widely regarded with disdain by Muslim scholars. Several reasons existed for their lack of popular support. First, the dynasty's clear bias to promote ethnically Arab military and civil officers, preferably from prominent old Arab families, earned the ire of groups newly converted to Islam. The Muslim principle of the "brotherhood of all believers" seemed to get mere lip service in the actual empire. Second, the Umayyads all too quickly assumed the attitude of a divinely appointed monarchical family, whose personal wishes were all too often presented as Allah's will. Despite the military victories of the era and their construction of important edifices like the Dome of the Rock mosque in

Jerusalem or the Great Mosque in Damascus, the Umayyads were widely viewed as self-aggrandizers who turned the cause of **jihad** to personal gain.

Expansion in the west culminated in 711 with the conquest of Spain. A Muslim army crossed the Pyrenees in 732 with an eye to winning Gaul, but was repulsed by an upstart Frankish warlord named Charles Martel. The Muslims retreated behind the Pyrenees and devoted their energies to furthering the spread of Islam among its subjects. Western Europe remained a confusing sprawl of Germanic warlords and shaky kingdoms, illiterate and only nominally Christian, distrustful of their aloof Byzantine cousins. It was also the poorest place on earth—surrounded, dwarfed, and threatened by an aggressive, energetic, and determined Islamic empire larger than anything they had ever heard of.

BARBARIAN KINGS AND SCHOLAR-MONKS

Medieval historians call the period in western Europe from the 4th to the 8th centuries the **Dark Ages**; to ancient historians it is **Late Antiquity**. Both groups are right. Or perhaps it is better to say that neither group is altogether wrong. For much of the period from 300 to 800 CE western Europe was a god-awful bloody mess of a place, filled to the rafters with poverty, famine and disease, nearly constant warfare, almost universal illiteracy, and a material standard of living that is horrifying to consider. And yet many of the institutional practices and cultural values of the earlier age were still alive, if in beleaguered and benighted form.

After the Western Roman Empire collapsed, its place was taken by a wild parade of warlord semi-states ruled by thuggish clan leaders. Some of these warlords offered a modicum of administration and security. Most, though, dedicated themselves to pillaging whatever food and material wealth they could find—or to retributive attacks on rivals who had already stolen what they themselves had been plotting at.

A 6th-century monk in Celtic England named Gildas described village life in the aftermath of Saxon raids this way:

> Sadly, the streets of our villages are filled with the ruins of once-high towers that have been pulled to the ground, with stones pried from fences or left over from the smashing of sacred altars, with dismembered pieces of human bodies that are so covered with lurid clots of blood that they look as though the people had been run through a press, and whose only chance for any kind of burial is to rot in the ruins of collapsed homes; all the rest will simply fill the stomachs of

ravenous beasts and birds. . . . To this very day not one of our villages is
what it used to be. Instead, all lie desolate, routed, and ruined. *(On the
Destruction of England, ch. 24, 26)*

Most of the people of western Europe, at least 90 percent of them, were reduced to subsistence farming. Probably one-half of all children born died before
reaching the age of five, and one-half of all females who made it to marriageable
age died before reaching the age of twenty-five, usually in child-birth. Tens of
thousands of homeless refugees, and perhaps even more, roamed through the
countryside at any given time, either having been driven from their homes by
new waves of settlers, in flight from marauders, or in search of new territories
where they could start afresh without rivals on the land. Meanwhile, the Mediterranean cities contracted into tiny hamlets—sometimes a mere 10 percent of
their former populations—and into corners of the settled urban area, leaving the
emptied quarters to decay into ghost towns. Manufacture and trade beyond the
immediate region became all but extinct. The sole exception was the thriving
commerce in slaves (see Figure 8.1).

Despite the miseries of the time, important aspects of Roman antiquity survived. Roman law remained in effect—inconsistently, to be sure, but not altogether forgotten. The Latin language remained the dominant tongue in the west,
and the barbarian kings did what they could to emulate and continue those elements of Roman tradition that they found useful. Intellectual life in the west
was limited to the Christian monasteries that dotted the landscape from the
4th century on, but displayed real zest and ingenuity. Thus while it was an age of
poverty and chaos, it was a creative chaos. Ultimately it saw the amalgamation of
the Roman, Germanic, and Christian cultures into the fascinating hybrid called
medieval society.

One of the first chroniclers of the medieval era, Bishop Gregory of Tours
(538–594), described the contemporary atmosphere memorably in the opening
prologue to his *History of the Franks*:

A great number of things keep happening—some good, some bad.
The people of the various petty princedoms keep quarreling with each
other in the fiercest way imaginable, while our rulers' tempers keep
bursting into violence. Our churches are assailed by heretics, then
retaken in force by our Catholics; and whereas Christian faith burns hot
in the hearts of many, it is no more than lukewarm in those of others.
Church buildings are pillaged by faithless pagans as soon as they
are gifted by faithful Christians. But no one has yet emerged who is
a sufficiently skilled writer that he can record these events in a

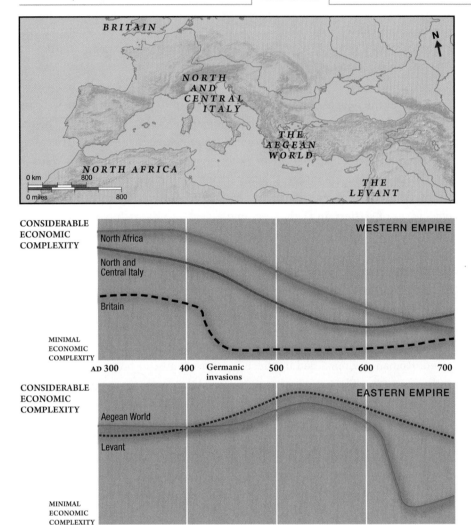

MAP 8.6   The Economy of Europe in the Dark Ages

* Adapted from Ward-Perkins, Bryan. *The Fall of Rome* (2006).

straightforward way, whether in prose or in verse. In fact, throughout the towns of Gaul the knowledge of writing has declined to such an extent that it has virtually disappeared.... [And so] I have undertaken this present work in an effort to preserve the memory of the dead and bring them to the attention of those yet to come; but my style lacks all polish, and I have had to devote too much of my attention to the clashes between the good and the wicked.

This period from the 4th to 8th centuries was one of the longest and most dire and challenging eras in Western history. Our sources for it are few—as books seldom get written in active war zones—but enough evidence survives to provide a basic outline of what occurred. The picture is not pretty.

DIVIDED ESTATES AND KINGDOMS

The Germanic peoples who streamed into western Europe confronted innumerable challenges, not the least of which was the terrain. Most of the European continent north of the Mediterranean coastline consisted of dense forest. Newcomers faced bitter resistance from the people who had already settled open areas, and so were forced to keep moving or to clear their own lands and begin farming from nothing. Moreover, various cultural traditions that had served the Germans well in the east served them ill in the more sedentary west.

One example is the early nomadic custom of dividing a man's estate equally between his surviving sons. This practice had provided for each new generation, because herds of animals could replenish their own numbers—but a western farm could not survive such division quite so easily. By the end of the second generation, if not earlier, the distributed lands were not sufficient to support a family. The most promising options, in such a case, were either to expand one's holding by clearing more forest at the perimeter (which worked in some cases, but in others seemed only to defer the problem) or to abandon the land altogether in search of new territory elsewhere. That move, however, exposed them to more hostilities, whether from previously settled peoples, other migrating bands, or warrior thugs. And once they found new places to settle, they faced the difficulty of clearing forests, digging wells, building homes, and beginning to farm, with only the tools they had managed to bring with them.[8] Under such conditions, most of continental Europe remained stubbornly mired in poverty until the 9th century.

The same problem of subdivision hobbled any sort of political development after 476: a warrior might turn himself into a king by forcing his will upon terrorized farmers, but he usually ended his life by dividing his kingdom among his heirs. One example will suffice. A brutal warlord named Clovis, a member of the Germanic group known as the Franks, carved out a sizeable kingdom for himself around the year 500 and made himself, briefly, the most powerful ruler in western Europe (see Map 8.6). When he died in 511 his realm was parceled out to each of his four sons: Theuderic, Chlodomer, Childebert, and Lothar. Theuderic,

---

[8] Until the 9th century, most northern farmers still relied on wooden implements, such as wooden shovels, wooden plow blades, and wooden pitchforks.

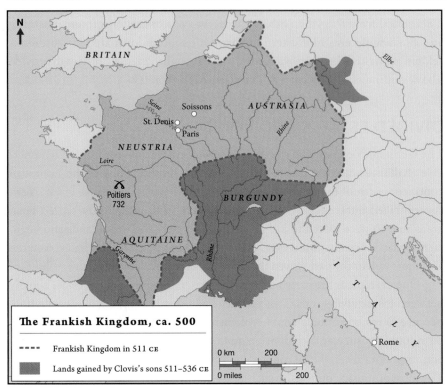

MAP 8.7   The Frankish Kingdom, ca. 500

however, went on to have two sons of his own; Chlodomer had three. And while Childebert had only daughters (who could not inherit, according to Frankish custom), his younger brother Lothar made up for him by producing seven boys. In only two generations, therefore, a single kingdom had split into twelve autonomous principalities, each with its own officials, tax system, laws, courts, weights, and measures. Any chance of stable governance quickly died out in such circumstances, but there is little evidence that many of the warlords were interested in even trying to provide it.

Gregory of Tours fills the four hundred pages of his *History* with tale after tale of savagery:

> This Rauching [a Frankish warlord] was extraordinarily vain—a man filled to bursting with pride, arrogance, and impertinence. He treated his servants as though he denied they were human beings at all. . . . For example, whenever a servant stood before him, as was usual, with a lighted candle while Rauching ate his meals, he would force the poor fellow to bare his legs and hold the lit candle between his knees

until it burned down to a stub. He would then demand that a new candle be lit, again and again, until the servant's legs were entirely scorched. If the servant cried out or tried to run, a drawn sword quickly stopped him, and Rauching himself would convulse with laughter as he watched the man weep. *(History of the Franks 5.3)*

Gregory relates another tale about Rauching. Two of his servants fell in love and, knowing that he would forbid their union, ran to a local priest for protection. The priest negotiated on their behalf and extracted a promise from the warlord that "he would allow the couple to stay united forever." Once the pair were back at his stronghold, Rauching ordered a massive tree to be felled and its trunk split in two lengthwise, with each half hollowed out, as one would do in making a pair of canoes. Rauching then bound the servants together, encased them in the rejoined hollow tree trunk, and buried them alive in a deep trench, saying with a roaring laugh, "See? I haven't broken my promise. I haven't 'split them up'!" (5.3).

An 8th century writer, Paul the Deacon, in his *History of the Lombards*, vividly described a different kind of horror—the prevalence of rape, and the efforts some women made to avoid it:

[Lombard women] used to put the flesh of raw chickens under the band that held up their breasts; and this, once the summer heat had spoiled and putrefied it, gave off a horribly foul odor. Thus when the Avars [another invading tribe] tried to rape them they found that they could not bear the stench—and thinking that the smell was natural to these women, they ran away, cursing loudly that all Lombard women stink.

Until a means was found to pass on undivided realms, little significant advance in government was possible. Most early Germanic kings and princes were itinerant; they traveled constantly, bringing whatever instruments of governance they had (records, copies of laws, accounts) with them. As often as not, individuals petitioning a ruler for justice had first to overcome a basic logistical problem: finding out where the king was, and then going to him.

THE BODY AS MONEY AND WOMEN AS PROPERTY

Given these difficulties, little lasting political development took place. Rule was personal, not institutional. Customs varied enormously from "kingdom" to "kingdom," from tribe to tribe, and even from clan to clan. As the Germans gradually settled the land and interacted with the old Roman populace, though, a degree of cultural assimilation occurred. Although easily 90 percent of the population remained illiterate, the old tribal customs that had been passed down orally for generations began to be written down in the 5th, 6th, and 7th centuries. These records provide our first nonliterary glimpses of Germanic values and practices.

Germanic law, such as it was, was constructed from the ground up, much like our modern system of torts. Individual conflicts were dealt with as they arose and were judged by some sort of group consensus, and each case, once settled, provided a precedent for similar cases in the future. This ad hoc construction explains the somewhat random nature of the earliest written codes; they were the result of compiled specifics, not of ideological blueprints put into action. Nevertheless, some sense of consistent values emerges from the codes. In most of the codes the issues of property, inheritance, marriage, and taxation are preeminent, which is to be expected.

The most striking feature of criminal law is the apportioning of compensatory payments for the physical injury of another, a system called **wergeld**. In these brutal times, to harm or kill another man was quite literally to threaten the existence of his entire family, which depended on his labor for food production and on his strength for physical protection. Murder or assault thus threatened the family, which all too often responded to this sort of crime by declaring a blood feud. Wergeld provided an alternative to endless vendettas. The system varied in its details from tribe to tribe, but the central idea remained the same: to compensate a victim, or his or her clan, by paying for the loss of a life, or for an injury to a vital or nonvital body part. Every part of the body was assigned a monetary value—so much for an arm, an eye, a foot, and so on, right down to the fifth toe on either foot.[9]

Germanic law regarded women not as property but as legal minors regardless of their age, under the more or less permanent guardianship of their fathers and husbands. Among the Salian Franks, for example, a group who ultimately settled in northern France in the 5th and 6th centuries, a woman who married against her father's will forfeited her rights to any family property and could be put to death by any family member. Among the Burgundians, who settled in eastern France at about the same time, a man could divorce his wife at any time and for any reason, so long as he returned her dowry and paid an additional sum as interest. Any woman who tried to leave her husband was to be drowned in a swamp. One exception to this Germanic rule was the Visigoths, who settled in Spain in the 6th century. Visigothic custom allowed an unmarried woman over the age of twenty to be a free adult, legally responsible for herself.

---

[12]   Wergeld may sound comical or horrifying, but also familiar; after all, our own personal-injury insurance policies follow the same general idea.

A girl was considered marriageable when she began to menstruate and was able, in theory at least, to produce children; this usually happened around the age of fifteen. Within marriage, strict division of labor between the sexes was the norm. While men did the plowing—an arduous task that generally required a man's physical strength—women performed most of the daily agricultural work from that point on: planting, weeding, fertilizing, and so on. Men focused on hunting, building, blacksmithing, felling trees, and clearing swamps. Men and women worked together to bring in the harvest, however.

A generation or two after settling in their respective parts of western Europe, most of the Germanic groups experienced a severe shortage of women. This happened for two reasons. First, relentless famine had forced the settlers to practice infanticide. In times of failed crops, which were many, this was an easy, if horrible, means of preserving the food supply. And since boys did the heavy labor, infant girls were the most frequent victims of infanticide. Second, many of those girls who survived childhood subsequently died in childbirth, as the strains of pregnancy and delivery on malnourished teenagers living in squalor commonly resulted in their death.

The shortage of women ironically caused an increase in their relative social "value," according to a crude formula of supply and demand, which the law codes came to reflect. By the 8th century, Germanic women had many more legal protections and freedoms than before. In marriage, men began to owe dowries to their brides, not the other way around, in order to secure a mate; this dowry became in many cases the bride's own property that she controlled directly and in her own name. The custom also arose whereby a husband owed his bride a **Morgengab**, or "morning gift," after their wedding night, to compensate her for her lost virginity. These developments hardly made Dark Age life significantly brighter, but they do illustrate some of the ways that Germanic culture adapted to its new circumstances.

CHRISTIAN PAGANISM

The most visible of the new circumstances was the Germans' gradual acceptance of Christianity. The traditional religion they had brought with them into the west was polytheistic and animistic: by offering prayers and gifts to the deities, they hoped to influence the workings of nature. Wotan and Thor were two of the most significant pagan gods, and they figured large in the tales of Germanic mythology. Wotan represented the forces of the Sun, Thor of Thunder and Lightning, Many of the German tribes encountered Christianity as early as the 4th century, as missionaries rushed westward to evangelize them. But the conditions of western Europe required missionaries to follow a different strategy than they had used in the cities of the eastern and central Mediterranean. Since continental Europe had no cities where the missionaries could address the hearts and minds of the multitude, they focused instead on the smallish number of Germanic rulers, princelings, and tribal warlords.

Aided (the sources assure us) by stupendous miracles, the missionaries converted this upper echelon of leaders and urged them to order the conversion of their clans and tribes. Dark Age writers like Gregory of Tours, Paul the Deacon, and Jordanes all relate fantastic tales of dramatic conversions of German rulers who then directed their victorious soldiers to receive baptism and join the cause of Christ. Of course, all that really happened in these forced baptisms—if anything happened at all—is that the rulers' subjects simply added Jesus to the long list of deities they continued to worship. Sincere in its way, no doubt, but hardly reason to regard them as Christian. Models of conversion from the top of society downward to the masses, usually either forced or enticed, can work, but they work slowly.

The Jelling Stone   This 10th-century Danish runestone is one of a series erected by King Harald Bluetooth (r. 958–986), who is traditionally regarded as the first of his people to convert to Christianity. The stones commemorate that conversion and offer atonement for his parents' pagan hostility to the faith. "Bluetooth" wireless technology is named after Harald, for the simple reason that one of its founders was reading a novel about the king at the time. The company's logo consists of the runic version of the letters H and B.

For many years and generations, and possibly for centuries, such Dark Age society was characterized by a curious, muddy amalgam of the two religions. When King Clovis of the Salian Franks ordered his followers to adopt Christianity by accepting mass baptism around the year 500, the Franks' conversion was real but incomplete. Jesus became for them a true deity but one of no more significance than the local forest god or one of their divine ancestors. Under these conditions, Dark Age Europe gradually produced a Christian religious culture that retained significant elements of pagan practice within it.

Christmas trees, for example, have nothing essential to do with the story of Jesus's birth. But the pagan Germans had a tradition of honoring the tallest tree in each forest as the unique domicile of the forest's ruling deity, and so they would honor the god by offering it gifts, decorations, and songs of praise. This pagan ritual slowly acquired a Christian gloss until, by the 9th century, the popular incorporation of tree worship into Christian practice was complete.[10] Another example is the popular celebration of bunnies and decorated eggs at Easter—neither of which appears in any Gospel version of Christ's Resurrection. Germanic peasant farmers owed a special tax to their tribal leaders at the onset of spring as an expression of gratitude for having helped the people to survive the perils of winter. Since theirs was a moneyless economy, they paid this tax with what they had at their disposal: baskets of eggs and springtime litters of bunnies. Residual pagan practices feature considerably less in most Eastern Orthodox forms of Christianity.

The long grip of hybrid versions of "Christian paganism" was indirectly abetted by the extraordinary popularity of monastic life. Many religions have ascetic and contemplative elements in them, and Second Temple Judaism fairly bristled with them. For their first three hundred years Christian missionaries were too busy in the streets and marketplaces of the eastern Mediterranean, spreading the Word (usually just ahead of the Roman police) to bother with the retired life of ascetic spirituality. Theirs was a calling to action, not meditation. But a Christian form of monasticism began in earnest in the 4th century. **Monasticism** rejected normal family and social life, along with the concern for wealth, status, and power. In their place, it favored a harsh life of solitude and spiritual discipline. What inspired this principled withdrawal from the world was, ironically, the gradual success of the Christian message itself.

By the 4th century Christianity had come a long way in the east. Although technically illegal and subject to periodic persecution until 313, Christianity had spread sufficiently that most easterners, especially those who lived in cities, were at least passingly familiar with it. The persecution under Diocletian had taken tens of thousands of lives, but it had highlighted both the number and the resolve of the Christians then alive. In turn, it earned them the grudging respect of many pagans. When Constantine I announced his own conversion and issued the **Edict of Toleration**, Christianity's hour had finally arrived.

POCKETS OF INTELLECTUAL LIFE

And this was precisely the problem for many Christians. How could they prove to God, and to themselves, that they had the same heroic commitment to him that their ancestors had possessed, ancestors who had quite literally risked their lives every day for Christ? To be a Christian after 313 involved none of the risk, the danger, and the suffering that it had carried before. After the Edict of Toleration, in fact, to be a Christian was easy, even fashionable.

---

[13]   As Christianity became more prominent in religious lives, its message of life renewed through the sacrifice and resurrection of Jesus harmonized with earlier pagan tradition and absorbed it.

For many faithful this proved intolerable, and so they intentionally sought out the loneliest, most rigorous, and most difficult way they could devise to love God—not out of spiritual masochism, but rather like an athlete who pushes herself to the limits of her ability in the pursuit of excellence. Individuals experiencing such desires went out into the deserts and forests, living in caves or on wind-blasted hilltops, exposed to the elements and wild beasts, scavenging for their food or begging it from passersby. Eventually, these ascetics began to live together in isolated communities where they tried to pattern their lives on those of the Twelve Apostles, as a sacred community united in their dedication to live as an idealized Christian mini-society unto itself.

Monasticism was extraordinarily popular in the 5th through 9th centuries, with hundreds of monastic houses established throughout the eastern and central Mediterranean, and it added a rich new element to a fast-Christianizing society. But when the movement came into western Europe it had rather a different impact. There the trickle-down model of evangelization had created a religiously hybrid world in which Christianity was poorly understood and haphazardly practiced. But when those individuals with deep, resonant, and knowledgeable commitments to the faith entered monastic life, they exacerbated the problem of popular religious ignorance, by removing from society the very individuals most capable of correcting and deepening the Christian life of the masses.

Hundreds of monasteries and convents were established in the early medieval era, from Ireland to Hungary, from Spain to Poland, from Sicily to Sweden (see Map 8.7). Many represented isolated pockets of intellectual and artistic life amid the general gloom of illiteracy and poverty. Perhaps 90 percent of these houses organized their daily lives according to the **Rule of Saint Benedict**, a communal handbook written by Saint Benedict of Nursia (480–547) to guide the monastery he had established at Monte Cassino in southern Italy. Benedict's Rule attracted so many adherents because it required relatively moderate discipline. It also had a balanced focus on the monks' physical and intellectual, as well as their spiritual, well-being. Benedictine monks were required to spend several hours each day in physical labor and in study as necessary adjuncts to their central function of worship. The physical labor, which primarily involved some sort of farmwork, helped to make each monastery self-sufficient. How else could a community cut itself off from the world if it could not feed itself and produce its own tools, clothing, and shelter?

But Benedict's insistence on study had the most important consequences for medieval Europe, for monasteries virtually monopolized book production. Novice monks received a carefully designed education that taught them to speak, read, and write Latin, as well as the basic elements of arithmetic, geometry, astronomy, and music. This training required the borrowing, copying, and commenting upon of the books of the western world's religious and secular learning. A constant stream of books thus flowed from monastery to

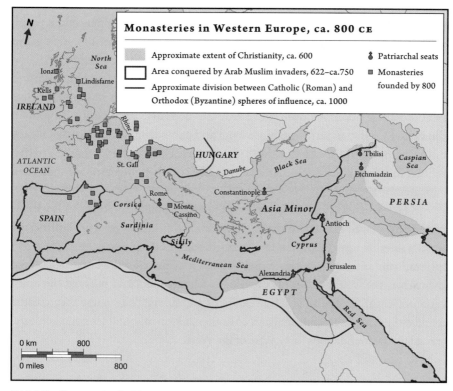

Monasteries in Western Europe, ca. 800 CE

Approximate extent of Christianity, ca. 600

Area conquered by Arab Muslim invaders, 622–ca.750

Approximate division between Catholic (Roman) and Orthodox (Byzantine) spheres of influence, ca. 1000

Patriarchal seats

Monasteries founded by 800

MAP 8.8   Monasteries in Western Europe, ca. 800 CE

Lindisfarne   The ruins of Lindisfarne Monastery and the opening-page of the Gospel of Matthew in the Lindisfarne Gospels, ca. 700.

monastery, creating western Europe's first libraries. We owe nearly the entire surviving corpus of classical Latin literature to the busy labor of copying and recopying by these monks. They preserved the poems of Virgil and Juvenal; the histories of Tacitus, Livy, and Suetonius; the speeches and letters of Cicero; and the plays of Seneca and Terence, among others. Once they had mastered the classical literature, monks moved on to reading, copying, and commenting upon the sacred Christian writings, preserving and extending the intellectual legacy of the faith. Until the start of the 12th century, nearly every single Christian scholar in western Europe either was a member of the Benedictines or had been educated by them.

In fact, when western Europe began to emerge politically from the Dark Age ruin, monks played a central role in the recovery. In the 8th century a new aristocratic warrior family rose to power in the northern Frankish territories. Resourceful, resilient, and ruthless, this family—known as the Carolingians—appointed themselves the would-be saviors of western Christendom and pursued the unification of Latin Europe with relentless focus and drive. The society they created marked the first successful amalgam of Roman, Germanic, and Christian culture, and it laid the foundations for the rise of the West.

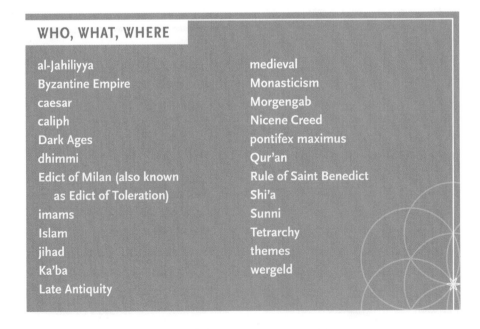

WHO, WHAT, WHERE

al-Jahiliyya

Byzantine Empire

caesar

caliph

Dark Ages

dhimmi

Edict of Milan (also known
    as Edict of Toleration)

imams

Islam

jihad

Ka'ba

Late Antiquity

medieval

Monasticism

Morgengab

Nicene Creed

pontifex maximus

Qur'an

Rule of Saint Benedict

Shi'a

Sunni

Tetrarchy

themes

wergeld

SUGGESTED READINGS

Primary Sources

Benedict of Nursia. *The Benedictine Rule.*
Boethius. *The Consolation of Philosophy.*
Gregory of Tours. *History of the Franks.*
Ibn Ishaq. *Life of the Prophet.*

Paul the Deacon. *History of the Lombards.*
Procopius. *The Secret History.*
The Qur'an.

Source Anthologies

Gregory of Tours. *The Merovingians* (2005). Edited and translated by Alexander Callander Murray.

Head, Thomas, ed. *Medieval Hagiography: An Anthology* (2001).

Smail, Daniel Lord, and Kelly Gibson, eds. *Vengeance in Medieval Europe: A Reader* (2009).

Swan, Laura. *The Forgotten Desert Mothers: Sayings, Lives and Stories of Early Christian Women* (2001).

Studies

Cook, Michael. *Commanding Right and Forbidding Wrong in Islamic Thought* (2001).

Crone, Patricia. *God's Rule: Government and Islam; Six Centuries of Medieval Islamic Political Thought* (2005).

———. *Meccan Trade and the Rise of Islam* (2004).

Donner, Fred McGraw. *Muhammad and the Believers: At the Origins of Islam* (2010).

Dunn, Marilyn. *Emergence of Monasticism: From the Desert Fathers to the Early Middle Ages* (2003).

Evans, J. A. S. *The Age of Justinian: The Circumstances of Imperial Power* (2001).

Geary, Patrick. *The Myth of Nations: The Medieval Origins of Europe* (2002).

Goldenberg, David M. *The Curse of Ham: Race and Slavery in Early Judaism, Christianity, and Islam* (2005).

Harmless, William. *Desert Christians: An Introduction to the Literature of Early Monasticism* (2004).

Hawting, G. R. *The First Dynasty of Islam: The Umayyad Caliphate, AD 661–750* (2000).

Heather, Peter. *Empires and Barbarians: The Fall of Rome and the Birth of Europe* (2010).

Kennedy, Hugh. *The Prophet and the Age of the Caliphates: The Islamic Near East from the Sixth to the Eleventh Century* (2004).

Khalek, Nancy. *Damascus after the Muslim Conquest: Text and Image in Early Islam* (2011).

Lawrence, C. H. *Medieval Monasticism: Forms of Religious Life in Western Europe in the Middle Ages* (2001).

Levy-Rubin, Milka. *Non-Muslims in the Early Islamic Empire: From Surrender to Coexistence* (2011).

MacLeod, Roy. *The Library of Alexandria: Rediscovering the Cradle of Western Culture* (2000).

Mottahedeh, Roy P. *Loyalty and Leadership in an Early Islamic Society* (2001).

Smith, Julia M. H. *Europe After Rome: A New Cultural History, 500–1000* (2005).

Wickham, Chris. *Framing the Early Middle Ages: Europe and the Mediterranean, 400–800* (2005).

———. *The Inheritance of Rome: Illuminating the Dark Ages, 400–1000* (2010).

Wood, Ian. *The Missionary Life: Saints and the Evangelisation of Europe, 400–1050* (2001).

For additional resources, including maps, primary sources, visuals, web links, and quizzes, please go to **www.oup.com/us/backman.**

CHAPTER 9

Reform and Renewal

750–1258

In middle of the 8th century, separated only by a few years, two palace coups took place two thousand miles from each other. Such events were commonplace in both realms and often involved blindings, beheadings, and poisonings—with at least one monarch ripped apart by having her limbs tied to four horses driven in four directions. At first, perhaps, these two seizures of power did not seem remarkable. But each set its society on a new course of development and brought their worlds into direct and lasting conflict. One brought the reign of Charlemagne, the other the golden age of Islam.

THE GREATER WEST, ca. 1200 CE

The centuries that followed witnessed much of the best and the worst of their societies' medieval era. They included unimagined prosperity, intellectual advance, artistic flourishing, religious revival, and political development—but also fiery hatred, social oppression, academic censorship, and xenophobia. They defined the broad division in Islam between Sunnis and Shi'a, still evident today, and the reinvention of Europe, with feudal society and medieval cities. Perhaps most notoriously they included the Crusades in the Holy Land, and also a new chapter in Jewish history.

◀ **Astrolabe** A 12th-century astrolabe from Muslim Spain. The increase in maritime trade across the Mediterranean by 1000 owed a lot to technical innovations introduced by Muslim and Jewish scientists, many of whom worked in Spain.

- Two Palace Coups
- The Carolingian Ascent
- Charlemagne
- Imperial Coronation
- Carolingian Collapse
- The Islamic Empire
- Sunnis and Shi'a
- The Qur'an and the Philosophers
- The Splintering of the Caliphate

- The Reinvention of Western Europe
- Mediterranean Cities
- The Reinvention of the Church
- The Crusades
- But Not a War against Islam
- Parliaments and the Mamluk Empire
- Judaism Reformed, Renewed, and Reviled

CHAPTER OUTLINE

TWO PALACE COUPS

The first coup took place in Damascus in 750, when a family known as the **Abbasids**, members of the Banu Hashim clan, which traced its ancestry back to the great-grandfather of the Prophet, rebelled against the Umayyad rulers of the Islamic empire. The Umayyad dynasty had never been popular. Despite building the shrine of the Dome of the Rock in Jerusalem and the Great Mosque in Damascus, they were seen (probably correctly) as more interested in power than in the faith. They only made things worse by reserving all positions of leadership in the empire for ethnic Arabs. Their prejudice led to severe economic and social trouble, as large numbers of Egyptians and Persians converted to Islam, abandoned their farms, and migrated to the cities, where they expected to receive preferment. The subsequent decline in agricultural production caused food prices to spike and imperial revenues to fall. The empire's cities swelled with disaffected populations, who found out the hard reality that membership in the **ummah**, or Islamic community, depended very much on the color of one's skin.

As unrest gained pace in the 8th century, the Abbasid clan in Khurasan, in northeastern Iran, began laying the groundwork for regime change. Although themselves Arab, the Abbasids championed a pluriethnic vision of Islam. They cagily sought support among the Shi'a who had taken refuge in Iran with false promises of elevating their choice to the caliphal throne after the coup. Finally, in 750, they struck. Led by clan patriarch al-Saffah ("the Slaughterer"), they routed the Umayyads on the battlefield, took control of the state, and promptly moved the capital eastward to their newly established city of Baghdad.[1] The Abbasids presided over the opening of the Islamic world to non-Arabs. Persians especially rose to prominence under the new regime, winning positions at court, in the provincial government, and in

---

[1]   Al-Saffah invited the remaining Umayyads to dinner. Just as the first course was being served, his agents sprang from their hiding places, knives flashing. Only one Umayyad family member escaped.

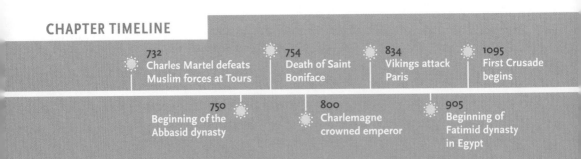

CHAPTER TIMELINE

732
Charles Martel defeats Muslim forces at Tours

754
Death of Saint Boniface

834
Vikings attack Paris

1095
First Crusade begins

750
Beginning of the Abbasid dynasty

800
Charlemagne crowned emperor

905
Beginning of Fatimid dynasty in Egypt

the Islamic schools. This began a sweeping process of cultural change, sometimes known as the "Persianization" of Islamic culture.

The second coup was much less bloody but no less epoch-making. The Frankish warlord-kings who had held sway over Gaul since Clovis's acceptance of Christianity around 500 were on the whole a sorry lot. These were the **Merovingians**. Impious, lecherous, suspicious, mostly illiterate, and generally hot-headed, they fought incessantly, plotted even more, and showed no persuasive interest in doing more with rulership than acquiring wealth and rooting out real or suspected rivals. From the mid-7th century on, they are known as the "do-nothing kings," whose ineffectiveness enabled local warlords and officials to usurp power for themselves.

The most successful of the usurpers was a family from northeastern Gaul known as the **Carolingians**. By the early 700s the founder of the dynasty, Pepin of Heristal, was serving as a regional Merovingian official but was in reality an all-but-autonomous ruler. He passed his position on to his illegitimate, though only, son, Charles Martel (d. 741), who added much of northwestern Gaul to the family domain. The secret to the Carolingians' effectiveness was a combination of vision, ruthlessness, and luck. The family early on developed a view of themselves as the self-appointed saviors of Christian Gaul and eventually of western Europe, destined like the biblical David to replace the rejected king Saul (that is, the Merovingian house), and establish a righteous and lasting realm.

For the next four or five generations the family advanced their dedication to uniting and strengthening western Christendom. One of the most dramatic events in this pursuit was Charles Martel's victory in 732 over Spanish Muslim forces that effectively stopped the Islamic advance into Europe. In 754 Charles Martel's son Pepin the Short completed the takeover of the Merovingian throne by persuading the papacy to recognize him as the true legitimate king of the Franks. The last Merovingian was deposed and the first Carolingian king enthroned.

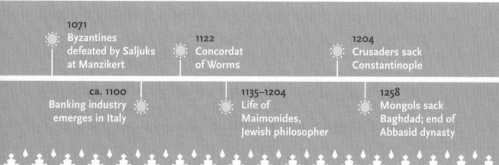

1071
Byzantines defeated by Saljuks at Manzikert

1122
Concordat of Worms

1204
Crusaders sack Constantinople

ca. 1100
Banking industry emerges in Italy

1135–1204
Life of Maimonides, Jewish philosopher

1258
Mongols sack Baghdad; end of Abbasid dynasty

THE CAROLINGIAN ASCENT

Pepin the Short (r. 754–768) became the king of the Franks by the acclaim of his people and the recognition of his title by Pope Stephen II (r. 752–757). He and his successors, Charles Martel and Charlemagne, stressed practical needs of connecting their realm and building an independent empire. The pope, for his trouble, gained in Pepin a military ally against the newest Germanic group to rip through Italy (the Lombards) and a tacit recognition that the Holy See was the arbiter of political legitimacy in Europe. Pepin accommodated Stephen by recognizing the pontiff's position as the secular ruler of the so-called Papal State, a wide swath of land across the middle of the Italian peninsula. With a strong ally and steady source of income, the papacy was able at last to exercise some genuine authority in the world, although the precise nature and extent of that authority remained uncertain for many years. Pepin energetically promoted his family's importance to championing the cause of Christianity.

There is something of a conundrum to Pepin's rise. The Carolingians were genuinely pious and dedicated to promoting the evangelization of barbarian Europe. Yet they owed their rise to power to their oppression of local churches. As early as Pepin of Heristal in the 720s, the Carolingians had ransacked the monasteries in their domains in order to raise the revenues they needed to pay their soldiers. Monasteries, after all, were the wealthiest institutions in western Europe, possessors of large estates well run with collective labor forces. Their sacristies were often filled with valuable items bequeathed by pious neighbors. Some of them also held deposits of cash or valuables from nervous owners who feared leaving them in their own homes.

The Carolingians presented their monasteries with a simple choice: These are barbarous times, and you can either give us your valuables to pay for our soldiers or you can be left alone to face certain annihilation by barbarian hordes or, even worse, the advancing Muslims. With their purses thus filled, the Carolingians' army swelled in size, enabling them to bring more and more of France under their authority. Charles Martel's great victory over the Muslims in 732, on the plain between Tours and Poitiers, solidified the family's heroic status and justified (in their own minds, at least) their manhandling of the monks. As the semiofficial *Chronicle of Saint-Denis* put it:

> The Muslims were marching to the city of Tours in order to destroy it, the Church of Saint Martin, and all the surrounding countryside, when Charles—that illustrious prince—opposed them at the head of his whole army. He set his soldiers in formation and fell upon

the enemy as ferociously as a hungry wolf falls upon a stag, until, by the grace of Our Lord, he had slaughtered on the field three hundred thousand of the enemies of Christianity, including their king Abd ar-Rahman. This was how he came to be called Martel ["hammer"], for he struck down his foes on the field as though he were a hammer made of iron, or steel, or any other type of metal. And the most amazing thing of all was the fact that he lost only fifteen hundred of his own men that day.

Success followed success, and by the end of Pepin the Short's reign almost all of modern France lay under Carolingian control.

What distinguished the Carolingians from other warlord families was their genuine dedication to transforming the societies they ruled. Pepin the Short built nearly as many monasteries as he ransacked and established churches and schools. He supported missionary work among the barbarians and at least attempted to develop an infrastructure of roads and bridges that would connect villages and towns. The Carolingians were also distinguished by their good luck: for five generations in a row they produced a single heir who inherited the family domain entire, without dividing it among siblings.[2] The greatest missionary of the age was Saint Boniface (680–754), an Anglo-Saxon monk who spent forty years preaching to the barbarians of the north, founding monasteries, churches, and schools with undiminished zeal (see Map 9.1). He had the ardent backing of the Carolingian court, "without which," Boniface wrote in a letter to a friend, "I could neither administer my churches and defend my clergy nor continue the fight against idolatry." Charles Martel, in fact, created four dioceses in southern Germany in his honor (at Salzburg, Regensburg, Freising, and Passau) and appointed him metropolitan, or supreme administrative officer among a group of bishops, over all German lands east of the Rhine River. In return for this support, Boniface made sure that all the bishops he appointed, from the Low Countries to Saxony, declared loyalty jointly to the papacy and the Carolingian ruler. The relationship between Rome and the Carolingians can be thought of as a partnership, although one in which the Carolingians had the dominant role.

---

[2]   The Carolingians did not rely on luck alone. They kept scores of mistresses and limited intimacy with their wives to the minimum needed to produce a male heir. Their method was not foolproof; in fact, several of the Carolingians did produce multiple legitimate heirs. Disease and warfare carried off most of them before political division occurred. In a few cases, a sudden assassination or imprisonment sufficed.

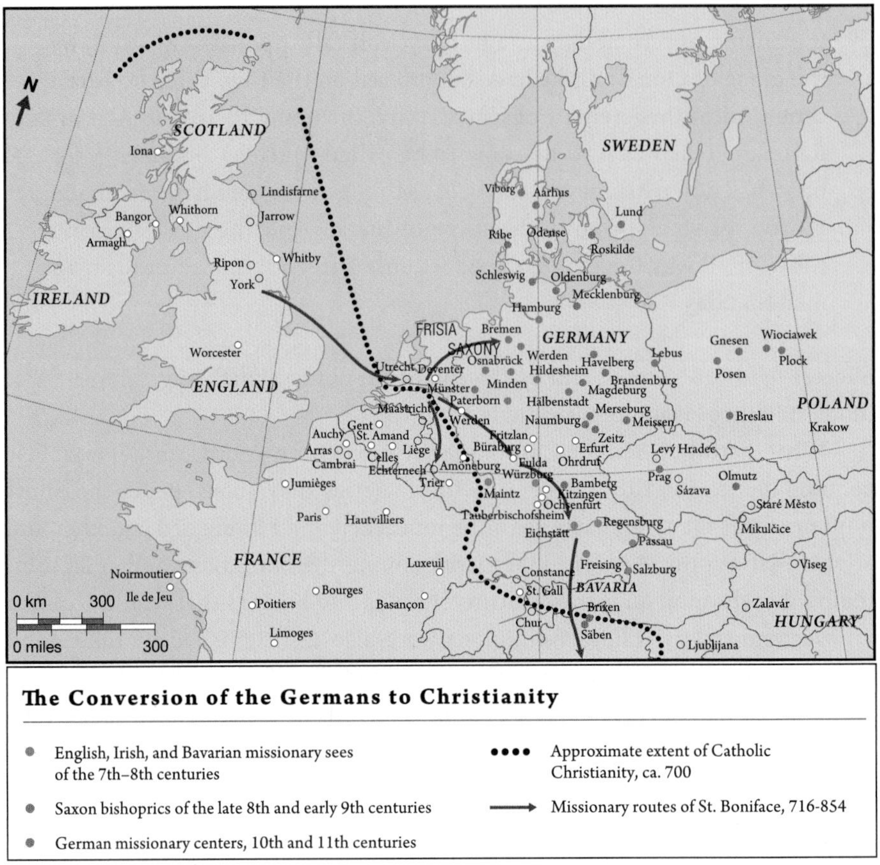

The Conversion of the Germans to Christianity

- English, Irish, and Bavarian missionary sees of the 7th–8th centuries
- Saxon bishoprics of the late 8th and early 9th centuries
- German missionary centers, 10th and 11th centuries
- •••• Approximate extent of Catholic Christianity, ca. 700
- ⟶ Missionary routes of St. Boniface, 716-854

MAP 9.1   **The Conversion of the Germans to Christianity**

CHARLEMAGNE

Pepin the Short died in 768, leaving two legitimate sons: Charles and Carloman. Carloman very conveniently died, however, leaving Charles (r. 768–814) as sole ruler of an undivided kingdom. Charles, known as Charlemagne ("Charles the Great"), spent the next forty years campaigning across Europe, expanding his realm into northeastern Spain, eastern Germany, Italy, Bohemia (part of today's Czech Republic), the Hungarian plain, and the northern reaches of the Balkans (today's Slovenia, Croatia and Bosnia and Herzegovina). His great goal was to unite Latin Europe under a single government with a comprehensive legal system, a network of churches and schools, a reliable basic infrastructure, and a regularized system of weights and measures (see Map 9.2).

Charlemagne's energy was prodigious. He also suffered from lifelong insomnia, which he inflicted on his courtiers:

> He habitually awoke and rose from his bed four or five times a night. He would hold audience with his retinue even while getting dressed or

MAP 9.2 **Charlemagne's Empire**

putting on his boots; if the palace chancellor told him of any legal matter
for which his judgment was needed, he had the parties brought before
him then and there. He would hear the case and render his decision
just as though he was sitting on the bench of justice. And this was not
the only type of business he would carry on at these hours, for he
regularly performed any one of his daily duties, whether it was a matter
for his personal attention or something that he could allocate to his
officials. (Einhard, *Life of Charlemagne*, ch. 24)

A promoter of education, he worked hard to educate himself too:

> He had the gift of easy and fluid speech and could express anything
> he wanted to say with extraordinary clarity. But he was not satisfied with
> the mastery of just his native tongue, and so he made a point of studying
> foreign ones as well; he became so adept at Latin that he could speak it as
> easily as his native tongue, and he understood much more Greek than he
> could actually speak. His eloquence was so great, in fact, that he could
> very well have taught the subject. And he energetically promoted the lib-
> eral arts, and praised and honored those who taught them. He studied
> grammar with Peter the Deacon, of Pisa, who was then an old man.
> Another deacon, a Saxon from Britain named Albinus and surnamed
> Alcuin, was the greatest scholar of his time and tutored the king in many
> subjects. King Charles spent many long hours with him studying
> rhetoric, dialectic, and astronomy; he also learned mathematics and
> examined the movement of heavenly bodies with particular attention.
> He tried to write too and had the habit of keeping tablets and blank
> pages under his pillow in bed,
> so that in his quiet hours he
> could get his hand used to
> forming the letters—but since
> he did not begin his efforts
> as a young man, but instead
> rather late in life, they met
> with little success. *(Life of Char-
> lemagne, ch. 25)*

The Sword of Charlemagne   Known as the Sword of
Charlemagne—even though it is at least one hundred
years too old to have been his—the sword was used
at the coronation ceremonies of all the kings of France
throughout the Middle Ages. Long held in the treasury of
the church of Saint-Denis, it is now housed in the Louvre.

A pragmatic streak led the Carolingians
to pursue a limited form of meritocracy; perhaps they had no real alternative. Anyone with a useful skill could
find service somewhere in the regime.
After all, the relentless traveling of the
royal court exposed them to a parade of
ineptitude. Everything from illiterate
priests to judges with no knowledge of
the law made the need for reform clear.
To the palace-capital at Aachen (Aix-
la-Chapelle, on today's French-German

borderlands), the court brought poets and theologians from Spain, historians and legal scholars from Italy, grammarians from Ireland, and Biblical exegetes from England. But they also scouted out skilled stonemasons, carpenters, metal smiths, scribes, weavers, tanners, musicians, coopers, and herbalists. Social background usually took a back seat to the more important issue of ability.

Charlemagne viewed power and status as commodities that he alone possessed and could parcel out at will. He governed his vast realm by delegating local, provincial authority to a caste of counts (*comites* in Latin) who represented the king and exerted power in his name; but these were not hereditary positions. The title of count was a job description, not a designation of social class. Charlemagne could appoint the lowest-born peasant as count, if he wished, and that count's position of honor would be equal to that of any count who claimed an aristocratic background. Ability and loyalty to the throne were what mattered most. The court held several assemblies each year, to which various counts and other officials were summoned. A typical summons read like this:

In the name of the Father, and of the Son, and of the Holy Spirit. Charles, the most serene, august, heavenly crowned, magnificent, and peaceful emperor, and also, by God's mercy, the King of the Franks and of the Lombards, to Abbot Fulrad.

You are hereby informed that I have decided to convene my General Assembly this year in eastern Saxony at the place called Stassfurt, on the Bode River. I therefore command you to come to this place on the fifteenth day before the calends of July—that is, seven days before the Feast of Saint John the Baptist—with all your men suitably armed and at the ready, so that you will be prepared to head out from that place in any direction I choose. In other words, come with arms, gear, and all the food and clothing you will need for war. Let every horseman bring a shield, lance, sword, knife, bow, and supply of arrows. Let your carriage train bring tools of every kind: axes, planes, augurs, lumber, shovels, spades, and anything else an army might need. Bring also enough food to last three months beyond the date of the assembly, and arms and clothing to last six.

I command, more generally, that you should see to it that you travel peacefully to the aforesaid place, and that as your journey takes you through any of the lands of my realm you should presume to take nothing but fodder for your animals, wood, and water. Let the servants belonging to each of your loyal men march alongside the carts and horsemen, and let their masters be always with them until they reach the aforesaid place, lest a lord's absence be the cause of his servants' evildoing.

Palatine Chapel   Interior of the Palatine Chapel at Charlemagne's imperial capital at Aachen.

Send your tribute—which you are to present to me at the assembly by the middle of May—to the appointed place, where I shall already be. If it should happen that your travels go so well that you can present your tribute to me in person, I shall be greatly pleased. Do not disappoint me now or in the future, if you hope to remain in my favor.

Clearly, the counts were kept aware that they owed their status entirely to the king's favor, not to any birthright of their own. Moreover, the king trained and sent out teams of *missi dominici* (literally, "dispatched royal agents" or "traveling lords"), who moved in regular circuits throughout the realm, reviewing comital records, holding open courts, and inviting the local populace to come forth with complaints about the job performance of the counts.

It was a primitive system of government but one that was meant to evoke the ruling style of the ancient Roman emperors, seeking a balance of centralized aims and local needs. The Carolingians admired the Roman idea of getting their subjects to see themselves as part of a larger civilization, although in the Carolingians' case the larger civilization was Latin Christianity, not Roman paganism. When building his palace complex at Aachen, Charlemagne ordered its chapel to be modeled on the Byzantine church of San Vitale that Justinian had built in Ravenna. And he had nearly identical marble pillars, stone columns, and glittering wall mosaics (and the appropriate skilled workmen) hauled north from Italy to do it.

IMPERIAL CORONATION

On Christmas Day in the year 800, Charlemagne was crowned augustus by Pope Leo III (r. 795–816). The significance of this was symbolic and also more than symbolic. The symbolic significance had to do with the date. The now-standard **anno Domini** system of dating—that is, reckoning the years from the purported time of Jesus's birth—was still a novelty. It had been created by a Syrian monk in the 6th century but had only become used in the west after the English scholar-monk Bede (d. 735) had promoted its use. By the time of Charlemagne's coronation, most literate people in Europe used the new system. Still, the bulk of the population probably still thought in terms of the old system (called annus mundi II) they had inherited from earlier times; and according to the old system the year 800 was actually the year 6000.

According to Einhard's *Life of Charlemagne*, which was written to order during the reign of Charlemagne's heir, Louis the Pious (r. 814–840), Charlemagne was surprised and incensed by the coronation. He would not have attended Mass even on Christmas if he had known what Leo what planning to do. But Charlemagne had been in Rome since early November, and the man who never slept would never have been caught in an unplanned coronation. More likely, some mishandled detail in the crowning ceremony caused his angry outburst. Regardless, Charlemagne probably took advantage of the calendrical quirk of the year 800/6000 to make his coronation signal the start of a bright new age in history.[3]

However, the significance of his coronation was far more than symbolic: it sent a political message to Byzantium. Seeking support for their claims to political legitimacy, Dark Age rulers like Clovis had frequently turned to the Greeks. The Byzantines, for their part, regarded the Latin westerners as ill-mannered and backward poor cousins, nominally members of the Christian family but hardly the sort of relatives one boasts about. Most Byzantines, in fact, regarded the loss of western Europe as a blessing in disguise. Charlemagne's coronation, however, changed everything. By assuming the imperial title, he effectively declared the Carolingian court independent of and equal to the Greek east. Moreover, by receiving the crown from the pope, the Carolingians established a way to pass on the imperial title in which the Byzantines had no role.

By assuming the imperial title, Charlemagne effectively declared the Carolingian court independent of and equal to the Greek east. Moreover, by receiving the crown from the pope, the Carolingians established a way to pass on the imperial title in which the Byzantines had no role.

Constantinople was not pleased with this declaration of independence but was powerless to do anything about it. Compounding matters, the throne in Constantinople was occupied at the time by a headstrong woman named Irene (r. 797–802), who had seized power by organizing a coup against her ineffectual

---

[3] Think of Charlemagne at his coronation as almost like a modern politician who coordinates speeches and ribbon-cutting ceremonies to coincide with significant anniversaries.

son Constantine VI. Charlemagne sent her an embassy and proposed marriage. If the marriage happened, his ambassadors urged, the eastern and western empires would unite, the growing rift between the Latin and Greek Churches would heal, and the Christian world could mount a powerful joint offensive against Islam. Irene was inclined to accept but she fell from power before she could give her answer.

Irene had been empress during the reign of her husband Leo IV (r. 775–780) and ruled as empress-regent while their infant son grew up. In 797, however, she had ordered her son to be blinded and left to die. She then assumed the gender-bending title of "emperor" (*basileos* in Greek), not "empress" (*basilea*). She was already unpopular, and her interest in marrying Charlemagne was the last straw and led to her overthrow. Several horrified Byzantine high officials plotted the coup. They seized Irene, cut off her hair, and forced her into a convent, never to emerge. Once in the convent, she seems to have accepted her fate with grace, seeing her life as a nun as a penance for her cruelty to her son. She died in 805.

Charlemagne, we are told, was so furious at this spoiling of his grand plan that he even formed a brief alliance with the Abbasid caliph in Baghdad, Harun al-Rashid (r. 786–809), to mount a two-pronged invasion of Byzantium. Nothing came of it. In the end, Charlemagne married twice. His first wife, Ermengarde, bore him six children; his second, Judith, produced two more.

CAROLINGIAN COLLAPSE

Carolingian luck ran out after Charlemagne's death in 814. At his death, Charlemagne's crown passed to his sole surviving heir, Louis the Pious (r. 814–840), but Louis had few of his father's gifts. Studious and well-meaning, he nevertheless lacked charisma and quick wit. He was also intensely straitlaced and moralistic—hence his nickname—and banished from the court all the dancing girls and mistresses who had made his father's sleepless nights less lonely. Instead of feasts, music, and gaiety in the imperial swimming pool, Louis enjoyed poring over plans to reform monastic life.[4] Even worse, Louis was determined to make up for his father's sexual libertinism by remaining staunchly faithful to his wife. As a result Louis was survived by three sons, all of whom hated him; after his death they divided up the kingdom and quickly went to war with one another.

The delicate sense of cultural unity across Latin Europe fostered by the earlier Carolingians now dissolved almost immediately into factionalism. The splintering of the empire could not be stopped, and within one hundred years of Charlemagne's death his empire had devolved into dozens of petty principalities.

---

4   Aachen is the site of a natural hot spring, over which Charlemagne had ordered his palace built.

The nicknames given to the late Carolingian princelings illustrate the decline. In no particular order: Charles the Bald, Louis the Stammerer, Charles the Simple, Louis the Blind, Charles the Fat, Louis the Child.[5] Civil war became incessant. The dozens of principalities soon shattered into hundreds of them, and Europe seemed likely to slip into another Dark Age.

Exacerbating the internal rot, new waves of invaders attacked Europe. Another nomadic group emerged from the central Asian steppe and marched into the plains of eastern Europe below the Danube River. These were the Magyars, the ancestors of today's Hungarian nation. They were a localized threat, however, encroaching only on the easternmost former members of the Carolingian state, although the people of northern Italy also had some reason to fear them. A much greater threat came from the north—the Vikings. Their hordes had begun to beset Latin Europe as early as Charlemagne's time; as the Carolingian state fractured, the invasions gained pace. What made the Viking threat so severe was the unpredictable nature of their attacks. Unlike the Magyars—a large, slow-moving land force—the Vikings raided in smallish groups of perhaps two dozen fighters per warship. Those ships, moreover, were designed to sail in as little as three or four feet of water, which meant that the Vikings could move upriver. Most of Europe's rivers flow northward and westward—opening directly on the Atlantic, the North Sea, and the Baltic Sea—in other words, directly in front of the Vikings' approach. The attackers were thus able to move with terrific speed and attack far inland. Viking warships attacked Paris in 834, during the reign of Louis the Pious, and even sacked Seville, the capital of Muslim Spain, about a decade later. There was no advance warning for these raids. The Vikings simply appeared all of a sudden, attacked and pillaged, and disappeared before any kind of defense could be mounted. And of course the incessant internal squabbling of the late mini-Carolingians only made the problem worse. Here is how a church council lamented the suffering of the time:

> Our cities are depopulated, our monasteries wrecked and put to the torch, our countryside left uninhabited. . . . Indeed, just as the first humans lived without law or the fear of God and according only to their dumb instincts, so too now does everyone do whatever seems good in his eyes only, despising all human and divine laws and ignoring even the commands of the Church. The strong oppress the weak, and the world is wracked with violence against the poor and the plunder of ecclesiastical lands. . . . Men everywhere devour each other like the fishes of the sea.

---

[5]   There was even a princeling named Bozo (although he was more capable than most of his peers).

In the words of the Old Norse poet Snori Sturluson (1179–1241), the Vikings "were like mad dogs or wolves, biting the edges of their shields, / and were as strong as bears or bulls. They killed men everywhere / and nothing could stop them—not fire, not steel." No wonder that scattered figures across Europe, gathering crowds of frightened followers around them, began to proclaim the end of the world.

And then the Muslims came again.

THE ISLAMIC EMPIRE

The Abbasid era (750–1258) is generally regarded as medieval Islam's Golden Age. From their magnificent new capital at Baghdad the caliphs transformed Islam's original Arab culture. The transformation also unleashed new problems, as that culture encountered western philosophy. With the inevitable backlash and the breakup of the empire, relations with western Europe were transformed as well. At the heart of Abbasid policy was the earnest, though cautious, welcoming of the involvement and traditions of the **malawi** ("clients," literally), the non-Arab Muslims. This new, open attitude was driven in part by simple pragmatism: by the mid-8th century, ethnic Arabs were no longer the numerical majority of Muslims. Taken together, Berbers, Egyptians, Kurds, Persians, and Syrians greatly outnumbered the relatively small nation of Arabs who still monopolized all positions of political, military, and religious authority.

Among the malawi, the largest single group by far were the Persians. The first wave of transformation under the Abbasids, therefore, was the intentional spread and promotion of Persian culture. Administrative integration came first. Persia, of course, had had long experience with administering a vast empire, going back to Cyrus the Great. Their tactic then had been a carefully controlled system of provincial governors called satraps; this same idea reemerged under the Abbasids as the network of new officials called **viziers**. A vizier (from Arabic *wazir*, meaning "helper" or "assistant") was the governor of a district and the personal representative of the caliph, a combination of administrator and ambassador.

To offset the inevitable danger of decentralizing imperial power, the Abbasids increased the number and extent of the state-owned estates (*sawafi*) within each province. They also increased the fiscal contributions owed by each province to Baghdad. With the new income, the Abbasids developed the city of Baghdad itself, improved the pay of the army, and continued developing the infrastructure that held the Islamic world together. Moreover, they withdrew from the viziers the authority to appoint local religious judges, or **qadis**, and monopolized control of all judicial appointments. Still, some loss of authority was inevitable. The viziers in Syria and Asia Minor bore the brunt of continuing the offensive against

Byzantium throughout the 9th and 10th centuries, a war they largely financed by themselves, which resulted in their increased autonomy from Baghdad.

SUNNIS AND SHI'A

The caliphs themselves remained more directly concerned, diplomatically and politically, with events in the east where restive groups of Shi'i Muslims began to rebel. The Shi'a had originally supported the Abbasids since they were in accord with the Abbasids' general call for the return of caliphal authority to members of Muhammad's family; but when the Shi'a found out that their particular line of that family would not be succeeding, they withdrew their support.

The rift between Sunni and Shi'i Muslims widened and grew more bitter with every generation. The dispute involved more than simply the Alids' claim to inherit the Prophet's mantle as leader of the Islamic community—a view that essentially defined Shi'ism during the Arab hegemony. Rather, an explicitly religious element entered the tradition. The death of the beloved Shi'ite leader Husayn ibn Ali al-Shahid, Ali's son, in battle against the Umayyad forces in 680, had inspired the creation of a passion narrative. Popular belief expected Husayn's return as the **Mahdi**—the "Guided One" who will emerge at the end of time and secure Islam's ultimate victory on earth. This belief now evolved into the Shi'ite doctrine of the "hidden imam," an imam, for the Shi'a, being the divinely appointed successor to Ali's line.

What differentiated the various sects of Shi'ism that emerged in Abbasid times was the number of true imams each group recognized, before the final imam went into hiding to await the moment of messianic return. The Shi'a, bound by their allegiance to Ali's descendants, thus incorporated the religious teachings and legal judgments rendered by those imams. In this way, their varying political programs transmuted into a web of traditions very much at odds with the Sunni majority.

The Abbasids were in a bind. In order to retain the support of the Islamic majority they had to champion Sunni orthodoxy, yet they owed the success of their coup against the Umayyads to the backing they had received from the Shi'a. Moreover, the open bias they showed for promoting Persians at court led to demands by other malawi groups for similar treatment. The rulers embraced as many aspects of the various malawi cultural traditions as could harmonize with Islamic teaching, whether Sunni or Shi'ite. The Persians, for example, had an ancient custom of veiling of their women whenever they appeared in public. This was done not to denigrate women but to express ethnic pride: inferior non-Persian men had no right to look upon a Persian woman. And since it seemed impractical to blind the empire's entire population of subject males, they veiled

Veiled Women   A late rendering of an early episode in Islamic history. This 17th-century fresco, from Safavid Iran, shows a scene of women mourning the dead, during one of the *riddah* wars of the first Islamic century (650–750 CE). The veiling of women, practiced by most Near Eastern peoples to some degree, was particularly associated with Persian culture, and it came to be the enforced norm within Islam after the Abbasid dynasty relinquished Arab Damascus and moved the capital east to Baghdad. The so-called Persianization of Islam then commenced. The Abbasids remained in power until the Mongols destroyed Baghdad in 1258.

their Persian women instead. It was a badge of honor, an expression of superiority. This practice harmonized well, however, with the Qur'anic demand for sexual modesty, and so became generally Islamized.

THE QUR'AN AND THE PHILOSOPHERS

A thornier problem arose from the very nature of the Qur'an. Many malawi had adhered to ancient Zoroastrian and Gnostic traditions, which found secret knowledge and multiple meanings in holy texts. The Qur'an's essence as the literal word of Allah seemed to operate against those traditions. Abbasid-supported jurists like Abu Hanifa [P] (d. 767), however, resolved this tension by reinterpreting the verse "Whether ye hide what is in your hearts or reveal it, Allah knows all" (3.29). This became a justification for **takiyya**—the intentional dissimulation of what one believes—since the Qur'an itself had both a literal meaning and also a number of hidden meanings, open only to interpretation by an initiated few. For Shi'i Muslims takiyya grew in importance from a bitter necessity during times of Sunni persecution to a fundamental and obligatory duty, the denial of one's faith as an expression of it. Another Zoroastrian idea absorbed into Islam was the notion of God as the Primeval Fire or Primordial Light, which then emanated out into the universe. By the middle of the 9th century the Shi'a had transformed this notion into their conception of the imam as the human epiphany of this Light.

On the Sunni side, some Yemeni and Bedouin tribes had long practiced a legalized form of concubinage. In *mut'a* (literally "pleasure" or "enjoyment"), a man married a woman for a prearranged period of time—a year, a month, a week, or even a single day—and paid her a prorated dowry in return for his "enjoyment" of her.[6] It is unclear how widespread the practice was in pre-Islamic times, but some evidence dates it as early as the 4th century among the Bedouin and possibly even earlier among some groups of Egyptian traders. Some later writers claimed that the Prophet himself had practiced it (al-Tabari, *Chronicle* 1.1775–1776). Sunni jurists rejected mut'a and the claim that the Prophet had ever been involved in it. But from the time of the legal scholar al-Shafi'i [A] (d. 819), a compromise allowed it, provided that the term of the marriage not appear in the written marriage contract. The Shi'a, in contrast, championed mut'a from the start (and still practice it widely today).

When Islam spread northward into the Levant and westward across North Africa, it encountered not only Judaism and Christianity but also the classical traditions of Greece and Rome. In an effort to curry favor with the new governors, groups of Christian scholar-monks in Syria began to translate works from the classical age into Arabic: Euclid's treatises on geometry, Plato's dialogues, the histories of Xenophon, the scientific and logical treatises of Aristotle were all translated. Intrigued by what they read or heard about, the caliphs maintained two principal centers for this translation in the late 8th and throughout the 9th century, both located in Baghdad. One was led by an Arab scholar named Yaqub al-Kindi [A] (d. 870) and the other by the Syrian Christian physician Hunayn ibn Ishaq [S] (d. 873). Hunayn ibn Ishaq also made the first translation of the Septuagint version of the Hebrew Bible into Arabic.[7]

The al-Kindi school focused on philosophical, literary, and logical texts, whereas the ibn Ishaq school tended to emphasize the Greek scientific and medical writings. Muslim scholars showed little interest in the Romans, whose intellectual works they regarded as derivative of the Greeks, although they did admire the Romans' adeptness with technology. But for every eager scholar wanting to

---

6   For a marriage of only one day, the marriage price could be as low as a handful of grain or dates.

7   By the time of the Abbasid takeover in 750 fully 50 percent of all Christians lived under Islamic rule. As they became Arabized, it became necessary to translate the Scriptures into Arabic.

pursue Greek knowledge, dozens of suspicious clergy cautioned against the ideas of unbelievers. The early Christian communities had exhibited a similar hesitation toward pagan Greek learning, until figures like Saint Augustine of Hippo and Boethius showed that classical learning posed no inherent threat to Christian orthodoxy. It could in fact help to clarify Christian ideas and beliefs. Resistance to the Greek tradition was as tenacious and passionate as the support expressed for it by scholars like al-Kindi.

Few of the great Muslim philosophers could read Greek; most depended on the translations made for the caliphal court. And like academics everywhere, some of them claimed more expertise than they actually had. Here is al-Kindi's thumbnail synopsis of Aristotle's *Metaphysics*:

> In the work called *Metaphysics* Aristotle sought to explain those things that exist yet do not possess matter; and how these things may co-exist with things that do have matter—and yet remain unconnected to matter and separate from it. He sought also to affirm the Oneness of God (the Great and Almighty), to explain God's many beautiful names, and to explicate how God is the causal agent of everything in the universe, making everything perfect—for God is the God of the universe, governing everything in His complete and perfect wisdom.

But Aristotle never said anything remotely like this. Was al-Kindi a charlatan? Certainly not. More likely, he wished to deflate clerical concerns about the dangers in seeking knowledge from non-Islamic traditions. He therefore tried to deflect criticism by making Aristotle sound like someone who would surely have been a Muslim if only he had been lucky enough to live in Islamic times.

This was cheating, of course, but at other times al-Kindi took brave stands:

> There is nothing shameful in admiring, and even in acquiring, the Truth, no matter where It comes from. To the student of Truth there is nothing that matters except Truth, and Truth is never cheapened or lessened by the person who states it, not even if he comes from a distant land and belongs to a backward nation. Indeed, Truth belittles no one and ennobles all.

Those interested in Greek philosophy thus faced a twofold problem: to show how a pagan discipline could explicate Islamic truth while preserving the authority of revelation. Does revealed truth need logical explication? Does offering one undermine the authority of the revelation?

Islamic thinkers had started to wrestle with these questions even before their discovery of the Greek tradition. From the Prophet's death in 632, Muslims and would-be Muslims had tried to answer a number of fundamental questions about the faith—the kinds of questions that anyone intrigued by the faith might raise. Was the Holy Qur'an created, or had it existed in heaven from all eternity? If it was present from the Creation, then why did Allah bother with the partial and imperfect Jewish and Christian revelations? And why does the Qur'an's message appear to change? How can it call first for Arabs to embrace Islam for repentance of their sins and to foster Arab brotherhood and unity, when later it calls Arabs to bring the message of Allah to the entire world?

> Those interested in Greek philosophy thus faced a twofold problem: to show how a pagan discipline could explicate Islamic truth while preserving the authority of revelation. Does revealed truth need logical explication? Does offering one undermine the authority of the revelation?

Another group of questions centered on Allah's attributes. In stating that Allah sees everything, hears our prayers, speaks, has knowledge, exerts will, and wields power, does the Qur'an imply that Allah is anthropomorphic—a kind of eternal man? And a third set of questions asked whether Allah's omniscience implies that every human's destiny is predetermined. Do we have free will, or has Allah, in knowing our ultimate fates, effectively set our ultimate fates?

The practical and immediate need to confront these matters resulted in a body of ideas and disciplines known as **kalam** (literally "speech" or "word," but

Truth Attainable by Rational Argument In this scientific manuscript from 13th-century Persia, two great rationalists, Aristotle and his pupil Alexander the Great, lead a discussion of the medicinal properties of certain animal organs and secretions.

usually translated as "theology"). Kalam was not philosophy and did not pretend to be. Instead, it was a method of inquiry into a limited number of specific issues that needed resolution, and its goal was to ease Islam's acceptance by cultures with long-established traditions that privileged rational thought. Reason, of course, is a universal trait. But the value placed upon reason, to the detriment of other ways of knowing, is a cultural one. As Islam spread, and as questions about the fundamental nature of Allah, his Qur'an, and man's free will were articulated, Sunni leaders resolved them by seeking a consensus among the community of scholars. This was the tradition known as **ijma'** ("consensus"), a principle that embraced the use of reason to resolve a religious question. But ijma' was not open-ended. Once the community's answer on any given questioned had been authoritatively expressed, the question was considered closed for all time. Tradition trumped any rethinking of any issue.

But the Christian-initiated translations of the Greeks posed another problem: as a result of their work, Muslim scholars encountered real philosophy (*falsafah* in Arabic), or open-ended rational inquiry. In philosophy, the answer given to any question does not close the matter; rather, it invites continual reappraisal. Philosophy is therefore as much an attitude of mind as it is any particular body of ideas, and it is not (ideally) an attempt to produce a desired goal. The liberal atmosphere of the early Abbasid years allowed philosophy to bloom, as the caliphs al-Ma'mun [A] (r. 813–833), al-Mu'tasim [A] (r. 833–842), and al-Wathik [A] (r. 842–847) encouraged new translations of and commentaries on the Western philosophical canon. They promoted as well the study of the philosophical and scientific traditions of Zoroastrian Persia and Buddhist India. In addition to the schools at Baghdad, these caliphs also opened a second center for liberal studies at Basra, in Iraq.

Opinions varied on the acceptability of the new cultural injections, but for the moment the inclusionists won. Prominent among these was a group of scholars known as the **Mu'tazilites** ("the Dissenters"). The Mu'tazilites had widely varying views but they shared a belief, or an inclination to believe, that whenever tradition and reason were in conflict, the scale tipped in reason's favor. Another way to describe the Mu'tazilites is as the party inclined to prevent ijma' from sealing off intellectual inquiry. For this reason alone, they were generally disliked and distrusted by most Sunnis; but what earned the Sunni's real ire was the Mu'tazilite position on the "createdness" of the Qur'an. The caliph al-Ma'mun, a strong Mu'tazilite sympathizer, even proclaimed this position the official doctrine of the state and required appointees to public office to swear allegiance to it. He triggered a violent revolt and died soon thereafter under suspicious circumstances.[8]

---

[8]   One tradition asserts that al-Ma'mun was resting by a river and asked some courtiers what he should eat. They just happened to have some dates at hand. He died on the spot, presumably poisoned.

THE SPLINTERING OF THE CALIPHATE

The cultural proliferation and ethnic egalitarianism of the Abbasids outraged many and inspired a predictable backlash. "O Lord," cried one offended Arab elitist, "the sons of whores have multiplied so much—please guide me to another land where I need not deal with bastards!" And as it happened, many were guided away from the cosmopolitan empire. The last Umayyads had fled as far as Spain, where they officially seceded from the empire and declared an independent kingdom of their own in 756. Other regions soon followed suit: Algeria broke away in 779; Morocco in 789; Tunisia in 800; Khurasan (northeastern Iran and part of Afghanistan) in 819; Sind (roughly the territory of today's Pakistan) in 867; and Egypt, too, in 868, only to have its rebels overthrown and succeeded by a new dynasty called the Fatimids in 905. So too did numerous smaller princedoms. Thus the cultural glories of the Abbasid Golden Age came at the cost of the political shattering of the empire (see Map 9.3).

Many issues played into the disintegration, only starting with concern about heretical ideas. Other issues were ethnic pride and racial bias, a sense of unfair commercial and tax policies, and frustration over the stalling out of strong jihad in favor of soft intellectualism. It is no coincidence that the splinter states became seedbeds for strict reform movements, such as the Almoravids and the Almohads. These sects, and others like them, called for halting what they regarded as the cosmopolitan rot that had beset Islam. They demanded a return to the militarism, discipline, and order of the great conquering age of the Prophet and his Companions. Only by restoring the active spirit of jihad, the reformists asserted, could the great cause of bringing Islam to the world be fulfilled.

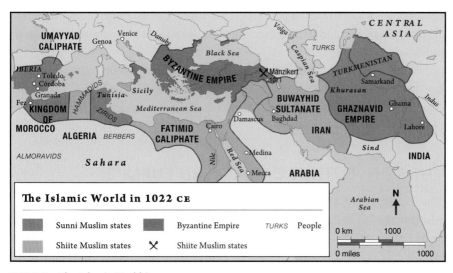

MAP 9.3   The Islamic World in 1022 CE

Two important developments coincided with the break-up of the Islamic empire. First, internally, Muslims had become the majority in two or three generations. Conversion, coercion, and emigration had caused the Jewish and Christian populations to shrink. Most Muslims states still recognized the legal rights of their non-Muslim subjects as dhimmis. But it is one thing to live in tolerance with foreign communities that vastly outnumber one's own, and it is quite another when one's own community has become the majority and the other groups suddenly appear as out-of-place foreigners. Acts of anti-Jewish and anti-Christian hostility became increasingly common through the 9th and 10th centuries, especially in areas experiencing temporary economic troubles. They became common features, too, of the reformist movements of the age. This was popular violence rather than state-run persecution in most cases, although the victims may not have appreciated the difference.

Second, this fracturing of the great Islamic empire coincided with the breaking up of the Carolingian empire in Europe. With western Europe entering another dark period, many of the splinter states saw an opportunity to expand commerce. After all, whether for dynastic, ethnic, or religious reasons, many of the splinter states disliked each other intensely and preferred to trade with Christian Europe than with their Islamic neighbors. Hence the new wave of Islamic attacks on Europe in the 9th and 10th centuries, coinciding roughly with the Magyar and Viking invasions. By 850 Muslim forces had conquered Sicily, parts of southern Italy, and the Balearic Islands, and they had made successful raids on Sardinia, Corsica, and the cities of Marseilles and Rome. But the Islamic attacks were not campaigns of conquest. Rather, they were attempts to carve out zones of interest, economic trading posts, and certain resources. And, as often as not, they were competing with one another to create these zones. For example, the Aghlabids of Tunisia seized Sicily in part in order to make sure that the Rustamids of Algeria did not get it.

All these developments transformed European and Muslim relations, which had been characterized by violence, distrust, and suffering. When the smoke cleared, Latin Europe and the Islamic world were each profoundly different places than they had been before.

THE REINVENTION OF WESTERN EUROPE

The Carolingian collapse was so spectacular and complete that it allowed Europe to reinvent itself in the 9th and 10th centuries—in the north via a new network of lords and vassals, bound by feudal bonds, and in the south by the growth of cities, powered by trade. The church, beset by corruption of astonishing proportions, responded with a reform movement of its own that remade the entire institution and put Christian life on a wholly new trajectory. The combination of these reinventions—social, civic, and spiritual—led directly to some of the greatest achievements of the medieval era. They also paved the way for the Crusades.

In France itself, the heartland of Carolingian power, the decay of the state and the pressure of foreign invasion caused farmers and their families to abandon their scattered homesteads and to take shelter in groups, under the protection of whatever strongman might exist in the district. Having little or nothing else to give in return for protection, they offered their labor. By this simple demographic shift, a society of individual farmers evolved into a new society based on **manors**—collective farms under the authority of lords. The lords owned the land and the major share of its annual yield, though the work was done by dependent farmers called **serfs**. Serfs were not slaves, although their daily lives differed little from slavery; lords could not buy and sell serfs as though they were mere property. Rather, serfs and lords were tied together by complex networks of mutual duties and rights. Serfs could not leave the manor, for example, or marry their offspring to someone from another manor, without their lords' permission. Lords were required to resolve disputes between serfs. The services owed back and forth made medieval manors like miniature communities, like agrarian states unto themselves.

The peasants brought varied backgrounds to their collective work, including knowledge of techniques like crop rotation, the use of wheeled plows, and the invention of horseshoes (which allowed quicker and more agile horses to replace lumbering teams of oxen as draught animals). Crop yields nearly doubled as a result. By living and working collectively, sharing labor, skills, and resources, farming on manors became much more productive. Crop surpluses became the norm, and western Europe became a food exporter for the first time in its history. It was largely to secure access to this food supply that the rump states of the broken Islamic empire began to compete for trading zones along the Mediterranean coast. And this trade allowed the new class of manorial lords to become rich—rich enough eventually to give up wooden manorial houses for stone castles (see Figure 9.1).

But the manorial lords lacked any real political legitimacy. They were, in many cases, of questionable ancestry and social status, men to whom war refugees had fled in desperation. These warlords (the Latin term is *milites*) used a variety of strategies to legitimate themselves. One popular option was simply to invent aristocratic genealogies for themselves, claiming descent from the Carolingians or some other early elite family. Another method was to form ties with other milites—a medieval equivalent of the modern practice of governments recognizing one another. By securing the support of other milites in the region, a warlord acquired at least a veneer of political authenticity.

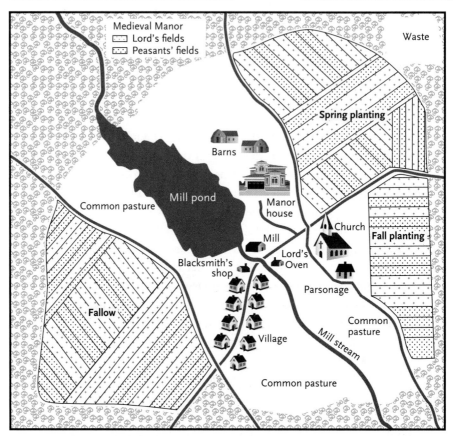

FIGURE 9.1 **A Medieval Manor**

These relationships between warlords had substance: some forms of military service, counsel, and economic assistance were invariably involved. Since each warlord differed in the amount of land or social recognition he commanded, these relationship slowly took on a hierarchical form, with a senior partner and a subordinate one—hence the terms **lord** and **vassal**, respectively. In forming a tie, a lord bestowed on the vassal dominion over the latter's allotted manor or manors, and the vassal in turn pledged to serve the lord loyally. In a public ceremony, the lord handed over a symbolic clod of earth, to represent the manors being bestowed. Since the Latin word for this land was *feudum*, these relationships were generally known as **feudal bonds**.

By the start of the 11th century, these connections had spread like a neural network across much of northern Europe; by the start of the 12th century they dominated it. Along with manors and feudal relations, they helped create a new society based on land tenure and ties of personal loyalty. Serfs worked for a landlord in return for the security and primitive justice he provided, while milites

Mediterranean Cities **307**

were bound to one another as lords and vassals. The system varied quite a bit from territory to territory. The feudal networks in France, for example, were significantly more elaborate, hierarchical, and complicated than those in England. When William the Conqueror (r. 1066–1089) seized the island in 1066 and parceled out the lands, he made it all but impossible for his vassals to redistribute the land to vassals of their own. Germany added its own twist, as great lords created feudal relations with high-ranking churchmen—abbots and bishops. Since these men would presumably not be producing heirs, there was little danger of the feudal lands becoming hereditary holdings.

MEDITERRANEAN CITIES

Mediterranean Europe followed a different trajectory. By long-standing custom, social position here had depended less on controlling land than on participating in the public life of the community: merchants, financiers, civic officials, and professionals formed the backbone of southern European life. Urban life had declined during the long centuries of the Dark Ages—some cities had collapsed to the point where they had only one-tenth of the ancient population levels—but revived under the short-lived stability of the Carolingians. Food surpluses from the new manors gradually made their way into urban markets. The Muslim attacks of the 9th and 10th centuries forcibly (and probably unnecessarily) opened those markets to trade with North Africa; cities like Barcelona, Genoa, Marseilles, Montpellier, Pisa, and Venice were the first to establish permanent commercial relations with the Muslim countries, and as a result they witnessed a dramatic rise in their wealth and power (see Map 9.4).

The Mediterranean accordingly roared back to life, much as the ancient Romans had first imagined, and from the 11th to the 15th century these cities were the economic powerhouses of Europe.[9] At the same time, the Byzantines' ground losses to the Muslims forced them to reorient their military and commercial attention northward, into the Slavic Balkan lands and the territories around the Black Sea. And as the Greeks gradually relinquished their control of the sea-lanes in the eastern Mediterranean, the Latin cities moved in aggressively. More cities joined in—Amalfi, Gaeta, Naples, Tarragona—and soon Latin Europe's commercial network, having expanded throughout the Mediterranean, spread around Spain, through the Gulf of Biscay, and into the North Sea. They brought lumber, minerals, wool, and metal ores to the manufacturing centers along the coast, transporting eastern silks, spices, metalwork, and dyed cloth back to the

---

[9] In the middle of the 12th century, the annual commercial tax revenue from the city of Palermo alone was four times that from the entire kingdom of England.

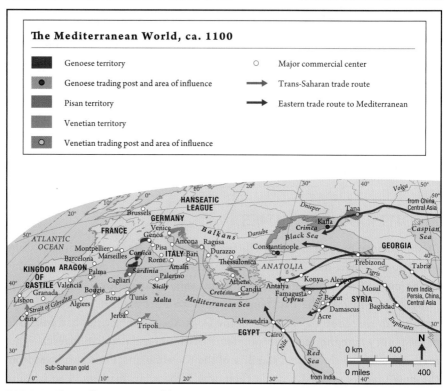

MAP 9.4   The Mediterranean World, ca. 1100

west. Developments in ship design led to larger and swifter commercial vessels, capable of delivering larger cargoes at less cost. Meanwhile the growing use of financial instruments like letters of credit reduced the danger of carrying large amounts of cash. By the late 11th century, an embryonic banking industry had already emerged in Italy.

Mediterranean cities quickly became multiethnic polyglot emporia, much as they had been during the Pax Romana. A visitor to 12th-century Barcelona or Pisa, for example, would find the streets and markets crowded with merchants. They came from Alexandria, Athens, Brussels, Famagusta, Lisbon, Palermo, and Tunis, and a dozen other places—with more than a sprinkling of Jews from all round the Mediterranean. The interaction between groups was regulated by complex systems of municipal and religious laws, ethnic customs, class privileges, and commercial traditions. Merchants of different ethnicities, cities, or particular social strata each had specific rights and privileges, negotiated between communal governments. In order to keep straight who was who, Mediterranean cities began to use dress codes to identify people. These **sumptuary codes** elaborately regulated styles of dress, types of fabrics, headgear, footwear, numbers of buttons,

Amalfi A panoramic photograph of Amalfi, a small town on the southern Italian coast that rose to great wealth and power in the 10th–12th centuries. This photo, from the late 19th century, shows how wealth and power did not always depend on or result in the physical growth of the city.

and the sorts of decorative badges, pins, and scarves each person could wear. The idea was not to shame groups but to establish the rules of their engagement.

The communicative calculus could be elaborate: a Muslim cloth merchant from Famagusta (in Cyprus), for example, conducting business in Montpellier with a Christian member of the jewelers' guild from Marseilles was entitled to a specific set of legal rights. One had to know who one was dealing with, or there was no deal. Moreover, since different groups often had different housing and dietary requirements, the custom quickly arose of segregating the cities: merchants from cities that did a lot of business with one another were awarded buildings, streets, or even whole neighborhoods to themselves. There they had special houses, butcher shops, alehouses, worship sites, so that each could live according to their own customs.

Most cities were governed by municipal councils and various administrative executives, most of whom in turn were drawn from the urban elites. This group consisted of local rural aristocrats, well-to-do merchants, the professional classes (bankers and lawyers, chiefly), and representatives of the leading artisanal and commercial guilds.

THE REINVENTION OF THE CHURCH

The Catholic Church also reinvented itself in the post-Carolingian centuries. It needed reform badly, for many forms of corruption had taken hold by the 9th and 10th centuries. The problem with the church, though, was not that it had "become corrupt." Rather, it had been corrupted by the milites, the secular warlords in Latin Europe. Simply put, the warlords, to raise funds for their armies, revived the old Carolingian practice of ransacking their own churches and monasteries. Many simply plundered and ran off with the spoils, but others conceived of a longer-term strategy for tapping into ecclesiastical wealth: they expelled the clerical leaders (often by killing them) and sold their positions to their military and political underlings and supporters. By placing their clients in ecclesiastical positions, the warlords secured a set percentage of the churches' annual revenues. In turn, they rewarded their followers with fancy titles, accoutrements, salaries, and prestige. This abuse was called **simony** and it was rampant, from village churches and small monasteries to large episcopacies and even the papacy. Few religious houses avoided the onslaught.

The chronicles of the 10th and 11th centuries abound with abominable behavior by warlord lackeys in Church position. The nadir was reached in Rome. During a period remembered as the "Pornocracy" (904–984), the Holy See was bought and sold numerous times among the leading families in Roman politics. Pope John XII (r. 956–963) was reported to have sold the bishopric of one town to a ten-year-old boy, as a birthday present from the boy's father.[10] The tradition of state control of the church dated back to the emperor Constantine and the Council of Nicaea. The more recent tyranny of the Carolingians had been stark, but they never abused the Church in the same way that the warlords now did. The fundamental reform required was to insist on the church's freedom from secular control. **Libertas ecclesie!** ("Freedom for the church!") became the demand of the reformers.

The reform movement began at the grassroots level, on the new manors, where the problem of simony was felt most acutely. To the peasants, simony not only looked bad but created a profound spiritual crisis. The Carolingians, after all, had struggled mightily to promote Christian education and to improve the quality of parish church life. As a result, by the mid- to late 10th century probably a clear majority of western peasants were meaningfully, knowledgeably Christian. And the one teaching they all knew was that they needed the sacraments in order to achieve salvation, especially baptism.

---

[10] John's favorite mistress, it was said, wore a papal crown, sat on a throne, and turned one wing of the palace into a whorehouse. He died in bed with a married woman.

But does a "priest" who got his job only by buying the title from a warlord actually have sacramental authority? Even if the "priest" does perform a Eucharist, are the bread and wine of that ceremony truly turned into the Body and Blood of Christ? And if not, is the ceremony of any value at all? If a peasant couple has a sickly infant whom they want to have baptized, is the baby truly baptized if the "priest" is a simoniac? The question was not theoretical: probably one-half of all children born in Europe at this time died before the age of five. Since Catholic doctrine maintained that only baptized Christians can be saved, the couple's baby would presumably suffer eternal damnation because of the illegitimacy of the "priest's" action. It gets more complicated, too: What if the priest in question had been properly trained for his vocation, but his ordination to the priesthood had been performed by a simoniac bishop? Or if that bishop's elevation to the episcopacy had been performed by a simoniac archbishop—perhaps by that ten-year-old boy appointed by John XII?

Outraged peasants understood one thing quite well: this problem existed because the milites had taken over the churches. Warlords no longer merely controlled the peasants' lives on the manors; their greed for church revenue now placed even the peasants' eternal souls in jeopardy. Demands for freeing the churches from the warlords' clutches therefore began on the manors, where the population could express collective complaint. These rallies for reform, called **Peace of God** assemblies, began as individual demonstrations. However, they multiplied in number, since peasants everywhere had essentially the same complaint and the same sole method of protest available to them. They thus took on the appearance of a movement—indeed, the first mass movement in Western history.

Movements need leadership. That leadership came from Europe's bishops. The reawakening of Europe's cities had revived the episcopacies as well. Although defined as the spiritual descendants of the Twelve Apostles, bishops had always been second-tier figures in the Latin Church. When over 90 percent of the population lived in the countryside, churchmen in cities lacked prestige—especially since hardly any cities in continental Europe were of any real size. In Charlemagne's time, for example, the city of Paris was only 7.5 acres (3 hectares) in area. By comparison, the university campus at which I teach is 75 acres (30 hectares) in area.

Monasteries had always been the real centers of power in Latin Christianity, going back to Saint Benedict in the 6th century. Most of the scholars drawn into the Carolingian court had been monks and abbots, and monastic wealth (when it was not plundered) was the largest accumulated treasure in most districts. As cities grew in size and number, the relative importance of bishops did too. And they seized on the Peace of God assemblies as a means to place themselves at the forefront of church reform. Bishops began to convene regional councils, scheduled and organized assemblies, arranged for large-scale public Masses, commissioned speakers, issued calls for specific milites to relinquish their strangleholds over their churches, and above all promoted themselves as the leaders of the reformed church. The more success they had in winning churches' freedom, the faster they rose in popular estimation.

By the time the reform reached the papacy (the last part of the church to be reformed) the bishops were clearly the dominant power brokers. But as the bishops took center stage, so too did the pope—who was, after all, the bishop of Rome.[11] The Church in the world had become the center, and the church removed from the world had moved to the margins. Europe's leading kings, however, were not enthusiastic about having an independent papacy. The second half of the 11th century was thus filled with diplomatic, rhetorical, and military wrangling between Rome and her rivals. Important turning points were the

pontificates of Leo IX (r. 1049–1054) and Nicholas II (r. 1059–1061). Leo spent much of his time as pope on the road, bringing the majesty of the office to the eyes of Europe's commoners for the first time, and Nicholas created the **College of Cardinals**—which subsequently acquired sole power to elect the next successor to Saint Peter. These two pontificates were, each in its own way, declarations of papal independence. By the time of Gregory VII (r. 1073–1085), military forces under the German ruler Henry IV (r. 1056–1106) invaded Italy and imprisoned the pope. When papal defenders from southern Italy raced to his rescue, they found that Henry had fled north. They sacked the city mercilessly, which forced Gregory to sneak out of Rome in disguise lest the outraged populace murder him.

Papal-reform Conflict The German emperor Henry IV, facing rebellion from his nobles, pleads with Countess Matilda of Tuscany to help persuade Pope Gregory VII to end the rebellion. This image appears in an 11th-century manuscript of *The Life of Matilda, Countess of Tuscany*.

---

[11] At first the overwhelming majority of popes came from monastic backgrounds. In the second thousand years of Christianity, more than 90 percent of popes were bishops before rising to the Holy See.

This was the tipping point in the papal-reform conflict, and all sides recognized a need to find a compromise. In 1122 it was reached: the **Concordat of Worms**, signed in that year, affirmed the papacy's independence. They recognized that only a free election by the College of Cardinals could legitimately select the pontiff. On the secular side, lay rulers vowed to accept the church's own appointees to clerical positions, but retained the right to bestow all the lands and revenues associated with those appointments. The great reform, everyone hoped, was finished.

THE CRUSADES

Between 1095 and 1291 Latin Europe fought a series of large-scale military campaigns to win back the Holy Land, which had been under Muslim control since 639. Numerous small-scale efforts continued after that but amounted to little. Nonetheless, the Crusades changed societies and regimes throughout the Mediterranean.

The Crusades are unique in Western history, for they are the only wars that were formally sanctioned and blessed by the church. To take part in them was considered not only morally justifiable but a positive spiritual action. These wars, the church proclaimed, pleased God and made one a better Christian—to the point that if a soldier died on crusade, he was assured forgiveness of all his sins and eternal salvation. (Assuming that he had had a penitent heart and pure motives.) The church called for crusades, preached them from the pulpit, formally inducted their leading fighters, and helped arrange their financing. As enthusiasm for crusades to the Holy Land waned in the 13th century, the crusades' mechanism of preaching and finance were brought to bear on conflicts elsewhere in Europe.

While a new phenomenon, the crusades were nevertheless a product of the centuries that had preceded them. If one disregards the religious motive that lay behind them, the crusades appear as simply the newest chapter in the centuries-old struggle for control of the eastern Mediterranean shore. These lands offered access to both the European economy, centered on the sea, and the overland Asian economy composed of the great silk and spice routes. Its geographical location made the Holy Land valuable long before it became holy. The Phoenicians and the Hittites fought over it. So did the Egyptians and the Sea

While a new phenomenon, the Crusades were nevertheless a product of the centuries that had preceded them. If one disregards the religious motive that lay behind them, the Crusades appear as simply the newest chapter in the centuries-old struggle for control of the eastern Mediterranean shore.

Peoples, the Hebrews and the Canaanites, and then the Persians and the Greeks, followed by the Greeks (under Alexander) and the Persians. The Romans came next, then the Persians again, the Byzantines after that, and then finally the Arabs under the Prophet Muhammad. And the litany of conflicts continues after the Crusades ended. In short, the Crusades had a larger context of East-West struggle that involved many more factors than religion alone. But the religious factor is what makes the Crusades unique. To find ways to justify warfare is one thing, but how did the Latin West ever develop the idea that Jesus wanted them to kill Muslims?

> In short, the Crusades had a larger context of East-West struggle that involved many more factors than religion alone. But the religious factor is what makes the Crusades unique. To find ways to justify warfare is one thing, but how did the Latin West ever develop the idea that Jesus wanted them to kill Muslims?

Part of the answer lies in the great reform effort, where intellectual reform was as important as institutional renewal. At the many councils convened during the 10th and 11th centuries, the church debated, among many other things, the theology of warfare. Under what conditions, if any, may a Christian legitimately use physical violence? Jesus had preached "Blessed are the peacemakers" and had accepted his own torture and death, but did that necessarily imply that Christians must never use any kind of force? Did the bravery of the martyrs of the first Christian centuries require all Christians to deny a right of self-defense when attacked? If one sees a criminal brutally assaulting a woman, is one committing an un-Christian act by pulling him off and beating him into submission?

Such questions were not just hypothetical. Latin Europe was overwhelmingly Christian by the late 11th century, but it was also a society organized for warfare—a secular hierarchy of warlords in the north and a congeries of maritime communes, each with its own militia, in the south. The reformed church needed to find ways to manage and restrain conflicts. One method it employed was the **Truce of God**, a solemn ban on warfare on holy days and on assaulting pilgrims. Those who violated the truce were excommunicated. Christian warfare was acceptable, the church decreed, only if it met three criteria: it must have a just cause, it must be fought in a just way, and it must be declared by a just authority.

By the end of the 11th century, many Europeans believed that warfare against Islam was indeed a just cause. After enduring centuries of persecution under the Romans, Christians in the Holy Land, across North Africa, and throughout the Mediterranean faced conquest by the followers of Muhammad. In creating the great Islamic empire, after all, Muslim armies had killed tens of thousands (and possibly hundreds of thousands) of Christians and Jews. Islamic law formally protected the rights of their subject Christians and Jews, but reality on the ground was often quite different. This is not altogether surprising. Under the early caliphs there had been a concerted effort to protect the empire's dhimmis, but as the years went by, churches and synagogues fell into disrepair as Muslims gradually became the majority group within the overall population. As Islamic unity then shattered into a maze of ethnic, sectarian, and dynastic rivalries, popular willingness to tolerate the non-Muslims in their midst only declined. The 10th and 11th centuries saw repeated popular attacks on Christians and Jews and sporadic state-run persecutions.

The popularity of pilgrimage as a Christian devotion complicated matters. For centuries waves of pilgrims had ventured from Europe to the Holy Land— with Muslim blessing—to worship at the sites associated with Christ. Pilgrimage, however, is by its very nature a public display of faith and therefore at odds with dhimmi law. Muslim ire focused on the European pilgrims traveling through their lands, less so on their own Christian subjects, and those pilgrims began to experience bitter street-level harassment and violence. Soon enough, though, intolerance of the dhimmis themselves took root in many places. Islamic reform groups like the Almohads and Almoravids in Spain and North Africa made no secret of their determination to crush the Christians and Jews living among them. In 1009 the Egyptian ruler al-Hakim (r. 996–1021) demolished the Church of the Holy Sepulcher in Jerusalem (the church built over what is believed to have been Jesus's actual tomb) and ordered every church and synagogue in his realm similarly destroyed. Christians across Europe were horrified but not altogether surprised. To take arms against such attacks therefore seemed to satisfy the requirement of a just cause.

Church of the Holy Sepulcher   What the crusaders were after: the tomb of Christ at the Church of the Holy Sepulcher in Jerusalem. The present chapel structure was built in the 13th century. Earlier buildings were damaged or destroyed by various attackers, the most notable being the Egyptian caliph al-Hakim in the early 11th century.

BUT NOT A WAR AGAINST ISLAM

There were eight major Crusades, all except the First Crusade ending in failure. The soldiers of the first campaign conquered the Holy Land in 1099 and carved four separate states out of it (see Map 9.5). These became nominally Christian states, although the overwhelming bulk of their populations were Muslims, Jews, and non-Latin Christians. Despite their violent creation, however, the states quickly developed internal policies that granted as much autonomy as possible to the native groups. The crusaders turned into surprisingly lenient rulers, as evidenced by the fact that thousands of Muslims and Jews migrated to the crusader states before they were crushed in 1291. While the Crusades aimed to wrest the Holy Land from Muslim control, they were not a general war on Islam itself. Christian trade with Muslims continued in the Mediterranean cities throughout the Crusades—and in fact increased steadily. Muslim sources of the age never present the struggles for the Holy Land in religious terms, and the Christian conquest of Jerusalem in 1099 triggered no groundswell of outrage outside of Palestine itself.

Nor were the Crusades a fight against Arabs. If the Crusades began with any specific enemy in mind, it was the Seljuk Turks whose arrival near the holy sites in the 1060s and 1070s did the most to interrupt the passage of pilgrims. The Abbasids had long courted the Turks, whose military might was considerable, and hoped to use them against Shi'i princes in Syria, Palestine, and Egypt who refused to obey Baghdad. The Turks were new to Islam, but they burned with the zeal often found among recent converts. With the caliphs' blessing they marched westward, defeated the Byzantine army at Manzikert in 1071, and spread throughout Anatolia, setting up an independent state. But many of the nomadic warriors refused to settle down and raided the Arab-led states to their south. The threat to the splinter states inspired them to crack down on their dhimmis in a show of force. The age demanded an expression of rigorous jihad, and it got it.

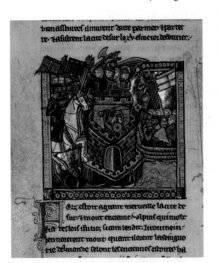

The Siege of Antioch (1098)
William of Tyre's *Histoire d'Outremer* ("History of Events across the Sea") is one of our best sources for the first two crusades and the internal life of the crusader states between wars. Here the siege of Antioch—the most strategically important battle of the First Crusade—is depicted.

Caught between Crusaders from the west and Turks from the east, the Byzantines survived by playing one side off the other. They no longer had the military might to assert themselves and became adept at diplomatic manipulation, acquiring for themselves a reputation for trickery and unreliability. The Crusaders came to despise the Byzantines as much as the Muslims, which explains the wild violence unleashed when the soldiers of the Fourth Crusade (1202–1204) sacked Constantinople.

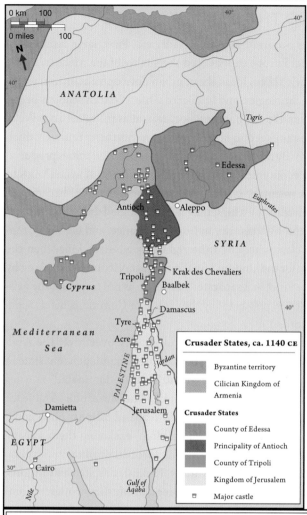

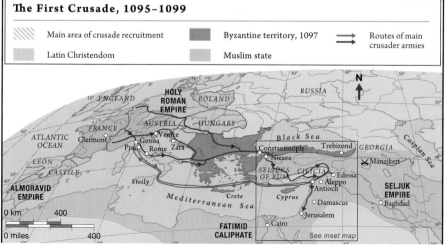

MAP 9.5   The First Crusade and the Crusader States

PARLIAMENTS AND THE MAMLUK EMPIRE

Several important changes occurred in the Crusader era. First, large numbers of Latin Christians from feudal Europe experienced the vitality of the Mediterranean. They brought back north with them ideas about urban development, manufacture and commerce, schools, technologies, and intellectual life. Western scholars began to learn Greek and Arabic and to use both intellectual traditions to advance Western thought. Cities were established in large numbers in northern Europe, which catalyzed economic growth. By the end of the Crusader era, in 1291, cities produced well more than half of the economic output of northern countries, which helps to account for the rise of parliamentary systems of government. As cities became the main providers of tax revenue to the kings, they also demanded a voice in the government. In the course of the 13th century in England, France, and Germany, representatives of the urban classes acquired the right to advise the king, then the power to initiate legislation for the king, and finally the authority to veto the king by controlling his purse. (They met in a separate "house" so as not to offend the aristocracy by their mere presence, just as today the House of Commons meets separately from the House of Lords.)

Second, the arrival of the Turks upset and ultimately overthrew the Arab rulers of the Middle East. In their place, the Turks created an independent state in Anatolia, called the Sultanate of Rum, and a second Turkish-dominated state in a reunited Egypt and Syria, called the Mamluk Empire. The **Mamluks** (Arabic for "slave") originated as an elite bodyguard unit for the Abbasid caliphs. Their name derives from the practice of seizing Christian children, enslaving them, raising them as Muslims, and putting them through an extraordinary military discipline and training. These slave-soldiers were culturally Turkish, despite their origins, and were independent of the tribal loyalties of the regular Muslim armies.[12] Nominally subject to the caliphs in Baghdad, these two states comprised the center of Islamic power (see Map 9.6). In 1258 Abbasid power disappeared entirely when the Mongols destroyed Baghdad; the Mongols' self-proclaimed drive for world domination ended when they were decisively defeated themselves by the Mamluks only two years later. Turkish hegemony over the Islamic world lasted in one form or another until the early 20th century.

Third, the Byzantine Empire effectively ceased to exist as a world power. When the Crusaders wrecked Constantinople in 1204, they held on to the empire for seventy years, parceling it out to themselves as fiefdoms. For three generations the mainly French usurpers plundered Greece and all her holdings, determined

---

[12]   The Mamluks were highly respected for their abilities—to the point that freemen were known to offer themselves as slaves in order to become eligible for service.

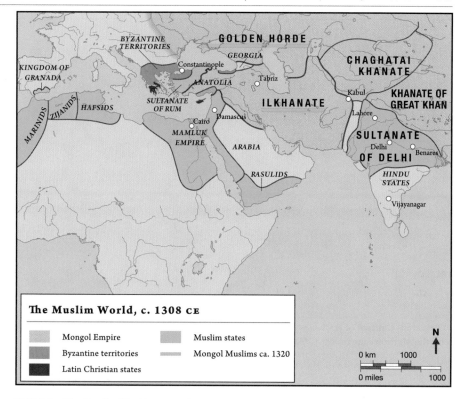

The Muslim World, c. 1308 CE

Mongol Empire	Muslim states
Byzantine territories	Mongol Muslims ca. 1320
Latin Christian states	

N

0 km   1000

0 miles   1000

MAP 9.6   The Muslim World, ca. 1308 CE

to crush the Orthodox Church and replace it with Roman Catholicism. By the time they were driven out, in 1278, the empire was in tatters and continued to live only as a weak confederation of four minor states. Using their diplomatic acumen, it managed to survive until its final defeat by the Ottoman Turks in 1453, but for much of its last two centuries the Byzantine Empire consisted of little more than the city of Constantinople itself.

JUDAISM REFORMED, RENEWED, AND REVILED

Scattered by the Romans in 70 CE, the nation of the Jews disappeared from history as a political entity. They were left stateless, exiled from their homeland, hounded by Christian evangelists, and still subject to persecution by the Romans. Yet the Jews survived—by adapting imaginatively to the societies where they lived, while clinging to the core of their traditions.

As a Mediterranean people, they scattered, predictably enough, around the sea basin (see Map 9.7). In most places local laws forbade them to own farmland, and hence the Jews of the Diaspora became even more heavily urbanized than

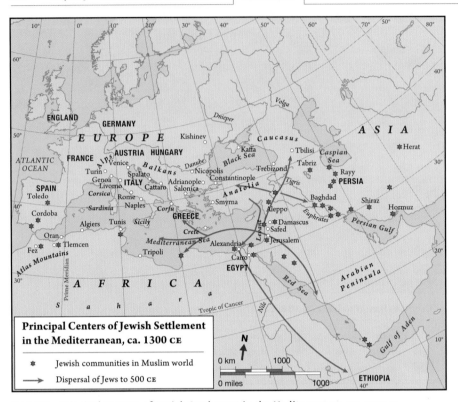

MAP 9.7   Principal Centers of Jewish Settlement in the Mediterranean, ca. 1300 CE

they had been before. Life in cities, moreover, offered them a modicum of safety, since they tended to live as discrete communities. In their own designated neighborhoods, they could have at least limited autonomy.

The class and sectarian rifts that had characterized life in Judea in Christ's time ceased to have meaning. They were all exiles now and the Temple was no more. The rabbinical strain of Judaism that traced its roots to the Babylonian Captivity hence became the norm for Jewish life. In city after city, Jews established their synagogues and schools, their butcher shops and eateries, and settled into lives as merchants and professionals.

As during their first exile in Iraq, the Jews quickly found that life as a religious minority presented challenges not addressed in the Torah. How should one live a Jewish life in a non-Jewish world? The rabbis therefore set to work to gathering, sifting, organizing, and commenting on the decisions handed down by earlier religious judges. At the same time new judgments were being rendered from one end of the Mediterranean to the other. These judgments and the precedents on which they rested were studied at the great rabbinical academies and eventually were codified in the **Talmud**. It had two parts—the Mishnah (the collected rabbinical laws, compiled around 200 CE by R. Judah ha-Nasi) and the Gemara (commentaries on the laws compiled around three hundred years later). Together, they formed the central pillar of medieval Jewish life. There were competing versions—one produced by scholars in Babylon (where the rabbinical tradition dated to the 6th century BCE) and another in Jerusalem.[13] Although both are considered valid, when the word Talmud is used, it generally refers to the Babylonian version.

Throughout the Middle Ages, most rabbis in Europe received their training at the academies in the Levant, either in Jerusalem or in Baghdad. An important new chapter of Jewish history began with the Carolingian collapse in the late 9th century. A number of late Carolingian princes, hoping to ignite some local manufacturing and commercial activity, invited Jewish communities to relocate from the Mediterranean and to settle permanently in northern Europe. They offered various enticements—legal autonomy under Carolingian protection, advantageous tax schedules, housing allowances, and so on. Once such guarantees were in place, scores of Jewish families, companies, and social networks migrated to the north and settled in the small towns that dotted the Rhine river valley and along the Seine.

For example, in 1084, shortly after arranging the legal founding of Speyer as a municipality, its lord, Bishop Rudiger, issued the following charter:

> In the name of the Holy and Indivisible Trinity, I, Rudiger, by the grace of God bishop of Speyer, having completed the task of establishing Speyer as a legally recognized city, determined to increase the city's honor a thousand-fold by bringing a community of Jews to live permanently within it; and so I invited in Jews from abroad and from Jewish communities in other towns. Moreover, I enclosed them within a fortified wall, lest they be too easily harmed by the rioting common people. . . . I gave them license and privilege to work at money changing according to their desire . . . and I bestowed upon them, from the church's holdings, a burial ground for their own possession and use. . . . As much as I am the ruler of Speyer's [Christian] residents, so is the archisynagogos for the Jews [therein]: he has power to judge all disputes and petitions brought before him. . . . In general, I have granted to the Jews of Speyer— as a crowning grace to my benevolence—statutes of such benefit to them as to be unequalled anywhere in Germany.

As decades passed, these small communities prospered and grew.

Although they remained in more or less continuous contact with the Mediterranean communities, northern Jews soon began to follow a different path of development from southern Jews. These different paths ultimately resulted in the

---

[13] Although called the Jerusalem Talmud, it was actually compiled by scholars in and around the city of Tiberias, along the western shore of the Sea of Galilee.

formation of two distinct Jewish cultural traditions—that of the **Ashkenazim**
in the north and the **Sephardim** in the south. The Ashkenazim were the most
geographically remote from their homeland, surrounded by a society that did not
welcome their arrival. They therefore turned inward, developing a brilliant culture that focused on preserving Talmudic tradition at all cost. The Sephardim,
comfortably Mediterranean, were in constant contact with Arab, Greek, and
Latin cultural developments, and they participated more directly in intellectual
exchange and changes in cultural norms. The stark contrast between Ashkenazic
and Sephardic Judaism became apparent when groups from both traditions migrated back to the Holy Land when it was under Crusader control. They wore
different styles of clothing, followed different liturgies and rituals, and spoke
different vernaculars.[14] Providing separate synagogues, butcher shops, markets,

Jewish Synagogue and Christian Church   During the long Reconquista of Spain from Muslim
control, many towns and villages changed hands numerous times. Mosques were turned into
churches, then back into mosques, then again into churches, over and over. Synagogues were
also built, taken over, handed back, reclaimed for another repeatedly. This 13th-century building in Toledo, in central Spain, was a mosque that was eventually converted into the church of
Santa Maria la Blanca. Skilled craftsmen of all faiths found work in the near-constant renova-
tion. In a handful of Christian churches in Spain, the vine-tracery patterns carved on arches
by Muslim stonemasons turn into Arabic lettering and spell out the *shahadah*: "There is no
god but Allah, and Muhammad is his prophet."

---

[14]   The southerners spoke early forms of Ladino, related to Old Spanish. The northerners spoke early forms
of Yiddish.

and housing for both communities challenged the ingenuity of the Crusader-state regimes and led to near-constant low-grade social friction.

North or south, east or west, medieval Jews lived in their separate districts in the cities. And these districts were frequently encircled by protective walls both to mark the territory of Jewish autonomy and to protect the Jews from angry Christian mobs. (The local rabbi possessed the key to the gate.) The church insisted that the only proper Christian response to the Jews was tolerance and coexistence—and that it was the church's special responsibility to protect the Jews. As Pope Innocent III (r. 1198–1216) put it in 1199:

> No Christian may use violence in order to force a Jew to receive baptism…for no one who has not willingly sought baptism can be a true Christian. Therefore let no Christian do a Jew any personal injury—except in the case of carrying out the just sentence of a judge—or deprive him of his property, or transgress the rights and privileges traditionally awarded to them. Let no one disturb the celebration of their festivals by beating them with clubs and hurling stones at them; let no one force from them any services which they are not traditionally bound to render; and we expressly forbid anyone … to deface or violate their cemeteries or to extort money from them by threatening to do so.

But a declaration like this is usually a recognition that such crimes did occur—which they did, frequently. Popular violence against Jews was a constant element of medieval life. Almost without exception, a papal call for a Crusade to the Holy Land triggered a popular uprising against the Jews. Most infamously, in 1096 rabid crowds murdered hundreds of Jews in Cologne, Mainz, and Worms. In the aftermath of these slaughters, the church took measures to prevent anti-Jewish violence whenever it summoned a Crusade, but those measures usually failed. Official forms of persecution existed too. In the city of Toulouse, for example, a representative of the Jewish community was required to stand on the steps of the Christian cathedral every year on Good Friday and be publicly slapped in the face by the bishop.

Despite the harsh circumstances confronting them, the Jews of the 9th to 12th centuries flourished. Their communities benefited from the economic growth of the era, which they had helped to produce. Their synagogues and schools brimmed with life, and many Jews played important roles in Christian society as advisers, teachers, translators, and intermediaries. Two of the greatest Jewish thinkers of all time emerged at this time too: Rashi (1040–1105) and Maimonides (1135–1204). Rashi lived in northern France and is regarded as the supreme commentator on the Talmud. To the present day, printed editions of the Talmud always include Rashi's line-by-line commentary on each page. Rashi's commentaries on the Bible were important not only to Jewish scholars but to certain Christian ones as well. Later Franciscan scholars like Saint Nicholas of Myra had a special affinity for his writings. Maimonides, by contrast, was Sephardic, growing up in Seville. The arrival in Spain of the Almohads, one of the brutal Sunni reformist sects, made life there untenable, so Maimonides traveled throughout the Mediterranean. He settled at last in Cairo, where he worked as a physician during the day and spent his nights writing legal texts, medical treatises, Biblical commentaries, and philosophy. His two major works were the *Mishneh Torah*—an enormous compilation of Jewish law, with commentary— and the *Guide for the Perplexed*, a brilliant but difficult analysis of the relationship between reason and faith.

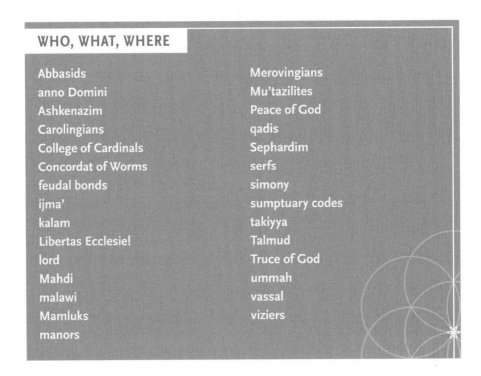

WHO, WHAT, WHERE

Abbasids	Merovingians
anno Domini	Mu'tazilites
Ashkenazim	Peace of God
Carolingians	qadis
College of Cardinals	Sephardim
Concordat of Worms	serfs
feudal bonds	simony
ijma'	sumptuary codes
kalam	takiyya
Libertas Ecclesie!	Talmud
lord	Truce of God
Mahdi	ummah
malawi	vassal
Mamluks	viziers
manors	

SUGGESTED READINGS

Primary Sources

al-Baladhuri. *The Origins of the Islamic State.*
Benjamin of Tudela. *Itinerary.*
Einhard. *The Life of Charlemagne.*
Ibn al-Haytham. *The Advent of the Fatimids.*
Ibn Ishaq. *The Life of Muhammad.*

Maimonides. *The Guide for the Perplexed.*
Rashi. *Commentary on the Torah.*
al-Tabari. *The History of al-Tabari.*
Theophanes. *The Chronicle of Theophanes the Confessor.*

Anthologies

Allen, S. J., and Emilie Amt, eds. *The Crusades: A Reader* (2003).

Constable, Olivia Remie, ed. *Medieval Iberia: Readings from Muslim, Christian, and Jewish Sources* (2011).

Dutton, Paul Edward, ed. *Carolingian Civilization: A Reader* (2004).

Lopez, Robert S., and Irving W. Raymond, trans. *Medieval Trade in the Mediterranean World: Illustrative Documents* (2001).

Shinners, John, ed. *Medieval Popular Religion, 1000–1500: A Reader* (2006).

Studies

Bachrach, Bernard S. *Early Carolingian Warfare: Prelude to Empire* (2000).

Beckwith, Christopher I. *Empires of the Silk Road: A History of Central Eurasia from the Bronze Age to the Present* (2009).

Chazan, Robert. *God, Humanity, and History: The Hebrew First Crusade Narratives* (2000).

———. *The Jews of Medieval Western Christendom: 1000–1500* (2007).

Constable, Olivia Remie. *Housing the Stranger in the Mediterranean World: Lodging, Trade, and Travel in Late Antiquity and the Middle Ages* (2003).

Cook, Michael. *Commanding Right and Forbidding Wrong in Islamic Thought* (2007).

Crone, Patricia. *Meccan Trade and the Rise of Islam* (2004).

Crone, Patricia, and Martin Hinds. *God's Caliph: Religious Authority in the First Centuries of Islam* (2003).

Davidson, Herbert A. *Moses Maimonides: The Man and His Works* (2004).

Friedmann, Yohanan. *Tolerance and Coercion in Islam: Interfaith Relations in the Muslim Tradition* (2003).

Griffith, Sidney H. *The Church in the Shadow of the Mosque: Christians and Muslims in the World of Islam* (2008).

Heather, Peter. *Empires and Barbarians: Migration, Development, and the Birth of Europe* (2009).

Hillenbrand, Carole. *The Crusades: Islamic Perspectives* (2008).

Jotischky, Andrew. *Crusading and the Crusader States* (2004).

Kennedy, Hugh. *The Prophet and the Age of the Caliphates: The Islamic Near East from the Sixth to the Eleventh Century* (2004).

McCormick, Michael. *Origins of the European Economy: Communications and Commerce, AD 300–900* (2002).

Moore, R. I. *The First European Revolution, c. 970–1215* (2000).

Peri, 'Oded. *Christianity under Islam in Jerusalem: The Question of the Holy Sites in Early Ottoman Times* (2001).

Ray, Jonathan. *The Sephardic Frontier: The Reconquista and the Jewish Community in Medieval Iberia* (2008).

Tolan, John V. *Saracens: Islam in the Medieval European Imagination* (2002).

Tyerman, Christopher. *God's War: A New History of the Crusades* (2009).

Wickham, Chris. *Framing the Early Middle Ages: Europe and the Mediterranean, 400–800* (2007).

———. *The Inheritance of Rome: Illuminating the Dark Ages, 400–1000* (2009).

For additional resources, including maps, primary sources, visuals, web links, and quizzes, please go to **www.oup.com/us/backman.**

Worlds Brought Down

1258–1453

THE GREATER WEST, ca. 1453

The 13th and 14th centuries were an age of unparalleled achievement and trauma. The earliest signs of a recognizably modern European world appeared—parliamentary government, an embryonic form of capitalism, universities, the emerging primacy of science, and the spread of literacy and vernacular culture. Modern technologies like mechanical clocks, eyeglasses, magnetic compasses, paper mills, and portolan charts came into use. So too, however, did "medieval" practices like the inquisition against heretics and the blood libel against the Jews. The Catholic Church assumed the basic institutional form it has today, but it also witnessed an extraordinary wave of popular mysticism and lay evangelism. Some even feared that lay revelation would displace the church as the mediator between God and man. Interest in science surged, in the confident belief that the cosmos was a rational structure whose deepest secrets could be discovered. At the same time, the greatest scientific mind of the age wrote to the pope to warn that the Antichrist, fast approaching, would appear in the guise of a scientist. Economically, Europe

◀ **The Triumph of Death**
Painted ca. 1562 by Pieter Bruegel the Elder (1525–1569), this picture represents the horrors of the warfare then starting to reengulf western Europe—the Wars of Religion. The "Triumph of Death" motif dates to the 14th century, when the Black Death poured over the entire Greater West. Bruegel gave it new and horrible life in this painting. "About suffering they were never wrong / the Old Masters," wrote W. H. Auden in his great poem "Musée des Beaux Arts."

- Late Medieval Europe
- Scholasticism
- Mysticism
- The Guild System
- The Mendicant Orders
- Early Representative Government
- Chivalry
- The Hundred Years' War

- The Plague
- Conquest of the Islamic World
- In the Wake of the Mongols
- A New Center for Islam
- Conservatism and Reaction
- The Ottoman Turks
- Persia under the Il-Khans

CHAPTER OUTLINE

finally overtook the Islamic world in wealth and ingenuity. Yet its very success carried within it the seeds of catastrophe. It also contributed to a growing willingness of society to ignore the teachings of the church.

The Islamic world similarly shone, even as it split permanently into three distinct civilizations. The Mongols brought the caliphate to a sudden and savage end, but their equally sudden withdrawal from the scene opened the door to new Muslim conquests, eastward into India and across the Red Sea into sub-Saharan Africa. Three new powerful states emerged—the Mamluks in Egypt and Palestine, the Ottoman Turks in Asia Minor and Syria, and the Safavids in Persia. Meanwhile Muslim Spain fell into a slow, painful decline. Sectarian differences continued, but the urgency of the conflicts between them abated. However, the Sufi movement, which the advance of the Turks westward had accelerated, remained a challenge for Islamic society.

The creative achievements of the age were extraordinary. This should come as no surprise: periods of tremendous affluence and power, and periods of horrific suffering, often inspire great imaginative leaps. The great figures of the late Middle Ages included poets and writers like Rumi [P] (1207–1273), Dante Alighieri (1265–1321), Hafez [P] (1315–1390), Yunus Emre [T] (1240–1321), Geoffrey Chaucer (1343–1400), and the anonymous compiler of the *Arabian Nights*; philosophers like Ibn Arabi [A] (1165–1240), Albertus Magnus (1193–1280), Saint Thomas Aquinas (1225–1274), Gersonides (1288–1345), William of Ockham (1288–1348), Ibn Khaldun [A] (1332–1406), and Hasdai Crescas (1340–1410); scientists like Thomas Bradwardine (1290–1349), and Nicole Oresme (1320–1382); artists like Giotto di Bodone (1267–1337); composers like Guillaume de Machaut (1300–1377); and political thinkers like Marsiglio di Padova (1275–1342). An age that produced these has a claim on anyone's interest. It is important to consider these two centuries together, for the ways in which societies responded to the shared horrors of the 14th century were largely shaped by what had happened in the 13th.

CHAPTER TIMELINE

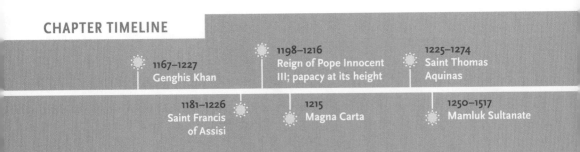

1167–1227
Genghis Khan

1198–1216
Reign of Pope Innocent
III; papacy at its height

1225–1274
Saint Thomas
Aquinas

1181–1226
Saint Francis
of Assisi

1215
Magna Carta

1250–1517
Mamluk Sultanate

LATE MEDIEVAL EUROPE

Latin Europe's history had been shaped by two opposed waves of development. The dual economic and cultural engine of the Mediterranean region spread its influence northward, bringing elements of cosmopolitan urban life, intellectual innovation, and cultural vibrancy into the European heartlands. Political leadership, however, came from the north, as the great monarchies of England, France, and Germany pushed their boundaries southward, drawn by Mediterranean commerce and the gravitational pull of the papal court. The cross-fertilization of north and south benefited each and fostered Europe's ability to reform and revitalize itself. In the contemporary Muslim world, by contrast, innovation came largely from outside, in the dominance of newly Islamicized new foreign rulers—the Ottoman Turks and their ethnic cousins, the Mongols and Tatars.

Feudal England, France, and Germany were the leading powers of the age. Their kings and princes dominated the political scene, and their soldiers provided the overwhelming bulk of the Crusaders. From the 11th to 13th centuries, they continually extended their power southward to reach the Mediterranean. Germany's emperors from the time of Otto I (r. 962–973) claimed sovereignty over northern Italy, and they showed themselves willing to compromise their authority over the German nobles in order to achieve it. France's Capetian dynasty, which came to power in 987 with little more than the city of Paris to its credit, engaged in five generations of aggressive diplomacy: through marriage, it brought more and more of central and southern France into the family domain. By the reign of Louis VII (r. 1137–1180), it reached as far south as the Pyrenees, though it still lacked a Mediterranean outlet—which finally came with Philip IV's (r. 1180–1223) Crusade against the Cathars in southern France and Louis IX's (r. 1226–1270) marriage to Margaret of Provence.

England's monarchs had pursued similar aims. At its zenith in the reign of Henry II (r. 1154–1189), the royal domain included England, Normandy, Brittany, Maine, Anjou, Gascony, and Aquitaine. As Henry's successors gradually

1258
Mongols annihilate
Baghdad

1347
Black Death arrives
in Western Europe

1453
Ottomans capture
Constantinople

1337–1453
Hundred Years' War

1370–1405
Reign
of Tamerlane

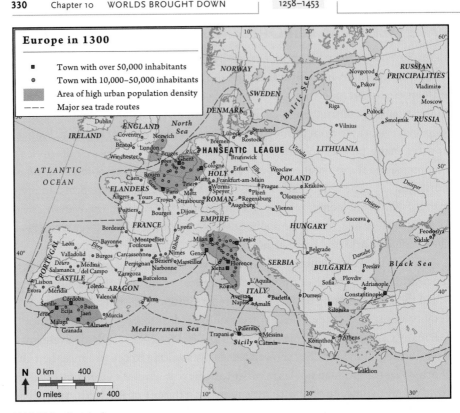

MAP 10.1   Europe in 1300

lost control of the French territories, they compensated by opening a strategic offensive in the Mediterranean marriage market. The countervailing wave was the northward spread of Mediterranean urban institutions and commercial techniques. Cities proliferated in the 12th and 13th centuries across feudal Europe. And they brought with them Roman law, notions of municipal citizenship, commercial and artisanal guilds, schools and universities, and even Mediterranean dress codes. These eased the interactions of the increasingly polyglot and ethnically varied cities (see Map 10.1).

The church, too, reached the zenith of its worldly power. The great Gregorian Reform had resulted in a sturdy, hierarchical organization—of priests, bishops, archbishops, and, at the summit, the Holy Pontiff. Popes like Innocent III (r. 1198–1216) and Gregory IX (r. 1227–1241) exercised a degree of power that no earlier popes had ever had. The new papacy based its authority on a principle called **plenitudo potestatis**—literally "fullness of power" but better translated as "ultimate jurisdiction"—which stressed the church's responsibility toward the world. On the Day of Judgment, it argued, every person must stand before God and be held responsible for his or her sins, but the members of the church must also be held accountable. Did your priest teach you the doctrines of the church?

Did he help guide you through life's challenges and temptations? Did he nourish you with the sacraments? Since the clergy bear some responsibility for every person's ultimate fate, the church must have a right to pronounce on the doings of our lives, particularly any aspect of life that carried a substantial moral component (admittedly a wide catchment area). Plenitudo potestatis did not assert the church's right to control individual lives, only its right to be heard.

SCHOLASTICISM

Through its bishops, the church oversaw the universities of Europe (see Map 10.2). This was the great age of **scholasticism**—really a curriculum rather than a philosophy. Scholastic learning was based on the conviction that the whole of the cosmos was rationally ordered: God, having created Man as a rational creature, has given him the ability, but also the responsibility, to determine the universe's operation. Not surprisingly, the rediscovered works of Aristotle took center stage. Scholastic writers specialized in a type of encyclopedia called a **summa**, which attempted to summarize all existing knowledge on a given topic. Scholastic

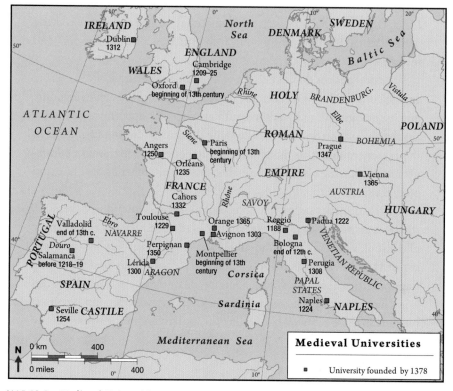

MAP 10.2   Medieval Universities

scholars believed in the unity of truth in all areas of human experience. Apparent inconsistencies in human knowledge are merely imperfections in our own understanding, not flaws in nature.

No one will ever award Albertus Magnus (1193–1280)—or his brilliant pupil Saint Thomas Aquinas (1225–1274)—prizes for prose style. They wrote in an annotated outline form: lists of questions followed by lists of answers, with subsections, objections, and counterassertions inserted wherever deemed appropriate. One might be reading lines of code for a computer program. For them, elegance lay in the thought behind the words, not the words themselves. Indeed, any stylistic flourishes that drew attention away from the ideas undermined the force of the argument. True beauty lay in the perfect rational ordering of God's Creation and in the perfectly rational representation of it in words. Here, for example, Aquinas argues that the soul does not die when the body does:

> Nothing in nature is destroyed by that which brings its existence to a perfected state. Now the perfection of the human soul consists in its acquisition of total knowledge and virtue—things attained by the withdrawal from the body. For knowledge is made perfect when it apprehends Ideas, Goals, Purposes, which are immaterial things; and virtue is made perfect when one does not give in to bodily passions but tempers and restrains them by reason. . . .
>
> Natural desires do not exist in vain. Humans naturally crave eternal existence; and while it is true that all creatures desire to keep living, only human beings rationally apprehend existence. To apprehend existence absolutely, as man does, is not the same thing as to desire to continue in the present moment, as dumb animals do. Therefore man seeks permanent existence for his soul simply because he apprehends absolute and eternal existence. . . .
>
> If the destruction of the body means the destruction of the soul, then it must follow that any weakening of the body entails a weakening of the soul. But in reality, if the soul is weakened in any way by a weakening of the body, that is only coincidental . . . and if our understanding flags or falters because of fatigue, injury, or weakness in the body—this is not necessarily fatigue, injury, or weakness in the understanding itself but only in those bodily faculties that the understanding utilizes. (*Summa contra Gentiles 2.79*)

The prose is bloodless (even more so in the original Latin). The point of it is to strip away rhetorical effect so that the beauty of God's Truth—in this case, the eternality of the human soul—can shine through, like sunlight through a windowpane.

Scholasticism represents a powerful moment in the history of Western culture, when it seemed possible to understand everything. The cosmos appeared to work with a formal perfection, and the limits of the human intellect seemed boundless.[1] But unlike the distant and indifferent Creator of the deists of a later time, the God of the scholastics was present, active, brilliant, and benign—an artist and scientist. The rational mind, Aquinas and others insisted, is not a tool but a beautiful gift through which we can perceive all the divine and hidden harmonies of life. This confidence overflowed into other areas of medieval life, like the construction of vast cathedrals and literary masterpieces like Dante's *Divine Comedy*. It would be a long time before the Western world was again so self-confident.

> Scholasticism represents a powerful moment in the history of Western culture, when it seemed possible to understand everything. The cosmos appeared to work with a formal perfection, and the limits of the human intellect seemed boundless.

The monastic wing of the church, for its part, remained wealthy and influential at the local level. Abbots, however, no longer numbered large among the power brokers in Rome, just as monastic schools had given way to the universities. Popes from the late 11th century on were almost always drawn from the pool of bishops—a trend that continues today. But monastic life underwent several reform efforts that brought new life to the calling. New orders—notably the Cistercians and the Carthusians—gained renown for sanctity and discipline, though they did not place much emphasis on scholarship as the Benedictines

Interior of Sainte-Chapelle, Paris The stained glass windows of Sainte-Chapelle (1246–1248) are a fine example of the vibrancy of Gothic Art. The pointed arches and ribbed vaulting of the Gothic style can be seen clearly.

---

[1] Scholasticism's confidence in the human intellect did not appear again in the West until the Enlightenment of the 18th century.

had done. Contemplative by design, these new orders were also sites of intense mystical experience.

MYSTICISM

Mysticism, or direct contact with God, was indeed among the most striking elements of the age. It was hardly a new phenomenon. The voices that had sent Abraham on his first wanderings in the Holy Land, the burning bush on Mount Sinai through which Moses heard God's commands, the warnings of the Biblical prophets—all these were God's piercing of the veil between the divine world and our own. In the Christian era, figures like Saint Jerome and Saint Augustine had had mystical revelations. God spoke to the masses countless times through the miracles of the saints. What was unique about the mystical experiences of the late Middle Ages was their sheer number. Many hundreds—even thousands—of people claimed to have had an irruptive experience of God, either in the form of visions or otherworldly voices. They included austere Carthusian monks and courtly poets, but also everyday peasants and town dwellers. At times, it seemed almost an epidemic, and historians have in fact looked for a clinical cause—such as prolonged famine, tainted food or water, or bacterial infection. But since claims of mystical experience stretched from Scotland to Portugal, from Majorca to Denmark, and from Belgium to Poland, a natural cause seems unlikely. None, at any rate, has ever been found.

Gero Cross A fine example of Gothic art. This crucifixion scene, carved in wood, was donated to the cathedral at Cologne by Archbishop Gero in the 14th century.

These revelations centered on Christ. People heard Christ, saw Christ, spoke with Christ, embraced Christ, and kissed Christ. Moreover, the Christ whom they encountered was not the stern, lordly King of Heaven and Judge of the Last Day (the most common images of Christ in early medieval art). Rather, he was the gentle, loving, tender-hearted Christ who suffered and died out of his love for all mankind. One mystic, an Englishwoman named Margery Kempe (1373–1438), speaking in the third person, describes how on a pilgrimage to Jerusalem

[she] wept and sobbed as plenteously as though she had seen Our Lord with her bodily eye, suffering His Passion at that time. Before her in her soul she saw Him verily by contemplation, and that caused her to have compassion. And when they came up on to Mount Calvary, she fell down because she could not stand or kneel, and rolled and wrestled with her body, spreading her arms abroad, and cried with a loud voice as though her heart would burst asunder; for, in the city of her soul, she saw verily and clearly how Our Lord was crucified.

After she returned to England, the sightings continue.

When she came home to England, [the visions] came seldom at first, as it were once a month, then once a week, and afterwards daily; and once she had fourteen [visions] in one day, and another day she had seven, and so on, as God would visit her, sometimes in church, sometimes in the street, sometimes in her chambers, sometime in the fields, whenever God would send them, and she never knew the time nor the hour when they would come.

Two aspects of the mystical epidemic stand out. First, people experiencing contact with God did not come away with new insights into theological mysteries or dramatic new interpretations of Scripture. They did not know how to live better, make the world a safer and more prosperous place, or unlock the secret meanings of life. Time after time, they described their experiences simply as intense waves of emotion. They felt an overwhelming sensation of God's love—as though God wanted only to remind people that he hadn't forgotten them. He sees their suffering and wants to reassure them that they are loved. Here is another Englishwoman, Julian of Norwich (1342–1416):

I have begged repeatedly to understand what God meant by these visions ever since I had them. Finally, after more than fifteen years, I received the answer, for I heard in my soul the following words: "Would you like to know the Lord's message in all this? Then learn this well: Love was His message. Who showed this message to you? Love did. What did He show you? Love. Why did He show it to you? Out of Love. Hold on to this idea and you will forever grow in your knowledge and understanding of Love; otherwise you will never know or learn anything."

And this is how I learned that Love was Our Lord's message. I saw with certainty that even before God created us He loved us, and that His Love has never slackened, and that His Love shall endure forever. All the works He has done have been done out of this Love; in this Love He has created all things for our good use; and in this Love our lives are everlasting. We began to exist at the moment of our creation, but the Love that made us was in God from the beginning of time. Our truest beginning is therefore in His Love, and all of this we shall see in God, without end.

Second, mysticism privileged women. Vastly greater numbers of women reported experiencing this sort of contact than men did, and it seems likely that even greater numbers of women experienced the visions without reporting them. Hildegard of Bingen (1098–1179) was a noble-born German abbess who dramatically described her visions in prose, painting, and in music. Hadewijch of Flanders (d. ca. 1245) composed a long sequence of poems and letters that described her own "mystical marriage" to Christ in the vocabulary of courtly love. Julian of Norwich, quoted above, was an educated commoner who at the age of thirty had sixteen separate visions. As a result, she became a recluse and devoted the rest of her life to puzzling out what had happened to her. Her *Revelations of Divine Love* is one the most moving of all mystical books.

Hildegard of Bingen   Hildegard was a famous and beloved abbess, a renowned mystic, and perhaps the first multimedia artist. She had mystical visions from the age of eight, although she never told anyone for more than thirty years. She became a nun and was eventually made abbess of her community of Bingen. When, in her late thirties, she admitted to her brother (who was a priest) that she had started having visions as a child and in fact still had them, he urged her to write. She wrote several books in which she tried to put into words what her experiences felt like and meant to her. When she decided that she could not describe her experiences in words, she put down the pen and took up a paint brush, composing dozens of ecstatic, expressive paintings. When that too proved insufficient, she composed music in the hopes that here at last she could describe what it feels like to be in God's intimate presence. Much of her music survives and is available on recordings. In the image presented here, she begins to write. The manuscript from which this image was photographed was destroyed in World War II.

While many mystics criticized contemporary problems in the church, none saw themselves as rebels against it. In fact, most took special care to champion orthodox doctrine. But while they spoke of their visions and their faith with a passionate intensity, it is possible to detect a grave dissatisfaction with the church and the world.

THE GUILD SYSTEM

The mystical exaltations may have had something to do with the economic vibrancy of the late Middle Ages. The medieval economy had grown at an impressive steady rate since the late 11th century. Fueled by agricultural surplus and the reopening of commercial ties with the Islamic world, it saw advances in financing, manufacturing, and shipping. But not everyone was pleased with this embryonic form of capitalism. The church, itself among the wealthiest of institutions, had a conflicted relationship with it, for capitalism functioned on the use of credit. Credit—that is, the loaning of money at interest—was morally suspect to many churchmen, since it entailed profiting from someone else's need. The very success of the economy raised the potential danger of materialism. The more money, possessions, property, and investments people had, the church feared, the more time they would devote to their management. God does not care about the value of our possessions, the church counseled, but about the value of our lives. Wealth is indeed better than poverty, but it is not intrinsically good.

> The very success of the economy raised the potential danger of materialism. The more money, possessions, property, and investments people had, the church feared, the more time they would devote to their management. God does not care about the value of our possessions, the church counseled, but about the value of our lives.

That did not stop people from pursuing wealth by an impressive array of new techniques. Among the most important innovations was the **guild** system. A medieval guild was not unlike a modern trade association or cartel: it set prices, quality standards, methods and volume of production, and wages paid to workers. It also assigned market shares to individual artisans or merchants. Each city had its own guilds, usually one for each artisanal industry (brewing, weaving and dyeing, metalwork), and another set for the commercial companies (finance, trading, shipping) that brought the goods to market. Guilds played important roles in urban life, funding charities, schools, and hospitals. Among the bylaws of the wine and beer merchants' guild at Southampton in the 13th century, for example, was this provision:

> Whenever the guild is in session the lepers at [the hospital of] La Madeleine shall receive in alms from

Two Master Craftsmen   Nanni di Banco (1383–1430) carved this relief of a stonemason and a woodcarver in honor of their guild.

the guild eight gallons of ale, as shall the sick in [the hospitals of] God's House and Saint Julian's. The Franciscans shall receive eight gallons of ale and four gallons of wine; and sixteen gallons of ale shall be distributed to the poor from whatever spot the guild meets at. . . . If any guild member should fall into poverty and cannot pay his debts, and if he is unable to work and provide for himself, then he shall receive from the guild one mark [of silver] every time the guild meets in session, in order to relieve his suffering.

Guilds not only complemented but at times nearly replaced the charitable functions of the church, which many feared had become too *plenitudo* of its own *potestatis*. The reach of the church in the late Middle Ages was extensive. It orchestrated Crusades, ran and policed the universities and cathedral schools, oversaw the workings of the marketplace, judged the activities of Europe's bedrooms, excommunicated kings and princes, warred with them on occasion, and staged councils to determine ever finer details of canon law. Many feared it had lost sight of its central mission of ministering to the people. This was the impetus behind the founding of the **mendicant orders**, groups dedicated to assisting the clergy in the performance of their evangelical mission. These orders grew rapidly in number, size, and popularity, and their astonishing success can be attributed to two principle factors—their unique dedication to serving the common people and the fact that they, unlike the clergy they assisted, opened their membership to women.

THE MENDICANT ORDERS

The two leading mendicant groups were the **Franciscans** and the **Dominicans**. The Franciscans, established by Saint Francis of Assisi (1181–1226) and approved by Pope Innocent III, dedicated themselves to preaching and service to the urban poor. They begged for alms and food and donated whatever they collected to the destitute. They preached a simple message of love, forgiveness, and charity. People flocked to them wherever they went. The Dominicans, on the other hand, aided the church's teaching mission. Too many faithful, especially in the countryside, still lacked proper religious instruction and so drifted into heresy. Heresies, in fact, enjoyed something of a golden age in the 13th and 14th centuries. Saint Dominic de Guzmán (1171–1221), an earnest Spanish cleric, established the order named after him (officially known as the Order of Preachers) in 1216 in the hopes of bringing the heretical back into the Catholic fold. He recognized that heresy was not the product of human evil or of Satanic mischief but was simply a consequence of the church's failure to provide appropriate religious education. In response, the Dominicans established schools across Europe, debated heretical ideas, and preached tirelessly.

The two most prominent heresies were Catharism and Lollardy, and both of them were profoundly critical of the church (see Map 10.3). The **Cathars**, the more eccentric of the two, posited two separate and equal gods, one absolutely good and the other absolutely evil. Trapped in the cosmic war between them, humans were condemned to a miserable cycle of reincarnation. To the Cathars the physical universe was the creation of the evil deity; our souls, by contrast, were created by the good god. We therefore participate in the cosmic struggle by overcoming our own physicality, the demands of the flesh, and the human concern for material wealth. Once we have achieved the appropriate spiritual state, we break the cycle of reincarnation and our souls are released from our bodies in a spiritual exaltation that tips the cosmic scale in favor of the universal good. The Lollards were almost dull in comparison.

Lollards condemned church corruption and worldliness. They believed in the right of nonpriests to preach, and they taught that to live according to the spirit of Christ was more important than to follow the many letters of the church's

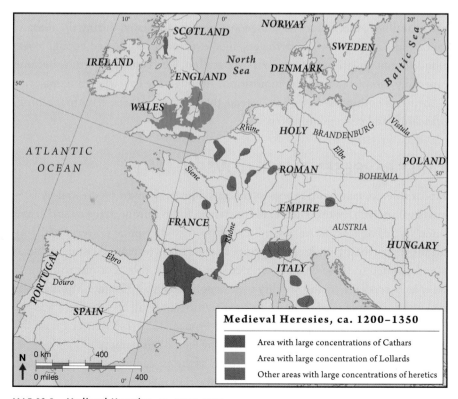

MAP 10.3   Medieval Heresies, ca. 1200–1350

laws. The Lollards had no common body of doctrines; they shared instead a general anticlericalism toward Rome, whose obvious wealth and involvement with earthly matters vitiated its spiritual authority in their eyes.

The Dominicans confronted these and other groups with relentless preaching and arguing. Dominicans were confident that the errant had only to hear Christian truth properly presented, and they would return to the church's embrace confidently and with gratitude. Of course, it did not always work out that way, which led to the development of a sterner educational tool—the inquisition. The **inquisition** began as a pedagogical program to counter heresy: determine what an individual or group actually believed, and then demonstrate its errors. Its origin lay in a principle of ancient Roman law analogous to our modern "probable cause" hearings. According to this principle, certain crimes are so detrimental to society that the state has a right, and indeed a responsibility, to investigate preemptively if there is a reasonable likelihood that the crime might be in the offing. Heresy fell into this category, because it imperiled the soul not only of the heretic; any innocent bystander might succumb.

Like other interrogation methods used in medieval times, inquisition did not shy away from using physical force, but it did not rely on force exclusively. The Inquisition of popular legend and Hollywood films, with black-hooded sadists plying red-hot pincers in dank dungeons, largely came later, during the Renaissance and Reformation. Nevertheless, medieval inquisitions used enough coercion and manipulation to earn a dark reputation. The Dominican friars became especially associated with the inquisition, although the overwhelming majority of them had nothing to do with it. Instead, they dedicated themselves to teaching, preaching, and peaceful ministry.

EARLY REPRESENTATIVE GOVERNMENT

Modern democracy has its roots in the parliamentary tradition created by late-medieval society. By 1300 nearly every state in Latin Europe, large or small, had some sort of representative assembly that possessed genuine power, usually by means of controlling the king's or prince's access to tax revenue. Aristocratic society responded to these changes with changes of their own. For one thing, new weaponry soon tested the nobility's monopoly on force. The late Middle Ages had no shortage of warfare, but the most significant of all the conflicts was the Hundred Years' War between England and France (1337–1453). Along with the Black Death, it sounded the death knell of the feudal aristocracy.

Noble courts were nothing new. As early as the 1st century CE Tacitus related, somewhat fancifully, how ancient Germanic warriors met with clan elders in a regular council he called a **comitatus** ("assembly"). But the late-medieval addition of representatives of the common people signified the real breakthrough. The governments' need for revenue drove the issue, but does not explain it entirely. Since Europe's nobles and churches remained exempt from taxation, the king's only recourse was to tax the free commoners in the cities. The urban classes responded positively, for the most part, provided that the king granted them in return a voice in the formation of government policy. By the 12th century such commoners' council held an advisory role in government, but by the 13th, when the urban manufacturing and commercial sectors represented the bulk of their realms' collective economic output, the cities' advisory role grew and became actual power to control the royal purse.

Mayor Taking the Oath of Office   In the mid-12th century norms surrounding the selection of mayors, and the powers they possessed, stabilized. Called by different names in different regions—*mayor* (England), *potestaat* (Flanders), *Burgomeister* (Germany), *podestà* (Italy)—they were elected officials with terms of office ranging from one year to life. Here the mayor of Bristol, England takes the oath of office, ca. 1479.

The transition was not always smooth. Constraints on royalty in England included the signing of **Magna Carta** in 1215 and the Provisions of Oxford in 1258, and both came about after high drama and much strong-arm maneuvering. In France, the Capetian kings from Louis VIII (r. 1223–1226) on were hobbled not only by their feudal obligations to the nobles but also by their practice of awarding land grants called "apanages" to the younger sons of each Capetian generation. As consolation prizes for not inheriting the crown, apanages were independent provinces that required their holder to perform no service to the throne. The Capetians therefore had even greater need to seek the financial assistance of the urban populace, which they did by developing the French parliament—the **Estates General**.

The German case was more complicated. The emperor Frederick II (r. 1215–1250) had inherited the German Empire from his father and the Kingdom of Sicily (which included southern Italy) from his mother, and frankly had little interest in Germany at all. His southern realm was wealthier and more cosmopolitan. Frederick encouraged urban growth within Germany but also issued, in 1231, the Constitutions in Favor of the Princes of Germany, which severely curtailed the power of those cities and indeed of his own feudal claims to privilege. He gave up a strong German monarchy in return for the German princes' leaving him alone to pursue his own goals in the Mediterranean. Nevertheless, his actions helped solidify the gains made in establishing the German parliament—known as the **Diet**.

By 1250 or thereabouts, the balance between the authority and status of the commoners and the nobles was changing dramatically. The milites ("warlords") had easily justified their emergence in the 11th century, with their monopoly on political power and privileged status. After all, they generated through their manors the largest portion of economic production in the realm. They alone could perform government service since they had a virtual monopoly, among the laity, on literacy; and they provided the dominant and most effective military service. But the rise of the urban economy had shifted economic dominance within Europe to manufacturing and commerce instead of agriculture, and the spread of literacy among city dwellers had opened up civil service to commoners. Government became professionalized, in other words, and men of noble birth began to shun the lesser offices of civil administration. That left room for commoners to enter and replace them. As two of the three struts that legitimated noble privilege gradually disappeared, voices began to murmur darkly about unjustified privilege.

CHIVALRY

The word *chivalry* derives from the French word for horsemanship and originally denoted skill at mounted shock combat: heavily armored knights astride thundering warhorses, bearing swords, lances, maces, and flails. Knights proved their worth at tournaments, fighting other knights in all-too-real contests in which many were killed. They sought not merely renown but position as a vassal to higher lords in search of loyal underlings. An 11th century text like the popular *Song of Roland* depicted its hero as the very summit of knightly perfection—an unsurpassed warrior loyal to his lord but to very little else. The fictional Roland exhibits no qualities other than his usefulness on a battlefield. By the 12th century, however, a significant change had occurred, and the ideal knight portrayed in literature was more a figure like Sir Lancelot, Sir Galahad, or Saint Perceval of the Arthurian tales. All were still champion fighters, but also models of **chivalry** in a new sense—comportment, noble demeanor, learning, and piety.

> The noble class felt the need to emphasize at every turn the chasm that separated it from commoners: the nobles were not different because privileged, they seemed to say, but were privileged because different.

They were sensitive to music and art, and above all chivalric lovers of virtuous noblewomen.[2]

As the 13th and 14th centuries came, and the aristocratic leadership of society began to give way to a new set of values, chivalry took on newer and more symbolic roles. Coats of arms, for instance, which had originally served the practical purpose of identifying battlefield participants, began to adorn everything a nobleman owned, from tableware and fireplace masonry to goblets, gloves, and stationery. Aristocrats not only patronized musicians and poets; they now endowed colleges, scholarships, chapels, and hospitals, and emblazoned them all with their names and heraldic signs. Genealogy became a passion of the elite, and its results (often fanciful) were published in books and embroidered on tapestries. Songs, tales, and histories enumerated their elevated sensibilities. Commerce and trade were denigrated as beneath the dignity of a lord. The noble class felt the need to emphasize at every turn the chasm that separated it from commoners: the nobles were not different because privileged, they seemed to say, but were privileged because different. And the difference was essential, not functional.

But the military role of the knightly class remained and sufficed to maintain the hierarchy. So long as mounted shock cavalry remained the premier fighting force, commoners might complain about abuses of privilege, but not about the very idea of privilege. In contrast, popular rebellions of the late Middle Ages—the three best known are the **Jacquerie** uprising in France (1358), the **Ciompi Rebellion** in Italy (1378), and the **Peasants' Revolt** in England (1381)—shared a common

Noble Warrior   Illuminated initial from English copy of the Letters of Pope Gregory I, 12th century. English scribes in the Middle Ages were particularly well known for the vitality and fluidity of the draftsmanship. This example, from a 12th-century copy of the Letters of Gregory I, shows a noble warrior—identifiable from his stance on top of a common foot-soldier, plus his brandishing of a fine sword—fighting a two-headed dragon. It is a brightly colored image, filled with hues of airy blue, green, gold, light copper, and red.

---

[2]   Lancelot's mistake was not in loving Lady Guinevere but in loving her with the wrong kind of love, adultery.

element: they questioned the very order of medieval society, not merely the abusive actions of a few elites within it.

> When Adam delved and Eve span,
> Who was then the gentleman?

asked an anonymous poet of the time. Though simply phrased, it was a radical question: When God created the world in all its original perfection, were there any "gentlemen"? Any privileged few who lived off the labor of the many? If not, then the existence of them now must be a distortion of God's original intent, which could be no other than a radical equality of all mankind.

The couplet was referred to in a sermon delivered by one of the leaders of the Peasant's Revolt, a priest named John Ball (1338–1381). The story is retold in the Historia Anglicana of Thomas Walsingham (d. 1422), with a fiery commentary:

> "When Adam dalf, and Eve span, who was thanne a gentilman?:
> From the beginning all men were created equal by nature, and that servitude had been introduced by the unjust and evil oppression of men, against the will of God, who, if it had pleased Him to create serfs, surely in the beginning of the world would have appointed who should be a serf and who a lord.

Ball ended by recommending

> uprooting the tares that are accustomed to destroy the grain; first killing the great lords of the realm, then slaying the lawyers, justices, and jurors, and finally rooting out everyone whom they knew to be harmful to the community in future.

In the 14th century several simple, inexpensive technologies developed in weaponry, which knocked the third and final strut out from under aristocratic claims to justified privilege. The two most significant weapons were the longbow and the crossbow, which appeared first in Wales and Scotland, where they were used to repulse the English armies of King Edward I (r. 1272–1307), and possibly even before that. Of course, the **longbow** is familiar today simply as the "bow and arrow," but prior to this century, bows were largely used by noble cavalry. The physical challenge of sitting astride a broad warhorse while fully armored, though, meant that knights' bows were relatively short in length and hence of limited power and range. The Welsh and the Scots, however, hit upon the idea of turning bows into infantry weapons instead, which allowed them to increase the length of the bow significantly. Longbows were often a full six feet (1.8 meters) long, and their arrows could pierce a suit of armor at a distance of two hundred yards (180 meters).

The **crossbow** was the medieval equivalent of a sawed-off shotgun, and it shot thick metal darts called *quarrels*. A ratcheted steel gear, turned by a steel crank, drew the bowstring; once released, the quarrel likewise could pierce plate armor and even shatter the bones it protected.[3] Crossbows date back to Alexander the

A World Turned Upside Down   The battle of Poitiers (1346), the first great battle in the Hundred Years' War. The English are on the left, with infantry longbowmen shown—inaccurately—in the front lines. Confronting them are the mounted knights of France. Much bloodshed ensued, ending in a surprise English victory. Similar slaughter occurred at Crécy (1356) and Agincourt (1415), although the war ended, in 1453, with a French victory.

---

[3]   In Spain, the crossbow may have been used as a surgical tool. A quarrel embedded in a soldier's bone could be removed by tying it to a quarrel shot by a crossbow in the opposite direction.

Great. The late medieval weapon, however, used a steel, not wooden, bow piece, which gave it tremendous force and required the crank to arm it. The crossbow was designed for close-range killing and holds the distinction of being the first weapon ever banned by the Catholic Church—not for its deadly force per se but because it allowed the unthinkable: with it, commoners could kill noblemen almost at will. This was more than social inversion, the church declared; it was an intrinsically immoral attack on God's ordering of society.

> The crossbow was designed for close-range killing and holds the distinction of being the first weapon ever banned by the Catholic Church—not for its deadly force per se but because it allowed the unthinkable: with it, commoners could kill noblemen almost at will. This was more than social inversion, the church declared; it was an intrinsically immoral attack on God's ordering of society.

THE HUNDRED YEARS' WAR

The **Hundred Years' War** (1337–1453) was the longest (although not continuous) war in Western history—and almost the longest in preparation. England and France had experienced fierce tensions and rivalries since 1066, when William the Conqueror crossed the English Channel with his army and conquered England. From this time on the English kings, as kings, were autonomous sovereigns but, as dukes of Normandy, also vassals of the throne in Paris. French kings were thwarted whenever they tried to curb the ambitions of their Norman vassals, however. And when the Norman kings managed to acquire even more French territories through strategic marriages—such as the marriage of Henry II (r. 1154–1189) to Eleanor of Aquitaine—the vassals stood more powerful and respected than the lords.

Matters came to a head when England's king Edward III (r. 1327–1377) claimed the French throne for himself. Legally, his claim was correct, as he was married to the last remaining heir of France's king Philip IV (r. 1286–1314). However, the French court would have none of it, found an alternative (a man named Philip of Valois), and the war began. On again, off again, the Hundred Years' War left the French countryside ravaged and her people dispirited (see Map 10.4). The English, who were vastly outnumbered, avoided pitched battles and instead sent innumerable small raiding forces, armed with longbows and crossbows. Their mission was to vandalize as much French territory as possible, terrorize the people, then return before the French could muster their enormous feudal army. The war matters primarily for the way in which it was fought, since the English weapons could pierce the French suits of armor and render mounted knights ineffective.

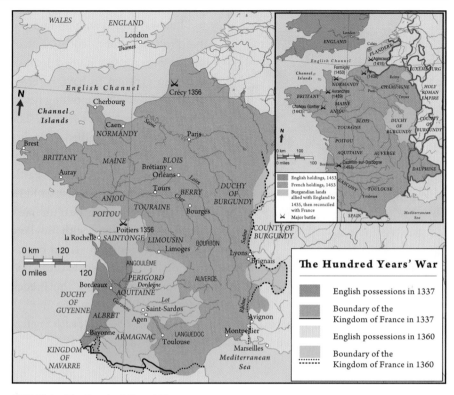

MAP 10.4 **The Hundred Years' War**

At stake was not simply dynastic territorial rights but an entire way of life. As one chronicler described an early English victory, at the battle of Crécy in 1356:

> The English [longbow] archers stepped forward and shot their arrows with great might—and so rapidly that it seemed a snow-blizzard of arrows. When these arrows fell on the Genoese [one of France's allies at the time] and pierced their armor, they cut the strings of their own weapons, threw them to the ground, and ran. When the king of the French, who had arrayed a large company of mounted knights to support the Genoese, saw them in flight he cried out, "Kill those blackguards! They're blocking our advance!" But the English kept on firing, landing their arrows among the French horsemen. This drove the charging French into the Genoese, until the scene was so confused that they could never regroup again.... [When the slaughter ended,] it became clear that the French dead numbered eighty banners, eleven princes of the realm, twelve hundred knights, and thirty thousand commoners.

Joan of Arc   An early image of Joan of Arc, showing her in armor but without her hair cropped.

The war ended with an improbable French victory, led by a charismatic peasant girl named Joan of Arc, who claimed to have received messages from Heaven telling her to drive the English from France. The French army briefly rallied under her leadership and scored several victories, until Joan was captured in battle and executed by the English in 1431. Shortly thereafter the Burgundians, who had been allied with England against the French, reversed course and sided with the French. With their newly combined forces, the French and Burgundians drove the English from the land, and in 1453 a permanent peace was settled. The first death knell of the feudal aristocracy had been sounded, however, despite the victory.

THE PLAGUE

Another, even direr death knell sounded across the Western world in late 1347, when a fleet of Genoese merchant ships returning from the Black Sea arrived in the harbor at Messina, Sicily. Aboard the vessels was a pack of rats carrying the bubonic plague. This disease originated in eastern Asia and had worked its way westward along the trade routes; the violent advance of the Mongol army under Genghis Khan (1167–1227) probably sped matters up considerably. Since the disease had never existed before in western Europe, the people had no biological means of fighting it off, and it took several centuries for the necessary antibodies to develop among the populations at large. Waves of the plague—known popularly as the **Black Death**—therefore returned to Europe until well into the 18th century.

This was the single worst natural disaster in Greater Western history, killing has many as fifty million people in less than three years—roughly one-third of the European and Muslim populations (see Map 10.5). The results were horrific. A Sicilian eyewitness recorded:

> At the start of November [in 1347] twelve Genoese galleys . . . entered
> the port at Messina. They carried with them a disease so deadly that any
> person who happened merely to speak with any one of the ships' members

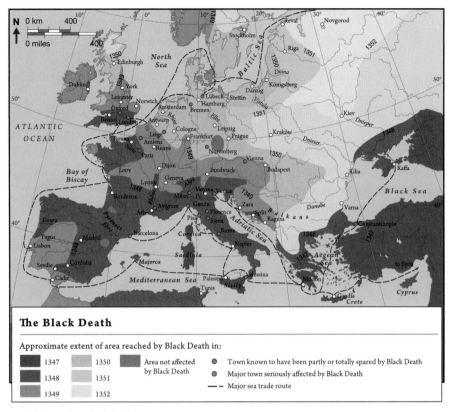

The Black Death

Approximate extent of area reached by Black Death in:

■ 1347	1350	■ Area not affected by Black Death
■ 1348	1351	
■ 1349	1352	

● Town known to have been partly or totally spared by Black Death
● Major town seriously affected by Black Death
- - - Major sea trade route

MAP 10.5   The Black Death

was seized by a mortal illness; death was inevitable. It spread to everyone who had any interaction with the infected. Those who contracted the disease felt their whole bodies pierced through with pain, and they quickly developed boils about the size of lentils on their thighs and upper arms. These boils then spread the disease throughout the rest of the body and made its victims vomit blood. The vomiting of blood normally continued for three days until the person died, since there was no way to stop it. Not only did everyone who had contact with the sick become sick themselves, but also those who had contact only with their possessions. . . . People soon began to hate one another so much that parents would not even tend to their own sick children. . . . As the deaths mounted, crowds of people sought to confess their sins to priests and to draft their wills, . . . but clergy, lawyers, and notaries refused to enter the homes of the ill. . . . Franciscans, Dominicans, and other mendicants who went to hear the confessions of the dying fell to the disease—many of them not even making it alive out of the ill persons' homes. *(Michele da Piazza, History of Sicily)*

In England:

> At the same time sheep began to die everywhere throughout the realm. In a single pasture one could find as many as five thousand carcasses, all so putrefied that no animal or bird would go near them.... Sheep and cattle wandered aimlessly through meadows and crop fields, for there was no one to go after them and herd them. As a result, they died in countless numbers everywhere, in ditches and hedges.... Moreover, buildings both large and small began to collapse in all cities, towns, and villages, for want of anyone to inhabit them and maintain them. In fact, many whole villages became deserted; everyone who lived in them died and not a single house was left standing. It is likely that many of these sites were never inhabited again. *(Henry Knighton, Chronicle)*

In Paris, another writer described a popular reaction to the crisis:

> Some said that the pestilence was the result of infected air and water,... and as a result of this idea many people began suddenly and passionately to accuse the Jews of infecting the wells, fouling the air, and generally being the source of the plague. Everyone rose up against them most cruelly. In Germany and elsewhere—wherever Jews lived—they were massacred and slaughtered by Christian crowds, and many thousands were burned indiscriminately. The steadfast, though foolish, bravery of the Jewish men and women was remarkable. Many mothers hurled their own children into the flames and then leapt in after them, along with their husbands, in order that they might avoid being forcibly baptized. *(Jean de Venette, Chronicle)*

The Spanish Muslim writer Ibn Khaldun [A] (1332–1406) summarized the ruin this way:

> It was as though humanity's own living voice had called out for oblivion and desolation—and the world responded to the call. Truly Allah inherits the earth and all things upon it. *(Ibn Khaldun, Muqaddimah)*

People tried every medicine, folk cure, and prayer they knew, all to no effect. In several instances townsfolk, who knew that the disease had something to do with rats, intentionally burned their entire towns to the ground in order to drive the rats away, but this of course only accelerated the spread of the contagion. By the time the plague had spread its way through nearly every corner of Europe,

Burying Plague Victims   A page from the Annals of Gilles de Muisit, late 14th century, in Tournai, showing crowds struggling to bury all the dead left in the in Black Death's wake.

it left behind piles of corpses so massive that people hardly knew what to do with them. Scores of "death ships" bobbed directionless on the seas, every person on board dead, with the victorious rats silently gnawing on their remains.

The consequences of such a catastrophe are almost unimaginable. The fatalities, coupled with the fear of interpersonal contact, halted agricultural and industrial production and severed all commercial ties. The death of so many farm animals had equally long-term effects: wool and dairy production all but ceased, and the loss of oxen and horses as draught animals meant that farming would be slow to restart. Once the immediate crisis passed, however, twin spirals of inflation and recession followed. Urban workers who had survived could demand higher wages for their labor, and this, combined with the general scarcity of goods, triggered rapid increases in prices. Rural workers faced a different problem. So many people had died that even decreased food production met local needs—and hence food prices dropped precipitously. When rural workers demanded lower rents for their work on the land, the landlords could therefore refuse. And the low crop prices hurt the farmers more than the decreased rents had helped them.

> Each return of the Black Death over the centuries left new iterations of the same miseries in its wake. No epidemic ever reached the hopeless severity of the first wave, since the gradual development of antibodies among the Europeans meant that fewer people died. But fear of the plague haunted the West for many generations.

So in general terms, urban workers who survived the Black Death profited from the decimation while rural workers were driven even deeper into poverty.

Each return of the Black Death over the centuries left new iterations of the same miseries in its wake. No epidemic ever reached the hopeless severity of the first wave, since the gradual development of antibodies among the Europeans meant that fewer people died. But fear of the plague haunted the West for many generations.

CONQUEST OF THE ISLAMIC WORLD

The 13th and 14th centuries witnessed the near-complete takeover of the Islamic world by a new wave of foreign conquerors, who dominated Muslim life for the next three hundred years, reconfiguring its map and introducing new cultural and social elements into Islamic identity. Leadership of Islam had long been monopolized by two groups, the Arabs and the Persians. While often in tension with one another, they had nevertheless worked out some sort of creative and nutritive cultural compromise. As the Abbasid state crumbled, however, ethnic and doctrinal conflicts arose between the populations of each rump state and its Arab or Persian rulers. The arrival of the newcomers, moreover, created at times cutthroat competition between the Muslim states. Neither of the groups of newcomers was monolithic: instead, each was a mongrel assemblage made up of numerous tribes and clans linked by language: the Mongols and the Turks.

The more destructive of the invaders were the **Mongols**, who began moving westward in the 12th century. No one knows the precise origin of the Mongols, or even if they have one. Ancient Chinese records trace them back to a group they called the Donghu (3rd century BCE), which was actually a confederation of various peoples speaking related dialects of an early version of the Mongolian language. But some scholars claim to see elements of early Turkish dialects in the Donghu as well. Certainly the Mongols, as they spread across Asia, maintained continuous contact with Turkish-speaking groups and absorbed elements of Turkish culture. (As the two groups gradually merged, they became known in the west as the Tatars.[4])

Nomadic peoples of the steppes found it natural to form occasional alliances and confederations—and to disband them just as casually. When gathered, these armies were often of considerable size. Fighting on horseback, they moved quickly and specialized in lightning strikes on other nomadic groups and small population centers. Siege machinery was largely unknown to them, which allowed fortified cities to withstand their assaults. The Mongols were a diverse group of tribes along the northern and northwestern borders of China, and the Chinese themselves had

---

[4]   The name Tatars derives from Latin *Tartarus*, "hell."

been traditionally among the Mongols' favorite targets for raiding. Centuries of such attacks had prompted the Chinese to build the Great Wall. While not impregnable, the wall repulsed attackers and migrants alike with sufficient success that it was a major reason for the seemingly endless waves of invaders and nomads who moved westward across Asia and into the Western world.

Under their brilliant but brutal commander Temüjin (ca. 1167–1227), the Mongols forged another of their periodic confederations. Better known by his title of Chinggis (Genghis) Khan, or "Universal Ruler," he broke through the wall in 1207 and subdued the northern half of China. The Chin emperor surrendered in 1214 and awarded Genghis Khan an enormous tribute payment of gold and silver coins. Sources say that it required three thousand horses to carry. At this point Genghis might have stopped his conquests, for in diplomatic records he referred to himself as the "supreme emperor of the east" and wrote to the Persian ruler in Khwarezmi (modern day) as the "supreme emperor of the west." The hapless Persian, however, rejected Genghis's peace offering and slaughtered all 450 members of the diplomatic embassy Genghis had sent. This called for revenge, and in 1219 Genghis Khan moved westward and quickly crushed what was left of the Persian state.

Khan left local rulers in place, so long as they swore unquestioning obedience to him, and he installed Mongol tax collectors in each region, to ensure a flow of revenue into his coffers. Some towns rebelled and slew these Mongol officials as soon as Genghis had moved on, which prompted the great Khan to return in wrath and annihilate entire populations. Once he was even reported to have ordered the killing of every living creature in a city, including its domesticated animals. Ali ibn Athir [K] (1160–1233), the great Kurdish historian, described the Mongols memorably in his *Universal History*:

> Even Antichrist, though He strike down all those who oppose him, will spare those who follow Him—but these Mongols spared no one, not even men, children, or women; they even ripped open the stomachs of women who were pregnant and killed their unborn children. ... These people came out of the lands of China and attacked cities ... in Turkestan ... and advanced on Samarkand, Bukhara, and other sites in Transoxiana. One of their armies made it as far as Khurasan and continued their campaign of conquering, pillaging, and ruining until they reached ... the borders of Persia, Azerbaijan, and Iraq, ... all of which they destroyed and wholly depopulated, except for a small remnant, in less than a year's time.

Coming as it does near the end of the *History*, ibn Athir's passage denotes the apocalyptic role he saw the Mongols to be playing. Surely the end of the world was nigh, if such malevolent power as the Mongols possessed could roll over the

The Siege of Baghdad   The conquest of Baghdad in 1258 by Genghis Khan's successor Hulagu, from a Persian manuscript of the 15th century.

world at will. Had he lived another quarter century, ibn Athir would have seen his worst imaginings realized.

The Mongol conquests were far greater than those achieved by any earlier people, or by any people since, but to call it an empire is inaccurate. The Mongols never achieved any sort of governance over the areas they laid waste and showed little interest in doing so. Genghis Khan died in 1227, and was succeeded by his third son, Ögedai (r. 1227–1241), who continued to push the borders of the Mongol-dominated realm further west until they reached Anatolia. Another branch of his army, moving north of the Black Sea, threatened Hungary, and even reached northward to the Baltic Sea and southward to the Balkans. Under Hulagu (r. 1217–1265), Ogedai's son and successor, the Mongols annihilated Baghdad in 1258. According to Muslim sources, as many as two hundred thousand people were killed in a week-long orgy of slaughter. The Mongols destroyed the royal library (one chronicle reports that the Tigris River ran black from the ink of all the books hurled into it) and burned dozens of mosques, schools, and hospitals. At the end, Hulagu had the Abbasid caliph, al-Musta'sim [A] (r. 1242–1258), rolled up in a Persian carpet and then trampled by Mongol horsemen. A contingent of Mongol soldiers then pressed further westward as far as Damascus, but were finally repulsed in 1260 at 'Ayn Jalut, near Nazareth, by a Mamluk army coming out of Egypt. At its height in 1279, the Mongol Empire covered some twelve million square miles (thirty-one million square kilometers) of land, nearly one-quarter of the Earth's land surface (see Map 10.6a,b).

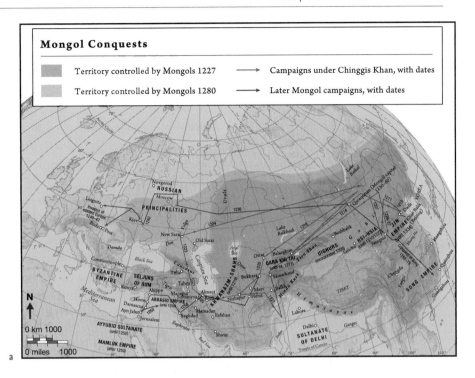

Mongol Conquests

- Territory controlled by Mongols 1227
- Territory controlled by Mongols 1280
- → Campaigns under Chinggis Khan, with dates
- → Later Mongol campaigns, with dates

a

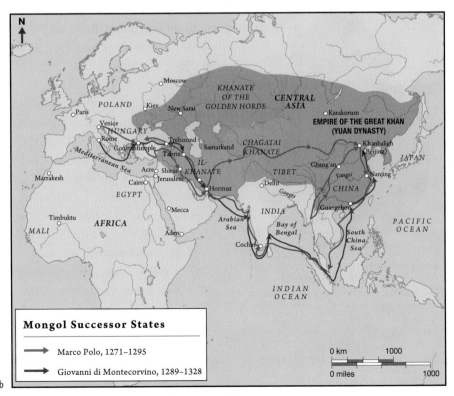

Mongol Successor States

- → Marco Polo, 1271–1295
- → Giovanni di Montecorvino, 1289–1328

b

MAP 10.6a,b   Mongol Conquests and Successor States

IN THE WAKE OF THE MONGOLS

The Mongols began to fight among themselves after the death of Genghis' grandson Kublai Khan (r. 1260–1294), and the enormous territory they held broke into a number of smaller though still considerable states. The most important of these were the Golden Horde, which dominated the southern Russian steppe; the Il-Khans, who held power over most of the previously Persian-controlled part of the Islamic empire; the Chagetai Khans, who controlled central Asia; and the Yuan dynasty, which held titular leadership over all the Mongol realms from their capital in Beijing.

Numerous Western states and individual rulers attempted to forge some sort of peaceful relations with the Mongols. Louis IX of France famously sent an emissary to Batu Khan (r. 1227–1255), the khan of the Golden Horde, congratulating him on his conquests and offering to bestow those lands on him officially in return for Batu's conversion to Christianity, becoming Louis's vassal, and paying him an annual tribute.[5] The church sent out teams of Franciscan missionaries with the unenviable charge of converting the Great Khans to Christianity. One

of these was Fr. Giovanni di Montecorvino (1247–1328), who established a church at Beijing, built a Christian school for 150 slave children he had purchased and manumitted, and translated the Psalms and the whole of the New Testament into Tatar for them. He sent back to Rome an extraordinary letter:

A Mongol Passport   An engraved safe-conduct pass issued from the court of the Mongol ruler Kublai Khan (1215–1294). Its bearer was guaranteed safety while traveling through the Mongol lands. The inscription reads: "By the strength of Eternal Heaven, an edict of the khan. He who has not respect [for the bearer of the passport] shall be guilty."

> I, Fr. Giovanni di Montecorvino, set out from the city of Tauris, in Persia, in the year of Our Lord 1291 and made my way to India, where I remained for thirteen months . . . and baptized about a hundred people. . . . I then continued my journey until I made it all the way to [China], the realm of the Great Khan who rules over the Tartars and to whom I presented the letter of our Holy Father the Pope, inviting him to adopt

---

[5]   Batu responded that he would teach Louis a lesson by burning Paris down around his ears.

the Catholic faith of Our Lord Jesus Christ. The Khan is too set in his idolatrous ways to change, although I must record that he has extended great friendship to us Christians in the years I have been living here in his realm. . . . I have built a church in [Beijing], where the Khan has his chief residence, . . . and in this church I have baptized some six thousand people, as near as I can reckon. . . . I believe it is possible that, if I had had two or three comrades to aid me, the Khan himself might have been baptized by now, and for this reason I beg that if any friars are willing to come this far and dedicate themselves to so great a task...then they will come. . . .

It has been twelve years since I had any news of the papal court, our Franciscan order, or the general goings-on in Europe. Two years ago a fellow from Lombardy came here—a surgeon—and spread the most vicious rumors about the papal court and other matters, but since these blasphemies are too horrible to be true I beg to hear the truth and pray that my fellow Franciscans, to whom I address this letter, do all they can to bring my request to Our Holy Father the Pontiff....As for myself, I have grown old and gray; even though I am only fifty-eight, toil and trouble have aged me. I have acquired a working knowledge of the language and script used by the Tartars, and have already translated the New Testament and the Psalter for them. . . . To the best of my knowledge there is no king or prince anywhere in the world who can compare to the Great Khan in terms of the vastness of his realm, the number of his subjects, or his wealth. But here I must now stop.

[Beijing], the eighth of January, in the year of Our Lord 1305.

The Great Khan referred to by Friar Giovanni was Temür Khan (r. 1294–1307), the son of Kublai Khan. Kublai, the grandson of Genghis Khan, had been the ruler of the Mongol Empire at the time of Marco Polo's supposed stay in China— "supposed" because not all scholars agree that Marco Polo actually made it to China. Temür Khan is not to be confused with Timur (r. 1370–1405), the Turkish founder of the Timurid dynasty, better known in English as Tamerlane. Two years later, Pope Clement V (r. 1305–1317) appointed Giovanni the archbishop of Beijing and sent him the assistants he had requested.

The "vicious rumors about the papal court" put about by the visitor from Lombardy, however, were not in fact too horrible to be true. Pope Boniface VIII (r. 1294–1303) had begun his pontificate with a splendid jubilee that brought as many as a million pilgrims into Rome; but papal stature had declined precipitously since then. Boniface, a rock-ribbed papal triumphalist, had provoked widespread ire by his insistence that "it is absolutely necessary to every single

Papal Gift   This is a copy of a now-lost original painting by Zhou Lang in 1342, depicting the arrival of a gift horse from Pope Benedict XII to the last Mongol ruler of China, Shundi. The gift was brought to the Chinese court by a Franciscan emissary named Fra Giovanni di Marignolli.

human being's salvation that he be subject to the Roman pontiff"—a declaration that he meant most literally. The claim was not new, but Christians across Europe chafed at the tone. Philip IV of France, who understood Boniface's claim to undermine his own desire to tax the French clergy, responded by issuing an arrest warrant for the pope, accusing him of everything from murder and bribery to devil worship and sodomy. When Philip's soldiers encountered Boniface at his vacation residence in Anagni, they slapped and beat the old man (Boniface was then nearly seventy) mercilessly; he died three days later of traumatic shock. Small wonder that Friar Giovanni, in Beijing, could hardly believe what his Lombard visitor had told him.

At the height of their power the Mongols controlled an almost unimaginably vast empire, from Beijing to the Euphrates River, and from Moscow to the Arabian Sea. In their wake, they left behind vast numbers of dead. In China alone, census records show that the population in 1200, before Genghis Khan's invasion, stood around 120 million people; in 1300 it figured only 60 million. Ibn Battuta [A] (d. 1378), the famous Spanish Muslim traveler, reported that Persia's population fell from 2.5 million in 1220 to a mere 250,000 in 1260. Some estimate that fully half of Russia's population died as a result of the Mongol conquests; one eyewitness to the destruction of the city of Kiev (the Russian capital at the time) described it this way:

> When the Mongols launched their next attack, upon Russia, they
> caused enormous destruction, leveling many cities and fortresses and

butchering countless men. They besieged Kiev, the capital, for a long time—and when they finally took it they put to death nearly everyone living in it. When my companions and I traveled through that area, we saw the skulls and bones of innumerable corpses lying everywhere on the ground. Kiev at one time had been a large and densely populated city, but now it hardly exists at all—a mere two hundred homes still stand, and every one of their inhabitants has been reduced to slavery. *(Giovanni di piano Carpini, 000, History of the Mongols)*

The Mongols had little interest in actual governance; they left most of the peoples under their control free to live according to their traditional laws and customs, provided that they sent taxes and tribute whenever asked and obeyed without question any new law that the khans decreed. The Mongols understood the significance of trade and were scrupulous about awarding and enforcing safe-passage guarantees to merchants (who paid handsomely for them). Beyond this, however, they showed no real concern for administration, relying simply on massive violent retribution against any group who resisted Mongol authority, to keep peace and order. Time and again, they slaughtered entire towns and villages, punishing collectively any infraction committed by anyone. Merchants and travelers moving across Asia commented repeatedly on the tranquility and order they saw everywhere throughout the Mongol-controlled continent, but as

Europe largely escaped the Mongols' wrath; the Islamic and Chinese worlds took the full brunt of it. The shock was sufficient to set Islamic history on an entirely new path.

Fr. Giovanni recognized in the ruins of Kiev, the tranquility was really the paralysis of brutalized people.

Europe largely escaped the Mongols' wrath; the Islamic and Chinese worlds took the full brunt of it. The shock was sufficient to set Islamic history on an entirely new path.

A NEW CENTER FOR ISLAM

The Turkish-led Mamluk Sultanate, consisting of Egypt and the Holy Land as far as the length of the Euphrates River, largely escaped the catastrophic violence of the Mongols. And so it became, for 250 years, the strong center of western Islamic civilization. The **Ottoman Turks** (tribal cousins of the Seljuk Turks of two centuries earlier) had arrived in force in the latter part of the 13th century, under their charismatic leader Osman (r. 1281–1324). They brought with them a new stability—and a new civilization facing both east and west. Centered upon Asia Minor, the Ottoman Empire was really a confederation of more or less independent realms, united in their recognition of the overlordship of the family of Osman. Among the most significant of these constituent realms was the Mamluk Sultanate.

Stretching from modern-day Libya on the African coast to northern Syria, the Mamluk Sultanate centered on the great cities of Alexandria, Cairo, Jerusalem, Damascus, Antioch, and Aleppo (see Map 10.7). It also lasted through two distinct periods that are sometimes, though incorrectly, called dynasties: the Bahri (1250–1382) and the Burji (1382–1517).

A **sultan** was a military officer, a general-in-chief, and the position was therefore open to advancement from within the army. Most sultans in fact gained office by selection from the leading generals. A few sultans did attempt to pass their position on to their sons, but usually the heirs were ousted by rival generals. The Bahri and the Burji were both foreigners to the region. The Bahri sultans were Kipchak Turks, an ancient people who had originated in Siberia and slowly migrated westward, reaching the Middle East around the middle of the 11th century, where they found employment in the highly disciplined ranks of the Mamluk soldiery. The Burji, by contrast, were ethnic Circassians, an obscure group from the Caucasus Mountain region who spoke Turkish in addition to their ancestral Adyghe language. (The name Circassian comes from the Turkish for "people from the Caucasus.") Both periods were characterized by short-lived sultanates: twenty-seven reigns in the Bahri era (an average of four years apiece) and twenty-six in the Burji (an average of 5.2 years apiece).

Islam had been an international multiethnic religion since the late 7th century, but political, religious, and social authority had been monopolized for

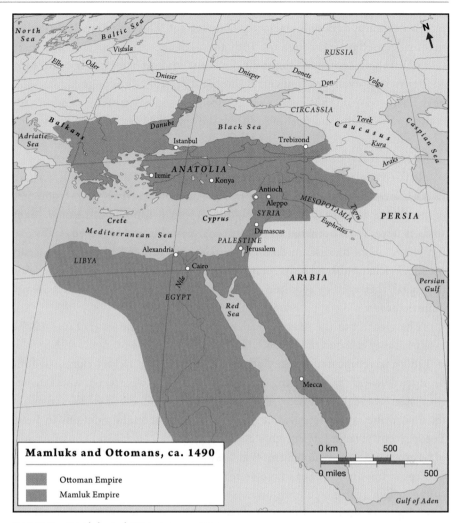

Mamluks and Ottomans, ca. 1490

Ottoman Empire

Mamluk Empire

MAP 10.7   **Mamluks and Ottomans, ca. 1490**

over six hundred years by just two groups, Arabs and Persians. The rise of the Mongols and Turks not only shattered those monopolies but drove the long-ruling societies into secondary status in their own homelands. They would not fully emerge from the political shadows until the 20th century. Moreover, Mamluk rule, occasioned as it was by military force, relied on force to sustain itself.[6] The atmosphere of violence both colored and contributed to a sense of failed jihad. The Crusaders had been driven from the Holy Land in 1291, it is

---

[6]   More than half the Mamluk rulers were assassinated or executed after mostly sham trials. More than half the remainder were forcibly deposed or resigned under threat of deposition.

true, but Islam as a geopolitical force was in retreat. The Christian Reconquista in Spain gained pace through the 13th and 14th centuries, and the survival of Constantinople continued to rankle, for Muslims had been trying to take the city for nearly seven hundred years. The great capital city of Baghdad had also been flattened. And the advance of the Mongols, some of whom had nominally converted to Islam, did nothing to slow the spread of Orthodox Christianity among the peoples of Russia and the Balkans, whom they dominated politically for several centuries.

In the Mamluk state, therefore, a concerted effort to restore a strong, authoritarian Islam continued. This was ironic, since many of the Mamluks—from some of the sultans down to the common soldiers—were Muslim in name only. Many soldiers never even bothered to learn to speak Arabic and regarded Arabs and Egyptians alike with disdain. In this regard, they were not unlike the supposedly Muslim Il-Khan ruling class in Persia, and, being largely uncommitted to religion in general, they thereby acquired reputations for religious tolerance that are not quite deserved.

The greatest of the Mamluk rulers was the first: Baibars (r. 1260–1277), who famously crushed the Seventh Crusade, defeated the Mongols at ʿAyn Jalut in 1260, and recaptured the city of Antioch in 1268—a victory that sealed the ultimate defeat of the remaining Crusader states. He also perfected what became the distinctive Mamluk system of granting lands to officers and soldiers in return for their military service. Not unlike the network of feudal relations in Latin Europe, only stripped of Europe's complex system of social and constitutional obligations, it left common farmers at the mercy of their Mamluk overlords. By 1300 or so fully one-half of whatever revenues each lord raised was owed to the sultan, which guaranteed him sufficient funds to keep adding new slaves to the army. Fortunately for the sultan, much of the spice trade from east Asia had been rerouted to avoid the Mongols and came instead by ship around the Arabian peninsula and up through the Red Sea, thus entering Egyptian markets directly. Until its collapse in 1517, therefore, Mamluk society remained extraordinarily wealthy, although the bulk of the wealth was monopolized by the ruling elite. In turn, the populace grew ever more dissatisfied with Mamluk governance as the decades passed.

CONSERVATISM AND REACTION

With so much wealth at their disposal, the Bahri and Burji did more than expand their armies: they also patronized art in rather showy but often brilliant ways. Sumptuously woven textiles and carpets became a hallmark of their courts (and highly prized commodities among the European well-to-do). Their palaces were showcases for decorative glass, enameled lamps and statuary, exquisite ironwork, and libraries filled with books of fabulously ornate calligraphy and jeweled bindings. Moreover, the Mamluks built scores of new mosques and religious schools (madrasas) and bestowed lavish endowments upon them. The Mamluks had a particular enthusiasm for Sufism, which the bulk of Sunnis had difficulty reconciling themselves to, and brought hundreds of Sufi masters and thousands of Sufi texts into their realm.

In a reaction against what they regarded as the gaudiness of Mamluk culture, much of the most vigorous intellectual life under the Mamluks was reactive and conservative and was found among the Arabs, Egyptians, Kurds, and Syrians, who smarted under the new regimes. The greatest figure of the era was Ibn Taymiyyah [K] (1263–1328), a prolific legal scholar whose works urged a return to the stripped-down essentials of Islam, insisted on conservative readings of the Qur'an and hadith, and raged against the dangerous influence of Sufism. (One of his favorite words is *bid'a*—"reckless innovation" or even "newfangled nonsense.") Taymiyyah insisted on the Qur'an's absolute authority and rejected any efforts to interpret its meanings apart from the most literal and exact. Although trained in kalam and philosophy, he rejected speculative thought as fundamentally un-Islamic and called for all Muslims to adhere to jihad against all the enemies of the faith—among whom he included the Mongols and the Shi'a. He also called on Muslims to reject the cult of Islamic saints, which he regarded as an impious absorption of Christian practice.[7] And perhaps most significantly for later centuries, he ardently championed the restoration of ethnic Arab leadership over international Islam.

The Black Death decimated the Islamic world just as it did the European, and the Mamluk Sultanate never fully recovered from the blow. In Cairo alone, as many as forty thousand people perished.

A Mosque Lamp A lovely oil-burning lamp made of enameled glass. Dating to the late 14th century, the lamp is Egyptian or Syrian in make.

---

[7] "Many of these saints' venerators do not even know that this is a practice derived from the Christians. May Christianity and its followers be accursed!" (*Kitab Iqitada*).

When the Burji dynasty replaced the Bahri in 1382 they made factionalism even worse by purging the Turkish elite and installing their Circassian fellows, through whom they ordered even heavier taxation of the common populace. The Burji likewise earned well-deserved reputations for graft and corruption that further alienated them from their subjects in Egypt and Syria. But so long as the Mamluk military machine stood supreme, there was little anyone could do about them.

By 1500, however, two things had occurred that brought Mamluk power to an end. First, the Portuguese had rounded the African continent and interjected themselves into the spice and silk trade coming out of India, thus depriving the Mamluks of desperately needed revenue. Second, the Ottoman Turks, whose enthusiastic embrace of gunpowder and cannons gave them a clear tactical advantage over all rivals, challenged Mamluk control of Syria and Palestine with an assault on Aleppo. This gained, the Turks pressed further southward, taking all of Syria in less than a year, and in early 1517 capturing Cairo itself, putting an end to the Mamluk era. The establishment of Ottoman power inaugurates Islam's modern era.

THE OTTOMAN TURKS

No one would have predicted it, but the Ottoman regime gave the Islamic world its lengthiest, stablest, and most prosperous rule. To a certain extent, they had the Mongols to thank for that. The Mongol devastation was so vast, and their extortion of wealth afterwards so extensive, that Iraq and Iran required at least a century to recover. Meanwhile the realm of the Seljuk Turks, who had dominated most of Anatolia since their victory over the Byzantines at Manzikert in 1071, had broken up into a sprawl of warring principalities, which the Ottomans were then able to pick off one at a time. The turning point was a severe defeat inflicted on the Seljuks by the Mongols in 1243 at Köse Dağ in northeastern Anatolia.

In 1453 the Ottomans under their leader Mehmed II [T] (r. 1451–1481) achieved what Muslim armies had dreamt of since the 7th century—the conquest of Constantinople, which they made their own capital. Only the Mamluks, far to the south, rivaled the might of the Ottomans. By 1500 even the Mamluks were in retreat, leaving the Ottomans as undisputed leaders of the Islamic world, a position they held until they finally fell from power in the aftermath of World War I. Through most of its long history, the Ottoman Empire comprised most of North Africa, the Hijaz (that is, the western coastal strip of Arabia including the holy cities of Mecca and Madina), Palestine, Mesopotamia, Syria, Anatolia, the Balkans, Hungary, and the Crimea. This was an area larger than the Byzantine Empire had ever been.

They had the advantage of arriving on the scene when everyone else (Mamluks excluded) was weakening. Under the Seljuks, much of the Greek Orthodox and Armenian Christian populations had been driven off the land by the Turkish leaders' need to award land parcels to their soldiers. Unattached Turkish frontier warriors and mercenaries (called *ghazis*, in Turkish) made things worse, massacring and enslaving Christians in roughly equal numbers in the 12th and early 13th centuries. Famines and disease took care of much of the rest.[8] By the time the Ottomans came to power, the Turks' scorched-earth policies had emptied most of the Anatolian countryside. Many of the displaced Christians relocated to the Balkan and Black Sea territories, where the Byzantines still exercised some control, while town dwellers preferred to emigrate into Latin Europe, especially Italy. Changes in the place-names of Asia Minor tell the story: Byzantine Sinope became Turkish Sinop; Trebizond was renamed Trabzon; Adrianople reemerged as Edirne; Pergamon became Bergama; Germanicopolis acquired the name Çankırı; Nicaea became known as İznik; and so on (see Map 10.8). Those Christians who remained faced punitive taxation and various forms of social discrimination, and occasionally some entire villages converted in order to gain a sounder footing under the new regime. By 1300 Asia Minor was overwhelmingly Muslim, and the Ottomans responded by building hundreds of new mosques, madrasas, hospitals—even temporary housing for new converts, as a means of instructing them in Islamic customs.

The Ottomans had an even stronger enthusiasm for Sufism than the Seljuks had, and they consequently brought in Sufi preachers in huge numbers. The Sufis

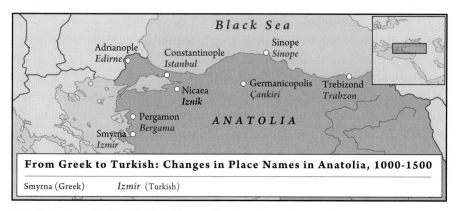

From Greek to Turkish: Changes in Place Names in Anatolia, 1000-1500

Smyrna (Greek)   *Izmir* (Turkish)

MAP 10.8   From Greek to Turkish: Changes in Place Names in Anatolia, 1000–1500

---

[8]   Warriors for hire flocked to 13th-century Anatolia from all around Europe and the Middle East.

bore special responsibility for converting the remaining Christians, which they did by emphasizing a kind of religious syncretism not seen since Roman times. Sermons drew direct parallels between the Twelve Apostles and the twelve Shi'a imams; others presented Allah, Muhammad, and Ali as an Islamic Trinity. The way had been prepared for these preachers by earlier figures like the great Sufi poet Jalal ad-Din Muhammad Balkhi [P] (1207–1273), better known in the West as **Rumi**, who penned thousands of verses, a number of sermons, and a famous collection of letters. Although he was a strict Muslim, Rumi's poetry frequently aimed at an ecumenical appeal:

> In search of Allah I ventured among the Christians and looked upon
>   the Cross,
> But I did not find Him there;
> I entered pagan temples and looked upon the idols,
> But I did not find Him there.
> I explored the mountain cave at Hira [the site of Muhammad's first
>   Qur'anic revelation]
> And even went as far as Kandahar, but I did not find Him there.
> So I made up my mind to climb to the top of Mount Caucasus,
> But there I found only a phoenix's nest.
> Turning around, I set out for the holy Ka'ba, the refuge of young
>   and old,
> But I did not find Him even there.
> Trying philosophy next, I looked for insight in the writings of
>   Ibn Sina,
> But I did not find Him there. . . .
> Finally, at last, I looked in my own heart, and found Him;
> He had been there all along. *(Quatrain 1173)*

His writings champion Islam but without disparaging other faiths. His approach seemed too gentle to many of his contemporaries, especially those Sunnis who were ill at ease with Sufi emotionalism. Yet the beauty of his poetry secured him an avid readership that lasts to the present day.

The unsettled nature of much Muslim life, as the Il-Khans plundered Iraq and Iran and as the Muslims in Spain continued to collapse in the face of the Reconquista, meant a continuous flow of immigrants into the Ottoman lands, which brought skilled labor and administrative talent to where they were needed. Judges, theologians, engineers, and civil bureaucrats, as well as farmers and artisans, poured into the region in large numbers. This enabled Ottoman society to stabilize quickly as a developed economic and political entity. And the Byzantine disappearing act opened Thrace, Macedonia, and the Balkans to Turkish expansion too. Under Murad I [T] (r. 1359–1389) the Turkish army added most of Bulgaria to the Ottoman domain as well, although Murad himself died shortly thereafter in battle against the Serbs at Kosovo.[9] In formalizing the peace accord after the fray, a prominent Serb princess married Murad's son and heir, Bayezid I; the union was reportedly an unusually happy one. Even more significantly, Serbian forces promptly joined up with Bayezid and helped him to attack Bosnia, Herzegovina, and parts of Hungary.

The stronger the Ottomans became, however, the more suspicious of them the Mongol Il-Khans in Persia and the Mamluks in Egypt grew. The popularity of Sufism among the Turks, and its sometimes troubling ecumenical traces, added to the popular hostility toward them. Bayezid I [T] (r. 1389–1403) went so far as to name his first three sons Musa [Moses], Issa [Jesus], and Mehmed [Muhammad], which was beyond the pale in most Sunni eyes. When the Ottoman rulers, mimicking the Mamluks, formed their own personal bodyguard of slave-soldiers (called janissaries, after the Turkish *yeniçeri*—meaning "new soldier"), many of whom were Greek Christians, they gave the appearance of being weak in their commitment to Islam; this rumor justified the attacks made on the Ottomans by the Mongols and Mamluks.

Despite those attacks, the Turks entered the 15th century as the clear leaders of international Islam. Turkish replaced Arabic and Persian as the language of diplomacy, and ethnic Turks filled the upper ranks of the civil and military hierarchies. When Constantinople was finally taken in 1453, it was renamed Istanbul and established as the new capital of the Turkish state. The move was doubly symbolic: not only did the Islamic world itself now stand triumphant over the Byzantines, but the Ottomans, unlike all earlier Muslim leaders, took up residence in the very city that straddled Asia and Europe. Islam would henceforth be a civilization on two fronts, facing both east and west, rooted in the faith that arose from Arabia but as much involved in Western ways as in Eastern. It was no coincidence that what enabled the great sultan Mehmed II (r. 1444–1446, 1451–1481) to finally achieve the conquest of Constantinople was his use of massive cannons that had been forged for him by engineers in Hungary. It was an eastern army with western technology.

> Islam would henceforth be a civilization on two fronts, facing both east and west, rooted in the faith that arose from Arabia but as much involved in Western ways as in eastern.

---

9   The battle of Kosovo only later became enshrined as a moment when Serbs heroically gave their lives against the Muslim infidel.

The Conquest of Constantinople   A fresco on the outer wall of a Byzantine church depicting the siege of the city by Suleiman the Magnificent. The massive cannons used by the Ottomans to break the defenses had been forged in Hungary by the ironworkers' guild, in hopes that Suleiman would settle for Constantinople and leave the Hungarians alone. They were wrong.

PERSIA UNDER THE IL-KHANS

The Mongols were themselves shamanistic, meaning that they followed tribal spiritual leaders who were in contact with the spirit world and worked as miracle healers. They were generally tolerant of other religions and did little to hinder the development of Christianity or Islam. There were, of course, exceptions. One early emir of Il-Khan Persia, Nawruz, issued a decree:

> All [Christian] churches shall be torn down, their altars destroyed, and all celebrations of the Eucharist shall cease; moreover all hymns of praise and ringing of bells to call Christians to prayer shall be abolished. I decree too that the leaders of all Christian and Jewish congregations shall be killed.

But although several prominent Mongols did convert to Christianity, Islam was far more successful in spreading its message among not only the Mongols themselves but their tributary peoples as well. Since the arrival of the Seljuk Turks in the 11th century, a significant number of Muslims were Turkish-speaking. This gave the Muslims a considerable advantage in proselytizing, for the long history of interaction between the Turks and Mongols had fostered widespread understanding of their respective languages. Moreover, groups of Turks had traditionally been among the Mongols' chief steppe allies in the occasional confederations of tribes that formed and dissolved over the centuries. Mahmoud Ghazan (r. 1295–1304), the ruler of the Il-Khan kingdom in Persia, converted to Shi'a Islam—probably as a political move. (Rumors had it that he continued to practice shamanism privately.) He now declared Islam the official religion of the Il-Khanate. Turkish gradually replaced Mongolian as the language of the Il-Khan state, and Turks and Mongols held the supreme political and fiscal offices. Ethnic Persians, however, continued to make up the bulk of the civil administration throughout Iraq and Iran.

A few cultural and intellectual highlights stand out in the Il-Khan period. Rashid ad-Din Hamadani [P] (1247–1318) was a physician and historian; his encyclopedic *Jami al-Tawarikh* ("Compendium of Chronicles") is one of the greatest of medieval world histories. Sa'di [P] (1184–1291) was a Sufi poet of considerable talent in both Persian and Arabic, although much of his fictional writing (for which he was widely admired) is marred by a surprisingly callous spirit. In one story from his book *The Rose Garden* (1.40), for example, he tells of a Chinese slave girl who rejects a Muslim prince's advances and is sent off, as a punishment, to be raped by a black slave "whose upper lip stood higher than his nostrils, whose lower lip hung down to his neck…and whose armpit stench smelled like pitch." Sa'di evidently intended this story, and others like it, to be humorous, but it is a humor based on cruelty. Hafez Shirazi [P] (1315–1390) is perhaps the best loved of all Persian poets down to the present day; his lyrical verses praised the beauty of the human form in language reminiscent of religious mysticism.[10]

The Tatars never enjoyed much popularity with the peoples of Iraq and Iran. Turkish managed to replace Mongolian as the official court language, and ethnic Persians still dominated the higher echelons of civil affairs. Too much of Il-Khan policy had been aimed at diverting wealth into Mongol hands, though, for there to be any popular base to their power. After 1335 there were no more Mongols in charge, since the Il-Khan line died out; this triggered a long series of civil wars between petty emirs. Adding to Persia's troubles, a new dynasty in China—the Ming—came to power, conquered Mongolia, and cut off the silk routes across central Asia. Persia's economy consequently went into a tailspin.

Another Tatar warlord, around 1400, named Timur the Lame, or Tamerlane (r. 1380–1405), briefly terrorized Iraq and Iran while trying to reestablish Tatar

---

[10] Scholars in Il-Khan Persia also translated Chinese medical texts and perfected blue-and-white ornamental tile work.

Tamerlane on the Move   This scene shows his invasion of India, ca. 1590.

supremacy. He cut a huge swath of destruction: Baghdad, Delhi, Isfahan (where he notoriously ordered forty thousand citizens beheaded and, feeling whimsical, had a pyramid made of their skulls), Aleppo, Damascus, and Iznik. He burned mosques, schools, and libraries everywhere he went, ordered all Christian churches torn down, and rounded up all the most skilled artisans and deported them to his own capital at Samarkand, where they were forced to finish their lives constructing palaces and monuments in his honor. No one mourned his passing, and it would take many generations for Iraq and Iran, already smarting from earlier Mongol atrocities, to recover from the damage he had inflicted on them.

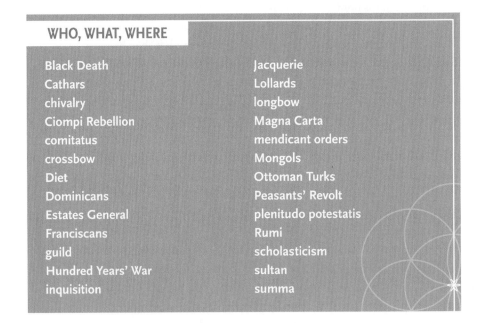

WHO, WHAT, WHERE

Black Death	Jacquerie
Cathars	Lollards
chivalry	longbow
Ciompi Rebellion	Magna Carta
comitatus	mendicant orders
crossbow	Mongols
Diet	Ottoman Turks
Dominicans	Peasants' Revolt
Estates General	plenitudo potestatis
Franciscans	Rumi
guild	scholasticism
Hundred Years' War	sultan
inquisition	summa

SUGGESTED READINGS

Primary Sources

Anonymous. *The Secret History of the Mongols.*
Anonymous. *The Arabian Nights.*
Alighieri, Dante. *The Divine Comedy.*

Chaucer, Geoffrey. *The Canterbury Tales.*
Froissart, Jean. *Chronicles.*
Ibn Battuta. *Travels.*

Ibn Khaldun. *The Muqaddimah.*
Ibn Taymiyya.

Kempe, Margery. *The Book of Margery Kempe.*
Rumi.

Anthologies

Aberth, John. *The Black Death: The Great Mortality of 1348–1350; A Brief History with Documents* (2005).

Dean, Trevor, trans. *The Towns of Italy in the Later Middle Ages* (2000).

Doss-Quinby, Eglal, Joan Tasker Grimbert, Wendy Pfeffer, and Elizabeth Aubrey, eds and trans. *Songs of the Women Trouvères* (2001).

Massoud, Sami G. *The Chronicles and Annalistic Sources of the Early Mamluk Circassian Period* (2007).

Murray, Jacqueline, ed. *Love, Marriage, and the Family in the Middle Ages: A Reader* (2001).

Studies

Aberth, John. *From the Brink of the Apocalypse: Confronting Famine, War, Plague, and Death in the Later Middle Ages* (2001).

Allsen, Thomas T. *Culture and Conquest in Mongol Eurasia* (2001).

Amitai-Preiss, Reuven. *Mongols and Mamluks: The Mamluk- Īlkhānid War of 1260–1281* (2005).

Arnold, John. *Inquisition and Power: Catharism and the Confessing Subject in Medieval Languedoc* (2001).

Beckwith, Christopher I. *Empires of the Silk Road: A History of Central Eurasia from the Bronze Age to the Present* (2010).

Blumenfeld-Kosinski, Renate. *Poets, Saints, and Visionaries of the Great Schism, 1378–1417* (2006).

Cahen, Claude. *The Formation of Turkey: The Seljukid Sultanate of Rūm; 11th to 14th Century* (2001).

Cohn, Samuel K., Jr. *Lust for Liberty: The Politics of Social Revolt in Medieval Europe, 1200–1425; Italy, France, and Flanders* (2006).

Dunn, Alastair. *The Peasants' Revolt: England's Failed Revolution of 1381* (2004).

Dyer, Christopher. *Making a Living in the Middle Ages: The People of Britain, 850–1520* (2003).

Goffman, Daniel. *The Ottoman Empire and Early Modern Europe* (2002).

Inalcik, Halil. *The Ottoman Empire: The Classical Age, 1300–1600* (2001).

Inalcik, Halil, and Donald Quataert, eds. *An Economic and Social History of the Ottoman Empire* (2005).

Leopold, Antony. *How to Recover the Holy Land: Crusading Proposals of the Late Thirteenth and Early Fourteenth Centuries* (2000).

Liu, Xinru. *The Silk Road in World History* (2010).

Pegg, Mark Gregory. *The Corruption of Angels: The Great Inquisition of 1245–1246* (2001).

Rouighi, Ramzi. *The Making of a Mediterranean Emirate: Ifrīqiyā and Its Andalusis, 1200–1400* (2011).

Rubin, Miri. *Gentile Tales: The Narrative Assault on Late Medieval Jews* (2004).

Sumption, Jonathan. *The Hundred Years War* (2000–2011).

For additional resources, including maps, primary sources, visuals, web links, and quizzes, please go to **www.oup.com/us/backman.**

TEMPLA DOMVM EXPOSITIS·VICOS·FORA·MOENIA·PONTES·
VIRGINEAM·TRIVII·QVOD·REPARARIS·AQVAM·
PRISCA·LICET·NAVTIS·STATVAS·DARE·COMMODA·PORTVS·
ET·VATICANVM·CINGERE·SIXTE·IVGVM·
PLVS·TAMEN·VRBS·DEBET·NAM·QVAE·SQVALORE·LATEBAT·
CERNITVR·IN·CELEBRI·BIBLIOTHECA·LOCO·

CHAPTER 11

Renaissances and Reformations

1350–1550

The Renaissance, the period in Europe roughly from 1350 to 1550, is one of the few eras in Western history that named itself. The cultural elite of the time believed they were living in an age of self-conscious revival. They were bringing back to life the ideas, moral values, art, and civic mindedness that characterized, they believed, the two high points of Western culture: Periclean Athens and Republican Rome. One of the first to use the term was the Italian writer, painter, and architect Giorgio Vasari (1511–1574), who celebrated a new epoch of civilized life. After a thousand years of medieval brutality and barbarism, Vasari claimed, Italian artists and thinkers

THE GREATER WEST, ca. 1550

◀ **Pope Sixtus IV** Sixtus IV (r. 1471–1484) is remembered for building the Sistine Chapel, establishing the Spanish Inquisition, and developing the Vatican Library. Record collection had long since become professionalized in the papal court; in fact, references to standing administrative offices with bureaucratic support date back to the 6th century, but a formal library was another matter. Sixtus saw the need for a centralized permanent collection of the church's manuscripts. Pope Nicholas V (r. 1447–1455) was the library's actual founder, but Sixtus greatly expanded and reorganized it and also made it available to scholars. Sixtus was a Franciscan, one of the last of his order to hold the papacy, but quickly became enamored of the pomp and splendor of the Renaissance court. He appointed a half dozen of his nephews to the College of Cardinals, including Giuliano della Rovere—the tall figure in the center—who later became Pope Julius II (r. 1503–1513), the target of Erasmus's great satire *Julius Excluded from Heaven*.

- "I Fixed upon Antiquity"
- Classicism, Humanism, and Statecraft
- The Political and Economic Matrix
- The Renaissance Achievement
- The Protestant Renaissance
- Erasmus: Satirist and Itinerant Scholar
- Martin Luther: The Gift of Salvation
- Rebellion against the Church: "Ninety-Five Theses"
- The Reformation Goes International
- Scholars and Activists
- Protestantism without Luther
- Calvin: Protestantism as Theology
- The Rebirth of Satire
- Utopias and Book Burnings
- Rabelais: The In-house Catholic Attack

CHAPTER OUTLINE

had bravely restored the lost perfection of art and philosophy as known to the ancients. An earlier Renaissance writer on education, Pier Paolo Vergerio (1370–1444), insisted that only the study of the classical liberal arts can lift society from the moral and spiritual decay of the medieval era. "Only those liberal arts," he proclaimed, "are worthy of free men; they alone can help us to attain virtue and wisdom ... [and fill in the gaps in our moral knowledge] which the ignorance of the past centuries has intentionally created."

Una rinascità—a "rebirth" of classical values that gave fresh hope and creative energy to Europe. It also led to the greatest eruption in Greater Western religion since the birth of Islam—the Protestant Reformation.

"I FIXED UPON ANTIQUITY"

Not everyone in the Renaissance shared Vasari's and Vergerio's sense of the near mythic magnificence of antiquity, and it took some time for the English version of the word *rinascità* to catch on. It did not acquire positive connotations in English until John Ruskin (1819–1900) used it in his famous study of architecture *The Stones of Venice* (1851): "This rationalistic art is the art called Renaissance, marked by a return to pagan systems" (1.1.23). Most of Vergerio's and Vasari's contemporaries were simply grateful to have been born after the filthy muddle of the Middle Ages. Francesco Petrarca (1304–1374), usually regarded as the first Renaissance man, expressed this nostalgia for the deep past of Rome and Athens. In an open letter written toward the end of his life, called the *Letter to Posterity*, he recalls his youthful studies:

> I had more of a well-rounded mind than a keen intellect, and was naturally inclined to every type of virtuous and honorable study but especially to moral philosophy and poetry. After a while, it is true, I began to neglect poetry in favor of sacred literature, in which I soon found a buried sweetness that I had previously acknowledged to be there but only in a perfunctory way; now however I found its sweetness so great

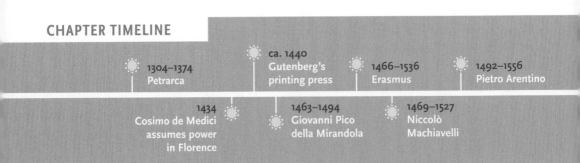

CHAPTER TIMELINE

1304–1374
Petrarca

ca. 1440
Gutenberg's
printing press

1466–1536
Erasmus

1492–1556
Pietro Arentino

1434
Cosimo de Medici
assumes power
in Florence

1463–1494
Giovanni Pico
della Mirandola

1469–1527
Niccolò
Machiavelli

that poetry became a mere afterthought for me. Out of all the subjects that intrigued me, I fixed especially upon antiquity—for the truth is that our own age repels me and has always done so. Indeed, were it not for the love of those I hold dear, I would rather have been born in any age but our own. I have spent most of my life thinking about other eras, in fact, as a way of ignoring my own, and that is why I have always loved the study of history.

> The three ideas most characteristically associated with the Renaissance—classicism, humanism, and modern statecraft—represent no essential break with medieval life at all. They may in fact be thought of as the culmination of medieval strivings.

However, the Renaissance—or the early part of it, anyway—shared more with its preceding age than it wanted to admit. The three ideas most characteristically associated with the Renaissance—classicism, humanism, and modern statecraft—represent no essential break with medieval life at all. They may in fact be thought of as the culmination of medieval strivings.

CLASSICISM, HUMANISM, AND STATECRAFT

The cult of classical learning and literature had its origins in early Western monastic life. Novice monks had long been directed to study the Roman poets Virgil and Horace, the historians Suetonius and Sallust, and the playwrights Terence and Seneca. It was their means to learn Latin before being granted access to the Scriptures and the patristic literature. The works of Aristotle, Ptolemy, Galen, and Euclid, moreover, had dominated university education from the start. But the great scholars of the Renaissance broadened this core canon by seeking out long-lost manuscripts; virtually anything by a classical author was of interest. Petrarca himself unearthed Cicero's *Letters to Atticus*, lying unused and unknown on a dusty library shelf in Verona for centuries, and brought out a new edition of it.

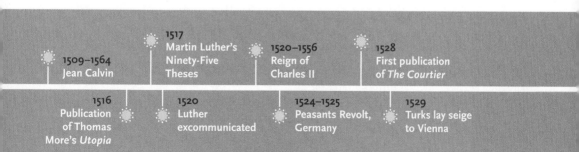

1509–1564
Jean Calvin

1517
Martin Luther's
Ninety-Five
Theses

1520–1556
Reign of
Charles II

1528
First publication
of *The Courtier*

1516
Publication
of Thomas
More's *Utopia*

1520
Luther
excommunicated

1524–1525
Peasants Revolt,
Germany

1529
Turks lay seige
to Vienna

What distinguished the Renaissance approach to the classics was a passionate conviction that they contained all that humans have best thought and best expressed. It was simply impossible not merely to be educated but to be a complete, satisfied, and accomplished human being without knowing the wisdom of the ancients. Pier Paolo Vergerio described the classical canon as "the only literature whose study helps us in the pursuit of virtue and wisdom, and brings forth in us those most sublime gifts of body and mind that ennoble men's spirit and that are properly regarded as second only to virtue itself as our most dignified attainment." This was more than mere affectation. Poseurs seldom engage in such intense archival and philological work. Renaissance scholars traveled through scores of libraries and archives, sifted through piles of manuscripts, corrected the minutest scribal errors, and commented prolifically on the cultural context and multiple meanings of a writer's text. Moreover, these scholars put their learning to use in works of their own, in every genre from poetry to stage drama, epistles to essays, histories to philosophical treatises.

The concern in this period to develop human potential, to value the particular, and to assert the inherent dignity of each person is called **Renaissance humanism**. The idea itself was not new, but the degree of emphasis placed on it was. The catastrophes of the 14th century, after all, had inspired many to doubt the values and assumptions of the high medieval era—the belief in a rationally ordered cosmos, a benevolent deity, the naturalness of a hierarchically structured society, the conviction that good will triumph over evil. The Black Death, after all, had shown no apparent concern to kill only the wicked, and the other calamities of the time had made people grow suspicious of systems of thought or social organization. What does one do, when everything a society takes for granted has been shown to be a sham? The world is a perilous place, a mad, painful jumble of impressions, sensations, thoughts, desires, fears, and inchoate longings. One struggles

The Cult of the Classics   Renaissance artists and writers regularly turned to classical Rome, and to a lesser extent to Periclean Athens, for inspiration, finding in these worlds the best models for the conduct of individual life and civil society. There was of course an element of affectation in this, but more generally it derived from a sincere conviction that the most practical guides to good living came from the pre-Christian world. This page from a new translation of Pliny's *Natural History* printed for a Florentine banker—Filippo Strozzi (1428–1491)—is a case in point. More than four years were spent on its production, and the costs involved totaled over 125 gold florins.

in vain to create anything like order or meaning. The best one can do is to find comfort, beauty, or value in the broken shards of the world scattered at one's feet. Humanism celebrated such simple pleasures: the precise arch of an eyebrow or the drape of a garment in a painting, the warm hue of sunlight entering a window, the sense of balance within an enclosure created by the artful placement of objects, the beautiful potential energy in a tensed coil of muscle. A focus on the particular called for a representational art, one attuned to the hard but transitory reality of objects in time. Medieval art had more widely used symbolic and allegorical representations.

Scholars in the Renaissance still wrote in Latin, but most of the creative literature of the age was in the vernacular. This too mimicked medieval practice, but reflected a different reason. In the Middle Ages, scholarship was written in Latin because it was the common tongue of the learned. Physicians in Spain could communicate with physicians in Hungary or Denmark; mathematicians in England could be read in Portugal or Poland. In the Renaissance, however, scholars wrote in Latin (or sometimes in Greek) out of a conviction in the intrinsic superiority of the classical languages. Latin and Greek, in the "pure" forms used in ancient times, were seen as uniquely capable of expressing complex thought. Imagine a demand today to make Shakespearean English the only form of English worthy of public discourse. Anyone who could read a computer manual in that language would be a rare person indeed—and not necessarily a better person because of it.[1]

The most famous of Renaissance descriptions of humanism came from Giovanni Pico della Mirandola (1463–1494), a brilliant polymath. His "Oration on the Dignity of Man" lays out the fundamental elements of the movement in elegant language:

> I read somewhere of a Muslim writer named Abdullah who, when asked to identify the most wondrous and awe-inspiring thing to appear on the world's stage, answered, "There exists nothing more wondrous than Man." Hermes Trismegistus expressed the same view when he wrote, "What a great miracle is Man, Asclepius!"
>
> But when I began to consider the reasons behind these opinions, every particular of their arguments for the magnificence of human nature failed to persuade me.

---

[1] Scholars sought to take the living Latin and Greek they had inherited and purge them of what they considered barbarisms and corrupt usages.

The unconvincing arguments include man's existence as a rational creature or as master of the physical world.

What strikes Pico della Mirandola as the essential and glorious point about humans is rather something else: to us alone has God given the freedom and ability to be whatever we want, to become whatever we desire, and to achieve whatever we wish. A flower has no choice but to bloom, wither, and die; a stone may serve as a building block, a projectile, or a hindrance in the road, but it has no destiny of its own, no yearning to become something. Humans alone, he insists, are free to be whatever we wish to be.

> You alone, being altogether without limits and in possession of your own free will, ... have it within you to establish the limits of your own nature.... Alone at the dark center of his own existence, yet united with God, Who is Himself beyond all created things, Man too exists beyond every created thing—and who can help but stand in awe of this great Fate forger? Even more: How is it possible for anyone to marvel at anything else?

To describe Man as, essentially, his own Creator was to flirt with heresy—and Mirandola did in fact run afoul of the church. To his credit, he admitted that he had overreached on several matters, issued a number of corrections and retractions, and announced his interest in becoming an obedient monk. He died suddenly at age thirty-one, however. Someone had slipped arsenic into his wine. His fate should not distract us, though, from recognizing the fundamentally religious nature of humanism. Humanism was not a secular philosophy. It sought to define the place of humanity in God's divine plan, to parse the relationship between Man and God, and so to glorify both.

> Humanism was not a secular philosophy. It sought to define the place of humanity in God's divine plan, to parse the relationship between Man and God, and so to glorify both.

The third major element of the Renaissance was statecraft. The concept of a state is a relatively modern one—and a legal fiction. A state as a thing in itself, independent of the people who comprise it and following its own norms and rules, requires a degree of abstraction. Simply to gather a number of people to live in the same space, after all, does not make a city. A city, by definition, is a legal entity, with power—the power to tax, for example, or to administer justice, to legislate, or to police miscreants. It exists on paper and in law, and it makes its powers available to those who dwell within it. Earlier notions of government had regarded the state as a network of personal relationships, but not necessarily as a distinct object. It had the king at the center, with his web of obligations and privileges to his nobles, his commoners, and the church. Exceptions to this model existed, of course, but until the 13th century they were in the minority.

Renaissance theorists and power brokers, taking their cue from late medieval writers like Brunetto Latini (1220–1294) and Marsiglio di Padova (1275–1342), thought of the state in a new way. The political state was a thing, a part of the natural world, and it functioned according to rules. Political leaders who understood this governed most effectively, because they could direct the state by means of its own internal logic. Statecraft therefore involved understanding systems of law, taxation, and economy. It involved the intricacies of diplomacy and negotiation, the mechanisms of crowd control, the manipulation of public opinion, and the knowledge of when to deceive or to exert force. Idealism had no part in it, and politics became a hard science rather than an expression of personal desire. For that very reason, however, it offered the perfect site for educated men of the

The Ambassadors   A powerful but somber piece by Holbein the Younger. Called *The Ambassadors*, it depicts a French nobleman dispatched to London on a diplomatic errand, together with his friend, a French bishop. Together they represent the active and the contemplative modes of life, with objects representing knowledge, power, and art in the background. The diagonally oriented object in the foreground, when looked at obliquely, is a skull representing Death.

Renaissance. Conscious of their abilities, and dedicated to the ancient Roman virtue of civic-mindedness, they could take their proper place within the world by mastering its rules and methods.

THE POLITICAL AND ECONOMIC MATRIX

Europe needed men of ability, Italy especially. Italy was by far the most developed urban society in Europe, followed closely by southern France and eastern Spain. Yet its political scene was a mess. The northern city-states, where the Renaissance began, had long been under the leadership of the German emperor, at least in name. His titular sovereignty dated to the 10th century, when Otto I subdued the region and gained the imperial crown. In the intervening three hundred years, emperors had brought armies over or around the Alps, intermittently but repeatedly, to assert their claims. And most of Italy's city-states opened their gates, bowed deeply, and paid their ritual and financial tribute. But once the armies were safely back in Germany, the Italians instantly returned to their independent republican ways.

The rise of the Hohenstaufen dynasty, however, had altered the rules of the game dramatically. Its joint rule over northern Italy and the Kingdom of Sicily (the result of a marriage alliance) included the southern third of the peninsula. That made urgent the need felt by many northerners to end permanently the imperial claims over their territories. Others, however, saw some utility in the on-again, off-again imperial connection, and so opposed autonomy. This scenario, in which the papacy became deeply involved, led to strife between and within each of the city-states. The Papal State, caught as it was between Hohenstaufen power bases to the north and the south, spent nearly the entire 13th century in diplomatic and military stratagems to break the power of the German/Italian/Sicilian connection. By the time of the 14th century's disasters, northern Italy was a mercenary's dreamscape. Wars large and small, palace coups, assassinations, plots, pillagings, enforced exiles, and institutional corruption had spread everywhere (see Map 11.1).

A unique feature of the Italian scene, however, helped pave the way for the Renaissance. Italian nobles tended to live within the cities, even though their rural estates were distant, and hence they played an active role in urban culture that nobles in Continental Europe did not. That included both ancient lineages and wealthy commoners whose riches had helped them purchase aristocratic titles. Moreover, the elitist bias against trade and commerce that characterized northern aristocratic society was much less virulent in Italy. Hence, by the start of the 15th century, an alliance had developed between the urban aristocrats and the mercantile and banking families of the bourgeoisie. This allowed them

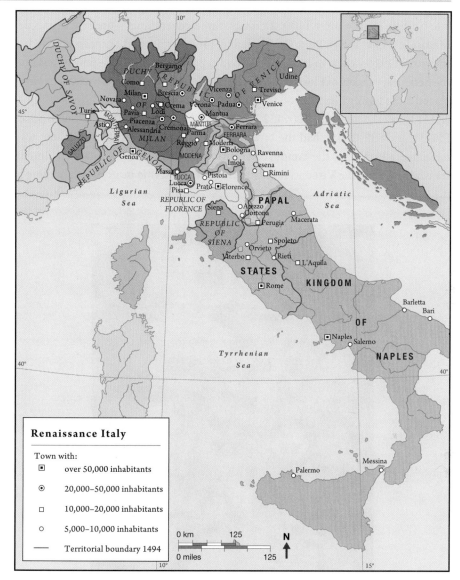

MAP 11.1   Renaissance Italy

to usurp republican government, to institute direct and often tyrannical control over the city-states. Most who did so, mimicking the 1st-century emperor Augustus, maintained the fiction and rituals of republican government while establishing despotic rule.

Most city-states thus had actual, if barely functioning, republican governments between 1350 and 1450 (the first half, roughly, of the Renaissance), but despotic governments from 1450 to 1550 (the second half). In Florence, for example, the Medici family, which had risen through the ranks in banking and textiles, gained a noble title shortly after 1400. Through three generations—under Cosimo de' Medici (r. 1434–1464), Piero de' Medici (r. 1464–1469), and Lorenzo de' Medici (r. 1469–1492)—they governed a pretend republic. In 1531 the family became the hereditary dukes of Florence (later elevated to the status of an archduchy) and placed three family members on the papal throne during the Renaissance—Leo X (r. 1513–1521), Clement VII (r. 1523–1534), and Leo XI (r. 1605). (A fourth pope, Pius IV [r. 1559–1565], had the birth name of Giovanni Angelo Medici but was unrelated.) In Milan, the famous Visconti and Sforza families followed similar trajectories, with the Visconti family taking the ducal title in 1369 and holding it

The Medici as the Magi Wealth has its privileges, among which has been the tradition of artists inserting portraits of their patrons into their religious paintings. Traditionally this was done by placing the patron somewhere within the frame of the original biblical story, but with this painting of the Three Magi coming to worship the child Jesus, the painter has gone one step further by portraying Lorenzo de' Medici and his family members as the Magi themselves. The imposition is apt, since the gifts brought by the Magi (gold, myrrh, and frankincense) were symbolic of the finance and spice trading that brought the Medici their enormous wealth. The painting is by Benozzo Gozzoli (1420–1497).

until the family line died out in 1447. At that point the Sforza family (of peasant origins, with several generations of mercenary soldiers thrown in) took over and governed by fiat until 1535. The d'Este family in Ferrara, who had led local politics since 1264, won a ducal title in 1452 (and another in 1471) and held on to power until 1597. Likewise the Gonzaga family in Mantua, where they ruled without stop from 1328 to 1708.

The concentrations of wealth and power in these city-states, and in others like them, made possible elaborate systems of patronage, which gave a tremendous boost to intellectual and artistic life. Again like Augustus, Renaissance despots put their resources to work in the public sphere. They commissioned scores of palaces, chapels, public fountains and market squares, mausoleums, fortifications, libraries and museums, schools, and hospitals. All were done in the newest styles and were richly decorated with paintings, sculptures, frescos, and tapestries—and they provided hundreds of opportunities for scholars, artists, and architects. Art was not for art's sake alone in the Renaissance. It expressed humanist values and aesthetics while serving to elevate the civic spirit. It also promoted the glory and wisdom of the patron whose support made the art possible.

The depressed economy contributed as well, since labor costs were comparatively low. The building frenzy of the 14th and 15th centuries therefore represented a jobs program: it bolstered support for the regimes by putting people to work. Manufacturing still limped along, since the shrunken population meant a decreased need for most goods; the demographic recovery was slow across Europe. The city of Toulouse, for example, had numbered thirty thousand in the early 14th century, and by the early 15th it had only eight thousand. Within Italy, Genoa had lost more than one-third of its population; Bologna and Milan had each lost half; Florence had lost three-fourths. Many towns did not regain their 13th-century populations until the 20th century. Moreover, the ongoing struggles against the Ottomans, who pressed their frontiers to the gates of Vienna, interrupted trade with Asia. Even with such drastically reduced numbers, the drift of rural poor into the cities ensured a constant labor surplus. Labor costs therefore were cheap, making the vast construction projects of the Renaissance possible.

The rich are with us always. Even in a depressed economy, concentrations of capital exist and often grow, so long as the possessor is lucky or clever (or corrupt) enough to seize the opportunities. In the Renaissance, those opportunities existed, especially in finance and armaments. With so much construction to perform and so much war to wage, those with capital were able to lend it at handsome rates of interest. Meanwhile manufacturers found markets always in search of weaponry and construction equipment. Venice's Arsenal—its shipbuilding factory—employed three thousand laborers at the start of the 15th century. Tax records from that time show that two-thirds of the city's merchants made at least six thousand ducats per year, and one-half of those fortunate merchants actually made well over twelve thousand. Seven merchants actually had annual incomes of over 140,000 ducats.[2] Such severe inequities in the distribution of capital ensured that rents and wages worked in favor of the elite. So did the power of the guild leaders and urban nobles. In Milan and Basel, a mere 5 percent of the population controlled one-half of each city's wealth. No wonder they had the ability to commission palaces, endow museums and libraries, dress in expensive silks and furs, and commission such splendid works of art. The Renaissance, for all its cultural glories, was a miserable time to be a poor farmer or a simple workman—which is precisely what the overwhelming majority of people were.

THE RENAISSANCE ACHIEVEMENT

Art and intellectual life tend to thrive when supported. The cult of patronage—that is, the eager support of painters, sculptors, poets, and scholars as a sign of one's cultivation—and the appreciation of individual talent gave a tremendous impetus to new forms of expression and the pursuit of knowledge. The influx of scholars and artists from the east also contributed, as the Ottomans closed in on the remnants of Byzantium. One Sicilian humanist, Giovanni Aurispa (1376–1459), rushed to Constantinople in the years leading up to the Turkish siege and came back with over two hundred manuscripts that might otherwise have gone up in flames. Copyists were hired by the hundreds in every city to get texts like these reproduced and circulated.[3] The invention of the printing press by Johannes Gutenberg in 1440 allowed books to pour over Europe like a tide. Aldus Manutius (1450–1515) was the most celebrated of humanist publishers; his printing house in Venice produced editions of well over a hundred Latin and Greek texts before his death.

Vernacular literature, or literature in local languages rather than Latin, also began to appear in print. This is important because most of the truly memorable literature produced in the Renaissance was in the common, not the learned, tongues. Petrarca's great sequence of sonnets and love-songs to his beloved Laura (the *Canzoniere*) have proved enduringly popular, while his Latin epic poem about the Roman general Scipio Africanus—called *Africa*—is turgid and lifeless. Much better is Ludovico Ariosto's (1474–1533) immense, and immensely

---

[2]   A Venetian ducat of that time was minted of roughly 3.5 grams of gold (one-eighth of an ounce). Gold, in 2012 U.S. dollars, has hovered around $1610 per ounce. A very rough estimate of the value of 6000 ducats, therefore, would be perhaps $1,200,000. In Shakespeare's play *The Merchant of Venice*, the amount loaned by Shylock to Antonio, on surety of "a pound of flesh," was half that amount.

[3]   By the start of the 15th century, Florence had opened the first lending library in Europe: one could actually borrow the books and take them home rather than having to read them on site, as before.

entertaining, mock-epic *Orlando Furioso* ("Crazed Roland"). It tells of the mad adventures of Charlemagne's knight Roland, who loses his mind when his beloved Angelica falls in love with a Muslim prince and moves to China. Then he turns into a one-man juggernaut, rampaging through Europe, Asia, and Africa and destroying everything in sight.

Not many Renaissance stage plays have lasted; only two are still widely read and produced today. Pietro Aretino (1492–1556), known in his lifetime as the "Scourge of Princes" for his scathing wit and willingness to blackmail the prominent when short of funds, wrote several brilliant bawdy comedies—along with a considerable amount of technically clever pornographic poetry.[4] The best, a comedy called *La cortigiana* ("The Woman Courtier"), tells of an upright wealthy citizen from Siena who receives an appointment as a papal cardinal. Traveling to Rome for his installation, he sees a beautiful young woman sitting at a window and decides he must have her as a mistress. The comedy ensues when a scheming con artist tries to teach the elderly man how to flatter and entice the young beauty—all the while pursuing a plan of his own.

The other great Renaissance comedy is *La mandragola* ("The Mandrake Root"), by Niccolò Machiavelli (1469–1527). The play, which appeared in 1518, tells of another upright elderly man, Nicia, newly married to a stunning but sexually shy beauty named Lucrezia. Unable to convince his bride to sleep with him, the foolish husband confides in a dashing young ne'er-do-well named Callimaco who, desiring Lucrezia for himself, hatches a plot. He tells Nicia that he has

ET DIST. SOL. ET LVNAE. 30

ad M B perpēdicularis. parallela igitur eſt CM ipſi LX. eſt autem & SX parallela ipſi M R; ac proptetea triangulum LX S ſimile eſt triangulo M R C. ergo vt S X ad MR, ita S L ad RC. ſed S X ipſius M Rminor eſt, quàm dupla; quoniā & X N eſt minor, quàm dupla ipſius MO. ergo & SL ipſius CR minor erit, quā dupla : & R multo minor, quā dupla ipſius R C. ex quibus ſequitur S C ipſius CR minoré eſſe, quā triplā. habebit igitur RC ad CS maiorem

H 2 rem

Greek to Me The Romans, being of a pragmatic bent, became expert innovators in engineering but showed relatively little interest in pure science, and hence the science inherited by the scholars of the Middle Ages was based firmly on, and consisted largely of commentary on, the science of the ancient Greeks. The page shown, from a book printed in Pisa, Italy, in 1572, depicts a passage from *On the Distances and Sizes of the Sun and Moon* by Aristarchus (3rd century BCE). The text and drawing examine the ratios of the diameters of the sun, Earth, and moon and calculate how they affect the light and dark portions visible during a lunar eclipse.

A 2008 performance of Aretino's *Songs of Lust*, set to modern music, was withdrawn in London after complaints about their obscene content.

learned, through careful study of ancient Greek scientific manuscripts, of a potion made from mandrake root. When given to a woman, it instantly enflames her with a lust that cannot be denied. The drug has an unfortunate side effect, however: the first man to have sex with the woman will die immediately afterward. Nicia declares that he wants Lucrezia, but not enough to die for it. Callimaco then announces, tremblingly, unwillingly, that he himself suffers from an unspecified mortal illness and has only a few days to live. So great is his admiration for Nicia and his desire to perform a useful service before he dies that he volunteers for the suicide mission.

La mandragola surprises most people who read or watch it. They usually come to the play knowing Machiavelli from another work of his, a small political treatise called *The Prince*. In 1499 the people of Florence had overthrown the Medici despot and restored republican government. Machiavelli, a Florentine, loved and served its republic with passionate dedication for thirteen years, from 1499 to 1512—as a diplomat, civil servant, and military overseer. Late in 1512, however, a counter plot restored Lorenzo de' Medici to power. Machiavelli was dismissed, arrested for conspiracy, tortured, and ultimately released. In retirement at his country estate, he then gave himself over to study and writing.

The Prince, although he never published it, was the first thing Machiavelli wrote. (He circulated it among a small circle of friends and dedicated it to Lorenzo de' Medici—probably in hopes of winning a position in the new government.) It is a notorious book, praised by some for its clear-eyed realism about how political power actually works and vilified by others as little more than a how-to manual for thugs. To modern readers, inured by long experience of politicians' lies, manipulations, and occasional crimes, the book no longer shocks. Stable society, Machiavelli argues, results more from stable order than from benevolent instability. Therefore a prince's first responsibility is to secure his own power, even if the exercise of that power is unjust. Ruthlessness should not be pursued for its own sake, but a wise prince will never rule it out altogether. A prince ought always to maintain an upright public appearance, but behind the scenes he should use any means at his disposal—including lying, cheating, stealing, or killing—in order to maintain power. Although *The Prince* never uses the phrase, its essential message is that in politics the end justifies the means.

Clear-Eyed Realist Niccolò Machiavelli (1469–1527) and a page from his philosophical masterpiece, *The Discourses on Livy*, in praise of republican forms of government.

Once the book was published, five years after Machiavelli's death, people read it with a shudder of horror. Machiavelli's defenders point to the chaotic state of Italian politics at the time, with French, German, Savoyard, and Spanish invaders at every turn. *The Prince*, they suggest, is simply a plea for a no-nonsense messianic figure who would restore Italian liberty. Perhaps. His letters, though, suggest that Machiavelli was a man of republican Florence, first, last, and always. He would have been delighted to see Ferrara, Mantua, Milan, Pisa, or Venice crushed by a foreign army if that were to Florence's gain. Complicating matters, he dashed off *The Prince* in a few weeks. Machiavelli then spent four years (1513–1517) composing his major work, *Discourses on Livy*, which elaborates a complex and passionate argument on the superiority of republican government over any other type of political organization.[5] "Governments of the people are superior to any government by a prince" (1.58).

Less controversial were Marsilio Ficino (1433–1499) and Baldassare Castiglione (1478–1529). Ficino was a celebrated philosopher who spent his career at the Medici court. He had mastered classical Greek as a young man and became a devout exponent of Neoplatonism. His greatest achievement, in fact, was a translation into Latin of the entire corpus of Plato's writings, which he completed in 1470 but did not publish until 1484 (having taken some time, meanwhile, to prepare for the priesthood). Until then, Plato had hardly been known in Latin Europe, and Western intellectual life had been long dominated by Aristotle. Ficino's other major works include a long treatise, *On Platonic Theology*, which explicates Christian doctrine on the immortality of the soul using Platonic ideas. He argues that the unique, characteristic destiny of the human soul is to investigate its own nature, but such investigation inevitably results (at least temporarily) in confusion and misery. Hence the ultimate goal of the soul is to rise above physicality, to become disembodied, and to achieve union with the divine. As a hybrid philosophical and mystical treatise, it is a stunning exercise. Ficino was the tutor of many Neoplatonists, most famously of Giovanni Pico della Mirandola, the author of the "Oration on the Dignity of Man."

Castiglione came from an ancient noble family near Mantua and spent his entire life in the circle of social and political elites. He served as a personal aide and confidante to the marquis of Mantua and then to the duke of Urbino and spent several years in Rome as an ambassador to the papal court, then several more as papal nuncio to the royal court of Spain in Madrid. He is remembered primarily for *The Courtier*, which is a kind of memoir written in the form of a fictional philosophical

---

5   "No properly run republic should ever find it necessary to overlook the crimes of any given citizen because of his supposed excellence" (Machiavelli, *Discourses* 1.24).

dialogue. In it he laments the passing of the Renaissance's golden era, when human-ism was at its height. By the 16th century Italy was overrun by ambitious foreigners, and courtly life as Castiglione had known it (or at least as he chose to remember it) had declined into a tawdry arena of power grabbing, money grubbing, and social climbing. He depicts fictionalized versions of the companions of his youth—elegant, charming, cultivated, effortlessly superior to everyone—who spend four evenings in an extended conversation about the qualities of an ideal courtier.

To Castiglione the courtier is above politics: he graciously advises any figure deemed worthy of attention but does not advocate any particular political phi-losophy. This marks a shift from the original ideal of humanism, which expected a passionate civic spirit from its adherents. Castiglione's figures expound on the need for courtiers to appreciate music and poetry, to excel at dancing, sports, and refined conversation, to understand the importance of fashion as well as affairs of state. In short, courtiers should exist beautifully, all the while exuding an air of nonchalance and unpracticed elegance. *The Courtier* was extraordinarily popu-lar, going through more than one hundred editions between its appearance in 1528 and 1616. Its significance lay in its elegiac mood: at a time when Europe's nobles were being displaced from political life, Castiglione consecrated for them the qualities that lifted them forever above the common rabble.

THE PROTESTANT RENAISSANCE

As the ideas and values of the Renaissance spread northward, they took on new styles, concerns, and emphases. Ultimately, if indirectly, they led to the shattering of the religious unity that had marked Latin Europe since the advent of Christianity.

It took some time for humanism to catch on in the north. The prolonged agony of the Hundred Years' War in England and France certainly impeded the spread of the new learning. So did the resistance of the universities of Paris and Oxford—both strongholds of Aristotelianism. As for Germany, intellectual life there had long been centered in the royal and aristocratic courts. The royal court at Munich, for example, had been a refuge for scholars like Marsiglio di Padova and William of Ockham in the 14th century, when both had fallen out of favor in Paris and Oxford, respectively. Now Germany had fractured into hundreds of principalities (nominally under the authority of the Habsburg dynasty—the weak successors to the crushed Hohenstaufens—but effectively autonomous), and its relatively few universities did not rush to embrace new ideas.[6] When humanism

---

[6]   Munich did not acquire a university until 1472. Even then, the university was at Ingolstadt, several miles away.

did finally begin to take root, around the year 1500, it did so in an altered form known as **Christian humanism**.

Like humanism in Italy, Christian humanism rejected scholastic system building and looked to the past for new models of thinking and behavior. However, Christian humanists showed a strong preference for texts and traditions that contributed directly to religious faith. Their goal was not to become better all-round individuals but better Christians. Consequently, they focused less on the writings of the ancient philosophers and poets and more on the early writings of the Christians—especially the New Testament itself. In the visual arts, the northern Renaissance likewise showed much less interest in depicting classical pagan themes. Rather, painters and sculptors avidly adopted Renaissance techniques to produce striking new presentations of biblical imagery. The Christian humanists were passionate reformers, dedicated to promote Christian education and practical piety through the preparation of newer and better texts. Their often-stated goal was backward looking: to restore Christian faith to its original purity as practiced in the apostolic community.

The Christian humanists were not yet anti-Catholic, only anticlerical. The shortage of priests had always been direr the further north one traveled in Europe, with exceptions in cities like Paris, London, and Mainz, but the problem had been persistently acute since the Black Death. Clergy at the grassroots level were in painfully short supply, and those who were available were often poorly trained. Hence northerners had developed strong traditions of lay piety. They focused less on the church's sacramental life and more on the simple reading of Scripture, the singing of hymns, and communal prayer. Religious fraternities and sororities abounded, offering many a life of organized piety, education, and moral rigor that deemphasized ecclesiastical dogma and ritual. The best

The Four Holy Men "A panel on which I have bestowed more care than on any other painting" is how Albrecht Dürer (1471–1528) described this powerful group portrait, completed in 1526. It depicts, from left to right, Saint John the Evangelist, Saint Peter (holding his ever-present key to paradise), Saint Mark, and Saint Paul the Apostle (who carries a copy of the Bible and a sword, the latter being a reference to his martyrdom). Dürer was a passionate supporter of the Lutheran Reformation, and the bottom portion of each panel (since lost) bore passages from Luther's German translation of the Scriptures. The intensity of the men's expressions and the classical simplicity of their dress testify to the spiritual earnestness of the Protestant Reformers—being awed and humbled by the magnificence of what they regarded as the rediscovered beauty and majesty of the Word.

known of these organizations was the Brethren of the Common Life, established in 14th-century Holland and spreading quickly across northern Europe. Its most famous alumni were Desiderius Erasmus (1466–1536) and Martin Luther (1483–1546).

ERASMUS: SATIRIST AND ITINERANT SCHOLAR

Erasmus was arguably the greatest of all humanist scholars, admired for the breadth of his classical learning, his quick wit and generous spirit, and the elegance of his writing. The illegitimate son of a Dutch priest in training and a physician's daughter, he grew up in Rotterdam and received his primary education at home. In 1483, however, both of his parents died in a new outbreak of the plague. Supported by the Brethren of the Common Life, Erasmus entered a series of monastic and lay-fraternal schools, where he was unhappy with the frequently dour discipline but delighted in their extensive libraries. In 1492, brilliant but penniless, he took monastic vows, entered an Augustinian house, and was soon ordained to the priesthood. He hated monastic life, though, and thought most of his fellow monks to be joyless and haughty automatons. Fortunately, a bishop from Cambrai, not far away in northern France, heard of Erasmus's brilliance and took him on as a personal secretary in 1495. The bishop urged Erasmus to pursue more formal study and sent him to the University of Paris.

Once he had finished his degree, Erasmus set out for England, where he had been invited to lecture at the University of Cambridge. Freed from the bishop's service, Erasmus spent the rest of his life as an itinerant scholar, lecturing at various universities and visiting one noble court after another. Chronically short of funds, he was offered many lucrative academic posts throughout his life but declined them all, preferring his freedom. He also rejected several offers to be appointed a Catholic bishop and two nominations to the College of Cardinals. He studied and wrote constantly, even while traveling. In fact, he claimed to have written much of his most famous work, *The Praise of Folly* (1509), while on horseback during a trip to England to visit his friend Thomas More. He died in Basel in 1536.

Despite such an unsettled life Erasmus produced an astonishing amount of writing. His letters alone fill eleven fat volumes in their standard edition. He wrote in three distinct voices. His most popular works were witty satires like *The Praise of Folly* that aimed to entertain people while nevertheless pointing out society's flaws and foibles. Folly here delivers a monologue on the crucial but unappreciated role she has played in human history. Everyone from kings and princes to peasants and peddlers, she claims, owe something to her for the simple reason that humans all prefer foolishness to common sense. Every page of history proves her point. In works like this, or his popular *Colloquies* (1518), Erasmus lampoons pedantic teachers, hypocritical clerics, greedy landlords, shrewish wives, petulant youths, preening nobles, untrustworthy merchants, and others with a wit that is pointed but almost never mean-spirited.

Erasmus's most notorious satire is a prickly piece called *Julius Excluded* (1513), a lengthy sketch depicting a confrontation at the Gates of Heaven between the recently deceased Pope Julius II (r. 1503–1513) and Saint Peter. Julius is drunk when he arrives and tries to unlock the gates with the key to his private money chest. Asked to account for his many sins, ranging from murder to sodomy, Julius replies that his sins were all forgiven "by the pope himself"—meaning, of course, Julius himself. When Saint Peter refuses to admit Julius into heaven on account of his excessive concern for

Erasmus of Rotterdam   Given the fact that he was the most traveled, best connected, and highly regarded religious scholar in Europe, there are surprisingly few contemporary portraits of Erasmus, the man who made a heroic last-ditch effort to reform Catholic Christianity before Martin Luther's break with Rome. This portrait, by fellow Dutchman Quentin Metsys (1466–1530), captures the quiet determination of the man. Despite his gift for satire and enjoyment of good (and sometimes bawdy) humor, Erasmus dedicated long years of work to exposing problems within the Catholic Church and promoting a spiritual rejuvenation that would keep all Christians within the arms of the church. His failure marks an important turning point, since most of the great reforms in the church in earlier centuries had been inspired from without. From Erasmus's time to the present, Catholic reform has been largely driven from within the institutional leadership.

worldly power and war making, the pope throws a fit, threatens to excommunicate Peter, and announces that he will raise an army to burst through the gates and take Paradise by force.[7]

Erasmus also composed a long series of moral polemics, earnest in tone yet intended for a general audience. In these books—like *Handbook of the Christian Soldier* (1503), *Education of a Christian Prince* (1516), and *The Complaint of Peace* (1517)—he condemns empty religious formalism and urges people to seek out the vital spirit of Christ as depicted in the Bible. They should live simply,

---

[7]   At one point the pope complains to Saint Peter, "You would not believe how *seriously* some people take little things like bribery, blasphemy, sodomy, and poisoning!"

honorably, peaceably, and with sincere conviction. These satirical and serious works were immensely popular: it has been estimated that, by Erasmus's death in 1536, some 15 percent of all the printed books purchased in Europe had come from his pen. In his third vein, Erasmus toiled at the most detailed and exacting textual scholarship—revised and annotated editions of the writings of the Latin fathers Saint Ambrose (d. 397), Saint Jerome (d. 420), and Saint Augustine (d. 430). He followed these projects with his masterpiece, a new critical edition of the Greek New Testament (1515), whose fifth and final version appeared in 1535. Known as the Received Version (*Textus receptus*), it was used by most early translators of the New Testament into English and other vernaculars. These works had a much smaller readership, understandably, but he regarded them as his chief legacy to the world.

MARTIN LUTHER: THE GIFT OF SALVATION

Among those who used Erasmus's New Testament as the basis for a vernacular translation was Martin Luther, the German monk whose agonized quest for salvation triggered the break with the church known as the **Protestant Reformation**. Like the humanists who sought to restore ancient morals, Luther sought to re-create what he believed to be Christian belief and practice as they had existed in the apostolic Church. He saw himself as a restorer, not a revolutionary, a liberator rather than an insurrectionist. The distinction is important, for it helped to set the stage for the brutal course the conflict ultimately took. Luther, a brilliant biblical scholar, had the gift of presenting his ideas in clear, forceful language that ranged easily in emotional pitch from exquisite descriptions of God's loving kindness to the coarsest verbal abuse of his foes (who consisted of anyone who disagreed with him). His charisma, energy, and passionate feeling were immense; he needed such powerful drive, for his ultimate goals—once he decided that compromise with the church was impossible—were nothing less than the complete overthrow of Catholic tradition and the resetting of the Christian clock, so to speak, fifteen hundred years back.

> Like the humanists who sought to restore ancient morals, Luther sought to re-create what he believed to be Christian belief and practice as they had existed in the apostolic Church. He saw himself as a restorer, not a revolutionary, a liberator rather than an insurrectionist.

Luther was born—proudly—of modest, laboring stock in northern Germany. His hardworking parents instilled piety and order in him from an early age, and when it came time for his education they sent him to a school run by the Brethren of Common

Life, the same group whose austere and rigid discipline had so disillusioned the young Erasmus. Hoping to establish his son in a legal career, Luther's father sent him to the University of Erfurt, but Martin was drawn instead to theology and the classical languages. In 1505, aged twenty-two, he shattered his father's hopes by taking vows as an Augustinian monk. A mere two years later he was ordained a priest.

His vocation brought him no peace, though. Belief in God tormented Luther, for he could see no way to please him. God's majesty was so immense, so vast, and so inconceivably great, that Luther found it impossible to believe that anyone could merit salvation. No one de-

A Restorer, not a Revolutionary   Martin Luther (1483–1546), in a portrait by Lucas Cranach the Elder (1472–1553). Apart from his work as an artist, Cranach was an early enthusiast for the printing press, and in time became one of Martin Luther's publishers. He is revered as a saint in both the Episcopal and Lutheran Churches in the United States.

serves to be saved, he believed, for the simple reason that no one can deserve to spend eternity in God's presence. How can anyone possibly claim to merit that? And yet that was precisely what Christian tradition told him to pursue—a life of prayer, repentance, good works, and devotion that would earn him the salvation Christ had promised to everyone who did so. Luther observed his monastic discipline with fanatical determination, even to the point where his abbot feared for his sanity. And yet the fear that nothing he did could possibly justify his standing before God never left him. So sharp grew his agony, he later wrote, that he began to despise God for having created a game that we cannot win—and then punishing us with eternal torment for losing it:

> Even as a blameless monk I still felt certain that in God's eyes I was a miserable sinner—and one with a very troubled conscience—for I had no reason to believe that God would ever be satisfied by my actions. I could not love a righteous God who punished the unrighteous; rather, I hated Him. I was careful never to blaspheme aloud, but on the inside, in the silence of my heart, I roiled and raged at God, saying, "Is it not enough for You that we, miserable sinners all, are damned for all eternity on account of original sin [the notion that, as a result of Adam and Eve's

misbehavior, all human beings come into the world with a moral stain upon them from birth]? Why do You add to our calamity by imposing the Ten Commandments on us as well? Why add sorrow upon sorrow through the Gospel teachings, and then in that same Gospel threaten us with judgment and wrath?"

But then came the breakthrough. Having been sent by his exhausted abbot to teach theology at the University of Wittenberg, Luther, in 1513, was preparing lecture notes on Saint Paul's Epistle to the Romans, a text he had read countless times before, when suddenly a new insight flashed through his mind:

> I pondered these words night and day until, at last, God had mercy on me and gave me to understand the connection between the phrases "The justice of God is revealed in the Gospel" and "The just will live through faith" [Romans 1.16–17]. I suddenly began to understand that God's justice—that is, the justice by which a just person may live for ever—is a gift of God won by faith. . . . All at once I felt reborn, as though I had entered Paradise through gates thrown wide open, and immediately the whole of Scripture took on a new meaning for me.

In other words, *of course* God knows that we do not "deserve" salvation. But salvation is God's gift to us, and he simply wants us to have it anyway.

After this flash of insight, the rest of the Scriptures' meaning lay open, as though Luther was seeing it for the first time. To be righteous in the eyes of God, one did not have confess one's sins to a priest, give alms to the poor, or earn indulgences by ritual devotions like pilgrimages or vigils. One did not have to follow disciplines like praying cycles of the rosary or not eating meat on Fridays. One attains righteousness simply by having faith in Christ; one must accept the salvation he offers as an unmerited gift. This idea became canonized in Luther's understanding as **justification by faith alone** (*sola fide* in Latin). It results not from our merit but from God's grace alone (*sola gratia*), as expressed uniquely through Christ's sacrifice on the Cross (*solo Christo*). Moreover, everything that God requires of us is expressed not through the teaching authority and tradition of the church but through the words of Scripture alone (*sola Scriptura*). Anything beyond biblical teaching is superfluous to salvation at best, and an impediment to it at worst. Few of these ideas were new. In fact, many of them had been enunciated by Saint Augustine (d. 430), the founder of Luther's own monastic order. But Luther carried them to a degree far beyond Augustine or any other theologian.

REBELLION AGAINST THE CHURCH: "NINETY-FIVE THESES"

Luther's theology offended the church because it made the church irrelevant. From the time of the Gregorian Reform in the 11th century, the church had developed its theology of salvation, with itself as intermediary. The church and the believer worked together to effect salvation, through teaching and ministry, the sacraments and pious action. The relationship was not a crude contract, although many saw it that way and had been making similar complaints since at least the second half of the 14th century.

What prompted Luther's rebellion against the church was not merely his new understanding of Scripture—for it was not, after all, new. Rather, it was his ire over the church's practice of selling **indulgences**, a donation to the church as a means of satisfying the requirements for the forgiveness of sin. From the 12th century on, Catholic doctrine had understood penance for sin to have four elements: contrition, confession, absolution, and satisfaction. One first has to repent honestly for what one has done; second, one must confess the sin fully to a priest; then, third, one receives absolution from that priest if the confession is sincere and genuine; and fourth, one must then make some sort of restitution for what one did. An indulgence—earned by some explicit act of charity or devotion—was a way of meeting the fourth demand. A special donation to the church was one way of earning the indulgence. Hence, while it was not an act of "purchasing forgiveness," it certainly could look like one—especially if the process was abused. And it was, egregiously, in Luther's time.

Many people had criticized the practice, including Erasmus. The Renaissance popes, as involved as ever in Italian politics, had waged wars against various despots, had tried to resist the advancing Ottoman Turks, and had expanded the church's network of universities across Europe. As a result, they were in constant and desperate need of funds, and many turned to the offering of indulgences as a reliable means of raising cash. An enormous campaign spread throughout Germany and Italy to raise funds for the construction of the new Saint Peter's Basilica in Rome (designed in part by Michelangelo and Bernini). In 1517 Martin Luther, just recently released from his spiritual tortures, witnessed the abusive and predatory selling of

Anti-Catholic Propaganda This anonymous woodcut of 1520 by a German satirist depicts the devil (complete with wings and clawed feet) sitting on a letter of indulgence and holding a money collection box. The devil's mouth is filled with sinners who presumably bought letters of indulgence in good faith, thinking they had been absolved from their sins.

indulgences in both places and was outraged. The symbolic starting point of the Protestant Reformation was not his biblical epiphany in 1513 but his Ninety-Five Theses—condemning the theology of indulgences.

The **Ninety-Five Theses** are simply a list of assertions that Luther declares himself prepared to argue—but the arguments themselves are not part of the text. This sort of posting bulletins of ideas was a common practice in universities of the time. Like the modern practice of publishing the prospectus of one's doctoral dissertation, it invited argument and discussion. He got it. Pope Leo X (r. 1513–1521) spent three years examining Luther's position and finally responded with a papal bull on June 15, 1520, called *Exsurge Domine* ("Arise, O Lord"). He condemned forty-one of the theses as heretical, and he gave Luther sixty days to reconsider his position and withdraw the offending statements. Luther answered back by publicly burning his copy of the bull on December 10, exactly sixty days after it was issued. After this, there was only one action Leo could take: On January 3, 1521, the pope excommunicated Luther. From this point on, little effort was made to mend fences. The people of Germany flocked to Luther's message by the thousands, and then by the tens of thousands. Within a few years the religious unity of Christian Europe was permanently sundered.

"The Pope is the Antichrist, and the Catholic Church is the most unruly of all crooks' lairs, the most brazen of all brothels, and the Kingdom itself of Sin, Death, and Hell," Luther wrote in a late book titled *On the Roman Papacy: An Institution of the Devil*. Pope Leo, for his part, dismissed Luther as "a German drunkard who will mend his ways once he sobers up." The language is not edifying. But once the rift between Luther and the church was opened, it developed quickly into an unbridgeable chasm. What began as an in-house theological dispute took on more and more political and social pressures. Two political issues were of special significance: the constitutional arrangement within Germany, and the threat posed by the Turks.

For two centuries the four hundred or so princes of Germany had enjoyed independence from imperial control, while the relatively weak Habsburgs went about adding to their domain in eastern Europe and by marrying available heiresses throughout the Continent. When Charles V (r. 1520–1556) came to the throne, he succeeded, by a genealogical quirk, to several lines of Habsburg-family legacies. These territories, when considered in the aggregate, put him in the unexpected position of having the German princes surrounded (see Map 11.2). His formal title(s), used on all his official records, ran as follows: "Charles, by grace of God the elected Holy Roman Emperor, forever August, King in Germany, King of Italy, Castile, Aragon, León, both Sicilies, Jerusalem, Navarra, Granada, Toledo, Valencia, Galicia, Majorca, Sevilla, Sardinia, Cordova, Corsica, Murcia, Jaen, the Algarves, Algeciras, Gibraltar, the Canary Islands, the Western and

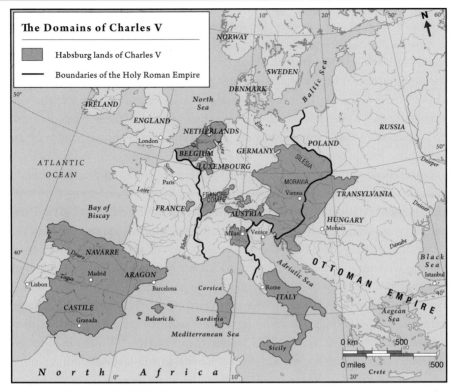

The Domains of Charles V

- Habsburg lands of Charles V
- Boundaries of the Holy Roman Empire

MAP 11.2   **The Domains of Charles V**

Eastern Indies, the Islands and Mainland of the Ocean Sea, etc. etc., Archduke of Austria, Duke of Burgundy, Brabant, Lorraine, Styria, Carinthia, Carniola, Limburg, Luxembourg, Gelderland, Athens, Neopatria, Württemberg, Landgrave of Alsace, Prince of Swabia, Asturia and Catalonia, Count of Flanders, Habsburg, Tyrol, Gorizia, Barcelona, Artois, Burgundy Palatine, Hainaut, Holland, Seeland, Ferrette, Kyburg, Namur, Roussillon, Cerdagne, Zutphen, Margrave of the Holy Roman Empire, Burgau, Oristano and Gociano, Lord of Frisia, the Wendish March, Pordenone, Biscay, Molin, Salins, Tripoli and Mechelen, etc."

By constitutional tradition, Charles had no cause to take advantage of his position by imposing his rule on the princes. However, since he was, as emperor, the defender of Catholicism, he considered seriously his obligation to combat the Protestant heresy. The princes, for their part, had good reason to support Luther: he had essentially given them control of the new churches.

Luther's *Address to the Christian Nobility of the German Nation* (1520) had laid out his vision for the organization and administration of his reformed church. Since there was no supreme spiritual authority—each believer needing only his Bible and his own conscience—the Protestant Church needed only secular administration and guidance. For that, Luther turned to the princes.

A prince who formally broke with Rome and converted to Lutheranism was entitled, Luther wrote, to confiscate the Catholic ecclesiastical lands, properties, and wealth within his principality and to lead the administration of the new reformed churches. The temptation was great, but most princes feared that seizing the extensive holdings of the churches and monasteries would cause Charles V to rush to Catholicism's defense. Hence, even though most of the nobles converted to Lutheranism, they hesitated to start plundering. But then the second political issue came into play.

The Turkish threat was complicated. Ottoman forces had driven deep into Europe, after taking Constantinople in 1453, in hopes of weakening Christendom. Charles V, naturally, spearheaded the effort to hold them at bay. Many Protestant princes hoped to form an alliance with the Ottoman sultan, Suleiman the Magnificent (r. 1520–1566), who had come to his throne at roughly the same time as Charles V came to his. Such a pact, they hoped, would leave Charles as the surrounded party and thereby neutralize his power. Diplomatic relations between Protestant rulers and Suleiman were extensive. The Turks had large numbers of Jews and Christians living within the European part of their empire, and for the time being, at least, they treated them with the tolerance required by dhimmi law. Dhimmi law did not protect Christian and Jewish buildings, however, and Suleiman advanced steadily. When the Turks overran Buda, the capital of Hungary, they delighted in destroying churches and synagogues throughout the city. Indeed, they set aflame a collection of Renaissance art as rich as anything in Florence or Milan.[8]

Suleiman's advance compelled Charles to mobilize his forces; but since the Turks were not yet threatening Habsburg lands directly, Charles bided his time. The Lutheran princes kept negotiating with Suleiman, to keep the pressure up. An alliance did not happen, but Suleiman concluded that Charles was too weak to offer any real resistance and so launched a fresh attack in 1526, quickly taking most of Hungary. After a brief pause he advanced his army as far as Vienna, to which he laid siege in 1529. At this point even the Protestants were worried. Luther published in that same year the pamphlet *On the War against the Turks*, in which he called for a united European front against the Ottomans yet rejected as un-Christian the notion of a Crusade. Suleiman's siege failed, however, and the Turkish advance was temporarily stopped.

With so much at stake in terms of geopolitics, it is not surprising that the rhetoric of the religious dispute became feverish. Catholics and Protestants at all levels of society hurled abuse at each other. Erasmus and Luther, for a while, maintained a

---

[8]   Buda—supposedly named after Bleda, Attila the Hun's older brother—much later incorporated with the small nearby town of Pest, to become today's Budapest.

civilized debate in print over theological issues like free will, the workings of divine grace, and the interpretation of Scripture. (The two men never met personally.) Other than that, though, most of the religious battle was in poisonous language. When large numbers of German peasants were persuaded by radicals to rise up in arms against their landlords in 1524 and 1525 in a rebellion known as the **Peasants' Revolt**, Luther responded savagely. While the peasants had been stirred by Luther's insistence on the dignity of all believers, he called on the princes to take bold action.

If his aim was to scare the peasants into submission, *On the Thieving, Murderous Hordes of Peasants* was a brilliant success:

> Therefore every one of you who can should act as both judge and executioner.... Strike them down, slay them, and stab them, either in secret or in the light of day ... for you ought always to bear in mind that there is nothing more poisonous, dangerous, or devilish than one of these rebels.... For baptism frees men's souls alone; it does not liberate their bodies and properties, nor does the Gospel call for people to hold all their goods in common.... Fine Christians these peasants are! There can hardly be a single devil left in hell—for I do believe they have all taken possession of these peasants, whose mad ravings are beyond all measure.... What a wonderful time we live in now, when a prince can better merit heaven by bloodshed than by prayer!

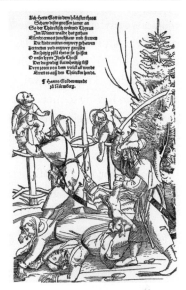

Turkish Atrocities   Throughout the 16th and 17th centuries the Ottomans made repeated efforts to expand their control in southeastern Europe, twice getting as far as the gates of Vienna. This woodcut depicts popular fears of Turkish savagery. "Such amusements are common in all wars," warned Erasmus in 1530, when this image was published. The Turks did commit atrocities like those shown here, but no more so than what European Catholics and Protestants inflicted on one another (and what both sometimes inflicted on the Jews) throughout the Wars of Religion.

Most of the rebels, denied Luther's expected support, laid down their weapons at once. The rest were quickly defeated in a battle at Frankenhausen in May 1525, and the revolt ended. The rebel leader, an apocalyptic firebrand named Thomas Müntzer, was executed. The cost of victory was high, however. As many as one hundred thousand people lost their lives.

After this, the "Protestantization" of Germany gained pace, as the princes rushed to support Luther's program and seized church lands and treasuries. Sincere religious conviction undoubtedly motivated them, but political and economic factors obviously were also at play. By formally adopting the Lutheran cause, princes acquired—with Luther's own blessing—the authority to appoint pastors to the new churches. This effectively placed the nobles in charge of the entire institution. Freed from having to meet their former fiscal obligations to Rome or to recognize the authority of ecclesiastical courts, the princes likewise ensured the obedience of the new Lutheran churches to noble demands. The policies they developed came to be summarized by the phrase *Cuius regio, eius religio* ("The religion of the ruler determines the religion of the land"). And most of the princes promoted the new *religio* in order to strengthen their grip on the *regio*.

THE REFORMATION GOES INTERNATIONAL

Like other reformers before him and since, Martin Luther believed that those who joined him in rebellion would agree with him on what to replace tyranny with. But things seldom turn out that way. People, it seems, unite more easily in opposition to a present evil than they rally around a new vision of future good. With its spread beyond Germany, especially in the legacy of Jean Calvin, Protestantism in fact thrived on divisions.

When Luther began his revolt, many among the pope's advisors recommended immediate and dramatic action. Luther, after all, seemed intent on tearing down the entire Catholic tradition. However, just as many others counseled a quietist approach. Once Luther validated the idea that people can interpret the Scriptures for themselves, they pointed out, they would soon disagree with Luther's interpretations as much as they disagree with Rome's. The rebellion would then splinter into countless factions and soon disappear under its own dead, fractured weight.

Each group of advisers was half right. At the start, Luther saw his actions as a much-needed campaign to correct flaws in Catholic belief and practice, not as a drive to destroy the church. He was a reformer, not a revolutionary. Dramatic counter-action was indeed called for, but not in the urgent sense recommended by the alarmists. As for the second group, they saw correctly the coming splintering of the reformers into rival groups, but their assumption that division meant failure was wrong. They had severely underestimated the extent of anticlerical feeling—and the intense resentment of the church's abuses and failings. By the time they realized their mistake, it was too late. Luther and his followers had flooded Germany with polemical pamphlets, sermons, hymnals, catechisms, and above all the Bible itself in translation.[9]

---

9   Luther and his followers understood the power of the new technology of printing.

It took a generation, more or less, for Luther's ideas to catch on outside of Germany. His basic ideas were known. How could they not be, considering the enormity of the scandal he had caused? However, Luther wrote most of his works in German—since vernacular Scripture reading and vernacular worship were so central to his theology. And translators did not rush to bring his works into other tongues. Luther had taken care to produce a number of pamphlets and broadsides in Latin, to encourage the spread of the revolt. His ongoing debate in print with Erasmus—the most revered scholar in the Christian world—also kept his program in the spotlight. Still, when Protestantism did start to spread, it did so on the heels of the spread of Christian humanism. Many saw that intellectual effort as preparation for the spiritual regeneration coming out of Germany.

Not all northern humanists were, or became, Protestant. Many of the most famous, in fact, remained staunchly Catholic. What contributed to the spread of Protestantism was not humanism itself but rather the dialogue between Renaissance and Reformation. It was the spirit of questioning, of returning to ancient sources. Many heard that dialogue and clung ever more fiercely to the Catholic tradition. Many others, though, who might otherwise never have thought it possible, heard in the debate a calling to a wholly new, and newly holy, path.

SCHOLARS AND ACTIVISTS

The best of the Christian humanist scholars were all dedicated Catholics: Guillaume Budé (1467–1540), Jacques Lefèvre d'Étaples (1455–1536), Cardinal Francisco Ximénez de Cisneros (1436–1517), and Joan Lluís Vives i March (1493–1540). Other writers—primarily Protestants like Ulrich Zwingli (1484–1531), Jean Calvin (1509–1564), and John Knox (1514–1572)—remain better known and were more historically significant because of their activities in the world. But pure scholars should have their due, too.

Budé was a classical linguist, one of the finest Greek scholars of his generation. Supported by the French royal court, he produced a Greek lexicon that remained the standard for scholars for nearly two hundred years. He was also the founder of the school that later became the Collège de France and of the library that ultimately grew into the Bibliothèque Nationale, both in Paris. Lefèvre, also a royal favorite, was an industrious writer of biblical commentaries as well as editions and translations of patristic texts. In 1530 he published the first ever translation of the entire Bible into French.

De Cisneros held immense power in Spain: he was the archbishop of Toledo, was twice the regent for the crown, and served as grand inquisitor at the high point of that institution's power in Spain. As a statesman Cisneros was blunt and direct even to the point of cruelty. He was not at all averse to ordering the forced baptism

Polyglot Bible A page from the Complutensian Polyglot Bible (1514–1517) published by Cardinal Francisco Cisneros, one of the great humanistic achievements of the Renaissance. The three main columns present the Biblical text in Hebrew, Latin, and Greek, while underneath are printed passages in Aramaic (Targum), where they survive, and alternative readings. The Complutensian edition was used extensively by the English translators who produced the King James Bible (Authorized Version) in 1611.

of the Moors of southern Spain and the burning of the Arabic manuscripts in the library at Granada. As a scholar, he was patient in the extreme: he spent fifteen years producing the Complutensian Polyglot Bible—an impressive work that reproduced, in parallel columns, the best texts then available of the entire Bible in Aramaic, Greek, Hebrew, and Latin.

Lluís Vives, a much more sympathetic figure, dedicated long years to social reform as well as to reform within the church. He was an earnest champion of education for women and welfare for the poor. The fourth-generation son of a *converso* family—that is, a family that had once been Jewish—he witnessed the Inquisition's execution of his father, grandmother, and great-grandfather.[10] And although he never wavered in his Christian commitment, he left Spain as soon as he could and never returned. After studying in Paris, he became a professor of philosophy at Oxford and spent his time between Oxford and the royal court in London, where he served as private tutor to the Tudor family.

PROTESTANTISM WITHOUT LUTHER

Among the Protestant humanists, the most influential were Ulrich Zwingli and Jean Calvin. Zwingli left behind over twenty volumes of writings—sermons, biblical exegesis, topical essays, some poetry—but little of this is read by anyone other than specialists. His impact was in the world of action rather than thought. He was born to a Swiss farming family and received a good though unremarkable education. In 1498 he enrolled at the University of Vienna, but was expelled for reasons no one has ever discovered. He was ordained a priest and spent several years as a military chaplain. A crisis of conscience, however, led him to withdraw

---

[10] Scholars use *inquisition*, with a lowercase *i*, to refer to the inquisitorial process in the Middle Ages. Uppercase *Inquisition* is reserved for the Renaissance, when what had been a medieval process turned into a formal institution.

from his post and take up duties as a simple parish priest in a small village in Switzerland. This position gave him ample time for self-education, and in a few years he had mastered Greek and acquired a usable knowledge of Hebrew.

By 1516 personal study of the Scriptures had inspired him to doubt the value of much Catholic doctrine and ritual. But he was too timid to admit his opinions in public until Martin Luther began his public work in 1517 with the Ninety-Five Theses. Zwingli then dedicated himself to the twin goals of supporting Luther's Reformation and securing Switzerland's independence from French, Italian, and imperial meddling. He formally broke with Rome, and by 1522 most of the German-speaking cantons of Switzerland had done the same and had placed themselves under Zwingli's leadership. He moved to Zurich, which became second only to Luther's Wittenberg as the unofficial capital of the Protestant movement.

Zwingli's brand of Christianity differed from Luther's in a number of specifics. In fact, Zwingli, who did not meet Luther personally until 1529, is one of the very first examples of a Protestant who broke away from the movement's founder. He died in battle against armies from the Catholic southern portion of Switzerland, and the embryonic church he had created became subsumed by the new church created by Jean Calvin.

A brief but violent interlude, however, preceded Calvin on the scene. Several dozen radical members of Zwingli's church at Zurich quit Switzerland and took up residence in exile at Münster, in northwestern Germany. Disgusted by what they considered the immoral joining of Protestant religion with secular government (Luther and the German princes, Zwingli and the Swiss town councils), they established themselves as an apocalyptic sect known as the **Anabaptists**.[11] Their name means "rebaptizers," for the group rejected infant baptism as meaningless by itself and called for a second baptism in adulthood. They also embraced a literal reading of Scripture, polygamy (although the extent of this is still debated), and the imminent approach of Christ's Second Coming. The sect came under the charismatic leadership of Jan van Leiden, who proclaimed himself the successor to the King David of Biblical times and his Münster church as the reincarnation of the Jerusalem Temple. Zwingli and Luther both denounced the group, as did all the Catholic rulers of the time. Persecutions followed as Münster was stormed by the Catholic prince (and bishop) of the city, the Anabaptists were tortured and executed, and their sympathizers across Europe were arrested.

---

[11]   Crushed by its enemies, the Anabaptist movement disappeared. The Mennonite church, founded by Menno Simons (1496–1561) of Holland, is a late offshoot that still survives.

By the time Jean Calvin established his own Reformed Church in Geneva, the conflict between rival Christianities had moved well beyond a war of words. Most of the Scandinavian territories (Finland was the exception) had declared for Lutheranism by the end of the 1520s. Lutheranism had also sunk deep roots in northern Germany and parts of Poland, Hungary, and the Low Countries. England was, for the time being, still staunchly Catholic, although Henry VIII's (r. 1509–1547) marital woes led him to break with Rome over the course of the 1530s (see Map 11.3).

MAP 11.3   **The Protestant Reformation, ca. 1580**

CALVIN: PROTESTANTISM AS THEOLOGY

At first glance, Calvin seems an unlikely revolutionary. Quiet, reserved, intensely bookish, he studied (under pressure from his father) for a legal career at the University of Bourges, where he fell under the spell of humanist classicism. At about the same time—somewhere around 1530—he had an evangelical conversion that changed his entire life. He described the event in the introduction to his later *Commentary on the Psalms*:

> All at once, God overpowered my mind, which at that point was far more incorrigible in such matters than one might expect in one so young, and opened it [to the Truth]. Having been given this sampling of, this introduction to, true godliness, I instantly burned with such a passion to have better knowledge of it that, even though I never abandoned my other studies entirely, I pursued them with much less drive than before.

If his account is accurate, his was an intellectual rather than mystical conversion, although it was no less passionate for that. True to his bookish nature, he turned almost immediately to writing the first edition (1535) of his main work, *Institutes of Christian Religion*, which he continued to revise until his death. (Its final and definitive editions appeared in 1559 in Latin and in 1560 in French.)

The *Institutes* was the first work to lay out the emerging theology of Protestant Christianity in a systematic, logical, organized way. Here is a representative passage, on how the Reformed Church uses discipline:

> It is necessary, likewise, to distinguish between different kinds of sins, for some are only minor infractions whereas others are enormous and enormously wicked crimes. In order to correct the latter, mere warnings and reproofs do not suffice, and one must resort to sterner measures—as Paul shows [1 Corinthians 5.1–5] when he does not allow himself to rest content after having condemned the man of Corinth who had committed incest, but immediately excommunicates the man after his conviction for the crime. Now we begin to see how the spiritual authority of the Church, which corrects sins according to God's Word, preserves our health, orders our lives, and establishes bonds of unity among us; for whenever the Church banishes from the community those guilty of adultery, fornication, theft, robbery, sedition, false witness, or any other crimes of that sort, or when it banishes those stubborn people who criticize God's Holy Judgment, even after having been admonished for lesser sins, it [the church] exercises no unauthorized rational power but only the jurisdiction that God Himself has given it. In order that no one may refuse to

recognize this judgmental power of the Church, or think that it represents only the opinion of the community of believers, God Himself bears witness that [the church's judgment] it is nothing less than His judgment of the case, and that what the Church does upon earth is ratified in Heaven. For the Church has by God's Own Word the authority to condemn the wicked and to receive the penitent back into the favor of the Church. Anyone who believes that the Church could even exist without this power to discipline is sorely mistaken—for how could we do without the very thing that God saw fit to give us? The reasons why this is necessary will be made clear in its action.   *(Institutes of Christian Religion 4.12.4)*

Martin Luther, like his model Saint Augustine, had been far too impulsive a writer ever to write anything like this.

Calvin shared Luther's central, defining notion of an infinitely majestic, all-powerful, and all-knowing God whose transcendent might and will is in absolute control of the entire cosmos. But Luther softened this commanding image by emphasizing the infinitely merciful, because unmerited, love that God feels for us. Calvin stressed instead the unfathomable mystery of God's justice. Since he is all-knowing, argued Calvin, God has known since the moment of Creation which human beings were to be saved and which were to be damned—and these fates are sealed absolutely by the sheer force of God's will. There is nothing any human being can do to alter his or her fate. Does this mean that many apparently "good" people will be punished in hell while many apparently "bad" people are rewarded in heaven? Yes, it does; but this, to Calvin, is simply the consequence of our complete inability to understand God's purpose, rather than a sign of God's supposed hypocrisy. We must remain faithful to the belief that God's ways are ultimately and supremely just, even if we cannot comprehend them. In essence, what Calvin called for was an attitude of radical humility before God, an absolute submission of the soul to the Almighty's wisdom, power, and righteousness.

Unlikely Revolutionary   Sketches of Jean Calvin (1509–1564), the founder of the Reformed (Presbyterian) Church, made in a notebook by one of his university students who preferred doodling to taking lecture notes.

But this is not an attitude of passivity. It is precisely because we cannot know whether we are among the **Elect** (his term for those predestined for salvation) that Calvin demands of his followers the strictest possible adherence to moral standards. To the Elect, he writes, good ethical behavior will come naturally and be the sign of their chosen status. To those who are not elected, their moral behavior will not affect their ultimate fate in the slightest—but they therefore have all the more reason to live according to a godly standard. The joy of such a life is in fact the only meaningful pleasure they will have before confronting the eternal torments of hell. Membership in good standing in the Reformed Church—Calvin's name for the branch of Christianity he established—is a likely indicator that one is among the Elect. Membership in the despised Roman Catholic Church or the Orthodox Churches is as likely an indicator as a life of gruesome sinfulness that one is not. But while being a Calvinist immeasurably improved one's odds of salvation, it alone determined nothing. The central concern of life therefore should not be the destiny of our individual souls but the fulfillment of God's purpose on the entire earth.

Calvin's teachings found receptive audiences all around Europe. Apart from its success in Switzerland, Calvinism became the dominant creed in Holland (where it became known as the Dutch Reformed Church), in Scotland (where it was called the Presbyterian Church), in parts of France (where Calvinists were called Huguenots), and in parts of England (where they were ultimately called Puritans). The theocratic state he established in Geneva earned a well-deserved reputation for severity, but Geneva also earned a reputation for modest, honest, and godly behavior. Calvinist communities emphasized simplicity and austerity in worship. Anything that smacked of Catholic ritual or hierarchical structure was eschewed. Instead, churches were communities of equals—joined together in prayer, Scriptural reading, hymn singing, and listening to sermons. How can there be a pecking order among the Elect? Sermons indeed form the centerpiece of Calvinist worship, since they are by nature ruminations on Scripture. Calvin himself was too gifted a scholar to insist on only literal readings of the Bible, although he tended to seek out symbolic or other interpretations only after considering the literal first.

Still other reformers and groups branched off to form new denominations, but these were considerably smaller in size and tinged with elements of ethnic or national rebellion. Lutheranism and Calvinism were the two with the greatest international appeal, and by the middle of the 16th century they had torn the religious fabric of Europe asunder. Only in the late 20th century, in the aftermath of two World Wars and the Holocaust, would there arise serious efforts to reconcile the fissures in Christianity.

THE REBIRTH OF SATIRE

Religious upheavals reflected developments in other aspects of cultural life. The conjunction of increasing literacy rates and the mass availability of printed texts generated a demand for literary entertainment unlike anything the Western world had experienced before. Not that the love of literature was itself new, but oral tradition could now give way to print on paper. Reading became a common pleasure of everyday life, no longer the reserve of scholars and monks. Printing houses across Europe poured out a steady stream of poetry, histories, stage dramas and comedies, travelogues, essays, memoirs, popular science tracts, and collections of letters and speeches.

Not everyone in Europe was reading Erasmus, Luther, and Calvin constantly—which is probably a good thing. In addition to Machiavelli and Aretino, three European writers stand out in the first half of the 16th century: Thomas More (1478–1535), Ulrich von Hutten (1488–1523), and François Rabelais (1493–1553). They could hardly have been more different in their personalities and life stories, but the most famous works of all three were satires.

Satire had been one of the most popular literary genres among the Romans. The English word satire, which appeared for the first time in 1509, in fact derives from Latin *satura* (denoting a witty poem that ridicules vice), not from Greek *satyricos* (which refers to the lewd stage comedies that accompanied tragedic festivals). A few Greek writers had practiced satire—Menippus (3rd century BCE) is the best example—but the Romans excelled at it. "Satire is all ours," once bragged Quintilian (36–96 CE), Rome's greatest literary scholar. But satire had all but disappeared during the Middle Ages. Levity about the world's idiosyncrasies and human foibles did not appeal very much to the monks who established the classical canon in their scriptoria. With the rise of classical humanism, however, satire came back to life. There were, after all, plenty of people to satirize: warmongering popes, fey aristocrats, affected scholars, grasping financiers, humanistic despots, self-absorbed artists.

UTOPIAS AND BOOK BURNINGS

Erasmus helped to revive prose satire with his *Praise of Folly*, and satire in prose, in fact, became the preferred style in the 16th century. His close friend Thomas More penned a popular though curiously dour *Utopia* (1516).[12] It consists of two parts, the first being an imaginary discussion between More and a traveler-adventurer named Raphael Hythlodaeus on the various ills then besetting Europe. High on the list are the enclosure movement, poverty, religious intolerance, the failure of

---

[12]   More is best known as the royal chancellor who refused to recognize Henry VIII's divorce and paid for it with his head.

systems of justice, and the propensity to war. In the second part, Hythlodaeus describes for More his travels to a "perfect society"—a far-distant island in the Atlantic named Utopia (which is an Anglicized version of the Greek phrase "no place").

Utopia is a crescent-shaped island, two hundred miles across, in which the population lives in scattered communities of about seventy-five thousand each. All goods are held in common; citizens take turns, in two-year shifts, farming the land and working at artisanal crafts; medical care and primary education are free and available to all. There are no lawyers; all wives are subservient to their husbands, to whom they must confess their sins once every month; and the penalty for pre- or extramarital sex is enslavement. There are a lot of slaves, consequently, who do most of the hard labor. Although meant as a satire, there is

Utopia   This woodcut by Ambrosius Holbein (1494–1519)—older brother of the famous artist Hans Holbein (1497–1543)—was the frontispiece for a 1518 edition of *Utopia*. Against a backdrop of the fictional island, Raphael Hythlodaeus describes the Utopian way of life to More.

nothing in *Utopia* to make a modern reader laugh, for More was largely humorless. (According to a family memoir he laughed at court jesters when they made pratfalls, but at little else.) He tried and failed on that score. *Utopia* remains a valuable book, though, not least for the insight it provides into its author's mind.

Far more successful as satire is the fictitious *Letters of Obscure Men* (1517) by Ulrich von Hutten, a swashbuckling imperial knight and occasional humanist writer. Born to a noble family in northern Germany, he grew up in a castle near the ancient settlement of Fulda. His parents dispatched him to a monastery when he was eleven, apparently to insure against his elder brother's claim upon the family estate. Six years later, in 1505, Ulrich escaped and wandered from city to city, leading a roguish life as an occasional student (he attended four universities in Germany), a poet, an amateur humanist scholar, and a willing sword for hire. Around 1509 he appeared in northern Italy, working as a mercenary soldier between stints at the universities of Pavia and Bologna. But by 1512 he was back in Germany serving as a Free Imperial Knight.

In 1515 the Duke of Württemberg killed a beloved cousin of his whose wife he had designs on. Ulrich responded by publishing blistering Latin poems that ruined the Duke's reputation and led ultimately to his overthrow. They made Ulrich famous, and in 1517 Maximilian I (r. 1493–1519) appointed him the poet laureate of the German Empire. In that same year, Ulrich became a passionate supporter of

Martin Luther and coauthored, with his humanist friend Johann Jäger (who used the pseudonym Crotus Rubeanus), the *Letters of Obscure Men*.

Filled with clever wit and broad, coarse humor, the *Letters* purport to be addressed to a prominent nobleman by fanatical Catholic monks and friars regarding why it is necessary to burn Jewish books like the Talmud and anti-Christian polemical literature. The diatribe is in reference to a real event: the debate, several years earlier, between the famed humanist scholar Johann Reuchlin and a group of zealous Catholic inquisitors who had argued for the same cause. (The title echoes the *Letters of Notable Men* that had passed between Reuchlin and his adversaries.) The *Letters* were written in intentionally bad Latin, making much of their humor impossible to convey in English. Reading them, it is clear that Ulrich never lost his hatred of Catholic monks, who might well respond to Protestantism and satire with book burnings, and this book is a settling of old debts. He gives his monks outrageous names like Brother Goatmilker and Brother Shitshoveller, attributes all sorts of lechery to them, and describes them nervously defecating under their robes during public debates. Ulrich's aim is less to defend the Jews (even though he was indeed an opponent of the book burnings) than to ridicule the pretensions and hypocrisy of the Catholics. The aristocrat who receives the letters—a real figure in Ulrich's time—also comes in for a lambasting. The monks sordidly declare their passionate relations with his wife.

A summary cannot relate the brilliant wordplay, sharp character depiction, and intellectual cleverness of the *Letters*. The book deserves to be better known and someday may find the translator it deserves. It was published anonymously, though its authorship was never in doubt. Ulrich spent his last years trying unsuccessfully to urge the independence of the German Empire from papal involvement. He contracted syphilis, and when the disease became acute he took refuge in Switzerland, near Lake Zurich, where he died in 1523.

RABELAIS: THE IN-HOUSE CATHOLIC ATTACK

The best-known of the three satirists was François Rabelais. Little is known for certain about his life. Born to a wealthy country lawyer, he received a sound education. A devout Christian, he entered the Franciscan order sometime around 1510 and about a decade later was ordained a priest. He traveled to libraries around France and earned a reputation as a first-rate classical scholar, but in 1524 he suffered the indignity of having his Greek books confiscated by one of his superiors, who thought they might lead to heresy. Rabelais successfully petitioned Pope Clement VII (r. 1523–34) in 1524 for release from his Franciscan order and to be allowed to join the Benedictines. Through his new order he studied medicine in Paris. However, since he disliked Benedictine life too, he broke his vows and moved to the University of Montpellier to continue his medical train-ing. He finished in record time, quickly sired two children with a local widow, and then moved on to practice medicine in Narbonne and Lyons.

In 1532 Rabelais published a brief satirical novel, *The Horrible and Terri-fying Words and Deeds of the Renowned Pantagruel, King of the Dipsodes*. When this proved unexpectedly popular, he followed it with three more volumes that continue Pantagruel's adventures while also providing, in another volume, the backstory of Pantagruel's father, Gargantua. The five books are now published together as a single work, *Gargantua and Pantagruel*. (A supposed sixth book, written by an opportunistic forger, appeared in 1564, eleven years after Rabelais's death.) Gargantua and Pantagruel are giants—enormous, misshapen, driven by inexhaustible appetites of body and mind, and delighting in broad scatological humor—and the same can be said of *Gargantua and Pantagruel* the novel. It is a **picaresque**, a vast sequence of discrete episodes. The closest it comes to offering a coherent story is a lengthy but loose narrative in Books 3 and 4 about their ef-forts to help a friend. (Another giant, named Panurge, wishes to locate an oracle known as the Sacred Bottle for help deciding whether to marry a girl whose fidel-ity is uncertain.) Though lively, the novel is shapeless, repetitive, and long.

What was its purpose? Rabelais certainly wanted to entertain his readers and make them laugh.[13] *Gargantua and Pantagruel* and the *Letters of Obscure Men* are the only truly funny books written in that unfunny century. Being satire, the laughs they raise come at someone's expense; we laugh because someone is being ridiculed. Both books have numerous targets, but they share one in particular, the Catholic clergy. If von Hutten attacks them from the Protestant side, Rabelais offers a Catholic in-house attack.

The wounds he inflicts, however, result not from rapier wit but a heavy two-handed broadsword. Much of Rabelais's humor is the clowning of a teenager who thinks he is clever when he is being gross. He mocks dry-as-dust scholastic theologians and pompous overfed monks by exaggerating their flaws a hundred-fold. He lambasts puritanical morality by having his heroes indulge in orgies of food, sex, and drink that would make a Roman emperor blush. Bodily functions stain every page. In one early passage (1.17), Gargantua caps off a drinking binge by untying his codpiece and peeing so much he floods the entire city of Paris, "drowning 260,418 people, plus women and children." Two other entire chapters (3.26, 3.28) consist of nothing more than a list of improvised nicknames for a character, all of them employing a variant of the word "scrotum."

---

[13] "Mirth is my theme, and tears are not; / For laughter is man's proper lot" is the famous ending couplet of Rabelais' verse preface.

Still, the verbal energy is extraordinary. Rejoicing in his freedom from Church Latin, Rabelais pours words onto the page in a kind of vernacular euphoria. The novel is a hymn to the French language and a celebration of human freedom: freedom to think, to scoff, to lust, to indulge in manic excess, to coin words, to imagine outrageous scenes, to offend, to risk boredom, and to delight in whimsy. Ultimately, it is about the freedom to hope for a better world than the one we live in. As a work of art it has failings, but as the expression of an irrepressible spirit it can never cease to fascinate. And that spirit is humanism.

WHO, WHAT, WHERE

Anabaptists

Christian humanism

Elect

indulgences

justification by faith alone

Ninety-Five Theses

picaresque

Peasants' Revolt

Protestant Reformation

Renaissance

Renaissance humanism

Satire

SUGGESTED READINGS

Primary Sources

Calvin, Jean. *Institutes of Christian Religion.*

Erasmus of Rotterdam. *Julius Excluded.*

———. *The Praise of Folly.*

Hutton, Ulrich von. *Letters of Obscure Men.*

Luther, Martin. *Address to the Christian Nobility of the German Nation.*

———. *The Freedom of a Christian.*

———. *Table Talk.*

Machiavelli, Niccolò. *Discourses on Livy.*

———. *The Mandrake Root.*

———. *The Prince.*

Rabelais, François. *Gargantua and Pantagruel.*

Vasari, Giorgio. *Lives of the Artists.*

Anthologies

Black, Robert, ed. *Renaissance Thought: A Reader* (2001).

Janz, Denis R., ed. *A Reformation Reader: Primary Texts with Introductions* (2008).

King, John N., ed. *Voices of the English Reformation: A Sourcebook* (2004).

Wiesner-Hanks, Merry. *The Renaissance and Reformation: A History in Documents* (2011).

Studies

Baylor, Michael G. *The German Reformation and the Peasants' War: A Brief History with Documents* (2012).

Benedict, Philip. *Christ's Churches Purely Reformed: A Social History of Calvinism* (2002).

Bolzoni, Lina. *The Gallery of Memory: Literary and Iconographic Models in the Age of the Printing Press* (2001).

Caffiero, Marina. *Forced Baptisms: Histories of Jews, Christians, and Converts in Papal Rome* (2011).

Diefendorf, Barbara B. *From Penitence to Charity: Pious Women and the Catholic Reformation in Paris* (2006).

Eisenstein, Elizabeth. *The Printing Revolution in Early Modern Europe* (2005).

King, Ross. *Machiavelli: Philosopher of Power* (2009).

Levi, Anthony. *Renaissance and Reformation: The Intellectual Genesis* (2004).

MacCulloch, Diarmaid. *The Reformation: A History* (2005).

Martines, Lauro. *Strong Words: Writing and Social Strain in the Italian Renaissance* (2001).

Mazzotta, Giuseppe. *Cosmopoiesis: The Renaissance Experiment* (2001).

McGrath, Alister E. *Reformation Thought: An Introduction* (2001).

Nauert, Charles G., Jr. *Humanism and the Culture of Renaissance Europe* (2006).

Oberman, Heiko A. *Luther: Man between God and the Devil* (2006).

O'Malley, John W. *Trent and All That: Renaming Catholicism in the Early Modern Era* (2000).

Ozment, Steven. *The Serpent and the Lamb: Cranach, Luther, and the Making of the Reformation* (2012).

Parks, Tim. *Medici Money: Banking, Metaphysics, and Art in Fifteenth-Century Florence* (2006).

Pettegree, Andrew. *The Book in the Renaissance* (2011).

———. *Reformation and the Culture of Persuasion* (2005).

Randall, Michael. *The Gargantuan Polity: On the Individual and the Community in the French Renaissance* (2008).

Stjerna, Kirsi. *Women and the Reformation* (2008).

Taylor, Barry, and Alejandro Coroleu. *Humanism and Christian Letters in Early Modern Iberia, 1480–1630* (2010).

Wiesner-Hanks, Merry E. *Women and Gender in Early Modern Europe* (2008).

For additional resources, including maps, primary sources, visuals, web links, and quizzes, please go to **www.oup.com/us/backman.**

ARMADA DE CAPITAIS QUE

do Luis   de gusmão   do Cao   de noronha

do mofia
sa

mão   de medosa   Leo   dacunla   afart   paulo

guo   caluo   afart   cata

lo doutor pou   bea do da
fazeda

CHAPTER 12

The Last Crusades

1492–1648

A ll wars are religious wars in one sense. "There are no atheists in foxholes," asserted a phrase popular in World War II. Even if untrue, it expresses a truism: for many people, the hard fact of death elicits something like religious dread.

THE AMERICAS IN 1600

ATLANTIC OCEAN

PACIFIC OCEAN

■ Spanish
■ Portuguese

Soldiers often take refuge in faith to survive war's horror. But are they drawn to fight in defense of their belief? As part of the religious realignment in Europe, wars left millions dead and much of Western society both economically and morally exhausted. The philosopher Thomas Hobbes (1588–1679) described life itself at this time as a tragic "war of all against all," in which existence was "solitary, poor, nasty, brutish, and short."

◀ **Passage to India** In 1497 the Portuguese explorer Vasco da Gama (1469–1524) rounded the southern tip of Africa and initiated Europe's first direct contact with the peoples of the eastern African coast; with the help of an Indian ship's pilot he met in the port city of Mombasa (in today's Kenya) the following year, he sailed directly across the Arabian Sea and landed in India. The Arab merchants who then dominated the region gave him a cold welcome, and three years later (1501) da Gama returned at the head of a fleet of warships and seized control of the city of Calcutta. This image from ca. 1558 shows the type of trade ship used by the Portuguese at this stage in their rise to global power. This was a carrack, recognizable by its three (sometimes four) masts, rounded stern, raised fore- and aftcastles, and most especially by its absence of heavy guns. Galleons were the premier warships by the middle of the century; carracks (some of which weighed more than a thousand tons, unloaded) were for transporting vast cargoes.

- The New World
- New Continents and Profits
- Conquest and Epidemics
- New Crops and the Enclosure Movement
- The Patriarchal Family
- Sexual Morality
- Enemies Within: Witches and Jews
- The Jews of the East and West
- Wars of Religion

- The Peace of Augsburg and the Edict of Nantes
- The Church of England
- The Thirty Years' War
- Wars of Religion: The Eastern Front
- The Waning of the Sultanate
- New Centers of Intellectual Life
- The Ottomans: From Strife to Warfare

CHAPTER OUTLINE

Moreover, Europe's religious realignments took place within the exciting, yet terrifying, context of an immensely broadened world. The first encounters with the New World brought epidemics that killed as much as 99.9 percent of indigenous Americans. At the same time, it brought demographic and moral changes to Europe, including population growth and a new idea of order rooted in the family. The "war of all against all" also became more specifically a war against others, including witches, Jews, and the East—where the tensions between Sunnis and Shi'a intensified as well. It also led to shifts of power between European nations, including England, the Dutch, and Spain.

THE NEW WORLD

For over four thousand years the entire known world had consisted of three continents: Europe, Africa, and Asia. From the start, the peoples of the Greater West had shown more restlessness and curiosity about the world than any other ancient culture. Phoenician travelers, beginning around 1200 BCE, had journeyed a bit beyond the Straits of Gibraltar and into the Atlantic. The Greeks had circumnavigated the British Isles by 300 BCE, and by the end of the 1st century CE the Romans had made contact with merchant-explorers from China. The latter ventured as far as the Euphrates River shortly after the time of Constantine the Great, around 360 CE, although much later the Ming dynasty closed China off from the outside world.[1] The first Christian missionaries had reached China well before the western Roman Empire fell in 476. Viking raiders had spread out through the Baltic, North, and Mediterranean Seas and had reached a corner of North America by the 10th century. The Muslim Arabs, followed by the Persians and Turks, had carved out vast realms on all three continents and developed techniques to map the

---

[1]   Under their great admiral Zheng He (1371–1433), Chinese fleets made it as far as the mouth of the Persian Gulf, to the Horn of Africa, and probably even up the Red Sea to Jiddah, not far from Mecca.

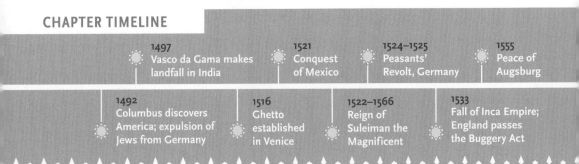

CHAPTER TIMELINE

1497
Vasco da Gama makes landfall in India

1521
Conquest of Mexico

1524–1525
Peasants' Revolt, Germany

1555
Peace of Augsburg

1492
Columbus discovers America; expulsion of Jews from Germany

1516
Ghetto established in Venice

1522–1566
Reign of Suleiman the Magnificent

1533
Fall of Inca Empire; England passes the Buggery Act

new territories. European stirrings in the Atlantic were thus only the latest phase in a centuries-long tradition of restlessness.

The Portuguese led the way. As early as 1415 their ships began to make contact with the coast of western Africa, down the expanse of what is today the country of Morocco. With the enthusiastic support of the royal Prince Henrique the Navigator (1394–1460), Portuguese fleets sailed next to the Azores and the Canary Islands. By 1445 they had reached the westernmost tip of the continent, at today's neighboring states of Senegal and Gambia. In the 1460s they began to curve eastward under the massive overhanging bulk of the Saharan expanse. Their ships crossed the equator in 1474, and in 1488 they reached the Cape of Good Hope at the southern tip of Africa. Only nine years later, in 1497, under the command of Vasco da Gama (1460–1524), the first European fleet made landfall in India (see Map 12.1). These were journeys of exploration and trade, not of conquest. Da Gama told the local ruler in Calcutta that he was

> the ambassador of the king of Portugal—the ruler of many lands and a man of such wealth that no one in this part of the world can compare; and that for sixty years this king's predecessors had dispatched ships to explore the seas in the direction of India, where they had heard that Christian kings like themselves lived. To connect with these Christian monarchs was the sole aim of their explorations, not to seek silver and gold—for the kings of Portugal possessed such tremendous wealth in these metals as to make them uninterested in whatever gold or silver was to be found in India or any other place.

Da Gama meant hardly a word of this, and it is doubtful his Indian host believed any of it. A genuine spirit of exploration for its own sake motivated those who put to sea and those who financed them. So, however, did an expectation of profit.

1571–1636
Mulla Sadra

1588
Defeat of the
Spanish Armada

1618–1648
Thirty Years' War

1632–1677
Baruch Spinoza

1572
Saint
Bartholomew's
Day Massacre

1598
Edict
of Nantes

1626–1676
Sabbatai Zvi

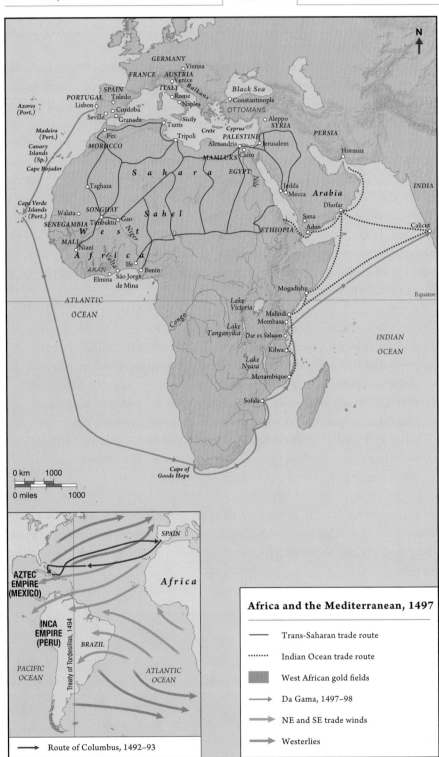

MAP 12.1   Africa and the Mediterranean, 1497

NEW CONTINENTS AND PROFITS

From the early 9th century sub-Saharan gold, spices, slaves, and ivory had been prized commodities in Mediterranean trade. Muslim merchants in Spain and Morocco had first brought these items to Europe, which accounts for the tremendous wealth of cities like Granada and Cordoba. (Tax records show that the Muslim inhabitants of Toledo alone held six thousand black slaves in the 10th century.) These were luxury goods enjoyed by the elites. When Christian forces drove the last Muslim rulers from Iberia in the 15th century, they took over control of this trade and determined to expand it. The commodities exchanged for these luxury items were predominantly textiles, metalwares, glazed pottery, glass, and paper. Not surprisingly, some of the coastal African peoples had embraced Islam in the intervening centuries, but this posed no bar to trade. Money mattered, not faith. When Vasco da Gama reached India in 1497, he mistook Hinduism for a quaint Eastern version of Christianity but identified precisely every precious stone and spice in the markets. Once in Calcutta, the Portuguese quickly established trading posts along the southwestern Malabar Coast of India. Within twenty years they had spread their commercial network to the Malay Peninsula, the Indonesian archipelago, and the Moluccas Islands; within another two decades, by 1542, they had reached Japan. Their first permanent trading post in China, at Macao, was established in 1555 (see Map 12.2).

> Money mattered, not faith. When Vasco da Gama reached India in 1497, he mistook Hinduism for a quaint Eastern version of Christianity but identified precisely every precious stone and spice in the markets.

Cristoforo Colombo's (1451–1506) innovation in 1492 was to propose reaching Asia by sailing directly westward rather than circumnavigating Africa to the south. Colombo was an Italian from Genoa, but he sailed under the Spanish flag of Ferdinand and Isabella. Such international arrangements were common, so no wonder just about every state ever associated with Colombo claims him as a native: to the Spanish he is Cristóbal Colón; streets and squares in Barcelona commemorate Cristòfor Colom; and the Portuguese proudly recall Cristóvão Colombo.[2] A few writers have argued that he was a Jew by ethnicity, but the evidence for this is extremely weak. Still, there is no reason, apart from lazy habit, to call him Christopher Columbus.

Every educated European since the 12th century had known that the world was round. Colombo was unprepared for the size of the globe, and so the length of his historic journey, but not the fact of it. And then he ran into an unexpected speed bump, the New World. Colombo never realized that the Caribbean islands

---

[2]   The English explorer John Cabot, who carried the Tudor flag as far as Newfoundland in 1497, was actually another Italian—Giovanni Caboto (1450–1508), from Venice.

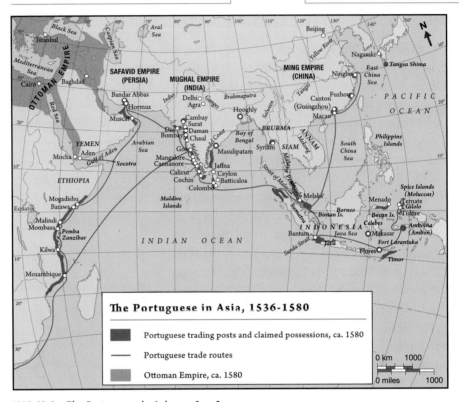

MAP 12.2 **The Portuguese in Asia, 1536–1580**

he had landed at were in fact the outer islands of two vast new continents. Despite four voyages to the New World, he believed to his dying day that he had sailed to islands just off the coast of Asia (see Figure 12.1). Such misjudgments do not lessen his achievement, however. The Atlantic passage was one of the greatest technical and human-adventure feats in Western history, and it had earth-changing consequences.

In his ship's log, Colombo duly recorded his first encounter with the indigenous people of the islands:

> When it became clear that they welcomed us, I saw that it would be easier to convert them to Our Holy Faith by peaceful means than by force, and so I offered them some simple gifts—red-dyed caps, necklaces of strung beads, and so on—which they received with great pleasure. So enthusiastic were they, in fact, that they began to swim out to our ships, carrying parrots, balls of cotton thread, spears, and other items to trade.... Still, they struck me as an exceptionally poor people, for all of them were naked—even the women, although I saw only one girl among them at the time. Every one of them I perceived to be young (that is, under

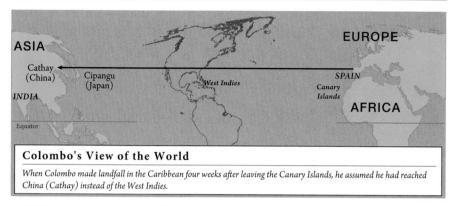

Colombo's View of the World

When Colombo made landfall in the Caribbean four weeks after leaving the Canary Islands, he assumed he had reached China (Cathay) instead of the West Indies.

FIGURE 12.1   Colombo's View of the World

the age of thirty), finely shaped and with handsome faces. . . . They appear to own no weapons and to have no knowledge of such, for when I showed them our swords they reached out and grabbed them by the blades, cutting themselves unexpectedly. . . . When I inquired, by pointing, about the scars visible on some of their bodies, they made me to understand, also by pointing, that people from another island had attacked them and tried to carry them off as slaves, but they resisted. . . . Overall they struck me as being clever, and I believe they would make good servants and could easily become Christian, since they have no religion of their own. They learned quickly to repeat the handful of words we taught them. If it please God, I intend to bring six of them home to Your Majesties, so that they might be taught to speak our language. Apart from the parrots, I saw no animals of any kind on the island.

Colombo's curiously unenthusiastic tone probably reflects his disappointment in the poverty of the people. Expecting the vast riches of China's silk and spice trade, he found instead naked islanders with nothing but ready smiles and a number of parrots. On subsequent journeys he discovered more of the natural wealth available, and his enthusiasm recovered noticeably. Within a few years other adventurers had reached both the North American and South American mainlands, and mapmakers began to appreciate that two entirely new continents had been found.

News of the discovery spread quickly across Europe, and soon wave after wave of explorers and adventurers set sail. In 1513 the Spanish admiral Vasco Núñez de Balboa (1475–1519), standing atop a hill in what is today's nation of Panama, became the first European to see the Pacific Ocean. Only six years later Fernão de Magalhães (Ferdinand Magellan, 1480–1521) set out to circumnavigate the entire globe, an astonishing feat that took three years and claimed the lives of 262 of his

The First Published Image of the New World
Cristoforo Colombo's first report to the Spanish kings of his discovery was published in Basel in early 1494; printed here is one of the illustrations that accompanied the Latin text. It shows Colombo arriving on the shore of "the island of Hispania" in a small landing craft. He offers a goblet as a peace offering to the inhabitants, who appear to be uniformly naked, male, and beardless, gathered at the shore to meet him.

initial crew of 280, including his own. Tales of the wealth available in the New World and in Asia set off a fiercely competitive wave of explorers, soldiers, and government representatives eager to stake out their claims (see Map 12.3).

Geographic location gave an immense advantage to the Atlantic seaboard nations of Europe: Portugal, Spain, France, the Low Countries, and England. The Mediterranean states, which had lived by maritime trade since 3000 BCE, were shut off from the New World bonanza since they could not pass the Straits of Gibraltar—which the Atlantic states had quickly sealed off like a cork in a bottle. Left to trade with Asia only through the Ottoman-controlled land routes, they began a long and slow commercial decline. This resulted in a fundamental change in the structure of the European economy, and by the end of the 16th century economic dominance had shifted away from the Mediterranean. The Atlantic states entered the 17th century as the economic and political powerhouses of Europe.

> The Mediterranean states, which had lived by maritime trade since 3000 BCE, were shut off from the New World bonanza since they could not pass the Straits of Gibraltar—which the Atlantic states had quickly sealed off like a cork in a bottle.

The sudden and massive influx of gold from the New World triggered the rise of the Atlantic commercial economies. This gold was seized chiefly from the Aztecs and Mayans of Central America and the Incas of what eventually became Peru and Bolivia. Credit for these seizures belongs above all to the army of **conquistadores** ("conquerors") led by Hernán Cortés (1485–1547), who subdued Mexico in 1521, and Francisco Pizarro (1471–1541), who vanquished the Incas in 1533. The conquerors' forces were astonishingly few in number: Cortés commanded an army of no more than six hundred conquistadores, and Pizarro had only 180. The Europeans' technological advantage is obvious: supplied with firearms, they could mow down the spear-carrying natives with considerable ease. But their victory had been made incalculably easier by an inadvertent biological warfare that preceded them on the scene.

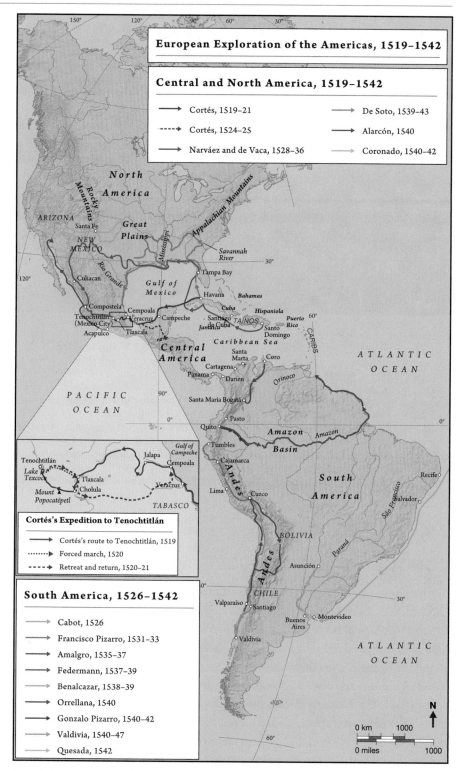

MAP 12.3 European Exploration of the Americas, 1519–1542

The Conquest of Mexico For a quarter century after Colombo's discovery of the New World, Spanish explorers and traders had established settlements only in the islands of the Caribbean; only a handful of expeditions had visited the mainland, to trade. Enough contact was made, however, for the transmission of European diseases like smallpox, influenza, and measles to the indigenous peoples of Central and South America, who, never having been exposed to them before, had no natural resistance to them. In many places throughout the New World as much as 90 percent of the population was killed before any European appeared directly on the scene. This painting, from the second half of the 17th century, illustrates the dramatic conquest of the Aztecs by Hernán Cortés in 1519. The Aztec empire had long been the most powerful (and violent) of the New World kingdoms. Cortés began his campaign with only six hundred soldiers—although he picked up many conscripts on his way to the Aztec capital of Tenochtitlan, shown here in the background—which was a sufficient number to bring down the once-great empire.

CONQUEST AND EPIDEMICS

Separated by a vast ocean, the peoples of Europe and of the New World had been exposed to different types of bacteria and viruses and had consequently developed different biological responses to them. The sailors who landed with Cristoforo Colombo on the island they called Hispaniola (today's Haiti and the Dominican Republic) brought with them the viruses for smallpox and measles. Neither disease had ever existed before in the New World, so they ran unchecked with horrifying effect. On Hispaniola alone, the population, which an early Dominican missionary (Friar Bartolomé de Las Casas, 1484–1566) had estimated to be three million strong in 1492, had fallen to a mere five hundred by 1538. That is a loss greater than 99.99 percent. In the opposite direction, some Europeans contracted a form of syphilis in the New World that seems never to have been present before in Europe. Within a few years, five million Europeans had died of it. Yet the impact on the New World was far greater.[3]

A Franciscan missionary, Friar Toribio de Benavente Motolinia (1484–1568), described how the natives "did not know how to treat the disease ... and consequently died in whole piles, like bedbugs. In many places, in fact, entire households died all at once, and since it proved impossible to bury so great a number of corpses, our

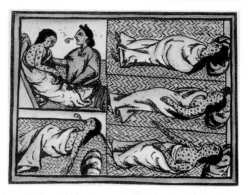

Smallpox Victims   The protracted isolation of the peoples of the Americas from the rest of the world made them vulnerable to a battery of diseases European colonists brought with them: the breath of a Spaniard was said to be sufficient enough to kill. These 16th-century illustrations, drawn by a native Mexican artist, depict smallpox victims. In the upper left panel a doctor attempts to treat his patient—undoubtedly he failed.

soldiers simply pulled down the houses over these people, letting their own homes serve as their tombs." Pizarro found similar circumstances favoring him when he stormed through Peru and Bolivia. Even a century later, in far-off Massachusetts Bay, smallpox and measles erased nine-tenths of the Native American population between 1617 and 1619. Such numbers are horrifying to imagine. Motolinia wrote that when Cortés led his men in triumph through the Aztec capital of Tenochtitlan—on the site of today's Mexico City—the soldiers could traverse the entire city stepping only on the corpses of smallpox victims, without ever once setting foot on the ground.

Such unintended suffering does not excuse the outright brutishness of the Europeans. In sailing to Africa, India, and China, the Europeans had shown no interest in conquest and colonization since they were able to acquire what they wanted—nonperishable luxury goods—by simple trade. Their technological advantage, in military hardware, over the sub-Saharan Africans was as great as it was over the indigenous New World peoples, but it did not prompt them to slaughter millions and seize their lands. The smallpox epidemic changed everything, and as a consequence the Europeans instantly developed a different attitude toward the land: here lay two vast and supremely wealthy continents that were, in effect, uninhabited—or near enough to uninhabited to persuade the conquistadores to finish the job. Moreover, the Protestant Reformation accelerated European interest in the New World. They saw not only an opportunity for evangelization,

---

[3]   Cortés was able to conquer Mexico in 1521 with only six hundred men-at-arms because 90 percent of the Aztecs had already been obliterated by smallpox by 1520.

but also a means to finance their struggles back home. The coincidence of the discovery of the New World's gold and silver deposits, and the bubbling over of the Catholic-Protestant rift into outright war in the 1540s, was too great to be entirely coincidental.

Once they had seized control of the gold and silver mines, the Europeans set to the large-scale production of cash crops like cotton, sugar cane, and tobacco. These commodities fetched high prices, retained consistent demand, and traveled well across the long distance from New World to Old. The annihilation of the local populace presented a problem, though, since all three crops were exceptionally labor intensive in their production. Without a large infusion of people to work the land, producing them was out of the question. There were only two ways to put people on the land in the numbers needed: settlement and slavery.

NEW CROPS AND THE ENCLOSURE MOVEMENT

It is one thing to explore and trade and another to settle. Europe's expansion could not have become the permanent development it did without demographic changes, including growing populations with reduced access to land ownership. These fundamental changes made it possible, and desirable, to export people—which is another way of describing overseas expansion.

After severe contraction in the late Middle Ages, Europe's population began to grow around 1500 and did so steadily for the next three hundred years (see Figure 12.2). A gradual decline in outbreaks of plague accounts for much of this, but so does improvement in the food supply. Famine has always been nature's principal method of population control. For the premodern world, steady growth in demographic numbers is a sure indicator of steady growth in the availability of food. Europe saw just such a steady growth from the 16th to 18th centuries, for two reasons. First, food exports to the Ottoman-controlled east declined. And second, Europe was introduced to new crops from North and South America—the most important being corn (maize), beans, tomatoes, and potatoes. It is unlikely that these were brought back with the intention of introducing new foodstuffs. Rather, they were probably loaded on ships as victuals for those making the journey back to Europe (see Map 12.4). Most Europeans disdained corn (maize), which they thought inedible for humans; they prized it instead as animal fodder. Tomatoes made exotic sauces and side dishes. Beans and potatoes, though, were radical innovations. By long-standing feudal customs, Europe's

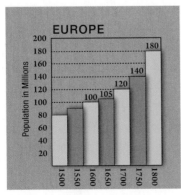

FIGURE 12.2   **Population Growth in Europe, 1500–1800**

manors remained dedicated to grain production, but beans and potatoes quickly dominated the peasants' individual garden plots. Gradually, fields normally left fallow were also given over to the new crops, which helped replenish the soil. Their high yields made them popular, not as market crops but as staples of the peasants' own diets. By the 17th century farmers on the Continent were eating as many as one to two dozen potatoes a day. Not the most satisfying of diets, but infinitely preferable to famine. Potatoes could also be distilled to produce vodka. Other grains that formerly went to peasant diets became available for distilling too.[4]

Increasing food supplies, however, meant declining agricultural prices. Small landholders who could not keep up with their rents therefore risked sliding back in debt bondage, and the manorial lords who lived off those rents faced severe potential drops in their own incomes as well. For many aristocrats, an answer to their trouble lay in the **enclosure movement**: By enclosing farmland—that is, by constructing a border of fences or thick hedgerows around it—landlords could evict their tenants, convert crop fields to meadows, and raise sheep or other herd animals instead. Their labor costs thus declined sharply, and the wool

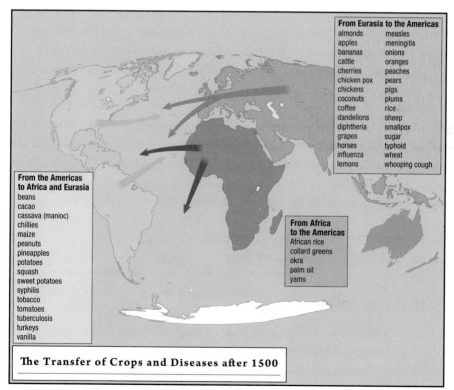

From Eurasia to the Americas

almonds	measles
apples	meningitis
bananas	onions
cattle	oranges
cherries	peaches
chicken pox	pears
chickens	pigs
coconuts	plums
coffee	rice
dandelions	sheep
diphtheria	smallpox
grapes	sugar
horses	typhoid
influenza	wheat
lemons	whooping cough

From the Americas to Africa and Eurasia

beans
cacao
cassava (manioc)
chillies
maize
peanuts
pineapples
potatoes
squash
sweet potatoes
syphilis
tobacco
tomatoes
tuberculosis
turkeys
vanilla

From Africa to the Americas

African rice
collard greens
okra
palm oil
yams

The Transfer of Crops and Diseases after 1500

MAP 12.4   The Transfer of Crops and Diseases after 1500

[4] The large-scale production of gin and whisky began—and so did greater alcoholism among the common people, with the usual social ills that accompany it.

generated by their sheep was self-renewing. Moreover, the steady rise in human population meant a steadily growing demand for textiles. In this way landed nobles improved their incomes significantly, but at the expense of the evicted farmers. Lacking the funds to purchase new lands of their own, rural workers had difficulty supporting themselves.

Thomas More had described the problem as early as 1516 in his *Utopia*, in which his narrator explains the rise of crime:

> It's because of sheep. These animals, so naturally mild and so easy to tend, can now be said to have become uncontrollable devourers, consuming even the people themselves; they empty homes, devastate crop fields, and turn whole villages into ghost towns. Anyplace where sheep can be raised to produce fine and rich wool, the nobles, gentry, and even the abbots (those supposed "holy men"!), not content with their rents and yearly fees, and feeling that it is not enough to live in luxurious laziness and do no actual good in the world, but choosing instead to bring actual harm into it, enclose all the land for pasture and put an end to farming. They demolish homes and level villages. The churches they allow to remain, of course, but only so they can use them as sheepfolds. As though they did not waste enough [land] already on coverts and private parks, these fine people are now destroying every human dwelling and letting every scrap of usable farmland run wild. *(Book 1)*

Evicted farm families had few options. The younger men could enter the military or merchant marine, and the females could seek positions as domestic servants, but for many the solution lay in seeking new fortunes abroad. The New World needed settlers in large numbers. It was a difficult decision, to travel thousands of miles from home, take up residence on a foreign continent, and begin the work of clearing the land afresh. But many chose to do so, because of population rise and land hunger. The feverish religious hostilities of the time, too, provided ample reason to quit the Old World for the New.

THE PATRIARCHAL FAMILY

Along with the Protestant reforms, these developments also led to a greater emphasis on the traditional family, with the husband firmly established at its head. But threats to family and state abounded, or were believed to abound, throughout the 16th and 17th centuries. And these threats, popularly believed to come primarily from witches and Jews, were considered so dire that society justified the most extraordinary measures to root them out.

Luther, Calvin, and the other Protestant leaders did not think of themselves as social reformers. When radicals like Thomas Müntzer (1488–1525) interpreted Luther's theology as a call to social rebellion, resulting in the Peasants' Revolt, Luther responded with characteristic vigor and called for the rebels' extermination. The Reformers, in fact, relied on existing social and political structures for their vision of a new Christendom: from feudal princes in Germany to urban elites in Switzerland, the existing social models provided the backbone of the Protestant campaigns.

And a strong backbone was needed, according to Luther, Calvin, and others. Human nature was too depraved, too ensnared in its own sinfulness, to be trusted. Figures of authority were needed to provide discipline. Protestant theology championed the notion of the "priesthood of all believers"—meaning that each individual could discern the teachings of the Bible for him- or herself. But only strong and demanding leaders could make sure that people lived according to the truths they read in Scripture. Hence Luther granted power to the German princes to enforce the teaching of the new Lutheran churches within their domains. Calvin established the town councils of the Elect to supervise, judge, and punish the Reformed citizens of Geneva and elsewhere.

Both men wrote extensive commentaries on the following passage from the New Testament:

> Let every person be subject to the governing authorities, for there is no authority except from God, and those authorities that exist have been instituted by God. Therefore whoever resists authority resists what God has appointed, and those who resist will incur judgment. For rulers are not a terror to good conduct, but to bad. Do you wish to have no fear of the authority? Then do what is good, and you will receive its approval; for it is God's servant for your good. But if you do what is wrong, you should be afraid, for the authority does not bear the sword in vain! It is the servant of God to execute wrath on the wrongdoer. Therefore one must be subject, not only because of wrath but also because of conscience. *(Romans 13.1–5)*

Since sinfulness is present in us from birth, disciplined authority needed to be as much a cornerstone of parenting as was love itself. Hence Protestant social ideology called for the patriarchal family as the fundamental unit of godly society. In that family, the man stood as the undoubted leader, charged with the protection and care of the whole household. The mother was subject to her husband's authority and given the special task of beginning the moral and spiritual education of their children. Luther and Calvin here drew on Saint Paul's Epistles: "Wives, be subject to your husbands as you are to the Lord. For the husband is the head of the wife just as Christ is the head of the church, the body of which He is the Savior. Just as the church is subject to Christ, so also wives ought to be, in everything, to their husbands" (Ephesians 5.22–24).

The Scottish Reformer and founder of the Presbyterian tradition, John Knox (1510–1572), wrote an infamous treatise called *First Blast of the Trumpet against the Monstrous Regiment of Women* (1558).

> To promote a woman to bear rule, superiority, dominion, or empire above any realm, nation, or city, is repugnant to nature; contumely [an insult] to God, a thing most contrary to His revealed will and approved ordinance; and finally, it is the subversion of good order, of all equity and justice. In the probation of this proposition, I will not be so curious as to gather whatsoever may amplify, set forth, or decor the same; but I am purposed, even as I have spoken my conscience in most plain and few words,

The Patriarchal Family   Cornelius Johnson (1593–1661) was a popular portraitist among the English aristocracy of the 17th century. This 1640 painting shows Arthur, 1st Baron Capell (1604–1649), together with his family. Capell was a staunch Royalist in England's Civil War, who personally escorted Queen Henrietta Maria to safety in France in 1646. Captured by Cromwell's forces in 1648, Capell was briefly imprisoned in the Tower of London before being executed. His eldest son, Arthur, shown at the far left here, joined what was left of the Royalist army even though he was only twelve years old at the time. This portrait shows the family posing before their formal garden. Note that of the three females in the picture, one (his wife, Lady Elizabeth Capell) is looking respectfully at her husband, the second daughter (Mary) is gazing at her baby brother, and the eldest daughter (Elizabeth) is looking slyly away to the right; only the males in the picture look directly at the viewer. Is it a coincidence that in this image, completed just before the outbreak of the Civil War, the Capell's garden is empty and storm clouds appear to be gathering over it?

so to stand content with a simple proof of every member, bringing in for my witness God's ordinance in nature, His plain will revealed in His word, and by the minds of such as be most ancient amongst godly writers. And first, where I affirm the empire of a woman to be a thing repugnant to nature, I mean not only that God, by the order of His creation, has spoiled [deprived] woman of authority and dominion, but also that man has seen, proved, and pronounced just causes why it should be. Man, I say, in many other cases, does in this behalf see very clearly. For the causes are so manifest, that they cannot be hid. For who can deny but it is repugnant to nature, that the blind shall be appointed to lead and conduct such as do see? That the weak, the sick, and impotent persons shall nourish and keep the whole and strong? And finally, that the foolish, mad, and frenetic shall govern the discreet, and give counsel to such as be sober of mind? And such be all women, compared unto man in bearing of authority. For their sight in civil regiment is but blindness; their strength, weakness; their counsel, foolishness; and judgment, frenzy, if it be rightly considered.

Husbands and fathers exercised their authority in a variety of ways. Physical discipline was permitted within certain limits, but men were expected above all to lead by setting examples of rigorous and godly behavior. To help them, most Protestant denominations offered some form of personal and family counseling. They also emphasized Bible reading within all family devotions. But since the godly family was the basic unit of godly society, the society itself had an intrinsic right to step in and exert authority when a parent failed. Public shaming, social ostracism, banishment from church life, and imprisonment were widely practiced.

SEXUAL MORALITY

At least in their first two or three generations, Protestant Christians placed a significantly sharper and more constant focus on sexual morality than their Catholic peers. Chastity before marriage and fidelity within it remained the moral ideal for all Christians, but Catholic Europe had long allowed a certain liberality in sexual matters, especially for men. Prostitution, while regulated, had been legal throughout Europe for centuries, for example, and no social stigma fell on the men who frequented prostitutes.[5] One way that Protestants sought to curb prostitution—apart from simply closing down the brothels—was through early marriage. With access to legitimate sexual release, they believed, men would not

---

[5]   Men had tended to put marriage off until they were established in a trade, which could take until their thirties.

be tempted to resort to illegitimate means. These earlier marriages helped account for the population increase that marked the century.

The era also witnessed new efforts to combat homosexuality. Same-sex eroticism had been regarded as a sign of weakness since Roman times. Christianity added the notion that the activity was immoral since it denied the procreative function that was sexuality's whole intent and purpose. Until the 13th century, however, homosexuality was not a criminal offense. By 1260 in France, homosexual acts became punishable by death. Comparable measures were instituted across Europe, at both the national and local levels, although it remains unclear how often such laws were enforced. Hostility to homosexuality increased with the need to rebuild the population after the Black Death as well. While Renaissance classicism brought more liberal attitudes, in Florence alone over 15,000 people were arrested for sodomy between 1432 and 1502 (though not all were convicted). The Spanish Inquisition arrested over 1,500 people on charges on homosexual acts between 1540 and 1700.

Protestantism's emphasis on Biblical truth (*sola Scriptura*) sharpened antihomosexual sentiments significantly, although formal condemnations came mostly at the local levels of government.[6] One notable exception was the Buggery Act passed by England's King Henry VIII (r. 1509–1547) in 1533, which remained in force until 1861, when the death penalty it called for was replaced by a sentence of life imprisonment.

> Forasmuch as there is not yet sufficient and condign punishment appointed and limited by the due course of the Laws of this Realm for the detestable and abominable Vice of Buggery, [whether] committed with mankind or beast: May it therefore please the King's Highness, with the assent of the Lords Spiritual and the Commons of this present parliament assembled, that it may be enacted by the authority of the same, that the same offence be from henceforth adjudged a felony, and that such an order and form of process therein to be used against the offenders as in cases of felony at the Common Law; and that the offenders being hereof convicted—by verdict, confession, or outlawry—shall suffer such pains of death, and losses and penalties of their goods, chattels, debts, lands, tenements, and [inherited properties], as felons do according to the Common Laws of this Realm; and that no person offending in any such offence shall be admitted to [the king's] clergy; and that Justices

---

[6] Just six passages from the Bible explicitly condemn homosexuality, and two are simply New Testament restatements of Old Testament proscriptions. The Scriptures record no direct teaching from Jesus.

of the Peace shall have power and authority within the limits of their commissions and jurisdictions to hear and determine the said offence, as they do in the cases of other felonies.

What makes any type of sexual activity a crime against the state instead of a matter of personal morality? In Protestant Europe, where the state had become the administrative head of the religious community, a sin against public morals was also a crime against civil society. Hence homosexuality—along with adultery, masturbation, foul language, gambling, and drunkenness—required a civil response. Protestants read the Bible as mandating the two-parent, heterosexual,

"A Jan Steen Household"   Jan Havickszoon Steen (1626–1679) was a prolific and popular genre painter of the Dutch Golden Age, who made a handsome living from his scenes of everyday life among common town and country dwellers. Sometimes comic, sometimes tragic, and sometimes a mixture of the two, his paintings were known for their attention to the crowdedness and chaos of domestic living—to such a point that even today a common Dutch colloquialism describes a messy, squalid space as "a Jan Steen household" (*een huishouden van Jan Steen*)—a phrase roughly comparable to the American expression "a pigsty." This painting is one of his moralistic images, showing the dangers of drunkenness. (Steen grew up in a family of tavern keepers, and knew what he was talking about—or rather painting.) Apart from the unbecoming postures of the two figures in the foreground and the uninviting physical scene, a woman and two companions (musicians?) are stealing the drunken pair's cloaks in the background.

married nuclear family. Any sexual activity outside that norm was in essence a threat to the godly state.

ENEMIES WITHIN: WITCHES AND JEWS

Popular belief in witchcraft had roots in pre-Christian classical, Germanic, and Celtic culture. Ancient and medieval beliefs differed from those of the early modern era, however. Earlier Europeans had held that some individuals (thankfully, not many) are simply born with an intrinsic ability to summon supernatural forces at will, which they used for good or ill. In contrast, people of the 16th and 17th centuries developed the belief that magical powers resulted from an explicit and conscious contract made between the witch (who could be male or female) and Satan. Witchcraft was now believed to be intentional—a power that an individual chose to acquire—rather than an innate, though freakish, ability possessed from birth. And that made popular fear of it all the stronger, especially given the era's particular emphasis on human weakness and sinfulness. If people could be so easily coaxed into a pact with Satan, then witchcraft could conceivably take over our world and bring about its ruin. A witch was not merely someone "possessed of powers" but someone actively engaged in evil, and the danger he or she represented required immediate action.

That action consisted of mania, arrest, trial, torture, and execution on a scale that is difficult to comprehend. Campaigns against witches began to increase markedly toward the end of the 15th century but became frenzied after 1560, once Europe's religious disputes turned violent. From 1560 to 1670, nearly two hundred thousand people across Europe were accused of witchcraft and subjected to judicial persecution or mob violence (see Figure 12.3). Roughly one quarter of them were executed. Those who confessed and repented—which required identifying other witches and agreeing to testify against them—were briefly imprisoned, frequently marked by a tattoo, fined, and released. Yet they were socially shunned for the rest of their lives. Germany, Switzerland, and eastern France had the most witchcraft trials per capita. And while there seems to be no substantial difference between the frequency of Protestant and Catholic prosecutions of witchcraft, it does appear that the Protestant-Catholic divide played a role: witchcraft mania struck most ferociously where Protestants and Catholics were most even in number. The witches who appeared in stage dramas like William Shakespeare's *Macbeth* were realistic characters to audiences, in addition to whatever symbolic role they played in the text. In the end, however, no country was immune to witchcraft.

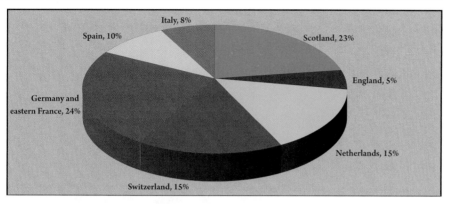

FIGURE 12.3   **Witchcraft Trials, 1450–1750**

Neither was any sex. Both men and women were believed capable of sell-ing their souls to Satan, although at least three-quarters of those arrested for witchcraft, and nearly 90 percent of those executed for it, were women. (Ire-land was the sole exception: roughly 90 percent of its prosecuted witches were male.) Popular assumptions about women's nature—as emotional, impulsive, passionate, demanding creatures—fueled the phenomenon. Women were re-garded as generally weaker than men, but especially in regard to sex. Ideas about sexuality, derived from ancient Greek medicine, held that female lust, once aroused, was insatiable.[7] Only a demonic lover like Satan, it was assumed, could satisfy a woman's sexual longing—and that was precisely the appeal used by the devil to ensnare his victims. Men who became witches were gener-ally assumed to have been enticed into it by women who had already given themselves over to satanic lust.

In this way, the witchcraft craze accords with the period's concern with sexuality in general. Ironi-cally, the era's emphasis on early marriage was directly related to its fear of unchecked sexuality. It demanded being the "godly wife and mother" responsible for her children's moral education, the subjection of wives to their husbands, and the sacralization of domestic life. A force as powerful and unpre-dictable as a woman's body needed to be firmly controlled—or else all hell, literally, could break loose.

> A force as powerful and unpredictable as a woman's body needed to be firmly controlled—or else all hell, literally, could break loose.

---

[7]   Many of the constraints placed on women—such as limiting their appearance in public or regulating their dress—were justified as protecting them from their own inability to control their passions.

Anne Hendriks, brulée à Amsterdam, A.° 1571.   Anne Heinrichs zu Amsterdam verbrent, A.° 1571.

Burning the Enemy Within   A convicted witch being executed in Amsterdam in 1571.

THE JEWS OF THE EAST AND WEST

The era was cruel to Jews as well. Late medieval hostility to Jews had resulted in a series of expulsion orders, first from England (1290), then from France (1306) and Germany (numerous times), and finally from Spain (1492) and Portugal (1497). Forced from one territory to the next, the Jews gradually concentrated in the Low Countries, Italy, North Africa, and the Ottoman Empire, where the **Ashkenazic** and **Sephardic** traditions of Judaism once again confronted one another (see Map 12.5).

For the host countries, the sudden increase in the Jewish populations aggravated social tensions and led many to segregate the Jews into **ghettos**. Regulations like these had been common since the 12th century. The surge in Jewish numbers within those districts, however, frequently led to new legislation limiting the Jews' freedom to move and act within the larger community. Venice established the first modern ghetto in 1516, but other cities were quick to follow.[8] Life in these communities was often difficult, since Jews from many backgrounds were thrust shoulder to shoulder, within a larger social context of economic decline and Christian hostility. The economic decline occurred largely because of the shift of economic power from the Mediterranean—where the Jews had taken refuge—to the Atlantic seaboard, which happened at the same time. Only those Jews who had migrated to the Low Countries moved into a society of economic growth.

---

[8]   The word *ghetto* likely derives from the Italian *borghetto*, meaning a "small borough" or "precinct."

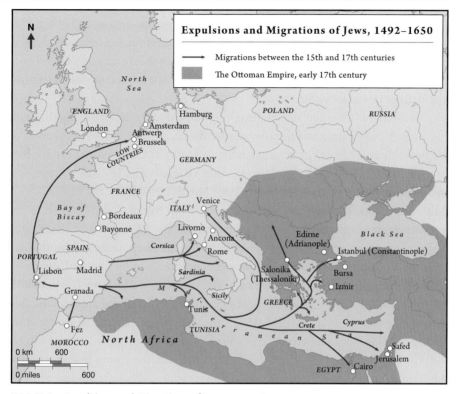

Expulsions and Migrations of Jews, 1492–1650

→   Migrations between the 15th and 17th centuries

■   The Ottoman Empire, early 17th century

MAP 12.5   Expulsions and Migrations of Jews 1492–1650

Not surprisingly, as most Jews' social and economic lives grew shaky in the 16th and 17th centuries, many found solace in new messianic movements, especially in the Ottoman state, which, after 1515, included the Holy Land. Jewish refugees from Europe generally received a cordial welcome from the Ottoman rulers Bayezid II [T] (r. 1484–1512) and Selim I [T] (r. 1512–1520), who encouraged Jews to settle in the Holy Land.[9] Many Jews, upon arriving in the Holy Land, expressed surprise at the squalor into which the cities had fallen. An Italian refugee, R. Obadiah of Bertinoro, sent a letter back to friend in which he estimates there being "only about seventy [Jewish] households in all of Gaza," while in Hebron he found "only twenty households, ... half of them coming from Spain and just recently arrived." In Jerusalem itself he found "only seventy households left, all of them poverty-stricken and with no means of support. ... Anyone who has food to last a year, or the means to procure it, is considered wealthy here."

In Italy, led by charismatic adventurers like Solomon Molcho (1500–1532) and David Reubeni (1490–1541), and in the Ottoman Empire, inspired by R. Isaac Luria (1534–1572) and R. Hayyim Vital (1543–1620), thousands of Jews believed in the

---

[9]   Spanish Jews set up the first printing press in the Ottoman state. Two Sephardic Jews, Joseph Hamon and his son Moses Hamon, served for a total of thirty years as personal physicians to the sultans.

imminent arrival of the long-promised messiah. These four figures, and others like them, preached a message of intense spiritual and social reform to prepare for the restoration of the Davidic Kingdom. These movements involved a minority of the Jews, but they were popular enough to make the rulers of their host countries concerned about the potential for social unrest.

Reubeni was an especially enigmatic figure, known today primarily through his diary. A curly haired and heavily bearded dwarf, he had a striking appearance. He probably came from the large Jewish community at Cranganore in India, but at some point he traveled to Khaybar, in today's Afghanistan. In 1522 he appeared in Sudan, speaking to crowds about a large Jewish kingdom in the east, supposedly ruled by his brother Joseph. For some reason, Reubeni also claimed to be a direct descendant of the Prophet Muhammad. His life's aim was to create a military alliance between European royalty and his supposed royal brother to open a two-front war upon the Ottoman Empire. In 1524 he went to Rome, entering the city while riding a white horse, and was received by Pope Clement VII (r. 1523–1534). With Clement's recommendation in hand, he approached the Portuguese king João III (r. 1521–1557), the rulers of Milan and of Venice, and finally the Habsburg emperor Charles V, each of whom promised some form of aid. (In Italy he made friends with Solomon Molcho, the son of Jewish parents who had converted to Christianity. Solomon reconverted to Judaism and, at Reubeni's encouragement, circumcised himself.) Reubeni's habit of complaining to these rulers about their treatment of native Jews, however, turned them against him. Sometime around 1531 he was arrested in Italy and sent to Spain, where he was tried by the Inquisition. No official record of his trial or execution survives, but a later chronicle records that in 1541 "a Jew from India who had come to Portugal" was put to death by the Inquisition at Llerana in southern Spain. His diary survives in the Bodleian Library in Oxford and was published in 1895.

When Sabbatai Zvi (1626–1676) came along and preached his own version of messianic deliverance, he found an enormously receptive audience. He was from Smyrna (modern Izmir, Turkey). **Kabbala**, a mystical interpretation of scripture developed by rabbis, had originated centuries before. In 1648, however, in fulfillment of a kabbalistic prophecy, Zvi declared himself the Messiah and ultimately moved to Istanbul, where he converted a Jewish scribe who promptly forged an ancient-looking revelation document from the patriarch Abraham.

> I, Abraham, confined for forty years to life in a cave, spent a long time in pondering when the miraculous time of deliverance might come, when suddenly, a heavenly voice cried out: "A son named Sabbatai will be born to Mordechai Zvi in the year 5386 [1626]. He, the great Messiah, will humble the Serpent and take his seat upon my throne."

Armed with this, Zvi preached to Jews throughout the Ottoman lands—Istanbul, Athens, Alexandria, Cairo, Gaza, Jerusalem, Aleppo—and gained followers everywhere. Jews as far away as Italy, France, Germany, and the Netherlands joined the movement. At least one entire community, at Avignon, made preparations to quit the city and move with all their belongings to Jerusalem, to join the anticipated new kingdom.

Zvi went so far as to issue a universal proclamation to all Jews:

> Sabbatai Zvi, the first-born son of YHWH, and the Messiah and Redeemer of all the people of Israel, to all the sons of Israel, sends Peace. Since you have been thought worthy to behold the great Day of Fulfillment promised by YHWH through His prophets, all your sorrows and lamentations must end and be turned to celebrations, your fasts be turned into feasts, and your tears must cease. Rejoice, instead, with psalms and hymns! Let your days of sadness and despair become days of jubilation! For I have appeared!

As unlikely as it sounds, the proclamation generated enormous excitement throughout the international Jewish world. Zvi's portrait began to be printed in Jewish prayer books (frequently appearing next to images of King David). His initials were carved on synagogue walls and embroidered onto flags, and prayers for him were inserted into Jewish liturgies.

A Messiah on His Throne
Sabbatai Zvi (1626–1676) was a Sephardic Jew who grew up in Smyrna (modern Izmir) in western Anatolia. A sensitive lad, troubled by violent mood swings, he began to experience mystical revelations in 1648 that intimated he was the long-expected messiah of the Jewish people. It is unclear how much he believed these revelations at first, and how many followers he acquired, but in 1665, after receiving a number of confirming signs that dispelled all doubt, he and his followers publicly proclaimed his messianic mission. This page from a prayer book, published in Amsterdam in 1666, shows him enthroned, with angels bringing him a heavenly crown. Note the lower image, which has him presiding over a table at which are gathered the representatives, presumably, of the Twelve Tribes of Israel. The Hebrew word *tikkun* in large print in the center of the image means the "restored harmony" expected to be provided by the messiah.

The speed of the Sabbatean cult's rise reflects the misery and difficulty of Jewish lives. Persecutions of the Jews grew in number and ferocity throughout the era, leading many to find hope only in a miraculous deliverance. Even a number of Christian groups enthused over the supposed Messiah's arrival, although they were probably more excited by the idea of the Jews leaving Europe than they were about their liberation. But the Ottoman ruler Mehmed IV (r. 1648–1687) grew concerned about

Zvi's popularity. Afraid that large numbers of Jews migrating to Israel would push for its independence, he began to pressure Zvi to stop his activity. Zvi responded, on September 16, 1666, by suddenly announcing his conversion to Islam—for which Mehmed rewarded him with great wealth, a prominent position at court, and several new wives. To Jews everywhere, the blow was devastating, and the Sabbatean movement fell apart instantaneously.

Most of the founders of Protestantism were surprised by the refusal of the Jews to convert to Christianity. For centuries, figures like Martin Luther believed, the Jews had bravely and correctly held out against the false teachings of the Catholics. "If I had been born a Jew," he wrote in *On Jesus Christ Having Been Born a Jew* (1523), "and if I had witnessed such idiots and buffoons [as the Catholics] trying to teach and administer Christian truth, I would as soon have turned myself into a pig as into a Christian." But surely, most Reformers confidently felt, once the beautiful Gospel truth was restored by the Protestants, the Jews would rush to accept it. Conversion would be their reward for enduring centuries of Catholic idiocy and persecution. "We will receive them with open arms, permit them to trade with us, to work with us, live among us, hear our Christian preaching, and witness our Christian way of life." When that failed to happen, the reaction was severe.

Luther himself penned many private letters to friends in which he railed against Jewish perfidy. He also released his wrath publicly in several viciously anti-Semitic tracts, the most notorious being *On the Jews and Their Lies* (1543):

> What ever shall Christians do with the damned, rejected Jews? We can hardly tolerate having them live among us as they do—for if we do, now that we know of their lies, hatred, and blasphemy, we will be complicit in their evil. We are powerless to convert them, but powerless too to put out the unquenchable fire of God's wrath, of which the prophets wrote. . . . Here is what I recommend. First, we ought to burn down their synagogues and schools, and bury underground whatever is immune to fire, so that no one ever again needs to see a single stone or cinder of them. . . . Their homes too should be set ablaze and destroyed. . . . Let all their prayer books and copies of the Talmud be taken from them, for it is by means of these that they propagate their idolatry, their lies, their foul cursing, and their blasphemies.

The tract goes on like this for two hundred pages. Luther was arguably no more anti-Semitic than many of his peers, but he was among the most influential and outspoken. His works may not have persuaded tolerant Christians to become otherwise—and it deserves pointing out that many individuals disagreed with Luther, in print. Yet his uniquely authoritative position among Protestants probably encouraged and confirmed many anti-Semites in the bigotry they already had.

The early modern era, in sum, was marked by harsh religious tensions compounded by severe economic dislocations. Small wonder, then, that so many dispossessed Christians fled to the New World. Small wonder, too, that so many dispossessed Jews fled to the Old.

WARS OF RELIGION

When societies employ force, they often justify their action by recourse to the divine. The ancient Hebrews, for example, considered some wars ethically justifiable as self-defense (*milhemet hovah*). Other wars, however, such as their conquest of the Promised Land from the Canaanites, they deemed to be a religious obligation (*milhemet mitzvah*), a manifestation of YHWH's victory over the false gods of the peoples of the Palestinian plain. The Greeks never entered battle, when they could help it, without first making offerings to the gods and looking for signs of heavenly favor or disfavor. They found divine revelation in everything from cloud patterns in the sky to the spray of blood in the sacrifice of an animal. In ancient Rome the constitutional authority to declare war laid not with the emperor, the consul, or the Senate but with the *fetiales*—the college of priests.

> Still, the church struggled for centuries to determine a Christian ethic for war. How can one justify even a war of self-defense when the greatest heroes of the church were martyrs? Can one be a soldier and a Christian at the same time?

Christianity posed a problem to medieval warriors (if they bothered to think about it), since Jesus's message had focused so intently on peace. He offered no resistance to those who sought to do him harm and forgave those who had already done it. Fortunately for the warlords, though, Dark Age–era Christianity emphasized Jesus as the stern Lord of Heaven, the All-Powerful Judge of Last Days, rather than the Prince of Peace. Still, the church struggled for centuries to determine a Christian ethic for war. How can one justify even a war of self-defense when the greatest heroes of the church were martyrs? Can one be a soldier and a Christian at the same time?

Medieval Muslims had less trouble with the matter: the Prophet himself had been an avid soldier, and the Holy Qur'an enjoined all believers, under certain circumstances, to take up arms for the faith. The Islamic empire had been achieved by the sword first and proselytizing later. The pious names (*laqab*) adopted by the early caliphs illustrate this attitude: al-Saffah ("the Slaughterer"), al-Mansur ("the Conqueror"), al-Muntasir ("the Victorious").

For Protestant Christians the moral sovereignty of the Bible posed no absolute bar to violence. They could point to Old Testament precedents, and the New Testament, too, opened the door to force. "Do not think that I have come to bring peace to the earth," warned Jesus. "I have not come to bring peace, but a sword.

For I have come to set a man against his father, and a daughter against her mother, and a daughter-in-law against her mother-in-law; and one's foes will be members of one's own household" *(Matthew 10.34–36).*

Most Christians do not read this passage as inciting conflict. It simply recognizes that commitment to the new faith can introduce dissension even within a family. But others noted that Jesus himself used violence on at least one occasion, described in all four gospels, when he encountered the money changers in the Temple: "Making a whip of cords, he drove all of them out of the temple ... [and] poured out the coins of the money changers and overturned their tables" (John 2.13–15). Moreover, the Gospel writers passed up the perfect opportunity to condemn all military activity—when crowds came to John the Baptist, asking what they needed to do in order to be saved. John replied not that soldiers needed to renounce the army but only that they should "not extort money from anyone by threats or false accusation, and be satisfied with [their] wages" (Luke 3.14).

Stories like this may not have been on everyone's mind in the 16th and early 17th centuries. Yet wars raged widely (see Map 12.6). The brief but bloody Peasants' Revolt in Germany in 1525 served as a kind of prologue to the other conflicts of the age, since it involved the four chief elements—religious conflict, economic conflict, social conflict, political conflict—characteristic of the era. The blows to Christian unity quickly reached France, but in England the adoption of Protestantism in fact signaled the end of a long civil war and the start of a new golden age. It took the Thirty Years' War in Germany, however, to embroil all of Europe.

THE PEACE OF AUGSBURG AND THE EDICT OF NANTES

The Protestant movement was only eight years old when the Peasants' Revolt erupted, but it had already progressed far enough to shred permanently any sense of Christian unity. Encouraged by Luther's open approval, the Protestant nobles responded in force and crushed the rebellion. The experience sharpened more antagonisms than it resolved, however, and set the stage for the coming battle with the emperor Charles V. The Catholic nobles in southern Germany—none of whom had stood up to support the peasants—feared the aroused might of their Protestant peers and looked to Charles to restore order.

But while they hoped for Protestantism's defeat, the Catholic princes were chary of Charles's ending up with more power in Germany as a result. When Charles finally began military action in the 1540s, support from the Catholic princes was at best occasional and at worst verged on treason. For this reason, the war quickly degraded into an inconclusive series of advances and defeats. Finally, when it appeared certain that neither side could gain a clear victory, Charles and

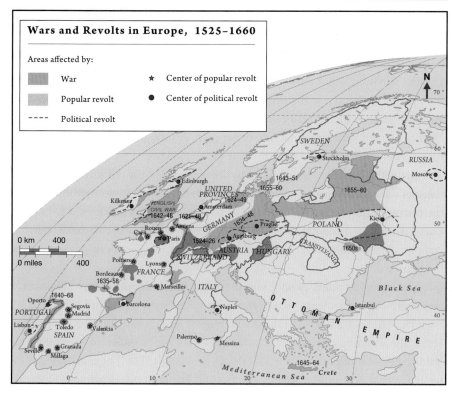

MAP 12.6   **Wars and Revolts in Europe, 1525–1660**

the Lutheran princes agreed to a compromise settlement. Known as the **Peace of Augsburg** (1555), it granted Lutheranism legal recognition and established *cuius regio, eius religio*, already encountered in chapter 11. With this policy, the religion of the local ruler determined the state religion of the principality, with certain guarantees offered to the rights of the religious minority.

Any hopes that the Augsburg compromise might serve as a model for other countries failed the first test, and in 1562 France became embroiled in a religiously charged civil war that raged for over three decades. The problem was that the Augsburg treaty had recognized the legal validity of Lutheranism but had not done so for Calvinism (since Calvin's version of Christianity had a negligible presence in Germany). And Calvin, who now lived across the Swiss border, in Geneva, longed to secure legitimacy for his followers back home.[10]

His chance came in 1562, when control of the French monarchy came up for grabs. The young King Francis II had died in 1560 after only one year on the throne, leaving his even younger brother, Charles IX (r. 1560–1574), to succeed

---

[10] By 1562 nearly one-fifth of the French population was Calvinist—primarily in the southern and eastern parts of the realm.

him. The question of the regency—that is, of someone appointed to run the government on Charles's behalf until he came of age—exposed political rivalries and religious antagonism as well. Each of the two leading noble families had ties to royalty, but one was Catholic and the other Calvinist. The Catholic faction was led by the duke of Guise, while the prince of Condé and Henri de Navarre led the Calvinists—who were called **Huguenots** in France. The queen mother, Catherine de' Medici, formed yet another faction of her own. Although essentially a court conflict between aristocratic rivals, the war quickly engulfed the whole population. The leaders of each faction appealed to the masses and turned a dispute over the *roi et loi* ("king and law") into a fight over *foi* ("faith"). Mob violence determined the course of the war almost as much as the actual armies did, for Catholics and Calvinists everywhere attacked each other. They ransacked each other's churches and plundered each other's shops and households. Clergy on both sides urged the fight onward.

The war's grimmest episode was the **Saint Bartholomew's Day Massacre**, a week-long orgy of violence that began as an assassination plot and turned into a mass riot (August 23–29, 1572). The Huguenot leaders had come to Paris to celebrate the wedding of Henri de Navarre, the Huguenot leader, to Marguerite de Valois, the sister of French king, Charles IX (r. 1560–1574). The marriage was intended to ease relations between Catholics and Protestants by uniting their causes in the royal family, but Catherine de' Medici hoped to put a decisive end to the fighting by plotting their murder. The murders spurred mobs to action, and soon crowds in other cities had joined in. When the killing finally ended, thousands of Protestants lay dead, the victims of shooting, strangling, knifing, and drowning. In addition to Paris, massacres took place in Angers, Bordeaux, Bourges, Gaillac, La Charité, Lyons, Meaux, Orléans, Rouen, Saumur, Toulouse, and Troyes—all cities that had reverted to Catholic rule. The riots sparked Protestant fury, predictably, and the Huguenots redoubled their efforts to bring down the royal house, aided now by sympathetic Protestants from Germany and the Netherlands. Catholic Spain responded in turn by sending its troops into southern France. France's civil war threatened to engulf all of Latin Europe.

The whole miserable struggle ended when the next French king, Henri III (r. 1574–1589), was murdered at more or less the same time as the Huguenot leader, the Duke of Guise. Henri de Navarre, married to Princess Marguerite, acceded to the throne. Although the Protestant champion, he made the cool calculation that France, being 80 percent Catholic, had to have a Catholic king. "Paris is worth a Mass," he reportedly declared, then announced his conversion to Catholicism. It took several years to convince the Catholics of his earnestness and to mollify the disappointment of the Protestants. In the end,

No "Restored Harmony" Here   On August 23, 1572, a plot to assassinate leaders of the Huguenot faction in Paris—probably but not certainly instigated by Catherine de' Medici—inspired a terrifying wave of mob violence by thousands of the city's Catholics against their Protestant neighbors. Some estimates put the number of Protestants killed in the riot as high as thirty thousand. The original target of the assassination plot, Gaspard de Coligny, the military leader of the Huguenots, can be seen hanging out of a window to the right. (He was only wounded, but was subsequently executed.) Catherine de' Medici is at the far back, toward the left, emerging from the Louvre and examining a pile of Protestant corpses.

though, he won the support of both and began a long reign that is widely regarded as one of the high points of French history—as Henri IV (r. 1589–1610). In 1598 he promulgated the **Edict of Nantes**, which guaranteed religious freedom, under certain restrictions, throughout the realm. This edict, together with the Peace of Augsburg, established a legal right to believe as one wishes—but in both cases freedom of religion was technically imposed on the people by the king, rather than arising from a demand bubbling up from the populace. In other words, it was a power of the monarch to impose, not a right claimed by the people. For a brief spell the Continent had achieved peace, but it had not attained tolerance.

THE CHURCH OF ENGLAND

Meanwhile, a different sort of religious settlement had evolved in England. There a civil war known as the **War of the Roses** (1455–1485) had erupted soon after England's humiliating defeat in the Hundred Years' War (1337–1453), as various factions fought to shift the blame for England's loss and to win the throne.[11] The War of the Roses never involved large numbers of commoners, but it decimated the English nobility. When the war ended in 1485, a relatively minor aristocrat named Henry Tudor became king, largely by attrition. Ruling as Henry VII (r. 1485–1509), he understood that he could make no elaborate claims of distinguished lineage or heavenly favor—and he did not attempt to do so. He governed modestly and frugally, making sure not to upset the delicate truce. Henry was quick to recognize the potential of the New World discoveries, though, and he invested heavily in developing England's meager maritime capability.

When his son Henry VIII (r. 1509–1547) came to the throne, the kingdom had begun its climb to wealth and power on the international stage. Portraits of Henry VIII convey an aura of manly vitality and newfound wealth altogether absent from portraits of his cautious father. They differed not only in personality but royal self-regard. Henry VIII's portraits exude confidence, swagger, and more than a touch of the gaudiness of the nouveaux riches—for that is precisely what the Tudor monarch was becoming. His marriage in 1509 to Catherine of Aragon, the daughter of the king of Spain, was a corporate merger of the two leading Atlantic seaboard powers. It promised to secure England's new dominant position in Europe for generations to come.

But then came the matter of divorce. Catherine, a pious, loving woman but without a robust physique, had produced several sickly children, and only one—a daughter, Mary—had survived infancy. By 1525, after sixteen years of marriage, it seemed likely that Catherine would not produce the male heir Henry so desperately needed. He decided to divorce her. This move offended Rome (since the marriage had happened only by means of a special papal grant in the first place), the royal house of Spain (since their princess was being publicly humiliated), and the German emperor (since he was Catherine's nephew, and was already smarting from his losses to the Lutherans in his realm). After much dramatic though failed diplomacy, Henry decided in early 1533 to break with the Catholic Church and establish the **Church of England**, or Anglican Church. It was a Protestant church with the monarchy as its supreme head.

Henry famously had six wives before he died. The first had given him Mary, the second produced his only son, Edward, and the third gave birth to another daughter, Elizabeth. Wives four and five gave him nothing but misery, and number six brought genuine affection and comfort to his last years. In creating the Anglican Church, however, Henry did more than establish yet another form

---

[11]   The War of the Roses took its name from the white and red roses on the respective heraldic badges of the noble houses of York and Lancaster.

of Protestantism; he brought England directly into the turmoil raging across Europe. Another version of Christianity was arguably the last thing Western culture needed at the time. Worse, it set the two countries leading the exploration of the New World and the new international economy at odds with one another. England and Spain, briefly united in Henry's marriage to Catherine and on the brink of becoming a joint superpower, instead remained bitter rivals through the rest of the century. Henry's action did result in an enormous increase in royal income, though. He ordered the suppression of every Catholic monastery in the realm and seized all their holdings—which may have amounted to one-fifth of the real estate in England and Wales. The Tudors used this wealth, along with their New World riches, to buy support in both houses of Parliament.

At Henry's death in 1547, the throne passed to his son Edward VI (r. 1547–1553). Only ten at his accession, he never emerged from the shadow of the regency council established for him. The steps made to eradicate Catholicism were undone when Edward fell ill and died, and the throne passed, after some intrigue, to his elder half sister, Mary (r. 1553–1558). Mary, as the daughter of the scorned Catherine of Aragon, was resolutely Catholic and determined to restore Catholicism. Her reign has entered popular memory as a nightmare of religious violence, earning her the nickname of "Bloody Mary." In reality, she was quite popular at first, especially with the many Catholics who still remained in the kingdom. Even many Protestants sympathized with her after her father's break with Rome. But her decision to marry Felipe of Spain in 1554 changed matters and dispelled any hopes that a peaceful religious settlement might be reached. (In Germany, the Peace of Augsburg was still a year away.)

A wave of political purges and religious persecutions marred her last three years on the throne, with roughly three hundred Protestant leaders hunted down as enemies of the crown and killed. Their stories were told—with more love for melodramatic detail than for historical accuracy—by John Foxe in his *Book of Martyrs*, first published in 1563. (Its actual title was *Actes and Monuments of these Latter and Perillous Days, Touching Matters of the Church*). The work is enormous, longer even than the Bible. And for a while it had nearly as much authority over English Protestants; a decree in 1570 ordered that a copy of it be placed in every cathedral church in England.[12]

Mary died childless, and the crown passed to her half sister, Elizabeth I (r. 1558–1603), in whose reign England reached the apogee of international power and prestige. Commonly regarded as England's golden age, this was the era of

---

[12]   Until the start of the 19th century, the three most widely disseminated books in England and America were the Bible (Authorized Version), John Bunyan's *A Pilgrim's Progress,* and Foxe's *Book of Martyrs.*

the poet-playwrights Christopher Marlowe (1564–1593), William Shakespeare (1564–1616), the pirate-adventurers Sir Francis Drake (1540–1596) and Sir Walter Raleigh (1552–1618), and the composers William Byrd (1543–1623) and Thomas Campion (1567–1620). Elizabeth secured a religious settlement that established the Anglican Church as the official faith, with the monarch as its supreme leader. This compromise was a hybrid of Catholic ritual and Protestant theology, and it proved amenable to a majority of her subjects. She placed legal restrictions on Catholic holdouts, but she was even sterner with the more radical wings of the Protestant movement, such as the Puritans, who began to see the New World as more inviting.

Elizabeth increased England's involvement in the new Atlantic economy, which brought her into direct conflict with Spain. She promoted the piracy campaigns of Sir Francis Drake against the Spanish fleets returning from the New World, laden with gold and silver. She also underwrote further exploration of North America. Given the already tense relations between England and Spain, Elizabeth's actions were sure to cause further trouble— which came in 1588 when Felipe II (r. 1554–1598) sent his famous armada to invade England. After the smaller, lighter English fleet defeated these massive warships, England's involvement in the hornets' nest of Continental politics only became more intense.

"The Only Defense of the Christian Faith" Engraving dated 1596 of England's Queen Elizabeth I (r. 1558–1603), showing her as erect and unyielding as the marble pillars on either side of her. She holds the usual signs of royal power (orb, scepter) but stands between two unusual other symbols: the falcon atop the left-hand pillar, feeding her young, and the falcon to the right, who rises as a phoenix. The inscription at the bottom (supplemented by a boilerplate poem beneath) lauds her as "the only defense of the Christian faith." The defeat of the Spanish Armada in 1588 had marked the highpoint of her popularity. Owing to economic troubles and a protracted war in Ireland, though, by the late 1590s she was losing control over her privy council and some of her popular regard with the masses, a slow slide that continued until her death. This image seems part of an effort to boost her public image.

Spain was also fighting at the time against the Netherlands, which had formed part of the Habsburg Empire. Smarting under Catholic rule, the staunchly Calvinist Dutch revolted against Felipe in 1566. They fought over religion, of course, but even more important was the money to be made in the New World. The Dutch resented having to send a portion of their earnings to Madrid, and they therefore sued for independence. England was happy to see Spain lose to the

Netherlands, and so gave the Dutch whatever overt and covert assistance they could afford.[13] The benefits proved obvious. With Spanish naval might curtailed, England established its East India Company in 1600. The Dutch founded their own East India Company in 1602, leaving them and England as the two most prominent European trading nations in the subcontinent. In North America, England built its first settlement in Virginia in 1607, and the Dutch colonized the southern portion of the island of Manhattan in 1612. Spain thus entered the 17th century in a state of severe economic decline.

THE THIRTY YEARS' WAR

These economic rivalries, political aspirations, and religious conflicts culminated in the last and bloodiest of the Wars of Religion: the **Thirty Years' War** (1618–1648), between Protestants and Catholics in Germany, drew in all of Europe. Like the other wars of the era, this conflict sprang from other motives than religious faith. Nor was the war inevitable, even though, with hindsight, it is easy to see it coming. Most of the European countries became involved in it, in one way or another. The war dragged on for so long in part because the Atlantic states profited from it: so long as the Germans remained mired in civil strife, they could not interfere with or compete against the English, Dutch, French, and Spanish who were busy plundering North and South America. All of the fighting took place in German territories, which makes sense given that the war was as much about Germany's constitutional problem as it was about religion (see Map 12.6).

Its effects were devastating: roughly one-fifth of the entire German population died. France and England both sent assistance to both sides of the conflict. When the Protestants were winning, they aided the Catholics; and when the Catholics were winning, they sent aid to the Protestants. The Dutch helped whichever side promised to help them keep their independence from Spain. Denmark entered the conflict with the aim of seizing northern German territory for itself. The king of Poland joined the fighting in order to defend the Catholic faith. He also claimed the throne of Sweden and hoped for papal and imperial recognition of his claim. The Swedes, for their part, fought to defend Protestantism—and to gain a military alliance with Orthodox Russia against Catholic Poland.

As with the Hundred Years' War between England and France, the significance of the Thirty Years' War lay in how it was fought rather than in the dreary narrative of which side won which battle in any given year. This was the first European-wide war. It was also the first war in which most of the fighting used modern

---

[13]   The playwright Christopher Marlowe served briefly as a spy for Elizabeth in Holland.

weapons based on gunpowder. Armed commoners now formed the overwhelming bulk of the armies, marching in formation, with lines of muskets flanked by cumbersome but mobile artillery. Under the command of cavalry officers still drawn from the upper classes, the armies were larger than any that had taken the field before. At the first battle of Nördlingen in 1643, for example, close to 50,000 soldiers took part, and 10,000 lay dead on the field by battle's end. Only two years later a second battle was fought on the same site, with 30,000 soldiers entering the fray and only 20,000 coming out alive. Similar slaughter took place at Breitenfeld in 1631, at Lützen in 1632, at Breda in 1634, at Thionville in 1639, at Jankau in 1635, and at Lens in 1648. Corpses lay rotting by the thousands in fields all across central Europe.

Among the most vivid testimonies to the war's savagery is a remarkable novel by Hans Jakob Christoffel von Grimmelshausen (1621–1676). Kidnapped by Hessian soldiers when he was only ten, he was captured in battle and redrafted into military service by several armies until the war's end in 1648. His novel, *The Adventurous Simpleton*, appeared in 1668 and tells of a young simpleton who, like

Armies before Professionalization   The small northern French town of Aire-sur-la-Lys had the misfortune of being near Calais, England's vital port entrance into France, and hence always fought over. Between the Hundred Years' War (1337–1453) and the Thirty Years' War (1618–1648) it was besieged nearly a dozen times. This painting from the latter conflict shows the crude makeup of mass armies: no longer the aristocratic-led cavalry, and not yet the professionalized infantry of the Age of Absolutism.

von Grimmelshausen, witnesses horrors and is pressed into service. An early scene sets the tone:

> At first I did not intend to force you, gentle reader, to accompany these soldiers to my father's homestead, for I know what evil things are about to happen there; but the nature of my story requires me to leave some record of the brutal acts performed, time and again, by those involved in the war here in our Germany.... After stabling their horses, the soldiers all set about their appointed tasks, the sum of which was the utter ruin and desolation of our farm. Some began to slaughter all of our animals and set them stewing or roasting, so that it appeared as though they were preparing a jolly feast; but others ransacked our house from top to bottom.... Whatever they did not want to cart away they tore to pieces. A few started to thrust their swords into the haystacks and bales of straw, to find any hidden sheep or swine they could add to the slaughter.... Our maid Ursula, shame to tell, was dragged into the stable and so roughed up that afterwards she refused to come out. Then they took one of our hired workmen and stretched him out flat upon the ground, and, prying his mouth open with a bit of old wood, they dumped a slop bucket full of shit and piss down his throat. They called this a "Swedish cocktail."

After rounding up other farmers in the neighborhood, the soldiers began interrogating them.

> First they took the flints out of their pistols, jammed the farmers' thumbs into the opened space, and used the pistols as thumbscrews to torture them as they would witches. One poor fellow, even though he had confessed to no crime at all, they thrust into the oven, and lit it. They wrapped a rope around another fellow's head and twisted it with a piece of wood until blood gushed from his mouth, nose, and ears.... I cannot report much about what happened to the women, young girls, and maidservants of the district, for the soldiers prevented me from seeing it; but I remember hearing pitiful screams coming from each corner of our house. *(1.4)*

Much of the novel's horror comes from Grimmelshausen's identifying the soldiers simply as *soldiers*. He often does not differentiate between Bavarians, Saxons, Austrians, Thuringians, Swedes, Dutch, French, Spaniards, Danes, Poles, Lutherans, Calvinists, or Catholics. They are all simply soldiers, there are no meaningful

Title Page of *The Adventurous Simpleton* (1668)   The first great German-language novel. Its author, Hans Jakob Christoff von Grimmelshausen (1621–1676), like the novel's main character, was abducted as a child and pressed into service in several armies throughout the Thirty Years' War. Unlike the novel's hero, Grimmelshausen never flew to the moon or visited the center of the Earth.

sides to the conflict, and the war is its own repellent cause and justification. But the novel offers more than scenes of savagery. Simpleton runs away from the army and finds his way through a dizzying series of unpredictable adventures. He turns himself into a populist highwayman à la Robin Hood; he impersonates a woman; he takes the place in high society of an aristocrat; he becomes a con artist and a religious pilgrim; he explores a utopian society of mermaids and mermen who live at the bottom of a lake in the Black Forest. At turns hilarious and horrifying, the novel depicts a treacherous world without order. It is a chaotic quest not for a Holy Grail but for simple human decency and the tiniest bit of stability in life.

Grimmelshausen wrote several other novels, each a sequel to his first, usually narrated by a minor character from *Simpleton.* The series recalls Geoffrey Chaucer's *Canterbury Tales* in its shifting kaleidoscope of experiences and views. Though little read today, Simpleton is the greatest German novel before Goethe, and it has never been surpassed as a depiction of war as collective insanity.

WARS OF RELIGION: THE EASTERN FRONT

Christian Europe was not the only theater of conflict. Events in the Middle East, too, turned violent in the 16th and 17th centuries, thanks to a similarly toxic mixture of religious, economic, and ethnic enmity. Three large, multiethnic states dominated the Islamic world around 1500: the Ottoman Empire, the Mamluk Sultanate in Egypt and Syria, and Safavid Persia. Twenty years later only two remained, and they challenged each other for leadership of the Muslim world for the next two hundred years.

Turks and Persians, heading up the Sunnis and Shi'a, respectively, were the standard-bearers of Islam. Ethnic Arabs held decidedly second-class status in both societies, and efforts to alter their position failed before the military might of the dominant regimes. Bayezid II [T] (r. 1481–1512) and his son Selim I [T] (r. 1512–1520) were anxious to continue the policy of aggressive Ottoman expansion and drove the Turkish army northward into the Black Sea, westward into the Balkans, southward toward Egypt, and eastward toward Persia. Bayezid even constructed a large naval fleet that defeated the Venetians in 1503 and left the Turks in command of the eastern Mediterranean sea-lanes. Bayezid had a more peaceful side to his personality, though, and took particular delight in managing the palace schools (sometimes even volunteering to examine students personally) and in fostering trade.

Selim—whose nickname Yavuz ("the Inflexible") describes his personality—began his reign with a near paranoid fear of Persian designs on his realm and spent his first two years in power executing forty thousand suspected Safavid sympathizers in Anatolia. Non-Muslims fared better under these two than did non-Sunni Muslims. Nearly a quarter million Jews emigrated to the Ottoman realm after the European expulsions and settled in Anatolia and Palestine. Like many of their predecessors and courtiers, however, Bayezid and Selim practiced an eclectic form of Islam. It was formally Sunni but tinged with a passionate admiration for **Sufism**.

The Turkish affinity for Sufism may have had its roots in the shamanistic cults of pre-Islamic times. But whatever its origins, it frequently set the Turks at odds with the more staid Sunni and Arabic majority they governed. Urged on by heavyweight scholars like Ibn Taymiyya [K] (1263–1328) after the fall of the Persianized Abbasids, Arab leaders in the 14th century had again placed the **'ulama** ("brotherhood," or "community") at the center of Sunni life. In this conservative view, the traditions of the Qur'an, **hadith**, and **sunnah** were paramount, and all forms of speculative theology and metaphysical innovation were denounced.

Ibn Taymiyya's career, together with those of his acolytes, can in fact be thought of as a small-scale Islamic analog to the Protestant Reformation:

- It demanded a strict return to the authority of early texts.
- It called for stripping away every aspect of religious life not specifically called for in those texts.
- It condemned as heretics all who disagreed with them or who used their ideas for other purposes.
- It was openly hostile to all forms of monastic life and to the cults of popular saints.
- It considered the earliest religious community (the Twelve Apostles for Luther, the Companions of the Prophet for Ibn Taymiyya) the most perfect in its observance of confessional life.

All of these traits were shared by the Sunni and Protestant reformers.[14] Ibn Taymiyya's party attacked Sufism as fundamentally un-Islamic, since it emphasized ecstatic union with God over strict observance of his laws. His immediate

---

14 In modern times Taymiyya inspired Muhammad ibn Abd al-Wahhab [A] (1703–1792), the founder of Wahhabism, the official doctrine of Saudi Arabia.

acolytes included Ibn Kathir [A] (1301–1372) and Ibn al-Qayyim al-Jawziyya [A] (1292–1350). Little had changed by the 15th century, except for the even deeper entrenchment of the conservative position.

THE WANING OF THE SULTANATE

The Ottoman economy peaked under Selim I's son and heir Suleiman I [T] (r. 1520–1566). Suleiman, the contemporary of Charles V in Europe, is known in Europe as "Suleiman the Magnificent." In the Muslim world, he is called "Suleiman the Lawgiver" in recognition of his work in codifying the great mass of legislation he inherited from his predecessors. He also made the imperial administration more efficient. He was a successful warrior as well, extending Ottoman power to Hungary.[15]

With the opening of the Atlantic trade, however, the Ottoman economy gradually slowed and stagnated. Population increase both fueled the initial growth and brought about the stagnation. When the economy was still expanding, immigration increased significantly. The arrival of the Jews formed only a part of this; a much greater factor was the influx of Muslims from Egypt and Syria and parts of Persia. Cities like Edirne, Trabzon, and Iznik grew by as much as 80 percent, while scores of others grew by 40 to 50 percent. Rural villages increased by 30 to 40 percent over the 16th century. Ultimately, overpopulation set in and was felt first in the countryside. Available farmland grew scarce, and local authorities responded by permitting the clearing of forests. Woodland, never abundant in much of the region, became even scarcer and contributed to a loss of commercial diversity. Adding to the trouble was the influx of gold and silver from the New World, which led to inflation. In 1580, for example, it took sixty silver Turkish coins to equal one gold ducat (then the international standard currency of account), but only ten years later it required 120. By 1640 it took 250. The price of basic commodities like wheat increased by a factor of twenty between 1500 and 1600.

As in Christian Europe, economic misery made religious and ethnic tensions worse. Popular resentment of ethnic and religious foreigners, especially of the relatively newcomer Sufis and Shi'a, increased. Street violence between factions forced local officials to take more direct and heavy-handed actions to keep the peace. But this required money. Over the 16th and 17th centuries, therefore, the power of the Ottoman sultanate waned. Provincial governors and urban or district commanders

---

[15]   Suleiman ultimately led his armies all the way to the gates of Vienna (which they failed to take).

Now It's Istanbul, Not Constantinople   A painting from 1537 showing a bird's-eye view of the now-Turkish capital of Istanbul. The picture still follows the medieval tradition of orienting maps with east at the top; a modern viewer needs to turn his or her head sideways to the left. The Hippodrome and the former Church of Hagia Sophia (now renamed the Ayasofya Mosque and renovated to include two minarets) are the two largest structures visible. Though subject to brutal pillage after its 1453 fall to the Ottomans, the city recovered quickly and became a welcoming refuge for Jews who fled the rising religious antagonisms of the 16th and 17th centuries.

first demanded the right to collect their own taxes and then used the revenue to finance their new political muscle.

The sultan's loss of fiscal and political power catalyzed the conservative trend in religion. **Madrasas** across the Ottoman state declared their opposition to any sort of speculative thought. Preachers condemned public morals for straying from the early 'ulama.[16] Even the natural sciences, which had been one of the glories of Islam in the medieval period, came under attack. When Murad III [T] (r. 1574–1595) had an astronomical observatory built in 1579, local preachers—mostly

---

[16] Especially popular targets for preachers were the new enthusiasms for coffee and tobacco, brought over from the New World.

Arabs—condemned it as an offense against Allah to attempt to unravel the secrets of the act of creation and hired mobs to tear it down.

NEW CENTERS OF INTELLECTUAL LIFE

The creative centers of intellectual life thus moved from the Ottoman center to Egypt and Persia. Cairo emerged as the vital site for scientific work. It was also the home of Ibn Khaldun [A] (1132–1406), whose great *Muqaddimah* ("Introduction to History") posited a new philosophy of history, based on materialism—or the pursuit of worldly goods rather than spiritual ends. Safavid Persia, by contrast, became the center for metaphysics. Its great achievement was a philosophical program known as **illuminationism** (*al-hikmat al-ishraq*), starting with a learned Sufi named Shahab al-Din Suhrawardi [P] (1155–1191). Its central figures were al-Amili [P] (1546–1622), Mir Damad [P] (d. 1631), and especially Sadr ad-Din al-Shirazi [P] (1571–1636)—better known in the Islamic world by the name **Mulla Sadra**. The author of *Transcendental Wisdom*, he remains the most influential thinker in the Persian philosophical tradition down to the present. A key feature of illuminationist, or ishraqi, thought is its effort to harmonize Sufism, Shi'ism, and rational philosophy.

Illuminationism was in fact a common feature of Greater Western philosophical thinking of the age, although European and the Middle Eastern thinkers arrived at it by different trajectories. In western Europe it is expressed in the philosophies of Baruch Spinoza (1632–1677) and Gottlieb Leibniz (1646–1716). Spinoza, a heretical Jew excommunicated by his Amsterdam synagogue, was also a heretical illuminationist. He argued for a highly original form of pantheism that asserted that God was Nature Itself (*natura naturans*, in his posthumously published masterpiece—the *Ethics*) and that every facet of and occurrence in nature (*natura naturata*) is a necessary consequence of God's existence. But the identification of God and Nature should not elicit an

> To Spinoza, human life has no divinely ordained purpose and the occurrences of nature possess no supernatural meaning; they simply *are*.

attitude of wonderment and awe from human beings. To Spinoza, human life has no divinely ordained purpose and the occurrences of nature possess no supernatural meaning; they simply *are*. The rational study of nature leads to no spiritual revelation, only to a rational understanding of God's manifestation within nature—which, Spinoza insists, is illumination enough for anyone.

Leibniz, by contrast, sees divine emanation everywhere. He rejects pantheism in favor of an idea to which he gave the awkward name of monadology; all forms of natural life are composed of fundamental units he calls monads, which contain within themselves all the qualities of the life-form they make up.

Spinoza   Baruch de Spinoza (1632–1677) was the greatest Jewish philosopher since Maimonides, although his ideas led to his receiving a writ of *herem*—a form of excommunication in Jewish law. The wording of the writ is striking. Its central portion reads as follows: "The leaders of this holy community, long familiar with the evil ideas and actions of Baruch de Spinoza, have tried repeatedly and by numerous stratagems to turn him from his evil ways; but we have failed to make him mend his wicked ways—in fact, we hear fresh reports every day about the abominable heresies he practices and teaches, and the monstrous deeds he continues to perform. . . . And [therefore] we have decided that the said Baruch de Spinoza should be excommunicated and expelled from the people of Israel. . . . [Wherefore], in accordance with the will of the Holy One (may He be ever blessed) and of this Holy Congregation, and in the presence of the holy scrolls of the Torah, with their 613 commandments, we hereby excommunicate, cast out, curse and damn Baruch de Spinoza with the same form of excommunication with which Joshua condemned Jericho, with the curse with which Elisha cursed the boys, and with all the curses which are written in the Book of the Law. Cursed be Baruch de Spinoza by day and cursed be he by night; cursed when he lies down and cursed when he rises up; cursed when he goes out and cursed when he comes in. The Lord will not spare him; His righteous anger and wrath will rage against this man, and bring upon him all the curses written in the Law. May the Lord blot out his name from under heaven, and condemn him to separation separate from all the tribes of Israel with all the curses of the covenant as they are contained the Law."

The concept is difficult to grasp—and Leibniz himself had difficulty in expressing it—but may be thought of, for organic matter at least, as something akin to a
particular life-form's unique genetic code. God himself, says Leibniz, is not present in nature, as Spinoza would uneasily have it, but his intent is present in the
system of monads. The study of nature does not bring us, therefore, into God's
presence, but it does illuminate for us the workings of his mind.

In Persia, illuminationism derived from the attempt to harmonize Islamic doctrine with classical Greek thought and the mystical elements of Zoroastrianism,
and hence to give Sufism a measure of intellectual respectability within the larger
Muslim world. Elements of illuminationism date to the 12th century but the theory
was given its fullest and most brilliant expression in the work of Mulla Sadra, the
greatest Muslim philosopher of the modern era. Mulla Sadra's most important book,
The Four Journeys of the Intellect (1638), maps out four stages in the route to spiritual
and philosophical enlightenment. He dissects the cognitive processes that lead from
the understanding of the physical world to a consideration of the essence of God and
the nature of the relationship of humans to the Creator. Illumination is both a divine
blessing and a technique of enlightenment, an aspect of spiritual discipline.

Sadra does not see God in creation like Spinoza; neither does he behold a
divine intelligence in it like Leibniz. Rather, he sees a mystical unity in creation
that parallels the unity of God himself and draws the enlightened believer into
a stronger desire for spiritual ascent, a return to the Oneness at the heart of all
things. Sadra thus pulls together and harmonizes Sufi mysticism, Aristotelian
rationalism, and Neoplatonic emanationism.

> Philosophy is the process of perfecting the human soul by coming to
> a true understanding of things-as-they-are, which is achieved—when it
> is achieved at all—through rational demonstration rather than intuition
> or appeal to prior authority. By means of philosophy, we come to resem-
> ble our Creator, and this allows us to perceive and ascribe a rational order
> to His creation.

Most of Arab Islam adhered to a staid and increasingly conservative form of
Sunni Islam, eschewing scientific and metaphysical innovation in favor of rigid
tradition. As early as the late 14th century Ibn Khaldun had observed that most of
the creative intellectual energy in the Islamic world came from non-Arabs. From
the *Muqaddimah*:

> All the great grammarians have been Persian, . . . all the great legal
> scholars. . . . Only the Persians still write great books and dedicate them-
> selves to preserving what is known. Thus, a saying attributed to the

Prophet himself rings true: "If Knowledge was suspended from the highest ceiling in heaven, the Persians alone would get it." ... All the intellectual arts, in fact, have long since been abandoned by the Arabs and become the sole preserve of the Persians.

The encouragement given to non-Arab Islamic and pre-Islamic traditions by the Ottomans thus stemmed from a sincere interest in promoting innovation and enquiry, but it also served a political purpose by providing a counterweight to the Arab-centric views holding sway from the Arab Peninsula through Palestine and Syria. It also provides another example of the interconnected nature of the cultural life of the Greater West.

THE OTTOMANS: FROM STRIFE TO WARFARE

Tensions between the Ottomans, their Sunni Arab base, and the Shi'i Safavids grew increasingly bitter. The Ottomans' economic stagnation worsened, while Safavid Persia not only carved out its own Islamic identity, but challenged the very notion that the center of Muslim civilization lay with the Arabs and Turks. The pulse of vital Islamic life, Persians insisted, had moved permanently eastward to Iran. The Persian **shah** (emperor) Ismail (r. 1501–1524), who believed himself divine, ordered the immediate conversion of all Sunnis in Iran to Shi'ism on penalty of death. And he made good on the threat by executing tens of thousands, confiscating their homes and goods, closing their mosques, and absconding with the funds for their schools. He also urged the Turkish people to overthrow the Ottomans. As a colorful warning to the Ottoman ruler (Bayezid II), Ismail had another political rival killed, had the skin removed from his corpse and ordered it stitched around a life-size straw figure of the man, and sent it to Istanbul.[17]

Predictably, wars broke out between the two states (see Map 12.7) and continued through the reign of Ismail's son Tahmasp I [P] (r. 1524–1576). Religious hatred intensified with each new reign. Ismail II (r. 1576–1578) played a role in Persia analogous to that of England's Mary Tudor. He tried to force the realm to reconvert to Sunni Islam, but the purges and persecutions he ordered became so bloody that his closest supporters poisoned him after only two years on the throne. Occasional persecutions of Iran's Jewish and Christian communities broke out in the 16th century, but in the 17th religious relations improved significantly. In general, as the Shi'a became more firmly established and were less involved in strife with Sunni holdouts, they eased up on oppression of Jews and Christians. Moreover, many Jewish immigrants from further west earned the shah's gratitude by

---

[17] Ismail kept his rival's skull—gold-plated and encrusted with jewels—and used it as a drinking cup.

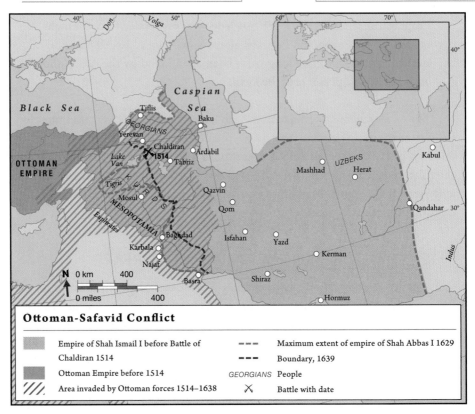

MAP 12.7   Ottoman-Safavid Conflict

introducing him to gunpowder and the casting of heavy artillery. The desire by rulers like Abbas the Great [P] (r. 1588–1629) to increase Iran's export of silk textiles and Persian rugs also opened the way for Armenian Christians, long expert in the crafts, to thrive under Safavid rule.

Ottoman relations with the west remained uneasy, especially with Habsburg Austria and Venice, their neighboring rivals for control of trade routes. The absence of a natural boundary between the Turkish and the Austrian realms kept mutual concerns for safety at a high level. And with the relative decline of Mediterranean trade relative to the Atlantic, control of the sea-lanes in and out of the Levant became all the more important. At the Battle of Lepanto in 1571 an alliance of naval forces led by Venice and King Felipe II of Spain defeated the Turkish fleet and decimated its corps of experienced officers. The so-called Long War (1593–1606) against Austria highlighted the need to modernize the Ottoman army with gunpowder weaponry, but resistance to Western technology among the Arab populace made this an unpopular development.

TABLE 12.1 **Sultanate of Women**

NAME	YEARS IN POWER	MOTHER OF	WIFE OF	ETHNICITY
Ayşe Hafsa	1520–1534	Selim I	Suleiman I	Tatar
Nur-Banu	1574–1483	Selim II	Murad III	Venetian
Safiye	1594–1603	Murad III	Mehmed III	Venetian
Hatice	1617–1621	Ahmed I	Osman II	Serb
Kösem	1623–1648	Ahmed I	Murad IV and Ibrahim I	Greek
Turhan Hatice	1648–1683	Ibrahim I	Mehmed IV	Ukrainian

Just as unpopular and destabilizing was the repeated phenomenon of women running the imperial government. The era of the 16th and 17th centuries in general—but especially the period of the 1640s and 1650s—is referred to as the **Sultanate of Women** (*kadınlar saltanatı* in Turkish; see Table 12.1). During the reigns of several weak-minded rulers, such as Ibrahim I (r. 1640–1648), and several minorities, such as that under Mehmed IV (r. 1648–1687), the leading members of the imperial harem effectively controlled the government. Taking the title of "queen mother" (*valide sultan* in Turkish), these women ran the state, directed foreign policy, and oversaw the fiscal system. What made matters worse, from the point of view of their disgruntled, mainly Arab, subjects, was the fact that most of these women were non-Muslim by birth and their embrace of Islam was therefore suspect. (The Ottomans made a point of marrying as many Christian-born wives as possible, as a nod to their Christian subjects.) In the 16th century the most prominent sultanas were Nur-Banu and Safiya, who either ran or helped to run the Ottoman state in the years 1574–1583 and 1595–1603, respectively. Both of Venetian descent, they restored relations with Venice after the battle of Lepanto and strengthened commercial ties between their empires. Two figures who especially stood out in the 17th century were Kösem, the Greek-born mother of Ibrahim, and her Turkish daughter-in-law Turhan Hatice, whose rivalry was as much personal as political and ended with Kösem's assassination in 1651.

The 16th and 17th centuries, in sum, were not necessarily more religious or more filled with religious hatred than earlier periods in Christian or Islamic history. However, religion became enmeshed in economic and ethnic rivalries of an unusually large scale. Money and the ties of blood intensified religious antagonisms until they reached a degree of fanaticism unlike anything that had existed before, with the possible exception of the medieval crusades. Such antagonisms would not reach this fever pitch again until the 20th century.

WHO, WHAT, WHERE

Ashkenazic	Mulla Sadra
Church of England	Peace of Augsburg
conquistadores	Saint Bartholomew's Day Massacre
Edict of Nantes	Sephardic
enclosure movement	shah
ghettos	Sufism
hadith	Sultanate of Women
Huguenots	sunnah
illuminationism	Thirty Years' War
Kabbala	'ulama
Madrasa	War of the Roses

SUGGESTED READINGS

Primary Sources

Diaz, Bernal. *The Conquest of New Spain.*

Grimmelshausen, Hans Jakob Christoffel von. *The Adventurous Simpleton.*

Las Casas, Bartolomé de. *A Short Account of the Destruction of the Indies.*

Montaigne, Michel de. *Essays.*

Mulla Sadra. *The Four Journeys of the Intellect.*

Anthologies

Diefendorf, Barbara B. *The Saint Bartholomew's Day Massacre: A Brief History with Documents* (2008).

Kors, Alan Charles, and Edward Peters, eds. *Witchcraft in Europe, 400–1700: A Documentary History* (2000).

Pryor, Felix, comp. *Elizabeth I: Her Life in Letters* (2003).

Symcox, Geoffrey, and Blair Sullivan. *Christopher Columbus and the Enterprise of the Indies: A Brief History with Documents* (2005).

Studies

Buisseret, David. *The Mapmaker's Quest: Depicting New Worlds in Renaissance Europe* (2003).

Bonney, Richard. *The Thirty Years' War, 1618–1648* (2002).

Briggs, Robin. *Witches and Neighbors: The Social and Cultural Context of European Witchcraft* (1996).

Clark, Stuart. *Thinking with Demons: The Idea of Witchcraft in Early Modern Europe* (1999).

Dale, Stephen F. *The Muslim Empires of the Ottomans, Safavids, and Mughals* (2010).

Diefendorf, Barbara B. *Beneath the Cross: Catholics and Huguenots in Sixteenth-Century Paris* (1991).

Dursteler, Eric R. *Renegade Women: Gender, Identity, and Boundaries in the Early Modern Mediterranean* (2011).

Fairchilds, Cissie. *Women in Early Modern Europe, 1500–1700* (2007).

Fritze, Ronald. *New Worlds: The Great Voyages of Discovery, 1400–1600* (2005).

Greyerz, Kaspar von. *Religion and Culture in Early Modern Europe, 1500–1800* (2007).

Hartz, Glenn. *Leibniz's Final System: Monads, Matter, and Animals* (2006).

Holt, Mack P. *The French Wars of Religion, 1562–1629* (2005).

Israel, Jonathan I. *European Jewry in the Age of Mercantilism, 1550–1750* (1989).

Kamen, Henry. *Spain, 1469–1714: A Society of Conflict* (2005).

Kaplan, Benjamin J. *Divided by Faith: Religious Conflict and the Practice of Toleration in Early Modern Europe* (2007).

Kleinschmidt, Harald. *Charles V: The World Emperor* (2004).

MacHardy, Karin. *War, Religion, and Court Patronage in Habsburg Austria: The Social and Cultural Dimensions of Political Interaction, 1521–1622* (2003).

Moris, Zailan. *Revelation, Intellectual Intuition, and Reason in the Philosophy of Mulla Sadra: An Analysis of the Al-Hikmah Al-'Arshiyyah* (2003).

Nadler, Steven. *Spinoza's "Ethics": An Introduction* (2006).

———. *Spinoza's Heresy: Immortality and the Jewish Mind* (2002).

Newman, Andrew J. *Safavid Iran: Rebirth of a Persian Empire* (2008).

O'Malley, John W. *Trent and All That: Renaming Catholicism in the Early Modern Era* (2000).

Parrott, David. *Richelieu's Army: War, Government, and Society in France, 1624–1642* (2001).

Peirce, Leslie. *Morality Tales: Law and Gender in the Ottoman Court of Aintab* (2003).

Pursell, Brennan C. *The Winter King: Frederick V of the Palatinate and the Coming of the Thirty Years' War* (2003).

Thomas, Hugh. *Rivers of Gold: The Rise of the Spanish Empire* (2004).

Wiesner-Hanks, Merry E. *Early Modern Europe, 1450–1789* (2006).

Wilson, Peter H. *The Thirty Years War: Europe's Tragedy* (2009).

For additional resources, including maps, primary sources, visuals, web links, and quizzes, please go to **www.oup.com/us/backman**.

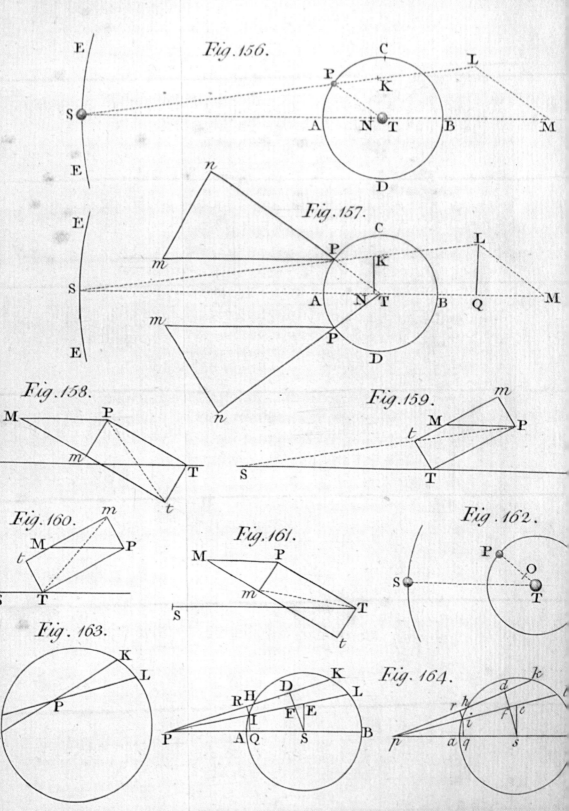

Fig. 156.

Fig. 157.

Fig. 158.

Fig. 159.

Fig. 160.

Fig. 161.

Fig. 162.

Fig. 163.

Fig. 164.

CHAPTER 13

Science Breaks Out and Breaks Through

1500–1700

In the 13th century a Franciscan scholar from England named Roger Bacon (1214–1294) gleefully tore into everyone around him who thought of themselves as scientists. He could, and did, find fault in anyone. Phrases like "damned fools," "ignorant asses," "inept buffoons," and "miserable idiots" pepper his writings in his own colorful Latin. Science, he argued, had been for too long a prisoner to philosophers who never thought to test their abstractions against the evidence of their senses.

THE GREATER WEST, ca. 1700

◀ **The Geometry of Gravity** Sir Isaac Newton's *Principia* (1687) was the closest thing the world had yet seen to a scientific Theory of Everything and dominated the field of physics until the start of the 20th century. This plate from the original edition illustrates some of Newton's theorems visually. The top image (Figure 156), for example, illustrates his thoughts on the gravitational interaction of three bodies: a central and fixed star, represented by the letter T, and two planets in orbit around it, P and S.

When a renowned figure like Albertus Magnus (1206–1280) came to lecture at the University of Paris and was received "like a second Aristotle," Bacon reacted bitterly: "Never before in the history of the world has there been committed a[n intellectual] crime as perverse as this."

Ironically, Bacon's assault on scientists marked the beginning of what we call today the Scientific Revolution. Bacon did not oppose grand theories in themselves. Rather, he believed that the only valid way to reach them was through observation. "Experimental science is the Queen of All Sciences, the goal of all

CHAPTER OUTLINE

- The Copernican Drama
- Galileo and the Truth of Numbers
- The Other Scientific Revolution
- The Council of Trent, 1546–1563
- The Society of Jesus
- Inquisition and Inquiry
- The Revolution Broadens
- The Ethical Costs of Science
- The Islamic Retreat from Science
- Thinking about Truth
- Descartes and the Quest for Truth
- Newton's Mathematical Principles
- The Choices for Western Society

our speculation," he wrote in his *Opus Maius* ("Large Study"). But even that was not sufficient. One had to master all the sciences—including mathematics, optics, astronomy, botany, and physics—before one could even begin to theorize about any one of them. Bacon spent many years achieving just that mastery, as well as learning Greek and Hebrew (and possibly a smattering of Arabic), in order to reach the grand synthesis that he believed only he could achieve. In the end, however, struggles within the Franciscan order forced Bacon into house arrest and silence; he never had the chance to elaborate his grand Theory of Everything.

In the 17th century Sir Francis Bacon (1561–1626) earned fame for his brilliance in law and philosophy, and he cultivated friendships among England's most wealthy and privileged people. Bacon (of no known relation to his medieval namesake) could, and did, flatter anyone. Bacon spent his last five years on the philosophical work that had always fascinated him. He planned a massive, comprehensive work to be called the *Great Instauration*—meaning the great refounding of the entire Western intellectual tradition—but completed only a handful of discrete books that were to form parts of the whole. His *Novum Organum* ("New Instrument") in 1620 reworked Aristotelian logic, while *The New Atlantis* in 1627 was a utopian fantasy. He envisioned, like Roger Bacon had several centuries earlier, a grand masterwork, a complete synthesis of human intellectual understanding. His focus, however, was on the process of analysis rather than on the gathering of data or the testing of hypotheses. Given facts A and B, what conclusions or assumptions can we validly draw from them—and how can we distinguish the valid from the invalid?

Both Bacons addressed the same problem, although from different angles: what are the intrinsic flaws in human thinking? What errors stand between us and Truth, and how can we overcome them? The world overwhelms us with data, impressions, facts, and observations, and our history overwhelms us with ideas, theories, opinions, and conjectures. We need a clear guide to dealing with all this input. How can we know that we are thinking properly?

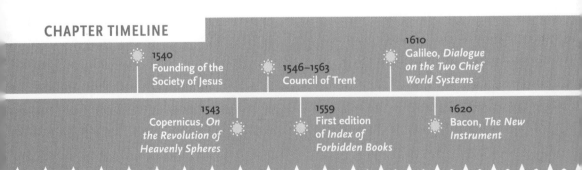

CHAPTER TIMELINE

1540
Founding of the
Society of Jesus

1546–1563
Council of Trent

1610
Galileo, *Dialogue
on the Two Chief
World Systems*

1543
Copernicus, *On
the Revolution of
Heavenly Spheres*

1559
First edition
of *Index of
Forbidden Books*

1620
Bacon, *The New
Instrument*

The **Scientific Revolution** of the 16th and 17th centuries was not a rejection of tradition, unlike Renaissance humanism, but a new phase in its development. The astonishing discoveries of the age placed science at the center of intellectual life in a way that was unique to the West. Fields like mathematics, medicine, and astronomy had always played important roles in intellectual culture. Plato's Academy, remember, expected everyone to master geometry before beginning philosophical study. However, in the 16th and 17th centuries they did more than place the sun at the center of the solar system, discover the universal law of gravitation, and defy the Inquisition and the Islamic retreat from science. They also came to define intellectual life and establish the standards by which it developed and was judged. The story from Bacon to Bacon helps to explain why.

THE COPERNICAN DRAMA

Science interested few people during the Renaissance; at best it formed a minor hobby for some. Like the classical Romans they emulated, Renaissance thinkers showed a keen interest in applied technology but spent little time on pure science. One partial exception was the great artist Leonardo da Vinci (1452–1519), whose curiosity about the natural world and eye for observation inspired him to make intricate drawings of human anatomy, various forms of plant and animal life, and types of machines. He even performed a few human dissections, on the sly. But while such work reflected a strong intuitive grasp of how things in the material world function, they are still not science—which may be one reason why Leonardo left these studies to private journals and notebooks. The only other Renaissance figure who may qualify as a scientist was the Swiss physician Philip von Hohenheim, better known by his nickname of Paracelsus (1493–1541). His understanding and practice of medicine was thoroughly medieval, although he did some pioneering experimentation with various chemicals and minerals in the treatment

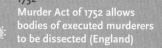

1637
Decartes, *Discourse on Method*

1687
Newton, *Principia Mathematica*

1660
Royal Society Founded (London)

1752
Murder Act of 1752 allows bodies of executed murderers to be dissected (England)

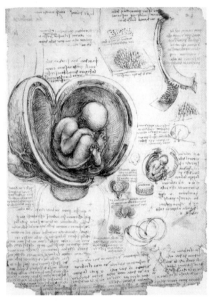

Drawing of a Fetus in a Womb   Leonardo da Vinci (1452–1519) performed as many as three dozen human dissections in his lifetime (he also dissected several cows and monkeys), which gave him unparalleled knowledge of the body. He prepared over two hundred detailed drawings for publication as a book on anatomy. As shown in this drawing of a fetus, he also wrote extensive notes. The book, *A Treatise on Painting*, was never published in his lifetime. This image also shows da Vinci's use of "mirror writing," which he used not for any secret purpose but simply because he was left-handed and found it easier to write this way without smudging the page.

of disease. His most significant discovery was the development of laudanum—a tincture of opium dissolved in alcohol that was used to treat a host of maladies until the early 20th century. Paracelsus is otherwise remembered primarily for the popular legends that arose around his involvement in alchemy.

The revival of pure science began with developments in astronomy. The revival sprang from a new model by Nicolaus Copernicus (1473–1543) of the motion of the planets, confirmed by careful calculations by Tycho Brahe (1546–1601) and Johannes Kepler (1571–1630). And it led Galileo to a direct confrontation between science and the church. Cosmology had formed a key component of Western science and philosophy from the beginning, going back to the ancient Greeks. The geocentric model handed down for two thousand years posited a static earth at the center of the universe, with the sun and other "moveable stars" (the planets) swirling about it in perfect circular orbits. The unmoving "fixed stars" comprised bright points on the ceiling of Creation. The universe was thus a single, finite, enclosed entity with mankind—Nature's masterpiece—at its center. Christians, to the extent they thought about such things at all, saw no reason to challenge the geocentric model, and indeed felt that it contributed to the Christian view of Man as God's supreme creation. Science was religion's handmaiden. God created the universe, in fact, in order to provide humans with a home. To study the workings of the natural world, therefore, was to most Christians a way of praising God and strengthening faith by deepening our appreciation of God's Creation. Throughout the Middle Ages in fact the church was the primary institution, and often the only one, promoting the study of science. When Western science revived in the 16th century, it did so once again hand in hand with Christian faith. It is a modern conceit that science advanced only when it divorced itself from religion; that divorce became finalized only in the 19th century. The Scientific Revolution therefore needs to be understood as an offshoot of religious history.

Flaws in the geocentric model were evident from the start. Even to the naked eye, the movement of the planets across the night sky was irregular: the transit of Venus (a mini-eclipse caused when Venus passes between Earth and the sun) was just one such irregularity. If the planets all move in ever-widening perfect concentric circles around a stationary Earth, how could the orbits of Venus and the sun intersect in this way? Over the centuries astronomers had come up with scores of intricate arguments to explain away the inconsistencies of the geocentric model, but with each new refinement the system seemed less and less viable.

Sometime around 1510 the German-Polish astronomer Nicolaus Copernicus (Mikołaj Kopernik in Polish) began to develop a different model that resolved many of the irregularities. This **heliocentric** model posited that the sun was the fixed center, and Earth was one of the planets in orbit around it. By 1514 he had begun to circulate his findings among a handful of friends. They spent years gathering more precise observational data, and Copernicus continued to refine his hypothesis. His book, *On the Movements of the Heavenly Bodies*, was not published until 1543, the year of his death.

When Western science revived in the 16th century, it did so once again hand-in-hand with Christian faith. It is a modern conceit that science advanced only when it divorced itself from religion; that divorce became finalized only in the 19th century. The Scientific Revolution therefore needs to be understood as an offshoot of religious history.

Copernicus had feared the book would set off a firestorm within the Catholic Church, but it did not. As early as 1536 a scientifically inclined cardinal, Nikolaus von Schönberg, had already written to him, encouraging his work:

> It was several years ago that I first heard of your skills, about which so many people were constantly speaking, and first developed such high regard for you. . . . What I learned was that you had not only mastered the knowledge of the ancient astronomers but had in fact created an entirely new cosmology according to which the Earth moves [in orbit] while the sun actually holds the most fundamental or central place in the universe. . . . At the risk of intruding upon your activities I want to urge you, with the utmost seriousness, to make these discoveries of yours known to scholars, and please to send me (as soon as is feasible) your writings on the workings of the universe, together with your data tables and anything else you may have that pertains to this important matter.

More criticism came from Protestant leaders, for whom the explicit teachings of Scripture carried more weight. Luther himself is often said to have condemned "that damned fool Copernicus" for challenging the authority of Scripture. (In reality, there is little evidence that Luther was fully aware of Copernicus's work.) Church condemnation did come, but not until some six decades later when the debate had shifted to Galileo's elaborations of the heliocentric theory and his claims for the scientific process that propounded it.

Copernicus had prepared for some resistance. In the preface to his book, he directly addressed the reigning pope, Paul III (r. 1534–1549). His book, he said, offered a simple hypothesis, an explanation of planetary movements that accommodated the available data far better than any permutation of the geocentric model. He closed with a dignified appeal to the church's concern for scholarly truth:

> I have no doubt that our most skilled and talented mathematicians will concur with my findings, so long as they are willing to investigate, with all the honest seriousness that scholarship requires, the arguments I have set forth in this book in support of my theories. But still, in order that everyone, both the learned and the nonlearned, may see that I hide from no man's judgment, I have decided to dedicate these findings of mine to Your Holiness, rather than to another, for even in this remote part of the world where I reside Your Holiness is regarded as preeminent in dignity for the position you hold, for your love of learning, and even for your interest in mathematics. . . . And if there should be any amateurs who (not letting their ignorance of mathematics stand in the way of a chance to pass judgment on such matters) presume to attack my theory because it contradicts some passage of Scripture that they misinterpret for their own purposes, I simply do not care; in fact, I dismiss their opinions as mere foolishness. . . . Mathematics is written for mathematicians. . . . I leave it to Your Holiness and all learned mathematicians to judge what I have written.

He defends his method more than his conclusions. What follows, in other words, is a set of mathematical proofs subject only to the critical review of mathematicians. He makes no theological or even astronomical claims, but argues only that his model conforms to the available data more precisely than earlier models.

Word of Copernicus's work spread quickly around Europe, and a number of scholars elaborated on the heliocentric theory. The Danish astronomer Tycho Brahe, for example, devoted his career to making ever more precise chartings of planetary movements and stellar positions. This improved data made possible the next major leap in astronomy, when Brahe's German pupil Johannes Kepler formulated three famous axioms of planetary motion. These axioms hold that the planets move in ellipses around the sun, that they move at nonuniform speeds, and that the

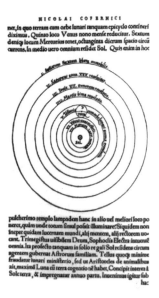

Nicolaus Copernicus   A portrait of Mikołaj Kopernik (Nicolaus Copernicus; 1473–1543) emphasizing his Catholic piety, and a page from his book *On the Revolution of the Heavenly Spheres*, which he published just before his death.

velocity of each planet throughout its orbit is in direct proportion to its distance from the sun at any given moment. Kepler had fought a childhood battle with smallpox that had left him very nearsighted. Unable to gather his own observational data, he used the mountain of astronomical tables and star charts left behind by his teacher. With these, he validated his model with a mathematical precision that few of his contemporaries could equal or even understand. Even Galileo initially ignored it.

GALILEO AND THE TRUTH OF NUMBERS

Galileo Galilei (1564–1642) was a genius in astronomy, mathematics, and physics, as famous in his day as Albert Einstein was in the 20th century. His achievements in any one of those fields alone would warrant his being remembered.[1] Trained in mathematics, which he later taught at the University of Padua, he learned astronomy largely on his own and with the use of his telescope. In *The Starry Messenger*, the first report of his astronomical discoveries in March 1610, he describes the most significant of his discoveries: the moons of Venus. The force of this discovery is often difficult for modern readers to appreciate. The geocentric model made no allowance for smaller bodies in orbit around the planets. Everything, in the classical view, orbited the Earth. Yet here was direct evidence against it.

---

[1]   Galileo was a skilled tinkerer too, renowned for his redesign of the telescope (invented by Hans Lippershey, of the Netherlands) and of the geometric compass (used by surveyors and artillerymen).

Galileo's Drawing of the Surface of the Moon   Galileo Galilei (1564–1642) developed but did not invent the telescope. He was not even the first to write about its uses for astronomy. By the time he published *The Starry Messenger* (1610), in which this sketch of the lunar surface appears, a Jesuit missionary in Beijing had already published a book about the telescope—in Chinese—for Wanli (r. 1572–1620), one of the last of the Ming Dynasty emperors. But Galileo did build the best of the early telescopes, and with it he made the then-astonishing discovery that the moon's surface was rough and pockmarked, as shown above.

The elaborate mathematical arguments of Copernicus and Kepler were easily ignored. By the astronomers' own admission, they were nothing more than conjectures, a way to make the numbers fall into neater computational alignment. Few people then alive even understood them. But Galileo's discovery was as solid and incontrovertible as the New World continents that Cristoforo Colombo had run into in 1492. Anyone with a telescope (and Galileo himself sold them, as a business venture, on the side) could look up in the sky and see Venus's moons for themselves. Galileo's findings were confirmed by none other than Christoph Clavius, the most prominent expert in mathematics and astronomy in the church, and the city of Rome gave Galileo a triumphant welcome in 1611.

Yet years later he was arrested and forced to recant. What had changed? Two factors principally, and Galileo shares in the blame for the first. In 1623 he published a treatise on comets in which he made a crucial mistake: he argued that comets were not physical objects but only optical illusions—tricks of refracted sunlight. Moreover, in putting forth this (wrong) hypothesis, he went out of his way (not unlike Roger Bacon) to insult astronomers who had asserted (correctly) that comets were in fact fiery solid bodies passing through the solar system far beyond the orbit of our moon. Several of those astronomers, however, were highly regarded clerics who taught at the church's college in Rome, and the papal court was in no mood to countenance such outright rudeness. Several years earlier, in 1616, the church had condemned the heliocentric model as contrary to Scripture, and Galileo was given a friendly warning to refrain from promoting or teaching Copernicanism. He complied, for the most part; but the offensive passages in his treatise on comets called for some sort of response.

If Galileo's first problem was scientific and political, his second concerned Scripture. What happens when scientific conclusions and Biblical statements are in conflict? In his letter to the Grand Duchess Christina, published in 1615, he argues that the Bible should be interpreted in a way that makes it compatible with the scientific finding. Here he invited a debate that Copernicus and Kepler had studiously avoided. They had presented heliocentrism as a mathematical theory only. Although aware that it contradicted Scripture, they offered no opinion about which form of truth was preferable. Galileo, however, brought the Copernican claims into direct open conflict with Scripture—and he made it clear that in his mind the Bible had to accommodate science, not vice versa.

That opinion, combined with his offensive mockery of the church's leading astronomers, turned the tide against him. Several clerics denounced him from the pulpit, and the scandal grew until Galileo was finally called before the Inquisition at Rome in 1632. Galileo's crime was not that he accepted the heliocentric theory; it was that he asserted it as incontrovertible truth. Science, Galileo held, was self-confirming. The Bible was not merely wrong, it was irrelevant. "The purpose of the Holy Spirit is to tell us how to get to Heaven," he wrote, "not to tell us how the heavens operate." And that is what brought on his condemnation.

> Galileo, however, brought the Copernican claims into direct open conflict with Scripture—and he made it clear that in his mind the Bible had to accommodate science, not vice versa.

Science and religion in the Greater West had always known tension, but the strain was proof of their close relationship. Apart from Jewish and Muslim scholars, every Western scientist of any note since the fall of the Roman Empire had been a sincere Christian, often at odds with the church but always identifying with it. And every Jewish and Muslim scientist had been a devout, if sometimes unorthodox, believer.[2] The first identifiable atheist—that is, one who expressly denies the existence of any deity whatsoever—in Greater Western history was not a scientist at all but a German seminary dropout. Matthias Knutzen (1646–1675) published three pamphlets in 1674 denying "God, any Authority from On High, and all sects and their ministers." All that is needed to live a moral life, he wrote, is "to harm no one, live honestly, and give each person his due."

Scripture, Galileo implied, allows room to maneuver; science, though, does not. The Church's position—and, to include the Protestants, the churches' position—was that two thousand years of tradition should not be overthrown because of some opaque mathematical formulas that relatively few people understood properly. The problem, essentially, was epistemological rather than theological: What exactly does it mean, "to *know* something"? At what point can mere humans justifiably declare that a given statement is universally true?

---

[2]   Copernicus and Galileo were both devout Catholics, and Brahe and Kepler were pious Protestants.

THE OTHER SCIENTIFIC REVOLUTION: THE COUNCIL OF TRENT, 1546–1563

Epistemology, or the study of nature of knowledge itself, implies teaching, which brings us to how Christian society responded to the challenges of the era. The Protestant Reformation is only the most obvious of the problems it confronted. Just as significant were the growth of modern monarchies, the early stages of capitalism, the missionary challenge of the New World, and the development of the new science. But the period's difficulties can be, and often have been, overstated. Seen in terms of the actual changes it prompted, the early modern crisis paled in comparison with the Middle Ages, when the church reinvented itself from top to bottom in order to help Europe emerge from the post-Carolingian ruin. The Roman Catholic Church of 1100, say, was a radically different institution from what it had been in 900, whereas the church in 1700 remained essentially what it had been in 1500; if anything, it was even more conservatively so. The reputed dying words of Pope Paul IV (r. 1555–1559) provide an apt epilogue to the Renaissance-era papacy: "Of all the pontificates since the time of Saint Peter, mine has been the most lamentable. Oh, how I regret everything that has happened. Pray for me!"

And yet they overstate the case. The church in fact responded vigorously, and, perhaps surprisingly, that response did not exclude the growth of science. One might even call it the other scientific revolution.

———————— + ————————

Reform was certainly needed, and figures like Erasmus and More had spent their lives calling for it. Even the most worldly of Renaissance popes recognized that many of the faithful were put off by the church and its cumbersome institutions. The problem was how to find reforms that would please everybody. Through much of the 14th and 15th centuries, when the Holy See was a political football of the Italian nobility, a movement arose to strengthen the role of general councils in ecclesiastical governance. The popes, many of them more concerned with their personal fates than with the office they held, opposed this "conciliarism" vehemently, but the resulting deadlock only aggravated the problems that both sides were supposedly trying to confront. The success of Protestantism produced urgent calls for a general council; papal dithering only made the calls more insistent.[3] But then, surprisingly, the Protestant juggernaut stalled. By 1540 every state in Europe that would become Protestant had done so; no new national-scale conversions were won by any of the major Protestant branches.

---

3   Pope Leo X (r. 1513–1521) famously dismissed Martin Luther at first as "some drunken German who will repent once he sobers up."

Beginning with Pope Paul III (r. 1534–1549), the court in Rome finally took the lead in bringing on reform. He appointed a commission of high-ranking clerics to investigate church abuses, whose final report, published in 1536, laid bare scores of problems in the administration of the church, the actions of the episcopacies, and shortcomings in parish life. In 1537 he issued a bull condemning the enslavement of the indigenous peoples of the New World; in 1540 he confirmed the formation of the Jesuits, a teaching and missionary order; and in 1542 he authorized the creation of the Holy Office—the Roman Inquisition. Last, after securing guarantees that its proceedings would be subject to papal approval, he called for a full ecumenical council to study and propose solutions to the general reform of Catholic life (which has come to be known as the **Counter-Reformation**). This **Council of Trent**, which convened (with a few intermissions) from 1546 to 1563, was the most important assembly of its kind until the Second Vatican Council of 1963–1965.

Although the religious revolt in northern Europe was obviously its trigger, the Council of Trent was more than a response to Protestantism; efforts at reform had begun long before Luther appeared on the scene. Nevertheless, the council's initial actions offered no hint of compromise but rather highlighted the differences between what it regarded as Catholic truth and Protestant lies. If anything, they asserted the Catholic position with even more force than before. The problem confronting the church, they believed, was not with doctrine itself but with the ways in which doctrine was taught to the people. The changes most needed were therefore in leadership and organization.

After Paul III, Pope Julius III (r. 1550–1555) devoted himself to personal pleasure—in particular, his infatuation with an illiterate, fourteen-year-old street beggar named Innocenzo. Julius moved Innocenzo into the Vatican palace (and the papal bedroom), awarded him several wealthy benefices, appointed him the abbot of the monastery of Mont Saint-Michel, and made him a cardinal. But the popes

Catholic Reform   Pope Paul III (r. 1534–1549), in an oil portrait by Titian (Tiziano Vecellio; 1490–1576) and the high pomp of the Council of Trent (1545–1563), which laid out the plan for the Catholic Counter-Reformation.

who succeeded him pressed the council to reach even farther in its ambition: Paul IV (r. 1555–1559) and Pius IV (1559–1565).[4] The Council ordered a streamlining of the church bureaucracy, outlawed ecclesiastical pluralism (the practice of a single individual holding appointments to serve in multiple parishes of dioceses), and heightened the responsibility of bishops to oversee the life of their provinces. Most important of all, it charged them with improving the education of their clergy and of the flocks they served. To assist them, the church helped to build hundreds of new parish schools to train teachers for them. At the higher levels, the church increased the funding for universities and reorganized curricula.

THE SOCIETY OF JESUS

Several new ecclesiastical orders joined the campaign and dedicated themselves specifically to education: the Ursulines ("Company of Saint Ursula"), founded in 1535 and papally approved in 1544, created a network of schools for girls across Europe and soon in the New World. More famous still was the Society of Jesus, commonly called the **Jesuits**, found by Saint Ignacio de Loyola (1491–1556) in 1540. "A Society founded for a single, central purpose—namely, to strive for the defense and propagation of the Faith, and for the progress of souls in Christian life and doctrine," the Jesuits dedicated themselves to preaching and teaching at all educational levels, although historically they have tended toward higher education. Founded as they were by a former soldier—Loyola, a Spanish noble and career military man, experienced a conversion while recuperating from severe battle wounds received in 1521—the Jesuits formed a compact and highly centralized organization. They took vows of poverty, chastity, and absolute obedience to their superiors, especially to the pope, and became the church's most successful tool in bringing Christianity to the outside world.

Within ten years of their founding, the Jesuits had established mission schools in India and Japan, and by 1600 they had extended their reach into South and North America and into sub-Saharan Africa. And since the Council of Trent particularly emphasized the doctrinal point that for Catholics, unlike Protestants, doing "good works" was an essential requirement of Christian living, the reformed church stepped up its involvement in charitable work among the world's poorest peoples. The combined efforts of these new orders, especially in their conflation of schoolroom teaching and service, helped gain many converts in the New World. They even returned many Protestant believers in southern Germany, parts of Bohemia, and throughout Poland-Lithuania to Catholicism.

---

4   Julius is the last pope known to have been sexually active and the last pope to have been explicitly homosexual.

Education requires books, however, and education in the Catholic faith faced a further obstacle: non-Catholic books were easily available too. The post-Trent church confronted the problem—or thought they had done so—by producing an **Index of Forbidden Books**. The first version of the *Index*, promulgated in 1559, was regarded as too severe in its strictures, and a revised and slightly moderated version appeared in 1564. The *Index* was continually updated over the centuries, with over forty editions published between 1564 and its suppression in 1966, making it the longest institutionalized censorship in Western history. It was also, arguably, the least effective, since few of the condemned books ever went out of print. In fact, the *Index* represented a perfect shopping list for individuals who wanted to read materials

Jesuit Missionaries   The Jesuits were pivotal in revitalizing the Catholic Church's evangelical and educational missions. In this 18th-century painting from Lima, Peru, the order's founder, St. Ignatius Loyola, appears in the center, flanked by two loyal followers, St. Francis Borja and St. Francis Xavier. At the bottom, figures representing Africa, Asia, North America, and South America bear witness to the extent of Jesuit missionary activity.

officially denied them. True, 90 percent of the books ever placed on the list were dense theological treatises that non-Catholics or lay Catholics were unlikely ever to read in the first place. Even so, the 1564 *Index* singles out quite an impressive list of writers. It condemned the works of Pietro Aretino, Sir Francis Bacon, Jean Calvin, Nicolaus Copernicus, Desiderius Erasmus, Henry VIII of England, Martin Luther, Niccolò Machiavelli, François Rabelais, and William Tyndale (an early translator of the Bible into English). Also forbidden were the Qur'an and the Talmud. Later editions added the *Essays* of Michel de Montaigne and the scientific writings of Johannes Kepler and Galileo Galilei.

Jesuit training emphasized all-round education, so that society members would be prepared for any educational or missionary challenge the papacy might throw their way. Even today, the training of a Jesuit takes up to thirteen years. Though grounded in classical humanism, Jesuit education branched off into mathematics and astronomy. Several of the leading scholars of the age were Jesuits. Fr. Christoph Scheiner (1573–1650) was a German astronomer who discovered sunspots independently of Galileo; he also wrote one of the first treatises on the physiology of the human eye. Fr. Alexius Sylvius Polonus (1593–1653) was a Polish astronomer like Copernicus and specialized in the design of ever more

refined telescopes. Although primarily an engineer, he nevertheless used his instruments, mastery of mathematics, and Copernican theory to compose a new
work on the design of the solar calendar.

Another influential Jesuit, Fr. Carlo Borromeo (1538–1584), was no scholar
but dedicated his career to promoting a better-educated clergy. Coming from a
wealthy aristocratic family (his mother was a Medici), he used his personal fortune
and the large income from his position as archbishop of Milan to found numerous
colleges and seminaries. He also established the Academy of the Vatican Nights, an
informal symposium to keep church leaders informed of the newest learning.

Most Jesuit astronomers accepted Galileo's work up through *The Starry
Messenger*. Fr. Roberto Bellarmine (1542–1621) did, even after he was made
a cardinal and placed in charge of the Inquisition. A theologian by training,
Bellarmine first attracted attention as a professor at the Roman College, where,
in addition to teaching priests-in-training, he wrote the four-volume *Disputation
Regarding the Controversies in the Christian Faith* (1593), in which he systematically confronted the theological positions of the leading strains of Protestantism. The English and German governments in fact endowed several university
professorships whose specific mission was to devise counterarguments against
Bellarmine's book.

When Galileo's work was investigated by the tribunal in 1610, Bellarmine understood the science well enough to accept his discoveries—and arranged for the
dropping of charges against him. He added a private warning not to proclaim Copernicanism publicly. Galileo followed the advice and pursued other research until
1623, when a cardinal who was friendly to him and supported his research—Maffeo
Barberini, another Jesuit—was elected as Pope Urban VIII (r. 1623–1644). Galileo
took this as a sign that the heliocentric theory was finally going to win public acceptance, and so he turned again from his work in physics to astronomy. By 1632
he had written his treatise *The Two Chief World Systems*, but he blundered. The new
treatise was written in the form of a dialogue between geocentric and heliocentric
astronomers, and even though Galileo was careful to make the heliocentrists capitulate at the end, he nevertheless made the old-style astronomers look foolish. Even
worse, he named the spokesman for the traditionalists Simplicio ("Simpleton"). He
should have known better. When Inquisitors petitioned to place Galileo on trial, an
irritated Urban allowed them to proceed.

As Galileo learned, tone matters. The church had promoted scientific work for
centuries and had a tradition of accepting ideas and discoveries not immediately
reconcilable with doctrine. It understood that knowledge proceeds by probing,
doubting, and testing. What matters is patience and humility. Galileo had sufficient
patience but lacked modesty when it came to his work. Other Catholic scientists of
the era presented new findings every bit as jarring to traditional sensibilities as

Galileo Galilei, by an Unknown Painter   To the right is a depiction of his trial by the Inquisition.

Galileo's, but presented them as discoveries in progress rather than indisputable truths. A German named Athanasius Kircher (1601–1680) was a pioneer of microbiology and linguistics.[5] An Italian physicist named Francesco Maria Grimaldi (1618–1663) made the first observations that led to the wave theory of light; he also compiled the first map of the lunar surface that described its geological features in detail. These men understood scientific research as a never-ending process, a slow groping toward truth, but one that can never declare final success. The infinite complexity of the universe precludes such hubris. But Galileo effectively altered the rules, or at least claimed that the rules were alterable and that pure truth—final and complete—was attainable. His revolutionary breakthrough was not heliocentrism in itself but the argument that the scientific method justifies itself, ratifies itself. Biblical authority and intellectual tradition mean nothing in the face of empirical data and rigorous mathematical logic. The separation of science from religion, in other words, was not a divorce. It was an annulment.

> Biblical authority and intellectual tradition mean nothing in the face of empirical data and rigorous mathematical logic. The separation of science from religion, in other words, was not a divorce. It was an annulment.

INQUISITION AND INQUIRY

Inquisition is a historical term, a word denoting a specific phenomenon of the past. One could even call it a technical term since it describes a precisely defined and regulated judicial process established by the Catholic Church in 1184. That process

---

5   Kircher was the first to describe microbes, and he correctly identified ancient Egyptian hieroglyphics with the Coptic language. He also wrote an entire encyclopedia of the Chinese language.

evolved over time, naturally, but even into the 19th century the word referred to a special type of investigation, conducted by ecclesiastical or secular authority, for the sake of public safety. To this extent, it is like the word "fascism"—a multifaceted but technically precise historical referent. But Inquisition, like fascism, is also a popular term, loosely used to describe almost any investigative process or institution that one deems profoundly unfair.

The Inquisition of the early modern era differed significantly from its medieval forebear. Pope Lucius III (r. 1181–1185) had established the Inquisition as a way of stopping the unjust execution of people for dissident religious beliefs. False beliefs within Christianity—heresy—was a sin against the church but was also a crime against the secular medieval state, and in the 12th and 13th centuries the aristocratic courts of Europe were quick to act against heretics—convicting them, killing them, and confiscating their property. The church took a dim view of heresy but championed the idea of intellectual free inquiry. Lucius's decree of 1184 helped to codify a strict, narrow definition of actionable heresy and brought state exercise of authority over heretics under the church's jurisdiction. As brutal and backward as the medieval Inquisition is to modern sensibilities, it is important to note that the number of people killed for dissident Christian beliefs across Europe declined sharply after the Inquisition's establishment.

Even so, ugly is ugly; and even without the use of physical torture (and most inquisitions never resorted to it) the threatening nature of the inquiry, its potential for unspeakable cruelty, was obvious and coercive. That ugliness grew, and the cruelty became a standard operating procedure, in the early modern era when the Inquisition was officially taken over as an institution of the governments. In the 16th and 17th centuries the monarchical states in France, Portugal, and Spain assumed control of it—as did the lesser princes in Germany, Italy, and the Low Countries—and used it to terrorize dissidents and control political opponents. Churchmen actively colluded in the process, certainly, but the notorious Inquisition of the time was as much an indicator of the loss of church power as it was an index of religious and intellectual intolerance.

Although some supported the idea, the Inquisition was not the weapon of choice for dealing with the Protestant Reformation. The Protestants, after all, declared their own separation from Rome and hence no longer came under the church's jurisdiction; later, the policy of *cuius regio, eius religio* granted a certain degree of toleration across the Catholic-Protestant divide. The Inquisition instead focused on three principal targets: witches, false converts from Judaism and Islam, and scientists. The witchcraft craze has been discussed. The issue of false converts was a complex one, arising from financial envy, racial prejudice, and unease about aristocratic stature. The conversion of nonbelievers to Christianity was a desire central to Christian aspirations since the dawn of the religion, but fanatical worries arose from the 15th century onward that many of Europe's converts were converts in name only—people who publicly proclaimed their Christianity but privately retained their Jewish or Muslim practice. Such suspects were referred to as crypto-Jews and crypto-Muslims.

The concern was not merely that they were religious frauds but that there was something intrinsic to their makeup. Some element in their collective bloodlines, it was feared, permanently tainted their Christianity and kept them from a genuine and full commitment. That would have been bad enough, for most of the bigots of the time; but what made matters even worse was the upward social mobility of the professional classes of the Renaissance and after. Noble families in economic decline often married wealthy, ambitious urbanites from the rising merchant economy. For them, the danger of exposing their pure noble blood to the inferior and possibly diseased elements in Jewish or Muslim blood set off a clamor of concern. Crypto-Jews and crypto-Muslims, in other words, were perceived as a threat to noble security and privilege as much as a threat to faith.

The last class of Inquisitorial victims, the proponents of the new science, are the most difficult to generalize about. Their names have become causes célèbres over the centuries. Giordano Bruno (1548–1600), a Dominican friar, mathematician, and cosmologist, provides the most dramatic example. Bruno had little training in science but much amateur enthusiasm for it. Seizing eagerly upon Copernican

Expulsion of the Moriscos from Spain   This painting by Pere Oromig depicts the expulsion of the Moriscos (suspected pseudo-converts from Islam) from the coastal town of Vinaròs, in eastern Spain, in 1609. Moriscos comprised nearly one-third of the population of this part of Spain at the time.

heliocentrism, he soon went further—without any good scientific reason for doing so. He argued that the universe is infinitely large, that the fixed stars were suns like ours that have planets of their own in orbit around them, and that the existence of life on these planets is a likelihood. He consequently denied the special nature of human beings as part of God's Creation, which was tantamount to denying the special role of Christ as the savior of humankind. His admirers over time have given him too much credit: he spun out so many ideas about science that the chance of at least some of them turning out to be true was high. He was an intelligent man, but it is a mistake to consider him a scientist in the sense that Galileo was. Nevertheless, he fell victim to the Inquisition. The court followed its usual tactic of delay, negotiation, and appeal; if Bruno would have only agreed to keep a low profile for a few years, he might well have been given his freedom. But he refused and was executed in a public square in Rome, with his ashes dumped into the Tiber River.

The most famous case of all is that of Galileo. Two inquiries into his science occurred, one in 1616 and another in 1633. The 1616 tribunal, led by Cardinal Bellarmine, reiterated the church's partial condemnation of heliocentrism and let Galileo go with a warning. Copernican theory could continue to be discussed and investigated, so long as it was presented only as a mathematical hypothesis instead of incontrovertible truth. Sixteen years later, having won further fame with his discoveries in optics, physics, and the study of tides, as well as his mathematical theory of infinite sets, Galileo breached his 1616 agreement. In his *Dialogue on the Two Chief World Systems*, he argued openly for the heliocentric model as the indisputable truth. Hence the Inquisition's action against him arose from the complaint that he had broken a contract with the church as much as from his scientific views. The formal judgment rendered by the tribunal reads as follows.

> Seeing that you, Galileo, . . . were denounced by this Holy Office in 1615 for asserting the truth of the false doctrine, maintained by some, that the sun is the unmoving center of the universe and that the Earth moves in orbit around it . . .
>
> And seeing that . . . it was agreed that if you refused to stop [proclaiming this theory as decided truth] this Holy Office could order you to abandon the teaching altogether . . . and that you could therefore be subject to imprisonment . . .
>
> And seeing that . . . your *Dialogue on the Two Chief World Systems* has recently been published . . . in which you try to give the impression that the matter is still undecided, calling it only "probable" . . . and that you confess that numerous passages of the book are written in such a way that a reader could in fact draw the conclusion that the arguments for [heliocentrism] are irrefutable . . .

We conclude, proclaim, sentence, and pronounce that . . . you have made yourself strongly suspected of heresy.

His punishment was house arrest and penance, and the Inquisition ordered his *Dialogue* to be burned. Galileo agreed and spent his last years in quiet work.[6] In 1638 he published his last major work, the *Discourses on Two New Sciences*, which treats problems of motion, acceleration, and mathematical theory. His trouble with the Inquisition was clearly related to, but not solely composed of, his belief in heliocentrism itself; rather, the immediate issue was his breaking of a sacred vow.

The more general and important issue, though, was in the debate about truth itself. Discussing Copernican theory was something the church's own astronomers did with enthusiasm. But to leap from enthusiasm to dogmatic certainty was

Measuring Acceleration   This model reproduces Galileo's experiment for measuring the acceleration of falling bodies. By placing bells at various places along the inclined plane and measuring time via the small pendulum at the plane's top, Galileo was able to show that the distance traveled by a ball rolled down the plane was always proportional to the square of the time elapsed. (A medieval scholar, Nicholas Oresme (1320–1382), had already determined that, but his discovery had been forgotten by Galileo's time.) More truly original was Galileo's determination, contrary to Aristotelian physics, that the speed with which objects fall is a vacuum—hence neutralizing the effects of air resistance—is independent of their mass.

---

[6]   The legend that Galileo at his verdict muttered under his breath "Even so, it moves" is most likely false. The first instance of it appears in a fanciful Spanish painting after his death.

something few were prepared to do, and the church believed it had a responsibility to warn people not to rush into making that leap. The case of Galileo and the Inquisition marks an important turning point in intellectual history—the rise of a belief in *quantification*. If the numbers in Theory A work more precisely and consistently than the numbers in Theory B, this belief goes, then Theory A is for that reason alone accepted as true. But is that really the case? By every imaginable quantitative index, the United States won the Vietnam War—but did it? Conversely, all of the numerical data published by Bernard Madoff for twenty years showed that his investment schemes were fraudulent—and yet knowledgeable investors still poured billions of dollars into his criminal business. Anyone who has ever argued that their scores on standardized exams do not reflect the reality of their knowledge and skills is holding to a position consonant with that of the Inquisition. Right or wrong, the Inquisition trusted God's Word more than it trusted mathematical formulas.

> Anyone who has ever argued that their scores on standardized exams do not reflect the reality of their knowledge and skills is holding to a position consonant with that of the Inquisition. Right or wrong, the Inquisition trusted God's Word more than it trusted mathematical formulas.

THE REVOLUTION BROADENS

It is unclear how much all of these discoveries and debates mattered outside the walls of academia and of the church. History books always present intellectual infighting as high drama, but outside the ivory tower academic squabbles often appear squalid or even silly. (Is it a coincidence that novels about life in academia are always comedies?) To a 17th-century peasant shoveling manure out of a cow stall, it probably did not matter whether that manure was at the fixed center of the universe or if it was in orbit around the sun. All he cared about was getting it out of the barn before the landlord came and beat him for not keeping up with his duties. But discoveries in other fields mattered a great deal at the time, because of their immediate practical value. Increasingly, too, they mattered because of ethical tensions as older taboos declined, especially in regard to Islam.

In medicine, William Harvey (1578–1657) identified the circulation of blood in the human body via the intricate system of heart, veins, and arteries. The existence of internal organs and tissues came as no surprise, but physicians had never understood their individual functions or their working together as a system. Harvey's work opened the door to comprehending the human body as an integrated organism. In chemistry, Robert Boyle (1627–1691), extrapolating from the atomic theory inherited from ancient Greece, described the molecular structure of compounds. In physics he both determined the role of air in the propagation of sound and derived **Boyle's law**, which states that the volume and pressure of a gas at constant temperature vary inversely. These discoveries helped in deriving new chemicals and stabilizing air pumps. In biology Robert Hooke (1635–1703) employed a compound microscope to discover the cellular structure of plants, which, when studied over time, gave hints of the actual process of growth. Organic life, Hooke was the first to assert, is an ongoing process of growth and decay according to natural principles. By analyzing fossils he came close to developing a full-blown theory of evolution almost two hundred years before Darwin.

All this points to an important development. If Galileo had effectively removed God from the workings of the physical cosmos, later scientists began to discover the structures that took the place of Providence. However useful these discoveries might have proved, could they compensate for the loss of a divine purpose in life? When one takes away the idea that the universe functions, however mysteriously, according to a heavenly plan, then one risks the fear of a random, meaningless existence. The poet John Donne (1572–1631) described this feeling

TABLE 13.1　Major Works of the Scientific Revolution, 1500–1700

1543	*On the Revolutions of the Heavenly Spheres*	Nicolaus Copernicus (1473–1543)
1543	*On the Makeup of the Human Body*	Andreas Vesalius (1514–1564)
1600	*On the Magnet and Magnetic Bodies*	William Gilbert (1544–1603)
1609	*The New Astronomy or Celestial Physics*	Johannes Kepler (1571–1630)
1610	*The Starry Messenger*	Galileo Galilei (1564–1642)
1614	*The Wonderful Law of Logarithms*	John Napier (1550–1617)
1619	*The Harmonies of the World*	Johannes Kepler
1620	*The New Instrument*	Sir Francis Bacon (1561–1626)
1628	*On the Motion of the Heart and the Blood*	William Harvey (1578–1657)
1632	*Dialogue on the Two Chief World Systems*	Galileo Galileo
1635	Academie française founded	
1637	*Discourse on Method*	René Descartes (1596–1650)
1653	*On the Arithmetical Triangle*	Blaise Pascal (1623–1662)
1658	*The Spirit of Geometry*	
1660	Royal Society of London founded	
1660	*New Experiments Physico-Mechanical*	Robert Boyle (1627–1691)
1661	*The Skeptical Chymist*	
1687	*Principia Mathematica*	Sir Isaac Newton (1643–1727)

of loss and confusion in "An Anatomie of the World" (1611), written for an aristo-cratic patron on the anniversary of the death of his wife:

> Then, as mankind, so is the world's whole frame
> Quite out of joint, almost created lame,
> For, before God had made up all the rest,
> Corruption ent'red, and deprav'd the best;
> It seiz'd the angels, and then first of all
> The world did in her cradle take a fall,
> And turn'd her brains, and took a general maim,
> Wronging each joint of th'universal frame.
> The noblest part, man, felt it first; and then
> Both beasts and plants, curs'd in the curse of man.
> So did the world from the first hour decay,
> That evening was beginning of the day,
> And now the springs and summers which we see,
> Like sons of women after fifty be.
> And new philosophy calls all in doubt,
> The element of fire is quite put out,
> The sun is lost, and th'earth, and no man's wit
> Can well direct him where to look for it.
> And freely men confess that this world's spent,
> When in the planets and the firmament
> They seek so many new; they see that this
> Is crumbled out again to his atomies.
> 'Tis all in pieces, all coherence gone,
> All just supply, and all relation;
> Prince, subject, father, son, are things forgot,
> For every man alone thinks he hath got
> To be a phoenix, and that then can be
> None of that kind, of which he is, but he.
> This is the world's condition now.

The poem expresses above all the pain that follows a great personal loss. Yet it succeeds because the dread of a shapeless and unintelligible universe was felt so widely at the time. "The world's condition now" seemed one of decay and doubt; ordered existence is so jumbled and out of joint that one does not even know "where to look for it." Even God himself, the poem laments, could do nothing to set matters aright, since "corruption ent'red, and deprav'd the best" before a divine order could be introduced.

Sic Transit Gloria Mundi   Done in Spain in 1655, this painting serves as a sly cautionary comment. A sleeping nobleman dreams of wealth, power, knowledge, art, beauty, and military prowess, only to have an angel enter the dream, holding a banner that reminds him that death is the end of all things.

It is a powerful poem that should be read whole; the passage here comprises perhaps one-sixth of it. Not all scientific discoveries, it asserts, are advances, for they come at a cost. Take the discovery of the circulation of blood. This breakthrough occurred not simply because William Harvey happened to come along and figure it out. It became possible only with the dissection of human bodies—corpses, mostly, but some still alive.

THE ETHICAL COSTS OF SCIENCE

Deep cultural taboos against the desecration of the body had forbidden dissections for millennia. These taboos predate Christianity and even Judaism. The elaborate funeral rites of the Egyptians and Mesopotamians, with their careful cleansing and wrapping of the body, the incantation of prayers and hymns, the presentation of offerings, the ceremonial burial or burning of the remains under the guidance of priests—all these document a powerful need to treat the dead with decorum. At the end of Homer's *Iliad*, Achilles drags Hector's dead body behind his chariot as he circles Troy. For Achilles it is a moment of triumph; for the reader or listener, it is a moment of moral horror: How can the great Greek hero behave so monstrously? Does Achilles even deserve our interest? To an ancient audience, the scene cast doubt on all that had gone before. In Sophocles' great tragedy *Antigone*, the drama turns on the treatment of the dead. Before the story begins, Antigone's brother Polyneices had led a rebellion against King Creon, who defeated the rebels on the battlefield and ordered that their corpses be left to rot in the field, "prey to the wild dogs and vultures." Antigone's tragedy is to be caught between the king's command and the laws of her religion, which demand proper burial rites for the dead. At the play's conclusion she chooses to bury her brother and accepts her own inevitable execution for disobeying the king.

William Harvey was able to make his great discovery because, by the 17th century, many Western states had come to believe that certain individuals *deserved* to have their bodies desecrated; it was a final supreme punishment for the worthlessness of their lives. After Harvey's breakthrough, detailed knowledge of the operation of the internal organs followed quickly, but these advances required a new horror: the careful cutting open of victims while they were still alive. Harvey himself participated in some of this. The wretches to whom this was done spent weeks, and sometimes months, in constant agony.[7]

Who were these miserable people? It varied from state to state, but in general the possibility of dissection after death awaited anyone convicted of murder, treason, or counterfeiting. Theft too opened the door to the cutting table, if the person one stole from was well-connected. (Heretics and witches did not need to fear the dissector's knife; they were burned at the stake. Besides, it was assumed that they were unnatural and so would not contribute to the understanding of normal human physiology.) A hardness of heart toward certain sectors of society had to exist before Harvey could make his discovery. Many people felt a concern that scientific knowledge can come at too high a price, ethically speaking, for the benefits it brings. Even today, people today seldom stop to wonder where the thousands of cadavers used each year in our medical schools come from. Individuals who donate their bodies to science make up only a fraction of the bodies used. The rest are the unclaimed remains of America's homeless population, donated by our county morgues. Practices vary from state to state in the United States. Illinois, for example, requires county medical examiners to keep unclaimed bodies for sixty days before releasing them to medical schools; Maryland requires a wait of only fourteen days. Medical examiners in New York, however, are allowed to release unclaimed cadavers within twenty-four hours.

---

[7] Physicians would make strategically placed incisions, then peel away layers of skin and muscle, in order to observe, for example, the full process of digestion from stomach to bowel.

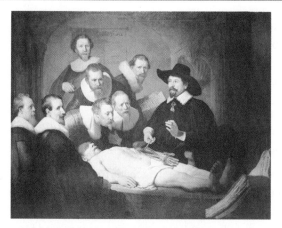 

Two Views of Human Dissection   On the left, Rembrandt van Rijn (1606–1669) shows a dignified exhibition of the start of a lesson on human anatomy; at this time, religious and civil law permitted a handful of dissections to be performed, under strictly regulated conditions. On the right, William Hogarth (1697–1764) shows a considerably more careless and cavalier approach, after Absolutist law permitted the dissection of those convicted of felonies.

But the picture becomes cloudier the more we look at it. Dissections actually were fairly common in the Middle Ages in the Mediterranean regions of Europe and in the Middle East. In Muslim Spain a physician named Ibn Zuhr [A] (1091–1161) performed dissections for research and several autopsies. He was in fact the first physician to deny that the human body was composed of four humors—though he found few people who believed him—and he invented the medical procedure now known as tracheotomy. A physician to Saladin himself, al-Baghdadi [P] (1162–1231), anatomized the corpses of a famine that struck Egypt in 1200, where al-Baghdadi had traveled in order to meet the great Maimonides.

In Christian Europe decrees forbidding the dissection of human remains for the purpose of transporting them to a distant burial site appeared as early as the 1160s, but these were not prohibitions of dissection generally. When in the Third Crusade (1189–1193) the German emperor Frederick Barbarossa (r. 1152–1190) drowned in a river in Asia Minor, his troops, wanting to bury him whole in Jerusalem, tried to preserve his body in vinegar. The human body, it turns out, does not pickle very well, and as Frederick decomposed, the crusaders buried his flesh, organs, and bones in three separate sites. By the late 13th century, in fact, dissections for the teaching of anatomy were standard in the leading medical schools such as the University of Montpellier. At the University of Bologna, another center for medical research and teaching, dissections were performed annually from 1315 on and were made available to the public. It was only in northern Europe that human dissections were both taboo and illegal, and those countries had a less developed scientific tradition. England forbade human dissections until the 16th century, and

Law in the Ottoman Empire   A page from a legal handbook, *The Confluence of the Currents (Multaka al-abhur)* by Ibrahim al-Halabi (1459–1549). Al-Halabi was from Aleppo and spent the first half of his long life in Syria and Egypt, studying and then teaching Hanafi law—one of the four main schools of legal thought in Islam. Around 1500 he moved to Istanbul and became the imam at the great mosque built by the sultan Mehmed II (r. 1451–1481). The *Multaka*, published in 1517 and shown here with some of its many annotations by later writers, remained the authoritative Hanafi text for the next three hundred years.

even after authorizing them on criminals, the law permitted a total of only ten per year throughout the kingdom.[8] Thus the acceptance of dissection came specifically in Protestant Europe, where it was reserved for social malefactors.

THE ISLAMIC RETREAT FROM SCIENCE

The ethical cost of science detached from religious faith may not have troubled the Muslim world in the same way as it did in parts, at least, of the Christian West. At least it seems that way, but science had largely disappeared from Muslim intellectual culture, displaced by legal and theological studies, historical writing, and poetry. From the 7th to the 11th centuries the Islamic world had excelled in every science—medicine, physics, astronomy, mathematics—on both the theoretical and practical levels, leaving Latin Europe far behind. By the 13th century, however, the Latin West had taken the lead. Throughout the Renaissance, much of the Islamic world was too engulfed in warfare and internal strife to continue supporting scientific academies and observatories. The arrival of the Ottomans and Mongols, the rise to power of the Safavids in Persia, and the political recalibrations all three caused drove intellectual effort into philosophical and historical pursuits in the effort to redefine the very nature of Islamic identity. The new conservative element in Islam, exemplified by Ibn Taymiyya in Damascus, dominated the curricula in the madrasas from the 14th century onward and kept the schools' focus intently on the Qur'an, hadith, and sunnah. Their goal was to produce pious and obedient Muslims, not to advance learning. Memorization of the traditional canon was the goal, not the pursuit of new knowledge. Except for Mamluk Egypt, science in the Islamic world stagnated in the early modern era.

This decline did not go unnoticed. The great scholar Mustafa Katip Çelebi [T] (1609–1657) famously bemoaned the shortcomings of his age:

> There are so many ignorant people ... their minds as dead as rocks, paralyzed in thoughtless imitation of the ancients. Rejecting and belittling all

---

[8]   The Murder Act of 1752 finally allowed the body of executed murderers to be available for dissection. France, Germany, and the Low Countries allowed the anatomization of anyone convicted of gross felonies.

new knowledge without even a pause to give it any consideration, they pass themselves off as learned men but really are just ignoramuses who know nothing about the world or the heavens.... The [Qur'anic] admonition— "Have they not contemplated the kingdom of Heaven and Earth?" [7.184]— means nothing at all to them, and they seem to think that to "contemplate the Earth and sky" means to stare at them like a cow.

He was not alone in his complaint. Even one of the Mughal emperors of Muslim India, Muhi ad-Din Muhammad Aurangzeb [P] (r. 1658–1707), lamented the fall in intellectual stature of Islam. In a diatribe against one of his early tutors, he harshly condemned what passed for education in the Muslim world:

> And what were some of the things you taught me? You taught me that France was a small island whose greatest king had previously been the king of Portugal, then of Holland, and then of England! You taught me that the kings of France and of Spain are just like our own petty provincial princes! ... God be praised! What impressive knowledge of geography and history you had! Wasn't it your duty to teach me about the ways of the world's nations—their exports, their military might, their methods of warfare, their customs and religions, their styles of government, their diplomatic aims? ... Instead, all you thought I needed to know was Arabic grammar and law, as though I was a judge or jurist.... By the time my education was finished I knew nothing at all of any science or art, except how to toss off some obscure technical terms that no one really understands!

Throughout much of the Ottoman Empire, frustration at the increasingly arid curriculum of the madrasas drove the more creative minds on to new schools known as *khanqas*, where the emphasis was on Sufi mysticism. Poetry, music, and metaphysical writing formed the core of this schooling, much of it powerfully imaginative and emotive. (Graduates from the khanqas frequently celebrated the completion of their studies by hurling the textbooks from their madrasa years into wells.) But science was still ignored. Memorization and transmission trumped exploration at every turn, leaving the European world unchallenged in its pursuit of scientific truth.

THINKING ABOUT TRUTH

Having severed its connection with the religious intellectual tradition, European science needed new standards. That includes standards of practice, criteria for determining the quality of evidence and argument, and principles for defining scientific truth. Without such agreement, scientific progress would be fitful at best, permanently hobbled at worst. Suppose one conducts an experiment several times and always achieves the same result. At what point may one legitimately conclude that this result is *always* the result—the natural and inevitable result of that experiment? Five times? Five hundred times? Five thousand times? When does it cease to be a mere result and become a conclusion? When does a general conclusion become an accepted scientific theory, and when does it finally become—the Holy Grail of research—a law of nature? Starting with Galileo and those who supported him, science had sloughed off its ancient standards and criteria but had yet to agree upon new ones to replace them. Even science, it turned out, needs a philosophy.

The 17th century was replete with efforts to establish this new philosophy, as new findings emerged from laboratories and lecture halls across Europe. Two of the most significant figures in this effort were Sir Francis Bacon (1561–1626) and René Descartes (1596–1650), and Isaac Newton (1642–1727) then made their ideas the foundations for mathematically precise scientific laws.

Francis Bacon we have already introduced. As the son of a career courtier, he grew up in high society, learned its manners, and became accustomed to its privileges. (His father, Sir Nicholas Bacon, had been the lord keeper of the Great Seal to Elizabeth I.) He worked as a lawyer and held a seat in Parliament. In 1589 he finally gained his first position in the royal administration and worked his way up, until, in the reign of James I (r. 1603–1625), he made it to the top of the pile, serving as lord chancellor and—a last plum—his father's old position as keeper of the Great Seal. But Bacon had expensive tastes. Even with all his income, he built up enormous debts, which may or may not have led to his taking bribes. Scandal swirled around him for several years as his enemies and creditors colluded to bring him down. In 1621 he finally fell from power in disgrace. Though he was allowed to keep his properties and aristocratic titles, he was barred from all political life and from most of privileged society.

A profoundly cautious man, except when it came to his spending habits, he advocated an uncompromising empirical approach to all knowledge, the gradual acquisition of discrete fact after fact, observation after observation, all of them subjected to repeated testing to insure their accuracy, until one has finally assembled enough data to hazard a general hypothesis. Mankind is prone to drawing hasty assumptions, he argued in *The New Atlantis*, and the only antidote is the patient accumulation of tested and retested facts.

Francis Bacon   Sir Francis Bacon
(1561–1626) in all his finery, before his fall.

Roger Bacon, the medieval Franciscan, had already identified four barriers to intellectual progress, errors so common as to be nearly universal:

> There are, in fact, four distinct impediments along the pathway to Truth—stumbling blocks, if you will, that get in the way of every man, no matter how learned he may be, and frustrate anyone who strives to reach the Truth. These impediments are: first, the precedents established by ill-equipped earlier authorities; second, long-established customs; third, the passionate sentiments of the ignorant masses; and fourth, our own habits of hiding our ignorance by the ostentatious display of what we think we do know.

Francis Bacon likewise identified four problems, which he called "illusions" (*idola* in Latin). Here he located the source of error in human nature, our own habits of thinking, the words we use, and tradition. While the correlation is not exact, he clearly had the earlier Bacon in mind:

> There are four types of illusions that bedevil the human mind— illusions to which, in order to keep them distinct, I have attached particular names. These are the illusions of the tribe, illusions of the den, illusions of the marketplace, [and] finally illusions of the theater. ...
>
> The *illusions of the tribe* are the fallacies inherent in human nature, ... [above all] the human tendency to consider all things in relation to itself, whereas everything that we perceive via our senses and reason is actually just a reflection of ourselves, not of the universe. The human mind resembles nothing so much as a flawed mirror, and like such a mirror it imposes its own characteristics upon whatever it reflects, and distorts and disfigures it accordingly.
>
> The *illusions of the den* are the fallacies inherent in each individual. Every mind possesses—in addition to the fallacies common to all men everywhere—its own individual den or cavern whose qualities intercept and corrupt the light of Nature as it receives it. This may result from each person's individual and unique disposition, from his education, his interaction with others, or his reading. ...
>
> There are also what I call the *illusions of the marketplace*, the illusions created by the daily interactions and conversations we have with each other—for we speak through language but words have been formed arbitrarily ... and they throw everything into confusion. ...
>
> Finally, the fallacies I call the *illusions of the theater*. By this term I mean those mistakes that creep into men's minds from the teachings of different

philosophies and from erroneous arguments. We must regard every philosophical system yet designed or imagined as nothing more than a play that has been staged and performed—a charade, in other words.

He saw scientific thinking as the careful piling up of individual bricks of knowledge to create a solid edifice. But Bacon himself never did any actual science; a wealthy aristocrat and career administrator, he was accustomed to telling other people how to do their jobs. Descartes, on the other hand, practiced what he preached.

DESCARTES AND THE QUEST FOR TRUTH

René Descartes received a good Jesuit education as a youth, but when he left school he was, he wrote, "filled with so much doubt and false knowledge that I came to think that all my efforts to learn had done nothing but increase my ignorance." In 1618 he met a gifted Dutch mathematician named Isaac Beeckman (1588–1637), and for entertainment they invented mathematical problems for each other. From this sort of play Descartes came to realize that geometric forms likes lines and curves, when marked on a graph, could be described by algebraic formulas. Thus was born **analytical geometry**, a discovery that set the trajectory for Descartes's intellectual life. As he began to elaborate on his original finding in 1619, he all but disappeared for nine years—moving from city to city, from France to Italy and the Netherlands, never telling anyone his addresses (which he changed regularly anyway), and gradually selling off the properties he had inherited from his parents. "To live well, live in secret" became a favorite personal motto. He emerged from self-exile in 1628 in the Netherlands, where he remained for twenty years, though still moving frequently. He moved to Sweden in 1649 at the request of its queen, who appointed him her tutor, but caught pneumonia and died in February 1650.

Descartes's greatest achievements were in mathematics and philosophy.[9] The invention of analytical geometry, apart from its inherent value, made possible the later discovery of calculus and mathematical analysis (differential equations and the like). His best-known work, however, remains the *Discourse on Method* (1637), which he wrote as an introduction to a volume of several scientific papers. In it he presents not only his own working method as a scientist but a creed, a set of principles that guide one to true knowledge, a hybrid of science and philosophy.

---

[9]   Descartes also made numerous advances in optics, meteorology, physics, and even physiology. As a young man, he dissected cows.

He vows "never to accept something as true which I did not distinctly know for myself to be true." Rather than encouraging skepticism and doubt, however, Descartes advocates passionately for certainty. Doubt is not a philosophy, but merely a tool—and Descartes detested thinkers like Montaigne who seemed to him to regard skepticism as the end point of human endeavor. For Descartes, it is the point at which one needs to start thinking the hardest. But what does "knowing" consist of? And what, precisely, is truth?

Descartes   René Descartes (1580–1666), the French mathematician and philosopher.

Descartes begins with a distrust of the senses. The data we gather about the world through our senses cannot be fully trusted for the simple reason that our sense perceptions are imperfect. That includes things we observe with our eyes, or the sensations that derive from touch or smell. Optical illusions are common; people often hear sounds or voices that are not actually present, or fail to hear those that are. Individuals who have lost a limb frequently report feeling an itch on a part of their body that is no longer there. Knowledge based on sense data, therefore, can never be entirely trusted, since it depends on a flawed system of observation—a fact that undermines the very foundation of experimental science. One can try to validate one's data by performing an experiment numerous times and gathering the data with scrupulous repetitive care. Nonetheless, logically speaking there is no absolute certainty that an experiment that repeatedly renders one result after five million consecutive attempts may not suddenly give a different result on the five-million-and-first.

True and absolute knowledge, if possible at all, must therefore derive from a different source than empirical observation. For Descartes that source is logic. Logical thought is itself an absolute reality, or, as he famously put it, "I think, therefore I am" (*Cogito ergo sum* in Latin). I can doubt everything I see, everything I hear, everything I touch, smell, or taste. I can even doubt whether I am alive. But even in the absence of all sense data, my thinking mind—all by itself—knows that I am doubting, knows that I am thinking about thinking, and therefore I know absolutely that I exist.

"Congratulations," one might say. "You exist. So what?" But Descartes's insight contains the germ of a revolution in scientific and philosophical thought. Absolute truth, he argues, is theoretical instead of physical, and the theoretical expression of physical reality is ultimately more real than any physical manifestation of it. Consider, for example, a circle. One can express the idea of "circleness" by drawing one on a piece of paper, but also by describing it in words. "A figure in two dimensions made up of all the points equidistant from a single central point." The description in words is one level of abstraction above the physical drawing on paper. But one can move to an even higher level of abstraction by describing a circle in algebraic notation, as a mathematical formula. This, to Descartes, is an absolute truth, because this formula will describe all circles, in every place and throughout all time. If scientific investigation seeks to understand the truth about circles, it must work at this abstract level. Only here can absolute truth exist and be understood.

> Descartes described an entire universe guided by an immense, internally consistent, and utterly logical set of laws and formulas that the human mind can grasp—and this way of thinking has dominated Western scientific life ever since.

Descartes described an entire universe guided by an immense, internally consistent, and utterly logical set of laws and formulas that the human mind can grasp—and this way of thinking has dominated Western scientific life ever since. Scientific research of all types—whether in physics, chemistry, microbiology, astronomy, medicine, or any other field—begins with an assumption that everything operates according to a set of natural laws. The goal of research is to peel back the covering of the universe and see the logical structure underneath. It may be a coherent structure of unimaginable complexity, but we do not doubt that it is there and that it makes rational sense.

Modern physics, for example, includes the laws of quantum mechanics and of general relativity. Both are universally accepted, and yet they seem to contradict one another fundamentally. Do physicists therefore give up their research grants with a shrug? "Physics . . . it was worth a try, but I guess it just doesn't work." Obviously not. They continue their work on the assumption that still another paradigm exists, one that we have yet to discover but which is absolutely out there, that reconciles our two apparently irreconcilable current systems.

John Donne had complained that the universe is "all in pieces, all coherence gone." Descartes was the first to argue convincingly that another type of system, based on fixed and unalterable natural laws, can take the place of Biblical and classical authorities—and that humans can figure them out. Just as the human mind exists within, but also beyond, the body, the abstract laws of nature exist within and beyond the physical universe. They guide it, shape it, drive it, and ennoble it with purpose.

NEWTON'S MATHEMATICAL PRINCIPLES

The first person to deliver on Descartes's promise was Sir Isaac Newton (1643–1727), the greatest scientist in Western history before Albert Einstein (1879–1955). He came from an undistinguished family and received a fairly standard education at a

boarding school. As a boy he enjoyed tinkering with machines, a hobby he continued throughout his life.[10] He earned a bachelor's degree in 1664 from Cambridge
University in classical studies, but by that time he had already started to teach himself mathematics and physics by reading the works of Descartes. When the plague
swept through England, he withdrew to his family's rural home, where he began his
work in optics and in the calculation of infinite series. The first resulted in his discovery that light can be broken into the spectrum of colors and has the properties of
a wave, and the second resulted in his discoveries of integral and differential calculus. Within two years he had become the leading mathematician of his age and
earned a prestigious professorship at Cambridge, where he remained for thirty
years. He spent his last thirty years in London serving as master of the Royal Mint
and president of the Royal Society.

Newton's greatest achievement was his *Philosophiae Naturalis Principia Mathematica* ("Mathematical Principles of Natural Philosophy"), published originally
in 1687. It is not light reading. Newton was a cranky, obsessive loner who loathed
being disturbed in his work, especially by people who could not understand the
complexity of his thinking—which was just about everyone. Only three hundred
copies of the first edition of the *Principia* were printed, which was probably well
more than the number of people capable of making sense of it. Newton insisted on
having empirical data as the basis for his high-flying mathematical formulations,
and hence the *Principia* skips from topic to topic, wherever there is sufficient data
to begin computing. Nevertheless, the variety and number of topics Newton addresses add up to a comprehensive theory about the physical world.

Its fundamental and astonishing idea is the theory of universal gravitation.
The idea that things such as apples fall to the ground was hardly startling news.
What prompted Newton's thinking was the question of why the planets do not
fall to the Earth's surface. Plainly there is evidently nothing holding them in
orbit in the sky. Physical theory had been based for centuries on the belief that
motion was an intrinsic quality of all matter. Water flows because that is what
water does; the atoms that propel our bodies forward are in constant movement
because movement is life itself. Death, in this view, is a cessation of natural movement. Newton argued instead that motion results from the interaction of objects,
and he showed that the interaction can be calculated precisely by taking into account their mass, velocity, and direction of motion. In this way he developed the
physical concept of force. But he then complicated matters by introducing another idea—what he called the "weight" (*gravitas* in Latin) or attraction that all

---

[10] Newton invented the reflecting telescope—one that uses a curved mirror rather than a second lens to
focus captured beams of light.

physical objects feel toward one another whether they are in a static or dynamic state. Thus was born the idea of gravity.

In his descriptions of gravity, which he further showed to be determined in permanent ratios according to mass, distance, and force, he produced a comprehensive explanation for physical actions as simple as an apple's fall from a tree and as complex as the elliptical orbits of the planets in the solar system. Descartes had shown the logical necessity of a universal set of natural laws governing all matter. Now Newton provided the mathematical formulas that those laws consisted of. The universe was not only internally coherent according to a single, though undeniably massive, set of laws, but those laws were knowable, calculable, and provable. When Newton died in 1727, he was given a hero's funeral and buried in Westminster Abbey.

THE CHOICES FOR WESTERN SOCIETY

The immediate impact of the Scientific Revolution was moderate, but it changed Western culture profoundly. The universe became in the popular mind less of a divine and glorious mystery and more of a fascinating mechanism, with all that is good and bad in that transition. The new tenets included the belief in a rational explanation for everything we experience, the considered reliability of an idea that is based on quantifiable evidence, and the habit of privileging the demonstrably logical over the intuitive. All came increasingly to characterize much of Western thought. Western society, being the most open to the rational exploration of the world and the exploitation of its potentialities, became poised to do just that (see Map 13.1).

> The immediate impact of the Scientific Revolution was moderate, but it changed Western culture profoundly. The universe became in the popular mind less of a divine and glorious mystery and more of a fascinating mechanism, with all that is good and bad in that transition.

Not that there were not sounds of alarm raised. When the Royal Society, England's premier institution for the promotion of science, was established in London in 1660, some warned that it was nothing short of the beginning of a Satanic apocalypse. One prominent Anglican clergyman, Robert South (1634–1716), denounced the members of the society in a sermon in 1667 as

> the profane, atheistical, epicurean rabble . . . who have lived so much in the defiance of God . . . a company of lewd, shallow-brained huffs [blowhards] making atheism and contempt of religion the sole badge of wit, gallantry, and true discretion. . . . The truth is, the persons here reflected upon are of such a peculiar stamp of impiety, that they seem to be

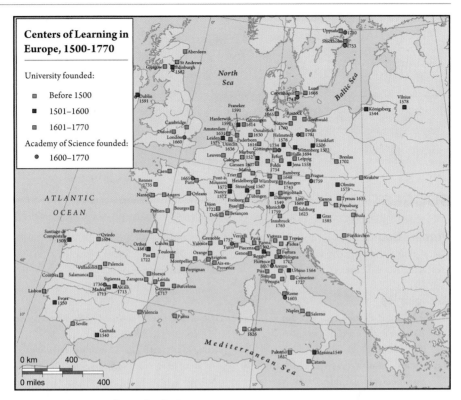

Centers of Learning in Europe, 1500-1770

University founded:

- Before 1500
- 1501–1600
- 1601–1770

Academy of Science founded:

- 1600–1770

MAP 13.1   Centers of Learning in Europe, 1500–1770

a set of fellows got together, and formed into a diabolical society, for the finding out new experiments in vice.

Developments in the Christian West and the Islamic West now sharply diverged. Europeans came increasingly to view the world as knowable, explorable, and understandable. In fact, it became something that the West could dominate. At the same time, the Islamic world took a pronounced inward turn, eschewing science and exploration in favor of a reexamination of tradition. Neither path was intrinsically right or wrong, but both resulted from conscious cultural choices and as the expressions of value. The consequences of those choices would be felt for centuries to come.

WHO, WHAT, WHERE

analytical geometry
Boyle's law
Council of Trent
Counter-Reformation
Epistemology

heliocentric
Index of Forbidden Books
Inquisition
Jesuits
Scientific Revolution

SUGGESTED READINGS

Primary Sources

Bacon, Francis. *Novum Organum.*

Descartes, René. *Discourse on Method.*

Galilei, Galileo. *The Starry Messenger.*

Hobbes, Thomas. *Leviathan.*

Anthologies

Donnelly, John Patrick, ed. and trans. *Jesuit Writings of the Early Modern Period, 1540–1640* (2006).

Finocchiaro, Maurice A., ed. and trans. *The Essential Galileo Galilei* (2008).

Hellyer, Michael. *The Scientific Revolution: The Essential Readings* (2008).

Jacob, Margaret. *The Scientific Revolution: A Brief History with Documents* (2009).

Studies

Biagioli, Mario. *Galileo's Instruments of Credit: Telescopes, Images, Secrecy* (2007).

Bireley, Robert. *Religion and Politics in the Age of the Counterreformation: Emperor Ferdinand II, William Lamormaini, S. J., and the Formation of the Imperial Policy* (2011).

Blackwell, Richard J. *Behind the Scenes at Galileo's Trial* (2006).

Brooke, John, and Ian Maclean, eds. *Heterodoxy in Early Modern Science and Religion* (2006).

Dear, Peter. *Revolutionizing the Sciences: European Knowledge and Its Ambitions, 1500–1700* (2009).

Evans, Robert J. W., and Alexander Marr. *Curiosity and Wonder from the Renaissance to the Enlightenment* (2006).

Feingold, Mordechai. *The Newtonian Moment: Isaac Newton and the Making of Modern Culture* (2004).

Gaukroger, Stephen. *The Collapse of Mechanism and the Rise of Sensibility: Science and the Shaping of Modernity, 1680–1760* (2011).

———. *The Emergence of a Scientific Culture: Science and the Shaping of Modernity, 1210–1685* (2006).

———. *Francis Bacon and the Transformation of Early-Modern Philosophy* (2001).

Godman, Peter. *The Saint as Censor: Robert Bellarmine between Inquisition and Index* (2000).

Henry, John. *Knowledge Is Power: How Magic, the Government, and an Apocalyptic Vision Inspired Francis Bacon to Create Modern Science* (2004).

Jardine, Lisa. *Ingenious Pursuits: Building the Scientific Revolution* (2000).

Lindemann, Mary. *Medicine and Society in Early Modern Europe* (2010).

Park, Katharine. *Secrets of Women: Gender, Generation, and the Origins of Human Dissection* (2010).

Park, Katharine, and Lorraine Daston. *Early Modern Science* (2006).

Shea, William R,. and Mariano Artigas. *Galileo in Rome: The Rise and Fall of a Troublesome Genius* (2003).

Spiller, Elizabeth. *Science, Reading, and Renaissance Literature: The Art of Making Knowledge, 1580–1670* (2004).

Tutino, Stefania. *Empire of Souls: Robert Bellarmine and the Christian Commonwealth* (2010).

For additional resources, including maps, primary sources, visuals, web links, and quizzes, please go to **www.oup.com/us/backman.**

CHAPTER 14

From Westphalia to Paris: Regimes Old and New

1648–1750

"Those who did not live in the 18th century before the [French] Revolution do not know life at its sweetest," declared the French career diplomat Charles de Tallyrand-Périgord (1754–1838). An egoist right to the tips of his fingers, Tallyrand knew what he was talking about. The period of the Ancien Régime ("Old Regime"), from 1648 to 1789, was a time of unparalleled privilege and delight for the European upper aristocracy. Its belief in absolute order spread throughout society as well, inspiring a demand for norms in the arts and even everyday life. While England's civil wars led to a constitutional monarchy, the Islamic world in fact grew more conservative. As international trade grew and a new economic system came into being, however, Europe faced a new round of crises and war. Urban manufacturing and commerce had long since become the main engines of economic life, but the landed

THE GREATER WEST IN THE AGE OF ABSOLUTISM

Peterhof
Potsdam
Schönbrunn
Versailles

○ Palaces built by Absolutist monarchs

◀ **Teaching Manners**
Enlightenment Europe placed profound importance on proper manners, one example being the publication of the first etiquette manuals for "proper" urban families. In this painting by Jean-Baptiste Chardin (1699–1779), a governess upbraids her charge for having dirtied his hat—presumably having dropped it on the ground during a tennis match.

CHAPTER OUTLINE

- The Peace of Westphalia: 1648
- The Argument for Tyranny
- The Social Contract
- Absolute Politics
- Police States
- Self-Indulgence with a Purpose
- Mercantilism and Absolutism
- Mercantilism and Poverty
- Domesticating Dynamism: Regulating Culture
- Decency and Modesty
- The Birth of Private Life
- The English Exception
- Civil War and Restoration
- Ottoman Might and Islamic Absolutism
- Safavid Pleasures
- The End of Order
- The Slave Trade and Domestic Subjugation
- The Return of Uncertainty

elite still enjoyed various rental incomes, judicial fees, annuities, ecclesiastical and governmental sinecures, and military revenues. That was more than enough for them to live in lavish comfort, especially given their most closely held privilege—exemption from paying taxes. While agreement between states brought peace, it too further concentrated wealth and power, and philosophy rose to the occasion with an argument for tyranny.

This was the **Baroque Age**, when fabulously ornate palaces, churches, summer residences, concert halls, libraries, museums, theaters, pleasure gardens, and private academies sprang up by the hundreds across Europe. Most were filled to bursting with paintings and sculptures and rang with the music written by liveried court composers and played by servant musicians—all for the enjoyment of the wealthy, powdered, perfumed, and brilliantly attired nobles. Their images, coats of arms, and marble-inscribed names bedecked everything in sight. The display sought not merely to impress but to overwhelm the viewer with its expressive power. And that meant the power not of the architect, artist, or composer, but of the nobleman whose authority and station made such glories possible. Europe's elites had always enjoyed their privileges, but seldom on this scale.

The all-encompassing grandeur was designed to stun the people into a state of paralyzed awe. But such a display was possible only by means of a brutal hoarding of wealth. Few periods in Western history ever saw a more intense concentration of power and wealth among the elites—or such widespread penury and suffering by the common people. The German poet Johann Wilhelm von Goethe (1749–1832) described Europe's peasant farmers as "caught between the land and the aristocracy as between an anvil and a hammer." Not a comforting image—especially when one realizes that Goethe did not make the observation out of sympathy for the commoners' plight, but merely as a recognition of what was and needed to be.

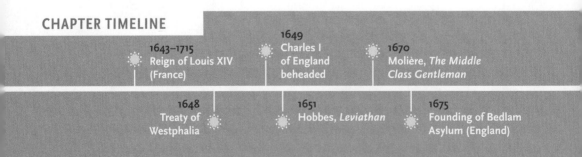

CHAPTER TIMELINE

1643–1715
Reign of Louis XIV
(France)

1649
Charles I
of England
beheaded

1670
Molière, *The Middle
Class Gentleman*

1648
Treaty of
Westphalia

1651
Hobbes, *Leviathan*

1675
Founding of Bedlam
Asylum (England)

THE PEACE OF WESTPHALIA: 1648

By 1648 most of Continental Europe was exhausted by over one hundred years of brutal warfare. Unable or unwilling to continue the carnage, all sides sued for peace. The **Peace of Westphalia** (1648) is an umbrella term for a collection of individual treaties that ended the hostilities. It rearranged political borders, created a framework of mutually agreed upon principles, and established a network of recognized sovereign governments. Over one hundred delegations had participated in the negotiations, which had taken seven years: sixteen nations, sixty-six German imperial principalities, and twenty-seven nongovernmental interest groups (such as churches, corporations, and guilds). This was the first general diplomatic congress in Western history, and it provided a model for subsequent international assemblies.

The peace dramatically revised the political map of Europe by splitting some states, joining others, carving out new independent entities, and moving many traditional boundaries (see Map 14.1). In so doing, it paid little attention to preserving ethnic domains. The goal instead was to produce a balance of power between the states created by the peace. If each new state was roughly equal in power to its neighbor, the thinking went, then wars would be less likely to break out between them. But to create such a balance, sheer acreage was not enough to consider; population density, economic and technological development, access to ports and rivers, and the availability of natural resources all had to be factored in. The resulting map shows several new states (an independent Denmark, Holland, Portugal, and Switzerland, for example) scattered amongst the larger territorial powers (Austria-Hungary, Bavaria, Brandenburg-Prussia, France, Poland-Lithuania, Spain, and Sweden). Moreover, countries now had a mechanism for creating alliances in order to check an ambitious neighbor. This eased tensions by allowing each state to control its own foreign policy in a meaningful way. Even small states like Denmark or Holland had strategic strengths that made them valuable allies. Threatening to withdraw their

1683
Ottoman siege of
Vienna repulsed

1689–1725
Reign of Peter the
Great (Russia)

1736
Fall of Safavid
Dynasty, Persia

1756–1763
Seven Years' War

1688
Glorious
Revolution,
England

1720
South Sea
Bubble

1755
Samuel Johnson,
*Dictionary of the
English Language*

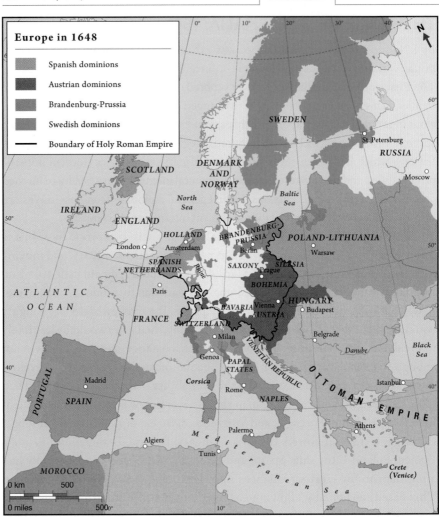

MAP 14.1   Europe in 1648

support from an alliance could make even a large state like France or Spain reconsider their policies.

The Westphalia treaties also reaffirmed the principle of religious establishment—the idea that the ruler of each state could determine its official religion (*cuius regio, eius religio*)—while guaranteeing the freedom of other faiths and denominations within certain prescribed limits. Strictly speaking, religious establishment meant more than a preference for any particular faith or denomination and was distinct from theocracy. Rather, it created a formal relationship between the state and the specific church. Religious establishment in the modern sense, in which the established church serves as an organ of the state, was a product of the Protestant Reformation: England established the (Anglican) Church of England

The Landed Gentry   Thomas Gainesborough (1727–1788) was the premier portraitist of
18th-century England, which was ironic since he had a profound dislike for the upper classes.
His speed was admired as much as his skill, which kept a constant stream of commissions
coming his way. In this dual portrait (1750) of Robert and Frances Andrews, a wealthy gentry
couple, Gainesborough slyly lets some of his disdain for his subjects show. The couple looks
distinctly out of place in the tranquil setting, like foreign objects imposed on the countryside.
Mrs. Andrews, then only eighteen, sits stiffly on an elaborate wooden bench. The area of her
lap was left deliberately unfinished, perhaps to allow for the inclusion of a baby in the future.
Mr. Andrews, aged twenty-four, has a look of forced nonchalance. Gainesborough has pushed
the couple to the side in order to spend more time painting the landscape (his real artistic
love). No workers, implements, or farm animals are on the scene, except for a small herd of
sheep far in the distance, which gives the land an eerily lifeless look.

in 1533, and the (Lutheran) Church of Sweden came into formal existence in
1536. Most of the states carved out by the Peace of Westphalia had in practice
established churches, although few had the formal legal structures uniting church
and state as did England and Sweden.

   This sprawl of new or heavily revised territorial states left most monarchs
without serious rivals for power. Where councils and parliaments had provided
a limited check on royal ambitions, few of these customs survived intact. The aristocracy remained wealthy, privileged, and secure in their control of the agrarian
countryside, but also unable to unite in opposition to royal aims. The new states
were professional bureaucracies—uninviting to most nobles, who found it more
to their liking to remain in their baroque palaces and chateaux than to crowd
into expensive cramped quarters in the busy capital cities. Moreover, individual
rulers could now consolidate extensive, centralized authority over their common
subjects, so long as they avoided using that power to threaten their neighbors.
In other words, the alliances and guarantees that aimed to prevent a king from
intimidating his neighbors actually helped him to tighten his grip on his own

subjects. In this way the peace helped to trigger the rise of royal **absolutism**, or a king's absolute power—not as a consciously deliberated policy, but rather as the unintended consequence of the quest for a balance of power.

THE ARGUMENT FOR TYRANNY

The argument for tyranny is a simple one, to its enthusiasts: it provides freedom. That may seem contrary to common sense, but the argument is sound. We define freedom by what we are free *from*. Many people, quite understandably, think of freedom as independence, or not being subject to control. To others, however, true freedom consists of freedom from chaos. The restoration of order after a long period of anarchy can thrill people with a sense of regained liberty—the liberty of a reliable, well-regulated tranquility.

The argument is an old one. The Archaic- and Classical Age Greeks celebrated their tyrants (*tyrannoi*, like Solon and Psistratus) and wrote them into their constitutions, as necessary correctives to democracy's occasional tendency to drive the cart into a ditch. The Roman Republic too allowed for constitutional dictatorship, a temporary though renewable grant of unlimited authority to revise the laws, reform government, and command the military. Julius Caesar had been a dictator—and a popular one at that until he appointed himself dictator for life, which made him effectively a king and all but assured his own assassination. In times of crisis, as when an airplane is spinning out of control or a ship is foundering in a storm, the rights to individual self-expression and self-determination do not further the cause of rescue. There is no time to hold elections, seek consensus, and let everyone on board freely express views about what to do. Instead, the argument goes, salvation requires a single firm hand on the controls and a single strong voice barking orders to an obedient crowd. Tyrants can make mistakes, of course, but they at least have the potential of saving the ship. Noisy, messy democracy and respect for independence of thought and action in such a plight only guarantees a crash.

The catastrophic wars of religion and civil wars before them, many now argued, were the result of liberalizing, mass-driven politics. In retreating from traditional authority since the 12th century, Europe had nearly committed suicide and had all but lost its collective mind in the crazed pursuit of witches. Only a restoration of patriarchal society, headed by noble male authority, could save the West from ruin. But this could not be done quietly or subtly. The aristocracy needed to parade its power, boast of it, and glorify it in everything it did. And the higher the aristocrat, the greater the need for spectacle. Kings, of course, needed to

> The aristocracy needed to parade its power, boast of it, and glorify it in everything it did. And the higher the aristocrat, the greater the need for spectacle.

parade their glorious position more than anyone else.[1] Jean Domat (1625–1696), a prominent jurist and royal favorite, justified the ostentation:

> Law grants the sovereign many rights, one of which must be the right to public display of anything that gives evidence of the grandeur and majesty needed to express the authority and dignity of his high and wide-ranging office.... God Himself [after all] wants monarchs to augment the authority He has shared with them, in ways that promote the awed respect of the people, and this can be achieved only by the grandeur conveyed by the brilliance of their palaces.

The Peace of Westphalia did not institute absolute monarchy in any formal sense, but it did establish the conditions that made its rise likely. Some early indicators of royal dictatorship had emerged even before the peace. In France the rapid concentration of power by the monarchy had begun under King Louis XIII (r. 1610–1643), whose chief minister—(Armand-Jean du Plessis) Cardinal de Richelieu (1585–1642)—summed up the problems confronting the throne when he first came to power in 1624:

> The Protestants acted as though they shared the state with you, the nobles, as if they were your equals rather than your subjects, and the governors of the provinces as though they were monarchs of their own offices. These scenarios set a bad example, one so harmful to the kingdom that even Your most loyal courts were influenced

Richelieu Armand-Jean du Plessis, Cardinal-Duc de Richelieu (1585–1642), was the sickly younger son of a low-ranking noble family, who grew to become the most powerful figure in the kingdom of France after the king himself. Richelieu believed firmly in the necessity of an absolutist monarchy; only a strong central monarch, ably guided and determined to exert his authority energetically, could maintain civil order. His rapid rise in the church and the French government went hand in hand. Consecrated a bishop in 1608, he became France's secretary of state in 1616; in 1622 he was made cardinal, and two years later he was Louis XIII's chief minister—a post he held until his death.

---

[1]   Privilege, in the Age of Absolutism, was not a consequence of power but the very essence of it.

by it and were driven—unreasonably—to build up their authority to the detriment of Your Own. Might I add that every individual seemed to measure his worth by the boldness of his presumption, . . . each one deeming the privileges he held from You valuable only to the extent that they satisfied his greedy fantasies. . . .

Sure in the knowledge of how much good a king can accomplish when he puts his power to proper use, I, in my confidence, dared to promise Your Majesty that You would soon regain control of Your state and that before much time elapsed Your wisdom and courage, together with God's blessing, would put the realm on a new path. I swore to Your Majesty that I would spare no effort and would use whatever power it pleased You to grant me to ruin the Protestants, to break the stiff-necked pride of the aristocracy, to return all Your subjects to Your dutiful service, and to restore Your name to the high position it deserves in foreign lands. *(Political Testament, ch. 1)*

Richelieu accomplished all this and more with a mix of careful negotiation and heavy-handed intimidation. He neutralized most of Louis XIII's foes thanks to his network of domestic and international spies, his ability to charm, and his willingness to bribe, and above all his ruthless conviction that only an all-powerful throne could keep France safe and strong. Richelieu's passion for order and security is as evident in his personal life as in his public policies, and in this he represents many of the qualities of the Age of Absolutism.

THE SOCIAL CONTRACT

Richelieu's dedication to a supremely powerful monarchy was instinctive, but more than one philosopher of the time reached a similar position. None of these thinkers directly created absolutism as a political force, but they help explain the sentiments that gave rise to it. The philosopher most closely associated with the theory of absolutism is Thomas Hobbes (1588–1679). Hobbes was not England's first philosopher, nor even her first political philosopher; he was, however, the first to write philosophy in English. A contemporary of René Descartes, with whom he corresponded, and Sir Francis Bacon, Hobbes spent most of his adult life as a tutor and secretary to William Cavendish, the second Earl of Devonshire, which left him ample time to take advantage of the earl's magnificent library. He had broad interests that included history, law, mathematics, and physics, as well as philosophy. Forced to spend time in exile in Paris after the arrest and subsequent execution of King Charles I in 1649 because of his strong royalist views, Hobbes returned in 1651 with the completed manuscript of his best-known work, *Leviathan*.

Although his own life was comfortable, Hobbes's philosophy owed much to the violence and misery of his age. He emphasizes the instincts for self-preservation and self-regard that are natural to all people. Our polite, civilized behavior toward one another is an acquired attribute, one that masks and hopefully controls our baser passions for food, wealth, power, pleasure, and status. The problem, he argues, lies in the finite nature of the things we desire. Seeking always to satisfy ourselves, we unavoidably live in a state of constant competition with one another. "The war of all against all," as he memorably put, corrodes our civilized veneer and leads us into periodic anarchies like the one Europe suffered after 1500. Moreover, people are unequal in abilities—some being stronger, others faster, still others more cunning, or more agile. The war of all against all therefore becomes a permanent state, with

> no place for industry, because the fruit thereof is uncertain; and consequently no culture of the earth; no navigation or use of the commodities that may be imported by sea; no commodious building; no instruments of moving and removing such things as require much force; no knowledge of the face of the Earth; no account of time; no arts; no letters; and which is worst of all, continual fear and danger of violent death; and the life of man solitary, poor, nasty, brutish, and short.

It is a pessimistic view of life. (A long-ago student of mine once submitted an essay on the horrors of the early modern era "in which life was, in Hobbes's view, 'solitary, poor, nasty, British, and short.'") But it is not altogether surprising, given the agonies Europe had experienced since the discovery of the New World, the Protestant Reformation, the Wars of Religion, civil wars, Inquisitions, and witchcraft mania.

Hobbes sees only one way out of the misery of the state of nature: limitless sovereign authority. Only by transferring our innate rights of self-determination to a governing authority entrusted with absolute power over the people can we hope to free ourselves from chaos. Interestingly, Hobbes does not much care whether the absolutist government is a monarchy, an oligarchy, or a democracy. All that matters is that the government, whatever its form, has unquestioned power to compel obedience. Unlimited and indivisible power to legislate, adjudicate, execute, and enforce, in a single sovereign entity, is the only way to live an ordered, peaceful, and prosperous life. Of course it also fails to prevent the abuse of that power; but Hobbes counters this charge with two assertions. First, no absolute tyranny can ever be worse than absolute chaos. And second, when people recognize their complete obedience to the Sovereign Authority, a stable and peaceful enjoyment of life really does result. Their total submission

The Social Contract   Title page of the first edition (1651) of *Leviathan* by Thomas Hobbes (1588–1679), the first work of political science in English.

Government, which bears responsibility for preserving social stability, may therefore legitimately assert its will on the community whenever it deems it necessary to do so. Renunciation of personal liberty, in other words, is the price of peace; but the truest form of freedom, Hobbes insists, lies in that very renunciation.

to the Sovereign Authority will temper any possible inclination that authority might have to abuse its power.

Leviathan is a difficult book to read. Its archaic English—all four hundred pages of it—defeats all but the most determined readers. (I have modernized its spelling and punctuation.) But it deserves attention. A darker yet more substantial work than Machiavelli's *Prince*, *Leviathan* elaborates what later became known as **social contract** theory. This theory holds that when people decide to live in community they enter a covenant with each other, compromising their individual free wills in return for the benefits of society. Government, which bears responsibility for preserving social stability, may therefore legitimately assert its will on the community whenever it deems it necessary to do so. Renunciation of personal liberty, in other words, is the price of peace; but the truest form of freedom, Hobbes insists, lies in that very renunciation.

Richelieu and Hobbes were not the only 17th-century figures to argue for absolutism, but they are the most interesting. Both men were brilliant, moody, and pessimistic about human nature, and each worked diligently to bring their ideas to fruition—Richelieu in deed, Hobbes on the page. Had they met, they might have recognized one another as kindred spirits despite their religious differences. For all his worldliness, Richelieu was a devout Catholic, and scholars still debate whether Hobbes was an atheist.[2] Each also had humane pursuits. Richelieu collected classical manuscripts (later donated to the Sorbonne, of which he was the

---

[2]   Can one be committed to Christianity while endorsing secular absolutism? Hobbes says yes, but was he just trying to avoid inflaming the still-smoldering religious antagonisms of his age?

chief executive), founded the Academie française (the premiere literary society in France), patronized painters and sculptors, and ardently promoted theatre. Hobbes dabbled in mathematics and physics, published his own translations of Thucydides and Homer, and wrote a vivid history of the English Civil War. Still, both men shared unsettling and ominous views about human nature and the hard realities of life. Their influence was profound, and the fears they articulated were shared by many—fears that allowed absolutism to take root and flourish. For a while on the Continent, it could enjoy even popular support.

ABSOLUTE POLITICS

The dominant dynasties, and the most representative, of the Old Regime were the Bourbons in France, the Habsburgs in Austria and (a separate branch of the family) in Spain, the Hohenzollerns in Brandenburg-Prussia, and the Romanovs in Russia. A web of intermarriages that in some cases went back generations or even centuries connected the royal families to one another. Even so, ties of affection were minimal and always gave way to politics. Standing armies became arms of the state, as royal families undertook vast building projects to display their rule. Mercantilism, the economic system to support their disastrous self-indulgence, also devastated much of the population.

Despite the supposed "balance of power" established at Westphalia, France was the dominant Continental state in every way. With somewhere between 15 and 18 million people, France around 1648 had twice the population of Spain and three times that of England. With its superior resources concentrated among the upper orders, all of whom lavished funds on the arts, French culture flowered. This was the age of the playwright Molière (1622–1673), the painter Nicolas Poussin (1594–1665), and the composer Jean-Baptiste de Lully (1632–1687). Young King Louis XIV set immediately to increasing the size of his army, in the hope of matching France's cultural clout with its military muscle.

Brandenburg-Prussia, by contrast, was a surviving remnant of the old Holy Roman Empire, steeped in tradition and pride but for the moment a poor, defenseless, war-shocked ruin. Much of the worst fighting of the Thirty Years' War had taken place here, leaving large stretches of the countryside desolate and many towns depopulated. Economic development came slowly, and most commercial, technological, and institutional innovations appeared here one or two generations after they had taken root in England, France, or Holland.

Habsburg Austria had a long genealogy going back to the Middle Ages, but the traumas of the 17th century had left much of its land depleted and demoralized. The Ottoman Turks advanced upon Austria almost as soon as the

Another Siege of Vienna   In 1683 the Ottomans again marched against the Habsburg Empire (their first effort having been in 1529). The Turks had an army of nearly one hundred thousand soldiers. The Habsburgs called on their Polish and Lithuanian allies to join in the defense and carried the day. In this painting by the Flemish artist Frans Geffels (1624–1694), the Turks have launched their assault on the city. The Poles and Lithuanians have not yet appeared on the scene. According to legend, as part of the celebration over their defeat of the Turks the Viennese bakers' guild created a new pastry: the croissant, which was designed to mimic the Islamic crescent, visible on the Turks' flag above the tent on the left. The idea is that every time one tears open a croissant, one is in effect calling the Turks a rabble of puff pastries.

Westphalia agreements were signed; by 1683 they had reached Vienna, which they besieged for two months before giving up.[3] (Forces from Poland, Russia, Venice, and the papacy joined the subsequent Austrian counteroffensive.) The Turkish defeat reenergized Austrian pride, an emotional swell that led to a sharp improvement in economic and social stability. This was the era of Austria's climb as a cultural capital, especially the cities of Salzburg and Vienna; the first Austrian composer of note, Heinrich Ignaz Franz Biber (1644–1704), almost single-handedly turned Salzburg into a pilgrimage site for music lovers. The background to the Romanov dynasty lay in a decade-plus of famines, civil wars, and foreign invasions known as the Time of Troubles (1601–1613).

Mikhail I Romanov (r.1613–1645) came to power just before the Thirty Years' War engulfed Europe and died before it ended, but he took advantage of Europe's deadly self-absorption to drive out the (Polish-Lithuanian) invaders besetting his country and solidified his control over all of Russia. When Piotr I (Peter the Great) came to power in 1689, he brought with him the style and techniques of autocratic rule that he had learned earlier when traveling in the west. Together they laid the foundation for a czarist state that would last until 1917.

---

[3]   The Turks used the ancient temple of the Parthenon in Athens as their main munitions storehouse. When Venetian artillery units took aim on it, the temple was blasted into the ruin it is today.

TABLE 14.1   **The Age of Absolutism**

AUSTRIA (HABSBURG)	BRANDENBURG-PRUSSIA (HOHENZOLLERN)	FRANCE (BOURBON)	RUSSIA (ROMANOV)	SPAIN (BOURBON)
Leopold I 1658–1705	Friedrich Wilhelm 1640–1688	Louis XIII 1610–1643	Mikhail I 1613–1645	Felipe I* 1621–1665
Josef I 1705–1711	Friedrich III 1688–1713	Louis XIV 1643–1715	Alexei 1645–1676	Carlos II* 1665–1700
Karl VI 1711–1740	Friedrich Wilhelm I 1713–1740	Louis XV 1715–1774	Theodore II 1676–1682	Felipe V 1700–1746
Maria Theresa 1740–1780	Friedrich II the Great 1740–1786	Louis XVI 1774–1792	Ivan V 1682–1689	Ferdinando VI 1746–1759
Josef II 1780–1790	Friedrich Wilhelm II 1786–1797		Peter I the Great 1689–1725	Carlos III 1759–1788
Leopold II 1790–1792	Friedrich Wilhelm III 1797–1840		Katerina I 1725–1727	Carlos IV 1788–1808
Franz II 1792–1835			Peter II 1727–1730	
			Anna 1730–1740	
			Ivan VI 1740–1741	
			Lizaveta 1741–1762	
			Peter III 1762	
			Katerina II the Great 1762–1796	
			Pavel 1796–1801	
			Aleksandr I 1801–1825	

*The last two Habsburg kings of Spain

POLICE STATES

Autocracy is not conceptually difficult to grasp, since dictatorships follow a few set patterns of development. The regimes of the 17th and 18th centuries were above all police states. Raw military muscle and the willingness to use it both secured and expressed their power. The king's army in France mustered merely 20,000 soldiers in 1661; by 1700 it numbered 400,000. The Prussian army in the Thirty Years' War had consisted mostly of unreliable mercenaries, with the result that Swedish forces had ravaged the countryside almost at will. After 1648 the Prussian monarch began to assemble a professional standing army of his own. It began small: between five and six thousand men. But by 1750 it had ballooned to 180,000. Control of the Austrian army was given to a professional military officer from France, Prince François-Eugène of Savoy (1663–1736), who oversaw its transformation from a ragtag mixture of old feudal forces and mercenaries into a national institution with modern methods of supply, training, and command. After only a few years' work, he had increased the size and quality of the Austrian forces to such an extent that they drove one hundred thousand Ottoman Turks eastward from Austrian lands by 1687, after which he turned the army around and expelled a French force from the west. Austria thus entered the 18th century with a professionalized army of nearly one hundred thousand men.

The transformation of the Russian military was even more dramatic. Long consisting of an informal conglomeration of semifeudalized noble cavalrymen known as **streltsi**, the army was disbanded and brutally purged of political rivals by Tsar Piotr I in 1698. Piotr was determined to bring Russia in line with Europe, in terms of economic and political development, and resolved not only to catch up with Europe but to do so by emulating it. He modeled his new army along French and Prussian lines, put his soldiers in Western-style uniforms, gave them Western weapons (muskets and artillery), and hired Western officers to train them.

These massive new armies drew from the lower orders of their respective societies for the rank and file; men from the urban and professional classes or the lower nobility dominated midlevel officer ranks. The highest ranks were still primarily the purview of the high nobility, but tended to include only those for whom the military was a lifelong career. Only Prussia used a military draft; in every other country, volunteers served. And there was no shortage of volunteers. The king's army offered commoners three meals a day, a salary, solid training, and the possibility of a pension after a certain number of years in service—things they had little or no chance of attaining on their own. These were "drum and bugle" armies, divided into companies that fought in formation using long, unbroken lines. Discipline was harsh and frequently brutal: beatings, fines, half rations, and imprisonment were common. The penalty for breaking ranks was flogging. Executions were common too. In Austria, Prince François-Eugène liked to perform them personally on soldiers who failed to obey orders on the battlefield. Piotr I once personally executed five soldiers accused of rebellion, after allowing others to prepare the way by torturing the men first.

The Peace of Westphalia, however, was largely successful in maintaining a relatively peaceful Europe. Conflicts remained, a couple of them even large-scale matters, but Europe between 1648 and the start of the French Revolution in 1789 was a much more peaceful place than it had been in the 140 preceding years. Most of the wars of the era arose from Louis XIV's grandiose plans to create a greater France, or more accurately to secure a number of extranational regions that might buffer France from external attack: the War of Devolution (1667–1668), the

Franco-Dutch War (1672–1678), the War of the League of Augsburg (1688–1697), and the War of the Spanish Succession (1701–1714). Louis came to regret his overreaching, although not until the very end of his life. On his deathbed, Louis is reported to have advised his heir (his great-grandson Louis XV): "Don't follow the bad example I've set."[4]

Why then were such enormous armies created? With fewer foreign and civil wars to fight, the soldiers were put to use policing their own populations. Soldiers marched the streets and plazas, stood in university lecture halls, observed church services, watched crowds entering and leaving theaters, policed the countryside, guarded government buildings, and monitored harbors. They guarded city gates, performed maneuvers in town squares, staffed prisons (one of the new inventions of the age), and inspected printing houses. Without such vast reserves of manpower, royal absolutism was unthinkable. Maintaining the

Prussian Military Discipline   By the middle of the eighteenth century, the Prussian line infantry made full use of flintlock muskets and bayonets, as well as drilling, which involved the rotation of the front and rear lines after each salvo. "If my soldiers were to think, not one of them would remain in the army," Frederick II of Prussia is reputed to have said. The painting above shows Frederick's forces charging directly into the fire of the Austrians at the Battle of Hohenfriedberg in 1745, which the Prussians won.

---

4   Louis on his deathbed: " I was too quick to start wars, and I kept them going out of vanity. . . . Be a peaceful ruler, and devote yourself above all to easing the suffering of your subjects."

military—paying salaries, providing weapons and uniforms, serving meals, offering housing, supporting pensioners—remained a central concern of every monarch of the 17th and 18th centuries. The costs even in peacetime were enormous; the occasional conflicts of the age drove the expenditures exponentially higher.

Old Regime monarchs also relied heavily on separate companies of royal commissioners and civil servants—called *intendants* in France, and known collectively as the **Directory** in Prussia—who traveled through the provinces and inspected the handling of royal and administrative affairs. These commissioners held jurisdiction over all matters relating to public finance (whether collecting it or paying it out), public safety, and justice. They also formed part of the kings' extensive networks of intelligence gatherers. Drawn chiefly from the urban professional classes, commissioners served the king personally and did not hold public office, and hence they received their own salaries directly from the royal purse. They were expensive supervisors to maintain, since the kings not only paid their salaries but also equipped them with trappings appropriate to a representative of the king. In Prussia, in fact, all government positions of high and middling rank were reserved for military personnel, which effectively excluded much of the traditional aristocracy from power. It also made the king's position all the more secure, since literally everyone who worked in his government received a salary directly from him. In return for their exclusion from government, the nobles received royal permission to reinstate serfdom on their estates.

SELF-INDULGENCE WITH A PURPOSE

Expensive too were the sometimes grand, sometimes grotesque, building projects of the age. Palaces and churches decorated with baroque profusion arose by the score, year after year, as did lecture and concert halls, libraries and museums, scientific laboratories, and academies. Louis XIV, stung by rebellions and resistance in Paris, moved outside the capital and began construction of the immense palace complex at Versailles, which became the permanent seat of power from 1682 on. And other rulers built their own imposing piles too.[5]

Versailles itself had been a small rural village of only a thousand inhabitants fifty years earlier. Louis's palace—known properly as the Château de Versailles—transformed the simple hunting lodge that had previously existed on the spot into a spectacularly vast edifice that housed the entire royal court. The Château possessed well over a half million square feet of floor

---

[5]   Friedrich II of Prussia built the palace at Potsdam, just outside Berlin; Piotr I of Russia built Peterhof; the Habsburgs in Austria established the palace of Schönbrunn, just outside Vienna.

The Château De Versailles   With 2,300 rooms, a roughly equal number of ornate windows, and over 600,000 square feet (55,000 square meters) of floor space, the Château de Versailles is by far the grandest public structure built in the Age of Absolutism. Intended to showcase royal splendor and the French culture that the king personified, every bit of material used to build, furnish, and decorate Versailles was produced in France. In this painting (1668) one can see the extensive park and gardens as well as the château itself.

space (55,000 square meters) divided among seven hundred rooms, most of them magnificent. Thousands of paintings, drawings, sculptures, tapestries, and precious objects lined the walls and adorned every room. The effect on a first-time visitor is overwhelming—not so much for its beauty (although it is indeed beautiful) as for the audacity of its grandeur.

Louis's decision to build a new home for his court was self-indulgent but with a purpose. By creating a single space for the royal government and by demanding the constant attendance of France's aristocrats, Louis was able to keep an eye on the nobles and keep them under his sway. Louis never forgot that his reign began with an aristocratic rebellion against him. Called the **Fronde**, this rebellion (1648–1653) had not targeted Louis personally; the king was only ten years old when the trouble began.[6] Instead, the Fronde was a reaction against the royal finance minister Cardinal Jules Mazarin (1602–1661), the successor to Cardinal Richelieu, who had imposed a tax on judicial officials and sought to curtail

---

[6]   *Fronde* is the French word for slingshot—a favorite weapon of the Paris rebels, who used them to shatter the upper windows of the royal buildings.

a number of aristocratic privileges. It took five years to quell the rebellion, and Louis resolved to keep a permanent eye on the nobles by requiring their presence under his own ornate new roof. To make his job easier, he had the palace lined with secret passages, one-way mirrors, and peepholes; and he maintained a large private staff to spy on the goings-on in every room. The Duc de Saint-Simon (1675–1755), whose keen-eyed *Memoirs* provides an irreplaceable view of life at court, summarized the key role of Versailles as a means of controlling the nobles:

> [Louis] loved splendor, grandeur, and opulence in everything and inspired similar tastes in everyone in his court, even to the point where the surest way to earn a royal favor—perhaps the honor of receiving a word from him—was to spend extravagantly on something like a horse and carriage.... There was a sly political purpose in this, for by making conspicuously expensive habits the fashion at court (even making them a sort of requirement for people of a certain rank) he forced the members of his court to live beyond their means, which inevitably brought them to depend on royal favors in order to maintain themselves. But this [habit of indebtedness] turned out to be a plague that gradually infected the entire country, for in no time at all it spread to Paris, then to the army, and finally to the provinces, and now a man of any social standing at all is judged solely by the costliness of his daily habits and the extravagance of his luxuries. Such foolhardiness—the result of vanity and ostentation—has brought vast worry in its wake and threatens to result in nothing short of a national disaster and utter collapse.

This was prescient: the story of the French economy in the 18th century is one of constant and compounded indebtedness, a fiscal rot of staggering proportions that ultimately brought down the entire regime. For the present, however, the spending continued at an astonishing pace.

It is doubtful that Saint-Simon ever spoke so boldly to the king himself about the danger. A far braver man was François Fénelon (1651–1715), a Catholic priest appointed in 1689 as tutor to Louis XIV's grandson. As part of his teaching Fénelon composed a novel in 1694, *The Adventures of Telemachus*, which describes the travels and education of the son of the famed Greek king Odysseus. The novel mounts a stinging attack on the ideas of divine-right monarchy and absolutism. "Good kings are quite rare," it says at one point; "in fact, the majority of them are rather poor." It also denounces as evil the pursuit of glory through war and the sickening love of luxury. Fénelon's book became hugely popular across Europe and was translated into a half dozen languages. (It also provided the plot for Mozart's 1781 opera *Idomeneo*.)

Louis XIV hated it but recognized the good effect Fénelon's tutoring had on his grandson, a famously spoiled brat. He was brave enough to speak out in a 1694 letter to the king:

> Sire, for thirty years now Your ministers have broken every ancient law of this state, in order to increase Your power. They have infinitely increased both Your income and Your expenses, but in the process have impoverished all of France and have made Your name hated—all for the sake of the luxury of Your court. For the last twenty years these same ministers have turned France into an intolerable burden to her neighbors through bloody war. Wanting nothing but slaves, we now have no allies. And in the meantime, Your people are starving and rebellion is growing. You are thus left with only two choices: either to let the rebellion spread, or to resort to massacring the very people whom You have driven into desperation.

In 1696 Fénelon was appointed archbishop of Cambrai, but the following year was relieved of his position as tutor.

MERCANTILISM AND ABSOLUTISM

Supporting the absolutist regimes was a varied set of economic policies known collectively as **mercantilism**. For about 250 years, from roughly 1500 to 1750, this was the prevailing model for understanding and managing the economic life of northern Europe: England, France, and the Netherlands were the chief centers of mercantilist thinking, with Austria, Germany, Spain, and Sweden comprising a second tier. The Mediterranean economy also contained mercantilist elements but was less dominated by them overall. Mercantilism, in general, defined economic wealth as tangible assets: the money in circulation, land and mineral resources, the available precious metals, the aggregate of physical goods that can be produced from nature's resources. Global wealth therefore is static. Since the Earth is not increasing in size, the amount of economically valuable material is therefore fixed, and the aim of commerce is thus to maximize the amount of valuable stuff—actual specie and goods—in one's possession. The two most efficient means of doing so are to increase the amount of bullion in one's possession, either through mining precious metals or by appropriating the bullion of others, and to export more commercial goods than one imports.[7] But either way,

---

7   In a closed system, one becomes richer than one's rivals by gathering more of the available "pieces" of wealth; the number of "pieces" in the system, however, remains constant.

Mercantilist Center   The town of Bristol was founded shortly before the Norman Conquest of 1066 and for a while was important chiefly at the launching place for English armies on their way to Ireland. The discovery of the New World raised its significance enormously, and by the 17th century Bristol was the second-largest and busiest port in the kingdom. Between 1600 and 1750 Bristol was the principal site from which English slave-traders shipped African slaves to the New World. This painting, ca. 1760, shows the busy quay, where goods were loaded and unloaded.

the world economy is a "zero-sum game"—meaning that growth is reduced to mere hoarding. Wealth is thus a matter of distribution rather than creation.

> Mercantilism, in other words, did not aim at the prosperity of an entire people, nor did it think that possible to achieve. Rather, its purpose was to concentrate wealth among as few individuals as possible.

Mercantilism thus champions **protectionism**—the blocking of imports by tariff barriers, usually, and, if necessary, by law. The system, since it was based on the idea of artificially manipulating the distribution of wealth, also welcomed the awarding of monopolies by government (in return for sizeable bribes and licensing fees), the fixing of prices and wages, the blocking of competition, and the imposition of high domestic taxes. In a world of finite wealth, the reasoning went, assets must be concentrated in a small number of hands. Only this could enable the grand expenditures such as those needed to defend the realm, administer the government, and maintain social order. Mercantilism, in other words, did not aim at the prosperity of an entire people, nor did it think that possible to achieve. Rather, its purpose was to concentrate wealth among as few individuals as possible. The absolutist regimes perfected their policies over the 17th and 18th centuries—and in the process drove their own subjects into the direst poverty. (It is worth pointing out, by way of illustration, that the economic policies of China in the late 20th and early 21st centuries include many mercantilist elements.)

The classic statement in defense of mercantilism came from Thomas Mun (1571–1641), an English merchant and member of the board of directors of the English East India Company. He wrote *England's Treasure by Foreign Trade* in 1630, although it was not published until 1664. In it he argues, among other things, for the forced lowering of domestic wages. If the people of England cannot afford to purchase food, clothing, and other consumer goods, he points out, then the government will have larger amounts of those commodities available for export, which brings more money into the royal purse.

Modern thinking commonly regards mercantilism as nonsense, which raises the question of whether people in the early modern era were economic idiots. In reality they were far from it. Given the social bias against commerce as a "common" activity, Europe's nobility and most of its intelligentsia gave little thought to how economies function. The very idea of an economy as an existing, organic system remained a foreign concept. Money, goods, land, and raw resources were things one could put in one's hand, feel the heft of, and know to be real. An economy, on the other hand, is an abstraction, an invisible system of interactions that obeys supposedly fixed laws. Producing, selling, and consuming goods are aspects of human agency, but the notion of "an economy" or "a market" as an autonomous thing that determines human action requires a conceptual leap. And few people in early modern Europe were capable of or interested in making such a leap. Merchants understood that a scarcity of goods—as when, for example, a drought results in decreased crop yields—meant that they could charge a higher price. However, they interpreted this not as a scientific "law of the market" but simply as a scenario they could exploit. When 16th-century Spain imported tons of gold bullion taken from the New World, the country expected to acquire enormous wealth. What it got instead was an inflationary spiral unlike anything Europe had ever seen, the collapse of the currency, and the ruin of vast stretches of the peninsula. Compounding the problem, the Spanish rulers spent this money on a colossal scale—on palaces, museums, churches, artwork, and the army—rather than investing it in wealth-generating industry.[8] But no one at the time, in Spain or elsewhere, would have agreed that there was any connection. *That*, they would

---

[8]   Spain did not fully recover as an economic power until the late 20th century.

have insisted, makes as little sense as asserting that eating of massive amounts of food could result in a dramatic loss of weight.

MERCANTILISM AND POVERTY

Mercantilism served two specific purposes. First, it generated impressive amounts of revenue for the leading merchants and financiers of the age, who benefited from monopolies, protectionist policies that banned foreign competition, and the relative decline of domestic markets—thanks to the poverty of the bulk of the population. With captive markets in overseas colonies, too, high prices could be demanded with impunity. Second, mercantilism produced enormous returns for the governments, which made money from bribes and monopoly licenses, high tariffs on imported goods, onerous taxation of the common people, and investment in the commercial activities of the leading mercantile firms. If mercantilism did not create prosperity for the nation, that was never its aim. All that mattered was the preservation of the state and the institutions it controlled.

> If mercantilism did not create prosperity for the nation, that was never its aim. All that mattered was the preservation of the state and the institutions it controlled.

Mercantilism had been at work in France and Spain since the 1530s, in England since the reign of Elizabeth I, and in most of the rest of Europe after 1648. Its effects were stark. In contrast to the baroque splendor of aristocratic palaces and ornate churches was the grinding, humiliating poverty of the peasantry, village laborers, and local artisans and craftsmen. A French official's report on conditions among the rural populace of Normandy in 1651 paints a brutal picture:

> The most consistent food source here are the rats that the people hunt, so desperately hungry are they. They also eat plant roots that the farm animals will not touch. One can scarcely find words adequate to describing the horrors one sees everywhere. . . . This report, in fact, actually understates those horrors, rather than, as one might think, exaggerates them, for it describes only the tiniest fraction of the suffering in this district, suffering so dire that only those who have actually seen it can understand its scope. Hardly a single day passes in which at least two hundred people do not die. . . . I attest to having personally seen whole herds of people—men and women, that is, not cattle—wandering the fields between Rheims and Rethel, rooting in the dirt like pigs, and finding nothing edible, but only rotting fibers (and even these are only plentiful enough to feed half the herd), they collapse in exhaustion and have no strength left to continue searching for food. . . . The rest survive on a

Peasant Life   A small Dutch farm family prays before sharing a single bowl of gruel. Note the absence of a table, but the presence of an open fireplace—a common site of accidents, especially involving infants. Two ladders serve as a staircase leading up to the sleeping quarters. Though small, the home is perfectly clean and well-ordered. The emphasis in this engraving (1653) is not on the harshness of peasant life but the spirit of simplicity and piety among the hardworking poor.

substitute for bread that does not deserve the name, made as it is from a mixture of chopped straw and dirt.

As dire as these conditions were, they were an improvement from the last years of the Religious Wars, for the simple reason that the people no longer had to avoid marauding bands of desperate soldiers from nearly every nation in Europe. Goethe's description of people "trapped between the land and the aristocracy as between an anvil and a hammer" takes on new vividness.

The question must be asked: Given such unspeakable suffering, why did people accept absolutist government—or at least not actively oppose it? The only answer is that things were even worse during the Religious Wars. One can hardly exaggerate the bloody, murderous horror that plagued Europe before 1648.

DOMESTICATING DYNAMISM: REGULATING CULTURE

European culture, too, was subject to a form of absolutism, but not simply as an extension of royal power. The whole of society became obsessed with rule making and breaking. Rules of etiquette, standards of spelling and usage, norms for musical composition and visual art, academic curricula, domestic architecture, even the subtle social demands of fashion—all these multiplied under the pressure to conform. All came to express explicit standards of value, certainty, decorum, and taste. Such standards have existed in every age, but they have seldom dominated life as they did in Old Regime Europe.

> The whole of society became obsessed with rule making and breaking. Rules of etiquette, standards of spelling and usage, norms for musical composition and visual art, academic curricula, domestic architecture, even the subtle social demands of fashion—all these multiplied under the pressure to conform.

The baroque style, which had emerged with the Catholic Counter-Reformation, had emphasized dynamic energy and raw emotional power. Roughly half the paintings by Peter Paul Rubens (1577–1640) glorify Catholic themes; most of the rest portray the magnificence of Europe's royals and high aristocrats. In music, the Baroque zenith was reached by the father-son team of Alessandro (1660–1725) and Domenico Scarlatti (1685–1757) and Antonio Vivaldi (1678–1741). Most music lovers today rank Johann Sebastian Bach (1686–1750) as the greatest baroque composer.[9]

Bach insisted that "all music should be for God" (*"Alle Musik soll für Gott sein"*). But as the style spread from Italy and Spain to the rest of Europe, its focus shifted to glorifying the monarchies. What else stood between the people and Hobbesian chaos? The courts slowly replaced the dynamism of the baroque with the controlled formal tone of **classicism**. In the visual arts this was the age of Nicolas Poussin (1594–1665) and Charles Le Brun (1619–1691); in theatre, of Pedro Calderón de la Barca (1600–1681), Pierre Corneille (1606–1684), and Jean Racine (1639–1699); in literature, of John Milton (1608–1674) and John Dryden (1631–1700). The strictures of formal classicism eased in the 18th century, but the insistence on proper composition, content, and form continued.

The Absolutist Age also saw the first comprehensive dictionaries of the European languages. Bilingual dictionaries, the sort to help English speakers learn French, or vice versa, had existed since the invention of the printing press. But dictionaries as normative reference works for native speakers and writers were another matter altogether. Nearly two dozen hastily produced English

---

[9]   In his own time, however, Bach was considered just a good provincial musician (especially as an organist). A figure of *real* stature would have composed operas, which Bach refused to do.

dictionaries had been published between 1550 and 1750, in a rush to capitalize on the dramatic spread of literacy made possible by print. Only with Samuel Johnson (1709–1784), however, was the extensive, critical, and prescriptive *Dictionary of the English Language* (1755) finally published.

Johnson's nine-year labor was a watershed event. A dictionary, after all, is a rulebook, one that asserts, for example, that the word *chair* is spelled C-H-A-I-R and in no other way—not chaar, chaire, chayr, chare, chaere, char, or any other phonetic estimation. (To date, for example, seven authentic signatures of William Shakespeare's have been found, and he spells his name differently each time.) It sets meanings and defines usage; it standardizes and regulates syntax.[10] Johnson's *Dictionary* succeeded where earlier efforts had failed, and it remained authoritative until the publication of the complete *Oxford English Dictionary* in 1928. In France, a team of scholars produced the *Dictionnaire de l'Académie française* in 1698. The *Vocabolario degli Accademici della Crusca* had appeared in Italy even earlier, in 1612, and the *Diccionario de la lengua española* arrived in 1780. The German language, by contrast, did not acquire a comparable dictionary until the Grimm brothers (of fairy-tale fame) began to compile their *Deutsches Wörterbuch* in 1838.

Ecstatic Divine Love   Gian Lorenzo Bernini (1598–1680) carved this famous statue of Saint Theresa of Avila in 1645. Theresa was a Carmelite nun whose mystical revelations formed the backbone of her books of confessional and theological writings. Her best-known books are *The Way to Perfection, The Inner Castle*, and her absorbing autobiography. In this last book (actually the first one she wrote) she describes one of her visions, this one of a heavenly angel: "In his hand I saw a long spear of gold, from the point of which a small flame showed. It was as though he thrust it repeatedly into my heart, piercing my innermost parts; and whenever he pulled the spear out it was as though he drew my heart out as well, leaving me all on fire with love for God. The pain was so great it made me moan—and yet this great pain was so sweet that I wanted it never to end."

---

[10]   Prior to Johnson, the spelling of English words was left to each writer's personal preference. So long as the reader could tell what word the writer meant, it meant little how the word used was spelled.

DECENCY AND MODESTY

If language needed standardization and control, so much more did daily behavior. Norms of social behavior had long been determined by local custom. Books of etiquette date back to the Middle Ages, when treatises on "courtesie" were required reading for the higher nobility of the late 12th and 13th centuries. Generalized works of etiquette for the urban classes, however, became increasingly common in post-Westphalia Europe. Richard Strathwaite (1588–1673) published a trilogy of guides—*The English Gentleman, The English Gentlewoman,* and *Description of a Good Wife*—that established norms of behavior that lasted a hundred years; Eleazar Moody's *School of Good Manners* (1715) was an enormously popular guide for parents who wanted to raise well-behaved children. In Italy, Baldassare Castiglione's *Il libro del cortegiano* (1528; in English as *The Book of the Courtier* in 1561) had established the norms for proper comportment in the Renaissance, but was overtaken in the 17th and 18th centuries by texts aimed at bourgeois society.

This is the society lampooned in the great comedy *The Middle-Class Gentleman* (*Le bourgeois gentilhomme,* 1670) by Molière (the pen name of Jean-Baptiste Poquelin [1622–1673]), whose very title is a part of the joke. A bourgeois commoner is attempting to behave with noble manners, as if one can become civilized by mimicking polite behavior. But a laughing matter in 1670 became serious business a generation later, as books on table etiquette, polite conversation, proper dress and comportment, and the rearing of well-behaved children grew in popularity. A French guide from 1729 helped explain the proper use of a new invention—the napkin:[11]

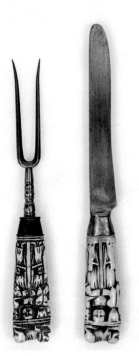

Table Knife and Fork Most Europeans had traditionally used only knives and spoons at table. Forks, though known since Roman times, were used only as kitchen tools, if at all. Renaissance Italy reintroduced the use of table forks, although it is unclear whether this resulted from the desire to emulate the Romans or to limit one's exposure to disease—since people commonly carried their own knives and forks with them in a box. As a rule, the farther north and west from Italy, the slower the adoption of the fork. In Germany and England especially, forks were long considered effeminate affectations; and the people of the American colonies did not embrace them until the late 18th century. The knife and fork shown here were made in Germany in the 17th century.

---

[11] Until the early 18th century, polite diners used the edges of the tablecloth to cover their laps and wipe their hands.

When at table one ought always to use a napkin, plate, knife, spoon, and fork; in fact it is now considered to be utterly improper to be without any one of these.

The proper thing is to wait until the highest-ranking dinner guest unfolds his napkin before unfolding one's own, but if everyone at table is a social equal, they should all unfold their napkins at the same time and without ceremony.

It is poor manners to use the napkin to wipe one's face, and even poorer manners to wipe one's teeth; but the grossest behavior of all is to use the napkin to blow one's nose.

This text from 1729 signals change in its very title: *La Salle: Les règles de la bienséance et de la civilité chrétienne* ("The Room: The Rules of Propriety and of Christian Civility"). And as for bodily comportment:

Decency and modesty demand that one keeps covered all the parts of the body, except the head and hands, when in society. Moreover, one should take every care never to touch with one's bare hand any part of the body that must remain properly covered; if one absolutely must do so, it must be done with the greatest discretion. A polite person simply must become accustomed to suffering small discomforts without twisting, rubbing, or scratching. . . .

When one needs to urinate, one should always withdraw to a private place—for it is permissible to perform natural functions (and this is true even for children) so long as one does it where one is not seen. It is nevertheless altogether impolite to emit wind from one's body—either from below or above—even if it is done without any sound.

Contrast an English guide from 1619, written in verse:

Let not your privy members be
laid open to be viewed;
it is most shameful and abhorr'd,
detestable and rude.

Retain not urine, nor the wind
which do thy body vex;
so [long as] it be done in secrecy,
let that not thee perplex.

The Teatro San Carlo in Naples   Built in 1737, then rebuilt after a fire in 1816, this is the oldest continuously used opera house in Europe. The original upholstery was blue; the red was used after a fire. Seen at the center here is the royal box, where members of the Bourbon dynasty sat. It was designed specifically for the staging of operas, with the auditorium built in a U-shape and tiered; an orchestra pit, so as not to overwhelm the singers; and all the backstage areas and equipment as needed for any theatrical production. Opera houses were expensive, and most of those built in the 17th and 18th centuries resulted from the patronage of royals and high aristocrats. By maintaining the system of tiered balconies as the reserve of the upper classes, the seats of the main floor could be opened to non-nobles. Thus opera, by its very popularity, helped to maintain the social system by embodying the privileged hierarchy while allowing the commoners to share in the delight made possible by aristocratic largesse.

Guidebooks laid out rules for conversation, letter writing, dress, the issuing of invitations, and behavior at occasions such as weddings, funerals, balls, and theaters.

Regulation reigned in other areas of life too. In music, most of the major compositional forms moved toward formal definition: fugues and sonatas initially, and eventually concertos and symphonies. Every opera had to have its text (libretto) approved by state censors before it could be staged, to make sure the plot carried no subversive messages. Just as significantly, popular pressure gradually demanded further norms in opera—such as the strict separation of comedy (opera buffa) and tragic opera (opera seria), the use of plots from classical drama or from French neoclassical theater, and the Italian language.[12]

---

[12]   Women were forbidden to take the stage in regular theater productions. Opera, however, offered them the chance to perform alongside men.

The period from 1680 to 1740 also saw the peak in popularity of castrati in the leading male roles. Castration before puberty prevented the natural deepening of the male voice, enabling the singer to sustain a high and flexible musical register. Moreover, the loss of testosterone production resulted in the weakening of the joints—which caused castrati to develop exceptionally long limbs and ribs. Their increased chest capacity allowed them extraordinary lung power, which aided their projection. So great was the demand for castrati and so lucrative were the potential rewards they could win that as many as three thousand young singers across Europe submitted to the operation annually during this peak period.

THE BIRTH OF PRIVATE LIFE

Aspects of domestic, even private, life became subject to innovative strictures, too. Societies were brought up on the idea of maintaining order at all costs. For most urban dwellers, living quarters by long tradition had been single open-space rooms above the workshop, tavern, or storefront in which they worked. The details of private life were conducted communally. Over the 17th and 18th centuries, however, domestic architecture took on interior walls, even among those with modest incomes. The activities of daily life—sleeping, cooking and eating, tending to hygiene, and socializing—were to be performed in discrete rooms. It is no accident that the word *privacy* was coined in the 17th century; before then, neither the word nor the concept existed. Even the human body became subject to a kind of control. Common people throughout the Middle Ages and Renaissance had worn simple garments that sheathed the body, whereas the 17th and 18th centuries saw the general introduction of underwear of various types. Henceforth, everyday dress for both men and women involved undergarments—not just to provide warmth but to support and control the body's movement. Cultural regulation like this was not imposed by government but arose naturally.

> Henceforth, everyday dress for both men and women involved undergarments—not just to provide warmth but to support and control the body's movement. Cultural regulation like this was not imposed by government but arose naturally.

As standards of expected behavior rose, manners improved, and aesthetic values became defined and codified. In turn, attitudes toward those who failed to observe the new niceties grew harsher. Aristocratic culture had always prided itself on the chasm that separated it from the dirty masses, but a sense of cultural elitism began to emerge among bourgeois Europeans at this time as well. As a result, efforts spread to instill better behavior among the lower orders, some of them altruistic, others not. Centuries-old peasant entertainments like carnivals (rural festivals that usually preceded Lent) were discouraged from the pulpit and judicial bench alike.

A Clean, Well-lit Place   The interior of a well-to-do burgher's house in 17th-century Holland. The Dutch prided themselves on their sense of order and balance. The family that lived here was obviously wealthy but not ostentatious. The woman in the front room plays a harpsichord; to the left of the door is a four-posted bed. Each room opens onto the other, and each is filled with light.

English Puritan ministers railed against the evils of taverns, dances, country fairs, and popular folk songs. Protestant ministers in Germany struggled to stamp out rural irregularities in communal worship.

In the cities, the urban poor were no longer objects of pity and almsgiving but were denounced in sermons, speeches, broadsides, and newspapers (another invention of the age) as lazy, deceitful, uncouth, and potentially dangerous. New institutions arose to deal with them: poor houses, hospitals (hospices, that is), and reformatories. These institutions performed the valuable services of removing the unsightly destitute from polite society, and then either rehabilitating them (if possible) by teaching them a craft or effectively imprisoning them. In 1676 Louis XIV went so far as to order every city in France to build and maintain a hospital for warehousing the worst off of the urban poor.

In England, people whose behavior violated basic norms but who had not broken the law frequently ended up in Bedlam. Although the hospital dates back to the 13th century, in 1675 it became the first asylum for the mentally ill.[13] The

---

[13]   In 1725 Bedlam was divided into separate wings for those considered curable ("patients") and incurable ("lunatics").

idea caught on, and asylums soon dotted the European landscape. So too did prisons. Prior to the 18th century, jails or dungeons were simply holding areas for those waiting until judicial punishment (execution, lashing, maiming, or a simple fine) was carried out. But after 1700 state after state preferred to remove criminals (in noncapital cases, at least) from society altogether, and lengthy incarceration became the punishment of choice. Those whose presence offended polite society became isolated, institutionalized, and removed from the scene.

THE ENGLISH EXCEPTION

England rose to the top tier of European nations in the second half of the 16th century. When Elizabeth I died in 1603, however, a constitutional crisis threatened to undo the internal stability of the realm and endangered England's position in the international economy. In response, the new Stuart dynasty asserted greater absolutism, but it ended in civil war.

Elizabeth, of course, had never married, and so the Tudor dynasty ended. After some intrigue, the throne passed to James Stuart, the great-grandson of Henry VIII's sister. This marked the beginning of the trouble-plagued Stuart dynasty, which lasted, with interruptions, until 1714. Being Scottish, James I (r. 1603–1625) faced rude resistance from the start despite the legitimacy of his succession.[14] More than ethnic prejudice was at work in this, however, for James was a passionate advocate of royal absolutism. Before coming to power in England he had published a tendentious book called *The True Law of Free Monarchies* (1598), in which he argues that since kingship existed "before any estates or ranks of men . . . [and] before any parliaments were held or laws made," it is therefore unnatural for a king's power to be checked in any way. The argument is as weak as James's stubbornness was strong, and the struggle to balance royal ambitions and Parliamentary rights ultimately characterized the history of the entire Stuart dynasty.

James restated his position in a speech to the English Parliament in 1610:

> The state of monarchy is the supremest thing upon earth, for kings are not only God's lieutenants upon earth and sit upon God's throne, but even by God himself they are called gods. There be three principal [comparisons] that illustrate the state of monarchy: one taken out of the word of God, and the two other out of the grounds of policy and philosophy. In the Scriptures kings are called gods, and so their power after a certain relation compared to the Divine power. Kings are also compared to fathers of families; for a

---

[14] James, who ruled as James VI in Scotland (r. 1567–1603), was the first to style himself the king of "Great Britain."

king is truly *parens patriae*, the politic father of his people. And lastly, kings are compared to the head of this microcosm of the body of man. . . . I conclude then this point touching the power of kings with this axiom of divinity, that as to dispute what God may do is blasphemy . . . so is it sedition in subjects to dispute what a king may do in the height of his power.

Colossally and ideologically vain, James I also had a near-pathological fear of assassination.[15] His childhood in Scotland had been filled with political deceits, palace intrigues, kidnappings, and numerous murder plots. The horror of his early years made him distrustful of those around him, and once in power in Edinburgh and London he resolved that institutions like parliaments, courts, and churches were mere service organizations of the monarchy rather than sharers of power. Although he had been brought up as a Catholic, James found that Anglicanism suited his self-regard, for it identified the king as undisputed head of the church. He embraced the faith and endorsed the Act of Supremacy, which asserted that only an avowed Anglican could ever sit on the throne in England. His greatest achievement was his support for a new English translation of the Scriptures intended specifically for his newly adopted church—the so-called **King James Bible**, known officially as the Authorized Version.

The seldom-read dedication to the King James Bible provides a good example of absolutist ideology. It begins:

Great and manifold were the blessings, most dread Sovereign, which Almighty God, the Father of all mercies, bestowed upon us the people of England, when first he sent Your Majesty's Royal Person to rule and reign over us. For whereas it was the expectation of many who wished not well unto our Sion, that, upon the setting of that bright Occidental Star, Queen Elizabeth, of most happy memory some thick and palpable clouds of darkness would so have overshadowed this land, that men should have been in doubt which way they were to walk, and that it should hardly be known who was to direct the unsettled State; the appearance of Your Majesty, as of the Sun in his strength, instantly dispelled those supposed and surmised mists, and gave unto all that were well affected exceeding cause of comfort; especially when we beheld the Government established in Your Highness and Your hopeful Seed, by an undoubted Title; and this also accompanied with peace and tranquility at home and abroad.

---

[15]   In childhood, James had seen more than one family member cut down. He regularly wore a heavy dagger-proof tunic under his royal garments.

But among all our joys, there was no one that more filled our hearts than the blessed continuance of the preaching of God's sacred Word among us, which is that inestimable treasure which excelleth all the riches of earth; because the fruit thereof extendeth itself, not only to the time spent in this transitory world, but directeth and disposeth men unto that eternal happiness which is above in heaven.

Then not to suffer this to fall to the ground, but rather to take it up, and to continue it in that state wherein the famous Predecessor of Your Highness did leave it; nay, to go forward with the confidence and resolution of a man, in maintaining the truth of Christ, and propagating it far and near, is that which hath so bound and firmly knit the hearts of all Your Majesty's loyal and religious

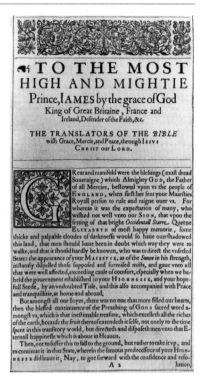

Divine Writ   Dedication page of the first edition of the Authorized (King James) Version of the Bible (1611).

people unto You, that Your very name is precious among them: their eye doth behold You with comfort, and they bless You in their hearts, as that sanctified Person, who, under God, is the immediate author of their true happiness. And this their contentment doth not diminish or decay, but every day increaseth and taketh strength, when they observe that the zeal of Your Majesty toward the house of God doth not slack or go backward, but is more and more kindled, manifesting itself abroad in the farthest parts of Christendom, by writing in defence of the truth, (which hath given such a blow unto that Man of Sin as will not be healed,) and every day at home, by religious and learned discourse, by frequenting the house of God, by hearing the Word preached, by cherishing the teachers thereof, by caring for the Church, as a most tender and loving nursing father.

James fervently believed in mercantilism and followed its tenets in order to escape financial dependency on the Parliament. Wanting to increase English power in North America, he established the colonies at Jamestown (1607) and

Plymouth (1620), in what would eventually become the states of Virginia and Massachusetts. He also tried, though unsuccessfully, to arrange a marriage between his son Charles and a Spanish princess. He awarded many monopolies and collected enormous licensing fees, which raised opposition from the gentry; but he compensated them by creating (and selling to the highest bidders—most of whom came from the gentry) an unprecedented number of new noble titles. The "baronetcy" was his signature invention, and he happily bestowed this honor on anyone who would pay his asking price of 10,000 pounds. Many purchasers came forward. When James first came to the English throne in 1603 the House of Lords had fifty-nine members; when he died in 1625 the House had more than twice that number. He also granted more than two thousand knighthoods.

CIVIL WAR AND RESTORATION

When Charles I (r. 1625–1649) became king, opposition to the Stuarts had grown to the point where Parliament openly demanded constitutional reforms. Charles had inherited his father's vanity and stubbornness, however, in addition to his titles, and had no intention of compromising royal prerogatives. Unfortunately for him, he also inherited England's involvement in the Thirty Years' War. Meeting commitments to numerous parties in that struggle placed ever-greater pressure on royal finances, but Parliament passed a Petition for Right (1628) that denied the crown additional taxes and restricted the king's judicial authority. The following year Charles summoned a new Parliament, immediately arrested nine of its leaders, and dissolved the assembly; no new Parliament met for eleven years, during which time Charles bullied new fees and levies from the provinces. By 1640 king and country were wholly estranged. When Parliament did convene again in that year, the legislators prepared a "Grand Remonstrance"—a lengthy list of formal complaints about royal abuses of authority. Charles's troops again stormed the Parliament, but were resisted. Civil war had begun.

The Parliamentary forces were disorganized at first but soon came under the leadership of Oliver Cromwell (1599–1658), a Puritan in religion and a member of the gentry by social status. Without much military experience, he nevertheless rose quickly through the officer ranks of the Parliamentary forces. He was one of the three or four most powerful figures on the scene when the army defeated Charles in battle and took him prisoner in 1645. Few people wanted to abolish the monarchy altogether, and most hoped to force the king to some sort of compromise. When news came that Charles was in secret negotiations with Royalist sympathizers to launch a Scottish invasion of England, however, patience was at an end. Parliament placed Charles on trial for treason in 1648, and when the tribunal returned a guilty verdict Cromwell was one of the signatories to the king's death warrant. Charles was beheaded on January 30, 1649.

But the people who had opposed the monarchy soon found that, having removed the king, they could not agree on what to replace him with. Dissension broke out almost immediately; after several tense weeks, Cromwell took over the government by general acclamation. For the next eleven years he governed the Commonwealth of England, Europe's most radical experiment to date in representative government. Despite his best efforts, Cromwell failed to put together an administration that could outlast him. When he died in 1658, the Commonwealth quickly fell apart, and Parliament summoned Charles I's exiled son, who had taken refuge in Holland, to return to England and restore the monarchy. Charles II (r. 1660–1685), a carefree hedonist by nature, agreed to certain limits on royal power and took the throne amid a general sense of celebration. After twenty years of government by dour Puritans, the people welcomed Charles's love of pleasure and laughter and his reopening of the theater houses.

The party was short-lived, however, since an outbreak of bubonic plague in 1665 and the Great Fire of London in 1666 destroyed much of the city and took tens of thousands of lives. Charles now adopted a more serious approach, although he never managed to keep his living expenses within the budget the Parliament had set for him. In 1672 he attempted to force through a royal declaration that removed all legal penalties from the practice of Roman Catholicism, but backed down when Parliament resisted. Doubts about Charles's own religious loyalty filled the rest of his years on the throne.

Charles had no legitimate heir, since his wife's pregnancies had all ended in miscarriages and stillbirths. (He had married a Portuguese princess, Catarina de Bragança, who was unpopular with the English on account of her Catholicism and her lasting inability to learn English.) And so the crown passed in 1685 to Charles's brother James II (r. 1685–1688), who was openly Roman Catholic and determined to introduce absolutism.[16] James's short reign was filled with dissension, since the Parliament refused to remove the legal strictures that limited Catholic rights. Even more worrisome was the new king's desire for a much larger standing royal army. England had traditionally never kept soldiers in uniform and on the public payroll during peacetime. James's proposal, moreover, appeared too much in line with the actions of the post-Westphalian monarchs across Europe and stirred the Parliament into dramatic action.

In 1688 a group of leading members of Parliament invited the Protestant ruler of Holland, Prince William of Orange, to invade their realm and depose

---

[16] Charles II was received in the Roman Catholic Church on his deathbed. James II had formally converted to Catholicism while growing up on the Continent during the Commonwealth.

James. (William was married to James II's daughter Mary.) William agreed. James initially thought he could defeat the invaders but soon realized otherwise, and so he fled the scene. He was soon captured by William's men, who, with William's consent, allowed him to escape to France—where he lived out his days in the court of Louis XIV. Since the coup proceeded without significant violence (James's soldiers deserted him en masse), it is known as the **Glorious Revolution**. Without shedding a drop of blood, England had staged a successful revolution, brought down an unpopular monarch, and brought to power a popular royal couple dedicated to Protestantism and constitutional rule.

OTTOMAN MIGHT AND ISLAMIC ABSOLUTISM

The Islamic world in the 17th and 18th centuries consisted of three empires that were also de facto absolutist states, although their regimes lacked the philosophical underpinnings found in Europe: the Ottoman Empire, Safavid Iran, and Mughal India (see Map 14.2). Language and culture distinguished them as much as political regimes. The Ottomans controlled the Arabic-speaking nations, the

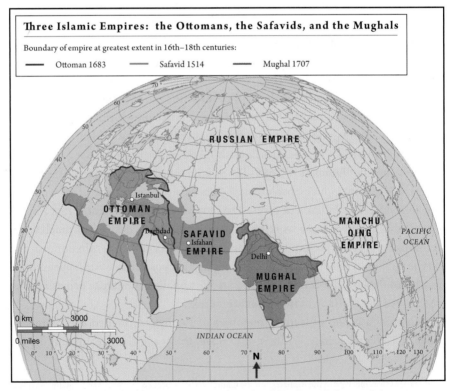

Three Islamic Empires: the Ottomans, the Safavids, and the Mughals

Boundary of empire at greatest extent in 16th–18th centuries:

—— Ottoman 1683   —— Safavid 1514   —— Mughal 1707

MAP 14.2   Three Islamic Empires: the Ottomans, the Safavids, and the Mughals

Safavids governed the Persian speakers, and the Mughal dynasty ruled over the numerous language groups of the vast Indian subcontinent. Important religious distinctions existed as well, with Sunni Islam dominating among the Arab peoples and Shi'ite Islam practiced by the bulk of Persian speakers. Though overwhelmingly Muslim, none of these states was religiously monolithic, for large Christian and Jewish populations continued to reside in them.

Ottoman military encroachments on Europe had continued well into the 17th century, and at least three times (1529, 1532, and 1683) their armies had advanced as far as Vienna. According to one tradition, the battle of 1683 was followed by a citywide celebration, for which the Viennese bakers' guild developed a new pastry—the croissant. This supposedly mocked the Islamic crescent that appeared on the Turkish army's banners. The powerful Ottoman forces were symbolically reduced to puff pastries.

After 1683 the Turks were put on the defensive for the first time in their history, a position exacerbated by the ascendancy of European merchant fleets in the Indian Ocean. Since they had previously lost control of the eastern Mediterranean at the battle of Lepanto in 1571, the new setbacks occasioned two new developments for the Turks. First, they gradually relinquished control over the furthest provinces of their empire—Morocco and Algeria, along the North African coast, which henceforth became independent states. To resist Spanish dominance in the western Mediterranean, these new states encouraged the "Barbary pirates" to attack ships on either side of the Gibraltarian Strait. Second, they delegated more power to provincial governors, with a system of tax farming that assigned local fiscal control to leading families. These steps were not, however, a complete capitulation of authority. Turkish autocracy had always differed from European absolutism in a fundamental way. Since the 15th century the monopoly of power was held by the dynastic house of Osman rather than by any specific individual. The sultan in Istanbul, as leader of the royal family, held primacy of place over his relatives, but power was rightfully held by every representative of Osman's line. The empire's system of government was therefore an oligarchical absolutism, but was no less absolutist for that.

Like that of its Western contemporaries, Ottoman absolutism was based on military might. The most important component of the army was the large corps of **Janissaries**, standing infantry units that resembled the military-religious orders of the Christian Middle Ages in their rigorous discipline, austerity, and spiritual vows. These "new soldiers" (the literal meaning of the Turkish word *yeniçeri*) were formed of Christian children from the Balkans and the Caucasus who were forced into military service and converted to Islam—just as had been the practice centuries before with the Mamluk slave-soldiers. They were sworn to celibacy during their years in the army, granted pensions and the right to marry upon retirement, and accorded exceptionally high social status. By the 17th century civil government was largely dominated by former Janissaries. At that time too the traditional practice of drafting Christian children into the corps (called *devşirme*) was abolished, as ethnically Turkish families sought to place their own children in the corps, in hopes of social advancement. Given the relative decrease in their military activity after 1683, the Janissaries were increasingly used (again like their European counterparts) as domestic police forces. In this role they maintained order, quelled revolts, and represented the ever-watchful eye of the sultan and his family.

SAFAVID PLEASURES

The Safavid dynasty in Iran had been established in 1501. It had established Shi'ism as the state religion and reasserted the Persian identity of the nation, after the Abbasid, Mongol, and Tatar interludes. The Safavids had emerged from a heterodox Sufi order and regarded themselves as either the earthly representatives of the Shi'i Hidden **Imam** or as the Hidden Imam himself. Given their religious origins, they were not likely to recognize any checks on their power. To be prudent, they complemented the religious basis of their claims to absolute authority by relying on the unwavering support of a large and potent army. Most of their army was composed of regular infantry units that served only as needed. More significant for maintaining the regime was a unique network of militant units known collectively as the **Qizilbash**. These companies—identifiable by the distinctive red-topped headpieces they wore (and from which they take their name)—regarded the Safavid ruler as divine. So great was their zeal that the Qizilbash customarily went into battle without any type of defensive armor. They were convinced that Allah and their Safavid lord's blessing would protect them from harm.[17]

Under the greatest Safavid **shah**, Abbas I [P] (r. 1587–1629), the Persians recaptured Baghdad and established commercial ties with both the British and Dutch East India Companies. Baghdad had never fully recovered from the devastation wreaked on it by the Mongols and may have held as few as fifty thousand people. An elaborate irrigation network had made the river valleys fertile since Sumerian times. Now that too lay in ruins, and most of Iraq had become a patchwork of scrubby pastoral zones loosely but violently controlled

---

[17]   The Qizilbash still exist as a distinct religious community in Afghanistan, Azerbaijan, Iran, and Pakistan. The third president of modern-day Pakistan, Agha Yahya Khan (1969–1971), was Qizilbash.

by rival tribes. But Baghdad itself still mattered as a forward defensive position against a renewed Ottoman offensive. Friendly ties with the East India Companies were vital, since conflicts over control of the sea-lanes had shifted commercial routes away from the Persian Gulf and toward the Red Sea, on the other side of the Arabian Peninsula. The shift threatened to cost the Iranians considerable revenue.

Like the European monarchs, the shahs centralized their nation's wealth as much as they did its political power, and they spent as lavishly on themselves as did Louis XIV. Magnificent palaces, pleasure gardens, libraries, astronomical observatories, and public adornments filled the cities. They built mosques and madrasas by the dozen and restored older centers of worship that had been damaged during the Mongol and Tatar years. In Iraq the holy shrines in the cities of Karbala and Najaf—dear to the Shi'a—were rebuilt and again became important sites of pilgrimage. Abbas II [P] (r. 1642–1666) extended his realm northward into Afghanistan, taking the strategic city of Kandahar from the Mughals, and ruled over a thriving and peaceable realm.

But the later Safavids gave in to the pleasures of their lavish lifestyle and spent more time enjoying themselves than in governing, which led to the dynasty's downfall in 1736. Several decades of turmoil ensued until, in 1796, a new dynasty took over—the **Qajar**—which held absolute power over Iran until 1925. The founder of the new dynasty, Muhammad Khan Qajar [P] (r. 1794–1797), had been castrated as a young boy by a rival for leadership of the Qajar tribe, and the experience contributed to his predilection for cruelty and violence.[18] While Muhammad was assassinated in 1797, the Qajar shahs still focused resolutely on maintaining their political power and the wealth that made it possible. Yet they also distanced themselves from the theocratic ideology of the Safavids. Religious and legal authority thus devolved from the court-appointed officials (qadis) of earlier times to the caste of scholars in shariah law produced by the madrasas. In the case of Shi'ite Islam, these were predominately clerics who held the title of **mullah** ("guardian"). Leadership of the mullahs fell to a higher office still, the **ayatollah** ("sign from God," literally). By the end of the 18th century, Iran had evolved into a dual absolutist state: political and military might was monopolized by the secular state under the autocratic control of the shah, while religious authority remained the preserve of an elite corps of mullahs led by their clerical superiors, the ayatollahs.

---

[18] Muhammad once ordered the blinding of twenty thousand men in a city that resisted his authority. He also had the Georgian city of Tbilisi burned to the ground and its entire Christian population put to death in 1795.

Isfahan   Isfahan, in central Iran, was the capital of Safavid Persia from
1598 to 1795. Located on a high plain just east of the Zagros Mountains, its
high elevation—comparable to that of Denver, in the United States—makes
for chilly winters. It snows usually once a year. Summers, though, are hot.
Shown in this image is the Shah Mosque, built in 1611 and considered one of
the great masterpieces of Persian architecture. The large square behind it
(the Naqsh-e Jahan Square) was built to serve a purpose analogous to that
of the Château de Versailles—that is, it housed all the Safavid rulers'
leading nobles and ministers of state, keeping them all in his direct sight.
The mosque itself comes off the square at a unique angle, so that the
towering entrance arch (called an *iwan*) and the central dome of the mosque
can both be seen from everywhere in the square. Visible to the right of the
great dome is a smaller, lower dome that marks the "winter mosque"—a
smaller, warmer site for use during the cold winters.

THE END OF ORDER

Absolutist Europe and constitutional England formed the center of a vast network of international trade (see Map 14.3). It proved a hybrid of commercial, colonial, mercantilist, and capitalist practices. It also turned on new markets,
sustained by slavery and domestic labor, and it added enough uncertainty on top
of sheer human misery to bring an end to order.

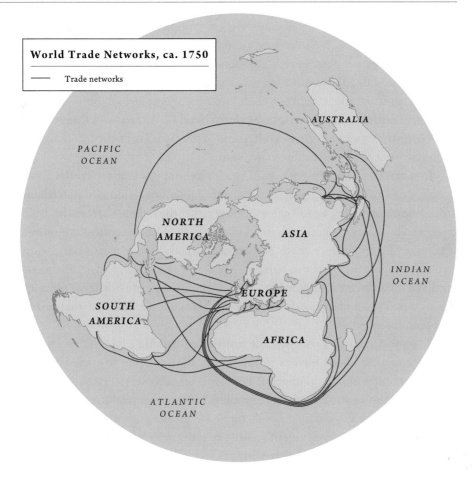

MAP 14.3   World Trade Networks, ca. 1750

Starting with Sweden in 1664, Europe's leading countries created royal or national banks that quickly developed systems of credit to finance manufacturing, commerce, and development. Strict mercantilism demanded the use of precious-metal coins, and aristocratic Europe's demand for Asian luxury goods never abated. Hence there was drainage of gold and silver from the West, which led to the introduction of paper money. Released from dependence on actual bullion, the new national banks dramatically increased loans, bonds, and other opportunities to invest. Credit now became available "on account," as promises to repay. National stock exchanges soon followed. Joint-stock companies like the British East India Company, the Dutch United East India Company, and the South Sea Company benefitted from the influx of investments. Their charters granted them monopolies on certain manufactures and trades, which allowed many to build impressive long-term returns. But involvement in this wealth creation was limited to those with excess capital, or wealth to invest, which was still a small percentage of the population. Mercantilist practices kept most laborers' wages at rock-bottom levels, and price controls and domestic taxes kept most skilled draftsmen from setting aside investment capital. As a result, most of the benefits of the international economy went to a small number of investors.

Investment was a new concept. The idea behind it—that capital itself, not people, can *do work*—is an abstraction that few fully understood. In purchasing stock, one is not buying a good or service, but rather the right to share in the profit generated by the future production and sale of those goods or services. Moreover, it takes money to produce goods and services, which usually means borrowing. In purchasing stock, one is also purchasing a share of a company's debt. Elaborate legal and financial arrangements can equally beguile and confuse those entering the market. The combination led frequently to speculative "bubbles" that ruined thousands of investors.

The most famous crash was the **South Sea Bubble** of 1720. The South Sea Company had been formed in London in 1711 in order to trade with the Spanish colonies in North America. To finance its activities, the company purchased England's national debt (then some 50 million pounds) in return for the right to exchange government bonds for shares in the company. Bondholders who despaired of the government's ability to redeem its bonds were thrilled by the possibility of New World riches and rushed to invest in the company. Soon a wave of speculation drove share prices to unprecedented heights, and the company encouraged the buying frenzy. It announced ever more spectacular ventures that it intended to undertake, like the manufacture of a (nonexistent) machine that could desalinate seawater—not to mention an ultrasecret "undertaking of great profit in due time to be revealed." Shares rose from 150 pounds each to over 1,000 pounds before the inevitable crash came and investors were wiped out.

THE SLAVE TRADE AND DOMESTIC SUBJUGATION

Among the most reliable investments were New World agriculture and the slave trade that enabled it. Until the 19th century, when settlers moved westward across the Great Plains, the New World did not produce food for export. Crops like potatoes, tomatoes, and corn (maize) were introduced into European farming and consequently were not shipped across the Atlantic. But sugar cane, cotton, and tobacco did not grow well in Europe. Being non-perishable, they could also be transported over-seas to generate enormous profits, but they were labor-intensive crops. The need for slaves thus grew, as did the demand for the crops. Throughout the 18th century be-tween seventy-five thousand and one hundred thousand African slaves were shipped across the Atlantic annually, until the slave trade was finally abolished (by France in 1793, England in 1807). Exact accounting is impossible, but somewhere around twelve million sub-Saharan Africans were brought to the New World in chains. The greatest number of them went to the Caribbean Islands, where they perished in hor-rifying numbers while working the sugarcane fields. Roughly a half million were sent to what eventually became the American South (see Map 14.4).

The profits generated by slave-produced New World agriculture were enor-mous. England's colonial profits rose from 10 million pounds to 40 million pounds between 1700 and 1776. France saw its revenues increase from 15 to 250 million livres in the same period. But the profits of the era were not distributed throughout society; they went to the highest social strata. Domestically, the rural economy was a ruin. As much as 20 percent of the European population lived in abject poverty.

The introduction of maize and potatoes alleviated famine in Europe, but also raised a new danger—alcoholism. Crops no longer needed for food could be con-verted into distilled spirits, which provided the poor with an escape from the drear-iness and hardship of their lives. Before, liquor distil-lation had primarily been a secret of monasteries, which used it to support themselves. By now, how-ever, the Protestant Reformation had advanced the knowledge of distillation across Europe. Gin became the hard liquor of choice among the poor, since it was so plentiful and cheap. By 1740, in England, gin production was nearly six times the nation's beer production—and all of it was drunk locally. The city of London alone had over six thousand gin shops, which sold cheap gin in bottles with rounded bot-toms. This meant that the bottles could not be set down without risking a spill, which in turn urged the buyer to drink the entire bottle. When the government in 1736 tried to reduce consumption by imposing a heavy tax on gin, crowds took to the street by the thousands until they won a repeal of the tax.[19]

Those poor not killed off by drink often succumbed to disease, since the physical conditions in which the poor lived were appalling. In the district of

> Gin became the hard liquor of choice among the poor, since it was so plentiful and cheap. By 1740, in England, gin production was nearly six times the nation's beer production—and all of it was drunk locally.

---

[19] As liquor became a favorite item for governments to tax, people operated their private stills at night, so that the smoke produced would not be seen. That is why homemade liquor is known as moonshine.

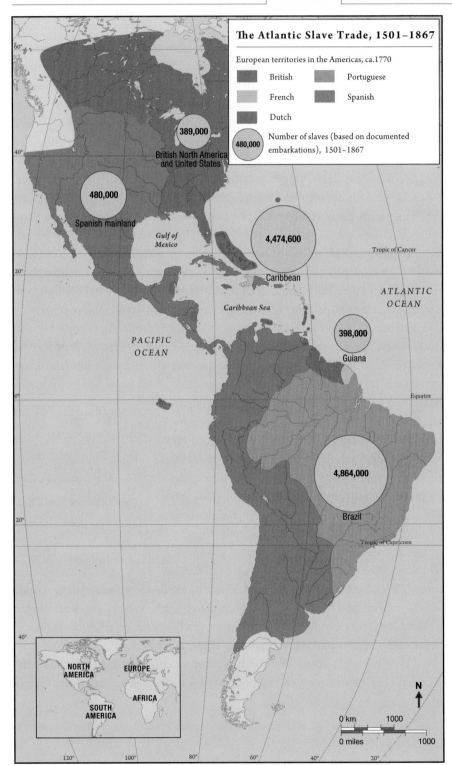

The Atlantic Slave Trade, 1501–1867

European territories in the Americas, ca.1770

British

French

Dutch

Portuguese

Spanish

480,000 Number of slaves (based on documented embarkations), 1501–1867

389,000
British North America and United States

480,000
Spanish mainland

Gulf of Mexico

4,474,600
Caribbean

Tropic of Cancer

Caribbean Sea

PACIFIC OCEAN

ATLANTIC OCEAN

398,000
Guiana

Equator

4,864,000
Brazil

Tropic of Capricorn

NORTH AMERICA   EUROPE

AFRICA

SOUTH AMERICA

N

0 km   1000

0 miles   1000

MAP 14.4   The Atlantic Slave Trade, 1501–1867

Brittany, in northwestern France, dysentery killed one hundred thousand in a single year (1779). Until the middle of the 18th century, only one-half of all children born lived to the age of ten, and only one-half of the females who made it to their tenth birthday survived until their fortieth. Pregnancy and childbirth were a death sentence for most of them.

Rural women became wage earners through the **putting-out system** of textile manufacture, which became increasingly widespread in the 18th century. Also known as **cottage industry**, this system transferred cloth production from towns to the countryside. Women had woven cloth for their families for centuries, but in the Middle Ages textile production had shifted to cities, where it came under the control of guilds that regulated production and set prices. The putting-out system returned the center of cloth making to the rural economy, as new merchants sought to avoid the urban guilds and improve profits. These entrepreneurs typically purchased bulk quantities of raw wool and cotton, which they distributed throughout rural districts, often following routes claimed by competing entrepreneurs. Then they retraced their steps, collecting the finished cloth from women and taking it to urban markets. Rural families needed this work desperately. Wages remained low, but by assigning tasks like carding or spinning to their children, countrywomen

The Working Poor   An example of cottage industry. In an attic room, an Irish family beats flax in order to expose the fibers contained within; once cracked open, the flax fibers are then soaked in water, removed, and spun by hand into linen thread.

were able to produce more finished cloth. Once redeemed, it often made the differ-ence between life and death.[20]

THE RETURN OF UNCERTAINTY

Given the miseries of the age, the passivity of the people in the face of the excesses of absolutist society is striking. Even the most dramatic political action, like England's civil war and revolution, was undertaken by bourgeois and aristocratic factions. The underclass had seldom known prosperity and independence—and so had grown not to expect them. Disruptions could still spark them into action, as the rebellions of the 11th and 14th centuries showed. Yet as long as absolutism kept the peace, as it generally did between 1648 and 1700, peasants complained of their lot but seldom rose up against it.

The reappearance of warfare after 1700 added just the uncertainty, inse-curity, and violence needed to trigger mass unrest. First came the War of the Spanish Succession (1702–1713). When King Carlos II died without an heir in 1700, France's Louis XIV and Austria's Leopold I—each of whom was married to a sister of Carlos's—greedily eyed the Spanish crown and its enormous overseas empire. Carlos's will had named an heir to the throne: the grandson of his sister, the closest male relative available. But Louis hoped to win the crown for himself before the young man, Felipe V, took power. Louis consequently invaded Spain; he also invaded the Spanish Netherlands, which brought him into a parallel war with England. The English army at this time was led by a career soldier named John Churchill, who defeated Louis's forces and brought the islands of Gibraltar and Menorca, plus France's New World territories of Newfoundland and Hudson's Bay, into England's possession.[21]

A subsequent conflict was the War of the Austrian Succession (1740–1748), which arose when ambitious outsiders challenged Maria Theresa's succession to the throne. Several countries joined into this fray, less to advance claims of their own than to do anything they could to weaken the Habsburg family in general. But the largest and most devastating conflict of the age was the **Seven Years' War** (1756–1763), which pitted Great Britain, Brandenburg-Prussia, and some smaller German principalities against an alliance of Austria, France, Russia, Saxony, and Sweden. This last war arose, in general, in response to the changes made to the Westphalian "balance of power" by the earlier two conflicts.

---

[20]   Cloth was the leading commodity in this system, but not the only one. Leatherwork, soap and candle making, and even metalwork formed part of the economy too.

[21]   His achievement resulted in his being created the First Duke of Marlborough, which raised the Churchills to the status of one of England's greatest noble families.

The War of the Spanish Succession had its North America parallel in Queen Anne's War. The War of the Austrian Succession correlated with King George's War. The Seven Years' War in Europe was matched with the French and Indian War. Together, these wars produced horrendous casualties. The Seven Years' War alone resulted in over a million deaths. Roused by the vast ruin of the countryside, the disruption of trade, the wasted expenditure, and the callous abuse of the peasantry, popular voices began to rise up and to demand change. Bread riots, calls for peace, and complaints over endless governmental deficits arose across Europe. Demonstrations against the treatment of the many by the very, very few sprouted from Ireland to Austria and from Sicily to Sweden. Surely something could be done to restore order. As the century progressed, new voices arose in response, voices dedicated to the idea that change was possible, necessary, and within reach. The world was a dark place that needed new light and hope.

WHO, WHAT, WHERE

absolutism

Ancien Régime

ayatollah

Baroque Age

classicism

cottage industry

Directory

Fronde

Glorious Revolution

Imam

Janissaries

King James Bible

mercantilism

mullah

Peace of Westphalia

protectionism

putting-out system

Qajar

Qizilbash

Seven Years' War

shah

social contract

South Sea Bubble

streltsi

SUGGESTED READINGS

Primary Sources

Fénelon, François. *The Adventures of Telemachus.*

Hobbes, Thomas. *Leviathan.*

Molière. *The Middle Class Gentleman.*

Tocqueville, Alexis de. *The Ancien Régime and the French Revolution.*

Saint-Simon. *Memoirs.*

Richelieu. *Political Testament.*

Anthologies

Beik, William. *Louis XIV and Absolutism: A Brief Study with Documents* (2000).

Gregg, Stephen H., ed. *Empire and Identity: An Eighteenth-Century Sourcebook* (2005).

Helfferich, Tryntje, ed. and trans. *The Thirty Years War: A Documentary History* (2009).

Wilson, Peter H., comp. *The Thirty Years War: A Sourcebook* (2010).

Studies

Bennett, Martyn. *Oliver Cromwell* (2006).

Bergin, Joseph. *Church, Society, and Religious Change in France, 1580–1730* (2009).

Casale, Giancarlo. *The Ottoman Age of Exploration* (2010).

Clark, Christopher. *Iron Kingdom: The Rise and Downfall of Prussia, 1600–1947* (2006).

Cracraft, James. *The Revolution of Peter the Great* (2006).

Dale, Stephen F. *The Muslim Empires of the Ottomans, Safavids, and Mughals* (2010).

Fowler, William M., Jr. *Empires at War: The Seven Years' War and the Struggle for North America, 1754–1763* (2005).

Harris, Tim. *Revolution: The Great Crisis of the British Monarchy, 1685–1720* (2006).

Hufton, Olwen. *Europe: Privilege and Protest, 1730–1788* (2001).

Hughes, Lindsey. *Russia in the Age of Peter the Great* (2000).

Ingrao, Charles. *The Habsburg Monarchy, 1618–1815* (2000).

Jones, Colin. *The Great Nation: France from Louis XV to Napoleon, 1715–99* (2003).

Levi, Anthony. *Louis XIV* (2004).

Linebaugh, Peter. *The London Hanged: Crime and Civil Society in the Eighteenth Century* (2006).

Martinich, A. P. *Hobbes* (2005).

Matthee, Rudolph P. *The Politics of Trade in Safavid Iran: Silk for Silver, 1600–1730* (2006).

Newman, Andrew J. *Safavid Iran: Rebirth of a Persian Empire* (2008).

Ormrod, David. *The Rise of Commercial Empires: England and the Netherlands in the Age of Mercantilism, 1650–1770* (2003).

Prak, Maarten. *The Dutch Republic in the Seventeenth Century: The Golden Age* (2005).

Quataert, Donald. *The Ottoman Empire, 1700–1822* (2000).

Rowlands, Guy. *The Dynastic State and the Army under Louis XIV: Royal Service and Private Interest, 1661–1701* (2002).

Smith, Jay M. *Nobility Reimagined: The Patriotic Nation in Eighteenth-Century France* (2005).

Streusand, Douglas E. *Islamic Gunpowder Empires: Ottomans, Safavids, and Mughals* (2010).

Szabo, Franz A. J. *The Seven Years' War in Europe, 1756–1763* (2007).

Wheatcroft, Andrew. *The Enemy at the Gate: Habsburgs, Ottomans, and the Battle for Europe* (2009).

Whisenhunt, William B., and Peter Stearns. *Catherine the Great: Enlightened Empress of Russia* (2006).

Zagorin, Perez. *Hobbes and the Law of Nature* (2009).

For additional resources, including maps, primary sources, visuals, web links, and quizzes, please go to **www.oup.com/us/backman.**

CHAPTER 15

The Enlightened
1690–1789

The **Enlightenment** is a term coined in the second half of the 18th century to describe an array of intellectual and cultural activities of the 1700s. Most of these new ideas, though not all of them, aimed to improve European life by setting its economic, political, religious, and social developments along paths dictated by reason and critical inquiry, rather than by tradition and blind faith. The **philosophes**—as the Enlightenment writers came to call themselves[1]—both continued and broadened the Scientific Revolution by carrying over the scientific method of inquiry from the functioning of the natural world to the human one. Their subject might be the mechanics of Absolutist government, the growth of legal traditions, the development of moral codes, the workings of a national economy, or the functioning of the mind or heart. Any field of human endeavor, when examined rationally, could be understood; and anything that could be understood could be improved.

At least it seemed that way for the first great figures of the Enlightenment, including John Locke, Pierre Bayle, Adam Smith, and Denis Diderot. For very different reasons, Voltaire and Jean-Jacques Rousseau found grounds for harsh

THE GREATER WEST IN THE ENLIGHTENMENT

SCANDINAVIA
DUTCH REPUBLIC
BRITAIN
HOLY ROMAN EMPIRE
PRUSSIA
RUSSIA
AUSTRIA
FRANCE
SPAIN
ITALY
OTTOMAN EMPIRE

◀ **A Meeting of a Masonic Lodge in Vienna, 1790** Mozart was said to be a member.

CHAPTER OUTLINE

- The Origins of the Enlightenment
- Learning from Our Worst Mistakes
- Locke and the Administration of the Commonwealth
- Bayle and Religious Toleration
- Free Markets and Rational Punishment
- Diderot and the Circulation of the Enlightenment
- Voltaire and the Limits of Optimism
- Rousseau: "Mankind Is Born Free"
- Jewish Enlightenment
- Haskalah and Hasidism
- The Jews and Europe's Ambivalence
- The Unenlightened
- Assessing the Enlightenment

skepticism—often directed at one another. Many Jews saw the Enlightenment as an opportunity to reassert their place in western Europe. In the face of widespread poverty and its consequences, however, the Enlightenment had uncertain answers, and assessing its impact is by no means simple. The Enlightened writers and publicists had widely varying interests but also widely varying aims. Historians have traditionally emphasized the role of the reformist wing of the movement, those figures who wanted to address abuses and excesses within existing society and government but without fundamentally replacing either. Another wing of the movement though was significantly more radical and sought either the destruction or wholesale replacement of the mores and institutions of the time. Whether moderate or radical, the men and women of the Enlightenment carried out the first major reform effort in centuries that aimed not to reestablish a supposedly better society of the past but to envision and create a wholly new world based on original ideas, practices, and values. Not since the 12th century had so many people devoted themselves so completely and excitedly to the thrill of the new.

THE ORIGINS OF THE ENLIGHTENMENT

The philosophes did not pursue ideas for their own sake; a pragmatic impulse drove the whole enterprise. The men and women of this movement were overwhelmingly public figures rather than dry university academics. (Many in the European professoriate agreed with the Enlightenment program, but few of them wrote well enough to play much of a part in it.) Like the "public intellectuals"

---

[1]   The term philosophes came into general use during the 1740s. Before that, the writers preferred to call themselves *les Lumières* ("the Enlightened Ones").

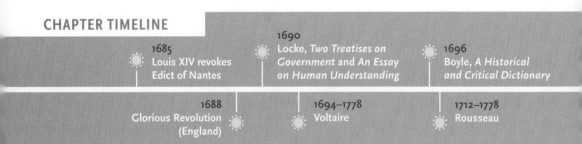

CHAPTER TIMELINE

1685 Louis XIV revokes Edict of Nantes	**1690** Locke, *Two Treatises on Government* and *An Essay on Human Understanding*	**1696** Boyle, *A Historical and Critical Dictionary*
1688 Glorious Revolution (England)	**1694–1778** Voltaire	**1712–1778** Rousseau

of today, they wanted to effect the immediate improvement of human life and to realize the all but certain promise of progress—if only the world would heed their message.

They found that message in response to a return of religious intolerance in France and a detested king of England. With John Locke, the Glorious Revolution and a limited form of democracy had a philosophical justification. With Pierre Bayle, religious freedom had its first great champion.

They were, as a group, the most self-confident thinkers since the scholastic writers of the 13th century. How could they be otherwise? Newton had proven that the universe is massively complex but rationally constructed; it functions according to a coherent system of natural laws. Mankind, as part of that universe, also obeys fixed laws—at least as a physical organism. If the rational mind can decipher the workings of the universe, how hard could it be to figure out the supposed mysteries of human activity and behavior? Why not develop new modes of action that are more in accord with rational principles? And how could such a scheme fail to bring about a better and more progressive world, one stripped of contradiction, idiocy, superstition, and intolerance? The work of the philosophes, in the words of one of them, Immanuel Kant (1724–1804), would help mankind to grow "out of its self-inflicted immaturity." Its immaturity results from man's failure "to use his own rational intelligence instead of being led along by someone else. . . . Dare to learn something! Anyone who persists in this immaturity, whether out of laziness or cowardice, makes it easy for others to think and act for him." The first stirrings of the movement arose in the 1690s, but its heyday was from 1740 to the outbreak of the French Revolution in 1789.

Like the leaders of most intellectual movements until the 20th century, the philosophes brimmed over with self-confidence and optimism. Their writings show the extraordinary breadth of their knowledge as well as the sharpness of

1713–1784
Denis Diderot

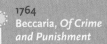
1764
Beccaria, *Of Crime and Punishment*

1779
Lessing, *Nathan the Wise*

1729–1786
Moses Mendelssohn

1776
Smith, *The Wealth of Nations*

their gifts for sarcasm and for tossing off witticisms that sound clever but say little. Consider just a sampler:

Diderot: "From fanaticism to barbarism is but a single step."
"What a delightful comedy this world would be, if only we played no part in it."

Hume: "Generally speaking, errors in religion are dangerous; those in philosophy only ridiculous."

Lichtenberg: "We call some actions vices simply because they are performed by ugly people."
"A book is a mirror: if an ass peers into it, don't expect an Apostle to peer back out."

Montesquieu: "[An author is] a fool who, not content with boring everyone around him during his lifetime, insists on boring generations yet to come."

Rousseau: "As long as he is not actually insane, a man can be cured of every folly except vanity."
"Those who are slowest to make promises are those who keep them most faithfully."

Voltaire: "Theology amuses me so. In it we see human insanity at its fullest."
"[Optimism] is an obsession with saying 'All is well' even when one is in Hell."

> The philosophes may have been the most influential group of talented amateurs in European history, not only because of their influence on their own age but because of the way they and their assumptions about human nature still affect us today.

With a few exceptions—David Hume (1711–1776) and Immanuel Kant, most notably—their knowledge was broad rather than deep, and at their worst they were infuriatingly flippant. Yet they brought to most of their work remarkable talents for clarity and shrewdness, and a dedication to practical reform. They wrote in many genres—essays, treatises, novels and stories, encyclopedia articles, letters, histories, poems, and stage dramas—to reach the broadest possible audience. The philosophes may have been the most influential group of talented amateurs in European history, not only because of their influence on their own age but because of the way they and their assumptions about human nature still affect us today.[2]

---

[2]   We are all, in the words of one of the philosophes' most earnest modern critics, still "Voltaire's bastards."

LEARNING FROM OUR WORST MISTAKES

Whatever else historians mean by the term Enlightenment, they do not mean a coherent set of ideas. Like the medieval scholastics they resemble, the philosophes represent a method of thinking rather than a body of thought. Their efforts all originated in the conviction that the bulk of human misery results from the irrationality of our actions, traditions, beliefs, institutions, and values. Simply remove the uncritical and witless assumptions that guide what we do with our lives; replace them with finely reasoned alternatives that can be logically supported, measured, and calibrated; and then watch mankind progress into a clearer, better, happier, and more productive life. The philosophes were not necessarily utopians. Hume, for example, for all his geniality of tone, should never be read by depressives. Yet they remained firm believers in man's ability always to make life better. One of the best-known pieces of literature produced by the Enlightenment—Voltaire's fable *Candide*—satirized the utopianism that had spread among some of the movement's truest believers.

Several factors triggered the Enlightenment, not the least of which were Louis XIV's reckless decision in 1685 to revoke the Edict of Nantes and the Glorious Revolution in England in 1688. The Edict of Nantes, promulgated in 1598 by France's king Henri IV, had established the official policy of religious toleration, and for nearly one hundred years this policy had preserved the peace between Catholics and Huguenots. Louis XIV knew little about religion (and was said by his sister-in-law never to have opened a Bible in his life). But he knew that he preferred a hierarchical Catholicism under royal control to a Protestant theology that privileged individual conscience over obedience to authority. At a stroke, Louis's action to revoke the edict stripped French Protestants of their legal rights. He seized the nearly one hundred cities placed under Huguenot control by the edict, drove their civic officials into exile, shut down their schools and churches, and banned all Protestant public activities. Forced to choose between conversion and banishment, approximately two hundred thousand French Protestants went into exile in Holland, England, and Brandenburg-Prussia. This renewal of persecution, coupled with fears about Louis's expansionist territorial aims, prompted the Holy Roman emperor Leopold I (r. 1658–1705) to cobble together a defensive alliance with England and the Low Countries (along with Sweden and several German principalities) called the **League of Augsburg**.

Meanwhile, in England, Parliament forced the detested Catholic king James II from the throne in 1688. Early in 1689 the Parliament drafted the Declaration of Rights that stipulated that henceforth all English monarchs were required to be Anglican, that freedom of speech was guaranteed, and that Parliament controlled the levying of taxes. The leaders of Parliament then offered the English throne to

James II's Protestant daughter Mary, who had married the Dutch stadtholder, or chief magistrate, William III of Orange. William was Louis XIV's nemesis and was determined to lead the forces of the league against France. Fighting began in 1689 and lasted for eight years. The Treaty of Rijswijk (1697) established a shaky peace, but the damage had been done: the horrors of the 16th and 17th centuries threatened to rise from the dead.

But the specter of the return of religious intolerance, of vain saber rattling, and of the economic misery created by flat-out war also sparked new efforts to rethink the attitudes of the age; hence the Enlightenment. Aristocratic and upper-middle-class readers had long enjoyed keeping up with new developments in science, but more and more thinkers were drawn to the critical investigation of human behavior. What is it that leads human beings, whether individually or communally, to act as they do? Is it possible to develop a science

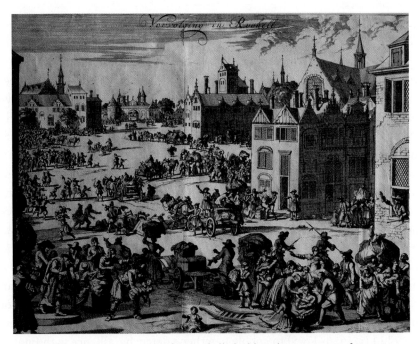

Persecution and Exile   The city of La Rochelle had long been a center of Huguenot life. After the Edict of Toleration was issued in 1598, direct persecution against French Protestants ceased but tensions remained. In 1622 the leaders of La Rochelle rebelled against King Louis XIII and were quickly put down; five years later, though, spurred on by English sympathizers, they rebelled again. This time Cardinal Richelieu came in person to oversee the siege of the city, which lasted fourteen months. Continued strife finally resulted in this scene from 1661, when three hundred Huguenot families were sent into exile. Louis XIV had risen to the throne in that year, and his intention to revoke the Edict of Toleration was well known.

of humanity? And if we can understand ourselves better, can we learn to avoid our worst mistakes?

LOCKE AND THE ADMINISTRATION OF THE COMMONWEALTH

The inquiry began with the publication in 1690 of John Locke's *Two Treatises on Government* and *An Essay Concerning Human Understanding.* Pierre Bayle's *Historical and Critical Dictionary* quickly followed in 1697. Locke (1632–1704) is commonly regarded as the first philosophe. Drawn initially to science, he studied medicine at Oxford University while reading philosophers like Descartes and Leibniz in his spare hours. In 1666 he met Lord Ashley, later the Earl of Shaftesbury, and joined his household as a general counselor. Locke provided medical care for the family, advised the earl on commercial and financial matters, arranged the marriage of the earl's heir, and oversaw the education of the Shaftesbury children. At one point Locke even performed a lifesaving operation on the nobleman. In 1672, when Shaftesbury became the lord chancellor of England, Locke was appointed to a secretarial position with the Board of Trade, an experience that seems to have sparked his interest in politics. When Shaftesbury fell from power in 1676 Locke moved to the Continent and spent the next decade living primarily in France and Holland, enjoying the support of various noble patrons, and working on the book that would become the *Essay on Human Understanding.*

But politics interrupted his studies once again when a number of the figures busily planning the Glorious Revolution made contact with him in Holland. At their urging, Locke quickly produced *Two Treatises on Government*, which provided a philosophical justification for Parliament's dismissal of James II and its transfer of the crown to William and Mary. In the treatises he attacks the notion of absolutist monarchy. In its place, his model sees all government as the expression of a social contract between the members of a community. This contract consists of recognizing that in choosing to live together, people tacitly agree to compromise their individual autonomy and to delegate to the government the power to adjudicate conflicts and administer the law.

But Locke, who spent his adult life among the propertied classes and enjoying their patronage, defined the central function of government as the administration of the commonwealth—which meant its property. He argued that all political rights begin with the "individual property interest"—that is, the ownership of property. Government is therefore legitimate only when it is composed of or chosen by individuals whose property comes under the state's jurisdiction. It is a moderate, limited form of democracy: only those people who own property, whether defined as land or commercial interest, have a rightful voice in determining the government's shape and activity. When a ruler such as James II violates the social contract, the propertied classes may justifiably resist him and even, as proved necessary in this case, remove him from office.

Locke's dictum that civil rights consist primarily of the rights to "life, liberty, and property" was cribbed by Thomas Jefferson when he wrote the American Declaration of Independence (1776). Jefferson, of course, altered Locke's position significantly, turning it into the better-known phrase "life, liberty, and the pursuit of happiness." Less well known is that Locke would probably have been horrified by the American revolutionaries, viewing them as rebels against the legitimate claims of the propertied men in England whom the colonists served. Some writers have asserted that Jefferson's change of phrase is itself an Enlightenment achievement: the invention of happiness. Such a concept could never have existed, the argument runs, until the philosophes placed the means of actually acquiring it within all men's and women's reach. "Happiness is a new idea here in Europe," wrote Louis Antoine Saint-Just (1767–1794), and some modern writers take him at his word. They shouldn't. Earlier writers like Aristotle, Saint Augustine, Geoffrey Chaucer, Giovanni Pico della Mirandola, or François Rabelais would have scoffed at the notion that no true concept of happiness existed in their times.[3]

Locke's understanding of government stands in sharp contrast to Thomas Hobbes's argument in *Leviathan*—the text to which Locke was implicitly responding. To Hobbes, the function of the state is to govern the people. Since we are all essentially equal in nature, our competing desires for self-fulfillment condemn us to constant competition, rivalry, and struggle, and government is therefore necessary to keep our hostile tendencies in check. Locke turns Hobbes's argument on its head: the essential role of the state is not to govern the people but to manage and administer its material wealth, or "property," as Locke put it. The state does not decide who gets which property; that would go against Locke's conviction that the private ownership of property is an intrinsic human right. The state does, however, set the terms by which those who already possess property may keep it, transfer it, and manage it—all of which it does by establishing laws regarding the rights of ownership, by setting taxes on property, and by setting inheritance norms. And Locke goes a step further. Since the state's fundamental function is to administer the collective property of the nation, only those who possess that property have the right to participate in government. Government

---

3   Saint-Just was a pornographer turned revolutionary who championed the despotism of Robespierre. He was known as the "Archangel of the Terror." Happiness, to him, was a well-oiled guillotine.

thus resembles a medieval guild, in which only those who engage in a particular craft or trade may set the rules for that craft or trade's activities.

BAYLE AND RELIGIOUS TOLERATION

Pierre Bayle (1647–1706) is the most enigmatic and beguiling of the philosophes. Born just before the Treaty of Westphalia, he came to public attention in 1686 with an attack on Louis XIV's decision to revoke the Edict of Nantes, called *An All-Catholic France*, which he followed with *A Philosophical Commentary* in the next year. This latter work is a touchstone—the first major treatise in Europe's history to champion the idea of religious toleration. The argument he makes for tolerance is, however, flawed. The question, as Bayle frames it, comes to this: Is it ever right to compel a person to change his belief even if the belief he holds can be proven false? He insists that the answer is no, since the choice of belief must be regarded as an intrinsic individual human right. Although he presents an array of real and imaginary case studies to buttress his position, he never confronts head-on the obvious counterargument: If a belief can be proven to be not only wrong but actually harmful, surely the morally correct thing is to stop unnecessary harm from being done. Adolf Hitler sincerely believed in the moral rectitude and historical necessity of annihilating the Jews of Europe. Was it therefore morally wrong to oppose him by force? Ought his beliefs to have been tolerated? Obviously not. Still, Bayle's work deserves note as a historical first.

Bayle continued his scholarly efforts with his most accomplished work—*A Historical and Critical Dictionary*, a sprawling, eccentric encyclopedia that began to appear in 1696. Despite its massive size, the *Dictionary* was by far the biggest "best seller" of all the philosophical works of Europe in the 18th century. Published in four fat folio volumes—more than three thousand pages—it is a wild collection of articles on topics ranging from ancient Greek philosophies to the erotica of Bayle's own time. It made, and still makes, delightful browsing, since Bayle allows himself to veer off on any tangent that holds his interest. Indeed, there are more tangents than text: over 90 percent of the *Dictionary* consists of lengthy footnotes, addenda, marginalia, spin-off mini-essays, and sometimes even footnotes to the footnotes. But the fun has a serious purpose. Time and again theodicy—the question of why evil exists—emerges as a central theme making the whole structure cohere.

Bayle examines the question philosophically, historically, theologically, linguistically, in art and literature, as a practical matter of law, even in a way that prefigures anthropology. "Mankind is evil and miserable," he writes; "everywhere one looks there are prisons, hospitals, gallows, and beggars. History, one might say, is nothing but the narrative of man's crimes and sufferings." But why is this so, if the world was created for us by an omnipotent and loving God? Bayle returns to the question over and over, but in bits and pieces, as though the question is too horrifying to contemplate for too long. If God is all-loving, he argues, he would destroy evil if he could—and yet evil obviously exists, so one must conclude that God cannot stop it. Bayle will have none of this, since it concludes in essence that God is not God. On the other hand, assuming that God could destroy evil if he wanted to, then he must not want to—in which case he is not all-loving. This too Bayle rejects. In the end, he suggests (though he never says so explicitly) that the question of evil has no rational explanation. The coexistence of an all-loving, all-powerful God and rampant, unremitting evil is simply a mystery that we must accept and acknowledge our inability to comprehend.

> In the end, Bayle suggests (though he never says so explicitly) that the question of evil has no rational explanation. The coexistence of an all-loving, all-powerful God and rampant, unremitting evil is simply a mystery that we must accept and acknowledge our inability to comprehend.

Yet this is not a failed exercise. Bayle's whole point is present here, though somewhat veiled. By his exuberant, continuous reexamination of the question, his implicit message is the fundamental and best argument for tolerance: the only proper human response to religious mystery is to recognize the inability of human beings to comprehend heavenly mysteries. No one can or should ever be so certain of his convictions that he deems it right to persecute those who disagree with him. We must tolerate, in other words, because we can never be sure.

Bayle is seldom read anymore, which is a shame. In his own time he was lauded as perhaps the greatest nonscientific mind in centuries. The German philosopher Gottfried Leibniz (1646–1716) described him as "one of the most brilliant men of our time, a man whose eloquence is as great as his intellect." Voltaire, in a generous mood, praised him as "the greatest master of logic who ever wrote." His influence on the later philosophes can hardly be overstated; and if he came to few positive conclusions in his work, that surely was part of his point.

FREE MARKETS AND RATIONAL PUNISHMENT

The Enlightenment drew writers from across Europe, but the movement's geographic centers were Amsterdam, Edinburgh, Geneva, The Hague, Leiden, London, and Milan. Paris was not an important center of this activity until Voltaire brought the new thinking there in the 1740s, when the political atmosphere proved more amenable to reform. From these centers the writers of the

Enlightenment poured forth a dazzling stream of ideas on every aspect of human life.

John Locke was interested in epistemology—the study of how we acquire knowledge and of what it means "to know" anything. However, as we have seen, he also provided a philosophical underpinning for forms of governance that draw their justification from the consent of the governed. His concern for rational foundations quickly spread from government to economics, with Adam Smith; to crime and punishment, with Cesare Beccaria; and to education, with Denis Diderot.

Adam Smith (1723–1790) published *The Wealth of Nations* in 1776 in order to prove the inevitable failure of mercantilism and the inevitable success of free-market capitalism. Mercantilism is wrong, he argues, for the simple reason that it is irrational: it assumes that people will passively accept their own poverty and oppression—all in order to support a regime that absorbs all available capital for its own ends. Capitalism, on the other hand, is based on a far more rational view of human motivation. It allows people the freedom to make their own economic choices and to reap the rewards of their own success. But in order for this to happen, markets must have open competition and freedom from price fixing. He therefore warns against cartels—powerful monopolies or agreements between firms—quite as much as against interference by the state.[4]

Smith thus redefined the notion of a **market**. The word no longer meant merely a physical site where commerce occurs, but rather a pattern of human behavior. Commerce was now seen as following set laws, since all individuals, in any free economic exchange, will act rationally in their own best interest. And these laws are based on the economic choices people make from among a limited supply of goods, along with the competition between firms for buyers—in other words, supply and demand:

> The natural effort of every individual to better his own condition, when suffered to exert itself with freedom and security, is so powerful a principle, that it is alone, and without any assistance, not only capable of carrying the society to wealth and prosperity, but of surmounting a hundred impertinent obstructions with which the folly of human laws too often encumbers its operations.

---

[4] "People of the same trade seldom meet together even for merriment or diversion, but that the conversation ends in some conspiracy against the public, or in some contrivance to raise prices."

Rational self-interest also guided the investigations of Cesare Beccaria (1739–1794) into economics and into law. His *Elements of Public Economy* (published posthumously, in 1804) anticipated some of Adam Smith's ideas on the need for economic policies that produced wealth for the entire populace by opening up markets to natural forces of competition, supply, and demand. His greatest work, however, was his study *Of Crimes and Punishments* (1764). A system of criminal justice, he argued, should aim to promote social security and order rather than to seek revenge upon malefactors. It thus ought to consider the causes of crime as much as punishment. After all, it is preferable for society to prevent crimes from happening than to punish their perpetrators after they have occurred. Hence any just society will actively seek to eradicate poverty, which Beccaria sees as the principle cause of crimes against property. For crimes against humanity, the aim of a judicial system should be to rehabilitate criminals who are emotionally unbalanced and to teach them to understand themselves, the consequences of their actions, and the paths to personal improvement.

Punishment of crimes is necessary, he insists, but is more effective when it is imposed in a rational way. Toward that end, punishments should be only as severe as necessary in order to promote social order. Anything more severe, he argues, is tyrannical and merely provokes attitudes of resentment and hostility that make the criminal all the more likely to commit another offense. Punishments must also be consistently applied. The certainty of punishment, not the severity of it, deters crime more effectively.

An 18th-Century Scene from an Italian Prison   The prisoner in the center of the image is being drawn up in the *strappado* torture.

Freeing individuals from corrupt and irrational practices, whether in politics, the marketplace, or civic life, will lead to the improvement of society for the simple reason that most of the Enlightened regarded human nature as essentially good. Though ineluctably based in self-interest, human behavior is also naturally social. We are equipped, in other words, with an ability to recognize in rationally chosen compromises an indirect means of satisfying self-interest. We are intrinsically good and when given freedom to act will consistently choose the good.

DIDEROT AND THE CIRCULATION OF THE ENLIGHTENMENT

Perhaps the most heroically energetic and resilient philosophe was Denis Diderot (1713–1784). While he was far from the best thinker or writer in the movement, he was perhaps the most important in getting Enlightened ideas into print and into circulation outside the closed society of the salons.[5] He was the central force behind the great *Encyclopédie*, the vast compendium of all the new learning in science, philosophy, economics, law, technology, art, and religion. Diderot was among the most utilitarian of the philosophes, a true believer in the cause of saving the world from tyranny, superstition, and ignorance. Here is how he himself put it, in the *Encyclopédie*'s entry "Encyclopedias":

> The aim of an encyclopedia is to gather in one place the knowledge scattered all over the world; to display the general content and organization of that knowledge to one's contemporaries; and to pass this knowledge on to later generations—so that the achievements of the past may be useful to the future; so that our children, by so improving their own minds, may become more virtuous and more happy; and so that we may not perish without having proved a benefit to all mankind. . . . For we have long had need of a rational age [such as ours], in which men would no longer look to classical authorities for the truth, but to the study of nature itself.

Despite its size—thirty-five volumes of print and images—or perhaps because of it, the *Encyclopédie* sold extremely well. Four thousand subscribers ordered copies before it was even in print. Thomas Jefferson purchased a set, and Empress Catherine of Russia, hearing of Diderot's financial woes,

---

[5] Diderot, like Ezra Pound later for modernism, had a wonderful ability to spot talent in others. He was tireless in encouraging, prodding, supporting, and publishing new authors.

purchased his entire library and hired Diderot, at a generous stipend, to be her "librarian" and guardian for the books. The books were shipped to Saint Petersburg after Diderot's death in 1784 and are now a special collection within the Russian National Library. But the *Encyclopédie* was not the only such effort; the 18th century, in fact, was a golden age for such enterprises. Just as 13th-century scholastics filled European libraries with *summas* on every topic, the Enlightened of the 18th gave birth to a glut of encyclopedias: Pierre Bayle's *Dictionnaire historique et critique* (1697), Ephraim Chambers's *Cyclopaedia* (1728), Gianfrancesco Pivati's *Nuovo dizionario scientifico e curioso, sacroprofano* (1744), Johann Heinrich Zedler's *Universal-Lexicon* (1754), and the first edition of the *Encyclopædia Britannica* (1768) are merely the best-known examples of this remarkable genre.[6]

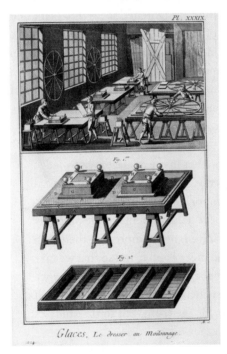 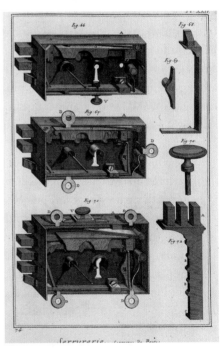

Pages from the *Encyclopédie*   The *Encyclopédie* reflects the personal interest of Denis Diderot in technology for its own sake and as a tool for social reform. The illustrations above depict scenes of sheet-glass manufacture and locksmithing.

---

6   Thomas Dobson's *Encyclopaedia* (1789–1798) was the first American encyclopedia. It copied much from the *Encyclopædia Britannica* and was soon replaced by the *Encyclopedia Americana*.

VOLTAIRE AND THE LIMITS OF OPTIMISM

As it happened, the two most influential of all the Enlightened were consider-ably less optimistic about human goodness and its ability to overcome the de-mands of society: François-Marie Arouet (1694–1778), who published under the pen name of Voltaire, and Jean-Jacques Rousseau (1712–1778). Both were prima donnas, but they differed profoundly in their origins, temperaments, aims, and styles.

Voltaire doubted the essential goodness of mankind, or at least of the lower orders of it. He believed in the possibility of human progress, but a progress firmly directed by a political and intellectual elite—of which he regarded himself and others like him as the indispensable leaders. The commoners, however, whether farmers in the countryside or laborers in the towns, he loathed as degenerate brutes incapable of rising above ignorance. Rousseau, on the other hand, came from those lower orders and held tightly to the conviction that goodness is the essential characteristic of all human beings. It is society itself that corrupts the individual—especially the privileged classes with whom Voltaire was so com-fortable. The power of the privileged, to Rousseau, derives from its enslavement and brutalization of the common man. Given these differences, it is no surprise to learn that the two men despised each other.[7]

Voltaire was born in Paris to a wealthy, bourgeois family. He was educated at the Jesuit Collège Louis-le-Grand, where he excelled in languages and law, and after graduation took a job as secretary to the French ambassador to Holland. This might have been the start of a successful government career, but his impulsive romantic entanglements and his habit of poking sarcastic barbs at his social superiors kept getting him in trouble. He was impris-oned twice—once in the Bastille after publishing sa-tirical verses about the prince regent—and released the second time only when he promised to flee the country. After an offhand witticism, a nobleman had Voltaire beaten by hired thugs—to which Voltaire responded by challenging him to a duel. But since Voltaire came from a lower social rank, his challenge enraged aristocratic society even more than the origi-nal insult. He remained in England for three years. His early writings, mostly poetry and stage dramas,

Voltaire (1694–1778)   The leading figure of the Enlightenment in France and tireless champion of free speech and religious toleration.

---

7   Rousseau, who died on July 2, 1778, is said to have died happy since he had lived long enough to learn of Voltaire's death on May 30.

however, were popular enough to keep him writing, although they make very poor reading today.

The years he spent in England marked the turning point in his life. Quickly learning English, he moved easily through educated society and met many of the most prominent figures in England's political and intellectual life. He observed English law and government, studied Newtonian physics, and avidly read the works of John Locke. The culmination of his experience was the grand state funeral given to Isaac Newton. Returning to Paris, Voltaire published his *Philosophical Letters on the English* (1733), which instantly propelled him to the front ranks of the intellectuals of his time. The *Letters* extol the rationalism of English life over the irrational, superstitious, and corrupt Continental world; he contrasts the modesty and gentleness of the Quakers with the rigid intolerance of the Calvinists, yet praises a constitution that permits both to practice their faiths freely despite the existence of an established Church of England. He marvels at the Quakers' absence of priests ("'We have none, my friend,' he replied, 'to our great happiness.'") and denounces the Presbyterians (who "wear the most severe expressions, . . . preach through their noses, and call [all other Christian denominations] 'whores of Babylon'"). He also praises the English for their judicial system, their open trade, their dedication to promoting science.

The *Letters* were a sensation with the reading public, which is why the government ordered the book to be banned and copies to be burnt. Voltaire went once again into exile, this time to a remote village, where he lived in the chateau of his mistress, the Marquise de Chatelêt. For the next twelve years he poured out a stream of pamphlets, plays, histories, poems, scientific papers, essays, and letters that made him the most prominent philosophe of the age. (The standard edition of his complete works today fills more than one hundred volumes.) His two principal concerns were religious toleration and freedom of speech. Political freedom meant little to him, since the unwashed masses neither needed nor deserved it. Besides, their educated superiors would profit less from democracy than from Enlightened ideas put into efficient practice by an absolutist regime guided by philosophes such as himself.

The death of the Marquise in 1749 left Voltaire deeply mournful, and he sought a new chapter in his life in Berlin. He accepted an invitation to reside with, debate with, and act as counselor to Frederick the Great of Prussia, the most rigidly absolutist ruler then in Europe. Yet his air of self-satisfaction, his sarcastic gaiety, and his inability to resist challenging all forms of authority (even those he was in agreement with) lead to a speedy falling out with the deeply serious-minded Frederick. After yet another brief imprisonment—this time in Frankfurt—Voltaire then went to Geneva and lived there just long enough to make himself unwanted. He moved at last to a brilliant estate at Ferney, near the French-Swiss

The Lisbon Earthquake   On November 1, 1755, a massive earthquake struck the city of Lisbon, followed by widespread fires and a tsunami. As many as sixty thousand of the city's two hundred thousand people died, and roughly 85 percent of the city's buildings were destroyed. This painting depicts the catastrophe in religious terms, with avenging angels swooping through the dark sky to cut down sinners amid popular calls to penance and renewed devotion.

border, where he remained for the last twenty years of his life. It was at Ferney that he wrote his best-known work, the novella *Candide* (1759).

The inspiration for the tale was a catastrophic earthquake that flattened Lisbon in 1755, killing perhaps as many as sixty thousand people and demolishing almost 90 percent of the city's buildings.[8] The tragedy shocked Europe, and the suffering of the survivors challenged many people's confidence in the rational ordering of the world and the conviction that man can understand it. *Candide*, for all its usual Voltairean humor, provides a first glimpse of the bitterness and pessimism that increasingly marked Voltaire's latter years. It also mercilessly satirizes the optimism of his rival philosophes—especially Rousseau, whom Voltaire regarded as vulgar, gullible, and naïve.

The novella tells of the title character and his thick-headed tutor Dr. Pangloss, whose fundamental teaching is that "everything is for the best in this, the best of all possible worlds." They stagger from one disastrous misadventure to another, in the search for Candide's lost love, the beautiful but vacuous Lady Cunegonde,

---

8   Experts today reckon the severity of the Lisbon quake as 9.0 on the Richter scale. (The strongest earthquake ever recorded was 9.5, in Valdivia, Chile in 1960.)

and for the mythical kingdom of El Dorado. Candide and Pangloss suffer through wars, famines, plagues, imprisonments and tortures, earthquakes, shipwrecks, and slavery with stoic resolve. Experiencing nothing but evil, they cling to their belief that everything happens for a reason and toward some positive end. By the end, Candide concludes that the most anyone can do is to tend to what is within one's reach. In the face of the world's evils, one must "cultivate one's own garden." Pangloss, however, remains unenlightened and optimistic.

ROUSSEAU: "MANKIND IS BORN FREE"

Jean-Jacques Rousseau, Voltaire probably would have said, was never enlightened to begin with. Rousseau shared Voltaire's enormous egoism but in every other way was his polar opposite. Born in 1712 to a working-class family in Protestant Geneva, Rousseau was orphaned at an early age and had a hardscrabble youth, working at odd jobs and sleeping wherever he could. In constant poverty and ill health, he developed a bitter and nervous temperament. Even after he had achieved renown and a modicum of wealth, he remained convinced that people were persecuting him. Almost entirely self-educated, Rousseau turned himself into a polymath by sheer will: he composed music, wrote novels, studied politics and philosophy, promoted new techniques of education, and acquired an amateur's knowledge of science. Brilliant but maladjusted, possibly paranoid, he spoke endlessly of his own virtue while complaining that no one understood him. He scolded everyone for their immorality, yet he had five children with his illiterate servant girl and placed each one in an orphanage. In his letters and his *Confessions*, one of the most fascinating autobiographies ever written, he at once exaggerates his own sins and exonerates himself anyway. Bad as he was, others were worse.

Jean-Jacques Rousseau (1712–1778)   Author of the *Discourse on the Origins of Inequality* (1754) and *The Social Contract* (1762), and a tireless enemy of Voltaire.

Yet this unstable misanthrope had a more profound influence on Western culture than any other figure of his time. At the heart of Rousseau's thinking was an unshakable belief in the fundamental goodness, decency, and equality of people. All the corruption and evil of this world, he insisted, was the fault of society—and not just the particular society of France in the *Ancien Régime*. It is the sheer fact of socializing, of living in community, that introduces injustice, pain, and unhappiness in human life. "Mankind is born free, but we see him everywhere in chains." That is the memorable opening of the *Discourse on the Origins of Inequality*, one of his best-known works. To live in community means to relinquish one's freedom, to accept compromises of one's desires and will. We may gain a degree of civility in the process, but civilization itself plants the seed of corruption in our souls. And we see this corruption in the unfair hierarchies of wealth, privilege, and power that exist.

Thus far, most of the Enlightened would have agreed. But Rousseau goes farther. Simply redistributing wealth and influence, he says, will not solve anything. The real problem is the concern for wealth and power that civilized life creates. Rejecting economists like Smith, Rousseau insists that the point of Enlightenment is to make people good, not rich. He similarly resists efforts like Diderot's to educate the masses in practical matters. To Rousseau, any philosophy that aims to help people enjoy material comfort and self-determination is wrongheaded, if not delusional. Human happiness, he insists, derives from a persistent pursuit of life's meaning. What is the good life, and what is happiness? Only by asking questions like these can hope to achieve either. Even if we never discover the answers, the very search for answers will make us better and happier. In the end, it is the effort to retain our humanity in the face of the world's brutality that gives life meaning and makes it endurable.

Rousseau does take some concrete positions. He rejects Locke's argument that ownership of property establishes a political right, since everyone, rich and poor alike, has surrendered freedom in entering the social contract. The only legitimate form of government will embrace the mandate of the majority—what he calls the General Will. As a believer in human goodness, Rousseau affirms that the General

> To Rousseau, any philosophy that aims to help people enjoy material comfort and self-determination is wrongheaded, if not delusional. Human happiness, he insists, derives from a persistent pursuit of life's meaning.

The Noble Savage   Jean-Jacques Rousseau did the most to popularize the idea of the **noble savage**—that is, the non-Europeans who are untainted by civilization's corrupting forces—but the notion was widespread before him. This handsome 1783 painting by Sir Joshua Reynolds (1723–1792) offers a romanticized portrait of a Tahitian native brought back to England by Captain James Cook.

Will must always be correct. It may not secure the highest economic yield (as Smith would ask), promote the best technical skills (with Diderot), or crush religious superstition (with Voltaire). It simply expresses the truest desire of the people, which will always promote the well-being of all. Our natural altruism, our concern for others, can guide social life once we overcome our shortsighted individual desire. Provided that the law governing society derives from and expresses the General Will, the freedom of each individual consists of obedience to it. Rousseau thus championed a radical democracy that offended the aristocracy while rejecting rational progress, which offended most of the Enlightened.[9]

Most of the Enlightened rejected religion absolutely. Some, however, took recourse to **deism**. Deists grudgingly believed in a single and possibly benevolent God who created the cosmos—but who plays no active role in it. Like a clockmaker, he builds his machine, winds it up, then sets it ticking. Deists like Hume, Voltaire, and Diderot insisted that the universe, from the moment of its creation, has operated solely according to rational principles. Since God plays no role in our lives, we owe him nothing more than a vague gratitude. More significantly, since God is unknowable, all dogmatic assertions are meaningless—which means that the teachings of all organized religions are without value. Churches—whether Catholic, Protestant, or Orthodox—have no right to command our obedience. A dual policy of religious freedom and of freedom from religious intolerance is essential to human progress. As Voltaire memorably put it:

> It is quite understandable that the fanatics of one sect want to wipe out the fanatics belonging to another, . . . but to have forced [someone like] Descartes to flee to Holland in order to avoid the wrath of the stupid . . . is an eternal shame upon our nation.

Later, in his popular *Philosophical Dictionary* (1764), he defends deists as people

> who do not claim to know how God punishes the wrong, or how He promotes the good, or how He forgives—for [the deist] is not presumptuous enough to boast that he knows God's nature; instead, the deist simply takes comfort in the knowledge that God is good and just.

The calm reasonableness of his tone, however, cannot make up for deism's obvious flaw: it is intellectually lazy. That helps explain why it failed to catch on with the general public. It accepts a divine Creator as a convenient cover, since science has failed to explain the universe's existence, only to cast the Creator aside and bolt for

---

9   In subordinating individual desires to the General Will, Rousseau has sometimes been seen as the creator, in theory, of fascist totalitarianism.

the nearest exit. Why would he go to the trouble of creating a universe only to show no interest in what happens in it? Deism does not even attempt an answer. Voltaire was even known to order servants to leave the room before letting conversation on religion begin. The lower orders, he felt, could never hope to understand his Enlightened ideas, so best not to irritate their ignorance by letting them overhear.

The deists deserve respect for their dedication to religious tolerance and their willingness to risk exile and imprisonment for its sake. But deism was the only major Enlightenment idea to disappear from European life after the 18th century.

JEWISH ENLIGHTENMENT

The promotion of reason and tolerance certainly appealed to Europe's Jewish populations. Many Jews supported the Enlightened goal of fighting superstition and ignorance, which were sources of anti-Jewish hatred. To secular Jews, an Enlightened world without religion would be a world without religious violence. And of violence they had had their fill.

By 1500 hardly any Jews still resided in western Europe, thanks to late-medieval and later expulsions in England (1290), France (1292), Spain (1492), and Portugal (1496). Most Continental Jews migrated east into Germany and then to Poland. The confederation then known as the Polish-Lithuanian Union dates back to 1385. By the 17th century it included what are today the nations of Poland, Ukraine, Belarus, Latvia, and Lithuania—and there they enjoyed a welcome and a degree of tolerance that they had seldom known in the west (see Map 15.1). Most of the exiled Sephardim migrated to Holland and the Ottoman Empire, although substantial numbers settled in southern Italy and North Africa as well. But matters changed when Poland became ensnared in political and social convulsions in the mid-17th century, including the so-called Polish-Swedish War (1600–1629) and the Northern War (1655–1660).[10] Fleeing once more from oppression, several hundred thousand Jews returned to western Europe, whose nations gradually—and grudgingly—revoked their bans on Jewish presence.

England was the last western country to revoke its ban, in 1655. Not everyone was pleased. The poet John Dryden (1631–1700), for one, complained in his best-known poem, *Absalom and Achitophel* (1681):

> The Jews, a headstrong, moody, murmuring race,
> God's pampered people, whom, debauched with ease,
> No king could govern, nor no God could please.

---

[10]   In the Khmelnytsky Rebellion of 1648 alone, well over a hundred thousand Jews were slaughtered by rampaging Cossack troops.

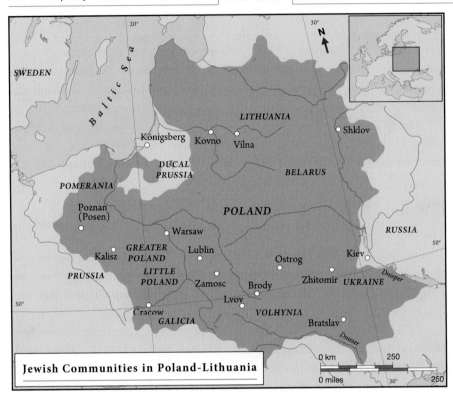

MAP 15.1   Jewish Communities in Poland-Lithuania

It is important to note, however, that the "Jews" here in fact represent the people of England. Dryden is using the Biblical tale of Absalom and Achitophel's rebellion against King David (2 Samuel) to describe the political struggle in England. David represents Charles II, whose followers were known as the Tories. Absalom and Achitophel stand for the Earl of Shaftesbury and the Duke of Monmouth, whose supporters were the Whigs. The poem's anti-Semitic overtone went down smoothly with Dryden's readers. Nonetheless, Jews had returned to an Enlightened Europe apparently dedicated to reform and reason.

Traditionally, most Jews had sought to secure a peaceful, though parallel, existence with Christian society. From their segregated communities, under the leadership of their rabbis, they had ventured out into the gentile world to conduct business. They could even engage, within limits, in the broader intellectual and social life—but returned at day's end to the community and its ritual life under the Law. Jews had retained their distinctive identity for centuries, wearing traditional clothing, observing dietary restrictions, performing their mitzvahs, keeping their languages alive, and perpetuating the traditions of Jewish intellectual life. Now many Jews were determined to reestablish Judaism in the west, not as a separate, segregated society but as an integral part of the new progressive world.

Amsterdam Synagogue   Emanuel de Witte (1617–1692) painted this interior view of the Portuguese Synagogue in the Dutch capital in 1680. This was the synagogue whose leaders excommunicated Baruch de Spinoza "with the excommunication with which Joshua banned Jericho, with the curse with which Elisha cursed the boys, and with all the curses which are written in the Book of the Law."

HASKALAH AND HASIDISM

The Hebrew term for enlightenment is **haskalah**, the name of one of the two main developments in European Jewish history in the 18th century. The Haskalah movement accepted the idea of assimilation, or seeking to integrate Jews into the main European populace and culture. Moses Mendelssohn (1729–1786), a Prussian autodidact who became Judaism's greatest philosopher since Maimonides, encouraged, if not complete assimilation, at least a dignified integration with gentile society. Israel Jacobson (1768–1828), the founder of Reform Judaism, deemphasized Jewish teachings that he regarded as merely ritual instead of moral or ethical and therefore essential. They recommended the decline of Jewish vernaculars like Yiddish and Ladino, which only kept Jews segregated from the European world, in favor of traditional Hebrew and the gentile vernaculars. Mendelssohn translated the entire Bible into German.

The **Hasidim** occupied the other end of the spectrum and the other end of Europe. Founded by the Polish rabbi Israel ben Eleazar (1696–1760), also known as the Ba'al Shem Tov ("Master of the Good Name"), Hasidic Judaism represented a revivalist spirit rather than a new set of ideas regarding observant life. The Hasidim (literally, "the Pious Ones") decried Ashkenazic rabbinic Jewish life as too rule-bound, soul-deadening, and formulaic. At the same time, they found the mystical-philosophical Kabbalistic elements of Sephardic Judaism too foreign. What R. Eleazar emphasized instead was a more vividly emotional and uplifting style of worship. Centered in the home instead of the synagogues, the Hasidim adhered strictly to Jewish Law but did so under the leadership of charismatic zaddikim ("holy men"), who led their congregations in joyous singing and dancing. The Hasidim maintained that sincerity of prayer, charity performed with warmth and eagerness, and sensitivity to God's ever-present reality are more pleasing in heaven than uninspired rituals. Eastern European Jews became known for the vitality of their worship and their communal lives. From these two developments—Haskalah and Hasidism—arose the Reform, Conservative, and Orthodox traditions of modern-day Judaism.

THE JEWS AND EUROPE'S AMBIVALENCE

Europeans were, as ever, ambivalent about the Jews. Most favored integration—that is, incorporating the Jews into society at least in terms of law and governance—but were opposed to outright assimilation, an idea that raised the uncomfortable notions of intermarriage and socializing on equal terms. The problem was described by Charles-Henri de Clermont-Tonnerre, in a debate in the National Assembly in 1789:

> We must deny everything to the Jews as a nation, but grant them everything as individuals. We must not recognize the authority of their judges—rather, they need to recognize the authority of ours. They should not be allowed to exist as a distinct political entity or power within our state; and accordingly we must not grant legitimacy to the discrete laws by which they have lived as a separate community. Each Jew, as an individual, must be a citizen [of France]. To any who say, "That is not what they want!" I can only reply: "If they do not want to be citizens, then they should say so openly, and be banished. It is insupportable to retain a polity of noncitizens within our state—a nation, as it were, within our nation."

Although many Jews did assimilate, they were not necessarily welcomed into the broader streams of society. Among the more paranoid of anti-Semites, the Jews' willingness to assimilate was proof of their supposed desire to attack Christian society from within. Friedrich II of Prussia issued an edict in 1744 that expelled all Jews from the city of Breslau, except for ten merchant and financial families. A similar enactment for the city of Berlin added that the few Jews who were allowed to remain in the capital could do so only on the condition that they refrain from marrying and bearing children. That was in 1750, the same year as when Maria Theresa of Austria evicted the Jews from the whole of Bohemia, only to invite them back, later, with the inspired idea of requiring them to pay a fee every ten years for the right to remain.[11] Nevertheless, numerous **Acts of Toleration** that offered full or partial constitutional rights to Jews were promulgated in country after country: Holland (1657), the British colonies (1665, 1740), Britain itself (1753), France (1781), Austria (1782), Spain (1789), and Hungary (1791).

But changes in law occur in advance of changes in popular opinion as often as they occur in response to them, and popular prejudices against Jews remained common across the Continent. The best hope for the future therefore lay not in the conversion or assimilation of the Jews but in the promotion of tolerance as a secular, civil virtue applicable to all regardless of faith. This was Spinoza's point when he wrote in his *Theological-Political Treatise* (1670) that all nations, even the Jews themselves, must surrender their self-appointed roles as the unique possessors of heavenly blessing, since "every man's happiness and true blessedness consists in enjoying the Good, not in indulging in the belief that he alone, to the exclusion of all others, is enjoying it. Anyone who thinks himself to be somehow more blessed and fortunate than his neighbors is therefore actually ignorant of both happiness and good fortune." Other Enlightened writers, notably Voltaire and Kant, ridiculed Judaism as a faith yet championed Jewish rights of full citizenship and had several Jews among their close friends.

The German playwright and philosopher Gotthold Lessing (1729–1781) wrote two plays that dramatized the plight of European Jewry—*The Jews* (1754) and *Nathan the Wise* (1779)—and presented (scandalously, for the time) Jewish characters who were more virtuous and kindhearted than their Christian neighbors.[12] In the latter play, which takes place during the Third Crusade, there is a scene in which the title character tells the Muslim warlord Saladin a parable. A wealthy, powerful, and noble-spirited man possessed a beautiful ring that enabled

---

[11]   In 1752, Maria Theresa promulgated a decree limiting all Jewish families to having a single son—or else face eviction.

[12]   Few Enlightenment plays appeal to modern tastes. Has anyone ever seen a production of Voltaire's *Oedipus* (1718), often cited as the greatest tragedy of the 18th century?

its wearer to enjoy God's special love and favor, and decreed that the ring shall be passed down the generations with each owner giving it to the son he loved the most. After several generations, one owner decided that he loved all three of his sons equally and so had two exact replicas of the ring made. None of the three heirs therefore knew for certain which ring was the original. In that situation, Lessing writes, the choices are stark: either the sons and their successors fight one another eternally, each certain that his own ring is the true one, or they decide to live together in peace in the hope that his ring is authentic and that its authenticity is proven by the excellence of its wearer's moral behavior. The parable is apt as a description of Lessing's hope for religious toleration and as a general expression of the spirit of the reformers. The only solution to religious strife, they maintained, is secular virtue.

THE UNENLIGHTENED

Competing ideas and tensions existed among the Enlightened about the lower orders of society as well, who still comprised the overwhelming bulk of the population. Some writers—Locke, Hume, Voltaire, and Kant especially among them—regarded the idea of radical democracy as sheer lunacy. But as poverty and its consequences spread, what was to be done? For Locke and Voltaire, to give common farmers and laborers a political voice equal to that of the educated and propertied was an offense to intelligence and good taste. To Hume, distinction by birth was as fixed as distinction by race. Just as "there never was a civilized nation of any other complexion than white," so too the notion of the civilized mass of common people was unimaginable. As for Kant, the only political or civic freedom he could envision was one of freedom of the Enlightened from the tyranny of the brutish common folk:

> In truth, only a ruler with a large and disciplined army at his disposal can say, "Debate as much you wish, but obey me!" An ironical fact thus emerges—that the greater the degree of civic freedom, the more limited the freedom of the spirit; but a lesser degree of civic freedom allows the [Enlightened] mind to grow to the utmost it is capable of doing.

As for Voltaire, he wrote movingly in his great *Treatise on Toleration*:

> It takes no great art, no specially trained eloquence, to show that all Christians should have tolerance for one another—but I am going one step further and asserting that all men should be regarded as brothers to one another. What? A Turk, my brother? A Chinaman, my brother?

A Jew? A Siamese? To which I respond: Yes! Absolutely! After all, are we not all children of the same Father, all created by the same God?

And yet Voltaire's personal letters and diaries, which fill 102 volumes in their standard edition, make plain that he despised Jews. Racial vituperation and caricature pour off their pages with numbing regularity. His anti-Semitism, like Martin Luther's in the 16th century, was certainly no worse than that of his contemporaries, yet his stature lent prejudice a shameful degree of legitimation. His views of the lower orders were no less odious. He finds them ignorant, brutish, foul-smelling, lazy, simplistic, incapable of understanding or appreciating the noble work of the philosophes.

The Simple Pleasures of Life   Louis Le Nain (1593–1648) was one of three French artist brothers, all of whom signed their works with only their family name, thus making it difficult to tell which brother painted which painting. The confusion is fitting, in its way, for the closeness and good cheer of the brothers is a common element in their paintings. Whether portraying a panel of city aldermen, a group of friends around a gaming table, or, as here, a peasant family listening to their grandfather play a song on his pipe, the Le Nain brothers show commoners' lives with dignity and grace.

Few of the philosophes or those who read them felt any shame about disregarding the lowest levels of society. Millions of peasants lived on the edge of poverty and famine. Those who could not pay their rent were driven from the land. In France alone nearly a quarter million peasants, on average, lost their farms per year over the 18th century and, having no place to go, migrated into the cities. Across Europe, from Ireland to Poland, between 10 and 20 percent of all city dwellers were indigent laborers who depended entirely on charity for survival. The possibilities this raised for crime led local governments to build ever more workhouses, where the indigent presumably could earn their keep by doing low-grade manufacturing labor. In reality, nearly a quarter of them died within six months of entering the poorhouse.

The number of these institutions across Europe more than doubled from 1700 to 1789, with the bulk of that increase occurring after 1740. (The population of Europe increased by only 30 percent over the same period.) With these demographic shifts came new social problems. By 1789 nearly one-fifth of all childbirths in Europe occurred out of marriage, a key factor in which was the number of poor women who entered domestic service to the better-off. In the German principalities, the rate of out-of-wedlock births quadrupled from 1700 to 1800. Many novels of the era, such as the immensely popular *Pamela, or Virtue Rewarded* (1740) by Samuel Richardson, narrate the drama of young girls in service at the mercy of their employers.[13]

Poverty grew more visible as it worsened, since the cities became choked with unemployed, starving crowds. The problem was exacerbated by disputes over whose responsibility they were. Traditionally, Europe's poor had depended on churches, religious confraternities, guild-supported hospices, and almsgiving by those lucky enough to have money to spare. Caring for the indigent was generally not regarded as a responsibility of the state. But the numbers of the wretched, and the social ills associated with their condition, became so acute that radical new approaches were needed.

Jonathan Swift (1667–1745) offered an ironic one with his famous essay "A Modest Proposal" of 1729, to deal with the teeming swarms of orphan children in Ireland:

> I am assured by our merchants, that a boy or a girl before twelve years old is no salable commodity; and even when they come to this age they will not yield above three pounds, or three pounds and half-a-crown at most on the exchange; which cannot turn to account either to the

---

[13]   Nor were servant girls the only victims of lecherous rakes. Richardson's richest novel, *Clarissa*, tells of the repeated attempts to seduce the virtuous maiden (of good birth) of the title.

parents or kingdom, the charge of nutriment and rags having been at least four times that value.

I shall now therefore humbly propose my own thoughts, which I hope will not be liable to the least objection. I have been assured by a very knowing American of my acquaintance in London, that a young healthy child well nursed is at a year old a most delicious, nourishing, and wholesome food, whether stewed, roasted, baked, or boiled; and I make no doubt that it will equally serve in a fricassee or a ragout.

His point was satirical, but the essay raises few laughs. A far more charitable and admirable man, Samuel Johnson, wrote that "a decent provision for the poor is a true test of civilization" and opened his own home to a parade of the needy. Yet even he reserved his charity for the "deserving poor"—those who could not care for themselves because of physical or mental debility. Like most of his contemporaries, Johnson expected the unhandicapped poor either to fend for themselves or to accept misery as man's natural condition.

The philosophes, for the most part, failed to do much better. Rousseau, as we saw, argues that man's natural compassion is corroded by the competition for material goods. Economic and social privilege therefore legitimate and perpetuate one another. When Voltaire received a copy of the *Discourse*, he thanked Rousseau for his "newest attack on the human race." His characteristic sarcasm might be dismissed as lighthearted, but a note Voltaire wrote in the margin gives his real opinion away: "Here it is—the philosophy of a wretch who wants nothing more than for the rich to be robbed by the poor."

> To most of the Enlightened, the uneducated laboring masses were simply a fact of nature, and no rational reform of society and civil life could change it.

The philosophes were not utterly heartless. They spoke fervently against the injustices that made the lives of common peasants and laborers worse. Gabriel Bonnot de Mably (1709–1785), for one, asserted the equality of all persons before the law, as well as the equality of their material needs—an early form of communism. But they did not see elevating the lowest strata of society as important, or even desirable. To most of the Enlightened, the uneducated laboring masses were simply a fact of nature, and no rational reform of society and civil life could change it. Even de Mably maintained that peasants were stupid and ignorant. They deserve sympathy, he argues, only because their poverty, which previously had been voluntary, had become institutionalized by absolutism. The philosophes, in sum, aimed at the rational reform of polite society. The great toiling bulk of mankind did not need liberty, wealth, and rights. They only needed better masters.

ASSESSING THE ENLIGHTENMENT

In the context of Europe's intellectual history, the significance of the Enlightenment can hardly be exaggerated. The philosophes generated new ideas, contributed enormously to culture, and inspired later generations to follow in their steps. They promoted political, social, and economic change, and their intellectual, and often personal, courage was extraordinary. But their failures, too, were many. Voltaire's *Candide* and Rousseau's *Emile*—both phenomenal successes in their time—are hard to read today as art. Diderot's plays are rarely performed. The 18th-century poets who are most read today were not part of the Enlightened program and often viewed it skeptically: in England, Alexander Pope (1688–1744) and Samuel Johnson (1709–1784); in Germany, Johann Wolfgang von Goethe (1749–1832) and Novalis (Friedrich von Hardenberg, 1772–1801); in Spain, Juan Meléndez Valdés (1754–1817). Only Edward Gibbon (1737–1794), among the philosophes, produced anything regarded today as literary art of the first rank. His great *History of the Decline and Fall of the Roman Empire* is still viewed as a masterpiece of English prose.

Readers of the Enlightened were numerous and avid. The *Encyclopédie* appeared in thousands of private and public libraries all over France, as did its English, German, and Italian counterparts in those countries (see Map 15.2).

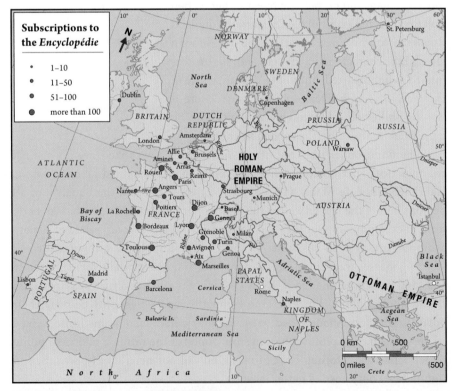

MAP 15.2   **Subscriptions to the *Encyclopédie*.**

Rousseau's *Emile*, like Voltaire's *Letters on the English* and *Philosophical Dictionary*, was known to tens of thousands. Lectures and public readings by Locke, Smith, Diderot, Beccaria, and others were enjoyed by untold numbers; and their ideas circulated through innumerable salon meetings. They fought against censorship by cleverly disguising their messages, by circulating to an extent under the governments' radar, by book smuggling across borders, and by the black market. But who exactly read these works and embraced their ideas, and what does that say about the sympathies of the Enlightened for others?

Some of the Enlightened's most fervent readers and supporters came from the aristocracy itself. Indeed, a number of the leading philosophes were themselves noble born, such as the Baron de Montesquieu. But it is a mistake to give them too much credit here. The relative size of the European aristocracy, as a demographic percentage, had declined significantly in the preceding two hundred years, owing to baronial war making and the absorption of smaller estates and baronies into larger ones. By the middle of the 18th century hereditary aristocrats made up a small portion of the European population, overall. Generally, the figure was 1–2 percent in England and France and increased as one moved eastward and southward through the Continent from there: 4–5 percent in Germany, 5–6 percent in Italy and in Austria-Hungary, 7–8 percent in Spain, and as much as 9–10 percent in Poland-Lithuania. Russia then provided a firm backstop with a return to a restricted 1–2 percent—although the bulk of these lived in western Russia's regions around Moscow and St. Petersburg, regardless of where their landholdings actually were.

Allowing for differences between countries, approximately 3–4 percent of the European population consisted of the hereditary aristocracy. The nobles found many of the philosophes' ideas worth investigating, but usually only those dealing with technical matters. It was one thing to improve agricultural yields, make mining more efficient, or develop better means to transport rural goods to urban markets. Beyond that, though, few dared or cared to venture. They expected legal privileges and monopolies, not open markets. Mercantilism and feudal privilege guaranteed their income, and Enlightened ideas attracted them only if they could increase their profit margins. Faced with runaway inflation, the nobles insisted with ever greater force on their rights and the seigniorial dues owed them by the peasants. These dues dated back to the 13th century and included payments to use the lord's utilities—namely his mill, oven, and winepress. (Needless to say, the peasants were forbidden to use anyone else's, for good measure.) Peasants commonly owed special taxes on commodities like salt. They had to build and maintain the roads—and then cart the nobles' goods to market.

All this revenue supported the maintenance of chateaux and country houses, fine carriages, the patronage of art and music, clothing of fine silks and ornament, plumed hats, powdered wigs, and (for the women) astonishing hairdressings and gowns. Opportunities for wealth were growing in the capitalist trade

A Feather in Your Cap?   This engraving from Denis Diderot's great *Encyclopedia* shows a group of women haberdashers making feather ornaments to adorn various wigs and gowns.

centered in the cities; but social prejudices made it difficult for aristocrats to sully themselves by doing business with common merchants. Making matters worse, a number of absolutist regimes (France and Spain, most notoriously) made it illegal for them to do so. Burdened by high costs, and with few alternate means of drawing income, many nobles fell into debt and relied on loans to maintain their standards of living.

Some nobles were drawn to Enlightened ideas about society, law, government, and religion—but they were very few. In general, countries with a higher proportion of nobility (Italy, Austria-Hungary, Spain, Poland-Lithuania) also had more impoverished nobles—who, in turn, felt more threatened by change. Noble readers of the philosophes in those countries were very few indeed. In England, France, and Germany, the nobles proved more willing to investigate Enlightened activity.[14] John Locke and David Hume owed much of their living to the patronage of society's greats. Immanuel Kant was revered by countless more Prussians than who actually read and understood him. Diderot had a few noble patrons who could be relied upon to help him out of his legal troubles; and the Baron de Montesquieu and the Marquis de Condorcet actively participated in

---

[14]   No fewer than thirty of the 160 author-contributors to Diderot's *Encyclopédie* were noble.

the Enlightened movement. But the overwhelming bulk of the aristocracy deeply distrusted more radical philosophes like Diderot and Rousseau and tried hard to marginalize or imprison them.

The main audience for the Enlightened, then, was the middle class—especially the upper strata of it, the professional classes. This comprised well-heeled financiers and merchants, industrialists, medical and legal professionals, and local civil servants. Many of these individuals were as wealthy as many aristocrats and lived lives of extraordinary material comfort. The Enlightened allowed them important roles in intellectual and artistic life that might enhance their reputations. **Salons**, learned societies, patronage of artists and composers, support for theatrical companies were more than just means to promote the new learning. They also controlled its funding and shaped its development. John Locke's wealthy patrons, for example, influenced the development of his political thought, with its stress on property rights; it is impossible to imagine those patrons supporting Rousseau in the same way.

By the 18th century this well-to-do middle class, the **bourgeoisie**, was large enough to support an ambitious campaign. The total population of France, for example, increased from roughly 22 million in 1700 to approximately 30 million in 1800—a gain of about 33 percent. But within that population the number of wealthy bourgeoisie increased 300 percent. Europe now had a highly developed urban culture. The greatest city of all was London, with just over a million people;

Example of an Enlightenment Salon   Here a group of philosophes gathers to hear a reading of Voltaire's play *The Orphan of China* (1755). It cannot have been painted by an eyewitness, since no one is asleep.

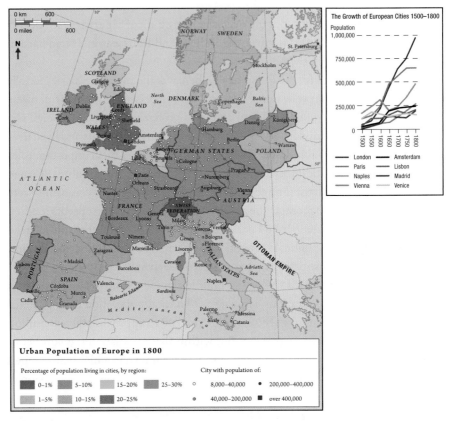

The Growth of European Cities 1500–1800

Urban Population of Europe in 1800

Percentage of population living in cities, by region:

		City with population of:
0–1%	15–20%	25–30%	○ 8,000–40,000	• 200,000–400,000
1–5%	10–15%	20–25%	◉ 40,000–200,000	■ over 400,000

MAP 15.3   Urban Population of Europe in 1800

Paris came next, with 600,000; the next tier was occupied by Berlin, Vienna, and Saint Petersburg, with about 200,000 each. Rome and Milan had slightly fewer, perhaps 150,000 each. Scores of smaller cities, too, could maintain universities, support scientific academies, offer lectures in public halls—and host salons and establish Masonic lodges (see Map 15.3).

> Freemasonry was thus an 18th-century version of keeping a private Facebook account. Here a controlled and closed circle of friends could stay in touch, trade ideas, and promote new projects.

Masonic lodges date to the 17th century, perhaps starting in Scotland. They were essentially private clubs, whose members were sworn to secrecy about their activities.[15] For a nobleman, mingling in public with commoners was social suicide. As Freemasons, however, nobles could socialize with well-to-do commoners, either to arrange business dealings or to support programs such as the Enlightenment. Freemasonry was thus an 18th-century version

---

[15]   Symbols like pyramids and illuminated eyes made Masonic lodges appear to descend from medieval guilds or secret societies like the Knights Templar. Some of this imagery appears today on U.S. currency.

of keeping a private Facebook account. Here a controlled and closed circle of friends could stay in touch, trade ideas, and promote new projects. In *War and Peace*, Leo Tolstoy sends his main character, Pierre Bezuhov, into the lodges in search of his own brand of enlightenment.

The Catholic Church condemned **freemasonry** as evil. The church saw it as a conspiracy to destroy the divinely ordained institutions that kept the world in order. (This response explains the nonsense in novels like *The Da Vinci Code*.) However, by 1750 Masonry had spread as far east as Poland and Russia, and as far west as the American colonies, where figures like George Washington and Benjamin Franklin were members. In Paris alone, in the 1770s, there were well over ten thousand Masons. Through such stratagems as these, Enlightened ideas spread much further than they could simply through book sales.

Most urban professionals clearly supported the scientific and aesthetic programs of the Enlightened. They favored breaking away from mercantilism and unleashing the free market—which is hardly surprising, since they were the ones most likely to benefit. They advocated Enlightened reforms in education as well, to promote science and technological development. None, however, spoke out in favor of public education for the masses. They desired instead vocational training for urban workers, with the elites in control of the curriculum, leaving higher matters like philosophy and political theory to leaders of the new society.

On political matters, the elites were divided. Enlightened despotism still seemed the best of all possible political worlds to many. This group advocated a thorough reform and improvement of the current systems of governance, but not a revolution. But by the 1770s the pendulum was swinging in favor of a clean break with the past, a destruction of the Old Regime, and the creation of a new form of republic. This is also the decade in which Voltaire's reign as the supreme philosophe began to give way to Rousseau's. But the radical philosophes disagreed with their moderate colleagues mostly in degree. Both political programs were based on the rationality of the human world. Humans might be essentially good (to the radicals) or at least potentially good (to the moderates). Either way, they had it within their power to create happiness here on earth, if only they adapted their behavior to the laws of nature.

> To critics of the Enlightenment, both then and now, the world hardly works according to universal laws. The very belief is itself unreasonable and a new form of oppression; it merely substitutes one system of human bondage for another.

To critics of the Enlightenment, both then and now, the world hardly works according to universal laws. The very belief is itself unreasonable and a new form of oppression; it merely substitutes one system of human bondage for another. In economics, they say, it encourages docile acceptance of what the masters of **laissez-faire** capitalism desire. Moreover, it gives those masters a morally odious excuse. They can claim to be unable to change the system that keeps them enriched and in power. This is just what Karl Marx argued in the 19th century, and Diderot and Rousseau may have hinted at it as well.

Were the Enlightened truly the champions of the common man? Most of them did not pretend to be. They wanted a world based on merit and reasoned argument rather than inherited privilege. If they saw themselves as the unique possessors of that merit, they were simply being human. Rousseau, above all, radicalized the Enlightenment by speaking passionately to the lower orders. He came from them, and he urged them to disregard the fancy theories of the powdered and pampered salons. He especially despised Voltaire as a hypocrite. Voltaire died rich, yet a bitter man, for he was never granted the peerage he so desperately desired. Lauded by all as a champion of freedom, he had been shunted aside by a vulgar upstart from Geneva. When Rousseau cast the light of his reason on the Enlightened, he found them wanting, and he called on the masses to take their fates into their own hands. He was fortunate to have died in 1778, for he never saw the results of that call.

WHO, WHAT, WHERE

Acts of Toleration
bourgeoisie
deism
Enlightenment
freemasonry
Hasidim
Haskalah

laissez-faire
League of Augsburg
market
noble savage
philosophes
salons

SUGGESTED READINGS

Primary Sources

Bayle, Pierre. *Historical and Critical Dictionary.*

Beccaria, Cesare. *On Crimes and Punishments.*

Diderot, Denis. *Encyclopedia.*

Hume, David. *An Enquiry Regarding Human Understanding.*

Locke, John. *An Essay on Human Understanding.*

———. *Two Treatises on Civil Government.*

Montesquieu, Baron Charles de. *The Spirit of the Laws.*

Rousseau, Jean-Jacques. *Confessions.*

———. *Discourse on the Origins of Inequality.*

———. *The Social Contract.*

Smith, Adam. *The Wealth of Nations.*

Voltaire. *Candide.*

———. *A Philosophical Dictionary.*

Source Anthologies

Hyland, Paul, ed. *The Enlightenment: A Sourcebook and Reader* (2001).

Jacob, Margaret C. *The Enlightenment: A Brief History with Documents* (2000).

Studies

Anderson, Fred. *Crucible of War: The Seven Years' War and the Fate of Empire in British North America, 1754–1766* (2000).

Berg, Maxine. *Luxury and Pleasure in Eighteenth-Century Britain* (2005).

Blanning, T. C. W. *The Culture of Power and the Power of Culture: Old Regime Europe, 1660–1789* (2002).

Blom, Philipp. *Enlightening the World: "Encyclopédie," the Book that Changed the World* (2005).

Buchan, James. *The Authentic Adam Smith: His Life and Ideas* (2006).

Dale, Richard. *The First Crash: Lessons from the South Sea Bubble* (2004).

Damrosch, Leo. *Jean-Jacques Rousseau: Restless Genius* (2007).

Doyle, William. *Aristocracy and Its Enemies in the Age of Revolution* (2009).

Feiner, Shmuel. *Haskalah and History: The Emergence of a Modern Jewish Historical Consciousness* (2004).

———. *The Jewish Enlightenment* (2003).

Groenewegen, Peter D. *Eighteenth-Century Economics: Turgot, Beccaria, and Smith and Their Contemporaries* (2002).

Hess, Jonathan M. *Germans, Jews, and the Claims of Modernity* (2002).

Israel, Jonathan. *Democratic Enlightenment: Philosophy, Revolution, and Human Rights, 1750–1790* (2011).

———. *Enlightenment Contested: Philosophy, Modernity, and the Emancipation of Man, 1670–1752* (2006).

———. *Radical Enlightenment: Philosophy and the Making of Modernity, 1650–1750* (2001).

McMahon, Darrin M. *Enemies of the Enlightenment: The French Counter-Enlightenment and the Making of Modernity* (2001).

Munck, Thomas. *The Enlightenment: A Comparative Social History, 1724–1794* (2000).

Pearson, Roger. *Voltaire Almighty: A Life in Pursuit of Freedom* (2005).

Porter, Roy. *The Creation of the Modern World: The Untold Story of the British Enlightenment* (2000).

Saul, John Ralston. *Voltaire's Bastards: The Dictatorship of Reason in the West* (1992).

Straub, Kristina. *Domestic Affairs: Intimacy, Eroticism, and Violence between Servants and Masters in Eighteenth-Century Britain* (2005).

Sutcliffe, Adam. *Judaism and Enlightenment* (2003).

Zaretsky, Robert, and John T. Scott. *The Philosophers' Quarrel: Rousseau, Hume, and the Limits of Human Understanding* (2009).

For additional resources, including maps, primary sources, visuals, web links, and quizzes, please go to **www.oup.com/us/backman.**

DÉCLARATION DES DROITS DE L'HOMME ET DU CITOYEN,

Décrétés par l'Assemblée Nationale dans les séances des 20, 21, 23, 24 et 26 août 1789, acceptés par le Roi.

PRÉAMBULE

LES représentans du peuple François, constitués en assemblée nationale, considérant que l'ignorance, l'oubli ou le mépris des droits de l'homme sont les seules causes des malheurs publics et de la corruption des gouvernemens ont résolu d'exposer dans une déclaration solemnelle, les droits naturels, inaliénables et sacrés de l'homme, afin que cette déclaration constamment présente à tous les membres du corps social, leur rappelle sans cesse leurs droits et leurs devoirs, afin que les actes du pouvoir législatif et ceux du pouvoir exécutif, pouvant être à chaque instant comparés avec le but de toute institution politique, en soient plus respectés, afin que les réclamations des citoyens, fondées désormais sur des principes simples et incontestables, tournent toujours au maintien de la constitution et du bonheur de tous.

EN conséquence, l'assemblée nationale reconnoit et déclare, en présence et sous les auspices de l'Être suprême les droits suivans de l'homme et du citoyen.

ARTICLE PREMIER

LES hommes naissent et demeurent libres et égaux en droits, les distinctions sociales ne peuvent être fondées que sur l'utilité commune.

II.

LE but de toute association politique est la conservation des droits naturels et imprescriptibles de l'homme; ces droits sont la liberté, la propriété, la sureté, et la résistance à l'oppression.

III.

LE principe de toute souveraineté réside essentiellement dans la nation, nul corps, nul individu ne peut exercer d'autorité qui n'en émane expressement.

IV.

LA liberté consiste à pouvoir faire tout ce qui ne nuit pas à autrui. Ainsi, l'exercice des droits naturels de chaque homme, n'a de bornes que celles qui assurent aux autres membres de la société la jouissance de ces mêmes droits; ces bornes ne peuvent être déterminées que par la loi.

V.

LA loi n'a le droit de défendre que les actions nuisibles à la société. Tout ce qui n'est pas défendu par la loi ne peut être empéché, et nul ne peut être contraint à faire ce qu'elle n'ordonne pas.

VI.

LA loi est l'expression de la volonté générale; tous les citoyens ont droit de concourir personnellement, ou par leurs représentans, à sa formation; elle doit être la même pour tous, soit qu'elle protège, soit qu'elle punisse. Tous les citoyens étant égaux à ses yeux, sont également admissibles à toutes dignités, places et emplois publics, selon leur capacité, et sans autres distinction que celles de leurs vertus et de leurs talens.

VII.

NUL homme ne peut être accusé, arrêté ni détenu que dans les cas déterminés par la loi, et selon les formes qu'elle a prescrites, ceux qui sollicitent, expédient, exécutent ou font exécuter des ordres arbitraires, doivent être punis; mais tout citoyen appelé ou saisi en vertu de la loi, doit obéir à l'instant, il se rend coupable par la résistance.

VIII.

LA loi ne doit établir que des peines strictement et évidemment nécessaire, et nul ne peut être puni qu'en vertu d'une loi établie, et promulguée antérieurement au délit, et légalement appliquée.

IX.

TOUT homme étant présumé innocent jusqu'à ce qu'il ait été déclaré coupable, s'il est jugé indispensable de l'arrêter, toute rigueur qui ne serait pas nécessaire pour s'assurer de sa personne doit être sévèrement réprimée par la loi.

X.

NUL ne doit être inquiété pour ses opinions, mêmes religieuses pourvu que leur manifestation ne trouble pas l'ordre public établi par la loi.

XI.

LA libre communication des pensées et des opinions est un des droits les plus précieux de l'homme; tout citoyen peut donc parler écrire, imprimer librement, sauf à répondre de l'abus de cette liberté dans les cas déterminés par la loi.

XII.

LA garantie des droits de l'homme et du citoyen nécessite une force publique; cette force est donc instituée pour l'avantage de tous, et non pour l'utilité particulière de ceux à qui elle est confiée.

XIII.

POUR l'entretien de la force publique, et pour les dépenses d'administration, une contribution commune est indispensable; elle doit être également répartie entre les citoyens en raison de leurs facultées.

XIV.

LES citoyens ont le droit de constater par eux même ou par leurs représentans, la nécessité de la contribution publique, de la consentir librement, d'en suivre l'emploi, et d'en déterminer la quotité, l'assiette, le recouvrement et la durée.

XV.

LA société a le droit de demander compte à tout agent public de son administration.

XVI.

TOUTE société, dans laquelle la garantie des droits n'est pas assurée, ni les séparation des pouvoirs déterminée, n'a point de constitution.

XVII.

LES propriétés étant un droit inviolable et sacré, nul ne peut en être privé, si ce n'est lorsque la nécessité publique, légalement constatée, l'exige évidemment, et sous la condition d'une juste et préalable indemnité.

AUX REPRESENTANS DU PEUPLE FRANCOIS.

CHAPTER 16

The War against Absolutism

1789–1815

In the minds of many, the French not least among them, the Revolution of 1789 is the prime divider of European history, the watershed moment that announced the dramatic and bloody beginning of the modern age. Of the drama and blood there is no doubt. The Revolution overthrew monarchy, abolished aristocracy and the decayed remnants of feudalism, instituted representative government, and asserted the innate human rights of liberty, freedom of expression, and equality before the law. It proclaimed the beginning of a new era of enlightened independence. Along the way it also slaughtered tens of thousands of victims, triggered a continental war, terrorized into silent obedience the very people it purported to free, ruined fortunes, and crushed forms of religious and cultural life that had buoyed human spirits through centuries of deprivation and struggle.

THE GREATER WEST, ca. 1800

It also led to an equally tumultuous and bloody aftermath that transformed the whole of Europe—and not just in the direction of liberty and modernity. The rise of Napoleon in France brought reform elsewhere, as he sought to expand his empire. Meanwhile an opening between Europe and the Turks invited parallel changes in Islam.

A REVOLUTION IN WESTERN HISTORY?

◄ **The Declaration of the Rights of Man and the Citizen** The central document of the French Revolution, enacted by the National Assembly on August 26, 1789.

Much of the vocabulary of modern political life derives from the Revolution. Factions are described as "left," "right," "centrist," or "radical";

- A Revolution in Western History?
- Revolutionary Road
- The Revolution Turns Radical
- Napoleon and the War Against Absolutism
- The Rush to Empire
- The Continental System
- How to Judge a Revolution
- Downfall
- Leaving the East Behind

CHAPTER OUTLINE

institutions promote their aims through "declarations" and "agendas"—which their opponents dismiss as "propaganda." The "will of the people," not the privileges of the mighty, is the touchstone for political rectitude. Even the ideology of a faction, including those dedicated to "terrorism," derives from the Revolution. So large does the Revolution loom in most Western minds that it is the first single political event given an entire chapter in most general histories of Europe. (In this respect it joins the two World Wars to form a triad of Most Important Events in Western History.)

> So large does the Revolution loom in most Western minds that it is the first single political event given an entire chapter in most general histories of Europe.

But other people disagree. For all its physical and philosophical carnage, after all, the Revolution changed nothing, they say. France began the year 1789 with a financially and morally corrupt political system. It persecuted millions in order to serve the interests of a self-regarding and indulgent minority, while wrapping itself in an aura of irreplaceability. And when the Revolution ended ten years later, with Napoleon in dictatorial charge, France had simply replaced one brutal regime with another. Much of France's subsequent political history, they argue, has consisted merely of a perpetual swing of the pendulum from one extreme to another: the French Republic (1792–1804), then Empire (1804–1814), then Second Republic (1848–1852), then Second Empire (1852–1870), then Third Republic (1870–1940), then Vichy and Nazi-occupied France (1940–1945), then Fourth Republic (1946–1958)—which was followed, in the aftermath of the definitive collapse of empire with the loss of Algeria, by a Fifth Republic (1958–present).

In 1989, on the eve of the bicentennial of the French Revolution, Britain's then-prime minister Margaret Thatcher was invited by the leading Parisian newspaper *Le Monde* to comment on the significance of the Revolution for advancing the cause of human rights in the world. She replied, with her customary directness, that she thought the Revolution had contributed nothing at all:

CHAPTER TIMELINE

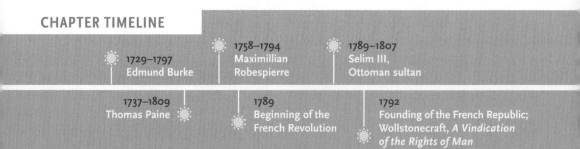

1729–1797
Edmund Burke

1758–1794
Maximillian Robespierre

1789–1807
Selim III, Ottoman sultan

1737–1809
Thomas Paine

1789
Beginning of the French Revolution

1792
Founding of the French Republic; Wollstonecraft, *A Vindication of the Rights of Man*

Human rights did not begin with the French Revolution.... [but] really stem from a mixture of Judaism and Christianity.... [Here in England we] had 1688, our quiet revolution, where Parliament exerted its will over the king.... It was not the sort of Revolution that France's was.... "Liberty, Equality, Fraternity"—[France's revolutionaries] forgot *Obligations* and *Duties*, I think. And then of course the "Fraternity" went missing for a long time. *(The Downing Street Years)*

Le Monde's angry headline the next day complained: "Thatcher Says Human Rights Did Not Begin in France."

So was the French Revolution one of the three most important events in Western history, or was it an inconsequential spasm of violence? Or is the truth somewhere in between? But if the latter, then why does the Revolution still elicit such powerful sentiments? Even in the eyes of its contemporaries, the Revolution appeared in widely varying guises. To Edmund Burke (1729–1797), one of the founders of modern political conservatism and a passionate champion of America's break from England, the Revolution showed only that the French people had proven themselves to be

the ablest architects of ruin that had hitherto existed in the world. In that very short space of time they ha[ve] completely pulled down to the ground, their monarchy; their church; their nobility; their law; their revenue; their army; their navy; their commerce; their arts; and their manufactures.... [There is a danger of] an imitation of the excesses of an irrational, unprincipled, proscribing, confiscating, plundering, ferocious, bloody and tyrannical democracy.... [In religion] the danger of their example is no longer from intolerance, but from Atheism; a foul, unnatural vice, foe to all the dignity and consolation of mankind; which seems in France, for a long time, to have been embodied into a faction, accredited, and almost avowed.

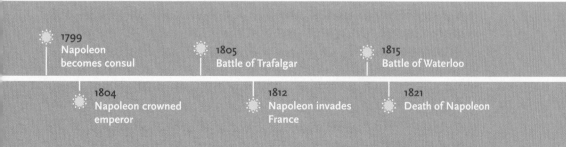

1799
Napoleon
becomes consul

1805
Battle of Trafalgar

1815
Battle of Waterloo

1804
Napoleon crowned
emperor

1812
Napoleon invades
France

1821
Death of Napoleon

TABLE 16.1   **Timeline of the French Revolution**

NATIONAL ASSEMBLY, 1789–1791	
June 20, 1789	Tennis Court Oath.
July 14, 1789	Storming of the Bastille.
Aug. 26, 1789	Assembly adopts The Declaration of the Rights of Man.
Oct. 5, 1789	Women's March on Versailles.
Nov. 2, 1789	All church property in France is nationalized.
Feb. 13, 1790	Suppression of monasteries and religious orders.
May 19, 1790	Feudalism abolished by National Assembly.
Feb. 28, 1791	400 nobles arrested at Tuileries Palace.
June 25, 1791	The royal family is caught trying to flee the country.
Sept. 14, 1791	Louis XVI formally accept new Constitution.
LEGISLATIVE ASSEMBLY, 1791–1792	
Oct. 1, 1791	National Assembly is dissolved; Legislative Assembly assumes power.
January, 1792	Food riots begin in Paris, last until March.
Feb. 7, 1792	Austria and Prussia form alliance to crush Revolution.
Mar. 20, 1792	Assembly adopt guillotine as official means of execution.
Apr. 20, 1792	France declares war on Austria and Prussia.
July 30, 1792	Austria and Prussia invade France.
Aug. 13, 1792	Louis XVI and family arrested after the storming of the Tuileries Palace.
NATIONAL CONVENTION, 1792–1795	
Sept. 20, 1792	Legislative Assembly dissolved. National Convention takes power.
Sept. 21, 1792	Monarchy abolished. French Republic declared.
Dec. 3, 1792	Louis XVI brought to trial.
Jan. 21, 1793	Execution of Louis XVI.
Apr. 6, 1793	Committee for Public Safety created.
June 10, 1793	Jacobins take control of Committee for Public Safety.
Sept. 5, 1793	The Reign of Terror begins.
Oct. 16, 1793	Marie Antoinette executed.
March 28, 1794	Death of Marquis de Condorcet in prison.
March 30, 1794	Danton executed.
May 8, 1794	Antoine Lavoisier executed.
July 28, 1794	Robespierre executed.
July 14, 1795	*Marseillaise* selected as the French national anthem.
Aug. 22, 1795	Constitution ratified.
Oct. 26, 1795	National Convention dissolved.
THE DIRECTORY, 1795–1799	
Nov. 2, 1795	The Executive Directory takes power.
May 10, 1796	Battle of Lodi.
June 4, 1796	Siege of Mantua.
Oct. 17, 1797	Treaty of Campo Formio.
July 21, 1798	Napoleon wins Battle of the Pyramids
Aug. 24, 1799	Napoleon leaves Egypt.
Oct. 9, 1799	Napoleon returns to France.
Nov. 9, 1799	Napoleon dissolves the Directory (18th Brumaire).
Dec. 24, 1799	Napoleon assumes power under title of Consul.

And yet the overthrow of the French monarchy led other Englishmen, like the young poets William Wordsworth (1770–1850) and Samuel Coleridge (1772–1834), to race to the Continent to witness firsthand the creation of a utopian new world. As Wordsworth wrote:

> Bliss was it in that dawn to be alive,
> But to be young was very heaven!—Oh! Times,
> In which the meager, stale, forbidding ways
> Of custom, law, and statute, took at once
> The attraction of a country in romance!
> When Reason seemed the most to assert her rights,
> When most intent on making of herself
> A prime Enchantress—to assist the work,
> Which then was going forward in her name!

Whether for the nobility of its aims or the vulgarity of its methods, the Revolution still fascinates and impassions.

REVOLUTIONARY ROAD

The great German poet Johan Wolfgang von Goethe (1749–1832) may not have had France in mind when he stated that "revolutions are never the fault of the people, but of the government," but the judgment fits the French case—at least as an immediate cause. The Old Regime was in fiscal free fall from 1750 on—long before the revolution turned radical.

Wars with Spain, Holland, Austria, and Prussia had drained money from the treasury at an astonishing rate, but the losses simply made war even more necessary: the crown, having already sucked every possible sou out of the domestic economy, needed more lands and people to plunder in order to maintain their place. Then, too, France had lent considerable support to the American Revolution, not from a desire to see democracy supplant monarchy everywhere but from a conviction that anything that undermined England's power indirectly favored France's. Crop failures plagued the kingdom at midcentury too, driving rent payers into arrears and their landlords into still-deeper debt themselves. When royal and aristocratic expenditures continued unabated, the result was a vast web of indebtedness. France had no national bank to regulate the fiscal rot, which forced the throne to live off short-term, high-interest loans from private sources. By the late 1770s fully 50 percent of the annual national budget went simply to paying the interest on the debt. Finance ministers came and went with steady regularity, some advocating fiscal restraint (a repulsive idea, to the court) and others supporting exuberant spending as a means of stimulating the economy. Heavier taxes were levied on the commoners to the point where massive protest loomed. No one seemed to know how to stop the downslide.

Louis XV (r. 1715–1774) had succeeded to the throne as a young child, and during the regency established for him (under the Duke of Orléans), much of the French aristocracy had worked tirelessly to secure and extend their privileges—especially exemption from having to pay most taxes. The ancient aristocratic-led system of legal courts (**parlements**) was reintroduced, and aristocratic councils replaced royal bureaucrats at every level of government. Louis tried to overturn these changes when he reached majority age. In 1771 he deployed the army to dissolve the parlements and oust the aristocratic governing councils; the next decade witnessed a continued back-and-forth between king and aristocracy that would have been unthinkable in the days of Louis XIV, but the gaping maw of national debt emboldened people to attempt the inconceivable. Meanwhile, Enlightened ideas about economic and social reform gained support at court as a means of forestalling disaster. Amid cries of alarm over royal tyranny trampling the traditional liberties of the nobles, Louis ordered a lifting of mercantilist policies restricting the grain trade, abolished the guild structure, and promoted religious toleration for France's eight million Protestants. All of this was bad enough, as far as the aristocracy was concerned—but then Louis announced his support, in 1775, for a comprehensive land tax. The announcement sparked a firestorm of complaint.

Calls for such a tax were nevertheless repeated throughout the 1770s and 1780s as the only possible way to address the crisis. Further royal steps included abolishing serfdom, condemning the use of judicial torture, and reforming the prisons, but these measures—though generally popular—required new debt financing, which only added urgency to the call for the nobles to relinquish their tax exemptions. By 1787, amid bread riots by the peasantry and loud denunciations of royal abuses of power, an aristocratic council demanded the reestablishment of the historical French legislative body known as the **Estates General**. This body, which had not met since 1614, had previously held jurisdiction over tax issues; the nobles calling for it to convene rested their hopes in a simple statistical fact: the legislature, being made up of three bodies (or estates)—one for the nobility, one for the clergy, and one for the commoners—was sure to ratify the aristocracy's position supporting tax exemption because every single one of the eight thousand–plus ecclesiastical offices represented in the clerical estate was held by a member of the nobility. No matter how loudly the **Third Estate**, the commoners, bellowed for reform, the abolition of the nobles' tax emption would lose by a two-to-one vote.

In the spring of 1789 elections were held around France to select the estates' delegates. Representatives of the commoners compiled detailed records of local

The Three Estates   French cartoon from 1789 depicting three fattened
members of the privileged classes riding atop a naked, chained, and
blindfolded commoner (who is also being spurred in a most
unfortunate place). The riders are an aristocrat, a bishop, and
a judge. The cartoon's message is clear.

grievances to be brought to Paris; these grievance notebooks (*cahiers des doléances*)
offer fascinating views of the attitudes and concerns of the common populace. An
example comes from a small commune on the river Orge, not far from Paris:

> The order of the Third Estate of. . . Dourdan, filled with gratitude
> for the fatherly kindness of Our King Who deems it fitting to restore
> our rights and customs of old, and setting aside for the moment our
> present sufferings and debilities. . . begs Him to accept this statement
> of our grievances, complaints, and remonstrances. . . . This estate for-
> mally petitions:
>
> That no citizen should ever lose his freedom except according to the
> dictates of the law; . . . that no letters nor other writings sent through the
> public mail be the cause of the detention of any citizen, except in the case
> of treason or conspiracy against the state; . . . that the property of all citi-
> zens be respected as inviolable; . . . that every poll tax be abolished. . . and

replaced by a tax on land and real property... and that the burden of this new tax be imposed equally on every class of citizen without distinction;... that the venality of civil offices be abolished;... that statutes limiting admission to officer status in the military to members of the nobility be rescinded;... that today's militia, which devastates the countryside, pulls workers away from their field labor, forces people into premature and ill-advised marriages [commoners could avoid being pressed into the militias by marrying], and subjects individuals to secret and arbitrary taxes, be abolished and replaced by a public, volunteer army. (*Archives parliamentaires de 1787 à 1860*, ed. Jérôme Mavidal and Èmile Laurent [Paris, 1862], ser. 1, vol. 3, pp. 250–254.)

But as the representatives gathered in Paris in June, the clerical and aristocratic estates decided to bar the Third Estate representatives from admission to the assembly—at which those representatives proclaimed themselves, together with the king, the sole legitimate government of France and began to write a new constitution. The Revolution, which had begun as a revolt of the nobles against the demands of the king and people for a land tax, had now become a popular movement to establish a constitutional monarchy that abolished aristocratic privilege.

The Oath of the Tennis Court, June 20, 1789   Representatives of the Third Estate gathered angrily on the largest available open space, a tennis court—for what came to be known as the Tennis Court Oath.

THE REVOLUTION TURNS RADICAL

To this point the Revolution had called merely for the reform of the state, not its destruction. By the end of 1789 the National Assembly, as the new government was called, had stormed the Bastille and freed the (surprisingly few) political prisoners held captive there, had abolished feudalism (although providing compensation for the nobles' losses), had issued a Declaration of the Rights of Man and Citizen, and had confiscated and sold all the ecclesiastical lands in the nation in order to pay off the royal debt. Nevertheless, the new government failed to win active national support. Across France most peasant farmers and laborers, presumably fearing an aristocratic backlash, did little more than seize the opportunity to destroy the local records that documented their particular obligations to their landlords, then quietly returned to their work while waiting for the political fracas in Paris to settle down. Rumors spread quickly of noble-backed gangs of thugs roaming the countryside seeking rebellion-sympathizing peasants to attack. A corps of six thousand Parisian women marched to Versailles and brought the royal family back into the city, both to prevent them from leaving the country and to enlist them in joining the new regime.

But it became clear throughout 1790 and 1791 that the Revolution in Paris was not winning the hearts and minds of the nation as a whole. And as it did, the leaders of the new government began to split into factions, each offering a more thoroughgoing platform of change in hopes of winning support. The two dominant parties were the Girondists and the Jacobins, the former favoring a reformed constitutional monarchy and the latter being dedicated to a more radical democracy—although it is difficult to identify specific political programs to any given faction, since policies, proposals, and personalities changed so rapidly among them.

In 1792, after three years of steadily decaying order, France was invaded by Austria and Prussia, who were determined to come to the aid not of Louis XVI but the ideal of absolutism. The military situation was dire, for although France's army was large, over two-thirds of its aristocratic officer corps had long since fled the country, leaving most of the military units leaderless. Even worse, most of those officers had joined the counter-Revolutionary forces. Sensing disaster, Louis and his family tried to flee the country but were caught at the border and brought back to Paris in chains. The Jacobins, by this time led by Maximilien Robespierre (1758–1794), a passionate ideologue who believed that anything standing in the way of the Revolution had to be eradicated, eventually seized control of the government through its leadership of the innocent-sounding Committee for Public Safety. But Robespierre and his committee believed fervently that the enemies of the Revolution would stop at nothing to undermine it, and so began to purge the new government's ranks of individuals and parties whose loyalty to the radical cause was suspect.

The Guillotine An 18th-century model of a guillotine. Intended as a humane means of execution, the guillotine inadvertently became the central symbol of the Revolution. Its first use was in 1792; the Reign of Terror ended with the beheading of Robespierre himself in mid-1794. Since estimates of the number of people guillotined during the Terror range from fifteen thousand to forty thousand, and since most executions took place in Paris itself, a dedicated spectator could have seen an average of twenty-five to sixty beheadings a day. And in fact great crowds of observers did show up regularly—so many that entrepreneurial vendors printed and sold programs of the daily schedule of beheadings.

The outbreak of pro-royalist rebellion in the far west of France convinced Robespierre that all the achievements of the Revolution to date were threatened. In a shockingly brutal wave of violence in the name of the supposed purification of society—known as the **Reign of Terror** (1792)—Robespierre's clique engineered the arrest of over three hundred thousand French men and women in only nine months, some forty thousand of whom were executed. Defending the harshness of his methods, Robespierre later wrote:

> If virtue is the wellspring of popular government in times of peace, then virtue combined with terror is the wellspring of such a government in time of revolution: virtue (without which all terror is fatal) *and* terror (without which all virtue is impotent). For terror is nothing more than swift, sure, and inflexible justice—indeed, it emanates from virtue and is not so much an independent principle as it is a natural consequence of the general idea of democracy when applied to our country's most urgent needs.... Subdue the enemies of liberty by terror [if you must]! You are right to do so, as founders of our Republic. Government, in a Revolution, is a despotism of liberty against tyranny. *(Report on the Principles of Public Morality, 1794)*

Machiavelli would have been proud of the sentiment, and perhaps envious of the superior style, had he lived to read Robespierre. But Robespierre was speaking in a context of catastrophic national emergency, since the Revolution was endangered by foreign invasion, aristocratic plots, and internal dissension. France's internal strife had to be quelled as quickly as possible in order to avoid annihilation.

Robespierre, who fell from power in 1794 and was himself guillotined, remains a divisive figure. Immediately after his death, his political enemies destroyed most of his papers and vilified him as a fanatical dictator—the portrait that long fixed his historical image. In the 19th century, however, groups representing the working-class French, then undergoing the horrors of the industrial revolution, revived his memory as a persecuted champion of the people. While his methods were harsh, they argued, his goals of eradicating the inequitable distribution of wealth in society and of ensuring the availability of education and work for all were admirable.[1]

The pace of revolution increased through the next two years. The government (renamed the National Convention) executed Louis XVI and criminalized the practice of Christianity, replacing it with the pallid cult of the Goddess of Reason. They adopted a new calendar that renamed all of the months of the year, forcibly introduced the metric system, confiscated the property of all "enemies of the Revolution," and instituted a national military draft. The draft was necessary since Britain, Holland, and Spain had joined Austria and Prussia in the invasion of the country. Spain wanted to defend absolutism; England, which had executed its own King Charles I in 1649 and lived to regret it, hoped mostly to keep France preoccupied with a land war so that it could not challenge England's primacy in the international sea-lanes. Holland's involvement was defensive, since France had launched a surprise attack on it in 1795, in order to provide a counterweight to England and to round up many of the French nobles who had fled to that country.

NAPOLEON AND THE WAR AGAINST ABSOLUTISM

As internal decay and external threat increased, and the Revolution's very existence seemed threatened, the Directory (yet another renaming and retooling of the central administration) summoned its most successful general to Paris to take control of the government, institute martial law, and restore order. His name was Napoleon Bonaparte (1769–1821).

Actually, his name was Napoleone di Buonaparte. Descended from a minor Italian baronial family, he was born and raised on the French-controlled island of Corsica. At the age of ten he moved to Autun in east-central France and enrolled in an elementary military academy, which he followed five years later with a course of study at the elite École militaire in Paris, where he trained to be an artillery officer; in 1785 he received his commission as a second lieutenant in the French army. When the Revolution broke out in 1789, he was back in Corsica and soon was involved in the civil struggle there between factions loyal to the monarchy, to the Jacobins, and to Corsican independence. He supported the Jacobin cause from the start and soon earned the rank of lieutenant colonel. By 1793 he

---

[1]   The British novelist Hilary Mantel indeed presents a sympathetic portrait of Robespierre in A *Place of Greater Safety* (2006).

was back on the Continent and leading campaigns against France's foreign invaders. His early successes on the field and his publication of a pro-Jacobin pamphlet brought him to the admiring attention of the Committee on Public Safety, which promoted him to brigadier general.

Robespierre's fall in 1794 resulted in Napoleon's brief fall from favor, but when he fought off a royalist challenge to the Directory the following year, his restoration was complete. Awarded the position of commander of the interior, Napoleon led the war against the Austrians, who were invading France via Italy. His successes led to another ambitious campaign into Egypt (where he had been sent by Directory leaders who, fearing Napoleon's growing prestige, wanted him out of Europe for a while), in an effort to weaken England's maritime commercial ties with India.[2]

His abilities as military commander made him a natural choice to take over the government once it reached its worst state of decay and strife; not that he was invited to do so. At some point during his Egyptian campaign he learned of the imminent collapse of the Directory and raced back to Paris with his troops in October 1799. A few weeks later, on November 10, 1799, he staged a coup d'état and became the dictator of France—although he had the sense to take the less ominous-sounding title of consul.[3] He initially shared power in a triumvirate that included the Abbé de Sieyès and Pierre-Roger Ducos, two holdovers from the Directory, although he dominated the government from the start. By 1802 all pretense of shared power was done away with, and Napoleon was the sole master of France.

The record of his accomplishments is lengthy and well known. After quelling France's internal conflicts and driving off her foreign invaders, Napoleon set himself to overhauling nearly every aspect of French civil life, problems he attacked with extraordinary energy and intelligence. His contemporaries, whether they admired him or hated him, marveled at his charisma and drive. "A man like me does not care if a million people die" in pursuit of a goal, he once declared. (At the time he said it, he meant it rhetorically; he later put the statement to the test on the battlefields, though.) He rewrote the national constitution and enshrined the notion of egalitarianism before the law and universal suffrage. He created the most fair and comprehensive taxation system France had ever had, abolished all feudal and local customs, and enacted a systematic law code for the entire country. This **Napoleonic Code** emphasized individuals' rights to property,

---

[2]   In legend Napoleon used the Sphinx as a practice target for artillery. Its nose and beard were in fact broken off in the 14th century on orders of a Muslim cleric—outraged that local farmers, to improve their harvest, had made ritual offerings to it.

[3]   According to the Revolutionary calendar, Napoleon become consul on the 18th of Brumaire—the title of a famous essay by Karl Marx.

standardizing the legal structures for contracts, leases, and establishing stock corporations. He also prohibited the creation of merchant guilds, industrial cartels, and trade unions. He then went on and constructed France's first system of national education, with primary and secondary schools (*lycées*) in every major town, established a teachers' training college in Paris, organized a network of military and vocational schools for those drawn to specific professions, and crowned the whole system with a national university.

Yet Napoleon could show pragmatism as well. He invited the exiled nobles willing to swear loyalty to the new constitution to return to France, a shrewd maneuver that brought vast amounts of stolen treasure back into the realm, along with the talent pool of many experienced military and civil officials. Another practical compromise was Napoleon's decision to restore the legal recognition and practice of Catholic and Protestant Christianity; although personally an Enlightened deist, he saw the value of religion as an instrument of social cohesion. While he guaranteed freedom of religious expression, he also arranged that all clergy received their pay directly from the central government, a move that kept Napoleon firmly in control of the churches.

All Men Are Created Equal   This allegorical drawing depicts reason and nature, represented by the two robed female figures on the left, celebrating the equality of whites and blacks in the new revolutionary order.   The black man holds the Rights of Man; on the picture's left demons of injustice flee to wreak havoc elsewhere.

Although he proclaimed himself a Republican, Napoleon did not permit all freedoms. He retained strict limits on freedom of speech and of the press, for example, which made it difficult for any individuals or parties to oppose his will or question his policies. (His defenders argue that the restrictions that Napoleon imposed were simply the standards of communications control to which he was accustomed from the army.) He also denied political rights to women: they were not allowed to vote, to enter contracts, or to hold bank accounts, and they remained the legal dependents of their fathers and husbands. Although he could be personally gallant toward the women in his private life (of whom there were many), he did not hesitate to state his opinion about the different positions of men and women in society. "A husband must possess absolute authority over his wife," he once declared, "and must have the right to say to her, 'Madam, you shall not go out of the house; you shall not go to the theater; you shall not pay a visit to such-and-such a person. And as for the children you bear—they are mine.'"

Napoleon relished his popular image as the savior of the Republic but he also believed in his unique personal authority. He had read much history in his school days and revered the Roman leader Octavian/Augustus, who had saved the Roman Republic by keeping its institutions and customs even while running them with an iron fist. His vision for France was along those lines. To the tips of his fingers and the end of his days, Napoleon believed in France's destiny to lead all of Europe and in his own destiny to lead France in the effort. But that meant addressing the problem of absolutism—for although it had been successfully stamped out in France, it still held sway in nearly every country in Europe, and each one of those regimes was determined to see France's Revolu-

Napoleon Enthroned   The oil portrait by Jean-Auguste Ingres (1780-1867) was first exhibited at the Paris Salon of 1806, where it had a chilly reception. Stiff and imposing, the figure of Napoleon holds the scepter of Charlemagne in his right hand. A stylized version of the German imperial eagle appears on the carpet at his feet. In the background over his left shoulder is a shield representing the states of Italy. Nothing about the painting is subtle – which helps explain its unpopularity.

tion fail. By 1804 he was ready to act. He arranged for an imperial coronation to be performed in Paris by the pope himself, and at the last moment he snatched the crown from the startled pontiff's hands and placed it on his own head.

There would be no question of his subordination to Rome. He was his own man, the ruler of his own state. But an emperor by definition needs an empire. And so he conquered Europe.

THE RUSH TO EMPIRE

As sheer narrative Napoleon's conquests make a long but straightforward tale, full of dramatic, impressive, frequently startling and moving episodes; but they are not conceptually difficult to grasp. In quick succession, between 1805 and 1812, he conquered the Netherlands, Bavaria, the Austrian Empire, northern Italy, the Rhineland Confederation, Saxony, Prussia, Poland, Spain, the Kingdom of Westphalia, and the Kingdom of Naples—nearly the whole of the Continent (see Map 16.1). A series of coalitions among various European powers against Napoleon had determined, more or less, the sequencing of these campaigns, but the general aim behind them was present in Napoleon's mind from the start. Megalomania and a desire for glory certainly played their part in this rush to empire. Napoleon's ego was as large as the continent he conquered, and many of the people of France shared his dream of domination. The French army was a truly national institution, being filled by conscription, and like the republic it fought for, it was organized as a meritocracy. Each victory on the battlefield therefore did more than score a military success; it validated the Revolution itself.

> The French army was a truly national institution, being filled by conscription, and like the republic it fought for, it was organized as a meritocracy. Each victory on the battlefield therefore did more than score a military success; it validated the Revolution itself.

The French in fact followed each victory with another revolution, toppling each opponent's government, abolishing its centuries-old feudal privileges, rewriting its constitution and civil laws, dismantling its mercantilist practices and dated tax codes, retooling its justice and educational systems, and establishing (often for the first time) freedoms of speech and worship. The justification for their work was simple: the nefarious and corrupt network of absolutist regimes in Europe, by the sacred ties established between them in 1648, would never allow the French Revolution to succeed, and therefore had to be destroyed. Since it had been established as a *system* for controlling Europe, absolutism anywhere on the Continent would always conspire to undermine republicanism anywhere else, even if only to discourage its growth within its own domestic borders.

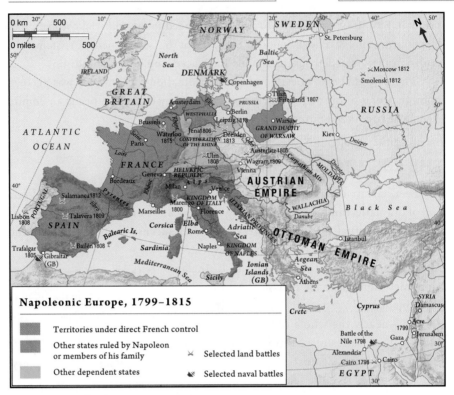

MAP 16.1   Napoleonic Europe, 1799–1815

The proof of this reality, to the French, lay in the unilateral invasions of their country as soon as the republic had been established. The conquest of Europe after 1805 therefore was not aggressive imperialism but defensive (though preemptive) anti-Absolutism.

Of course, it was easy to concoct such an excuse. Did the French truly believe it? Did Napoleon himself? Or was this mere after-the-fact rationalizing? This is the crucial issue for those who, from Napoleon's time to our own, try to form a judgment about the emperor. Admirers of Napoleon saw (and see) him as the bold man of action. To them, he brought down a near-universal tyranny; in sweeping away its dead traditions, he made possible the creation of a modern Europe based on individual rights and the championing of merit over inherited privilege. His detractors saw (and see) a power-mad glory hound who simply replaced one form of tyranny with another. At most they did (and do) grant him his military genius and his better-than-average gift for self-justification.

Across Europe, in country after country, Napoleon did dismantle the old order and attempted to install the new—although he was also careful to install a loyal member of his own family as the new king. We see a glimpse of his aims, for example, in a letter he sent in 1807 to his brother Jerome, whom he had installed as the king of Westphalia—the very site of the formal birth of absolutism:

> My chief concern is for the well-being of your [new] subjects, not only as it affects your standing and my own, but also because of the impact it has on the whole condition of Europe. Do not listen to anyone who says that your subjects, being so long accustomed to servitude, will fail to feel gratitude for the freedoms you bring to them—for the common people of Westphalia are more aware than such individuals would have you believe, and your rule will never have a secure basis without the people's complete trust and affection. Quite simply, what the German people desire and pressingly demand is that men without rank but of genuine ability will have an equal claim upon your favor and advancement, and that every trace of serfdom and feudal privilege... be done away with. Let the blessings of the Napoleonic Code and of public trials that use juries be the centerpiece of your administration. . . . I want all your subjects to enjoy liberty, equality, and prosperity alike and to such a degree as no German people has yet known. . . . Everywhere in Europe—in Germany, France, Italy, Spain—people are longing for equality and liberal government. . . . So govern according to your new constitution. Even if Reason and the Enlightened ideas of our age did not suffice to justify this call, it still would be a smart policy for anyone in your position—for you will find that the genuine support of the people is a source of strength to you that none of the absolutist monarchs neighboring you will ever have.

If genuinely felt, the sentiments Napoleon expresses here suggest an idealism behind his conquests that might mitigate the harsher conclusions made about his character. Even so, it is difficult to overlook the fact that his conquests came at the high cost of approximately three million battlefield deaths.

THE CONTINENTAL SYSTEM

He replaced mercantilism everywhere with a new set of economic policies that he termed the **Continental System**. This system had two aims. First, it sought to create an integrated Continental economy by establishing permeable borders for the transfer of goods, services, and labor across Europe; by encouraging freedom of movement and assuring individual rights to property, the plan hoped to awaken a dormant entrepreneurial spirit. People no longer held in place by outdated customs would be free to seek opportunities wherever they might occur and thus create the truly meritocratic society Napoleon claimed to desire. But the second aim of the Continental System was both its real purpose and the cause of its own failure: to bring about the collapse of Britain by imposing a strict trade embargo on it. Soon after proclaiming himself emperor, Napoleon had made several attempts at a naval attack on Britain, but these attempts had all ended in failure—most notably at the Battle of Trafalgar (1805). The Continental System essentially closed all European ports to British shipping and redirected all Continental trade to markets within the continent itself. The overseas colonies of all Continental powers were likewise sealed off from British commercial contact. The hope was that Britain, unable to acquire sufficient raw materials for its industries and denied access to its most significant markets, would weaken to the point of collapse, at which point Napoleon's administration could sweep into London and take over.

The system succeeded at neither goal. The embargo against Britain actually helped to turn the island into an economic superpower, because it effectively removed all competition from England's aggressive expansion into global markets. Without any rivals on the scene, the British were able to extend their domination across southern and eastern Asia. France could hardly encourage Europeans

Unfettered Trade   Cartoon depicting a happy British merchant conducting trade with Nanjing and Beijing without competitors, as a result of the Continental System imposed on Europe by Bonaparte.

to trade solely with other Europeans while their armies were tearing apart the countryside. Moreover, he needed capital to keep funding the war effort; this need for cash is what led to the sale of the vast French-held territories in the central part of what became the United States—the Louisiana Purchase (1803). England's dominance at sea, well established in the Atlantic Ocean by 1805, became world-wide with Napoleon's ultimate fall in 1815. England proved able, in fact, to block most Continental shipping even along the European coastline, which forced the system's trade to proceed strictly over land, which was much more costly. Neither did the system work to generate an economically united Europe. The vast and complicated work of de-absolutizing the Continent—reallocating property, writing constitutions, instituting new civil law codes—while pressing the military campaigns ever further to the east, made it impossible to direct sufficient funds toward creating the new manufactures, supply lines, markets, currency exchanges, and tariff structures needed to make the system succeed.

The system did result in one significant change, however. By dismantling feudal ties and encouraging the freer movement of labor across Europe, Napoleon's policies accelerated the most important demographic shift of the era, namely the rise of **urbanism**. In 1800 only 2 percent of the Continental population lived in a city; by Napoleon's downfall in 1815 this percentage had doubled. (Some countries, such as Italy, had considerably higher degrees of urbanization. Others, such as Poland, were almost entirely agrarian.) This leap was made up not only of rural migration into cities but of peoples migrating from one country into another. Polish former peasants appeared in German cities; Hungarian farm laborers took up residence in Austria and Italy; Spanish workers appeared in France. Many of these individuals, barred by language or ethnic prejudice from obtaining jobs in skilled trades, ended up as domestic laborers—cooks, maids, footmen, servants, gardeners. Those lucky enough to belong to the middle class thus became able for the first time to employ large corps of domestic staff, as the swelling of urban population drove down the cost of such labor. By 1810 in Paris, for example, roughly one-fifth of the entire urban population worked in domestic service, and most of these were in service to middle-class, bourgeois families rather than upper-class high society.

Immigration like this, on this scale, produced profound social changes. For the bourgeoisie, the standard of daily living rose remarkably. Freed from doing their own cooking, cleaning, house tending, and child rearing, they were able to indulge themselves in a more comfortable existence of leisure. For the immigrants, their own family relations tended to break off, since it was predominantly individuals, not entire families, who moved into the towns to find employment. The cities thus swelled with isolated job seekers rather than cohesive family units. Young women unable to find work in domestic service or in other trades

Urban Workers   "Street scenes" is the title of this illustration from an early 19th century German periodical published in Stuttgart, a city whose population more than tripled over the course of the century. Shown here, clockwise from upper left, are a milkmaid, fishmonger, coachman, fruit seller, organ grinder, and figurine-seller.

were therefore reduced to prostitution as a means of survival. By 1815 Paris alone had over thirty thousand active prostitutes, and London had twice as many. The social ills that frequently attend prostitution—violence, alcohol or drug addiction, disease, abandoned children—soon followed. Young men unable to find work frequently drifted into crime too, and the dramatic rise in urban crime led to the formation of modern police forces. Awareness of the rising troubles in the cities also inspired the governments of the early 19th century to begin compiling official statistics on population growth, degrees and patterns of poverty, the need for housing and urban infrastructure, the lack of education, and access to clean water and sewers.

Napoleon's wars, in the end, altered Europe's history every bit as much as the Revolution altered France's. The positive achievements or gains of the era may or may not be directly credited to the Revolution, but the absolute and irreversible clearing away of the Old Regime by Napoleon made those achievements possible. (And that holds whether or not it was truly his personal goal, and not merely an excuse for a love of dictatorship.) Europe after 1815 was an altogether different place from what it had been in 1789.

> Napoleon's wars, in the end, altered Europe's history every bit as much as the Revolution altered France's. The positive achievements or gains of the era may or may not be directly credited to the Revolution, but the absolute and irreversible clearing-away of the Old Regime by Napoleon made those achievements possible.

HOW TO JUDGE A REVOLUTION

Within weeks of the Storming of the Bastille in 1789, the British statesman Edmund Burke (1729–1797) began writing *Reflections on the Revolution in France*. Published in 1790, the book takes the form of a letter written to a friend and sets out Burke's reasons for believing that the Revolution would end in abject failure and misery. He may have predicted correctly, but had he truly known how to judge a Revolution? For the pamphleteer Thomas Paine (1737–1809), justice, not stability, is the true index of political legitimacy.

Mankind, Burke argues, is inherently conservative—meaning that our natural instinct is to hold securely what we value and to desire to pass those things on to our heirs. These values include but are not limited to property and wealth: morals, religious beliefs, emotional connections, and notions of identity also constitute the human legacy and are worth keeping. But an impulse to conserve does not preclude change, he asserts. A stable society will always allow a degree of freedom and experimentation, and even encourage them, and will leave a path open for individuals to achieve on their own merits. Burke insists, however, that the fairest and strongest society will be one that evolves from, rather than breaks with, its past. "A spirit of innovation is generally the result of a selfish temper and confined views. People will not look forward to posterity, who never look backward to their ancestors."

Even more important, Burke argues that inequality among people is not intrinsically evil. Indeed, it cannot be so, since it is natural. Some people are simply smarter than others; some run faster; some are more skilled with their hands; some are given to contemplation rather than action. He is not speaking of any individual's metaphysical worthiness, only of their unique, specific characteristics. To insist that everyone is equal is to lie in order to appear kindhearted. Social and economic distinction, therefore, are natural. A well-regulated society will not allow social inequality to be oppressive, he contends, and yet any society that does away with social inequality is itself oppressive:

> Even more important, Burke argues that inequality among people is not intrinsically evil. Indeed, it cannot be so, since it is natural.

> Believe me, Sir, those who attempt to level, never equalize. In all societies, consisting of various levels of citizens, some description must be uppermost. The levelers, therefore, only change and pervert the natural order of things. . . . The Chancellor of France, at the opening of the Estates, said, in a tone of oratorical flourish, that all occupations were honorable. If he meant by that only that no honest employment was disgraceful, he would not have gone beyond the truth. But in asserting that anything is honorable, we imply some distinction in its favor. . . . Do not imagine that I wish to confine power, authority, and distinction to blood and names and titles. No, Sir. There is no qualification for government but virtue and wisdom, actual or presumptive. Wherever they are found, they have, in whatever state, condition, professions or trade, the passport of Heaven to human place and honor. . . . Everything ought to be open, but not indifferently, to every man.

Burke suggests that we need to think in terms of degrees of freedom and model our government after the social structure that is natural to any given community. Gradual but constant evolution is the best guarantor of stability—and Burke shares (although he would have denied it) Hobbes's notion that government's primary function is to provide stability, not justice. He does not oppose justice as a principle, but he sees it as the consequence of a stable society rather than as a vague ideal to be pursued at any cost. In pursuing such heady though foggy-minded ideals as liberty, equality, and fraternity, Burke belives, the Revolution was doomed at its birth. Moreover, he concludes his *Reflections* with a prediction:

> When the leaders choose to make themselves bidders at an auction of popularity, their talents, in the construction of the state, will be of no service. They will become flatterers instead of legislators—the instruments, not the guides, of the people. If any of them should happen to propose a scheme of liberty, soberly limited and defined with proper qualifications, he will be immediately outbid by his competitors who will produce something more splendidly popular. Suspicions will be raised of his fidelity to the cause. Moderation will be stigmatized as the virtue of cowards, and compromise as the prudence of traitors, until, in hopes of preserving the credit which may enable him to temper and moderate, on some occasions, the popular leader is obliged to become active in propagating doctrines and establishing powers that will afterward defeat any sober purpose at which he ultimately might have aimed.

A revolution, in other words, *any* revolution, will always fail because those who lead it are united only in their opposition to what they have overthrown. Once the work of creating a new government begins, unity will end. Former partners in revolution will become rivals in politics. To win out over each other, the rivals will keep offering the public increasingly generous, popular, and radical promises. Soon, angry accusations of being an "enemy of the revolution" will fly through the air, arrests and executions for treason will multiply, and riots will ensue. The revolution will spin out of control until finally someone comes along who, in order to save the gains made by the revolution, restores order by force. That means "propagating doctrines and establishing powers" that will undermine the entire enterprise by creating a new version of the very order that the revolution overthrew. In other words, the revolution spins from Louis XVI to the Estates General, to the Girondists, to the Jacobins, to Robespierre and the Terror, to civil war, to Napoleon—from autocracy to autocracy. Burke published his book in 1790 before any of this happened, and he died in

1797 before seeing the end of the process, but he seems to have predicted each stage perfectly.

Others saw the Revolution differently. In England, Thomas Paine wrote *The Rights of Man* (published in two parts, 1791–1792), in which he rebutted Burke's analysis. Paine asserted that human rights are innate, granted by Nature rather than bestowed by government; therefore any state that restricts or subverts the rights of its citizens may be opposed and brought down.[4] Government can retain its legitimacy only by supporting the intrinsic rights of its citizens. It was in this spirit that Paine grew distrustful of Napoleon and ultimately abandoned France, calling the emperor "the completest charlatan that ever lived."

Paine had immigrated to America in 1774 as an enthusiast for the colonies' push for independence and stayed there until 1787, when he returned to London. In 1792 Paine went to Paris to witness the Revolution firsthand and was elected to serve in the National Assembly even though he could speak no French. Robespierre

France as a Storm-Tossed Ship   This 1796 British map fancifully depicts Revolutionary France as a ship in distress. Note the broken prow-mast and the cut-away anchor in the Bay of Biscay; two aft-sails have become unmoored; and a storm brews ahead even while the ship founders on rocks at the bottom.

---

4   *The Rights of Man* was so popular and caused such scandal in London that Paine was tried in absentia for sedition against the crown.

hated him and arranged for his arrest in 1793. Released the following year, Paine remained in France until he returned to America in 1802.

Another initial supporter of the Revolution was Mary Wollstonecraft (1759–1797), a reformer for women's rights, who responded to Burke with two passionate tracts. *A Vindication of the Rights of Man* (1791) and *A Vindication of the Rights of Woman* (1792) dismissed Burke's notion of liberty as a smokescreen to protect the interests of the propertied classes, when it is the rights of the lower orders that must be respected. She argued that traditional society has brutalized women and degraded them to a subhuman level, leaving the only rational choice for reform to be the destruction of all existing social mores and the political regimes that support them. Wollstonecraft too rushed to Paris to witness the Revolution, in 1793. Within two years, though, she grew disillusioned with the violent turn of events, and, after a disastrous romantic liaison added personal misery to her political disappointment, she returned to England.

Reactions to the Revolution across the Continent likewise ranged widely. The Absolutist regimes responded by sending their armies into France, but among the general population of Germans, Italians, Dutch, Piedmontese, Spaniards, and even Russians there were many who cheered the French on. Ludwig van Beethoven famously admired Napoleon and intended to dedicate his Third Symphony to him, until the imperial coronation in 1804 led him to tear the dedicatory epistle to shreds. The poet Johann Wolfgang von Goethe (1749–1832) was too conservative and elitist to support revolutionary egalitarianism; in fact, he served as an advisor to German forces fighting French troops in 1792 and 1793. Yet when he met Napoleon in 1806, he declared *"Voilà, un homme!"* ("Behold, a Man!") and accepted with pleasure the emperor's award

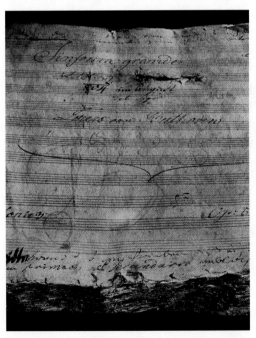

Beethoven's Third Symphony   First page of the manuscript of Ludwig von Beethoven's Third Symphony. According to legend, Beethoven had been an early admirer of Bonaparte and had intended to dedicate the symphony to him, but was enraged when Napoleon crowned himself emperor. He reportedly crossed out Napoleon's name so angrily that he tore a hole in the manuscript, as shown.

of the Cross of the French Legion of Honor, which he continued to wear for the rest of his life. While Napoleon clearly fascinated his non-French contemporaries, and while many of them welcomed liberation from the absolutist regimes he toppled, most of them chafed against rule by Napoleon's Revolutionary agents. The French conquests, in fact, helped trigger a rise in nationalistic fervor across Europe. Peoples humiliated by Napoleon's quick victories reacted by expressing a desire to unify and establish ethnically and culturally based states to forge their own destinies, rather than follow the path laid out for them by Napoleon.

DOWNFALL

Napoleon's brilliance as a charismatic leader, military commander, administrator, and legal and social reformer were extraordinary, but so were his deficiencies. He had little understanding of naval warfare and no understanding at all of economics. He trusted his own judgment over that of his advisers. He underestimated the extent to which ethnically based national identity mattered to the peoples of Europe. Worst of all, he had no interest in the things he did not understand, and so gave them insufficient attention. All of these weaknesses played a role in his ultimate military defeat and fall from power.

The Continental System never worked. Europe's coastline, all 3,100 miles (5,000 kilometers) of it, proved impossible to police, and merchant-smugglers were resourceful when it came to avoiding the harbor police. Moreover, by ceding control of the sea-lanes to the British, the Continental System simply allowed the British to secure international markets in the Americas and Asia that proved so lucrative as to turn Britain into an economic superpower. Britain also used its capital to invest in domestic infrastructure, such as networks of roads and canals, to facilitate further development. The Continent, subsumed as it was in war and reconstruction, could not match such investment. Until 1810 British goods slipped through the trade barriers and were readily available across Europe. Even the wasteful War of 1812 between Britain and America—fought over the issue of British searches of American vessels to make sure they were not trading with France—did not weaken the British position with respect to the Continent.

Napoleon also miscalculated when he overthrew the Spanish king Ferdinand VII in 1808 and replaced him with his own older brother, Joseph Bonaparte. The dismantling of absolutism in Spain failed when Napoleon ordered the suppression of roughly two-thirds of the monasteries and convents in the realm and confiscated their property. The displaced Spanish nobility allied with the disenfranchised clergy to lead resistance against the invaders. Unable to defeat the Bonapartist forces in open battle, the Spanish fighters waged instead a guerrilla war that kept a large number of French troops (over three hundred thousand of them) mired in an unwinnable conflict when they were sorely needed elsewhere in Europe. Small wonder that Napoleon complained of his "Spanish ulcer."

Meanwhile, family troubles added to his indigestion. Although an energetic womanizer, Napoleon dearly loved his wife Josephine; but like England's Henry VIII in the 16th century, Napoleon agonized over his wife's supposed failure to give him a son. Convinced that he needed an heir to continue his life's work, he reluctantly arranged for a Parisian bishop to annul his marriage to Josephine in 1810, so he could remarry. Pope Pius VII (r. 1800–1823) refused to perform the annulment, which is why Napoleon turned instead to a local bishop (who, like all the French clergy, was on Napoleon's payroll). He set his sights initially on the younger sister of Tsar Aleksandr I of Russia (r. 1801–1825), whose two daughters had recently died, leaving the succession to the throne in doubt; rather than invade Russia—then the last substantial absolutist state in Europe—Napoleon hoped simply to acquire it as a dowry. Aleksandr, however, refused the match even though he was, at the time, Napoleon's ally in a grand (and delusional) plan: they hoped to drive the Ottoman Turks from Europe and carry the conquests of a unified Catholic and Orthodox Christendom as far as India.[5]

Aleksandr was a complicated character himself—emotional, idealistic, contradictory, and given to dramatic shifts of mood. His relations with Napoleon went from initial revulsion to implacable opposition of "the oppressor of Europe and the disturber of the world's peace." Yet he was dazzled by Napoleon's brilliance when they met, and he became unswervingly loyal in return for his help in bringing Finland and Poland under tsarist rule. The pact against the Turks soon followed. Aleksandr even insisted on his love for Napoleon after French forces had invaded Russia in 1812; only the French sacking of Moscow turned that love back to hatred.

Napoleon married instead Marie-Louise, the daughter of the Austrian emperor Franz II (r. 1804–1835), who soon gave him the son he so desperately wanted. The birth of this son (also named Napoleon) signified an important change in people's perceptions of the emperor—even among the French. The destroyer of inherited privilege had himself produced an heir to whom he intended to pass on the government of all of Europe. Anti-Napoleon pamphlets began to circulate, and some government advisors began to urge the emperor to restrain his ambition. One of those advisors, his former foreign minister Charles-Maurice de Talleyrand, even started to negotiate secretly with Franz II over how France might be governed if Napoleon should fall.

---

5   Leo Tolstoy provides extraordinarily sensitive portrayals of Napoleon and Aleksandr in *War and Peace*.

In June 1812 Napoleon invaded Russia with an army of roughly six hundred thousand men—perhaps the largest single force ever mustered in European history to that time. Russia responded by avoiding direct clashes while maintaining a rearguard action, drawing the French further and further into the enormous landmass. In September Napoleon entered Moscow, after pounding through Russia's last defensive stand at the battle of Borodino. He found the capital virtually deserted and two-thirds of it aflame. Hopelessly exposed and left unsupplied, the French marched back to Paris, hoping to make it back before the brutal Russian winter set in. Aleksandr's forces harassed the French enough to slow them down miserably, and the onset of winter did the rest of the damage.[6]

Napoleon was able to hold on to power for two more years, but his position in Europe, and even in France, was never the same. Overthrown by the Republic and imprisoned initially on the Mediterranean island of Elba, he escaped but was defeated by the British at the battle of Waterloo in 1815. He was then imprisoned on the island of Saint Helena in the middle of the South Atlantic, more than a thousand miles from any mainland. He died, fittingly, of a cancerous ulcer on May 5, 1821. (Rumors of Napoleon's murder by arsenic poisoning have been thoroughly disproven.)

Napoleon's legacy continues to divide people. No one doubts his exceptional talents and charismatic energy, but few people accept uncritically his own judgment of himself—in the memoirs he dictated during his seven years on Saint Helena:

> [My] imperial government was a kind of Republic... [because I was] summoned to take control of the government by the voice of the nation itself.... There has never been, in fact, a king who was more truly a "people's sovereign" than I was.... If I were to return [to power] I would establish my empire once again upon the ideals of the Jacobins, for Jacobinism is a volcano that threatens all orders of privileged-based society. I could reproduce it easily even in Prussia... and with the power of Prussia at my disposal I could use [Jacobinism] as a club to smash Austria and Russia.

As for his miserable end:

> My body is in the hands of wicked men but my soul is free. I am prouder here on Saint Helena than if I were sitting again on my throne, appointing kings and handing out crowns.... If I had succeeded [by

---

6   Only forty thousand of the original six hundred thousand made it back from Russia to France by December; most of the dead fell victim to starvation, exposure, and exhaustion.

Charting a Disaster   A striking image (called a cartogram), created by Charles Joseph Mainard in 1869. It grafts a chart onto a map, showing the depletion of Napoleon's army as it marched from Poland to Moscow and back. The constantly narrowing line represents the decline in French forces heading east (brown) and then returning west (black). The line below the main figure tracks the temperature of the brutal Russian winter. Edward Tufte (1942-), a pioneer in the field of data visualization, describes Mainard's cartogram as the "best statistical graph ever drawn."

adding a reformed Russia to my empire] I would have been remembered as the greatest man ever to have lived.... [But my] martyrdom will strip away my reputation as a tyrant.... In time [I will acquire] a crown of thorns.

He made permanent some of the most important achievements of the Revolution—the equality of all people (or men, at least) before the law; the rights of personal

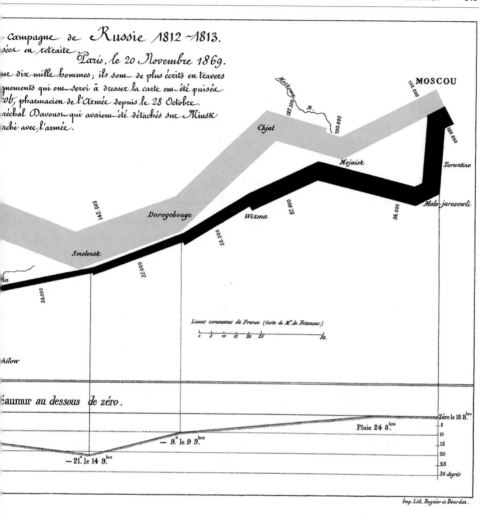

Campagne de *Russie* 1812 ~1813.

...sée en retraite

Paris, le 20 Novembre 1869.

...ur dix mille hommes; ils sont de plus écrits en travers

...gnements qui ont servi à dresser la carte ont été puisés

...ob, pharmacien de l'Armée depuis le 28 Octobre.

...réchal Davoust qui avaient été détachés sur Minsk

...rché avec l'armée.

MOSCOU

Kowno

Chjat

Mojaisk

Tarantino

Dorogobouge   Wixma   Malo-jarosewli

Smolensk

...ra

...hilow

Lieues communes de France (Carte de M.r de Fezensac)

...aumur au dessous de zéro.

Zéro le 18 8.bre

Pluie 24 8.bre

— 9.° le 9 9.bre

— 21.° le 14 9.bre

Imp. Lith. Regnier et Dourdet.

freedom of thought, belief, and expression; the individual right to property; the abolition of serfdom. He created Europe's first national system of public education. He established a fair and rational system of taxation. And then he brought those reforms to the nations he conquered. But in the process he created an imperial tyranny. His wars cost millions of lives. Among the French alone, perhaps 20 percent of all deaths that occurred between 1799 and 1815 resulted from his military actions.

In the end, he showed little remorse. He believed above all in France's destiny to lead Europe and in his own destiny to lead France. To have achieved anything less would have been tragic, and to have failed to answer the cause of glory would have been worse than death. "Death, after all, is nothing," he declared; "but to spend one's life defeated and without glory is to die anew every day."

LEAVING THE EAST BEHIND

The Ottoman Empire underwent profound decentralization during the 17th century. It also confronted a new threat from Romanov Russia, which expanded aggressively southward to the Black and Caspian Seas. By 1774 Russia's Catherine the Great (r. 1762–1796) had extended her control to a narrow strip along the northern rim of the Black Sea, where she founded the port city of Odessa. Only nine years later she annexed the whole of the Crimean peninsula and even briefly held a portion of Romania (see Map 16.2). For the Ottomans, having already lost much of eastern Europe and the Balkans area to the Austrian Habsburgs, these setbacks seriously undermined the strength of their empire and triggered a number of internal reforms—not all of them welcome. For the moment, the most pressing need was to reform the military.

The Janissaries had dominated the Turkish army since the 13th century but had long since been surpassed in organization, training, and overall might by the Western national armies. The Janissaries, in fact, had become an elitist and conservative force in the empire, interested primarily in securing their privileges and maintaining the status quo. The ruler Selim III [r. 1789–1807] brought in military

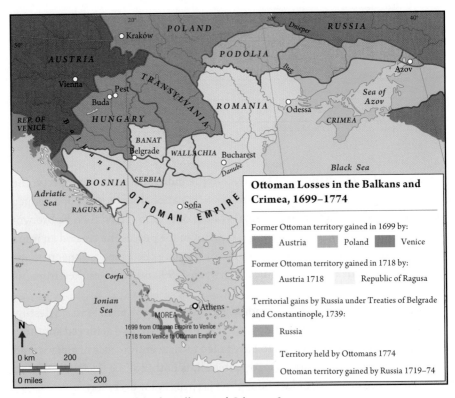

MAP 16.2 **Ottoman Losses in the Balkans and Crimea, 1699–1774**

advisers from the French Republic, who helped him to abolish the semifeudal structure of the army, established foundries for the building of modern artillery weapons, retrained the infantry, and provided new instruction in naval warfare. Selim also established a separate printing press solely for the publication of technical manuals, engineering texts, and up-to-date geographical atlases. Angered by these new developments, the Janissaries rose in revolt in 1807, assassinated Selim, and installed a cousin, Mustafa IV [T] (r. 1807–1808), who ruled briefly until he was murdered by his own brother, Mahmud II [T] (r. 1808–1839).

Mahmud tried to continue the reforms begun by Selim III, but with mixed success. Aspects of public finance were modernized, along with provincial legal practices. For example, local governors had long enjoyed their administration of provincial Courts of Confiscation. These courts gave local officials the right to personally confiscate the property of convicted criminals—and the practice triggered the amount of abuse one might expect from such an arrangement. Mahmud closed these courts entirely. He tried to develop a modern navy as well. The Turks had become maritime nonentities ever since losing the battle of Lepanto in 1571, and since then the empire had seen its control of the shipping routes in the Persian Gulf and the Indian Ocean lost to the British.

The French Revolution had inspired these attempts at reform, and the Turkish opening to Western ideas and technologies contributed to a fashionable vogue for Turkish culture in the West—as in the Turkish setting of Mozart's opera *Die Entführung aus dem Serail* (*The Abduction from the Seraglio*, 1782). The Revolution also invited elements of Western culture to take new root in the Islamic world. Ottoman mosques began to incorporate baroque styles of decoration; summer palaces adopted rococo designs. Perhaps most striking, Turkish wall paintings began to copy the European fashion for depicting dramatic battle scenes— complete with dashing generals astride rearing warhorses, crowds of infantry dead on the field, air thick with artillery smoke. The paintings did not merely introduce representational figures, to the exclusion of more traditional geometric and Arabesque patterns; they also vividly depicted human triumphs, sufferings, joys, pleasures, and despairs. Developments in French poetry, French theater, and French dress were eagerly reported by Turkish writers. Even the 18th-century craze for breeding tulips and creating elaborate gardens to house them caught on with the Ottomans.

Napoleon's campaigns through Egypt and Syria brought the cultural romance to a quick end, and after most of the Habsburg state had fallen to his forces, the Ottomans began to fear they were next. They were saved by the on-again, off-again alliance between Napoleon and Aleksandr of Russia, which ultimately drew French attentions away. But the lesson had been learned, and the push to modernize dominated the rest of the 19th century. The government gave a name

to the movement: **Tanzimat** ("reorganization"). Its central planks would be economic development and the integration of the empire's non-Muslims and non-Turks into civil society, by granting them civil liberties and promoting a new type of egalitarianism in Islamic society. These efforts, however, faced determined resistance by Arab groups interested instead in establishing their own ethnically based nationalism.

In its own way, the history of the Ottoman world curiously paralleled that of the Europeans in the 18th century: attempts to dismantle outdated systems of privilege were followed by reform efforts based on notions of equality and the increased social and economic interaction of ethnic groups. And these in turn were resisted by nationalistic forces determined to develop on their own. Napoleon's downfall in 1815 brought a reprieve; but dramatic action would be needed.

The Tulip Period This late 18th century Turkish manuscript painting shows a crowd, mostly female, relaxing in a park. It appears in a work called "The Book of Women" and represents—although it does not come from—the so-called Tulip Period in Turkish history (1718-1730), when Ottoman society consciously oriented itself in favor of Enlightened Europe. Notable here are the social mixing of men and women, the Western-style building in the background, the absence of veils (and the visibility of the women's hair), the woman in the foreground smoking a pipe, and the beardless man accompanying her.

WHO, WHAT, WHERE

Continental System
Estates General
Napoleonic Code
parlements

Reign of Terror
Tanzimat
Third Estate
Urbanism

SUGGESTED READINGS

Primary Sources
Bonaparte, Napoleon. *Memoirs.*
Burke, Edmund. *Reflections on the Revolution in France.*

De Las Cases, Emmanuel-Auguste. *The Life, Exile, and Conversations of the Emperor Napoleon.*

Robespierre, Maximilien. *Virtue and Terror.*

Sieyès, Abbé de. *What Is the Third Estate?*

Walter, Jakob. *The Diary of a Napoleonic Foot Soldier.*

Anthologies

Blaufarb, Rafe. *Napoleon: Symbol for an Age; A Brief History with Documents* (2007).

Dwyer, Philip, and Peter McPhee, eds. *The French Revolution and Napoleon: A Sourcebook* (2002).

Larsen, Anne R., and Colette H. Winn, eds. *Writings by Pre-Revolutionary French Women* (2000).

Studies

Bell, David A. *The First Total War: Napoleon's Europe and the Birth of Warfare as We Know It* (2008).

Birn, Raymond. *Royal Censorship of Books in Eighteenth-Century France* (2012).

Brown, Howard G. *Ending the French Revolution: Violence, Justice, and Repression from the Terror to Napoleon* (2007).

Censer, Jack, and Lynn Hunt. *Liberty, Equality, Fraternity: Exploring the French Revolution* (2001).

Cole, Juan. *Napoleon Napoleon's Egypt: Invading the Middle East* (2007).

Doyle, William. *The Oxford History of the French Revolution* (2002).

Dwyer, Philip G., ed. *Napoleon and Europe* (2003).

———. *Napoleon: The Path to Power* (2008).

Edelstein, Dan. *The Terror of Natural Right: Republicanism, the Cult of Nature, and the French Revolution* (2010).

Englund, Steven. *Napoleon: A Political Life* (2004).

Faroqhi, Suraiya. *The Ottoman Empire and the World around It* (2006).

———. *Subjects of the Sultan: Culture and Daily Life in the Ottoman Empire* (2005).

Hanson, Paul. *Contesting the French Revolution* (2009).

Hathaway, Jane. *The Arab Lands under Ottoman Rule, 1516–1800* (2008).

Israel, Jonathan. *A Revolution of the Mind: Radical Enlightenment and the Intellectual Origins of Modern Democracy* (2009).

Kates, Gary. *The French Revolution: Recent Debates and New Controversies* (2005).

Lawday, David. *The Giant of the French Revolution: Danton; A Life* (2011).

Masters, Bruce. *Christians and Jews in the Ottoman Arab World: The Roots of Sectarianism.* (2004).

———. *The Origins of Western Economic Dominance in the Middle East: Mercantilism and the Islamic Economy in Aleppo, 1600–1750* (2008).

McPhee, Peter. *The French Revolution, 1789–1799* (2002).

———. *Living the French Revolution: 1789–99* (2009).

———. *Robespierre: A Revolutionary Life* (2012).

Mousset, Sophie. *Women's Rights and the French Revolution: A Biography of Olympe de Gouge* (2007).

Murphey, Rhoads. *Ottoman Warfare, 1500–1700* (1999).

Scurr, Ruth. *Fatal Purity: Robespierre and the French Revolution* (2007).

Simonetta, Marcello, and Noga Arikha. *Napoleon and the Rebel: A Story of Brotherhood, Passion, and Power* (2011).

Tackett, Timothy. *When the King Took Flight* (2004).

Woloch, Isser. *Napoleon and His Collaborators: The Making of a Dictatorship* (2001).

For additional resources, including maps, primary sources, visuals, web links, and quizzes, please go to **www.oup.com/us/backman.**

CHAPTER 17

Industrialization and Its Discontents

1750–1850

M an has been a tool user since the Neolithic Age. From the time of the first stone implements, the brute labor needed for subsistence was performed by men and women, and sometimes children, holding tools in their hands. The Bronze and Iron Ages were in fact defined by tools.

The next major leap came with harnessing animals to larger tools like plows and wagons. By the Middle Ages both the water-wheel and windmill captured the energy of the natural world, putting it to use in everything from milling grain to producing paper. The Renaissance created tools of increasing sophistication—telescopes and microscopes come quickly to mind—but as late as 1750 most goods were overwhelmingly the result of tools held in human hands. This was especially true of food and textiles—the two commodities that humans consume the most over their life spans. Through the centuries, labor had become more efficient, and the West had learned new ways to use natural resources. But human labor, with all its limitations, still defined economic activity. Well into the 18th century, it required the labor of eight people to feed and clothe ten people. That is an improvement on the roughly 9.5:10 ratio of Sumerian times, but still backbreaking physical labor, twelve hours a day.

The industrial revolution changed that forever. It also led to crushing conditions and the cultural movement known as Romanticism.

INDUSTRIALIZATION IN THE GREATER WEST, ca. 1850

SWEDEN
BELGIUM
UNITED KINGDOM
GERMANY
FRANCE
SWITZERLAND

Level of industrial output per capita (100=UK in 1900)
0–15
16–30
60–75

Increase in level of industrial output per capita 1830–1850
○ 50–100%
● over 100%

◀ **Interior of a Typical Coal Miner's Home, 1880s** Coal fueled the Industrial Revolution, and mining it was one of the most brutal and dangerous jobs of the 19th century. This photo depicts a typical one-room tenement of a coal miner's family, ca. 1889.

- England's Head Start
- Innovation and Infrastructure
- Trying to Catch Up to England
- Trying to Catch Up to Europe
- "The Sick Man of Europe"
- Life in the Industrial Age
- Riots and Reform
- Women and Children Last
- The Romantic Generation

CHAPTER OUTLINE

ENGLAND'S HEAD START

Starting in Britain in the second half of the 18th century, power-driven machines altered Western life profoundly, permanently, and absolutely. Industrialization created new economies, new cities, and new social relations, and it brought all of these changes on with startling speed. And the people of the time were quick to recognize the implications of mechanization.

The early English Romantic poets William Blake (1757–1827) and William Wordsworth (1770–1850) described the effects on industry on the human soul and the natural world as dire and ruinous. In a brief poem that serves as a prologue to his long epic *Milton*, Blake refers to an ancient legend that Jesus, in his youth, had visited England. Blake asks:

> And did those feet in ancient time
> Walk upon England's mountains green?
> And was the holy Lamb of God
> On England's pleasant pastures seen?
> And did the Countenance Divine
> Shine forth upon our clouded hills?
> And was Jerusalem builded here
> Among those dark Satanic mills?
>
> Bring me my bow of burning gold:
> Bring me my arrows of desire:
> Bring me my spear: O clouds, unfold!
> Bring me my chariot of fire!
> I will not cease from mental fight,
> Nor shall my sword sleep in my hand
> Till we have built Jerusalem
> In England's green and pleasant land.

CHAPTER TIMELINE

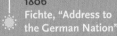

1765
Development of the spinning jenny

1799
First documented use of the phrase "industrial revolution"

1818
One-third of the German states join Custom Unio

1769
First water-powered spinning machine

1806
Fichte, "Address to the German Nation"

The "dark Satanic mills" possibly refer to the massive grain mills that lay only a few miles from Blake's home in London, but in a larger sense they describe the smoke-billowing factories then spreading across all of England.

The first documented use of the phrase **industrial revolution** to describe a new economy driven by factories and a growing workforce appears in a letter written in 1799 by a French diplomat visiting England, who saw industrialization as a positive development. (He also claimed that the English had stolen the idea from the French.) Nevertheless, awareness of the changes brought by machine power was everywhere. As Friedrich Engels wrote in *The Condition of the Working Class*

Dark Satanic Mills   *Coalbrookdale by Night* (1801) by Philip James de Loutherbourg. The Madeley Wood furnaces shown here were owned by the Coalbrookdale Company, which was the first industrial firm successfully to use coke as a fuel. Coke is the residue from a controlled burning of coal with a restricted supply of oxygen; it burns at a significantly higher temperature and produces higher-grade metals in the smelting and refining processes.

1819
Peterloo Massacre, England

1824
Glasgow Young Men's Society for Religious Improvement founded

1826
Janissaries abolished in Ottoman Empire.

1832
Cholera epidemic kills hundreds of thousands in Europe

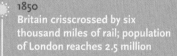

1850
Britain crisscrossed by six thousand miles of rail; population of London reaches 2.5 million

in England in 1844, "An industrial revolution was a revolution which at the same time changed the whole of civil society."

Like so much of the West's economic history, the basis of the industrial revolution lay in demographic change, or a growing population. Improvements in food production and advances in medicine had combined to spur a consistent increase in the European population ever since the 16th century; in the late 18th and early 19th centuries, though, the rate of increase grew dramatically. Larger domestic populations meant larger potential markets for manufactured goods. At the same time, Europe's international contacts meant increased opportunities to acquire raw materials and new targets for selling goods. The expansion of literacy, too, meant a more highly skilled labor force.

To take advantage of these conditions, one needed money—or access to it. It took financing to start private commercial ventures on a large scale. The mercantilist systems on the Continent had made that all but impossible. But when Napoleon demolished that system, national banks and stock exchanges came into existence, and financial markets could provide the capital, or funds for investment, needed. By 1815 most of Europe was ready to industrialize. England, though, had a fifty-year head start. Having avoided the burden of absolutism, left unaffected by the turmoil of the French Revolution, and intentionally ignored during the Napoleonic era, it had become an economic superpower.

> By 1815 most of Europe was ready to industrialize. England, though, had a fifty-year head-start. Having avoided the burden of absolutism, left unaffected by the turmoil of the French Revolution, and intentionally ignored during the Napoleonic era, it had become an economic superpower.

England's population in 1780 had stood at roughly eight million people; by 1850 it had grown to eighteen million. By 1880 it had reached twenty-six million.[1] This created a large demand for goods like food, clothing, furniture, and housewares; it also provided cheap labor. According to the "Iron Law of Wages" made popular by the English economist David Ricardo (1772–1823), population growth always outpaces industrial productivity, and that fact drives labor wages down to subsistence levels—what he termed "natural wages." Cheap labor was the primary fuel propelling the industrial economy forward, and it remained so into the 20th century.

New technologies from the Scientific Revolution and the Enlightenment had dramatically improved crop yields. A single acre of farmland in 1750 produced around fifteen bushels of wheat, but by 1850 it produced twenty-seven bushels. Careful breeding of animals had resulted in sheep that in 1850 produced twice as much wool annually as they had done in 1750, and cows produced more milk as

---

[1]   The engine of growth was the countryside, where improved medical care had lowered the mortality rate of children and mothers. The smallpox vaccine was available after 1790.

Agricultural Management   Thomas Weaver (1774-1843) painted this scene of Thomas Coke, 1st Earl of Leicester (1754-1842), inspecting a flock of sheep on his thirty thousand acre estate at Norfolk. Coke had enclosed most of his lands and encouraged the "scientific agriculture" of the time by experimenting with new types of feed and fertilizer and new techniques of animal breeding.

well. Higher productivity caused a decline in prices, which meant, theoretically, more disposable income for the purchase of manufactured goods. England, in simple terms, had an active market economy in the 18th century, as the Continent would not until well into the 19th. In Spain, France, the German states, eastern Europe, and Russia, agricultural economies were still at the subsistence level. The overwhelming majority of the people (as many as 90 percent in some territories) ate what they produced and made their own clothes. In the absence of any "disposable income," or spending money, economic demand was nonexistent.

England had achieved its unique status by eliminating its small-scale farmers. Big landowners had driven most of their farmers off the land through a combination of increased rents, buyouts, and evictions; they then consolidated this land into large-scale holdings that they could farm more efficiently. Or they could "enclose" the land and give up crop farming altogether, in favor of raising sheep and cattle for wool and dairy products. Acres of land that might have needed two hundred people to farm now needed only twenty to tend the herds and flocks. This decreased the landowners' labor costs while increasing their incomes. Instead of a countryside dotted with small farmers, England became divided among a small class of large landholders and a more numerous class of agricultural laborers who worked for wages.

Wage workers now used their incomes to purchase commodities that peasants had once made for themselves. Money had taken root as the foundation of the national economy. That new industrial economy, based on money, is capitalism. It is a system based on markets—on the supply of and demand for money, goods, and services.

Clothing was, after food, the most important purchase most people made. Even today, textiles make up the second-largest commodity consumed worldwide. The growth of the population naturally meant a need for more textile production. For England, which had been a mass wool producer since the Middle Ages, the new demand was especially for cotton—which was available from the southern United States. If enough American raw cotton could be brought to England, and if England could arrange its industrial capacity correctly, it could not just meet all domestic needs; it could also produce finished cloth for export. And political turmoil on the Continent left the English without any competitors on the international market. England had outlawed slavery in the 18th century, but that did not stop them from doing business with the slave-owning American South. American cotton and British wool formed the basis of industrial expansion.

> England had outlawed slavery in the 18th century, but that did not stop them from doing business with the slave-owning American South. American cotton and British wool formed the basis of industrial expansion.

INNOVATION AND INFRASTRUCTURE

Social and cultural factors played a role too. First, by the 18th century Britain was largely free from powerful guilds. Guilds had been central to the development of the medieval economy, but they were ill suited to a capitalist system, since their control of prices and production levels undermined the free play of supply and demand. In Habsburg Austria, for example, if demand rose for a given commodity, then the guilds that controlled the commodity would not necessarily increase production. After all, a guild derived much of its profits from government subsidies and membership fees rather than from commerce itself. Without an incentive to increase production, there was little reason to experiment with new technologies that might produce more goods more efficiently. England's remaining guilds were too weak and marginal to check market forces.

Second, an entrepreneurial culture had taken root in England in the 17th century (as it had done in Holland too) that encouraged economic growth. On the Continent, the nobility often believed that manufacture and commerce were "common" pursuits, beneath the dignity of an aristocrat. That class-based prejudice existed among the British, but to a far lesser degree. So long as he conducted his business in a dignified and gentlemanly way, an English lord's reputation did not necessarily suffer—which made access to capital for industry easier. Moreover, the English constitution had developed in such a way as to center real power in the House of Commons, whose members largely were drawn from the bourgeoisie, which was most interested in promoting trade. Third, the British legal system encouraged business by establishing the rights of property and allowing tradesmen to take out patents on the technologies they developed. Secure in the right to the rewards of one's own innovation, manufacturers, financiers, and shippers were more willing, and eager, to innovate.

While the manufacturing sector in England was spurred to new life, it quickly realized the limits of its means of production. Consider the textile industry. The putting-out system, which hired people to work in their own homes, had sufficed for a while, but the new demand for cloth far outpaced its ability to produce. Adding more carders, spinners, and weavers to the system helped, yet by the middle of the 18th century a drive to find more efficient machines had begun. England by this time controlled a vast colonial empire whose many millions of subjects needed everything from clothes to furniture, beer to kitchen utensils, housewares to agricultural tools. Entrepreneurs had ample incentives to increase their output; demand for goods like textiles, after all, was *elastic*: lower prices produced greater demand. Investment in new technology, such as the flying-shuttle loom, alone doubled a single weaver's ability to produce cloth. But now that weaving capacity had increased, there was incentive to increase the capacity of spinners to produce thread for the weavers. This led in 1765 to the development of the spinning jenny, a machine that could spin more than one spool of yarn at a time.

The most dramatic innovation, however, came in 1769 with the first water-powered spinning machine, which was quickly replaced by spinning machines and looms operated by steam engines. The application of steam power to textile production truly revolutionized the industry and began a social and economic revolution. Such machines, running continuously, day after day, could produce quantities of finished cloth previously unimaginable—and given the economies of scale, such production was highly profitable. They remained highly profitable, too, even though their productivity led to a decline in the price of the cloth. Early industrial factories driven by steam were immense, noisy, dangerous, and hot places that were miserable to work in; but the machines, if properly tended, never tired. By 1810 amounts of finished cloth that in 1750 had required over two hundred skilled workers to produce needed only a dozen semiskilled machine operators. With factory cities fast filling with displaced farm populations looking for work, the downward pressure on wages made it possible for entrepreneurs to invest large sums in machinery while still reaping huge profits. These and other innovations

Spinning Machines   Quarry Bank Mill, in Cheshire, England, was the largest textile mill in Britain by 1830. Originally water-powered, the spinning machine (called the "mule") was driven by steam engine after 1810. Until the practice was outlawed in 1847, the Quarry Bank Mill relied heavily on unpaid child labor.

changed completely the way large numbers of people worked and lived, and they shaped much of the rest of the 19th century.

The final necessary ingredient, in order to launch Britain's industrial revolution, was its development of the national infrastructure—the roads and waterways that brought the nation together. Without the ability to move bulk quantities of raw materials into the new factories and to efficiently ship large inventories of finished goods out to market, the producers' innovations were all for naught. Here geography favored the British. While large enough to support a population of tens of millions, Britain was yet a small enough island that the idea of uniting it with a comprehensive transport system seemed feasible. Investments in coastal barges, and in expanding harbors to accommodate them, enabled the movement of coal—the chief fuel of industry—around the island. Smaller river barges allowed shipments to move up and down the rivers, while a new network of interior canals connected rivers to one another. By 1815 the British had constructed some four thousand miles of canals, linking up their counties to such a degree that goods could be moved easily from any place in the realm to another. New networks of roads, and ultimately of railroads, completed the task, making Britain's physical infrastructure the most extensive and efficient in the world.

It had to be, given the enormous weight of the raw materials needed in the factories. Coal was available in enormous quantities, as was iron ore. Only the lack of means to move these resources efficiently had impeded their full use. Coal burns at a higher temperature than wood (the most common fuel in use before the 19th century), which made it more effective in steam production. Moreover, a by-product of coal called coke burns at an even higher temperature still, making it the fuel of choice for refining iron ore into usable iron, and ultimately for producing steel. Britain's coastal and river barges moved coal and coke by the hundreds and thousands of tons. The development of wrought iron made it possible, in the 1820s, to move heavy freight overland by railcars driven by steam engines.

An English engineer developed the first steam engine capable of pulling a train. Trains themselves had been in use for well over a century by that time, but they had been pulled along the tracks by teams of horses and had been used principally for transporting loads of coal from the mines. With the new steam-powered engine, freight could be moved anywhere affordably—so long as the tracks were in place. England thus began constructing an elaborate system of railroad tracks from mines and quarries to factories and markets all across the country. By 1830 a mere one hundred miles of track existed, but within twenty years a network of more than six thousand miles of track crisscrossed the country (see Map 17.1).

The unique combination of Britain's natural and cultural geography, its ability to inspire and capitalize on new technologies, and its legal and economic adaptability set the nation decades ahead of Continental Europe. Through the rest of the 19th century, it struggled to respond to the social problems created by industrialization, even while continuing to innovate and develop new technologies. Its challenge was to maintain its now dominant position in the world.

TRYING TO CATCH UP TO ENGLAND

The diplomats who redrew the political map of Europe at the **Congress of Vienna** in 1815 showed little enthusiasm for developing an industrial economy. More than anything, the statesmen, who represented more than two hundred separate states and princely houses, wanted to turn back the clock—if possible, all the way back to 1648 and the Treaty of Westphalia. Most of the parties favored the restoration of monarchical governments across Europe, along with the economic and social programs that had traditionally supported them. Too much had changed, however, to allow that. Whatever its faults, the Continental System had freed people from serfdom and encouraged their migration to manufacturing and commercial centers—enough that the majority of the people wanted to move ahead into the new economic world opened up by Britain.

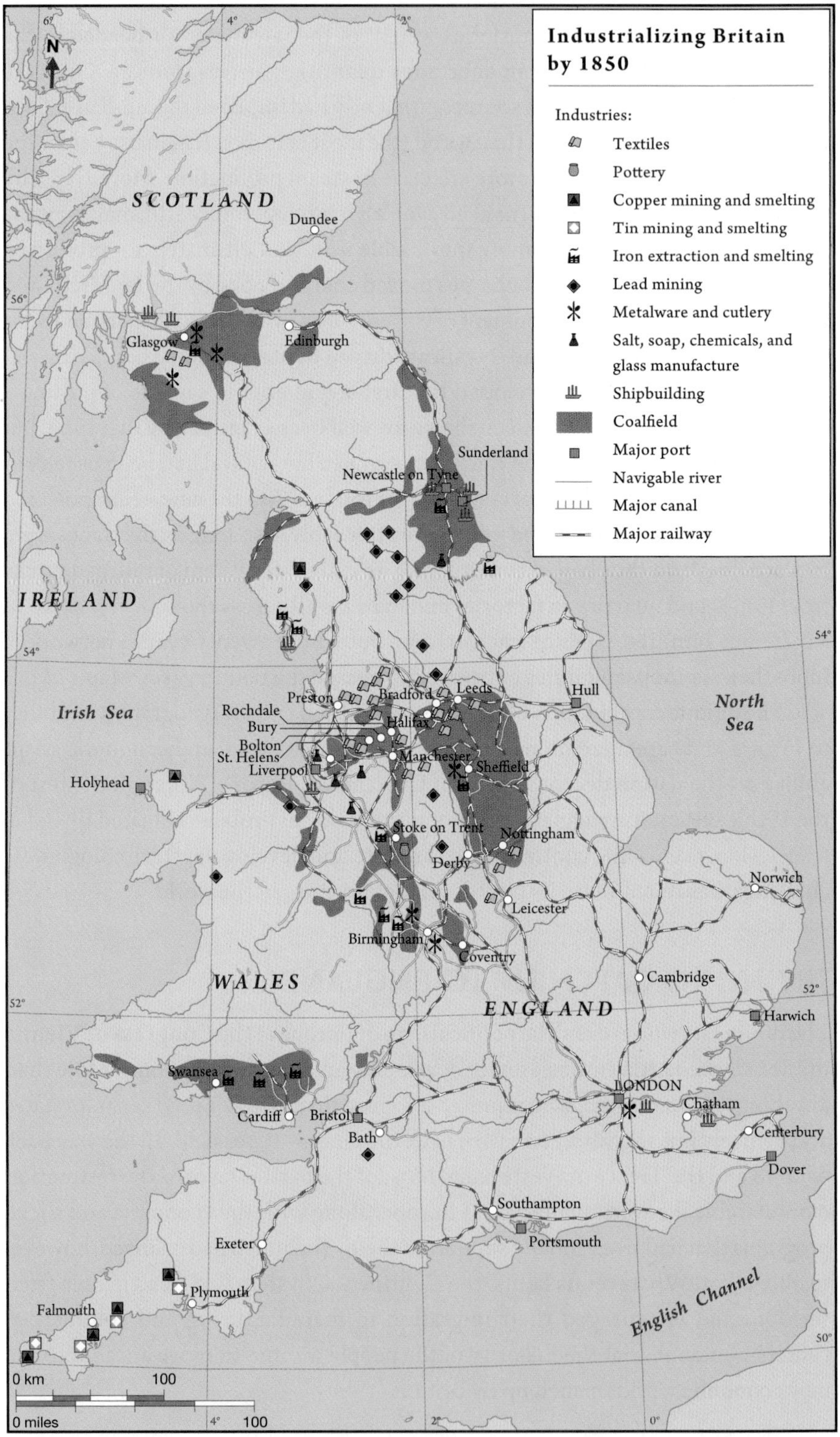

Industrializing Britain by 1850

Industries:
- ⬭ Textiles
- ◖ Pottery
- ▲ Copper mining and smelting
- ▢ Tin mining and smelting
- ⛏ Iron extraction and smelting
- ◆ Lead mining
- ✳ Metalware and cutlery
- ⬧ Salt, soap, chemicals, and glass manufacture
- � Shipbuilding
- ▨ Coalfield
- ◼ Major port
- — Navigable river
- ⎅ Major canal
- ⊸⊸ Major railway

MAP 17.1 **Industrializing Britain by 1850**

European industrialization differed from the British version in profound ways. First, Britain's commanding lead in international markets meant that Continental industry aimed instead to serve domestic markets. The European population, after all, was large enough to merit such attention, and by carefully assigning tariffs and import quotas, the Continental states could protect their newer industries from British competition. Second, the post-1815 states played even more central roles in industrialization than the government had done in England. The Continental governments not only built infrastructure but invested directly in the fledging industries—especially heavily capitalized industries like railroads—and in the building of factories. Third, important general differences emerged in the way each Continental country industrialized. France, for example, tended to favor the production of luxury items like glassware, china, and fine housewares; in Germany specialty domestic commodities predominated, like linens, timepieces, tools, and kitchenwares, as well as state-used commodities like ships and weaponry.

Once again, demography and geography played important roles in the ways industrialization progressed. In France, for example, the population grew at a healthy rate, but considerably slower than its neighbors (see Figure 17.1). In 1700 the French population was somewhere near twenty million, and by 1850 it had grown to approximately thirty-five million, a steady but otherwise unremarkable growth rate of not quite 2 percent annually. Over the same period, Britain's population had leaped from five million to twenty million (a growth of nearly 5 percent per year), while Germany's had increased from fifteen million to thirty-four million (about 3.5 percent per year). This meant that the need to increase food production that had driven the British rush to industrial production was lacking in France. Their traditional means of feeding themselves sufficed, which enabled the French to focus on luxury goods, niche markets that had smaller gross sales but higher profit margins.

This served France well, for the maintenance of a traditional peasantry on the land had kept the urban labor pools from growing excessively large,

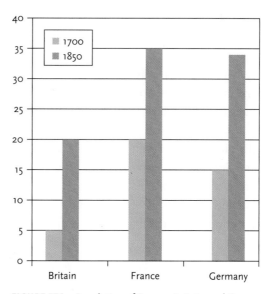

FIGURE 17.1   Population of France, Britain, and Germany, 1700–1850

as had happened in England. But it came at the price of France—once Europe's largest and most prosperous economy (even though the wealth was hoarded at the highest levels)—becoming a second-tier commercial power.[2] Indeed, France's more measured industrial development resulted in generally less dire social disruptions, compared to those suffered by the British and Germans, and the basic structures of much of French life in the countryside survived until the end of the 19th century.

The Congress of Vienna had consolidated Germany's three-hundred-plus independent territories to a mere three dozen larger entities. This augured well for German industrial growth, especially given the rapidly expanding population, but the reigning conservative impulse after 1815 inclined each new state to adhere strictly to its own laws and customs. Merchants wanting to move goods across territorial borders had to contend with multiple sets of tolls and tariffs, multiple laws and jurisdictional systems, and multiple currencies; few were willing to make the effort. Germany therefore began to industrialize, although on a regional rather than a national level. The consequently lower levels of investment capital available meant that few entrepreneurs could afford expensive coal-fired machinery and had to rely on water-powered factories. This in turn meant that Germany's first factories were limited to areas in mountainous regions with access to fast-flowing streams, like Saxony and Silesia. Led by Prussia, one of the three dozen German principalities, a Customs Union (*Zollverein*) was created in 1818 and had enrolled one-third of the German states within twenty years, creating not a full-fledged free-trade zone but a set of streamlined partnerships. Members agreed to observe Prussian customs and regulations, in order to promote industry. In this way, Prussian leadership in the move toward eventual German reunification can be seen decades before the political movement itself took root. The Customs Union hired British equipment and engineers to develop the German coal industry and train them to build and maintain a railroad system. By 1850 nearly four thousand miles of rail track had been laid in Germany, and industrial development had progressed to such a degree that one could say that industrialization brought about the unification of Germany.

Many European states failed to industrialize at all after 1815: Austria, Italy, the Netherlands (though not Belgium), Poland, Portugal, Russia, Scandinavia, and Spain. The reasons for this failure were unique to each territory, but most involved some combination of a lack of natural resources, a shortage of capital, and a disinclination of labor to adopt new skills and technologies. In Austria and Spain, for example, geography worked against them. Fully two-thirds of the area of the

---

2   French cities like Bordeaux, Lyons, Montpellier, and Vienna, formerly busy centers of trade, became sleepy provincial towns.

Austrian-Hungarian Empire consisted of major mountain ranges that impeded infrastructural development. In Spain, the majority of the peninsula consisted of a hot upland plain, called the *meseta*, that was poor agricultural land, with few metal or mineral resources and little water. In Italy—which after 1815 was still divided into over a dozen petty kingdoms and principalities—intense regional pride and a cultural disinclination to change frustrated efforts to unify and industrialize. Though agriculturally rich, and with long-established traditions of artisanal crafts and professional (that is, financial, legal, and medical) expertise, few Italians valued the ideas of industrialized labor and mechanized production. What industrial production did exist, such as power-driven silk weaving in Lombardy, was performed on a part-time basis; seasonal female laborers simply filled in their days between the planting and harvesting of their crops. Even as late as 1861, in unified Italy's first national census, there were three times as many Italian farmers as there were industrial workers, and the majority of those workers were women working part-time.

Europe lagged behind Britain in railroad development, as in everything else, but did its best to catch up. In 1830, when England had established its first hundred

Italian Farm Workers   Italy was among the last of the western European countries to industrialize. These Italian farm workers, photographed sometime in the early 1900s, were still using oxen to pull their mower, long after other countries had introduced more modern techniques.

miles of track, France had a mere twenty miles of track to compare—and there was none anywhere else on the Continent. Belgium, however, began to construct a system immediately and by 1835 had established a network that covered the entire (although admittedly small) country. By 1850, though, things had changed. Germany, which by 1840 was funneling one-third of all its industrial investment capital into the railroads, had developed a grid of over 3,600 miles of track, and France's rail line had grown to roughly 1,800 miles. Underdeveloped Austria, by contrast, had a mere 850 miles of track, and Italy had not even half of that amount (see Map 17.2). The general picture that emerges suggests that railways proved most successful when connecting areas already starting to industrialize, but they

MAP 17.2   Industrializing Europe by 1870

themselves were seldom enough to initiate industrialization. And furthermore, whereas industrialization greatly expanded national economies, the wealth it generated exacerbated rather than relieved social inequities.

TRYING TO CATCH UP TO EUROPE

The Muslim world after 1800, for the most part, had only one of the many elements that had been essential to trigger industrialization in Europe: a growing population. The other elements—investment capital, an openness to technical innovations, secure access to raw materials, a reliable transport infrastructure, flexible market economies, and a system of government amenable to entrepreneurialism—were in short or irregular supply.

Census records for the Ottoman state are spotty, although the general pattern seems clear: after a dramatic downturn in population during the 18th century, the 19th saw strong population growth, from roughly seven million at the start of the century to about twenty million by its end. The growth was not evenly spread, however, with the lion's share of it happening in the empire's European provinces. (Generally speaking, the further east and south one traveled in the Ottoman Empire, the lower the population density.) This increase took place within a shrinking imperial geography, since Morocco, Algeria, and Tunisia had all broken away from Ottoman control by 1835 (see Map 17.3). As a result, the population density effectively doubled. Moreover, the political and social scene grew unsteady as the Ottoman Empire's hold over the western half of the Islamic world weakened.

Historians, especially European historians, tend to portray the Ottoman state as in a gradual but nonstop decline after 1700. Certainly the defeat of their last great campaign to take Vienna in 1683 was a watershed, and territorial retreat against the Austrian-Hungarians and the Russians was disheartening. Yet as late as 1750 the Ottomans were still the rulers, in terms of area, of the largest state in the Western world. The empire showed great resilience and was open to many reforms. Indeed, the 18th and 19th centuries were marked, if anything, by continuous waves of reform as the rulers labored to address the myriad ethnic, religious, economic, and social problems confronting it. This was not blind flailing. Taking their cue from the great Spanish Arab scholar Ibn Khaldun (1332–1406), whose ideas inspired many of the enacted or merely proposed reforms (and whose famous book *The Introduction to History* [*Muqaddimah*] was translated into Turkish at this time), the Turks crafted a variety of reforms that would hold together the fabric of Islamic society. These considered the interplay between the attractive forces of religious allegiance, economic interdependence, and political tradition on

> Yet as late as 1750 the Ottomans were still the rulers, in terms of area, of the largest state in the Western world.

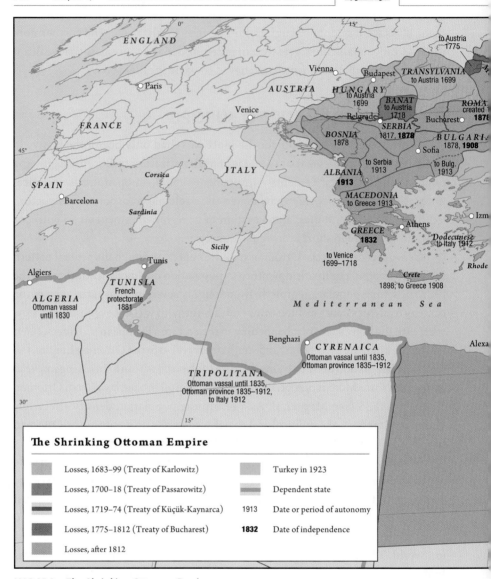

MAP 17.3 **The Shrinking Ottoman Empire**

the one hand and the divisive, centrifugal forces of ethnic or tribal localism, social division, and technological underdevelopment on the other.

Numerous Turkish writers of the time, echoing the efforts of their Enlightenment contemporaries in Europe, commented on the reform efforts emanating from the Istanbul court. One was Sari Mehmed Pasha (d. 1717), the son of a grocer who rose ultimately to the position of imperial treasurer, who saw the fundamental problem in the empire as the blurring of distinctions between the Muslim ruling class and their tax-paying non-Muslim subjects:

DOLIA
land 1699

to Russia
1785
  Odessa

KHANATE OF CRIMEA
1774; to Russia 1783

Azov

RUSSIA

BESSARABIA
to Russia 1812

Black   Sea

Sinope

Batumi

to Russia
1826

Tiflis

DAGESTAN
(tributary to 1723)

*Caspian
Sea*

Trabzon

bul

to Russia
1878

GEORGIA

Ankara

Erzerum

ARMENIA
1918–20

KARABAKH
tributary to 1730

ANATOLIA
Kayseri

Konya

Diyarbakir

KURDISTAN

AZERBAIJAN
tributary to 1730

Anatalya

Aleppo

SYRIA
French mandate
1920

Mosul

Tehran

LEBANON
French mandate
1920
Damascus

LURISTAN

British
protectorate
1878

Cyprus

IRAQ   Baghdad

PERSIA
(IRAN)

PALESTINE
British mandate
1920

Jerusalem

*TRANS-
JORDAN*
British mandate
1920

EGYPT
British occupation
1812

Suez

KUWAIT

Neutral zone
1920

British
protectorate
1899

EL HASA

*HEJAZ
1916*

*Red
Sea*

Tropic of Cancer

N

0 km   200

0 miles   200

The admission of non-Muslims to the military ranks must be stopped,
for nothing but trouble can result when those who are not descendants of
cavalry officers are turned suddenly into cavalry officers. . . . Provincial
town dwellers and farmers deserve to be protected, and their welfare increased by doing away with all [governmental] abuses; at the same time
we should bend every effort to helping the people become prosperous—
but it would be wrong to indulge the non-Muslims too much. (*The Book of
Advice for Viziers and Governors*)

This did not bode well for the Christians and Jews in the empire. And while Mehmed Pasha's opinions were not official policy, the unease in the empire frequently resulted in popular hostility against religious minorities.

Another watershed was Napoleon's 1798 invasion of Egypt. This had been a short-lived conquest, but the event showed clearly how Muslim military might was falling behind that of Europe. Thereafter, periodic separatist movements arose throughout the Ottoman Empire, which were usually encouraged by Russia and Austria-Hungary. These setbacks forced the Turks to invest time and money in rebuilding the military that they would otherwise have committed to developing their industrial capacity. They settled on a strategy of replacing their traditional patchwork system of administration—one that had insured as much of each province's local customs as possible—and instead mandated a single system of law, granted citizen status to all, and abolished tax exemptions for privileged groups. In the early 19th century the ruler Selim III (r. 1789–1807), having witnessed the might of the French forces, tried to modernize the Turkish army along European lines but was stopped by a revolt of the Janissaries. His successor, Mahmud II (r. 1808–1839), took the drastic step of abolishing the Janissaries altogether in 1826. In their way, these reforms were progressive and echoed the egalitarian sentiments then current in European thinking, but they were anathema to much of the Muslim populace, most of whom angrily rejected the notion of equal status before the law for their non-Muslim neighbors.

"THE SICK MAN OF EUROPE"

Ottoman trade with Europe took place under the aegis of a group of trade agreements known somewhat ominously as **capitulations**. These agreements had previously been occasional arrangements that guaranteed Turkish and European merchants access to one another's markets for a mutually agreed-on period of years. By 1815, however, most capitulations overwhelmingly favored the Europeans. In fact, they did little more than grant European traders the right to enter Ottoman markets at will—in return for vague European promises to aid the Ottomans diplomatically in their territorial disputes with Austria-Hungary and Russia. Moreover, most capitulations ceded jurisdiction over all foreign traders and visitors to the foreigners' resident diplomats, and granted jurisdiction over foreigners whose home countries had no ambassador in Istanbul to whatever countries did have diplomatic representation there. They even allowed selected foreign governments to extend their own trading privileges to Christian and Jewish subjects of the Ottoman state.

The net effect of these capitulations was twofold. First, the empire's Mediterranean trade fell almost entirely into the hands of the Europeans precisely at the time when Europe began to industrialize. (Commerce in the Black Sea, Red Sea, Persian Gulf, and Indian Ocean remained in Muslim hands and usually exceeded, in annual revenue, the amount lost in the Mediterranean to the Europeans.) Second, popular resentment of Christians and Jews, whether Ottoman subjects or not, flared up significantly along with popular displeasure at what the empire's Muslim subjects regarded as the ruling dynasty's weakness and corruption.

A French traveler through the Middle East at the end of the 18th century summarized his impressions of relations between the Turks' Muslim and non-Muslim subjects this way:

> [Christian and Jewish merchants in Egypt] are confined to separate quarters where they live among themselves and have hardly any communication with the outside world; they dread such contact, in fact, and emerge from their neighborhoods as seldom as possible in order to avoid the insults thrown at them by the common people . . . and the bullying of the Mamluks. . . . Living as they do in a kind of perpetual imprisonment, they are constantly fearful—that perhaps an outbreak of plague will force them to blockade themselves in their houses, or perhaps a revolt somewhere will cause their neighborhood to be plundered, or perhaps the leader of some Islamic faction will extort money from them.

His view of relations in Damascus was no better:

> Turks, in fact, never speak of the [Muslim] people of Damascus without mentioning that they are the biggest troublemakers in the whole empire. . . . But they are quick to add too that the Christians there are more vile and troublesome than anywhere else. . . . The Damascene Arabs, for their part, hate the Christians too, and this hatred is fomented by their continual contact with Mecca . . . for Damascus is the general meeting point for all Islamic pilgrims coming from the north of Asia, just as Cairo is for the Muslims coming out of Africa. . . . Most European travelers and merchants agree . . . that the empire's Greek Christian subjects are a wicked, deceitful, abject, and insolent lot, whether they prosper or not. . . . For since the Turks treat the Greeks with the haughtiness and contempt they usually reserve for slaves, the Greeks cannot help becoming what they are regarded as. Forced constantly to lie, or to avoid violence by sly behavior, they indulge in obsequious flattery, deceit, and cheating of every kind.
>
> (C. F. Volney, *Travels in Egypt and Syria* [1785])

Even allowing for the traveler's ready stereotyping, the strain between communities is palpable.

Numerous efforts to revive the economy emanated from the court at Istanbul, but all failed. The Ottomans invested heavily in steamships, which increased the productivity of maritime trade, but were slow to develop railroads. Whatever rail lines they had in the 1800s were almost entirely limited to their European provinces; Anatolia, Palestine, and Egypt remained undeveloped in this regard. Farming methods did not undergo the transformative change they did in Europe, largely because most of the arable land remained in individual family farms; they were never consolidated into the larger holdings necessary to make the expense of new technology bearable. Without a corresponding increase in production, rural society did not develop the market economy characteristic of Europe. In terms of manufacture, the empire never successfully freed itself of the guild structure, and hence incentives to increase production failed to materialize despite the continuing interest in Ottoman goods like silks, carpets, and textiles. The most noticeable change in the manufacturing sector of the 19th century was the

Industrialization Comes to the Ottomans   A silkweaving mill in Bursa, Turkey, in the late 19th century. Note the younger girls who tended the boiling basins where the older and more-skilled women extracted and cleaned the silk. Silk manufacture had been a specialty in Bursa since the 16th century. Since Islamic tradition forbade, and generally still forbids, Muslim men to wear silk—they regard it as effeminate—silk cloth was primarily an export commodity, and a highly profitable one.

increase in the percentage of women in the workplace, but their labor was by hand. Mechanization was insignificant.

Without local market economies, access to investment capital, incentives to increase production, and a reliable infrastructure for transport, the empire could not industrialize and hence had no chance to catch up with the fast-growing European economy. As the "sick man of Europe"—as Westerners began to call the Ottoman state in the 19th century—Istanbul's hold over even its reduced empire continued to slip, prompting more efforts by the provinces to secede. The most famous and significant of these secessions was Greece's successful revolt in 1832.

LIFE IN THE INDUSTRIAL AGE

Until the industrial revolution the word "unemployment" did not exist in English. In earlier centuries the word "unemployed" had been widely used, but almost always in relation to an object instead of a person: tools might lie unemployed on a workman's shelf; a workman himself, however, never "was unemployed." He was simply poor. Daniel Defoe, in his great *Journal of the Plague Year* (1756), described the ghostly emptiness of the London city streets with a reference to "coaches . . . left unemploy'd for five or six days"; yet people themselves, even the poorest among them, were seldom without work to do. Industrial society, however, was rife with unemployment. It indeed depended on it, for surplus labor kept wages down to a level that justified the capital risk of entrepreneurship.

But unemployment was only one of the dire new developments created by industrialization. Hardly a single aspect of Western society remained unaffected. Everything from the role of the state to the structure of the family, from women's roles in society to the material standards of living, from the urban landscape to school curricula, and more, were altered in one way or another. Much of 19th-century history, in fact, can be read as a long effort to adapt to the changes brought on by the industrial revolution.

The easiest change to quantify is the increase in urban development—although the word "development" may be misused here. What occurred was largely the unchecked, uncontrolled, riotous, and blighted increase in the number and size of cities wherever the mechanization of labor took root. In 1800 Europe had a mere twenty-two cities with populations of 100,000. By 1850 that number had grown to forty-seven. The populations of cities both old and new likewise skyrocketed. By 1850 London's population stood at an astounding 2.5 million people, making it easily the largest city in Europe. Paris had roughly 1.5 million; Berlin and Naples each had a half million; Vienna held approximately 400,000; and Brussels held 250,000 (see Map 17.4). These leading cities had ballooned not only with industry

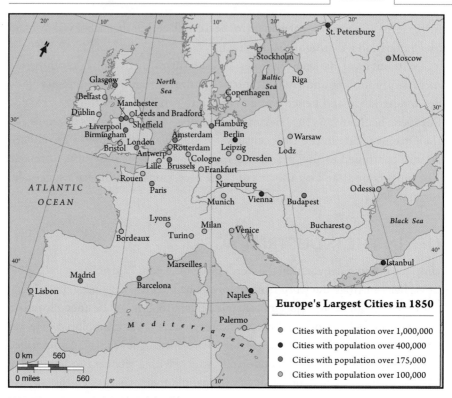

MAP 17.4   Europe's Largest Cities in 1850

but also with the financial and government administrations needed to manage it. There were lesser, though still large, centers—like Barcelona, Budapest, Hamburg, Lyons, Palermo, Rouen, and Stockholm. But even with these, the capacity to cope with such unprecedented increases in numbers failed miserably. For everyone except the reasonably prosperous—perhaps the top 15 percent of the urban population—living conditions ranged from the bad to the almost unspeakably awful.

Workers, the unemployed, migrants, and their families were squeezed into filthy hovels with poor sanitation, little warmth, and inadequate supplies of fresh water to drink. Lacking any kind of sewage system, people relieved themselves in chamber pots and simply flung the refuse into the street.[3] Chemical smog and coal smoke filled the air; prostitution and violent crime were rampant. In the worker slums of Lille (population in 1872: 158,000) fully one-third of the population lived in cellars. In Stockholm several thousand poor families, who lived primar-

---

[3] By the mid-19th century, the ratio of urban inhabitants to flush toilets was still an alarming 200:1 in most industrial cities.

Shantytown   The word *shantytown* originated in North America and came into general use in the middle of the nineteenth century to denote the ramshackle dwellings of poor Irish immigrants. It quickly was taken over, however, to describe the slum areas that sprang up outside industrialized cities. This scene presents a dewy-eyed vision of one such shantytown in Germany. The poor are clearly poor, but almost picturesquely so. Notice the well-dressed genteel couple in the center, who are handing out money to the children.

ily in the hilly areas surrounding the archipelago that makes up the center of the city, actually lived in holes they had dug in the ground. Census records from 1847 show that in one Irish working-class neighborhood in London, St. Giles, no fewer than 461 people lived jammed together in only twelve houses. Cholera and tuberculosis (then called consumption) were endemic and according to some estimates accounted for over 50 percent of all deaths in factory cities in the 19th century. A single wave of cholera in 1832 killed 32,000 people in Paris alone and another 7,000 in London; worse still, the same epidemic carried off 250,000 in Russia. The effects of tuberculosis were even more dire.

Local and national governments responded with housing codes, the expansion of sewage systems, and efforts to control crime, but were seldom able to keep pace with the misery. Factory workers, vulnerable to reduced wages created by the great abundance of labor, generally earned too little to support their families, and consequently women and children had to work too. In textile manufacturing, in fact, fully one-half of the pre-1850 labor force was made up of women and children as young as seven. Conditions for the workers were often dismal. Work days were frequently twelve or even fourteen hours in length, and discipline could be brutal.

An English woman who worked hauling carts of coal out of a mine shaft described her work to a government-inquiry panel in this way:

> I was married at 23, and went into a colliery when I was married. I used to weave when about 12 years old; can neither read nor write. I . . . make sometimes 7 [shillings] a week, sometimes not so much. I am a drawer [cart puller], and work from 6 in the morning to 6 at night. Stop about an hour at noon to eat my dinner; have bread and butter for dinner; I get no drink. I have two children, but they are too young to work. I worked at drawing when I was in the family way. I know a woman who has gone home and washed herself, taken to her bed, delivered of a child, and gone to work again under the week. . . .
>
> [When hauling coal] I have a belt round my waist, and a chain passing between my legs, and I go on my hands and feet. The road is very steep, and we have to hold by a rope; and when there is no rope, by anything we can catch hold of. There are six women and about six boys and girls in the pit I work in; it is very hard work for a woman. The pit is very wet where I work, and the water comes over our clog-tops always, and I have seen it up to my thighs; it rains in at the roof terribly. My clothes are wet through almost all day long. . . .
>
> My cousin looks after my children in the day-time. I am very tired when I get home at night; I fall asleep sometimes before I get washed. I am not so strong as I was, and cannot stand my work so well as I used to. I have drawn till I have [worn the] skin off me; the belt and chain is worse when we are in the family way. [My husband] has beaten me many a times for not being ready [to have sex]. I [was] not used to it at first, and he had little patience. . . .
>
> I have known many a man beat his drawer. I have known men take liberties with the drawers, and some of the women have bastards.
>
> *(Parliamentary Papers, 1842, vol. 15)*

In France, factory workers were long required to carry a document called a *livret* ("booklet"), which was a kind of worker's passport. Foremen and superiors in a factory regularly wrote comments in an employee's livret, citing his or her mistakes, tardiness, poor attitude, breakages, or ill discipline. Applicants for factory jobs were required to produce their booklets for their prospective employers to review.

Apart from the demeaning nature of these conditions, industrial work also fostered economic and social dependency, since workers lived more or less at the mercy of their employers. Textile factories often provided housing for their unmarried female workers—the cost of boarding being deducted from their

a

b

Engraving from *A Treatise on the Winning and Working of Collieries* by Matthias Dunn (1848) It shows a boy pulling a loaded cart through a shaft in a Welsh coal mine (a). Children sometimes started to work in the mines as young as age seven. Below, a woman drags a heavy load of coal up an incline, assisted by two children (a boy and a girl, apparently) at the rear (b). From the coal region of Midlothian, in Scotland, ca. 1848.

wages—which meant that many women literally spent their whole working lives on the job site. Children sent to work in their youth ended up crippled and deformed, unable to care for themselves in their adult years. One observer of the child workers in the cotton mills left this vivid description:

> When I visited Bradford, in Yorkshire, in 1838, being desirous to see the condition of the children—for I knew that they were employed at very early ages in the worsted business . . . I asked for a collection of cripples and deformities. In a short time more than 80 were gathered in a large courtyard. They were mere samples of the entire mass. I assert

without exaggeration that no power of language could describe the varieties, and I may say, the cruelties, in all these degradations of the
human form. They stood or squatted before me in all the shapes of the
letters of the alphabet. This was the effect of prolonged toil on the tender
frames of children at early ages. (*Parliamentary Debates, 3rd ser., vol. 245*)

All that was left for one thus ruined was to join the public welfare rolls. Given
such wretched conditions, it is not surprising to learn that alcoholism became
rampant—although it is a shock to discover that the problem was so extensive that
in many cities the businesses staggered their scheduled paydays in order to minimize the number of drunks on city streets at any given time. Neither is it surprising
that workers and indigents alike began to riot. Labor strikes and demonstrations
shook northern England as early as 1811. In France the silk-weaving center of
Lyons erupted in worker rebellions in 1831 and again in 1834—the latter revolt
resulting in several hundred deaths and the arrest, conviction, and deportation of
approximately ten thousand city dwellers.

RIOTS AND REFORM

A riot over starvation wages by linen weavers in Silesia (then part of Prussia, today
located in Poland) in 1844 gained such renown that the Romantic poet Heinrich
Heine (1797–1856) commemorated their struggle in verse. "The Silesian Weavers"
appeared in 1844, in the immediate aftermath of the revolt. Many of his poems were
set to music by Franz Schubert and Robert Schumann. Karl Marx was also a fan and
was the first to publish Heine's "Germany—A Winter's Tale" (also 1844). It is easy
to see how lines like these, from "The Silesian Weavers," would appeal to Marx:

> Doomed is our king, the rich man's king,
> who remained unmoved by our suffering
> and snatched the last penny out of our hands
> before giving us over to his thuggish bands.

In Manchester, the "Peterloo Massacre" occurred in 1819 when private militias hired by the local factory owners showed up at a popular demonstration of
workers. Speakers there were calling for universal suffrage and secret ballots as
the only means of getting the government to address urban problems effectively.
When the most popular of the speakers, a firebrand named Henry Hunt, began
his speech, the militias swung into action:

> The commanding officer then approaching Mr. Hunt, and brandish-
> ing his sword, told him that he was his prisoner. Mr. Hunt, after enjoining

the people to tranquility, said, that he would readily surrender to any civil officer on showing his warrant, and Mr. Nadin, the principal police officer, received him in charge. Another person, named Johnson, was likewise apprehended, and a few of the mob; some others against whom there were warrants, escaped in the crowd.

A cry now arose among the military of "Have at their flags!" and they dashed down not only those in the cart, but the others dispersed in the field; cutting to right and left to get at them. The people began running in all directions; and from this moment the yeomanry lost all command of temper: numbers were trampled under the feet of men and horses; many, both men and women, were cut down by sabers; several, and a peace officer and a female in the number, slain on the spot. The whole number of persons injured amounted to between three and four hundred. The populace threw a few stones and brick bats in their retreat; but in less than ten minutes the ground was entirely cleared of its former occupants, and filled by various bodies of military, both horse and foot. Mr. Hunt was led to prison, not without incurring considerable danger, and some injury on his way from the swords of the yeomanry and the bludgeons of police officers; the broken staves of two of his banners were carried in mock procession before him. The magistrates directed him to

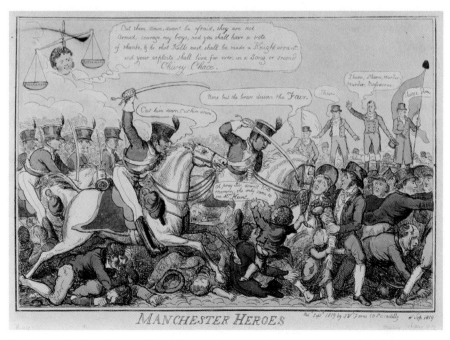

Cutting the Workers Down to Size   Cartoon showing police putting down the labor strikers at the Peterloo Massacre in 1819, in Manchester.

be locked up in a solitary cell, and the other prisoners were confined with the same precaution. The town was brought into a tolerably quiet state before night, military patrols being stationed at the end of almost every street. *(Annual Register)*

Unrest continued to grow throughout the century, giving rise to passionate debate over what to do about the myriad negative consequences of industrialization.

Not all was doom and gloom, however. Private charities and organized efforts to relieve urban suffering proliferated by the thousands across Europe.[4] A private enterprise called the Society for the Diffusion of Useful Knowledge appeared in 1824, dedicated to teaching the masses everything from new job skills to personal hygiene. In Paris the church-run Society of Saint Vincent de Paul formed in 1835 to provide clothing, food, and rudimentary education to workers and transients. Meanwhile the French government-funded network of night schools, called Polytechnic Associations, made vocational training available to over one hundred thousand people by 1850.

WOMEN AND CHILDREN LAST

Women were affected by industrialization in ways that men were not. Initially, women made up more of the workforce, at least in some industries: England's textiles factories, in fact, notoriously hired women and children to a disproportionate degree. Women and children made up as much as 75 percent of the labor force in some areas. A woman received less than half the wages a man did in factory work. Working women in the 19th century also differed from their forebears in a significant way: they lived apart from their families. In rural areas, women had put in as many hours of daily labor as men did, but since workplace and domestic space were the same, no fundamental division between work and family existed. In many factories, the female laborers were single girls or women who had left the family farm in search of work. Cut off from their traditional social units, they had to forge new connections in a strange and dangerous new urban setting. Married women with one or two children were often able to rely on new friends or neighbors to help with childcare while they put in long hours at the factory. But as her family increased in number, it grew increasingly difficult for a woman to keep working, no matter how badly the family needed her wages, and so she dropped out of the workplace. Factory owners were quick to seize on the

---

[4]   London was the site of nearly five hundred relief organizations by midcentury.

Women at Work in a French Textile Mill   Everyone looks healthy, happy, and, well, industrious.

children themselves as replacement workers; children earned less than half of even the discounted wages of women, after all. It took the Factory Act in 1833 to restrict and regulate (though not ban) child labor.[5]

Unmarried women were vulnerable to sexual exploitation, either from demanding factory bosses, seducing boyfriends, or criminal attackers. Public health workers recorded that approximately one-third of all the babies born in an industrial city in England or France in the 1820s and 1830s were born out of wedlock. Throughout France, an average of thirty thousand newborns were abandoned at foundling hospitals and orphanages annually. Thousands more each year—although no one can know the precise number—were victims of infanticide. Prostitution formed another aspect of exploitation. Industrial cities swarmed with it. After all, factory work and employment in domestic service to the wealthier families could absorb only a fraction of the working-class women packed into urban slums.[6] Many of those with no other means to support themselves turned to sex work. Paris had roughly thirty thousand streetwalking prostitutes in the

---

[5]   The Factory Act outlawed child labor for those under the age of nine. It set a maximum limit of nine hours of labor a day for children aged nine to thirteen.

[6]   The word *slum*, according to a popular though dubious folk etymology, emerged in the Industrial Revolution as a slang variant of the word *slime*, to describe the filthiness of the hovels into which workers were packed.

Workhouse   The St. Marylebone Parish Workhouse was established in 1730. By 1834 it had acquired several new and enlarged buildings. Refugees from the Irish Potato Famine drove its occupancy to over 2200. This photo dates to 1901, after a new wave of construction added two five-story blockhouses to the site. During World War I it also housed Belgian war refugees.

1830s; London had over twice that number. Concerns about the spread of disease rose accordingly.

In order to deal effectively with the social consequences of industrialization, Western governments began to create special bureaus for the collection of data: commissions on public health, on housing, on working conditions, on urban crime, on municipal codes and infrastructure, all appeared for the first time in the early 19th century, and the data they gathered form the basis of our understanding of the problems Europe faced as its economy mechanized. But the states were not the only institutions involved. Private charities, trusts, and societies formed by the hundreds, each usually dedicated to a particular urban problem. Catholic religious orders established scores of hospitals, old-age homes, soup kitchens, and orphanages. Protestant groups instituted Bible-reading societies, evangelical gatherings, temperance societies (to fight the alcoholism rampant among the industrial poor), and workhouses. In Scotland, the "Glasgow Young Men's Society for Religious Improvement"—a forerunner of today's YMCA—was formed in 1824 to provide healthy alternatives to urban crime, alcohol, and sexual license.

Private religious groups inaugurated the idea of Sunday schools as places where young people could gather to study the Scriptures and sing hymns. Half of all British working-class children received reading instruction at Sunday schools. Among the many problems facing the slums was a dire shortage of places of worship. In Berlin, for example, the churches in the city, combined, could seat about twenty-five thousand people on any given Sunday, but there were well over eight hundred thousand people living in Berlin. Without churches, the faithful had to extemporize. Some whole denominations emerged, either as completely new phenomena or as revitalized versions of older denominations, and most of them depended on a heightened emotionalism that responded to the desperate needs of the people. Among these new denominations were the Methodist, Quaker, and Baptist branches of Protestant Christianity. In the United States, itself beginning to industrialize in the North, some of the new denominations included the Latter-day Saints (the Mormons) and the Seventh-day Adventists; the second half of the century saw the establishment of the Jehovah's Witnesses and the Salvation Army.

THE ROMANTIC GENERATION

Romanticism was the most pervasive and influential cultural phenomenon in the first half of the 19th century. Everyone agrees on that. What few historians can easily do, however, is state exactly what Romanticism was. Between 1899 and 1932 a brilliant historian named Henri Pirenne (1862–1935) published the massive seven-volume *History of Belgium*, and when he reached the 19th century and came to the topic of Romanticism he briefly halted. A careful scholar, given to detail and precision, he indulged himself and came up with 152 separate definitions of it. Rather than compete with Pirenne, it may be better to back away from precision and describe Romanticism—vaguely, perhaps, but not inaccurately—as a generational mood that tended to prefer emotion and instinct over structural order and rational thought. Just as reference to the '60s generation calls up images of attitude, aesthetic style, political concerns, and social rebellion, so too does the term "Romanticism" denote sentiments about human life, nature, and the workings of the world.

Of course, not every young person in the United States in the 1960s wore long hair, experimented with drugs and "free love," listened to an electrified Bob Dylan, marched on Washington to protest the war in Vietnam or in support of civil rights, or sought to create a new social order by establishing communes. Neither did every young adult in the first decade or two of the 19th century wear long hair, experiment with opium and Byronic free love, listen to Beethoven, set out to join Greece's nationalist rebellion against the Ottoman Empire, or seek a new social order by overthrowing bourgeois values in favor of an anarchic utopia of like-minded souls in communion with one another. But individuals in each era did so—enough to give each age its identity.

We can see the Romantic temperament expressed most clearly in the arts, especially in literature. Compare a few lines of Samuel Johnson (1709–1784) and William Wordsworth (1770–1850). The differences between the poems are stark:

> Where then shall Hope and Fear their objects find?
> Must dull Suspense corrupt the stagnant mind?
> Must helpless man, in ignorance sedate,
> Roll darkling down the torrent of his fate?
> Must no dislike alarm, no wishes rise,
> No cries attempt the mercies of the skies?
> Enquirer, cease, petitions yet remain,
> Which Heaven may hear, nor deem religion vain.
> Still raise for good the supplicating voice,
> But leave to heaven the measure and the choice,
> Safe in His power, whose eyes discern afar
> The secret ambush of a specious prayer.
> Implore His aid, in His decisions rest,
> Secure, whate'er He gives, He gives the best.
> Yet when the sense of sacred presence fires,
> And strong devotion to the skies aspires,
> Pour forth thy fervours for a healthful mind,
> Obedient passions, and a will resigned;
> For love, which scarce collective man can fill;
> For patience sovereign o'er transmuted ill;
> For faith, that panting for a happier seat,
> Counts death kind Nature's signal of retreat:
> These goods for man the laws of Heaven ordain,
> These goods He grants, who grants the power to gain;
> With these celestial Wisdom calms the mind,
> And makes the happiness she does not find. *(Johnson, "The Vanity*
> *of Human Wishes," ll. 343–368)*

Johnson's carefully measured, stately rhythms and strong rhymes bespeak order and stoic calm, even while the poem asserts the supreme need to reconcile the infinite longings of the heart with the world's harsh and finite realities. Happiness does not exist outside of ourselves, like an as-yet undiscovered continent; but we can attain something like it, the poem hints, by the calm acceptance of our limits, hopeful under the eye of a mysterious but loving God.

Wordsworth's poem, in contrast, follows a regular but less rigid metrical scheme, avoids rhyme altogether, and emphasizes throughout the world's sensuous delight:

> O there is blessing in this gentle breeze,
> A visitant that, while he fans my cheek,
> Doth seem half-conscious of the joy he brings
> From the green fields, and from yon azure sky.
> Whate'er his mission, the soft breeze can come
> To none more grateful than to me; escaped
> From the vast City, where I long have pined
> A discontented Sojourner—Now free,
> Free as a bird to settle where I will.
> What dwelling shall receive me? in what vale
> Shall be my harbour? underneath what grove
> Shall I take up my home? and what clear stream
> Shall with its murmur lull me into rest?
> The earth is all before me: with a heart
> Joyous, nor scared at its own liberty,
> I look about; and should the chosen guide
> Be nothing better than a wandering cloud,
> I cannot miss my way. I breathe again;
> Trances of thought and mountings of the heart
> Come fast upon me; it is shaken off
> That burthen of my own unnatural self,
> The heavy weight of many a weary day
> Not mine, and such as were not made for me. *(Wordsworth,*
> *The Prelude, 1.1–23)*

The poet feels more than he thinks, exults rather than analyzes. He sets out from the hated City into the world of wild nature where he can breathe again, confident that he cannot fail to find his way.

Both poems are magnificent, but they work on the reader in different ways—and that difference is the result of Romanticism. Another pairing—this time in the field of music—might start with the floating melodic piano line that introduces the well-known chorale by Johann Sebastian Bach, "Jesu, Joy of Man's Desiring." Its lovely, long, regular run of eighth notes contrasts with the four-note blast that begins Ludwig von Beethoven's Fifth Symphony. This is not to say that Bach's music lacks passion or that Beethoven's lacks structure (although many early critics and musicians complained of exactly that, when attempting to play Beethoven). Rather, these two passages of music affect the ear and stir the soul in different ways—intentionally. Bach's music is sublimely beautiful and moving—and yet one is always aware of its cool, intricate structure. Beethoven's music can astonish us with its power—and yet part of its effect arises from the uneasy sense it inspires that Beethoven himself is at times barely in control of the surging passionate wave he is unleashing. Romanticism exalted, and exulted in, that sense of passionate abandon.

Romanticism, or forms of it, appeared broadly throughout Western culture, in philosophy, popular attitudes, painting, and politics, as well as poetry and music. Indeed, it is this very all-pervasiveness that makes Romanticism difficult to pin down. How can one summarize coherently a culture shared by personalities as vastly different as Charles Baudelaire (1821–1867), the decadent French poet, and Otto von Bismarck (1815–1898), the "Iron Chancellor" of the German Empire?[7] In its most general sense, Romanticism was an intellectual reaction against the 18th-century Enlightenment ideals of order, discipline, and reason. To analyze human nature scientifically, the new generation felt, was to cheapen it by reducing people to machines. The human heart, in a clinical sense, can be studied as a matter of medical science—but the passions it houses are mysterious, darkly powerful, beyond reason.

> To analyze human nature scientifically, the new generation felt, was to cheapen it by reducing people to machines. The human heart, in a clinical sense, can be studied as a matter of medical science—but the passions it houses are mysterious, darkly powerful, beyond reason.

Moreover, the Enlightened view of the world had resulted in a bloody revolution and millions of dead from Paris to Moscow. It was thus hard to justify maintaining its core tenets about the rational reform of society and the inevitability of progress. At the same time, Romanticism rejected the mechanized horrors of industrialism and the bourgeois values that championed it. Industrial capitalism, after all, gave every appearance of valuing commodities more than people, of regarding human beings merely as workers, consumers, and nothing more. For Thomas Carlyle (1795–1881), as he expresses in his essay "Signs of the Times" (1829), it cheapened existence itself by cynically squashing every humane value and attribute:

> Were we required to characterise this age of ours by any single epithet, we should be tempted to call it, not an Heroical, Devotional,

---

[7]   Baudelaire: "To say 'Romanticism' is, in essence, to say 'Modern Art.' It is to speak of intimacy, spirituality, color, the aspiration to the infinite—as expressed by every tool available to the arts." ("The Salon of 1846")

Philosophical, or Moral Age, but, above all others, the Mechanical Age. It is the Age of Machinery, in every outward and inward sense of that word; the age which, with its whole undivided might, forwards, teaches and practises the great art of adapting means to ends. Nothing is now done directly, or by hand; all is by rule and calculated contrivance. For the simplest operation, some helps and accompaniments, some cunning abbreviating process is in readiness. Our old modes of exertion are all discredited, and thrown aside. On every hand, the living artisan is driven from his workshop, to make room for a speedier, inanimate one. The shuttle drops from the fingers of the weaver, and falls into iron fingers that ply it faster.... There is no end to machinery. Even the horse is stripped of his harness, and finds a fleet firehorse yoked in his stead. Nay, we have an artist that hatches chickens by steam; the very brood-hen is to be superseded! For all earthly, and for some unearthly purposes, we have machines and mechanic furtherances; for mincing our cabbages; for casting us into magnetic sleep. We remove mountains, and make seas our smooth highway; nothing can resist us. We war with rude Nature; and, by our resistless engines, come off always victorious, and loaded with spoils.

The poem by Heinrich Heine quoted earlier, "The Silesian Weavers," imagines a group of women tending an industrial loom as they weave a death shroud for the German nation; witch-like, they weave a trio of curses into the cloth— denouncing God, the king, and the hellish industrialized country they have all become victim to.[8] To rebel against mechanization, utilitarianism, middle-class values, and bourgeois respectability was, in the early 19th century, a declaration of the freedom of the soul. To a lesser extent, Romanticism was also a nationalistic response against French predominance in the political and cultural spheres, and hence was a rebellion against the Napoleonic era.

Because of its rebellious nature, Romanticism was very much a young person's movement. Most of the writers commonly associated with Romanticism— Friedrich Schelling (1775–1854), Stendahl (Marie-Henri Beyle; 1783–1842), Lord Byron (1788–1824), Percy Bysshe Shelley (1792–1822), John Keats (1795–1821), Thomas Carlyle (1795–1881), Mary Shelley (1797–1851), Aleksandr Pushkin (1799–1837), Victor Hugo (1802–1885), Mikhail Lermontov (1814–1841)— were all under the age of forty (and many under the age of thirty) in 1815. The older Romantics were Johann Wilhelm von Goethe (1749–1832), William Blake

---

[8] Heine: "O Germany, we're spinning out your pall, / Weaving our triple curse through it all."

(1757–1827), William Wordsworth (1770–1850), Samuel Taylor Coleridge (1772–1834), and Novalis (Georg Philipp Freiherr von Hardenburg; 1772–1801). Generalization about so broad a range of writers is difficult, but they did share a tendency to privilege the instinctive, impulsive, creative spirit in humans over the rational and analytical.

The Romantic generation believed in "genius"—meaning by this word an individual's imaginative capacity, the passionate and spiritual instinct that allows us to feel connected to nature and to one another. The only true happiness people can attain in life, it follows, is to live in intimate harmony with our sensations and passions. This is not necessarily to promote hedonism; the desire to please and serve others can be as sincerely felt a passion as sexual lust or any other selfish impulse. Indeed, most of the Romantics believed that ethnic and cultural groups possessed a kind of collective genius—a shared spiritual intimacy that allows members of a race to understand one another intuitively.

This sense of cultural cohesion strongly influenced a development later in the century, nationalism, when native groups broken apart artificially by the Treaty of Vienna struggled to reunite. They sought a world of organic states brought to spiritual perfection by their unique identities. The German Romantic philosopher Johann Gottlieb Fichte (1762–1814) put it thus, in his "Address to the German Nation" in 1806:

Encountering Wild Nature   A work by Theodore Chasseriau (1855) depicting Macbeth and Banquo as they encounter the three witches, in Shakespeare's *Macbeth*.

Men who speak the same language are joined to each other by Nature herself, through countless invisible bonds, long before any human art begins; such men understand one another and can always make themselves understood with perfect clarity; they belong together, and they possess a single, indivisible nature. . . . Only when a [united] people is left to itself, so that it can create and develop in harmony with its own unique genius, and only when every individual within each group develops himself in accord with that shared genius—while also in harmony with his own individual genius—then, and only then, does the divine creative spirit manifest itself as it ought.

To remain in contact with the intuitive, passionate self—whether the individual or the collective self—was the only guarantee of a satisfying life to the Romantics. Life should be mysterious, at least to some extent. Reason is a tool to be deployed whenever needed, they felt, but it does not define humanity; to those who allow Reason to dictate their entire view of life and regard every activity and observation as an opportunity for analysis, the Romantics respond with an urgent alarm to wake up from their methodical dullness before they effectively turn into machines themselves.

The dangers were many, and they threatened all of society. "Only the material, the immediately practical, not the divine and spiritual, is important to us," wrote Carlyle. "The infinite, absolute character of Virtue has passed into a finite, conditional one; it is no longer a worship of the Beautiful and Good, but a calculation of the Profitable. . . . Our true Deity is Mechanism." Industrialization not only brought penury and suffering to millions at the bottom of the economic scale, it also cheapened everyone's lives by reducing them to a mechanical, bureaucratic, institutionalized monotony. When the machines take over, the Romantics urged, our souls die.

WHO, WHAT, WHERE

capitulations	industrial revolution
Congress of Vienna	Romanticism

SUGGESTED READINGS

Primary Sources

Babbage, Charles. *On the Economy of Machinery and Manufactures.*

Carlyle, Thomas. "Signs of the Times."

Engels, Friedrich. *The Condition of the Working Class in England in 1844.*

Ricardo, David. *On the Principles of Political Economy and Taxation.*

Anthologies

Breckman, Warren. *European Romanticism: A Brief History with Documents* (2007).

Frader, Laura Levine. *The Industrial Revolution: A History in Documents* (2006).

Wu, Duncan, ed. *Romanticism: An Anthology* (2005).

Studies

Allen, Robert. *The British Industrial Revolution in Global Perspective* (2008).

Berend, Iván. *History Derailed: Central and Eastern Europe in the Long Nineteenth Century* (2003).

Bilenky, Serhiy. *Romantic Nationalism in Eastern Europe: Russian, Polish, and Ukrainian Political Imaginations* (2012).

Burnette, Joyce. *Gender, Work, and Wages in Industrial Revolution Britain* (2008).

Clark, Gregory. *A Farewell to Alms: A Brief Economic History of the World* (2008).

Cohen, Deborah. *Household Gods: The British and Their Possessions* (2006).

Crump, Thomas. *A Brief History of the Age of Steam: The Power That Drove the Industrial Revolution* (2007).

Flanders, Judith. *Inside the Victorian Home: A Portrait of Domestic Life in Victorian England* (2005).

Holmes, Richard. *The Age of Wonder: How the Romantic Generation Discovered the Beauty and Terror of Science* (2009).

Hudson, Pat. *The Industrial Revolution* (2007).

Landes, David S. *The Unbound Prometheus: Technological Change and Industrial Development in Western Europe from 1750 to the Present* (2003).

McLane, Maureen N. *Romanticism and the Human Sciences: Poetry, Population, and the Discourse of the Species* (2006).

Mokyr, Joel. *The Gifts of Athena: Historical Origins of the Knowledge Economy* (2004).

Pollard, Lisa. *Nurturing the Nation: The Family Politics of Modernizing, Colonizing, and Liberating Egypt, 1805–1923* (2005).

Pomeranz, Kenneth. *The Great Divergence: China, Europe, and the Making of the Modern World Economy* (2001).

Richardson, Alan. *British Romanticism and the Science of the Mind* (2005).

Sunderland, David. *Social Capital, Trust, and the Industrial Revolution, 1780–1880* (2007).

Swade, Doron. *The Difference Engine: Charles Babbage and the Quest to Build the First Computer* (2002).

Weightman, Gavin. *Industrial Revolutionaries: The Making of the Modern World, 1776–1914* (2009).

Wrigley, E. A. *Energy and the English Industrial Revolution* (2010).

For additional resources, including maps, primary sources, visuals, web links, and quizzes, please go to **www.oup.com/us/backman.**

The Birth of Modern Politics

1815–1848

The diplomats who convened at the Congress of Vienna (1814–1815) did more than redraw the map of Europe. They also tried to turn back time by returning European politics to the familiar rule of kings. The high idealism of the French Revolution, they felt, had resulted in nothing to recommend it. What was needed was to reestablish an older tradition that, while perhaps not perfect, did at least have the benefit of stability in its favor. They feared the revolutionary virus and a country's capacity to wreak havoc on its neighbors—two dangers associated with France. Hoping to contain and eradicate both, they crafted a long series of decrees, treaties, and protocols. These agreements created a new balance of power between the nations by reconfiguring international borders and by introducing a measure of constitutional government under royal leadership.

CIVIL UNREST IN THE GREATER WEST, 1819-1831

They also brought about a philosophical division between conservatism and liberalism, the two sets of beliefs that would dominate most of European political development for the next two centuries. By midcentury, however, both views were challenged by social upheavals and by Marxism, a new philosophy of history and revolution. And none of these fully encompassed changes in family life and the budding rights of women.

◀ **Revolutionary Fervor** A sacred call to "Brotherhood" inspires the people from all Europe in their march against monarchy, privilege, and social hierarchy. To Karl Marx, the rebellions of 1848 offered the promise of worker solidarity; to his dismay, nationalist passions got in the way.

- Conservatism in Power
- Royalism and Nationalism
- The Moral Component of Conservatism
- The Challenge of Liberalism
- Industrial Capitalism and Its Critics
- The Real Revolution of 1848
- Karl Marx and Revolution
- The Collapse of the "Concert of Europe"
- Women and the Cult of Domesticity
- Popular Magazines and the Novel

CHAPTER OUTLINE

CONSERVATISM IN POWER

The restoration of monarchies was the fundamental strategy of the diplomats. This is hardly surprising, since the royal families driven from power by Napoleon had spent the intervening years plotting their return. Complicating matters, though, was the fact that many of the dynasties created by Bonaparte—such as the new Duchy of Warsaw and the Kingdom of Piedmont-Sardinia—had acquired a certain amount of popular support. Representatives of five major powers dominated the **Congress of Vienna**: Austria, Britain, France, Prussia, and Russia. Further complicating matters was the new political division between liberalism and conservatism.

The main figure of the Congress, though, was Klemens von Metternich (1773–1859), an Austrian aristocrat and the chief diplomat for the Habsburg emperor. Metternich had been born in the age and social milieu of absolutism and aristocratic privilege, and throughout his long and active life he never wavered in his conviction that the people of Continental Europe were not ready for democracy. He did not disagree with democracy in principle, but believed that it worked only in certain highly limited circumstances. Above all, Metternich insisted, a politically stable democratic society arose only from gradual, evolutionary change in political structures. The radical surgery represented by political revolution was guaranteed to fail and to bring misery to any society that attempts it. (Metternich met Edmund Burke briefly in 1794, during a visit to England; the men took an immediate, instinctive liking to one another.)

The issue for Metternich was not the desire of the powerful to maintain their status but the impatience of revolutionaries who believed they could pass over periods of organic growth that were in fact essential before democracy could begin. Metternich wrote in his *Memoirs*:

> The nature of Man is unchanging. The principal needs of any society are always and ever shall be the same; any differences that appear to exist between human societies are simply the result of the varying influences (different climates, different fertility of soil, existence as an island as

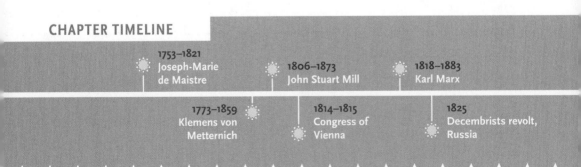

CHAPTER TIMELINE

1753–1821
Joseph-Marie
de Maistre

1806–1873
John Stuart Mill

1818–1883
Karl Marx

1773–1859
Klemens von
Metternich

1814–1815
Congress of
Vienna

1825
Decembrists revolt,
Russia

opposed to a continental territory, etc.) that Nature has effected upon them. Such influences undoubtedly have consequences far beyond the fundamental material realities of life: they can establish and shape unique needs of the most advanced kind, and can even determine the laws of a society and influence the development of its religion. . . . It is true of institutions as well; their origins are frequently obscure, but they then progress through stages of evolution until they reach a developmental peak, only at last to decay. Like Man himself, and following the same natural laws, they have a period of infancy, then of youth, then of full adult vigor and intelligence, then of decline. But throughout this natural process they retain at all times two key elements that never relinquish or see a diminution of their everlasting power—namely, the dictates of religious and social morality, and the limits established by geography.

Conservatism thus values tradition and stability above the individual. As Metternich saw it, it was realism, pure and simple, a common-sense recognition that human life takes place within a physical and cultural geography to which it must adapt. Not all things are possible, and therefore to desire all things is impractical. Change is of course possible, but only when it comes about gradually.

Although the conservatives carried the day at Vienna and remained in power throughout Europe for most of the next thirty years, not everyone shared their dream of return to a stable past. In the first place, these others argued, the stable old order revered by conservatives had been neither stable nor ordered. The most wretched misery, confusion, and resentment had always roiled just beneath the surface. It was merely that the aristocrats had paid no attention to any of it until the revolutionaries took their privileges away. Besides, a monopoly of privileges by social elites does not constitute a cultural tradition, or at least not a tradition that is worth preserving. What the opponents of the Treaty of Vienna wanted, therefore, was a new alternative, a society built upon a different notion. Liberalism—as this opposing political view came to be called—assumed the intrinsic goodness of all

1830
Conservatives lose power in Britain; uprisings throughout Europe.

1838
Beginning of Chartist movement

1857
Matrimonial Causes Act (Britain)

1834
New Poor Law

1848
Rebellions throughout Europe; publication of *The Communist Manifesto*

1861
Mrs. Beeton's Book of Household Management

Diplomats at the Congress of Vienna in 1815   To a man, they were all members of their countries' aristocracies, and the Treaty they produced reflected that fact.

people and argued that people, if left to manage their own lives, would choose what is good, honorable, and fair. Liberals called therefore for civil liberties, equality under the law, the right to vote, and a free market economy.

Conservatism and liberalism alike were newly coined words. The word conservatism appeared in English for the first time in 1835. The adjective "conservative" dates back to Chaucer, but it was used in a political sense beginning only in 1830 when it appeared in an article by John W. Croker (1780–1857) in the *Quarterly Review*: "attached to the Tory, and which might with more propriety be called the Conservative, party." The word "liberalism" was coined in 1819 by Lady Morgan (Sydney Owenson), when she wrote admiringly of a friend that "he is worthy of a conversion to Liberalism."[1]

Croker, an Irish statesman and member of the British Parliament, is best remembered for a blisteringly hostile review he wrote of the poem "Endymion," by John Keats. So ferociously did Croker attack the poem that Keats's fellow poet Lord Byron quipped that it may have accounted for Keats's early death. This from Byron's *Don Juan*, canto XI:

> John Keats, who was killed off by one critique,
> Just as he really promised something great,

---

[1]   John Henry Newman on religion, in his *Apologia Pro Vita Sua*: "The more serious thinkers among us are used . . . to regard the spirit of Liberalism as the characteristic of the destined Antichrist."

If not unintelligible,—without Greek,—
Contrived to talk about the gods of late,
Much as they might have been supposed to speak.
Poor fellow! His was an untoward fate.
'Tis strange the mind, that fiery particle,
Should let itself be snuff'd out by an article.

Of course, not just the vocabulary of politics was changing. The 19th century crackled with intellectual energy as people from Dublin to Istanbul, from Lisbon to Moscow, struggled to find new ways to order civic life. The profoundest and most intriguing drama of the age came not from the political struggles between monarchists, conservatives, liberals, socialists, and anarchists (to choose just five of the leading factions across the continent). It was the intellectual wrestling between the emerging new political traditions and developments in economics, science, philosophy, art, and religion. Like a child's kaleidoscope that changes shape with every turn of the wrist, the cultural landscape of Western civilization shifted, and was forced to shift, with every new development in the understanding of the world, the human heart, and the human mind. Like other creatively chaotic periods in history—the era of Second Temple Judaism, for instance, or post–Dark Age Greece, or the Europe of the 14th and 15th centuries—the 19th century demanded the thinking through of everything afresh. To a surprising degree, we are still engaged in their struggles.

> Like a child's kaleidoscope that changes shape with every turn of the wrist, the cultural landscape of Western civilization shifted, and was forced to shift, with every new development in the understanding of the world, the human heart, and the human mind.

ROYALISM AND NATIONALISM

The English educator Thomas Arnold (1795–1842) wrote in a letter to a friend in 1840 that "the principle of Conservatism has always appeared to me to be not only foolish, but to be actually *felo de se* [an attack upon itself]: it destroys what it loves, because it will not mend it." None of those who attended the Vienna congress would have agreed—or would have dared to say so, even if they did. One conviction dominated the assembly: only strong centralized governments, guided by noble traditions, served by professionalized bureaucracies, and backed by large national armies, could pull Europe back from the brink of disaster. But an entirely new and urgent issue presented itself, and it worked against the neo-royalist platform of the congress: the need to industrialize, and to do so quickly. Industrialization required investment and entrepreneurship, and the people most interested in entering the new economy demanded more—recognition of the rights of personal property, a role in shaping government policies, and a relatively free market. Capitalism in the new era existed to serve itself first. The government benefited only secondarily from taxation, which provided it with reliable revenue but without impeding innovation and economic growth.

The congress kept the two aims of strong monarchical government and an industry-friendly economy in sight, but did so to the exclusion of other considerations. When the diplomats put their pens to the map of Europe, they took into account royal desires, military capabilities, industrial resources, access to markets and harbors, and agricultural potential. The so-called Holy Alliance of the five major powers represented at Vienna swore to support one another:

> Any state which undergoes a change of government due to revolution by that fact alone ceases to be a member of the European Alliance. . . . And if on account of that change other states are threatened, the European Powers bind themselves, by peaceful means or if necessary by arms, to force the guilty state back into the bosom of the Great Alliance.

All this produced a sprawl of states that were roughly equal to one another in military and economic potential (see Map 18.1). States thus existed in a balance of power that would discourage any one state from provoking its neighbor. To an extent the congress succeeded, since Europe avoided international war until 1860.

However, the congress failed, or refused, to consider a critical desire of the mass populations, the desire for nationalism. Most wanted to unite along ethnic lines and thereby create nations that expressed ethnic and national *genius*—the collective consciousness of a distinct culture. The lines drawn in Vienna dismembered such desires. The Polish people, for example, were forced into an unnatural division, with their people dispersed between Prussia, Russia, and Austria-Hungary. The Italians, politically riven since the end of the Roman Empire, remained divided into a dozen principalities. For nearly fifty years, Europe's reformers looked back at the Congress of Vienna as a gathering of callous reactionary elites parceling out the family silver to one another, while the legitimate desires of the people were crushed.

The policies of the new regimes were indeed conservative. They restored the royal families to power in Austria-Hungary, France, Prussia, Russia, and Spain; they also restored a dozen lesser princes to small buffer-zone states between the major powers. The returned monarchs quickly brought back all the facets of absolutism that they could get away with. Austria's Franz I (r. 1804–1835), for example, censored every medium of public communication and set up elaborate networks

MAP 18.1   Europe in 1815

of spies and informants in order to stamp out any hint of radicalism.[2] France's
Louis XVIII (r. 1814–1824) abolished the Estates General and established in its
place a two-chambered legislature made up of a Chamber of Peers (the aristocracy) and the Chamber of Deputies. Membership in the latter was restricted to
the wealthiest bourgeois, those most likely to inaugurate France's industrial development. Prussia's Friedrich Wilhelm III (r. 1797–1840) gained territories in
the 1815 settlement, especially the early industrial centers of the Ruhr valley in

---

[2]   A somber, brooding personality, he was Franz I of Austria but Franz II of the Holy Roman Empire. That
    old empire, however, was dissolved and carved up in the 1815 accords.

the Rhineland and Westphalia, making Prussia for a while the leading German state in Europe. But he also cracked down sharply on any form of rebellion or demand for reform. In Spain, Ferdinando VII (r. 1814–1833) nullified the liberal constitution drawn up in 1812 by the Napoleonic regime, reinstated the Inquisition, imprisoned the leaders of the Spanish Parliament, and declared a return to divine-right absolutism. Even dismembered Italy made several attempts to overthrow the restored regimes, the largest occurring in 1821.

Popular opposition to conservatism resulted in numerous crackdowns. In 1817, for example, amid celebrations to mark the three hundredth anniversary of Martin Luther's rebellion against the Catholic Church, university students in Wartburg demanded a loosening of government controls over education. They ended up being chased and clubbed by police, and the governments of the German Confederation imposed strict new censorship regulations over student publications. They installed overt and covert surveillance networks on campuses everywhere, with commissioners whose job was to preserve the ideological stability of the universities.

Lord Byron   The great Romantic poet Lord Byron (1788-1824), portrayed in fanciful Turkish garb by Thomas Phillips in 1813 after his return to England from a two years' trip to the continent and as far east as Constantinople. After publishing the first volume of Childe Harold's *Pilgrimage*, as he put it, "I awoke one morning and found myself famous." For the rest of his short life Byron was a famous for his scandalous love-life as he was for his poetry. In his last two years, however, he dedicated himself to as great cause: the liberation of Greece from Ottoman rule. He died at Missolonghi, while leading a rebel band on a campaign to attack Lepanto.

In 1821, Greek patriots rose up against the Ottoman Turks, whose control over Greece had been reconfirmed at Vienna. When the Russian tsar Aleksandr I (r. 1801–1825) sent troops to aid the rebels—Turkey's loss being Russia's gain—the conservative alliance pressed Russia to stop. All official aid to the Greeks was indeed halted, but by this point, under the influence of Romanticism, popular sentiment across Europe had swung strongly in favor of the Greek cause. When the poet Lord Byron popularized the Greek drive for independence with his own personal heroics, public pressure on the Ottomans and their conservative supporters increased; Greece subsequently won its independence in 1828. The ruins of the Parthenon became a symbol of that struggle. Between 1801 and 1812 the former British ambassador to Greece, Thomas Bruce, the Earl of Elgin, under an agreement with the Ottoman government, removed a large number of statues and marble friezes from the Parthenon in Athens, shipped them to London, and sold them to the British government. These "Elgin Marbles," once cleaned and secured in the British Museum, were enormously popular but controversial. The Greek government, formally established and internationally recognized as of 1830, denied that Lord Elgin's supposed authorization to take the sculptures was genuine, insisted that the Ottoman government had had no right to allow such a thing anyway, and demanded the Elgin Marbles' immediate return to Greece. Nearly two hundred years later, they are still pressing their case.

In Spain, the continued presence of antiroyalists inspired a new wave of repressive measures. These culminated, in 1823, with over two hundred thousand French troops being sent into the country in defense of the Bourbon dynasty. In Russia, the death of Aleksandr I in 1825 triggered an attempt to create a liberal government by a group of rebels known as the Decembrists. The new tsar, Nicholas I, put them down with great severity and inaugurated the most conservative government in all of the West. The new century seemed off to a poor start.

THE MORAL COMPONENT OF CONSERVATISM

Liberal-minded people, including historians, tend to portray conservatism as a reactionary movement. They see it as an effort by elites to retain their privileges at the expense of common people, common sense, and natural progress. There is something to be said for that view of the post-Vienna crowd, but in the end it is neither accurate nor just. A core of strong ideas lay at the heart of conservatism—ideas that deserve to be taken seriously. Many of those ideas can be traced back to Edmund Burke's *Reflections on the Revolution in France*, which is commonly regarded as one of the foundational texts of political conservatism. Another important source for conservatism was the *Essay on the Generative Principle of Political Institutions* by the French-Savoyard diplomat Joseph-Marie de Maistre (1753–1821).

> More so than liberalism, conservatism has a philosophical basis, one that emerges from a central ethical question: How should people live? In particular, how should people live when living together?

More so than liberalism, conservatism has a philosophical basis, one that emerges from a central ethical question: How should people live? In particular, how should people live when living together? Conservatism recognizes the rights of individuals, but also the responsibilities that individuals have toward one another. It emphasizes the mutual duties that bind us together and create a cohesive society; in a conflict between individual desires and social requirements, the claims of society reign supreme. Those social claims have any number of origins— cultural tradition, religious conviction, economic requirement, and political or social security, among them; and any successful and legitimate government must work within the parameters established by them. These forces are perhaps not as immutable as a mountain range, but they can hardly be ignored.

Conservatism thus values traditions—including religion, established norms of morality, and social continuity. Its ethical goal is the preservation of the group rather than the gratification of the individual. As its name suggests, conservatism *conserves* something, preserves it, and desires its continued existence: and the "it" is, in a word, tradition. Burke makes the point:

> If civil society be the offspring of convention, that convention must be its law. That convention must limit and modify all the descriptions of constitution which are formed under it. Every sort of legislative, judicial, or executory power are its creatures. They can have no being in any other state of things. . . . Government is not made in virtue of natural rights, which may and do exist in total independence of it. Government is a contrivance of human wisdom to provide for human wants. Men have a right that these wants should be provided for by this wisdom. Among these wants is to be reckoned the want, out of civil society, of a sufficient restraint upon their passions. Society requires not only that the passions of individuals should be subjected, but that even in the mass and body, as well as in the individuals, the inclinations of men should frequently be thwarted, their will controlled, and their passions brought into subjection. This can only be done by a power out of themselves. . . . But as the liberties and the restrictions vary with times and circumstances, and admit of infinite modifications, they cannot be settled upon any abstract rule; and nothing is so foolish as to discuss them upon that principle.
>
> To avoid therefore the evils of inconstancy and versatility . . . we have consecrated the state, that no man should approach to look into its defects or corruptions but with due caution; that he should never dream of beginning its reformation by its subversion; that he should approach to the faults of the state as to the wounds of a father, with pious awe and trembling solicitude. . . . Society is indeed a contract. Subordinate contracts for objects of mere occasional interest may be dissolved at pleasure—but the state ought not to be considered as nothing better than a partnership agreement in a trade of pepper and coffee, calico or tobacco, or some other such low concern, to be taken up for a little temporary interest, and to be dissolved by the fancy of the parties. It is to be looked on with other reverence; because it is not a partnership in things subservient only to the gross animal existence of a temporary and perishable nature. It is a partnership in all science; a partnership in all art; a partnership in every virtue, and

in all perfection. As the ends of such a partnership cannot be obtained in many generations, it becomes a partnership not only between those who are living, but between those who are to be born. *(Reflections on the Revolution in France)*

Similarly, Joseph-Marie de Maistre emphasized the organic nature of authentic political constitutions, which he saw as the by-product of social development, rather than the creation of human minds:

The more we study the role of human agency in the development of political constitutions, the more convinced we become that it plays the smallest of roles and is in fact a mere tool [of the larger social development]. To my mind there remains no reason to doubt the absolute truth of these four propositions: first, that the basic principles underlying all political constitutions exist prior to the laws themselves; second, that any [legitimate and enduring] constitutional law is, and must be, the natural development or sanction of a pre-existing, though unwritten, right; third, that the most essential, intrinsically constitutional, and fundamental rights are those which remain unwritten—and indeed cannot be put in written form without endangering the state; and fourth, that the inherent weakness and vulnerability of any constitution is directly proportional to the extent that it exists in written form. *(Essay on the Conservative Principle of Political Institutions)*

Conservatism does not, on the whole, deny the need for change, but it is deeply skeptical of humans' ability to create entire new systems of religious belief, economic policy, political action, and social order. Such things, conservatives maintain, require time-tested, gradual development. As Burke had emphasized, revolutionary passions are ultimately self-defeating and leave misery in their wake. Napoleon's career was not one of tragic failure but of stupidly predictable failure, since what he had tried to accomplish was not natural. His downfall therefore did not result from his having been corrupted by power but from his having been a revolutionary in the first place. Conservatism appealed, and still appeals, to minds inclined to accept that the world has its own ways and that our abilities to reshape it to our liking are limited. The world as it actually exists is not egalitarian. Attributes like talent, intelligence, skill, beauty, wealth, and social position are simply not dealt out in equal measures to all people; hierarchies exist everywhere in nature and are, therefore, natural. Egregious abuses of privilege ought of course to be opposed. But opposition to hierarchy itself, and not just to its occasional abuses, is unnatural, historically uninformed, and philosophically indefensible.

The conservative governments of the early 19th century hardly wished to halt the course of history. Rather, they wanted to insure that the shock of industrialization did not obliterate all that was good and necessary in the European tradition. For there was no doubt about the need to industrialize. The process had begun before the signatures were dry on the Treaty of Vienna. But industrial capitalism seemed to conflict with the traditional society championed by the conservatives, since it valued individual enterprise and innovation. Capitalism depends on the freedom of capital and labor to move, the breaking of old customs and institutions, and the cool, calculating mentality of business—ledgers, inventories, market forces, interest rates, supply routes, tax incentives. The challenge was to achieve the economic benefits of industrial development without jettisoning the values—king, country, church, tradition—of the old order.

Consider, for example, the vast numbers of urban poor. Since the industrial economy profited from the enormous surplus of available labor, factory owners had no incentive to alleviate suffering—at least not until the social unrest created by their misery affected the workplace. The conservative governments recognized the need for public support for the poor, but tried to tailor these welfare programs in ways that would return the indigent to village societies. According to the Poor Law, originally enacted in England in the 16th century, a welfare

A New Institution but an Old Order   John Croker is credited with coining the term 'Conservatism.' He also established a British institution that came to be closely associated with it—the Athenaeum Club. Originally intended as a quasi-academic club—a club for men "of eminence in science, literature, the arts, and public service," according to house rules—it soon attracted British peers, Anglican bishops, and Cabinet members. It admitted its first female member in 2002.

recipient received a monthly payment in the parish where he was born. The idea behind this plan was that the traditional networks of family, friends, church, and local squire would assume the responsibility of tending to his or her needs; the government's role was in essence to complement, but not to replace, traditional and natural methods of caring for the poor.

The moral component of conservatism had a powerful appeal. The role of government, as conservatives saw it, was to maintain and support a moral life, and they opposed efforts to insert the state into roles best left to individuals and the organic communities to which they belong. The obligation to aid the poor is immediate and personal, conservatives maintained: if I am aware of a family in my neighborhood that is in dire need of help, then I have a personal duty to come to its aid if I can. To hold that the government ought to provide aid for all the indigent is foolhardy, for it is the most indirect, inefficient, and impersonal way of bringing assistance where it is needed. It is also morally wrong, since it means my passing along the problem to someone else. In its insistence on local solutions to local problems, and on personal responsibility instead of government initiative, conservatism appeals to the desire for moral behavior and social connection.

THE CHALLENGE OF LIBERALISM

As strong as conservatism's appeal was, it lost ground to the steady opposing pull of liberalism. The second of the three main political traditions of the modern West (socialism being the third), **liberalism** regards the primary function of government to be the promotion of freedom instead of order. By 1830, as industrialization rushed ahead, the conservatives' hold on government weakened across Europe, and they even lost control in several nations. Rapid urbanization on the Continent made it difficult to contain and suppress the demands for social reform and political participation. These demands from the laboring population coalesced into the liberal alternative.

True to its name, liberalism has proven more changeable over the last two centuries, freely discarding some values while taking on new convictions, as conditions warranted. However, it has retained its dedication to freeing individuals from undue control. If conservatism rests on the foundation of preserving the best of society's past, liberalism, in general, seeks to liberate individuals from the strictures of inequality, injustice, and intolerance. As John Stuart Mill (1806–1873), liberalism's answer to Edmund Burke, wrote in a letter to a newspaper, "A Liberal is he who looks forward

> If conservatism rests on the foundation of preserving the best of society's past, liberalism, in general, seeks to liberate individuals from the strictures of inequality, injustice, and intolerance.

for his principles of government; a [conservative] looks backward" (*Morning Star*, July 6, 1865). Compare a cutting comment from a prominent conservative periodical: "What lurking conspirator against the quiet of his native government . . . has failed to ask and receive the protection of our Liberals?" (*Blackwood's Magazine*, February 1828). Or this retort from a Canadian newspaper of 1832: "We shall first notice the slanderous imputations cast upon the Liberals, that they are a discontented set of men, ever on the watch to find occasion of complaint and clamour" (*The Liberal*, September 20, 1832).

At least from the time of John Locke in the late 17th century, liberals have asserted the fundamental equality and goodness of human beings:

> To understand political power right, and derive it from its original, we must consider, what state all men are naturally in, and that is, a state of perfect freedom to order their actions, and dispose of their possessions and persons, as they think fit, within the bounds of the law of nature, without asking leave, or depending upon the will of any other man.
>
> A state also of equality, wherein all the power and jurisdiction is reciprocal, no one having more than another; there being nothing more evident, than that creatures of the same species and rank, promiscuously born to all the same advantages of nature, and the use of the same faculties, should also be equal one amongst another without subordination or subjection, unless the lord and master of them all should, by any manifest declaration of his will, set one above another, and confer on him, by an evident and clear appointment, an undoubted right to dominion and sovereignty. (*Second Treatise of Civil Government, ch. 2*)

If people are individually good and equal, then the good society is achieved by leaving them alone as much as possible, to act freely. Any action by government that would curtail individual freedom, then, must be justified by extraordinary argument, since it upsets the natural good ordering of the world. To take the example of the conservative Poor Law, liberalism finds it unacceptable. In tying the welfare recipient to his home parish, the law restricts his freedom of movement, his freedom to seek employment or education, and his freedom to determine his own fate. After the liberals came to power in 1830, they enacted the new Poor Law of 1834, so that welfare payments followed the recipient if he chose to move from one location to another, in search of work or for any other reason. It was a costlier and less efficient system of administration, to be sure—but it maximized the citizen's freedom to act.

Part of the difficulty for liberalism has been the very nature of freedom: it requires identifying what it is we are free from. The debate has beset political thinking ever since Thomas Hobbes made his arguments in favor of absolutism in the early 17th century. As formulated in the 19th century, liberalism meant above all freedom from control by government. This is hardly surprising, given Europe's experience of hierarchy, privilege, and monarchical tyranny, and considering that the strongest support for liberalism came from the new middle class, the **bourgeoisie**. Their newfound economic muscle depended precisely on individual freedom and the rights of property. Their position is easily expressed: so long as one does not coerce others, one ought to be left alone to do what one pleases with one's own property. Society has no right to force an entrepreneur to manage his property in a certain way, just as the entrepreneur has no right to force his workers to accept low pay or miserable working conditions. Freedom of choice is all. A worker who does not like the pay or demands of any given workplace is free to walk away from it and pursue a better situation elsewhere. Better yet, he can cultivate his own entrepreneurial goals. Moreover, any worker who *is* willing to accept a job at low pay, harsh hours, and miserable conditions should be free to do so.

For this reason, 19th-century liberalism championed **laissez-faire** capitalism, or capitalism without government intervention: a deregulated economy was the only way to insure the freedom of every individual to do as he saw fit. Hence liberals opposed wage- and working-condition regulations, fought against high taxes, and resisted the idea of labor unions, even while they encouraged the free movement of the poor who received government assistance. That free movement, of course, is part of what guaranteed the surplus of labor that kept costs at rock-bottom levels.

The Bourgeoisie   A group of French bourgeoisie riding in a horse-drawn tram, 1880.

In 1840, legislation was proposed that would reduce factory workdays from twelve hours to ten. In response, a public-relations campaign insisted that government regulation of the marketplace was ill-considered and harmful:

> There are few subjects upon which more erroneous sentiments prevail, than as to the proper objects and limits of legislation. Thus, in our attempts to improve, by legislation, the condition of the poor, we have not only multiplied the number, but reduced them to a state of degradation before unknown. By our poor laws and our charities, we have pauperised, and almost ruined the country. . . . In our commerce and manufactures also, the effects of legislation have been equally mischievous. By our well meant, but injudicious attempt to foster and protect, we have constantly been driving capital from productive into unproductive channels, encouraging the smuggler, checking our commerce, and stunting our manufactures; and our efforts to procure to the operatives a fair remuneration for their labor, has always ended in a reduction of their wages, or in depriving them altogether of employment. Thus, after repeated failures, we have been, in some degree, schooled into knowledge, and have purchased our experience at the usual price. Modern legislation is indeed improving, though the improvement is rather of a negative nature, and consists not so much in passing better laws, as in repealing bad ones. It may be confidently predicted that all further improvement will be of the same kind, and thus, in matters of commerce and manufactures at least, we shall approach continually to a condition of complete and unrestricted freedom. *(London, "Battle of the 10-Hour Day Continues")*

Liberalism has tended to see the world as in constant flux, in contrast to the emphasis on time-honored customs and institutional structures found in conservatism. Since the world is continually changing, the only sensible way of ordering it is to privilege meritocracy, opportunity, and innovation. Let creative minds create, without censorship; let individuals determine their own political fates, through free elections; let people with ideas and drive be free to exercise them and reap the benefits of their success, in free markets.

INDUSTRIAL CAPITALISM AND ITS CRITICS

It was not the plight of the urban poor under industrial capitalism, therefore, that led to the political defeat of the conservatives in 1830. Instead, it was the plight of the entrepreneurs, who wanted to free the new economy from what they regarded as the archaic paternalism of the aristocratic order. The solid middle class of the 19th century joined forces politically with another emerging group, skilled laborers—those whose technical expertise with new machinery allowed them to rise to higher wage levels. Together, they demanded greater clout through the extension of **suffrage**—the right to vote.

In England, the process occurred peacefully, with the conservatives voted out in 1830. In France, by contrast, it took yet another popular rebellion to pull the nobles from power. The reigning Bourbon king, Charles X (r. 1824–1830), had made himself hated by dissolving the liberal-leaning parliament, ordering new elections, and rigging them so that only candidates he had preapproved could win. His timing was rotten, since France had just suffered through a miserable winter and shortages had doubled the cost of most foodstuffs. Spontaneous, angry food riots took places in most of the larger cities. Fearing revolutionary violence, Charles abdicated and passed the crown to his cousin Louis-Philippe (r. 1830–1848)—the last king France would ever have. He granted a new charter that doubled the number of Frenchmen who had the right to vote, but even this number still represented a mere 1 percent of the population (compared to about 8 percent

The New Voters   When the British House of Lords vetoed, in 1831, yet another draft of the Reform Bill that extended the vote to working-class men and re-drew the lines of the country's electoral districts, crowds of demonstrators took to the streets across the nation. The London protestors shown here are carefully presented as proud workers who are loyal to the monarchy.

in England). The outlook for liberal reforms in France looked bleak, except for one thing. Louis-Philippe became not just more conservative as the years went by but also more unpopular, until finally in 1848 he abdicated.[3]

Liberal-led rebellions broke out in 1830 in other parts of Europe too, although the protests failed to effect much real change. Factory workers in the German territories, for example, smashed industrial equipment and demonstrated in factory yards to protest their low pay and long hours. Disaffected Belgians (actually French-speaking Walloons) in the heavily industrialized Netherlands took to the streets and demanded better working conditions, a recognition of their ethnic and linguistic identity, and a new constitution. Disaffected university students and junior military officers campaigned for reform in Poland, seeking a reunification of all Polish people (divided by the Treaty of Vienna among Prussia, Austria, and Russia) and a national constitution—to which Russia responded with an armed attack.

Spain's clash between conservatives and liberals was also violent. The restored Bourbon king, Ferdinand VII (r. 1813–1833), was a diehard absolutist who made only the mildest of compromises with constitutionalism. When he died without a male heir, his throne passed to his daughter Isabella II (r. 1833–1868), who in her early years seemed amenable to a modest reform program. Her claim to the throne was challenged, however, by her ultraconservative pro-absolutist uncle, named Carlos—whose followers were therefore known as "Carlists." The Carlists fought bitterly to restore divine-right monarchy, the authority of the Catholic Church, and traditional society, even at the expense of economic development. Wars with the Carlists hardened Isabella's attitudes, until in her later years she herself had become a royal absolutist. Finally, in 1868, she abdicated the throne after some of her more reform-minded generals voiced their unhappiness against her drift into autocracy. Isabella had twelve children, although doubts remain to this day about their biological father. Her husband, Francisco, was widely reported to be homosexual, and Isabella publicly complained about his supposed effeminacy. She spent her last years in comfortable exile in Paris, but the struggle between Spain's conservative traditionalists and liberal constitutionalists continued into the 20th century with the bloody civil war of the 1930s.

What the reformers demanded throughout the 1830s and 1840s can be easily summarized: expanded suffrage, decreased taxes, confirmed property rights, deregulated trade and workplaces, and curtailed labor unionization. These issues served the bourgeoisie's interests. As the industrial economy developed, however, becoming more diversified and specialized, so too did the bourgeois class that

---

3 Louis-Philippe fled to England in disguise and carrying a passport identifying him as one "Mr. Smith."

promoted it. Usually only the great merchants, leading industrialists, and most prominent financiers had access to political power. The rest of the middle classes, from lesser merchants to lawyers and physicians and down to office clerks and school teachers, toiled away without any direct political influence.

Beneath the bourgeoisie was the great mass of the laborers, skilled and un-skilled, working long, rigorously enforced shifts in the factories. These came to be known as the **proletariat**—a pejorative term that derived from the Latin, and whose colloquial meaning was "those who smell." They were regarded as the lowest and most vulgar sort of humans, who contributed nothing to the better-ment of society except the next generation of workers. (The word *proletarius* in ancient Rome colloquially designated a "stunt cock," a slave whose sexual service gratified his male and female owners.) As reported in a news magazine of the time:

> The proletariat, which has not morally and physically any thing to lose, has allied itself to this revolutionary tendency.... This word, which has lately become familiar to all readers of German and French literature, signifies the lowest and poorest classes, those in fact who are totally des-titute of property. *(The Daguerreotype, October 16, 1847)*

The bourgeois reformers aimed less at alleviating the proletariat's misery than at improving the efficiency of the economy. Limiting the work week to a maximum of sixty-nine hours for workers aged fourteen to nineteen, for example, reduced the number of jobless poor who received public assistance. Funds for welfare pay-ments and housing subsidies were also redirected to workhouses, where the poor received room and board in return for long hours of unskilled drudgery.[4]

The bourgeois were not necessarily heartless or grasping, and many of them donated generously to the poor. However, much like the early conservatives, they believed that charity was a personal moral duty, not the rightful function of civil government. Many hundreds of private charitable institutions were founded in the first half of the century: orphanages, hospitals, organizations like the YMCA and the Society for the Prevention of Cruelty to Animals, medical clinics, vocational schools (called polytechnics), athletic and hygienic programs, Sunday schools, mu-sical societies, and lending libraries. The problems created by industrialism, how-ever, far outstripped the ability of private, volunteer kindness to address.

Angered by the slow pace and self-serving nature of liberal reform, the urban poor began to organize to demand swifter and more far-reaching reforms. In 1838 the London Working Men's Association drafted a "People's Charter," a petition that they circulated among laborers in city after city, ultimately collecting over six million signatures. This became known as the **Chartist movement,** and it

---

4   Charles Dickens dramatized the starvation level accommodations of the workhouses in *Oliver Twist*.

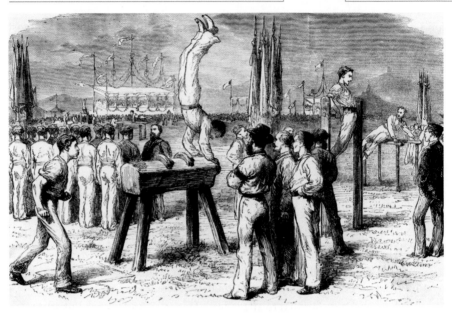

Gymnastics Class   A sketch (1872) illustrating the popular craze for athletics and fitness at the end of the 19th century in Europe. The scene shown here depicts a gymnastics festival in Bonn, Germany.

provided a model for labor protests across Europe. The Chartists made six essential demands:

1. universal suffrage (though for men only)
2. annual elections
3. secret ballots
4. elimination of the requirement to own property in order to qualify for public office
5. fair redistricting of electoral maps; and
6. guaranteed salaries for those serving in government.

Without the last, only the rich could afford to enter public service.

Chartism thereby helped to redefine liberalism. What society needed, the Chartists insisted, was not only personal freedom from undue governmental control but freedom as well from the unjust control of people's lives by unfettered capitalism. Just as the power of government needs to be checked by constitutional restraints, lest it devolve into tyranny, so too does the industrial economy require regulation. Otherwise, it will become a system of economic slavery. It took several decades for the new

> What society needed, the Chartists insisted, was not only personal freedom from undue governmental control but freedom as well from the unjust control of people's lives by unfettered capitalism.

ideas to flourish—starting with yet another round of protests, strikes, street riots, and violent clashes with states and industries.

THE REAL REVOLUTION OF 1848

After at least a decade of discontent, urban workers and the homeless poor across the Continent rose up in violent protest in 1848. With only a handful of exceptions—Britain, the Netherlands, Russia, Scandinavia, and the Ottoman Empire—every Western government confronted mass rebellion of some sort. To some critics, the wave of uprisings looked suspiciously organized, but most regarded them as spontaneous bursts of rage, with each explosion giving encouragement to the next. Demonstrators filled the streets and squares, blockaded roads, smashed factory windows and equipment, and looted and burned stores. Speeches and broadsheets proclaimed the end of political and economic elitism and called for the transfer of power to new governments chosen by full and open democratic processes.

Coming as they did in the aftermath of several consecutive crop failures and growing concern of European-wide famine, these revolts frightened everyone.[5] The French king, Louis-Philippe, had forbidden public assemblies as early as 1835, in an effort to forestall political agitation. But in 1847 the leaders among the radical reformers organized a broad network of large-scale "private banquets," at which reformers plotted their moves and incited their audiences to increase their activity. The decision in January 1848 by the French premier François Guizot (1787–1874) to suppress these banquets triggered an uprising in Paris, which in turn triggered uprisings across Europe (see Map 18.2). Guizot declared himself "an unflinching enemy of universal suffrage—I regard it as the certain ruin of democracy and liberty."

Within a matter of days the protestors had forced Louis-Philippe to abdicate, and a new constitutional republic was established (the Second Republic, in France's back-and-forth political narrative). For the president of the new government, the Republican leaders chose Louis-Napoleon, the nephew of the great emperor. He began modestly. In accepting the new post, he assured the assembly:

> I am guided by no ambition. . . . Having grown up in free countries and learned from the school of hard knocks, I will remain forever faithful to the duties [entrusted to me]. . . . I vow to devote myself entirely, unreservedly, to strengthening this Republic by guiding it to develop wise laws, honest goals, and great and noble deeds, and my greatest honor will be to hand over to whomever succeeds me, after four years in

---

[5]   Alexis de Tocqueville described France as "a society cut in half—those who possessed no property were united in envy, and those who did possess anything were united in terror."

MAP 18.2   Centers of Revolution, 1848

office, a stable government, with its liberties intact and its genuine progress assured.

Only four years later, however, Louis-Napoleon declared the Second Republic dead, restored autocracy, and took the imperial title of Napoleon III
(r. 1852–1870). Thus was born France's Second Empire.

In Italy, the uprisings took many forms. The northern city of Milan, rebelling
against Austrian rule, began the year with a popular effort to give up smoking

tobacco since the taxes on it were so onerous. The no-smoking demonstration worked too well, however: Austrian soldiers went on a retributive rampage and killed over sixty people. Outrage over the imperial response triggered unrest throughout the peninsula. In Rome, rebels assassinated the prime minister of the Papal State, causing Pope Pius IX (r. 1846–1878) to flee south, where he went into hiding with the temporarily exiled Duke of Piedmont and King Ferdinando II of Naples. Revolutionaries in Palermo succeeded briefly in forming a new government and issuing a constitution. Uprisings throughout the German-speaking territories, including Habsburg Austria, were notable for their insistence on the unification of Germany into a single state. They did not achieve it, but the crowds in Vienna did manage to force Klaus von Metternich, the chancellor, from office. Riots in Berlin resulted in the deaths of hundreds at the hands of Prussian soldiers. Despite promises from the king to introduce a liberal constitution, a conservative new legislature was put into place instead, one that proved the starting point for the career of a new military figure and diplomat, Otto von Bismarck.

The narrative of 1848 is so confusing, in part, because there were as many motives as rebels. Aristocrats feared the unbridled absolutism desired by Louis XVIII of France and Franz I of Austria; industrial capitalists opposed the undermining of property interests through taxation and regulation; urban workers rebelled against horrid work conditions and wretched pay; and the poor took to the streets to demand rescue from famine, crime, and disease. Europe's transition into a modern, developed industrial economy left everyone, it seemed, vulnerable and aggrieved. What brought on such a state of affairs? And how could a stable future be created from so much misery, distrust, and sheer rage? For the time being, most European states retreated in another brief era of law-and-order conservatism.

KARL MARX AND REVOLUTION

The first major figure to suggest an interpretation of this staggering era was a scholar-turned-journalist named Karl Marx (1818–1883). A German Jew, Marx had earned a PhD in philosophy from the University of Jena in 1841, but failed to win an academic position in Germany and turned to journalism. After he was accused of treason in 1844 for supposedly seditious criticisms of the government, Marx, who was then living in Paris with his young family, renounced his Prussian citizenship and made his way to London. Early in 1848 Marx published ***The Communist Manifesto***, coauthored with his close friend Friedrich

Title Page of the First Edition of Karl Marx's Masterpiece, *Capital: A Critique of Political Economy* (**1867**) "I assume from the start that the reader is willing to learn something new and to start thinking for himself." (Preface)

Engels (1820–1895), and shortly thereafter he returned to Germany to participate in the uprisings of that summer.

Marx returned to England in 1849, disappointed in the failure of the rebellions but confident in the eventual victory of reform. He had already laid out a general theory of history in a book called *The German Ideology* (1846), and he spent his remaining years refining his ideas and working to promote economic and social reform. He had relatively little success in his own lifetime, either as a scholar or as a political activist, but he became arguably the single most influential political thinker of the 20th century. Only then were his ideas adopted—in severely reshaped form—by communist parties around the world.

Marxism is essentially a theory about history, and like its creator it is profoundly optimistic. Like Rousseau before him and the Romantics of his own time, Marx believes in the essential goodness of human nature; it is the world that plants the seed of corruption in the heart. All human conflict is at root a conflict over things—gold, lands, animal herds, estates, inheritances, cities, tax revenues, harbors, mines, and trade routes. Clashing ideas and values are real, but secondary, and in fact are usually little more than rationalizations for the conflict over wealth.

> Like Rousseau before him and the Romantics who followed him, Marx believes in the essential goodness of human nature; it is the world that plants the seed of corruption in the heart.

Marx calls this process **historical materialism**. Economic matters, in simplest terms, are the fuel that drives history forward. In all ages, he argues, change has come about through the conflict between those who produce the bulk of society's wealth with one technology and those who produce it under alternative technologies. In a nomadic, pastoral society, for example, ownership of the animal herds decides social status and hence political power. But when that society transitions into agrarian life, a new technology of wealth production is created, namely crop farming; control of land now determines economic value and therefore social status. The conflict between these modes of existence drives the change from a tribal society governed by unwritten customs to a bureaucratic state governed by written laws and contracts (such as land deeds). The rise of manufacturing and commerce propels the development of urban life and yet another stage of historical growth, especially as the urban economy eclipses the rural economy as the main producer of aggregate wealth. Hence the development of parliaments, with power in the hands of representatives from the urban economic elite. In each case, material life shapes social existence. Liberalism's emphasis on limiting society's claims on individual wealth and property therefore creates a society of free individuals.

But liberalism, in Marx's view, makes a fundamental and grievous error: it privileges the very things that we need to do away with—individual happiness and private property. Liberal notions of justice aim to protect us from one

Historical Materialism on Vivid Display Steelworkers, idealized.
William Scott Bell (1811-1890) painted this mural at Wallington Hall,
Northumberland. A viewer can almost hear the men singing a Disneye-
sque tune as they swing their hammers in unison. No smoke, no dirt,
no misery. A little girl even sits contently by while her father nobly
toils. The coke-fueled heat coming out the furnace by which she sits
could reach 2000 degrees Fahrenheit (1200 degrees Celsius).

another, to restrict one person's ability to take or interfere with another person's
property. And this means, Marx insists, that liberalism is essentially a philosophy
of separation, whereas true human happiness consists of community, fellowship,
and shared prosperity. Once we see liberalism as it really is, we will seek to move
past it and to create a harmonious future without selfishness.

Simply put, we must show the world what it is actually fighting
over—for this, in the end, is what people need to recognize, whether
they want to or not. In order to reform society's way of thinking, we must
first help it to realize the way it is actually thinking already; we must
awaken the world from its dreamy image of itself and show its actions for
what they truly are. . . . Once we have accomplished this, the world will
see that it can actually possess what it has hitherto only dreamed of
[namely, a truly happy and stable society].

So he wrote in a letter to a friend in September 1843.

Marx saw that the motivating forces in history are economic and technological. That insight surprises few readers today, but in its time it was strikingly original. What remains controversial is Marx's conclusion: the production and distribution of wealth determines culture. Marx argues that the struggle to control the means of production determines everything about a society from its political values to its laws, religious life, morals, and intellectual outlook. The process is not even conscious—it does not need to be. Since the class that controls the dominant means of production also controls the state, it can perpetuate its position, just as it promotes its religious and moral values. The leading role in the economy played by industrial capitalists, for example, finds its political expression in the House of Commons, which represents its interest. It also finds its ideological expression in the cultural values of hard work, entrepreneurial drive, and free markets. As for religion, Marx holds that Christianity seems almost tailor-made to create a mass of docile workers: "Blessed are the poor"; suffering ennobles the soul; the affairs of this world do not really matter; reward comes in the next life; "turn the other cheek" to one's oppressors; and love one's enemies. He calls these teachings "slave morality."

> Marx argues that the struggle to control the means of production determines everything about a society from its political values to its laws, religious life, morals, and intellectual outlook. The process is not even conscious—it does not need to be.

But Marx insists that the painful cycle can be broken. Interrupting the march of capitalism will allow human altruism to emerge from its suppressed state. Indeed, the cycle is destined to be broken. The key is the transfer of economic and political power to the great mass of the proletariat.[6] That transfer culminates and concludes the historical process begun ages ago when the first nomad cut furrows in the earth and planted seeds. Marx does not, as some suggest, argue that its outcome is inevitable, but it is predictable. The interplay of economic, technological, and social forces produces the opportunities for social change; but human will and action are required to inaugurate each new development. To Marx, European capitalism in the middle of the 19th century had reached another decisive historical moment.

Since industrial capitalism, he argues, is incapable of self-reform, its death is imminent, but that death will not occur on its own. The struggle to wrest power and pass it to the workers may take a long, concerted effort—and may require force. As he wrote in *The German Ideology*:

> A revolution is required because the ruling class cannot be overthrown in any other way, but also because the working class that

---

6   It was Marx who popularized the word *proletariat*.

dislodges it needs a revolution itself—a revolution that will purge the proletariat of the accumulated [cultural] trash of its past. Only thus can the workers rebuild society.

The act of revolution, in other words, creates the revolutionaries it needs to complete its own process. Marx abhors violence and never advocates it; he calls only for labor strikes, mass demonstrations, relentless political pressure, and the like. His rhetoric is always dramatic, but a call to confrontation is not the same thing as a call to arms.

THE COLLAPSE OF THE "CONCERT OF EUROPE"

Did the uprisings of 1848 significantly alter the political or economic trajectories of Europe? After all, no governments fell from power as a result. Some writers insist that the year nevertheless marks a turning point: the severe economic and social problems catalyzed by industrialization had become impossible to ignore. One could no longer assume that the free market, left to itself, would set society along the path to a natural balance of prosperity, opportunity, and order. Henceforth, both conservatives and liberals would have to compromise their convictions with a practical commitment to economic regulation and government-sponsored social welfare. In this view, the second half of the 19th century represents a series of efforts to strike the right form of compromise.

Such writers also point to 1848 as the point of collapse of the "concert of Europe" created by the Congress of Vienna in 1815. When King Friedrich Wilhelm IV of Prussia (r. 1840–1861) was confronted with armed insurrection in Berlin, he agreed to create a national assembly for Prussia and dissolve his absolute authorities. He thus catalyzed similar settlements for all of the German territories. Moreover, debates over whether to include the ethnic Germans residing in the Austrian-Hungarian Empire brought Austria and Prussia to the brink of war. The possibility of the Habsburg Empire's ethnic Germans seceding from the megastate encouraged the nationalist hopes of the Magyars (ethnic Hungarians), Croats,

> To Marxists, the vast movement of history, like the current of a broad and powerful river, was toward the revolution of the proletariat, the destruction of capitalism, and the evolution of a new, classless society of freedom.

Slovenians, and Czechs, which the Habsburgs quelled only with extreme force. Russia quickly became involved in the dispute, which in turn ignited Turkish concerns. A regional conflict threatened to expand into an international war. The failure of the 1815 settlement was all but officially recognized by the resignation of Klemens von Metternich as the Habsburg's minister of foreign affairs in April 1848—even before most of the year's dramas had occurred.

Other writers regard 1848 not as a pivot point for European history but simply as a road sign confirming the path that Europe was already on. The rebellions and violent responses may have accelerated developments, but they did not fundamentally change the direction of history. To Marxists, the vast movement of history, like the current of a broad and powerful river, was toward the revolution of the proletariat, the destruction of capitalism, and the evolution of a new, classless society of freedom. Events like 1848 encouraged them to believe in the inevitability of **communism**. As *The Communist Manifesto* proclaims (in the English edition prepared by Engels himself):

> Hitherto, every form of society has been based, as we have already seen, on the antagonism of oppressing and oppressed classes. But in order to oppress a class, certain conditions must be assured to it under which it can, at least, continue its slavish existence. The serf, in the period of serfdom, raised himself to membership in the commune, just as the petty bourgeois, under the yoke of feudal absolutism, managed to develop into a bourgeois. The modern laborer, on the contrary, instead of rising with the progress of industry, sinks deeper and deeper below the conditions of existence of his own class. He becomes a pauper, and pauperism develops more rapidly than population and wealth. And here it becomes evident, that the bourgeoisie is unfit any longer to be the ruling class in society, and to impose its conditions of existence upon society as an over-riding law. It is unfit to rule because it is incompetent to assure an existence to its slave within his slavery, because it cannot help letting him sink into such a state, that it has to feed him, instead of being fed by him. Society can no longer live under this bourgeoisie, in other words, its existence is no longer compatible with society.
>
> The essential condition for the existence, and for the sway of the bourgeois class, is the formulation and augmentation of capital; the condition for capital is wage-labor. Wage-labor rests exclusively on competition between laborers. The advance of industry, whose involuntary promoter is the bourgeoisie, replaces the isolation of the laborers, due to competition, by their revolutionary combination, due to association. The development of Modern Industry, therefore, cuts from under its feet the very foundation on which the bourgeoisie produces and appropriates products. What the bourgeoisie, therefore, produces, above all, is its own grave-diggers. Its fall and the victory of the proletariat are equally inevitable.

The revolution of 1848 therefore accelerated historical change. Constitutions may have been jettisoned and franchises rescinded; nationalist aims were thwarted,

The Dream of Universal Brotherhood   A fanciful painting from 1848 showing the nations of Europe all marching, under a heavenly blessing, toward a statue symbolizing human rights. Note the sprawl of broken, discarded crowns and aristocratic shields in the foreground.

workers brought to heel, and the poor forced to submit. But the very success of the powerful and propertied ensured the ultimate success of the revolution. Common workers could now believe in the inevitability of victory, whether or not that victory appeared in a Marxist form, and that belief was the real revolution of 1848. The movement was only in embryonic form by midcentury, with Marx and Engels busily analyzing the workings of politics and economy in print, while organizing and rallying workers into labor unions and political factions in meeting halls. But the communist model they created eventually became the third dominating political and social vision of the modern era, after conservatism and liberalism.

WOMEN AND THE CULT OF DOMESTICITY

It was not only Marxist writers who felt that the dramas of 1848 had changed nothing or little. Millions of women across Europe smarted under new industrial cruelties and old social biases alike. They experienced a feverish jolt of optimism at the turn of the 19th century at the prospect of a reformed and enlightened society that would value them, if not as equals, at least as deserving members of society with legitimate claims, concerns, and demands. Not all were miserable, and it would be foolish to assume that social prejudice defined all of their lives.

The Enlightenment of the 18th century, nevertheless, entailed a critical reexamination of women's roles in Western life.

As it happened, few of the influential figures of the Enlightenment gave the subject of women any sustained thought. Locke, Kant, Herder, Montesquieu, Beccaria, Smith, Hume, Gibbon, and Condorcet say almost nothing about women in their published works, and most of them had little space for women in their private lives too. Diderot, who married for love, created several sympathetic female characters in his plays and novels—the best being a fictionalized portrait of his own sister in the novel *The Nun* (*La religieuse*; 1760)—but never dealt in earnest with the idea of reforming society's treatment of women. The only philosophe to discuss women in society at any length at all was Rousseau. And his views hardly gave hope to those seeking a better position for women in the Enlightened future.

By the second half of the 18th century, most women's lives had not altered significantly from what they had been a hundred years previously. Most women were legally controlled by their fathers until they married, at which point they came under the legal control of their husbands. Customs varied from country to country in regard to dowries, inheritance rights, and property ownership. Little formal education was available, except for those capable of hiring private tutors. Marriage and childbirth were the central events in most women's lives. Peasant and working-class girls usually married in their early twenties, but were considered marriageable by age sixteen; they were usually given to husbands anywhere from five to fifteen years older. By her mid-thirties an unmarried woman was considered a spinster, according to English law. By the end of the 19th century, the British government sent annual shipments of spinsters to its overseas colonies, especially to India, where they might find work as governesses or teachers.

Most women lived in or near poverty. On the Continent, perhaps one-fifth of all people, male and female, faced flat-out starvation-level poverty. Most of these were drawn to cities in search of employment, and their numbers increased under industrialism. Perhaps another 30–40 percent of the population were barely able to support themselves. They had food to survive on and a roof over their heads, but little else. Women brought in extra money by spinning, needlework, laundering, or other simple services, while remaining at home with their children—and that often meant the difference between survival and destitution for their families. One reason for their poverty was the increased cost of living. Taking account of only the basic necessities—housing, food, clothing, and fuel for cooking—the average cost of living for most Europeans increased roughly three to four times faster than wages over the entire 18th century. In Spain alone, the ratio was five to one. These dire conditions helped sustain the practice of female infanticide, despite laws forbidding it; male infants were usually killed only in cases of serious sickness or disability. When poor families could not bring themselves to euthanize infants they could not support, they handed them over instead to orphanages and workhouses.

Women formed a large segment of the workforce and indeed came to dominate certain manufactures. On average, however, they earned only about 40 percent of what male wage earners received, and efforts to unionize labor hardly helped. In fact, these efforts were driven in part by attempts to drive women from the workplace altogether, so that more men could find employment. Industrialism brought another change to family life as well—the physical separation of work space and domestic space. Throughout most of human history, the home was also where one worked—either a farm or a small shop above which the shopkeepers lived. But the factory economy now meant that one went away to the job, while home was a refuge after a long day's labor. The effort to push women out of the job market and "back into the home" thus defined the home as a woman's terrain. It

Domesticity Critiqued   A typically bleak view of family relationships by Edgar Degas (1834-1917). The Bellelli Family, shown here, depicts Degas' aunt with her husband and two daughters. The mother's formal, stiff posture and grim expression, etched sharply against a relatively blank background, contrasts with the distracted, unfocused image of the father, whose busy desk and cluttered background suggests self-involvement. The contrast between the postures of the daughters indicates their divided loyalties in a desolate scene of family alienation. Degas painted this large canvas—it measures roughly six feet by eight feet—while studying in Italy as a young man. His views on marriage never changed.

was also part of a new **cult of domesticity.** For working-class women, programs taught personal hygiene, basic literacy, and simple craftwork like sewing, basket weaving, and shoemaking.

Sex and illegitimacy ran rampant. In Europe, it has been estimated that one of every six deaths across the industrialized world resulted from sexually transmitted disease. The majority of unwed mothers were of the working class, but the fathers of their children came from every social level. Many of the problems of urban society were regarded as moral failings, as opposed to flaws in the economic or political systems. They were also widely blamed on women for making the supposedly unnatural choice of working outside the home, rather than nurturing their families.

> Sex and illegitimacy ran rampant. In urban Europe, it has been estimated that one of every six deaths across the industrialized world resulted from sexually transmitted disease.

Among middle-class women, the cult of domesticity took on even greater sentimentality. Proper society emphasized the importance of the home as a place of refuge, comfort, and nurture for hard-working husbands and fathers. Novels became the most popular genre of popular literature, overtaking poetry, and the overwhelming majority of them dealt with domestic themes: the discovery of love and its culmination in happy marriage and a cozily elegant domestic life.

POPULAR MAGAZINES AND THE NOVEL

Among the most popular new publications of the age were magazines for middle-class women like *La Belle Assemblée, Bell's Court and Fashionable Magazine Addressed Particularly to the Ladies,* and *Wives' and Widows' Gazette of Fashions,* which began to appear in large numbers in every country. These offered advice on fashions, décor, family relationships, home economics, sheet music, and dress patterns, along with serialized fiction and sentimental poetry. Also popular were guidebooks to maintaining happy, efficient, economical, and comfortable homes. The leading example, *Mrs Beeton's Book of Household Management* (1861), became one of the best-selling books of the century.[7] Isabella Beeton was only twenty-five when she published the first edition of this massive book of over 1,100 pages. (She died only four years later of a uterine infection after the birth of her fourth child; her first two had already died.) She made her purpose plain at the start:

> What moved me . . . to attempt a work like this, was the discomfort and suffering which I had seen brought upon men and women by

---

[7] Over two million copies of *Mrs Beeton's Book of Household Management* sold in the United Kingdom in ten years—more than all the novels of Charles Dickens in his lifetime, combined.

household mismanagement. I have always thought that there is no more fruitful source of family discontent than a housewife's badly-cooked dinners and untidy ways. Men are now so well served out of doors—at their clubs, well-ordered taverns, and dining houses—that in order to compete with the attractions of these places, a mistress must be thoroughly acquainted with the theory and practice of cookery, as well as be perfectly conversant with all the other arts of making and keeping a comfortable home.

Even more blunt is the first page of the opening chapter:

> As with the Commander of an Army . . . so it is with the mistress of a house. Her spirit will be seen through the whole establishment; and just in proportion as she performs her duties intelligently and thoroughly, so will her domestics follow in her path. Of all those acquirements, which more particularly belong to the feminine character, there are none which take a higher rank, in our estimation, than such as enter into a knowledge of household duties; for on these are perpetually dependent the happiness, comfort, and well-being of a family.

While the bulk of its pages consist of cooking recipes, Mrs. Beeton also offers detailed advice on cleaning, first aid, and the oversight of domestic servants; what surprises many modern readers is the attention she gives to legal matters, as in chapter 44:

> In civil cases, a wife may now give evidence on behalf of her husband; in criminal cases she can neither be a witness for or against her husband. The case of assault by him upon her forms an exception to this rule. The law does not at this day admit the ancient principle of allowing moderate correction by a husband upon the person of his wife. Although this is said to have been anciently limited to the use of "a stick not bigger than a thumb," this barbarity is now altogether exploded. He may, notwithstanding, . . . keep her under restraint, to prevent her leaving him, provided this be effected without cruelty.

The millions of middle-class women who read Mrs. Beeton, and other authors like her, prided themselves on their domestic efficiency and propriety.

So too did the popular literature of the age. Not only did novels become the most popular literary genre of the 19th century; the majority of both their readers and authors were women. This marked a sharp shift of opinion from the 18th century, when the new genre was blamed for spreading lax morals. Novels

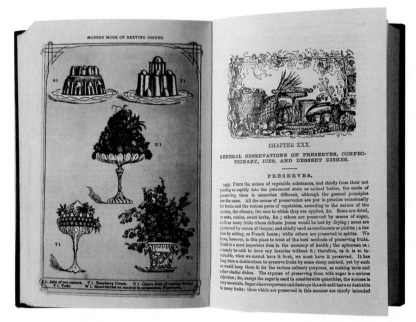

Guidebook to Happiness   *Mrs. Beeton's Book of Household Management*, published in 1861 when the author was only twenty-five years old, offers an antidote to Degas' gloomy outlook on the family (see page 695). Over 1,100 pages, it guides readers through everything necessary to create a happy, orderly, comfortable bourgeois home. Isabella Beeton died in 1865, from complications in the birth of her fourth child.

dangerously misled young women, it was said, filling their hearts and minds with fantasies of idle romance. As late as 1801, the father-daughter team of Robert and Maria Edgeworth wrote in their popular guide *Practical Education*:

> With respect to sentimental stories, and books of mere entertainment, we must remark, that they should be sparingly used, especially in the education of girls. This species of reading cultivates what is called "the heart" prematurely, lowers the tone of the mind, and induces indifference for those common pleasures and occupations which, however trivial in themselves, constitute by the far the greatest portion of our daily happiness.

Compare this with Thomas Broadhurst's *Advice to Young Ladies on the Improvement of the Mind and Conduct of Life* only a few years later, in 1810:

> She who is faithfully employed in discharging the various duties of a wife and daughter, a mother and a friend, is far more usefully occupied than one who, to the culpable neglect of the most important obligations,

is daily absorbed by philosophic and literary speculations, or soaring aloft amidst the enchanted regions of fiction and romance.

Popular novelists like Jane Austen (1775–1817) or the Brontë sisters (Charlotte [1816–1855], Emily [1818–1848], and Anne [1820–1849]) published their books under male pseudonyms. Jane Austen even took to hiding her manuscripts under piles of knitting and sewing, lest any household visitors discover her life as an author. In 1856 the great writer George Eliot (another woman: Mary Anne Evans [1819–1880]) published a delightfully vindictive article, "Silly Novels by Lady Novelists," in the *Westminster Review*. Eliot castigates writers who

> have evidently never talked to a tradesman except from a carriage window; they have no notion of the working-classes except as "dependents;" they think five hundred a-year a miserable pittance; Belgravia and "baronial halls" are their primary truths; and they have no idea of feeling interest in any man who is not at least a great landed proprietor, if not a prime minister. It is clear that they write in elegant boudoirs, with violet-coloured ink and a ruby pen; that they must be entirely indifferent to publishers' accounts, and inexperienced in every form of poverty except poverty of brains.

But not all the novels were silly. George Eliot's own novels—especially her masterpiece, *Middlemarch*—depict England's rural and village settings with uncommon delicacy and intelligence. In France, the novels of George Sand (Amantine Dupin, Baroness Dudivant [1804–1876]) provide sympathetic portraits of agrarian and working-class men and women who struggle against poverty and social prejudice. Italy's Matilde Serao (1856–1927) published a series of novels in the 1880s whose melodramatic plots were laced with a powerful social conscience driven by her work as a journalist and newspaper editor. Rosalía de Castro (1837–1885), from northwestern Spain, was primarily a poet, but her novels detail with dignity and precision the lives of the rural poor. Austrian novelist Bertha von Suttner was the first woman ever to win the Nobel Peace Prize, for her passionate antiwar novel *A Farewell to Arms* (*Die Waffen nieder*; 1889).[8] Annette von Droste-Hulshoff (1797–1848), from an old aristocratic family from the region of Westphalia, is best known in Germany for her religious poetry, but also wrote a disturbing novel called *The Jew's Beech Tree* (*Die Judenbuche*; 1842), which may be the first murder mystery in modern fiction.

---

[8]   The first woman ever to win the Nobel Prize in Literature was Sweden's Selma Lagerlöf (1909).

If women found acceptance, however grudging, on the shelves of booksellers, they still faced determined opposition when it came to legal rights. Even privileged women faced great obstacles. An Englishwoman named Caroline Norton (1808–1877) came from a respectable family with military and colonial connections; her two sisters each married into the nobility, and she wed a prominent barrister and member of Parliament. Her husband, however, turned out to be a violent drunkard whose jealousy prompted him to suspect the lovely Caroline, unfairly, of constant infidelity. His verbal and physical abuse were unrelenting—especially during his many bouts of alcoholic stupor. To make extra money, Caroline began to publish poetry and novels, which were well received and led to friendships with many prominent writers and statesmen. In 1836, unable to take any more violence, she left her husband. Her husband in turn abducted their three children (all sons), refused to let her see them, and sued to gain possession of all her book royalties—arguing successfully in court that everything belonging to a wife is the rightful possession of the husband. For six years she was forbidden to see her boys and received none of her book earnings. In 1842 their eldest son died in a horse-riding accident, after which her husband relented and allowed her occasional visits to the remaining two boys. She had no legal grounds for divorcing her husband—wife beating not being against the law then—and did not become free until his death in 1875.

Caroline Norton devoted many years to the struggle for changes in the laws regarding marriage and divorce. The culmination of her efforts came with the Matrimonial Causes Act of 1857, which gave women the legal ability to initiate divorce; they could also retain possession of a share of the couple's wealth. The act reaffirmed their right—originally granted in 1839, also thanks in part to Caroline Norton—to shared custody of their minor children. Norton wrote a pamphlet-length letter, addressed to Queen Victoria herself—

> the one woman in England who *cannot* suffer wrong; and whose royal assent will be formally necessary to any Marriage Reform Bill which the Lord Chancellor, assembled Peers, and assembled Commons, may think fit to pass, in the Parliament of this free nation; where, with a Queen on the throne, all other married women are legally *NON-EXISTENT*.

She concluded:

> Nevertheless, so long as human nature is what it is, some marriages must be unhappy marriages, instead of following that theory of intimate and sacred union which they ought to fulfill: and the question is,

therefore, what is to be the relation of persons living in a state of alienation, instead of a state of union,—all the existing rules for their social position being based on the first alternative,—namely, that they are in a state of union,—and on the supposition that marriage is indissoluble, though Parliament has now decided that it is a civil contract? Divorced or undivorced, it is absolutely necessary that the law should step in, to arrange that which is disarranged by this most unnatural condition. It becomes perfectly absurd that the law which appoints the husband legal protector of the woman, should not (failing him who has ceased to be a protector, and has become a very powerful foe) itself undertake her protection. She stands towards the law, by an illustration which I have repeatedly made use of,—in the light of an ill-used inferior; and she is the *only* inferior in England who cannot claim to be so protected. *("A Letter to the Queen on Lord Chancellor Cranworth's Marriage and Divorce Bill" [1855])*

Britain stood ahead of the curve, compared with the Continent, in recognizing the legal rights of women.

By the end of 1848 Europe was tiring of revolutions, and with good reason. The overthrow of absolutism and the forced march of industrialism had been wrenching experiences. The people had demanded the restructuring of the state and the reconsideration of longstanding social traditions. Conservatism and liberalism offered new paths out of the chaos; but while significantly distinct from earlier notions of political order, they were not revolutionary. Indeed, conservatism presented itself as the upholder of traditionalism, while liberalism offered itself as the intelligent way to control and channel the forces of change.

The real revolutionary developments of the midcentury were the challenges of Marxism and the campaign for the rights of women. Both were changes of the mind and heart as much as calls to transform the state or workplace. It would take another two or three generations for these changes to take root, but their effects on daily life were dramatic, permanent, and inescapable. These changes, when they came, permanently altered family structures, moral values, notions of state power and obligation, and religious life—as good a definition as any of what *revolution* really means.

WHO, WHAT, WHERE

bourgeoisie	cult of domesticity
Chartist movement	historical materialism
communism	laissez-faire
The Communist Manifesto	liberalism
Congress of Vienna	proletariat
conservatism	suffrage

SUGGESTED READINGS

Primary Sources

Beeton, Isabella. *Mrs. Beeton's Book of Household Management.*

Burke, Edmund. *Reflections on the Revolution in France.*

Maistre, Joseph-Marie de. *Considerations on France.*

———. *Essay on the Generative Principle of Political Constitutions.*

Marx, Karl. *Capital.*

———. *The Communist Manifesto.*

———. *The 18th Brumaire of Louis Napoleon-Napoleon.*

———. *The German Ideology.*

Metternich, Klemens von. *Memoirs.*

Mill, John Stuart. *On Liberty.*

———. *The Principles of Political Economy.*

Norton, Caroline. *English Laws for Women in the 19th Century.*

Tocqueville, Alexis de. *Recollections.*

Anthologies

Leroux, Robert, and David Hart, eds. *French Liberalism in the 19th Century: An Anthology* (2012).

Marx, Karl. *Selected Writings* (2000). Edited by David McLellan.

Tucker, Robert C., ed. *The Marx-Engels Reader.*

Studies

Alexander, Robert. *Re-writing the French Revolutionary Tradition: Liberal Opposition and the Fall of the Bourbon Monarchy* (2007).

Berend, Ivan T. *History Derailed: Central and Eastern Europe in the Long Nineteenth Century* (2005).

Boime, Albert. *Art in an Age of Counterrevolution, 1815–1848* (2004).

———. *Art in an Age of Civil Struggle, 1848–1871* (2008).

Cohen, G. A. *Karl Marx's Theory of History: A Defence* (2001).

Dénes, Iván Zoltán. *Conservative Ideology in the Making* (2010).

Devigne, Robert. *Reforming Liberalism: J. S. Mill's Use of Ancient, Religious, Liberal, and Romantic Moralities* (2006).

Fortescue, William. *France and 1848: The End of Monarchy* (2005).

Gross, Michael B. *The War against Catholicism: Liberalism and the Anti-Catholic Imagination in Nineteenth-Century Germany* (2005).

Kahan, Alan S. *Liberalism in Nineteenth-Century Europe: The Political Culture of Limited Suffrage* (2003).

Kertzer, David I., and Marzio Barbagli, eds. *Family Life in the Long Nineteenth Century, 1789–1913* (2002).

Langewiesche, Dieter. *Liberalism in Germany* (2000).

Leopold, David. *The Young Karl Marx: German Philosophy, Modern Politics, and Human Flourishing* (2007).

Liang, Hsi-Huey. *The Rise of Modern Police and the European State System from Metternich to the Second World War* (2002).

Pitts, Jennifer. *A Turn to Empire: The Rise of Imperial Liberalism in Britain and France* (2006).

Popkin, Jeremy D. *Press, Revolution, and Social Identities in France, 1830–1835* (2001).

Rapport, Michael. *1848: Year of Revolution* (2009).

Sack, James J. *From Jacobite to Conservative: Reaction and Orthodoxy in Britain, c. 1760–1832* (2004).

Sked, Alan. *Metternich and Austria: An Evaluation* (2008).

Sperber, Jonathan. *The European Revolutions, 1848–1851* (2005).

———. *Revolutionary Europe, 1780–1850* (2000).

Vick, Brian E. *Defining Germany: The 1848 Frankfurt Parliamentarians and National Identity* (2002).

Wolff, Jonathan. *Why Read Marx Today?* (2002).

Zamoyski, Adam. *Rites of Peace: The Fall of Napoleon and the Congress of Vienna* (2008).

For additional resources, including maps, primary sources, visuals, web links, and quizzes, please go to **www.oup.com/us/backman.**

CHAPTER 19

Nationalism and Identity

1801–1903

THE GREATER WEST, 1871

O ne of the most dramatic and ubiquitous cultural developments of the 19th century was the phenomenon of passionate, urgent concern for national identity. What does it mean to be
a member of a particular ethnic or cultural group? What makes
one English, German, Hungarian, Polish, or Serbian? Can a foreign immigrant ever be truly assimilated into a new culture? Into
a political state, yes—but that is another matter entirely, a question of mere citizenship. Can an ethnic Russian truly become
Irish, however? Is it possible, or even desirable, for a Dutch man or woman to
become French—and if so, is not some element of his or her "Dutchness" lost in
the process? Attempts to answer questions like these altered the map of Europe.
In turn, those changes led to renewed questions and divisions within European
Jews and a crumbling Ottoman Empire.

It seems odd that questions of identity still haunted peoples who had
lived together for over a thousand years; the explanation lay in the innumerable configurations of their joint existences. Political borders designating
states and countries in past centuries had been drawn variously along dynastic lines, religious lines, geographic lines, lines of military conquest, lines
demarcating zones of economic interest, linguistic lines, negotiated lines of
convenience, and lines based on nothing in
particular. The willful drawing and redrawing of political boundaries at international
congresses like Westphalia and Vienna, or at
scores of local meetings over the centuries
to settle regional disputes, had the effect for
many of making states seem artificial at best

◀ **Fighting for the Nation**
A Greek rebel against Turkish
rule, shown carrying banner
and sword. The image
illustrates the linkage
between Romantic passion
and political nationalism.

- Nationalism in Theory
- Nationalism in Practice: Germany
  and Italy
- Frustrated Nationalism: Hungary
  and Ireland
- Assimilation and Zionism
- Islamic Nationalisms
- Reforming Islam

CHAPTER
OUTLINE

and irrelevant at worst. If the "country" to which one owes political obedience and personal loyalty can be altered by something as small as a signature on a treaty, then how can one honestly feel any sense of deep identification with it? Given such persistent arbitrariness, the absence of any sure sense of communal identity becomes less of a surprise (see Map 19.1).

The upheavals of the late 18th and early 19th centuries only added to the confusion. As late as 1815 just under 10 percent of Europe's population lived in cities with populations above fifty thousand; only fifty years earlier than that, however, the figure had been closer to 2–3 percent. The threefold increase in urban population meant more than a quantitative growth in absolute numbers, for urban populations tend to greater ethnic complexity than rural ones. Farming societies, in other words, are more typically homogenous in their ethnic makeup than urban societies, and so the rise in the number and size of cities meant a concomitant increase in ethnic heterogeneity. Napoleon's Continental System had erased, for a while, at least, the legal barriers to peoples' free movement from one territory to another, as they sought opportunities to learn new skills and access new markets. The result was the presence of sizable communities of resident foreigners in cities across Europe: ethnic Poles living in Berlin or Paris, ethnic Sicilians residing in Milan or Hamburg, ethnic Greeks taking up new lives in Madrid or Genoa, ethnic Portuguese residing in Rotterdam or Lille. When the Continent began to industrialize at speed, post-1815, the pluri-ethnic character of urban life became even more pronounced. Under these conditions, when a city like Munich became home to a confusing sprawl of cultural groups, what did "being German" or "being Bavarian" mean?

NATIONALISM IN THEORY

Edward Augustus Freeman (1823–1892), one of England's great historians in the 19th century, confronted the question in an essay entitled "Race and Language" (1879):

CHAPTER TIMELINE

1801
Act of Union between England and Ireland

1829
Catholic Emancipation Act (Ireland)

1831
Rifa'a al-Tahtawai, *The Essence of Paris*

1845–1852
Irish Potato Famine

1805–1848
Rule of Mehmet Ali Pasha in Egypt

1830
Greece wins independence; Bulgaria secures autonomy from Ottomans

1839–1876
Tanzimat in Ottoman Empire

[What of] those parts of the world where people who are confessedly of different races and languages inhabit a continuous territory and live under the same government? How do we define nationality in such cases as these? The answer will be very different in different cases.... They may form what I have already called an *artificial nation*, united by an act of its own free will. Or it may be simply a case where distinct nations, distinct in everything which can be looked on as forming a nation, except the possession of an independent government, are brought together, by whatever causes, under a common ruler. The former case is very distinctly an exception which proves the rule, [such a] nation is something different from those nations which are defined by a universal or at least a predominant language. We mark it as an exception, as something different from other cases. And when we see how nearly this artificial nation comes, in every point but that of language, to the likeness of those nations which are defined by language, we see that it is a nation defined by language which sets the standard, and after the model of which the artificial nation forms itself.

Freeman mentions Switzerland as an example of an artificial nation—one composed of several groups, each of which maintains its own language. He sees other examples in the Ottoman and Austrian-Hungarian empires of his time:

While in each Western country some one of the various races which have settled in it has, speaking roughly, assimilated the others, in the lands which are left under the rule of the Turk, or which have been lately delivered from his rule, all the races that have ever settled in the country still abide side by side. So when we pass into the lands which form the Austr[ian]-Hungar[ian] national government, another fragment is ruled by civilized strangers, a third is trampled down by barbarians. The existing states of Greece, Romania, and Serbia are far from taking in the

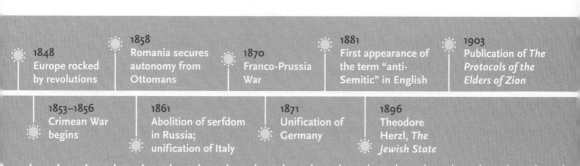

1848
Europe rocked by revolutions

1858
Romania secures autonomy from Ottomans

1870
Franco-Prussia War

1881
First appearance of the term "anti-Semitic" in English

1903
Publication of *The Protocols of the Elders of Zion*

1853–1856
Crimean War begins

1861
Abolition of serfdom in Russia; unification of Italy

1871
Unification of Germany

1896
Theodore Herzl, *The Jewish State*

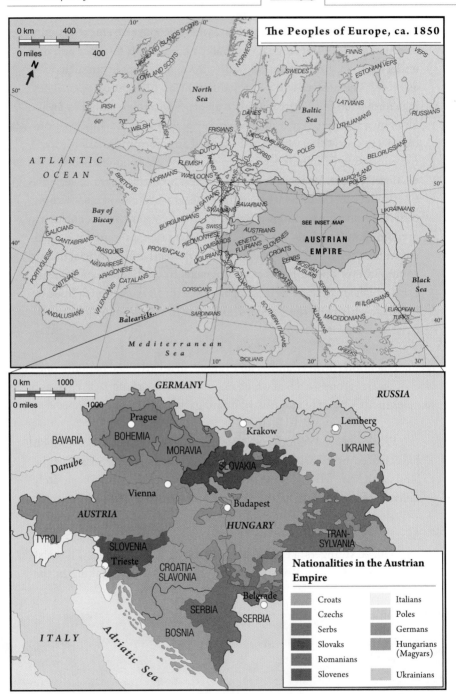

MAP 19.1   The Peoples of Europe, ca. 1850

whole of the Greek, Romanian, and Serbian nations. In all these lands . . .
there is no difficulty in marking off the several nations; only in no case
do the[se] nations [correspond] to any existing political power.

To Freeman, language defines national identity. But other possibilities exist.
To some writers, one's nationality comprised race, loyalty to a unique political
vision, religious practice, or even native cuisine. Rudyard Kipling (1865–1936),
tireless champion of British imperialism and at one point the most popular writer
in the English-speaking world, identified nationality and sentimentality; one's
nation is simply the place to which one remains loyal in one's heart.

> Our hearts where they rocked our cradle
> Our love where we spent our toil,
> And our faith, and our hope, and our honor,
> We pledge to our native soil.
>
> God gave all men all earth to love
> But since our hearts are small
> Ordained for each one spot should prove
> Beloved over all.

The search for national identity was intrinsically Romantic—self-fascinated, intuitive, multifaceted (and, inevitably, contradictory), and awe-inspiring—and
informed numerous aspects of Romantic thought and expression, from historical
writing like E. A. Freeman's to the political essays of Ernst Renan (1823–1892)
and the poetical-philosophical works (not to mention the music) of Richard
Wagner (1813–1883). Like Romanticism, the influence of nationalism spread
throughout the 19th century. Unlike Romanticism, the fascination with national identity continued to be felt throughout the 20th century as well, all too often in odious and destructive ways.[1]

However it is defined, **nationalism** was and re-mains a potent force. It may in fact be the most vital element in modern political history. The word im-plies more than mere patriotism, although it includes that notion. Nationality in
the 19th-century sense suggests a collective consciousness, a growing awareness
that the members of an individual nation-group share a depth of feelings, values,
and attitudes toward the world. Together, these sentiments give meaning to their

> However it is defined, nationalism was and remains a potent force. It may in fact be the most vital element in modern political history.

---

[1] George Orwell: "Nationalism is power-hunger tempered by self-deception."

Scots This lithograph of Queen Victoria's "Four Highlanders" was printed in 1869. Victoria lost her mother and her husband in 1861 and went into deep and prolonged mourning, during which time she lived primarily in Scotland.

aggregate existence and may in fact be the only way to realize a fully meaningful life. In the United States this conviction took the form of a belief in America's manifest destiny to move westward across the Great Plains and extend the national borders to the Pacific coast. In Europe it took the form of popular desire to eradicate the artificial political lines drawn in 1815 and replace them with organic states composed of the political and geographical union of all members of specific national groups: a Germany made up of the aggregate of all ethnic Germans; an Italy that unites all ethnic Italians into a single state; an independent Hungary that gathers all Magyars under an autonomous government of their own.

But the word "nation" did not always have this populist meaning. In the 16th and 17th centuries it was widely used to designate the aristocracy in most countries—that is, the people born into privilege, the people who mattered. That is why the declaration made in 1789 by the revolutionaries locked out of the meeting of the Estates General in Paris—that "we are the nation"—was so radically decisive. Rousseau had argued that a nation composed of all of its people in equal membership would create not only a more just society but a decidedly more powerful, dynamic, and harmonious one. Here the *volonté générale* ("general will") of its constituents would find the freest and most perfect expression. This idea carried through into the Industrial Age, though differing political camps put it to different uses. To most conservatives, nation meant culture, language, and tradition—the political and social norms that bound people together under the paternal care of ancient hierarchies. To liberals, the word described the egalitarian gathering of people under a constitution that recognized rights, guaranteed the claims of property, and promoted individual freedom. To Marxists, a nation was a fiction, an imagined grouping used by capitalists to control industrial production and promote the interests of the bourgeoisie. It is part of the complexity of nationalism that all of these views were, and are, to some extent correct.

The political narrative of 19th-century nationalism is episodic: it took decades either for discrete territories to unite into a single nation or for a subjugated land to break away from foreign domination and establish its independence. The most prominent political successes were the unifications of Germany and of Italy, while the most significant political failures were those of Hungary and of Ireland.

NATIONALISM IN PRACTICE: GERMANY AND ITALY

Germany as a unified political state had not existed since the 13th century, and Italy had ceased to exist as a single nation as many as eight centuries before that. The Congress of Vienna had reshuffled the German territories into a confederation of thirty-eight states and the Italian peninsula into roughly a dozen autonomous petty principalities. The desire for unification was present from the start, although it was hardly universal. The middle classes in both places were the prime movers for unification, for they stood to benefit the most: only by pooling the peoples' resources, they recognized, could the Germans or Italians catch up to industrialized England. National banks were needed to provide financing for start-up manufacturers, for example, and extensive systems of transport and communication had to be established. Moreover, they needed to be established quickly. To those of the working class, a unified state seemed the only feasible way to rein in the abuses and inequities of industrial capitalism. Both groups thus saw national union as the most promising path to both economic growth and social reform. Conservatives in both places balked at both developments and fought to protect their provincialism. The strong Romantic pulse of the young generation, however, inclined them to explore and exalt the collective genius of their cultures at large. It thus complemented the ledger-book mentality of the entrepreneurial class in its press for national union.

The Prussians had taken the early lead in the German Confederation by reforming their military along meritocratic lines. Reorganizing the officer corps signaled the end of the dominance of the old aristocracy (called **Junkers**) in Prussian society and paved the way for other reforms: cities won the right to control their own finances, and German universities were opened to competitive admission. By 1848, tired of conservative foot-dragging and impatient of initial liberal efforts at reform, workers and bourgeois alike proposed schemes for German nationhood at a meeting of the Frankfurt Assembly.

Most of the delegates came from professional circles and confronted a pressing question: Did unification mean the union of all ethnic Germans everywhere or simply of those Germans residing in German-governed principalities? German populations living in Czech-dominated Bohemia, for example, or in Habsburg-controlled Austria, wanted to be included in a "Greater Germany" but could not do so without risking active resistance from their rulers. The Prussian king Friedrich Wilhelm IV (r. 1840–1861) was offered, but declined, the crown of a "Lesser Germany" that omitted those extraterritorial nationals. Not that his refusal had anything to do with the extraterritorial nationals; he refused the crown simply because it had been offered by the people. A true conservative, he declared that the only crown he could ever wear was one that he placed upon his own head, lest he appear to condone liberal attitudes:

> This crown [that you offer] is no real crown.... [It] humiliates whoever wears it.... It smells of the gunpowder of the revolution of 1848—the most ridiculous, stupid, and vile (although not, thank God, the most evil) uprising of this century.... Let me state it outright: If the [true] crown of the united German nation, a crown with a one-thousand-year-old heritage ... should ever be bestowed again, it will be I and my peers—alone—who bestow it. Woe to those who assume authorities to which they have no right. *("Proclamation of 1849")*

Instead of an early union of the Lesser Germany, what came out of the Frankfurt Assembly was an even weaker version of the former German Confederation.

One thing remained clear: the debate over German unification boiled down to a political rivalry between Prussia and Austria, since either one of these seemed likely to take the lead in a single Greater Germany. As one of the Frankfurt delegates put it:

> There is no avoiding the fact that the whole issue of a united Germany comes down to a simple choice between Prussia and Austria. German life in these two states certainly has its positive and negative characteristics—in the first, the focus is on national union and reform, while in the second the focus is upon mere, and ultimately destructive, dynastic power. In this way, the whole issue of "Germany" is not about a constitution but about power, pure and simple. The monarchy in Prussia thinks about the whole of the German people, while that in Austria never will. *("Speech to the Frankfurt Assembly" [1848] by Johann Gustav Droysen)*

Historians still debate the consequences of the failure at Frankfurt. At the very least, unification, with the support of a broad cross-section of the people, happened only later. Yet it was also caused by a new political alliance between the Prussian monarchy and the military. This direct military element, some argue, forced German nationalism onto a unique path that led unavoidably to Nazism and Hitler. (Historians call this debate the Sonderweg controversy, after the German for "unique path.")

———— + ————

Unavoidably or not, the Prussian military did in fact take over the cause of unification. Under the leadership of Prime Minister Otto von Bismarck (1815–1898), a deeply conservative, complex, and brilliant figure, Prussian arms bullied and beat its neighbors into submission.[2] Bismarck started a war with Denmark (1866) in order to seize the disputed principalities of Schleswig and Holstein, then provoked a "Seven Weeks' War" against Austria (also 1866), which gained another half-dozen territories, while securing Venice (previously under Habsburg control) as his Italian ally. He then engineered the Franco-Prussian War (1870–1871), which returned, among other areas, the Alsace-Lorraine region to German control (see Map 19.2). Bismarck, who regularly wore a military uniform but never served in the army himself, is most frequently remembered for his statement that "the great issues of our time will not be resolved by speeches and parliamentary votes (that was the mistake of the revolutionaries of 1848 and 1849) but by blood and iron." Yet he also declared that "anyone who has ever looked straight into the glazed eyes of a soldier dying on a battlefield will think twice before starting a war."

Bismarck himself had little nationalistic feeling for a "Greater Germany"; his loyalty was first and foremost to Prussia. But since German unification seemed inevitable, he chose to bring it about in his own way, with Prussia very much the dominant element. Bismarck gambled that the German people would support his militarism in return for his championing of liberal social programs that he personally found odious: health insurance, unemployment insurance, and retirement pensions—anything that avoided actual regulation of the marketplace. He was right. Germany became not only a single nation—the

Otto von Bismarck in 1864.

Otto von Bismarck Prussian diplomat and Prime Minister who engineered the unification of Germany.

---

[2]   Bismarck neither enjoyed nor glorified war; he was simply willing to resort to it when there seemed no other way to achieve what he desired.

The Unification of Germany

■ Habsburg Empire	▬ Border of German Customs Union (Zollverein) 1842
■ Prussia 1815	▬ Southern border of North German Confederation 1867
■ Territory added to Prussia 1815–66	▬ Border of German Empire 1871
■ Territory added to Prussia/German Empire 1871	

MAP 19.2   The Unification of Germany

Second Reich (the first being the medieval empire established in the 10th century)—under Bismarck, but also became both an unfettered industrial-capitalist economy and a social-welfare state. On January 18, 1871, at the end of the Franco-Prussian War, which destroyed the power of the French emperor Napoleon III, the Prussian king Wilhelm II became the emperor of Germany with the following proclamation:

> I, Wilhelm . . . do hereby declare that I have concluded that it is my solemn duty to our common Fatherland to answer the call of the united German princes and free cities and to assume the German imperial

title ... while fully conscious of my responsibility to protect the rights not only of the empire of its loyal German subjects, to maintain peace, and to assure the independence of the German nation (which depends, in its turn, on the united strength of its people). I assume this title in the hope that the German people will be freely able to reap in lasting peace the rewards of its strenuous and selfless wars, within national boundaries that will grant the Fatherland safety from renewed French aggression—a safety that has been lacking for centuries. May God grant that I and my successors on this imperial throne will ever add to the wealth of our empire not by military conquest but through the blessings and gifts of peace, in the realm of national prosperity, freedom, and morality.

It is as concise a summary of nationalist sentiments as one could hope to find.

Once united, Germany accelerated its industrial development and efforts to "Germanize" the population. The first development is self-explanatory: the construction of new factories (especially in steel manufacture, railroads, and arms)

Nationalism and Power   The Krupp Steel Works factory in Essen, Germany. Founded in 1810 as a foundry for producing railway equipment, the Krupp factory turned to manufacturing cannons and other armaments in midcentury. Weaponry quickly became its primary manufacture after 1870. By 1900 Krupp was the largest company in Europe, with over seventy-five thousand employees across the Germany, roughly one-third of whom worked in the original plant at Essen.

and the building of both commercial and military fleets that could challenge England's dominance on the high seas. "Germanization" of the countryside involved the forced assimilation of ethnic minorities and the resettlement of ethnic Germans on farmland confiscated from groups such as the Danes, French, Lithuanians, and Poles. The languages spoken by these groups were forbidden in schools, books, newspapers, theaters, concert halls, museums, courtrooms, the military, and most other public sites.

Bismarck, a devout Pietist Lutheran, also targeted Catholicism as an intrinsically non-German religion. This anti-Catholic campaign was known as the **Kulturkampf** ("culture battle") and lasted from 1871 to 1878. Among the measures the government took were the banning of the Jesuit Order and the breaking of diplomatic relations with the Vatican. Internally, the Reich forbade Catholic priests from mentioning any political issue in the pulpit; clergy found guilty of "political preaching" faced two years' imprisonment.[3] The government also closed roughly one-third of all monasteries. It is difficult to know the extent to which the Kulturkampf targeted Catholics and how much it aimed to undermine the Polish communities now living under the authority of the Reich; Bismarck certainly had little sympathy for either group. In either case, however, it backfired: Catholic representation in the Reichstag doubled over the seven years of government oppression.

——————— ✦ ———————

Italy's unification equaled Germany's in drama, but it was a drama of a different sort. Political decentralization had not particularly bothered most Italians through the centuries; fragmentation and localism had so long been the norms of Italian life that they were seldom questioned. This sort of particularism, in fact, had preserved much of what was best loved in Italian life—local customs, local cuisines, local dialects, and a strong sense of local identities. Until well into the 19th century, few people on the peninsula thought of themselves as Italians. Instead, they were Beneventans, Florentines, Lucchesans, Neapolitans, Perugians, or Venetians—or, for those with a more regional sense of identity, Ligurians, Sicilians, or Tuscans. The strongest impulse toward national identity came from resentment of foreign domination. At least since the 13th century, the Italian peninsula had been dominated by a shifting matrix of European powers: Angevins, Austrians, Catalans, French, Germans, Savoyards, and Spaniards. In the 16th century Machiavelli had penned *The Prince* as a desperate plea for a native uprising against the foreigners (at that point primarily the French) tearing apart the countryside. The chief villains in the 19th century were the Habsburg

---

[3] By 1878 nearly two thousand Catholic clergy had been either jailed or exiled, including fully one-half of all the bishops in Prussia.

Austrians in the north and the Bourbon French in the south, both of whom had been either placed or ratified in power by the despised Treaty of Vienna. In 1827 the Romantic poet Alessandro Manzoni (1785–1873) published his only novel, often considered Italy's greatest, *The Betrothed* (*I promessi sposi*), which dramatized, among other things, the suffering inflicted on northern Italy by foreign usurpers. (The same author's *Adelchi* (1822) dramatizes the overthrow of a Lombard prince by Charlemagne, the great but meddlesome 9th-century emperor.) The novel is set in the 17th century, when the region around Manzoni's birthplace of Milan was controlled by Spanish forces, but it alludes directly to the dominance of the Austrians in the 19th—a theme of his stage dramas as well.

Popular rebellion broke out in hundreds of small riots and demonstrations.

I MANGIA-MACCARONI

Neapolitans Two Neapolitan youths in an archetypal pose, eating maccheroni. Naples is the Italian peninsula's largest port city. Commonly thought of as a place of squalor and crime, it was (and still is) the fourth largest urban economy in Italy, and the first Italian city to have a railway line. When Naples joined the Kingdom of Italy in 1861, national unification was complete.

"Italian patriotism is like the patriotism of the ancient Greeks," wrote a prominent Neapolitan official in 1850; "it consists of love for a single town, not for a whole country. Conquest by foreigners is the only thing that ever unites Italians. Left to themselves, they will always split into smaller groups." Another proponent of unification, Giuseppe La Farina (1815–1863), wrote that

Italy's independence should be the aim of every spirited and intelligent man, for neither our schools, commerce, nor industry will ever flourish or develop so long as Austria's boot remains on our necks.... To gain freedom politically we must drive out the Austrians who dominate us. To gain freedom intellectually we must drive out the Austrians who keep us the slaves of the Holy See. And to create a national literature, too, we must drive out the Austrians who keep most of our people illiterate.... Everything tends toward political unification. Our science, industry, commerce, and arts require it. No great advancements are possible unless we first bring together the skills, minds, capital, and labor of our great nation.... Woe to anyone who dares to get in our way!

The only open question, in most Italians' minds, was whether the unified country would be a monarchy (favored by many in the north) or a democracy (the general preference of those in the south). Diplomatic leadership came from the north in the persons of Vittorio Emmanuele II, the king of Piedmont-Sardinia (r. 1849–1861)—which was one of the misshapen countries created in 1815—and his chief minister, Camillo Benso, the count of Cavour (1810–1861). Military and populist leadership, however, came from the south in the person of Giuseppe Garibaldi (1807–1882), a charismatic adventurer who pursued the cause of liberating enslaved peoples everywhere from Tunisia and Brazil to Italy, the United States, and France.[4]

Garibaldi had defeated the Bourbon-controlled south by the end of 1860, while Cavour (with some help from the French) had neutralized Habsburg power in the north by roughly the same time. By 1871 the last remnants of foreign resistance had been overcome, and Vittorio Emmanuele journeyed to Rome and assumed the title of king of Italy (see Map 19.3). The only remaining problem was the Holy See. The pope was not only spiritual leader of the Catholic Church but also the political ruler of part of central Italy since the Middle Ages. His domain had long since been reduced, geographically, but Pope Pius IX (r. 1846–1878) refused to relinquish any aspect of his secular authority and so became "the prisoner of the Vatican." The dispute continued until 1929, when a concordat signed by the Holy See and the Italian government finally ended the matter. But Italy was united only in name. The north remained the center of economic might, with its banks, industry, and commercial links; the south, by contrast, was overwhelmingly rural and poorly educated. Since Italy's political leadership invariably came from the north, the economic disparity between north and south, and the unequal leverage of political power between them, would hamper Italian development for decades.

Wittingly or unwittingly, France played a significant role in the unifications of Germany and of Italy. Napoleon III (r. 1852–1870), who as Louis-Napoleon Bonaparte had served as president of the Second Republic, dreaded another uprising of the common peasants and laborers. Now emperor, he pushed hard for France's industrial and commercial development, even while doing all he could to centralize political authority into something as close to absolutism as he could manage.[5] The goal was to encourage a carefully controlled type of nationalism, one in which popular loyalty was not only to the country but to the state itself. By mobilizing the government behind industrial expansion, he hoped, people would

---

[4]   Garibaldi offered his services in the American Civil War—on two conditions: President Lincoln would abolish slavery immediately and make him commander-in-chief of the Union army. Lincoln politely declined.

[5]   Napoleon III created the infamous penal colony at Devil's Island off the coast of French Guiana—immediately sending 240 of the Republican leaders who had opposed his coup d'état.

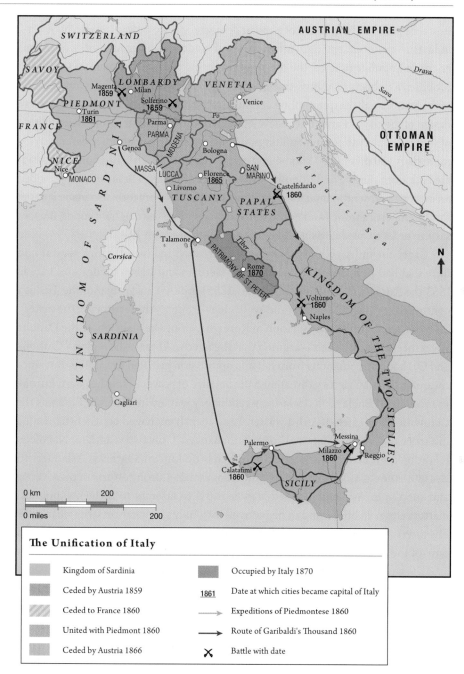

MAP 19.3   The Unification of Italy

associate prosperity not with individual entrepreneurship outside of state regulation but with the government—and especially with the ruler at its head.

The emperor controlled state finances, commanded the military, determined foreign policy, and dictated domestic affairs to an impotent national assembly whose existence preserved the fiction of popular democracy. Two policies dear to his heart—industrial development and urban renewal—advanced because of innovations he made in public finance, the most notable being his establishment of the Crédit Mobilier, a publicly held investment bank whose capital financed the construction of the Suez Canal, the quintupling of France's miles of rail lines, and the wholesale redesign of the city of Paris. The redevelopment of the city center involved demolition of well over thirty thousand buildings, wiping out entire neighborhoods, and laying more than 120 miles (200 kilometers) of new roads. A dozen broad boulevards radiated out from the Arc de Triomphe, in the heart of the city. These not only provided an esthetic and sentimental focal point to the city; their breadth also made it easier for the emperor's troops and police units to fan out into the neighborhoods, if necessary, in order to quell uprisings like those of 1848 (see Map 19.4).

Eager for military glory, Napoleon III rushed inadvisedly into several conflicts that had pervasive consequences for German and Italian unification. Late in 1853 the Russian tsar Nikolai I (r. 1825–1855) ordered his army into the Turkish-controlled regions of Moldavia and Wallachia—roughly the territory of the eastern and southern part of today's nation of Romania, along the plain where the Danube River meets the Black Sea—arguing that the need to liberate the regions' Catholic and Orthodox populations from Islamic oppression justified the action. But since the quick Russian victory threatened the balance of power in southeastern Europe, France joined England in declaring a retaliatory war against Russia. This was the **Crimean War** (1854–1856), a wasteful and ineptly managed conflict that ended in a truce that left international borders unchanged. Only two years later Napoleon III ordered French military action into then little-known Southeast Asian territories later known as Vietnam and Cambodia. France's strong efforts in the Crimea and success in Asia emboldened Napoleon III to attempt to influence political matters closer to home, and so he plunged into Italy's unification struggle in 1859. His interests were divided: as a devout Catholic he wanted to preserve the autonomy of the Vatican, but as a nationalist he sincerely wanted to see a unified Italy. And the hard-nosed politician in him sought to wrest some territorial concessions from Cavour in return for military assistance against Austria. In the end, the hard-nosed politician won. French troops helped drive the Austrians from the region around Venice, and for their trouble Cavour and Vittorio Emmanuele II granted France, in 1860, the city of Nice and the area of the French Riviera.

Had Napoleon III ceased his adventures at that point, his reign would have been remembered much more positively than it now is. Instead, he first undertook a bizarre campaign to conquer Mexico. His forces were defeated by a Mexican nationalist force in a battle at Puebla, which took place on May 5, 1862. Worse, he then stumbled into a direct conflict with Otto von Bismarck.[6] The Franco-Prussian War (1870–1871)

---

[6] Although French troops remained in Mexico until 1867, Cinco de Mayo lives on as a national holiday.

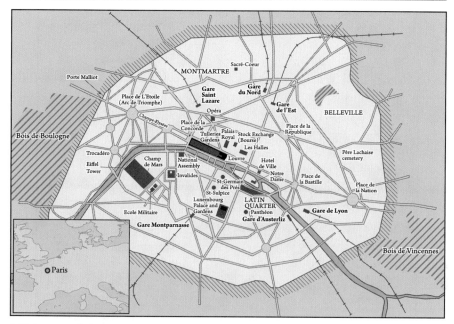

MAP 19.4   Paris in 1890

proved a disaster for France. The Prussian military outmatched France's army, and Bismarck outwitted Napoleon III diplomatically and militarily at every turn. The southern German states of Baden, Bavaria, Hesse, the Palatinate, and Würtemberg all rushed to join Prussia in defending the Fatherland, and after only three months of fighting the French army fell and the emperor himself was captured. Germany declared victory and its imperial unification, and Napoleon III was deposed. France then declared the start of its Third Republic (1870–1940), while the disgraced former emperor fled into exile in London, where he died in early 1873.

FRUSTRATED NATIONALISM: HUNGARY AND IRELAND

Nationalist passions may have been ubiquitous, but victories were not. Two of the most notable failed efforts of the 19th century—although they succeeded in the 20th—occurred in Hungary and Ireland.

Hungary had not been independent since 1526, when the Ottomans crushed the Magyar army and killed the Magyar king at the battle of Mohács. The remaining independent Hungarian nobles had split over what to do next. Some elected a new Hungarian monarch and formed a rump mini-kingdom that lasted only a brief time before being absorbed into the Ottoman Empire, while the others threw their support to Ferdinand I (r. 1526–1564) of Habsburg Austria. Hungary remained divided between Habsburgs and Ottomans until 1687, when a vast military alliance organized by Pope Innocent XI (r. 1676–1689) and

Hungarian Patriot   Lajos Kossuth (1802-1894), the great national champion of Hungarian independence, called for his country's freedom from Austria in a stirring speech to the Hungarian Diet in 1848. "Gentlemen!" he cried, "The fate of our nation is now in our hands...God has placed each one of you in the position of arbiter of the life or death of Hungary!" This drawing shows Lossuth, after his speech, in one of his many appearances around Hungary calling for recruits to the nation's militia.

known as the Holy League (Austria, the Holy Roman Empire, the Venetian Republic, Poland-Lithuania, and Russia, plus others) routed the Turkish army at a second battle of Mohács. Soon virtually all of the Hungarian homeland lay under Habsburg control. The century and a half of Austrian-Ottoman fighting had left much of Hungary in ruins, with many of its cities depleted or flattened and much of its urban population lost to emigration.

Austrian rule, autocratic and frequently brutal, weighed heavily on the Hungarians. Hardly a decade passed without a nativist rebellion somewhere in the Magyar lands. The Habsburgs responded in true absolutist style by destroying strongholds, choking off supplies to cities, forbidding the publication in the Magyar language, and keeping the peasantry (fully 90 percent of the population) dirt-poor.[7] The temporary dismantling of absolutism under Bonaparte gave fresh hope to the people not only by ridding them of a detested monarchy but also by presenting an opportunity

---

7   Hungary refused to use German in government councils or for public records. It thus has the honor of being the European country with the longest tradition of spoken Latin anywhere.

for economic development. Hungary's traditionally diversified subsistence farms gave way to large-scale monoculture that could provide food and materiel to Napoleon's eastward-heading army; the French also developed local roads, bridges, and transport vehicles. The enthusiasm created by the resulting economic boom, combined with the subsequent crushing of political hopes at the retrograde Congress of Vienna in 1815, catalyzed Magyar pride and resentment and sparked new demands for the creation of an autonomous Hungarian state. Led by charismatic leaders like István Széchenyi (1791–1860) and Lajos Kossuth (1802–1894), the Hungarians pushed continually to overthrow the Habsburgs. While they succeeded briefly during the raucous uprisings of 1848–1849 (during which Kossuth dramatically issued the Hungarian Declaration of Independence), Habsburg power was restored by force, with the assistance of tsarist Russia. Kossuth was driven into exile and died abroad. Magyar nationalist hopes lived on, but would not fully revive until the ultimate collapse of the Habsburg Empire in World War I.

By contrast, many of the Irish actually wanted to remain under foreign control. After centuries of British rule and misrule, enough Anglo-Irish Protestants had lived in Ireland long enough to regard the island as their native country. Although a minority of the total population, they were yet sufficiently numerous that the legitimacy of their claims could not be altogether dismissed. But the development of parliamentary government meant that, if Ireland were to gain political autonomy, the Protestants would always remain a minority—and thus, they feared, never receive fair representation in government or full equality before the law. To many loyalists the solution was to deny representation and equality to the Catholic majority by rejecting Irish home rule and prohibiting Catholics from participation in government. Irish nationalism, as it entered the 19th century, thus progressed in two stages—first the struggle for Catholic emancipation, then the fight for home rule. Protestants in Ireland opposed both campaigns.

Since the 16th century, royal writ had effectively restricted political rights in Britain to those willing to take the **Oath of Supremacy**—that is, to recognize the monarch as the supreme head of the church within the realm. This law barred Catholics from holding public office; moreover, anyone who refused to take the oath could be arrested for treason. With very few exceptions, the law had effectively forbidden Irish Catholics to play any part in their own government. Rebellions against England had broken out regularly in the 17th century but were crushed by England's superior armed forces. Legal assaults usually followed on the heels of the military ones. By 1700, for example, Irish Catholics were forbidden to purchase new land or to inherit it from a Protestant, and the law required Catholic landholdings to be subdivided among all surviving sons upon a landholder's death. Over genera-tions these maneuvers undermined Catholic land tenure, turning the Irish majority from free owners to tenants-at-will who could be turned out by their Protestant landlords on a whim. Catholics could not vote, sit on juries, serve in the military, or work as schoolteachers or police. The Anglo-Irish Protestant minority therefore had a monopoly on economic and political power over the entire island.

A brief relaxation of the legal persecution in 1778 produced such a powerful anti-Catholic backlash within England that riots engulfed London, leaving more than four hundred people dead and hundreds more injured. These are known as the "Gordon Riots" (1780), named after Lord George Gordon (1751–1793), who in his position as head of the Protestant Association had led the effort to over-turn the easing of legal oppression of the Catholics. Leading a mob of fifty thou-sand, Gordon tried to present a petition against the legal reforms to Parliament. Blocked from entry into Parliament, the mob then went out of control, destroy-ing Catholic chapels, pillaging the homes of London Catholics, and setting fire to Newgate Prison. It took several days for the English army to quell the riots. Gordon escaped briefly to Holland but afterwards took up residence in Birming-ham, where he converted to Orthodox Judaism. In 1788 he was arrested and sent to Newgate Prison, where he died five years later.[8] Hatred and mistrust across religious lines remained deeply engrained as Ireland entered the 19th century.

England recognized that Catholic emancipation would have to be granted eventually, or else the island would never cease to rebel. As a means of retaining control, however, the English now proposed an **Act of Union**, whereby the nomi-nally independent Irish Parliament (composed solely of Protestant Anglo-Irish since the 17th century) was subsumed into the British Parliament. The Irish were slow to warm to the idea, but eventually they agreed, and in 1801 the union took place. Catholic emancipation followed a generation later. By 1829, therefore, Irish Catholics had secured the right to vote and to serve in government. Their smaller numbers, in both the House of Lords and the House of Commons, however, meant that they were unable to form a sufficiently large bloc to affect policy.

Disputes about the nature of Irish nationalism continued to rage. To the ma-jority Catholics, more than half of whom still spoke Gaelic rather than English, the Protestant Anglo-Irish were not Irish at all. By blood, language, law, religion, and custom they were English and therefore foreigners on Ireland's soil. To the Protestants, national identity meant more than biological ethnicity or religious commitment. A nation could be as legitimately defined by dedication to a set of ideals and values—as the example of the United States showed. In the 1790s, in fact, a Protestant lawyer named Theobald Wolfe Tone (1763–1798), inspired by

---

[8]   The Gordon Riots provide the backdrop to Charles Dickens's novel *Barnaby Rudge* (1841).

the French Revolution, had mounted a campaign for Ireland to solve its political troubles by creating a nonsectarian democratic republic. Enlightenment idealism, he hoped, would dissolve the hatreds that had filled and ruined Irish life. Wolfe Tone went so far as to negotiate a French invasion of the island that would over-throw the parliament in Dublin and establish the new Enlightened Ireland. (The French forces were repulsed quickly, and Wolfe Tone was arrested and convicted of treason. He killed himself while in prison awaiting execution.) The failure of his vision meant that Ireland's competing national identities continued their bloody rivalry throughout the 19th century.

——————— ✦ ———————

Industrialization only worsened matters. Because of its ties to England, Ireland experienced a wave of industrialization earlier than the European con-tinent, though it never advanced far enough to challenge English manufacturing might. (The English saw to that.) Textile factories predominated, for the produc-tion of fine Irish linens, along with breweries and distilleries. These factories were scattered across the country but were found most frequently in counties where the Anglo-Irish Protestants predominated.[9] Most Irish still worked the land and never shared in the prosperity of the factory-owning class. Moreover, farm prices fell dramatically after 1815, when the barriers to trade with the Con-tinent fell, so most farmers fell into ever worse poverty, widening the economic gap between the Catholic majority and the Protestant minority. Manufacturing wealth and agrarian poverty were a volatile mix; the rural poor grew angrier and more violent and even began to organize themselves into networks of underground movements. For the Anglo-Irish, their industrial prosperity meant that they had even more to lose in the event of a successful nationalist rebellion.

The 1820s and 1830s saw repeated attempts at reform. Some of these efforts, like the Catholic Emancipation Act of 1829, which gave Catholic Irishmen (and only men) the right to vote for their own representatives in government, had salu-tary effects. Others, like the temperance movement, seemed a mixed blessing. By 1842 five million people in Ireland had publicly sworn themselves to total absti-nence from alcohol, a figure large enough to worry the owners of the heavily capital-ized breweries and distilleries. By 1844 distillery revenues across Ireland had fallen by 50 percent from what they had been only twenty years earlier. Ireland's popula-tion in 1844 was roughly 8.5 million, so the number of pledge takers represented

---

[9]   One landlord described his Catholic tenants and factory workers as "ignorant, prejudiced, vulgar, brutal [people] unacquainted with . . . an efficient police, kind or indulgent landlords, or a respectable clergy."

Conspirators   An Irish cartoon featuring a group of rebels swearing-in (and toasting) a new recruit to the cause of "Captain Rock"—a euphemism for the cause of Irish nationalism.

more than half the country. Landlords began to fear sober tenants, who might thereby organize into a movement, more than drunken rowdies.

Given the slow emergence of something like an organized Irish majority and the willingness of the British to institute at least some reforms, a successful campaign for Irish independence might have come about by midcentury, but then catastrophe struck—the Great Famine (1845–1852). The fungus-like potato blight (*Phytophthora infestans*) is believed to have come to Ireland in 1844 from South America aboard ships transporting guano, a natural fertilizer widely used in western Europe at the time. The blight in fact infected much of western Europe, not just Ireland. Conditions in Ireland, however, allowed the disease to reach its maximum and most deadly effect. By 1845 fully one-third of the entire Irish population lived on potatoes, combined at best with bacon, buttermilk, and cabbage, since potatoes grew so abundantly as to allow even the poorest farmers with the tiniest landholdings a subsistence diet.[10] The blight—for which no cure is known even today—not only wiped out entire crops but infected the soil itself and guaranteed the loss of subsequent plantings as well even if one brought in fresh seed potatoes. Perhaps half of the 1845 harvest was lost, and the blight destroyed three-quarters of the 1846 harvest. Only in 1852 did the blight run its course, leaving Ireland permanently changed and Irish-English relations permanently scarred. In general, the blight was deadlier the farther to the south and the west one traveled (see Map 19.5).

---

[10]   Farm families, especially in the west, ate as many as twenty potatoes per person daily.

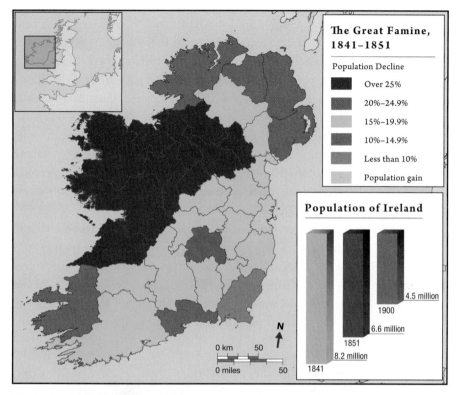

MAP 19.5   **The Great Famine, 1841–1851**

Somewhere between 1 and 1.5 million Irish died of starvation during the famine, and a slightly larger number, perhaps as many as two million, were forced to emigrate—mostly to America and Canada, in addition to from Britain itself. Nearly one-third of the westward-sailing emigrants died before reaching their new homes, however, making the total mortality figures all the more horrific. The blight itself was a natural disaster, but one made considerably worse by British mismanagement of the crisis. The British blocked international relief efforts and refused to commit to long-term public works projects that would have enabled Irish workers to purchase foodstuffs from abroad. To Irish eyes, though, the two most odious of Britain's actions throughout the crisis were to continue shipping into England large quantities of the unblighted potatoes to make up for England's own native losses and to refuse to redirect Irish grain crops (which provided the raw material for the distilleries and breweries owned by the Anglo-Irish) so that they could feed the people instead. As John Mitchel (1815–1875), a young Irish nationalist, bitterly wrote: "The Almighty, indeed, sent the potato blight, but the English created the Famine."

As John Mitchel (1815–1875), a young Irish nationalist, bitterly wrote:

"The Almighty, indeed, sent the potato blight, but the English created the Famine."

Sir Charles Trevelyan (1807–1886), assistant treasury secretary at the time, was responsible for orchestrating Britain's response to the crisis. A dedicated civil servant who went on to hold several important positions in the British Empire, Trevelyan nonetheless was a poor choice for dealing with Ireland's suffering, simply because he seemed to approve of it. "The judgment of God sent the calamity to teach the Irish a lesson," he wrote in a pamphlet, *The Irish Crisis* (1848), that was intended to justify his inaction; indeed, he wrote openly that "th[e] calamity must not be too much mitigated. . . . The real evil with which we have to contend is not the physical evil of the Famine, but the moral evil of the selfish, perverse and turbulent character of the [Irish] people." For his service during the Famine, Trevelyan was knighted by Queen Victoria.

In the midst of this horror, the Revolutions of 1848 rocked Europe. Ireland's version of it lasted only a single day before being put down, but the implications of possible revolt loomed large in British minds afterward. Like the leading voices at Westphalia in 1648 or at Vienna in 1815, the leading political figures in Britain resolved to contain the revolutionary impulse and sought any means to forestall Irish independence. The issue of home rule did not emerge again as a live political issue until the 1880s.

The Face of Horror   The suffering of the Potato Famine in Ireland is starkly portrayed in this painting from 1850 by George Frederick Watts (1817–1904).

Within Ireland, two essential demographic facts shaped matters. First, many of the most desperate, angry, and radical of the Irish had either died or emigrated. This may explain the political quiescence of Ireland after midcentury, since the presumed leaders of any populist movement were absent. Second, the enormity of the disaster, coupled with some easing of British restrictions on land tenure for Catholics, meant that those Irish who did remain on the land were able to increase their holdings: individual farms grew from as few as five acres to fifteen, or a hundred, or even more, which meant that something beyond mere survival was possible. Industrialization declined overall throughout the island but focused more intensely on the northern counties, such as Ulster, where a large shipbuilding industry took root. In other words, postfamine Ireland was less populous overall, more secure in its resources, and more ethnically and religiously demarcated. For the time being, peaceful order and relative calm and prosperity trumped the urgent demands of the frustrated Irish version of nationalism.

ASSIMILATION AND ZIONISM

The Psalmist's oath in exile has been a mainstay of Jewish prayers and aspirations for centuries: "If I forget you, O Jerusalem, let my right hand wither; let my tongue stick to my palette if I cease to think of you, if I do not keep Jerusalem in memory even at my happiest hour" (Psalms 137.5–6).

Driven into Diaspora by the Romans, the Jews' dream of returning to Palestine remained constant, even if it seldom expressed itself in a mass movement. Some individual and small-group emigration trickled into the region, and on occasion it swelled—at it did, for example, after the establishment of the Crusader states in the 12th century and with the consolidation of the Ottoman Empire in the 16th and 17th centuries. For the most part, though, the bulk of Europe's Jews since the Diaspora chose either to coexist with mainstream Western society or to assimilate, while awaiting the messiah.

While there is no absolutely necessary link between the return to Zion and the appearance of messiah, most Talmudic and **midrashic** writers over the centuries assumed a connection between the phenomena. By the start of the 19th century most Jews expected the two events to happen concurrently. In 1845, however, a European conference of Reform rabbis proclaimed that the appearance of the messiah and the return to Zion could happen separately. The exploits of several would-be messiahs over the years, such as Sabbatai Zvi (see chapter 12) and Jacob Frank (1726–1791), had made many Jews skeptical of messianic claims but still dedicated to the notion of return to the Holy Land.

During the Enlightenment many Jews, especially the more well-to-do, embraced the rationalism of the age, in the hope that in a Europe without religion there would be no religious hatred. Some of these Jews abandoned Orthodoxy, accepted Western gentile forms of dress, diet, and thought, and joined the world of the salons. The great philosopher Moses Mendelssohn (1729–1786) is perhaps the best example of an assimilated, Enlightened Jew. Still others went so far as to accept baptism as a means of gaining entry to mainstream society— like the parents of Karl Marx and of the British statesman Benjamin Disraeli (1804–1881).

Most Western countries had given Jews—officially, at least—something like full civic and political equality by 1871: they struck down guild restrictions that had prohibited Jewish involvement in certain industries and crafts; they opened Europe's universities to Jews; and they permitted Jews to participate in newly emerging professions like journalism. Under the Ancien Régime Jews had not been permitted to reside in Paris; by 1880 more than forty thousand Jews lived there—nearly two-thirds of all the Jews in France. Throughout Germany, Jewish populations in cities of at least twenty thousand inhabitants quadrupled between 1815 and 1871. In Berlin alone the Jewish population increased from three thousand to thirty-six thousnad over that period.

Most Jews in western Europe prospered in these years. Tax rolls tell the tale. England, for example, had admitted roughly ten thousand Jewish immigrants between 1750 and 1815, most of them simple peddlers; yet by 1850 virtually all of their families had achieved middle-class status. In Germany, 80 percent of all Jews reported incomes that made them solidly middle-class.

Wie sich der Chanukaleuchter des Ziegenfellhändlers **Cohn** in Pinne zum Christbaum des Kommerzienrats **Conrad** in der Tiergartenstraße (Berlin W.) entwickelte.

Assimilation: An Evolutionary Perspective   An anti-assimilationist cartoon. Jews cannot become assimilated into the German nation without losing their Jewish identity.

Given their urbanization, Jews figured large as business leaders, journalists, physicians, and lawyers.[11] Many Jews launched political careers as well. Adolphe Crémieux (1796–1880) served in France's Chamber of Deputies and twice held the position of minister of justice; Gabriel Riesser (1806–1863) became Germany's first Jewish judge. Benjamin Disraeli, mentioned before, was England's first (and still the only) Jewish prime minister.

Romantic nationalism, however, quickly ended the Enlightened dream of a single, unified, rationalized human community, and Jews were once again seen as alien. Resistance to Jewish advancement occurred at the popular level, and it rose as rapidly as the Jews themselves did within society. But racial discrimination, not religious opposition, defined the new anti-Semitism. Marx may have been one of the first Westerners to write publicly about "the Jewish Question," but he was hardly the first to raise it. In 1844 a Frenchman named Alphonse Toussenel (1803–1885) published a vile attack titled *The Jews—Kings of Our Time: A History of Financial Feudalism*, which was quickly followed by Arthur de Gobineau's (1816–1882) *Essay on the Inequality of the Human Races* (1855), one of the first books to argue for the inherent superiority of the "Aryan race."

These books represent the start of a century-long parade of anti-Semitic literature in Europe that culminated in an infamous forgery, *The Protocols of the Elders of Zion* (1903). This Russian work, soon translated into every major European language, purports to represent the blueprint for an international Jewish conspiracy to take over the world. In English the terms anti-Semitic and **anti-Semitism** were coined in 1881, appearing first in the London journal *The Athenaeum* with the laconic observation that "anti-Semitic literature is very prosperous in Germany."[12] Being disproportionately visible in industrial, urban Europe, the Jews were disproportionately blamed for its miseries. That meant everything from low wages and miserable housing for workers to self-satisfied, bourgeois elitism.

> Being disproportionately visible in industrial, urban Europe, the Jews were disproportionately blamed for its miseries.

The Jews' very success was seen as proof of their insidious intent. Surely it cannot be a coincidence that Jews own businesses, publish newspapers, fill the ranks of the medical and legal professions, manage theaters, and help write the laws? Either the Jews are engaged in an international conspiracy or they are simply mean and grasping. In either case, the bigots concluded, we tolerate the Jews at our peril. But not all criticism of assimilation came from outside. Many Orthodox

---

[11] Jews made up 10 percent of all lawyers in the city of Würtemberg. In Vienna in 1870 fully 40 percent of all medical students were Jewish.

[12] A German journalist named Wilhelm Marr appears to have invented the word anti-Semitism in 1879.

Jews viewed warily the rise of secularism. Jewish schools now taught secular subjects—geography, mathematics, and European languages—that pushed aside the traditional focus on the study of scripture and the Talmud. The Jewish High Rabbinical Court in Paris in 1808 had asserted the authority of civil law over religious law; in effect, Jews should be French citizens first and observant Jews second. In 1818 authorities in Hamburg issued a new prayer book written in German, not Hebrew, and printed from left to right, unlike Hebrew. It also introduced practices like choirs, organ playing, sermons in the local language, and integration of the sexes, and it dropped from the weekly prayers all references to a Jewish return to Zion.

These tensions resulted in new efforts to establish at long last a Jewish state. Two fundamental convictions form the basis of those efforts, known as **Zionism**. One is the belief in the Jews' unique claim to possession of the Holy Land—a claim as old as the Abrahamic Covenant. The other is recognition of the historical fact that the Jews, despite two thousand years of effort, will never be wholly accepted into Western society. The Viennese journalist Theodor Herzl (1860–1904), who organized the First International Zionist Congress, summed up this view in a powerful pamphlet titled *The Jewish State* (1896):

> The anti-Semitism of today should not be confused with the persecutions that Jews have faced in the past, for while it does have a religious tinge to it in some countries, the principle focus of this new aggression is different. In most places where anti-Semitism thrives, in other words, it does so because of the [civil] emancipation of the Jews. . . . Maybe, if we would be left in peace for a generation or two, we could possibly assimilate completely into the peoples who surround us, but the simple fact is that they will not leave us in peace. Instead, they manage to tolerate us for a short time, but then their hostility returns—again and again. For some reason our prosperity irritates the world, probably because for so many centuries it had grown accustomed to regard us as the most contemptible of the poor. Society's stupidity and mean-heartedness have made it blind to the fact that prosperity has actually weakened our Jewish identity by eradicating those customs that used to distinguish us. . . . We are a single people—our enemies have united us even without our consent. This has happened before. Suffering has brought us together, and in that union we recognize our strength. Surely we are strong enough to found a state of our own, one that will be a model for all states.

The Zionist movement found most of its support among the Jews of eastern Europe. These Jews, in the 19th century, made up roughly two-thirds of the

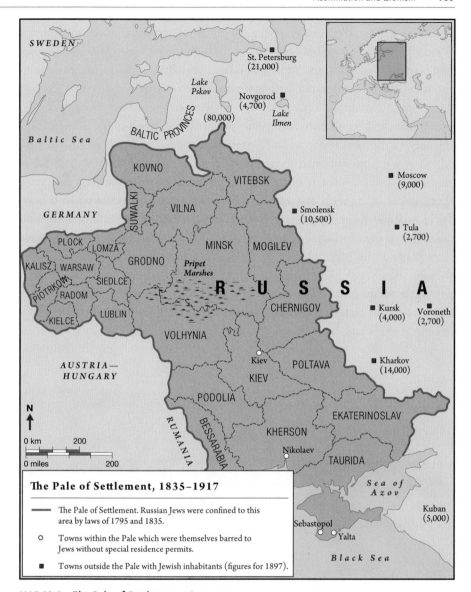

MAP 19.6   The Pale of Settlement, 1835–1917

entire world's Jewish population, so success here was essential to the ultimate spread of Zionism (see Map 19.6).

Anti-Semitism in eastern Europe—including the area known as the **Pale of Settlement**—was particularly vicious. The Russian tsar and king of Poland Aleksandr II (r. 1855–1881), despite his liberalizing tendencies, was widely unpopular and the subject of numerous assassination attempts. In fact, in 1881 members of the revolutionary Narodnaya Volya ("Will of the People") Party did kill him. Although no Jewish individuals or groups had been involved, popular sentiment blamed the murder on the supposed international Jewish conspiracy. Wave after wave of **pogroms** now rolled through the region, cutting down Jews, destroying synagogues, and setting Jewish books aflame. As a result, more than three million Jews migrated farther westward into eastern and central Europe, desperate and hungry, carrying only the possessions they had on their backs. To these exiles and the eastern European Jews who welcomed them, Zionism was the only solution to the hatred and bigotry that had permeated Jewish history.

Slowly, groups of Jewish settlers also began to return to the Holy Land. Between 1881 and 1914 nearly one hundred thousand Jews had taken up residence there, either living with distant relations and friends or purchasing land from Turkish landlords or Palestinian freeholders. Zionist organizations in Europe created their own financial networks that made capital available to would-be settlers. Many of the Turks who sold their lands were absentee landlords, and some were public officials determined to withdraw from a decaying Ottoman state with their purses full. These were fully legal purchases of property, but that fact did not appease many of the roughly seven hundred thousand Palestinians who lived in the area and dreamed of a free homeland of their own.

The Aftermath of a Pogrom The aftermath of an anti-Jewish pogrom in Russia, 1881. Survivors pick through the remnants of a Torah scroll, prayer books, and other items in a pillaged synagogue.

ISLAMIC NATIONALISMS

Nationalism roiled throughout the Islamic world just as in Europe. The Ottoman state had expanded far into Europe, with a diverse religious and ethnic makeup, and through the centuries it had likewise struggled to guarantee a degree of religious toleration while preserving Islamic religious law, guarding the holy cities, and maintaining the pilgrimage routes that led to them. Moreover, the flexible structure of Ottoman administration had allowed non-Turks to serve in government and even to rise to positions of political and social prominence. But in the 18th century the empire went on the defensive against expansionist powers in Russia, Austria, and revolutionary France. And with the rise of industrial Europe, the empire as a unifying force for Muslims weakened dramatically, to be replaced by ethnically based nationalist sentiments. The Ottoman gift for accommodation proved no match for the newfound commercial and military might of European states, and the tardy reform efforts of figures like Selim III (r. 1780–1807) crumbled in the face of the increasingly urgent demands for local control over local fates.

Greece wrested her independence from the Ottomans in the 1820s. In the following decade France, which had already humiliated the Muslims during Napoleon's Egyptian and Syrian adventures, invaded Algeria and carved it away from Ottoman rule. At the same time, Tunisia and Egypt instituted political and economic reforms in an effort to secure their independence. The region of Bulgaria had gained autonomy by 1830, with Romania not far behind. Off to the east, the Caucasus territories of Abkhazia, Georgia, Batumi, and Kars were wrenched away by Russia. By 1878 the Ottomans remained in control of only Anatolia, Iraq, Palestine, and the Hijaz—the coastal strip of Arabia that lay alongside the Red Sea, including the holy cities of Mecca and Medina. Persia had long since established itself as an independent—indeed a rival—state under the Safavids and then the Qajars. What had once been a universal Islamic empire stretching from the Atlantic Ocean to India was thereby reduced to a single Middle East state, kept alive by a shaky alliance between its Turkish and Arab leaders.

———————— ✦ ————————

Nationalistic passions were both fed and challenged by several new strains in Islamic thought. In the 19th century Russian intellectual life was divided between liberals and Slavophiles—that is, between those who promoted Western-style reforms on the one hand and those who urged a return to Russian cultural and religious tradition on the other; 19th-century Islamic thought was divided as well. While many believed that new Muslim countries could be aligned with Europe without abandoning their Islamic character, others advocated instead a thorough turning away from the Greater West and delving deeper into Islamic tradition. An example of the first was the pro-Western reform promoted in Egypt under the dynasty established by **Mehmet Ali Pasha** (r. 1805–1848), more commonly known in the West by the Arabized version of his name, Muhammad Ali Pasha. An example of the second was the intensely conservative reform championed by the dynasty of Muhammad ibn Saud (r. 1744–1765), a tribal prince from a small oasis town in central Arabia.

Mehmet Ali, an ethnic Albanian, arrived in Egypt from Ottoman-controlled Greece at the head of an army as part of the Ottomans' campaign to regain control of Egypt after Napoleon's forces had withdrawn. He assassinated most of his Mamluk rivals for power, which made him popular with the Egyptian masses, and subsequently drove the remaining Mamluk soldiers into the desert. By 1805 he had taken the title of *wali* ("governor") of the country and ruled independently, even though he publicly claimed obedience to the ruler in Istanbul. His most important innovation was a popular army. Mehmet understood the growing weakness of the regime in Istanbul and believed that Egypt was the site for a renewal of Islamic power: its economic might, coupled with its proximity to the holy cities of the Arabian Peninsula, made it the natural successor as leader of the Islamic world. But in order for Egypt to assume that leadership, he believed, the Egyptians themselves had to form the basis of the state, and hence he remodeled the army.

> Mehmet understood the growing weakness of the regime in Istanbul and believed that Egypt was the site for a renewal of Islamic power: its economic might, coupled with its proximity to the holy cities of the Arabian Peninsula, made it the natural successor as leader of the Islamic world.

By 1820 he had conscripted thirty thousand Egyptians and turned them into a disciplined force, and by the end of his life in 1848 the army numbered 150,000 or more. This was the first truly Egyptian military force—with ethnic Egyptians making up the rank and file and gradually staffing the officers' ranks as well—since the days of the pharaohs. Mehmet wanted a modern army too, with modern weaponry, and so he established close ties with industrialized England, from whom he acquired not only modern rifles and artillery but also military trainers to instruct his soldiers. He also put together a new navy with ships purchased from England, France, Italy, and Greece. By 1830 he had constructed his own new shipyard at Alexandria, which began to produce a steady stream of frigates and men-of-war. Once his navy was fully developed, Mehmet launched a combined land and sea attack against the Ottomans, taking Jerusalem, Acre, Damascus, Beirut, and Aleppo in quick succession until, by peace treaty in 1833, he ruled all of Palestine and Syria in addition to Egypt. He also sent a force into Arabia itself, and briefly controlled both Mecca and Medina.

Mehmet Ali ruled as an autocrat but reorganized and professionalized the government along Western lines, with a central cabinet composed of ministries

Negotiating with the Europeans   David Roberts (1796-1864) produced this lithograph of the great social reformer Muhammad Ali Pasha (r. 1805-1848) receiving European dignitaries in his palace at Alexandria, Egypt. Roberts spent several years in Egypt and the Middle East drawing sketches from which he later produced color prints, which he published in nine hugely popular volumes.

of war, finance, foreign relations, education, and commerce. In trade, he directed Egypt's exports away from the Ottomans and toward Europe. He supported the introduction of cotton cultivation along the Nile, and soon Egyptian cotton began to be shipped to the factories of England. As soon as the engineering skill was available, Mehmet Ali also constructed his own textile plants and sugar refineries, too. He appointed European administrators and civil engineers to improve the sanitation of cities, and he hired Europeans to head new military academies and polytechnic (vocational) schools.[13] Newspapers were introduced, appearing in both Arabic and French. New centers for translating European technical manuals into Arabic were set up, along with publishing houses to produce the works.

REFORMING ISLAM

The opening up to Europe helped to inspire an intellectual and cultural revival in Egypt known as **al-Nahda** ("awakening" or "renaissance"), which some writers describe as an Islamic Enlightenment. Most of the thinkers associated with

---

[13]   In the 19th century, roughly one-tenth of the urban populations in Egypt died each year from infectious disease.

al-Nahda believed that Muslim society faced being surpassed by Europe's economic, military, and technological might and thus needed to open its arms and minds to ideas from the outside world. As in their great medieval empire, Muslims could actually strengthen and deepen their culture, they believed, for customs from abroad could be harmonized with Islamic values.

The first great figure in the movement was Rifa'a al-Tahtawi (1801–1873). He had been sent to Paris, along with a corps of younger students, by Mehmet Ali Pasha in 1826 in order to learn French, study Western ideas, and develop closer understanding between Europe and the Islamic world. After a stay of five years, Tahtawi wrote a celebrated memoir (*The Essence of Paris*) in which he recounts his group's excitement at learning Western law, philosophy, mathematics, and science. He read Voltaire, Rousseau, and Montesquieu. He wrote volumes on social theory, citizenship and political rights, and moral philosophy. After returning to Cairo, he established the School of Languages (1835), which not only instructed students in languages but also served as a central clearinghouse for ideas about secular government, national identity, and cultural pluralism. Tahtawi believed passionately in the integration of Islam and European culture. This was possible, he argues, because Europe had separated its religion from its political and civic traditions. Key to this integration, he contends, is the notion of **citizenship**—a form of group identity that is not determined by race, creed, or ethnicity. Rather, one chooses to join a community and acts as a member in good standing of it. A nation, in the modern sense, Tahtawi urges, consists of people who share not just an allegiance to a vision of the past but a vision for the future.

> A nation, in the modern sense, Tahtawi urges, consists of people who share not just an allegiance to a vision of the past but a vision for the future.

The other major school of Islamic thought, however, thoroughly rejected, condemned, and demonized modernization. The clerics and writers known ultimately as **Wahhabis** were conservatives and traditionalists, but nationalists too in their way. Named for a mirthless cleric from central Arabia, Muhammad ibn Abd al-Wahhab (1703–1792), the Wahhabi movement declared that the overwhelming majority of Muslims throughout the entire world—Sunni, Shi'a, and Sufi—had fallen into a state of spiritual ignorance and moral barbarism. What had caused this religious desolation? Ignorance of the meaning of the Qur'anic concept of *tawhid*—the "unity" of God. Interpreting this concept in the strictest possible fashion, Wahhabis emphasized that God is the One, the Only, the Creator, the Divine. Any act of religious observance that diverted attention from him was an abomination. Acts such as charity to the poor or the veneration of shrines bestowed on human beings or physical spaces the devotion owed solely to God. As al-Wahhab once wrote:

It is well-known that the Messenger of God (Peace be upon him!) obliged the faithful to observe *tawhid* many years before obliging them to the Pillars of Islam. . . . *Tawhid* is supreme among religious duties, more important than prayer, alms, fasting, and pilgrimage.

Anything and everything that distracts the soul from recognizing the Supreme One is an abomination. Wahhabism accepts as historical facts the miracles performed by Islamic saints, but it forbids veneration of the saints who performed them or the shrines where they are entombed. That would be idolatry. To give alms to the poor is a religious requirement, but it is idolatrous to do so out of love for the poor rather than love of God. Only by returning to a pure and martial faith—ideally to practices in existence during the lifetime of the Prophet himself—could the moral horror of the modern world be erased and an authentic Muslim society established.

Abd al-Wahhab never articulated a full body of teachings on government. Drawing his inspiration from the 14th-century conservative jurist Ibn Taymiyya, he stressed the moral responsibility of the ruler to destroy all forms of idolatry—if necessary, by force. Any ruler who adhered to Wahhabi ideals and enforced its strict moral code would be acceptable. Al-Wahhab taught that every true Muslim (meaning his followers) must refuse to obey political and clerical authorities who do not maintain the proper attitude toward tawhid. It was not until well after his death in 1792 that his clerical successors began to formulate a coherent set of ideas regarding governance; most drew their main ideas directly from Ibn Taymiyya. Ibn Taymiyya had identified "innovation in religion" as a second abomination, equal to that of idolatry, and called for relentless state action to stamp it out in all its forms. His Wahhabi acolytes did the same in the 19th century.

The Arab prince Muhammad ibn Saud enthusiastically embraced the teachings of the Taymiyya-Wahhabi sect in the middle of the 18th century. Ibn Saud was an ambitious figure, determined to free Arabia from foreign control and create a new Arab-led society that would restore Islam's greatness and purge it of the vile "innovations" that had crept into its practice through the centuries. Two enemies, as he saw it, stood out among many—the Ottomans and the Sufis. By 1765, when Ibn Saud died, he had conquered much of central Arabia and parts of the east. His succeeding son, grandson, and great-grandson extended the conquests, until by 1818 nearly the entire peninsula, including the holy cities, was under their control (see Map 19.7). At this point, the Egyptian reformer Mehmet Ali, acting with the blessing of the Ottoman ruler in Istanbul, launched his own attack on Arabia, to wrest the holy sites from Saudi control and liberate them from Wahhabi doctrine and practice. He succeeded for a time, but Saudi determination and the fast-growing sense of Arab nationalism won control back for them in 1824. This Second Saudi State lasted from 1824 to 1891.

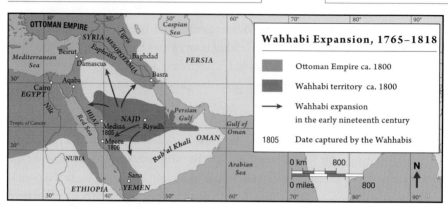

MAP 19.7   Wahhabi Expansion, 1765–1818

A key element of Wahhabism, based on the Taymiyyism of the 14th century, is the notion that only Arabs can reform and save Islam. The religious revelation vouchsafed to the Prophet Muhammad called first for the unification of the Arab tribes and only afterward for bringing the Prophet's message to all mankind. Islamic reform movements throughout history have had an ethnic or nationalist element, beginning with the Shi'a tradition, which asserted the primacy of religious authority among those directly descended from the Prophet. In medieval times, the Abbasids urged the Persianization of Islamic life in order to unify groups embracing the faith. The Almoravid and Almohad movements of the 11th and 12th centuries called for a restoration of rigorous jihad under leadership by the Berbers of North Africa. The arrival of the Seljuk Turks triggered the start of a conservative Sunni crackdown on the Shi'a (though under Turkish leadership), but also broadened the appeal of the Sufi movement. The Mongols and Tatars had no doubts about who was meant to control and reform the Islamic world. And the arrival of the Ottoman Turks encouraged a new openness to non-Islamic culture—although under the Ottomans' own strict control. In the 14th century Ibn Taymiyya was the first figure of note to call for the restoration of Islamic leadership to those to whom Allah himself had granted it, the Arabs. In its 19th-century Wahhabi version, Saudi-based Arab nationalism simply completed a historical cycle that restored leadership to the people who had been privileged to wield it first.

> In its 19th-century Wahhabi version, Saudi-based Arab nationalism simply completed a historical cycle that restored leadership to the people who had been privileged to wield it first.

The fast-crumbling Ottoman Empire, for its part, tried to counter the pro-Western nationalism exemplified by Egypt and the Wahhabi nationalism of the Saudis. The empire's Tanzimat (Turkish for "reform"), which flourished from

1839 to 1876, represented a last-ditch effort to hold onto power.[14] Its essence was to promote civic secularism while protecting religious pluralism. Especially within its shrunken political borders, the Ottoman realm was too diverse, both ethnically and religiously, to conflate religion and civic life. So the Ottomans proposed, if anything, a different kind of nationalism—one based not on race or creed but on secular government and religious freedom. They built more schools, reorganized curricula, and encouraged newspapers and magazines. They enacted

ARMÉE OTTOMANE

SADIK-BEY
Colonel d'infanterie, aide de camp de
S. M. I. le Sultan.

RIZA-BEY
Commandant de cavalerie, aide de camp
de S. M. I. le Sultan.

CHEFKET-BEY
Lieutenant-colonel d'artillerie.

Uniformed Secularism   Portrait of three leaders of the increasingly secular and professional Turkish army. The religiously trained and motivated Janissaries had been disbanded in 1826, after they had attempted a coup. The great reform era known as Tanzimat ("Re-organization") lasted from 1839 to 1876, during which the empire attempted to integrate its non-Muslim subjects more fully into society, while modernizing its institutions and legal processes. In the end, the empire fell victim to the intense nationalist passions of the nineteenth century.

---

[14]   Tanzimat failed to sustain the empire, but it helped to lay the foundations for the modern nation of Turkey after World War I.

laws promising equality for all subjects regardless of faith. They even appointed Christians and Jews to reform councils to advise the government, as well as to the Supreme Judicial Council, which acted as an appellate court. The fact that the Arab world violently rejected these reforms and called for an end to Ottoman power shows the depths of nationalist passions.

WHO, WHAT, WHERE

Act of Union
al-Nahda
anti-Semitism
citizenship
Crimean War
Junkers
Kulturkampf
Mehmet Ali Pasha

midrashic
nationalism
Oath of Supremacy
Pale of Settlement
pogroms
Wahhabis
Zionism

SUGGESTED READINGS

Primary Sources

Bismarck, Otto von. *Memoirs.*

Fichte, Johann Gottlieb. *Address to the German Nation.*

Herzl, Theodor. *The Jewish State.*

———. *Old New Land.*

Mazzini, Giuseppe. *The Duties of Man.*

Renan, Ernest. *What Is a Nation?*

Seacole, Mary. *Wonderful Adventures of Mrs. Seacole in Many Lands.*

al-Tahtawi, Rifa'a. *The Emancipation of Muslim Women.*

———. *The Essence of Paris.*

Anthologies

Kurzman, Charles, ed. *Modernist Islam, 1840–1940: A Sourcebook* (2002).

Spencer, Philip, and Howard Wollman, eds. *Nations and Nationalism: A Reader* (2005).

Studies

Aksan, Virginia H. *Ottoman Wars, 1700–1870: An Empire Besieged* (2007).

Akşin, Sina. *Turkey from Empire to Revolutionary Republic: The Emergence of the Turkish Nation from 1789 to the Present* (2007).

Anderson, Benedict. *Imagined Communities: Reflections on the Origin and Spread of Nationalism* (2006).

Baron, Beth. *Egypt as a Woman: Nationalism, Gender, and Politics* (2007).

Bayly, C. A. *The Birth of the Modern World, 1780–1914* (2003).

Ceylan, Ebubekir. *The Ottoman Origins of Modern Iraq: Political Reform, Modernization, and Development in the Nineteenth-Century Middle East* (2011).

Çiçek, Nazan. *The Young Ottomans: Turkish Critics of the Eastern Question in the Late Nineteenth Century* (2010).

Clark, Christopher. *Iron Kingdom: The Rise and Downfall of Prussia, 1600–1947* (2009).

Eichner, Carolyn J. *Surmounting the Barricades: Women in the Paris Commune* (2004).

Eley, Geoff. *Forging Democracy: The History of the Left in Europe, 1850–2000* (2002).

Elon, Amos. *The Pity of It All: A Portrait of the German-Jewish Epoch, 1743–1933* (2003).

Fahmy, Khaled. *All the Pasha's Men: Mehmed Ali, His Army, and the Making of Modern Egypt* (2002).

Frankel, Richard E. *Bismarck's Shadow: The Cult of Leadership and the Transformation of the German Right, 1898–1945* (2005).

Gellner, Ernest. *Nations and Nationalism* (2009).

Gerwarth, Robert. *The Bismarck Myth: Weimar Germany and the Legacy of the Iron Chancellor* (2005).

Gross, Michael B. *The War against Catholicism: Liberalism and the Anti-Catholic Imagination in Nineteenth-Century Germany* (2005).

Hall, Catherine, Keith McClelland, and Jane Rendall. *Defining the Victorian Nation: Class, Race, Gender, and the British Reform Act of 1867* (2000).

Harvey, David. *Paris: Capital of Modernity* (2005).

Hewitson, Mark. *Nationalism in Germany, 1848–1866: Revolutionary Nation* (2010).

Khuri-Makdisi, Ilham. *The Eastern Mediterranean and the Making of Global Radicalism, 1860–1914* (2010).

Langewiesche, Dieter. *Liberalism in Germany* (2000).

Lerman, Katharine Anne. *Bismarck* (2004).

Offen, Karen. *European Feminisms, 1700–1950: A Political History* (2000).

Pollard, Lisa. *Nurturing the Nation: The Family Politics of Modernizing, Colonizing, and Liberating Egypt, 1805–1923* (2005).

Porter, Brian. *When Nationalism Began to Hate: Imagining Modern Politics in Nineteenth-Century Poland* (2002).

Smith, Anthony D. *The Ethnic Origins of Nations* (2009).

———. *Nationalism: Theory, Ideology, History* (2002).

Wawro, Geoffrey. *The Franco-Prussian War: The German Conquest of France in 1870–1871* (2005).

Wetzel, David. *A Duel of Giants: Bismarck, Napoleon III, and the Origins of the Franco-Prussian War* (2003).

For additional resources, including maps, primary sources, visuals, web links, and quizzes, please go to **www.oup.com/us/backman.**

CHAPTER 20

The God Problem

1799–1907

"God is dead." Many people know this quotation from the German philosopher Friedrich Nietzsche (1844–1900), if only from having seen it scrawled on bathroom walls, where it often comes with a rejoinder: "Nietzsche is dead—God." However, Nietzsche's statement was not, as many readers assume, a bold declaration of intellectual freedom after centuries of superstition and thought control. For him, the death of God was tragic, perhaps the worst calamity ever to befall mankind. His insight highlights the dilemmas of one of the 19th century's most striking changes: secularization, or the declining power of religious beliefs and institutions and the subsequent decline in religious practice. The ascendancy of secularism resulted from many factors but derived in large part from two of the century's greatest scientific achievements, in a new theory of earth's history and Darwin's theory of evolution by natural selection. It affected how a new generation studied the Bible itself, as part of a movement called *historical criticism*, and it drew intense and conflicted responses from all faiths across Europe.

THE VOYAGE OF THE BEAGLE, 1831–1836

◀ **God Is Not Dead**   Prayer card (1867) depicting pilgrims to the grotto at Lourdes, France, where a vision of the Virgin Mary occurred to St. Bernadette Soubirons. At top, Christ displays his Sacred Heart while bestowing a blessing on the church. Pilgrims look through a protective fence at the grotto—at the back of which stands the figure of Mary.

NIETZSCHE: A COSMOS WITHOUT GOD

The son, grandson, and great-grandson of Lutheran pastors, Nietzsche was steeped in Christian tradition—and like so many of his peers, he had left his faith behind by his mid-twenties. Yet rather than rejoicing in the

- Nietzsche: A Cosmos without God
- Who Killed God?
- The Theory of Creation
- Evolution by Natural Selection
- The Bible and History
- The Protestant Churches' Response
- The Catholic Counterattack
- The War on Modernism
- Modernism, Secularism, and the Jews
- The Islamic Exception

CHAPTER OUTLINE

power of the rational mind released at last, he saw only ruin and misery. In his 1882 book *The Gay Science*, he cast the dilemma as a parable.

> Have you heard the tale of the lunatic who lit his lantern early one morning and ran into the marketplace shouting out, "I want to find God! I want to see God!" Since many in the crowd around him did not believe in God, he stirred them to laughter.
> "Is God lost?" asked one.
> Another replied, "Maybe He has lost His way, like a little child?"
> "No, surely He is simply hiding, or has gone on holiday!"
> "Perhaps He emigrated instead!"
> They all jeered and laughed, but the lunatic stood his ground. Piercing them with his eyes he cried out, "Do you want to know where God has gone? I'll tell you: We have killed him! Yes, you and I—we murdered Him! . . . God is dead and will remain so, and we are the ones who killed Him. What comfort is there now for us—we, the worst of all murderers! The holiest and most powerful force ever to have existed has bled to death, cut open by our knives, and there is no one who can wipe the bloodstain from our hands. What water can possibly wash it away? What rites of atonement, what sacred mysteries would have to be invented [to purify us]? Is not the deed we have done too much for us to bear? Must we not become gods ourselves now, simply to appear worthy of our action?

At this, the crowd grows silent. They had not, Nietzsche saw, considered the implications of their unbelief or their mockery:

> At length the lunatic hurled his lantern to the ground, where it smashed into pieces and its light went out. Then the lunatic said, "I have come too early; it is not yet my time. News of the Great Event is still

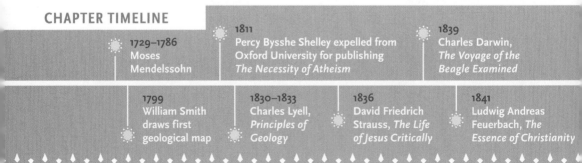

CHAPTER TIMELINE

1811
Percy Bysshe Shelley expelled from Oxford University for publishing *The Necessity of Atheism*

1839
Charles Darwin, *The Voyage of the Beagle Examined*

1729–1786
Moses Mendelssohn

1799
William Smith draws first geological map

1830–1833
Charles Lyell, *Principles of Geology*

1836
David Friedrich Strauss, *The Life of Jesus Critically*

1841
Ludwig Andreas Feuerbach, *The Essence of Christianity*

approaching, still on the move, and hasn't yet reached their ears. Just as lightning and thunder require time [to reach men's awareness], as starlight does too, so do deeds require time before men can perceive them and understand—and the meaning of this particular deed is still further from these men than even the most distant stars. And yet they themselves did it!"

It is said that the lunatic later pushed his way into several churches and struck up a funeral prayer, crying "May God rest in eternal peace!" Each time, when he was led outside and asked to explain himself, he replied only, "What are churches now but the tombs and mausoleums of the Lord?" *(The Gay Science, no. 125)*

A cosmos without God, Nietzsche understood, is purposeless and without meaning. The universe becomes a vast sprawl of indifference. An act of creation meant that life exists for a reason. If there is no Creator, all that exists is a random gathering of molecules—beautiful, perhaps, but in the end pointless and spiritually void. Worst of all, human life has no intrinsic value. I may be kindhearted and charitable, with love for everyone around me; or I may selfishly hoard material goods, seize whatever sexual pleasures I desire, and smash the skulls of anyone I wish to harm. It makes no difference at all. The world will continue on its way, and all my actions, whether "good" or "bad," will be forgotten. It certainly is "nicer" to be kind than to be selfish—but niceness is no substitute for God. If human existence is a mere crack of light between eternities of darkness, then why not take whatever pleasures one desires while one can? This is, after all, the only opportunity one will ever have to experience them.

> Nietzsche was not the first philosopher to consider the implications of a Godless universe, but he felt those implications so deeply that his writings still have the power to shock, enthrall, enrage, and horrify readers.

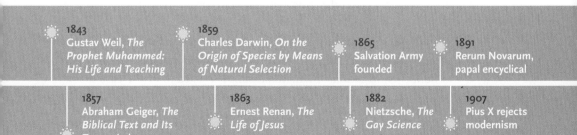

1843
Gustav Weil, *The Prophet Muhammed: His Life and Teaching*

1859
Charles Darwin, *On the Origin of Species by Means of Natural Selection*

1865
Salvation Army founded

1891
Rerum Novarum, papal encyclical

1857
Abraham Geiger, *The Biblical Text and Its Transmission*

1863
Ernest Renan, *The Life of Jesus*

1882
Nietzsche, *The Gay Science*

1907
Pius X rejects modernism

Nietzsche   Friedrich Nietzsche
(1844–1900), the philosopher of the
death of God.

Nietzsche was not the first philosopher to consider the implications of a Godless universe, but he felt those implications so deeply that his writings still have the power to shock, enthrall, enrage, and horrify readers. He is one of the very few philosophers to whom people respond viscerally. But that was his aim—to shake us out of our intellectual complacency and force us to confront painful questions. If "God is dead," this is precisely why we have to start thinking harder than we have ever done. And without delaying a single instant.

The 19th century marks a watershed in European history, the period when Western culture began to turn decidedly secular. Since the dawn of Western history in 3000 BCE, religion had formed an essential part of the bedrock of its culture. Religious doubters, rebels, skeptics, heretics, and critics existed in every faith and every age, but genuine nonbelief was rare. How else could one explain the existence of the world than by a god? From ancient Greece forward, virtually all leading scientists—from Aristotle to Newton—were people of religious conviction. Philosophers from Plato to René Descartes (1596–1650), Baruch Spinoza (1632–77), Immanuel Kant (1724–1804), and Georg Friedrich Hegel (1770–1831) all retained passionate, if sometimes quirky, convictions about God. Even the most irreligious of the Enlightened, Voltaire, acknowledged the existence of a divine creator. **Atheism** existed, and indeed the word dates back to the 16th century, but its usage was limited to "godlessness" in the moral sense—of "godless" behavior.[1] Except for Nietzsche, almost everyone yet mentioned in this book accepted the existence of one or more deities—and based ethical behavior at least partly on that belief.

What, then, had happened? Why did the rejection, or mere absence, of religious belief suddenly become so prominent in European society? In 1811 the Romantic poet Percy Bysshe Shelley (1792–1822) was expelled from Oxford University when he was discovered to be the author of a pamphlet called *The Necessity of Atheism*. In 1877, however, the Russian writer Leo Tolstoy (1828–1910) could have one character describe another, in his novel *Anna Karenina*, as

> an odd, uneducated fellow, one of those wild "modern" people one meets so often these days, a "freethinker" raised from birth with notions of nonbelief, negation, and materialism. . . . It used to be the case that a

---

[1]   The words secularism, agnosticism, and atheism (in the sense of disbelief) were all coined in the second half of the 19th century.

"freethinker" was someone who had been brought up with the ideas of religion, law, and morality, and had reached the state of freethinking after long years of personal pain and struggle. But now there is this new kind of ready-made freethinker—the ones who grow up without ever even hearing that there once were such things as moral laws and religious convictions, and that these were the authorities in life. These new folks, now, simply grow up in a world where all this is rejected out of hand—which is to say, they grow up as savages. *(Anna Karenina 5.9)*

From the passionate and risk-taking rejection of God to a world in which it simply does not occur to many to wonder about God's existence is quite a leap into the dark. Or into the light, depending on one's point of view.

WHO KILLED GOD?

The decline of Christianity in 19th-century Europe resulted from a host of factors. Industrial capitalism figures large. The working class wrenched millions of Europeans from their rural parishes and deposited them in dense and wretched urban settings, in which there was little or no organized religious life. Forced to work twelve to fourteen hours a day in factories, six days a week, with few churches or clergy members available, many of the working poor simply lost the habit of attending church. And given widespread illiteracy, there was insufficient Bible reading or private devotions to compensate. In cities from Manchester to Milan, and from Oporto to Prague, thousands of gleaming new churches were built or revamped, yet these lay overwhelmingly in tidy middle-class precincts that few working-class people could reach—and those people would have felt distinctly out of place and unwelcome even if they could have reached them.

Another cause of unease was the institution of the "established church," meaning the legal proclamation of a specific Christian tradition as the official faith of a nation. United Italy designated Roman Catholicism as its state religion; England had its Anglican Church and Scotland its Presbyterian Church. Each of the provinces of united Germany had its own national church, and the alliances between governments and the Orthodox Churches in eastern Europe and Russia date back to the Middle Ages. Popular discontent with a government's policies frequently resulted in popular dissatisfaction with the church. Meanwhile the bourgeois classes that benefited most from the industrial economy came to represent the centers of power within each government.

Less directly involved, though still a factor, was prosperity itself. 19th-century Europe witnessed a proliferation of new department stores, exhibition halls,

Temple of Consumerism   The grand staircase at Le Bon Marché department store in Paris. The founder of the store was Aristide Boucicaut (1810-1877), who credited much his success to his promotion of his store as a place where proper bourgeois women could meet without chaperones.

The untimely death of deeply loved relations, friends, or romantic partners has proved through the centuries to be a powerful impulse to religious meditations. Without the painful presence of death, once a constant in life even with the best available medical care, it became easier to avoid thinking about it.

museums, sports venues, theaters, music halls, and restaurants.[2] All these challenged the traditional role of churches as centers of community. As church became a once-a-week, Sunday-mornings-only affair, religious enthusiasm waned. And for those millions who did not share in the prosperity of the age, taverns and bodegas provided some relief from their miseries. Meanwhile, many of the most enthusiastic believers, both Protestant and Catholic, lay or clerical, left Europe to pursue missionary work overseas, often in Africa or eastern Asia.

Another contributing factor to secularism may have been modern medicine. Physicians became able to treat and cure a broader array of ailments; vaccines mitigated the horrors of cholera and smallpox; and improvements in food production and distribution lessened famine. Child mortality decreased, life expectancy increased, and more and more people lived longer and healthier lives. These were undeniably positive developments, but they contributed to secularization by lessening the presence of death in peoples' lives. This is not a trivial point. Among the middle classes who had access to modern medical care, it was not uncommon to attend only a handful of funerals in a lifetime—usually later in life when older relatives died. For comparison, England's Queen Anne (r. 1702–1707) had eighteen pregnancies, thirteen of which ended in miscarriages; four children were born but died before the age of two. Her sole surviving child died just days after his eleventh birthday. The untimely death of deeply loved relations, friends, or romantic partners has proved through the centuries to be a powerful impulse to

---

2   The first two department stores were Bainbridge's in Newcastle-upon-Tyne and Le Bon Marché in Paris; both opened in 1838.

religious meditations. Without the painful presence of death, once a constant in life even with the best available medical care, it became easier to avoid thinking about it.

Until the late 19th century, too, religious houses had been the main providers of social services throughout Europe: they had run hospitals and orphanages, provided education, organized soup kitchens and almshouses, and offered palliative and charitable care for the elderly and destitute. The liberal nation-states, however, gradually took over most of these roles as the century progressed, which effectively marginalized the active presence of religious life in society. From the point of view of the disaffected, churches—especially established churches—were institutions that enjoyed their tax exemptions and government subsidies while apparently catering to the well-to-do middle and upper classes. But they played a constantly declining role in most people's lives and lost popular support.

The advance of liberalism, especially after 1848, also had an indirect philosophical effect. By promoting toleration of differing traditions and dissenting views as a civic virtue, it implicitly allowed and perhaps even encouraged the circulation of ideas that directly challenged religion's traditional position of cultural authority. By making a virtue of welcoming dissent, liberal society unintentionally added to the growing sense of distance from their religious roots felt by millions. And the religious and social debates of the age reached ever increasing numbers of people thanks to the proliferation of newspapers and magazines in the second half of the century. Finally, by inviting religious plurality, liberal Europe created a marketplace of ideas that provided encouragement to many but also fostered confusion when it came to people's religious convictions. The midcentury **Oxford movement** in England, for example, aimed to confront the problem of Anglicans who no longer adhered to the traditions of Anglican Christianity because they no longer really understood them. A parallel development in Protestant Germany was the so-called Neo-Lutheran movement. Denominational and nondenominational Sunday schools began to proliferate to combat religious ignorance or indifference.[3]

Toleration contributed to the rise of **secularism** by redefining civic virtues. The earliest secularists did not present themselves publicly as enemies of Christianity but rather as champions of nonpartisanship. George Jacob Holyoake (1817–1906), the most prominent early campaigner for civic secularism in England, described his position in this way:

> Secularism is not an argument against Christianity; it is one independent of it. It does not question the pretensions of Christianity; it

---

[3]   The first known Sunday school, at Surrey Chapel in London, opened around 1800 and enrolled as many as three thousand children by 1860.

advances others. Secularism does not say there is no light or guidance elsewhere, but maintains that there is light and guidance in secular truth, whose conditions and sanctions exist independently, and act forever. Secular knowledge is manifestly that kind of knowledge which is founded in this life, which relates to the conduct of this life, conduces to the welfare of this life, and is capable of being tested by the experience of this life. *(Origin and Nature of Secularism, 1896)*

Holyoake was briefly imprisoned for blasphemy in 1842. The secularist cause was given formal order by the creation of groups like England's National Secular Society, founded in 1866, and Germany's Freethinkers' League (*Freidenkerbund*), established in 1881.

The last person imprisoned for blasphemy in England was John William Gott (1866–1922), a salesman in the garment trade. Gott's crime was not rejection of Christianity but mockery of it. In 1921 he had published a series of crude pamphlets, one of which depicted Jesus dressed like a circus clown, standing on the backs of two donkeys as he entered Jerusalem. Condemned to nine months' hard labor, Gott completed his sentence but, his health broken, died shortly after his release.

THE THEORY OF CREATION

Secularism found a target in one of the most notorious false beliefs of its time— the date of Creation. It found new weapons, too—in science's attempts to trace history in the earth and in evolution by natural selection.

James Ussher (1581–1656) was a brilliant and saintly Anglo-Irish Protestant scholar, the archbishop of Armagh and primate of all Ireland who helped calm the Irish religious and political scene during the panicked violence of the English Civil War; unfortunately, he is remembered today chiefly for a single ridiculous idea. In 1648, the same year when the Peace of Westphalia put an end to the Wars of Religion and inaugurated the age of absolutist governments, Ussher published a lengthy study of biblical history entitled *The Annals of the Old Testament*, which attempted to work backward through the detailed chronologies given in the Hebrew Bible and thereby calculate the likely dates of the most important events it describes. The ancient Jews, Greeks, Romans, and early Christians all used different calendars, some lunar, some solar, and all originating at different points. This made the task immensely complex—especially since Ussher correlated their particulars with the astronomical tables of Johannes Kepler and the calendrical measurements used by the ancient Egyptians and Persians. After years of painstaking research, Bishop Ussher opened his *Annals* with the solemn announcement that God began his six-day labor of Creation, as related in the initial chapter of Genesis, at sunset on the evening preceding Sunday, October 23, in the year 4004 BCE—making the world around him exactly 5,652 years old.

His conclusion was remarkable more for its precision than for its originality; attempts to determine the date of Creation by means of the Bible's many genealogies and royal lists were as old as the Bible itself. The Jewish calendar's Year 1—the year *before* God began his work of Creation—corresponds to the year 3760 BCE, and the astronomer Johannes Kepler calculated Creation to have occurred in 3992 BCE. Isaac Newton himself, a half century after Ussher, concluded that the Creation took place in the year 4000 BCE. The belief that the world in the 19th century was approaching six thousand years old was surprisingly widespread, and Ussher's chronology was commonly printed inside editions of the Authorized (King James) Version of the Bible until the early 19th century.[4] In the United States an edition known as the Scofield Reference Bible, which included the King James Version and an annotated update of Ussher's chronology, appeared in the years immediately prior to the American entry into World War I. It sold more than two million copies before the middle of the 20th century and became the foundation of the Christian-fundamentalist challenge to the theory of evolution.

The theory of the 4004 BCE Creation never had official recognition from any of the mainstream Christian churches in the West, and it came under direct attack from the work of three British scientists: two geologists, William Smith (1769–1839) and Sir Charles Lyell (1797–1875), and the biologist Charles Darwin (1809–1882). Smith was the self-educated son of a village blacksmith; apprenticed to a surveyor working to map out canals for the great industrial boom then underway, he developed a passionate interest in geological formations and fossils. He taught himself map drawing and in 1799 produced a geological map of the area around the city of Bath in Somerset. It showed consistent relationships between the various strata of stone and their fossil remains, illustrating the development over time of the entire region.

The success of this map, and the enthusiasm it raised among other geologists, inspired Smith to his greatest project—a map of the entire geological structure of Britain, which he published in 1815. Smith's maps, and the detailed data he published along with them, pointed to rock strata composed of like materials and containing similar fossils. These can be connected to create a picture of the formation of the land. In other words, he provided clear evidence that the British

---

[4]   Ussher identified 2348 BCE as the date of Noah's Ark and the Great Flood and 1491 BCE as the year when Moses led the Exodus of the Jews from Egypt.

A Map that Changed the World   William Smith published his geological map of Britain in 1815, which made clear that the the island emerged gradually over time, rather than appeared whole from a single act of creation. Unfortunately, others plagiarized his map and subsequent books, and he fell into debt. He spent two years in debtors' prison, and afterward worked as a surveyor. Above is a detail of the map showing southwest England and part of Wales.

Isles emerged from sequential development over long periods of time rather than all-at-once creation.

Sir Charles Lyell was in many ways the antithesis of Smith. Born to a prominent Scottish family of lawyers and civil servants, Lyell went to Oxford University, traveled extensively, moved easily in society, married a famous beauty who was also a scientist, and held a professorship at King's College London. A gregarious, charming, and generous man, he made his career less by conducting field research (his eyesight was poor) than by synthesizing the investigations of others. His most important work was the three-volume *Principles of Geology* (1830–1833), which, surprisingly, became a bestseller.

Lyell's main contribution was the popularization of the theory called **uniformitarianism,** originally proposed by another Scottish geologist, James Hutton (1726–1797). The theory stated that geological change consists of the slow accumulation of smaller changes—and these changes continue to happen in the present. The idea seems self-evident today, but it was a radical challenge to a world that believed that the earth's entire history covered less than six thousand years. Lyell's theory demanded hundreds of thousands of years for the physical record to make sense. The fact that Lyell himself was known to be a deeply committed Christian gave his theory additional force; it was well known that he accepted his own theory only because the evidence for it was so overwhelming. And he continued to expand and revise this theory through twelve editions of *Principles* and through six editions of a subsequent study called *Elements of Geology*.

EVOLUTION BY NATURAL SELECTION

The young English naturalist Charles Darwin read Lyell's *Principles of Geology* while on a five-year voyage (1831–1836) aboard the HMS *Beagle*, exploring the coasts of South America and its outlying islands. Several papers that he delivered after his return to England, along with the publication of his travelogue *The Voyage of the Beagle* (1839), established his reputation as a scientist and writer of rare gifts. He and Lyell became lifelong friends, and their relationship grew ever closer despite Lyell's resistance to Darwin's great contribution—his **theory of evolution by natural selection**. Some of the fundamental ideas behind it had been around for several years; yet no one had pieced them together with as much geological support and analysis as Darwin. Moreover, although other scholars had suggested that species change over time, none had come up with an explanation for why they did so. Darwin supplied a powerful one, and it is the central idea behind the science of biology today.

Darwin's theory, worked out in detail in the years after his voyage, dealt wholly with the animal world, but it clearly implied that human beings evolved in a similar manner. Darwin posited natural selection as the means by which evolution occurs. First, nature produces a superabundance of offspring in each generation. A single grain of wheat, for example, produces a wheat shaft that contains dozens of new grains, or a single female salmon lays hundreds of eggs that are then fertilized by the millions of sperm cells produced by the male salmon. Second, this superabundance results in a contest among those offspring for the resources necessary for life. This contest will favor individuals who have a unique ability that gives them an advantage over their rivals. And third, this preferred characteristic, whatever it might be, is then passed on to its offspring. Eventually, this will allow the species to develop into a new form.

> As many more individuals of each species are born than can possibly survive; and as, consequently, there is a frequently recurring struggle for existence, it follows that any being, if it vary however slightly in any

manner profitable to itself, under the complex and sometimes varying conditions of life, will have a better chance of surviving, and thus be *naturally selected*. From the strong principle of inheritance, any selected variety will tend to propagate its new and modified form.   *(The Origin of the Species, ch. 1)*

Even though Darwin could observe the effects of natural selection, he did not have a scientific basis for explaining how it actually happened. Today, the science of genetics tells us how that inheritance takes place. All living things and all their organs are made up of tiny cells, and all cells carry within them genes—which they pass on to the next generation. However, this basic unit of heredity may change, and the accumulation of slow changes, as in geology, may change a species.

Darwin spent fifteen years working out the details of his theory—which he finally published as **On the Origin of Species by Means of Natural Selection** in 1859. Darwin ended the book with a plea that it be seen as a celebration of life rather than as an attack on cherished assumptions:

Authors of the highest eminence seem to be fully satisfied with the view that each species has been independently created. To my mind it

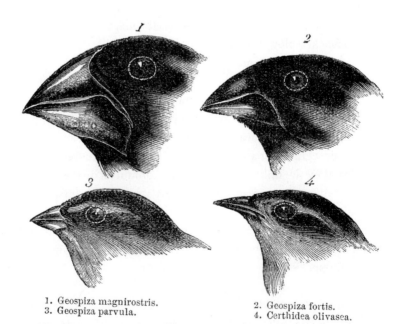

1. Geospiza magnirostris.
3. Geospiza parvula.
2. Geospiza fortis.
4. Certhidea olivasea.

Endless Forms Most Beautiful   Prints made from drawings by Charles Darwin (1809-1882) while on his trip to the Galápagos islands, published in his *Voyage of the Beagle* (1839). Here he shows some of the variation in the beaks of finches.

accords better with what we know of the laws impressed on matter by the Creator, that the production and extinction of the past and present inhabitants of the world should have been due to secondary causes, like those determining the birth and death of the individual. When I view all beings not as special creations, but as the lineal descendants of some few beings which lived long before the first bed of the Silurian system was deposited, they seem to me to become ennobled. Judging from the past, we may safely infer that not one living species will transmit its unaltered likeness to a distant futurity. And of the species now living very few will transmit progeny of any kind to a far distant futurity. . . . As all the living forms of life are the lineal descendants of those which lived long before the Silurian epoch, we may feel certain that the ordinary succession by generation has never once been broken, and that no cataclysm has desolated the whole world. Hence we may look with some confidence to a secure future of equally inappreciable length. And as natural selection works solely by and for the good of each being, all corporeal and mental endowments will tend to progress towards perfection.

It is interesting to contemplate an entangled bank, clothed with many plants of many kinds, with birds singing on the bushes, with various insects flitting about, and with worms crawling through the damp earth, and to reflect that these elaborately constructed forms, so different from each other, and dependent on each other in so complex a manner, have all been produced by laws acting around us. These laws, taken in the largest sense, being Growth with Reproduction; inheritance which is almost implied by reproduction; Variability from the indirect and direct action of the external conditions of life, and from use and disuse; a Ratio of Increase so high as to lead to a Struggle for Life, and as a consequence to Natural Selection, entailing Divergence of Character and the Extinction of less-improved forms. Thus, from the war of nature, from famine and death, the most exalted object which we are capable of conceiving, namely, the production of the higher animals, directly follows. There is grandeur in this view of life, with its several powers, having been originally breathed into a few forms or into one; and that, whilst this planet has gone cycling on according to the fixed law of gravity, from so simple a beginning endless forms most beautiful and most wonderful have been, and are being, evolved.

Within the scientific community, Darwin's theory of evolution carried the day. Even Lyell eventually endorsed it. His problem was not with evolution itself but with the idea of natural selection. It seemed to undermine the notion of a heavenly plan; it could even dismiss the need for a Creator altogether. Others, however, saw no reason why Darwin's work had to be regarded as an attack on religion. A popular novelist and historian of the day, Charles Kingsley (1819–1875), who was also an Anglican priest, sent Darwin a letter immediately after its publication:

> [It] is just as noble a conception of Deity to believe that He created primal forms capable of self development into all forms needful ... as to believe that He required a fresh act of intervention to supply the lacunas which He Himself had made. I question whether the former be not the loftier thought.

Not only could the Anglican priest accept so "non-Christian a theory as evolution"; he delighted in it.[5]

A famous debate took place at the Oxford Association for the Advancement of Science in 1860 between Darwin's most vocal champion, Thomas Huxley (1825–1895), and Samuel Wilberforce (1805–1873), then the bishop of Oxford. Darwin did not attend. His work on *The Origin of Species* had been so all-consuming that his health broke down while he was completing it. Angry words flew across the stage, and the crowd roared and jeered; in the end, both sides declared victory. While inconclusive, this debate set the tone for the war of words that ensued in lecture halls, pulpits, newspapers and magazines, common rooms, and at dinner tables across England and the Continent.

For many people, opposition to evolution was visceral. By validating the notion of an earth that was hundreds of millions of years old, they felt, it removed God from the creation of life. It seemed not only to contradict biblical tradition but to be holding it up to ridicule. Darwin's later book *The Descent of Man* (1871) stated explicitly what *The Origin of Species* had only implied: human beings themselves were the product of evolution and had emerged from more primitive species.[6] Cartoonists rushed

---

[5] "What can be more delightful to me," Kingsley is said to have replied at an aristocratic dinner, "than to know that Your Ladyship and I sprang from the same toadstool?"

[6] Darwin never claimed that humans are descended from apes. Instead, humans and apes are descended from a remote common ancestor. 'Some ancient member of the anthropomorphous subgroup gave birth to man,' he writes in ch. 6 of *The Descent of Man*. This subgroup includes a variety of apelike creatures, such as the gorilla, chimpanzee, and orangutan (and their forebears).

to depict Darwin derisively as an ape-man. His bald head, strong facial features, and flowing white beard—which he had grown to cover some of the effects of his long illness—were well suited to caricature.

The notion of all earthly life as a struggle for existence seemed coldly harsh. That the fittest survive at the expense of the rest seemed irreconcilable with a loving Creator. The Bible's apparent evidence that the world was created in 4004 BCE could be set aside easily enough by interpreting its dates as merely symbolic. Abraham did not literally live to be 175 years old (Genesis 25.7), it might be said; the high number of years attributed to him simply symbolized great age and wisdom. However, Scripture repeatedly asserts that the loving God made the cosmos as a thing of supreme beauty and order, all set in motion according to his divine plan. This was tough to square with the arbitrary ruthlessness of Darwin's world-as-battlefield. If the Bible's most fundamental traditions and moral teachings can be set aside as mistaken, then what is left?

Ape-man   Darwin suffered from ill health most of his life adult life (he ultimately died of heart disease), and the intense exertion of writing his *Origin of Species* nearly killed him. During a long convalescence he grew out his beard, which together with his advancing baldness gave him a distinctive look that was easily and sometimes cruelly caricatured. Here he is shown as half man and half monkey, trying to teach another monkey about its identity.

THE BIBLE AND HISTORY

Can the authority of the Scriptures be salvaged? It all depends on how one reads them, answered a new group of biblical scholars on the Continent. These new scholars referred to their work as **higher criticism** or **historical criticism** in order to differentiate it from the type of literary work that seeks to establish improved editions of texts corrupted through faulty copying and printing. Instead, they sought to determine the origins of the biblical texts in time and place.

The Gospel of Matthew, for instance, places unique emphasis on proving how Jesus's acts fulfill Hebrew prophecy. For the new scholars, this suggests that Matthew wrote his book specifically for a Jewish audience—and further, that he may have originally written the text in Hebrew or Aramaic instead of the Greek in which we have it. Specific episodes of Jesus's life are repeated across the first three Gospels. This suggests not only that the Gospels borrowed from one another but hints at the existence of an otherwise unknown, missing collection of source material (now known to biblical scholars as "Q") from which they drew.

Some reevaluation of religion may have been expected after the convulsions of the Scientific Revolution and the Enlightenment, which had challenged so many aspects of religious tradition. But the goal of this new type of criticism was not mere appreciation. It was closer to forensic analysis—of a sort that one might find at the scene of a crime or in a courtroom.

The first great scholar of this sort was Friedrich Schleiermacher (1768–1834), a Lutheran pastor and professor of theology at the newly established University of Berlin. Schleiermacher did some early work in historical criticism, but he is best known for training the generation of critics that followed, many of whom became associated in one way or another with the University of Tübingen in southern Germany. His pupil David Friedrich Strauss (1808–1874) ignited a scandal when he published *The Life of Jesus, Critically Examined* (1836), in which he stripped Jesus's life of all its miraculous aspects. He argued that tales of Christ's astonishing deeds, and indeed his resurrection, were simply literary devices—magical set pieces drawn from centuries-old mythological tales.

In wanting to persuade readers that Jesus was in fact the Messiah promised in Jewish prophecy, Strauss argues, the writers of the Gospels simply invented episodes of spiritual derring-do, like plot devices in a film script, that echoed episodes from the Old Testament. Thus the scene of Jesus's walking on the water to join his disciples on their fishing boat never actually occurred; it is rather a fictional echo of both the Noah's Ark story and the tale of Jonah and the whale—but with salvation coming over the water's surface, instead of God's wrath. The tale of the Virgin Birth, according to Strauss, was nothing more than an effort to give Jesus as remarkable an entrance into history as they could muster.

More daring still, he insists that even the accounts of Jesus's resurrection from death are just adaptations of earlier legends, like the deaths and resurrections of Mithras or Osiris, that early Christian followers found useful in winning converts. While he professed to admire "the Jesus of history" even though he rejected "the Christ of faith," Strauss unsettled readers across Europe. A reviewer of the English translation, Lord Shaftesbury (1801–1885), called Strauss's volume "the most pestilential book, I think, ever vomited out of the jaws of hell."

Stripping away all supernatural elements to discover "the historical Jesus" became the rallying cry of the new scholarship. Five years later another German academic, Ludwig Andreas Feuerbach (1804–1872), published a dense volume called *The Essence of Christianity* (1841) that mounted an even more radical attack on biblical faith. To Feuerbach, the Christian God is little more than an exercise in wish fulfillment by the entire culture. Since we can imagine supreme virtues like justice, goodness, generosity, and love, he argues, we create a Being that unites these virtues and indeed personifies them. For most people, to deny the existence of the Being would be tantamount to denying the virtues themselves; and since we cannot live without believing in ideals, we create, out of our own need, the Supreme Ideal, which is God.

To long for something is to feel that it is necessary, and our sensibilities long for a personal God. But the longing for a personal God is genuine, heartfelt, and profound only when it is a longing for a single entity—only a single God can satisfy it.... Whatever we feel strongly enough is necessary we feel strongly enough to be real.... Our desire says, "A personal God must exist"—that is, it is unacceptable that God should not exist; our satisfied feeling [therefore] simply says, "He exists.".... Our longing demands a crafted, sympathetic, personal God, a single One, and a historically true One. *(The Essence of Christianity, ch. 15)*

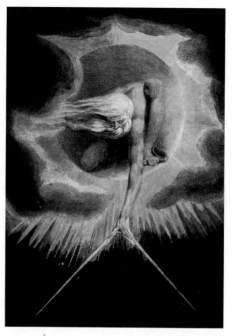

Supreme Ideal   William Blake (1757–1827) engraved and printed versions of this image numerous times. Called *The Ancient of Days*, it illustrates a biblical verse (Proverbs 8.25) and was used by Blake as the frontispiece to his work *Europe: A Prophecy* (1794). It depicts God in the process of forming the universe, holding out a compass to mark the perfection of his creation.

To Feuerbach, even the pared-down and demythologized Jesus of historical criticism is evidence of our instinctive need to believe and to seek some firm rooting for the belief.[7]

The next blow came from France. In 1863 Ernest Renan (1823–1892) published *The Life of Jesus*, the first full-scale attempt at a biography of the "historical Jesus." Renan had studied for the priesthood but lost his faith—as a result, ironically, of the curriculum at his seminary. As he came to master Biblical Hebrew, Renan saw that the traditional attributions of date and authorship for many of the Old Testament texts were incorrect. The five books of the Torah could not possibly have been written by Moses, for instance, since the books show countless

---

[7]   Strauss and Feuerbach were both translated into English by Marian Evans—who later gained fame as the novelist George Eliot (1819–1880).

Ernest Renan   Ernest Renan (1829–1892), author of *The Life of Jesus.*

signs of different authorship and of an anachronistic Hebrew vocabulary. Some texts, like parts of Deuteronomy, were clearly written many centuries after the earliest sections of Genesis. And the difficulties multiply as one progresses through the rest of the Hebrew Bible. Differences in vocabulary and grammar alone show that the book of Isaiah, for instance, has at least two and possibly three separate authors. The book of Daniel was written in its present form nearly four hundred years after the events to which it supposedly bears eyewitness.

The problem of multiple authorship challenged the tradition of accepting the Bible as the literal word of God. But even the faithful of a more liberal bent were puzzled. Would biblical books written centuries later than others therefore supersede the books that came before? If so, then why retain the earlier works at all? Worse still, historical criticism drew many similar conclusions about the New Testament. Renan's book became an international bestseller, and it has never been out of print down to the present day.

Higher criticism of the Bible quickly became a popular phenomenon, with books by new scholars (and by a few charlatans) appearing almost monthly, in every country in Europe. The German scholar (and close friend of Karl Marx) Bruno Bauer (1809–1882) declared half of the Epistles of Saint Paul in the New Testament to be forgeries. A Dutch scholar named Allard Pierson (1831–1896) declared Jesus's Sermon on the Mount to have been plagiarized from Jewish wisdom literature. Edwin Johnson (1842–1901), an Englishman, argued that there was no reliable evidence for the very existence of Jesus. Another German, Adolf von Harnack (1851–1930), perhaps the greatest Protestant theologian of the 19th century, announced that the Gospel of John should be disregarded altogether as a historical source, since "its author acted with the freedom of an absolute monarch, switching events around at will and showing them from perverse angles, inventing [Jesus's] speeches and dialogues out of whole cloth, and presenting [Jesus's] greatest thoughts in entirely fictive situations."

A French priest, Alfred Loisy (1857–1940), began his scholarly career teaching at one of France's most prestigious Catholic seminaries, the Institut Catholique de Paris, but quickly ran into trouble. A gifted professor of Greek and Hebrew, he put forth a fivefold argument: Moses did not write any of the Torah; the opening chapters of Genesis on the creation of the world must be read as allegory instead of history; the Old and New Testaments must be judged separately in regard to their historical accuracy; the religious teachings presented in the

Bible represent a development over time rather than a single, eternal doctrine; and, for purposes of determining historical truth, the Scriptures are no more authoritative or exempt from criticism than any other ancient texts. By 1893 he was compelled to resign from his seminary post and take up teaching at a public college. Loisy continued to publish, and to land in trouble. Finally, in 1908, Pope Pius X (r. 1903–1914) excommunicated him.

Historical Criticism by itself did not lead to the rapid development of secularism in Europe, but it followed on the heels of other major social upheavals and scientific challenges. Coming as it did after industrialism, modern geology, and evolutionary theory, its contribution to the spread of religious doubt appeared increasingly large and dire. Mainstream Christian churches encouraged the faithful to seek out biblical wisdom. But where does a believer turn when the churches, perhaps through no fault of their own, cannot keep pace with the age, and the Scriptures themselves are of uncertain authority? How does one balance a commitment to a tradition of revealed Truth with a willingness to explore new ideas and new ways of thinking? Even more fundamentally, was it still possible to be a Christian believer and remain intellectually honest?

> Historical Criticism by itself did not lead to the rapid development of secularism in Europe, but it followed on the heels of other major social upheavals and scientific challenges. Coming as it did after industrialism, modern geology, and evolutionary theory, its contribution to the spread of religious doubt appeared increasingly large and dire.

THE PROTESTANT CHURCHES' RESPONSE

Communities often respond to crisis by pulling in opposite directions: some in the community embrace new ideas, while others reaffirm established certainties. Depending on the circumstances, either reaction can make sense; and in some cases, both reactions might. The Christian churches of the 19th century, like the governments of the age, had to confront upheavals unlike anything they had dealt with previously. The wars of religion in the 17th century had been brutal, and yet they were conflicts over which version of Christian revelation was the true one. For all their horror, they were at least conflicts between groups of genuine conviction. But how does one deal with the explicit *denial* of revelation and the argument that there is no truth to be fought over? If the teachings of Christianity are not heaven-sent truths, does faith have a future? "Yes, indeed," answered the mainstream churches, both Protestant and Catholic. "No, not really," answered more and more Europeans as they sank comfortably into their increasingly secular lives.

Take just two examples of the resulting tug-of-war. In England, the Anglican reaction to the triple blow of industrialism, science, and historical criticism was slow and measured, for the most part, with occasional outbursts of energetic activity. Rural society felt relatively little impact. Small village parishes still formed the backbone of the community, and attendance at services remained high. But life in the cities was another matter altogether. As with the state, the church devoted a greater percentage of its resources to serving the fast-growing middle-class sections of the towns than to the downtrodden workers' slums. "Proper society" mattered more.[8]

A national census in 1851 revealed two surprising facts: for the first time ever, more people in England lived in towns than in the countryside; and second, attendance at religious services was in sharp decline. Of the country's 17.9 million people, 5.2 million identified themselves as active Anglicans, 4.5 million were "Dissenters" or "Non-Conformists" (the terms for anyone who was a Protestant Christian but not an Anglican), and a mere 380,000 were Roman Catholics. That meant more than 7.2 million English people, or 40 percent of the nation, effectively declared themselves either nonpracticing Christians or nonbelievers.[9] Only five years later, another survey showed, less than 20 percent of Londoners attended church. There is little evidence of overt hostility to religion among the workers and urban poor, since we have few records that come from them directly. (One Evangelical Christian reformer, Hannah More [d. 1833], had long advocated teaching the masses how to read but not to write, lest their unhealthy thoughts begin to circulate.) This suggests that their nonappearance at church resulted from either a lack of opportunity or indifference.

The Nonconforming churches and the more Evangelical sectors of Anglicanism did a better job of serving the urban poor than did the Church of England. Nonconformist denominations included the Baptist, Congregationalist, Methodist, and Presbyterian churches, as well as the newly established (1865) sect known as the Salvation Army. These denominations tended to place more emphasis on biblical teaching and puritanical morality, and less on institutional tradition and formal liturgy, than the Anglicans and Catholics, which made it easier for them to establish themselves in poorer districts. Group worship could take place in homes and meeting halls and did not rely to such an extent upon large church buildings as the centers of community. These denominations benefited somewhat from class antagonisms; the very fact that they were Nonconformist—that is, that they consciously disassociated themselves from the

---

[8]   In 1833, Parliament voted more money to maintain the royal stables at Windsor Castle than to provide elementary schools for the general public.

[9]   "It is not that the Church of God has lost the great towns," wrote one Anglican clergyman; "it has never had them."

Preaching the Gospel   An itinerant preacher in India, late 19th century. As Christianity began to lose place to secularism within Europe, missionaries focused more of their energies on spreading the Christian message abroad, in Africa and Asia.

Church of England—formed part of their appeal. By rejecting the established church, parishioners were in some ways declaring opposition to the middle class that made up most of its members and to the aristocracy that made up most of its highest officials. But popular participation in the Nonconformist churches declined in the second half of the 19th century at roughly the same rate as in the Anglican Church.

Being so strongly based on a tradition of biblical reading that tended toward the literal, these groups had particular difficulty with the intellectual challenges posed by historical criticism and the rise of modern science. For many of these people, the loss of unquestioned biblical authority meant the collapse of faith itself. The novelist George Eliot (Marian Evans), who was raised an Evangelical, identified her loss of faith precisely with her doubt of Scriptural inerrancy. Dissenters engaged energetically in missionary work in the fast-multiplying British colonies in Africa and India; yet that meant that many of their most talented and charismatic men and women were drawn away from the home front.

The Anglican Church itself was torn over the rise of secularism. To conservative Anglicans the answer lay in a rigid opposition to modern science and historical criticism. Samuel Wilberforce, the bishop of Oxford who had debated evolution with Thomas Huxley, dismissed Darwin's *Origin of Species* in one of the book's earliest reviews:

> Now we must say at once and openly. . . that such a notion [as evolution by natural selection] is absolutely incompatible not only with single expressions in the Word of God but with the whole representation of that moral and spiritual condition of man which is its proper subject matter. Man's derived supremacy over the earth; man's gift of reason; man's free-will and responsibility; man's fall and man's redemption; the incarnation of the Eternal Son; the in-dwelling of the Eternal Spirit,—all are equally and utterly irreconcilable with the degrading notion of the brute origin of him who was created in the image of God. . . . Man is not and cannot be an improved ape. *(Quarterly Review 108:258–260)*

The Church of England suffered greatly from the growing rift between "Low Church, "High Church," and "Broad Church" Anglicans. The Low Church consisted of the Evangelicals—those parishioners with the least interest in preserving strict liturgical and ritual tradition, basing their theology solidly on the literal meaning of the Scriptures. The High Church consisted of just the opposite—the Anglicans most dearly loyal to ritual, hierarchy, and tradition. The Broad Church was made up of the most liberal Anglicans, who remained most open to liturgical reform, evolutionary theory, and historical criticism. Wilberforce belonged to the High Church wing, but in his review of Darwin he championed unreservedly the authority of Scripture over any amount of scientific evidence to the contrary.

Secularism won out over each of the three branches in roughly equal amounts—though for different reasons. The Low Church lost numbers through its refusal to accept modern intellectual life; the High Church lost the working class that felt alienated from "proper society." And the Broad Church lost members precisely because its intellectual openness to evolution and historical criticism inadvertently helped the idea of a Godless universe to succeed.

In Germany the challenge to religion included an unexpected political element. A royal decree by Friedrich Wilhelm III (r. 1797–1840) known as the Prussian Union of 1817 had not only gathered the autonomous Lutheran Churches into a single national entity but had folded the Reformed (Calvinist) Churches into the mix. It thereby created a kind of Protestant superchurch called the Evangelical Christian Church. Coming as it did on the three hundredth anniversary of the start of the Protestant Reformation, the union aimed to breathe new life into Christian worship, but the move was controversial from the start. Many Calvinist ministers resisted their forced assimilation into what they regarded as a too-liberal Lutheran tradition. In turn, many Lutheran clergy objected that much of what was most distinctive about Lutheran worship was lost. But matters became even more dire as Prussian political power, led by Otto von Bismarck, overwhelmed the other German states and created a united Germany.

As opposition to the Reich became impossible, popular resentment found expression through opposition to the official Evangelical Church, usually through the simple choice not to attend Sunday services. Many thousands of Germans who found it impossible to accept the established church yet who refused to relinquish regular worship emigrated to the United States in the 1840s and 1850s. Among those who remained behind, many rallied to a reform movement they called **Neo-Lutheranism**, which aimed not only to reaffirm the distinctive Lutheran heritage but also to address the problems of Darwinian theory and historical criticism.

Neo-Lutherans were not a uniform theological bloc, and in fact they quickly divided into schools of thought that were roughly analogous to Low, Broad, and High Anglicanism. Since traditional Lutheranism placed such a high premium on the authority of Scripture, great numbers of the Neo-Lutherans insisted all the more strongly on the belief in Scriptural inerrancy and the body of Scriptural interpretation established in Martin Luther's *Book of Concord*; these became known as the Confessional Lutherans and most closely resembled the Scripturally-based Low Church wing of Anglicanism; they notably championed the rejection of modern science and textual criticism. Other Neo-Lutherans, however, were more analogous to the High Church Anglicans; they privileged the institutional tradition of Lutheranism and the need to remain united against a hostile world. Still others believed that traditional faith and the new sciences could be harmonized—or at least that harmony was worth attempting. These Neo-Lutherans became known as the Erlangen school—after the university where many of their leading scholars were trained—and parallel the Broad Church leaders in the Church of England.

Whatever their intellectual and moral merits, the three Neo-Lutheran groups failed to staunch the hemorrhage of Christians from communal worship. No book of Christian theology, traditional devotional literature, or biblical commentary published in German in the 19th century came close to selling as many copies as Strauss's *Life of Jesus, Critically Examined* or Feuerbach's *Essence of Christianity*.[10] Even within the Lutheran liturgies of the century, the slow advance of the

---

[10] The German translation of Darwin's *Origin of Species* outsold Luther's *Book of Concord*.

secularist worldview could be seen. The Apostles' Creed had long been one of the foundational documents of Protestant Christianity. This ancient statement of faith was given special approbation by Martin Luther in the 16th century because it did not contain the declaration about the "one, holy, catholic, and apostolic Church" that was found in the Nicene Creed:

> I believe in God, the Father Almighty,
> > maker of heaven and earth.
> And in Jesus Christ, his only Son, our Lord,
> > who was conceived by the Holy Spirit,
> > and born of the virgin Mary,
> > suffered under Pontius Pilate,
> > was crucified, died and was buried.
> > He descended into hell.
> > On the third day He rose again from the dead.
> > He ascended into heaven
> > and sits at the right hand of the Father.
> > From thence He will come to judge the living and the dead.
> I believe in the Holy Spirit,
> > the holy Christian church,
> > the communion of saints,
> > the forgiveness of sins,
> > the resurrection of the body,
> > and the life everlasting. Amen.

But the Prussian Synod of 1846 authorized a revised version for the established Evangelical Christian Church. This version removed three elements deemed no longer acceptable, given the advances of modern science and critical analysis: the Virgin Birth, Christ's descent into hell, and the bodily resurrection of the saved on Judgment Day.

Arguments over these matters dominated church life in Germany through the middle decades of the century. In 1892 a Lutheran minister in Württemberg, Christoph Schrempf, caused an even greater scandal when he acknowledged from the pulpit that he could no longer, in good faith, recite any part whatsoever of the Apostles' Creed. When a group of offended university students complained to one of their divinity professors—Adolf von Harnack (1851–1930), a leader in historical criticism—about Schrempf's audacity, Harnack responded that, while the Creed deserves respect for its antiquity and historical significance, it could not and should not be believed by any educated Christian.

THE CATHOLIC COUNTERATTACK

Industrialism affected Catholic Christianity less than it did the Protestant variety. Catholics made up a high percentage of industrial workers across Europe and generally brought with them ingrained habits of communal identity. Irish immigrants, for example, filled many of northern England's largest factories, just as Polish, Czech, and Hungarian workers flocked into German manufacturing cities. And as immigrants, their minority status heightened their sense of solidarity. Catholic migrant workers tended to live in congregated clusters, which led easily to the development of full parish life. Moreover, the Catholic Church was relatively quick to condemn the excesses of industrial capitalism and the wealth disparities between the bourgeoisie and the working poor. That meant that fewer Catholics fell away from their faith because of their church's supposed association with the capitalist elite.

The supreme expression of the church's warnings about unchecked capitalism appeared in 1891 when Pope Leo XIII (r. 1878–1903) issued the encyclical **Rerum Novarum** ("Of New Things"). The Church recognized the intrinsic rights of private property but insisted on the equal right of workers to form labor unions. Without a system of collective bargaining, Leo argues, the industrial capitalist economy gives a morally unacceptable permanent advantage to the wealthy.

> Let workers and employers therefore make free agreements, and in particular let them agree freely as to wages; nevertheless, there remains

Noble Workers   Giuseppe Pellizza da Volpedo (1868-1907) was an artist who dedicated most of his short life to promoting the rights of the working class in Italy and advocating for socialism. His best-known work, *The Fourth Estate* (1901), commemorates a labor strike in Milan. The prominent role given to a woman in the picture was radical even among Italian progressives of the era.

a fundamental requirement of natural justice older and more authoritative than any arrangement between man and man—namely, that wages
ought not be so low that a frugal and well-behaved worker cannot support himself or his family. When a worker is forced, by need or by fear of
something even worse, to accept wages lower than this threshold by an
employer who refuses to pay more, the worker is nothing more than a
victim of violent injustice.

At the same time he insists, in a swipe at Marxism, that the relationship
between workers and owners must not be and need not be one of conflict.

> The great error [of Marxists] is to insist on the idea that each class is
> inevitably hostile to the other, and that capitalists and workers are fixed
> by a law of nature in a state of perpetual conflict. This view is so
> wrongheaded and contrary to reason that in fact its exact opposite is
> true—for just as the harmony of the human body derives from the
> proper arrangement of its various parts, so too does nature ordain that in
> human society the various classes should dwell in harmonious accord.
> This is what produces the balance in a body politic. Each class needs the
> other, for capital cannot survive without labor, and labor cannot survive
> without capital.

The Catholic social movement, of which Rerum Novarum was merely one
part, had begun in the 1820s as soon as industrialization took root on the Continent, which insulated the faith from the slow pull of involuntary secularism. **Social
Catholicism** was founded on the idea that the challenge to Christian society
under industrialism was structural rather than per-
sonal. The question, in other words, was not "How
do we help the poor?" but "How do we combat poverty?" Liberal economics in the industrialized state
did not merely fail to eradicate poverty but actually
caused it—and hence the response had to be principled and ideological as well as activist.

Clergy in Belgium, France, and Germany
preached steadily against the systemic flaw of
unregulated capitalism. In 1825 the first full-
length moral indictment of industrial society ap-
peared: *Regarding the Faith and Its Relations with the Civil and Political Order,* by
a French priest named Hugues de Lamennais (1782–1854). A German priest
and later bishop of Mainz, Wilhelm Emmanuel (Baron von Ketteler, 1811–1877),

entered the fray immediately after his ordination, preaching on workers' rights and the need for state regulation of the marketplace. He called for the legalization of labor unions throughout Europe. In 1869, at a bishops' conference in the ancient German city of Fulda, he argued passionately that the problem of industrial capitalism was vastly more significant than any of the intellectual conflicts then confronting Christian society. Poverty, he insisted, not Charles Darwin or David Friedrich Strauss, was the real scourge of the age. In England, Henry Edward Manning (1808–1892), a convert from Anglicanism, regularly preached sermons on the rights of laborers; in 1889 he helped negotiate a settlement to the dockworkers' strike that paralyzed commerce in London. After he was made a cardinal in the church, Manning became a close adviser to Pope Leo XIII and indeed helped him to write Rerum Novarum.

The Catholic Church had less success against political nationalism, especially in Italy. The campaigns to create a unified Italy found their main obstacle in the pope himself. Since the early Middle Ages the Roman pontiff had been not only the spiritual leader of all Catholics but also the political ruler of the Papal State—a large territory in the middle third of the Italian peninsula. Believing that its civil domain was vital to the financial support of the worldwide church, Pope Pius IX (r. 1846–1878) steadfastly opposed every effort to create an Italian nation. The longest-reigning pope in history (after Saint Peter himself), he became a virtual prisoner in the Vatican Palace when Vittorio Emmanuele II's soldiers seized Rome in 1860. Pius compensated for his loss of political sovereignty by summoning the First Vatican Council (1869–1870), the convocation best known for pronouncing the dogma of papal infallibility.

The infallibility of the pope had been a traditional assumption among Catholics since the Middle Ages, but it had never been formalized as an official teaching. The Vatican Council determined that the dogma of infallibility, already established by tradition, needed formal definition in order to provide a guarantee of the church's authority against the intrusion of new ideas upon Catholic faith. Here they were thinking not of the challenges of Darwinian evolution or modern physics but the implications of historical criticism.

Scholarly analysis of the Scriptures, they wanted to assert, can validly contribute to the appreciation of the biblical text but can never replace the interpretive authority of the church. The pope, as head of the church, must have recourse to the exercise of absolute authority over it in the definition of its central beliefs—at least in certain circumstances. Pius IX's political travails in Italy made him increasingly conservative, and although he remained revered for his piety and gentle nature, his last years in office were marked by a deepening isolation from the world outside the palace walls. The church seemed in these years to enter a period of withdrawal and retrenchment.

THE WAR ON MODERNISM

Pius's successor, Leo XIII, resolved to bring the church back into direct engagement with the world. Though no less conservative than Pius had been, Leo revitalized the church's campaign to secure the rights of workers and the poor. He introduced the idea of **subsidiarity**, by which he meant that problems ought generally to be resolved locally. This principle, which governed Catholic social teaching throughout the 20th century, had two aims. First, it sought to preserve the dignity of persons and to help them recognize their own moral responsibilities. And second, it sought to safeguard against an overreaching centralized government.

The church responded slowly to the scientific discoveries and Scriptural analysis of the century. Leo was a natural diplomat and had the gift of knowing his own intellectual limits, and so he set out not to respond to the intellectual assaults on Catholic tradition but to prepare the groundwork for such a response. His most important effort in this regard was the encyclical *Providentissimus Deus* ("The God of All Providence," 1893), which effectively established two guiding principles. First, the truths of science and Scripture can never contradict each other once they are fully known and understood. Since both are gifts from God, they must ultimately exist in harmony; apparent contradictions between them merely indicate where our understanding is imperfect. Second, the study of the Scriptures should be welcomed at all times. It merely requires an honest spirit that seeks a better understanding of God's word, rather than a malicious spirit that desires only to point out textual inconsistencies for their own sake.

Leo's successor would have none of it. Pius X (r. 1903–1914) railed against all forms of intellectual novelty—which he grouped under the heading **modernism**. He was kindly, pious, and generous but temperamentally ill-equipped to deal with innovations; he regarded any new idea as a direct threat to the faith and stubbornly refused to consider it. Soon enough, he would not allow new ideas to be considered. In two decrees issued in 1907, *Lamentabili Sane Exitu* ("With lamentable consequence") and *Pascendi Dominici Gregis* ("Feeding the Lord's flock"), he formally condemned sixty-five teachings that he deemed irredeemably anti-Catholic. Calling them a **Syllabus of Errors**, he ordered all clerics to swear a loyalty oath that explicitly rejected every tenet of modernism. The oath, which was required of all clergy until 1967, ran in part:

> I proclaim that God, Who is the origin and the end of all things, can be known with certainty by the natural light of reason; . . . that the teachings of the Faith have been handed down to us from the Apostles, through the orthodox Fathers, and always with exactly the same meaning and the same intent; . . . I declare my complete opposition to the

errors of the modernists, who claim that there is nothing divine in sacred tradition [of the church]. . . . I firmly maintain and shall maintain to my last breath the belief of the Church Fathers in the sacred gift of Truth— Truth which most certainly exists, has existed, and always shall exist in the apostolic succession of bishops. . . . And I vow that I will keep these promises faithfully, wholly, and sincerely, keeping them inviolate, and in no way ever deviating from them in teaching or any other way. . . . All these things I do promise and swear, so help me God.

He followed up by instituting a clerical purge. He recommended the establishment of oversight committees (called *sodalitia*, or "fellowships") in every diocese in the church worldwide. These he charged with the detection of modernism and empowered to censor all clerical publications, and he entitled them to work in complete secrecy.[11] Accordingly, scores of books were banned and dozens of priestly careers ended—some by expulsion from clerical orders and some even by excommunication. In time the entire École biblique in Jerusalem, founded by a Dominican priest in 1890, was condemned and briefly closed.

The effect of these measures was easy to imagine: much of Catholic intellectual life stagnated. It did not recover until after World War II, with the establishment of the Second Vatican Council (1962–1965). To many in the broader Western society, the church's war on modernism seemed a painful embarrassment, not merely a flat-out inability to understand modern scientific and textual thinking but a petulant refusal by pious ideologues to think or to allow others to do so. Victims of the purges under Pius X—like the French scholar Alfred Loisy (1857–1940), the English Jesuit George Tyrell (1861–1909), or the Austrian lay theologian Friedrich von Hügel (1852–1925)—became martyrs to intellectual freedom, for their supporters. Loisy was defrocked and excommunicated, while Tyrell was expelled from the Jesuit order and excommunicated. Both men were denied a Catholic burial. And the Roman Catholic Church entered the 20th century with a growing popular reputation as the enemy of thinking.

> To many in the broader Western society, the church's war on modernism seemed a painful embarrassment, not merely a flat-out inability to understand modern scientific and textual thinking but a petulant refusal by pious ideologues to think or to allow others to do so.

---

[11]   Some censors went so far as to intercept private mail and to review a suspect's book purchases at local shops. Many kept notes in secret codes.

MODERNISM, SECULARISM, AND THE JEWS

In the 18th century, Jewish biblical scholars who worked to harmonize their tradition with the principles of the Enlightenment became known as **maskilim** ("the enlightened ones"). Their aims were twofold: to strain out irrationalities from Jewish observance, thereby broadening its appeal to the irreligious Enlightened society; and to revitalize Scriptural study among Jews for its own sake. The zenith of maskilic efforts was the publication of a new edition of the Torah by Moses Mendelssohn (1729–1786) between 1780 and 1783. Mendelssohn's edition included a parallel German translation (written, though, in Hebrew letters) and highly detailed technical notes on linguistic problems in the Masoretic text. What Mendelssohn left out of his edition were the rabbinical commentaries on legal and ritualistic issues raised by the text that had been traditionally included in Hebrew Bibles from the 13th century on. Mendelssohn's great work had many mistakes and shortcomings, but it nevertheless represented a major breakthrough—a Torah that aimed above all to be read as a text and not as a guide to daily observance.

After the Congress of Vienna imposed a new political order on Europe in 1815, Jewish excitement over the new Torah continued to grow. Soon new editions of the books of the Prophets (*Nevi'im*) and of the Writings (*Ketuvim*) appeared, all prepared along Mendelssohn's model. Dense scholarly books on the fine points of Hebrew grammar, synonyms, particles, and toponyms were published with surprising frequency; soon entire academic journals dedicated to the study of Hebrew philology and literature were founded. An entire new academic field began to emerge—in Germany, first of all—called the *Wissenschaft des Judentums* ("Jewish sciences"). It was not long before non-Jewish and non-German scholars took notice. When the historical development of the Hebrew language became better understood, the development of the biblical texts themselves over time became clearer—the phenomenon that triggered historical criticism and eventually the modernist crisis among Christians.

One of the greatest of the early Wissenschaft scholars was Abraham Geiger (1810–1874), a Reform rabbi from Frankfurt am Main who spent most of his scholarly career at Breslau, in Prussia (today's city of Wroclaw, in Poland). Geiger founded two important journals (and filled the first volumes of each with many of his own researches). In his masterpiece, *The Biblical Text and Its Transmission* (*Urschrift und Übersetzung der Bibel*, 1857), he laid out the most detailed argument yet published on the development of the Bible over centuries. It addressed the presence of competing versions on the text, as well as the variations between the numerous translations and editions of it over time. To Geiger, the Bible and indeed all of Jewish tradition possess an unfixed, fluid nature: "Every age, every cultural movement, and every personality in our history has brought ideas of its own to bear on the Bible." Moreover, they will continue to do so. Geiger hoped that the efforts of historical criticism would lead the Jews on to the next phase of development, seeing in their tradition's adaptability the secret of its endurance. We do not know what Geiger thought of Darwinian theory, but his views on the evolution of Judaism are interestingly consonant with it, whether intentionally or not. A loose German translation of *Origin of Species* was published in 1860, with a much better version coming a decade later.

What was *not* part of Geiger's intention was the secularizing effect of his scholarship on many of Europe's Jews. Most of the new scholars were, or soon became, Reform Jews rather than Orthodox, and their work contributed directly to the firm establishment of the Reform tradition. The Wissenschaft school did not start the secularizing trend. The movement away from Orthodoxy had begun at least a century earlier, in the early 18th century. Yet Orthodox leaders failed to respond to developments effectively. It may be that they regarded the rise of anti-Semitism or the suffering of the industrialized poor as the more pressing problems; certainly nationalistic passions from one end of Europe to the other gave them reason to pause. But the fact remains that Jewish Orthodoxy by and large dug in its heels. Like Catholic conservativism, it fought against the new scientific understandings of religious tradition by simply saying no.

Surprisingly few Orthodox rabbis took on the Darwinian challenge, though. Instead, they just ignored it. Judaism had never accepted the notion of original sin and the Fall of Man—the idea that human life is a devolution from an earlier state of spiritual perfection. Thus, few Jews felt that mankind's arising from primitive beginnings threatened their tradition. Moreover, Orthodoxy had never insisted on a literal interpretation of the Six Days of Creation, which left the door open to accepting geological time.

Once again, social and economic changes led to the spread of secularism or nonobservance, but here the role of industrialization is less important than it was for Christian Europe. Over the course of the 19th century, Europe experienced two major waves of immigration—of Jews fleeing the troubled Ottoman Empire, and of Jews escaping the pogroms in Czarist Russia. The overall European population doubled to more than 400 million, and the number of Jews went from roughly 3 million to 8 million. Close to 5 million, however, lived specifically in eastern Europe, and most of them were poor—victims either of the weak economic development of the area, of their own refugee status, or of legal barriers to advancement.[12] Given their dire condition, many emigrated yet again, further west into cities like Warsaw (30,000 in 1800, 300,000 in 1900), Berlin (12,000 in

---

12 Most secondary schools at the time restricted Jewish enrollment to no more than 5 percent of the student body.

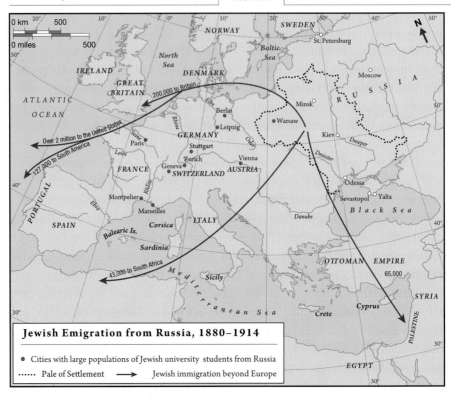

MAP 20.1 within the map:

Jewish Emigration from Russia, 1880–1914

- Cities with large populations of Jewish university students from Russia
- ······ Pale of Settlement ⟶ Jewish immigration beyond Europe

MAP 20.1 Jewish Emigration from Russia, 1880–1914

1800, 140,000 in 1900), and Vienna (2,000 in 1800, 150,000 in 1900). There they followed the classic immigrant pattern of hard work, education, and advancement through subsequent generations to reach professional status—doctors, lawyers, journalists (see Map 20.1). Secularization, as a consequence, resulted from the drive to succeed and gain acceptance.

The family of Karl Marx fit this pattern, as did those of Theodor Herzl (1860–1904) and Sigmund Freud (1856–1939). What was unusual in their cases was simply the degree of secularism and assimilation that they had achieved. Describing the same phenomenon among Jewish immigrants to the United States, Moses Weinberger (1854–1940), a popular Orthodox writer, lamented in 1887:

> How awesome is the strength of America! In a single year it transforms "Rachel, wife of Reb Jaakov" into "Mrs. Jacobs" and "Reb Baruch, cobbler and shoemaker" into "Mr. Bennett, Shoe Manufacturer." The Enlightenments of Berlin and Europe put together did not accomplish as much in half a century.

A separate movement among 19th-century Jews is known variously as Secular Judaism, Secular Zionism, Humanistic Judaism, or Cultural Zionism. This was not, as it might sound, a vision of Jewish identity shorn of religious convictions. Rather, it emphasized a fundamental unity of identity across the religious lines that divided the multiple Jewish traditions—Orthodox, Reform, and Conservative Judaism, plus the many subgroups and outcroppings belonging to each. Among the early leaders of this mission was Asher Ginsberg (1856–1927), a Russian Jew better known by his pen-name Ahad Ha'am. Ahad Ha'am clashed with Theodor Herzl over the issue of establishing a Zionist state in Palestine, thinking it was impractical. But he did want to help organize and maintain a Jewish presence in Palestine, one that would symbolize for all Jews everywhere their ancestral linkage. It would establish, in his words, "a Jewish state and not merely a state made up of Jews." Seeing the growing divisions among Jews as a greater problem, for the moment at least, than the vulnerable position of Jews in Western society, Ahad Ha'am devoted his life to calling all Jews to recognize their fundamental and eternal connectedness.

THE ISLAMIC EXCEPTION

The rapid growth—imposition, really—of Wahhabism was the major development in Islam in the 19th century. Scientific study in the Muslim world had long since turned inward; it consisted of endless commentaries on codified bodies of knowledge, rather than in exploring new areas of investigation. Europe had pulled ahead of the Arabic-speaking world in science as early as the 13th century, and the Scientific Revolution of the 17th century widened the gap almost beyond bridging. Few of the advances and discoveries of the 19th century made much of an impact in the Islamic world, or indeed were even known there, and so they presented nothing like the threat to traditional faith they did in the West. Darwin's *Origin of Species* remained virtually unknown; it appeared in an Arabic translation for the first time only in 2009. The closest available version of Darwinian theory was an edition of Thomas H. Huxley's popularization, in English, in which certain key terms were printed in boldface, with Arabic footnotes at the bottom of each page. It was published in 2008.[13] The scientific vacuum this represented made it easier for Wahhabism's form of anti-intellectualism to take root.

> Few of the advances and discoveries of the 19th century made much of an impact in the Islamic world, or indeed were even known there, and so they presented nothing like the threat to traditional faith they did in the West.

Not all Muslim societies experienced the same distancing from modern science. Some embrace it wholeheartedly, at least in theory, while their actual

---

[13]   A 2009 poll in Egypt found that only 9 percent of the adult population both knew of evolution and believed in it.

involvement is somewhat marginal. Others, however, remain staunchly opposed. They see the systematic structure of scientific thinking as an attempt to confound the complete freedom of action retained by Allah. In a few instances, opposition to science lasted until well into the 20th century. In Iran, for example, dissection of corpses remained forbidden in medical schools until the 1920s. And at the leading Islamic university in Egypt (al-Azhar) the Copernican heliocentric model was not officially accepted until 1961.

Historical Criticism found no friendlier audience among Muslims, although efforts began in Europe to apply its tenets to the Qur'an. In 1843 Gustav Weil (1808–1889), a German Jewish scholar of Arabic and Turkish who worked as the librarian of the University of Heidelberg, published *The Prophet Muhammad: His Life and Teaching*, the first-ever work to apply critical methods to the origins of Islam. Apart from the Qur'an and *hadith*, Weil had access only to a single other source—the life of the Prophet written by Ibn Hisham (d. 833), an edited version of an even earlier biography of the Prophet written by Ibn Ishaq (d. 767), whose text was then unknown in the West. He followed this with an even more ambitious volume titled *A Historical-Critical Introduction to the Qur'an* (1844) and an essay titled "Biblical Legends among the Muslims" (1849), which details the ways in which rabbinical writings influenced Islamic tradition.

Al-Azhar University, Cairo, ca. 1910   Founded in the 10th century, Al-Azhar is one of the oldest universities in the world. For nearly a thousand years its curriculum—Islamic law and jurisprudence, Arabic, grammar. logic, and philosophy—barely changed.

These works sparked enough interest that soon a fairly large corps of scholars, mostly German and British, ventured into the field, and a stream of editions, translations, and historical-critical analyses were published. Sir William Muir's (1819–1905) *Life of Mahomet and the History of Islam to the Era of the Hegira,* in four volumes, appeared between 1858 and 1864. It was followed by the *Prolegomena to the Historical Origins of Islam* by Julius Wellhausen (1844–1918), *Muslim Studies* by Ignaz Goldziher (1850–1921), the ten-volume *Annals of Islam* (1905–1907) by Leone Caetani (1869–1935), and the series of works by the controversial Belgian Jesuit scholar Henri Lammens (1862–1937). With the exception of Lammens, all of these scholars professed admiration for Islam and Arab culture, and they dissected the early Muslim texts to show how Islam evolved historically. Like the Gospels when it came to Jesus, they found, the earliest Islamic texts that discuss the Prophet come roughly a century after his death. They should hence be read not as authoritative contemporary evidence but as after-the-fact attempts to sculpt a narrative by those who had emerged as leaders of the movement. Most Muslims around the world heatedly rejected these ideas.

To many in the Islamic world most strongly opposed to the new science and criticism, their opposition was not merely a knee-jerk rejection of innovative thinking. Rather, it was a rejection of European political imperialism—which was beginning to take place precisely at the end of the 19th century as new scholarly texts were coming into print. Indeed, many Muslims regarded those works as the intellectual front of the imperialist war itself; many still do.

WHO, WHAT, WHERE

atheism

higher criticism

Historical Criticism

maskilim

modernism

Neo-Lutheranism

On the Origin of Species by
    Means of Natural Selection

Oxford movement

Rerum Novarum

secularism

Social Catholicism

subsidiarity

Syllabus of Errors

theory of evolution
    by natural selection

uniformitarianism

SUGGESTED READINGS

Primary Sources

Darwin, Charles. *The Descent of Man.*

———. *On the Origin of Species.*

Feuerbach, Ludwig. *The Essence of Christianity.*

Geiger, Abraham. *The Biblical Text and Its Transmission.*

Goldziher, Ignaz. *Muslim Studies.*

Leo XIII, Pope. *Rerum Novarum.*

Lyell, Charles. *Principles of Geology.*

Newman, John Henry. *Apologia Pro Vita Sua.*

Nietzsche, Friedrich. *The Gay Science.*

Renan. Ernst. *The Life of Jesus.*

Strauss, David Friedrich. *The Christ of Belief and the Jesus of History.*

———. *The Life of Jesus Critically Examined.*

Wellhausen, Julius. *Prolegomena to the Historical Origins of Islam.*

———. *Prolegomena to the History of Ancient Israel.*

Anthologies

Fritzsche, Peter, trans and ed. *Nietzsche and the Death of God: Selected Writings* (2011).

Guy, Josephine, ed. *The Victorian Age: An Anthology of Sources and Documents* (2001).

Herbert, Sandra. *Charles Darwin and the Question of Evolution: A Brief History with Documents* (2011).

Studies

Artigas, Mariano, Thomas F. Glick, and Rafael A. Martínez. *Negotiating Darwin: The Vatican Confronts Evolution, 1877–1902* (2007).

Bernardi, Peter J. *Maurice Blondel, Social Catholicism, and Action Française: The Clash over the Church's Role in Society during the Modernist Era* (2008).

Brown, Callum G. *The Death of Christian Britain: Understanding Secularisation, 1800–2000* (2009).

Browne, Janet. *Charles Darwin: A Biography.* (2003).

Burrow, J. W. *The Crisis of Reason: European Thought, 1848–1914* (2002).

Chiron, Yves. *Saint Pius X: Restorer of the Church* (2002).

Crews, Robert D. *For Prophet and Tsar: Islam and Empire in Russia and Central Asia* (2009).

Ford, Alan. *James Ussher: Theology, History, and Politics in Early-Modern Ireland and England* (2007).

Hill, Harvey. *The Politics of Modernism: Alfred Loisy and the Scientific Study of Religion* (2002).

Jodock, Darrell. *Catholicism Contending with Modernity: Roman Catholic Modernism and Anti-Modernism in Historical Context* (2010).

Koltun-Fromm, Ken. *Abraham Geiger's Liberal Judaism: Personal Meaning and Religious Authority* (2006).

Larsen, Timothy. *Crisis of Doubt: Honest Faith in Nineteenth-Century England* (2009).

———. *A People of One Book: The Bible and the Victorians* (2011).

McLeod, Hugh. *Secularisation in Western Europe, 1848–1914* (2000).

O'Connor, James, trans. *The Gift of Infallibility: The Official Relatio on Infallibility by Bishop Vincent Ferrer Gasser at Vatican Council* (2008).

Prusak, Bernard P. *The Church Unfinished: Ecclesiology through the Centuries* (2004).

Schultenover, David G., ed. *The Reception of Pragmatism in France and the Rise of Roman Catholic Pragmatism, 1890–1914* (2009).

Winchester, Simon. *The Map That Changed the World: William Smith and the Birth of Modern Geology* (2001).

Young, Julian. *The Death of God and the Meaning of Life* (2003).

———. *Friedrich Nietzsche: A Philosophical Biography* (2010).

For additional resources, including maps, primary sources, visuals, web links, and quizzes, please go to **www.oup.com/us/backman.**

CHAPTER 21

The Modern Woman

1860–1914

Throughout the second half of the 19th century, ever-increasing numbers of women across the Greater West began to agitate for equal rights, most particularly the right to vote. Calls for better treatment of women date back to the 14th century at least, but usually from solitary voices. Now the issue of women's rights was the subject of more widespread expectation and demand.

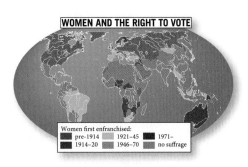

WOMEN AND THE RIGHT TO VOTE

Women first enfranchised:
pre-1914 | 1921–45 | 1971–
1914–20 | 1946–70 | no suffrage

The first major step forward occurred in the labor protests of the early 1800s, when European women formed the majority of the workforce in certain industries. These women expected an improvement in their lot as part of the rise of workers' rights, but their hopes were beaten down for the most part and had to wait for another generation or two. The first bill before the British Parliament to extend suffrage (the right to vote) to women was presented in 1867 and defeated by an overwhelming vote of 194 to 74. Ironically, the very industrial system that had kept women down before 1860 gave them the means to press forward in the latter decades of the century. These changes in the workplace, during the Second Industrial Revolution (see chapter 22), combined with the development of political liberalism to enable the call for women's suffrage and ultimately the rise of broader demands for women's rights, in the **feminist movement**.

THE APPETITE FOR REFORM

◀ **The New Woman** Promotional poster for production of *The New Woman* (1894), a play by Sydney Grundy, in London.

The hunger for reform was acute. Popular attitudes regarding women's place in society ranged widely, but the majority emphasized their fundamental duty to maintain the family

- The Appetite for Reform
- Whose Rights Come First?
- Suffragists and Suffragettes
- Love and the "Modern Woman"
- School, Work, and the New Woman
- Women, Islam, and Nationalism
- Honor Killing and Genital Cutting

CHAPTER OUTLINE

and household and insisted on the unnaturalness of their interest in civil society, politics, and intellectual life. As the popular London weekly newspaper *The Saturday Review* put it in 1871:

> The power of reasoning is so small in women that they need adventitious help, and if they have not the guidance and check of a religious conscience, it is useless to expect from them self-control on abstract principles. They do not calculate consequences, and they are reckless when they once give way, hence they are to be kept straight only through their affections, the religious sentiment, and a well-educated moral sense.[1]

The sanctity of the family as the fundamental unit of society, in this view, trumped any demand by women for civic equality. Hence opposition to female suffrage was primarily moral—which set it apart from the economic and class-based arguments levied against the demands of male workers and commoners. Hundreds, if not thousands or even more, of pamphlets, sermons, domestic guidebooks, novels, melodramatic stage-plays, sentimental popular songs, mawkish paintings, and family-oriented magazines pressed the point continually.

Industrialization had separated the work space from the domestic space, and among the middle class this led to a heightened popular vision of the home as a place of refuge. A wife, as overseer of the domestic safe haven, both supplied and tended to the essential emotional cohesion of family life; but until divorce laws were reformed she did so from a position of legal powerlessness. To those pressing for reform, both female and male, the liberal capitalist ideology that distinguished between the male-identified public sphere and the female-identified home front was the fundamental problem. The solution, therefore, was not merely to remove the barriers that excluded women from the man's world of commerce and government;

---

[1]   Another example: "No woman can or ought to know very much of the mass of meanness and wickedness and misery that is loose in the wide world. She could not learn it without losing the bloom and freshness which it is her mission in life to preserve."—*The Saturday Review*

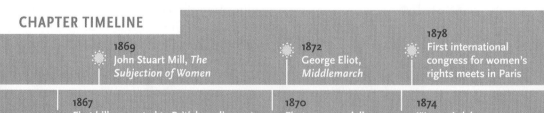

CHAPTER TIMELINE

1869
John Stuart Mill, *The Subjection of Women*

1872
George Eliot, *Middlemarch*

1878
First international congress for women's rights meets in Paris

1867
First bill presented to British parliament to extend suffrage; Russia and Finland open their universities to women

1870
First commercially produced typewriters

1874
Women's labor and trade; unions legalized in France

Family Values   Queen Victoria (r. 1837-1901), Britain's longest reigning monarch, enjoyed huge popularity in the first half of her reign, but the death of her husband, Prince Albert, in 1861 sent her into a protracted seclusion and left her with an increasingly dour demeanor; her popularity surged again after 1876 when she assumed the title of Empress of India and stood as the resolute champion of British imperialism. In this early family portrait, Victoria and Albert watch affectionately over five of their children. They eventually had nine, before Albert's death.

it was to end the very notion of separate female and male spheres of belonging and action. As one Englishwoman recalled, in a biography of her suffragist mother published in the 1930s:

> To remain single was thought a disgrace and at thirty an unmarried woman was called an old maid. After their parents died, what could they do, where could they go? If they had a brother, as unwanted and

1880
Naphey, *The Physical Life of Woman*; France allows girls to attend secondary school

1893
Helene Stöcker, "The Modern Woman"

1903
Women's Social and Political Union formed in Britain

1906
Universal suffrage in Finland

1913
"Cat and Mouse Act" passed in Britain

1923
Huda'i Sha'arawi founds Egyptian Feminist Union

permanent guests, they might live in his house. Some had to maintain themselves and then, indeed, difficulty arose. The only paid occupation open to a gentlewoman was to become a governess under despised conditions and a miserable salary. None of the professions were open to women; there were no women in Government offices; no secretarial work was done by them. Even nursing was disorganized and disreputable until Florence Nightingale recreated it as a profession by founding the Nightingale School of Nursing in 1860.

This was Louisa Garrett Anderson (1873–1923), an early feminist whose mother, Elizabeth Garrett Anderson (1836–1917), had been Britain's first-ever female licensed physician.

The same point was made at greater length by the political philosopher John Stuart Mill (1806–1873) in his book *The Subjection of Women* (1869):

> There is no country of Europe in which the ablest men have not frequently experienced, and keenly appreciated, the value of the advice and help of clever and experienced women of the world, in the attainment both of private and of public objects; and there are important matters of public administration to which few men are equally competent with such women; among others, the detailed control of expenditure. But what we are now discussing is not the need which society has of the services of women in public business, but the dull and hopeless life to which it so often condemns them, by forbidding them to exercise the practical abilities which many of them are conscious of, in any wider field than one which to some of them never was, and to others is no longer, open. If there is anything vitally important to the happiness of human beings, it is that they should relish their habitual pursuit. This requisite of an enjoyable life is very imperfectly granted, or altogether denied, to a large part of mankind; and by its absence many a life is a failure, which is provided, in appearance, with every requisite of success. But if circumstances which society is not yet skilful enough to overcome, render such failures often for the present inevitable, society need not itself inflict them. The injudiciousness of parents, a youth's own inexperience, or the absence of external opportunities for the congenial vocation, and their presence for an uncongenial, condemn numbers of men to pass their lives in doing one thing reluctantly and ill, when there are other things which they could have done well and happily. But on women this sentence is imposed by actual law, and by customs equivalent to law. What, in unenlightened societies, colour, race, religion, or in the case of a conquered country,

nationality, are to some men, sex is to all women; a peremptory exclusion from almost all honourable occupations, but either such as cannot be fulfilled by others, or such as those others do not think worthy of their acceptance. Sufferings arising from causes of this nature usually meet with so little sympathy, that few persons are aware of the great amount of unhappiness even now produced by the feeling of a wasted life.

Mill never used eight words to say something when he could think of eighty; but his perception was sharp and his character essentially sympathetic. His argument throughout *The Subjection Is Women* is primarily **utilitarian**: women have proven themselves talented and resourceful in spite of the appalling constraints placed on them by centuries of cultural tradition, and therefore it can only benefit society to put these proven skills to full use by allowing women to participate in civic life. Mill was enough a man of his era to maintain that women ought not to enter the workplace, since that would remove them from their domestic responsibilities, yet he advocated full political rights for them and equality before the law. Early feminists like Anderson and Mill moved against the tide of their times. The cofounder of the magazine *The Economist*, Walter Bagehot

Dangerous Liaison   *Interior*, by Degas (1869), presents a disturbing vision of male-female relations. The narrow bed, simple furnishings, and the prominent display of a sewing box suggest this is a scene of a prostitute and a customer in a hotel room. (In Paris at that time prostitutes often carried sewing boxes, both as an indicator of their profession but also, and more practically, so they could repair their clothing after a customer's rough assault.) The disheveled woman has turned her back on the man, who stands, dark and menacing, against the door.

(1826–1877), offered just one response, and Mill's advocacy for women's suffrage nearly caused a permanent rupture of his relations with his own father.[2]

Things were no better for women on the Continent. French law declared as a bedrock legal principle the notion that "a wife owes obedience to her husband." German law granted every husband the sole right to decide when the breastfeeding of his infant son by his wife should end. (The nursing of daughters, presumably, was not sufficiently important to merit regulation by the state.) As late as 1900, German law denied all parental rights over her children to any woman who remarried after her husband's death; her new husband, the children's stepfather, assumed sole legal authority over them. Social pressures limited the movements that proper middle-class women could make in the world, while allowing men to roam freely, with predictable results. By the end of the 19th century nearly 17 percent of all the children born in France annually were illegitimate, and nearly one-quarter of all adult female deaths either resulted directly from or were complicated by sexually trans-mitted diseases.[3] In nearly every major statistical category—life expectancy, education, employment, and income, above all—women on the Continent lagged behind men, especially in the working class; it was only a matter of time before calls were raised to do something about it. Reformers in Britain and the United States led the way, with Scandinavian activists close behind. In order to protect women's health and secure their rights under the law, they quickly realized, two things stood out as strategic necessities—suffrage and education.

> By the end of the 19th century nearly 17 percent of all the children born in France annually were illegitimate, and nearly one-quarter of all adult female deaths either resulted directly from or were complicated by sexually transmitted diseases.

WHOSE RIGHTS COME FIRST?

Opposition came in many forms and from many directions, some of them surprising. That most men in Europe opposed women's suffrage comes as no surprise. Neither does the opposition mounted by most of the mainstream churches, which dismissed ideas of the "modern woman" as an abrogation of the traditional roles of wife and mother. But large numbers of intelligent, talented, and ambitious women also refused to go along with the call to equal rights—such as the nurse and organizer Florence Nightingale (1820–1910) and the novelist Mary Ward (1851–1920). And often their reason was not so much lack of sympathy for women as passion for reform on behalf of others.

---

[2] Bagehot: "The light nothings of the drawing room, and the grave things of the office, are as different from one another as two human occupations can be."

[3] French law forbade unwed mothers to bring paternity suits against the fathers of their children.

Nightingale, whose opposition to the women's movement was particularly fierce, shared many of the attitudes of contemporary males about female abilities and weaknesses. She had served heroically in the Crimean War of the 1850s, tending to thousands of wounded British soldiers. After the war she established a school in London that launched modern nursing as a profession; she also helped raise funds for the grand Royal Buckinghamshire Hospital outside the city. A deeply pious and determined woman, she maintained throughout her life that the cause of women's rights paled in comparison with the world's other sufferings. In fact, as she wrote to a friend in December 1861, it seemed to be nothing more than middle-class self-absorption:

> Now just look at the degree in which women have sympathy—as far as my experience is concerned. And my experience of women is almost as large as Europe. And it is so intimate too. I have lived and slept in the same bed as English countesses and Prussian *Bauerinnen* [peasant girls]. No Roman Catholic *Supérieure* [mother superior] has ever had charge of women of the different creeds that I have had. No woman has excited "passions" among women more than I have. Yet I have no school behind me. My doctrines have not taken hold among women. . . . No woman that I know has ever *appris à apprendre* [attempted to understand]. And I attribute this to want of sympathy. . . . It makes me so mad, the Women's Rights talk. . . . Women crave for being loved, not for loving. They scream out at you for sympathy all day long, [but] they are incapable of giving any in return, for they cannot remember your affairs long enough to do so. . . . I am sick with indignation at what wives and mothers will do [out] of the most egregious selfishness. (Quoted in Cook, *The Life of Florence Nightingale, 1820–1910,* 1913)

To Mary Ward—who published two dozen novels under her married name, Mrs. Humphrey Ward—suffrage represented a perversion of female character. As she wrote in a magazine editorial in 1889, suffrage reform was an effort to fit women into roles to which they were not suited by nature or by Christian faith:

> As voters for or members of School Boards, Boards of Guardians, and other important public bodies, women now have opportunities for public usefulness which must promote the growth of character, and at the same time strengthen among them the social sense and belief. But we believe that the emancipation process has now reached the limits fixed by the physical constitution of women, and by the fundamental difference which must always exist between their main occupations and those of men. . . . Nothing can be further from our minds than to seek to depreciate the position or the importance of women. It is because we are

keenly alive to the enormous value of their special contributions to the community, that we oppose what seems to us likely to endanger that contribution. We are convinced that the pursuit of a mere outward equality with men is for women not only vain but demoralizing. It leads to personal struggle and rivalry, where the only effort of both the great divisions of the human family should be to contribute the characteristic labour and the best gifts of each to the common stock.

The first significant gains in women's rights, ironically, appeared in states along the European periphery, although these were rights separate from suffrage itself. Tsarist Russia opened its universities to women in 1867, for example, as did Finland. The United States formally allowed women to enroll in its universities the following year, and Sweden did so the year after that.[4] In 1872 Sweden

Female Physician   Emily Shanks (1857-1936), a British-Russian painter who lived in Moscow until 1914, painted this scene of a female physician conducting an ear exam. Women were allowed to study medicine informally in Russia as early as the 1850s, but the first MD degree was not granted until 1867 when Nadezhda Suslova (1843-1918) became the country's first licensed female physician.

---

[4]   By 1880 fully one-third of all university students in the United States were women.

outlawed arranged marriages that did not have the expressed consent and agreement of the bride. The first women's labor and trade unions in France were legalized in 1874, and by 1900 the law allowed women to practice law. In Russia, roughly one of every ten licensed physicians was female by 1914.

An obvious questions arises: Why were the dominant European states—the states with the most developed economies, highest literacy rates, most established democratic systems, and most elaborate and sophisticated networks of communication—the last states to extend suffrage to women? The women's rights movement, after all, had actually arisen originally in those leading nations. Calls for women's full legal and political equality date back to the Enlightenment of the 1700s in England and France. To pick just a sampler, Jeremy Bentham's *Introduction to the Principles of Moral and Legislation* (1781), the Marquis de Condorcet's *In Support of the Rights of Citizenship for Women* (1790), and Mary Wollstonecraft's *Vindication of the Rights of Women* (1792) all called for universal suffrage, equity in property rights, and reform of marriage and divorce laws. And the leading feminist writer in Sweden, Hedvig Nordenflycht (1718–1763), was calling, more tamely, for improved education for females. Many women of the 19th century in fact agreed with Florence Nightingale's opinion that the world had far more pressing issues to deal with than the plight of European women.

Harriet Martineau (1802–1876), for example, one of the founders of modern sociology, thought the feminist leaders of her time to be downright dangerous; her political passions focused on abolishing the slave trade, extending suffrage to working-class men, and improving educational opportunities for women. Public health issues and poor relief, not political rights for middle-class women, were what mattered. Martineau's first two books, *Illustrations of Political Economy* (1832) and *Poor Laws and Paupers Illustrated* (1834), focused on the economic injustice of industrial capitalism and became bestsellers, ironically leaving her financially secure for life. She never married (although she nearly wedded Charles Darwin's brother, Erasmus). Her three-volume study *Society in America* (1837) is one of the classic works of early sociology. The result of two years of travel in the United States, it offers a sharp critique of American values and practices. The chapter "The Political Non-Existence of Women" describes how American women are given "indulgence rather than justice" and have few prospects in life other than marriage. Toward the end of her life, Martineau signed petitions calling for female suffrage but refused to call herself a suffragist.

The delay in bringing female suffrage to Belgium, Britain, France, Germany, Holland, and Italy was due not only to stubborn male opposition. For many passionate reformers, the problems of the working poor were simply more dire. Not everyone agreed, and certainly not Beatrice Webb (1858–1943), coauthor with her husband, Sidney, of *The History of Trade Unionism* (1894) and *Industrial Democracy* (1897) and a founder of the socialist Fabian Society. To her, the prospect of two oppressed individuals, one denied the vote and the other dying of starvation, created an obvious moral choice for action. A noted German activist of the era, Anna Maier, in her autobiography (1912) described the plight of her life in distinctly economic rather than sexual terms. To Maier, economic oppression trumped sexual prejudice and had to be dealt with first:

> My father was a weaver and my mother a spooler, although whenever necessary they did any work they could find. I was the youngest of twelve children and learned at an early age what it is to work. . . . [From the age of six] I had to get up at five o'clock every morning to do some spooling before running off to school. My clothes were rags. After a morning at school I hurried home to do some more spooling before having lunch, and then I returned to school for the afternoon lessons, after which I went back to more spooling. . . . When I was thirteen my mother took me by the hand and we went to the manager of a nearby tobacco factory, to see if he would give me a job. He refused, but my mother begged him to take me on since my father had recently died and we were desperate, and so he hired me. . . . The way workers were treated at the factory was hellish. The older women berated the young girls and sometimes even beat them. . . . Years went by, and eventually a new newspaper, the *Arbeiterinnen Zeitung* ["Women Workers' Daily"], started to be published; one of the older women smuggled a few copies into the factory. . . . When a friend loaned me a copy I had to hide it at work and could not even let my mother see it at home. I learned many new things and met many new people. . . . When some men founded a workers' organization they said women could not join, but when a party agent came . . . I asked him if I wasn't enough of an adult worker to be a member. I remember that he was embarrassed at first, but he finally spoke up: "When do you want to start?" I joined, and remain a member to this very day.

The gradual success of antipoverty programs and the legalization of labor unions indirectly helped the cause of women, for as they alleviated the sufferings of the working poor, they freed up energies to pursue other goals.

SUFFRAGISTS AND SUFFRAGETTES

Suffragists and suffragettes were not the same thing. They pursued the same end—women's right to vote—but their methods differed. In simplest terms, **suffragists** worked peaceably and within the legal system for women's rights, whereas

suffragettes favored confrontation, aggressive action, and, whenever they thought it necessary, even violence in order to change society. Britain's National Society for Women's Suffrage formed in 1867 and provided a model for similar groups that sprung up quickly on the Continent—like the VVV (*Vereeniging voor Vrouwenkiesrecht*, or "Society for Women's Legal Rights") in Holland. In 1878 a loose network of these associations convened the first international congress for women's rights in Paris, where they embraced the terms feminist and suffragist and charted out strategies for their cause. These drew heavily on their observations of (male) electoral politics of the age, which included fostering political alliances and courting sympathetic members of the press. Earlier campaigns by women to promote the abolition of slavery and alcohol had given them vital experience at shaping public opinion. But in the end these early feminist organizations proved more successful in enrolling members than in bringing about significant reform. Constitutional change is a slow-moving business, especially when it faces entrenched resistance.

The denial of female suffrage lingered into the 20th century, which resulted in a dramatic change in some reformers' tactics. Led by the redoubtable Emmeline Pankhurst (1858–1928) and her three daughters, Christabel (1880–1958), Sylvia (1882–1960), and Adela (1885–1961), the new group called themselves suffragettes. These activists broke away from the main suffragist association in Britain in 1903 and established the Women's Social and Political Union (WSPU). The WSPU was a distinctly more militant organization; its motto was "Deeds, not words." The suffragettes provoked anger and outrage everywhere they went. Unaffiliated with any political party, they nevertheless attended and intentionally disrupted political

Redoubtable Suffragette   Emmeline Pankhurst addressing a crowd of men.

meetings by the score; they protested outside Parliament and sometimes chained themselves to its doors; some vandalized shop windows and churches.[5]

Pankhurst herself engaged in little overt violence other than trying to force her way into Parliamentary meetings (for which she was imprisoned for six weeks)—and once slapping a policeman in order to be arrested. But she declared that "the condition of our sex is so deplorable that it is our duty to break the law in order to draw attention to the reasons why we do so." In a speech in the United States in 1913, she described her experience and the WSPU's tactics:

> I do not come here as an advocate, because whatever position the suf-
> frage movement may occupy in the United States of America, in England
> it has passed beyond the realm of advocacy and it has entered into the
> sphere of practical politics. It has become the subject of revolution and
> civil war, and so tonight I am not here to advocate woman suffrage. Amer-
> ican suffragists can do that very well for themselves. I am here as a soldier
> who has temporarily left the field of battle in order to explain—it seems
> strange it should have to be explained—what civil war is like when civil
> war is waged by women. . . . I am here [also] as a person who, according to
> the law courts of my country, . . . is of no value to the community at all; and
> I am adjudged because of my life to be a dangerous person, under sentence
> of penal servitude in a convict prison. So you see there is some special in-
> terest in hearing so unusual a person address you. I dare say, in the minds
> of many of you—you will perhaps forgive me this personal touch—that
> I do not look either very like a soldier or very like a convict, and yet I am
> both. . . . We have brought the government of England to this position, that
> it has to face this alternative: either women are to be killed, or women are
> to have the vote. I ask American men in this meeting, what would you say
> if in your State you were faced with that alternative, that you must either
> kill them or give them their citizenship,—women, many of whom you re-
> spect, women whom you know have lived useful lives, women whom you
> know, even if you do not know them personally, are animated with the
> highest motives, women who are in pursuit of liberty and the power to do
> useful public service? Well, there is only one answer to that alternative;
> there is only one way out of it, unless you are prepared to put back civili-
> zation two or three generations; you must give those women the vote. Now
> that is the outcome of our civil war.

---

[5]   One suffragette committed suicide by running into the path of a racehorse owned by the royal family, to draw attention to the plight of women.

Ultimately, she was arrested several dozen times before Parliament finally granted unrestricted women's suffrage in 1928.

Suffragettes on the Continent followed similar measures. In France, Hubertine Auclert (1848–1914) became infamous, and triggered a wave of copycat protests, when she smashed a ballot box in a municipal election in Paris to express her disgust at being unable to vote. Madeleine Pelletier (1874–1939), a physician and France's first female licensed psychiatrist, made her mark by agitating not only for suffrage but for women's rights to contraception and abortion (then a taboo subject) and by protesting the normative ideas of femininity by dressing as a man, complete with cane and bowler hat.[6] Moreover, she continued to provide abortion services despite their illegality. A German socialist, Clara Zetkin (1857–1933), edited a radical newspaper (*Die Gleichheit*, "Equality") and invited arrest by taking a public position against World War I.

Many imprisoned suffragettes protested their arrests by going on hunger strikes, hoping to win sympathy for their cause by sacrificing themselves even to the point of death. Governments quickly responded by ordering forced feedings, a brutal process in which the woman was bound to a chair, had rubber tubing pushed down her throat or through her nostrils and into her stomach, and then had a loose porridge poured into her. Worse still, the British government passed the "Cat and Mouse" Act (officially, the Temporary Discharge of Prisoners for Ill Health Act) in 1913. This ordered police to release from prison any hunger-striking suffragette, only to rearrest her after she had regained her health on the outside. The forced feedings and repeated arrests swung public sympathy toward the women prisoners—especially when their sufferings were made public. In her memoir (1914), Lady Constance Bulwer-Lytton (1869–1923) wrote of disguising herself as a poor seamstress in order to avoid receiving preferential treatment because of her noble status. The harsh treatment she received in prison resulted in a stroke that left her right

Rallying for Women's Suffrage
German poster in support of Women's Day (March 8, 1914), a rally on behalf of women's suffrage. The German government banned this poster soon after its appearance, and most copies have been destroyed.

---

6   Asked once why she dressed as a man, Pelletier responded, "I'll show my breasts when men start wearing pants that show their pricks."

arm paralyzed. She taught herself to write with her left hand and produced *Prisons and Prisoners* in a year.

But extreme actions, even terrorist ones, cost the movement public sympathy, too. To chain oneself to the houses of Parliament was one thing; to set fire to the homes of Parliamentarians was another. In February 1913 a group of WSPU members burned down the home of David Lloyd George, then the chancellor of the exchequer. Lloyd George privately supported women's suffrage but officially opposed it in 1913, for fear that it might disrupt preparations for the coming World War. The following year another suffragette took an axe to a painting of Venus by Diego Velázquez (1599–1660) in the National Gallery in London. She claimed that she was merely doing to one beautiful woman what society was doing to all.

As dedicated as the suffragists were, and as brave and selfless as at least many of the suffragettes were, winning the vote ultimately resulted more from the economic conditions in Europe after World War I. Before that, only Finland (1906) and Norway (1913) had universal suffrage; Denmark passed it in 1915. After the war, women were enfranchised in half of Europe (see Map 21.1).

LOVE AND THE "MODERN WOMAN"

Helene Stöcker (1869–1943) was a leading German feminist who advocated suffrage but devoted most of her prodigious energy to women's sexual health. That issue turned out to be an increasing part of redefining a woman's role. It also went hand in hand with the growing availability of information about sex throughout society—and growing controversies over birth control. It was also just one part of the redefinition of female identity—in literature, education, and public perception.

Stöcker founded the Society for the Protection of Mothers in 1905 (later renamed the German Society for the Protection of Mothers and for Sexual Reform) and edited two journals—*Mutterschutz* ("Care for Mothers") and *Die neue Generation* ("The New Generation"). Through these she campaigned for publicly available sex education, including contraception and abortion, and advocated for the legal rights of children born out of marriage. In 1906 she published *Women and Love: A Manifesto for Emancipating Women and Men in Germany*, which described her plan to reinvent male-female relationships, preferably within marriage but not necessarily so. Her goal, she insisted, was not just to pursue equality for its own sake; it was to help relationships between men and women to become more true, more intimate, and more rich. The greatest harm of the gender inequity of the age was not the legal injustice of it, she argued, but the emotional aridity of the relationships it fostered and even encouraged.

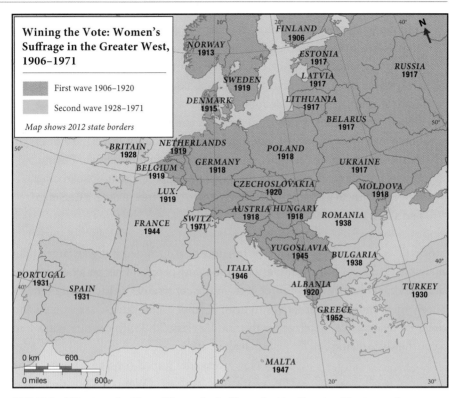

MAP 21.1 **Winning the Vote: Women's Suffrage in the Greater West, 1906–1971**

Stöcker envisioned a world in which any woman who wanted to do so could rise above the traditional path of being a dutiful daughter, then a quiet, uncomplaining wife, and then a loving selfless mother. If a woman wanted, she could pursue an independent life filled with emotional, intellectual, and sexual richness. Stöcker's essay "The Modern Woman" (1893) put the case with her typical candor:

> I am describing a unique species, ... the modern woman, ... who sets out from the shelter of her father's household ... in order to gain financial independence, the prerequisite of every freedom. ... The modern woman does not wish to become man-like but only to become a happier, because a more free, person, one who continues to grow in her unique womanly way. She long ago gave up the childish complaint that she was not born male; rather, she has learned to appreciate her unique feminine strength as a rare gift, a thing set apart, something beyond traditional categories. ... [The modern woman] is born for love. With the fires of her nature—with all her heart, soul, and sensuality—she craves

intimacy, and she needs it more than a man does. . . . She yearns to give and receive love as a woman, not simply to sit quietly by while clever men talk to one another. . . . She craves freedom too, and just as intensely. Only these two things, love and freedom, combined, can grant her the kind of inner peacefulness found among truly liberated people. She therefore maintains a critical distance, a composure, in order to avoid being overwhelmed by her intense youthful sensuality, lest, after a brief thrill, she end up making herself and another truly miserable. But she knows one thing all too well: The greatest happiness that life can offer develops only in a relationship between two fully free people, a free man and a free woman. Of this there is no doubt.

Stöcker's concern was for a kind of freedom that included but was larger than mere political rights. She wanted, as did so many people of her generation, to re-define sexual identity so as to free it from the constraints of Victorian morality. Surely there must be alternatives to brutish labor for working-class women and dreary if respectable marriage for the middle class. The 19th century witnessed a constantly growing call for just such alternatives.

Not everyone joined in the chorus. The "Woman Problem" or "Woman Question" was analogous to nationalism: just as the air was filled with passionate discussions of the "Englishness" of the English, the "Germanness" of the Germans, or the "Spanishness" of the Spaniards, so too were many people intent to define the essential qualities of womanhood. Advances in science were of little help here, since Darwinian evolution appeared to reduce human life to a set of predetermined biological functions. And related sciences did not seem any more enlightened.

> Stöcker's concern was for a kind of freedom that included but was larger than mere political rights. She wanted, as did so many people of her generation, to redefine sexual identity so as to free it from the constraints of Victorian morality.

A popular American medical guide of the 1880s, *The Physical Life of Woman: Advice to the Maiden, Wife, and Mother,* by Dr. George Napheys, asserted that "the vast majority of women" possess only "moderate" sexual appetites, and "only in very rare instances do women experience one tithe of the sexual feeling which is familiar to most men. Many of them are entirely frigid, and not even in mar-riage do they ever perceive any real desire." A German gynecologist, Dr. Otto Adler, estimated in 1904 that "as many as forty percent" of all women experience no sexual desire in their lifetimes. Anatomists who studied the brain announced confidently that men are by nature between 12 and 20 percent more intelligent than women. Intellectual work, they proclaimed, when performed by women, diverts bodily energies away from their natural reproductive mission. An Englishwoman studying medicine at Girton College in 1888 summarized the attitude of physicians around her, in an anonymous article in the *Westminster Review*, as a sarcastic warning:

> Women, beware! Beware! You are on the brink of destruction! You have hitherto been engaged only in crushing your waists [by wearing corsets], now you are attempting to cultivate your minds! You have been merely dancing all night in the foul air of ballrooms; now you are beginning to spend your mornings in study. You have been incessantly stimulating your emotions with concerts and operas, with French plays and French novels; now you are exerting your understanding to learn Greek and solve propositions in Euclid. Beware! Oh, beware!! Science pronounces that the woman who studies—is lost!

Knowledge of sex, and confusion about it, abounded. Condoms, which had been used in Europe at least since the early 18th century, were readily available at taverns, pharmacists, and outdoor markets.[7] Other methods of contraception included cervical caps and diaphragms (made of vulcanized rubber after 1850), and herbal abortifacients like Queen Anne's lace, which consisted of the crushed seeds of flowering wild carrots. The most commonly used methods were presumably coitus interruptus and what is known today as the "rhythm method." Abortion was illegal everywhere in Europe but was generally available—at a high price and at considerable risk to health. Christian churches, too, felt the need to determine and enact official positions on contraception. Most had always condemned abortion, but doctrines on contraception were another matter. Until such measures became widely available, starting in midcentury, the churches had felt no need to take a definitive position except to condemn coitus interruptus as the "sin of Onan"—a reference to the tale in Genesis 38. Onan was the brother of Judah, and according to the custom of the times Onan had a responsibility, after Judah's early death, to wed and provide offspring for Judah's childless widow. When Onan instead "spilled his seed on the ground" by interrupting the sexual union with his sister-in-law, God condemned him to death for disobedience to the Law. Whatever the cause, birth rates among the middle class declined significantly between 1850 and 1914. In Britain, for example, one-quarter of all families

---

[7] Condoms occasionally were sold at concession stands in theaters. The German army after 1870 handed them out to soldiers when they were about to go off duty.

had eight or more children in 1825. By 1925 fully one-half of all families had only one or two children each, while one family out of every six was childless.

The distribution of information about birth control ("family management" or "family limitation," as it was known at the time) was highly contentious. Western countries struggled with the tension between traditional morals and the free exchange of scientific knowledge. In the United States, President Theodore Roosevelt (r. 1901–1909) spoke for many when he called family limitation "one of the most unpleasant and unwholesome features of modern life." But women's demand for reliable contraception continued to grow. Dr. Aletta Jacobs (1854–1929), Holland's first female physician, established Europe's first birth control clinic in Amsterdam in 1882, dispensing information about contraception and the materials for it. A German physician in Breslau (today's city of Wrocław, Poland), Dr. Richard Richter, published the first treatise on the use of intrauterine devices in 1909. Alarmed by this proliferation of materials, social critics in Germany began to express concern that the ensuing labor shortage would invite immigration by "alien people—especially Slavs and perhaps the eastern European Jews too."

Male Antimasturbation Device
Masturbation had long been criticized in European culture as a sin or a personal failing, but it only became regarded as clinically unhealthy in the early 18th century, when a series of pseudo-scientific works warned of its supposedly harmful effects. In Victorian times, concerns about the dangers of masturbation grew so extensive that many parents began to employ physical methods to prevent their sons from indulging in the fearful practice. This piece dates to 1880. Made of copper, it was worn on a belt to protect boys both from masturbation and from unintentional nocturnal emissions.

Ignorance of sexual matters was nevertheless widespread and, to an extent, deliberately imposed. If the moral code of "proper society" forbade the discussion of sex and tried to control the distribution of scientific knowledge about it, then it is not surprising that many men and women began their sexual lives without any accurate understanding of what they were beginning. Experts still warned that masturbation was medically harmful to both men and women, since it depleted the body of "vital fluids and energies." That depletion supposedly left the body, according to a medical guide of the time, more vulnerable to "seminal weakness, impotence, dysury [painful urination], *tabes dorsalis* [syphilitic myelopathy], pulmonary consumption, dyspepsia, dimness of sight, vertigo, epilepsy, hypochondriasis, loss of memory, manalgia [catatonia], fatuity [dementia], and death."

Much of Western society held two contradictory beliefs at once—in the sexual rapaciousness of women and in their natural sexlessness. The explanation lay in the widespread view that there are two types of women.[8] Assuming that most women—proper women, in society's eyes—had no interest in sex, many felt there was no need to educate them about it, and the consequence was entrenched ignorance.

✦

Many of the era's greatest works of literature are dedicated to exploring female identity in both its generalized essentials and its individual quirks. These are great works of art—and their authors are all male. Women writers also explored female character in depth, but generally with less of a singular focus on a specific woman, as in the works written by men, and generally with less artistic success. George Eliot's *Middlemarch* (1872) was undeniably the greatest novel written by a European woman in the late 19th century; the first in the 20th century by a woman to have truly changed the very shape of the novel was Virginia Woolf's *Mrs. Dalloway* (1925). No doubt the more modest growth in the intervening fifty years has many causes—and no doubt the underappreciation of novels and plays written by women in their time has contributed to our ignorance in our own.

Literature of Female Identity: A Sampler

Madame Bovary (1857), by Gustave Flaubert

Anna Karenina (1878), by Leo Tolstoy

The Portrait of a Lady (1881), by Henry James

Fortunata and Jacinta (1887), by Benito Pérez Galdós

Hedda Gabler (1890), by Henrik Ibsen

Tess of the d'Urbervilles (1891), by Thomas Hardy

The New Woman (1893), by Bolesław Prus

Effi Briest (1894), by Theodor Fontane.

In the intervening fifty-plus years, women in every Western country continued to produce excellent fiction (Willa Cather and Edith Wharton in the United States, for example) but were their aims any less revolutionary, and if so, why? It is an important question. Why, at the very time when the status of women in Western society was being most passionately and universally debated, were women novelists, poets, and playwrights stimulating any less of a debate? No doubt the deep involvement of so many women in suffragist and suffragette

---

[8] As one medical writer in Oxford put it: "Nine out of ten women are indifferent or actively dislike [sex]; the tenth, who enjoys it, will always be a harlot."

work partially explains the lack; the times called for action, not novels or poems. Moreover, political themes seldom make for enduring literature.

Sex itself may provide another explanation. Not gender, but actual sex. European fiction and drama from 1850 to 1914 was dominated by the **realist** and **naturalist** schools, which aimed for a fuller and more detailed depiction of daily life. It lingered on its characters' gritty surroundings, the sounds and smells of the cities they inhabited, the sense of despair and misery created by wretched food, hard labor, and oppressive social mores. A goal of these writers was to depict the whole array of pressures, demands, irritations, and longings that shape human lives. One of the greatest naturalist writers in France, Émile Zola (1840–1902), wrote a series of twenty novels with interlocking characters, families, settings, and events in an effort to portray the entire panorama of French life during the Second Empire. His descriptions of social snobbery, grueling manual labor, inadequate housing, the ruin of alcoholism, prostitution, marital bliss, and marital despair are often unnervingly vivid.

Nana   *Nana*, by Edouard Manet (1832-1883). Painted for the 1877 Salon at Paris but rejected for its immoral character, Manet's large canvas (almost nine feet tall) presents another scene of a prostitute and her client. What offended viewers about this picture was not its subject-matter (which was fairly common by that time) but the fact that the young woman appears to have no shame about her profession; indeed, she has turned toward and is smiling prettily at the viewer. The fact that her customer, though only half shown, is clearly a member of respectable bourgeois society probably did not help either.

Many realist and naturalist writers depicted sexual relations with a candor that often set the Victorians' teeth on edge. Though tame by 21st-century standards, the frank sexuality in European literature from 1850 to 1914 may have been off-putting to women writers—something they did not wish to attempt, or felt that they could not do. Even Virginia Woolf, as late as her death in 1944, allowed no sex to enter any of her books.[9] Women writers already worked in the face of enough social prejudices. Did they feel that writing frankly about sexual feelings might be too much? No one can say for sure.

---

[9]   Woolf's most subversive novel, the time-shifting, gender-bending fantasy *Orlando*, published in 1928, was inspired by her lesbian affair with Vita Sackville-West. But it contains no trace of eroticism.

> **Literature of Sexuality: A Sampler**
> *L'Assommoir* (1877), by Émile Zola
> *Ghosts* (1881), by Henrik Ibsen
> *Miss Julie* (1888), by August Strindberg
> *The Kreutzer Sonata* (1889), by Leo Tolstoy
> *Jude the Obscure* (1895), by Thomas Hardy.
> *Sister Carrie* (1900), by Theodore Dreiser
> *The Sacred Fount* (1901), by Henry James

SCHOOL, WORK, AND THE NEW WOMAN

As the European industrial economy continued to expand, the late 19th century saw explosive growth in public education across the West. Even factory workers at the low end of the pay scale needed to be functionally literate and numerate, if only so that they could read the regulations governing the shop floor. Prior to the revolutions of 1848, most Western states had established only public secondary schools. Elementary education was thought to be needed only by the relatively well-to-do, who hired private tutors for their young children, which left poor working-class youths free to be exploited in the factories. When the 19th century began, only Germany had a system of state-run primary schools; France created its system in 1833. For most working-class girls, formal education ended there. France did not open its secondary schools to girls until 1880, and by the end of the century there were only three dozen such schools for girls in the entire country, and the schooling was not made compulsory until a few years later. Germany's first secondary school for girls appeared in 1872. In Britain, primary schooling became compulsory in 1880 but was not run by the state until 1902. In the Netherlands compulsory state-run schools did not exist for either boys or girls before 1901, but private primary and secondary education had long been among the best in Europe. Usually the creation of public primary education systems followed within a decade of the outlawing of child labor.

Secondary education expanded rapidly too, as the economy created a demand for better-educated workers. Careers in civil service, law, and medicine opened up too. New careers as railway engineers, train staff, postal workers, shipping clerks, harbormasters, civil servants, accountants, public works supervisors and staff, secretaries, teachers, journalists, and legal aides all appeared in the late 19th century—and all needed preparation. Public schools provided new opportunities for women, since the education of children seemed to many to be a natural extension of women's traditional role as caregivers. The United

States led the way, with fully two-thirds of all primary and secondary school teachers being female by 1890. Europe's figures did not measure up, but the majority of primary school teachers in each country were women. So great was the demand, in fact, that entire colleges for training teachers were created; along with special colleges for medical training, they were the first cracks in the walls that kept women out of the university system. Aside from professional colleges, the first colleges for women were established in the 1870s and 1880s—such as Newnham College in Cambridge or Lady Margaret Hall in Oxford—but were not formally accepted into their university systems until well into the 20th century. Overall, the numbers of women in all areas of education continued to grow until, on the eve of war in 1914, perhaps as many as 12–15 percent of European undergraduate students were female.

A different and special chapter in the development of education opened with the career of Maria Montessori (1870–1952), the first female licensed physician in Italy. Her training in psychology led to an interest in the education of mentally handicapped children. In 1896, with the support of the Italian minister for education, she worked with a group of special-needs children whom the state schools had dismissed as uneducable. Using her own experimental methods, she produced an impressive result: within three years, her eight-year-old students outscored public school students in reading and writing. This led to her opening a new elementary school in a rough neighborhood in Rome in 1907, where she wanted to see what effect her methods would have on mainstream students.

Montessori's methods were controversial among educators, and remain so today, but produced consistently superior performance in every category, including social behavior, up to the age of twelve. Her method was based on the notion of self-directed education, or "spontaneous self-development." She believed that children, being naturally inquisitive, learn better by being allowed to explore at their own rate than by being drilled with data according to a state plan. As she wrote in *Education for a New World*, the teachers in her schools thus acted more as facilitators or guides than as deliverers of knowledge:

Maria Montessori (1870–1952)
Educational reformer and the first woman to receive a medical degree in Italy.

Scientific observation has established that education is not what the teacher gives; education is a natural process spontaneously carried out by the human individual, and is acquired not by listening to words but by experiences upon the environment. The task of the teacher becomes that of preparing a series of motives of cultural activity, spread over a specially prepared environment, and then refraining from obtrusive interference. Human teachers can only help the great work that is being done, as servants help the master. Doing so, they will be witnesses to the unfolding of the human soul and to the rising of a New Man who will not be a victim of events, but will have the clarity of vision to direct and shape the future of human society.

Schools using her methods, whether officially affiliated with the International Montessori Association or not, began to spring up across Europe and especially in the United States.

——————— ✛ ———————

Meanwhile, the numbers of women in the workplace also increased. The development of the telegraph and telephone systems created a need for well-trained operators, while machines like the typewriter (invented in 1829, with the first commercially produced typewriter appearing in 1870) virtually created the modern business office, with its attendant pools of secretaries, clerks, and administrative managers. Women thus became essential, if "inferior," elements of the modern commercial economy. Newspapers and magazines dedicated to them multiplied exponentially. Hundreds of popular songs, plays, and paintings focused on the **new woman** of the start of the century, whether to celebrate, lampoon, or pillory her. Some were gently playful, as in the popular stage play *The New Woman* by Sydney Grundy, or in this anonymous poem of 1898:

> Rock-a-bye baby, for father is near.
> Mother is "biking"—she never is here!
> Out in the park she's scorching all day
> Or at some meeting is talking away!
>
> She's the king-pin at the women's rights show,
> Teaching poor husbands the way they should go!
> Close then your eyes; there's dishes to do.
> Rock-a-bye baby, 'tis Pa sings to you!

The reference to "biking" alludes to a popular new invention: the chain-driven bicycle. Earlier bicycles had employed direct drive—that is, the pedals were attached directly to the hub of the large front wheel. Though capable of significant speed, these early bicycles were notoriously unstable and required a man's strength to pedal. Chain-driven bicycles, however, suited women and were quickly adopted as a new means of locomotion that was doubly important. They enabled, in those pre-automobile days, a wider degree of maneuverability, and they symbolized, in their very propulsion, the spirit of independence shown by the new woman.[10]

Free to move her own person, to control her own sexual life, to attend school, to pursue a career, and to seek a new kind of fulfillment in life, the New Woman entered the 20th century full of hope.

> The finest achievement of the new woman has been personal liberty. This is the foundation of civilization; and as long as any one class is watched suspiciously, even fondly guarded, and protected, so long will that class not only be weak, and treacherous, individually, but parasitic, and a collective danger to the community. Who has not heard wives commended for wheedling their husbands out of money, or joked because they are hopelessly extravagant? As long as caprice and scheming are considered feminine virtues, as long as man is the only wage-earner, doling out sums of money, or scattering lavishly, so long will women be degraded, even if they are perfectly contented, and men are willing to labor to keep them in idleness! Although individual women from pre-historic times have accomplished much, as a class they have been set aside to minister to men's comfort. But when once the higher has been tried, civilization repudiates the lower. Men have come to see that no advance can be made with one half-humanity set apart merely for the functions of sex; that children are quite liable to inherit from the mother, and should have opportunities to inherit the accumulated ability and culture and character that is produced only by intellectual and civil activity. The world has tried to move with men for dynamos, and "clinging" women impeding every step of progress, in arts, science, industry, professions, they have been a thousand years behind men because forced into seclusion. They have been over-sexed. They have naturally not been impressed with their duties to society, in its myriad needs, or with their own value as individuals. The new woman, in the sense of the best woman, the flower of all the womanhood of past ages, has come to stay— if civilization is to endure.

So declared *The New Womanhood*, a best-selling manifesto of 1904 by Winnifred Harper Cooley. This hymn of victory to come is likewise expressed in fictional

---

[10]   Bicycles helped get rid of the Victorian corsets and stays that had for so long restricted and deformed women's movements.

form in *The New Woman* (1893), by one of Poland's greatest novelists, Bolesław Prus (1847–1912).

WOMEN, ISLAM, AND NATIONALISM

Yet another book championed the rights of women and called for an end to their social seclusion, free access to education, and a guarantee of full political equality. In fact, it was also entitled *The New Woman* and appeared between Prus's novel and Harper Cooley's manifesto. It was *Al-Mar'a al-jadida*, published in Cairo in 1901, by Kasim Amin (1863–1908). His call was not alone, but it quickly ran into struggles over Arab nationalism and the Ottoman decline.

Amin's father was a Kurd and his mother an Egyptian; apart from four years in France in the 1880s, he spent the whole of his brief life in Egypt.

Spirit of Independence Advertisement for the Grand Manège Central, a popular bicycling track and park in Paris, ca. 1890. The American suffragist Susan B. Anthony (1820-1906) once declared: "I think [the bicycle] has done more to emancipate women than anything else in the world. It gives women a feeling of freedom and self-reliance. I stand and rejoice every time I see a woman ride by on a wheel. . . the picture of free, untrammeled womanhood."

An aristocrat, and wealthy, he worked for a time as a lawyer and was one of the cofounders of Cairo University, which he served as vice president and secretary general. While in Paris, Amin had made contact with the great Islamic reformer Muhammad Ali, who inspired his conviction that Islam needed to remake itself in order to adapt to the modern world. Otherwise, it risked losing out to the conservative Wahhabi movement, which regarded every social innovation as an affront to sacred tradition.

To Amin (more so even than to Muhammad Ali himself) the most urgently needed reform was to improve the social status of women in Muslim society. He called for four essential changes—allowing women's access to education, a constitutional guarantee of political equality, abolition of the customary wearing of the veil, and reform of marriage laws in order to deny husbands their right to repudiate a wife at will and to take multiple wives. To make his full argument required two books, and *The New Woman* had been preceded in 1899 by the legal treatise *The Emancipation of Women* (*Tahrir al-mar'a*). These were bold positions to take even in the Islamic Enlightenment atmosphere of turn-of-the-century Egypt, and Amin stirred up considerable opposition (although he was ultimately admired within Europe after *The Emancipation of Women* appeared in a German translation in 1928). For several years he engaged in a public debate with conservative jurists on these issues, but he soon devoted the bulk of his time to the establishment of Cairo University (1908), which Amin and his cofounders intended to be a Western-style university emphasizing liberal thought. It could therefore serve as a complement, even a counterbalance, to the religiously based al-Azhar University, which dated back to the year 972.

For conservative Muslims, especially those of Arab ethnicity, modernization violated both the spirit of the faith and the dictates of nature; authentic Islamic identity and Western notions of human rights, democracy, and social progress, they insisted, were fundamentally incompatible.

As in Europe, the question of women's status in the Islamic world was related to the issue of nationalism. Tanzimat efforts (1839–1876) to modernize the Ottoman superstate proved in the end to be impossible. For conservative Muslims, especially those of Arab ethnicity, modernization violated both the spirit of the faith and the dictates of nature; authentic Islamic identity and Western notions of human rights, democracy, and social progress, they insisted, were fundamentally incompatible. For many others, especially those who welcomed the socially liberalizing aspect of Tanzimat but rejected its insistence on the continuation of Ottomanism, the future lay in local autonomy, independence from both the universalizing claims of Ottoman political overlordship and ethnically Arab religious supervision. They wanted to break free of both constraints and establish instead new provincial societies that were free to define their own Islamic and national identities. Abu al-Qasim al-Shabbi (1909–1934), a Tunisian poet and social critic of the era, put it bluntly: "Everything the Arabs have produced throughout all the long centuries of their history is colorless and utterly devoid of inspiration."

Writers experimented with new literary forms, especially the novel, because of its ability to express criticism of social ills and depict the struggles of individuals against various forms of oppression. As in Europe, the travails of women were a theme for many novelists and playwrights, including Taha Husayn (also spelled Hussein; 1889–1973), Mahmud Taymur (1894–1973), and Tawfiq al-Hakim (1898–1987). In al-Hakim's 1934 play based on *A Thousand and One Nights*, Scheherazade's storytelling helps her survive her murderous husband, and she achieves a mystical union with the ancient goddess Isis.

The reformers pressed especially for girls' rights to education and the reform of marriage practices to prohibit forcing girls into arranged marriages against their wills. Namik Kemal (1840–1888), an Ottoman court official turned playwright and journalist, championed girls' education in countless articles and essays. Ahmed Midhat (generally known as Midhat Pasha; 1822–1884) edited a daily newspaper in Istanbul, *Tercüman-ı Hakikat* ("The Interpreter of Truth"), that promoted social reform and distributed a weekly supplement designed especially for schoolchildren. Midhat also wrote over one hundred

Huda'i Sha'arawi   Sha'arawi was a social reformer and founder of the feminist movement in Egypt, and author of *Harem Years: Memoirs of an Egyptian Feminist.*

books of history, popular science, and social reform, reaching an enormous audience. But the best-known feminist of her time was the Egyptian reformer Huda'i Sha'arawi (1878–1947), who organized a women's self-help society and the Union of Egyptian Women-Intellectuals. She also founded the Egyptian Feminist Union, in 1923, and served as its president until her death. Sha'arawi focused her prodigious energies on political involvement, speaking at conferences across Europe and organizing feminist demonstrations throughout Egypt. In addition to her *Memoirs*, she published two feminist journals called *The Egyptian Woman*—one in French (*L'Égyptienne*) and one in Arabic (*al-Misriyya*).

A few schools for girls opened in the 1880s and 1890s and received public funds, but more girls were probably enrolled in private or missionary schools than in the state-run system. Illiteracy remained a problem for both boys and girls, however; as late as 1914 perhaps only 10 percent of the Ottoman population could read and write. In general, reforms were most successful in those countries that had both close commercial and diplomatic relations with Europe and a higher percentage of non-Muslims among their populations: Egypt, Lebanon, Palestine, and what would eventually become the nation of Turkey. The countries of the Arabian Peninsula, Iraq, and Iran, however, saw little change. In Bengal, in the northeastern corner of India, a woman named Rokeya Sakhawat Hussein (1880–1932) opened the first high school for Muslim girls in 1909. At the same time, conservative ways remained deeply entrenched. As late as 1908, in fact, the slave trade remained legal throughout much of Ottoman society, so long as the slaves in question were non-Muslim females. The American ambassador to Constantinople during World War I famously noted that Armenian girls could be purchased in Turkish cities for as little as eighty cents apiece.

HONOR KILLING AND GENITAL CUTTING

As nationalist aspirations among peoples long ruled by the Ottomans rose, certain ethnic and cultural practices not formally part of Islamic teaching began to revive. Two of these are significant in regard to women: honor killing and genital cutting. Neither is accepted by mainstream Islamic tradition today, whether Sunni or Shi'ite. Both, however, were widely practiced in the Islamic world and experienced a resurgence during the Ottoman breakup.

Honor killing has a long history in many parts of the Islamic world, dating back to well before the arrival of the Prophet, but it is hardly a custom unique to Arab culture. The ancient Romans practiced it: the paternal authority (*patria potestas*) of the head of a family entitled him, and in fact demanded of him, that he preserve the good honor and repute of his household by eliminating those whose licentiousness brought dishonor to the clan. Many of the pre-Christian Germanic tribes demanded that families protect the moral uprightness (*mundium*) of their clans by killing those unmarried females who lost their virginity.[11] To the Arabs, Egyptians, and Kurds who followed the practice, two distinct concepts of honor predominated. Male honor (*hasab*) was both

Modern but Pure   Some unliberated women sunbathing near Istanbul, ca. 1900. The modernizing Tanzimat reforms of the mid-nineteenth century paid little attention to promoting the rights of women in the Ottoman state. As late as 1908 there was still an active slave-trade in females, even though slavery had been officially abolished in the 1840s and 1850s.

---

[11]   The Salian Franks allowed any member of the family to kill a wayward female. Early Burgundians ruled that a woman who had sex outside of marriage was to be drowned in a swamp.

hereditary and personal, the reputation held by virtue of one's birth and family status as well as one's personal integrity; like a bank balance it could increase or decrease according to one's behavior and the actions of the family one headed. Female honor (**'ird**), by contrast, was solely personal. More akin to the English-language concept of "purity" than "honor," moreover, it was a quality that a woman either possessed or did not, and its value only decreased. Once lost, it was lost forever. But the moral stain of the loss of 'ird spread to the members of the woman's family—which justified the action needed to restore the family's hasab: the killing of the sinner. Honor killings in the last decades of Ottoman rule remained hidden from view and difficult to quantify. Those who perpetrated or witnessed such killing did not consider it a crime, and hence they saw no need to report it to authorities. The Turks themselves, to whom honor killing was more culturally foreign, did not wish to stir up the anger of their non-Turkish subjects by investigating such deaths too intently.

Female circumcision was most widely and openly practiced in the northeastern quadrant of Africa—Egypt, Ethiopia, Somalia, and Sudan—and in many parts of the Middle East. The custom was publicly condemned but long remained a secret practice in northern Arabia, southern Jordan, and the Kurdish regions of Iran, Iraq, Syria, and Turkey. Secret, but not rare. As many as 80–90 percent of females in some of these regions either submitted or were forced to submit to some form of circumcision. Men who frequently went off on lengthy trading journeys relied on circumcision as a way of guaranteeing their wives' fidelity. In the most extreme cases nearly the entire vaginal opening was sewn shut, in addition to the more customary removal of the clitoris.

The practice predates Islam and probably originated from a mixture of motives—hygienic, aesthetic, and moral. The hygienic argument held that circumcision allowed for easier and fuller cleansing of the body after menstruation or childbirth; the aesthetic argument maintained that the procedure enhanced the beauty of the female form. The moral argument was the most nefarious, as it remains today. The moral motive insisted that circumcision promoted chastity before marriage and fidelity within marriage. Because it denied women the ability to experience pleasure, it thus removed temptation. The Islamic position on genital cutting is open to interpretation. A verse in one collection of the hadith of the Prophet Muhammad relates that when Muhammad encountered a woman in Medina who worked as a ritual circumciser, he said to her. "But do not mutilate—it is better for the woman and more desirable for her husband [to cut less rather than more]." This would seem at least to permit the practice, but legal scholars have long debated the authenticity of the verse.[12]

---

[12] Most Islamic scholars today soundly reject female circumcision, yet the practice remains widespread.

The call for the emancipation of women in the Islamic world, then, required bravery and countercultural determination unlike anything faced by women in western Europe. But in both cases the call was met with considerably more indifference and hostility than sympathy. To alter the position of women in society meant to change the definition of the nation itself at a critical moment. In Europe, the ideological dream of the nation was about to be realized in global empire. In the Islamic world, the dream of national independence, after four hundred years of political subjection to the Turks, seemed about to end. The call for emancipation arose at the same time across the Greater West but was heard only in Europe—and only after its imperial dreams had set the world afire.

WHO, WHAT, WHERE

feminist movement
'ird
naturalist
new woman

realist
suffragettes
suffragists
utilitarian

SUGGESTED READINGS

Primary Sources

Bulwer-Lytton, Constance. *Prisons and Prisoners.*

Martineau, Harriet. "The Political Non-Existence of Women," in *Society in America.*

Mill, John Stuart. *The Subjection of Women.*

Norton, Caroline. *English Laws for Women in the Nineteenth Century.*

Reid, Marion Kirkland. *A Plea for Woman.*

Shaarawi, Huda. *Harem Years: The Memoirs of an Egyptian Feminist.*

Stöcker, Helene. *Women and Love: A Manifesto for Emancipating Women and Men in Germany.*

Verbitskaya, Anastasia. *The Keys to Happiness.*

Source Anthologies

Badran, Margot, and Miriam Cooke, eds. *Opening the Gates: A Century of Arab Feminist Writing* (2004).

Nelson, Carolyn Christensen, ed. *A New Woman Reader: Fiction, Articles, and Drama of the 1890s* (2000).

Patterson, Martha H., ed. *The American New Woman Revisited: A Reader, 1894–1930* (2008).

Studies

Ali, Kecia. *Sexual Ethics and Islam: Feminist Reflections on Qur'an, Hadith, and Jurisprudence* (2006).

Bartley, Paula. *Emmeline Pankhurst* (2003).

Bush, Julia. *Women against the Vote: Female Anti-Suffragism in Britain* (2007).

Capaldi, Nicholas. *John Stuart Mill: A Biography* (2004).

Friedmann, Yohanan. *Tolerance and Coercion in Islam: Interfaith Relations in the Muslim Tradition* (2003).

Haeri, Shahla. *Law of Desire: Temporary Marriage in Shi'i Iran* (2002).

Hatem, Mervat F. *Literature, Gender, and Nation-Building in Nineteenth-Century Egypt: The Life and Works of 'A'isha Taymur* (2011).

Keddie, Nikki R. *Women in the Middle East: Past and Present* (2006).

Kertzer, David I., and Marzio Barbagli, eds. *Family Life in the Long Nineteenth Century, 1789–1913.* (2002).

Logan, Deborah Anna. *Harriet Martineau, Victorian Imperialism, and the Civilizing Mission* (2010).

———. *The Woman and the Hour: Harriet Martineau's "Somewhat Remarkable" Life* (2002).

Malone, Carolyn. *Women's Bodies and Dangerous Trades in England, 1880–1914* (2003).

Marchand, Suzanne, and David Lindenfeld, eds. *Germany at the Fin de Siècle: Culture, Politics, and Ideas* (2004).

Offen, Karen M. *European Feminisms, 1700–1950: A Political History* (2000).

Phillips, Melanie. *The Ascent of Woman: A History of the Suffragette Movement and the Ideas behind It* (2003).

Pugh, Martin. *The Pankhursts: The History of One Radical Family* (2008).

Roberts, Mary Louise. *Disruptive Acts: The New Woman in Fin-de-Siècle France* (2002).

Stansell, Christine. *The Feminist Promise: 1792 to the Present* (2010).

Tosh, John. *A Man's Place: Masculinity and the Middle-Class Home in Victorian England* (2007).

For additional resources, including maps, primary sources, visuals, web links, and quizzes, please go to **www.oup.com/us/backman**

Midi le jour, Minuit la nuit

CHAPTER 22

The Great Land Grab

1880–1914

There is, it seems, no end to empires. To individual megastates, yes—but to empires themselves, no. We have already had a parade of them: the Akkadians, the Midians, the Hittites, the Assyrians, the Babylonians, the neo-Babylonians, and the Persians—empires all, and all only by the end of our first chapter. Subsequent chapters presented the Athenian, the Alexandrian, the Roman, the Parthian, the Byzantine, the Umayyad, the Carolingian, the Ottonian, the Abbasid, the Seljuk, the Mamluk, the Mongol, and the Ottoman empires. Then came the empires of Tamerlane and Charles V. The Venetian Empire in the Mediterranean. The Aztec, Incan, and Mayan Empires of the pre-1492 New World. The Spanish Empire in the Americas. The Safavid Empire in Iran. The Mughal Empire in India. The Polish-Lithuanian Empire. Napoleon's Empire. The Austrian-Hungarian Empire. France's Second Empire. Russia's Romanov Empire. Until one begins to list them, one hardly realizes the extent to which Greater Western history appears to be dominated by them.

Is it possible that this is not accidental? Might empires, in fact, be the norm of human political life—the default position, so to speak? Many have thought so. Especially at the dawn

EUROPEAN COLONIES AND PROTECTORATES, 1914

◀ **The White Man's Burden**
A French colonial officer in West Africa attempts to teach his pupils how to tell time by a watch. Several girls are attentive, but the boys present are happily distracted by a playful monkey. The cartoon is uncritical, even affectionate, and exudes an atmosphere of patience on the part of the officer. The children are like school-children everywhere—some studious, some mischievous. But no sign of oppression or resentment is visible. Neither are any African adults, who presumably are somewhere else, working for colonial masters who are far less kindly and patient.

- "The White Man's Burden"
- The Second Industrial Revolution
- Looking Overseas
- Missionary Europe

- A Gilded Age
- Western Ways: Emulation and Resistance

CHAPTER OUTLINE

of the 20th century, this thought seemed to drive the European nations and others as well into headlong competition to cover and to covet the earth. Belgium, Britain, France, Germany, and Italy all took part. So, more modestly, did Japan and the United States. Ever since, it has been commonplace to condemn Europe and America for the global landgrab they indulged in. **Imperialism**, say critics, is evil, a harsh and soulless crushing of cultures considered "Other"—and European and American imperialism, by virtue of those territories' technological advantages over their victims, are uniquely evil. Racism and exploitation, a greed that flat-out ignored the peoples and interests of the rest of the world, is what lay behind the Western feeding frenzy. There is much to say for this view. Critics of European imperialism can literally point to the graves of millions who died in the mad dash to make rich Europe even richer. But the period from 1880 to 1914 was also a time of resistance to empire, as reformers, activists, politicians, journalists, writers, critics, and commoners of all stripes cried out in horrified dismay at what their society was becoming or had already become. It was the time of a Second Industrial Revolution and the Gilded Age it enabled.

"THE WHITE MAN'S BURDEN"

Karl Pearson (1857–1936), a prominent British mathematician and ardent champion of the British Empire, saw imperialism as simply the best use of the earth's resources. In an essay called "National Life from the Standpoint of Science" (1900), he wrote:

> History shows me one way, and one way only, in which a high state of civilization can be produced—namely, the struggle of race with race, and the survival of the physically and morally fitter race. If you want to know whether the lower races of man can evolve a higher type, I fear the only course is to leave them to fight it out among themselves.... Let us suppose that we could prevent the white man, if we liked, from going to lands

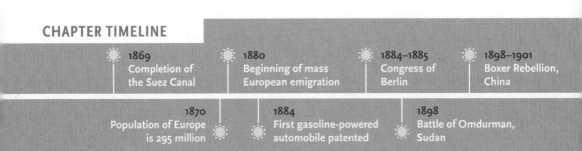

CHAPTER TIMELINE

1869	1880	1884–1885	1898–1901
Completion of the Suez Canal	Beginning of mass European emigration	Congress of Berlin	Boxer Rebellion, China

1870	1884	1898
Population of Europe is 295 million	First gasoline-powered automobile patented	Battle of Omdurman, Sudan

of which the agricultural and mineral resources are not worked to the full; then I should say, "A thousand times better for him that he should not go, than that he should settle down and live alongside the inferior race."

Aside from its obvious racism, Pearson's argument was essentially amoral, and supporters of any of the empires mentioned above would likely have agreed. It runs something like this. The earth offers only finite amounts of natural resources, but the constantly increasing human population has constantly increasing needs. Given those needs, the right to access and exploit resources belongs to whoever is in the best position to get the most value from them. A society that has failed, for whatever reason, to put its resources to proper use has effectively renounced its right to control them. And any foreign group that exploits those materials for productive gain is not only right to do so but also benefits the society shunted aside. Imperialism is therefore best understood as a vital instrument in the evolution of human civilization, and its benefits far exceed any harm it causes. Pearson again:

> The struggle for existence between the white man and the red man in America, painful and even terrible as it was in its details, has given us a good far out-balancing its immediate evil. In place of the red man, who contributed practically nothing to the work and thought of the world, we have a great nation, mistress of many arts, and able, with its youthful imagination and fresh, untrammeled impulses, to contribute much to the common stock of civilized man.
>
> The great function of science in national life is to show us what national life means, and how the nation is a vast organism subject to the great forces of evolution. . . . Is it not a fact that the daily bread of our millions of workers depends on their having somebody to work for? That if we give up the contest for trade routes, free markets, and waste lands, we indirectly give up our food supply? Is it not a fact that our strength depends on these and upon our colonies, and that our colonies have been

1899
Rudyard Kipling, "The
White Man's Burden"

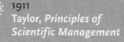

1903
Ford Motor
Company founded

1911
Taylor, *Principles of
Scientific Management*

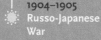

1901
Naoroji, *Poverty
and Un-British
Rule in India*

1904–1905
Russo-Japanese
War

1914
Population of Europe is 450 million;
over 90 percent of Africa partitioned
among European states

won by the ejection of inferior races, and are maintained against equal races by respect for the present power of our empire?.... The path to progress is strewn with the wreck of nations; traces are everywhere to be seen of the slaughtered remains of inferior races, and of victims who found not the narrow way to perfection. Yet these dead people are, in very truth, the stepping-stones on which mankind has arisen to the higher intellectual and deeper emotional life of today.

The thought is odious, even vile. But does that mean it is incorrect?

To believe in the innate superiority of one's race or culture is nothing new. The ancient Persians had no doubt about the inferiority of every culture they overran. To the ancient Greeks the word for "barbarian" (*barbaroi*) applied to any non-Greek ethnic group; neither Charlemagne nor Tamerlane considered any of his conquered peoples to be his equal. And Napoleon was confident in France's divine mission to lead the world. The nations that set out after 1880 to dominate the globe shared the same confidence in their rights to rule others. But a new element crept into their thinking. The imperialism of the late 19th and early 20th centuries differed from earlier imperial adventures in this one important regard: the European champions of imperialism thought of their actions in Darwinian terms—as a necessary step in the evolutionary development of the entire human species. This was **social Darwinism**, the misuse of Darwin's theory of evolution by natural selection to justify competition among societies. It was all the more self-confident because of what many Europeans regarded as its scientific certitude. Belief in the "survival of the fittest" justified their actions as morally necessary—the best, or even perhaps the only, means by which human civilization itself could advance.

In the words of Rudyard Kipling's most famous poem (1899), imperialism was "The White Man's Burden":

> Take up the White Man's burden—
> No tawdry rule of kings,
> But toil of serf and sweeper—
> The tale of common things.
> The ports ye shall not enter,
> The roads ye shall not tread,
> Go mark them with your living,
> And mark them with your dead!

> The imperialism of the late 19th and early 20th centuries differed from earlier imperial adventures in this one important regard: the European champions of imperialism thought of their actions in Darwinian terms—as a necessary step in the evolutionary development of the entire human species.

Take up the White Man's burden—
And reap his old reward:
The blame of those ye better,
The hate of those ye guard—
The cry of hosts ye humour
(Ah, slowly!) toward the light:—
"Why brought ye us from bondage,
Our loved Egyptian night?"

Take up the White Man's burden—
Ye dare not stoop to less—
Nor call too loud on Freedom
To cloak your weariness;
By all ye cry or whisper,
By all ye leave or do,
The silent, sullen peoples
Shall weigh your Gods and you.

THE SECOND INDUSTRIAL REVOLUTION

An empire is a machine—an ordered system of tools, institutions, and communications to govern people and administer goods. And that is a much more difficult thing to accomplish than the military conquests that lead up to it. Military conquest, after all, is nothing more than a bloodstain on a map, however great or small the area. An empire is so much more. Genghis Khan butchered millions of people in the process of getting tens of millions more to obey him out of sheer terror, but what he "created" was no more an empire than the atomic bombing of Hiroshima was an urban-development plan. True empires require engineers, jurists, civil officials, industrialists, financiers, teachers, missionaries, skilled laborers, and the infrastructures that can connect them efficiently and reliably. From 1870 to 1914 western Europe developed an abundance of all these, in what is known as the **Second Industrial Revolution**. And the natural resources needed to fuel and feed that revolution lay increasingly overseas—as did the new shape of empire.

The first wave of industrialization had focused on the production of consumer goods—textiles and food, especially, with housewares and furniture running second. All were fueled by the new energy technologies of coal and by high-grade refined iron. The Second Industrial Revolution was essentially a continuation of the earlier process but with a focus instead on producing capital goods—goods used to produce other goods, such as steel, heavy machinery, chemicals, electrical power, and refined petroleum. Many of these are the "capital"

Industrial Warfare "If you want to make a pile of money, invent something that will enable these Europeans to cut each others' throats with greater facility," was the advice given by a friend to Hiram Stevens Maxim (1840-1916), an American inventor who patented his Maxim Gun, the first portable automatic machine gun, in 1884. Capable of firing ten rounds per second, it gave an incalculable advantage to the British in their imperial expansion. In its first battlefield use, in southern Africa in 1893, a mere four British gunners were able to repel an attack by three thousand African warriors.

of industrial capitalism, or resources in the hands of factory owners. Many are also public goods, like automobiles and radios, open to everyone and bringing people together. Other key developments of this period were the telegraph and telephone, lighter and stronger steamships and railroads, subways, the internal combustion engine, the airplane, and modern weaponry—like repeating rifles, artillery, and machine guns. The chemical industry produced soaps, detergents, dyes, photographic plates and films, medicines, gasoline and other petroleum products, synthetic textiles, paints, fertilizers, and explosives.

When the French chemist Louis Pasteur (1822–1895) discovered germs—the microorganisms that cause many diseases—he established an entire new science, which in turn led to two critical innovations. One was *pasteurization*, in which foodstuffs are heated to destroy the bacteria that cause spoilage. The other was *immunology*, the study of vaccines and other means to protect people from disease. He perfected a vaccine against rabies by 1885, and by the end of the century scientists had developed vaccines against cholera, diphtheria, and typhus. Joseph Lister (1827–1912), an English chemist, developed the first successful antiseptic and the process of disinfection.[1] Their work helped launch modern medicine, as did Madame Marie Skłodowska-Curie (1867–1934). Curie, who won the Nobel Prize in physics (1903) and again in chemistry (1911), established radiology, the study of radioactivity, and her work led to the development of X-rays.

While railroads had been in use for decades, it wasn't until the 1880s that they overtook canals as the dominant means of transporting cargo in Europe. Once advances in steel production dramatically reduced the cost of laying and maintaining rail lines, the cost of shipping cargo along those lines decreased as well, which spurred further production of goods. The development of electrical grids, telegraph and telephone networks, and radio systems enabled communication at speeds never before known. It felt like a whole new era in human development. "The economic changes that have occurred during the last quarter of a century— or during the present generation of living men—have unquestionably been more important and more varied than during any period of the world's history," crowed an enthusiastic American economist, David Ames Wells (1828–1898).

Karl Friedrich Benz (1844–1929) patented the first gasoline-powered automobile in 1884, but it was Henry Ford who revolutionized personal transportation. He founded the Ford Motor Company in 1903, with its innovative assembly-line model. Mass production became the norm, or at least the desired one. With plentiful cheap oil, high-grade steel machinery, and endless quantities of electrical power, goods could be produced literally around the clock. By 1900, the half dozen leading European nations produced two-thirds of all the manufactured goods on the planet. Modern transportation and communication allowed these goods to reach markets around the world, and they brought back to Europe the resources to produce more goods, which in turn stimulated new cycles of production and consumption (Map 22.1).

New technologies appeared with stunning rapidity. In the United States alone nearly a million patents were issued for inventions between the end of the Civil War (1865) and the start of World War I—everything from pneumatic braking systems (1872) and the phonograph (1877) to the telephone (1879), light bulb (1880), jackhammer (1890), radio (1893), semiautomatic rifle (1898), safety razor and electric vacuum cleaner (1901), airplane (1903), helicopter (1907), dental braces (1910), and the backless bra (1914). So quickly were new industries created that in a single five-year period, 1896–1901, the volume of stocks sold on the New York Stock Exchange increased by a factor of six. Not only did new technologies appear constantly, the amount of time taken to bring those technologies to general use shortened dramatically. The telephone, invented in 1879,

---

[1]   Listerine, the antiseptic mouthwash named for Joseph Lister, was originally marketed as a floor cleaner and a treatment for gonorrhea.

Share of World Manufacturing Output, 1900

Europe 63%

Rest of the World 29.1%

India 1.7%

China 6.2%

Industrialization and Manufacturing in Europe, 1870–1914

Industry in 1870		Industry in 1914	
	Coal mining	▫	Steel
‖‖‖	Iron working	⚒	Shipbuilding
≡	Textile production	⚗	Chemicals
——	Major railway lines, 1914	⚡	Electrical industry

MAP 22.1 **Industrialization and Manufacturing, 1870–1914**

had become a standard business necessity across Europe and the United States by 1900. The automobile was a novelty item at first, but with the development of the petroleum industry it was soon transforming entire cities. Petroleum also supplied the asphalt on which automobiles ran.

Charting a New Course   The first automobile maps appeared in 1900 in both France and Germany. In both countries, bicycle tire manufacturers, all of whom quickly started manufacturing tires for cars, sponsored or created automobile maps to encourage people to buy their new products. In 1910, the French tire company Michelin published its first road map of France, which included information on local attractions and restaurants.   Shown above is the cover of this early Michelin Guide, bearing an advertisement for Renault automobiles.

Modern management techniques must be counted among the innovations of the era. Called **scientific management** by its founders, this set of ideas aimed at a single goal: to improve the efficiency of the manufacturing workplace by increasing the productivity of labor. Machines, after all, could be set to function at a constant rate for as long as they were fueled and maintained, but workers were less predictable. Some were more intelligent and skillful than others, some more energetic and diligent, and some more highly motivated and determined; still others were lazy, inconsistent, awkward, and slow. To even out these differences, scientific management sought to break down manufacturing into small, distinct steps. Rather than have a hundred furniture makers each build an entire dining table, one worker could plane lumber for the tabletop, the next join the pieces, the third trim the edges, the fourth shape the table legs on a lathe, and so on, step by step, over and over, again and again. Finally, the finished dining tables emerged from the assembly line—identical, at a steady pace, and with maximum efficiency. In *The Principles of Scientific Management* (1911), Frederick Winslow Taylor (1856–1915) called for the minute study of workers' physical movements in order to design steps with perfect efficiency. The point was to get workers to adapt themselves to the machines they operated.

This was time management: the efficiency of the machines set the pace of manufacture. It still sometimes called for intelligent, highly skilled workers, but Taylor also saw that many tasks could be performed by any worker regardless of skill, intelligence, or motivation. At times, in fact, industry could exploit workers' lack of education or intellectual sharpness. The booming steel industry, he

Unscientific Management   This still from Charlie Chaplin's masterpiece
"Modern Times" (1936) illustrates how human labor was made to accommodate
the workings of machines in industrial manufacture. The machine itself became
the workers' boss, and occasionally (as here, with Chaplin trying to rescue a
fellow worker trapped in the gears) it not only directed the workers' lives, but it
consumed them.

noted, had a particular need for dullards, since the handling of pig iron (iron
ore at the intermediate stage of the smelting process) called for more brawn
than brains:

> Now one of the very first requirements for a man who is fit to
> handle pig iron as a regular occupation is that he shall be so stupid and
> so phlegmatic that he more nearly resembles in his mental make-up the
> ox than any other type. The man who is mentally alert and intelligent is
> for this very reason unsuited to what would, for him, be the grinding
> monotony of work of this character. Therefore the workman who is
> best suited to handling pig iron is unable to understand the real science
> of doing this class of work. He is so stupid that the word *percentage* has
> no meaning to him, and he must consequently be trained by a man
> more intelligent than himself into the habit of working in accordance
> with the laws of this science before he can be successful. The writer
> trusts that it is now clear that even in the case of the most elementary
> form of labor that is known, there is a science, and that when the man

best suited to this class of work has been carefully selected, when the science of doing the work has been developed, and when the carefully selected man has been trained to work in accordance with this science, the results obtained must of necessity be overwhelmingly greater than those which are possible under the [traditional] plan of "initiative and incentive."

The condescending tone is on display throughout the book. Even Taylor balked at calling workers mere appendages to machinery, but that is the essence of his management science and the key to his vision of efficiency.[2]

One of the chief problems with improved industrial capacity was over-production. When manufactures outpaced consumption, prices tumbled and profits slumped or even disappeared. The problem was noted as early as the 1820s, when the word "depression" was used for the first time in its economic sense.

The Suez Canal   Crowds watch the first ships to sail through the Suez Canal on November 17, 1869, in this print from a German magazine. The canal was designed by a French engineer, Ferdinand de Lesseps (1805-1894), the same man who later formally presented (though he did not design or build) the Statue of Liberty, to President Grover Cleveland of the United States.

---

[2]   At Harvard Business School, founded in 1908, *The Principles of Scientific Management* was the core textbook until the start of the Great Depression in 1929.

Every advance in technology, it seemed, only made the problem worse by making it easier to produce and deliver more goods. Modern railroads and steamships could cross continents, oceans, and soon even the most daunting natural barriers. The Transcontinental Railroad crossed America in 1869, the same year the Suez Canal was completed, cutting in half the time needed for ships to sail from Europe to India. The twelve-mile-long Simplon Tunnel through the Alps, along the Swiss-Italian border, sped people and goods between northern and southern Europe. Never before in Western history were so few people able to feed so many, with less than 10 percent of the population engaged in farming. This freed more workers to seek employment in cities, which pushed wages down, but production levels remained so high that food prices fell even faster.

A growing population lessened the risks of a rapid fall in prices, or deflation. The birthrate in most of western Europe declined sharply between 1870 and 1914, especially among the bourgeois and skilled-labor classes. This decline was due in part to the availability of contraception but probably even more to the (slowly) growing alternatives to motherhood available to women. Advances in medicine brought about an even sharper decline in mortality, with the net result that a European population of 295 million in 1870 ballooned to over 450 million by the start of World War I—a gain of 60 percent in a single generation. Such impressive growth ensured steadily expanding markets for goods of all sorts. Even this was not enough, however. Markets, like the homes they supplied, filled to bursting with a seemingly never-ending stream of household goods, foodstuffs, appliances, tools, and decorative objects. As production grew in pace, the only solution to declining profit margins was to find ever more markets to flood with commodities. That meant looking overseas.

LOOKING OVERSEAS

Overseas resources were definitely within reach. Commercial contacts with Africa, India, eastern Asia, and the South Pacific islands had continued since the late 16th century, so the routes, harbors, and geography were mostly familiar. Now the telegraph, radio, and telephone enabled regular contact with far-flung territories, and modern weaponry gave Europeans a decisive battlefield advantage. The West seized roughly one-quarter of planet Earth (and roughly one-third of its human population) in an astonishingly short span of time.

The unification of Germany in 1870 was the trigger event. German industrial capacity had grown rapidly under Bismarck's leadership—so quickly that even the expense of a large military and extensive social programs did not slow economic expansion. Moreover, since Germany had been a comparative latecomer to industrialization, its factories benefited from newer technologies. Germany was also one of the few countries in Europe to have a rising birthrate, which meant that the population was younger than in Britain, France, or Italy. The rush of youthful energy and optimism seemed to be on Germany's side. All it lacked was overseas connections.

News from Around the World   The White House became wired for telegraph and telephone in the 1880s. (Computers were introduced during President Jimmy Carter's term.) Here a trio of engineers monitor the telegraph system bringing news of the Spanish-American War in 1895.

A second trigger was Reconstruction, the remaking of the American South after the Civil War. The South had long been among the principal suppliers of raw cotton for European textile factories, but the catastrophic Civil War (1861–1865) had essentially cut off those supplies. In the postwar decades American policy aimed primarily at developing domestic industry, and this inward turn not only meant a decrease in the export of raw materials; it also increased competition on world markets by introducing American finished goods. Like Germany, America was a young nation filled with energy and ambition, and it soon became a major producer of everything from textiles and foodstuffs to steel, machinery, weapons, automobiles, and electrical appliances.

America also invested in education. The Morrill Act of 1862 (renewed and expanded in 1890) granted states the right to sell or develop federal lands for the creation of colleges and universities. These land-grant colleges meant continued innovation in arts, engineering, and sciences.[3] America's growing military might was also a factor. Though still recovering from the Civil War, American fighting forces, once fully modernized, had the potential to rival the great European powers, especially on the sea-lanes. In response, Europe had to seize the moment.

> Though still recovering from the Civil War, American fighting forces, once fully modernized, had the potential to rival the great European powers, especially on the sea-lanes. In response, Europe had to seize the moment.

The British led the way by transforming their long commercial domination of India into full-scale exploitation, led by the privately held British East India

---

3   The first land-grant university created from scratch was Kansas State University in 1863.

Company. India produced cotton on a massive scale, which compensated for the loss of American cotton, while its enormous population was a potential market. An uprising against British control in 1857 led to a sharp military crackdown, after which the entire subcontinent was formally declared a colony (1858) of Her Majesty Queen Victoria (r. 1837–1901). So great a prize was India that for nearly a dozen years the British scarcely looked elsewhere for further colonial adventures. With Germany's and Italy's unifications, however, that had to change. The Continent was now awash with goods, and prices plummeted. The Long Depression (1873–1896), known in its time as the Great Depression until a still greater one struck in 1929, was marked by severe deflation and loss of profits. In the United States the price of cotton fell by 50 percent; grain fell to only a third of its previous value. Declines in Europe were at times even worse, owing to panics on the Vienna, Paris, and London stock exchanges. Since decreasing production was unthinkable, the answer was two-pronged. First, increase access to markets abroad by seizing them; and second, seek protection by discouraging competition within an industry and by government subsidies. Firms joined or cooperated, forming cartels, to thwart the natural workings of the market.

Until the 1870s few governments, whether Liberal or Conservative, favored outright colonialism. In 1852 the British prime minister Benjamin Disraeli, a Conservative, had dismissed England's handful of colonies as "a millstone around our necks" that cost far more to protect and maintain than they produced.[4] But by the mid-1880s newspapers were describing the race to extend Western industrial might throughout the entire world. "When I left the Foreign Service in 1880," wrote one British diplomat, "nobody thought about Africa. When I returned to it in 1885, the nations of Europe were almost quarreling with each other as to the various portions of Africa which they should obtain." A contemporary French official expressed his amazement, saying, "We are witnessing something never before seen in history—the actual partition of a foreign continent [Africa] by a handful of European countries." He quickly added, however, that "France, of course, is entitled to the largest share in these spoils."

An international congress met in Berlin in 1884–1885 to lay out the legal framework for European expansion into Africa. Organized by Otto von Bismarck, the **Conference of Berlin** included Austria-Hungary, Belgium, Denmark, France, Germany, Italy, the Netherlands, the Ottoman Empire, Portugal, Russia, Spain, and Sweden (in union with Norway at the time). The United States was invited

---

[4]   William Gladstone, a Liberal, declared that "the lust-love of territory have been among the greatest curses of mankind."

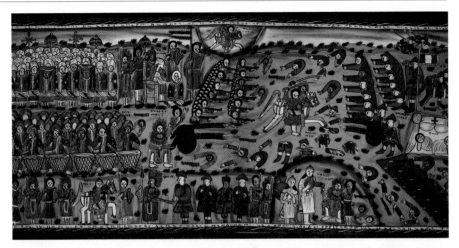

Repulsing the Europeans   Italy was a latecomer to European imperialism. The Italians invaded Ethiopia (one of the few parts of Africa not yet taken) in 1895. In a decisive battle at Adowa, at the northernmost point of the country, an Ethiopian army, armed with the latest Western military technology, crushed the ill-placed and ill-trained Italian forces. This painting by an unknown Ethiopian artist, depicts the victory over the Italian soldiers—identifiable here by their red headgear.

but did not attend. Of course, no African countries were invited; none, in fact, were even informed of the congress' intentions. The conference did not actually divide Africa among the European powers. It merely established the standards by which any European country could claim an African territory against another European rival. Yet its effect was immediate: in the ensuing scramble, France extended its traditional hold over central North Africa by seizing the territory of French West Africa (today's Benin, Burkina Faso, Ivory Coast, Guinea, Mali, Mauritania, Niger, and Senegal) in 1895. Italy invaded Ethiopia in the same year, but was beaten off; a few years later, however, the Italians captured Somalia and eventually Libya. With government backing, a British businessman and diamond merchant, Cecil Rhodes (1853–1902), used his position as prime minister of the British Cape Town Colony in southern Africa to instigate the Boer War (1899–1902), a conflict with the then Orange Free State and the Transvaal Republic (forerunners of the Union of South Africa), where a large deposit of diamonds had recently been discovered.[5] One result was the extension of British sovereignty northward into what came to be called Rhodesia (today's Zambia and Zimbabwe). Portugal seized Angola and Mozambique. Germany secured Cameroon, Namibia, and Tanzania. By 1902, fully 90 percent of Africa had been

---

[5]   Rhodes, an ardent imperialist, once declared, "If I could, I would annex other planets."

partitioned among the dominant European states; only Ethiopia and Liberia remained independent (see Map 22.2).

The rush to carve away parts of Asia was no less feverish or violent, but generally not as successful. Direct commercial relations, circumventing the Ottoman middleman, had gone on since the 16th century with permanent trading posts established from India to the Malay Peninsula and from southern China to Japan. The Dutch were the first, and periodically among the most vicious, European nation to take full political control of an Asian country. The government-chartered Dutch East India Company had been established in 1602 with an awarded monopoly on the movement of goods into and out of Indonesia. The British East

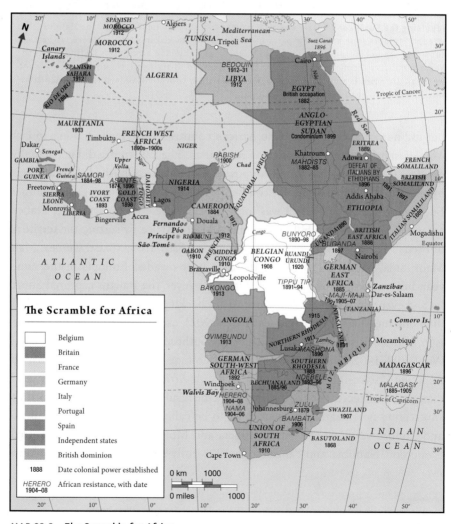

MAP 22.2 **The Scramble for Africa**

India Company held sway over most of India, by grant of Parliament, from the second half of the 18th century onward. In the early 19th century Britain then expanded further east and seized control of Burma before turning south and taking Malaya.

The Europeans sometimes turned to even nastier measures, as when the British forced the Chinese to accept India-grown opium in lieu of money to pay for Chinese silks and tea. By 1840 opium addiction was so widespread in China that the emperor attempted to deny the British entrance to Chinese harbors, which prompted so-called gunboat diplomacy to force the opening of the ports. The First Opium War (1839–1842) ended with China forced to cede to Britain permanent control of the harbor at Hong Kong.[6] France moved aggressively into Southeast Asia in the 1850s and 1860s, using the murder of a Spanish missionary by a group of resentful Vietnamese as an excuse to colonize much of southern Vietnam. By 1883 France was in control of the northern regions of Vietnam, along with much of Cambodia. Ten years later it added Laos to French Indochina (see Map 22.3).

All that remained up for grabs by 1890 were the outlying islands of the South Pacific. Britain snatched up Fiji and a few surrounding sites, while Germany seized the Marshall and Samoan Islands. France moved into Tahiti and into New Caledonia, an archipelago off the eastern coast of Australia. The biggest prize in the Pacific, however, was the widespread group of Philippine Islands. These had long previously belonged to Spain, but a successful revolution in 1898 brought about a short-lived period of independence. In that year the United States ended its brief but bloody conflict with Spain—the Spanish-American War of 1898, fought over the issue of control of Cuba and Puerto Rico. Among other things, the peace treaty gave the Philippines to America. Not all Americans were enthusiastic about taking up colonial responsibilities so far from home. Rudyard Kipling composed "The White Man's Burden" at this time precisely to rouse Americans to imperialist action. The United States and the Philippine Republic signed a peace treaty after three years of fighting (1899–1902); warfare continued in some of the outer islands, however, as late as 1913. In 1934, Congress guaranteed Philippine self-rule in ten years. World War II intervened, however, and Philippine independence did not become a reality until 1946.

Only Japan managed to retain full independence, which it did largely by becoming an imperialist power itself. Rapid industrialization had begun in 1868 after the Meiji Restoration overthrew a backward-looking network of feudal

---

[6]   Hong Kong remained the last outpost of the British Empire in Asia; it was not restored to Chinese control until 1997.

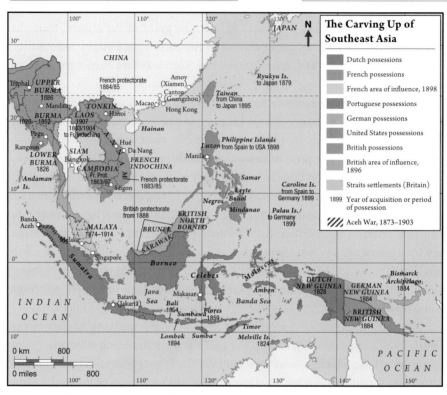

MAP 22.3   **The Carving Up of Southeast Asia**

regimes and restored the imperial dynasty, but the new government was intensely aware of Japan's weakness: it had no modern navy. Moreover, Japan had
ample agricultural land but virtually no metal ore for mining. That meant that
the nation could industrialize only by importing raw materials and exporting finished products, and it had to unload its ships in reliable markets. With so many of
the Pacific and East Asian markets snapped up by Europe, Japan had to carve out
its own colonial zones, which brought it into conflict with Russia.

The Russo-Japanese War (1904–1905) was fought for control of Manchuria,
Korea, and the island of Sakhalin. The first two were prized as rich in resources and
heavily populated; the latter was the sole major source of petroleum in East Asia.
This was primarily a naval war, with a handful of battles for control of ports. Japan's
victory surprised most observers, but the treaty that ended the war awarded Japan
no territory and released Russia from having to pay for the costs of the conflict.[7]
Riots erupted across Japan in response to the news and fostered a powerful sense of

---

[7]   President Theodore Roosevelt won the Nobel Peace Prize for helping to negotiate a peace treaty between
       Japan and Russia.

Japanese Victory   Japanese victory at the Battle of Tsushima, the decisive naval battle of the Russo-Japanese War (1904-1905). Japan's forces annihilated two-thirds of the Russian imperial fleet.

betrayal. Doubting that it would ever receive a fair hearing on the international scene, the imperial government, with popular backing, decided to turn aggressive. Five years after the war, Japan annexed the Korean peninsula; Russia agreed to withdraw from Manchuria, opening the way for further Japanese expansion. Japan continued to develop its military might, and when World War I ended in 1918 the Japanese quickly seized Germany's Asian colonies.

JAPANESE EXPANSION IN NORTH ASIA, 1870–1905

Japanese Empire, 1870
Territory acquired, 1874–1910
Japanese sphere of influence from 1905

MISSIONARY EUROPE

Western Europe's global land grab was without precedent in history. The political and economic factors behind it, importantly, were buttressed by an often convoluted set of religious and humanitarian motives. Armies of missionaries traveled before, with, and after the troops, spreading Christianity and attempting to quell the long-standing tribal hatreds and class and ethnic rivalries that they encountered wherever they went. With their various Christian moralities in tow, missionaries confronted a parade of cultural practices they found not only foreign but authentically horrifying. In much of east Africa, for example, the tradition of female genital cutting aroused particular disgust. The stoning of women for alleged adultery or the enslavement of children elicited a special sympathy. The Hindu folk practice of *sati* also demanded some sort of response: in parts of old India, a widow was thrown alive onto the burning funeral pyre of her deceased

Doing God's Work   Missionaries conducting a baptism ceremony in the Congo. By 1900 there were approximately nine million Christians in Africa; by the year 2000 that number had grown to nearly four hundred million. The continent's traditional religions have declined dramatically. Africa north of the Sahara Desert is now overwhelmingly Islamic, but south of the desert it is chiefly Christian.

husband so that she could accompany him into the life beyond. If imperialist subjugation was the price of putting an end to such practices, missionaries preached, then it was a price worth paying.

Writing a quarter century later about Britain's seizure of Egypt in 1882, Sir Evelyn Baring (1st Earl of Cromer, 1841–1917), Britain's first colonial governor of that country, offered a classic defense of imperialism. It needed to be done as much for Egypt's benefit as for Britain's, since the Egyptians had proven themselves to be incapable of running their own affairs. And if it needed doing, then better the British than anyone else:

> Egypt may now almost be said to form part of Europe. It is on the high road to the Far East. It can never cease to be an object of interest to all the powers of Europe, and especially to England. A numerous and intelligent body of Europeans and of non-Egyptian orientals have made Egypt their home. European capital to a large extent has been sunk in the country. . . . In addition to these peculiarities, which are of a normal character, it has to be borne in mind that in 1882 the [Egyptian] army was in a state of mutiny; the treasury was bankrupt; every branch of the administration had been dislocated; the ancient and arbitrary method,

under which the country had for centuries been governed, had received a severe blow, whilst, at the same time, no more orderly and law-abiding form of government had been inaugurated to take its place. . . . History, indeed, records some very radical changes in the forms of government to which a state has been subjected without its interests being absolutely and permanently shipwrecked. But it may be doubted whether any instance can be quoted of a sudden transfer of power in any civilized or semi-civilized community to a class so ignorant as the pure Egyptians, such as they were in the year 1882. These latter have, for centuries past, been a subject race. Persians, Greeks, Romans, Arabs from Arabia and Baghdad, Circassians, and finally, Ottoman Turks, have successively ruled over Egypt, but we have to go back to the doubtful and obscure precedents of Pharaonic times to find an epoch when, possibly, Egypt was ruled by Egyptians. Neither, for the present, do they appear to possess the qualities which would render it desirable, either in their own interests, or in those of the civilized world in general, to raise them at a bound to the category of autonomous rulers with full rights of internal sovereignty. If, however, a foreign occupation was inevitable or nearly

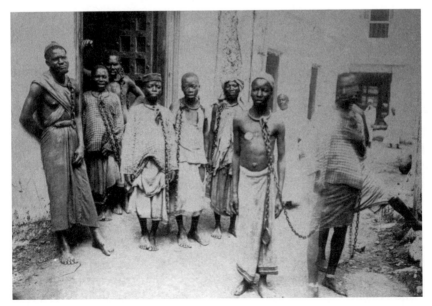

Slaves in Chains   Slavery was officially abolished in Zanzibar in 1873. Until then it had been the busiest slave market in eastern Africa, with as many as fifty thousand slaves a year passing through its ports; most of these were sent to the Persian Gulf region.

inevitable, it remains to be considered whether a British occupation was preferable to any other. From the purely Egyptian point of view, the answer to this question cannot be doubtful. The intervention of any European power was preferable to that of Turkey. The intervention of one European power was preferable to international intervention. The special aptitude shown by Englishmen in the government of Oriental races pointed to England as the most effective and beneficent instrument for the gradual introduction of European civilization into Egypt. *(Lord Cromer, Modern Egypt, 1908)*

Nothing can justify the orgies of violence and theft that attended empire building, yet European control did put an end to the international slave trade. It also attempted to halt practices like female circumcision in Africa, sati in India, and foot-binding in China. At the same time, one can argue that imperialism simply replaced one form of slavery with another. Perhaps no number of schools, hospitals, railroad systems, newspapers, and democratic institutions—all legacies of European rule—can offset cultural murder.

A GILDED AGE

The Europeans' technological superiority gave them the most lopsided military victories in human history. Some of them had nearly a carnival atmosphere, resembling nothing so much as our modern video games. And once in power around the globe, the Europeans instituted many of the practices of **command economies**—economies that aim to provide the highest possible yield for whoever held the raw materials and captive markets. It brought at home the chilling self-confidence of a "gilded age."

Shooters simply mowed down the resistance with seemingly endless numbers of clicks—except that Europe's remote controls consisted of real weapons. Remington and Winchester breechloading rifles, elephant guns, Jarmann M1884 repeating rifles, Kropatschek 11-millimeter carbines, Maxim and Gatling machine guns, and seven-pound field artillery—all these squared off against warriors armed with little more than spears and arrows. The results were horrifying and became horrifyingly familiar.

In 1897 a French force of only 32 Europeans and 507 African mercenaries massacred a native army near Sokoto, in today's Nigeria, that numbered more than 30,000. Two years later only 320 Senegalese fighters, under French command, wiped out over 12,000 Sudanese troops. And in 1908 a company of 389 French soldiers annihilated a 10,000-man army from the kingdom of Ouaddai, near today's province of Darfur along the Chad-Sudan border in east-central Africa.

The British scored their one-sided victories as well, including the campaign to conquer Sudan in 1898. Sudan itself was of relatively little value to the British in terms of natural resources. The country, upriver from Egypt, mattered principally for strategic purposes: those who controlled Sudan could impede traffic along the Nile. The Sudanese fighters, known as Dervishes, numbered over 50,000 and met the English at Omdurman, now a suburb of the Sudanese capital of Khartoum. The well-armed British were aided by a flotilla of gunboats that had steamed up the river. Winston Churchill (1874–1965), the future prime minister, served there as a second lieutenant and described the battle in an 1899 memoir:

> [The infantry] fired steadily and stolidly, without hurry or excitement, for the enemy were far away and the officers careful. Besides, the soldiers were interested in the work and took great pains. But presently the mere physical act [of repeated firing] became tedious. . . . But at the critical moment the gunboat arrived on the scene and began suddenly to blaze and flame from Maxim guns, quick-firing guns, and rifles. The range was short; the effect tremendous. The terrible machine, floating gracefully on the waters—a beautiful white devil—wreathed itself in smoke. The river slopes of the Kerreri Hills, crowded with the advancing thousands, sprang up into clouds of dust and splinters of rock. The charging Dervishes sank down in tangled heaps. The masses in the rear paused, irresolute. It was too hot even for them. . . . And all the time out on the plain on the other side bullets were shearing through flesh, smashing and splintering bone; blood spouted from terrible wounds; valiant men were struggling on through a hell of whistling metal, exploding shells, and spurting dust—suffering, despairing, dying.

The carnage lasted for five hours and left ten thousand Dervishes dead, fifteen thousand wounded, and another five thousand captured; the British lost fewer than fifty men. Churchill's vivid memoir mentions, but does not quantify, how many British gunmen suffered the effects of carpal tunnel syndrome from pulling the triggers of their weapons so many times.

Industrial Warfare   Lord Kitchener, major-general of Britain's imperial troops in Africa, defeated the Mahdist forces (an Islamic messianic group) in battle at Omdurman, in Sudan, in 1898. The British killed over ten thousand Mahdists and wounded another thirteen thousand, while suffering only forty seven losses themselves. According to an eyewitness: " . . . It was not a battle but an execution . . . The bodies were not in heaps—bodies hardly ever are; but they spread evenly over acres and acres. Some lay very composedly with their slippers placed under their heads for a last pillow; some knelt, cut short in the middle of a last prayer. Others were torn to pieces."

Lopsided advantages like this did more than ensure battlefield success; they altered the perceptions of warfare itself and of the participants as well. The Europeans appeared not simply as the victors. Rather, a society that could engineer such stunning conquests must in some sense be superior. As for its victims, a nation that clings to spears and arrows in an age of steel and gunpowder may not deserve massacre and foreign oppression, but it can hardly be surprised when they result. Such, at any rate, was the attitude of many in the West. An officers' manual for British forces fighting in Sierra Leone described "the weird and treacherous surroundings, and the nerve-wracking effects of the climate" in the region. It contrasted the "cunning savages . . . like the wild animals of [their] own forests" with "the stern discipline and enthusiastic *esprit de corps* of the British army" under the command of "that indispensible factor in the machine of West African warfare—the British officer." European readers more often felt wonder and pride than revulsion.

Even the Europeans, however, were disgusted by the excesses of King Léopold II of Belgium (r. 1865–1909). Léopold, who had long been keen to develop colonial holdings in Africa, cast his eye on the vast natural wealth of the Congo: "To open to civilization the only part of the globe where it has not yet penetrated, to pierce the darkness which envelops whole populations, is a crusade, if I may say so, a crusade worthy of this century of progress." Unable to stir the Belgian parliament into action, he hit on the idea of establishing instead a private company, the International African Association, to help the Congolese "develop." He hired the scurrilous British explorer Henry Morton Stanley (1841–1904) to represent the Association and get local tribal rulers to sign

The Horror   A photo of Congolese with their hands chopped off, the common punishment for failure to meet rubber-collection quotas. "The baskets of severed hands, set down at the feet of the European post commanders, became the symbol of the Congo Free State. . . . The collection of hands became an end in itself. Force Publique soldiers brought them to the stations in place of rubber; they even went out to harvest them instead of rubber. . . They became a sort of currency. They came to be used to make up for shortfalls in rubber quotas, to replace. . . the people who were demanded for the forced labour gangs; and the Force Publique soldiers were paid their bonuses on the basis of how many hands they collected."

friendship pacts with it, but the pacts turned out to be sales contracts—giving ownership of the entire region to Léopold. He found himself in possession of thirty million people and an area of 900,000 square miles (2.3 million square kilometers). The Congolese were brutally whipped and beaten, forced to harvest rubber, palm oil, and ivory (the three most profitable products of the region). Workers who failed to meet their quotas were punished by having their hands chopped off.

Léopold's thugs were organized into the "Force Publique," whose savagery was so methodical that they kept accounts of the number of hands they had severed. They were expected to produce a hand for every bullet they fired, lest they be charged with wasting military resources. Hands became, in fact, a form of currency, redeemable for bonus payments at the end of each month.[8] An estimated five to eight million Congolese were murdered during Léopold's reign, with an equal number dying of starvation and disease.

In 1908, after proof of the Belgian cruelties was published (1904) by a British diplomat, the Belgian Parliament forced Léopold to relinquish control of the Congo and placed it under the authority of the Belgian state. Yet Léopold was among the wealthiest people in the Western world and remains a popular

---

8   Severed hands were delivered to officials throughout the 1890s at nearly a metric ton per day.

figure in Belgian history. Among Belgians today, he is remembered for the large number of public buildings he constructed with his wealth, including the Musée de Congo in Tervuren. Now known as the Royal Museum for Central Africa, it contains thousands of artifacts of Congolese life. It makes no mention, however, of the savagery that brought them to Belgium and reduced the Congolese population by one-half. To this day, the museum's website states only that "to promote Belgium's work of 'development and civilization' in Congo . . . Léopold II hoped to build some form of museum or 'showcase.'"

* * *

On the last day of December in the year 1900 Mark Twain (Samuel Clemens; 1835–1910) penned a brief "Salutation-Speech from the 19th Century to the 20th," which appeared the next day in the *New York Herald*. Like most of the American writer's late work, this piece is marked with a sharp, bitter humor. In it, he regrets the era he has lived through and holds little hope for the century to come:

> I bring you the stately matron named *Christendom*, returning be-draggled, besmirched, and dishonored from pirate-raids in Kiaw-Chow, Manchuria, South Africa, and the Philippines, with her soul full of mean-ness, her pocket full of boodle, and her mouth full of pious hypocrisies. Give her soap and a towel, but hide the looking-glass.

Western society needed a thorough cleansing, and a younger Mark Twain might have hoped one was possible. But the imperial, gilded, rapacious world he lived in offered no reason for optimism.

Government and chartered companies "expropriated" (that is, stole) lands, crop fields, mines, flocks, and businesses at will. They forced locals to work at re-duced wages, and they seized mineral rights and monopolized control of imports and exports. They dismantled support for centuries-long commercial routes, since neighboring territories were likely to be subjects of a rival European power. They also built tariff barriers that kept competitors' goods out of domestic markets. They ensured that their colonies sold only the goods produced by their imperialist mas-ters, at whatever price those masters set.

Their goal was clear: to maximize profit for the European power in control of each region, its government, its officials, and its merchants. The imperial age thus strongly resembles the absolutist era—but with a difference. Compared to mercan-tilism, it worked better, because it covered a broader area and its tools of oppression were more deadly. The larger the empires grew, too, the greater was the need to protect business interests. Mining and manufacturing, and the banks used to back them, were seen as too big to allow to fail.

England's industries found it difficult to compete with Continental rivals, but no matter: they simply consolidated into larger and larger corporations in the hopes of improving profits. Many banks and investment houses consolidated as well and worked out special relations with the government-led Bank of England. In this way, Britain gradually exposed itself to crushing debts, and the shakiness of the entire structure increased the need for government manipulation. In fact, it was partly in order to write off debt from the construction of the Suez Canal that the British decided in 1882 to annex it.

> The imperial age thus strongly resembles the absolutist era—but with a difference. Compared to mercantilism, it worked better, because it covered a broader area and its tools of oppression were more deadly.

The command economies of imperialism and its repeating cycles of boom and bust effectively locked out underdeveloped nations within Europe from international markets. Unable to compete or secure funding for their own industrialization, many of these countries—Greece, Ireland, Italy, Norway, Poland, Sweden most notably—lost tens of millions of their people through emigration between 1880 and 1914. Approximately one-half of these emigrants made their way to the United States, with the other half divided between Australia, Canada, and Latin America (see Map 22.4).

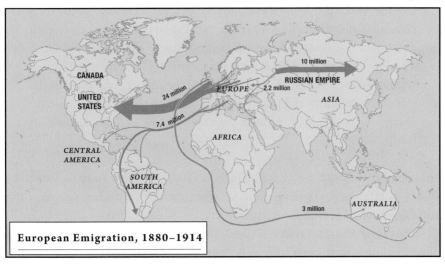

European Emigration, 1880–1914

MAP 22.4   European Emmigration, 1880–1914

WESTERN WAYS: EMULATION AND RESISTANCE

Once in control of their colonies, the Europeans encountered consistent but relatively minor unrest. Their technological edge made resistance seem futile to most of their subjects, many of whom were accustomed to rule by small numbers of tribal elites. Although they smarted under European oppression, they nonetheless benefited from the disappearance or at least the neutralization of longstanding tribal and clan conflicts.

Some colonial subjects emulated Western ways as a means to modernize their societies. They prized Western education, technology, and civil government, and they sought to promote improved understanding between rulers and ruled, even though the treatment they received from their European governors was shoddy. "However well-educated and clever a native might be," wrote a British military officer in India, "and however brave he may prove himself, I believe that no rank we can bestow on him would cause him to be considered an equal of the British." Contrast that with an 1871 speech by Dadabhai Naoroji (1825–1917), an Indian statesman who served in the British Parliament from 1892 to 1895:

> The introduction of English education, with its great, noble, elevating, and civilizing literature and advanced science, will for ever remain a monument of good work done in India and a claim to gratitude upon the Indian people. . . . Britain may well claim credit for law and order, which, however, is as much necessary for the existence of British rule in India as for the good of the Indian people; for freedom of speech and press, and for other benefits flowing therefrom. . . . [But] the benefits are more than counterbalanced by evils inseparable from the system of a remote foreign dominion. . . . Commonsense will suggest this to any thoughtful mind. These evils have ever since gone on increasing, and more and more counterbalancing the increased produce of the country, making now the evil of the bleeding and impoverishing drain by the foreign dominion nearly or above £30,000,000 a year. *(Poverty and Un-British Rule in India, 1901, pp. vi–viii)*

His book *Poverty and Un-British Rule in India* (1901) brought to popular attention within Britain the devastating effect of colonialism on the Indian people, while still expressing hope for a shared prosperity.

The case of Mohandas Gandhi (1869–1948) is instructive.[9] Born to a prominent provincial Hindu family near Bombay (today's city of Mumbai), he traveled to London

---

9 Mahatma, as Gandhi is also known, is a Hindu honorary title meaning "Great Soul."

in 1888 and studied law at University College London for three years. He spoke fluent English, adopted Western dress and manners (though he hated British cooking), and hoped to make a living as a barrister back in British India. His career faltered, however, and he took a position in British South Africa, where his encounters with racism and discrimination turned him gradually against the empire. For a time, Gandhi exhibited a measure of Western-style race prejudice, too: "Kaffirs [a derogatory term for black South Africans] are as a rule uncivilized.... They are troublesome, very dirty, and live almost like animals," he wrote in the newspaper he founded while in South Africa, the *Indian Opinion*. On another occasion he asserted, "We believe as much in the purity of race [as white South Africans do].... We believe also that [whites] should be the predominating race." He finally returned to India in 1915, renounced Western dress, embraced strict Hindu asceticism (for example, taking a vow of lifelong celibacy), and began the nonviolent protest campaign against British rule in India for which he became famous.

The Young Gandhi   Mohandas Gandhi (1869-1948) seen here as a barrister in South Africa. Remembered, of course, as the champion of India's independence from Britain and as the apostle of non-violence, Gandhi also campaigned tirelessly for the rights of women. He wrote in *Young India* (1930), a newsweekly he published from 1919 to 1932: "to call woman the weaker sex is a libel; it is man's injustice to woman. If by strength is meant brute strength, then, indeed, is woman less brute than man. If by strength is meant moral power, then woman is immeasurably man's superior. Has she not greater intuition, is she not more self-sacrificing, has she not greater powers of endurance, has she not greater courage? Without her, man could not be. If nonviolence is the law of our being, the future is with woman. Who can make a more effective appeal to the heart than woman?"

The largest sustained rebellion against the Europeans, the **Boxer Rebellion** (1898–1901), occurred in China. It began when a millennial Buddhist sect from northern China opened a campaign of violence against European missionaries and native Chinese who had converted to Christianity. The rebels came largely from the peasantry and called themselves the society of the Yihequan, meaning "Righteous and Harmonious Fists." They believed themselves the sanctified saviors of China from foreign imperialism, fighters whose religious rituals made them invulnerable to Western guns and cannon. The Yihequan believed they would be reincarnated as "spirit warriors"—an entire ghost army that would rout the Western corrupters of China's world. They opposed Western culture as much as Western colonial rule and hence had much in common with other nationalist movements around the globe.

Later Chinese nationalists were ambivalent about the Boxers and remain so today. They admired the patriotism the rebels evinced but wanted to distance themselves from both the Boxers' low origins and unorthodox religious convictions. After uprisings in the countryside, the Boxer forces, perhaps a quarter million strong, moved into Beijing and other cities, in order to target missionaries, merchants, and diplomats. They killed several hundred Westerners, along with several thousand Chinese Christian converts. The empress dowager of the weak Qing dynasty was personally sympathetic to the Boxers but was compelled by her treaties with the Europeans to help put them down. In the end, the Boxers were routed by an alliance of soldiers from the five leading European states (Austria-Hungary, Britain, France, Germany, and Italy) plus forces from Japan, Russia, and the United States. To avenge the murdered missionaries and converts, the Eight Army Alliance committed widespread atrocities, including murder, rape, and arson, against civilians.

Mark Twain again: Soon after his toss-away "Salutation to the 20th Century," he wrote a parody of the "Battle Hymn of the Republic." In it he curses the imperialist greed that, he believed, had overtaken Western society. It had made his whole working life nothing but an "era of incredible rottenness." The aftermath of the Boxer Rebellion—which he had publicly supported—was particularly galling to him.

> Mine eyes have seen the orgy of the launching of the Sword;
> He is searching out the hoardings where the stranger's wealth
>   is stored.
> He hath loosed his fateful lightnings, and with woe and death
>   has scored;
> His lust is marching on.
>
> I have seen him in the watch-fires of a hundred circling camps,
> They have builded him an altar in the Eastern dews and damps;
> I have read his doomful mission by the dim and flaring lamps—
> His night is marching on.
>
> I have read his bandit gospel writ in burnished rows of steel:
> "As ye deal with my pretensions, so with you my wrath shall deal;
> Let the faithless son of Freedom crush the patriot with his heel;
> Lo, Greed is marching on!"

We have legalized the strumpet and are guarding her retreat;
Greed is seeking out commercial souls before his judgment seat;
O, be swift, ye clods, to answer him! Be jubilant my feet!
Our god is marching on!

In a sordid slime harmonious, Greed was born in yonder ditch,
With a longing in his bosom—and for others' goods an itch—
As Christ died to make men holy, let men die to make us rich—
Our god is marching on.

His daughter advised him that this scornful rendition of a much-loved hymn was too bitter and was certain to offend his readers. He never published it.

WHO, WHAT, WHERE

Boxer Rebellion
command economies
Conference of Berlin
imperialism
scientific management

Second Industrial
Revolution
social Darwinism

SUGGESTED READINGS

Primary Sources

Baring, Evelyn. *Modern Egypt.*

Gandhi, Mohandas. *An Autobiography: The Story of My Experiments with Truth.*

Hobson, J. A. *Imperialism: A Study.*

Taylor, Frederick Winslow. *The Principles of Scientific Management.*

Anthologies

Bowman, William D., Frank M. Chiteji, and J. Megan Greene, eds. *Imperialism in the Modern World: Sources and Interpretations.*

Brown, Judith M., ed. *Mahatma Gandhi: The Essential Writings.*

Fischer, Louis, ed. *The Essential Gandhi: An Anthology of His Writings on His Life, Work, and Ideas.*

Martin, Susan K., Caroline Daley, Elizabeth Dimock, Cheryl Cassidy, and Cecily Devereaux, eds. *Women and Empire, 1750–1939: Primary Sources on Gender and Anglo-Imperialism.* (2009).

Naoroji, Dadabhai. *Poverty and Un-British Rule in India* (1901).

Smith, Bonnie G., ed. *Imperialism: A History in Documents* (2000).

Studies

Appleby, Joyce Oldham. *The Relentless Revolution: A History of Capitalism* (2010).

Bickers, Robert, and R. G. Tiedemann, eds. *The Boxers, China, and the World* (2007).

Broadberry, Stephen, and Kevin H. O'Rourke, eds. *The Cambridge Economic History of Modern Europe* (2010).

Cannadine, David. *Ornamentalism: How the British Saw Their Empire* (2002).

Curtin, Philip D. *The World and the West: The European Challenge and the Overseas Response in the Age of Empire* (2002).

Delmendo, Sharon. *The Star-Entangled Banner: One Hundred Years of America in the Philippines* (2004).

Deringil, Selim. *The Well-Protected Domains: Ideology and the Legitimation of Power in the Ottoman Empire, 1876–1909* (2011).

Drayton, Richard. *Nature's Government: Science, Imperial Britain, and the "Improvement" of the World* (2000).

Ferguson, Niall. *Colossus: The Rise and Fall of the American Empire* (2004).

———. *Empire: The Rise and Demise of the British World Order and the Lessons for Global Power* (2003).

Gelber, Harry G. *Opium, Soldiers, and Evangelicals: Britain's 1840–42 War with China and Its Aftermath* (2004).

Hanioğlu, M. Şükrü. *Preparation for a Revolution: The Young Turks, 1902–1908* (2001).

Harrington, Peter. *Peking, 1900: The Boxer Rebellion* (2001).

Jasanoff, Maya. *Edge of Empire: Lives, Culture, and Conquest in the East, 1750–1850* (2006).

Karabell, Zachary. *Parting the Desert: The Creation of the Suez Canal* (2004).

Kern, Stephen. *The Culture of Time and Space, 1880–1918* (2003).

Lelyveld, Joseph. *Great Soul: Mahatma Gandhi and His Struggle with India* (2012).

Linn, Brian McAllister. *The Philippine War, 1899–1902* (2000).

Meyer, Karl E., and Shareen Blair Brysac. *Tournament of Shadows: The Great Game and the Race for Empire in Central Asia* (2006).

Pomeranz, Kenneth. *The Great Divergence: China, Europe, and the Making of the Modern World Economy* (2001).

Silbey, David J. *A War of Frontier and Empire: The Philippine-American War, 1899–1902* (2007).

Watts, Sheldon. *Epidemics and History: Disease, Power, and Imperialism* (2000).

Wesseling, H. L. *The European Colonial Empires, 1815–1919* (2004).

Xiang, Lanxin. *The Origins of the Boxer War: A Multinational Study* (2002).

For additional resources, including maps, primary sources, visuals, web links, and quizzes, please go to **www.oup.com/us/backman.**

CHAPTER 23

From Nihilism to Modernism

1880–1939

Not all Westerners at the start of the 20th century were greedy, grasping imperialists, and not all believed in their historical destiny and in social Darwinism. What Mark Twain called an "era of incredible rottenness" also had some of the most intense soul-searching and self-criticism the West had seen since the 17th century. The analysis was thoroughgoing and biting: it was creative, scientific, poetic, religious, and philosophical. At times it bordered on being obsessive. No single outlook or set of ideas defined it, although elements of confusion and doubt, and of the loss of old certainties, were predominant. It took the form of new styles in painting and sculpture, bold experiments in music, even bolder dissections of the human mind, and innovations in fiction and drama. It also challenged basic assumptions about truth and value.

THE GREATER WEST IN A TIME OF UNCERTAINTY, 1880–1939

Even the sciences discovered that some of their most fundamental beliefs about space, time, and motion were doubtful if not flat-out wrong. In philosophy the confident idealism of midcentury, as evidenced by a writer like Georg W. F. Hegel (1770–1831), gave way to thoroughgoing uncertainty about the nature of reality, a more radical individualism, and a renewed interest in logic and language. And both developments suggest a turning away from the world and toward the self, in philosophy's attempts to produce order. Even

◀ **A Certain Horror** *The Scream*, by Edvard Munch (1893). Munch's diary described the picture's origins: "I was walking along a path one evening, the city [of Oslo] was on one side, the fjord on the other. I was tired and felt ill, so I stopped and looked over the fjord. The sun was setting and the clouds were as red as blood. I felt a scream passing through the world, and could even hear it, or so it seemed. So I painted this picture."

- Sickness unto Death
- A Wave or a Particle?
- Relativity and Space-time
- The Will to Power
- Logic and Language
- From Phenomenology to Existentialism
- The Illness of Western Society
- Sexuality and Psychoanalysis
- Beyond the Pleasure Principle
- Modernism and Irony
- The Artistic Truth Within

CHAPTER OUTLINE

architecture and home decoration visibly rejected 19th-century mass production and imperial grandeur and gave way to arts-and-crafts movements that emphasized individuality, originality, and personal expression.

SICKNESS UNTO DEATH

In politics, socialists, anarchists, feminists, commonsense democrats, isolationists, and even some conservatives loudly protested the imperialist frenzy. Many had seen the march to empire coming as early as midcentury, with developments like the Crimean War and the Louis-Napoleon's proclamation of the Second French Empire. Karl Marx, in 1852, saw the new aggressiveness as an effort to emulate the glories of 1805–1812, but its heart was nothing more than the pursuit of money. Bonaparte, Marx sneered, at least could have claimed some sort of justification for his violence. Europe's new aggressors were marked by nothing more than "passions with no truth in them; truths with no passion in them; unheroic pseudo-heroes; history without events; [and] a series of developments driven forward by nothing more than the calendar."

Not all opponents of imperialism were revolutionaries like Marx. George Bernard Shaw (1856–1950) denounced empire building in essays, lectures, pamphlets, and plays like *The Man of Destiny* (1895, about Napoleon), *Caesar and Cleopatra* (1898), and *John Bull's Other Island* (1904, about the Irish Question). Shaw was no democrat; he was far too skeptical about the intelligence of common people. Yet he championed a moderate form of socialism that would free people from the concern for wealth that drove imperialism.

In the United States, the Anti-Imperialist League formed in 1898 to oppose annexation of the Philippines. To the League, this violated the principle of government by consent of the people, enshrined in the Declaration of Independence. Otto von Bismarck, ever eager to expand Germany's power within Europe, had no interest in imperialist adventures outside the Continent and resisted them with all his might—which led to his dismissal by Emperor Wilhelm.

CHAPTER TIMELINE

1881
Ibsen, *Ghosts*

1885
Haggard, *King Solomon's Mines*

1886
Nietzsche, *Beyond Good and Evil*

1889
Van Gogh, *Starry Night*

1891
Wilde, *The Picture of Dorian Gray*

1899
Freud, *Interpretation of Dreams*

1900
Max Planck formulates quantum theory

1901
Husserl, *Logical Investigations*

Many leading intellectuals, too, like the classical scholar and parliamentarian Theodor Mommsen (1817–1903), denounced imperialism as simply a waste of time and energy.

Industry still demanded more materials, more products, and more markets. Yet to critics it seemed to cheapen people's lives. Oscar Wilde (1854–1900), the playwright and novelist, dismissed as a cynic someone "who knows the price of everything, and the value of nothing." Mass production meant crass production. It was fine to devote a nation's talent and treasure to spreading literacy and scientific knowledge among the masses. What good was it, however, if those skills went only to produce cheap housewares, kitschy art, and shallow pulp fiction?

Books became the dominant form of popular entertainment, with novels surpassing poetry as the favorite genre. Max Pemberton (1863–1950) wrote many adventure stories aimed at working-class audiences. His most successful was *The Iron Pirate* (1896), about a steam-driven frigate that terrorizes the Atlantic. H. Rider Haggard (1856–1925) was even more successful, with novels like *King Solomon's Mines* (1885) and *She* (1887).[1] The latter tells of an English scholar of antiquities who travels to an uncharted kingdom "in darkest Africa," ruled by a mythical immortal beauty. "God help English literature," wrote one critic of the time, "when English people lay aside . . . the works of Defoe, Swift, Thackeray, Charlotte Brontë, [and] George Eliot . . . for the penny-dreadfuls of Mr. Haggard."[2] The pressure of the marketplace drove down standards in popular music as well. The invention of the phonograph and radio, while good things in themselves, meant that people no longer had to learn to play instruments in order to have music in their lives. They could simply turn on the machine to hear whatever they wished. Light popular songs crowded out more serious and

---

[1]   H. Rider Haggard's novels later became the models for the Indiana Jones movies.

[2]   Cheap adventure novels were called penny dreadfuls, because they appeared in magazine installments costing only a penny.

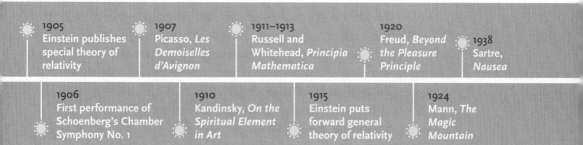

1905	1907	1911–1913	1920	1938
Einstein publishes special theory of relativity	Picasso, *Les Demoiselles d'Avignon*	Russell and Whitehead, *Principia Mathematica*	Freud, *Beyond the Pleasure Principle*	Sartre, *Nausea*

1906	1910	1915	1924
First performance of Schoenberg's Chamber Symphony No. 1	Kandinsky, *On the Spiritual Element in Art*	Einstein puts forward general theory of relativity	Mann, *The Magic Mountain*

Low Culture   A group of friends listening to a gramophone, Béziers, France, ca. 1910.

challenging music. Culture, it seemed, was being split into high and low—and low culture was winning out.

Many writers, critics, and artists at the end of the 19th century therefore reacted by championing the high. "Art for art's sake" became their rallying cry. Art had to be dedicated to nothing but itself; it had to pursue beauty, truth, and deep feeling on their own terms, without any concern for the masses. "Nothing is truly beautiful unless it is useless," wrote the French critic Théophile Gautier (1811–1872). "Everything that is useful is actually ugly since its usefulness derives from its answering to a human need—and human needs are ignoble and disgusting.... The most useful thing in a house [after all] is the toilet."

The preface to Oscar Wilde's novel *The Picture of Dorian Gray* (1891), served as a manifesto for this passionate aestheticism:

> The artist is the creator of beautiful things. To reveal art and conceal the artist is art's aim ....
>
> Those who find ugly meanings in beautiful things are corrupt without being charming .... Those who find beautiful meanings in beautiful things are the cultivated. For these there is hope ....
>
> There is no such thing as a moral or an immoral book. Books are well written, or badly written. That is all.

... It is the spectator, and not life, that art really mirrors. Diversity of opinion about a work of art shows that the work is new, complex, and vital .... We can forgive a man for making a useful thing as long as he does not admire it. The only excuse for making a useless thing is that one admires it intensely.

All art is quite useless.

Wilde's career reached its zenith in his stage comedy *The Importance of Being Earnest* (1895); but his fall, after a conviction for "gross indecency" with his homosexual lover, inspired a keen self-investigation. Written in 1897 while in his prison cell, his *De Profundis* ("Out of the Depths") recognizes the need for moral seriousness and the pursuit of goodness in life. This farewell letter/essay was not published until 1905—five years after his death in Paris. Without this sense of spiritual purpose, life is cast adrift. And this very aimlessness permits the greed, power wielding, and self-serving hypocrisy of late Victorian society. In the words of the Danish philosopher Søren Kierkegaard (1813–1855), it was "the sickness unto death" and the principal curse of modern European life.

Wilde ends *De Profundis* with a resolve not to despair of his fall from fame and fortune but to live henceforth transforming every experience of life into goodness—the truth of beauty lies in the determination to ennoble life with meaning, rather than merely to adorn it, as before, with cleverness and wit:

Religion does not help me. The faith that others give to what is unseen, I give to what one can touch, and look at .... When I think about religion at all, I feel as if I would like to found an order for those who cannot believe .... And agnosticism should have its ritual no less than faith. It has sown its martyrs, it should reap its saints .... Its symbols must be of my own creating. Only that is spiritual which makes its own form. If I may not find its secret within myself, I shall never find it. If I have not got it already, it will never come to me. Reason does not help me .... But, somehow, I have got to make both of these things just and right for me.

Wilde accepts the challenge to make one's own meaning, one's own beauty, one's own truth, since he sees that the soul is made stronger by the effort itself. But Meaning, Beauty, and Truth—all capitalized—will never actually be achieved or attained. And for a very simple reason: because they do not exist.

A WAVE OR A PARTICLE?

Many intellectual currents accepted, or even urged, the notion that there were no fixed moral or material truths. They rejected the solid bourgeois certainties of the 19th century—belief in a rational, coherent, material universe, in nationalism and progress, in philosophical idealism, and in universal moral and aesthetic values. But they did not reject these assumptions carelessly or out of pique. Years of grinding work in laboratories, libraries, studies, and artists' studios lay behind this radical and seemingly abrupt break with the past. And the first signs of major change occurred in the sciences.

Europeans in the 19th century commonly regarded physics as the least interesting of all sciences. It seemed a professional dead end; after Sir Isaac Newton, all that remained to do was to clear up a few minor things or add a few points to the general picture. Newton's three laws of motion, as laid out in the *Principia Mathematica*, had established classical mechanics (the movement of matter); his law of universal gravitation explained nature's fundamental force. The cosmos operated according to fixed laws and mathematical formulas. Alfred North Whitehead (1861–1947), the great British mathematician and philosopher, described the start of his career as "an age of successful scientific orthodoxy, undisturbed by much thought beyond the conventions . . . [and] one of the dullest stages of thought since the time of the First Crusade." The discovery of a new energy, electricity, stirred things up for a while, but James Maxwell (1831–1879), a Scottish physicist, soon calmed things down again. Maxwell showed how electricity, magnetism, and light are all manifestations of the same force—electromagnetism. The rest of physics, it seemed, was merely a matter of adjusting a few details.

But then a spate of new discoveries popped up, discoveries that could not be fitted into the Newtonian framework. In fact, they seemed to attack it. On November 8, 1895, Wilhelm Röntgen (1845–1923) discovered X-rays while experimenting with electrical current passing through a vacuum tube.[3] These rays were yet another elemental force, but they could not be explained by the standard model. Then came the electron, discovered by 1897 by J. J. Thomson (1856–1940) at Cambridge University in England. Before Thomson, atoms were believed to be the smallest particles in nature—the fundamental building blocks. As Thomson deflected cathode rays through electromagnetic fields, he found subatomic particles less than 0.0005 times the mass of the smallest atom, hydrogen. The very next year Madame Curie discovered another element, radium, that somehow emitted radiation—and with it another new form of energy, radioactivity. Suddenly the universe, at

---

[3]   The "X" in X-rays derived from the mathematical sign for an unknown. Röntgen received the first ever Nobel Prize in physics, in 1901.

X-ray Vision   Cartoon of a "beach idyll" when seen via the new technology of X-rays, discovered by Wilhelm Röntgen in 1895. Certainly not what most of us were thinking of when as youngsters we longed to have X-ray vision.

the smallest of levels, looked stranger than it had since the time of Copernicus, Kepler, and Galileo.

These discoveries showed the universe to be immensely more complex than anyone understood. But they were nothing compared to what came next. All of classical physics, and even the newer discoveries, had relied on the *ether*. This medium had neither mass, nor weight, nor color; it was uniform, odorless, and tasteless; it was imperceptible to touch or measurement; it offered no physical resistance. Yet it had to exist, because all of those atoms and energies had to move *through something*. Otherwise atoms and energies could not interact, just as swimmers rely on water in order to move through the sea or a pool. The ether ensured that all movement, all changes in momentum and direction, and all interactions of force and counterforce would proceed smoothly and perfectly. But then came Max Planck (1858–1947) and Albert Einstein (1879–1955), and our understanding of the universe would never be the same.

Planck and Einstein seldom performed experiments; they both preferred to work out on paper the theories behind other people's data. Planck's first breakthrough came in 1900, after a group of physicists who were trying to coax the maximum brightness out of light bulbs with the least possible electricity sent the accumulated data of their experiments to him. He came up with an astonishing conclusion: the data could be explained only by introducing into the calculations a fixed unit of energy—a kind of packet of light energy, called a *quantum*. One could have x amount of light energy, or $2x$, or $3x$, and so on, but nothing in between. Light was not, therefore, a continuous wave of energy but instead a torrent of finite bits.

To make matters even more confusing, these quanta of light (the plural of quantum) behaved like physical particles possessing mass, even as they also had the characteristics of waves. Planck turned to this conclusion, he later wrote, "as an act of despair." It was the only way to make mathematical sense out of the data, even though it upset the foundations of all of physics. In this he was remarkably like Copernicus four hundred years earlier, who had to wreck the system he had inherited in order to make his numbers crunch better. Planck had reluctantly invented a new physics based on quanta, a **quantum theory**. Most physicists rejected his claims at first, even though they could find no fault in his reasoning. Once Einstein confirmed Planck's theory, however, most fell into line.[4]

Not even Einstein, however, was prepared for the next step. Matter, too, appeared to behave as both wave and particle. That is the basis of how quantum developed over half a century or more, to reveal the inner workings of atoms and molecules. Scientists could make sense of the properties of the different chemical elements that, before, had just seemed handed down like a table in a reference book. They could better understand reactions between atoms and molecules, unleashing a new scientific revolution in chemistry, physics, and biology   to the point that we can now look deep into the brain or hold entire computers in our hands. Yet they could make predictions about only the *probability* that any one particle would be anywhere. That "wave-particle duality" is also the basis of the *uncertainty principle*, which sets limits on what one can know about a particle at a given moment. If uncertainty has become as powerful a metaphor as relativity, no wonder Einstein rebelled against quantum theory. Besides, he had made some sweeping and precise predictions of his own.

European culture had earlier periods of uncertainty about how to know what was true, but now the very idea of fixed truth seemed to be false. Nothing quite like this had happened before, and it crossed scientific and artistic lines.

RELATIVITY AND SPACE-TIME

Einstein finished the task of reinventing physics in 1905 when he published what came to be known as his special theory of relativity. His general theory of relativity followed in 1915. They are difficult, but it is important to understand the basics—and not solely in order to appreciate the science. **Relativity** could in fact stand for the entire cultural and intellectual ferment of the early 20th century. It could stand for the relativity of aesthetic values, of philosophical terms, and of literary judgments. Artists and poets did not derive their ideas from Planck and Einstein, although many were keenly aware of them, but there are parallels all the

---

4   Speaking of one holdout against quanta, Plank recalled, "He's a perfect example of the type of theorist we do not need . . . the kind who says 'The facts don't fit my theory; too bad for the facts.'"

same. European culture had earlier periods of uncertainty about how to know what was true, but now the very idea of fixed truth seemed to be false. Nothing quite like this had happened before, and it crossed scientific and artistic lines. As the American historian, political writer, and novelist Henry Adams (1838–1918) wrote in a letter (1903) to a British friend (Charles Gaskell):

> Forty years ago, our friends always explained things and had the cosmos down to a point, [with] Darwin and Charles Lyell. Now they say they don't believe there is any explanation, or that you can choose between half-a-dozen, all correct . . . . Every generalisation we settled forty years ago is abandoned . . . . Science has given up the whole fabric of cause and effect. Even time-sequence is beginning to be threatened. I should not at all wonder if someone should not upset time. As for space, it is upset already. We did that sixty years ago, with electricity.

The **special theory of relativity**, or special relativity, maintains that all measurements of space and time are relative. This is not just a matter of perspective, like looking at a draftsman's ruler or waiting in line. A ruler may be twelve inches in length, but if one looks at it from a distance or at an angle it appears considerably shorter. An hour spent waiting at the Registry of Motor Vehicles seems infinitely longer than an hour spent listening to Mozart. Einstein's results are something else again. Consider a man bouncing a basketball. Suppose it moves with perfect regularity and in a perfectly vertical line—three feet down, three feet up, over and over, exactly one bounce per second. The ball therefore travels a total of six feet per second. But now imagine that the man is standing on a flatcar on a train that is moving down the track as he bounces the basketball. To an observer watching from a platform thirty feet away, the ball moves not in a vertical line but at an angle to the vertical because of the horizontal movement of the train. Moreover, the ball turns out to travel at a different speed—say, five feet diagonally down and five feet diagonally up, for a total of ten feet per second.

The special theory shows that this is not simply a difference of perspective. The ball does not just "seem" to be traveling at one speed and not the other; the special theory holds that the ball is actually traveling six feet per second *and* ten feet per second, depending on the observer, *at the same time*. Time and space are elastic and should be conceived as different facets of a single dimension that Einstein called **space-time**.[5]

---

[5] Einstein's special theory of relativity is the basis of the idea that nothing can go faster than the speed of light.

Space-time A photo of the Andromeda galaxy (also known as M31) taken through a Celestron 80ED telescope with a one-hour exposure. Andromeda is a spiral galaxy roughly 2.5 million light-years from Earth and contains over a trillion stars. Andromeda and our own Milky Way galaxy are drawing nearer to one another and will collide in about 4.5 billion years.

The **general theory of relativity**, or general relativity, describes gravity's relationship to space-time. Newton had posited gravity as an attraction between all particles with mass, but he offered no insight into what gravity actually is. After all, why would two bodies hundreds of billions of miles apart feel attracted toward each other? Newton admitted defeat on this question and happily returned to his calculations on how great the force would be. To Einstein, gravity is not a force at all. It is simply the name we give to an experience we have of space-time. A person in a stationary elevator can "feel gravity." It is the sensation of the floor of the elevator, preventing him from falling into the Earth's core (or at least into the basement). But if now the elevator began to accelerate upward, even if there were no Earth below pulling the person down, he would feel the exact same sensation of the floor pushing upward. In fact, he could not tell if the elevator was moving or not. Einstein called this relationship of motion to gravity the *equivalence principle.*

In general relativity, every vantage point in the universe, whether moving or stationary, is as valid as every other vantage point. The laws of physics will look the same in each. There is no fixed and absolute center to anything: to space, to motion, to "gravity," to time. Everything is relative. From the point of view of a spectator, a football thrown by a quarterback appears to arch smoothly upward, reach a zenith, then arch smoothly downward into the receiver's arms. That is true, says Einstein—but it is also true that the ball travels in a straight line through a space-time that is curved. It is the curvature of space-time that gives the impression of the ball's rising and falling. Adding to the wonder and confusion of it all, adds Einstein, it is also true, from a different vantage point, that the ball is not moving at all. The curved space-time of the universe rushing past it gives the impression of the ball in flight. Each observation is equally valid.

Planck received the Nobel Prize in Physics in 1918, Einstein in 1923. Their ideas have been confirmed by thousands of experiments and to unimaginable degrees of precision. They were sufficient to upend the entire scientific understanding of the cosmos, but taken together they add yet another level of confusion: quantum theory and general relativity, as we currently understand them at least, cannot both be true—or at least they have so far resisted the unity of a single theory that gives the right answers. Much of the research done in the hundred years since Planck and Einstein has been devoted to reconciling them. Einstein himself spent the last twenty years of his life trying to determine a "unified field theory" that would harmonize these theories. Efforts continue in ways more open to the paradoxes of quantum theory than Einstein himself ever was, with string theory today.

While immensely sophisticated and math-ematically complex, these ideas quickly entered 20th-century culture. Everything thought by scien-tists for three thousand years had been shown to be false, and the two new truths that prove it actually conflict with one another. A story like that is hard to keep secret. What people took away from the new physics was the broader idea of relativity—no fixed points, no absolute time, no absolute space. And the more we learned about the universe, the more immense, confusing, unexpected, and for some more frightening it seemed to be. An English physicist, Paul Dirac (1902–1984), described the instant popularity of Planck's and Einstein's work this way:[6]

> What people took away from the new physics was the broader idea of relativity—no fixed points, no absolute time, no absolute space. And the more we learned about the universe, the more immense, confusing, unexpected, and for some more frightening it seemed to be.

> It is easy to see the reason for this tremendous impact. We had just been through a terrible and very serious war.... Everyone wanted to forget it. And then relativity came along as a wonderful idea leading us to a new domain of thought. It was an escape from the war.... Relativity was a subject that everybody felt himself competent to write about in a general philosophical way. The philosophers just put forward the view that everything had to be considered relative to something else, and [then] they rather claimed that they had known about relativity all along.

Dirac was being ungenerous to philosophers, but he was right to point to the sim-ilarities between modern science and contemporary philosophy. There too, the focus was on the futility of finding absolute and permanent truth. Unlike the physicists, though, the philosophers simply gave up.

---

6   Dirac was also the first physicist to put forth the idea of antimatter.

THE WILL TO POWER

Like physics, philosophy in the 20th century was insightful and brilliant. Like physics, too, it has often been exceedingly difficult to understand. Often, however, it has been depressing, and that is not an unfortunate side effect. It is the work's very point. Coming down from the heights of idealism, its thrust has been the randomness, contingency, and disorder of life. Modern philosophy has argued for the inability of our minds to comprehend reality—and the slipperiness of language in trying to discuss it. It is not a pretty picture.

The fundamental division is between analytic and rationalist philosophies. **Analytic philosophy** stresses the need for close and careful reasoning. Analytic philosophies have had a dizzying array of names, including symbolic logic, logical positivism, functionalism, and eliminative materialism. **Rationalist philosophy** stresses instead the movement of the human mind itself. Rationalist philosophies, too, have splintered into a vast number of specialties, including phenomenology, existentialism, hermeneutics, neo-Marxism, structuralism, and post-structuralism. In general, the analytic philosophers have been English speaking, while rationalist philosophy has dominated Continental thought. What they share is a 19th-century inheritance—a purposeless universe and a view of human life that is, in the absence of a divine Creator, without essential function or meaning.

The key figure in the new bleakness was Friedrich Nietzsche (1844–1900), the prophet of God's death. Although little known in his lifetime, Nietzsche's work advanced the nihilistic philosophy of the age, even though he himself rejected the extreme skepticism known as **nihilism**. To Nietzsche, human life without God is tragically meaningless. Every individual's existence is a cold crack of light between two eternities of darkness, and nothing that happens during that brief crack matters in any absolute sense. We are simply random gatherings of molecules that cohere and experience consciousness for a short time before dissolving again into nothingness. Not a very sunny view. "Hope in [a supposed] reality is the greatest evil that can befall anyone," he writes, "for all it does is prolong one's agony." But Nietzsche's point is to rouse us to action, not to drive us to collapse in despair. This is exactly where he parts company with the nihilists: we should not simply accept the world's randomness but actually do something about it. Let's not make the agony of our existence even worse by being stupid while we are here. Let's not tell ourselves comforting lies or live by values we do not genuinely believe in. Instead, we should have the courage to face awful reality as it is and live authentically while we live.

> To Nietzsche, human life without God is tragically meaningless. Every individual's existence is a cold crack of light between two eternities of darkness, and nothing that happens during that brief crack matters in any absolute sense.

How do we know what is authentic? As usual, it is easier to identify what is false than what is true. One thing that is clearly false, Nietzsche argues, is the Western belief in democracy and the equality of mankind. In our heart of hearts, he demands, we know that we do not believe in this idea. One has only to look around—at one's coworkers, at crowds on a bus, at the people lined up in grocery stores, at mobs gathered at a ball game. If we are honest, we will admit to ourselves that most people are stupid. In contrast, democracy makes sense only if one assumes that people are all equally capable of making intelligent decisions about how to govern society. We should therefore throw democratic ideas and institutions on the trash heap. Go ahead and admit it, Nietzsche urges. Life is already brief, purposeless, and meaningless. Why spend the little time we have living in a political system that gives fools an equal share of influence? Why should

Believing in Democracy   A group of night-school students, many of them new immigrants, saluting the American flag. Note that the flag has only forty-eight stars; Alaska and Hawaii both gained statehood in 1959. (Arizona became the 48th state in 1912.) Roughly a quarter-million immigrants received citizenship per year through the 1920s and the first half of the 1930s. Fear of Fascist and Communist infiltration drove down the number to a fifth of that from 1935 to 1945, but by 1950 that number rose to a quarter-million per year again. The number of new citizens per year then held steady at that level until 1970, when it began another period of rapid growth.

we refuse to acknowledge what we all actually think? Just to be nice? That sounds pleasant, he says, but niceness is no basis for a philosophy, except to fools:

> What bizarre distortions and lies people put up with! It never ceases to amaze anyone who has eyes to see. "Oh, look! Isn't everything around us so cheery and free, so easy and simple! Isn't it wonderful how we have given ourselves a free pass to experience everything that is superficial! . . . And oh! how we figured out from the dawn of time how to keep ourselves ignorant so that we might enjoy a degree of freedom and escape from care, feel ourselves to be brave and cheerful, and to actually enjoy existence!" *(Beyond Good and Evil [1886])*

What is another idea to reject? Christianity. All religions to Nietzsche (the child of a family of Lutheran ministers) are just emotional security blankets.

And Christianity—at least in what he saw it in its late 19th-century form—is particular guilty because of its very niceness. The Christianity of his time, he finds, preaches what he terms a "slave-morality" of meekness and passivity, of self-denial and contempt for strength. As he put in a late book,

> I say that [this] Christianity is the greatest single curse on mankind, [its] most gargantuan and deep-seated depravity, . . . the most enduring blemish on the human race, . . . for it favors everything that is weak, base, and malformed . . . . Some call it the "religion of compassion,"' but I say that compassion negates all the fundamental instincts that contribute to the vitality and meaning of life! *(The Twilight of the Idols [1888]).*

Nietzsche was not as resolutely anti-Christian through most of his life as most people think. He hated Victorian piety as intellectually soft, but he retained an emotional attachment to, though not an actual belief in, the intellectually and morally rigorous Christianity he had grown up with.[7] His rants on the need to annihilate every vestige of Christianity date to the last two years of his life, when the onset of his mental illness was undeniable: he signed letters as "Nietzsche Caesar," filled wastebaskets with torn up money, declared his intention to establish a world government, and vowed to murder all anti-Semites.

Regardless, reading Nietzsche is a visceral experience. He shouts, curses, and ridicules. He uses coarse language and offers ugly analogies. He aims to shock. His books offer no calm, rational arguments; instead they consist of series of independent passages, each written at a white heat and usually in a single burst of inspiration. He writes in a confrontational and emotional style, like a firefighter trying to hurry people out of a burning building that is on the brink of collapse. Life is a state of continual emergency, and Nietzsche understood that we are our truest selves during emergencies. We may not be our best selves, but we are truest to what we value most. We are willing to be selfish if selfishness is called for and ready to bark out orders if necessary. We are focused on what has genuine meaning to us.

Nietzsche offers no solace to his readers and insists that we stop pretending that everything is fine. We must stop telling ourselves that everything is in God's hands, that history is progress, that democracy and capitalism will make the world better, that all people are created equal, and that Christian platitudes can relieve

---

[7]   Nietzsche, the prophet of the death of God, it turns out, was sentimentally fond of Christmas trees.

human suffering. We must stop saying that the West is right to bring "civilization" (not to mention schools, electricity, and railroads) to the savages around the earth. The only things he recognizes as absolutely good are the desire for life and the urge to create. There is hope of an ennobling life, with purpose, only in the instinctive human yearning to renew existence.

Thus he champions the **will to power**—the passionate striving to make meaning and leave a mark on the world. The phrase sounds ominously like a prelude to 20th-century fascism—and it has often been interpreted that way. Yet Nietzsche, despite his love of violent vocabulary and strident prose, was neither a fascist nor a sadist. (As a medical orderly during the Franco-Prussian War he regularly fainted at the sight of blood.) By the will to power, he meant the *creative drive* or *creativity*. In one of his notebooks, he discusses his philosophical ideas in relation to recent discoveries in physics:

> The triumphant idea of force—namely, the thing by means of which our physicists have invented God and God's invention of the world—needs elaboration. It needs an interior element, one I call "the will to power." An insatiable desire to enact power, to wield it and use it, to spur creation.

Nietzsche envisions a world in which those with the will to power would emerge as natural leaders, whether in politics, intellectual life, or art. These **supermen** (*Übermenschen*) would do a better job of it than the general masses. They would also provide inspiration and models for people everywhere to tap into their own creative drives. Such a scheme might make for a messy, conflict-prone world—but, Nietzsche asks, isn't that the world we live in now? In the world of supermen, the conflicts would at least be noble ones. We could set aside the shameful struggles over wealth and social status and the hypocritical moralism of Mark Twain's era of incredible rottenness.

THE RHODES COLOSSUS
STRIDING FROM CAPE TOWN TO CAIRO.

Super-man?   Cecil Rhodes (1853-1906) as viewed by Punch magazine (December, 1892) as the colossus of British imperialism in Africa, from Cairo to Cape Town. "I would colonize the moon, if I could," he once said.

LOGIC AND LANGUAGE

Western philosophers after Nietzsche had experienced the death of God and of classical physics. They had witnessed the unnerving strangeness and relativity of the universe develop from a rarified scientific theory to a general world view. Many, too, were disgusted by the aggressive, industrial, and imperialistic culture around them. This seemed, on the whole, to be the greatest and most thorough fracturing of the European mind since the 17th century, when John Donne complained, "'Tis all in pieces, / All coherence gone." What were they to do? In general, they turned their gaze away from the world and toward the inner tools we use to try to make sense of it. If the world makes no fixed sense, they argued, then we should turn attention to the question of how logic and language ever made us think there was a real order to the cosmos in the first place. The very word "reality" in 20th-century culture, both high and low, started regularly to appear inside quotation marks.

In the Anglophone tradition, major Analytical philosophers, such as Bertrand Russell (1872–1970) and his student Ludwig Wittgenstein (1889–1951), focused on the structures and functions of logic and language.[8] These are, after all, the

Making Sense out of the Shards of Reality   *Logicomix: An Epic Search for Truth* is a graphic novel by Apostolos Doxiadis, published in 2009, that narrates and illustrates Bertrand Russell's attempt to find some form of absolute truth in the philosophical foundations of mathematics. Here he debates (and as in real life, was tormented by) his most brilliant student, Ludwig Wittgenstein.

---

[8]   Wittgenstein was an Austrian Jew who wrote most of his work in German; but since he both studied and later taught at Cambridge University, lectured in English, and wrote at least some of his work in English, I include him among the Anglophone philosophers. Certainly his lifelong emphasis on the relationship between logic and language places him in that tradition. Indeed, he is one of its main shapers.

tools with which humans try to create a reality out of a messy universe. Idealism had regarded the world, much like Newtonian physics, as a vast, comprehensive, interlocking system. Analytical philosophers, by contrast, approached the topic more modestly. Given that there is no grand system, what sense can we make out of the shards of reality within our grasp? If, for example, there are no universal standards of goodness, justice, or beauty, is there any legitimacy in holding simple beliefs about them? If goodness is relative, then why is it good to offer help to people in need? Why is it just to punish harshly someone who commits a violent crime but to punish less severely someone who commits a nonviolent one? If beauty is a relative construct, then can it be said that a piano sonata by Beethoven is "better" than a tune by a Dixieland jazz band? To answer these questions, the analytical philosophers insisted, one must not investigate the ideal concepts of Goodness, Justice, and Beauty—a hopeless activity, in any case. Instead, one should analyze specific propositions about people in need, about behavior (and misbehavior), and about art.

Take those sentences again. What do they propose? Does goodness consist in the help *given* to people in need or simply in *offering* help? Must the people receiving help *know* that they need it? Suppose they need help but do not know it, or do not desire it. Can any assistance offered them still be considered good? If so, under what conditions, and why? The only way to understand an act of goodness, then, is to wrestle with meanings. In the second proposition, about crime, one must wrestle not only with the adjective *just* (as in "it is just to punish violent offenders") but also with the phrase *it is*. What do we mean when we say that something "is" something else? For example, when we say, "Snow is white," are we stating that snowness and whiteness are identical? If so, then is it also true that the white sheets on my bed are made of snow? Or are we saying that snow uses whiteness, possesses it, shares it, or enacts it? What, exactly, *is* the meaning of *is*?

Methods like these use language in order to understand language, which risks philosophy itself becoming a kind of mere wordplay. To avoid that, many analytical philosophers turned instead to the tools of mathematics and symbolic logic. Reduce language whenever possible to sets of mathematical symbols and turn sentences into formulas. Their philosophical writings became highly technical. For example, Wittgenstein describes a relation between two hypothetical statements (*propositions* in the preferred analytical term to use) in this way:

> We must not say, "The complex sign '*aRb*' says '*a* stands in relation R to *b*;'" but we must say, "That '*a*' stands in a certain relation to '*b*' says that *aRb*."

Such thinkers sought greater precision in philosophical thinking, but precision usually came at the expense of accessibility. In Russell's 1905 essay "On

Denoting," to choose another example, he defined the proposition "x is a mountain" as the symbol Mx, and the proposition "x is golden" as the symbol Gx. He could then confidently state "A golden mountain does not exist" in this way:

$$\sim[(\exists x)(Mx \ \& \ Gx) \ \& \ \forall y((My \ \& \ Gy) \rightarrow y = x)]$$

This may be correct, but who can tell? Russell also wrote, along with Alfred North Whitehead (1861–1947), a three-volume work on the foundations of mathematics. Titled *Principia Mathematica* (1911–1913) after the great work by Sir Isaac Newton, it uses just this type of symbolic logic throughout more than a thousand dense pages in order to come to the conclusion—now logically proven as never before—that one plus one equals two.[9] Analytical philosophy did not intentionally keep common people at a distance, but it often came across as disdainful of nonspecialists. These philosophers employed a highly technical style because they saw themselves as scientists rather than humanists.

FROM PHENOMENOLOGY TO EXISTENTIALISM

Continental philosophers could be just as brilliant and just as opaque, but in a very different way. They studied the ways in which we experience things—a method known as **phenomenology**. While there may or may not be a universal ideal called Beauty, we have all experienced beautiful things—a sunset, a Bach cantata or a favorite song, a poem, whatever. Analytical philosophers might busy themselves dissecting the phrase "Cantata 199 by Bach is beautiful." Phenomenologists instead set out to study how we experience the music. What physiological effects does it produce as we listen? What memories does it invoke? What thoughts do we have during its performance? What is the flow of our emotions as one passage leads into another—or our sensation(s) after the music stops?

Phenomenology is based on the belief that, whereas the world may or may not be rationally ordered, our reactions to it are—or at least they can be. Phenomenology is *subjective*, meaning that it begins from the point of view of someone's experience. It is also *intentional*, meaning that it examines the how and why of the experience. The great figure at the turn of the century was Edmund Husserl (1859–1938), a German-speaking Jew born in what is now the Czech Republic. He spent his career at the universities of Göttingen and of Freiburg. His two-volume *Logical Investigations* (1900–1901) set the tone for Continental philoso-

---

9 As Russell dryly put it on the last page of the third volume of his master work, this now-certain truth that $1 + 1 = 2$ "may prove useful."

phy for the entire century. Among those who were either directly or indirectly his students were Martin Heidegger (1889–1976), Edith Stein (Saint Teresa Benedicta of the Cross, 1891–1942), Jean-Paul Sartre (1905–1980), Hannah Arendt (1906–1975), Karol Wojtyła (Pope John Paul II, 1920–2005), and Jacques Derrida (1930–2004).

As Husserl described it, phenomenology was based on two key ideas. First, we can only truly know our perceptions of things rather than the things themselves. Perhaps the thing itself may not exist; all we can say for certain is that we have a perception of it.[10] Second, our perceptions have a structure. With phenomenology, therefore, we no longer philosophize about the world but about ourselves only. Nevertheless, it turns out we are pretty fascinating. Our perceptions, emotions, memories, intuitions, and modes of thinking are endlessly complex, but they betray hitherto unknown structures and patterns. Phenomenology emphasizes the ways in which humans are hardwired to interpret experience. Our minds, to borrow a somewhat dated computer analogy, are not blank disks that the world fills with data; rather our mental disks are formatted in particular ways that determine how the data will be stored, reclaimed, and used. Husserl's ideas led in time to the notion of **structuralism**: our lives occur within sets of structures that shape our every experience. These structures can be biological, cultural, economic, geographical, historical, linguistic, political, psychological, religious, or even sexual. Together, they provide a kind of scaffolding from which we view and participate in the world.

Another philosophy to develop from phenomenology is **existentialism**. Existentialists agree with the structuralist foundation of phenomenology. However, they believe, this does not by itself explain everything about human nature—or even about any individual human's nature. We still have choices. As a white, male, middle-aged, middle-class, Christian, university-educated, Midwestern-born but now Boston-based, heterosexual, politically liberal, suburban, American, married history professor, I might be predisposed to react in a predictable way in any new situation. Yet I still have unique personal desires and inclinations, and I can exert a free will. I can make of my life what I want of it, to a degree. The structures into which I was born, or into which I have grown, determine probabilities, not certainties. My lived life, my "reality" (those quotation marks again), is whatever I make of my existence. In the formula made famous by Jean-Paul Sartre, "existence precedes essence": my nature is the product of

---

[10]   Husserl's insight harmonizes with Einstein's: all that exists is our perception of space-time.

my choices in life, not vice versa. It is easy to trace these ideas back to Nietzsche, the great champion of the creative will, and it is easy to see, ironically, how the existentialist view proved so attractive to religious thinkers of the 20th century, especially Protestant Christian ones. Karl Barth (1886–1968), Rudolf Bultmann (1884–1976), Paul Tillich (1886–1965), and Reinhold Niebuhr (1892–1971) are leading examples.

To Sartre, however, the existentialist view of life entails a certain horror. Life is contingent and depends on our choices and actions in order to come into being; reality is what we make. And awareness of that inspires an overwhelming sense of moral duty that he described as a philosophical nausea. *Nausea* is, in fact, the title of Sartre's best-known novel, published in 1938. Written in the form of a diary, it relates the anxieties of a young historian trying to finish a book about an 18th-century political figure. The novel contrasts the Enlightenment era that he studies—with its confidence in reason, order, and progress—and the directionless confusion of the young historian's personal life in the 20th century. The result is anxiety and despair. The awareness of having to create his own reality is too much for him.

> I live alone, absolutely alone, never speaking to anyone.... When living alone, one forgets what it is to speak. Possibilities in life disappear along with one's friends. Events float past one; sometimes someone suddenly appears, says something, then goes away.... All I can get out of these tragic solitudes of mine is a small amount of a kind of empty purity.

He admires but is frightened by people who live in the world.

> People who live in the world have figured out how to look at themselves in the mirror and see themselves as they appear to their friends.... The Nausea isn't inside me—it's out there. I can feel it, in the walls, in my suspenders. It's everywhere around me.... Nothing really happens in life. Scenes changes, people come and go, that's all. Days follow one another, days after days, with no rhyme or reason, an endless, monotonous sequence.... Everything changes, though, when you talk about life, though hardly anyone notices, because people think we speak the truth. As though there was a single true story in life! Things happen the way they happen, but we talk about them altogether differently.

Toward the end, the narrator starts to recognize that life's meaninglessness can present an opportunity to create a meaning of his own. He can choose to think, to act, and to feel. "The feeling of Nausea hasn't left me," he concludes, "and I don't

Sartre Demonstrating against Racism After 1945 Sartre became a political activist in the Marxist vein, and although he never formally joined the Communist Party he was nevertheless an ardent, if naïve, supporter of Stalin, China's Mao Zedong, and Cuba's Fidel Castro. Here he joins a group of youths protesting discrimination against France's growing immigrant population.

expect it to; but it's no longer a burden, a sense of sickness, or a passing spasm. It is me."

Existentialism is a call to duty. It demands that we take action and make something of the world, or at least of our lives in it, and many of the leading existentialists led lives of deep commitment to political and social causes. On the other hand, it could also be used to lend an aura of faux sophistication to lives of shallow languor; to do nothing intentionally, like the narrator in *Nausea*, as an expression of one's philosophical depth.

> Existentialism is a call to duty. It demands that we take action and make something of the world, or at least of our lives in it, and many of the leading existentialists led lives of deep commitment to political and social causes.

THE ILLNESS OF WESTERN SOCIETY

Sartre's novel appeared in 1938, but its anxiety had roots in Western society back at least to the 1880s. Crowded into industrial cities, choking on coal smoke and chemical fumes, urban Europeans began to show a new degree of concern simply for their health. They spent long hours at hard physical labor or hunched over desks in clerical offices. Governments churned

A Scout Is Clean   "A scout is clean" in mind, body, and deed, according to the regulations of the Boy Scouts organization founded by Robert Baden-Powell (1857-1941), a retired lieutenant general in the British Army. His *Scouting for Boys: A Handbook for Instruction in Good Citizenship* (1908) was one of the bestselling books of the 20th century. The rapid rise of the Boy Scouts and the Girl Scouts (Girl Guides, in Britain and Canada) illustrates the patriotic passions of the era. This trading card—distributed, ironically, in packages of cigarettes—comes from 1929.

out hundreds of reports on public health; newspapers reported on outbreaks of diseases. Public schools began to distribute milk and lunches to students; they more often included physical exercise in their daily curricula. The movement to create public parks and sporting fields grew; so did amateur leagues for soccer, rowing, boxing, and racing. Popular guides like *Mrs. Beeton's Book of Household Management* (see chapter 18) covered hygiene, first aid, nutrition, and exercise. New associations like the Boy Scouts and Girl Scouts promoted fitness and outdoor activity, while bicycling clubs and gymnasia promoted new sports like basketball and tennis. The better-off paid equal attention to mental health. Spas dotted the map, and the new field of psychology burgeoned.

Many critics of turn-of-the-century culture used the imagery and language of illness to describe what they saw around them. European society was "disintegrating, corroding, as a result of the decay of civilized life," proclaimed the first edition of *Le Décadent*, published in Paris in 1886. Henrik Ibsen's drama *Ghosts* (1881) suggested a moral rot in European culture analogous to advanced syphilis, prompting one critic to describe the play as an open sewer. Arthur Schnitzler used the same metaphor in his 1900 play *La Ronde* ("A Circle Dance"), in which pairs of lovers meet in various locales around Vienna, before or after their sexual encounters. Schnitzler's lovers come from every social class, from the Austrian aristocracy to lowly prostitutes, and they portray the moral decadence that so many thought endemic to the time. The novels *Against the Grain* (*À rebours*,

1884) by J. K. Huysmans and *The Picture of Dorian Gray* (1890) by Oscar Wilde both chronicle, in lushly lurid language, the physical and spiritual decay of their protagonists. The popular Welsh writer Arthur Machen (1863–1947) exploited themes of degeneration and sickness in horror stories like "The Great God Pan" (1894) and fantasy novels like *The Hill of Dreams* (1907). Tuberculosis—generally known as "consumption" at the time—appeared time and again in novels, plays, and operas whose heroes, antiheroes, and love interests waste away in settings of physical and emotional rot. *La Bohème* "The Bohemian Girl"; 1896), an opera by Giacomo Puccini (1854–1924), traces the doomed love of a consumptive artist in a Parisian garret in sumptuous music. The novel *Buddenbrooks* (1901), by Thomas Mann (1875–1955), chronicles the decline of German society through several generations of a physically and spiritually sickly mercantile family. Mann's *Tristan* (1903) and *The Magic Mountain* (1924) are set in a tuberculosis sanatorium.

European medicine identified women as vulnerable to hysteria. This supposed female disorder—named after the Greek word for the uterus—accounted for everything from nervousness and loss of appetite to general irritability and abdominal pain. Several medical journals reported that as many as one-quarter of all women were afflicted. Plays and novels of the time are filled with scenes of female fainting and otherwise inexplicable discontent. Along with rest and avoiding any activity that might rouse emotions, one common treatment was a "pelvic massage." (The physician would keep this up until the women experienced a "hysterical paroxysm," to rebalance their nervous energies.)[11]

One of the chief causes of hysteria, experts announced, was the tendency of women to veer from their traditional roles as wives and mothers. The development of a woman's mind through education redirected the natural energies and fluids that kept the womb healthy, causing it to atrophy. "If we wish woman to fulfill the task of motherhood, she cannot possess a masculine brain," wrote the eminent German neurologist Paul Julius Möbius (1853–1907). "If a woman's female abilities were developed in the same way as those of the male, her maternal organs would suffer and [she would] end up as a repulsive and useless hybrid."

With so many voices bearing witness to the illness of Western society, it is not surprising that other voices answered—with some unexpected diagnoses and treatments all their own. Political and social critics denounced the policies that had given the West control of much of the world but had cost it its soul. Chemistry had to reinvent itself after the discovery of new particles and new forms of energy. Physics replaced the Newtonian order with two new systems, quantum

---

[11] Doctors turned eagerly to electric vibrators to treat more patients with hysteria per day. "Aids that every woman appreciates," ran the slogan in a catalog that sold the devices.

theory and relativity, that seemed to contradict one another. Philosophy almost gave up on the external world to focus on our modes of perception, and literature described a culture suffering from terminal illness. And a new science of the mind emerged: psychology.

SEXUALITY AND PSYCHOANALYSIS

Where there is illness, there will be physicians, or those acting as such, to treat the afflicted. Psychology emerged in the 1870s and grew rapidly both in sophistication and in popularity. The existence of an unconscious or subconscious mind dates at least to 1889, with the work of the French psychologist Pierre Janet (1859–1947), and allusions to a mind within the mind can be traced back to the Enlightenment. But the idea gained new power with the work of Sigmund Freud (1856–1939).

After completing his medical studies, Freud specialized as a neurologist and general psychologist. In 1886 he married and set up a private practice in his hometown of Vienna. Freud first used hypnosis as a means to access the inner thoughts of his patients, but he noticed that its effects were temporary; besides, most of his patients spoke quite freely without it. He developed instead **psychoanalysis**, the technique of encouraging free association, and he saw meaningful patterns not only in what his patients said but also in what they avoided saying. From this he developed the concept of *repression*: certain thoughts were being held back not only from open expression but even from the patients' conscious thinking. And many of these repressed thoughts turned out to be sexual. Freud hypothesized that neuroses resulted from the patient's inability to address basic erotic instincts.

By the late 1890s, Freud had begun to elaborate a new theory of consciousness. For Freud, our waking minds are in continual dialogue with our unspoken urges, and equally powerful social and cultural norms regulate those instinctive drives. In Freud's terminology, one's conscious mind, the *ego*, was a product of and a counterbalance to two additional processes. One was our biological instinct for sexual pleasure, the *id*. The other was the ethical conscience, the *superego*—consisting of social norms, religious teachings, and cultural values. Freud realized that he could test his theory by studying not only his patients' free-associative ramblings but also their unconscious ones—in their dreams. What is a dream, after all, but our minds still thinking and talking while our bodies rest?

In 1899 he published what he considered his greatest work, *The Interpretation of Dreams*, which argues that dreams originate as wish fulfillment. Common moral standards dictate that one ought not to act on every sexual impulse. In response, our superegos repress these feelings without our conscious effort. To Freud, however, these impulses are never annihilated; they simply find expression

Freud's Couch   This is the original couch used in Sigmund Freud's psychoanalytic practice in Vienna, where much of the clinical work was done that led to the formulation of his theories of the human mind.

in indirect ways—chiefly through our dreams. But even in the dream state, our superegos remain active, which explains why erotic desires are often expressed in our dreams through disjointed images, dialogues, or sensations. Our ids also find delight and release in racy jokes (when in safe company) and "Freudian slips" of the tongue. (The formal term is *parapraxis*—plural *parapraxes*.)

Freud's *Three Essays in the Theory of Sexuality* in 1905 insisted on sex as the primal and primary human instinct, and it provoked a storm of protest. Victorian society was never as prudish as people often think it was; polite society did not relish open discussions of sexual matters, but it permitted them within the limits of propriety. *Three Essays* rankled not simply because it dealt with sexuality but because of what it said about sex.

Freud describes infantile sexuality as progressing through stages. The first is an intense focus on the delight derived from bodily contact with one's parents, in nursing or cuddling. The second, the "anal stage," finds relief in control of the lower digestive tract. In the third stage, the child becomes fascinated with the genitals. This "Oedipal stage,"

> To a class-obsessed world like Freud's, the notion that a duke experiences the same mental processes as a ditch-digger was unpardonable.

however, was the most shocking of all. In Freud's theory, when a child becomes aware of genital pleasure, a complex chain reaction sets in—culminating in a son's desire to supplant his father as the object of his mother's attention. In the parallel "Electra" stage, a daughter desires to supplant her mother in her father's affection. It is not that all children desire to have sexual intercourse with their parents. Rather, at some basic level, one's parents are the source of physical pleasure from the moment of one's birth, and hence we associate body pleasure with our parents. At puberty, however, our bodies begin to feel an entirely new type of pleasure stimulus, one which our species is hardwired to dissociate from our parents. (This is what he meant as a taboo.) Learning to accept this new body pleasure as something wholly distinct from the body pleasure we associate in our minds with our parents is part of the inner conflict of adolescence.

Freud labored for years to earn acceptance of his theories. Despite his growing clinical practice and dedicated disciples, the psychological world resisted his focus on the role of sex in shaping human nature. Most people are still uncomfortable with his model. Freud is saying, after all, that everyone is driven by instinct; everyone's conscience represses true nature; everyone's consciousness has the same fundamental structure. To a class-obsessed world like Freud's, the notion that a duke experiences the same mental processes as a ditchdigger was unpardonable.

The turning point came in 1909, when Freud accepted an invitation to deliver a series of public lectures in the United States, later published as *Five Lectures on Psychoanalysis*. They helped correct the popular image of him as a sex-obsessed madman. His *Introductory Lectures on Psychoanalysis* (1917) also secured his reputation. His polite manner and the straightforward, accessible rigor of his thinking won people over and made them willing at least to consider his approach.

Many people wrote to Freud, from this time on, with questions or entreaties. One of his most famous letters (1935) was this response, in English, to an American woman's inquiry about her son:

> Dear Mrs. [X].
> I gather from your letter that your son is a homosexual. I am most impressed by the fact, that you do not mention this term yourself in your information about him. May I question you why you avoid it? Homosexuality is assuredly no advantage, but it is nothing to be ashamed of, no vice, no degradation, it cannot be classified as an illness; we consider it to be a variation of the sexual function produced by a certain arrest of sexual development. Many highly respectable individuals of ancient and modern times have been homosexuals, several of the greatest men among them (Plato, Michelangelo, Leonardo da Vinci, etc.). It is a great

injustice to persecute homosexuality as a crime and cruelty too. If you do not believe me, read the books of Havelock Ellis.

By asking me if I can help, you mean, I suppose, if I can abolish homosexuality and make normal heterosexuality take its place. The answer is, in a general way, we cannot promise to achieve it. In a certain number of cases we succeed in developing the blighted germs of heterosexual tendencies, which are present in every homosexual; in the majority of cases it is no longer possible. It is a question of the quality and the age of the individual. The result of treatment cannot be predicted. What analysis can do for your son runs in a different line. If he is unhappy, neurotic, torn by conflicts, inhibited in his social life, analysis may bring him harmony, peace of mind, full efficiency, whether he remains a homosexual or gets changed. If you make up your mind he should have analysis with me—I don't expect you will—he has to come over to Vienna. I have no intention of leaving here. However, don't neglect to give me your answer.

Sincerely yours with kind wishes,

Freud

P.S. I did not find it difficult to read your handwriting. Hope you will not find my writing and my English a harder task.

BEYOND THE PLEASURE PRINCIPLE

As his fame grew, Freud continued to revise his conclusions. Most significantly, he argued that an instinct toward aggression challenges sex for primacy. Aggression originates as the instinct for self-preservation. In a life-or-death situation, people will resort to violence. Aggression also represents an expression of the sexual instinct: to secure access to a mate, human behavior ranges from competitive mating rituals to actual violence. Every act of creation is also an act of destruction. To grow a crop, one must first rip out existing plant life.

In 1920 he published *Beyond the Pleasure Principle*, a treatise on what he called the "death drive." This drive represents the counterweight to the life-generating sexual impulse, but is also in some ways just another expression of it. Sexual enjoyment involves stimulation of our physical senses and mental energies—and yet there is a countervailing pleasure in the calming of the senses after great excitement. We experience the pleasure of relaxation not only after a bout of sex but also after a hectic day's work or battling heavy traffic. The desire for death is the purest and most complete craving for calm after the strain and clamor of life. It is a longing to return to the inanimate state from which we all originate.

Freud came slowly to the theory of aggression. In fact, it took a world war to convince him of humanity's innate barbarism. His work challenged, thrilled, amused, and revolted people, and it still does. Psychologists today have moved far beyond Freud's original model and have rejected much of it; it is seldom taught in psychology departments. However, the effect of his ideas is still felt throughout Western culture. He stands with Darwin, Marx, and Einstein as one of the most influential thinkers of the last two hundred years. (Imagine *that* conversation!) He can even be called a structuralist, since he believed that human consciousness has an order. We think, react, value, and believe according to principles whose workings follow logical patterns. At the same time, he is an irrationalist, since he sees human nature as at the mercy of forces it can neither understand nor control. We are masses of sensation, fear, longing, and anger. What we call reason—even civilization itself—is only the imperfect casing we have erected to contain and control these instincts.

Freud insisted that Western civilization was sick—literally, clinically sick. He saw neuroses all around him, in depressions, phobias, anxiety disorders, and psychoses. He began by analyzing and treating individual cases, but the horrors of the new century led him to psychoanalyze the culture itself. His late book-length essay titled *Civilization and Its Discontents* (1929) could with justice be called "Civilization and Everyone in It." It argues that to be civilized *is* to be unhappy. Civilized behavior begins in not giving expression to our most fundamental instincts. It means not having sex with every attractive person we encounter, not striking every person who raises our anger, and not always saying what we feel. It is the superego given social form. But no degree of civilized conduct can extinguish our creative and destructive instincts:

> Civilization exacts a heavy toll on man's sexuality and his instinct for aggression.... [Our natural instincts] are not to love our neighbor but to indulge our aggressive impulses upon him—whether, that is, to hurt him for labor, to use him to satisfy our sexual desires, to seize his possessions, to humiliate him, hit him, torture him, kill him.

And then the cage door snaps shut:

> Who has the audacity to deny this, in the face of all the facts of history?

For Freud, civilization cannot bring happiness. After five thousand years of effort, mankind appears no less unhappy than in the days of Hammurabi

The Death-Drive   Freudian theory had long insisted that Eros—the sexual drive—was the main motivating force in human life, but the experience of World War I led Freud to posit the existence of a second fundamental instinct—Thanatos, the death drive, by which he meant both the instinct of aggression toward others and the innate desire for the thrill of risk. This 1915 painting, *The Charge of the Lancers*, is by Umberto Boccioni, a leading artist of the Futurism movement.

the Babylonian. We are better fed, better educated, and possess more creature comforts, but could such things mask our true desires and our truest selves? Civilization itself seems an example of the comforting lie that Nietzsche warns against. Freud hardly wants to see a return to barbarism—although he lived to see it, with the rise of the Nazis and his subsequent escape to London. He wants only to relieve as much of the pain of civilized life as possible. And the only way to do so was to alleviate the crushing control of the superego. To Freud, the end of the 19th century saw the West trapped in a hypocritical sexual morality, an outworn religious culture, a decayed social structure, brutal imperialist governments, and callous capitalism. Society itself suffered from a neurosis that was to develop in the mid-20th century into a full-blown case of mass psychosis.

MODERNISM AND IRONY

Modernism was a movement from roughly 1860 to 1950 that began with the visual arts in Europe, with the group known now as the postimpressionists. It spread to literature, architecture, and finally to music. Like the Romanticism that characterized the start of the century, **modernism** resists easy definition since it reached so many different spheres. The sheer number of figures who made up the movement sets it apart from the past. Unlike other cultural eras and movements— art for art's sake, classicism, decadence, Enlightenment, impressionism, Romanticism, symbolism—the term modernism offers no hint of its core ideas or values. After all, it means nothing more than "the new." That, already, however, was a distinctive cry. The American poet and critic Ezra Pound (1885–1972) coined a slogan for a generation he called upon them to "make it new."

The closest thing to a manifesto of modernism appeared in 1863, in "The Painter of Modern Life," an essay by the French poet Charles Baudelaire (1821–1867) that defended Constantin Guys (1802–1892). Guys, as Baudelaire sees it, is determined to cast off old ways of expression and would demand radically new responses from viewers as well. Shock is part of the point, Baudelaire is honest enough to admit, but only a part. New techniques, expertly employed, will also produce new perspectives on truth and beauty: "He is in search of something indefinable—something we may perhaps term *modernity*." Many artists of the time painted even contemporary scenes with figures cloaked in medieval dress or Asian finery (then a popular fashion). "This is, on the face of it, utter laziness— pure and simple!"

The craft of art lies not in perpetuating old standards of beauty but in seeking out new ones. It risks mistakes of judgment in the quest to find new pleasures and new insights. Baudelaire cannot resist an example sure to offend his readers—an image of a common prostitute. To produce that image, painters would be false to their artistic calling if they used the same techniques as a Renaissance artist painting fabled Greek and Roman courtesans. The result would be more than historically inaccurate; it would be an artistic abomination.

Modernism demands the new, but it also rejects modernity. It rejects the inherited attitudes about how artists should work—in structure, technique, and presentation. And yet it also rejects the impersonality of conformist, mass-produced, and mass-consumed culture. The same ambivalence applies to the public at large. While nearly every leading modernist desired a wider following, most of them also railed at popular taste. They wanted an art and literature that could be understood and appreciated not just by the wealthy or the aristocracy, but they often dismissed the very audiences who viewed, read, or listened to their art.

The vogue of the misunderstood genius has a long history, and a great many modernists did not fit the image at all. However, they often set themselves apart

TABLE 23.1 **Modernism: Leading Artists**

VISUAL ARTISTS	LITERATURE	MUSIC
Paul Cézanne, 1839–1906		
Henri Rousseau, 1844–1910		
Paul Gauguin, 1848–1903		
Vincent van Gogh, 1853–1890	Joseph Conrad, 1857–1924	
Georges Seurat, 1859–1891	Constantine Cavafy, 1863–1933	
Gustav Klimt, 1862–1918	William Butler Yeats, 1865–1939	
Wassily Kandinsky, 1866–1944	Luigi Pirandello, 1867–1936	Claude Debussy, 1862–1918
Henri Matisse, 1869–1954	Marcel Proust, 1871–1923	Aleksandr Scriabin, 1872–1915
Piet Mondrian, 1872–1944	Hugo von Hofmannsthal, 1874–1929	Arnold Schoenberg, 1874–1951
Pablo Picasso, 1881–1973	Rainer Maria Rilke, 1875–1926	Charles Ives, 1874–1954
Georges Braque, 1882–1963	Thomas Mann, 1875–1955	Maurice Ravel, 1875–1937
Amadeo Modigliani, 1884–1920	E.M. Forster, 1879–1970	Béla Bartók, 1881–1945
Marcel Duchamp, 1887–1968	Robert Musil, 1880–1942	Igor Stravinsky, 1882–1971
Juan Gris, 1887–1927	James Joyce, 1882–1941	Anton Webern, 1883–1945
Giorgio de Chirico, 1888–1978	Virginia Woolf, 1882–1941	Alban Berg, 1885–1935
	Franz Kafka, 1883–1924	Sergei Prokofiev, 1891–1953
	William Carlos Williams, 1883–1963	Leo Ornstein, 1893–2002
	D. H. Lawrence, 1885–1930	Paul Hindemith, 1895–1963
	Ezra Pound, 1885–1923	Virgil Thomson, 1896–1989
	Aaron Copland, 1900–1990	Fernando Pessoa, 1888–1935
	T.S. Eliot, 1888–1965	Dmitri Shostakovich, 1906–1975
	H.D. [Hilda Doolittle], 1886–1961	Olivier Messiaen, 1908–1992
	Djuna Barnes, 1892–1982	John Cage, 1912–1992
	Federico García Lorca, 1898–1936	Benjamin Britten, 1913–1976
	Bertold Brecht, 1898–1956	
	Ernest Hemingway, 1899–1961	

from and sometimes at odds with mainstream popular culture. One can count on a single hand the leading modernists who came from working-class origins, although a few others pretended to have humbler backgrounds than they actually did.

Disdain for mainstream culture was felt passionately. To Baudelaire, respectable European society was "utterly worn out, brutalized, and greedy" and incapable of genuine feeling. The playwright Bertolt Brecht, too, complained:

> Whenever anyone goes to conventional stage drama, he says of it, "Oh yes, I've felt that way too; that just how I experience things; that's real life . . . . That's what great art is. Everything is so clear and self-evident. I cry when everyone else cries and laugh when everyone else laughs."

He wanted to create a new type of drama that solicits a very different reaction:

> "Who ever would think that way? You can't do that! It's too strange;
> it's beyond belief; and it has to stop!"

James Joyce, the author of *Ulysses* (1922), summed up his own attitude in a letter: "Writing in English is the most ingenious torture ever devised for sins committed in previous lives. The English reading public explains the reason why."

THE ARTISTIC TRUTH WITHIN

There was more to modernism than contrariness. In the visual arts, painters and sculptures aimed to reproduce the "truth within" rather than just external appearance. They sought personal visions of the realities beneath the surface. Art became less representational and more intuitive, symbolic, and impressionistic—more expressive of the artist's response to the world than of the world itself. It parallels the philosophical currents of the age, sometimes consciously so. The composer Arnold Schoenberg pronounced that the purpose of art was "to express oneself *directly*—not one's taste or upbringing, or one's intelligence, knowledge, or skill. Not all the *acquired* characteristics, but that which is *inborn* [and] *instinctive*."

The primitive self, driven by passion and instinct, is the only self that matters to art—because it is the source of art. Most of the modernists felt naturally drawn to the irrational, intuitive, and primitive. Paul Gauguin abandoned Europe (not to mention his wife and five children) to live in Tahiti and to create a new art. Pablo Picasso was fascinated with tribal African masks. Such writers as Constantine Cavafy and Rainer Maria Rilke shared a passion for ancient Greek mythology. Mann's four-volume novel *Joseph and His Brothers* (1930–1943) reimagined the very roots of mythology in the Biblical tale. Schoenberg, Igor Stravinsky, and Sergei Prokofiev drew for their music on ancient folktales and songs.

Modernism broke with established forms in the quest to express subjective experience. Painters and sculptors abandoned the representational art they had inherited in favor of highly personal expression. Vincent van Gogh's *Starry Night* (1889) draws its power from its refusal to portray the sky as it appeared outside his asylum window, so that he could express instead the state of his troubled mind. Picasso could paint exquisite representational art, but representational painting did not allow him to express what he wanted. His breakthrough, *Les Demoiselles d'Avignon* ("The Young Ladies of Avignon," 1907), portrays naked prostitutes along the Carrer d'Avinyó, a street in Barcelona then notorious for its sordid nightlife. Two of the women wear African masks and savage expressions while the remaining three scowl. All five stare blankly and disdainfully at the viewer—presumably their next customer—as though challenging his right to be there. Their bodies are shown from at least two separate perspectives, which breaks their forms into geometric shapes and flat fields of color. The painting makes viewers feel as though they are under attack. No wonder so many people hated it, starting when it was first exhibited, in 1916.[12] Picasso knew he had produced a masterpiece and so kept it in his private collection.

The Russian-born émigré Wassily Kandinsky (1866–1944), who spent most of his adult life in Germany and France, was the most direct and eloquent theorist

Four Modernist Works   *Left: Les Demoiselles d'Avignon* (1907) and *Sketch of Igor Stravinsky* (1922) by Pablo Picasso, *Right: Composition No. 4* by Wassily Kandinsky, and *Starry Night, Saint-Rémy* (1889) by Vincent van Gogh.

---

[12]   The painter Henri Matisse reportedly flew into a rage at Les Demoiselles d'Avignon, feeling that Picasso was mocking Modernism.

of Modernism after Baudelaire. At the age of thirty he gave up a successful career as an economist, after being moved by an exhibit in Munich of paintings by Claude Monet, the impressionist. (Kandinsky had been offered a prestigious professorship at the leading university in Estonia.) He decided almost instantaneously to enroll instead in art school. His 1910 book *On the Spiritual Element in Art* has never been equaled as a meditation on art by a practicing artist. Kandinsky wrote about art so well because, as a late convert to it, he had thought about it so much. He asked why it matters, why it is worth giving up a profitable career for, and why it can elevate the soul even in a time of deepening confusion and despair. Art, to him, is as much religion as aesthetics, in a world that no longer has a place for metaphysics:

> The spirit strengthens itself and develops itself just as the body does; and just as a body can weaken and become worn out, so too can the spirit. The essential, life-generating force within every artist is precisely like the "talent of gold" described in the Gospel story—it is the priceless thing that must not be buried away, and any artist who lets his talents decay without putting them to use is like the "lazy servant" of the story.... Art is a force that has a goal: it must be made to serve the development and refinement of the human soul.

Art, in other words, supplants religion (as Nietzsche had already insisted); it is the only remaining means of achieving anything like spiritual salvation:

> An artist must train his soul as much as he trains his eye.... And above all he must have something to say; to master a technique, to gain control over physical form is not the goal of art. Art's only real goal is to adapt form to spiritual meaning.

This is precisely why abstraction is not only acceptable but necessary. The only eternal realities that the spirit can attain and understand, the only transcendent truths available to us, are those experienced through aesthetic bliss. And that art follows no rules but its own:

> Abstract forms, or representational forms that have been partially abstracted, can take the place of determinedly physical objects in almost any painting.... For "beauty" in art is nothing more nor less than the expression of the soul's desire. Whatever seems beautiful to our souls is beautiful in art.

Modernists like Kandinsky thought of art as the only substitute for religious faith, the only spiritual lifeline available in a world otherwise devoid of hope or meaning beyond our meager selves.

Composers like Arnold Schoenberg, Igor Stravinsky, and Alban Berg jettisoned tonality—the basis of 18th- and 19th-century music in familiar chords. They developed instead twelve-tone music, which treated equally the notes of the scale. The result was an intentional dissonance that struck many new listeners as an assault. Fistfights broke out at the first performance of Schoenberg's Chamber Symphony No. 1 (1906), and rioting crowds sometimes spilled out into the streets.[13]

Poets like Rilke and William Butler Yeats experimented with blank verse and unmetered rhythms, but they still mostly adhered to traditional forms until the start of World War I. And the novel was among the last literary genres to undergo transformation. As early as 1900, Henry James focused more on the interior lives of the characters than on their explicit actions. In *The Ambassadors* (1903) and *The Golden Bowl* (1904), he carefully dissects their characters' motives and reactions. Luigi Pirandello, from the novel *The Late Mattia Pascal* (1904) to his plays *Six Characters in Search of an Author* (1921) and *Henry IV* (1923), explores the uncertain nature of individual identity and morality. The character of Pascal, trapped in a loveless marriage and a dead-end job, trudges through existence only for the sake of his twin daughters. When they unexpectedly die, he sets off alone on a holiday to deal with his mourning—only to find out that his shrewish wife (and her own shrewish mother) have declared him missing and, later, dead. Freed at last from his old existence, Mattia changes his name, acquires a fortune through gambling, and travels across Europe enjoying life for the first time. But feelings of guilt creep in. He fakes his assumed character's death and returns home—only to find that his wife has remarried and is now happy. He can longer exist either as Mattia or as his alter ego.

In 1906 the Austrian writer Robert Musil published *The Confessions of Young Törless*, about psychological and sexual sadism in a military academy. It

> Modernists like Kandinsky thought of art as the only substitute for religious faith, the only spiritual lifeline available in a world otherwise devoid of hope or meaning beyond our meager selves.

---

13 The riot at the premiere of Stravinsky's Rite of Spring (1913) resulted from the crowd's anger at what they considered the brutish choreography of the ballet, not just the music.

was one of the first novels to explore explicitly Freud's ideas about the conflict between the irrational instinct and the conscious mind. As with poetry, however, the main break with the novel's past occurred after the start of the war in 1914. Writers like James Joyce, Virginia Woolf, and Ford Madox Ford now introduced stream-of-consciousness narratives, a nonchronological order of events, and unreliable narrators.

Modernist art emerged from a perceived need for a rupture with tradition, in order to explore the disordered inner reality of existence. Little of it is comic, since the turn-of-the century generation did not find much that was funny in instinctive drives or in the impossibility of permanent meaning. For T. S. Eliot, the poet and critic, the artist actually has to quell all emotion when creating art: "Poetry is not a turning loose of emotion, but an escape from emotion; it is not the expression of personality, but an escape from personality. But, of course, only those who have personality and emotions know what it means to want to escape from these things." The artistic and intellectual life of the 20th century began in uncertainty, aimless yearning, and despair. And it got worse.

WHO, WHAT, WHERE

analytic philosophy	rationalist philosophy
existentialism	relativity
general theory of relativity	space-time
modernism	special theory of relativity
nihilism	structuralism
phenomenology	supermen
psychoanalysis	uncertainty principle
quantum theory	will to power

SUGGESTED READINGS

Primary Sources

Baudelaire, Charles. "The Painter of Our Time."

Eliot, T. S. "Tradition and the Individual Talent."

Freud, Sigmund. *Civilization and Its Discontents.*

———. *The Interpretation of Dreams.*

Kandinsky, Wassily. *On the Spiritual Element in Art.*

Rilke, Rainer Maria. *New Poems.*

Sartre, Jean-Paul. *Nausea.*

Shaw, George Bernard. *Caesar and Cleopatra.*

———. *John Bull's Other Island.*

Wilde, Oscar. *De Profundis.*

———. *The Importance of Being Earnest.*

Anthologies

Marino, Gordon, ed. *Basic Writings of Existentialism* (2004).

Otis, Laura, ed. *Literature and Science in the Nineteenth Century: An Anthology* (2009).

Rainey, Lawrence, ed. *Modernism: An Anthology* (2005).

Studies

Fawaz, Leila Tarazi, and C. A. Bayly, eds. *Modernity and Culture: From the Mediterranean to the Indian Ocean* (2001).

Garff, Joakim. *Søren Kierkegaard: A Biography* (2007).

Gay, Peter. *Modernism: The Lure of Heresy from Baudelaire to Beckett and Beyond* (2010).

———. *Schnitzler's Century: The Making of Middle-Class Culture, 1815–1914* (2002).

Holmes, Deborah, and Lisa Silverman, eds. *Interwar Vienna: Culture between Tradition and Modernity* (2009).

Jodock, Darrell. *Catholicism Contending with Modernity: Roman Catholic Modernism and Anti-Modernism in Historical Context* (2000).

Kragh, Helge. *Higher Speculations: Grand Theories and Failed Revolutions in Physics and Cosmology* (2011).

———. *Quantum Generations: A History of Physics in the Twentieth Century* (2002).

Paret, Peter. *German Encounters with Modernism, 1840–1945* (2001).

Perelberg, Rosine Jozef, ed. *Freud: A Modern Reader* (2005).

Pippin, Robert B. *Nietzsche, Psychology, and First Philosophy* (2011).

Porter, Bernard. *The Absent-Minded Imperialists: Empire, Society, and Culture in Britain* (2006).

Preston, Aaron. *Analytic Philosophy: The History of an Illusion* (2010).

Singer, Barnett, and John Langdon. *Cultured Force: Makers and Defenders of the French Colonial Empire* (2008).

Weller, Shane. *Modernism and Nihilism* (2011).

Young, Julian. *Friedrich Nietzsche: A Philosophical Biography* (2010).

Zahavi, Dan. *Husserl's Phenomenology* (2003).

For additional resources, including maps, primary sources, visuals, web links, and quizzes, please go to **www.oup.com/us/backman.**

L.532a

CHAPTER 24

The World at War (Part I)
(1914–1918)

THE WORLD AT WAR, 1914–1918

Major clashes, 1914-1918

T he day after the signing of the armistice that ended World War I, the British novelist D. H. Lawrence (1885–1930) wrote to a friend with a gloomy warning:

> I suppose you think the war is over and that we shall go back to the kind of world you lived in before it. But the war isn't over. The hate and evil is greater now than ever. Very soon war will break out again and overwhelm you.... The crowd outside thinks that Germany is crushed forever. But the Germans will soon rise again. Europe is done for.... The war isn't over. Even if the fighting should stop, the evil will be worse because the hate will be dammed up in men's hearts and will show itself in all sorts of ways.

He had good reason to be pessimistic. The war that ended in November 1918 had been the cause of more bloodshed and horror than any conflict in Western history—and of more than in all human history after the psychotic conquests of Genghis Khan seven hundred years earlier. Three empires—the Austrian-Hungarian, the German, and the Ottoman—lay in ruins. Two others—the British and the American—had been knocked staggering.

Along the war's three hundred-mile-long western front, in northern and eastern France, entire towns and villages had been obliterated, crop fields and mines devastated, and roads

◀ **Armed to the Teeth** The Krupp armaments factory in Essen, Germany, 1912.

- The Run-Up to War
- The Balance of Power
- A New Map of Hell
- The War in the Trenches
- The Home Front
- Officers and Gentlemen
- Russia's Revolution
- Bolshevism and the Laws of History
- Exporting Revolution
- How Not to End a War
- Young Turks

CHAPTER OUTLINE

and bridges ruined. Millions of corpses lay buried or rotting in the sun. Some sixty-five million soldiers had taken part. By the time the war ended, ten million of them lay dead, another twenty-one million of them had been wounded, and still another million remained missing. The deaths were shared by all: on the side of the Axis powers, 1.8 million Germans and 1.2 million Austrian-Hungarians; on the side of the Allies, 1.7 million Russians, 1.4 million French, and nearly a million British. The late-coming Italians lost 460,000 soldiers, and the even later-coming Americans lost 115,000. The rest of the dead consisted primarily of Serbs, Turks, Romanians, Poles, Czechs, Slovaks, and Arabs.

By the war's end, the political map of the West had already changed, with America's entry into a European war, a revolution in Russia, and the birth of what would become the Soviet Union. It was to change still more after the war, with a harsh peace treaty, the resentment of the losers, and the end of the Ottoman Empire.

THE RUN-UP TO WAR

With hindsight, one can see the war coming as early as 1905, but not as the result of any presumed inevitable march of political events or economic developments. The popular demand for war simply rose continually. World War I was willed into being by a Europe drunk with nationalistic pride, with each nation eager to claim its victor's cup in the social Darwinian battle of life. Militarism had been on the rise across Europe ever since German unification in 1870, and it had to be. The "balance of power" codified by the Treaty of Vienna in 1815 had presupposed a permanently fragmented German people, but unification had tipped the scale heavily in Germany's favor. Some sort of direct action was necessary, and that action found expression in the rapid development of

> World War I was willed into being by a Europe drunk with nationalistic pride, with each nation eager to claim its victor's cup in the Social Darwinian battle of life.

CHAPTER TIMELINE

1899–1902 Boer War	**1905** Failed revolution in Russia	**1914** Beginning of World War I
1900–1914 Fifteen million Europeans emigrate overseas	**1908** Young Turks lead constitutional reform in Turkey	**1915** Germany sinks Lusitania; beginning of Armenian genocide

military might—put to use in the colonization of Africa and much of Asia. And once the imperialist land grab was completed, the massive military remained.

Europe around 1900 was armed to the teeth, much as in the Age of Absolutism by 1715. As armies swelled and stockpiles of weapons ballooned, pressure built up to put them to use. In capitalist terms, unexercised muscle was a wasted resource. In Germany the Colonial Society, a nationwide group that championed imperialism, issued vague but insistent calls for war. "Peace is rotten," declared the Berlin-based poet Georg Heym (1887–1912) in a private notebook. He hoped for a war, "any war, even an unjust one," and in that same year (1912) he published a disturbing paean to it. Opening "He is risen that was long asleep," the poem describes the awesome, mythic power of War as it sweeps across the countryside, smashing towers, obliterating cities, devouring woods and fields. The nightmarish effect of "War," however, derives not from Heym's powerful description of War's terrible strength, but from his admiration of it.[1]

The popular journalist-lawyer Heinrich Class (1868–1953) was a member of another patriotic group, the Pan-German League. He wrote in the same year:

> If any nation has just cause to seek to expand its sphere of influence, it is the German one, whose population is rapidly growing, whose industry needs new markets, and whose overall economy needs new land from which to derive new resources.... We need these things and we need them now, and we need to acquire them by any means whatsoever.... We must engage in a proactive politics abroad—in fact, let us state it bluntly: we must be aggressive.... To begin with, any expansion within Europe can only come from direct conquest since neither France nor Russia will be so obliging as to give away part of their territories to us.... Another consideration is whether or not southeastern Europe might do

---

[1] He is risen that was long asleep, Risen now from caverns deep, He stands in the twilight, unknown, and grand, And crushes the moon in His black hand.

1916
Start of Arab
revolt

1918
End of World
War I

1920
Treaty between Allied powers and
Turkey abolishes Ottoman Empire

1917
Bolsheviks assume
power in Russia

1919
Paris Peace Conference;
Treaty of Versailles

for us, specifically the parts of the Austrian Empire and of the Balkans generally where the Slavic peoples (a "sub-German people," if I may put it thus) currently reside.

The Germans were not alone in their ardor for conflict. French politicians, writers, university students, and workers smarted from their defeat in the Franco-Prussian War of 1870. Demoralized by the Dreyfus Affair, they urged restoration of the country through military glory.[2] Only victory on the field, they declared, could restore national honor. In Britain, too, many people looked eagerly forward to a contest that would settle, once and for all, the intense competitions begun with the founding of the German Reich. British confidence ran at high level. After all, the country had not had a serious military setback since the American Revolution. British forces in the last twenty years had put over three hundred million people around the world under their control.

Not everyone had war fever, of course. Trade unionists and socialist reformers in all countries were among the loudest voices condemning the march to conflict. Members of the clergy also spoke up frequently against the militarist wave. One of the best known opponents of war was Norman Angell (1872–1967), the Paris-based editor of the *Daily Mail*, who in 1909 published a pamphlet called *Europe's Optical Illusion.* (It appeared in expanded form the following year as *The Great Illusion.*) Angell speaks the language of business. He argues that, aside from purely moral issues, a European war would be disastrous simply because the economies of the countries had become too interdependent. Unlike manufacturing, the finance industry crossed too many international borders to survive a conflict. Credit was extended in such an extended web, he argues, that any prolonged disruption to a single commercial sector would be felt everywhere (see Map 24.1). Angell sees an appeal to economic interests as the only argument that might succeed in a society that so romanticizes bloody conflict:

> War has no longer the justification that it makes for the survival of the fittest; it involves the survival of the less fit. The idea that the struggle between nations is a part of the evolutionary law of man's advance involves a profound misreading of the biological analogy. . . .

---

[2] Alfred Dreyfus (1859–1935) was a French army captain unjustly accused of passing military secrets to the German embassy in Paris in 1894. His two trials, both of which ended in his conviction, were the cause of intense national debate and scandal since Dreyfus was a Jew and the charges against him were at least partially motivated by anti-Semitic hatred. He was fully exonerated in 1906 and reinstated in the army with the rank of major. Nevertheless, he had already endured five years of imprisonment in solitary confinement at the penal colony on Devil's Island in French Guiana and after his exoneration he was wounded in an assassination attempt. He retired from the army in 1907 but re-enlisted when World War I broke out and served throughout the conflict, earning promotion to the rank of lieutenant colonel.

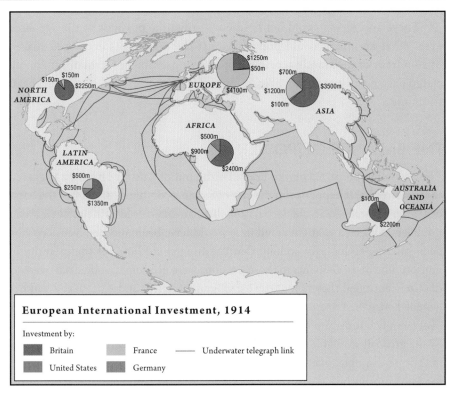

European International Investment, 1914

MAP 24.1   European International Investment, 1914

Are we, in blind obedience to primitive instincts and old prejudices, enslaved by the old catchwords and that curious indolence which makes the revision of old ideas unpleasant, to duplicate indefinitely on the political and economic side a condition from which we have liberated ourselves on the religious side? Are we to continue to struggle, as so many good men struggled in the first dozen centuries of Christendom— spilling oceans of blood, wasting mountains of treasure—to achieve what is at bottom a logical absurdity, to accomplish something which, when accomplished, can avail us nothing, and which, if it could avail us anything, would condemn the nations of the world to never-ending bloodshed and the constant defeat of all those aims which men, in their sober hours, know to be alone worthy of sustained endeavor?

Back in England, Angell continued to campaign against the slaughter. He later served briefly as a member of Parliament, was knighted in 1931, and in 1933 received the Nobel Peace Prize.

These arguments could not hold out against the passions of the age, however. What argument could prevail against the sentiments expressed shared by hundreds of thousands across Europe? As a prominent German general declared once hostilities in fact began, "Even if it all ends in ruin, it has been beautiful to see."

THE BALANCE OF POWER

The assassination of Archduke Franz Ferdinand of Austria-Hungary triggered the catastrophe. It happened in the city of Sarajevo, on June 28, 1914, at the hand of a bitter nineteen-year-old Serb nationalist named Gavrilo Princip. But if it had not been this event that triggered it, it would have been another. Tensions had been running so high for so long that anything could have set the calamity in motion. The main elements in these tensions were economic. Industrial overproduction continued throughout the carving up of Africa and Asia, and it had not lessened once the European empires had achieved full size. The result was a cycle of economic booms and busts between 1885 and 1914 that was made even worse by the growing availability of cheap transportation. Petroleum and electricity allowed, for example, massive imports of American, Argentinean, and Canadian foodstuffs to Europe. Against this threat, Europeans could either erect punitive tariff barriers or prop up their native industries with subsidies. To varying degrees, they did both. Manufacturers formed cartels to regulate output and fix prices. Banks organized themselves into consortia to set interest rates and control the movement of capital.

Not Looking Back A photo of European immigrants on a dock in New York Harbor around 1900. The father points to the land that will be their new home.

State interventions and cartel manipulations not only distorted markets but solidified the divide that separated Europe's rich, developed nations from its poorer, undeveloped ones. Ireland, Greece, Portugal, Poland, and the Scandinavian countries could not compete internationally, and their sharp economic declines drove more and more of their populations abroad. Between 1815 and 1900 over forty million people had already emigrated from Europe—primarily to the United States, Canada, Argentina, Brazil, and Australia. Almost fifteen million more did so between 1900 and 1914 (see chapter 23). Only Belgium and the Netherlands experienced a net gain in population through migration. Artificial controls in the markets also hardened the distinction between the wealthy and the poor within each industrialized country. With little capital available for smaller businesses, labor wages stagnated from 1900 to 1914, while prices for most consumer goods rose.

The widening gap between rich and poor led to the rise of trade unions and the creation of the Labour Party in Britain, which by 1906 held twenty-nine seats in Parliament. Germany, in contrast, avoided strong labor unions by initiating a broad network of social welfare programs, like workman's compensation and retirement pensions. These programs lured workers away from radicalizing, but they were expensive. Coupled with the huge new military expenditure and generous subsidies to industrialists, they left the central governments of the European empires increasingly vulnerable. Each boom-and-bust cycle after 1900 only made matters worse, until the system practically cried out for resolution.

The leading states created alliances that they hoped would preserve economic and military balance. These alliances often changed, as each boom-and-bust cycle altered the relative strengths of each partner. One year's ally might be next year's diplomatic and commercial rival (see Map 24.2). But the alliances generally tried to counterbalance the economic and military weight of the German Empire. Britain aimed above all to secure its naval superiority. It wanted to maintain sufficient

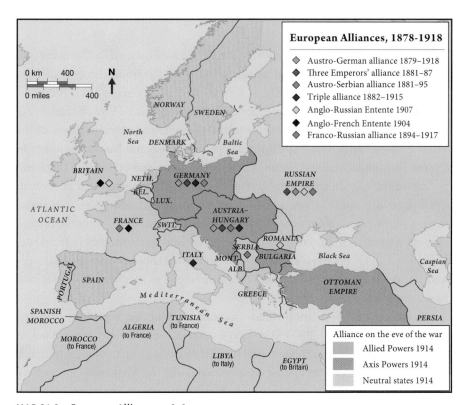

MAP 24.2   European Alliances, 1878–1914

Gold Miners, South Africa   South Africa has rich natural deposits of
diamonds and gold, the desire for which lured the British to wage the two
Boer Wars (1880-1881, 1899-1902). A recent geological survey reports that
the country has as much as 50 percent of the world's known gold reserves.

strength to battle any two European nations combined—usually Germany and
any country with which it could be allied. In the Anglo-French Entente of 1904,
also known as the Entente Cordiale, for example, France recognized British interests in Egypt and Suez in return for British recognition of French interests in
Morocco. The Anglo-Russian Entente of 1907 (sometimes erroneously called the
Triple Entente) settled border disputes between British and Russian zones of influence in Afghanistan and Persia. These agreements, and others like them, did
not create actual military alliances, yet they did pave the way to them by preemptively removing points of contention. Germany, for its part, responded to these en-
tentes by forming pacts of its own with Austria-Hungary and the Ottoman Empire.
Surging nationalism among many of the Slavic and Arab peoples living under
Habsburg and Ottoman rule, respectively, weakened those empires dramatically.
And the cost of putting down their rebellions helped to keep the two states near
bankruptcy as the century began.

Relations between Britain and Germany had grown especially strained
during the Boer War (1899–1902). The Germans took the side of the Afrikaners against the British, who were determined to extend their colonies in South
Africa, once huge deposits of gold were discovered in the Afrikaner Orange Free
State. Britain won a modest victory in the war, but it came at a heavy price in men,

material, and prestige. Germany enjoyed the Britons' embarrassment and the apparent vulnerability of British forces.

Relations worsened several years later, thanks to the blundering of Kaiser Wilhelm II, who had a long track record of putting his foot in his mouth. In an interview with England's *Daily Telegraph* on October 28, 1908, he described the British people as "mad as March hares." He claimed to have personally drawn up the battle plan that helped the British win a campaign against the Afrikaners and to have forwarded it to his "revered grandmother" Queen Victoria. Public opinion in Britain was outraged, and the German Reichstag took action to limit the emperor's authority on the international scene. Subsequent crises in North Africa and the Balkans, in the context of the fast-decaying Habsburg and Ottoman Empires, brought matters to a fever pitch.

In 1905 the German chief of general staff, Alfred Graf von Schlieffen (1833–1913), had developed a detailed battle plan in the event of a two-front war with France and Russia. Kept secret for nine years, the **Schlieffen Plan** called for a rapid strike at France via Belgium and Luxembourg, in order to circumvent French defenses. It would attack Paris from the north and score a quick victory before Russian forces could marshal in the east. When the Austrian archduke was assassinated in June 1914, the Habsburg state declared war on Serbia, which called in its ally Russia, which in turn prompted Austria to summon its ally Germany. Dreading its two-front vulnerability, Germany took preemptive measures by declaring war on France and putting the Schlieffen Plan into effect. Belgium, however, was a neutral country without any alliances at all.[3] To aid this innocent victim and to uphold international law, Britain, on September 4, 1914, declared war on Germany. Within a matter of three months, a provincial crisis in the Balkans had swelled into a global conflict.

World War I pitted the Axis powers of Germany, Austria-Hungary, the Ottoman Empire, and Bulgaria against the Allied forces of the British Empire, France, Russia, Serbia, Belgium, and Luxembourg. Eventually Japan (1914), Italy (1915), Romania and Portugal (1916), Greece, and the United States (1917) joined the fray, on the side of the Allies. The empires drew on all their dominions for soldiers and material support, leading to further conflict around the globe. Casualties mounted quickly, and colonial subjects seized the opportunity to rise up against their imperial masters. By 1916 the Axis and Allied powers both resorted to forced conscription. And resistance to the draft, combined with events in the colonies, shook up societies far from the war's center in Europe.

---

[3]   In fact, the 1831 treaty that established Belgium as an independent nation had explicitly forbidden it to form alliances.

TABLE 24.1   **World War I (1914–1918)**

June 28, 1914	Archduke Ferdinand of Austria-Hungary murdered in Sarajevo.
August 4	Germany invades Belgium.
August 26–30	Russia invades Germany and is defeated at battle of Tannenberg.
September 4–10	German advance on Paris halted at 1st battle of the Marne.
October 18	Trench warfare begins.
February 19, 1915	Allied campaign against Gallipoli begins (lasts until January 1916).
May 7	Germany sinks the *Lusitania*.
May 23	Italy enters war, joining the Allies; German counter-offensive drives Russians from most of Poland.
October 3–5	Allied troops land at Salonika.
February 21, 1916	Battle of Verdun begins. Lasts until 15 December.
April 23	Start of Easter Rebellion in Dublin.
June 6	Arab Revolt begins.
June	Russian forces against Austria suffer one million casualties.
July 1	Battle of the Somme (lasts until 18 November). Allies lose 600,000 soldiers.
August 27	Romania enters the war.
November 28	First German air-raid on London.
February 1, 1917	German U-boats begin unrestricted attacks.
March 11	British forces capture Baghdad.
March 15	Russian tsar is overthrown, forced to abdicate.
April 6	U.S. enters the war on the Allied side.
November 16	Vladimir Lenin and his Bolsheviks come to power in Moscow.
December 9	British capture Jerusalem.
January 8, 1918	President Wilson announces his 14 Points.
March 3	Treaty of Brest-Litovsk: Russia withdraws from the war.
June	Re-unified German army advances to within 60 miles of Paris.
August	British victory at Amiens.
October 30	Ottoman Empire and Austrian-Hungarian Empire surrender.
November 11	Austria and Germany sign armistice agreements with Allies, ending the war.
January 12, 1919	Paris Peace Conference begins.
June 28	Treaty of Versailles is signed.

A NEW MAP OF HELL

The narrative of the war is dismal to recount. Most Western accounts of the war emphasize the importance of the western front—the long, entrenched line along the French-German border, from Belgium to Switzerland—but other fronts proved equally as significant and deadly. World War I was fought in seven separate arenas: on the western front, on the eastern front with Russia, in northern Italy, in the Balkans, along the periphery of the Ottoman Empire, in the European colonies, and at sea. Each had its own unique horrors. And each left nations obliged to mobilize "the home front" to share those horrors (see Map 24.3).

On the western front, the initial German advance through the Low Countries was halted a few miles short of Paris at the First Battle of the Marne (1914). More than two million soldiers took part in all, roughly one-quarter of whom died or were wounded. After this defeat, the Germans withdrew to a line that ran in a rough arc from Ypres in Belgium, through Soissons in northern France, and down to Verdun in northeastern France. This line moved little over the years and became a site of trench warfare that claimed over three hundred thousand French and German lives before the war's end. More than a half million more were wounded. Both sides tried to break the deadlock by mounting major offensives—most notably at Verdun (1916), at the Somme (1916), and at Passchendale in Belgium (1917). These gained little territory but left hundreds of thousands of corpses lying on the muddy fields. A final effort to break the standoff came in 1918, with the Second Battle of the Marne, when German forces made a last-ditch effort to get through Allied lines and seize Paris. This too resulted only in more slaughter—a quarter-million dead, all told.

The eastern front saw a handful of initial Russian victories, as they rushed forward while German forces became mired in the west. Before long, however, Germany repelled the Russian advance, and by the end of 1915 a German and Austrian counteroffensive drove the Russians out of Poland. Fighting in 1916 pummeled Russia's forces with extremely heavy losses, and 1917 brought another shock—the Russian Revolution and the fall from power of the tsar. This led to Russia's formal withdrawal from the war. The Treaty of Brest-Litovsk, formalized on March 3, 1918, freed Vladimir Lenin's Bolshevik forces to concentrate on securing their control over Russia itself.

The war in northern Italy was fought primarily between the Italians and Austrians. This third front, along Italy's northeastern border with Austria, did not open until Italy joined the war in 1915, and Allied hopes that it might break the deadlock elsewhere were soon dashed. No fewer than a dozen fierce campaigns were fought near the Isonzo River in the Italian Alps. Fighting ended with an Austrian surrender in October 1918.

The Axis armies marched into the Balkans early in the war, and by October 1915 they routed the Serbian forces and seized the Serb capital of Belgrade. They then joined with Ottoman and Bulgarian forces and took Romania. An effort to conquer Greece failed, and the last years of the war were spent in trying to quell rebellions among the Serbians and Bosnians.

For decades, the Ottoman Empire had been dismissed as "the sick man of Europe." However, despite predictions of its speedy collapse, Ottoman forces surprised the Allies with their resilience. The Turks held off a major Allied

MAP 24.3   World War I, 1914–1918

invasion (composed largely of soldiers from Australia, New Zealand, Canada, and South Africa) at Gallipoli, on the Dardenelles straits, for eight months in 1915. In the plain between the Tigris and Euphrates rivers, the British hoped to launch a sudden strike straight into Baghdad; the Turks stopped the Allies at Kut al-Amara. More than 20,000 British soldiers died in the siege of Kut and another

10,000 were marched off across the desert as prisoners of war, two-thirds of them dying along the way.

The Turkish economy, however, could not keep Ottoman forces supplied, which left the empire severely weakened. The Allies capitalized on this by organizing the **Arab Revolt**, an uprising of Middle Eastern Arab tribes against Turkish rule.

Colonial Troops Many of the combatants in World War I came from the European colonies. Here, for example, is a photo of a Ugandan color guard on march (under a British officer, of course).

Lieutenant Colonel T. E. Lawrence (1888–1935), the British officer popularly known as Lawrence of Arabia, played a pivotal role. The revolt aimed to replace Ottoman imperial rule with autonomous Arab countries. Unknown to Lawrence, however, the British and French governments had already agreed secretly to divide up the Middle Eastern dominions between themselves. This pact, known as the **Sykes-Picot Agreement** (1916), arranged for Britain to receive what is today southern Iraq, Jordan, and most of what is now Israel. France received northern Iraq, today's Syria and Lebanon, and the southeastern corner of today's Turkey. Imperial Russia, a junior partner in the arrangement, was to receive the city of Istanbul (Constantinople) and the Bosporus—but Russian claims were nullified by the Bolshevik Revolution of 1917.

A small amount of fighting took place in the German colonies in Africa and Asia, but few troops were available to defend these far-flung territories, and imperial Germany surrendered most of its colonies shortly after the war began. Only the colony at German Southwest Africa, today's Namibia, held out until 1918.

There was only one pitched naval battle in the entire war. At the Battle of Jutland in June 1916, British and German naval forces fought to a draw, leaving the British in control of the North Sea. More significant were the attacks of German submarines, or U-boats, on international shipping. German strategy was to cut off the resupply of Britain: it imposed an embargo on all ships, of whatever origin, carrying any civilian or military goods to the United Kingdom. In practice, this meant attacking British and American ships. The U-boats proved highly effective, but at the cost of slowly drawing America into the general conflict.

In 1917, Germany declared its intent to engage in unrestricted maritime attacks; Russia withdrew from the war, and Germany reallocated its hitherto split forces along the single western front. All this brought America into the war in April 1917. When it became clear that the American entry would only prolong the slaughter, all sides agreed to an armistice. The Treaty of Versailles formally ended the war on June 28, 1919—five years, to the very day, after the assassination of the Austrian archduke in Sarajevo.

THE WAR IN THE TRENCHES

The narrative of the war and its strategies is important. So are the political wrangling and diplomatic schemes surrounding them. One can view the entire century as a long, drawn-out consequence of the Great War. But two elements of the war deserve special notice—the experience of common soldiers and the customs of the military officers who commanded them.

Along most of the western, eastern, and Italian fronts, the war quickly devolved into a brutal war of attrition. Battlefronts moved little, which meant that the physical desolation of these areas was severe. The western front especially was dominated by trench warfare—parallel lines of muddy ditches, separated by a "no man's land" of landmines and barbed wire. From these ditches, soldiers fired machine guns, threw grenades and canisters of poison gas, tended mortar batteries, and occasionally charged one another with bayonet-fitted rifles. Most trenches were between seven and eight feet deep and perhaps four feet wide. Proper drainage was not possible under such conditions, so soldiers lived daily in water-and-urine soaked mud up to a foot deep. Worse still, trenches ran in zigzag patterns rather than straight lines, in order to minimize the damage from grenades and artillery shells. The patterns also limited a sniper's ability to fire down a long line of crowded men. Yet they meant that most soldiers lived day in and day out seeing only walls of mud on all sides. The mounds of filth and piles of corpses encouraged a large rat population, which spread disease. Well behind the trenches were various supply camps; even further behind was the heavy artillery. Most higher-ranking officers took up stations somewhere behind the artillery, often separated from the fighting by several miles.

> Most trenches were between seven and eight feet deep and perhaps four feet wide. Proper drainage was not possible under such conditions, so soldiers lived daily in water-and-urine soaked mud up to a foot deep.

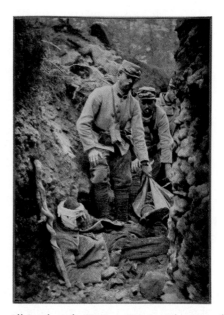

All Dead on the Western Front   "The Price of Victory" reads the original caption to this candid news photo of French soldiers in a trench near Argonne, in northern France, in June 1915. The pipe-smoking central figure steps casually over a wounded comrade as he helps to carry out a corpse.

It was too much heavy firepower in too concentrated an area. Opposing trenches were sometimes so close that enemy soldiers could converse with one another. Artillery barrages intended to weaken the enemy's position fell all too often on the gunners' own comrades, and clouds of poison gas needed only the mildest of breezes to bring the fumes on the very soldiers who had released them. By 1916 cheaply made gasmasks were standard issue for all soldiers, but they never provided any real protection. Chlorine gas left countless soldiers blinded, with permanently blistered faces and scarred lungs.

Siegfried Sassoon (1886–1967), one of the greatest of World War I poets, famously described the horrors of trench warfare in his poem "Attack":

> At dawn the ridge emerges massed and dun
> In the wild purple of the glow'ring sun,
> Smouldering through spouts of drifting smoke that shroud
> The menacing scarred slope; and, one by one,
> Tanks creep and topple forward to the wire.
> The barrage roars and lifts. Then, clumsily bowed
> With bombs and guns and shovels and battle-gear,
> Men jostle and climb to, meet the bristling fire.
> Lines of grey, muttering faces, masked with fear,
> They leave their trenches, going over the top,
> While time ticks blank and busy on their wrists,
> And hope, with furtive eyes and grappling fists,
> Flounders in mud. O Jesus, make it stop!

The heavy weaponry—giant howitzers and concrete machine-gun pillboxes, especially—was designed for defensive rather than offensive purposes. That left both sides unable to move forward even if they did score an occasional victory.[4] Small wonder that photographs of battlefields often look like blasted moonscapes.

Small wonder too that officers' reports on both sides, trying to show evidence of progress for their home offices, rarely spoke of strategic gains. Instead of territory, they used a grim tally of corpses as indices of achievement. On the eastern front, woefully ill-equipped Russian soldiers faced unending volleys of

---

[4]   At Verdun, in 1915, 1.5 million Allied soldiers died to advance the battlefront a mere three miles—thirteen deaths for every inch of ground gained.

Ghostly Battlefield   Soldiers of the 10th Field Artillery Brigade, Australian 4th Division, on march near Ypres, France, in October 1917.

Axis artillery shells and machine-gun fire. The tsar's officers could respond only by ordering wave after wave of soldiers into the barrage, in the hope that, eventually, the Germans and Austrians would run out of ammunition. Russian losses mounted so quickly that when rebels rose up against the tsar, in 1917, the army joined with them. At the time of the Treaty of Brest-Litovsk, the truce between Russia and the Axis, nearly four million Russian soldiers were held as prisoners of war by Germany and Austria.

In the face of these grim realities, it became more and more difficult to sustain popular support for the war effort. The war was, after all, initially touted everywhere as certain to be over by Christmas 1914, a mere six months after it began. In reality, as November's freezing rains gave way to a gray and bitter December, all that had happened was over a million senseless deaths. At the same time, the playwright George Bernard Shaw published a pamphlet, "Common Sense about the War." He argued that it was every patriotic British soldier's duty to rise from the trenches, turn about-face, and shoot his own officers for their incompetence and moral idiocy.

Shaw's outrage stemmed in part from how officers were placed in command. At the start of the war, only 250 of the more than 12,000 officers in the British regular army had earned their positions by promotion from within the ranks. The rest had acquired their posts thanks to aristocratic status, family connections, or

British public school ties. They had little military experience or knowledge of military affairs, but the social elite was supposedly better suited to command. No wonder their blunders brought on so many deaths. In March 1915 an army study reported with concern that twelve thousand members of the upper classes or graduates of elite schools were actually serving as common soldiers. By the end of the year, almost all had been reappointed to the officers' corps.

Soldiers captured in battle became prisoners of war, held according to standards set by the Hague Conventions of 1899 and 1907. These international agreements called for prisoners to receive the same standards of housing, diet, medical attention, and general treatment as soldiers serving the host country. Not all prisoners were so lucky. When the war ended, Germany held roughly 2.5 million prisoners, while Britain and France each held approximately three-quarters of a million. The United States had about 50,000 in its possession. Most of these received adequate to fair treatment. But prisoners in the non-European theaters of the war fared far worse. At least one-third of the Allied soldiers captured by the Ottomans died during their imprisonment. Disease, malnutrition, thirst, and forced labor were the main causes. The Turks generally established their prisoner-of-war camps far from the battlefronts—in the Balkans, the Middle East, or

Armenian Genocide   Starvation, dehydration, exposure, and forced marches killed most of the victims of the Armenian tragedy, 1915–1916. The government of Turkey does not deny the deaths of 1.5 million Armenians; it insists rather that they were the result of wartime happenstance instead of an intentional policy.

in Mesopotamia. And they forced their prisoners to march hundreds of miles to the camps—ostensibly to reserve transport vehicles and fuel for the war effort. But the forced march of prisoners across mountains and through deserts, without enough food and water, produced predictable results.

The worst single chapter of this grim history was the death of as many as 1.5 million Armenians—victims of massacre, deportation, forced march, and starvation. This Armenian genocide began with the arrest in Istanbul of 250 leaders of the Armenian community in April 1915, right after the Allied raid at Gallipoli. They were suspected of complicity in a plot to bring down the Ottoman state. From that point on, Armenian populations across eastern Anatolia were subject to torture, burnings, drownings, and even injections with morphine and typhoid fever. No official record has ever been found in the Ottoman archives directing a conscious campaign of annihilation. To this day, the Republic of Turkey denies the accusation of genocide, although Turks do not dispute the deaths of the Armenian people. But the evidence is overwhelming.[5] Hundreds of thousands of corpses lay strewn along the roads and tracks from the Armenian highlands to the Syrian desert.

THE HOME FRONT

Mobilizing the home front was every bit as vital as mobilizing the military, especially since none of the countries were prepared for a long war. France had entered the conflict with only a one-month supply of ammunition. The Germans, confident of a quick victory, never bothered to requisition winter boots and coats for their infantrymen until winter had set in.[6] Retooling the industrial economies for war thus became a top priority. The transition involved nationalizing industries, rationing most consumer goods, forbidding labor strikes, and raising capital by selling war bonds. To keep society in line, most states instituted some form of censorship and mounted extensive propaganda campaigns. Britain's Defense of the Realm Act (1914), for example, empowered the government to censor newspapers, read private mail, search homes without a warrant, and imprison or deport anyone guilty of unpatriotic utterances.

In every country the compulsory military draft left a severe shortage of laborers in fields and factories. The German Reichstag not only forbade labor strikes but even made it illegal for any able-bodied man to be unemployed. Women had to step in to keep domestic production going. Food shortages

---

[5]   As early as August 18, 1915, the *New York Times* reported that Turkish acts were "a plan to exterminate the whole Armenian people."

[6]   The winter of 1914–1915 was a bad one on the western and eastern fronts. Soldiers complained that even grenades froze together in their supply crates.

became common; in Germany alone over 750,000 civilians perished from star-vation or complications from malnutrition. State investment in manufactur-ing, however, tended to go to the same large industrial and agricultural firms as before the war began. At least, it was thought, they could operate on a large enough scale to meet wartime needs. But the close relationships between them and the government raised alarms about war profiteering at the expense of small businesses and common workers.[7]

Women's Work   Workers taking inventory in a British munitions factory during World War I. The extraordinary amount of munitions used in the war necessitated continuous production. As millions of men went into active service, women in all the involved countries stepped up to fill the factory positions.

---

[7]   The so-called Spanish Flu epidemic that spread across the entire world between January 1918 and December 1920 was the worst natural disaster since the Black Death in the mid-14th century and the smallpox pandemic in the New World in the 16th century. The origin of the flu virus is thought to have been somewhere in north-central Kansas. From a military installation there, Fort Riley, it likely spread among American soldiers who brought the virus into Europe. By the time the virus ran its course, the disease had spread globally, even into the Arctic, and may have killed as many as one hundred million people—approximately 5 percent of the global population. Despite its name, there was nothing Spanish about the flu. The virus received its name because Spain's non-involvement in World War I meant that it was the only European country not to be under news-censorship, and so the first detailed reports of flu appeared in that country.

The steady war propaganda kept the public in support of the war for quite some time, even in the face of mounting fatalities. In fact, the longer the war dragged on, the greater the effort was to rally support. Only the nature of the propaganda changed—from early enthusiastic posters to cartoon depictions of the enemy as bloodthirsty savages.[8] However, thousands on all sides took public stances against the conflict. Their reasons differed. Some argued along class lines, others along economic or racial lines; still others staked out a moral position against all forms of militarism. In Britain, over fifteen thousand individuals officially registered for "conscientious objector" status, as permitted by the Hague Conventions, risking social ostracism and even imprisonment.

By 1917 tens of thousands of French soldiers mutinied against directives to begin another frontal assault on German trenches. They objected to a new tactic called a "creeping barrage." Soldiers were to charge forward just a few feet behind successive waves of artillery shells, which would give them cover. Instead, the barrages killed the very troops they were supposed to be helping. In the end, roughly 25,000 soldiers underwent courts-martial for mutiny, and roughly one-tenth were convicted. Most of these received harsh imprisonments, and several hundred were executed.

In November 1914 a group of 101 British suffragists signed their names to an "Open Christmas Letter" addressed to "the Women of Germany and Austria":

> Sisters,
>
> Some of us wish to send you a word at this sad Christmastide, though we can but speak through the Press. The Christmas message sounds like mockery to a world at war, but those of us who wished and still wish for peace may surely offer a solemn greeting to such of you who feel as we do. Do not let us forget that our very anguish unites us, that we are passing together through the same experiences of pain and grief.
>
> Caught in the grip of terrible circumstance, what can we do? Tossed on this turbulent sea of human conflict, we can but move ourselves to those calm shores whereon stand, like rocks, the eternal verities—Love, Peace, Brotherhood.
>
> We pray you to believe that come what may we hold to our faith in Peace and Goodwill between nations; while technically at enmity in obedience to our rulers, we owe allegiance to that higher law which bids us live in peace with all men.

---

[8]   A poster announced the start of war: "The Great Game Has Begun!"

Though our sons are sent to slay each other, and our hearts are torn by the cruelty of this fate, yet through pain supreme we will be true to our common womanhood. We will let no bitterness enter in this tragedy, made sacred by the life-blood of our best, nor mar with hate the heroism of their sacrifice. Though much has been done on all sides you will, as deeply as ourselves, deplore, shall we not steadily refuse to give credence to those false tales so freely told us, each of the other?

We hope it may lessen your anxiety to learn we are doing our utmost to soften the lot of your civilians and war prisoners within our shores, even as we rely on your goodness of heart to do the same for ours in Germany and Austria.

Do you not feel with us that the vast slaughter in our opposing armies is a stain on civilization and Christianity, and that still deeper horror is aroused at the thought of those innocent victims, the countless women, children, babes, old and sick, pursued by famine, disease, and death in the devastated areas, both East and West?

As we saw in South Africa and the Balkan States, the brunt of modern war falls upon non-combatants, and the conscience of the world cannot bear the sight.

Is it not our mission to preserve life? Do not humanity and common sense alike prompt us to join hands with the women of neutral countries, and urge our rulers to stay further bloodshed?

Relief, however colossal, can reach but few. Can we sit still and let the helpless die in their thousands, as die they must—unless we rouse ourselves in the name of Humanity to save them? There is but one way to do this. We must all urge that peace be made with appeal to Wisdom and Reason. Since in the last resort it is these which must decide the issues, can they begin too soon, if it is to save the womanhood and child-hood as well as the manhood of Europe?

Even through the clash of arms we treasure our poet's vision, and already seem to hear:

A hundred nations swear that there shall be
Pity and Peace and Love among the good and free.

May Christmas hasten that day. Peace on Earth is gone, but by re-newal of our faith that it still reigns at the heart of things, Christmas should strengthen both you and us and all womanhood to strive for its return.

We are yours in this sisterhood of sorrow.

The author of the letter was Emily Hobhouse (1860–1926), a longtime social activist. Hobhouse got her start in public life when she campaigned against the brutal conditions that she had witnessed in British concentration camps in South Africa during the Boer War. The Christmas Letter created a rift among suffragists, since many of them supported the war. Despite their differences, however, most suffragists agreed to set aside the issue of women's rights until the war was over and to dedicate themselves to humanitarian work in the meantime.

A group of 150 German suffragists responded in March 1915 with an open letter (in English) of their own:

> To our English sisters, sisters of the same race, we express in the name of many German women our warm and heartfelt thanks for their Christmas greetings, which we only heard of lately.
>
> [Your] message was a confirmation of what we foresaw—that women of the belligerent countries, with all faithfulness, devotion, and love to their country, can go beyond it and maintain true solidarity with the women of other belligerent nations, and that really civilised women never lose their humanity.

OFFICERS AND GENTLEMEN

Every war introduces new weapons and new technologies of communication and transport and confronts new and usually unforeseen challenges. However, it takes time to understand the innovations and translate them into military tactics. As the saying goes, commanders are always fighting the last war. When World War I began, none of the top officers on either side of the conflict was familiar with trench warfare, submarine warfare, or aerial warfare. None had experienced poison gas or the gargantuan howitzers of modern artillery. Joseph Joffre (1852–1931), the French commander in chief at the outbreak of hostilities, had never even commanded an army before. His entire career up to that point had consisted of working as a military engineer. King George V read concerned reports from his general staff about the incompetence of the chief commander of the British Expeditionary Force, General John French. The leading commanders on all sides

> When World War I began, none of the top officers on either side of the conflict was familiar with trench warfare, submarine warfare, or aerial warfare. None had experienced poison gas or the gargantuan howitzers of modern artillery.

had inherited a tradition that still mimicked the military strategy and tactics used by Napoleon Bonaparte—a fast-moving infantry, pressing ever forward, complemented by portable artillery. This had worked brilliantly for Bonaparte at Austerlitz in 1805—but not in 1915, when the German field commander, Erich von Falkenhayn, earned the nickname "the Blood Miller of Verdun."

Mistakes in command, even elementary ones, marked the war effort on all sides. Miscommunication between the German and Austria-Hungarian leaders, for example, left their realms exposed to Russian advance. Each had expected the other to protect the Russian front while they pressed ahead in Belgium and Serbia, respectively. The confusion allowed Russia's forces to advance through all of Poland before they were stopped. At the eight-month siege of Gallipoli (1915–1916), civilians were assigned to the minesweepers that were supposed to clear the waterways in preparation for the Allied attack—crews that, unsurprisingly, fled once they came under heavy Ottoman artillery fire. As a result, one-third of the Allied battleships were sunk. On the Italian front officers launched twelve direct assaults against dug-in Austrian alpine units that held a clearly superior uphill position—protected by minefields, barbed wire, machine-gun nests, and artillery units. Fully one-half of all of Italy's 600,000 casualties in the war were suffered right here.

Just as sobering were the losses in the air and at sea. Both the airplane and the submarine made their military debut and proved vital to the outcome of the

Flying above the Pyramids   Airplanes were used almost entirely for reconnaissance in the first year of the war, since their engines could not carry the additional weight of bombs. Pilots were not even issued parachutes, at first, since those too proved too heavy for most engines. Guns were of little use until they could be synchronized with the propellers, lest they shoot off their own blades.

conflict. France put 68,000 airplanes into service; 52,000 were destroyed in battle. The design of the planes had to be kept simple, since many pilots went into battle after as little as a single week's instruction. Airplanes and airships were used initially for surveillance, but commanders quickly got the idea of dropping explosives. However, early airplanes did not fly at high altitudes, which left them vulnerable to enemy ground fire. Airplanes had their most dramatic effect in the Arab Revolt against the Turks, since the Ottomans had little heavy artillery and had dedicated it to other theaters. T. E. Lawrence described a battle at Megiddo in Palestine toward the end of the war, when British and Australian forces trapped a division of Turkish soldiers in a narrow defile, then strafed them from the air:

> When the smoke had cleared it was seen that the organization of the enemy had melted away. They were a dispersed horde of trembling individuals, hiding for their lives in every fold of the vast hills. Nor did their commanders ever rally them again. When our cavalry entered the silent valley the next day they could count ninety guns, fifty lorries, and nearly a thousand carts abandoned with all their belongings. The RAF lost four killed. The Turks lost a corps.

Despite Allied victories, lives were seen as wasted. Americans were reluctant to join a war that the officer and political class either was not trying to win or was too incompetent to lead. More than that, complaints ran, members of the labor and rural classes were regularly ordered into the worst of the fighting; so were recruits from colonial territories. In Australia today, commemoration of the slaughter at Gallipoli is a more emotionally powerful holiday than Armistice Day itself. The French mutinies of 1917 resulted from the officers' belief that they could pinpoint artillery barrages, from miles away, to provide cover for advancing infantrymen—which was absurd on the face of it.

Siegfried Sassoon, the soldier-poet, protested the war with a letter read in Parliament on July 30, 1917, published subsequently in the *Times* of London:

> I am making this statement as an act of willful defiance of military authority because I believe that the war is being deliberately prolonged by those who have the power to end it. I am a soldier, convinced that I am acting on behalf of soldiers. I believe that the war upon which I entered as a war of defense and liberation has now become a war of aggression and conquest. I believe that the purposes for which I and my fellow soldiers entered upon this war should have been so clearly stated as to have made it impossible to change them and that had this been done the objects which actuated us would now be attainable by negotiation.

I have seen and endured the sufferings of the troops and I can no longer be a party to prolonging these sufferings for ends which I believe to be evil and unjust. I am not protesting against the conduct of the war, but against the political errors and insincerities for which the fighting men are being sacrificed.

On behalf of those who are suffering now, I make this protest against the deception which is being practiced upon them; also I believe it may help to destroy the callous complacency with which the majority of those at home regard the continuance of agonies which they do not share and which they have not enough imagination to realize.

Despite government censorship, news about the war and its horrors circulated widely. After the initial elation in 1914, a popular attitude of grim resignation and determination set in. The war was no longer popular, but few saw any alternative, once it had begun, except victory. When Russia pulled out of the conflict and American entered it, in late 1917, fear arose that the war would drag on interminably. After the Allied victory at the Battle of the Somme, the exhausted Germans were ready to submit.

RUSSIA'S REVOLUTION

Reaching from Germany and Poland in the west to China and Japan in the east, Russia comprises one-sixth of the world's land mass. It is an enormous territory, made up largely of flat grassland with an icy northern fringe and no natural internal boundaries in its western reaches and of forests, steppes, and fertile valleys interspersed with mountainous stretches in its eastern expanses. It is also vast, open, and despite its large population chiefly an empty space. It is a land of extensive ethnic and cultural diversity, marked by long distances, poor communication, an adverse climate, and above all defensiveness and vulnerability. It lacked both an effective government and any natural borders to keep enemies out.

Despite reformist victories, autocratic ineptitude and the miseries of World War I brought an end to tsarist rule and the start of civil war. By 1920 Vladimir Lenin (1870–1924) and his Bolshevik party had won and established a Communist rule that would govern Russia until 1991.

---   +   ---

For long centuries the people of Russia suffered waves of invasion from all sides. According to tradition, Russia's history begins with an invasion of Swedish Vikings who established the first Kingdom of Kievan Rus' in the ninth century. Subsequent invaders included the Kumans, Pechenegs, Khazars, Slavs, Byzantines, Poles, Lithuanians, Germans, and French. Still other attackers included the Huns, Chinese,

Mongols, and Turkish peoples of the east. Without adequate means to defend themselves, Russia's rulers traditionally relied on two tactics. One was to relinquish territory by retreating; this forced invaders to maintain long supply lines while exposing
them to often brutal winters. The other tactic was to hurl wave after wave of common
soldiers at the attackers, in order to use up the invaders' stores of ammunition.

With a few exceptions, the Romanov rulers held tight to autocracy and
resisted efforts to reform. The development of democratic traditions, capitalist economies, industrialization, and liberal societies in the West frustrated
and frightened Russia's rulers more than they inspired them. If Bonaparte had
not been enough to convince Russia of Europe's dangerousness and untrust-
worthiness, the Crimean War in the 1850s was. Through the second half of the
19th century, nevertheless, pressure for reform did increase. The question was how
to reform. Many Russians supported Western-style reforms like human rights, democracy, and economic development; others hoped for a uniquely Russian version
of change, something homegrown and rooted in tradition. The tension between
these competing notions of change underlay much of Russia's social and cultural
development of the era. It provides the backdrop for the parade of great literary artists Russia produced: Aleksandr Pushkin (1799–1837), Nikolai Gogol (1809–1852),
Mikhail Lermontov (1814–1841), Ivan Turgenev (1818–1883), Fyodor Dostoevsky
(1821–1881), Leo Tolstoy (1828–1910), and Anton Chekhov (1860–1904).

Bloody Sunday   Tsarist soldiers firing on demonstrators at the Winter Palace in Saint
Petersburg, Russia, on "Bloody Sunday," January 9, 1905.

Calls for reform gained momentum in the 1860s and 1870s. Serfdom was abolished in 1861, and independent judiciaries with trials by jury were established. But in 1881 a terrorist assassinated Tsar Aleksandr II, which led his successor, Aleksandr III (r. 1881–1894), to strengthen the police state. He reached out for popular support by promoting a **Pan-Slavism** that masked an obsessive hatred of Jews, with the result that anti-Jewish pogroms became common and vicious. Aleksandr also tried to force rapid industrialization; his signature project was the Trans-Siberian Railroad, begun in 1891. Russia's loss in the war with Japan in 1905, combined

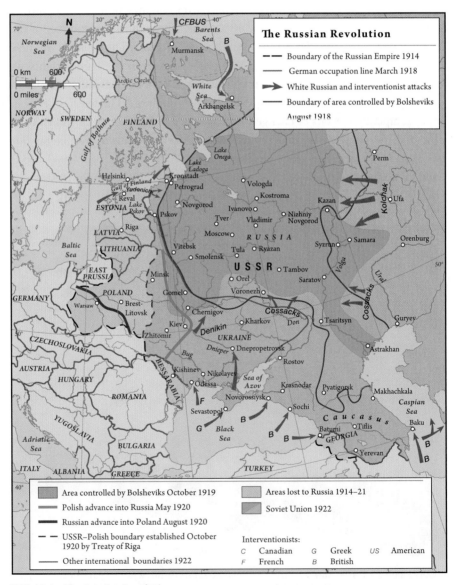

MAP 24.4 The Russian Revolution

with a failed attempt at revolution in Moscow and Saint Petersburg, led the next tsar, Nikolai II, to dismiss the Russian parliament.

The deaths of millions of poorly trained and ill-equipped soldiers, several years of horrendous crop failures, and the collapse of the currency led to a wave of food riots and labor strikes in early 1917. Unlike in 1905, the army supported the rebels this time, and the government fell. But as with revolutions elsewhere, most notably in France in 1789, the people could not agree on what government would replace the old administration. They were united only in their opposition to the tsar and to World War I. A dizzying array of rival parties quickly formed, and each party was just as quick to raise an army of its own. For two years a civil war raged across Russia. Liberals fought against Socialists against pro-tsarist Whites against pro-peasant Greens against Anarchists against Mensheviks against Bolsheviks (see Map 24.4).

The **Mensheviks** and Lenin's **Bolsheviks** were factions within the Communist movement behind rival leaders. The Bolsheviks won in part because they understood the depth of the popular desire for radical agrarian reform—how desperately the peasants wanted Russia's farmland redistributed. They won, too, because they believed unapologetically in the use of violence and terrorism to achieve their ends.

BOLSHEVISM AND THE LAWS OF HISTORY

Lenin possessed the unwavering drive and personal discipline of a true zealot.[9] Lenin's real name was Vladimir Ilyich Ulyanov, and his father had worked for the imperial bureaucracy as a provincial school inspector. He converted to radicalism as a youth and spent much of his young adulthood in Europe, where he made contacts with a network of dedicated reformers. (He became a Marxist in 1890 or 1891, during his study of the law as an extramural—that is, nonmatriculating—student at the University of Saint Petersburg.) Lenin sympathized with poor workers and farmers but never identified with them. He saw himself instead as a Romantic leader of the masses, a passionate intellectual superior to those whom he led.

His elitism carried over into his political thinking as well. Lenin's party positioned itself as a vanguard party: they held all authority and ruled the masses directly, rather than, as some Marxist groups had called for, establishing a government by public referendum. He championed a separate group of professional revolutionaries whose ideological purity would ensure the success of the revolution. It would also conveniently legitimize whatever tactics the party elite chose

---

[9]   Lenin's older brother was executed in 1887 for a failed attempt to assassinate Tsar Aleksandr III. The hanging of his brother turned Lenin against the tsarist state.

to employ. The incorruptibility of the Bolshevik leaders, he was convinced, would prevent them from being seduced by the trappings of the power they so ruthlessly reserved for themselves.

Lenin had to alter Marxist theory in order to make it fit the Russian situation, and the changes he made helped set the tone for much of the 20th century's international politics. Marx had argued that the inevitable transfer of wealth and power to the working class would and could happen only in an industrial society. Industrial capitalism as he saw it, for all its evil, was a necessary stage en route to Communist freedom. The proletarian class who would inherit the earth consisted first and foremost of urban laborers. Russia by 1920, however, had not become an industrialized society by any stretch of the imagination. Dirt-poor farmers and unskilled laborers still made up easily 80 percent of the population. Lenin as an intellectual needed to tweak the Marxist formula so that historical development could leapfrog over the industrial stage and straight to socialism.

Lenin wrote his most interesting books during his two-decade European exile before coming to power, when he was trying to establish himself among the revolutionary elite. His first significant publication was *The Development of Capitalism in Russia* (1899). Stuffed with statistics and charts, it is his most technical and forbidding work, but it is an important one. It is here that he

reworks Marxist theory by arguing that Russia's agricultural production already had all the labor specialization, class structure, and market competition called for by Marx. Lenin also extends his argument against **populism**. Populism, as he sees it, is moral compromise dressed up as common sense. True reform means centralizing all authority among professional revolutionaries, for the servitude of the masses allows them to be co-opted by capitalist landowners.

In the 1890s there were widespread calls within Russia for land reform—all within a structure of social democracy that would preserve the rights and citizenship of the elite. Lenin would have none of that. He insisted that only the

Russian Peasants Russian villagers pose for a photographer in this picture from the 1890s. Their wooden huts with thatch roofs can be seen, as well as the simple dirt roads that were the norm. In spring these became nearly impassable as the melting snow turned them into rivers of mud.

revolutionary caste can lead the masses to freedom, and it can do so only by ignoring the opinions of those they lead. As he put it in *What Is to Be Done?* (1902):

> The history of the world shows that workers by themselves can achieve nothing more than a trade-union level of consciousness.... Socialist theory, however, emerged from the coalescence of the philosophical, historical, and social theorizing of the intellectual classes, those educated members of the propertied classes. In terms of their social backgrounds, both Marx and Engels, the very founders of modern scientific socialism, belonged to the educated bourgeoisie. In Russia too the theoretical foundations [of revolutionary Marxism] were established independently of the labor movement, as an organic, inevitable consequence of the thought trajectory of the revolutionary socialist intelligentsia.

The leaders of the revolution, in other words, are of not the same stock as the workers they control, and they should not apologize for it.

Lenin's next major publication was *Materialism and Empiriocriticism: Critical Comments on a Reactionary Philosophy* (1909). It represents Lenin's only attempt at genuine philosophical writing. A number of Russian thinkers living in Europe had fallen away from Marxism after 1900, seeing it as too dependent on a materialist and determinist view of the world. Surely there is more to human existence than objective economic forces and inexorable laws of historical inevitability. What about human individuality? Human will? The power of instinct and passion? The human tendency to irrational longing and the desire for beauty? Is there, in the end, no room for the human spirit in philosophizing about human life? Lenin responds with an emphatic *no*.

No other book betrays more of Lenin's thin, hard, and brittle personality. He argues that there are only two real possibilities in a philosophical view of the world—materialism and idealism. There is the world of objects, things, bodies, atoms, molecules, and natural forces on the one hand, and there is the world of theories, Platonic forms, abstract ideas, and impersonal notions on the other. Any philosophy that attempts a middle position or claims somehow to transcend the poles is either short-sighted or just plain verbal tomfoolery. His point is reminiscent of Thomas Hobbes in *Leviathan*: a society can consist only of absolute chaos or absolute order, and any position in between is simply the sweep of the pendulum on its way from one extreme to the other. Materialism, Lenin concludes, must be the truth, since it alone is supported by modern science. Physical reality exists outside of human thought for the simple reason that the universe existed before human beings did—millions of years before, in fact. Moreover, human thought emerges from the human brain, which is itself a physical object. No brain, no thought; materialism alone has verifiable existence.

Lenin's argument is neither elegant nor original, but he presents it with evangelical intensity. The theory of **dialectical materialism**, or of the pendulum swings of history in a firmly materialist world, is actually a fairly minor aspect of Marx's own thought. But with Lenin it appears front and center as the force driving history forward—to the confrontation of the proletariat and the bourgeoisie. There is no way for human beings to avoid this force, any more than they can avoid Newton's universal laws. Just as all molecules are subject to gravity, all humanity is driven by dialectical materialism.

> Materialism, Lenin concludes, must be the truth, since it alone is supported by modern science. Physical reality exists outside of human thought for the simple reason that the universe existed before human beings did—millions of years before, in fact.

Most of Lenin's contemporaries lambasted the book as cold, crude, and shallow. He seemed determined to ignore anyone else's ideas, even Marx's. Although the book quickly sank from view, it was revived in the 1930s by a new leader of the Bolshevik regime, Josef Stalin—whose ability to regard people as mere objects was even more pronounced than Lenin's.

EXPORTING REVOLUTION

Lenin's most interesting book was inspired by the experience of World War I. *Imperialism, the Highest Stage of Capitalism* was published in Saint Petersburg in 1917. Lenin wrote it while living in Zurich in 1916, as he watched World War I unfold in all its tragedy from a safe distance in neutral Switzerland. Lenin here confronts a significant problem: Karl Marx had not foreseen imperialism. According to Marx, industrial capitalism would result in a consolidation of economic power among the most prominent members of the bourgeoisie. Once this institutional lock on further economic development was in place, the proletarian revolution would take place.

Lenin had to address why a revolution had not occurred to stop imperialism before it began. His adroit answer also buttresses his earlier contention—that agrarian Russia could bypass the industrial stage and still effect a Marxist revolution. In late capitalism, he argues, finance and industry form a union of their own that shuts out all competition. Once it has taken over an entire national economy its profits become stagnant, which drives the cartel overseas in search of new markets and larger profits. By investing its capital abroad, the cartel divides the world between the imperialist industrial nations and the colonized countries that are locked out of industrial development. Because the undeveloped nations depend on monopolistic capital, they assume the role of the proletariat as the actors in the revolution. Lenin asserts that imperialism is neither an aberration nor an accidental consequence of capitalism; it is actually the *goal* of capitalist societies, and the Great War of 1914 is the initial stage of the revolution yet to come. And the agents of the revolution will be the agrarian workers of the undeveloped periphery—meaning Russia.

Once the Bolsheviks took control of the government, Lenin and his comrades indeed led the country as a vanguard. He introduced two final major revisions of Marx's thought. First, he insisted on violent action in order to bring the revolution to fruition. And second, he insisted on the need to export the revolution to the colonized nations living under capitalist rule. Just as Bonaparte had believed that absolutism had to be crushed everywhere in order to preserve the revolution in France, Lenin concluded that revolutionary Russia needed to promote the rising up of oppressed rural workers everywhere.

> Just as Bonaparte had believed that absolutism had to be crushed everywhere in order to preserve the revolution in France, Lenin concluded that revolutionary Russia needed to promote the rising up of oppressed rural workers everywhere.

For the time being, however, that was not possible, Lenin declared. The Bolsheviks had to get Russia in order first. In 1920 they instituted a complete state takeover of the land and whatever manufacturing base the country possessed. They conscripted labor, confiscated all foodstuffs and goods, and began an emergency redistribution of provisions. The following year, however, Lenin announced a new policy of state socialism. Now the government retained control of finance, transportation, and industrial output but allowed the rest of the economy to return to a modest degree of private enterprise. Peasants contributed a certain percentage of their crops to the state, but they were free to sell the rest on an open market. Traders were allowed to buy and sell as they pleased. In essence, Lenin throughout the 1920s introduced a "mixed" system—socialism in the large-scale economy and capitalism in the small, local economies.

Politically, Communist Russia was a dictatorship led by a Bolshevik party of some half million members, and Lenin himself reigned supreme. He maintained the "ideological purity" of the party—by which he meant keeping the party subservient to his authority—by instituting regular purges. Spying and terrorism began on a massive scale, along with a network of forced labor camps. "Let us cleanse the Russian land of every type of harmful insect . . . by which I mean the

Lenin in the Vanguard   Lenin addresses a Moscow crowd in 1918.

rich, the miscreants, the lazy—all those not dedicated entirely to the revolution-ary cause."[10]

The Bolsheviks wiped out, by imprisonment, extermination, or both, the entire professional class of financiers, entrepreneurs, civic officials, engineers, and administrators, seeing them as unreliable. They abolished the Russian Orthodox Church, confiscated its possessions, and forbade all religious ceremonies and religious education. An internal security bureau, the forerunner of the KGB, strictly censored all publications, broadcasts, and public addresses. Mandatory public education introduced the new generation to socialist ideals and the correctness of the Leninist model of communal existence. Lenin himself remained in complete control until his death in 1924, but he seemed diminished as a personality. His strength was as a firebrand, attacking old systems, rather than as the administrator of a bureaucracy, even a ruthless one. His final four years are filled with complaints: "Russians are lousy workers compared to those in the West." "Treat the Jews in the Ukraine with an iron rod . . . . Transfer them to the front, and never let them into government offices." "Tell every member of the Security Bureau to kill anyone who does not show up to work because he wants a stupid Christmas celebration."

---

[10]   "One out of every ten lazy workers," Lenin proclaimed, "should be shot on the spot."

Still, despite the horrors of the civil war and of Lenin's brutal governance, daily life for most Russians was probably better in the 1920s than it had been under the tsars. Food and shelter become more available, as did some forms of education and medical care. This says more about the miserable failure of the Romanovs than about the success of the Bolsheviks, but the fact remains. Visitors from the West brought back to Europe breathless reports about Marxism as a new path of development. The West could and should consider that path, they said, as it rebuilt from the ruins of World War I. The spike in Western interest in Marxism came immediately after the conflict ended in 1918, and it helped set the stage for the misery that followed.

Emancipated Women   A Soviet propaganda poster in honor of the heroines of socialist labor. It proclaims, "What the October Revolution brought to the female worker and the peasant woman."

HOW NOT TO END A WAR

The United States entered World War I on April 6, 1917, "to make the world safe for democracy," in the words of President Woodrow Wilson (r. 1913–1921). Wilson had recently won election to a second term, largely on the platform of having kept America out of the conflict, though in a state of "armed neutrality." In reality, the country had never been altogether neutral. Between 1914 and 1916, American trade with the Allies had increased fourfold, and most of the goods sold had been war material—weapons and ammunition, military rations, and supplies like tents, boots, and uniforms. U.S. banks had extended the Allies more than two billion dollars in loans and credits, which meant that only an Allied victory would ensure repayment. Britain and France's debt alone equaled $45 billion in today's dollars. When the British imposed a naval blockade on Germany's Baltic coast, American ships never even attempted to challenge it.

Germany launched its U-boats into the Atlantic primarily to interdict American supplies to the Allies, an action that provoked American anger but failed to rouse the country to join the fight. Even when a German U-boat, in May 1915, sank the *Lusitania*—a British transatlantic passenger liner that had 128 Americans on board—and Germany refused to apologize, the U.S. position

Creating a New World Order   The main protagonists at the Paris Peace Talks:
Vittorio Emanuele Orlando of Italy, Britain's David Lloyd George, Georges
Clemenceau of France, and U.S. president Woodrow Wilson.

did not change.[11] An intercepted telegram from Berlin to the German ambassador in Mexico City, in January 1917, added fuel to American outrage. The Zimmermann telegram (named for the diplomat who had sent it) showed that Germany had offered military aid if Mexico was willing to declare war, in order to regain the territories lost in 1845 when the United States annexed Texas. One month later, when the Russians overthrew the tsar and pulled out of the conflict, Germany was able to gather its forces for a single massive campaign against the western front. America finally stirred to action.

After armistice was declared on November 11, 1918, the difficult work of ironing out a permanent peace settlement began. The actual settlement punished the losers, angered both sides, and practically ensured anything but permanent peace. The collapse of the Ottoman Empire was just one more sign that although the old order was gone for good, the grounds for resentment still simmered.

The Allied leaders—President Wilson, British prime minister David Lloyd George, French prime minister Georges Clemenceau, and Italian prime minister Vittorio Orlando—met in Paris along with teams of diplomats, historians, lawyers, and economists amid high hopes. Negotiations deadlocked almost instantly. The United States maintained that no single country had caused the war and so

---

[11]   Germany claimed that the *Lusitania* was carrying war supplies to Britain—and, as it turns out, it was.

every participant shared responsibility; all, therefore, had to compromise on territorial concessions. Wilson pressed especially hard for a political redivision of central and eastern Europe to respect ethnic nationalities. The French, however, considered themselves the victims of German aggression. The overwhelming bulk of the fighting on the western front, after all, had taken place on French soil. The only acceptable option was to punish Germany so that she could never again threaten France. The British took a position somewhere between the two. After months of talks and no progress at all, the governments finally agreed out of exhaustion and frustration to France's demands.

The **Treaty of Versailles** (1919) actually consists of five separate treaties, one with each of the Axis powers (Germany, Austria, Hungary, Bulgaria, and Turkey), and each one created as many problems as it resolved. The treaty with Germany—the Treaty of Versailles proper—proved the most controversial. France insisted on, and won, vast concessions. Germany was stripped of all overseas colonies and internationally held funds, which were duly reapportioned among Belgium, Britain, France, and Italy. The regions of Alsace and Lorraine were ceded to France, and the rest of Germany west of the Rhine River was given over to a new international body dedicated to world peace and cooperation, the League of Nations. Germany's borders were in essence pushed back to what they had been in 1871. The German military was limited to one hundred thousand soldiers and was denied aircraft, heavy artillery, and warships.

Most galling of all to the Germans were articles 231 and 232 of the treaty, which forced Germany to accept guilt for the entire war:

> Article 231: The Allied and Associated Governments affirm and Germany accepts the responsibility of Germany and her allies for causing all the loss and damage to which the Allied and Associated Governments and their nationals have been subjected as a consequence of the war imposed upon them by the aggression of Germany and her allies.

> Article 232: The Allied and Associated Governments recognize that the resources of Germany are not adequate, after taking into account permanent diminutions of such resources which will result from other provisions of the present Treaty, to make complete reparation for all such loss and damage. The Allied and Associated Governments, however, require, and Germany undertakes, that she will make compensation for all damage done to the civilian population of the Allied and Associated Powers and to their property during the period of the belligerency of each as an Allied or Associated Power against Germany.

These articles obliged Germany to make reparations for all civilian losses to the Allied powers, which a separate commission reckoned at a sum of 226 billion reichsmarks (roughly $680 billion in today's currency). This was an impossible sum, since so much of Germany's accumulated wealth had been confiscated. The treaty, after all, had taken away territories that supported most of the nation's industrial capacity—75 percent of its iron ore deposits, 30 percent of its steel production, and nearly 30 percent of its available coal.

As stringent as it was, the treaty represented far less than France had originally wanted. Criticism of the pact emerged almost instantly. The British Parliament and the U.S. Congress refused to ratify it, which left France feeling exposed, with unreliable allies. A leading British economist who had in fact been a delegate to the peace conference, John Maynard Keynes (1883–1946), repudiated the treaty. In his *Economic Consequences of the Peace* (1919), Keynes had a gloomy prediction not only for Germany but for the entire Continent:

> The essential facts of the situation, as I see them, are expressed simply. Europe consists of the densest aggregation of population in the history of the world. This population is accustomed to a relatively high standard of life, in which, even now, some sections of it anticipate improvement rather than deterioration. In relation to other continents Europe is not self-sufficient; in particular it cannot feed itself. Internally the population is not evenly distributed, but much of it is crowded into a relatively small number of dense industrial centers. This population secured for itself a livelihood before the war, without much margin of surplus, by means of a delicate and immensely complicated organization, of which the foundations were supported by coal, iron, transport, and an unbroken supply of imported food and raw materials from other continents. By the destruction of this organization and the interruption of the stream of supplies, a part of this population is deprived of its means of livelihood. Emigration is not open to the redundant surplus. For it would take years to transport them overseas, even, which is not the case, if countries could be found which were ready to receive them. The danger confronting us, therefore, is the rapid depression of the standard of life of the European populations to a point which will mean actual starvation for some (a point already reached in Russia and approximately reached in Austria). Men will not always die quietly. For starvation, which brings to some lethargy and a helpless despair, drives other temperaments to the nervous instability of hysteria and to a mad despair. And these in their distress may overturn the remnants of organization, and submerge civilization itself in their attempts to satisfy

desperately the overwhelming needs of the individual. This is the danger against which all our resources and courage and idealism must now co-operate.

Europe after the war did indeed have difficulty feeding itself, and not just Germany. For a time the Allied countries could draw on the resources of their colonies. Now, however, the collapse of the Ottoman and Habsburg Empires gave fresh hope to colonized peoples throughout the world. They might finally achieve freedom from all European control. Germany, meanwhile, was forced to swallow a humiliating treaty that left a legacy of resentment and betrayal.

> Now, however, the collapse of the Ottoman and Habsburg empires gave fresh hope to colonized peoples throughout the world. They might finally achieve freedom from all European control.

The settlement with Austria was not as punitive as that with Germany, although the Austrians felt that it was. Austria and Hungary became separate countries, much to the rejoicing of the Hungarians, and an autonomous Czechoslovakia was established. A short-lived kingdom of Serbia, Croatia, and Slovenia soon evolved into the federated state of Yugoslavia; smaller territorial concessions were made to Italy and Romania. Austria itself was thus reduced to a landlocked republic and was forbidden to unite with Germany into a larger German state. The Hungarians celebrated independence from Vienna and were left with an ethnically cohesive state. However, they resented losing control of the Slovak, Slovenian, and Balkan peoples—who had at one time made up 60 percent of their subjects (see Map 24.5).

YOUNG TURKS

The demise of the Ottoman Empire both was and was not a consequence of the war. The revolt in 1908 of a faction called the **Young Turks** had already led to a constitutional reform that reinstated the Turkish Parliament and severely limited the power of the monarchy. A number of peripheral territories, primarily in the Balkans and much of today's country of Libya, had already taken advantage of the political disorder and managed to win independence from Istanbul. While the rebellion contributed to a shrinking of the empire, it nonetheless produced a more stable and reform-minded government.

The Young Turks were not democrats, although they posed as such when negotiating with the Western powers. Interested above all in promoting pan-ethnic Islamic nationalism, they overthrew the sultan Abdul Hamid II in 1909 and replaced him with his half brother Mehmed V (r. 1909–1918). The Young

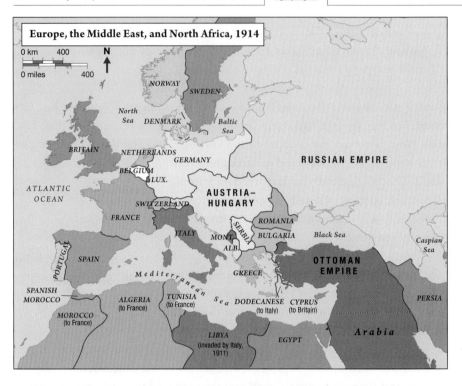

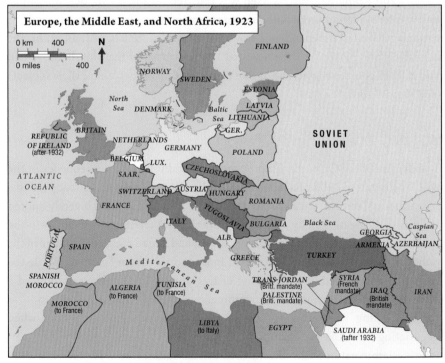

MAP 24.5   Europe and the Middle East in 1914 and 1923

Turks had modernizing ambitions, and some of them, at least, hoped to govern a united Islamic world under a secular regime, seeing this as the best hope of resolving the religious sectarianism among Muslims. The position of non-Muslims under Young Turk rule was uncertain. Indeed, the policies of the Young Turks were contradictory, which prompted groups like the Armenians and Jews to seek to break away from Turkish rule altogether. The Young Turk administration, not the sultan, entered the war on the Axis side.

The Arab Revolt had weakened Turkish power even further, by causing most of the Middle East to rise up against Istanbul. Defeat in the war meant the effective end of the empire, and the ensuing political confusion meant that it took until 1920 to formalize a peace treaty with the Allies. The treaty cut away even further at the Turkish dominion. Greece was awarded sites in Thrace, while Italy received control of Rhodes and the Dodecanese Islands. Independent republics of Armenia and Kurdistan were carved out of the eastern reaches of the empire (although all three were short-lived), and all the Arab territories were given over to the Allies. Syria became a French Mandate, while Iraq, Palestine, and Transjordan became a British Mandate.

Arab Delegates to the Paris Peace Conference   Prince Faisal stands in the foreground; just over his left shoulder, in Arab headdress, is Col. T.E. Lawrence (Lawrence of Arabia). Contrary to promises of independence made earlier to the Arabs, Britain and France retained control of much of the Middle East after the collapse of the Ottoman state.

Turkey was left, in essence, with only those territories that were primarily Turkish in population. The settlement hurt Turkish pride, which was further harmed by international accusations of guilt for the Armenian genocide. A new leader, Mustafa Kemal Atatürk (1881–1938), took advantage of wounded Turkish nationalism to promote a new Republic of Turkey with a curious blend of liberal and reactionary elements. He was committed to secularism and republican government, but rigidly determined to defend Turkey against any criticism from outside.

The Great War ended, at last, with bristling resentment, constrained economies, and damaged national pride on all sides. The coming years did not look hopeful.

WHO, WHAT, WHERE

Arab Revolt
Bolsheviks
dialectical materialism
Mensheviks
Pan-Slavism

populism
Schlieffen Plan
Sykes-Picot Agreement
Treaty of Versailles
Young Turks

SUGGESTED READINGS

Primary Sources

Angell, Norman. *The Great Illusion: A Study of the Relation of Military Power to National Advantage.*

Graves, Robert. *Goodbye to All That.*

Jünger, Ernst. *Storm of Steel: From the Diary of a German Shock-Troop Officer on the Western Front.*

Keynes, John Maynard. *The Economic Consequences of the Peace.*

Lenin, Vladimir. *Imperialism, the Highest Stage of Capitalism.*

———. *The State and Revolution.*

———. *What Is To Be Done?*

Shaw, George Bernard. *Common Sense about the War.*

Anthologies

Neiberg, Michael S., ed. *The World War I Reader: Primary and Secondary Sources* (2006).

Shevin-Coetzee, Marilyn, and Frans Coetzee. *World War I: A History in Documents* (2010).

Weinberg, Robert, and Laurie Bernstein. *Revolutionary Russia: A History in Documents* (2010).

Studies

Akçam, Taner. *A Shameful Act: The Armenian Genocide and the Question of Turkish Responsibility* (2007).

Azak, Umut. *Islam and Secularism in Turkey: Kemalism, Religion, and the Nation State* (2010).

Bass, Gary Jonathan. *Stay the Hand of Vengeance: The Politics of War Crimes Tribunals* (2002).

Bein, Amit. *Ottoman Ulema, Turkish Republic: Agents of Change and Guardians of Tradition* (2011).

Bloxham, Donald. *The Great Game of Genocide: Imperialism, Nationalism, and the Destruction of the Ottoman Armenians* (2007).

Campos, Michelle. *Ottoman Brothers: Muslims, Christians, and Jews in Early Twentieth-Century Palestine* (2010).

Ceadel, Martin. *Living the Great Illusion: Sir Norman Angell, 1872–1967* (2009).

Englund, Peter. *The Beauty and the Sorrow: An Intimate History of the First World War* (2011).

Fitzpatrick, Sheila. *The Russian Revolution* (2008).

Hanioğlu, M. Şükrü. *Atatürk: An Intellectual Biography* (2011).

Herwig, Holger H. *The First World War: Germany and Austria-Hungary, 1914–1918* (2009).

Kévorkian, Raymond. *The Armenian Genocide: A Complete History* (2011).

Kramer, Alan. *Dynamic of Destruction: Culture and Mass Killing in the First World War* (2009).

McMeekin, Sean. *The Berlin-Baghdad Express: The Ottoman Empire and Germany's Bid for World Power* (2010).

———. *The Russian Origins of the First World War* (2011).

Philpott, William. *Three Armies on the Somme: The First Battle of the Twentieth Century* (2011).

Sharp, Alan. *The Versailles Settlement: Peacemaking after the First World War, 1919–1923* (2008).

Strachan, Hew. *The First World War.* Vol. 1, *To Arms* (2003).

Suny, Ronald Grigor, Fatma Müge Göçek, and Norman M. Naimark, eds. *A Question of Genocide: Armenians and Turks at the End of the Ottoman Empire* (2011).

Thompson, Mark. *The White War: Life and Death on the Italian Front, 1915–1919* (2010).

Zürcher, Erik J. *The Young Turk Legacy and Nation Building: From the Ottoman Empire to Atatürk's Turkey* (2010).

For additional resources, including maps, primary sources, visuals, web links, and quizzes, please go to **www.oup.com/us/backman.**

CHAPTER 25

Radical Realignments

1919–1939

THE GREAT DEPRESSION
IN THE GREATER WEST

Decline in industrial
production of over 30%
Decline in industrial
production of up to 30%

The Greater West entered the postwar era with little confidence and many worries. Europe remained politically unstable and economically vulnerable, and the Middle East churned with new turmoil and resentment toward Europe. America largely wanted to wash its hands of "foreign entanglements," to quote an old warning from George Washington in his presidential farewell address, and a new government in Moscow declared its goal of liberating the world from capitalist oppression. Desolation and confusion reigned. The immediate crisis, however, was economic. Most of Europe emerged from the war either bankrupt or perilously close to it. "The military crisis may be over," wrote the French poet Paul Valéry (1871–1945) in 1919, "but the economic crisis is still here with us in all its ferocity."

Apart from the dislocation of their overseas colonies, the European countries had lost their dominance in many international markets to relative newcomers—Australia, Canada, Japan, and the United States. Even worse, most of Europe's governments were deeply in debt. They had financed the war by selling billions of dollars in bonds and by borrowing both public and private funds from the United States. England and France responded to their debt problem, initially, by simply printing more money; but when bondholders objected to receiving repayment in devalued currency, they stopped. The United States, for its part, refused to accept the

◀ **Force of Will** Never a great orator, Mussolini compensated by being a passionate one. His expressive nature came across to many as buffoonish and insincere. An egoist who despised democracy and Christianity as refuges for the weak, he likened himself to a Nietzschean "superman" but lacked the positive qualities Nietzsche had expected in such a figure.

- History for Beginners
- Parceling Out Nations
- New Rights and New Economies
- The Great Depression
- The Search for Someone to Blame
- Modernism, Experiment, and Trauma
- The Rise of Fascism: Italy and Spain
- Nazism in Germany
- Oppression and Terror in Russia
- A New Deal?
- Appeasement and Pacifism

CHAPTER
OUTLINE

new currency, too. The United States emerged from the war in better economic and political shape than any other participant. Even so, America found it difficult to convert back to a peacetime economy and struggled with inflation that reached as high as 18 percent in 1919–1920.

Everything seemed in flux even before the beginning, in 1929, of the great economic crash called the Great Depression. Educators were revisiting the entire history of Western civilization. Attempts to create an international League of Nations foundered; national aspirations were emerging on the peripheries of Europe and in the Middle East; and runaway inflation set the stage for economic unrest. The tyrannies of Fascism and totalitarianism further threatened peace. Amid all this, modern literature entered a new stage with its own experiments and trauma.

People across Europe and America cried out for an explanation, which resulted in a growing popular interest in history. American colleges and universities responded with what came to be called "Western civilization" courses that followed the story from Mesopotamia to the Treaty of Versailles.

HISTORY FOR BEGINNERS

How on earth had the Western world got itself into such a mess? Europe, after all, was the cradle of democracy, modern science, Western Christianity, and philosophy. It had given birth to Michelangelo, Leonardo da Vinci, Shakespeare, Cervantes, Rembrandt, Bach, Mozart, Goethe, Voltaire, Pushkin, and Tolstoy. It had produced both industrial genius and the most trenchant criticism of industrialization. Europe had the world's highest literacy rates and standards of living. Its technological development was unmatched. Though still hampered by legal and social prejudices, women played a larger public role in it than in any other society on the globe. A vigorous and determined press enabled citizens to stay informed. Yet this civilization had now sunk to an extraordinary depth of savagery.

CHAPTER TIMELINE

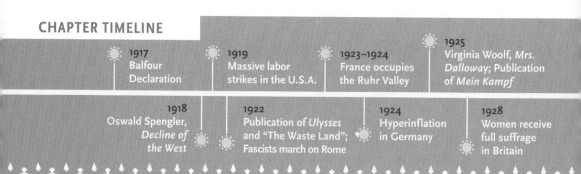

1917
Balfour Declaration

1919
Massive labor strikes in the U.S.A.

1923–1924
France occupies the Ruhr Valley

1925
Virginia Woolf, *Mrs. Dalloway*; Publication of *Mein Kampf*

1918
Oswald Spengler, *Decline of the West*

1922
Publication of *Ulysses* and "The Waste Land"; Fascists march on Rome

1924
Hyperinflation in Germany

1928
Women receive full suffrage in Britain

People across Europe and America cried out for an explanation, which resulted in a growing popular interest in history. American colleges and universities responded with what came to be called "Western civilization" courses that followed the story from Mesopotamia to the Treaty of Versailles. While these courses did not shy away from the horrors of war, they emphasized the positive achievements of three millennia—monotheism, democracy, education, and prosperity. At the same time, literature and philosophy departments crafted "great books" and "great ideas" surveys of Western culture. Such courses presumed that the Western way of life still offered the best chance for a bright future. Before long, the courses created at the University of Chicago and at Columbia University established models that were quickly adopted by other schools around the country. The fundamental problem, they urged, was not with Western values themselves but with the perverting radical misrepresentations of them. Capitalism is not at fault; only the most unchecked and rapacious form of it. Democracy is not the culprit either; if anything, it was the too-limited and constrained versions of it that led to the trouble. The answer, therefore, was to pursue more and better capitalism, more and better democracy.

Survey courses of this type did not appear in Europe's universities, principally because Europeans already knew their history better than most Americans knew theirs; but European curricula moved sharply away from the nation-based focus of their history departments and placed new emphasis on the histories of other countries and cultures. Still, a two-volume history by a sickly German loner became almost overnight the most talked-about book in Europe. In universities, coffeehouses, public libraries, and private studies everywhere, everyone read it and debated it. The book was *The Decline of the West*, by Oswald Spengler; a first volume appeared in 1918, a second four years later. In it, Spengler identifies ten different morphological types of cultures, of which three are at work in the three thousand years of Western history. He argues that Western civilization has evolved through these three major phases of development—the Magian, the Apollonian, and the

1929
Start of the Great Depression;
Lateran Agreement between
Vatican and Italy

1933
United States abandons
the gold standard; Hitler
appointed Chancellor

1936–1939
Spanish Civil War

1939
World War II in
Europe begins

1932
Unemployment in
Germany over 43 percent

1936
The Great Purge in Soviet Union; John
Maynard Keynes, *The General Theory
of Employment, Interest, and Money*

1938
Munich Conference gives
Sudetenland to Germany

Faustian. Spengler describes these, respectively, as the belief in magic (including the major religions), the striving for order (classical Greece and Rome), and the pursuit of power and knowledge (the modern West). For him, Europe in the early 20th century had reached the end of its Faustian period, after which life ceases to be creative and vital and becomes bureaucratic and superficial.

His argument is not wholly original; an earlier form of it had been made by an Italian scholar named Giambattista Vico (1668–1744) in the 18th century. Vico, however, had emphasized the cyclical nature of civilizations: after the inevitable collapse of any society, it begins a new cycle by a return to another, though different, primitive stage. Spengler, in contrast, sees no necessary relationship between phases; when one phases ends (usually after a period of roughly one thousand years) a new one begins; but no one can predict which phase will succeed any previous one. History is a constant and random reconfiguration of cultural types around the globe.

Spengler's book proved popular not for the strength of its arguments but for the resonance of its gloomy outlook with the prevailing mood of postwar Europe. Indeed, once Europe recovered some stability in the 1920s, interest in Spengler evaporated until the gloom of yet another postwar era (in the late 1940s this time) made him once again a figure of interest.

Rival visions of history were quick to appear. For H. G. Wells (1866–1946), a popular novelist and science-fiction writer, hope for the future remains—so long as we remain dedicated to educating all people.[1] Catastrophes like the Great War occur only when ignorance and prejudice reign supreme, he assured readers. Wells published *The Outline of History* in 1920. In its 1,300 pages he argues for an evolutionary view of history. Mankind, he says, is in a continual state of adaptation. Although periods of crisis and ruin may occur, human history progresses upward—or it will if we let it:

> The need for a common knowledge of the general facts of human history throughout the world has become very evident during the tragic happenings of the last few years. Swifter means of communication have brought all men closer to one another for good or for evil. War becomes a universal disaster, blind and monstrously destructive; it bombs the baby in its cradle and sinks the food-ships that cater for the non-combatant and the neutral. There can be no peace now, we realize, but a common peace in all the world; no prosperity but a general prosperity. But there can be no common peace and prosperity without common historical ideas. Without such ideas to hold them together in harmonious co-operation, with nothing but narrow, self-ish, and conflicting nationalist traditions, races and peoples are bound to drift towards conflict and destruction. This truth, which was apparent to

---

[1] "Human history becomes more and more a race between education and catastrophe."—H. G. Wells.

that great philosopher Kant a century or more ago—it is the gist of his tract upon universal peace—is now plain to the man in the street. Our internal policies and our economic and social ideas are profoundly vitiated at present by wrong and fantastic ideas of the origin and historical relationship of social classes. A sense of history as the common adventure of all mankind is as necessary for peace within as it is for peace between the nations.

Even more massive works appeared, too. Arnold Toynbee's (1889–1975) *A Study of History* (twelve volumes, starting in 1934) and Will Durant's (1885–1981) *The Story of Civilization* (eleven volumes, starting in 1935) made bookshelves groan across the world.

The war was only one reason for the sudden fascination with history. The other was fear of Marxism. To many oppressed laborers and struggling émigrés, the Bolshevik success in Russia gave a jolt of encouragement, just as the American Revolution had inspired reformers in 18th-century France. Radical change seemed within grasp and worth pursuing. Across Europe workers' rights had been rolled back during the war, including the right to unionize, and that convinced many workers that the labor struggles of the previous century had to be fought anew. Capitalism, it seemed to them, was as likely to regress as to reform. Labor strikes across Europe and America prompted a broad array of legal and extralegal crackdowns by Western governments.

Concern about the "Red Menace" was especially strong in the United States, where fears of Bolshevism reached near-panic levels. In 1919 alone came the Seattle General Strike, the Boston Police Strike, the Pennsylvania Steelworkers' Strike, and the United Mineworkers' Strike. It is easy to see why Western civilization courses placed such emphasis on the rise of modern democracy and the strength of economic liberalism. They displayed a special fascination with the American and French Revolutions, as twin birthplaces of freedom, and they focused on capitalism's self-correcting powers, as guarantors of prosperity and justice. The pure "Western tradition," they argued, still represented humankind's best hope as long as it was allowed to work.

A renewed passion for history also characterized Arab society. While Arab chroniclers and memoirists had always been numerous,

Worker's Paradise   Bernard Shaw's faith in human nature was bitterly shaken by World War I, and in the mid 1920s he lost faith in democracy and drifted into admiration for strong leaders. An early enthusiast for Mussolini, he visited Russia in 1931 and returned full of enthusiasm for Stalin.

and some had earned a wide readership, no Arab historian of any note had emerged since Ibn Khaldun in the 14th century. The breakup of the Ottoman world, however, coupled with the surging nationalism of the ethnic Arabs seeking independence, inspired an energetic new wave of historical writing. Most of these works say more about the time in which they were written than about the eras they ostensibly discuss, though, since they tend to view earlier ages through the prism of 19th-century imperialism and colonialism. The medieval Crusades, for example, had been regarded for centuries in the Muslim world as a series of bitter but local frontier wars of relatively minor importance. No full-length Arab-language history of the Crusades, in fact, had ever even been written; the wars for the Holy Land had always taken a backseat to the conflicts that really mattered—those between the Arabs and the Turks, between the Arabs and the Persians, and between the Arabs, Persians, and Turks combined against the Mongols. In the aftermath of 19th-century imperialism and global conflict, however, Arab writers reinterpreted the Crusades dramatically. Suddenly these frontier skirmishes stood out as the first of Western Christianity's war upon Islam, the start of a determined crime spree to strangle Islam in its crib and seize control of the Arab lands.

PARCELING OUT NATIONS

President Woodrow Wilson had arrived at the Paris Peace Conference with an outline of how to structure the peace settlement and lay the foundations for postwar rebuilding. But the plan, known as the **Fourteen Points**, quickly proved unworkable. So, it soon proved, did Europe's economy.

Wilson's main ideas—apart from preserving free movement on the seas and free trade between countries—were to redraw Europe's political boundaries. After the collapse of the Habsburg, Ottoman, and Romanov Empires, he sought to recognize the ethnic and nationalist aspirations of the peoples in central and eastern Europe. He also hoped to create an international **League of Nations** that would arbitrate disputes, oversee demilitarization, and provide for collective security. But creating new borders faced two difficulties. First, the movement of peoples in the preceding hundred years made it impossible to establish countries without ethnic minorities. Europe's populace was now intermixed (see Map 25.1). Second, political rivalries between the dominant nations frustrated efforts to build stable new countries. The contours of Poland, for example, resulted from a desire to establish a buffer zone between Russia and Germany. Byelorussian, German, Jewish, and Ukrainian minorities made up at least a third of the new country's population, and no fewer than twenty-five political parties formed, each with a different constituency and a different vision of Poland's future. Similar problems confronted the newly created Bulgaria, Czechoslovakia, Hungary,

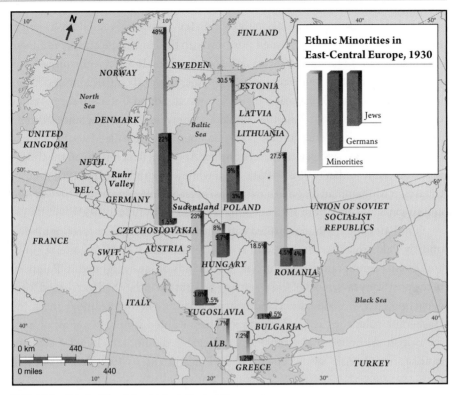

MAP 25.1   Ethnic Minorities in East-Central Europe, 1930

Romania, and Yugoslavia. Compounding their problems, the new states of eastern Europe were industrially undeveloped. Anywhere between 60 and 80 percent of their populations was still engaged in primitive farming.

Many of the same problems existed outside of Europe. The League of Nations had parceled out the former Ottoman Empire to Britain and France, since it judged the Middle East to be unready to stand on its own. Britain took control of Iraq, Palestine, and Transjordan, while France was given Lebanon and Syria. Britain also oversaw Arabia, Egypt, and Iran. The creation of these not-quite independent states, or **mandates**, outraged their inhabitants. Not only did they violate promises made by the Allies during the war, they seemed simply to substitute one form of foreign imperialism for another. Moreover, the Western powers took little notice of local conditions, including culture and religion. The Turks had at least understood the difference between Shi'a and Sunnis; between ethnic Arabs, Armenians, Kurds, Palestinians, Syrians, and Turkmen; and between the various tribes. In establishing a unified British Iraq, for example, the League of Nations fused distinct territories that the Ottomans had governed as independent provinces.

Global politics and dynastic rivalries within the Arab world complicated matters. Britain, for example, had established close ties with the Hashemite clan, a prominent Arab family said to be the last direct descendants of the Prophet Muhammad, and planned to install its leader, Faisal ibn Ali, as ruler of a unified Palestine and Transjordan. The **Balfour Declaration** in 1917, however, bound Britain to support a national Jewish homeland in Palestine. Caught between opposing allegiances, Britain divided Palestine and Transjordan as autonomous units, installed Faisal as king of Iraq (r. 1921–1933), and placed Faisal's brother Abdullah ibn Hussein on the throne as ruler of Transjordan (r. 1921–1951). Meanwhile a descendant of the 19th-century tribal emir Muhammad ibn Saud emerged as the leader in Arabia itself. This was Abd al-Aziz ibn Saud (emir from 1915 and king of Arabia from 1926 to 1953).

The Palestinian Mandate roiled with tensions between the native population (mostly Palestinian Arabs, but with sizable Jewish and Christian communities) and Zionist immigrants from Europe. Thousands of Jews migrated to Palestine in the postwar years, most of them settling on lands that they had purchased from departing Turks or Palestinian landowners pursuing a better life under one of the Hashemite rulers or the Saudi dynasts; others wanted simply to get away from the British. Although these transfers were legal, it did not take long for concern to arise about Jewish "displacement" of the Palestinians. By 1922 Britain decided

White City   Ben-Yehuda Street in Tel Aviv was famous for its Bauhaus-style architecture, which was used during a construction boom in the 1930s when thousands of Jewish refugees poured into the city. The neighborhood takes its nickname from the local practice of covering the exteriors of buildings with heat-reflecting white plaster.

to slow the migration of Jews into the region, in order to appease its millions of Muslim subjects. The Arabs opposed Jewish settlement (at this stage, at least) less out of resistance to the idea of Zionism than as a cudgel with which to beat the British. These developments pleased no one and set the stage for decades of turmoil.

NEW RIGHTS AND NEW ECONOMIES

Most European countries received new constitutions or significantly revised existing ones, and the most significant revision was the extension of the vote to women. The campaigns for female suffrage had taken a backseat to the war, but calls for the vote rose anew before the ink on the peace treaty was dry. Women received the right to vote in the new Czechoslovakia in 1918, in Germany in 1919, in Austria and the United States in 1920, and in Poland in 1921. Limited rights of suffrage were introduced in Britain and Hungary in 1918 and 1925, respectively; British women received full rights in 1928. Women in France and Italy were denied the vote until 1945, however, and Switzerland rejected female suffrage until 1971. Delays were largely the fault of the Liberal parties, who warned that women would vote overwhelmingly for Conservatives.

Economic concerns dominated the postwar years. Except for the regions around the old western front, the war had left most of Europe's factories intact. These factories needed to be retooled for commercial manufacture from their wartime activities, but they did not need to be rebuilt from the ground up. Industrial production could therefore begin again as soon as capital and raw materials became available. France, for the moment, was almost entirely dependent on German reparations and American credit for capital. Britain and Belgium also relied heavily on German payments but were better prepared to relaunch their manufacturing base. A problem blocked their path, however. Republican president Warren G. Harding (1921–1923) placed high tariffs on imports in order to protect American businesses. This meant that Europeans could not sell their products and

RÉPUBLIQUE FRANÇAISE

EXPOSITION COLONIALE
INTERNATIONALE
PARIS
1931

IMP. DE VAUGIRARD - PARIS. 1928   J. de la Népère

Selling the Empire   Paris hosted the International Colonial Exposition in 1931, one of the last large-scale celebrations of imperialism. This poster invites visitors to delight in the colorful costumes and quaint handcrafts of France's happy underlings.

thereby earn the money they needed to pay off their American creditors. For Britain and Belgium, it also meant a greater reliance on their colonies and Middle Eastern mandates, while Germany turned instead to trade with eastern Europe and Communist Russia.

Inflation set in as governments let their currencies depreciate in order to make their goods cheaper and more competitive. The tactic worked, to an extent, but the falling currencies made it harder for Europeans to purchase American goods—which in turn triggered concerns for U.S. growth. Instability in the markets threatened to impede economic recovery. When Germany failed to make a reparation payment to France in 1923, the French took drastic action. Fearing that its ties with Russia might enable Germany to recover its prewar economic dominance on the Continent, and worried that America and Britain never ratified the Versailles Treaty and thus were unreliable allies, the French sent an army into the Ruhr Valley. There it seized German factories and effectively held the German workers and their families for ransom, while demanding payment in full of Germany's entire reparations debt.

Germans everywhere were outraged, and the Weimar government urged Ruhr citizens to stay at home and refuse to work for the French. When talks failed to resolve the dispute, Berlin responded by wildly printing trillions of marks—and declared the reparations bill "paid" with worthless currency. Feverish hyperinflation followed.

A single U.S. dollar in January 1924 purchased four German marks; by September a dollar equaled nearly 4.5 *trillion* marks. Personal savings, life-insurance policies, bond holdings, and pensions were wiped out instantaneously. Germans who received their pay in cash found that it lost half its value by the time they reached a shop in which to spend it. In October 1923, Betty Scholem, a woman living in Berlin, wrote to her son, the famous Jewish scholar Gershom Scholem, then living in Switzerland, describing conditions:

Play Money By November of 1923 hyperinflation had made German currency worthless. At more than four trillion marks to the U.S. dollar, the money had more value as fuel for kitchen stoves and fireplaces than as currency.

Streetcar fare is twenty million marks, and tomorrow it will probably be fifty. You can't even imagine what it is like. My God, it's like witnessing a witches' Sabbath, only a million times more wicked. As you know, we sell women's magazines to [a certain friend]. A few days ago her husband sent us a cashier's check for five million marks—but when we went to the local branch of their bank, here in Berlin, to pick it up, they charged us forty million marks in transfer fees! ... [Some other friends of ours] went out to lunch and had rabbit. It cost 1.75 *billion*.

One needed a wheelbarrow full of marks to purchase a single loaf of bread.

The United States responded to the crisis with a plan created by the director of the federal Bureau of the Budget, Charles G. Dawes—who won the Nobel Peace Prize in 1925 and became vice president under President Calvin Coolidge. This massive bailout restructured reparations—which of course had not really been paid at all—so that Germany had a chance to meet its obligation without crippling its own economic development. The currency was stabilized within a year, but the issue of reparations and the moral stain of responsibility for the war continued to rankle Germans. Even as the economy improved, voters responded to candidates who announced their determination to do something about the "guilt payments" and restore Germany's honor.

Several years of impressive growth across Europe began in 1925. With order restored to markets and the threat of new French-German hostilities removed, relief and hope filled the air. Within four years, in fact, western Europe reached its prewar levels of industrial production. Radios, telephone systems, automobiles, phonographs, tractors, motion pictures, televisions, and gas lighting were manufactured. A new era was dawning, with an infinite number of new technologies and products on the horizon. Or so it seemed to governments and private banks, which lent money for new businesses at previously unimagined rates. Entrepreneurs drew investment from all quarters. But two underlying economic problems festered. First, machines like gasoline-powered tractors and combine harvesters, together with new chemical fertilizers, made agriculture more productive than ever. But that meant that prices could easily collapse just when farmers were taking on debt to purchase the machinery. Second, the rush of investment in new technologies and manufactures left less capital for established industries. For the time being, these were potential problems only. All they needed, however, was the right jolt, or series of jolts, to become a full-blown catastrophe.

THE GREAT DEPRESSION

Not everyone shared in the economic growth of the mid-1920s. In the United States, which was by then the largest and most influential economy in the world, the top 5 percent of the population received nearly 35 percent of all income, while 70 percent of the nation lived in or near poverty. Disparities in total wealth were even more lopsided. In Europe, matters varied from country to country. France, for example, had traditionally championed small and medium-sized companies over large firms, and so it was less at risk from stock-market fluctuations. Britain, too, had a less inequitable concentration of wealth than the United States, because it had had an income tax since 1798. Germany did not yet have one, since the Kaiser had preferred to fund the Great War on debt, fearing that a tax on wealth would anger the wealthy.

The web of debt nevertheless ensnared every Western country: governments owed other governments, banks owed other banks, and companies owed other companies. And the web grew more dangerous as people became more hopeful for the future. With so many exciting new products, people felt that the potential for riches was almost limitless. Urged on by zealous stockbrokers, they were therefore willing to invest their entire savings—and to borrow more in order to invest. For a while, all that cash did prompt growth; but rising stock prices quickly turned into a bubble, and when the bubble burst, stocks and bonds lost value, and credit dried up.

On Black Tuesday, October 29, 1929, on the New York Stock Exchange, prices tumbled. It was the beginning of the **Great Depression**. Banks and companies failed by the tens of thousands, throwing millions of people out of work. Farmers who had invested in new machinery only to see the agricultural prices fall could not make their loan payments and lost their farms. In order to staunch the flow of red ink, American banks all but stopped lending to Europe. This meant that credit-dependent countries like France and Germany could not purchase American goods, which in turn added to America's woes. Popular culture demonized bankers and portrayed them as incompetent, self-serving, soulless, or corrupt tricksters—or a combination of all four.[2]

The largest commercial bank in Austria came close to liquidation, which triggered a panic among European banks. Assets were frozen, which meant that depositors could not access their own savings, and lines of credit were cut off. Fearing a repeat of the miseries of the early 1920s, governments made the mistake of trying to stabilize currency rates rather than stimulating consumption and production by injecting new money into the system. Pressure placed on currencies by the Depression led most Western countries to abandon the **gold standard** (see Map 25.2). This monetary system, introduced in the West by Britain in 1821 (and adopted by the United States in 1873), pegged a currency to the price of gold, so that a British sovereign, a German mark, or an American dollar always bought the same amount of the precious metal. Since worldwide supplies of gold, and the demand for it, were relatively constant through the 19th century, currency values and exchange rates remained stable. The problem with the gold standard, though, was that gold prices alone did not reflect any given currency's actual value at any particular time: inflation and interest rates also played a part. In the run-up to World War I most Western governments needed to print money rapidly in order to cover their military costs—and this

---

[2]   Bank robbers like Pretty Boy Floyd (Charles Arthur Floyd) or Bonnie and Clyde (Bonnie Parker and Clyde Barrow) became popular-culture heroes.

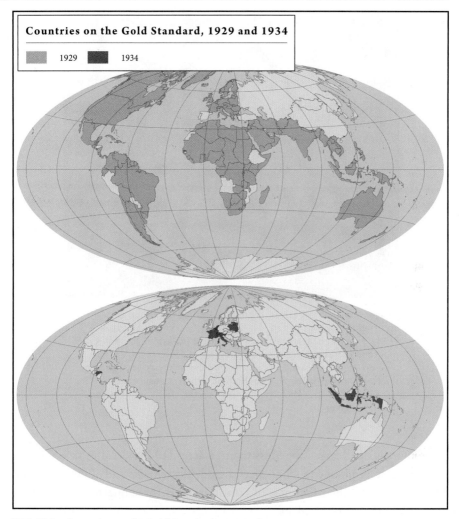

Countries on the Gold Standard, 1929 and 1934

1929   1934

MAP 25.2   **Countries on the Gold Standard, 1929 and 1934**

forced up both interest rates and the inflation rate. The United States abandoned the gold standard in 1933.[3]

The statistics are grim. Banks failed; many of these were purchased, at bargain prices, by larger banks—which recouped their expenses by confiscating the homes, farms, and businesses of the failed banks' borrowers. Millions of Americans lost their homes, their farms, and their jobs. Unemployment reached as high as 25 percent, three years into the crisis. In Europe, the numbers were even worse. Over 40 percent of the German workforce was unemployed. In France, where

---

[3]   By 1933, in the United States alone more than five thousand banks failed.

Hunger Marchers   A series of protests against food shortages occurred throughout Britain during the Depression of the 1930s. The largest single demonstration took place in 1932. A group of three thousand protestors set out from Glasgow in Scotland, and by the time the march reached London there were as many as one hundred thousand involved. The metropolitan government summoned a police force of seventy-five thousand to break up the crowd before it could reach Parliament.

three-fourths of all farms were less than 25 acres (10 hectares) in size, farmers had no way to produce enough to meet their debt payments and often were lucky to be able to feed their families. In Poland roughly three-quarters of a million farmers lost their farms to debt.

The decline in international trade hit the shipping industry especially hard. The Dutch shipping industry declined by two-thirds in three years, while parts of coastal northern England and Scotland had unemployment rates of 90 percent or more. With tax revenues plummeting and the need for social services rising, Western governments leaned harder on their colonies. They cut salaries and wages for foreign workers, increased rents and taxes, and cut back on expenditures like road building, schools, health care, and a host of social services. Local resentments flared.

Manufacturing output declined by nearly 40 percent worldwide between 1929 and 1933. The effects were felt everywhere, but as always they were felt most stingingly among the urban and rural poor. Unemployment was particularly high among young people, those aged sixteen to twenty-six, who had little to do except sit idly in cafes and parks and nurse their resentment. Many of these made easy

TABLE 25.1   **Unemployment Rates during the Great Depression, 1929–1936**

	BRITAIN	GERMANY	SWEDEN	USA	NETHERLANDS
1929	10.4	13.1	10.7	3.2	5.9
1930	16.1	22.2	12.2	8.7	7.8
1931	21.3	33.7	17.2	15.8	14.8
1932	22.1	43.7	22.8	23.6	25.3
1933	19.9	26.3	23.7	24.9	26.9
1934	16.7	14.9	18.9	26.7	28.0
1935	15.5	11.6	16.1	20.1	31.7
1936	13.1	8.3	13.6	16.9	32.7

targets for recruiters from radical and reactionary political groups. Both Communist and Fascist parties relied on these feelings to gain followers.

THE SEARCH FOR SOMEONE TO BLAME

Ideology and its appeal are a recurring theme in fiction of the 1920s and 1930s. The German writer Thomas Mann (1875–1955) powerfully depicted this sort of seduction in two novellas; both "Disorder and Early Sorrow" (1925) and "Mario and the Magician" (1929) illustrate this bitter hopelessness. Less well known in the English-speaking world is the novelist Hans Fallada (1893–1947), whose *What Now, Little Man?* (1932), *A Wolf among Wolves* (1937), and *Iron Gustav* (1938) present the miseries of life in Depression-era Germany with unforgettable power. Fallada's books gave such a powerful description of life in the Weimar Republic that later the Nazi propaganda minister, Josef Goebbels, took an interest in using them as a way of justifying the Nazi regime; Goebbels tried to blackmail Fallada into writing an anti-Semitic and pro-Nazi novel. Fallada, who detested the Nazis and their anti-Semitism, avoided filling the request for a few years. In 1944, however, Goebbels had Fallada arrested and placed in an insane asylum until he produced. *The Drinker*, published ultimately in 1950, was instead an autobiographical work criticizing Fallada's own difficulties with drug and alcohol addiction. He died in 1947, leaving behind the manuscript of his greatest novel, *Every Man Dies Alone*, his indictment of the entire Nazi era. It was published shortly after his death.

A journey through the Congo turned André Gide (1869–1951), the French writer, against Western imperialism and led him to become, briefly but passionately, a Communist. "Communism," he wrote, "is the only promise for the salvation of mankind; I would lay down for it in an instant, to make it succeed." Membership in Britain's Communist Party (the CPGB) increased dramatically after the 1929 crash, especially in the heavily hit industrial towns and coalfields of the north and west, where local newspapers began to refer to certain localities as "Little Moscows" because of their active Communist groups. Another site popularly regarded as a haven of Communism was the Jewish neighborhood in the East End, in London.

Popular and official attitudes toward Europe's Jews worsened. Jews were singled out either as presumed leaders of socialist cells or as corrupt merchants and financiers. In Poland, employers were ordered to test their workers and apprentices for their knowledge of Polish—and thus to root out Yiddish-speaking Jews. The government of Austria forced all Jewish-owned banks to close, while the government in Romania ordered Jewish companies of any sort to take on Christian partners or else forfeit their ability to obtain credit. The Greek state rescinded its contracts with Jewish businesses. In Britain, formal actions regarding Jews were confined to policy debates over Zionism and Palestine, but the tone of those debates was often ugly. According to the *Times* of London Zionist Jews were "pushing, grasping, and domineering," while the *Morning Post* bemoaned the fact that British citizens were being "compelled to pay for establishing a national home" for Jews. An Anglican clergyman

"The Biggest Rogue in All the Land"   As Nazi anti-Semitic racism goes, this cartoon is relatively mild. It contrasts the upright, healthy, hardworking, and noble Aryan youth with the supposedly decrepit, slovenly, money-grubbing Jew.

observed in 1920 that nearly all the British then living in Palestine were "obsessed by the notion that Zionism is incipient Bolshevism."[4]

Among the charges leveled against Jews everywhere was the rumor that they were benefiting from a crisis: birthrates across Europe fell sharply after 1929, as married couples feared they could not feed many mouths. But fewer children—who previously had worked on family farms, in factories, or in odd jobs—meant lower incomes for poor families. Some political circles saw the decline as part of the decline of the nation, and they singled out the Jews as a factor in both developments. Regarded as a race of financiers and merchants, they were blamed for economic woes everywhere, and as one of the few groups with population growth, they were seen as "taking over" society by biological means. Not everyone felt this way, of course, but complaints remained widespread throughout the Depression.

Henry Ford (1863–1947), founder of the Ford Motor Company, spoke for many when he wrote about the supposed dangers of "the International Jew" (1920) in the Michigan newspaper he owned, *The Dearborn Independent*:

> In Russia [the Jew] is charged with being the source of Bolshevism, an accusation which is serious or not, according to the circle in which it is made; we in America, hearing the fervid eloquence and perceiving the prophetic ardor of young Jewish apostles of social and industrial reform, can calmly estimate how it may be. In Germany he is charged with being the cause of the Empire's collapse and a very considerable literature has sprung up, bearing with it a mass of circumstantial evidence that gives the thinker pause. In England he is charged with being the real world ruler, who rules as a super-nation over the nations, rules by the power of gold, and who plays nation against nation for his own purposes, remaining himself discreetly in the background. In America it is pointed out to what extent the elder Jews of wealth and the younger Jews of ambition swarmed through the war organizations—principally those departments which dealt with the commercial and industrial business of war, and also the extent to which they have clung to the advantage which their experience as agents of the government gave them.
>
> In simple words, the question of the Jews has come to the fore, but like other questions which lend themselves to prejudice, efforts will be made to hush it up as impolitic for open discussion. If, however, experience has taught us anything it is that questions thus suppressed will sooner or later break out in undesirable and unprofitable forms.

---

[4] As late as 1938 the *Weekly Review* declared that the goal of Zionism "though not definitely avowed, is to secure world domination for the members of its race."

Ford's warning seems unnervingly prescient, although not in the sense he meant it:

> The Jew is the world's enigma. Poor in his masses, he yet controls the world's finances. Scattered abroad without country or government, he yet presents a unity of race continuity which no other people has achieved. Living under legal disabilities in almost every land, he has become the power behind many a throne. There are ancient prophecies to the effect that the Jew will return to his own land and from that center rule the world, though not until he has undergone an assault by the united nations of mankind.

A new generation, raised to believe in the unique injustice of their suffering, came of age determined to rescue their honor as well as their livelihoods. And they were willing to take desperate action.

The agonies of the Depression, in sum, added to concerns for Western decline left over from the war. A new generation, raised to believe in the unique injustice of their suffering, came of age determined to rescue their honor as well as their livelihoods. And they were willing to take desperate action.

MODERNISM, EXPERIMENT, AND TRAUMA

The war, the wretched peace treaty, a revolution and a civil war, the Red Menace, the Ruhr Valley disaster, hyperinflation, the Depression—all these traumas strengthened modernism in the arts, which now seemed prophetic (see chapter 23). The Irish poet William Butler Yeats (1865–1939) summed up the atmosphere in "The Second Coming" (1920):

> Things fall apart; the centre cannot hold;
>   Mere anarchy is loosed upon the world,
> The blood-dimmed tide is loosed, and everywhere
>   The ceremony of innocence is drowned;
> The best lack all conviction, while the worst
>   Are full of passionate intensity.

The proud confidence of the imperial age had given way to anxious doubt. Without a fixed center, life's only point of reference becomes the personal, but individual weaknesses and quirks leave its viewpoint uncertain. Still, if our consciousness is all we have, we would be wise to investigate it. Interwar modernism did precisely that, in complex, enduring art characterized by innovations and experiment.

This second generation of modernists was born after 1880 and therefore reached intellectual and artistic maturity during or after the war. For them, Freud's theories about human nature being driven by forces we imperfectly control resonated loudly. These impulses for creation and destruction, Eros and Thanatos (death), helped shape the literary and artistic culture of the 1920s and 1930s.

Paul Valéry, the French Symbolist poet and essayist, described the crisis of his generation in 1919 as "A Crisis of the Mind":

> No one can say what [ideas or values] will be alive or dead tomorrow, whether in literature, philosophy, or art; no one knows what ideas or forms of expression will be inscribed on [our culture's] casualty list, or what new things will take their place. Hope remains, of course.... but Hope is merely what we call the mistrust of what is obvious to any mind that thinks.... The facts are clear and pitiless: thousands of young writers and artists have died; the dream of a united European culture is lost; knowledge has been shown to be unable to save anyone or anything; science is gravely wounded, and what we might call its moral ambitions are shamed by the brutal applications to which we put it. Idealism barely survives,... realism lies hopeless and defeated,... faith has lost its way,... even the skeptics have lost their doubts,... and there is no one left who is the master of his own thoughts.

Valéry's gloom was characteristic of the postwar movement. The modernists, for all their playfulness, produced little work that can be called comic. Art's break with the past, combined with a loss of enthusiasm for the future, led to a fascination with the present moment. Literature kept returning to the inner thoughts of actors and viewers as they struggle, usually in vain, to free themselves from the horrors of the world.

A high point in modernism occurred in 1922, when three artistic masterpieces appeared: the novel *Ulysses*, by James Joyce (1882–1941), the poem "The Waste Land," by T. S. Eliot (1888–1965), and the film *Nosferatu*, by Friedrich W. Murnau (1888–1931). *Ulysses* depicts the events of a single crucial day in the life of Leopold Bloom, an assimilated Irish Jew living in Dublin. He visits the post office, attends the funeral of a friend, stops in the National Library, attends to a business errand, eats lunch, walks along the beach, and visits a friend who is giving birth in a hospital. Along the way Bloom encounters a young aspiring writer named Stephen Dedalus, with whom he forms an unexpectedly close bond. They drink together in a pub; Bloom then follows a drunken Stephen into a brothel in order to watch over him, and helps him after Stephen gets into a scuffle with a policeman. After he and Stephen part, Bloom returns home to his wife, Molly, who has spent the afternoon with her lover, and collapses into bed. A magnificent long stream-of-consciousness monologue by Molly closes the novel.

Joyce narrates this day with a riot of innovations. Patterned on Homer's epic *The Odyssey*, the novel presents Bloom as a modern-day Odysseus (Ulysses in Latin), with Stephen as his son Telemachus, and the unfaithful Molly as his ever-faithful wife, Penelope. Each chapter employs a different style and a new set of motifs and imagery. One chapter—the visit to the brothel—is written as a play, complete with stage directions. It enacts not only the two men's activities but also their thoughts and fears. Another section appears in the dry question-and-answer form of a Catholic catechism. A third episode shatters the narrative into nineteen vignettes of minor characters, who function as a chorus commenting on the main action. Yet *Ulysses* tells a traditional, or indeed mythical, tale of middle-aged loss, sadness, and longing. Stephen, Bloom's symbolic spiritual son, is a frustrated artist who rails against the political and religious bonds that shackle Irish society.[5] Molly, meanwhile, reawakened to sexuality after her afternoon love affair, meditates on the role that love and loneliness have played in her life. She claims in her soliloquy that she and Leopold have not had intercourse in a decade, but she resolves to tell Bloom in the morning about her infidelity and to renew their marriage.

James Joyce The greatest of the Modernist literary artists, Joyce was denigrated by many of his more elitist peers as a mere commoner trying to mingle with his betters. Virginia Woolf admired aspects of Joyce's talent but decided in the end that his work was too filled with low, tawdry realities. His novel *Ulysses* is "an illiterate, underbred book it seems to me," she sniffed; "the book of a self-taught working man, [and] we all know how distressing they are, how egotistic, insistent, raw, striking, [and] ultimately nauseating."

Ulysses is a virtuoso performance and, for many, the supreme modernist novel. Its technical experimentations are not merely vehicles for displaying Joyce's talent; they are part of the point. The realist novel is dead, *Ulysses* proclaims. It is dead not only because nothing new can be done in that genre but because there is no reality to portray outside the perspectives of each individual character. Even those perspectives, however, cannot be fully trusted. Stephen and Leopold's states of mind are continually interrupted by impulses, hallucinations, visions, and suppressed memories; Molly's musings on the decade-long absence of sex in her marriage (a consequence of the trauma of their son's death) may just as

---

5   For Stephen in *Ulysses*, "History is a nightmare from which I am trying to awake."

likely be self-delusion as self-confession, a way of justifying to herself her infidelity. One cannot be sure. And that is one of the book's many hidden revelations.

Following hard on *Ulysses*'s footsteps was T. S. Eliot's "The Waste Land." Like many of Eliot's poems, it was composed in fragments over the course of many months and possibly several years. Shifting between different voices, multiple situations, and abrupt jumps in time, it is filled with obscure literary, historical, and mythical allusions. The poem makes for difficult reading, and its overall effect is of collage.

> The realist novel is dead, *Ulysses* proclaims. It is dead not only because nothing new can be done in that genre but because there is no reality to portray outside the perspectives of each individual character.

> April is the cruelest month, breeding
> Lilacs out of the dead land, mixing
> Memory and desire, stirring
> Dull roots with spring rain.
> Winter kept us warm, covering
> Earth in forgetful snow, feeding
> A little life with dried tubers.
> Summer surprised us, coming over the Starnbergersee
> With a shower of rain; we stopped in the colonnade,
> And went on in sunlight, into the Hofgarten,
> And drank coffee, and talked for an hour.
> Bin gar keine Russin, stamm' aus Litauen, echt deutsch.
> And when we were children, staying at the archduke's,
> My cousin's, he took me out on a sled,
> And I was frightened. He said, Marie,
> Marie, hold on tight. And down we went.
> In the mountains, there you feel free.
> I read, much of the night, and go south in the winter.

Imagine a vast museum filled with all the treasures of Western art, literature, and music. Imagine video clips of all the major historical events, plus newspapers, music hall songs, excerpts of autobiographies, and recordings of burlesque performances. "The Waste Land" is what you might have if you picked through the ruins of such a museum after a catastrophic explosion and fire—shards of memories, bits of newsprint, fragments of sculptures, scraps of painted canvas, torn pages from volumes of verse. After the wreck of civilization, the poem suggests, the artist must piece together his own set of references and touchstones, to create his own ordering of the world. The reader does not "understand" the poem in the traditional way, since no one can recognize without help the origins of all the bits of charred ruin, but one knows that a catastrophe has occurred and that the museum will never again exist as it once did. Even the jumble of oddments, though, stirs deep emotions. Reading "The Waste Land" is astonishing. How can something that seems at first to make so little sense have such overwhelming power?

Nosferatu, also released in 1922, revises the legend of the vampire Dracula as it had been popularized in the 1897 novel by Bram Stoker. The film relocates the story from Stoker's contemporary England to a fictional Baltic port city in northern Germany in the 1830s. A representative of a German manufacturing firm is sent to Transylvania to meet with a new client, one Count Orlok, who of course turns out to be a vampire. He attacks the businessman in his sleep but does not kill him, as he usually does with his victims. Why? The businessman had shown Orlok a portrait of his wife back in Germany, and the vampire is smitten. He follows the business-man back to Germany and purchases the house directly across the street from the happy couple—all the while planning his attack and satisfying his bloodlust by kill-

Count Orlok   The role of Count Orlok, the vampire in *Nosferatu* (1922), was played by Max Schreck (1879–1936). A favorite of playwright Berthold Brecht's, Schreck spent most of his career in theater, but he also appeared in a silent film version of Shakespeare's *Merchant of Venice* (1923).

ing dozens of other innocents. The wife, suspicious of her new neighbor, realizes what Orlok is when she reads a book on vampires. It informs her that the only way to kill a vampire is for a virtuous woman to offer herself to him as a sacri-fice. One night she does so, for the sake of humanity, and Orlok, in his orgiastic en-joyment of her blood, fails to notice the rising of the sun. It vaporizes him.

Visually stunning, the film can still enthrall. Its distorted physical sets, un-natural lighting (white trees against a black sky, for instance), and oblique camera angles give it an unsettling awkwardness. These mirror and heighten the psychological discomfort felt by the film's protagonists but also by its viewers. As with *Ulysses* and "The Waste Land," the formal technique not only propels the story but is an intrinsic element of it. Orlok represents the unfulfilled human soul, condemned to an existence it did not choose and in pursuit only of its own desire. What it desires most is what will kill it. The Freudian echoes may or may not be intentional on the filmmakers' part. Either way, the film shows how much the interwar modernist movement had absorbed Freud's theories and made them its own. Orlok neither understands nor controls his impulse to bloodlust. On his first evening with the businessman in Transylvania, he nearly gives the game away when he leaps out of his chair to lick the blood when his guest accidentally cuts his hand while slicing bread. When the man's wife willingly submits to the vampire's attack, she sets the scene for Orlok's rapturous acquisition of both Eros and Thanatos.

Nosferatu is in large part an allegory of the rise of modern capitalist Germany, a society expanding its borders and pursuing its dream of wealth. It is the Germany that marched headlong into the Great War.

The fact that the film relocates the novel's setting to northern Germany in the 1830s is significant. The fictional city is an amalgam of two Hanseatic port cities that were vital to German trade. Germany in the 1830s had just established the Customs' Union (*Zollverein*), which presaged the German Empire under Bismarck. The seed of industrial capitalism, in other words, had just been planted. *Nosferatu* is in large part an allegory of the rise of modern capitalist Germany, a society expanding its borders and pursuing its dream of wealth. It is the Germany that marched headlong into the Great War.

These masterpieces aside, the second wave of modernism proved to be more varied, inclusive, and popular than the first. The most visible change was the prominence of women writers and artists among the avant-garde. Freed from the struggle for the right to vote, women emerged as important figures in modernist cultural life. Among all women modernists, however, pride of place belongs to Virginia Woolf (1882–1941), one of the 20th century's greatest writers.

Woolf was born into a prominent and famously complicated family; privately educated, she grew up in an atmosphere of extraordinary intellectual stimulation.[6] The death of her mother in 1895, when she was thirteen, was the first great emotional shock in Virginia's life and triggered an inward turn in her consciousness and behavior. The death of her father in 1904 resulted in a full-blown nervous breakdown; she recovered gradually but spent the rest of her life on the

---

[6]   Woolf's father, Sir Leslie Stephen (1832–1904), a well-regarded author and journalist, was the chief editor of the *Dictionary of National Biography*.

TABLE 25.2 **Women in Modernist Cultural Life**

Editors, Publishers, Critics	Painters and Sculptors
Sylvia Beach (1887–1962)	Camille Claudel (1864–1943)
Adrienne Monnier (1892–1955)	Natalia Goncharova (1881–1962)
Rebecca West (1892–1983)	Georgia O'Keefe (1887–1986)
Poets	**Short–story Writers**
H.D. (Hilda Doolittle, 1886–1961)	Katherine Mansfield (1888–1923)
Marianne Moore (1887–1972)	
Novelists	**Composers**
Djuna Barnes (1892–1982)	Alma Mahler (1879–1964)
Ivy Compton-Burnett (1884–1969)	Nadia Boulanger (1887–1979)
Edith Södergran (1892–1923)	Germaine Tailleferre (1892–1983)
Virginia Woolf (1882–1941)	Lili Boulanger (1893–1918)

edge of mental instability. She attempted suicide at least once, in 1913. She killed herself in 1941, when World War II and a resurgence of manic depression made her fear losing her mind once and for all.

Woolf's greatness as a novelist lay in her unique combination of technical virtuosity and intense emotion. Starting with her third novel, *Jacob's Room* (1922), and through to her two masterworks *Mrs. Dalloway* (1925) and *To the Lighthouse* (1927), she employs stream-of-consciousness monologues, unpredictable shifts in time and perspective, unreliable narrators, and at times a complete absence of plot. In this way, she focuses instead on the inner lives and intricate, unspoken bonds between her characters. Very little ever "happens" in a Woolf novel. The plot of *Mrs. Dalloway* consists simply of the preparations over a single day, in an upper-middle-class London family, for a dinner party that evening. Yet Woolf captures an astonishing range of emotions, impressions, memories, and longings among various family members. And these inchoate threads of feeling intertwine in intricate patterns. Few novels depict such emotional richness so quietly and yet so successfully.

Virginia Woolf One of the great writers of the 20th century, Woolf had produced most of her best writing before the start of the Great Depression: *Jacob's Room*(1922), *Mrs. Dalloway* (1925), *To the Lighthouse* (1927), among her novels, and *The Common Reader*(1925) and *A Room of One's Own* (1929) among her non-fiction.

Yet Woolf's novels can leave the reader with a feeling of incompleteness. Emotional life ends only when life itself ends, and the close of each Woolf novel does not feel like an ending at all. The same characters will awaken the next morning, and their inner maelstroms of sensation, regret, delight, and doubt will begin all over again. That, of course, is part of the modernist point: we are *beyond* ideas, plans, beliefs, and convictions. Life is by definition aimless, since no one can be certain of the target at which we should aim. Woolf skillfully depicts the emotionally corrosive effects of prejudice against women, but nowhere does she propose a specific idea of how to combat it. Woolf occasionally allowed her name to be added to petitions and helped her husband, Leonard Woolf, with some of his correspondence in his own political career. Otherwise, her political activities extended no further than conversation among her writer friends. Despite her professed admiration for the suffragists and the urgency of the political issues of the 1920s and 1930s, there is no evidence that she ever bothered to cast a vote in any election.

> The generation that came of age during those horrendous times, however, felt modernism's creative aimlessness and self-exploration to resonate profoundly with their own aching uncertainty.

But then neither did Joyce nor Eliot. Second-generation modernism emphasized the unfixed, shifting nature of reality. They viewed most systems of belief and intellectual constructs with ironic detachment. Before the Great War and the Great Depression, modernism found few avid supporters and was at best an interesting marginal culture phenomenon. The generation that came of age during those horrendous times, however, felt modernism's creative aimlessness and self-exploration to resonate profoundly with their own aching uncertainty.

THE RISE OF FASCISM: ITALY AND SPAIN

Fascism is the cult of power—the belief that force, directly applied to achieve a specific end, is the best form of government. Of course, all governments are in the business of reining in the actions of the people they govern; governments place limits on our daily activities, our business dealings, the ways in which we pass estates on to our heirs, the substances we are permitted to eat, drink, smoke, or inject, the people we are allowed to marry. We agree to controls on our personal freedom in return for the stability and order of communal life. But *control* implies *force*, and no government can long survive without possessing the ability to make the populace feel its sting. Good government therefore consists of knowing the right amount of force to apply, and when, and towards what end.

For an astonishing number of Europeans in the 1930s the best form of government, and perhaps the only form of government possible, considering the enormity of the West's troubles, was one in which the state abandoned any pretence of moderation, shared authority, or the consent of the governed and simply assumed the direct, open, and unchallenged exercise of its own will. This was *Fascism*—a word that derives from the name of one of the ancient symbols of

Roman power, the *fasces*: a long, tightly bound bundle of birch rods, from which the blade of a battle-ax emerges toward the upper end. It was not a weapon but the symbol of one.[7]

As an ideology, Fascism differed in several ways from earlier forms of authoritarian government like royal absolutism, although the differences probably did not matter much to its victims; prisoners getting their faces crushed against stone walls have other things on their minds. Absolutism had been founded on the simple conviction that *someone* had to exert absolute external control on society; the absolute control mattered more than the identity of the person wielding it. Neither did it matter, in theory at least, what the absolute ruler did with that power: whatever the ruler wanted to do was the right thing to do.

In Fascism, however, the identity of the dictator was everything, for Fascism embraced the Romantic notion of the collective soul of a national group—the mystical shared spirit (or *genius*, in the 19th-century sense of the term) of a people that expressed their deepest needs and longings. As the living embodiment of that spirit the Fascist leader knew—in his blood and sinews as much as in his mind—what his people desired, needed, hoped for, and feared, and for that reason his actions *were* the nation's actions. He did not impose his will on the people, as in absolutism, but rather expressed their will—and the more forcibly, the better. Fascist leaders emphasized their mystical connection with the nation and presented their rule as the organic expression of the general will.

> Fascist leaders emphasized their mystical connection with the nation and presented their rule as the organic expression of the general will.

Italy's Benito Mussolini (r. 1922–1943) was Europe's first Fascist leader, coming to power after he and a large band of his followers staged a "March on Rome" in opposition to the rise of socialist parties across Italy. The war had displaced millions of Italian farmers and laborers, many of whom felt drawn to radical socialist and Communist parties in the immediate postwar years; nationwide strikes became common and threatened to cripple the already-damaged economy. The Fascists had their origins in those war veterans who were proud of their service and felt that the radical elements in society were undermining the Italian way of life. Mussolini, after a youthful involvement in socialist politics,

---

[7]   Carried by the bodyguards of Roman magistrates, the fasces represented the republic's authority over its citizens and the notion of strength through unity.

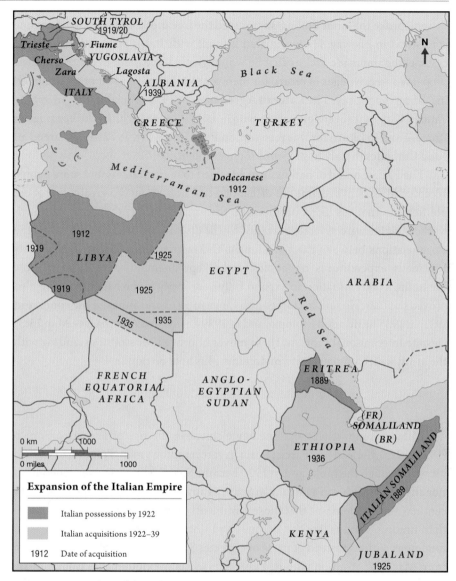

MAP 25.3 Expansion of the Italian Empire, 1922–1939

drew many leaders of his new party from the special-forces units that had fought in the Alps. In 1922, after the threat of yet another general strike, the Fascists marched on Rome by the thousands, determined to take over the government if it was not handed over to them voluntarily. The king chose not to resist and received Mussolini, appointing him the leader of the new government.

Mussolini ran Italy with a combination of terror and traditionalism. Using his special corps of thuggish loyalists, the Blackshirts, he crushed all political dissent, broke the labor unions, suppressed the free press, and brutalized anyone who stood in his way. He ingratiated himself with Italy's economic and aristo-cratic elites and made it clear that he would gladly leave them in control of their property and privileges in return for their political support. Most of them agreed, including the papacy. The **Lateran Agreement** of 1929 officially recognized the Vatican City as a sovereign nation within Italy—indeed within the confines of Rome—and in return for this recognition Pope Pius XI (r. 1922–1939) urged all good Catholics in Italy to support his government.

The Fascist brand of nationalism appealed to many Italians, but more people accepted Mussolini's regime out of fear of retaliation, or out of a greater fear of the political alternatives like Communism, than out of true enthusiasm. Although workers' rights were severely curtailed by the disbanding of labor unions and the close relations between the government and industrial leadership, the Fascists' enormous expenditures on public works kept unemployment relatively low. Mussolini's determination to expand Italy's authority in the Mediterranean also proved popular. He sent his forces into Libya in 1923 and annexed the country in 1931; in 1935 he invaded Ethiopia, and in 1939 he invaded Albania (see Map 25.3). Despite international protests, these moves improved Mussolini's standing with the army, which was central to maintaining his hold on power.

Military support was also the key element in the rise of Francisco Franco (1892–1975), the leader of Fascist Spain. A career military man, Franco had worked his way through the ranks and in 1920 became Spain's youngest-ever general. Na-tionalist sentiments ran as strong in Spain as anywhere else in Europe in the 19th century; the problem was that those sentiments were regional and divisive rather than uniting. Groups like the Basques and Catalans regarded themselves as au-tonomous nations instead of parts of a greater Spain. They sought independence from Madrid, not union with it. Passionate in his conviction that Communism represented the greatest evil of the modern era, Franco believed in monarchy, the Catholic Church, and Spanish (by which he meant Castilian) cultural tradition—and he was determined to eliminate everything that threatened them.

Spain had endured two bloody but inconsequential civil wars (1833–1840 and 1872–1876) that left it with a weak constitutional monarchy and a deeply divided parliament. Industrialization and the loss of Spain's last colonies (Cuba, Guam, the Philippines, and Puerto Rico) to the United States in the Spanish-American War of 1898 had added new strains to the situation, causing Spain to enter the 20th century with even stronger centripetal momentum than in the 19th. Officially neutral in World War I, the government in Madrid had made an ill-fated attempt to conquer Morocco as a salve to wounded pride. In 1923 the army, under the command of a liberal general named Miguel Primo de Rivera, had staged a coup and tried to institute republican reform. This new regime recognized the rights of workers to form unions and admitted moderate socialist parties to the political process. But these concessions had triggered a conservative backlash by Spain's landowning elite and industrial leaders, and in 1930 Primo de Rivera was forced to resign, which opened the door to yet another civil war—and the rise to power of the Fascists.

The **Spanish Civil War** of 1936–1939 began after a six-year experiment with a republican form of government that aggressively pursued a liberal agenda. Franco quickly emerged as the champion of conservative interests. The bulk of the army sided with Franco, while most of the naval and air forces supported the Republicans, which turned the war into a struggle between the inland plains on the one hand and the coastal perimeter on the other. The war drew the attention of anti-Fascist groups across Europe, and tens of thousands of volunteers from Britain, France, the United States, and elsewhere joined the Republicans. So too did a small but highly influential contingent of officers and airmen from the Soviet Union, whose involvement helped to radicalize many of the Republican fighters—a trend that only added urgency to the Fascist cause. The bitterness of the struggle intensified the political divisions: the liberals became increasingly revolutionary, while the conservatives grew increasingly reactionary.

Witness the description of Barcelona in George Orwell's *Homage to Catalonia* (1938):

> Practically every building of any size had been seized by the workers and was draped with red flags or with the red and black flag of the Anarchists; every wall was scrawled with the hammer and sickle and with the initials of the revolutionary parties; almost every church had been gutted and its images burnt. Churches here and there were being systematically demolished by gangs of workmen. Every shop and cafe had an inscription saying that it had been collectivized; even the bootblacks had been collectivized and their boxes painted red and black. Waiters and shop-walkers looked you in the face and treated you as an equal. Servile and even ceremonial forms of speech had temporarily disappeared. Nobody said *Señor* or *Don* or even *Usted*; everyone called everyone else "Comrade" or "Thou," and said *Salud*! instead of *Buenos dias*. Tipping had been forbidden by law since the time of Primo de Rivera; almost my first experience was receiving a lecture from a hotel manager for trying to tip a lift-boy. There were no private motor-cars, they had all been commandeered, and the trams and taxis and much of the other transport were painted red and black. The revolutionary posters were everywhere, flaming from the walls in clean reds and blues that made the few remaining advertisements look like daubs of mud. Down the

The Horror of War   The bombing of a small Basque town in 1937 (by Nazi and Italian Fascist airplanes, acting on behalf of the Nationalist forces led by Francisco Franco) inspired Pablo Picasso to paint his great mural *Guernica*, which he exhibited at the World's Fair in Paris of that year. Using a gloomy black, gray, and white palette, he layered images of horror on top of each other in the center of the scene (note the human skull and the attacking bull located inside the image of the shrieking horse), which he counter-balanced with images of dismemberment along the base and figures of women in pain and despair at either side. Even after a lifetime of seeing reproductions of the painting in books, to stand before the original painting, now housed permanently at the Museo Nacional Centro de Arte Reina Sofia in Madrid, is an unforgettable experience.

Ramblas, the wide central artery of the town where crowds of people streamed constantly to and fro, the loud-speakers were bellowing revolutionary songs all day and far into the night.

The war ended on April 1, 1939, with a decisive Fascist victory. More than half a million people had perished in the fighting, and in the years that followed many tens of thousands more disappeared in retaliatory attacks by the Fascists against their political enemies. The new regime outlawed all competing political parties and imposed strict censorship of the media and school curricula. It mandated the use of Castilian Spanish, promoted conservative Catholicism, and built a network of concentration camps where criminals and political enemies were imprisoned, tortured, and killed.

NAZISM IN GERMANY

The Weimar government was all but powerless in the face of Fascism's rise in Germany. The Nazi Party, formally the National Socialist Party, was in fact only one of many extremist factions that had formed throughout Europe almost immediately after the signing of the Versailles Treaty. Nor was its extremism limited to Fascism. Under Josef Stalin, Communism in Russia became a brutal means of social control.

Adolf Hitler (1889–1945) joined the Nazis in 1919 (he was the fifty-fifth member) and took control of the party in 1921. In November 1923 Hitler and his followers attempted a coup in Munich that they hoped would provide a springboard to seizing power in Berlin—an uprising they thought would mimic Mussolini's March on Rome. The effort collapsed immediately, but a sympathetic judge sentenced Hitler to a mere nine months in prison. He emerged from his cell with a bulky manuscript that he soon published: *Mein Kampf* ("My Struggle"), published in two volumes (1925–1926). The book is odious, rambling, and filled with venom. But whatever personal demons haunted Hitler's mind, his book resonated with the bruised and embittered egos of many Germans.

Mein Kampf devotes most of its pages to a theory of the superiority of the German race, on the basis of which it promotes two strategic goals. The first goal was **Lebensraum**—"living space," literally. By this term Hitler meant not just the return of ethnically German territories carved away from the nation by the Versailles Treaty; he also meant the right of Germany to expand into eastern Europe and the Balkans at the expense of the inferior Slavic peoples who resided there. His second goal was to promote an organic, classless, national community of the Germanic people. It would unite them in spirit and blood and would express its spiritual unity in Nazism and its leader. It insisted that the spiritual purity of the German "folk" (*Volk*) could be achieved only by removing from its midst the polluting presence of Communists, homosexuals, the physically and mentally handicapped, and above all the Jews.

Amid the desperate conditions of postwar Germany, Hitler appealed to ever growing numbers of disaffected and resentful Germans. His skill as a speaker and the brilliance of his propaganda director, Josef Goebbels (1897–1945), made Hitler's political rise seem unstoppable. The impact of the Great Depression provided the last boost needed to bring the Nazis to power. In the national elections of 1928, the Nazis were still a minor, though growing, power; in the next election cycle of 1930 (one year after the onset of the Depression), they became the second largest party in Germany.

My Space After sending in their troops into Poland in 1939, the Nazis were quick to reorganize the administration of their new territories and to resettle the land with ethnic Germans. The new administrative districts were called "Reichsgaue"—an intentionally archaic-sounding term in German intended to promote the (false) notion of a Germanic historical claim to the land. Here a healthy (and suspiciously tidy-looking) young German tries to look as though she is as connected to the Polish soil as the crops she is pretending to care for.

From this point, the Nazis quickly turned to the use of violence, blackmail, and intimidation in order to strengthen their hand. Hitler purged the party of any possible rivals to his personal rule. The personality cult of "the Leader" (*der Führer*) promoted by Goebbels grew in intensity, and the desire to cleanse Germany of moral guilt for World War I intensified too. Finally, in January 1933, after a new round of elections, the Nazis emerged as victors, and Hitler won appointment as chancellor of the nation. In September he delivered a speech that summarizes the Nazi view of politics and German history:

> In 1919 when the Nazi Party came into existence in order to replace the Marxist-democratic republic with a new nation, the very idea seemed hopeless and foolish—especially to those pseudo-intellectuals who, with their shallow understanding of history, looked upon us with a simpering and pitying smile. Most of them knew that our nation was about to fall upon evil times, because they recognized that the men in charge of the November Republic were both too evil and too inept to lead our great nation. What they did *not* know, however, was that our party would *never* fall victim to the ideas and sentiments that caused *them* to run from the attacks of Marxism for the last fifty years. . . . We were ready from the start for the long and difficult struggle to build up a party that would destroy Marxism. . . . The former leaders, the bourgeois leaders, of society talked endlessly of "quiet progress" . . . while we held hundreds and thousands of demonstrations. . . . They blathered about democracy, but kept away from the people. National Socialism, on the other hand, talked about authority, but engaged with the people, wrestled with the people, as no movement in German history had ever done. . . .
>
> As the sole legitimate possessor of state power, our party understands that it is responsible for the entire course of German history. . . . We may reject the principles of democracy and parliamentary government, but we passionately believe in the peoples' right to govern themselves. Parliaments, we insist, do not express the will of the masses, but actually pervert and violate that will. The will of the people finds its only true and effective expression in its most gifted leaders. . . . Power and its ruthless application can accomplish much.

The appeal of such a message was deep, for it offered a chance to rewrite history as well as to chart a new future. And the people of Germany desperately desired to do both.

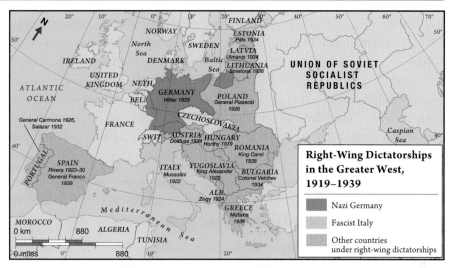

MAP 25.4   Right-Wing Dictatorships in the Greater West, 1919–1939.

Fascism's appeal was wide-reaching (see Map 25.4). Austria had at least two Fascist parties of note—the Fatherland Front and the Home Defense Force; Belgium's Rexist Party grew large enough to hold one-tenth of the seats in the national parliament; Britain had fifty thousand members in its Fascist Union, led by Oswald Mosley. In Croatia the Fascist Insurrection Party was led by the loathsome Ante Pavelic, and in Finland the Lapua Party of Vihtori Kohsola nearly seized power in a coup in 1932, while Ioannis Metaxis presided over Greece's Fascist Party of Free Believers and in Hungary Ferenc Szálasi led the Arrow/Cross Party. The National Union Party, under its leader Vidkun Quisling, came briefly to power in Norway, while Portugal's Fascist group was under the leadership of António Oliveira de Salazar. Poland's Fascist Falanga Party (deriving its name from the ancient Greek phalanx) and its leader Bolesław Piasecki spouted torrents of anti-Semitic bile that rivaled anything uttered by Hitler. Corneliu Codreanu was the charismatic, anti-Semitic head of Romania's leading Fascist party, known primarily as the Iron Guard but occasionally using the names Everything for the Fatherland, the League of Christian Defense, and the Legion of the Archangel Michael.

> In all of these countries, Fascism appealed to two very distinct groups: the poor, who wanted retribution against real and perceived enemies, and the industrial and financial elites, who craved social and economic stability.

Even France itself felt the tug towards Fascism, producing as it did an abundance of extremist parties: the Cross of Fire (led by François de la Rocque) which may have had as many as a million members, French Action (led by Charles Maurras), the French Popular Party (under Jacques Doriot), French Solidarity (headed by Jean Renaud), and the Young Patriots (led by Pierre Taittinger). It may be the case, in fact, that France avoided becoming a Fascist country only because it had so many Fascist parties, which kept splitting the votes between themselves. In all of these countries, Fascism appealed to two very distinct groups: the poor, who wanted retribution against real and perceived enemies, and the industrial and financial elites, who craved social and economic stability.

OPPRESSION AND TERROR IN RUSSIA

Fascism and Communism stood as opposite ends of the political spectrum in the 1920s and 1930s, and each presented itself as the only defense against the other. Yet they resembled each other closely in methods of social control—so closely that observers as early as 1926 coined the word **totalitarianism** to describe their shared form of political oppression. Like the Fascist groups across Europe, Russia's Communist regime under Josef Stalin (1879–1953) was an intensely centralized society. The Bolshevik Party held all authority and openly used systematic police terror to dominate and manipulate the general population.

Stalin had come to Lenin's attention early in the century and by 1912 was appointed to the Bolshevik Central Committee. An enthusiast from the start for Lenin's insistence on the use of violence against political enemies, Stalin indulged his taste for cruelty, and for the rest of his life he relied on assassinations, purges, enslavement, and intimidation to achieve his ends. After Lenin's death in 1924, Stalin resolved to increase Russia's industrial and agricultural output by any means necessary, and that meant dismantling the economic structures created by Lenin's New Economic Policy. That policy had called for the nationalization of large-scale economic activities while allowing for small-scale private production in local markets. Stalin railed against the independent peasant farmers (*kulaks* in Russian) as enemies of the state and called for their immediate liquidation. State officials massacred hundreds of thousands of farmers and their families, confiscated their lands in order to form new collective farms under the direct control of the government, and forced the rest into exile and starvation. Many millions more perished of famine and exposure.

Stalin relentlessly blamed all food shortages and failures to meet the goals of his vaunted Five-Year Plans on conspiracies led by corrupt officials, lazy workers, inept engineers, political rivals, and, of course, their Jewish financial cronies. Starting in 1936 in the **Great Purge** he orchestrated a series of show trials in

Building Socialism   Women and children were also sent to the gulag during Stalin's murderous reign. Here a group of prisoners work at digging a canal out of the frozen Russian ground.

which phony evidence was used to prove false charges against these "enemies of socialism"—and then to justify their execution. By the next year he did away with even the show trials. He simply ordered mass arrests and confinements in a vast network of brutal concentration camps that stretched across Russia from Moscow to Siberia—the **gulag** (an acronym for the Russian phrase meaning "Central Administration of Corrective Labor Camps").[8] From 1938 to Stalin's death in 1953, roughly one million prisoners died in these camps. Some were starved and worked to death; others were simply beaten to death or shot. And perhaps another million or more died after being sentenced to internal exile.

The Bolshevik regime had improved the social and political status of Russian women by establishing a high-level Women's Department within its ranks, granting women the right to seek divorce, and securing access to abortion ser-

---

[8]   By the time World War II began, Stalin had already murdered 90 percent of his generals and 80 percent of his colonels. That left the army at a decided disadvantage.

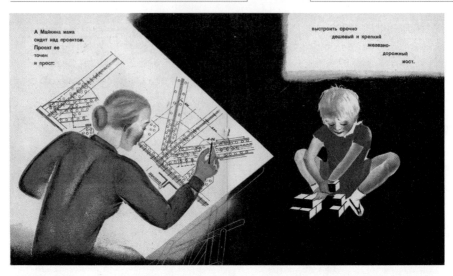

Working Mother   This image comes from a children's book called *Mommy's Bridge* (1933). The book aimed to show that women working to create a socialist state could do so without fear of failing as mothers. Stalin emphasized a cult of motherhood in order to encourage women to produce more little socialists.

vices. Stalin rolled back many of these gains, but less out of opposition to women's rights in theory than from a need to stem a demographic hemorrhage. He killed so many millions that the nation had difficulty maintaining a national work-force. He therefore ordered improved health care available to women (although access to birth control was tightly restricted), and education focused on improv-ing literacy rates. The number of female engineers, physicians, and civil officials rose significantly; the lower ranks of the Party itself became in time filled with female members. At the same time, Stalin redefined the family. What Marx had dismissed as an outdated bourgeois institution was officially rehabilitated as a "school for socialism." To encourage large families, Stalin bestowed a new award—that of the "Heroic Mother" (*Mat'eri Geroi*)—on women who produced ten children. Propaganda posters of the 1930s vividly depict all these changes in the significance of women to the socialist dream.

A NEW DEAL?

When Hitler became chancellor on January 3, 1933, his aims could hardly have been clearer. *Mein Kampf* had spelled them out in rambling detail, and the thug-gish tactics used by his uniformed and civilian supporters gave overwhelming evidence of the Nazis' willingness to beat, murder, rob, and swindle to accom-plish those aims. Whatever else might be said about Hitler, he seldom shied away from speaking his mind. Why, then, did the nations of the West give him more or less free rein for six years to do whatever he wanted? Before looking for answers, it is important to emphasize the continuing economic crisis.

The steps needed to confront the Depression seemed clear enough: only spending on public projects like highways, dams and levees, electrical grids, schools, and parks could put enough people to work that it would spark economic recovery. The creation of welfare-state programs could offer nonworking sectors of the population, such as children and the elderly, essential services like housing and health care. This was in fact how Hitler enabled Germany's recovery. Massive investment in rebuilding the military and constructing large-scale projects like the Autobahn system (the highways) all but eradicated Germany's sky-high unemployment rate by 1937. In the United States, Franklin Delano Roosevelt's torrent of new programs known as the **New Deal** followed the same basic path. It put millions of men and women back to work, provided price supports for cash-strapped farmers, offered unemployment insurance and retirement benefits to those no longer working, and made welfare payments to dependent mothers and their children.

Opposition to such schemes was widespread, however, and in many countries the opposition undercut recovery. Some of the opposition was simply personal: those with capital and incomes did not relish paying higher taxes—often dramatically higher—in order to benefit others. Much, however, was a matter of principle, since government intervention on such a scale smacked of socialism. Two brilliant economists squared off in the debate and set the terms for much of the philosophical divide between liberalism and conservatism for the rest of the 20th century—John Maynard Keynes (1883–1946) and Friedrich Hayek (1899–1992).

Keynes was the author of *The Economic Consequences of the Peace* (1919). After his bitter experience at the Paris Peace Conference, he moved between Cambridge, where he was a fellow at King's College, and London, where he advised the Treasury on economic matters. He was also associated with the group of writers, artists, and philosophers (including Virginia Woolf) who became known as the **Bloomsbury Group**. In 1936 he published his greatest work, *The General Theory of Employment, Interest, and Money*, which some have called the most important work of economics of the 20th century. Believing that unemployment was the single most severe problem posed by the Depression, Keynes argues in *The General Theory* that market forces alone cannot solve the problem. As profits decline, wages will fall indefinitely to restore profits, given enough time, and in unacceptably unpredictable ways. The rehiring of displaced workers and the taking on of new laborers will always be the last step taken by businesses on the mend. Moreover, Keynes adds, many failed or failing businesses will simply never return; some might reinvent themselves and produce new manufactures and services that rely less on labor—but this will only extend the problem. The solution to endemic unemployment, he maintains, is direct government action. The wages earned by labor will allow them to spend more, and the return to normal demand levels for products and service will mean a return to normal prices and profits to businesses.

Friedrich Hayek was born in Vienna, then the still-vibrant capital of the Austrian-Hungarian Empire. His family was wealthy and academic, and he fought bravely in an artillery unit on the Italian front. His personal sense of the loss of the comfort, stability, and refinement of the prewar era never left him. After the war he studied law and economics at the University of Vienna, earned a doctorate, and published his first book, on monetary theory, in 1929—the year of the crash. On its strength Hayek was appointed a professor at the London School of Economics, where he taught until 1950. He later taught at the University of Chicago (1950–1962) and the University of Freiburg (1962–1968), and in 1974 he received the Nobel Prize in Economics. Hayek challenged Keynes both theoretically and empirically, book for book, article for article, lecture for lecture, throughout the 1930s and 1940s. Their rivalry was without personal animosity, but the differences between the two men were profound.

Hayek endorsed the pre-1848 vision of classical economic liberalism, one that asserted the prime importance of individual liberty, personal responsibility, and the sacrosanct rights of property. A free market, he insisted, was the best and ultimately the only reliable guarantor of all three. Government intervention is a violent interruption of a natural process and leads only to demands for further interruptions. Think of how erecting a levee or a dam on a river may protect a floodplain: it may protect that particular plain, but it only passes the problem of river flow further downstream—where more calls for action will result in still more levees and dams, built at ever greater expense. Eventually, the river becomes unmanageable and a disaster vastly greater than that posed to the initial floodplain will occur. Better to recognize that rivers sometimes flood, and one should not build homes below the high-water level. Period. Hayek, a somewhat stiff and formal personality, would probably not have used such a homespun analogy, but in a private moment he might have approved.

In his two most famous attacks on Keynesian economics, *The Pure Theory of Capital* (1941) and *The Road to Serfdom* (1944), his conclusion is stark: government intervention in a free economy, no matter how well intentioned, is the first step toward totalitarianism—whether of the liberal (Communist) or conservative (Fascist) variety. "When economic power is centralized as an instrument of political power it creates a degree of dependence scarcely distinguishable from slavery," he famously wrote; "it has been well said that, in a country where the sole employer is the state, opposition means death by slow starvation."

APPEASEMENT AND PACIFISM

How evil does a regime like Fascism have to be before other countries will take preemptive action against it? Who may take such action—only the Fascist state's immediate neighbors? How is it that the churches of Europe, both Catholic and Protestant, failed to make immediate, unqualified, and repeated condemnations of immoral regimes preaching doctrines of hatred and violence? Why did the Western world respond to Fascism by tolerating it? This is the essential, urgent question posed by the 1930s, and it still rankles millions of people.

Why did the Western world respond to Fascism by tolerating it? This is the essential, urgent question posed by the 1930s, and it still rankles millions of people.

There is no single answer. The guiding policy of the West toward Hitler in the 1930s was called **appeasement**—the granting of political and territorial concessions in order to preserve peace—and each Western country appeased Hitler in different ways and for different reasons. And because of the continued economic crisis, the stakes were high. Each nation debated how to confront the Nazi danger without risking a slide of its own into totalitarianism.

France had perhaps the easiest choice to make, since it had really no choice at all. After World War I and the Depression, France could not even feign a direct challenge to Hitler's aggression. It took instead a purely defensive posture by building a barricade along the French-German border—the **Maginot Line**, named after the minister of war, André Maginot. An interlocking chain of artillery casements, machine-gun pillboxes, tank formations, barbed wire, minefields, and concrete bunkers, it was a variation on the trench networks of World War I—and proved in the end to be just as ineffective. The point, though, is that France could do little else.

The causes of American appeasement were rather more complicated. First, a strong popular sentiment in favor of isolationism dominated the 1930s. The Paris Peace Conference had spoiled the hopes of many regarding their country's ability to influence Europe for the better, and the crushing urgency of the Depression—which had left nearly one-half the U.S. population in dire poverty—demanded immediate, unwavering attention. Senate Republicans led the case for nonintervention, by establishing a special commission to examine America's involvement in World War I. Its 1936 report concluded that munitions manufacturers had influenced the U.S. decision to enter the war, out of a simple but coldhearted desire for profits. Outrage at these "war profiteers" fueled noninterventionist passions across America.

But another factor mattered just as much, namely the concern over aggressive Communism. While the full extent of Stalin's humanitarian crimes remained unclear, enough was known to make Washington wary. Hitler clearly sought to force his will over central Europe, but Stalin wanted the entire world under his boot-heel. Given a choice between evils—which many in Washington thought was all they had, in the 1930s—it might make strategic and even moral sense to prefer a strong Nazi Germany as a barricade against a Stalinist Europe.

The causes of British appeasement were perhaps the most complicated of all. Most people in Britain agreed that the Versailles Treaty had been a disaster and that the refusal of the Parliament to ratify it had been correct. But if the West had been wrong in 1919 to strip Germany of its peripheral territories, how could it oppose Germany's desire to have those territories restored? So long as Hitler's demands called only for rolling back an unfair treaty, many British concluded, they were not worth foiling at the cost of another war. For example, Hitler repeatedly demanded the return to Germany of the Ruhr Valley (of 1923–1924 fame). Britain, loath to quarrel yet again with France, at first hesitated and denied the claim, citing the treaty as justification. But when German demands became more shrill and Hitler declared his willingness for war, if necessary, Britain relented. In 1936 it agreed to allow the Nazi regime to take control of and remilitarize the district.

Munich Conference   Negotiations between Neville Chamberlain and Adolf Hitler, with attendants, in September 28, 1938, to resolve the issue of Nazi claims to control the Sudetenland region in Czechoslovakia. After returning home from this meeting, Chamberlain spoke to a crowd outside 10 Downing Street: "My good friends, this is the second time in our history that there has come back from Germany to Downing Street peace with honour. I believe it is peace for our time. We thank you from the bottom of our hearts. And now I recommend you to go home and sleep quietly in your beds." World War II broke out almost exactly one year later.

For the moment, tensions calmed, but then Hitler began the gamble again the following year by calling for Germany's right to unite with Austria (the *Anschluss*). Similar demands, similar arguments, similar threats—and once again, British compliance. Then in 1938 Hitler insisted on the return of the Sudetenland—the predominantly ethnically German part of what was then northern Czechoslovakia. Once again the British prime minister Neville Chamberlain (r. 1937–1940) had to explain his position on the floor of the Parliament in March 1938:

> The position that we had to face in July was that a deadlock had arisen in the negotiations which had been going on between the Czechoslovak Government and the Sudeten Germans and that fears were already entertained that if it were not readily broken the German Government might presently intervene in the dispute. For His Majesty's Government there were three alternative courses that we might have adopted. Either (1) we could have threatened to go to war with Germany if she attacked Czechoslovakia, or (2) we could have stood aside and allowed matters to take their course, or, finally, (3) we could attempt to find a peaceful settlement by way of mediation. The first of those courses we rejected. We had no treaty liabilities with Czechoslovakia. We always refused to accept any such obligation. Indeed, this country, which does not readily resort to war, would not have followed us if we had tried to lead it into war to prevent a minority from obtaining autonomy, or even from choosing to pass under some other Government.
>
> The second alternative was also repugnant to us. However remote this territory may be, we knew, of course, that a spark once lighted there might give rise to a general conflagration, and we felt it our duty to do anything in our power to help the contending parties to find agreement.
>
> We addressed ourselves to the third course, the task of mediation. We knew that the task would be difficult, perhaps even perilous, but we felt that the object was good enough to justify the risk.

Chamberlain substitutes the word "mediation" here for "appeasement," which actually had a positive connotation at the time—a sense of reasonableness and diplomatic maturity. Only after World War II did it acquire its current taint.

Another English word entered common use in the West in the 1930s, carried over from French—**pacifism**. It appeared first in 1902 to describe French social reformers who opposed the military buildup that culminated in World

War I. From 1919 on, however, it denoted any principled and total rejection of violence as a means of resolving disputes. In the preface to his play *Heartbreak House* (1919), George Bernard Shaw described prewar Europe as a time and place where "there was only one virtue, pugnacity; only one vice, pacifism. That [combination] is an essential condition of war."[9] In an early treatise dedicated to the subject, the social critic P. S. Mumford wrote in his *Introduction to Pacifism* (1937, that "the Pacifist believes: 1. That war, i.e. mass murder, as a political policy is morally wrong, and consequently will never produce good results.... 2. That security for nations, ideals, or personal freedom can be obtained only by nonviolent resistance." Pacifism therefore meant not merely the preference for peace but the belief that any form of violence is intrinsically evil.

The most famous name among British pacifists of the time was the novelist and critic Aldous Huxley (1894–1963), best remembered today for his novel *Brave New World* (1932), in which he warned of the harmful effects of society's growing dependence on technology. Urged on by figures like him, the Student Union of Oxford University in 1935 swore a public oath that it "would not take up arms in defense of King and country... under any conditions whatsoever," should conflicts with Nazi Germany, Fascist Italy, or Communist Russia come to war. This "Oxford Oath" circulated through Cambridge University as well before coming to the United States. By the end of 1936 no fewer than sixty thousand American undergraduates had also taken the pledge, starting at Columbia University and Brown University.

Britain found itself in a bind—caught between loathing and distrust of Hitler on the one hand and a grudging willingness to consider his demands on the other. Despite urgent warnings in Parliament from Churchill and others, the ruling Conservative Party hoped to the very last that nations could deal with even a tyrant like Hitler with caution and reasonableness. Many in the country, and in Britain's closest ally, the United States, feared Stalin even more and hoped against hope that Hitler could be used as a foil against him. And leading groups of the generation that would do the actual fighting, if it came to that, had already announced their refusal to fight at all.

In the face of all this, Churchill rose in Parliament on October 5, 1938, with a stirring speech against any further appeasement or pacification. He ended with a quote from the Bible (Daniel 5.27):

> The Prime Minister desires to see cordial relations between this country and Germany. There is no difficulty at all in having cordial

---

9   Winston Churchill wrote in his 1930 memoir *My Early Life* that he had "always been against the Pacifists during [a] quarrel, and against the Jingoes at its close."

relations with the German people. Our hearts go out to them. But they have no power. You must have diplomatic and correct relations, but there can never be friendship between the British democracy and the Nazi Power, that power which spurns Christian ethics, which cheers its onward course by a barbarous paganism, which vaunts the spirit of aggression and conquest, which derives strength and perverted pleasure from persecution, and uses, as we have seen, with pitiless brutality the threat of murderous force. That power cannot ever be the trusted friend of the British democracy.

What I find unendurable is the sense of our country falling into the power, into the orbit and influence of Nazi Germany, and of our existence becoming dependent upon their good will or pleasure. It is to prevent that, that I have tried my best to urge the maintenance of every bulwark of defense—first, the timely creation of an Air Force superior to anything within striking distance of our shores; secondly, the gathering together of the collective strength of many nations; and thirdly, the making of alliances and military conventions. . . . It has all been in vain. Every position has been successively undermined and abandoned on specious and plausible excuses. We do not want to be led upon the high road to becoming a satellite of the German Nazi system of European domination. In a very few years, perhaps in a very few months, we shall be confronted with demands with which we shall no doubt be invited to comply. Those demands may affect the surrender of territory or the surrender of liberty. I foresee and foretell that the policy of submission will carry with it restrictions upon the freedom of speech and debate in Parliament, on public platform, and discussions in the Press. . . .

But [the British public] should know the truth. They should know that there has been gross neglect and deficiency in our defenses; they should know that we have sustained a defeat without a war, the consequences of which will travel far with us along our road; they should know that we have passed an awful milestone in our history, when the whole equilibrium of Europe has been deranged, and that the terrible words have for the time being been pronounced against the Western democracies: "Thou art weighed in the balance and found wanting."

The Nazi regime made an enormous gamble after 1933. It bet its survival on the belief that the nations of the West would acquiesce so long as Nazi demands were couched in terms of the Versailles Treaty. The six years of breathing space accorded Hitler by the policies of appeasement and the popular call for pacifism were all he needed to rebuild Germany's military system and to turn it into the most awesome fighting force in Europe. On September 1, 1939, Hitler took his decisive step by sending his army into Poland—the first territory outside any conceivable German claim to legitimate dominion. At that point it was at last undeniable that Nazi aims were pan-European. Within three days, World War II had begun.

WHO, WHAT, WHERE

appeasement	Lateran Agreement
Balfour Declaration	*Lebensraum*
Bloomsbury Group	League of Nations
Fascism	Maginot Line
Fourteen Points	mandates
gold standard	New Deal
Great Depression	pacifism
Great Purge	Spanish Civil War
gulag	totalitarianism

SUGGESTED READINGS

Primary Sources

Hayek, Friedrich A. *The Road to Serfdom.*
Hitler, Adolf. *Mein Kampf.*
Keynes, John Maynard. *The General Theory of Employment, Interest, and Money.*
Orwell, George. *Homage to Catalonia.*
Spengler, Oswald. *The Decline of the West.*
Toynbee, Arnold J. *A Study of History.*
Valéry, Paul. "A Crisis of the Mind."
Wells, H. G. *The Outline of History.*

Anthologies

Aster, Sidney, ed. *Appeasement and All Souls: A Portrait with Documents, 1937–1939* (2005).
Crew, David F. *Hitler and the Nazis: A History in Documents* (2006).

Studies

Berend, Ivan T. *Decades of Crisis: Central and Eastern Europe before World War II* (2001).
Bosworth, R. J. B. *Mussolini's Italy: Life under the Fascist Dictatorship, 1915–1945* (2007).
Brendon, Piers. *The Dark Valley: A Panorama of the 1930s* (2009).
Caldwell, Bruce J. *Hayek's Challenge: An Intellectual Biography of F. A. Hayek* (2003).
Diepeveen, Leonard. *The Difficulties of Modernism* (2002).
Evans, Richard J. *The Coming of the Third Reich* (2004).

———. *The Third Reich in Power, 1933–1939* (2005).

Fitzpatrick, Sheila. *Everyday Stalinism: Ordinary Life in Extraordinary Times—Soviet Russia in the 1930s* (2000).

Geifman, Anna. *Death Orders: The Vanguard of Modern Terrorism in Revolutionary Russia* (2010).

Gregor, A. James. *Marxism, Fascism, and Totalitarianism: Chapters in the Intellectual History of Radicalism* (2008).

Griffin, Roger. *Modernism and Fascism: The Sense of a Beginning under Mussolini and Hitler* (2011).

Hagedorn, Ann. *Savage Peace: Hope and Fear in America, 1919* (2007).

Hodgson, Keith. *Fighting Fascism: The British Left and the Rise of Fascism, 1919–39* (2010).

Hoffmann, David L. *Stalinist Values: The Cultural Norms of Soviet Modernity, 1917–1941* (2003).

Kennedy, David M. *Over Here: The First World War and America Society* (2004).

Kitchen, Martin. *Europe between the Wars: A Political History* (2006).

Lampe, John R. *Balkans into Southeastern Europe: A Century of War and Transition* (2006).

Lampe, John R., and Mark Mazower, eds. *Ideologies and National Identities: The Case of Twentieth-Century Southeastern Europe* (2004).

North, Michael. *Reading 1922: A Return to the Scene of the Modern* (2001).

Overy, Richard. *The Twilight Years: The Paradox of Britain between the Wars* (2009).

Paxton, Richard O. *The Anatomy of Fascism* (2005).

Pfannestiel, Todd J. *Rethinking the Red Scare: The Lusk Committee and New York's Crusade against Radicalism, 1919–1923* (2003).

Pine, Lisa. *Education in Nazi Germany* (2011).

Romero Salvadó, Francisco J. *The Spanish Civil War: Origins, Course, and Outcomes* (2005).

Steiner, Zara. *The Lights that Failed: European International History, 1919–1933* (2007).

———. *The Triumph of the Dark: European International History, 1933–1939* (2011).

Thomas, Hugh. *The Spanish Civil War* (2001).

Tubach, Frederic C. *German Voices: Life during Hitler's Third Reich* (2011).

Wapshott, Nicholas. *Keynes Hayek: The Clash That Defined Modern Economics* (2011).

Weitz, Eric D. *Weimar Germany: Promise and Tragedy* (2009).

Widdig, Bernd. *Culture and Inflation in Weimar Germany* (2001).

Worley, Matthew. *Oswald Mosley and the New Party* (2010).

For additional resources, including maps, primary sources, visuals, web links, and quizzes, please go to **www.oup.com/us/backman.**

"THIS WORLD CANNOT EXIST HALF SLAVE AND HALF FREE"

SACRIFICE FOR FREEDOM!

CHAPTER 26

The World at War (Part II)

1937–1945

THE WORLD AT WAR, 1937–1945

Major clashes

Fifty to sixty million deaths. Adolf Hitler's invasion of Poland on September 1, 1939, inaugurated the war in Europe, and Japan's attack on the U.S. naval base at Pearl Harbor, Hawaii, on December 7, 1941, triggered war in the Pacific. World War II ended in 1945 with the unconditional surrenders of Germany in May and Japan in September. It was ruin run wild over three continents. More than 110 million soldiers participated; twenty-seven million of them perished. Six million Jews, almost all of them civilians, were murdered in the Nazi concentration camps; another twenty to twenty-five million civilians from among all the other combatants' nations died of starvation or exposure, in air raids or artillery shelling, or were deported to the death camps. In one way or another the war involved most of the nations on Earth, and the great powers formed into two camps—the Allies (led by Britain, France, the Soviet Union, and the United States) and the Axis (Germany, Italy, and Japan, principally).[1]

◀ **Fight for Freedom** A patriotic call to duty in wartime Britain (note the Anglican collar on the clergyman at left—already wholly in shadow). The threatening figure brandishing the whip is artfully drawn: he could be interpreted as either a Nazi German or a Stalinist Russian. Aimed at the British, this poster was produced by the U.S. government.

The largest, bloodiest, most destructive, and most expensive conflict in human history, World War II nearly wiped out entire races and entire cities. Along with its unparalleled atrocities, however, a recognition of the need for justice after the war led to the attempt to treat the atrocities as war crimes. And along with the atomic bomb, the postwar years also brought the recognition of international

- A Place in Memory
- The War in Europe
- Wars in the Pacific
- Atrocities and Holocaust
- Making Amends
- The United Nations and Human Rights
- Atomic Fissures
- Women in, and against, Fascism
- World War II and the Middle East
- Arab Nationalism and Growing Zionism

CHAPTER OUTLINE

law in the United Nations. Women had seen the pace of their gains fall with the Great Depression and Fascism, but they also played an active role in wartime. So did territories on the peripheries, in Africa and the Middle East. In the process, they felt evolving definitions of Arab nationalism and Zionism—the drive for a state of Israel.

A PLACE IN MEMORY

Unlike the start of World War I, no jubilant crowds greeted this conflict. Popular sentiments were decidedly grim. After Hitler took the Sudetenland from Czechoslovakia, and the West had acquiesced, few people doubted that a horrible conflict was imminent, and the last six months before the war were filled with desperate strategic maneuvers. Britain and France, fearing the worst, promised to defend Greece, Poland, Romania, and Turkey in case of Nazi aggression. Hitler countered by forging the "Pact of Steel" with Fascist Italy, in May 1939. In Moscow, meanwhile, Stalin was exasperated at the West's delay in protecting eastern Europe and so began his own furtive negotiations with Hitler. In a surprise nonaggression pact signed in August 1939, each side vowed not to attack the other and to remain neutral in the event of war elsewhere. And Stalin counted on that pact. He needed every last month and week of delay, in order to replenish the officer corps that he had decimated with his purges.

The news stunned Europe and the United States, since the ideology of each nation was so opposed to the other. What the West did not know was that a secret clause in the Nazi-Soviet Pact arranged for the two countries to divide the lands of Poland, Estonia, Latvia, and Lithuania. At some future date, their conquest was to be undertaken by either Germany or Russia—and that future arrived more quickly than even Hitler and Stalin may have guessed.

---

[1]   Counting the pre-1939 Sino-Japanese War between China and Japan, estimates of the dead may reach as high as eighty million.

CHAPTER TIMELINE

1937
Japan invades China

August 1939
Nonaggression Pact between Germany and USSR

June 2, 1940
German army captures Paris

1942
Final Solution put into effect

1938
Virginia Woolf, *Three Guineas*

September 1, 1939
Germany invades Poland

December 7, 1941
Japanese attack on Pearl Harbor

World War II holds a special place in memory. To the people of Russia, where by far the greatest number of victims fell, it is called the "Great Patriotic War" to honor their extraordinary suffering. To them, the eastern front marked the center of the conflict, and the battle for Stalingrad was the turning point of the entire war. Western Europe recalls instead the Nazi seizure of Holland, Belgium, and France; the battle of Britain; the Normandy Invasion; the North African and Italian campaigns; and the final march on Berlin.

In China, which remained apart from the broader conflict, it is the "War of Resistance" against Japan, while in Japan it is either the "Japan-China Incident" or simply the "China Incident." (After all, neither country ever issued a formal declaration of war.) Japanese historians long described the war against America and her allies as simply one facet of the "Greater East Asian War"—a broad independence movement that aimed to free East Asia of Western meddling. (Japanese officials later drew a parallel with China's own description of its Tiananmen Square massacre of 1989 as an "incident.") Americans speak of World War II, but a widely read history written in the mid-1980s referred to the struggle as the "Good War." That goodness lay, at least in nostalgic memories, in the moral clarity of America's involvement—as a conflict between obvious Good and obvious Evil. By whatever name the war is known, it left scars on the hearts and minds of all who participated in it (see Figure 26–1).

> Americans speak of World War II, but a widely read history written in the mid-1980s referred to the struggle as the "Good War." That goodness lay, at least in nostalgic memories, in the moral clarity of America's involvement—as a conflict between obvious Good and obvious Evil.

THE WAR IN EUROPE

The broad narrative of the war divides easily into three stages—Nazi success after success, decisive battles in Russia and against Italy, and Allied success in France and Germany. From 1939 to 1942 Germany quickly overran, in order,

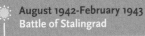
August 1942-February 1943
Battle of Stalingrad

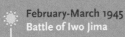
February-March 1945
Battle of Iwo Jima

August 1945
United States drops atomic bombs on Hiroshima and Nagasaki; Japan surrenders

1948
Universal Declaration of Human Rights

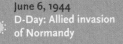
June 6, 1944
D-Day: Allied invasion of Normandy

May 1945
Germany surrenders

1945
Nuremberg and Tokyo War Crimes Trials begin; UN established

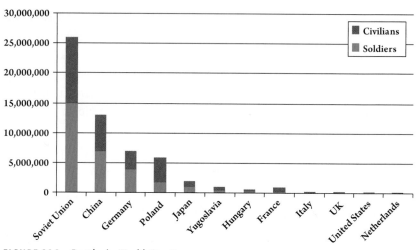

FIGURE 26.1   **Deaths in World War II**

Poland, Denmark, Norway, Holland, Belgium, and France. The Nazis made the fullest possible use of Germany's advantages in technology and numbers to break through defensive barriers at speed. Their **Blitzkrieg** ("lightning war") strategies concentrated heavy but mobile firepower (tanks and aircraft especially) and rapid troop movement in small areas. Having split their opponents' forces, the Germans then rapidly advanced straight ahead rather than contending with the divided flanks, which forced the shattered defense forces to attempt to regroup against a fast-moving enemy.

Time and again, in the first three years of the war, Nazi strategies forced their opponents to capitulate before they ever had a chance to mount a counter campaign. In less than two months in 1940, before the French army could even muster, the Nazis raced through the Low Countries, circumvented the Maginot Line altogether, and occupied Paris. The city surrendered on June 22. An infamous film clip shows a jubilant Hitler, who arrived in Paris shortly thereafter, celebrating the crushing of an era established by the hated Versailles Treaty. Roughly two-thirds of France remained under Nazi occupation for the next four years, while a Nazi-controlled puppet regime under Field Marshal Philippe Pétain (1856–1951) governed southern France from its temporary capital in the city of Vichy. Meanwhile, Poland had been divided with Stalin according to the Nazi-Soviet Pact, which allowed the Nazis to round up Jews for the labor camps rapidly being built in the east. The "ethnic cleansing" of Europe had begun.

In the second half of 1941 Hitler stood at the apogee of his power. True, his attempt to force Britain's capitulation through air raids from August to

October 1940 had failed, ending his dream of conquering Britain. He had also been drawn against his will into fighting in the Balkans and North Africa, thanks to Mussolini's amateurish efforts to establish Fascist control of the central Mediterranean. Yet he was confident enough in late 1941 both to invade Russia in June and to declare war on the United States in December. These events mark the beginning of the second phase of the war in Europe.

Hitler in Paris After the collapse of French defenses, the Nazi army seized control of France in a matter of a few weeks. Here a triumphant Hitler poses with Albert Speer (1905–1981), his Minister of Armaments and War Production, and Arno Breker (1900–1991), his favorite sculptor, before the Eiffel Tower.

The campaign into Russia, called Operation Barbarossa, caught Stalin by surprise and progressed rapidly. Barbarossa was the largest single military action in Western history, involving three million German soldiers (75 percent of the entire Nazi army and 66 percent of its total air power), who went east against nearly five million soldiers of the Soviet Red Army. Stalin's forces were already established in the half of Poland ceded to him by Hitler in 1939, and so the initial Blitzkrieg strikes occurred there. After breaking through the Russian ranks, the Germans pressed a three-pronged attack: to the northeast, against Leningrad (Saint Petersburg); due east, toward Moscow; and to the southeast, to Stalingrad (Volgograd). Each of the three campaigns ended in Nazi defeats. The Nazis reached Leningrad in September of 1941 but were unable to storm the city. Instead, a miserably protracted siege lasted over two years, until January 1944, during which more than a million city dwellers died of starvation, cold, and disease. The Nazis themselves incurred extraordinarily high casualties, as they were exposed to brutal winters for which they were unprepared and poorly resupplied.[2] The battle for Moscow, from October 1941 to January

---

[2] Nazis dropped over one hundred thousand bombs and more than two hundred thousand artillery shells on Leningrad.

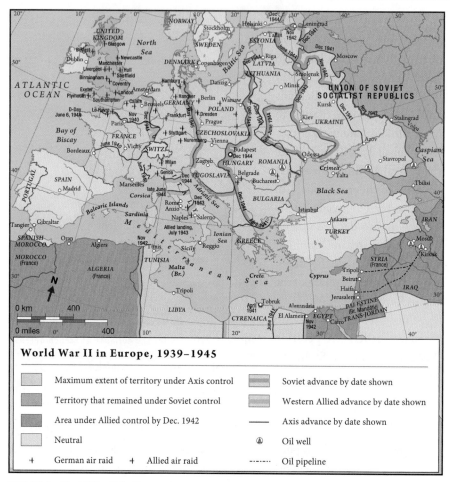

MAP 26.1   World War II in Europe, 1939–1945

1942, ended with a decisive Russian victory, however, as did the battle for Stalingrad, from August 1942 to February 1943 (see Map 26.1).

Matters worsened for the Germans quickly thereafter. The Allies in the west moved steadily through North Africa and turned north, invading Sicily and the Italian mainland in the late summer of 1943. The Fascist government toppled Mussolini and imprisoned him, though he quickly escaped, with German help; he was later captured trying to flee to neutral Switzerland and was lynched by a mob in Milan. Italy then broke with the Axis and joined the Allied side, which set the stage for the third and final stage of the war—which began with the Allied invasion of Normandy on D-Day, June 6, 1944.

The Nazis had long anticipated an invasion but were surprised at the precise location and date when it did finally come. Nevertheless, their defenses were strong. An Allied force of 130,000 men, made up primarily of U.S. and U.K. soldiers, landed on the beaches, while another 20,000 parachuted far behind the Nazi defenses to cut off reinforcements. Though enormously costly in lives, the D-Day landing proved a huge success, and that year Allied forces liberated Holland, Bel-

D-Day Allied troops landing on the beach at Normandy on D-Day, June 6, 1944.

gium, and France, while their troops in Italy pressed continually northward. Gradually, as 1945 began, Allied armies from the west and the south and Russian forces moving in rapidly from the east closed in on Germany and then on Berlin itself. The war ended in May 1945 after Adolf Hitler committed suicide in his Berlin bomb shelter, and his remaining circle of high officials surrendered unconditionally.

WARS IN THE PACIFIC

The war in the Pacific began on December 7, 1941, when Japan attacked the U.S. naval base at Pearl Harbor in Hawaii, but tensions between the two countries had been rising for at least twenty years before that. Japan had long feared domination from the mainland, from China or Korea, and the coal-powered American maritime rivals added a new threat. Only by rapid industrialization, and the means to deliver its manufactures to world markets, could Japan feel protected. But the islands of Japan have little in the way of mineral ores—which forced them to look for outside sources of raw materials, fuel to process and ship them, and secure markets in which to sell them.

Japan's imperialist adventures had begun in 1904–1905 with the Russo-Japanese War. This war had been fought principally for control of the island of Sakhalin off the coast of Russia, where sizeable deposits of oil were known to exist. In 1910 Japan forcibly annexed Korea too, which had much-needed natural resources and a large population that could serve as a captive market. When World War I broke out, Japan formed an alliance with Britain and laid claim to Germany's east Asian and Pacific Island colonies—which it duly received. Japanese sailors also fought briefly in the Great War in the Mediterranean, against the Ottomans. By this point Japan was fully in the grip of militarism, every bit equal to that of Europe prior to 1914. When the Great Depression hit in 1929, the military took an even more active role in government, touting itself as the only real solution to the economic problem. Its solutions in the 1930s focused on stirring up trouble in China in order to justify direct military action (see Map 26.2).

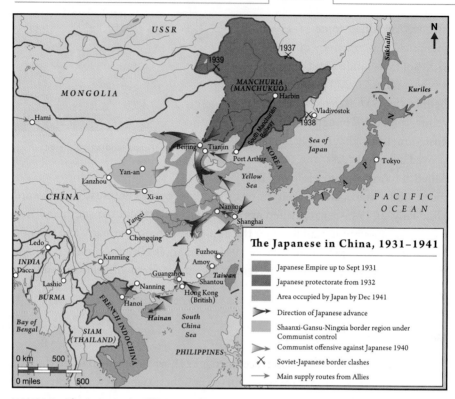

MAP 26.2   The Japanese in China, 1931–1941

Two "incidents" provided all the justification Japan needed. In September 1931 the Japanese staged a supposed Chinese terrorist attack on the South Manchurian Railway, which was then under lease to Japan. They placed a small bomb a short distance from a little-used piece of track and detonated it. The explosion caused only minor damage, but it attracted the attention of nearby Chinese soldiers, who hurried to investigate. The sudden "onslaught" of Chinese forces provided a pretext for Japanese action—and the seizure of all of Manchuria within five months of the faked terrorist attack.[3] The United States condemned Japan's action and vowed never to recognize any government established in Manchuria by Tokyo.

The second incident triggered the start of the Second Sino-Japanese War (1937–1945) and was a murkier affair. It occurred in July 1937 at the Marco Polo Bridge (the Lugou Bridge in Chinese, or Roku in Japanese), a long stone bridge over a tributary of the Hai River located a dozen miles southwest of Beijing. The bridge formed part of the rail line that linked Beijing with the rest of the province

---

[3]   An exhibit in the Yushukan Military and War Museum in Tokyo still blames the 1931 Manchurian Railway bombing on Chinese militias.

and was thus of great strategic importance. The Chinese government, as a courtesy, had long allowed any nation that had trade legations in Beijing to place armed guards along this rail line. These guards had the right to perform occasional maneuvers—but Japan was the only country actually to do so. Either by plan or by accident, a squad of Japanese soldiers performed night maneuvers without informing local Chinese officials as they were supposed to do. One of the Japanese soldiers disappeared, and when Chinese officials began to search for him and to investigate the matter, Japan claimed that a cover-up conspiracy was under way and used this as a pretext for a full-scale invasion of Beijing and the entire province.

When the United States condemned the aggression, announced economic sanctions, and ultimately cut off oil and steel to Japan, the Japanese military began the preparations that led ultimately to the attack on Pearl Harbor.

> In broad outline, Japanese imperialism differed little from the European variety. Japan, too, believed in its innate superiority over other cultures, its superior claim to the world's resources, and its destiny to prove that superiority through force.

In broad outline, Japanese imperialism differed little from the European variety. Japan, too, believed in its innate superiority over other cultures, its superior claim to the world's resources, and its destiny to prove that superiority through force. Like the Europeans, the Japanese also showed themselves capable of horrific, wanton violence on occasion. In the First Sino-Japanese War of 1894–1895, a Japanese army division found the mutilated corpses of some of their compatriots who had been wounded and captured by the Chinese in an earlier battle. Infuriated, the division attacked the coastal town of Port Arthur (now Lushunkou) and massacred nearly the entire population, both military and civilian—an estimated population of five to six thousand. A mere three dozen survivors faced the grim task of burying the dead.

Militarism gained pace in Japan as the nation's population grew—forty-five million in 1900, sixty-five million by 1930. The greater numbers of people, combined with the Depression, highlighted the fundamental fact that Japan alone among developed nations could not feed itself.[4] For the generation that fought in World War II, imperial might and the martial spirit that sustained it were the best guarantors of prosperity and proof of the peoples' superior nature.

As with the war in Europe, the war in the Pacific falls neatly into three stages. The years from 1937 to 1941 mark the first stage, when Japan imposed its will throughout eastern and southeastern Asia, snatching up former German colonies and adding new ones through their campaigns in China. The second stage consists of the start of the war with the United States in 1941 to the Battle of

---

[4]   Japan today remains the only industrialized nation that survives on imported food.

Midway in 1942. Midway Island lay roughly 1,500 miles (2,400 kilometers) west of Hawaii; though small, it had great strategic value because of its location midway between Hawaii and Japan. When Japan attempted a joint naval and amphibious assault on it, a smaller American force successfully fended off the attackers—and turned the tide of the war (see Map 26.3).

The final stage ran from 1942 to the Japanese surrender in 1945, as the Allies pressed in on the Japanese Empire from all sides. A ferocious battle to take the garrison island of Iwo Jima in February-March 1945 was the most notorious single episode in the campaign. Iwo Jima lay 750 miles due south of Tokyo and was the site of strategic airfields that the Japanese used to resist American air attacks on Japan itself. Of the roughly 18,000 soldiers stationed there, only two hundred survived and were captured; the rest perished in the assault. The United States attacked with a force of 70,000, nearly 7,000 of whom perished; another 20,000 were wounded. Overall, it was a heavier U.S. toll than in the invasion of Normandy on D-Day. The war ended suddenly with the American decision to

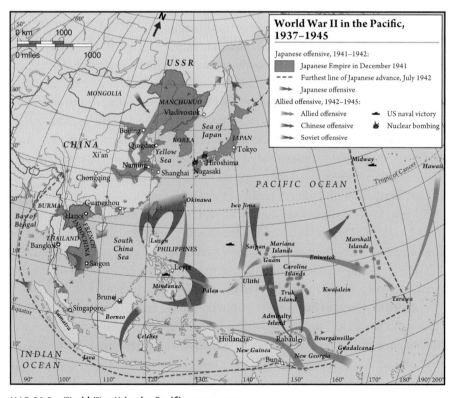

MAP 26.3 World War II in the Pacific, 1937–1945

drop atomic bombs on Hiroshima and Nagasaki in August 1945, and the Japanese government surrendered.

ATROCITIES AND HOLOCAUST

All wars have their atrocities, but technology has made modern warfare particularly grisly. From the introduction of gunpowder weapons and the creation of mass armies, the frequency and scale of massacres in wartime have increased dramatically. The mere pressing of a button or the pulling of a trigger can produce carnage to equal that at Thermopylae or Actium, Hastings or Hattin, Breda or Lepanto. For one generation, World War I seemed the summit of human horror; but airplanes and armored vehicles came into wide use only toward the end of that conflict, and World War II began with even more destructive weapons. Ironically, interwar recovery efforts made those weapons possible, thanks to the heavy investment in industry. The roll call of massacre sites is a long one: Auschwitz, Babi Yar, Dresden, Hiroshima, Katyn, Manila, Nagasaki, Nanking, Novi Sad, Port Arthur, and Treuenbrietzen are simply the best-known episodes. We know as much as we do about the atrocities in part because the Nazis kept meticulous film and documentary archives of their own activities. In part, too, the Allies insisted on international tribunals for investigating and prosecuting war crimes.

> From the introduction of gunpowder weapons and the creation of mass armies, the frequency and scale of massacres in wartime have increased dramatically. The mere pressing of a button or the pulling of a trigger can produce carnage to equal that at Thermopylae or Actium, Hastings or Hattin, Breda or Lepanto.

Four episodes, out of thousands, give a sense of the heartless savagery of the war. First was the Nazis' program to improve the gene pool of the Aryan race by euthanasia. Known as the "T4 Project," this campaign targeted native Germans with any major form of physical or mental handicap. Hundreds of thousands of such ethnic "mercy killings" and forced sterilizations took place.[5] (Exceptions were made for wounded war veterans.) The project took its name from the address of its administrative center in Berlin—4 Tiergartenstrasse—and began in 1939, shortly before the invasion of Poland. Officially closed in 1941, to cover up its

---

[5]   Between 1933 and 1939 the Nazis sterilized roughly three hundred thousand undesirables. The T4 Project aimed to be a less costly way of achieving the same "racial hygiene."

Persecuting an Orthodox Jew Poland was the site of heroic resistance against the Nazis and also a center of intense anti-Semitism. In this photo from 1941 a group of sneering Nazi soldiers cut the beard off an elderly Jew.

actions, the T4 project unofficially operated almost to the end of the war, and another two hundred thousand people were killed. Hitler recruited physicians, engineers, chemists, and administrative personnel with great care, in order to make sure that their ideological zeal matched their technical expertise. His chancellors Philipp Bouhler (1899–1945) and Viktor Brack (1904–1948) served as administrative heads, and Dr. Karl Brandt (1904–1948), oversaw the review, selection, and disposal of the victims. In the end, the Nazis' official T4 records report that some seventy thousand men, women, and children were put to death in a half-dozen sites built especially for the program; in the Nuremberg trials that followed the war, evidence of an additional 150,000 victims emerged. Initially, the victims were killed by lethal injections—but the process took too long and the poisons became too costly once the war began, so Brandt recommended custom-designed gas chambers instead. Bouhler was arrested at the war's end but committed suicide before he could be tried; Brandt and Brack were tried, convicted, and executed for crimes against humanity.

T4 was prologue to a still greater tragedy—the systematic murder of six million Jews, the **Holocaust**, or Shoah (Hebrew for "catastrophe"). Nazi hatred of the Jews was fanatical, but unlike other anti-Semitic episodes in Western history the war on the Jews had primarily a racial rather than a religious basis. The Jews, it was feared, polluted the Aryan race. First, their mere presence in Europe fouled the atmosphere and corrupted the culture; second, by intermarriage they weakened the racial purity of the Germanic people; and third, their supposed championing of both the hated ideologies of Communism and untrammeled capitalism gave them a dangerous degree of control over the material lives of the people. Hitler had made it clear in *Mein Kampf* what he intended to do about the Jewish problem, if he ever had the chance. "We must free ourselves from the forces that now control our public life.... Our first objective must be to wipe out Jewish society as it currently exists."

The Jewish population of prewar Germany had been roughly 500,000; another 200,000 were added when Hitler annexed Austria. Just over half of these had fled the Nazis before the start of the war. When Hitler swept into Poland, however, some two million more Jews came under his control, and the increased numbers added to the frenzy of Nazi hatred. The solution to the Jewish problem, they concluded, was to ship Jews to concentration camps where they could be forced to labor on behalf of the Germans. Although the **Final Solution** of exterminating the Jews was not decided upon until later in 1941, it was clear that the half dozen main camps were set up to kill.

A report written by two escapees from Auschwitz-Birkenau, Alfred Wetzler (1918–1988) and Rudolf Vrba (1924–2006), describes the scene that met them when they arrived at the camp in early 1942:

> By the middle of May a total of four Jewish male transports had reached Birkenau from Slovakia. All received the same treatment as ourselves. From the first and second transports, 120 of us were sent to Auschwitz on orders of the Auschwitz camp command, which had asked for doctors, dentists, university students, and professional administrators and clerks. After one week at Auschwitz 18 doctors and nurses, as well as three clerks, were selected from the 120 professionals. The doctors were assigned to the Auschwitz hospital and the three clerks, including myself, were sent back to Birkenau. Two of my companions, . . . both of whom have since died, went to the Slovak block. I went to the French block, where we were given administrative work. The remaining 99 persons were sent to work in the Auschwitz quarry, where they perished within a short time.
>
> Shortly afterwards a so-called hospital was established in one of the buildings. This was the notorious Block No. 7. I was assigned there as head-nurse at first; later I became the manager. . . . This hospital was nothing other than an assembly point for those awaiting death. All prisoners unable to work were sent here. Naturally, there could be no question of medical treatment or nursing. Every day about 150 people died and their corpses were sent to the Auschwitz crematorium.
>
> At the same time the so-called "selection" was started. The number of prisoners who were to be gassed and their bodies burned was determined twice weekly, on Monday and Thursday, by the camp doctor. Selectees were loaded on a truck and taken to the birchwood. Those who reached there alive were gassed in the big barrack built for the purpose and located next to the hole for burning bodies, and then were cremated in that hole. Approximately 2000 from Block No. 7 died each week, of which about 1200 deaths resulted from "natural causes" and about 800 from "selection." Death reports on those dying from natural causes were made out and sent

to camp HQ at Orianenburg. Selectees were marked up in a book labeled "Special Treatment." I was manager of Block No. 7 until 15 January 1943, during which time I could observe what was going on. About 50,000 prisoners were destroyed during that period, either from "natural causes" or through "selections."

This report, quoted here in its official English translation for the courts, was among the most valuable pieces of evidence presented at the Nuremberg Trials.

The Nazis killed Jews everywhere they found them, but eight camps formed the main sites of industrialized murder: Auschwitz-Birkenau, Belzec, Bergen-Belsen, Chelmno, Lublin/Majdanek, Mauthausen, Sobibor, and Treblinka. Six of the eight (those apart from Bergen-Belsen in Germany and Mauthausen in Austria) are in Poland, where the Nazis shipped their victims from across Europe (see Map 26.4). Those Jews deemed fit for labor received temporary reprieves and were set to work. The rest faced quick annihilation in gas chambers, followed by cremation in special ovens built for the purpose.

For a time, the English language failed before the scale of the evil; a new word was needed for a crime of this magnitude. Fittingly, a Polish Jew, Raphael

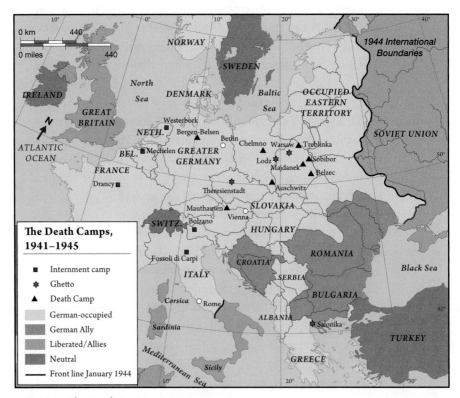

MAP 26.4   **The Death Camps, 1941–1945**

Lemkin, coined the term **genocide** in 1944. Lemkin (1900–1959) had been a public prosecutor in prewar Poland, and in 1939 he joined the army to fight against the Nazis. Wounded in battle, he escaped to Sweden and eventually to America, where he subsequently taught law at Duke, Yale, and Rutgers universities. He served as an adviser to Robert H. Jackson, the U.S. Supreme Court judge who later served as chief counsel at the Nuremberg Trials.

Six million Jews died in the Holocaust—the great majority in a single eighteen-month spasm of psychotic violence from late 1942 to mid-1944. By the time it ended, when advancing Russian and Allied troops closed in on Germany, the Jewish societies of Austria, Germany, Lithuania, Poland, Romania, and the Ukraine had been all but annihilated.

Auschwitz Jewish children in the death-camp at Auschwitz.

Jews were not the only victims of the Nazi's industrialized murder scheme. Somewhere between two and three million Russian prisoners of war died in the camps, as did two million Polish Gentiles who had resisted Nazi power or impeded the Germans' roundup of Jews. Other victims included homosexuals, the physically disabled, the Roma (Gypsies), Freemasons, and Jehovah's Witnesses; this last group was persecuted less for their religious beliefs than for their refusal to serve in the German army.

Six million is also the rough tally of Chinese killed while fighting Japan during the 1941–1945 war alone. If one adds the war of 1932–1937, the tally reaches twenty million. The Chinese-Japanese conflict had many causes

TABLE 26.1 **Non-Jewish Victims of the Concentration Camps**

Soviet POWs	2,000,000–3,000,000
Poles	2,000,000
Roma (Gypsies)	350,000
The Disabled	250,000
Freemasons	120,000
Homosexuals	15,000
Jehovah's Witnesses	4,000

and frequently reached feverish pitches of intensity. The most notorious of atrocities in this conflict was the **Rape of Nanjing.** In the weeks following the Marco Polo Bridge Incident (December 13, 1937), a large force of 150,000 Japanese soldiers advanced on Nanjing, then the capital of China. Accounts of what happened differ—and the Japanese either destroyed or removed their records on the affair, as American forces drew closer to Tokyo in 1945. Enough evidence, however, survives to make it clear that somewhere around 250,000 Chinese civilians were slaughtered by the Japanese army, all in a period of only five to six weeks. Another 20,000–50,000 Chinese women and girls were raped, most of them repeatedly. Civilians were shot, stabbed to death, or beheaded. Others were doused with gasoline and set aflame. Hundreds were plowed, alive, into ditches and covered with tons of dirt. In the end even the Japanese commanding officer, General Iwane Matsui (1878–1948), expressed confusion and regret over how it had all happened; his soldiers, it seemed, had simply gone briefly mad.

The Rape of Nanjing   In just six weeks, after taking the then-capital of Nanjing in December 1937, Japanese soldiers beat, raped, tortured, and killed as many as three hundred thousand Chinese men, women, and children. To many ardent nationalists in Japan, even today, none of this ever happened. Most Japanese today acknowledge that a gruesome battle took place, but they place the number of the dead at only one-tenth of the real casualties and attribute even those deflated numbers to regular battlefield occurrences.

Another crime was the Japanese abduction and sexual enslavement of a quarter million women and girls to serve as prostitutes, or **comfort women**, for their soldiers. These women were taken overwhelmingly from the occupied territories, although there is evidence that some Japanese women—primarily the relatives of critics of the government—were also forced to work throughout the empire. The official purpose of the "comfort stations" was, first, to control the spread of sexually transmitted diseases among the soldiers, by giving them access to a regulated sex trade. Second, it was said to protect against espionage by foreign agents posing as prostitutes. It seems likely that the basic aim was more elemental—to curry favor with the soldiers by giving them what they would have simply taken anyway.

The program began as early as 1932, when the first comfort station was introduced in Shanghai at the start of the Second Sino-Japanese War. The government actively recruited women to work in the brothels, even to the point of placing advertisements in newspapers; but as the empire and the army grew, volunteers no longer sufficed. By 1937, civilian agents hired by the government to manage and provide for the military brothels resorted to fraud and kidnapping. Ultimately, many tens of thousands of Chinese, Indonesian, Korean, Malay, Philippine, Thai, and Vietnamese women were abducted, raped, and humiliated. Although several Japanese prime ministers have apologized for the abuse of women during the war, the government still denies any legal liability for the military brothels. It holds that the total number of comfort women was no larger than twenty thousand—none of whom, it insists, were forced into the work.

MAKING AMENDS

How does a nation make amends for horrors? Can crimes of the magnitude of those committed in World War II be atoned for or forgiven? Who has the right to judge? One result of the war was the creation of a setting where such questions could be debated and decided on the basis of international law. The **Nuremberg Trials** of German leaders and **Tokyo Trials** in Japan did more than set the stage.

The idea of international law dates to the Treaty of Westphalia in 1648 but started to assume

> Nazi Germany and Imperial Japan were not the first nations to commit war crimes; nor were they the only ones to commit appalling acts in World War II. Germany and Japan were unique in that their crimes were conceived, implemented, and administered by the state as conscious elements of national policy.

its modern character in the 19th century, with the growth of multinational businesses and modern empires. The Allies, however, had planned at least since early 1942 to bring the Nazis to justice for war crimes, and they had worked out the mechanisms for doing so long before Germany actually surrendered. The Tokyo Trials were another matter. Although the Allies agreed in principle to bring charges against the leaders of Imperial Japan, the joint process was preempted by General Douglas MacArthur (1880–1964), who used his position as supreme commander of the Allied Powers in the Pacific to order the arrests of nearly forty Japanese leaders and to begin their prosecution. The tribunal worked out the details as it conducted its work.

Nazi Germany and Imperial Japan were not the first nations to commit war crimes; nor were they the only ones to commit appalling acts in World War II. Germany and Japan were unique in that their crimes were conceived, implemented, and administered by the state as conscious elements of national policy. At Nuremberg, the Allies placed twenty-four top Nazi officials on trial, twenty-one of whom were convicted; subsequent trials of lower-tier officers convicted 142 of 185 defendants. Still more trials took place in several of the concentration camps, adding hundreds more to the list of criminals brought to justice before the trials closed in 1956. Most of the guilty were either hanged or imprisoned for life, although several of the most prominent defendants, like Herman Göring (1893–1946, the head of the German Air Force, or *Luftwaffe*), committed suicide before their executions could be carried out.

Göring on Trial   Hermann Göring (1893–1946) was the commander-in-chief of the Nazi air force (*Luftwaffe*) and Hitler's designated successor. Convicted of crimes against humanity at the Nuremberg Trials, he committed suicide the night before he was to be hanged. In a late conversation with an interviewer he boasted that " people can always be talked into doing what their rulers want. It's easy—all one has to do is tell them that they are being attacked, and then blame it on unpatriotic pacifists who are exposing everyone to harm. It will work in any country."

These courts marked a crucial point in the establishment of fundamental standards of international justice. As one of the leading judges at the trials, Robert H. Jackson (1892–1954), declared in his opening statement for the prosecution on November 21, 1945:

> Never before in legal history has an effort been made to bring within the scope of a single litigation the developments of a decade, covering a whole continent, and involving a score of nations, countless individuals, and innumerable events. Despite the magnitude of the task, the world has demanded immediate action. This demand has had to be met, though perhaps at the cost of finished craftsmanship. In my country, established courts, following familiar procedures, applying well-thumbed precedents, and dealing with the legal consequences of local and limited events, seldom commence a trial within a year of the event in litigation. Yet less than eight months ago today the courtroom in which you sit was an enemy fortress in the hands of German S.S. troops. Less than eight months ago nearly all our witnesses and documents were in enemy hands. . . .
>
> I should be the last to deny that the case may well suffer from incomplete researches, and quite likely will not be the example of professional work which any of the prosecuting nations would normally wish to sponsor. It is, however, a completely adequate case to the judgment we shall ask you to render, and its full development we shall be obliged to leave to historians. . . . At the very outset, let us dispose of the contention that to put these men to trial is to do them an injustice, entitling them to some special consideration. These defendants may be hard pressed but they are not ill used. . . . If these men are the first war leaders of a defeated nation to be prosecuted in the name of the law, they are also the first to be given the chance to plead for their lives in the name of the law.

While few people complain about the trials' outcomes, the manner in which they took place raises questions about the quality of their justice. As pointed out at the time—for instance, by Supreme Court Justice William O. Douglas (1898–1980)—the laws defining war crimes were written after the atrocities had been committed. The trials were therefore ex post facto ("after the fact"), appearing more like revenge rather than fair judgment.[6] Some critics even condemned the processes as sophisticated lynchings. Both Winston Churchill and the American secretary of the Treasury, Henry Morgenthau Jr. (1891–1967) were adamantly

---

[6] Göring, presented with a copy of the indictment against him, penned the comment, "The victor is always the judge, the defeated is always the accused"—with his signature.

opposed to the trials. Churchill simply advocated summary executions without any kind of trial whatsoever. Morgenthau's position had more nuance. He pointed out that Stalin in his show trials of the 1930s had written the laws under which the defendants were charged, appointed the judges and prosecutors, and determined the place for the proceedings. For the Allied Powers to do so could give the impression of a similar sort of rough justice. It did not help matters that Stalin made a point of repeatedly endorsing the Nuremberg trials in public. In the end, many of the accused, along with the German nation as a whole, recognized that some form of atonement, even an imperfect one, was necessary for the atrocities committed.

The Tokyo Trials were a different matter. At least since the battle at Midway Island in 1942, the Imperial Japanese government had carefully searched out and destroyed documents regarding their crimes, and in the weeks before their surrender in 1945, they undertook a mass purging of their records. Above all, they wanted to protect the emperor Hirohito and his family from any possible legal charge. Second, they wanted political and military leaders to claim plausible deniability about their role in criminal action. The tribunals therefore operated with distinctly inferior standards of evidence: documents could be submitted to the courts, for example, without their authenticity or provenance clearly established. "The tribunal shall not be bound by technical rules of evidence," declared the foundation charter of the Tokyo Trials, "and it shall admit any evidence which it deems to have probative value."

The tribunals forbade the cross-examination of some witnesses for the prosecution. Tribunals disallowed hearsay evidence (third party accounts rather than those of eyewitnesses) that contradicted the hearsay evidence presented by prosecutors, and they adopted a new standard for "negative criminality." Here they condemned Japanese officials for not preventing actions that were legal when they were performed. In the end, the Allies and nearly every nation under Japanese rule after 1932 staged trials of over ten thousand Japanese officials, more than half of whom were convicted, and roughly one thousand were executed.

THE UNITED NATIONS AND HUMAN RIGHTS

The **United Nations (UN)** set in formal order the standards and procedures for maintaining peace and international law. Established in 1945, this organization of member nations established a special tribunal for hearing specific cases as well as the permanently standing International Court of Justice and International Criminal Court. War crimes and crimes against humanity came under the jurisdiction of the International Criminal Court.

To prevent further war crimes and to establish a sounder basis for trials when they should occur, the United Nations on December 10, 1948, approved the **Universal Declaration of Human Rights**, whose drafting and promotion

Creating a New World Order   Delegations from the United States, UK, USSR, France, and China meet in Washington, D.C., at the Dumbarton Oakes Conference in August 1944 to draft the charter of a new international institution—what would become the United Nations. The five chartering countries became the permanent members of the Security Council.

were chiefly the work of Eleanor Roosevelt (1884–1962), the wife of President Franklin Delano Roosevelt. It was the first, and is still the most important, statement of global rights in history. Until 1990, when forty-five Muslim nations withdrew from the Universal Declaration and provided a substitute for it, the declaration provided a standard for justice recognized, officially at least, around the globe. (We return to the Cairo Declaration on Human Rights in Islam in chapter 30.)

The key articles of the Universal Declaration assert:

Article 1: All human beings are born free and equal in dignity and rights. They are endowed with reason and conscience and should act towards one another in a spirit of brotherhood.

Article 2: Everyone is entitled to all the rights and freedoms set forth in this Declaration, without distinction of any kind, such as race, color, sex, language, religion, political or other opinion, national or social origin, property, birth or other status. . . .

Article 3: Everyone has the right to life, liberty and security of person.

Article 4: No one shall be held in slavery or servitude; slavery and the slave trade shall be prohibited in all their forms.

Article 5: No one shall be subjected to torture or to cruel, inhuman or degrading treatment or punishment.

Article 6: Everyone has the right to recognition everywhere as a person before the law.

Article 7: All are equal before the law and are entitled without any discrimination to equal protection of the law. . . .

Article 9: No one shall be subjected to arbitrary arrest, detention or exile.

Article 10: Everyone is entitled in full equality to a fair and public hearing by an independent and impartial tribunal, in the determination of his rights and obligations and of any criminal charge against him.

Article 11: (1) Everyone charged with a penal offence has the right to be presumed innocent until proved guilty according to law in a public trial at which he has had all the guarantees necessary for his defense. (2) No one shall be held guilty of any penal offence on account of any act or omission which did not constitute a penal offence, under national or international law, at the time when it was committed. . . .

Article 13: (1) Everyone has the right to freedom of movement and residence within the borders of each state.

Article 14: (1) Everyone has the right to seek and to enjoy in other countries asylum from persecution. . . .

Article 16: (2) Marriage shall be entered into only with the free and full consent of the intending spouses. . . .

Article 18: Everyone has the right to freedom of thought, conscience and religion; this right includes freedom to change his religion or belief, and freedom, either alone or in community with others and in public or private, to manifest his religion or belief in teaching, practice, worship and observance.

Article 19: Everyone has the right to freedom of opinion and expression; this right includes freedom to hold opinions without interference and to seek, receive and impart information and ideas through any media and regardless of frontiers.

Article 20: (1) Everyone has the right to freedom of peaceful assembly and association. . . .

Article 21: (1) Everyone has the right to take part in the government of his country, directly or through freely chosen representatives. (2) Everyone has the right of equal access to public service in his country. (3) The will of the people shall be the basis of the authority of government; this will shall be expressed in periodic and genuine elections which shall be by universal and equal suffrage and shall be held by secret vote or by equivalent free voting procedures.

Article 23: (1) Everyone has the right to work, to free choice of employment, to just and favorable conditions of work and to protection against unemployment. (2) Everyone, without any discrimination, has the right to equal pay for equal work. . . .

Article 26: (1) Everyone has the right to education.

The UN General Assembly adopted the declaration by a nearly unanimous vote: Czechoslovakia, Saudi Arabia, South Africa, the Soviet Union, and Yugoslavia abstained.

Their respective policies of female subjection, apartheid, and rejection of private property and free speech contradicted its central tenets. While sincerely supported by the nations that signed it, the declaration bears the marks of its Western and Enlightenment origins. It could have been written by Rousseau himself—personal safety, political participation, due process, equality before the law, and social egalitarianism. The Enlightenment had championed education but never asserted an individual right to it; Voltaire, for one, would have been horrified at the prospect of teaching the masses to read. That difference sets the declaration ahead of its 18th-century forebears.

> While sincerely supported by the nations that signed it, the declaration bears the marks of its Western and Enlightenment origins. It could have been written by Rousseau himself—personal safety, political participation, due process, equality before the law, and social egalitarianism.

The declaration marked an important step into a better world than the one that had given birth to it. Before long the Cold War between Communist nations and nations to the west raised tensions, which made it impossible for the declaration to be a binding treaty. Eleanor Roosevelt and her colleagues had to settle for its acceptance as universal guidelines or standards of behavior. Subsequent regional treaties such as the European Convention for the Protection of Human Rights and Fundamental Freedoms (1953) and the African Charter of Human and Peoples' Rights (1981), however, based their articles on the declaration and made its principles binding.

ATOMIC FISSURES

Harry S. Truman, U.S. president from 1945 to 1952, gave the orders to drop the atomic bomb on Hiroshima on August 6, 1945, and another on Nagasaki just three days later. The Japanese government capitulated the day after the Nagasaki attack, with surrender taking effect on August 15.

Without unconditional surrender, Truman had warned, Japan would face "the inevitable and complete destruction of [its] armed forces and just as inevitably the utter devastation of the Japanese homeland." It can hardly have been a surprise that the Americans had long been at work on a weapon of unparalleled destructiveness. The **Manhattan Project**, as the secret program to develop an atomic bomb was known, had begun in 1939 under the scientific direction of J. Robert Oppenheimer (1904–1967). It was generally and correctly assumed that Nazi Germany was trying to develop atomic weapons as well. While Hitler would hardly have kept Emperor Hirohito informed of their progress, Japan six years later must have suspected that the United States might be attempting something of dramatic scale. After all, nuclear physicists in Japan had undertaken their graduate studies in the United States with some of the very scientists involved in the Manhattan Project.

Hiroshima and Nagasaki were important but not vital hubs of industry, shipping, and military communications, and neither had been the site of any fighting or bombing prior to that August. The Americans wanted "untouched" targets, the better to assess the effectiveness of their new weapons. According to the *U.S. Strategic Bombing Survey*, a report on the bombs' effectiveness:

> The morning of 6 August 1945 began bright and clear. At about 0700 there was an air-raid alarm and a few planes appeared over the city. Many people within the city went to prepared air-raid shelters, but since alarms were heard almost every day the general population did not seem to have been greatly concerned. . . .

After the all-clear sounded, persons began emerging from air-raid shelters and within the next few minutes the city began to resume its usual mode of life for that time of day. It is related by some survivors that they had watched planes fly over the city. At about 0815 there was a blinding flash. Some described it as brighter than the sun, others likened it to a magnesium flash. Following the flash there was a blast of heat and wind. The large majority of people within 3,000 feet of Ground Zero were killed immediately. Within a radius of about 7,000 feet almost every Japanese house collapsed. Beyond this range and up to 15,000–20,000 feet many of them collapsed and others received serious structural damage. Persons in the open were burned on exposed surfaces, and within 3,000–5,000 feet many were burned to death while other received severe burns through their clothes. In many instances clothing burst into spontaneous flame and had to be beaten out. Thousands of people were pinned beneath collapsed buildings or injured by flying debris.... The people appeared stunned by the catastrophe and rushed about as jungle animals suddenly released from a cage.... Pandemonium reigned as the uninjured and the slightly injured fled the city in fearful panic.

Hiroshima's population then stood at around 350,000, Nagasaki's around 250,000. The bombs killed about 20 percent of each city's population instantly

Atomic Destruction   Nagasaki after the atomic bombing.

and turned their cityscapes instantly into moonscapes.[7] Within five years of the bombings, an equal number people died from the effects of radiation as had died in the explosions themselves—a total of perhaps a quarter million—while many tens of thousands more suffered from radiation wounds and diseases for decades to come.

Why not give Japan an explicit warning, or even a preview by detonating the bomb on a deserted Pacific island? Was it truly necessary to incinerate 70,000 people in Hiroshima and another 40,000 in Nagasaki, most of them civilians? As recalled by Henry Stimson (1867–1950), the American secretary of state:

> We carefully considered such alternatives as a detailed advance warning, or a demonstration, in some uninhabited area. But both of these suggestions were discarded as impractical. They were not regarded as likely to be effective in compelling a surrender of Japan, and both of them would involve risks. Even the New Mexico test did not give final proof that any given bomb was certain to explode when dropped from an airplane. Quite apart from the generally unfamiliar nature of atomic explosives, there was the whole problem of exploding a bomb at a predetermined height in the air by a complicated mechanism which could not be tested in New Mexico. Nothing would have been more damaging to our effort to obtain Japan's surrender than a warning or a demonstration followed by a dud. . . . Furthermore, we had no bombs to waste. (*"The Decision to Use the Atomic Bomb," Harper's Magazine, February, 1947*)

Stimson's matter-of-fact tone masks the complexities of the issue. Japan had expressed a possible willingness to surrender in the spring of that year and passed word to Josef Stalin, who had offered to serve as intermediary with the Americans. But Stalin never forwarded the Japanese offer to Washington, in the hope that by prolonging the struggle in the Pacific, he might strengthen his own hand in East Asia. In fact, he was already racing to send his troops, recently relieved of battle in Europe after the Nazi surrender, across the massive Russian countrywide into Japanese-controlled Manchuria. On August 8, only two days after the bombing of Hiroshima, 1.5 million Soviet troops invaded Manchuria and presumably would have continued into Japan itself. The prospect of Stalin replacing Imperial Japan as the supreme lord of eastern Asia was untenable to the United States, which proceeded to drop their second atomic bomb on Nagasaki the very next day—as much as a warning shot across the Soviet bow as a final blow against Hirohito.

---

[7]   Most of the dead were killed either by the force of the explosions or from "flash burns" caused by the tremendous heat they generated, reaching 7,000°F (3,900°C).

Arguments that the bombings were necessary in order to spare the millions of lives that would have been lost in a conventional attack cannot be wholly dismissed, but neither can they be taken at face value. There is no way of knowing for certain what would have happened had America simply continued its conventional advance. The question therefore changes. America could certainly have defeated Japan without the atomic bombs—but could it have reached Tokyo before Stalin's troops did? By August 1945, it was clear that the Russians had no intention of withdrawing from eastern Europe. Were the Allies ready to confront a Stalin also in control of East Asia?

Except for the iconic images of the mushroom clouds over the two cities, photos and film of the devastation were strictly controlled or suppressed altogether. America may have wished to avoid comparison with images then circulating of the Nazi death camps. Photos of mangled, bloodied, and charred bodies, the government feared, might raise doubts about the legitimacy of American actions precisely when the country faced the possibility of continuing the war against the Communist regime.

Some scientists in Russia, in fact, had been engaged in nuclear research since the early 1930s, but Stalin's government was intensely focused on practical industrial development, so little of this "pure research" was therefore given sufficient funding or encouragement. What changed Stalin's mind was a letter in 1942 from a Russian physicist that pointed out a singular fact: no American, British, or German physicist had published any research on nuclear fission in scientific journals since 1939. Clearly something was up. Why else the sudden and total silence from the most brilliant scientists in the West? Stalin began to give priority to nuclear research in Russia, though progress was slow until after 1945, when Russian troops reached Berlin and started transporting truckloads of German physicists back to Moscow.[8] With the help of these new recruits, the Soviet Union developed its first atomic bomb in 1949. Britain became an atomic power in 1952 and France in 1960. As the postwar tensions between the West and the USSR rose higher and higher, they did so in a frightening new context of potential mass annihilation.

> As the postwar tensions between the West and the USSR rose higher and higher, they did so in a frightening new context of potential mass annihilation.

---

[8] A German-born British physicist named Klaus Fuchs (1911–1988), whose hatred of Nazism inspired him to join the British Communist Party in 1933, began passing sensitive scientific material to Russia as early as August 1941. An early member of the British team investigating the building of an atomic bomb, he eventually was welcomed into the Manhattan Project in 1943. Transferring to Los Alamos itself in 1944, Fuchs kept Stalin's scientists informed of the general developments in atomic research. His espionage continued until 1949. He was tried by the British in 1950 and sentenced to fourteen years in prison. Released in 1959, Fuchs emigrated to Communist East Germany and continued his nuclear research until his death.

WOMEN IN, AND AGAINST, FASCISM

By the 1930s Western women had secured political equality and the right to vote. They found the challenge of *social* equality more stubborn, however; or perhaps they simply settled for what they had newly earned. The Roaring Twenties had seen youthful hedonism and the appearance of major literary and artistic talents. The Depression and the totalitarian threat, in contrast, pressed most women back into the home. Yet when war came, women were in the thick of it.

Nazi ideology, based on a somewhat mythical traditionalism, had made women's place in society clear: it emphasized women's duty to produce more Aryan children in order to offset the growth of Jewish and Slavic peoples. As Hitler put it in a speech to the Nazi Women's League in September 1934:

> The catchphrase "Emancipation for Women!" was coined by Jewish intellectuals, who also shaped the whole of the so-called women's movement. But surely no German woman needs emancipation in an era as full of promise as our own.

ТРАКТОР В ПОЛЕ — ЧТО ТАНК В БОЮ!

Fighting Fascism on the Farm   This Soviet poster from 1942, with the words "A Tractor in the Field Is Worth a Tank in Battle," proclaims the importance of farm work and of women workers. The poster's calm, reassuring image ignores the wartime devastation that Hitler's armies were then creating in the Soviet Union.

Remilitarization and the revival of heavy industry under the Nazis put men back to work. As in Fascist Spain, however, women were essentially driven from the workplace. (Women did, however, supply much of the clerical and lower administrative staff of the regime.) Italy differed from her totalitarian allies. There, women not only had owned and run businesses and estates, but many worked in factories and served in the civil service. Expectations about their domestic roles did not alter much, but a public life was widely considered acceptable as well. Communist Russia experienced the most dramatic change in women's roles, since the ideology insisted on a radical equality of gender roles. Women worked in factories, toiled on the land, ran offices, and served as bureaucrats, at least on the lower levels. In fact, they served on something like an equal level with men—although also equal to men in their lack of freedom. In order to accelerate industrial production, Stalin outlawed abortion in 1936 and increased state aid to families with young children, so that women could afford to remain in the workplace. When war finally broke out, women in Russia saw active combat.[9]

In western Europe a more complex picture emerged. The poor economic conditions of the 1930s undermined many of the political gains made by women after 1918, since government revenue had declined so precipitously. In Britain, for example, unemployment benefits were withheld from all women who worked as domestic staff—as cooks, maids, and housecleaners—and from women who worked out of their own homes as seamstresses, launderers, or typists. Consider a woman who lost a clerical or manufacturing job and was compelled to take a position in domestic service at dramatically reduced pay. If she accepted, she was ineligible for unemployment insurance, since she was employed; but if she declined, she was ineligible since she was not actively seeking work. As conditions worsened, married women who lost their jobs were denied unemployment payments as well, whether their husbands were working or not. In Austria, government statistics on unemployment regularly consisted only of men who were out of work, since women were regarded as workers but not as employees. And that, too, ate into welfare payments and other social benefits.

Although Mussolini boasted that Fascism had created a utopia, Italian women in the 1930s experienced unending want, oppression, and despair. Most trade unions were broken, and labor strikes were outlawed—which made it difficult for any workers, much less women, to show discontent. Government funding for education, health programs, and unemployment faced regular cuts to make room for military expenditures. The Italian military made up over 30 percent of government costs in the 1930s and approached 40 percent when war finally came. As conditions worsened, birthrates fell. Women either put off marriage or did what they could to avoid pregnancy (contraception was forbidden). The Italian birthrate fell 30 percent between 1911 and 1941, and this came amid a decline in overall population thanks to heavy emigration.

Women had featured prominently in the pacifist campaigns of the 1930s too. Taking up where the antiwar groups of World War I had left off, many women's groups that had formed to pursue suffrage turned to the cause of avoiding war. The **Women's International League for Peace and Freedom** (WILPF) convened

---

[9] By 1940 women made up almost half of the workforce in Russia. Just over one hundred thousand were decorated for valor after service in artillery and tank units or in the signal corps.

for the first time in the Netherlands, in The Hague, in the spring of 1915; it later moved its headquarters to Geneva, Switzerland, where it still resides. Its founders were an American, Jane Addams (1860–1935); two Germans, Anita Augsburg (1857–1943) and Lida Heymann (1868–1943); and a Dutchwoman, Dr. Aletta Jacobs (1854–1929).[10] The WILPF campaigned for equal rights for all citizens, economic justice, and greater understanding and empathy between peoples.

Members were divided, sometimes passionately, on whether socialism had to be a part of the movement for peace and freedom—but the real crisis confronting it was Fascism. To work tirelessly for peace and fairness in the long term is one thing. What should one do, however, when aggressive, violent evil has burst upon the scene? Some activists and writers formed a new group, the Women's Congress against War and Fascism (WCWF). Founded in Paris in 1934, it advocated the use of force as a last resort against international Fascism. Given the general popularity of appeasement, however, anti-Fascist groups like the WCWF came under suspicion of possible connections with Communism.

The decade's most famous statement in favor of pacifism was *Three Guineas* (1938) by Virginia Woolf. Woolf was then at the height of her fame as a novelist and had long been active in, and publicly associated with, women's issues. The bitterness of *Three Guineas* is understandable, even appropriate, although in the end it works against Woolf's aims. The book offers three essays, each written in the form of a letter (to a different person in each case) who has asked the author for a financial contribution to a social cause. The first cause is a drive to enlarge and refurbish a women's college at Cambridge University; the second, to help professional women advance in their careers; and the third, "to prevent war by protecting culture and intellectual liberty." The third essay, which is as long as the first two combined, is not only Woolf's statement of radical pacifism but an attempt to decode the root cause of all war. She sees war as the extreme expression of a uniquely male desire for aggression. To offer direct resistance to Fascism is simply to extend the male need to dominate, to beat down, to control, and to rule.

Women and Pacifism   Pacifist protestors at Radcliffe College, April 1941.

In a footnote Woolf equates two newspaper articles that appeared in the same issue of the *Daily Herald* (August 1, 1936). One article quotes a member of Parliament urging "the House of Commons to stand up to

---

10   Jane Addams became the first American to win the Nobel Peace Prize in 1931. Another leader of the WILPF, Emily Greene Balch (1867–1961), received the prize in 1946.

dictators (i.e. Hitler)"; the other reports a British woman's suit against her estranged husband for financial support: He "insists that I call him *Sir*," the woman complains. "I also have to clean his boots, fetch his razor when he shaves, and speak up promptly when he asks me questions." Both stories, in Woolf's argument, show the universal brutality of male dominance and chest-thumpery. In fact, the primary target of her scorn, apart from the loutish husband, is the British member of Parliament who advocates action against Hitler.

Woolf contrasts male brutishness with female nurturing and civilizing; she sees the role of guardian of civilized behavior as the special calling of the "daughters of educated men." The lower orders, both male and female, she dismisses as the "ignorantsia." Woolf recognizes the evil of Fascism but sees it as latent in all male aggression—overt or covert, political or social, extreme or mild. She condemns the Nazis for their ugly habit of burning books even while she celebrates her call to women, in the college-fund essay, to

> Woolf recognizes the evil of Fascism but sees it as latent in all male aggression—overt or covert, political or social, extreme or mild.

> burn the college to the ground. Set fire to the old hypocrisies. Let the light of the burning building scare the nightingales and incarnadine the willows. And let the daughters of educated men dance round the fire and heap armful upon armful of dead leaves upon the flames. And let their mothers lean from the upper windows and cry, 'Let it blaze! Let it blaze! For we have done with this "education"!'

Was Woolf's thoroughgoing pacifism heartfelt but naïve? She had visited Germany and Italy with her husband, Leonard Woolf, only a few years earlier and had seen the monstrosity of the regimes at firsthand. The fact that Leonard was Jewish brought the danger of Hitler home. As far as actual resistance to the evil, she vowed only, along with Leonard, to commit joint suicide should Nazi armies set foot in England. The Germans never did land, but Virginia took her life in 1941, when she felt the return of her recurring mental illness and depression. Leonard survived until 1969.[11]

Friedrich II von Hohenzollern, the 18th-century Prussian monarch, once said of warfare that "if it is properly done, it will pass entirely unnoticed by

---

[11] Helena Swanwick (1864–1939) made the case for pacifism more compellingly in *The Roots of Peace*, published the same year as *Three Guineas* and unfortunately now out of print.

civilians, women, and children." For a time the idol of Voltaire, he was probably trying hard to sound like a philosopher himself, rather than the brute he was. His own wars, after all, left scores of thousands of noncombatants dead or despairing. War as it is actually practiced seldom spares the innocent, and at least since medieval times one of the more reliable strategies makes use of just that fact to erode morale among the opposition and to undermine a society's support for conflict by bringing the battlefield directly into their homes.

World War I had been a partial exception. At least along the western front, only a small number of British, French, German, and Italian women witnessed any fighting or were direct casualties of it, though millions of them suffered the loss of loved ones. But World War II was different. The battlefronts were too numerous and too mobile, and air assaults like the London Blitz or the Allies' fire-bombing of Dresden respected neither gender nor age. No matter which side they were on, and whether they supported the war or not, women were involved from start to finish.

Britain called its women to active service almost immediately once fighting began in 1939, requiring every woman aged eighteen to fifty to register either for military or civil service. By 1941, as soon as the Blitz was over, unmarried British women aged twenty to thirty were drafted directly into one of the noncombat units. In the countryside, women were called into the "Land Army" to maintain food production; in the cities somewhere between 80 and 90 percent of all adult females worked either in industry or directly in the war effort. They served as clerks, radio operators, drivers, warehouse and shipping personnel, instructors, nurses, or searchlight handlers. In Italy, women served as nurses and physicians, teachers, and military staff, although the Fascist regime restricted other types of work to males. Men still dominated industry and farming. France, however, whether Occupied or Vichy, pushed women into traditional household roles as much as possible.

American women probably made the greatest social and economic gains during the war years. Women filled factories, offices, the professions, and schools in record numbers in the 1940s. And one area of particular significance was journalism. Women had long worked in the U.S. news industry, whether print or radio, but usually in behind-the-scenes positions like clerks, production assistants, and general staff; the Women's National Press Club had formed as early as 1919. When female correspondents began losing their jobs during the Great Depression, Eleanor Roosevelt organized weekly press conferences to which only women journalists were invited. The practice sent out a symbolic message and preserved at least a few dozen jobs for women in Washington. When the war came, nearly 150 women journalists became accredited war correspondents and photographers. They reported from foreign battlefields, military bases and ships, hospitals and concentration camps across Europe and East Asia.

We Can Do It!   American women at work constructing B-17 bombers, August 1942, at the Douglas Aircraft Company in Long Beach, California.

Women received only 50–75 percent of the pay men earned for the same work. It did not matter whether they worked in offices, schools, factories, the military, journalism, hospitals, or scientific labs. It did not matter whether they worked alongside men or in place of men who had entered the military. They were also largely expected, and even forced, to give up employment after 1945, as men returned from war. Many of women's gains disappeared after the war ended, setting the stage for the domestic era of the 1950s. Yet women in every country contributed mightily to the war effort—and just as much to the effort to promote peace.

WORLD WAR II AND THE MIDDLE EAST

While not active in the conflict, the peoples of the Near East were profoundly affected by World War II, and their aspirations affected both Allied and Axis strategies. The war also led to growing tensions among European mandates, Arab nationalism, and a Jewish homeland.

The Muslim lands that already existed as autonomous nations—Egypt, Iran, and Turkey most notably—declared neutrality in the conflict but were drawn in nonetheless. The Fertile Crescent regions that existed as European mandates (Lebanon and Syria, under France; Palestine, Jordan, and Iraq, under Britain) were important factors in Allied strategies from the start. Egypt, technically independent since 1922, had endured a British military occupation that aimed above all to keep the Suez Canal open—and popular sentiment against the British presence rose throughout the 1930s. When the war began in 1939, Egyptian hopes of freedom from British influence led the nominal ruler, King Farouk I (r. 1936–1952), to open negotiations secretly with Berlin, offering to join the Axis if Britain should be driven from the region. German forces under Field Marshal Erwin Rommel (1891–1944) advanced almost to Cairo before being turned back at the battle of El Alamein in late 1942, which dashed the prospect of a British withdrawal.

Iran too was a neutral power. Under Reza Shah Pahlavi (r. 1925–1941) it was engaged in an array of ambitious modernization projects. Public schools, modern hospitals, a national system of trains and buses, a comprehensive radio and telephone grid, the University of Tehran—all were paid for with revenues from oil. But oil in wartime becomes a weapon, and neither the Allies nor the Axis wanted Iran's oil to fall to the other side. Roughly a thousand German nationals resided in Iran in the early years of the war; most were engineers and businessmen developing a local steel industry in return for oil. When Reza Shah rejected Allied demands that he deport the Germans, both British and Soviet forces invaded the country and forced him to abdicate in favor of his son, Mohammad Reza Shah Pahlavi (r. 1944–1979), who immediately aligned himself with the Western Allies. Mohammad remained in power until the Iranian Revolution of 1979 toppled him and instituted the Islamic Republic.

Turkey likewise faced pressure from both Allies and Axis governments but remained neutral until the last year of the war, when it seemed clear that Nazi Germany would fall. Like Egypt, the country joined the Allies simply to earn the right to participate in the UN end-of-war negotiations for a permanent settlement. By holding to a neutral position for so long, Turkey was able to advance its internal development as a secular democracy and so to serve as a bridge between the West and the Middle East.

The Fertile Crescent itself was under French and British rule. Nations did not exist here—only an administrative grid of Western mandates and regional governors who tried to manage an interlocking yet fluid array of tribes, clans, and sects. The Ottomans had known better and had not tried to force the Arabs into larger units. France and Britain governed their mandates by allying themselves with self-selected conservative elites—landowners, clerical leaders, leading merchants, tribal chieftains, and military officers. All expressed, and in some cases genuinely felt, a willingness to work with their European masters. In return, Europe tacitly recognized their positions as leaders, ready and fit to take over whenever the Europeans left.

Syria, technically, was enemy territory to the Allies after 1940, since the Nazi seizure of Paris had left control of Syria to the puppet-regime of Vichy, which took its orders from Berlin. Hitler began to use Damascus at a staging and refueling site for planes bringing Iraqi oil to Germany, and this in turn led to the British decision to invade. Aided by "Free France" forces in exile, Britain took control of Syria in July 1941 and held it until the end of the war. When the war ended, however, Syria declared itself an independent republic, wrote a constitution, and elected a prime minister. Newly liberated France responded by bombing Damascus (in May 1945) and reasserting its rights under the UN mandate.

New Allies Mohammad Reza Pahlavi, the shah of Iran from 1941 to 1979, established close ties with the US and UK, who supported him in return for his help in bringing Iranian oil to Western markets. Reza Pahlavi wanted to bring Iranian life into line with modern European, secular, and democratic society. Here he confers with U.S. President Franklin D. Roosevelt at the Tehran Conference in late 1943.

Britain opposed the French claim and wanted to secure an advantageous position with the new Syrian Republic. First, it pressured France to withdraw its troops (done by April 1946). Second, it recognized the republic's claim to a "Greater Syria" that extended its borders to the Mediterranean. Finally, Britain promised to do all it could to prevent further Jewish immigration into Palestine; at the same time, Britain was formally committed to a Jewish homeland there.

ARAB NATIONALISM AND GROWING ZIONISM

Arab nationalism differed from its European models, in that it emphasized shared language and culture over shared territory. Autonomy from the West meant more than an independent form of government. Secularism was a means to an end, rather than an ideal. Most Arabs, whether Sunni or Shi'i, were devout Muslims and desired to recreate an Islamic caliphate—though only in the sense of a symbolic spiritual realm. But most declared allegiance to secularism in order to placate Western concerns for the many Jews and Arab Christians that lived in the region. As one writer expressed it:

> The nationalism we are talking about is nothing more than Love— the feeling that binds a man to his family. For our country is simply a large household, our nation a large family. Nationalism thus makes the heart glad and the soul joyful, just as any form of love does, and whoever feels

this joy shares it with everyone who feels the same. It raises one beyond oneself and brings one closer to spiritual perfection. *(The Battle for Our Destiny, 1958)*

The writer was Michel Aflaq (1910–1989), an Arab Christian from Damascus who founded the **Ba'ath Party**—which he envisioned as the representation of secular **Pan-Arabism**, combined with socialist ideals of state-sponsored care for the masses. To Ba'ath supporters, and many other "nationalist" groups of the 1930s and 1940s, the "nation" of the Arabs implied something larger than any political arrangement and should not be thought of in Western political terms; the Arab nation, to them, was a spiritual state, an elevated sense of communal and cultural identity, a renewal of the original, founding community of the united Arab *peoples*.[12]

Britain had established a pro-Western monarchy in Iraq with the elevation of King Faisal I (r. 1921–1933), who maintained good relations with Britain. After a brief coup that was caused in part by the effects of the Depression, Faisal's grandson took over and ruled as Faisal II (r. 1939–1958). They hoped to foster a sense of political unity among the peoples living in Iraq. Ethnic, sectarian, and even geological divisions, unfortunately, stood in the way. As it had been determined by the UN mandate, Iraq consisted of two oil-rich zones, one in the north and one in the south, with an arid desert zone in between and centered on the ancient capital of Baghdad. The Kurds live in the north, the Iranian-allied Shi'a in the south, and the Ba'athist, pan-Arab, Sunnis in the arid middle. Without the resources of the north or south, the Sunni middle could hold Iraq together and impose its will only by force.

Palestine was both the most and least significant of the mandate territories. In earlier centuries its religious importance had matched its commercial significance: it bridged the Mediterranean-based economy of the West and the caravan-route-based economy of Asia. Trade routes, however, had long since moved, with the development of modern shipping, rail, and air-cargo traffic. The Suez Canal, opened in 1869, and the Trans-Siberian Railroad, completed in 1916, opened still more routes for goods. When Mark Twain visited Palestine in the latter half of the 19th century he described it as a barren expanse of dust, rocks, and weeds that was almost devoid of habitation. As he famously put it in *The Innocents Abroad* (1869):

> The further we went the hotter the sun got, and the more rocky and bare, repulsive and dreary the landscape became. There could not have been more fragments of stone strewn broadcast over this part of the world, if every ten square feet of the land had been occupied by a

---

[12]   The Arabic word ba'ath means "renaissance."

separate and distinct stonecutter's establishment for an age. There was hardly a tree or a shrub anywhere. Even the olive and the cactus, those fast friends of a worthless soil, had almost deserted the country. No landscape exists that is more tiresome to the eye than that which bounds the approaches to Jerusalem. The only difference between the roads and the surrounding country, perhaps, is that there are rather more rocks in the roads than in the surrounding country.

Conditions had changed by the mid-20th century, of course, and the most dramatic change was the growing Jewish presence. Between 1869 and 1923 roughly fifty thousand Russian and European Jews had immigrated to the Holy Land, where they purchased farmlands, pastures, homes, and businesses from departing Turks and emigrating Arabs. Another sixty thousand arrived by 1932; and during the early years of Hitler's rule, while the West pursued appeasement, perhaps 150,000 more Jews came. The British did all they could to restrict immigration during the war, to avoid upsetting their Arab subjects. The British also saw it as a first step toward resolving the tensions between Arab claims and the founding of a Jewish state.

The Jews were still a minority in the Holy Land in 1945, although they constituted a majority in Jerusalem and several other cities. The Jews who moved into Palestine included poor farmers and laborers, but also large numbers of professionals—physicians, lawyers, business managers, engineers, teachers, labor organizers, and scholars—and their skills transformed the landscape. New industries, schools, and trades appeared on the scene, health care improved, malarial swamps were drained, and transportation and communication networks were established. New political and legal institutions were introduced as well. Unlike their Arab neighbors, the Jews formed modern political parties based

Exodus to Nowhere The SS *Exodus 1947* was a packet steamer that carried 4,500 German Jews, most of them Holocaust survivors, to the Holy Land. Britain was then still in possession of the Palestinian Mandate and had a determined policy not to worsen their relations with the Arabs by allowing increased Jewish immigration, and hence when the *Exodus 1947* reached port in Haifa, British authorities refused to let them disembark. Taking control of the ship, British officials sought other sites to unload the passengers but no place seemed suitable—and so they made the decision to return them to Germany. The predictable uproar occurred, and the fate of the Jews became international news for months on end. With the formal creation of the nation of Israel in 1948, all bars to the group's repatriation were removed, but by then half of the original 4,500 had either died or fled.

on ideology—pro-labor, pro-business, pro-socialist, secular, or religious. These organizations unified the populace across the region. Palestinian Arabs remained wedded to a more traditional tribal and clan-based social organization. The Jews, in other words, developed a Western variety of political nationalism that proved more effective than the cultural and spiritual variety of nationalism familiar to the Arab world. This powerful sense of nationhood, and the legal and institutional practices that operated within it, combined with the immense emotions produced by the Holocaust, which demanded a safe homeland for the Jews. Together, they created the unstoppable drive toward a State of Israel in 1948.

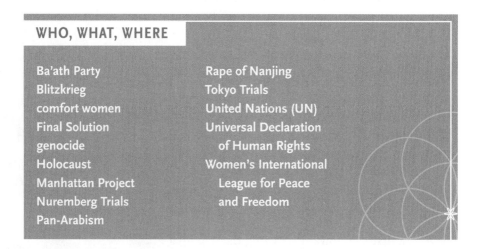

WHO, WHAT, WHERE

Ba'ath Party
Blitzkrieg
comfort women
Final Solution
genocide
Holocaust
Manhattan Project
Nuremberg Trials
Pan-Arabism

Rape of Nanjing
Tokyo Trials
United Nations (UN)
Universal Declaration
 of Human Rights
Women's International
 League for Peace
 and Freedom

SUGGESTED READINGS

Primary Sources

Gilbert, G. M. *Nuremberg Diary.*

Levi, Primo. *Survival in Auschwitz.*

Stimson, Henry L., and McGeorge Bundy. *On Active Service in Peace and War.*

Swanwick, Helena. *The Roots of Peace* (1938).

Woolf, Virginia. *Three Guineas* (1938).

Zweig, Stefan. *The World of Yesterday.*

Anthologies

Coetzee, Frans, and Marilyn Shevin-Coetzee, eds. *The World in Flames: A World War II Sourcebook* (2010).

Goldensohn, Leon. *The Nuremberg Interviews* (2005).

Laqueur, Walter, and Barry Rubin, eds. *The Israel-Arab Reader: A Documentary History of the Middle East Conflict* (2008).

Madison, James H. *World War II: A History in Documents* (2009).

Marrus, Michael R., comp. *The Nuremberg War Crimes Trial, 1945–46: A Documentary History* (1997).

Martel, Gordon, ed. *The World War Two Reader* (2004).

Simmons, Cynthia, and Nina Perlina. *Writing the Siege of Leningrad: Women's Diaries, Memories, and Documentary Prose* (2005).

Studies

Bass, Gary Jonathan. *Stay the Hand of Vengeance: The Politics of War Crimes Tribunals* (2001).

Bellamy, Chris. *Absolute War: Soviet Russia in the Second World War; A Modern History* (2008).

Bix, Herbert. *Hirohito and the Making of Modern Japan* (2000).

Carpenter, Stephanie. *On the Farm Front: The Women's Land Army in World War II* (2003).

Evans, Richard J. *The Coming of the Third Reich* (2003).

———. *The Third Reich at War, 1939–1945* (2008).

———. *The Third Reich in Power, 1933–1939* (2005).

Friedländer, Saul. *Nazi Germany and the Jews.* Vol. 1, *The Years of Persecution, 1933–1939* (1998).

———. *Nazi Germany and the Jews.* Vol. 2, *The Years of Extermination, 1939–1945* (2008).

Gelvin, James L. *The Modern Middle East: A History* (2011).

Glendon, Mary Ann. *A World Made New: Eleanor Roosevelt and the Universal Declaration of Human Rights* (2002).

Gregor, Neil. *Haunted City: Nuremberg and the Nazi Past* (2008).

Hasegawa, Tsuyoshi. *Racing the Enemy: Stalin, Truman, and the Surrender of Japan* (2006).

Hitchcock, William I. *The Struggle for Europe: The Turbulent History of a Divided Continent, 1945 to the Present* (2004).

Knox, Macgregor. *Common Destiny: Dictatorship, Foreign Policy, and War in Fascist Italy and Nazi Germany* (2009).

Laucht, Christoph. *Elemental Germans: Klaus Fuchs, Rudolf Peierls and the Making of British Nuclear Culture, 1939–59* (2012).

Mawdsley, Evan. *Thunder in the East: The Nazi-Soviet War, 1941–1945* (2007).

Megargee, Geoffrey P. *War of Annihilation: Combat and Genocide on the Eastern Front, 1941* (2007).

Merridale, Catherine. *Ivan's War: Life and Death in the Red Army, 1939–1945* (2007).

O'Shea, Paul. *A Cross Too Heavy: Pope Pius XII and the Jews of Europe* (2011).

Pike, Francis. *Empires at War: A Short History of Modern Asia since World War II* (2011).

Rees, Laurence. *World War II behind Closed Doors: Stalin, the Nazis, and the West* (2008).

Steiner, Zara. *The Lights That Failed: European International History, 1919–1933* (2007).

———. *The Triumph of the Dark: European International History, 1933–1939* (2011).

Thorpe, Julie. *Pan-Germanism and the Austrofascist State, 1933–38* (2012).

Totani, Yuma. *The Tokyo War Crimes Trial: The Pursuit of Justice in the Wake of World War II* (2009).

Vaizey, Hester. *Surviving Hitler's War: Family Life in Germany, 1939–48* (2010).

Weikart, Richard. *Hitler's Ethic: The Nazi Pursuit of Evolutionary Progress* (2011).

Wendehorst, Stephan E. C. *British Jewry, Zionism, and the Jewish State, 1936–1956* (2011).

Wette, Wolfram. *The Wehrmacht: History, Myth, Reality* (2007).

Wintle, Michael, and Menno Spiering, eds. *European Identity and the Second World War* (2011).

For additional resources, including maps, primary sources, visuals, web links, and quizzes, please go to **www.oup.com/us/backman.**

CHAPTER 27

The Theater of the Absurd

1945–1968

It was no easy thing to survive the first half of the 20th century and still believe in the goodness of mankind, the inevitability of progress, or a loving God. And in fact millions of people ceased to believe in all three. An immense task of rebuilding once again confronted the West. Hundreds of thousands of corpses needed burial, and millions of wounded and displaced people needed care. Billions of tons of rubble had to be cleared.

THE GREATER WEST, ca. 1950
— "Iron Curtain"

Rivers and fields had to be re-opened. Whole cities had to be fixed up or entirely reconstructed. Homes, schools, hospitals, factories, offices, sewage systems, communications networks, roads, subways, theaters, waterways, airports, harbors, train stations, rail lines, power grids, warehouses, and places of worship all demanded attention. The agricultural sector, too, needed to be reestablished. The destruction was immense, even awe-inspiring.

The Italian novelist Elsa Morante (1912–1985), who was half Jewish, spent part of the war hiding in the Apennine Mountains from the Nazis. She described the physical and emotional desolation of the time in a wrenching novel called *History* (*La storia*, 1974). It depicts the brutality of everyday

◀ **Postwar** On November 27, 1944, more than three hundred RAF bombers all but obliterated the city center of Freiburg im Breisgau, in far southwestern Germany. The home of one of Europe's great universities, Freiburg was the hometown of such notables as the philosopher-theologians Hannah Arendt, Walter Benjamin, Martin Heidegger, Edmund Husserl, Karl Rahner, and Edith Stein. In this stark photo, a lonely resident—still dressed in proper clothes for polite society—searches for food after the bombing.

- Setting to Work
- Alienation and the Absurd
- The Cold War and Decolonization
- Decolonization
- The Welfare Society and the Economic Boom
- Social Conservatism, Economic Liberalism, and the Postwar Boom
- A Generation of Rebellion
- Turning Point: 1967–1968
- The Female Factor
- Women, Islam, and the State
- The Structures of Thought

CHAPTER OUTLINE

life in war-torn Rome—searching for food and cast-off clothing, trying to find a safe place to sleep amid ruins, running from looters and rapists. Morante evokes the horror of the war not by narrating large-scale scenes of battle but by describing small, even intimate, betrayals of trust and decency. The main character, a shy southern Italian woman named Ida, is raped by a passing Nazi soldier; while Ida's travails form the bulk of the narrative, Morante goes out of her way to present the death of the soldier who raped her in a sympathetic light. (An Allied bomb lands directly on his transport, and he is obliterated.) When Ida encounters a train filled with Jews on their way to the death camps, she singles out of the noise within the closed car the sound of several children singing a song—and rushes to the door in order to join in with the doomed children.

The effect is all the more powerful because of the smallness of its scale. Ida's quest is both material and ethereal: to survive, keep her children safe, and restore some kind of normal life, but also to make sense of horrors. Suffering that does not *mean something* is unbearable. "Man in his fundamental nature needs to explain the world into which he was born," Morante writes. "This is what separates him from other animals. Every last person, even the least intelligent and the lowest of the world's castaways, explains the world to himself from childhood on, and this is what enables him to keep living. Without it, all would be madness."

Many in Europe never found safety or meaning, and an aura of persistent gloom lasted long after the war. It influenced literature with the idea of "the absurd." Millions of others, however, rolled up their sleeves and set to work. They rebuilt nations and economies. They faced down the tensions and violence of the Cold War—a world divided between the West and Communism—by moving away from imperialism as well as into a "second wave" of feminism. Some of the same tensions stirred conflict and change in Islamic states as well. They also created new systems of literature and philosophy that, it just so happened, described thought and language as systems.

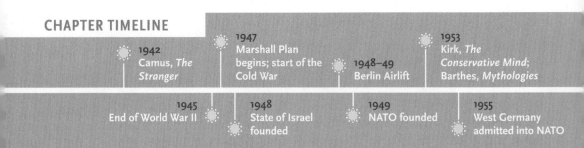

CHAPTER TIMELINE

1942
Camus, *The Stranger*

1947
Marshall Plan begins; start of the Cold War

1948–49
Berlin Airlift

1953
Kirk, *The Conservative Mind*; Barthes, *Mythologies*

1945
End of World War II

1948
State of Israel founded

1949
NATO founded

1955
West Germany admitted into NATO

SETTING TO WORK

The refugee crisis called for attention first. Roughly fifty million refugees and several million prisoners of war had to be repatriated—that is, sent home. The difficult process was made even more confusing by new national boundaries and by Stalin's unwillingness to withdraw his troops from eastern Europe. Germany was divided into zones of Allied control. Brutal forms of ethnic cleansing became commonplace in the east, as ethnic minorities were shuffled from one location to another. In Poland, for example, the non-Polish population constituted one-third of the nation before the war; it was reduced to a mere five percent (see Map 27.1). Wartime criminals, collaborators, and postwar looters were sought out for punishment. Judicial punishments and mob justice reached many who had collaborated with the Nazis. In Belgium alone over six hundred thousand people (roughly 8 percent of the population) were prosecuted.

Europe could not feed itself. Agricultural production in 1945 was less than half its prewar level, and strict rationing was put in place everywhere. Lacking markets in which to sell, and having no fuel with which to operate their machinery, farmers refrained from growing crops and turned instead to raising livestock. Shipments of food from the United States helped to keep people alive, but rationing continued in many countries well into the 1950s. The **Marshall Plan**, named after U.S. secretary of state George Marshall (1880–1959), began in 1947. It provided cash, credit, raw materials, and technical assistance to jump-start industrial production.[1]

Marshall described the agricultural crisis in a public lecture he delivered at Harvard University in June of 1947:

> The farmer has always produced the foodstuffs to exchange with the city dweller for the other necessities of life. This division of labor is the basis of modern civilization. At the present time it is threatened with breakdown.

---

[1] Within five years the Marshall plan provided over $13 billion dollars in aid—worth more than $100 billion dollars today.

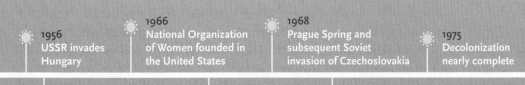

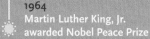
1956
USSR invades
Hungary

1966
National Organization
of Women founded in
the United States

1968
Prague Spring and
subsequent Soviet
invasion of Czechoslovakia

1975
Decolonization
nearly complete

1964
Martin Luther King, Jr.
awarded Nobel Peace Prize

1967
Six-Day War

1969
Organization of the Islamic
Conference founded

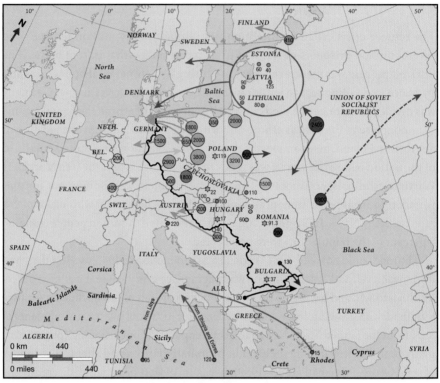

Displaced Peoples in East and Central Europe, 1942–1955

● Baltic peoples ● Czechs ● Finns ● Germans ● Greeks ○ Hungarians ● Italians ○ Poles ● Romanians
● Russians ◇ Russians forcibly repatriated ● Turks ✡ Jewish emigration to Israel 1945–50 in thousands
(300) Number of refugees in thousands (with color of peoples)   —— "Iron Curtain" 1948

MAP 27.1   Displaced Peoples in East and Central Europe, 1945–1952

The town and city industries are not producing adequate goods to exchange with the food-producing farmer. Raw materials and fuel are in short supply. Machinery is lacking or worn out. The farmer or the peasant cannot find the goods for sale which he desires to purchase. So the sale of his farm-produce for money which he cannot use seems to him an unprofitable trans-action. He, therefore, has withdrawn many fields from crop cultivation and is using them for grazing. He feeds more grain to stock and finds for himself and his family an ample supply of food, however short he may be on clothing and the other ordinary gadgets of civilization. Meanwhile people in the cities are short of food and fuel. So the governments are forced to use their foreign money and credits to procure these necessities abroad. This process exhausts funds which are urgently needed for reconstruction. Thus a very serious situation is rapidly developing which bodes no good for the world. The modern system of the division of labor upon which the exchange of products is based is in danger of breaking down. The truth of the matter is that Europe's requirements for the next three or four years of foreign food and other essential products—principally from America—are so much greater than her present ability to pay that she must have substantial additional help or face economic, social, and political deterioration of a very grave character.

Under Stalin's orders the nations of eastern Europe, now under Communist control, declined U.S. assistance and denounced it as a disguised effort to reestablish economic imperialism. In the West, the aid provided by the Marshall Plan jump-started the economy as hoped, and industrial capacity returned quickly to prewar levels. By the mid-1950s western Europe was again exporting manufactured goods around the globe. Currencies had stabilized, and Europe began a long period of steady growth that allowed it to perform a great social experiment—the modern welfare state.

Full Speed Ahead "The Open Road of the Marshall Plan," a German poster promoting the rebuilding effort.

ALIENATION AND THE ABSURD

The determination and hard work of so many people did not translate, however, into optimism. Gloom predominated, even among the war's victors. In fact, much of European culture and at least some in America hardly believed what it saw—a vast ruin of shattered hopes and beliefs. The notion of **absurdity** summed up, for many, the meaningless of existence and the inscrutability of fate. The French-Algerian writer Albert Camus (1913–1960), the first great writer of postwar Europe, made the quest for meaning in an absurd world an emblem of his generation.

> To Camus that is the drama of life, and its tragedy. A world that can continue to exist after sixty million deaths is a world in which no individual life has real meaning.

As he sees it, we can bear the unhappiness of today because we have some hope for tomorrow. That uncertainty, or ambiguity, is endurable. But it still leaves a tension, however, that can be resolved only by a lie: we believe that our lives matter, but if we are honest we must acknowledge that they do not. To Camus that is the drama of life, and its tragedy. A world that can continue to exist after sixty million deaths is a world in which no individual life has real meaning. We do not choose to come into this world, but we are powerless to leave it, short of suicide. Life is thus reduced to mere existence—and the absurdity of it all.

Camus enjoyed enormous success with his first novel, *The Stranger* (1942), and he followed it with more novels, plays, critical essays, and philosophical works. He won the Nobel Prize in Literature in 1957, before dying in an automobile accident. His brilliant career, his reputation as a man of action,[2] and his remarkable good looks made him a cultural icon. He was the alienated modern man as smoldering romantic hero—a brooding James Dean with advanced degrees in philosophy and a war record to boast of.

In *The Stranger* the protagonist, Meursault, argues with a priest who is trying to redeem his soul after he commits a murder:

> Something inside me snapped. I do not know why. I began to scream at him, as loudly as I could, berating him, telling him his prayers were wasted on me. I seized him by the collar of his cassock and let fly with all the anger and passion in my heart: *You're so confident about everything, aren't you? But there's not a belief in your head that is weightier than a hair, a single hair on a woman's head!* The poor fellow couldn't even be sure he was alive, since he was living like one already dead. And he thought *I* was the one with an empty existence! But I knew the truth—about me, about everything—better than he ever did; I knew my life and the death that was coming for me. Yes, that was all, is all. But I had as strong a grip on it as it had on me. . . . I had done this, but not that; a third thing, but not a fourth—and so what? It was like I had been waiting just for this moment, this crack of light at dawn, to win my vindication. Nothing mattered, nothing, and I knew why. . . . What did it matter that some people died, or that a mother loved her child? What could his God, or the lives that people choose for themselves, or the fates they think they control, possibly mean to me?

Camus summarizes the problem of absurdity in *The Myth of Sisyphus* (1942):

> I do not know if the world has any transcendent meaning, but I do know that if such meaning exists I cannot know it; it is impossible for me to know it. What can a meaning outside of my own existence possibly

---

2   Camus had been a member of the Resistance during World War II.

mean to me? I can understand things only in human ways—the things that I touch, the things that press back against me. These things I understand. But I also know that I cannot reconcile my desire for absolute truth and unity with the impossibility of reducing the world to a rational, understandable principle. What truth about these things can I state without lying? Without invoking a sense of hope that I do not possess—a hope that means nothing outside my own existence?

The Philosopher as Rock Star   Albert Camus dedicated his life to attacking the nihilism and despair that Nietzsche had warned of. "Do not wait for the Last Judgment; it takes place every day."

Camus ultimately pulled back from nihilism, that denial of all meaning to life, in the 1950s, when he devoted himself to political action. He campaigned energetically for human rights on behalf of the United Nations. His dedication to action, however, resulted in (or was a result of) a severe case of writer's block, which cut short his literary and philosophical career. Deciding that "courage is the only moral virtue," he championed the rights of the poor and oppressed around the world, campaigned against admitting Fascist Spain into the United Nations, protested the brutality of the Soviet regime, and advocated an end to capital punishment. He never renounced his ideas about the absurdity of life. He simply decided that he could still try to create a better existence for himself and others.

Much of Western literature and philosophy took up the themes of absurdity and alienation. The view of life that they portrayed was grim—from the philosophy of Camus's contemporary Jean-Paul Sartre to the plays and novels of the Irish writer Samuel Beckett (1906–1989) and or the French-Romanian playwright Eugène Ionesco (1909–1994). Many of the plays and novels were comic, but the laughter they produced was nervous and never far from despair.

THE COLD WAR AND DECOLONIZATION

To some politicians and military commanders, the fall of Berlin in 1945 should not have been the end of the war. Worries about Stalin's Russia and the role it would play had emerged as early as 1943 and were an important factor in the closing military strategies of the Allies. Communism under Lenin and then Stalin had always been feared, but Communist Russia had looked inward during the run-up to the war. Now that the war had left Stalin in possession of half of Europe locked behind an **Iron Curtain**, his long-stated goal of exporting revolution to other nations now was put into effect. An American general, George Patton, proclaimed his readiness in 1945 to keep his tank divisions rolling eastward until they brought Moscow to its knees, and he had his share of supporters.

Winston Churchill, too, wanted to continue on to Russia after Hitler's defeat—which explains why the British voted him out of office in the first postwar election. They were grateful for his role in saving the country from the Nazis, but they wanted no part in a new war with their former ally in the east. To many observers, President Truman's decision to drop the atomic bombs on Hiroshima and Nagasaki was motivated at least in part by Russia. It was, they felt, a warning to Russia not to expand its role in the east as it had done in Europe.

The **Cold War** between the Soviet bloc and western European nations allied with the United States received its name from Bernard Baruch (1870–1965), a wealthy American financier and presidential adviser who was appointed in 1946 to the UN Atomic Energy Commission. He advocated a World Atomic Authority that would have complete control over atomic weapons. By this point, however, Stalin's scientists had begun work on their own atomic program. Baruch borrowed the term from George Orwell; the British writer had used it to describe the "peace that is no peace" that would exist if two atomically armed countries opposed one another. Neither nation would dare to use its weapons, and yet neither would dare to disarm. Orwell coined the term in 1945, before Stalin had begun the Soviet nuclear program. Baruch applied it to the high-tech rivalry that became real when Russia tested its first atomic bomb in 1949.

The Cold War unfolded in three main stages. The years from 1947 to 1962 marked the first and most hostile stage. The United States and Western Europe were determined to prevent any revival of Fascism by promoting democracy and capitalism. They naturally viewed Soviet expansion with suspicion. Most Russians, however, had no doubts that the West was the real aggressor. How many times had a European power invaded Russia? Hitler had been only the most recent would-be conqueror, in a line that stretched back through Kaiser Wilhelm, Napoleon, Selim III, Charles XII of Sweden, and the Polish-Lithuanian Confederation of the 17th century. In fact, it ran all the way back to the Crusades and the age of the Vikings. Yet when had Russia ever invaded Europe? After 1945, Russia at last possessed a buffer zone of European states that allowed it to export its Communist ideals while remaining somewhat safe from attack.

The second stage of the Cold War stretched from 1962 to 1979. This was the era of **détente**, when the USSR and the West tried to ease tensions between them by diplomacy, cultural exchange, and treaties to limit arms. West Germany played an important role here by pursuing closer relations with Communist East Germany. A younger generation increasingly warned of the dangers of the weapons buildup.

We pick up the final phase of the Cold War in chapter 29. It began with the Soviet invasion of Afghanistan in 1979, the effort to suppress the Solidarity reform movement in Poland, and the rise to power in Moscow of Mikhail Gorbachev in 1985. Gorbachev's willingness to tear down the Berlin Wall in 1989 began the end of the Cold War—a process that both sides declared complete in 1991.

Throughout the initial phase of the Cold War, each side aggravated tensions. The United States and Russia supported separate sides in the Greek Civil War of 1946–1948. Stalin blockaded West Berlin

The Berlin Airlift   In June 1948 the Soviet Union imposed a land-blockade on Berlin in the hope of bringing the Allied-controlled western half of the city under Soviet control. This was the first major crisis of the Cold War. The Allies responded by delivering food, water, clothing, and other supplies by air. By the time the blockade ended in May 1949, over 200,000 flights had delivered roughly 5,000 tons of supplies a day.

(1948–1949) in an effort to starve the city until it accepted Soviet rule; the Allies responded by dropping over two hundred thousand planeloads of food.[3] The United States created the **North Atlantic Treaty Organization (NATO)**, a defensive alliance to protect Western Europe. The Soviet Union saw it instead as a marshalling of forces to attack Russia, and with every country added to the alliance, the battlefront moved closer and closer to the Soviet border (see Map 27.2). Even such peaceable institutions as the International Monetary Fund (IMF) and the World Bank (both started in 1946) struck Moscow as aggressive, for they aimed to promote capitalism.

The Korean War (1950–1953) pitted the U.S.-backed South Koreans against the Communist-led North Koreans. Stalin's death in 1953 led to a temporary calming of hostilities, but these roared back to life with the **Cuban**

---

[3]   During the Berlin Airlift, an average of one plane every three minutes delivered food to the German capital.

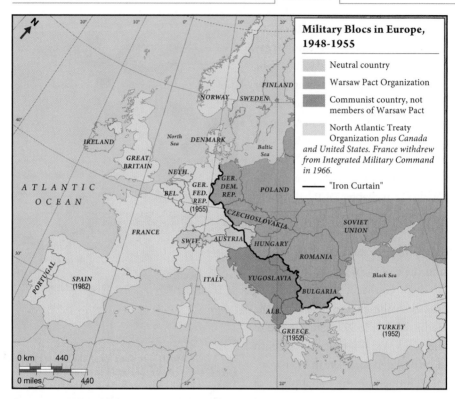

Military Blocs in Europe, 1948-1955

- Neutral country
- Warsaw Pact Organization
- Communist country, not members of Warsaw Pact
- North Atlantic Treaty Organization *plus Canada and United States. France withdrew from Integrated Military Command in 1966.*
- —— "Iron Curtain"

MAP 27.2   **Military Blocs in Europe, 1948–1955**

Missile Crisis of 1962, when the USSR's new leader, Nikita Khrushchev (1894–1971), built military bases in Cuba equipped to launch nuclear missiles. After two weeks of intense negotiations, threats, and a U.S. blockade of Cuba, Khrushchev withdrew the missiles. The world had come within minutes of a full-scale nuclear war. After this close escape, both sides agreed to ease hostilities and, if possible, to limit the spread of nuclear weapons.

DECOLONIZATION

This was also the era of **decolonization**, when Europe gave up, willingly or unwillingly, the bulk of its overseas territories. Independence movements had already picked up their pace when the Depression made it harder for the imperial nations to afford their overseas involvements. First, the former colonies of the Ottomans gained freedom (though often only a partial freedom, under a government named by the Europeans), followed by those of the Japanese Empire.[4] The European-held colonies followed. First came those in south Asia.

---

[4]   Japan had held Burma, Cambodia, parts of China, Laos, and Vietnam for only a decade, after seizing them from the Europeans who had held them much longer.

Burma, India-Pakistan, Indonesia, and Sri Lanka all gained freedom in the late 1940s. In the 1950s the decolonizing wave passed to Southeast Asia, and in the 1960s it came at last to Africa. By 1975 the process was virtually complete (see Map 27.3).

A host of problems confronted each of the newly independent countries, often before the ink had dried on their new charters. One problem was particularly prevalent in Africa: the political borders of the new nations did not correspond to ethnic, religious, or cultural boundaries. The borders of Somalia, for example, consisted only of the extent of Italian military conquest. The new "country" after the Italian withdrawal did not exist in any meaningful way for the native peoples, who found themselves lumped together in a state not of their own choosing. Nigeria was formed from no fewer than 420 distinct ethnic and tribal groups. While Kenya, for instance, had a more traditional structure to it, the problem of borders accounted for much of the political instability in African nations.

Independence from Europe also did not translate directly into economic self-sufficiency. Too many natural resources had been stripped away, in cases such as Cambodia, the Congo, and India. Elsewhere resources remained monopolized by foreign corporations or the descendants of the colonizers, who often remained

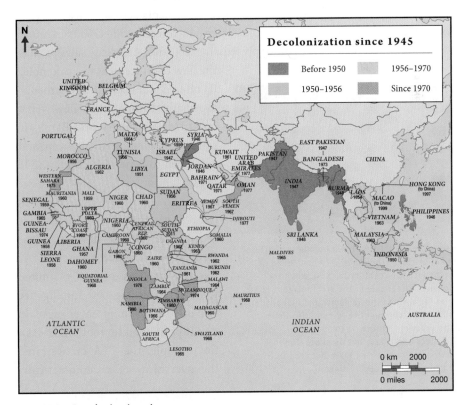

MAP 27.3   Decolonization since 1945

in what was for them their homeland. Even as the 20th century drew to a close, Africans and Asians of European descent and their associates held much of the productive land, mineral resources, and commercial properties in the former European colonies. They also dominated political life. In Zimbabwe, for instance, white citizens made up a mere 1.5 percent of the total population but as late as 1987 were guaranteed 20 percent of the seats in parliament. The Dutch East Indies, colonized in 1602, had been seized by Japan in World War II, and after the war the independent nation of Indonesia began to draft a constitution. The Dutch, however, waged a four-year war (1946–1950) to reestablish control; they were willing to compromise on sovereignty but fought bitterly to retain possession of the profitable trades in coal, coffee, oil, rubber, and spices. In the end, as many as eighty thousand Indonesians were killed and several million were displaced from their homes, especially on the islands of Java and Sumatra.

Decolonization also added to the rivalry between the West and the Soviet Union. In nearly every former colony hundreds, if not thousands, of diplomatic, economic, and military agents worked to encourage the new country to join their paths of development. Communism appealed strongly among the poorest and most powerless of the freed peoples and to many left-leaning intellectuals. Its message of economic equality resonated with desires to settle old scores with the West. Khrushchev supported independence movements across Africa and Asia but lacked capital for direct investment. Hence he offered trade credits in return for the raw materials that could supply Russia's factories. America's sales pitch to the new countries was more complex. It offered substantial investment—especially through the newly-chartered IMF and the World Bank—in return for guarantees to keep markets open to American goods and to resist Communism.

To keep an eye on Soviet attempts to spread their influence, the United States developed the **Central Intelligence Agency (CIA)**. Its mission was officially limited to the gathering of intelligence but in practice it often engaged in direct political intervention. In Iran, for example, the CIA orchestrated the overthrow of a democratically

Cleaning House   The United East India Company, chartered by the government of The Netherlands, had controlled Indonesia from the late-16th century to 1800, when the government took over direct rule of the archipelago. Seized by imperial Japan in 1941, Indonesia demanded independence after the war but the Dutch fought to re-establish their colony. After two years of fighting, Indonesia won independence in December 1949. In this photo, Indonesian workers remove the portraits of the three hundred Dutch governors who had ruled the country since 1595.

elected new prime minister, Muhammad Mosaddegh, in 1953, when he nationalized the oil industry and its petroleum reserves. For good measure, they also had Mussadegh arrested by the new government of Muhammad Reza Pahlavi, who ruled as shah until his own overthrow in the Iranian Revolution of 1979. Such actions did not endear the United States to many, but were considered necessary to stop Soviet expansion. In Korea (1950–1953) and Vietnam (1955–1975) the confrontation of Communist and Western interests reached the point of military action. Neither war ended satisfactorily for either side.

THE WELFARE SOCIETY AND THE ECONOMIC BOOM

While trying to contain Communist expansion, Europe also devised programs to put economic development back on track and to prevent a reemergence of Fascism. These programs aimed at the creation of **welfare states**—societies in which the central government, funded by heavy taxation, provided all essential social services. They did this out of two central convictions: that education, health care, and a secure retirement are human rights and that people who have their basic needs met will not be tempted by radicalism.

The welfare state differed in each country. In France, for example, the government focused on protecting children through education, family allowances, and childcare assistance. The British placed special emphasis on security for adults through health care, unemployment insurance, and pensions. The fundamental goal of maintaining stable life for all citizens remained the same, though. The United States did not travel as far down this road as western Europe did, but it went farther than many people today remember. By the 1960s it offered a broad range of social benefits—Social Security for retirees, unemployment insurance, health care for the elderly and the indigent (Medicare and Medicaid), assistance with securing mortgages through the Federal Housing Administration (FHA), and access to college education (the GI Bill, Pell Grants, and loan guarantees)—even while undertaking massive infrastructure projects like the interstate freeway system and while subsidizing the oil and automobile industries.

Sir William Beveridge (1879–1963), a prominent economist, stated the British case for social welfare in 1942, in a report to Parliament called *Social Insurance and Allied Services* but known commonly as the Beveridge Report. He called on three essential principles:

> The first principle is that any proposals for the future, while they should use to the full the experience gathered in the past, should not be restricted by consideration of sectional interests established in the

Subsidized Housing   Architects and urban planners review plans for creating more high-rise housing in a poor district in postwar Glasgow (1953). Post-colonial immigration increased demand for housing in western Europe's bigger cities, and the development of the welfare state gave high priority to providing housing.

obtaining of that experience. Now, when the war is abolishing land-marks of every kind, is the opportunity for using experience in a clear field. A revolutionary moment in the world's history is a time for revolutions, not for patching. . . .

The second principle is that organisation of social insurance should be treated as one part only of a comprehensive policy of social progress. Social insurance fully developed may provide income security; it is an attack upon Want. But Want is one only of five giants on the road of reconstruction and in some ways the easiest to attack. The others are Disease, Ignorance, Squalor and Idleness. . . .

The third principle is that social security must be achieved by co-operation between the State and the individual. The State should offer security for service and contribution. The State in organising security should not stifle incentive, opportunity, responsibility; in establishing a national minimum, it should leave room and encouragement for voluntary action by each individual to provide more than that minimum for himself and his family.

Beveridge was arguing that the purpose of the state is to remove want, disease, ignorance, squalor, and idleness—as opposed simply to guaranteeing an individual's freedom to do so on his or her own.

This marks a significant change in 19th-century liberalism. Yet as early as 1848 liberalism had insisted on the state's responsibility to intervene. Free-market capitalism, for all its positive elements, gives profound advantages to some parts of society and not others. Intervention should thus be seen as re-establishing the freedom of the majority rather than curtailing the freedom of the minority. In protecting workers, for example, the state is simply correcting the imbalance that the marketplace gives to company owners. Workers must have the right to form unions and negotiate collectively for wages and work conditions, because company owners otherwise control labor. Another example is progressive taxation—requiring those with higher incomes to pay higher percentages of that income in tax. In this way, the state breaks up self-perpetuating concentrations of wealth, so that a larger number of people gain the freedom to achieve success themselves.

The postwar welfare state extended such thinking. No one is free who is born into want, disease, ignorance, and squalor—and no such person can achieve freedom. Even idleness, Beveridge thought, is not simply a vice. It is imposed by unemployment, lack of education, and lack of opportunity. Removing these bars to freedom, liberalism argued, is the responsibility of the state. The purpose of government is to care for its citizens rather than to preserve owners' rights to control their property. Higher taxes on the wealthy are needed to pay for basic services.

> Even idleness, Beveridge thought, is not simply a vice. It is imposed by unemployment, lack of education, and lack of opportunity. Removing these bars to freedom, liberalism argued, is the responsibility of the state.

Not everyone was pleased. F. E. Hayek in the 1930s and 1940s warned of the "road to serfdom" (see chapter 25). Economic freedom was to Hayek the engine of all other freedoms, and any interference in capital, goods, services, and labor invited totalitarianism. (After reading a subsequent report by Beveridge in 1944 called *Full Employment in a Free Society*, Hayek declared that Beveridge knows "no economics whatever.") A leading American theorist who dissented from welfare-state orthodoxy was Russell Kirk (1918–1994), the author of *The Conservative Mind: From Burke to Santayana* (1953).[5] Kirk's brand of conservatism emphasizes morality, tradition, and right living: "All culture arises out of

---

[5] "When religious faith decays, culture must decline, though often seeming to flourish for a space after the religion which has nourished it has sunk into disbelief."—Russell Kirk

religion." No amount of wealth or poverty can stand in the way of living by, and for, shared values. Nevertheless, Kirk insisted that the rights of private property were essential to freedom, since without the means to support oneself one cannot be truly free; attacks on property, as represented by the taxation required for the welfare state, undermined freedom.

British voters reelected the Conservative Party, then still under the leadership of Churchill, in 1951 largely out of fear of the welfare state. While welcome in the abstract, the welfare society was proving expensive to sustain. As the party's manifesto put it:

> The attempt to impose a doctrinaire Socialism upon an Island which has grown great and famous by free enterprise has inflicted serious injury upon our strength and prosperity. Nationalisation has proved itself a failure which has resulted in heavy losses to the taxpayer or the consumer, or both. . . . Our finances have been brought into grave disorder. No British Government in peace time has ever had the power or spent the money in the vast extent and reckless manner of our present rulers. Apart from the two thousand millions they have borrowed or obtained from the United States and the Dominions, they have spent more than 10 million pounds a day, or 22 thousand millions in their six years. No community living in a world of competing nations can possibly afford such frantic extravagances. . . . A Conservative Government will cut out all unnecessary Government expenditure, simplify the administrative machine, and prune waste and extravagance in every department. . . . British taxation is higher than in any country outside the Communist world. It is higher by eight hundred millions a year than it was in the height of the war. We have a population of fifty millions depending on imports of food and raw materials which we have to win by our exertions, ingenuity, and craftsmanship. . . . We are a hard working people. We are second to none in ability or enterprise so far as we are allowed to use these gifts. We now have the only Socialist Government in the Empire and Commonwealth. Of all the countries in the world Britain is the one least capable of bearing the Socialist system. . . . We must free ourselves from our impediments. Of all impediments the class war is the worst. At the time when a growing measure of national unity is more than ever necessary, the Socialist Party hope to gain another lease of power by fomenting class hatred and appealing to moods of greed and envy. . . . There is no means by which this Island can support its present population except by allowing its native genius to flourish and fructify. We cannot possibly keep ourselves alive without the individual effort, invention, contrivance, thrift, and good housekeeping of our people.

While successful in the short run, this line of thinking was too colorless. There had to be more to the conservative program than an argument that the nation could not afford the liberal program. After four brief years, the British returned the more liberal Labour Party to power in 1955 and gave the welfare state a renewed endorsement. It was not until Margaret Thatcher took the leadership in 1979 that conservatism reemerged as a powerful force in British life.

SOCIAL CONSERVATISM, ECONOMIC LIBERALISM, AND THE POSTWAR BOOM

Germany lay divided into the democratic Federal Republic of Germany (FDR), or West Germany, and the Soviet-dominated Democratic Republic of Germany (GDR), or East Germany. West Germany, aided by the Marshall Plan and various UN programs, achieved a stunning economic and political recovery under Konrad

Adenauer (1887–1967), its chancellor from 1949 to 1963. Adenauer led the Christian Democratic Union (CDU), the party that has dominated German politics for the last sixty years. He was polite but reserved, and he could be coldly autocratic, especially in his later years, yet his vision for Germany was generous, welcoming, and humble regarding the sins of the Nazi past.

Adenauer was determined to create a prosperous and decent society that would integrate with the rest of western Europe. He set German-French relations on a better course by agreeing to the transfer of the Saarland to France, and he started the effort to reconcile Germany with the new State of Israel. He acknowledged the horror of the Holocaust, offered unconditional and repeated apologies, and extended reparations and aid to the fledgling Jewish state. By 1955 he had restored West Germany's

Konrad Adenauer   The tag-line on this photo reads: "Together with the Chancellor, all Germans eye with worry their capital city." Adenauer was one of the founders of the Christian Democratic party in postwar West Germany and served as Chancellor of the Federal Republic from 1949 to 1963. He oversaw the reconstruction of the nation and its economy, restored diplomatic relations with Britain, France, and the US, advocated restitution to all Jews, and was a resolute champion of the new state of Israel. Participants in a television poll in 2003 named him "the greatest German of all time."

reputation so much that NATO welcomed it into the alliance. At home Adenauer set in motion the welfare state. Education, health care, pensions, and unemployment insurance all became hallmarks of the Christian Democrats. Austria, Belgium, Italy, the Netherlands, and Norway for many years were (and in some instances, still are) dominated by Christian Democratic parties. Other nations with prominent Christian Democrat parties include Czechoslovakia, Denmark, France, Hungary, Ireland, Luxembourg, Portugal, Poland, Romania, and Sweden.

Christian Democrats have figured large in most western European nations— and in fact in most developed non-Communist countries worldwide since World War II. As an ideology, **Christian Democracy** is a hybrid of social conservatism and economic liberalism. It blends forward-looking economic growth with a regard for traditionally Christian moral values. The movement started in the 19th century with a Catholic twist. Pope Leo XIII's encyclical *On New Things (De Rerum Novarum)* had discussed the impact of industrial capitalism on society (see chapter 20). Yet the thrust of most Christian Democrat parties has been moral, not theological—the importance of family, help to the poor and oppressed, communal identity, and social justice. After World War I many Protestant groups joined forces with the early Christian Democrat parties, out of concern for the rise of secularism across European society. They affirmed the Christian heritage of their societies, not in order to exclude other religious communities but to challenge secular ethics and Communism.

On the economic front, Christian democracy staked out a position midway between free-market capitalism and socialism. Commercial competition is generally good, it holds, but needs to be used for the benefit of society as a whole, and that requires regulation. Unchecked capitalism creates wealth, but the problems of the 20th century resulted not from lack of wealth but from its unequal distribution. Hence the welfare state. Substantial and indexed taxation, with tax rates increasing with income levels, exists both in order to fund essential services and to engineer a society that has less income disparity. To a significant degree, however, western Europe could afford its welfare structure because the United States provided the cost of military defense through direct aid and subsidization of NATO.

With the state providing for their basic needs, western Europeans could spend more of their incomes on the new consumer goods that rolled off factory lines: televisions, automobiles, refrigerators, laundry machines, record players, mass-produced cigarettes and alcohol, motorcycles, electric coffee makers, vacuum cleaners, hair dryers, power tools, gas and electric ovens. High taxes naturally reduced "disposable income," the money left over to buy such items, but a new tool kept the purchases coming—consumer credit. Credit has been the fuel for capitalism since the 13th century, but it had always been limited to governments, banks, investment houses, companies, merchants, and entrepreneurs. Now that consumers too could purchase items on credit, consumption could keep pace, and more so, with production, assuring manufacturers of steady demand for their products. Demand spurred continuous production and continual innovation, which in turn generated profits that could be taxed to fund the welfare state.[6]

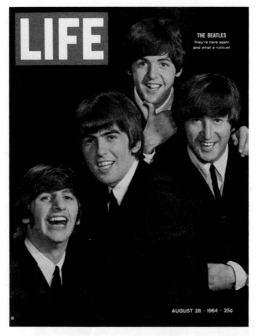

"Can't Buy Me Love"—But You Can Buy the Album   On August 28, 1964 *Life* magazine ran this photo of the Beatles on its cover. "They're here again—and what a ruckus!"

It worked well, until the late 1960s. As long as the economies kept growing, so did tax revenues, and governments remained solvent. But economic growth depended on the growing postwar population, the **baby boom**. It demanded more goods—more food and toys, more athletic equipment, more clothing, more schools and school supplies, more stereo systems, and more ways to care for all of them. But when the population increase leveled off, so too did demand for goods. Prices tumbled and profits along with them. To continue funding the welfare state, taxes rose and credit became tighter. The miracle of the West suddenly appeared vulnerable.

A GENERATION OF REBELLION

Ballooning public costs also contributed to that vulnerability. Welfare spending grew steadily through the 1960s until, as early as 1964, it strained budgets across western Europe and the United States. In Britain, annual costs for social services

---

[6]   The first true credit card, the Diners Club Card, appeared in 1950, and American Express brought out its card in 1958. Sweden introduced the Eurocard in 1960. France's Carte Bleue appeared in 1967.

rose 50 percent between 1964 and 1970. With the U.S. military shield protecting Europe from the Soviet Union, western states were still able to sustain their generous welfare programs with ease. In the United States, however, the combination of social spending and military costs threatened ruin. For millions of baby boomers coming of age in the 1960s, the economy and society appeared to be unraveling, along with the political system that oversaw it. As America entered the war in Vietnam, it seemed to many to have lost its moral authority as well. A generation of rebellion began to question received values and to protest against unjust norms and failed policies.

A Generation in Rebellion   University students in Paris, in 1968, seized the buildings of the Sorbonne in protest against the Cold War and the failures of the welfare state. The photos visible here are portraits of Karl Marx, Friedrich Engels, Josef Stalin, and Mao Zedong. Workers across the nation joined in a general strike, which nearly brought down the government of Charles de Gaulle. De Gaulle agreed to hold new elections to the National Assembly, but as he did so he marshaled the French army outside Paris. The rebellion broke up soon thereafter. The motives of the rebels are still debated. Clearly many were Communists or Socialists, but many also seem to have joined in a spirit of unfocused anarchy. One of the many graffiti left behind by the students on the walls of the Sorbonne read: "We do not want a world in which the price for a guarantee of not starving to death is to die of boredom."

In western Europe, however, the rebellious 1960s had a different focus. Heavy public investment in higher education continued. Britain created dozens of public universities in the 1950s and 1960s, which British students attended for free. Discontent arose not from denied access to education but from social prejudices that preserved old privileges. One could be brilliantly educated at a new "red brick" university—yet one could get the best jobs or most promising careers, many believed, only if one had attended the private universities of Oxford and Cambridge.

France too expanded access to its universities, but at a much slower rate—and with preferred treatment for the middle class. As late as 1968 only 4 percent of university students nationwide came from the working class. Italy invested in fewer new universities but admitted students in large numbers and also helped pay for their tuition; the average student-to-faculty ratio rose higher than 200:1. The quality of their education, or at least the perception of its quality, declined proportionally. By 1968 only half of university graduates were able to find work in the fields of their study. The liberalization of higher education across western Europe, in other words, had failed to alter ingrained social privilege and class stratification.

Similar complaints arose about economic strata. In 1967 in West Germany, despite twenty years of reform, the top 2 percent of the population still owned more than one-third of the nation's wealth—a pattern that echoed the inequity of the era before World War I. France and Britain had comparable concentrations of wealth. Western society, overall, was better off than ever before, but the ideal of social justice, many complained, had been sold out. People had ceased to be thinking and feeling actors on the world stage and had become mere consumers.

Western society, overall, was better off than ever before, but the ideal of social justice, many complained, had been sold out. People had ceased to be thinking and feeling actors on the world stage and had become mere consumers.

The 1960s were also the age of **civil rights** struggles in the United States—the struggles for equal access for African Americans to transportation, lunch counters, jobs, schools, and every other part of society. Dr. Martin Luther King Jr. (1929–1968) was a powerful moral force who advocated the use of civil disobedience to obtain these goals. He won the Nobel Peace Prize in 1964. His shocking assassination in 1968 did not deter other groups, including Hispanic Americans, American Indians, and gays and lesbians, from also advocating for their own rights in the face of sometimes enormous hostility. Major civil rights laws were passed by the U.S. Congress starting in 1964. But the decade also saw immigration conflicts in western Europe. Millions of Africans, South Asians, and Muslim Arabs migrated into Europe during decolonization. They came for many different reasons. Some feared the instability of the postcolonial societies and their underdeveloped economies. Others felt a keen sense of cultural identity with the withdrawing Europeans. Still others were openly recruited by Western powers that, after eighty million war deaths, faced the hard work of rebuilding. Jobs were plentiful in western Europe, and economic futures in Africa, Asia, and the Middle East seemed uncertain, so why not migrate?

Germany had the greatest need for workers, given the scale of reconstruction and given that half its population was captive behind the Iron Curtain. Konrad Adenauer invited "guest workers" (*Gastarbeiters*) from Turkey to work in construction and in factories. In 1964 the FDR's labor minister, Theodor Blank (1905–1972), commemorated the arrival of the one-millionth Turkish guest worker:

> These million workers contribute vitally to the steady growth of German industry, the maintaining of stable prices, and upholding

Germany's reputation on the world marketplace. . . . To judge from available statistics, our native labor pool will continue to shrink for the foreseeable future. . . . We are in fact wholly dependent on the guest workers to keep our economy moving forward. . . . In fact we can no longer even imagine economic life without them, a situation that entitles them to share in the benefits of our [welfare] society.

Tensions between the guest workers and their German hosts were growing, he acknowledged, but "the coming together of people from different backgrounds and cultures has worked—and for that we owe our guest workers our gratitude."

But popular resistance to immigration kept growing. In 1982 a group of professors at the University of Heidelberg went so far as to publish an open letter that warned of

the infiltration of our German people by millions of foreign immigrants and their families—the infiltration of our language, our culture, our national traditions. . . . In many workplaces and neighborhoods, in fact, our German people are made to feel like strangers in their own land.

In Britain, immigrants included Indians, Pakistanis, Arabs, Africans, Chinese, and Southeast Asians. Throughout the 1960s a Conservative British politician, Enoch Powell (1912–1998), warned of the growing expense of the welfare state. He is best remembered, however, for a speech in the spring of 1968 on the threat of immigration:

In 15 or 20 years, on present trends, there will be in this country three and a half million Commonwealth immigrants and their descendants. That is not my figure. That is the official figure given to parliament by the spokesman of the Registrar General's Office.

There is no comparable official figure for the year 2000, but it must be in the region of five to seven million, approximately one-tenth of the whole population, and approaching that of Greater London. Of course, it will not be evenly distributed from Margate to Aberystwyth and from Penzance to Aberdeen. Whole areas, towns and parts of towns across England will be occupied by sections of the immigrant and immigrant-descended population.

As time goes on, the proportion of this total who are immigrant descendants, those born in England, who arrived here by exactly the same route as the rest of us, will rapidly increase. Already by 1985 the native-born would constitute the majority. It is this fact which creates the extreme urgency of action now, of just that kind of action which is hardest for politicians to take, action where the difficulties lie in the present but the evils to be prevented or minimised lie several parliaments ahead. . . .

For reasons which they could not comprehend, and in pursuance of a decision by default, on which they were never consulted, they found themselves made strangers in their own country. They found their wives unable to obtain hospital beds in childbirth, their children unable to obtain school places, their homes and neighbourhoods changed beyond recognition, their plans and prospects for the future defeated; at work they found that employers hesitated to apply to the immigrant worker the standards of discipline and competence required of the native-born worker; they began to hear, as time went by, more and more voices which told them that they were now the unwanted. On top of this, they now learn that a one-way privilege is to be established by Act of Parliament; a law which cannot, and is not intended to, operate to protect them or redress their grievances, is to be enacted to give the stranger, the disgruntled and the agent provocateur the power to pillory them for their private actions. . . .

As I look ahead, I am filled with foreboding. Like the Roman, I seem to see "the River Tiber foaming with much blood". That tragic and intractable phenomenon which we watch with horror on the other side of the Atlantic but which there is interwoven with the history and existence of the States itself, is coming upon us here by our own volition and our own neglect. Indeed, it has all but come. In numerical terms, it will be of American proportions long before the end of the century. Only resolute and urgent action will avert it even now. Whether there will be the public will to demand and obtain that action, I do not know. All I know is that to see, and not to speak, would be the great betrayal.

Powell's "Rivers of Blood" speech set off a stormy debate. While many Britons denounced his comments as racist, most rallied to his cause. The argument against immigration was the same one used by societies dating back to Roman efforts to block Germanic tribesmen from overwhelming the empire in the 3rd century CE: too many, too fast. Mass assimilations can be difficult for the host society, as they are for the immigrants themselves. Popular support for Powell's comments swelled, because immigration was seen as a threat to the welfare state.[7] Powell argued that welfare programs could continue at steady levels even while reducing Britain's basic tax rate (just over 40 percent in 1968)—but only if the country avoid military entanglements abroad and reduce the immigrant population. Those were two big ifs.

---

[7]   In polls between 1969 and 1974, Enoch Powell was repeatedly identified as the single most admired politician in Britain.

Migrant Labor   An immigrant from Portugal arrives in Britain, in search of a better life. He was lucky to get out. A repressive quasi-Fascist regime, led by António de Oliveira Salazar, ran Portugal from 1932 to 1974.

TURNING POINT: 1967–1968

Cold War tensions had eased somewhat after the near-catastrophe of the Cuban Missile Crisis, but they roared back to life in 1967 and 1968. They were fueled by three events—the Six-Day War in the Middle East, the Soviet invasion of Czechoslovakia, and the Tet Offensive against American forces in Vietnam.

Relations between Israel and her Arab neighbors had remained difficult, since the Arab states refused to recognize Israel and continued to call for its destruction. Border clashes occurred regularly, and members of the **Palestinian Liberation Organization (PLO)** regularly carried out terrorist attacks on Israeli citizens and property. Rivalries and disagreements between the Arab states, however, impeded any sort of collective action against Israel until 1967, when alliances between Egypt, Jordan, and Syria left Israel surrounded by declared enemies. Fearing invasion from all sides, Israel launched the **Six-Day War**. Air strikes and rapid troop movements paralyzed the Arabs' military capabilities, and in only six days Israel seized the Gaza Strip, the Golan Heights along the Israeli border with Syria, the Sinai Peninsula, and the entire West Bank. It also took possession of the eastern part of the then-divided city of Jerusalem (see Map 27.4).

The speed and completeness of the Israeli victory deeply embarrassed the Arab nations, including the eight countries that had provided armed assistance: Algeria, Iraq, Kuwait, Libya, Morocco, Saudi Arabia, Sudan, and Tunisia. Apart

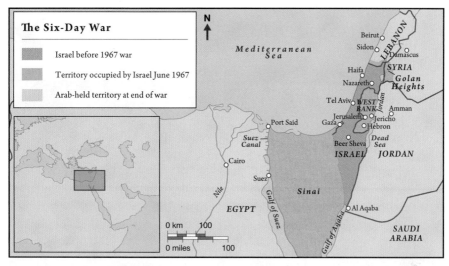

The Six-Day War

- Israel before 1967 war
- Territory occupied by Israel June 1967
- Arab-held territory at end of war

N

Mediterranean Sea

Beirut
Sidon
Damascus
LEBANON

Haifa
Nazareth

SYRIA
Golan Heights

Tel Aviv
Jerusalem
Gaza
WEST BANK
Jordan
Amman
Jericho
Hebron

Port Said

Suez Canal

Cairo

Suez

Beer Sheva
Dead Sea

ISRAEL   **JORDAN**

Nile

Gulf of Suez

Sinai

EGYPT

Al Aqaba

Gulf of Aqaba

SAUDI ARABIA

0 km   100
0 miles   100

MAP 27.4   **The Six-Day War**

from what it meant to the combatants and local populations, the war had important implications for the Cold War. Arab popular opinion quickly decided that the stunning defeat was possible only through secret U.S. intervention on Israel's behalf. Although America staunchly supported the state of Israel prior to the war, most Arabs had regarded the British and French as the biggest meddling outsiders. After the war, much of Arab popular resentment turned toward the United States.

The following year, on the night of August 20, 1968, Soviet tanks rolled into Czechoslovakia and put an end to the liberalizing reforms of its Communist government. Czechoslovakia had been Communist since 1948, but a new leader, Alexander Dubcek (1921–1992), hoped to create a less repressive form of government, a "socialism with a human face." Reforms instituted early in 1968 (known as the **Prague Spring**) permitted independent political parties; this appalled the Soviet ruler, Leonid Brezhnev (1906–1982), who ordered the military intervention. The action was more threatening than violent, but it sent a chill throughout Europe; the USSR, after all, had killed over twenty thousand

> The attack on Czechoslovakia was the first direct experience of Soviet brutality for the generation that came of age in the late 1960s, and it made clearer than ever the perilous state of the world.

civilians in its 1956 invasion of Hungary. Even the most liberal of western Europeans could not easily deny the brutality of Communist government or try to dismiss that brutality as something unique to Josef Stalin's rule. Under Stalin's successor, Khrushchev, and then again under Khrushchev's successor, Brezhnev,

The Prague Spring   "Ivan, go home!" shouted this young Czech woman to the Soviet soldiers who rode their tanks through the streets of Prague in 1968. The invasion of Czechoslovakia was a turning point in the Cold War, since it challenged Communist sympathizers across Europe and America to reconsider their idealistic view of the Soviet Union.

the leadership in Moscow had shown its willingness to secure and expand its dictatorial authority. The attack on Czechoslovakia was the first direct experience of Soviet brutality for the generation that came of age in the late 1960s, and it made clearer than ever the perilous state of the world.

Also in 1968, a surprise wave of attacks by the troops of North Vietnam against the U.S.-supported government in South Vietnam nearly toppled the American-backed regime in Saigon. Called the Tet Offensive, these attacks targeted roughly 120 separate towns and cities in the south and left 10,000 South Vietnamese and American soldiers dead and another 35,000 wounded. America had become directly involved in Vietnam in 1955, when President Eisenhower deployed several hundred military advisers to the regime in Saigon. By 1963 U.S. troops were still as few as 16,000, but under President Lyndon Johnson the military presence escalated dramatically, passing the half million mark by 1968. The sharp impact of the Tet Offensive made it abundantly clear that, even with increased numbers and superior technology, the United States could look forward to no quick and easy victory in Vietnam. Chinese and Soviet support for the Communist North Vietnamese further assured a long and drawn-out war (see Map 27.5).

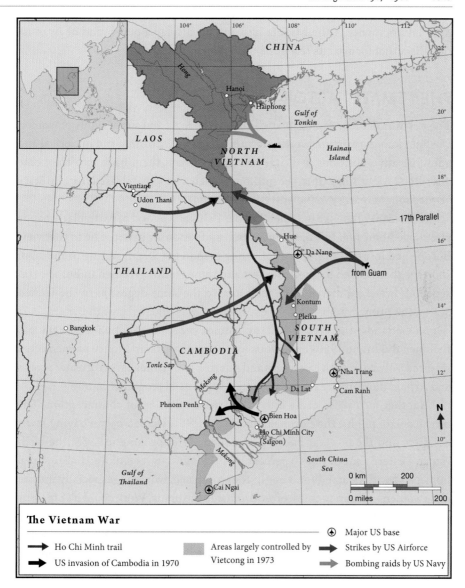

MAP 27.5   The Vietnam War

The 1967–1968 turning point drove home some harsh realities. The economic bonanza of the postwar years was coming to a halt, and that threatened to unravel the safety net provided by the welfare state. The Cold War turned out not to be merely a strategic game between bureaucrats and armchair generals; the threat was real and deadly. In the United States the struggle for civil rights showed that prejudices and racial hatreds still roiled, while conflicts in Europeans over immigrants threatened hard-won social stability everywhere.

And developments in the Middle East put on display a new brand of Arab nationalism that focused its resentment on the United States.

THE FEMALE FACTOR

The postwar decades saw dramatic shifts in the legal and social rights of women. Despite women's wartime work in farming, in manufacturing, and in clerical and administrative positions, cultural pressures pushed them back into the home after 1945. At the same time, the millions of men who were released from military service sought reentry in the postwar economy.

Americans often like to remember the 1950s as a period of particularly happy and stable home life. In Europe, privation and rationing gave the lie to that view. Europe had lost tens of millions of young men in the war, resulting in the labor shortage that had led to guest workers and immigration. Women in Europe consequently were not driven from their jobs to the same degree as in the United States; the primary injustice they experienced was unequal pay. In Britain, Italy, the Netherlands, and West Germany, women received only two-thirds the pay that men did in the 1950s and 1960s for the same work; in France women often received only half. With low wages and salaries, companies earned greater profits and so paid more in taxes—which in turn kept social programs running.

Another factor also came into play—the availability of contraception. The birth-control pill hit the European market in 1961, women began having fewer children, and the postwar baby boom ended. After peaking in 1955, the birthrate in western Europe fell 40 percent by 1975. With fewer children to care for at home, and with demand for labor in the workplace, women—especially middle-class women—began to think of work outside the home. Work could be a lifelong career, rather than a way to support oneself until marriage.

By 1970 fully one-half of European mothers had stopped having children by the age of twenty-seven or twenty-eight, which meant that forty years of productive work still lay ahead of them, if they were interested. And they *were* interested. They wanted careers, not merely jobs, and they demanded equal pay for equal work. The rise of feminism thus aimed specifically at economic justice. Men still predominated in heavy industry and manufacturing, but new careers opened up in schools and universities, in health care, in management, in journalism, and in law. Women were drawn to these "white collar" careers in large numbers.

The movement for equality for women in the 1960s and 1970s came to be known as **second wave feminism**. Feminism's first wave, starting in the 19th century, had a single goal—the right of women to vote. Crusaders for contraception were then relatively few, and they were seen as radicals. The second wave focused on personal life, sexual health, access to abortion and contraception, equal rights in the workplace, the availability of child care services, gender roles in society, and the portrayals of women in popular culture. Since then, a third wave of feminism, from the 1990s to the present, has had two main streams. One was a broadening of the movement to include the poor and ethnic minorities. The other was an examination of the very concepts of gender, race, and sexuality.

The second wave scored signal achievements. In the United States, new institutions dedicated to improving women's lives were established—from the Presidential Commission on the Status of Women (1961) to the National Organization for Women (1966), the National Abortion Rights Action League (1968), and the Coalition of Labor Union Women (1974). The Supreme Court in 1965 struck down states' bans on the sale of contraception, and in 1973 it upheld women's right to abortion. The first shelters for battered women opened their doors. Universities across the nation created programs in women's studies. Laws and procedures regarding rape were revised with a new emphasis on the protection of rape victims. Military academies admitted women applicants, while female undergraduates in colleges outnumbered males by 1978.

Feminism in western Europe did not have the vibrancy of America's reform movement, largely because the extensive welfare-state structures had already achieved—at least on paper—many of its goals. The new French constitution of 1946, for example, had mandated equal legal rights for men and women, and

Second Wave Feminists   Italian women march in front of the Coliseum in Rome to protest the country's divorce laws, in 1974. The banner reads: "Movement for the Liberation of Women."

women were already vital to the workforce. While discrimination persisted, especially in pay, political instability seemed the more immediate problem. Between 1946 and 1958 the French government went through no fewer than twenty-seven cabinet reshufflings, which made it difficult to mount any extended campaigns for reform. Only in 1968 was the first national organization for women's rights formed—the Mouvement de Libération des Femmes (MLF). Even then, the MLF saw itself as a network of psychologists, psychoanalysts, philosophers, and legal scholars rather than a group of activists. Practical, hands-on reform had to wait until the 1971 formation of Choisir ("Choice"), a group that advocated for contraception and abortion rights.

In West Germany too, the welfare state had addressed many women's issues. That assumption helps explain why no government between 1945 and 1961 had a single woman in a cabinet-level post. As Franz Josef Würmeling, the West German minister for the family and social affairs, put it in 1961:

> The [German] family has responded to the economic constraints of our time in two main ways: with housewives and mothers taking jobs outside the home, and then limiting the number of children they have. . . . But for housewives and mothers to work outside the home is not a solution; it is in fact a compulsive evil.

In Britain feminist concerns were the program of the Labour Party, along with social welfare and reform. Labour was in power from 1945 to 1951 under Clement Atlee (1883–1967), then again from 1964 to 1970 and 1974 to 1976 under Harold Wilson (1916–1995). The laws regarding abortion, contraception, divorce, education, and sexual preference were all liberalized, but a vital feminist movement failed to appear.

WOMEN, ISLAM, AND THE STATE

The status of women in postcolonial Islamic society played out between the opposing forces of modernization and traditionalism. The ideologies of the Cold War did not affect Muslim states directly, since atheistic Communism held no appeal, but the political conflict mattered to them very much. Three broad issues had a particular impact on women: national identity, the role of Islamic law in civic life, and the nature of state government.

First, national identity. The states created out of European decolonization sometimes crossed, and sometimes divided, traditional ethnic borders. Creating a sense of national identity thus represented a challenge to traditional social structures and values. Some factions believed that Western-style pluralism could be harnessed to produce a modern democratic society based on individual rights and capitalism even while retaining the core values of Islam. This reformed tradition, they believed, would allow Islamic states to remain open to the West and rid Muslim life of centuries-old norms regarding women, while still retaining an authentic religious identity.

One example of this reform-minded strain emerged in Turkey. There the secular constitution ensured equal treatment of women before the law, moderated customs regarding marriage and divorce, and allowed women economic freedom, access to education, and freedom of dress. In Algeria after liberation in 1962, men and women came to possess full and equal civil rights. Lebanon also experimented with democracy, civil rights, religious pluralism, and greater participation and freedom for women in public life. Conflicts with Israel and Syria kept Lebanon a fragile society, but the capital city of Beirut became known in the 1960s and 1970s as the "Paris of the eastern Mediterranean." In Iran, too, under the autocratic regime of Shah Muhammad Reza Pahlavi, westernizing policies opened the state to economic development, the growth of a vivid cosmopolitan culture, and an easing of restrictions on female participation in society. No political freedom existed, of course, and the rewards of economic development were hoarded by the Shah and his cadre. But Iranian society seemed set on a liberalizing trajectory, prior to the Islamic revolution of 1979.

Learning New Ways   An Iranian teacher assists one of her students during class, late 1960s.

Other factions in response raised the second issue of importance to women—the role of Islamic law, or **shariah**. They argued that Islam cannot be harmonized with Western ways, and the only correct path was complete rejection of Western values and the embrace of ancient Islamic practices. In the words of one conservative reformer, Mona Fayyad Kawtharani, ancient practices like the veiling of women represent resistance to the West.[8] Ethnic and tribal traditions also contributed, but civic rights and social freedoms for women became ideological statements. After the overthrow of the shah and the declaration of Iran as an Islamic Republic, in 1979, the fundamentalist new regime ordered women to relinquish Western styles of dress, forbade them from venturing out in public without an accompanying male family member, and pressed them back into domestic life.

The role of religion in national life thus became crucial to determining women's fates. The Organization of the Islamic Conference (OIC) formed in 1969 to present a united Islamic face to the world. With fifty-seven member states, it is the largest international organization in the world after the United Nations itself, and it came to reject the UN Declaration on Human Rights (1948) because of its basis in secular values. The OIC's **Cairo Declaration on Human Rights**, adopted in 1990, states in its preamble that the only valid foundation for human rights is in faith:

> Convinced that mankind which has reached an advanced stage in materialistic science is still, and shall remain, in dire need of faith to support its civilization as well as a self-motivating force to guard its rights;
>
> [and] believing that fundamental rights and freedoms according to Islam are an integral part of the Islamic religion and that no one shall have the right as a matter of principle to abolish them either in whole or in part or to violate or ignore them inasmuch as they are binding divine commands, which are contained in the Revealed Books of Allah and which were sent through the last of His Prophets to complete the preceding divine messages;
>
> and [believing] that safeguarding those fundamental rights and freedoms is an act of worship whereas the neglect or violation thereof is an abominable sin, and that the safeguarding of those fundamental rights and freedom is an individual responsibility of every person and a collective responsibility of the entire *Ummah*;
>
> [We do] hereby and on the basis of the above-mentioned principles declare as follows.

---

[8]   As a sign of its rejection of Western ways, a society could accept a simple head scarf, the head-to-toe burka, or something in between.

Among the Declaration's highlights:

Article 1: (a) All human beings form one family whose members are united by submission to God and descent from Adam. All men are equal in terms of basic human dignity and basic obligations and responsibilities, without any discrimination on the grounds of race, colour, language, sex, religious belief, political affiliation, social status or other considerations. . . .

Article 2: Life is a God-given gift and the right to life is guaranteed to every human being. It is the duty of individuals, societies and states to protect this right from any violation, and it is prohibited to take away life except for a Shari'ah-prescribed reason. . . .

Article 5: The family is the foundation of society, and marriage is the basis of its formation. Men and women have the right to marriage, and no restrictions stemming from race, colour or nationality shall prevent them from enjoying this right. . . .

Article 6: (a) Woman is equal to man in human dignity, and has rights to enjoy as well as duties to perform; she has her own civil entity and financial independence, and the right to retain her name and lineage. (b) The husband is responsible for the support and welfare of the family. . . .

Article 9: (a) The quest for knowledge is an obligation, and the provision of education is a duty for society and the State . . . . (b) Every human being has the right to receive both religious and worldly education from the various institutions of education and guidance, including the family, the school, the university, the media, etc. . . .

Article 10: Islam is the religion of unspoiled nature. It is prohibited to exercise any form of compulsion on man or to exploit his poverty or ignorance in order to convert him to another religion or to atheism.

Article 11: (a) Human beings are born free, and no one has the right to enslave, humiliate, oppress or exploit them, and there can be no subjugation but to God the Most-High. (b) Colonialism of all types being one of the most evil forms of enslavement is totally prohibited. . . .

Article 12: Every man shall have the right, within the framework of Shari'ah, to free movement and to select his place of residence whether inside or outside his country and, if persecuted, is entitled to seek asylum in another country. . . .

Article 19: (a) All individuals are equal before the law, without distinction between the ruler and the ruled. (b) The right to resort to justice is guaranteed to everyone. . . .

Article 22: (a) Everyone shall have the right to express his opinion freely in such manner as would not be contrary to the principles of the Shari'ah. (b) Everyone shall have the right to advocate what is right, and propagate what is good, and warn against what is wrong and evil according to the norms of Islamic Shari'ah. (c) Information is a vital necessity to society. It may not be exploited or misused in such a way as may violate sanctities and the dignity of Prophets, undermine moral and ethical values or disintegrate, corrupt or harm society or weaken its faith. (d) It is not permitted to arouse nationalistic or doctrinal hatred or to do anything that may be an incitement to any form of racial discrimination.

Article 25: The Islamic Shari'ah is the only source of reference for the explanation or clarification to any of the articles of this Declaration.

The Cairo Declaration recognizes the innate dignity of all people. It asserts their rights to live in peace, to own property, and to receive health care and an education. It also protects people from enslavement and war; and it prohibits anyone from taking another's life "except for a Shari'ah-prescribed reason." But since "the Islamic Shari'ah is the only source of reference for the explanation or clarification to any of the articles of this Declaration" (article 25), exceptions exist to almost every one of its guarantees. As far as women are concerned, the OIC's declaration recognizes that "woman is equal to man to human dignity, and has rights to enjoy as well as duties to perform," but that is not the same thing as saying that a woman has equal rights—as the UN declaration explicitly declares.

The third issue affecting women's status was the debate regarding the role of the state itself. In order to hold together their ethnically plural nations, with diverging interpretations of the role of religion in national life, postcolonial governments have relied on centralized authority. Propping up their militaries and police structures has proved expensive, however, and many Muslim governments have pushed hard for economic development. "Strongmen" with authoritarian regimes have included the shah in Iran, Hafez al-Assad in Syria (r. 1971–2000), General Muhammad Zia ul-Haq in Pakistan (r. 1978–1988), or Muammar al-Qaddafi in Libya (r. 1969–2011). In each case, wealth has been hoarded by elites rather than distributed throughout society, and countries without oil have been mired in poverty. In the poorer states—Afghanistan, Bangladesh, Jordan, Libya, Pakistan, Syria—lack of economic opportunity drove women into isolation within the home, so that they could not compete with men for available jobs.[9]

---

[9]   Even in oil-rich Saudi Arabia, wealth is so centralized that millions of women and men live in poverty.

THE STRUCTURES OF THOUGHT

Catastrophes can have their beneficial aspects. They can sweep history's slate clean; they can trigger a willingness to rethink basic assumptions. Something like this happened in the late Middle Ages, when the Black Death carried off one-third of Europe's population. People questioned why God would permit so much suffering, how society had responded, and what truly matters in life. All these questions contributed to the great Renaissance of the 15th and 16th centuries. In the ancient world, the destruction of the Temple in Jerusalem and the Jews' being hauled away to Babylon in slavery, in 586 BCE, inspired the creation of rabbinical Judaism, the Oral Torah, and the revival of Jewish thought. In the 20th century, the blow of two World Wars, the Depression, the Holocaust, and the threat of global nuclear annihilation again stimulated thought about fundamental questions in life.

The intellectual and artistic life of the second half of the 20th century in the West has been rich. The experimental spirit of modernism has combined with new developments in science, linguistics, technology, and psychology. If much of this work has been bleak and despairing, it also contains intense feeling and ironic, if unsettling, humor. **Structuralism**, most notably in the 1950s through 1970s, had a particular focus on language. The **post-structuralism** that followed is more skeptical of systems of thought. Both, however, are difficult to define once and for all. The writing style of their leading thinkers is often difficult, too, and highly technical.

Such a style of prose is not accidental. The massive expansion of higher-education systems in the postwar era resulted in the professionalization of philosophy. Philosophers, in short, became academics. Their investigations were not conducted with popular audiences in mind, and they could write in a way that few others could understand. Consider just a sampling. For Jürgen Habermas (b. 1929) in Germany, critical theory can still speak directly to the role of the individual in politics, but most individuals would be lost reading it:

> Under the functional aspect of reaching understanding, communicative action serves the transmission and renewal of cultural knowledge; under the aspect of coordinating action, it serves social integration and the establishment of group solidarity; under the aspect of socialization, it serves the formation of personal identities. *(Habermas, The Theory of Communicative Action, 1981)*

For Hilary Putnam (b. 1926), an American philosopher, the very idea of explanation is in question. He works in a tradition that scrutinizes every term, in a specialized and technically precise language:

On the internalist view, we recall, explanation depends on factors internal to the body of knowledge (on structuring the body of knowledge so that the parts stand in appropriate logical and epistemic relations) *except*, of course, for the truth of the statements comprising the explanans. (Putnam, The Threefold Cord: Mind, Body, and World, 1999)

Despite its difficulty, post-structuralism has allowed feminists, ethnic minorities, and others to look for the hidden assumptions in the critical thinkers of the past. Perhaps the most famous stream within post-structuralism, however, began with Jacques Derrida (1930–2004). His theory of "deconstruction" involves close readings of past thinkers. Even to quote it is daunting, so we must first get a better handle on structuralism.

Structuralism emerged in response to the collapse of belief in values portrayed by the absurdists, such as Camus and Beckett. It emphasizes the structured ways in which we see, participate in, and comprehend the world. The world itself may be incomprehensible, said the structuralists, but our perceptions of it are not. They arise from structured systems of language, thought, and social interaction.

> The world itself may be incomprehensible, said the structuralists, but our perceptions of it are not. They arise from structured systems of language, thought, and social interaction.

Structuralism has its roots in the work of a Swiss linguist, Ferdinand de Saussure (1857–1913). Saussure argued that all languages are arbitrary systems. They are *systems* because they are held together by self-dependent rules of grammar, syntax, and etymology; they are *arbitrary* because they bear no necessary relation to the world they describe. Consider a book. English speakers centuries ago, when books were invented, could have selected *any* combination of letters or sounds to denote the new object. But *B, O, O,* and *K* are what they settled on. And that choice had all sorts of side-effects: a person who sells books became a BOOK-SELLER, and his or her place of business became a BOOKSTORE. Someone who learned a great deal from reading books became BOOK-SMART. Saussure's point is that the relationships that matter are not those that connect the words to the things they describe, like B-O-O-K to a book. They are the relationships that connect words together. All our statements—all of our "speech acts," as some linguists call them—say as much about our language itself as about the world.

Claude Levi-Strauss (1908–2009) emerged in the 1950s and 1960s as the most brilliant of structuralist anthropologists. Levi-Strauss maintained that the differences between cultures are local variations of shared human traits. Human actions, desires, emotions, and ideas emerge from a single, though complex, structure of instinctive needs. Every human society, for example, abhors the idea of incest. This is no coincidence. But cultural norms about incest can still vary enormously. In the West, biologists might talk about the danger to the species from marrying too closely within a family. (Incest, they would say, "narrows the gene pool." If the environment changes and wipes out people with just some genes, then everybody is gone.) Other societies would have very different words and practices. To Levi-Strauss, human beings all perceive the world in certain ways; I see this pen, that piece of paper, this desk, that lamp. Yet we interpret it in different ways, thanks to the connections we make. Just as Saussure said about words, we define things in relation to one another. Levi-Strauss made his life's work showing the hidden parallels that exist across cultures.

As we saw in earlier chapters, Sigmund Freud and Karl Marx describe, in their different ways, patterns in human life. Freud wrote about the lures of Eros and Thanatos, Marx about class conflict and modes of production. Not surprisingly, then, structuralists of the 1960s and 1970s revived their ideas. The French literary theorist Roland Barthes (1915–1980) showed in *Mythologies* (1953) the cultural values in ordinary middle-class life. Everything from fashion magazines to televised wrestling matches, from advertisements for household cleaning prod-

ucts to striptease shows, has hidden meanings that can be decoded. A poem, a novel, or an essay has hidden meanings too. The point is not what the author tried to say, but what he could not avoid not saying. A text, as Barthes put it, represents the "death of the author."

The belief in hidden systems or codes in all human activity carries a risk. If humans can only operate within limits, even without awareness of them, then is it possible to be a free moral agent? Or are human beings instead just a part of the vast system of the world? And if so, can we be held morally responsible for our actions? The question is not just theoretical. A number of early structuralists, especially in France, had unsavory pasts. Louis Althusser (1918–1990), a Marxist philosopher, resisted efforts to reform the Communist Party after

Consuming Hidden Meanings   A modishly dressed young Swede shows off her Levi's shopping bag in 1973, in Stockholm. The image of a woman's bottom that adorns the bag—also displayed on a poster in the store window—is a play on the phrase "skin-tight jeans". The advertisement is intended as playful rather than demeaning, as it reflected the spirit of sexual liberation among the young generation of the late 1960s and early 1970s. Cheeky chic.

Stalin's death; he also strangled his wife. (In court, he explained that he was massaging her neck absentmindedly, and when he stopped he realized she was dead. He was sentenced to a mental institution.) He also added his name to a petition in 1977 that called for the repeal of "age of consent" laws, so that adults could legally have sex with children under the age of fifteen. Other figures had even more sordid pasts. An earlier German philosopher whose ideas influenced structuralism, Martin Heidegger (1889–1976), had affairs with two of his Jewish graduate students shortly before joining the Nazi Party, which he served for twelve years. Paul de Man (1919–1983), a Belgian literary critic schooled in structuralism, wrote over two hundred pro-Nazi articles.

But ideas should be judged for themselves, not for the individuals who derive them. Structuralist thinking at its best helped to assuage the bleakness felt by the postwar generations. It reoriented the mental map of Western intellectual life. It was, in its way, an antidote to modernism. And, with Jacques Derrida, it provided the antidote by creative but sympathetic readings of many of the great modernists. The horrors of the century shattered faith in progress, goodness, meaning, and purpose in life for millions of people. Structuralism rebuilt some essential scaffolding in a ruined landscape. People still wanted something to believe in.

WHO, WHAT, WHERE

absurdity
baby boom
Cairo Declaration on
    Human Rights
Central Intelligence
    Agency (CIA)
Christian democracy
civil rights
Cold War
Cuban Missile Crisis
decolonization
détente
Iron Curtain

Marshall Plan
North Atlantic Treaty
    Organization (NATO)
Palestinian Liberation
    Organization (PLO)
post-structuralism
Prague Spring
second wave feminism
shariah
Six-Day War
structuralism
welfare states

SUGGESTED READINGS

Primary Sources

Barthes, Roland. *Mythologies.*

Camus, Albert. *The Myth of Sisyphus.*

———. *The Stranger.*

Kirk, Russell. *The Conservative Mind.*

Lévi-Strauss, Claude. *The Savage Mind.*

Powell, Enoch. *Freedom and Reality.*

Anthologies

Hanhimäki, Jussi, and Odd Arne Westad, eds. *The Cold War: A History in Documents and Eyewitness Accounts* (2003).

Pierson, Christopher, and Francis G. Castles, eds. *The Welfare State Reader* (2007).

Prince, Althea, and Susan Silva-Wayne, eds. *Feminisms and Womanisms: A Women's Studies Reader* (2004).

Winkler, Allan M. *The Cold War: A History in Documents* (2011).

Studies

Azoulay, Ariella. *From Palestine to Israel: A Photographic Record of Destruction and State Formation, 1947–1950* (2011).

Barrett, Roby C. *The Greater Middle East and the Cold War: US Foreign Policy under Eisenhower and Kennedy* (2010).

Fraser, Derek. *The Evolution of the British Welfare State: A History of Social Policy since the Industrial Revolution* (2009).

Gaddis, John Lewis. *The Cold War: A New History* (2005).

Geller, Jay Howard. *Jews in Post-Holocaust Germany, 1945–1953* (2005).

Grossmann, Atina. *Jews, Germans, and Allies: Close Encounters in Occupied Germany* (2009).

Harrison, Brian. *Seeking a Role: The United Kingdom, 1951–1970* (2011).

Hilton, Matthew. *Consumerism in Twentieth-Century Britain: The Search for a Historical Movement* (2003).

Judt, Tony. *Postwar: A History of Europe since 1945* (2005).

Lüthi, Lorenz. *The Sino-Soviet Split: Cold War in the Communist World* (2008).

Palier, Bruno, ed. *A Long Goodbye to Bismarck?: The Politics of Welfare Reforms in Continental Europe* (2010).

Patten, Howard A. *Israel and the Cold War: Diplomacy, Strategy, and the Policy of the Periphery at the UN* (2012).

Pugh, Martin. *Women and the Women's Movement in Britain, 1914–1959* (2000).

Roth, Benita. *Separate Roads to Feminism: Black, Chicana, and White Feminist Movements in America's Second Wave* (2004).

Sturrock, John. *Structuralism* (2003).

Wendehorst, Stephan E. C. *British Jewry, Zionism, and the Jewish State, 1936–1956* (2011).

Westad, Odd Arne. *The Global Cold War: Third World Interventions and the Making of Our Times* (2007).

Zubok, Vladislav M. *A Failed Empire: The Soviet Union in the Cold War from Stalin to Gorbachev* (2008).

For additional resources, including maps, primary sources, visuals, web links, and quizzes, please go to **www.oup.com/us/backman.**

CHAPTER 28

Something to Believe In

1945–1988

Europe's movement away from Christian religious observance accelerated in the second half of the 20th century.
The revolt was intuitive rather than intellectual. Many who
had survived World War II simply concluded that no god
would allow such suffering, and any god who would allow it
did not deserve worship. Others retained their belief but not
their former practice; with entire cities in ruins, there were
not enough churches left standing. Still others felt that
Europe could not afford the time for churchgoing. The task of rebuilding was
too important—and once the economies did begin to hum along, there were too
many opportunities to "get ahead." Millions of Europeans felt trapped by the tension between the United States and the Soviet Union. Regardless of what happened with missiles, few doubted that Europe itself would once again become a
battlefield and responded to the knowledge with despair.

PREDOMINANT RELIGIONS OF THE GREATER WEST, ca. 1988

Predominant/state-supported religion:
Roman Catholicism / Sunni Islam
Orthodox and other Eastern Churches / Shiite Islam
Protestantism / Judaism

Yet amid secularism and spiritual anxiety, there was also revival. As attendance in churches declined, both Catholic and Protestant thinking became more
diverse. Pope John XXIII began the most sweeping Catholic reform in centuries,
with concern for the plight of Jews after the Holocaust and for Catholics behind
the Iron Curtain. Protestantism saw a "new
orthodoxy" in Europe, but also new modes of
worship and new spiritual energy in the United
States and the Third World. Postwar realities
also brought on important changes in Jewish
and Islamic observance across the Greater
West. Jews fractured into new denominations

◀ **Believing in Prosperity**
The 60s generation, Italian-
style. Postwar youths, full of
energy and brio, secure in their
comfort and care, but already
showing signs of rebellion
against conformity.

- Religious Observance
  and "Spiritual Anxiety"
- Science and Secularism
- The Catholic Reformation
- Postwar Protestantism
- The Fundamentals of Protestantism

- Jewish Revival—And Conflict
- International Judaism and
  the Myth of Israel
- Islamic Revolutions
- Ba'athism and Brotherhood

CHAPTER OUTLINE

and contested histories of Israel, and the tensions between traditional Islamic cultures and modernity sparked another revolution.

RELIGIOUS OBSERVANCE AND "SPIRITUAL ANXIETY"

One factor in the decline of religious observance was the welfare state. The governments of western Europe assumed much of the social role formerly filled by churches. Meanwhile eastern Europe under Communism suppressed churches altogether. Soviet regimes confiscated church lands, buildings, and bank accounts. They forbade religious education and practice and imprisoned anyone who offered resistance. Technology played a role too. Modern transportation and communication meant that people did not have to make friends with their neighbors in order to have a social life. Parishes as a social institution went into decline, and people who still wanted a religious life could go "church shopping."

Many people ceased active religious life out of sheer frustration and anger. While countless Christians were brave and generous during the 1930s and 1940s, the sad fact is that most church leaders failed to respond to the threat of Fascism. Most of them, in fact, had made compromises of one sort or another with Franco, Hitler, and Mussolini. How could the moral leadership of Christian Europe have failed so wretchedly? Whatever the reasons, the generation that survived the war in Europe turned away from traditional Christian practice. Much of the baby-boom generation that came of age in the 1960s therefore grew up without ever knowing it.

In 1950 western Europeans overwhelmingly identified themselves as Christians and claimed to attend church regularly. By the end of the century, all that had changed. While most people still identified as Christians, they tended to mean it in a cultural sense only, without regular practice—often defined as attending ordinary religious services (not counting weddings, baptisms, and funerals) at least once a month for a whole year. By 2010, for example, in Austria only 18 percent of the population attended church; in Belgium, only 7 percent;

CHAPTER TIMELINE

1945 "Stuttgart Confession of Guilt"	1954 European Organization for Nuclear Research established	1968 Papal encyclical, *Humanae vitae*
1952 International Humanist and Ethical Union founded	1962–65 Second Vatican Council	

in France, Germany, and Hungary, only 12 percent. Only 30 percent of Italians attended Mass, as did only 20 percent of Spaniards. Only 10 percent of the British were practicing Christians. For Protestants and Catholics alike, the trends pointed downward (see Figure 28.1).

These are only national averages. Christian practice in most countries still thrives in rural areas, villages, and small towns—but not in large cities. In Paris, as little as 2 percent of the population attends services; in Milan, by the turn of the millennium, the figure had sunk to 5 percent. Barcelona's three hundred churches, if crammed to capacity, could hold 450,000 faithful; but the city's

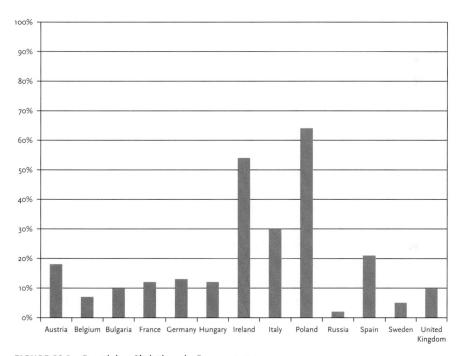

FIGURE 28.1   **Practicing Christians in Europe: 2010**

1975
European Space Agency founded; UN
Resolution 3379 condemns Israel

1987
Benny Morris, *The Birth of the Palestinian
Refugee Problem, 1947–1949*; Hamas founded

1973
Yom Kippur
War

1979
Peace treaty between Egypt and
Israel; Iranian revolution

population is 1.8 million, and the churches are virtually empty, apart from tourists. Moreover, the figures do not describe an important demographic shift. Many practicing Christians in Europe—perhaps one-tenth of the total—are recent immigrants from Africa.

Was the decline in religious culture a positive or a negative development? Was it an awakening to reason after two millennia of superstition, or was it a loss of cultural identity? However one interprets the trend, its historical significance is undeniable. Christianity, for good or ill, has been a foundation stone of Western culture and identity. While its decline does not foretell the end of Western life, it does indicate a momentous change.

> Christianity, for good or ill, has been a foundation stone of Western culture and identity. While its decline does not foretell the end of Western life, it does indicate a momentous change.

The change was noticed from the start. Paul Tillich (1886–1965), a German Protestant theologian, identified the "spiritual anxiety" of the postwar era. Every era, he argued in 1952, has its own unique form of anxiety. The ancient world's spiritual crisis was the fear of death, for which Christianity was the cure. The Christian era's crisis was guilt for not living up to God's expectations. But now, to Tillich, the spiritual crisis was different—a crisis of meaninglessness. To live without purpose, as Tillich asserts in *The Courage to Be* (1952), is not to live at all:

> The anxiety of meaninglessness is anxiety about the loss of an ultimate concern, of a meaning which gives meaning to all meanings. This anxiety is aroused by the loss of a spiritual center, of an answer, however symbolic and indirect, to the question of the meaning of existence. . . . The breakdown of absolutism, the development of liberalism and democracy, the rise of a technical civilization with its victory over all enemies and its own beginning disintegration—these are the sociological presupposition for the third main period of anxiety. In this [era] the anxiety of emptiness and meaninglessness is dominant. We are under the threat of spiritual non-being.

A secular world, in Tillich's eyes, is a soulless one. The West after the loss of faith knows that this is true, yet feels powerless to do anything about it.

SCIENCE AND SECULARISM

Advances in science, generally speaking, did not cause the loss of faith. Although it took some time to understand ideas like evolutionary theory and Einstein's relativity, most mainstream Christian denominations absorbed them. Smaller groups resisted any compromise with Biblical literalism, but mostly in the United States. European Christians, both Protestant and Catholic, were, if anything, invigorated by the intellectual challenge.

The sheer volume of new discoveries is not surprising, since government and industry invested so much money in the sciences. The Cold War was the era of "big science," involving everything from the space race to subatomic particle colliders, from cancer research to genetic engineering, and from biochemical processes to digital microprocessing.[1] Spending on scientific research in Europe

TABLE 28.1 **Breakthroughs in Science, 1950–1998**

1952	Polio vaccine developed by Jonas Salk.
1953	Francis Crick and James Watson model DNA molecule.
1962	Thomas Kuhn publishes *The Structure of Scientific Revolutions*.
1963	Tectonic plate theory confirmed.
1964	Louis Leaky identifies *Homo habilis*.
1965	Cosmic microwave background radiation (echo of Big Bang) detected; Noam Chomsky posits theory of generative grammar.
1968	ARPANET (precursor of Internet) established.
1969	First microprocessor; Neil Armstrong lands on the Moon.
1970	Stephen Hawking and Robert Penrose prove the universe must have had a beginning in time.
1971	Biologists identify the gene that controls an organism's sense of time
1972	Astronomers identify the first-ever confirmed black hole; Stephen J. Gould presents theory of evolution by punctuated equilibria.
1973	First successful experiment of recombinant DNA; Development of TCP/IP, allowing diverse computer networks to communicate with each other.
1796	Confirmation of theory of a genetic component in development of cancer.
1977	First transmission of television signals on optical fibers.
1978	Mary Leaky discovers fossilized human footprints 3.5 million years old.
1981	Programmers at Microsoft Corporation develop MS-DOS operating system.
1982	Experimental proof of Einstein's predicted "spooky action at a distance" theorem.
1984	Discovery of Homo erectus skeleton, 1.6 million years old.
1987	Genealogical model shows how all human mitochondrial DNA can be traced back to a common African maternal ancestor.
1988	Etienne Baulieu develops the RU-486 abortion pill.
1990	Tim Berners-Lee invents the World Wide Web.
1993	First evidence published of a possible genetic role in homosexuality in humans.
1995	Discovery of first extra-solar planet; first complete sequencing of a genome of a living organism (hemophilus influenzae); first preventative treatment for sickle cell anemia
1996	First lander/rover on Mars; Java programming language released.
1997	First cloning of an adult mammal: Dolly, the sheep; Fermilab reports discovery of the Top Quark.
1998	The expansion of the universe is discovered to be accelerating; construction begins, in orbit, on the International Space Station; vaccines discovered for Lyme disease and for rotavirus.

---

[1] Few may have noticed the invention of the microprocessor the same year that Neil Armstrong became the first man to walk on the moon.

and the United States quintupled between 1945 and 1980 (even after adjusting for inflation); so did the number of scientists and engineers engaged in research. Spending on so vast a scale produced results, of course. But the gains in knowledge are remarkable all the same.

Given the high costs of scientific research, these achievements could not have occurred without the support of governments and other institutions. In nuclear physics, for example, leadership belonged to the European Organization for Nuclear Research (known as CERN, an acronym of its original French name—Conseil Européen pour la Recherche Nucléaire), established in Geneva in 1954. Funded by twelve governments, CERN had an operating budget in 2010 of approximately 650 billion dollars. The European Molecular Biology Laboratory, established in 1974, conducts research at five principal sites, with a 2010 operating budget of $170 million. The European Space Agency (created in 1975), with a 2010 budget of five billion dollars, is headquartered in Paris. The Institute for Reference Materials and Measurements, based in Belgium, maintains the standardization of units of measure; it was created in 1957 as the Central Bureau for Nuclear Measurements. Supervising a dozen other groups is the Joint Research Council of the European Union, with expenditures in 2010 of roughly five hundred million dollars.[2]

Scientific Breakthrough   ENIAC, the first digital computer (1946).

---

[2]   Publicly funded research and development in 2005 was approximately $275 billion.

But few believers abandoned their faith after learning about quasars, DNA, stem cells, or the fossils of human ancestors. Besides, secularization is not the same thing as irreligion. It does not mean atheism or hostility to faith. Rather, most secular Europeans since the 1960s have been indifferent to organized religion, making it difficult to keep tradition going.

Groups dedicated to a secularized society proliferated after World War II. The International Humanist and Ethical Union, formed in Amsterdam in 1952, brought together over a hundred smaller groups across Europe. The union, which claims a membership of five million people around the world, promotes a secular basis for society but recognizes the right to freedom of belief:

> Humanism is a democratic and ethical life stance, which affirms that human beings have the right and responsibility to give meaning and shape to their own lives. It stands for the building of a more humane society through an ethic based on human and other natural values in the spirit of reason and free inquiry through human capabilities. It is not theistic, and it does not accept supernatural views of reality.

In 1956 several thousand secularists came together in Oslo and formed the Norwegian Humanist Association to campaign against the established Lutheran Church. The British Humanist Association came together in 1967 (although its origins lay in the 19th century); among its chief aims is to maintain the strict separation of church and state. Activists in Stockholm created the Swedish Humanist Association in 1979. The European Humanist Federation brought together several smaller institutions when it formally organized in Berlin in 1993. Now based in Brussels, it participates actively in the work of the European Union. Membership in such groups has grown steadily, and their chief goals have been to remove religion from civic life and to encourage reasoned interpretations of science, government, ethics, and society.

The great bulk of Europe's secularization, however, has resulted from waning participation in organized faith. It was not an intellectual rebellion or a conscious rejection, but a fading away. Even in staunchly secular France (with church attendance only 12 percent), the majority self-identifies as Christian.

Three factors head the list of probable causes: the nature of capitalist society, religious pluralism, and antagonism toward institutional churches. First, life in the West offered unending opportunities for work, leisure, and entertainment— cinemas, television, sports events, restaurants, cafes, radio, museums, theaters, concerts, parks. These took over part of the social function of churchgoing, just as the welfare state assumed the caring role of churches. Second, the many religious choices eroded a strong sense of religious identity, especially among Protestants. So did intermarriage. Since at least the 1960s, fewer and fewer people say that they can

No Time for Church   Scottish flags wave atop one end of Wembley Stadium in London for a football match between England and Scotland, in 1955. The popularity of professional sports—aided by the construction (often at public expense) of vast stadiums and by the advent of television coverage—is one of many factors that has contributed to the secularization of Europe.

differentiate between the teachings of various denominations. The third factor was consciousness of the churches' real and perceived failings. For many who came of age in the late 1960s, the institutional churches had much to answer for.

THE CATHOLIC REFORMATION

A series of crises rocked the Roman Catholic Church throughout the 20th century and contributed to the loss of lay members. Especially painful for many Catholics was the Church's response to Fascism and the Holocaust—or rather its lack of one. Pope Pius XII (r. 1939–1958), though personally opposed to Fascism, charted a moderate course in opposing Mussolini and Hitler; officially, the Vatican remained neutral throughout the war. Pius feared a military assault on Catholic communities across Europe or even on the Vatican itself if it took public positions on political matters. Many Jews looked to Rome to take a strong moral position, and Pius secretly protected thousands, in churches and monasteries as well as in the Vatican. In the end, roughly 80 percent of Rome's Jewish population received direct aid from the Church in avoiding capture by the Nazis via their Fascist allies.

Still, Pius never unmistakably condemned the ongoing Holocaust. The closest he came was in a radio speech on Christmas Day in 1942. Near the end of his talk, he called for the restored promise of honesty, fairness, generosity, and mercy toward all of God's people:

> Humanity owes such a vow to the innumerable dead who lie buried on battlefields: the sacrifice of their lives in their fulfillment ought to be a holocaust for a new and better social order. Humanity owes such a vow to the unending cries of mothers, widows, and orphans who have had the light, comfort, and sustenance of their lives torn from them. Humanity owes such a vow to the innumerable exiles whom the hurricane of war has blown from their homes and left stranded in foreign lands: they can lament with the Prophet [Jeremiah], "Our inheritance has been handed over to strangers, our homes to foreigners" [Lamentations 5.2]. Humanity owes such a vow to the hundreds of thousands of people who, without any just cause and only on account of their nationality or race, have been sent either to their deaths or to a gradual decline. Humanity owes such a vow to the many millions of noncombatants—women, children, the sick, the elderly—to whom the aerial bombardments (whose horrors we have repeatedly condemned from the start) have destroyed lives, goods, possessions, houses, hospitals, and places of worship without discernment or sufficient care. Humanity owes such a vow to the rivers of tears and bitterness, to the clouds of sorrow and torment, which have proceeded from the deadly ruin of the present conflict, darkening the heavens and calling out for the descent of the Holy Spirit—that It might free the world from the spread of violence and terror.

Even this moving invocation does not specify the suffering of the Jews. His description of persecution and his quotation from Jeremiah might be veiled references to the Jews, but many Catholics wanted something more from their leader. Pius was no anti-Semite, but to his critics he is the pope who failed to speak out. To them the church—or at least the papacy—lost moral authority.

After the war, Pius encouraged the rebuilding of Europe and the creation of the European Union of 1957 (see chapter 29). He also focused on the plight of Catholics behind the Iron Curtain. His positions on the State of Israel mixed altruism and stubbornness.[3] The crux of the conflict was Jerusalem, which the Vatican maintained should be an internationally controlled city. Pius's legacy

---

3   Pius showed concern for everyone suffering from persecution and war, but he refused to recognize Israel. The Vatican finally recognized Israel late in 1993.

regarding Judaism is complex, and it will become clear only when the archives of his pontificate are fully available to researchers.

Pius XII's successor was Pope John XXIII (r. 1958–1963), who dedicated his pontificate to **aggiornamento**, or bringing the church up to date. John believed that the church needed to confront head-on the rift between the practices of the church and the lived realities of everyday Catholics. He convened the **Second Vatican Council** (known as Vatican II), which met from 1962 to 1965. John did not live to see the conclusion of the council, but his spirit dominated its proceedings. The council's work was wide ranging. It refined the relations between the papacy and bishops. It reformed the liturgy, to allow greater lay participation. It expressed regret for the centuries-long hostilities between the Catholic and Orthodox Churches. It renewed a spirit of missionary work around the globe. And it rededicated the church to seeking union, whenever possible, with the Protestant and other churches.

Most controversially, the council rejected the tradition of blaming the Jews for the killing of Christ:

> True, the Jewish authorities and those who followed their lead pressed for the death of Christ; still, what happened in His passion cannot be charged against all the Jews, without distinction, then alive, nor against the Jews of today. Although the Church is the new people of God, the Jews should not be presented as rejected or accursed by God, as if this followed from the Holy Scriptures. All should see to it, then, that in catechetical work or in the preaching of the word of God they do not teach anything that does not conform to the truth of the Gospel and the spirit of Christ. Furthermore, in her rejection of every persecution against any man, the Church, mindful of the patrimony she shares with the Jews and moved not by political reasons but by the Gospel's spiritual love, decries hatred, persecutions, displays of anti-Semitism, directed against Jews at any time and by anyone. *(Nostra Aetate, "In Our Time")*

Many bishops had opposed the change. Except for a few individuals, they were motivated not by anti-Semitism but by a desire to uphold another tradition—the church's "infallibility," or freedom from error. How could the central ritual of the church, the Mass, have been wrong when for centuries it had blamed the "perfidious Jews" for the Crucifixion? The reformers won the day, however.

The end of Vatican II did not stop further reforms. Pope Paul VI (r. 1963–1978), John XXIII's successor, instituted the Mass in languages other than Latin, by simple decree. For liberal-minded Catholics, the work of the council and then the reforms of Paul offered hope for a faith adapted to the needs of contemporary society. In

Adapting to the Needs of Contemporary Society   Roman Catholicism, though still the single largest branch of Christianity, has struggled to keep abreast with the social and cultural changes since World War II—and has in fact debated whether or not it should do so. The reforms of the Second Vatican Council (1962–1965) displeased many Catholics, many of whom thought the council had compromised too much with modernity, and many others who felt that it had not reformed nearly enough. Shown here is a Mass on behalf of the then gravely ill Pope John Paul II (r. 1978–2005), at Our Lady of Angels Cathedral in Los Angeles.

sheer numbers, however, they were proved wrong. Attendance at Mass continued its steep decline, and pursuit of the priesthood fell off at a startling rate. Conservative Catholics attributed the decline to the reforms themselves. They argued that, in the attempt to make the church relevant to the modern world, it had cut itself off from its roots. Liberal Catholics pointed to two other issues—the church's ban on contraception and its refusal to allow women to be priests.

The debate over artificial contraception had been around for a long time, at least since the 12th century, but it became urgent with the availability of the birth-control pill in 1961. Paul VI spent several years investigating the science behind the new method. He also reviewed church doctrine on the nature of sexuality and the purpose of marriage. He set up advisory committees that included laymen and laywomen, both married and unmarried. He reviewed the documents of Vatican II and consulted with both physicians and theologians. Finally, in 1968, he issued *Humanae Vitae* ("Of Human Life"), perhaps the most famous papal encyclical in history.

The encyclical recognizes (in an innovation) that sex has a twofold purpose. Besides producing offspring, it expresses love. All the more reason, then, that marriage is the only licit venue for sex, for without a lifelong commitment, sex is reduced to coupling. Marriage does more than unite a man and woman into "one flesh." It unites the married couple with the loving God who brought them together:

> Marriage, then, is far from being the effect of chance or the result of the blind evolution of natural forces. It is in reality the wise and provident institution of God the Creator, whose purpose was to effect in man His loving design. As a consequence, husband and wife, through that mutual gift of themselves, which is specific and exclusive to them alone, develop that union of two persons in which they perfect one another, co-operating with God in the generation and rearing of new lives.
>
> The marriage of those who have been baptized is, in addition, invested with the dignity of a sacramental sign of grace, for it represents the union of Christ and His Church.

Married love, then, is a human analogue to the Holy Trinity itself. *Humanae Vitae* consequently rejects all forms of artificial contraception and insists that "each and every" act of sexual union must be left open to the possibility of new life.

The crowds stayed away in droves. Studies of European Catholics from 1970 on showed that a major factor in their falling away from church attendance was the church's stance on contraception. A clash was perhaps inevitable—even more so with the rise of second wave feminism. To many women, *Humanae Vitae* resentenced them to lives of endless reproduction just when they were winning their freedom to pursue other goals.

Of secondary significance was the issue of women's ordination as priests—secondary because fewer women were interested in pursuing the priesthood than in avoiding pregnancy. The church's traditional position was that Jesus, in selecting his twelve apostles, had chosen only men, and so only men were called to priesthood. The church therefore did not have the authority to ordain women, even if it wanted to do so. At Vatican II many bishops and their theological advisers argued against this strict interpretation of the Gospel. The apostles, they pointed out, were also all married men and all Jewish. Did it not then follow that the church does not have the authority to ordain anyone other than Jewish husbands to the Catholic priesthood? Moreover, the New Testament clearly distinguishes between the apostles and bishops. The church would have none of this, however. Paul VI and his successor, John Paul II (r. 1978–2005), insisted that the priesthood is a uniquely male calling, and the question is closed.

Vatican II was the most thoroughgoing reform of the church since the Renaissance. But the legacy of the Council is still debated. To conservatives, the council is to blame for the church's European decline; it substituted modern fashions for a two-thousand-year tradition. To liberals, the council failed to enact enough reform; it left the same old patriarchy, perhaps with a friendlier face. In either case, the results are still to be seen Sunday after Sunday, in row after row of empty seats in the pews.

POSTWAR PROTESTANTISM

The story of postwar Protestantism is also one of loss, and yet Protestant Christianity grew as fast in the postcolonial Third World as it faded in Europe. Moreover, when it came to spiritual energy, the United States became a leader in the Protestant world.

Attendance at and active membership in church life declined at roughly the same pace and to the same extent as with Catholic Europeans. Protestantism in Europe, however, experienced a fragmentation that the Catholic Church did not. The decline began in the 19th century, gained pace with the disillusionment of World War I, and turned severe after World War II. By 1989, when the Soviet Union began to disintegrate, it became apparent that Protestant Christianity had survived four decades of Communist persecution in eastern Europe better than it had survived in the postwar west. This tenacity of faith in the east perhaps resulted from the persecution itself, as Protestants resisted the official state atheism. In the west, Protestantism faced many of the same factors that affected Catholic Christians—modern capitalism, religious pluralism, and frustration with the institutional churches.

The Protestant churches, as institutions, had been organized along national lines since the 16th century. Many, in fact, had been established as the official churches of their countries, led by national councils and ruled (at least symbolically) by the monarchies. The blow that the World Wars dealt to nations, and to nationalism, thus affected the churches as well. In Nazi Germany, a National Socialist brand of Lutheranism, the "German Christian" movement, had received official support. The German Evangelical Church (EKD, for Evangelische Kirche in Deutschland), formed in 1933, had roots in the World War I era. Some six hundred thousand members strong, the EDK had supported Hitler and defrocked all Lutheran ministers of Jewish descent. It also established a "research institute" charged with preparing a new translation of the

Nazi Resister   Lutheran pastor and theologian Dietrich Bonhoeffer.

New Testament—one that would eliminate all references to the Jewishness of Jesus and his apostles and turn them all into Aryans.

Although the EKD survived until the end of the war, there was heroic resistance to it. A group of Lutheran, Calvinist, and Moravian theologians and pastors met in Barmen (the birthplace of Friedrich Engels, ironically enough) and formed the Confessing Church. As a religious group, they did not denounce Nazism itself but only the Nazification of their faith in the EKD. Nevertheless, several leading figures in the Confessing Church became prominent activists against the Nazi regime, most notably the Lutheran pastors Hermann Maas (1877–1970) and Dietrich Bonhoeffer (1906–1945). Maas, an ardent Zionist from his youth, risked his life many times to shield Jews from arrest and helped many to flee Germany.[4] Bonhoeffer campaigned actively against the Nazi regime and in 1943 even joined the conspiracy of some German intelligence officers to assassinate Hitler. Bonhoeffer was arrested and died in the Flossenbürg concentration camp on April 9, 1945, only three weeks before the end of the war.

Uneasy over their churches' collusion with the Nazis during the war, and left without a clear leadership after it, German Protestantism lost momentum. The faithful had enough to do clearing rubble, finding food and shelter, reviving the economy, reorganizing the state, and (until the Berlin Wall was erected in 1961) maintaining a connection with their countrymen and family members living under Soviet control. Churchgoing, to many of them, was hardly a priority. In October 1945 ecumenical figures from outside Germany persuaded the Protestant leaders to issue a somewhat tepid and vague acknowledgement of their failures during the Nazi years; known as the "Stuttgart Confession of Guilt," it acknowledged that "enormous wrong befell many peoples and countries on account of us," but insisted, "We fought for many years, in the name of Jesus Christ, against the mindset that exemplified the Nazi's violent regime." The leaders' shortcomings, the "Confession" said, consisted of "not standing up for our beliefs more courageously, not praying more faithfully, not believing more joyfully, and not loving more ardently." The murders, pogroms, book burnings, arrests, deportations, and concentration camps of the previous twenty-five years are never mentioned.

---

[4]   Israel placed Hermann Maas on the list of "Righteous among the Nations" at the official Yad Vashem Holocaust Memorial in Jerusalem.

This is no time, the leaders seemed to say, for looking back. Besides, the main Protestant denominations were undergoing some painful rifts. Theologians and church leaders across the Continent began reinterpreting their traditions. They sought to expunge ideas that, in their eyes, had contributed to the two World Wars—national pride, belief in progress, support for liberal capitalism, confidence in "justification by faith" and the guidance of the elect. Among the most important of these new schools of thought was Protestant **neoorthodoxy** (sometimes known as dialectical theology). Its founder was the Swiss Calvinist theologian Karl Barth (1886–1968); Dietrich Bonhoeffer was also active before his arrest. So later were the Swiss writer Emil Brunner (1889–1962), the Frenchman Jacques Ellul (1912–1994), and the Americans Reinhold Niebuhr (1892–1971) and William Stringfellow (1928–1985).

> Neoorthodoxy tried to restore the transcendent mystery of God, but it prepared the way for its own end. Europe's struggling Protestants craved a more immediate, approachable, and comforting deity.

Neoorthodox thought is difficult, and intentionally so. Protestant theology up to that point, it assumed, had made God too easy to understand. It had made him a Protestant minister "writ large," as Bonhoeffer put it. Neoorthodoxy emphasized instead the absolute strangeness and "complete Otherness" of God. Unlike the confident liberal Protestant writers of the 19th century, Barth and his followers stressed that God's nature could not be known. The human intellect will never be up to the task—and thus we are helpless in the face of God's will. He will save whom he chooses to save. Try as we might, we will never be able to understand or predict whom he will choose. Neoorthodoxy tried to restore the transcendent mystery of God, but it prepared the way for its own end. Europe's struggling Protestants craved a more immediate, approachable, and comforting deity.

In Britain, the decline of religious life also became apparent after the war. Economic straits meant less money for the support and maintenance of church buildings, and the sunny tone of much Anglican preaching seemed out of place. The loss of empire also meant the decay of prestige for the Church of England and its head, the archbishop of Canterbury. Just as Britain ceased to be a political superpower, so too did mainstream Anglicanism and Episcopalianism lose ground.

THE FUNDAMENTALS OF PROTESTANTISM

In Africa, Asia, and South America, Protestant communities ceased to look to Europe for leadership. Missionary work in the Third World increased steadily starting in the 1950s, bringing many new faithful into the fold. It also affected the substance of the faiths themselves. As described by an Anglican missionary to India, William Robertson (1894–1955):

> Christianity is not a product of the West. Its divine Founder lived in an Eastern land. The great churches of its glorious youth with that roll of doctors and martyrs belonged chiefly not to Europe but to Africa and the East. We must therefore desire to go to a land like India as little as possible as Westerners. We must give every encouragement to the clothing of the catholic faith and the worship that enshrines it in Indian garments. Our vision must be that of a real Indian Church.
>
> Our ideal is to live in simplicity as far as possible in the Indian way. Our hope is that if we are faithful God will enable us to make some contribution to the Church in India by helping forward the naturalizing of her theology and worship . . . .
>
> Our hope is that our Ashram will be so Indian in character that many Hindus will feel at home in it, and will readily stay with us. Hospitality will always be part of our programme, and we hope to have accommodation for a number of guests. We hope also to undertake works of social service, and some of us may teach in schools. It has been suggested that we should visit the prison, the leper asylum, and the hospitals. In this way rather than in preaching we believe that we can show forth the spirit of Jesus, our Lord. *(From Love's Redeeming Work: The Anglican Quest for Holiness, by Geoffrey Rowell, Kenneth Stevenson, and Rowan Williams, 2004)*

By the end of the Cold War, the number of practicing Christians outside of Europe vastly exceeded the number within Europe. And they stamped the faith with elements of their native cultures.

Despite upheaval in the 1960s and 1970s, the United States never experienced the severe popular decline in Christian practice seen in Europe.[5] America was also the site of three important developments—Pentecostalism, fundamentalism, and evangelicalism. All three are styles of worship rather than separate denominations, and all three took root in the mainstream Protestant churches.

Pentecostalism takes its name from the descent of the Holy Spirit upon the original twelve apostles, as told in the New Testament. Taking the appearance of tongues of flame, the Spirit filled the twelve with heavenly grace; and the sign of this gift was that they could suddenly speak in foreign tongues. Pentecostalism first appeared in the last years of the 19th century, a revival movement among poor

---

[5] The nation with the highest proportion of active Christians today is Nigeria, where 85 percent of the Christian population attends church regularly.

rural groups in the American South. It is at root a mystical union with God. The believer is seized by a spiritual ecstasy, speaks aloud in unrecognizable speech, and often receives or performs miraculous healings. It preaches of a second baptism "in the Holy Spirit," and it celebrates a surrender of the believer's heart to the Resurrected Christ. As such, Pentecostalism is openly, even proudly, anti-intellectual in its approach—based on a conviction that traditional Protestantism has tied itself into knots by a dependence on rational inquiry. By the 1960s and 1970s it entered mainstream Protestantism as a charismatic reform that has proved highly popular. Moreover, Pentecostal missionaries in the 1980s and 1990s found many welcoming audiences in South America and parts of Asia, especially China, where it now forms the fastest-growing Christian movement. But it has failed to take root in Europe.

Mystical Union with God   Worshippers at a Pentecostal revival in Brazil. The explosive growth of Pentecostalism has been in a statistical sense, one of the major success stories in recent Christian history. Its appeal has been particularly strong in South America. Estimates of the worldwide Pentecostal population are difficult to make, since Pentecostalism is more a style of worship than a discrete denomination; figures range from two hundred to five hundred million.

The key element of **fundamentalism** is "Scriptural inerrancy." It too is a mode of worship rather than a distinct denomination, and scholars trace its origins to 19th-century debates in the United States over Darwinian theory and the Biblical record.[6] It can mean the strictest and simplest type of literalism when reading the Bible, but more commonly it insists merely on the presence of a fundamental Truth in every Scriptural passage. For example, when the Bible states that Abraham lived 175 years (Genesis 25.7), it is not talking about calendar years; it is simply proclaiming that obedience to God guarantees a heavenly blessing—in this case, long life. Fundamentalism rose to the forefront of several Protestant denominations in the 1980s and was embraced by large sectors of the Republican Party. Morally earnest, fundamentalism has an element that urges personal and societal reform before the approach

---

6   The publication in 1910–1915 of a twelve-volume anthology of pamphlets called *The Fundamentals: A Testimony to the Truth* is often taken as the symbolic start of the movement.

of Armageddon—Jesus's return and the final battle between good and evil, which certain fundamentalist groups describe as the "Rapture."

Evangelicalism, too, emphasizes the work of the Holy Spirit in the world and the centrality of Biblical truth. However, it retains more of the traditional elements of Protestant denominations than Pentecostalism does—and less millennial urgency than fundamentalism. Evangelicals also focus more on *ecumenicalism*, or bringing Protestant churches together. They seek simply to enliven what they regard as staid forms of Protestant worship. Evangelicalism is the only trend of the three that has gained any footing within Europe, where it tries to bring energetic Christian worship back into Anglican, Calvinist, and Lutheran life. The World Council of Churches formed in Amsterdam in 1948, to staunch the spiritual loss in Europe.

In sum, European Protestantism in the later 20th century struggled to disassociate itself from the elements that, for many people, had made it complicit in two world wars. It attempted to do so both in a highly intellectualized way, with dialectical theology, but also with a stripped down version of evangelicalism that emphasized feeling over intellect and a return to Biblical basics. Neither attempt succeeded in Europe, and the vital centers of Protestant Christianity thus passed beyond Europe's borders. In the United States, Latin America, Africa, and Asia, the faith has adapted itself to local worship traditions, giving it new life in new forms.

JEWISH REVIVAL—AND CONFLICT

World Jewry experienced both elation and sorrow in the years after Israel's success in the Six-Day War. Although still surrounded by hostile neighbors, Israel had proven its might and extended its borders to more easily defensible positions. Jews from throughout the Diaspora migrated in a large new wave, especially from Muslim countries, now that the fledging state seemed likely to survive (see Map 28.1). More than 90 percent of the quarter-million Jews living in Morocco, for example, returned to the Holy Land within a decade of the 1967 war, while virtually the entire Jewish population in Libya (roughly 35,000) did the same.

Not all Arab Jews showed such confidence in Israel. The quarter-million or so Jews in Algeria, for example, migrated instead to France, with some continuing on to the United States. Their Sephardic traditions and greater degree of religious observance changed the tone of French Jewish life. Yet tens of thousands poured into Israel from Iraq and Iran, and the small number of Jews remaining in Egypt were essentially forced out by the government of Gamal Abdul Nasser

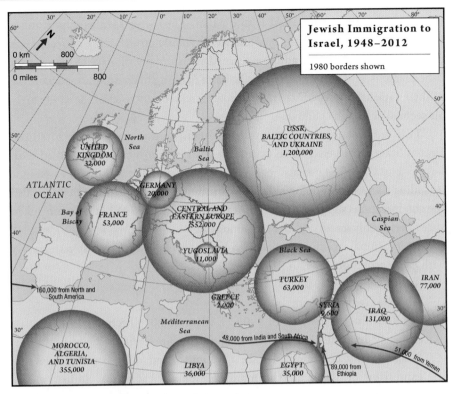

MAP 28.1   Jewish Immigration to Israel since 1948.

(r. 1956–1970). For the first time, many Jews arrived from the United States and western Europe as well.

The new wave of immigrants profoundly altered Israeli society. The nation had been founded earlier in the 20th century largely by refugees and immigrants from the Ashkenazim of central and eastern Europe. Many were secular, and they brought with them a passionate Zionism and a commitment to socialism. The new arrivals of the 1950s, 1960s, and 1970s were different. The North African Jews were Sephardic, spoke Ladino and Arabic rather than Yiddish and Hebrew, were highly observant, and were generally blue-collar laborers eager for an opportunity to prosper. Meanwhile the Oriental Jews (immigrants from the Arabian Peninsula, Iraq, and Iran) and the Jews returning from the United States and western Europe were educated professionals and entrepreneurs. A new money-driven consumer culture developed in challenge to the older, idealistic communal identity.

Israel's compulsory military service was still an engine of social integration. Yet strong prejudices between many of these groups polarized society. Survivors of the Holocaust and their descendants often regarded the Sephardim and the

Jews from the prosperous West with disdain. They were seen as opportunists who wanted to connect with their Jewish roots only now that the suffering was over. Sephardic religious traditions seemed alien and out of place to many established Israelis, and so did the Sephardic habit of living in communities according to their national origin. Moreover, the commercial orientation of the newer arrivals seemed crass and shallow.

This reorientation of Israeli life had significant consequences. First, the United States replaced France as the Western nation most closely allied with Israel.[7] The United States also became the chief supplier of military assistance, by selling its most technologically sophisticated weaponry to Israel. (It was also the chief weapons supplier to several Arab states in the 1970s, but it usually made sure to offer only its second-tier technology.)

International opinion turned decidedly against Israel—most notoriously with UN Resolution 3379, in 1975:

> The General Assembly,
>
> Recalling its resolution 1904 (XVIII) of 20 November 1963.... that "any doctrine of racial differentiation or superiority is scientifically false, morally condemnable, socially unjust and dangerous" and its expression of alarm at "the manifestations of racial discrimination still in evidence in some areas in the world, some of which are imposed by certain Governments by means of legislative, administrative or other measures",
>
> Recalling also that, in its resolution 3151 G (XXVIII) of 14 December 1973, the General Assembly condemned, inter alia, the unholy alliance between South African racism and Zionism,
>
> Taking note of ... the principle that "international co-operation and peace require the achievement of national liberation and independence, the elimination of colonialism and neo-colonialism, foreign occupation, Zionism, apartheid and racial discrimination in all its forms, as well as the recognition of the dignity of peoples and their right to self-determination",
>
> Taking note also of Resolution 77 (XII) adopted by the Assembly of Heads of State and Government of the Organization of African, ... which considered "that the racist regime in occupied Palestine and the racist regimes in Zimbabwe and South Africa have a common imperialist origin,

---

[7]   America was home to six million Jews, more than lived in the Holy Land itself, and American public and private economic aid to Israel grew rapidly.

forming a whole and having the same racist structure and being organically linked in their policy aimed at repression of the dignity and integrity of the human being",

Taking note also of the Political Declaration and Strategy to Strengthen International Peace and Security and to Intensify Solidarity and Mutual Assistance among Non-Aligned Countries, . . . which most severely condemned Zionism as a threat to world peace and security and called upon all countries to oppose this racism and imperialist ideology,

Determines that Zionism is a form of racism and racial discrimination. *(http://www.un.org/documents/ga/res/30/ares30.htm)*

This diplomatic shift had many causes, including anti-Americanism as a consequence of the Cold War and the war in Vietnam. Moreover, yet another war had been fought in the Middle East on October 6, 1973. On Yom Kippur, the holiest day in the Jewish calendar, united Egyptian and Syrian forces had launched a surprise assault on Israel. Caught unawares, the Israeli forces nearly fell, but after two weeks they managed to drive off their attackers and advanced far toward Cairo and Damascus before agreeing to a cease-fire. The war did not change territorial borders very much, but it destroyed Israel's aura of invincibility, assuaged hurt Arab pride, and emboldened anti-Israel forces to push for the UN resolution. Under pressure from the United States, the UN ultimately revoked Resolution 3379 in 1991. It is the only revoked declaration in UN history.

Within Israel, by the mid-1970s the majority of the population consisted of the non-European immigrants of the previous decades or their offspring. That change placed the earlier settlers in the minority for the first time. One consequence was a sharp shift to the political right, since Arab and Oriental Jews generally took a more hard-line stance toward the Arabs. The conservative Likud Party, led by Menachem

U.S. and Israeli Assault This Egyptian political cartoon, published in the run-up to the Yom Kippur War in September 1973, shows a joint U.S.-Israeli bomb falling on the home of an Egyptian boy. In reality, the war began when Egypt and Syria launched a surprise two-front assault on Israel.

Begin (r. 1977–1983), now rivaled the Labor Party for dominance, and Israel's governments for the next twenty-five years were coalitions. Neither Likud nor Labor could win an outright majority. In an effort for peace, Egypt's President Anwar Sadat (r. 1970–1981) boldly traveled to Jerusalem to deal directly with the government. Begin and Sadat had a surprisingly good rapport and, aided by U.S. president Jimmy Carter (r. 1977–1981), signed a peace treaty in 1979.

The political shift reflected a second major development in Israel, religious conflict. Israel had had a diverse population from the start. In 1948, at the nation's founding, about 10 percent of Israel's citizenry was Arab; by 2010 Arabs comprised nearly 20 percent of the population, not counting Palestinians residing in the occupied West Bank and Gaza Strip. The Jews themselves were divided between wholly secular Jews (roughly 20 percent), those who identified as nonobservant but believing Jews (50–55 percent), observant Orthodox Jews (15–20 percent), and *Haredim* (or Ultra-Orthodox) Jews (5–10 percent). Between 5 and 7 percent of Israel's citizens are Christian; another 1–2 percent of the citizens are Druze. But Israel's constitutional system of proportional representation has meant that small and even fringe parties have figured in every governing coalition.

Together with the virtual deadlock between Labor and Likud since the 1970s, the divisions make it difficult to unify the government behind any plan to resolve the conflict with the Palestinians. Moreover, the Ultra-Orthodox have demanded, as the price of their joining any coalition, control of the ministry that determines and enforces religious law regarding marriage. (Israel has no civil marriage.) That has largely meant strict Orthodoxy on marriage law. Many Reform immigrants, converts, and children of a Jewish father and non-Jewish mother have found, to their surprise, that the government does not legally recognize them as Jews at all—even though it grants them citizenship.

INTERNATIONAL JUDAISM AND THE MYTH OF ISRAEL

International Judaism has undergone a wide range of changes and evolutions. Nearly one-third of all Jewish marriages in the United States and in western Europe since the 1970s have been mixed, and the majority of families resulting from those mixed marriages have become culturally or religiously Christian by the third, and sometimes by the second, generation.[8] Reform Jews, whether observant or not, have proved the most willing to enter mixed marriages, Orthodox and Conservative Jews the least. Reform Jews in the west have also been quickest

---

[8]   In the United Kingdom, fully half of all Jewish marriages were mixed by the year 2000.

to accept homosexuality as a normal aspect of human life, regardless of Biblical and halakhic (rabbinical legal) condemnations of it. They have been the first to allow women to enter the rabbinate as well.[9]

Conservative Judaism, in contrast, permits men and women to sit together during worship but accepted female rabbis only starting in the late 1980s. Conservative Judaism also initiated the formal ritual of a bat mitzvah for girls, to correspond to the centuries-old bar mitzvah for boys. Both rituals take place at the traditional coming of age at thirteen years. The bat mitzvah, begun only in 1922 in the United States, proved popular and was gradually accepted by all major Jewish traditions, although the Orthodox held out against it the longest. Orthodox Judaism rejects women rabbis as contrary to halakha and tradition, but several rabbinical schools since 2000 allow women to participate in rabbinical study and to qualify as educators. In recent decades several new versions of Judaism have emerged in the West: Humanistic, Liberal, Reconstructionist, Renewal, and Tradition Jews have all emerged since the 1970s.

Rabbi Naamah Kelman   Born in New York City in 1955, Kelman moved to Israel in 1976 to pursue graduate studies. She received ordination as a Conservative rabbi in 1992, making her the first woman rabbi in Israel. Since 2009 she has served as dean of Hebrew University in Jerusalem.

Jews of every denomination have also endured continued persecution, and Jews trapped behind the Iron Curtain faced some of the worst of it. Under Stalin and Khrushchev, thousands of synagogues, schools, Jewish newspapers, theaters, and youth clubs were all closed. By the middle of the 1960s there were fewer than a hundred synagogues in the entire USSR. More than a million Jews left eastern Europe and Russia in the 1990s, heading chiefly to Israel and the United States. As late as 2002, in Russia proper, Jews made up less than one-fifth of 1 percent of the total population. Lower birth rates combined with emigration to reduce what had once been the center of Jewish population to the tiniest fraction of what it had been.

Hundreds of thousands asked to emigrate to Israel but were denied exit visas on the excuse that they had access to information vital to state security. And in fact Jews were prominent in many professions. In the 1960s a mere four thousand were allowed to repatriate to the Holy Land. In Poland and Czechoslovakia, where Soviet officials often appointed Jewish members of the Communist Party to administrative positions, anti-Communist rebellions took on an ugly anti-Semitism. The Soviets could always blame, and did blame, government failures on Jews in positions of power. Romania's dictator Nicolae Ceauşescu (1918–1989), in power

---

[9] The first woman rabbi, Regina Jonas (1902–1944), was killed at Auschwitz after two years caring for fellow concentration-camp prisoners and delivering lectures on Jewish history and law.

from 1965 until his death, held his Jewish subjects for ransom; he granted them exit visas only in return for large cash payments to support his lavish lifestyle.

An unexpected challenge to Jews everywhere came from within Israel itself, starting in the 1980s, with the young scholars and journalists known as the **New Historians**. Mostly born in Israel, they came of age just when the thirty-year hold (a common practice internationally) expired on government records pertaining to the establishment of the state of Israel. With access to these declassified documents, historians like Benny Morris (b. 1948), Tom Segev (b. 1945), and Avi Shlaim (b. 1945) offered fresh—and to many older Israelis, treacherous—views of Zionism.

The standard history up until then had described the early Zionists as peaceful idealists. These stout pioneers longed to settle in the Holy Land side by side with their Arab neighbors. When Hitler came to power, they spared no effort to save their doomed European compatriots, but could do nothing in the face of such evil. And when the nation of Israel was formally proclaimed in 1948, these Zionist heroes watched in surprise as their good Palestinian neighbors suddenly abandoned the land. Surrounding Arab states had ordered it, promising a glorious return once Arab armies trounced the inexperienced Jewish forces. But when that plan failed, the Zionist victors had no alternative but to claim the abandoned land as Jewish territory. "We did not have real history in this country," argued Segev; "we had mythology."

The debate began in earnest in 1987, with the publication of Benny Morris's study *The Birth of the Palestinian Refugee Problem, 1947–1949*. Here Morris argues that the seven hundred thousand Palestinians who fled the Holy Land at the time of Israel's war of independence did so for a variety of reasons—but the chief cause was the Israeli army, which forced village after village to flee. Morris sees no evidence of a central policy of ethnic cleansing. Rather, he insists that Palestinians were expelled in location after location, on orders of commanders on the ground, depending on their strategic needs in the war.

Another New Historian, Ilan Pappé (b. 1954), entered the fray in 1988. His *Britain and the Arab-Israeli Conflict, 1948–1951* maintains that the British colonial government had favored the establishment of a Palestinian Arab, not a Jewish, state. Most disturbing of all was Tom Segev's *The Seventh Million: The Israelis and the Holocaust* (1993), which criticizes the Zionist leaders of the 1930s for caring more about the establishment of Israel than about helping the Jews facing mass murder under the Nazis. To older Israelis, this was inexcusable slander.

The debate was intense, and it remains so today. Morris and his peers insist that they want only to discover the truth about their nation. A permanent peace settlement, they say, can come about only if both sides confront honestly the strengths and weaknesses of their claims to the land. But to their critics, the New Historians

Palestinian Refugees   Palestinian refugee camp in Gaza, 1967.

are mounting an assault on Zionist belief itself—the belief in a unique Jewish identity and a unique Jewish fate, both tied to the Holy Land. The impact of the New Historians probably would not have been so great had not Jewish identity already been so endangered by secularization, assimilation, mixed marriages, and divisions among denominations. To attack the "myth of Israel" was, to many, to attack Judaism itself. Without that, what does it mean to be a Jew? As more records become declassified, the historical picture changes and takes on more detail. But this remains only half the story. Modern Arab archives remain largely closed to researchers—and absolutely closed to Jews. Until full access is available to all, the truth of what happened to those seven hundred thousand Palestinians, how, and why will be unknown. A just and permanent settlement of the Israeli-Palestinian dispute will be impossible.

> To attack the "myth of Israel" was, to many, to attack Judaism itself. Without that, what does it mean to be a Jew?

Jews around the world, but especially in Israel and France, faced yet another threat starting in the 1970s: terrorism. It started with the surprise attack on the Israeli athletic team at the 1972 Olympic Games held in Munich. Small acts of violence were then commonplace, but organized and well-funded campaigns of guerrilla violence became the preferred strategy of those opposed to Israel.

ISLAMIC REVOLUTIONS

The idea of revolution holds an uneasy place in classical Islamic teaching. Unlike the English word *revolution*, which is morally neutral ("digital revolution," anyone?), the most frequent Arabic terms are decidedly negative. *Al-fitnah* ("rebellion"), *al-ma'siyah* ("disobedience"), and *al-riddah* ("apostasy")—all imply efforts to overturn a divinely established order. Misrule is no justification for revolution; only impiety is. A ruler may be autocratic, corrupt, and venal, but unless he has violated religious law and damaged the spiritual well-being of the community, he must be obeyed. To oppose a ruler who is guilty of impiety is not "revolution" but jihad. But even a righteous jihad poses dangers, since the anarchy it produces if it fails might lead believers astray. It is best to accept any government that does not flout the basic tenets of the faith, no matter how inept or despotic it may be. Thus Ibn Taymiyyah (d. 1328), the inspiration for the modern Wahhabi movement, justified rebellion against the Mongols (who had described Genghis Khan as the Son of Allah) but insisted on acceptance of the despised Mamluks.

In the 18th century, in response both to the Enlightenment and to European incursions into the Islamic world, a new word entered the popular vocabulary. *Al-thawrah* ("uprising") implied secular insurrection against a foreign regime and thus had an element of nationalist sentiment. Wahhabi groups across North Africa and throughout the Middle East used this term when calling for Arab rebellion against the Ottoman Turks and their European enablers. Both the Arab struggle under Muhammad ibn Saud (d. 1765) against the Turks and the Egyptian insurrection against the British in 1919 were described by contemporaries as *al-thawrah*.

The Islamic world of the late 20th century was filled with political upheavals and refusal to settle for an unacceptable status quo. The 1950s saw military coups d'état in Egypt, Iran, Iraq, and Pakistan. Uprisings in the 1960s occurred in Libya, Syria (four times), and Yemen. Still more revolts came in the 1970s in Iran, Iraq, Lebanon, Pakistan, Syria, and Yemen. The 1980s were relatively quiet, with civil insurrection only in Lebanon and Yemen, but the 1990s saw rebellion in Lebanon, Pakistan, and Yemen. And these were only the successful uprisings; scores more failed revolts took place in every country. It is an impressive record of determined opposition.

Still, what was the status quo against which they rebelled? And why was it unacceptable? There are two obvious explanations and another two that are less obvious. All four are colored by profound religious concerns.

First was the issue of nationalism and the emotional residue of European imperialism and the Cold War. Many Muslim states were the creation of Europe. The imperialist countries left not only international borders but as often as not new nativist regimes and new constitutions to prop them up. European motives were seldom altruistic. If a government was willing to oppose the spread of Communism, open its country's markets to Western commerce, and keep oil production going, then the West cared little how corrupt and oppressive it might be. The result was a series of pro-Western autocracies that were widely viewed by their Arab subjects as puppets. They were also constant targets for ambitious new leaders who wanted to show their eagerness to confound the West and to stoke Arab pride.

Time magazine in 1973 described Muammar al-Qaddafi, who had seized power in Libya in 1969, this way:

> The leadership of the 100 million Arabs is, in the famous words of Egypt's Gamal Abdel Nasser, "a role wandering aimlessly about in search of an actor to play it." Now that Nasser is dead, now that his successors are gray and conventional, it is the implausible figure of Muammar Gaddafi that has acquired the role of an Arab Parsifal. He is a mere 31 years old, handsome, devout, ardent, even fanatical. "The Arabs need to be told the facts," he is fond of saying. "The Arabs need someone to make them weep, not someone to make them laugh." Nasser once told the young Gaddafi: "You remind me of myself when I was your age." Gaddafi was profoundly moved. To be the new Nasser is his obsession—to succeed where Nasser failed.

The new Arab leaders, while anti-Western in their public stances, were often eager to retain good relations with Europe and the United States privately, in order to preserve the flow of Western dollars. By Islamic standards, their false piety was cause for legitimate revolt.

Second was the issue of Israel. With the possible exception of Jordan, few of the Arab countries cared about the plight of the Palestinians, whom popular prejudice among the broader Arab populace regarded as poor, backward rustics. But other countries cared very much about using them as a cudgel with which to beat the Israelis. Repeated defeats at the hands of the Israeli Defense Force wounded Arab pride. It also threatened to undermine the legitimacy of the national governments. As Islamist groups repeatedly pointed out, the Qur'an itself (3.110–112) had proclaimed of the Arabs:

> You are the best nation formed out of mankind, commanding what is good, forbidding what is evil, and believing in Allah. If only the People of the Book [Jews and Christians] had had faith, it would have been well for them. Some of them do have faith, but most of them are perverted transgressors. They will never be able to do you any serious harm, only minor annoyance. When they come out to fight you, they will turn their backs [to flee], and will

not be succored. Shame is their lot, pitched over them [like a tent] wherever they might go.... They have incurred Allah's wrath, and humiliation covers them [like a blanket]—all because they rejected Allah's signs, impiously killed His prophets, and have continually rebelled and transgressed.

That was a hard pill to swallow after seven straight military defeats. The need to take the lead in opposing Israel, and to be seen to take the lead, became a central plank of Middle Eastern politics. Any regime that faltered or failed in this regard paid a price in popular discontent.

A third explanation is less obvious: decolonization let loose long-simmering ethnic and tribal rivalries. These contests frequently played themselves out as power struggles within nations, but from the 1970s on they took the form of angling for leadership of the broader Islamic world. Ethnic Arabs had not been in such a role since the late 8th century, when power passed to the Persians. In the 14th and 15th centuries, leadership in the Muslim world passed to the Ottoman Turks, who held it until World War I. Wahhabism originated in the 18th century as an intellectual movement to restore Arab primacy, but the Arab states began to adopt it after World War II. The rebel

Demonstrating for Pan-Arabism   Gamal Abdel Nasser was the president of Egypt from 1956 to 1970 and one of the leading statesmen for the pan-Arab movement. Among his achievements was a brief formal union of Egypt and Syria into a single United Arab Republic. Formed in 1958, the union ended when Syria withdrew in 1961. Here, an Egyptian crowd, carrying Nasser's portrait, protest the Syrian secession.

leaders who managed to hold onto power through the 20th century consistently presented themselves as leaders of a pan-Arab movement to guide Islam into the new age. The state-run media in ethnically Arab countries referred to the 1979 uprising in Iran as *al-shawrah al-Iraniyyah* ("Iranian secular rebellion"). They wished to deny both the ethnic Persians and the dominant Shi'a of that country the honor of leading an "Islamic revolution."

Which brings up, at last, the fourth issue—Islam's relationship with modern culture. Islamic modernism had emerged in the 19th century, when progressive religious scholars were eager to adapt Islamic life to technological and secular society. These modernizers included the Young Turks at the Ottoman court, the Islamic Enlightenment in Egypt, and writers as broadly based as Beirut, Damascus, and Baghdad. The ideas associated with Islamic modernism fell into disrepute, however, in the 20th century. Religious and nationalist conservatives rejected modernism out of hand because of its pro-Western taint. The enduring problems in the Islamic world, to the conservatives, did not need a Western solution but rather a traditional Islamic one, rooted in ancient values and customs.

> The enduring problems in the Islamic world, to the conservatives, did not need a Western solution but rather a traditional Islamic one, rooted in ancient values and customs.

The theocratic government established in Iran after the overthrow of the shah in 1979 offered one variation on this theme. As the Ayatollah Khomeini put it in his best-known book, *Islamic Government*:[10]

> Islamic government is a government of law. In this form of government, sovereignty belongs to God alone and law is His decree and command. The law of Islam, divine command, has absolute authority over all individuals and the Islamic government. Everyone, including the Most Noble Messenger(s) and his successors, is subject to law and will remain so for all eternity—the law that has been revealed by God, Almighty and Exalted, and expounded by the tongue of the Qur'an and the Most Noble Messenger(s). If the Prophet(s) assumed the task of divine vice-regency upon earth, it was in accordance with divine command.

Free-market capitalism, with its emphasis on individual freedom and the rights of property, did not fit well with a conservative Islamic view that championed community and egalitarianism. Better suited to Muslim values, and specifically to Arab ones, was the political ideology known as Ba'athism.

---

[10]   "In Islam," wrote Khomeini, "government has the sense of adherence to law; it is law alone that rules over society."

BA'ATHISM AND BROTHERHOOD

Ba'athism is at root a form of Islamic socialism. It calls for a state-run capitalism in which the government, or the Ba'athist Party, provides essential services to all citizens. Ba'athism originated in Syria in the 1940s and gained popularity in the postwar decades. Although a secular political ideology, it complemented the conservative religious movement of the Wahhabis. Like them, it emphasized the unique role of the Arabs in securing a new future for international Islam. Its mission was to turn back the course of history to the social and cultural ideal of the first Arab caliphate.[11] This vision may or may not have been a genuine political goal; what mattered was Arab unity as an expression of religious culture.

The desire to restore an Islamic culture of the past meant first the rejection of Western ideas, values, and civic norms. Democracy, equal rights for women, freedom of speech, and the separation of religion and government appear not as universal ideals but as Western customs incompatible with Islamic culture. Hence the decision to replace the UN Declaration of Human Rights with the Cairo Declaration (see chapter 27), which, as we saw in the last chapter, subordinates all claims of human rights to shariah. Hence too the 1988 charter of **Hamas**, a conservative religious-political Palestinian group that devoted itself equally to charitable campaigns and social work among the Palestinians and to a terrorist war upon Israel.

Hamas, which originated as an offshoot of the Egyptian **Muslim Brotherhood**, took as its slogan the declaration that "Allah is our goal, the Prophet [Muhammad] our model, the Qur'an our constitution, jihad our method, and death for Allah's sake our most sublime conviction." Its well-known view on the Palestinian issue is expressed clearly in its founding charter.

> In the name of Allah the Merciful and Compassionate . . .
>
> "You are the best nation" [Qur'an 3.110].
>
> [Hamas] is a free-standing Palestinian movement; ever loyal to Allah, it embraces Islam as its way of life and aims to raise Allah's flag over the entirety of Palestine. Those who follow other religions [of the Book] may continue to live in the secure enjoyment of their lives, property, and personal rights, even though without Islam disagreements arise, injustice spreads, and corruption thrives, leading to never-ending strife and war . . . .
>
> Ours is a global movement, worthy to fulfill our role because of the clarity of our ideals, the loftiness of our purpose, the exalted nature of our goals . . . .

---

[11]   The Ba'athist Party's constitution proclaimed "a single Arab nation from the Persian Gulf to the Atlantic Ocean, a nation with an eternal mission."

Marching to Annihilate the Zionist Enemy   Hamas members and sympathizers rally in Gaza City on the first anniversary of the death of Abdel Aziz al-Rantissi (1947–2004), the group's co-founder. Rantissi helped to popularize the false notion that the Holocaust was the result of a secret Jewish conspiracy with the Nazi leaders; the conspiracy, he claimed, aimed to drive more Jews to emigrate to Palestine while making the rest of the world feel sorry for them and thereby allow the creation of Israel. Many Palestinian leaders, including Mahmoud Abbas, the current president of the Palestinian Authority, have endorsed the idea. (In fact, Abbas used an elaborated version of the theory for his Ph.D. dissertation.)

> We are one element in the jihad-struggle to confront the Zionist invasion.... The Prophet (may Allah's prayer and peace be ever upon him!) himself said: "The hour of judgment will not come until the Muslims fight the Jews and kill them all—such that every tree and stone will say "Oh Muslim, servant of Allah! There is a Jew hiding behind me. Come kill him!'"... There is no solution to the Palestinian problem except by *jihad*.

Less well known is its position regarding modernism:

> Our movement began at a time when true Islam had all but disappeared from Arab life: its laws had been broken, its teachings ignored, its values altered. Wicked people had seized power, and under them there was nothing but oppression and darkness .... Homelands were usurped, people sent into exile and made to wander aimlessly through the world; justice disappeared and lies took its place. Nothing was as it should have been—which is the case whenever true Islam is driven out ....

In order to bring up the generations in an authentic Islamic way, it is necessary to teach the duties of religion, to study the Qur'an and the Prophet's traditions in their completeness, and to learn Islam's history and ways from authentic sources . . . .

We respect [nationalist] movements, understanding the conditions and circumstances that gave birth to them, and so long as they reject both the Communist East and the Crusading West we encourage them in their work . . . . We detest opportunism and seek only the good of all people. We reject material wealth and celebrity, seeking no return from any human being.

Such groups commanded significant popular support, but less for their anti-modern stance than for their anti-Zionism. A unified pan-Arab movement, they confidently believed, emboldened by a pure and disciplined application of traditional Islamic morality, could not fail to achieve the annihilation of the Zionist enemy. And success would be the crowning achievement of the Arab campaign to regain its rightful place at the head of international Islam. This is why Israel's repeated military victories in the 1960s and 1970s stung: while the Zionist state continued to thrive at the physical center of the Arab lands, Arab dreams to regain their status remained frustrated.

Groups like the Muslim Brotherhood and Hamas shared that frustration with political parties like the Ba'athists. They wished to revitalize a past vision of Islamic-Arab greatness rather than pursue a new one. They sought not a revolution but a restoration.

WHO, WHAT, WHERE

aggiornamento	neoorthodoxy
evangelicalism	New Historians
fundamentalism	Pentecostalism
Hamas	Second Vatican Council
Muslim Brotherhood	

SUGGESTED READINGS

Primary Sources

John XXIII. *Pacem in terris.*

Paul VI. *Humanae vitae.*

Tillich, Paul. *The Courage to Be.*

————. *Theology of Culture.*

Anthologies

Bonhoeffer, Dietrich. *Conspiracy and Imprisonment, 1940–1945* (2006).

Hahnenberg, Edward P. *A Concise Guide to the Documents of Vatican II* (2007).

Studies

An-Na'im, Abdullahi Ahmed. *Islam and the Secular State: Negotiating the Future of Shari'a* (2010).

Asad, Talal. *Formations of the Secular: Christianity, Islam, Modernity* (2003).

Bauman, Zygmunt. *Modernity and the Holocaust* (2001).

Bethge, Eberhard. *Dietrich Bonhoeffer: A Biography* (2000).

Calvert, John. *Sayyid Qutb and the Origins of Radical Islamism* (2010).

Campos, Michelle U. *Ottoman Brothers: Muslims, Christians, and Jews in Early Twentieth-Century Palestine* (2011).

Gerlach, Wolfgang. *And the Witnesses Were Silent: The Confessing Church and the Persecution of the Jews* (2000).

Heschel, Susannah. *The Aryan Jesus: Christian Theologians and the Bible in Nazi Germany* (2010).

Hockenos, Matthew D. *A Church Divided: German Protestants Confront the Nazi Past* (2004).

Jenkins, Philip. *God's Continent: Christianity, Islam, and Europe's Religious Crisis* (2009).

Karsh, Efraim. *Fabricating Israeli History: The "New Historians"* (2000).

Lamb, Matthew L., and Matthew Levering, eds. *Vatican II: Renewal within Tradition* (2008).

Morris, Benny. *Righteous Victims: A History of the Zionist-Arab Conflict, 1881–2001* (2001).

————. *The Birth of the Palestinian Refugee Problem Revisited* (2004).

O'Malley, John W. *What Happened at Vatican II* (2010).

Roy, Olivier. *Holy Ignorance: When Religion and Culture Part Ways* (2009).

Sánchez, José. *Pius XII and the Holocaust: Understanding the Controversy* (2002).

Segev, Tom. *One Palestine, Complete: Jews and Arabs under the British Mandate* (2001).

————. *1967: Israel, the War, and the Year That Transformed the Middle East* (2008).

————. *The Seventh Million: The Israelis and the Holocaust* (2000).

Taylor, Charles. *A Secular Age* (2007).

Warner, Michael, Jonathan VanAntwerpen, and Craig Calhoun, eds. *Varieties of Secularism in a Secular Age* (2010).

Young, Julian. *The Death of God and the Meaning of Life* (2003).

For additional resources, including maps, primary sources, visuals, web links, and quizzes, please go to **www.oup.com/us/backman.**

CHAPTER 29

Global Warmings

1989–2001

In late 1989 Mikhail Gorbachev, the general secretary of the Soviet Union from 1985 to 1991, opened the Berlin Wall. The collapse of the Soviet Union followed quickly thereafter. As winter came and 1990 began, another Soviet-bloc country emerged into freedom almost every month: East Germany, Bulgaria, Czechoslovakia, Romania, Lithuania, Latvia, Estonia, Poland, Hungary.

WORLD POPULATION, 1950–2000

Country where population increased by:
0–50% | 100–150% | 200–250% | over 300%
50–100% | 150–200% | 250–300%

Soon even nations within the Russian Confederation declared their independence, most notably Ukraine and Georgia. Every emergent state, and eventually Russia itself, announced its intent to write a new constitution, to dismantle its state-run economy, and to adopt democracy and free-market capitalism. The transitions were rocky, but people everywhere spoke optimistically of a "postideological era." The ideological battle between East and West belonged, it seemed, to the past. Western values and ideas had become the norm (see Map 29.1).

A surprise international bestseller, *The End of History and the Last Man* (1992) by Francis Fukuyama, argued that with Communism's failure the battle for human hearts and minds was ended. Conflicts still lay ahead, but they would be mere economic or territorial disputes, not philosophical ones:

> What we may be witnessing is not just the end of the Cold War, or the

◄ **The End of History?** And the walls came tumbling down. . . . German youths celebrate the opening of the Berlin Wall on November 9, 1989. Ironically, that date is also the anniversary of other crucial events in German history: the end of the Revolution of 1848, the declaration of the Weimar Republic (1918), Adolf Hitler's failed "Beer Hall Putsch"—his first attempt to seize power in the country (1923), and the Kristallnacht attacks by the Nazis upon Germany's Jews (1938).

- One Year, Four Crises
- The United States of Europe
- Feminism's Third Wave
- Women and the Global World
- Islam and Its Discontents
- But Why Terrorism?
- Economic Globalization

CHAPTER OUTLINE

passing of a particular period of postwar history, but the end of history as such: that is, the end point of mankind's ideological evolution and the universalization of Western liberal democracy as the final form of human government.

The debate between differing visions was settled—or so it seemed.

However, triumph soon gave way to profound tensions. Open markets and democratic government, it turned out, are difficult to institute overnight. Outgoing government figures in many ex-Soviet nations made private deals to share power, sell off national industries and public resources, and arrange guarantees of immunity from prosecution for crimes committed while in power. With price controls lifted on consumer goods, inflation skyrocketed. The opening of secret-service archives triggered disputes over the settling of old scores with informants. The need to secure nuclear weapons and fissile-material laboratories raised concerns for safety. Many earnest, and many overearnest, emissaries from Western churches rushed in to win godless former-Communist souls for Christ, numb to local desires to revive their Orthodox traditions.

The end of the Cold War and the independent demands of peoples and nations thus introduced a host of new challenges. Globalized capitalism and the enormous influence of the United States as the only remaining superpower raised both hopes and fears that the norms of the West would become universalized. Among the most immediate concerns were the debates over how to promote economic development while protecting the environment and how to protect the rights of women and the poor without imposing, or appearing to impose, Western cultural values that were at odds with those of non-Western states. These concerns dramatically and suddenly complicated relations within the Greater West as the Muslim states struggled to determine their own relations with modernity. Trouble emerged right from the start in 1989.

CHAPTER TIMELINE

1984
Luce Irigaray, *An Ethics of Sexual Difference*

1992
Francis Fukuyama, *The End of History and the Last Man*

1989
Publication of *Satanic Verses* leads to uproar in the Muslim world; *Exxon Valdez* environomental disaster; Ayatollah Khomeini dies; Berlin Wall breached

1993
Treaty of Maastricht creates European Union

ONE YEAR, FOUR CRISES

A popular video game called World in Conflict, released in 2007 by software developers in Sweden, is set in 1989 and presents the fictional scenario of the Soviet Union, in a last desperate gamble to stay in power before collapse, invading western Europe. That done, the Soviets promptly attack the U.S. city of Seattle in order to immobilize the Americans' missile-defense mechanisms; the United States responds by unleashing a tactical nuclear strike on the Soviet forces, annihilating the city in the process. Meanwhile, China enters the fray as a Soviet ally, and the war quickly becomes global in scale.

The scenario is unlikely, if not preposterous, but not because of its attribution to the USSR of a military strength that it simply did not possess at that time. A more realistic scenario for the game would have been for the threat to world peace to come from China and parts of the Islamic world, for that is where signs of discontent with world developments were most visible, most determined, and most violent.

In the wake of Communism's fall what remained to do, it seemed at first, was to set to work bringing the world into the golden dawn of prosperity, freedom, and progress. Freed of the need for Cold War nuclear deterrence, people spoke of a "peace dividend." Now governments could balance their books, lower taxes, promote economic growth, and even expand social services. It was heady optimism unlike anything the West had seen since before the two World Wars. Hundreds of thousands rushed into western Europe, fleeing poverty and oppression, and were received as heroic survivors of despotism. Manufacturing

> Freed of the need for Cold War nuclear deterrence, people spoke of a "peace dividend." Now governments could balance their books, lower taxes, promote economic growth, and even expand social services. It was heady optimism unlike anything the West had seen since before the two World Wars.

1995
UN Women's Conference
in Beijing; WTO founded

1999
Euro currency introduced; Good Friday accord
signed; "Battle of Seattle" against WTO

2000
World population 6.1 billion

2001
Terrorist attacks on the
United States

The Fall of Communism in Eastern Europe and the Soviet Union

Former republics of the Soviet Union gaining independence in 1991	Independence from Soviet Union declared 1991; at war with Russia, 1994–2000	▬ Boundary of the former Soviet Union to 1991
Boundary of Russian Federation after December 1991	Former Warsaw Pact country holding free elections, 1990–1992	🌿 Violent ethnic conflicts

MAP 29.1   **The Fall of Communism in Eastern Europe and the Soviet Union**

companies from the West saw huge potential markets in the East. Churches looked to the millions who had been denied religious life for forty years.

Three other events in that remarkable year of 1989 presaged a less rosy future. First, the leader of the Islamic Republic of Iran, the Ayatollah Ruhollah Khomeini (1902–1989), ghoulishly declared a death sentence on a British novelist, Salman Rushdie (b. 1947), and offered $3 million to any Muslim who murdered him. Earlier that year Rushdie had published a novel, *The Satanic Verses*, that Khomeini—without having read it—declared blasphemous:

> I would like to inform all courageous Muslims throughout the
> world that the author of the novel *The Satanic Verses* . . . as well as those

publishers who were aware of its contents, are hereby sentenced to death. I call upon all pious Muslims to execute them all, quickly, wherever they might find them, so that afterwards no one will dare to insult the holiness of Islam. Anyone who is killed in carrying out this sentence will be regarded as a martyr and will go directly to heaven.

The novel takes its title from a dream sequence in which the fever-stricken main character imagines that the Prophet Muhammad has made a deal with three ancient pagan deities to insert some of their pseudo-revelations into the text of the Qur'an. Even more repugnant to some Muslims was an episode set in India, in which the prostitutes in a certain brothel have all taken the names of the Prophet's wives as pseudonyms.

Khomeini died four months after pronouncing the death sentence, but his call spurred fanatics into action. The novel's Japanese translator, a recent convert to Islam, was stabbed to death; its Italian translator, knifed in Milan, survived; its Norwegian publisher was shot in the back four times, but also survived. A mob set fire to a hotel where the novel's Turkish translator was participating in a literary conference; thirty-five people burned to death. The Turkish translator himself escaped the fire, but several of the firefighters beat him senseless. Rushdie stayed in protective custody with the British government for nine years, and the death sentence remains, although Iran has agreed not to pursue it. Iranian officials announced in 1998 that they have "no intention, nor is it going to take any action whatsoever, to threaten the life of the author of *The Satanic Verses* or anybody associated with his work, nor will it encourage or assist anybody to do so."

A handful of would-be assassins do not represent an entire religion or culture, but the reaction of the Muslim world alarmed the West. The Union of Muslim Organisations, Britain's largest Islamic group, petitioned Parliament to ban the distribution of the novel.[1] Thousands of Muslims poured into the streets in protest, and a crowd in the town of Bolton staged a public burning of the book. Bookshops were vandalized and firebombed, and hundreds more received bomb threats. The Organisation of the Islamic Cooperation, a group for coordinating policy between Muslim states at the United Nations, requested all its member states to ban the book. In May 1989 a crowd of twenty thousand burned an effigy of Rushdie in Parliament Square in London. The Islamic Union of Students' Associations in Europe also endorsed the demand for Rushdie's murder. Numerous other Islamic groups opposed the killing, but on legal rather than moral grounds.

---

[1]   Within a year of publication, *The Satanic Verses* was banned in nineteen countries, including Egypt, Saudi Arabia, and South Africa.

Demonstrating Against *The Satanic Verses* Ayatollah Khomeini's call for the assassination of novelist Salman Rushdie prompted dozens of demonstrations worldwide, both for and against the *fatwa*. In this photo, Khomeini supporters in Tehran declare their support for the *fatwa* with the assertion that freedom of speech does not extend to religious insult.

They argued that Khomeini's fatwa, or Islamic legal pronouncement, had not followed the proper guidelines, and anyway a fatwa could not be enforced in a non-Islamic country such as Britain.

The Rushdie affair brought home the anger of many Muslims worldwide at Western values. The Khomeini regime had instituted public whippings, stonings, beheadings, and firing squads for its enemies. "Those who attempt to undermine or ruin our Republic in the name of democracy," Khomeini warned, "will be suppressed; they are worse than the Jews of Banu Qurayza, and must be hanged." (The reference is to a group of 7th-century Jews from Medina, some eight hundred of them, who had opposed Muhammad's rise and were consequently captured and beheaded.) The Iranian Revolution pursued not only a separate path of development for Islamic nations but active opposition to the West's "oppressive, un-Islamic" ways of life.

Arab states feared the Iranian Revolution as both Shi'a and Persian, and therefore a threat to Arab and Sunni dominance. Iran and its neighbor Iraq fought a bitter eight-year war (1980–1988) that left hundreds of thousands dead. But rejection of the West's politics, economy, popular culture, and moral values proved popular, and militant organizations had at least the tacit support of the broader population—and even several governments. Soon news and debates in the West regularly referred to such names as Islamic Jihad, Party of God, Party of Islam, and Party of Liberation. Like the nations in which they were founded, most of these institutions are of recent origin; many of their founders are still active. All promote a restoration of conservative Islamic values, but not all promote anti-Western violence. Many of these groups are quite small, with only a few hundred members. But some claim membership in the hundreds of thousands.

Until the Rushdie affair, the West had generally regarded developments in the Islamic world as regional concerns, of interest only as they affected Israel or the price of oil. Muslim immigration into Europe and the United States still worried relatively few. But the tens of thousands of angry European Muslims on the streets of Berlin, Copenhagen, The Hague, London, Paris, Rome, and dozens of smaller cities provided a wake-up call. This might not be the "end of history" after all.

— ⁕ —

The second alarming incident of 1989 was the grounding of the *Exxon Valdez*, an oil tanker, in Prince William Sound, Alaska. The tanker was plump with 55 million gallons (over 200,000 cubic meters) of heavy, thick crude oil from Alaska's far-northern Prudhoe Bay when its hull was crushed against a reef.[2] It created an environmental disaster greater than anything the United States had experienced. The responsibility lay with the Exxon Corporation; an Alaskan court ordered it to pay over a quarter billion dollars in compensation and another five billion dollars in punitive damages. To finance its payments, Exxon received a multibillion-dollar line of credit from the J.P. Morgan investment bank, which invented a new kind of financial instrument in order to provide the capital. They

Environmental Disaster   The work to clean up the oil spilled by the *Exxon Valdez* took years. Here workers use high-power sprays on coastal rocks and the beach. Technologies for cleaning up after oil spills are today essentially the same as they were in 1989.

---

2   The *Valdez* released somewhere between 11 and 32 million gallons (42,000 to 120,000 cubic meters) of oil into the sound.

called it a **credit default swap**, and it was to play a role in a still larger disaster—the economic collapse of 2008.

The spill showed that the oil industry's recovery and cleanup techniques were ineffective, and so was the government's oversight. Immediate efforts included a controlled burn of the oil and the application of a chemical dispersant; both had only modest success owing to bad weather conditions. In fact, the dispersant created underwater plumes of oil that could no longer be reached. Mechanical skimmers arrived after a delay and began to collect oil from the water's surface. The rocky shorelines suffered heavy contamination, which crews addressed with high-pressure sprays of scalding water. Workers and volunteers spent thousands of hours cleaning by hand the sea birds, seals, and otters that were coated with thick sheens of oil. The loss of wildlife was immense; the hot water sprays also killed the plankton that form the first link in the marine food chain. Even twenty years later, marine and coastal wildlife were dramatically reduced in numbers. While the sound itself now appears surprisingly clean, as much as 20,000 gallons of oil still lie beneath the surface. Many local plant species and the animal populations that feed on them have declined over 90 percent and show little likelihood of recovering.

The spill awakened millions in the West to the threat that industrial development can pose to the environment (see Map 29.2). Concerns about pollution were hardly new, but they took on new urgency after a 1973 boycott by the **Organization of Petroleum Exporting Countries** (OPEC) drove gasoline prices to record levels. The first Green Parties appeared on the political scene in Belgium and West Germany, where they won parliamentary seats. Debates about Western dependency on oil, its effects on the environment, and the dangers of what seemed the only real alternative—nuclear energy—continued. After a drought in 1988, government officials spoke for the first time of global warming, a sweeping change in the earth's climate. Britain's prime minister Margaret Thatcher in 1988 called for political action to combat climate change, but promoted nuclear energy as the solution. The *Valdez* oil spill accelerated calls for international action.

The first significant step was the UN Conference on Environment and Development, or Earth Summit, held in Rio de Janeiro in 1992. Its Rio Declaration called environmental protection an "integral part of the development process," one that "cannot be considered in isolation from it." It also committed nations to "the essential task of eradicating poverty as an indispensable requirement for sustainable development." Critics complained that the two goals were contradictory, at least in the short term, since only economic development could overcome Third World poverty. The demand to reduce carbon emissions from fossil fuels while also resisting the spread of nuclear energy, critics said, was simply unrealistic. Transportation of goods and people alone accounted for 40 percent of carbon emissions. For all its ecological drawbacks, oil is effective, relatively inexpensive,

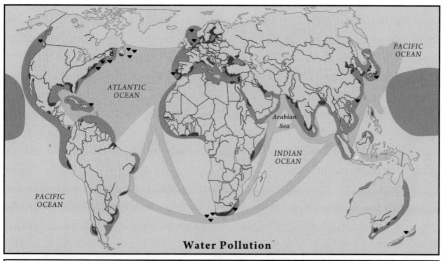

Water Pollution

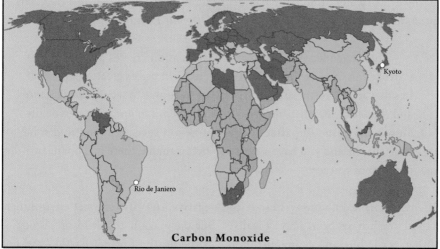

Carbon Monoxide

Water Pollution and Carbon Monoxide Emissions Worldwide

▼ Offshore dumpsite for waste

   Great Pacific Garbage Patch

   Severe pollution

   Moderate pollution

   Area of frequent oil pollution

Emissions of CO_2 in tonnes per person per year (2008):

   over 10   1–5

   5–10   under 1

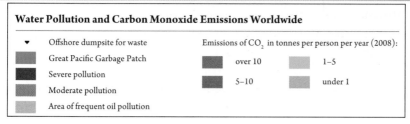

MAP 29.2   **Water Pollution and Carbon Monoxide Emissions Worldwide**

and easy to move. One can have economic health or environmental health, critics insisted, but not both.

The conflict between economic development and environmental preservation came to a head with the document known as the **Kyoto Protocol**, an international response to global warming in 1997. Thomas Malthus (1766–1834) had raised a related issue as long ago as 1826, in his *Essay on the Principle of Population*. To Malthus, human history has always been the contest of a growing population for the finite material goods of the earth. "The power of population is indefinitely greater than the power in the earth to produce subsistence for man." When the tension between the two powers becomes too great, nature alleviates it by famine and disease. Knowingly or not, those who argued most for environmental protections were Malthusians. They believed that human and economic catastrophe could be averted only by protecting the environment.

Others took the opposite view, insisting that economic growth was the answer to the ecological problem. In two books, *The Ultimate Resource* (1981) and *The Resourceful Earth* (1984), the American economist Julian Simon (1932–1998) laid the intellectual foundation for many conservative leaders at the end of the century. For Simon, the competition for scarce resources in a free market promotes innovations, as he wrote in *The Ultimate Resource*:

> The basic idea is that growth in population creates a demand that provokes an increase in prices. The increase in prices creates opportunities that attract businesses and scientists to be able to satisfy the demand and thus increase their income. Most of them fail and they personally absorb the costs. But after a while, some are successful and find solutions. At the end you have a situation better than if there had not been a problem of scarcity.

If environmental doomsayers were too negative, the "free-market environmentalists" may have been naïve idealists. But once again the "end of history"—either as the birth of a capitalist utopia or the death of planet Earth—had not yet arrived.

——————— ✦ ———————

A third crucial event of 1989 occurred in China. In April, students at Beijing University used the funeral of a popular dissenting politician as an occasion to demonstrate for reform in Tiananmen Square. Over one hundred thousand people joined the demonstration, which soon became a direct challenge to the government. The demonstrators in the square were peaceful and stopped short of calling for the Communists to leave office; rather, they demanded democracy, freedom of speech, freedom of association, an end to political cronyism, and increased funding for education. As the crowd swelled, demonstrators issued a call for university students and faculty throughout China to boycott classes. Urban

Tank Man   The identity of this lone figure, staring down a column of tanks en route to Tiananmen Square, is still unknown—and he may well be grateful for that fact, given the continuing crackdown on dissidents by China's ruling elite.

workers, who generally supported the government's economic liberalization but had begun to experience inflation, voiced support for the students.

Violent rioting broke out in several cities, though not in Beijing itself. The government portrayed the demonstrators as plotting to overthrow the state, which only strengthened student resolve. On June 4, the army took action, both within Beijing and across the nation. Estimates of the number of protestors, onlookers, and soldiers killed nationwide ranges from 241 (the official government reckoning) to as many as five thousand, as estimated by the local branch of the Red Cross. Thousands, and possibly tens of thousands, were wounded.

The government tried to control how these events appeared to the world, but too late. Satellite phones and radio and television broadcasts had leaked too many reports and videos. The benign image that the regime had presented was stripped away, to reveal a brutal autocracy with the power of tanks and fact-twisting propaganda:

> This turmoil was not a chance occurrence. It was a political turmoil incited by a very small number of political careerists after a few years of plotting and scheming. It was aimed at subverting the socialist People's Republic. By making use of some failings in the work of the Chinese

government and the temporary economic difficulties, they spread far and wide many views against the Constitution, the leadership of the Chinese Communist Party and the People's Government, preparing the ground for the turmoil ideologically, organizationally and in public opinion. . . .

Even under this circumstance, the Party and the government exercised great restraint towards the students' extremist slogans and actions and had all along given due recognition to the students' patriotic enthusiasm and reasonable demands. At the same time, the Party and the government warned the students not to be made use of by a handful of people and expressed the hope for solving the problems through dialogues and by normal, democratic and legal procedures. . . .

A group of ruffians banded together about 1,000 people to push down the wall of a construction site near Xidan and seized large quantities of tools, reinforcing bars and bricks, ready for street fighting. They planned to incite people to take to the streets the next day, a Sunday, to stage a violent rebellion in an attempt to overthrow the government and seize power at one stroke.

At this critical juncture, the martial law troops were ordered to move in by force to quell the anti-government rebellion. . . . Over 1,280 vehicles were burned or damaged in the rebellion, including over 1,000 military trucks, more than 60 armoured cars, over 30 police cars, over 120 public buses and trolley buses and over 70 motor vehicles of other kinds. More than 6,000 martial law officers and soldiers were injured and scores of them killed.

Such heavy losses are eloquent testimony to the restraint and tolerance shown by the martial law enforcement troops. For fear of injuring civilians by accident, they would rather endure humiliation and meet their death unflinchingly, although they had weapons in their hands. It can be said that there is no other army in the world that can exercise restraint to such an extent. *(Official Report of the Editorial Board of the Truth about the Beijing Turmoil, Beijing Publishing House, 1990)*

In response to the crackdown, the European Union and the United States embargoed the sale of weaponry to China, and the World Bank suspended all developmental loans to Beijing. Billions of dollars in foreign investments were canceled, and international tourism to China fell by 25 percent.

Communist and Maoist ideology no longer convinced most Chinese, but the Party could still command obedience by appeals to nationalism. The Party presented itself as the only sure guarantor of stable economic reform and the protector of national pride. The Communists in effect played a double game. It showed a friendly face to the outside world and courted international investment. Yet internally it portrayed the Chinese people as the victims of misunderstanding and imperialist aggression. The Party now stood as the paragon of patriotism. When the 2000 Olympic Games were awarded to Sydney, Australia, instead of Beijing, China's press condemned the decision as another example of entrenched pro-Western bias.[3]

The rise of radical Islamism, the debate between environmentalism and economic development, and the flourishing of Arab and Chinese nationalism have shaped Western life ever since. The Cold War may have ended in 1989, but a profoundly unsettled world took its place.

> The rise of radical Islamism, the debate between environmentalism and economic development, and the flourishing of Arab and Chinese nationalism have shaped Western life ever since. The Cold War may have ended in 1989, but a profoundly unsettled world took its place.

The post-1989 changes in fact echoed many of the experiences of the post-1815 era, when an economic and social time lock opened, and an accelerating wave of aggressive capitalism rushed in. Scores of huge fortunes were amassed almost instantly, as people with access to capital snatched up privatized state monopolies while the bulk of the populations, unaccustomed to and suspicious of Western-defined "market forces," found themselves with no means to support themselves. Unemployment in Poland, for example, hit 20 percent, and an investigative report from members of the European Union classified fourteen percent of the nation as "severely materially deprived." The gross national product (GNP) of Ukraine collapsed 50 percent within ten years of the Soviet breakup, while hyperinflation threatened to make the national currency useless; even after another decade (that is, by 2009) more than one-third of the adult population was unemployed. Hungary lost three-fourths of its export markets when protectionist measures closed access to its former trading partners; the national trade deficit soon grew to nearly triple the amount of total exports.

Soon enough, the predictable backlash occurred, and currents of political ultraconservatism emerged across eastern Europe that advocated a return to centralized control. Intense nationalistic sentiments rose, which prompted many nonmajority populations—especially large numbers of Jews—to emigrate. Right-wing coups were attempted in Georgia, as people denounced the

---

[3] "Give China a chance!" had been the slogan for Beijing's 1993 bid to host the 2000 Olympic Games.

corruption and cronyism of democratically chosen administrations. Assassinations and attempted assassinations poisoned the political atmospheres.

The West responded by injecting capital through the IMF, increasing private investment, bringing at least some of the nations (Bulgaria, Estonia, Hungary, Latvia, Lithuania, Poland, Romania) into the European Union and most of the same into NATO. The economic malaise improved through the 1990s as a result, but improvement came at the cost of leaving the not-included nations feeling exposed and vulnerable, especially in the face of renewed political swagger from Russia's leader, Vladimir Putin.

THE UNITED STATES OF EUROPE

The idea of uniting Europe in a single superstate can be traced back at least to Charlemagne in the early 9th century. Several medieval popes had imagined it. Habsburgs had probably fantasized about it. Napoleon almost achieved it. Hitler almost destroyed the place in his sick attempt make it happen. But the idea existed outside the minds of would-be dictators too.

Unification's appeal lay into the hope that it might be the one force powerful enough to contain nationalist passions, and it expressed the idea that European civilization stood for more than material progress. At the Continent's center, German thinkers have traditionally been at the forefront of the call to unification.

> Unification's appeal lay into the hope that it might be the one force powerful enough to contain nationalist passions, and it expressed the idea that European civilization stood for more than material progress.

The Romantic writer Novalis (the pen name of Georg Freiherr von Hardenberg; 1772–1801) had prophesied that "blood will stream over Europe until the nations fully understand this terrifying madness that drives them in circles." Novalis believed in the power of culture and art to save Europe. His contemporary Justus Friedrich von Schmidt-Phiseldek (1769–1851), a German politician and writer, had warned that unless Europe united into a large confederation it would soon lose its place on the international stage. The young but robust United States would rise not only as an economic power but also as the symbolic leader of Western life. Another German, Julius Fröbel (1805–1893), had raised an even sharper alarm. If Europe did not unite, he had warned, it would become a battleground in a war between the United States and Russia.

Nietzsche had devoted a long section of *Beyond Good and Evil* (1886) to the question of national and civilizational identity:

> No matter what you wish to call the thing by which Europe is made distinctive—its "civilization," "humanization," or "progress"—or if you

simply call it (without praise or blame) Europe's political "democrati-zation," there is an overarching physiological process occurring, indeed accelerating, behind all the moral and political theorizing around it: namely, Europeans are becoming more and more alike, more and more detached from those elements of climate and class that lead to the creation of separate races.... An essentially super-national, free-wandering European man is emerging, one who physiologically possesses as his defining trait a superfluity of the ability to adapt. (*Chapter 242*)

Because of the pathological soul-estrangement created by the utter insanity of nationalism ... and because of the short-sighted sleight-of-hand performed by today's politicians (who got to where they are pre-cisely by playing off this madness), ... people are overlooking or perhaps (willfully?) misunderstanding the most obvious thing in the world: namely, that *Europe wants to unite.* (*Chapter 256*)

The aspiration to unite was cultural, moral, esthetic, and even spiritual. At stake were shared values and beliefs, a commitment to human rights, civic-minded-ness, reason, and personal freedom. Politics and the economy played their roles, but what mattered most was the idea of Europe as a civilization, not just a com-mercial entity.

How much the horrors of the 20th century changed things. The leaders of western Europe, after years of wrangling, agreed in March 1957 to the first step toward union—the **Treaty of Rome**, which established the European Economic Community (EEC). The treaty's preamble proclaimed its purpose:

> Determined to lay the foundations of an ever-closer union among the peoples of Europe,
>
> Resolved to ensure the economic and social progress of their coun-tries by common action to eliminate the barriers which divide Europe,
>
> Affirming as the essential objective of their efforts the constant im-provement of the living and working conditions of their peoples,
>
> Recognising that the removal of existing obstacles calls for con-certed action in order to guarantee steady expansion, balanced trade and fair competition,
>
> Anxious to strengthen the unity of their economies and to ensure their harmonious development by reducing the differences existing between the various regions and the backwardness of the less favoured regions,
>
> Desiring to contribute, by means of a common commercial policy, to the progressive abolition of restrictions on international trade,

Intending to confirm the solidarity which binds Europe and the overseas countries and desiring to ensure the development of their prosperity, in accordance with the principles of the Charter of the United Nations,

Resolved by thus pooling their resources to preserve and strengthen peace and liberty, and calling upon the other peoples of Europe who share their ideal to join in their efforts, they announced the creation of the EEC.

More of a corporate merger than a cultural confluence, the EEC created a competitive commercial bloc that could hold its own on the world market.

The EEC's goals were to help postwar recovery and to counterbalance American economic power. Two other groups, the European Coal and Steel Community and the European Atomic Energy Community, were merged with the EEC in 1967, creating the European Community. Already it sounded less like a chamber of commerce and more like an association of cultures.

The next step to full integration came late in 1993, when a treaty signed a year earlier at Maastricht, in the Netherlands, took effect. This treaty established the **European Union** (EU), as not a single institution but as a united group of independent European nations. This flexible web of institutions would provide a process for coordinating policies formed at the level of member states:

The European Union (EU) is not a federation like the United States. Nor is it simply an organisation for co-operation between governments, like the United Nations. It is, in fact, unique. The countries that make up the EU (its "member states") remain independent sovereign nations but they pool their sovereignty in order to gain a strength and world influence none of them could have on their own. Pooling sovereignty means, in practice, that the member states delegate some of their decision-making powers to shared institutions they have created, so that decisions on specific matters of joint interest can be made democratically at the European level.

From the six members of the original European Economic Community of 1957 (Belgium, France, West Germany, Italy, Luxembourg, and the Netherlands), the EU grew steadily (see Map 29.3). It now numbers twenty-seven member

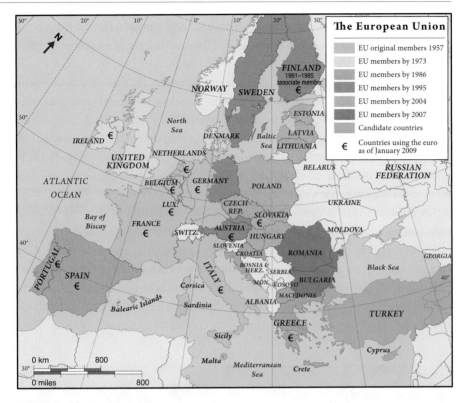

MAP 29.3   The European Union

states, with another five official candidates for membership. Each nation must meet three criteria before joining:

- It must have a democratic government that recognizes human rights and the rule of law.
- It must have a free-market economy.
- It must meet administrative standards to participate seamlessly with other member states.

Of those standards, the most crucial is the ability to limit governmental debt to an acceptable percentage of GNP. Once a member, each country may choose to join in a common currency—the euro—which was introduced in 1999. By eliminating or reducing bureaucratic barriers, the EU promoted the free movement of workers, goods, services, and capital. All these, combined with the low price of oil caused by Middle East overproduction, made the 1990s an economic boom time. Still-developing economies in countries like Greece, Ireland, and Portugal benefitted from substantial investment in new manufacturing and financial ventures.

Unified Europe was not without problems. More people flowed from poor nations into wealthy ones than euros flowed from wealthy nations into poor ones. This meant rising unemployment in countries like Britain, France, and Germany; it also meant uncertain growth in countries like Greece, Portugal, and Spain. Labor surpluses put downward pressure on wages in the developed countries, since by far the most migration took place among the working class. Meanwhile the developing nations took on excessive debt in proportion to their growth. For the time being, however, the availability of cheap capital, which included substantial investments from the United States and China, made the decade feel more prosperous than it was.

A more immediate problem was the social assimilation of so many new foreign workers. Concern about immigration had become an issue as early as the late 1960s, but the creation of the union put increased numbers on the move. And this was the movement of Europeans within Europe rather than the migration of Africans or Asians into Europe. It was also chiefly the migration of individuals rather than entire families. Since many such workers sent parts of their pay back to their families, they often could afford only crowded and squalid housing. They

Roma   The Roma people, or Gypsies, originated in Romania but are now widely dispersed across Europe, and they remain largely unwelcome immigrants. Here a group of Gypsy women sit on a street corner in Berlin. The Roma were another group singled out for elimination by the Nazis. Estimates of the number of Gypsies killed in the death camps range from 300,000 to 1.5 million.

remained socially isolated in their host countries and struggled for acceptance. They were also the first workers to be laid off during bad times. The need for their wages back home, however, often kept them in their host countries where they looked for new work. The emotional strain on these workers, not to mention on their distant families, was great.

When a recession hit, the unemployed in Britain alone grew from 1.6 million workers to 3.0 million between 1990 and 1993. The downturn contributed to the rise of reactionary popular movements in Europe. Neo-Nazi skinheads led race riots and railed against "foreigners," both European and non-European. "France for the French!" became the cry of the far-right National Front Party, which by the middle of the decade was earning 15 percent of the vote. The French government, eager to capitalize on anti-immigrant passions, in 1996 chartered aircraft to fly undocumented workers back to their native countries. In Austria and the Netherlands as well, immigration was the crucial issue in determining the outcome of elections.

FEMINISM'S THIRD WAVE

The 1990s were a crucial period in the history of Western women, too. The collapse of Communism introduced eastern European women to the ideas of modern feminism. And the expansion of the EU to include countries like the Czech Republic, Hungary, and Poland provided opportunities for women to migrate westward in search of work and a new life. However, that only heightened awareness of the differences between national cultures when it comes to women's rights and roles.

For every move toward liberalization in the 1990s, there was an equal trend toward conservatism. In both Ireland and Italy, efforts to liberalize laws pertaining to divorce met powerful resistance from traditional-minded women's groups. While homosexuality to most people was no longer a pathology or a crime, the "gender wars" brought thuggish attacks on homosexuals. Other disadvantaged groups in society—from ethnic minorities to the physically disabled, from underrepresented religious groups to the urban poor—demanded more attention to their own agendas.

——————————— + ———————————

This was the decade of feminism's third wave, and while its active center was firmly fixed in the United States, much of its intellectual leadership came from Europe. The two leading figures were French-speaking. Luce Irigaray (b. 1932), a Belgian psychoanalyst, became especially influential as her books appeared in

English translation. Both *An Ethics of Sexual Difference* (1984, in English in 1993) and *Speculum of the Other Woman* (1974, in English in 1985) display her eclectic ideas and methods. (She holds two doctorates—one in philosophy, another in linguistics—and is also a certified psychoanalyst.) Her central theme is the struggle to create an authentic understanding of femaleness. For her, ideas of gender are socially constructed around a system of binary relations. Every aspect of Western culture, Irigaray writes, right down to the use of gendered nouns and adjectives in Western languages, presents the male as the norm. Everything that is "She," meaning "not He," fails to comprehend fully the Otherness of the female. Business practice, too, tends to use male experience as the default. Would men ever have thought of maternity leaves had women not fought for them?

> Every aspect of Western culture, Irigaray writes, right down to the use of gendered nouns and adjectives in Western languages, presents the male as the norm.

Is Irigaray too cavalier in seeing a "gendered nature" in everything?[4] In one essay she criticizes the sexual tyranny of men, in often technical language:

> It is important to rediscover the uniqueness of female sexual delight.... Are not these women being de-personalized, abandoned without vitality, sensations, perceptions, gestures or images of their own, things expressive of their own true identity? For women, at least two types of orgasms exist—one that is attuned to the male sexual economy ...; but there is another more in harmony with women's true identity, their true sexual nature. There are many women who feel nothing but guilt and unhappiness, who are paralyzed and dismissed as frigid, simply because they cannot enjoy their true sensations, their true sexuality ... , within the norms established by the phallocratic sexual economy. Such women could embrace sexuality if they were allowed to pursue a norm of sexual delight more attuned to their bodies and their sex.

To Irigaray's critics, the relentless focus on language defeats any practical social change. In the last decade, however, she has been involved in several studies for the EU investigating the conditions of women's lives. She has also played a role in developing possible legislation for the European Parliament.

---

4   "Is $E = mc^2$ a gendered equation?" Irigaray once asked. "It may be." She explained her reasoning: "The equation is sexist because, like male-ness, it is hierarchical. In privileging the speed of light over all other speeds, it enacts a form of domination that is expressive of gendered relations."

If Irigaray made her name by drawing attention to language, Julia Kristeva (b. 1941) made hers by rejecting "essentialism." To this Bulgarian-French sociologist and literary critic, there is no such thing as femaleness in the first place. Rather than a fixed essence, Kristeva writes, femaleness is an ongoing process. All that one can do is to take a snapshot of it at any particular moment in time. She herself attempted such a snapshot in an unfortunate early book called *About Chinese Women* (1975), in which she praised Chairman Mao's Cultural Revolution. But process, to Kristeva, is also crisis. She posits an instinct called the *semiotic* that underlies self-consciousness. Resembling Freud's concept of the id, the semiotic consists of the unspoken—the thing that we are trying to say when we use language but can never get quite right. Our lived experiences, she argues, can never be completely described in language, since language is fixed in time. Think of a photograph of a speeding car. The photograph can present a perspective of the car's shape and color, but it can never tell us what it is like to drive the car, what makes it move, or how to operate it. Reality is always more complex, yet also more immediate and simple, than language can convey. It is more dynamic, yet also more static and reassuring, more richly mysterious and compelling, yet also more familiar and calming.

Kristeva calls the gap between language and reality the *space of abjection*. For her, this space is the domain of women, ethnic minorities, gays, lesbians, and the poor, since the language and value systems that create our "snapshot" of experience are inevitably male, white, heterosexual, and prosperous. To be outside the dominant structure is therefore to live in continuous crisis.

To her critics, Kristeva also distances herself from the everyday problems of women in the world—discrimination, violence, unequal pay, and control over sexual reproduction. Unless it is dedicated to programs for social change, they argue, feminism risks becoming only an interesting academic specialty. To discuss the space of abjection does little to improve the lives of Portuguese girls trapped in French textile sweatshops. It cannot help Turkish daughters who fear "honor killing" at the hands of their own fathers or brothers in Germany. Admirers of the third wave, however, have a reply: this is exactly what we are talking about. Why should women *have* to justify feminism through its results? No one, after all, discounts intellectual fields like literary criticism, art history, mathematics, or astronomy for not addressing social problems. Criticism of the irrelevance of third wave writers, they say, is simply another form of sexism.

WOMEN AND THE GLOBAL WORLD

Feminism as practical action did not cease in the 1990s. In fact, it went global. Under the leadership of institutions like the **UN Women's Conference**, the call to recognize women's rights as human rights grew louder. Meetings in

Third Wave Feminism in India   India's centuries-old caste system has proven resilient to change, which has led many oppressed groups to join forces. In this photo members of the National Federation of Dalit ("untouchable") community unite with reformers on behalf of women's rights.

Mexico City (1975), Copenhagen (1980), and Nairobi (1985) recognized the different priorities of Western and non-Western women. Western speakers, in general, had addressed economic, legal, and political rights, while representatives from the non-Western countries emphasized disease, hunger, poverty, and violence. The difference did not show a lack of caring or understanding. It showed instead how much Western women had achieved—on fundamental issues still faced every day by women in Africa, Asia, and Latin America.

A rousing call to action came in the 1995 conference held in Beijing. Hillary Rodham Clinton (b. 1947), then the First Lady of the United States, enumerated the plain horrors confronting women around the globe:

> It is a violation of human rights when babies are denied food, or drowned, or suffocated, or their spines broken, simply because they are born girls.
>
> It is a violation of human rights when women and girls are sold into the slavery of prostitution for human greed—and the kinds of reasons that are used to justify this practice should no longer be tolerated.
>
> It is a violation of human rights when women are doused with gasoline, set on fire, and burned to death because their marriage dowries are deemed too small.

It is a violation of human rights when individual women are raped in their own communities and when thousands of women are subjected to rape as a tactic or prize of war.

It is a violation of human rights when a leading cause of death worldwide among women ages 14 to 44 is the violence they are subjected to in their own homes by their own relatives.

It is a violation of human rights when young girls are brutalized by the painful and degrading practice of genital mutilation.

It is a violation of human rights when women are denied the right to plan their own families, and that includes being forced to have abortions or being sterilized against their will.

If there is one message that echoes forth from this conference, let it be that human rights are women's rights and women's rights are human rights once and for all. Let us not forget that among those rights are the right to speak freely—and the right to be heard.

The rising ethnic pluralism in Europe probably did more than the Internet to increase awareness of women's global plight. Poverty and violence are harder to ignore when they happen here rather than thousands of miles away.

The "United States of Europe" began to resemble the United States itself, not only as an institution but also in its cultural pluralism. And not everyone was pleased.

ISLAM AND ITS DISCONTENTS

Militant Islamism continued to spread throughout the 1990s and caused sharp political ruptures in North Africa and the Middle East. With the exception of Iran, most of the foment came from nongovernmental groups. Indeed, most militants opposed their own governments as much as they resented what they regarded as Western neocolonialism. These groups turned to terrorist tactics as their main form of political action, fearing that no other tactic could bring reform. The danger lay not only in the attacks themselves but also in the response of Arab governments. These states hoped to co-opt popular support for Islamic groups by manipulating the passions stirred up by the Israeli-Palestinian conflict.

The funeral of Ruhollah Khomeini in 1989 was a riot of religious enthusiasm. Tens of thousands lined the streets of Tehran, weeping and beating their breasts. Hundreds of thousands more repeated the scene in city after city. When the open coffin was brought out of the mosque in Tehran, people surged forward in a frenzy. Hoping to touch the body or to grab a piece of its shroud, they nearly tore the corpse to pieces. The scene played endlessly on European and American media, driving home viscerally the new religious energy in parts of the Islamic world. Uproar followed in Algeria and Tunisia, where the governments cracked down on Islamist parties that had gained majority support among the poor masses.

In Algeria, for example, the Islamic Salvation Front (FIS) won local and national elections with its calls for government by Islamic law, or shariah. The Algerian government voided the elections and declared martial law, triggering a civil war (1991–1992) that killed one hundred thousand. Fearing comparable scenes in their own countries, the governments of Egypt and Tunisia also suppressed Islamist groups. In Egypt President Hosni Mubarak placed every mosque under direct government control, in an effort to root out radical clerics. In Turkey, the Rifah (or Welfare) Party rose quickly, scoring local electoral victories in 1994 and two years later electing Necmettin Erbakan as prime minister.

Erbakan had the demeanor of an academic, which he was (he was a professor of mechanical engineering), but his political convictions were those of an Islamist radical. A personal manifesto that he had published, called *Millî Görüş* ("A National Vision"), warned of a decline in Islamic moral standards as a result of Muslims' too-close relations with the corrupt West. He rejected the idea of Turkey joining the European Common Market, which he disparaged as a joint Catholic and Zionist conspiracy to engulf and assimilate the Islamic world. His policies antagonized the overwhelmingly secular Turkish army, however, which pressed him to resign after only twelve months in office. Also appearing on the scene in 1994 was the Taliban (literally "students"), a group of young radicals in Afghanistan. Some had fought against the Soviet invasion; by 1996 they were in control of the country with their own ultraconservative interpretations of shariah.

Finding the legal paths to power blocked, many of these extremist groups turned to violence and made the 1990s a golden age of terrorism. The most frequently used techniques were car bombings and shootings, although by the end of the decade suicide bombings became increasingly common as well. And the victims were global. Colombia suffered the greatest number of terrorist attacks, all connected to the trade in illegal drugs. Other hot spots included India, Indonesia, Pakistan, and Sri Lanka.

The greatest number of attacks came from domestic rather than foreign enemies. Algerians fought against their own government, separatists in Northern Ireland against the United Kingdom, Kurdish rebels against the Turkish state, and Basque separatists in the Spanish capital of Madrid. In only a handful of cases was terrorism directed outward against foreign nations. Those cases, however, included Libya's brutality in France and Britain, Israel's struggle with the Palestinians, and the horrific attack on the United States on September 11, 2001 (see Map 29.4).

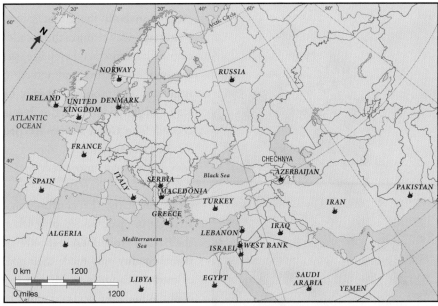

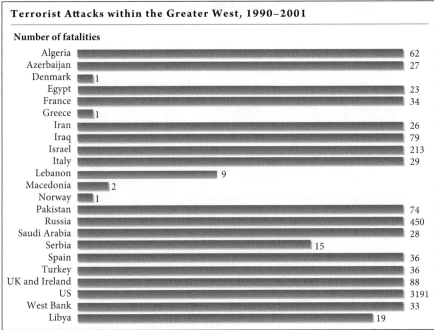

Terrorist Attacks within the Greater West, 1990–2001

Number of fatalities

Algeria	62
Azerbaijan	27
Denmark	1
Egypt	23
France	34
Greece	1
Iran	26
Iraq	79
Israel	213
Italy	29
Lebanon	9
Macedonia	2
Norway	1
Pakistan	74
Russia	450
Saudi Arabia	28
Serbia	15
Spain	36
Turkey	36
UK and Ireland	88
US	3191
West Bank	33
Libya	19

MAP 29.4   Terrorist Attacks within the Greater West, 1990–2001

BUT WHY TERRORISM?

Fringe-group terrorism seldom works. In the short term it terrifies, even paralyzes, whole populations; but it also steels their resolve not to give in to the terrorists' aims. The conflict in Northern Ireland, for example, was resolved only after terrorist

Day of Infamy   September 11, 2001. Terrorists from Osama bin Laden's group known as al-Qaeda hijacked four U.S. airliners and intentionally flew them into chosen targets. One plane crashed into the Pentagon in Washington, D.C. Two others took down the towers of the World Trade Center in lower Manhattan. The fourth crashed in rural Pennsylvania when the passengers stormed the cockpit. In this photo, the south tower has already collapsed, and the north tower has just been hit by the airplane targeting it. More than 2,700 people died, and 2,200 more were injured.

groups on both the Catholic and Protestant sides, tiring of the decades of conflict, renounced violence, surrendered their arms, and agreed to negotiate. The process proved to be long and difficult, but it finally succeeded. The **Good Friday Accord** (or Belfast Agreement), signed in May 1998, went into effect in December 1999, ending eighty years of strife. Similarly, the constitutional struggle in Spain ended only when the Basque group ETA realized that their brutality only made their goal of more freedom from Madrid less likely. When they declared a halt to terrorism in 2006, negotiations for greater autonomy began at once; by 2011 a permanent settlement had been made. If terrorism worked, Israel would have been brought to her knees decades ago.[5]

Why then did terrorism spread so viciously at the end of the 20th century? Two schools of thought predominate, one pointing to economic and the other to political factors. The economic theorists argue that the poor are attracted to terrorism out of desperation. They are recruited to become suicide bombers by wealthy elites, who use terrorism against a declared enemy as a tool to gain power and influence among their own people. These groups also build strength by courting popular support through social work and by appealing for aid outside of their country. Sustained terrorist campaigns, after all, require money—lots of money.

For example, Hamas, the Palestinian group founded in Gaza in 1987 by a poor religious scholar named Shaikh Ahmed Yassin (1937–2004), acquired financial backing from the Muslim Brotherhood. Yassin quickly brought physicians into the leadership and set to work providing free health services to the Gazan poor, which helped establish a popular base. Tens of millions of dollars annually (an estimated 50 percent of its money) comes from Saudi Arabia; perhaps

---

[5]   State-run terrorism, of course, is another matter. Testimonials could be given by any number of people—the ancient Assyrians, Attila the Hun, Genghis Khan, Tamerlane, and Stalin come to mind.

another 10 percent comes from the government in Iran. Ironically, Hamas in its first years also received financial backing from the Israeli government, which had sought to draw support away from the PLO under Yasser Arafat. As it gained financial heft, however, Hamas supplemented its charitable work with armed terrorism. Most recent Western estimates of Hamas's funding place it in the range of $400 to $500 million dollars a year.

The case of **al-Qaeda**—the group behind the September 11, 2001, assault on the World Trade Center and the Pentagon in the United States—is similar. Its founder, Osama bin Laden (1957–2011), was born to wealth, a member of the Saudi royal family. He expanded his fortune through owning and managing several large construction companies. A longtime religious conservative, bin Laden fought against the Soviet Union in Afghanistan with the mujahideen, and his politics became radicalized during the first Gulf War (1989), when he objected to "infidel armies" in the land of the Prophet. From this point on, he called the United States the greatest of the four "enemies of Islam" against which he dedicated his life. The other three were Jews, Shi'i Muslims, and unspecified "heretics."

IRA Funeral Masked members of an IRA (Irish Republican Army) honor guard carry the coffin of one of their colleagues, Bobby Sands, who died on hunger strike in a British prison in 1981. Sands had been a low-ranking member in the Provisional IRA and was arrested on a charge of illegal possession of weapons. When he and nine other IRA cellmates began their hunger strike they attracted considerable media attention—as a result of which Sands was elected a member of the British parliament to represent a district at the western edge of Northern Ireland, even though he was in prison. Sands died after sixty-six days without food.

The second leading theory sees political and social conditions as terrorism's richest source. Repressive governments and discriminatory societies, this line of thinking goes, create their own terrorists as individuals come to feel the need for dramatic action. The **Irish Republican Army** (IRA) in Northern Ireland is the best example. Originating in the 1910s, the IRA had as its goal a single objective—to overthrow what it regarded as 750 years of English tyranny over the Irish people. IRA fighters saw themselves as champions of Irish freedom and of Catholic vengeance on Protestant persecutors. Consider, too, the Kurdish PKK (Partiya Karkerên Kurdistan, or Kurdistan Workers' Party), which Abdullah Öcalan (b. 1948) founded in 1978. Nursing an intense resentment of the Republic of Turkey, the PKK fought to gain independence for the Turkish Kurds. It also had the long-term aim of a united Kurdistan, made up of the Kurds in northern Iran and Iraq too. Financial support poured in from Syria, which hoped to profit from Turkey's trouble. Later the bulk of its funding came from extortion, racketeering, and the drug trade.

> If a strong-armed regime can persuade its subjects that the real cause of their misery is foreign meddling, then the repressed people will lash out against that enemy. In this scenario the tyrannical authority casts itself as the true champion of the people, its only alternative to corruption and humiliation from abroad.

However, a political explanation of terrorism must be more subtle than a simple formula like "terrorism as revenge." If a strong-armed regime can persuade its subjects that the real cause of their misery is foreign meddling, then the repressed people will lash out against that enemy. In this scenario the tyrannical authority casts itself as the true champion of the people, its only alternative to corruption and humiliation from abroad.

In the case of Syria, for example, which is perhaps the most repressive Arab regime of the last forty years, the Assad family has held control, even though it represents the small, and largely detested, Alawite minority. In fact, it has turned its minority status into its strength, by building up a national myth, thanks to a steady diet of anti-Semitic and anti-American propaganda. Only the Assads, they repeat, can hold at bay the strife between Arab tribes and sects within Syria. Only they can stand up to Zionists and Western imperialists.

In an editorial published in *Tishreen* (September 16, 2003), Syria's largest and state-run newspaper, Ghazi Hussein declared that the Holocaust was an invention of the Jews—a plan they had hatched with the Nazis. Why arrange to have six million fellow Jews killed? So that the world will feel sorry for the survivors and allow them to create the Zionist state:

> Zionism lurks in the darkest chapter of [Israel's] history, and invents fictions about Jewish suffering in the "Nazi Holocaust" which it then inflates astronomically.... The fundamental problem is not the fact that

the Zionists attempt to re-write history but that Zionist groups use this false history to deceive international opinion, win the world's sympathy, and then engage in blackmail. . . . Two goals are paramount to Israel and the Zionist organizations that support it: to get more money out of Germany and the other European entities, and to use the myth of the Holocaust as a sword held over the necks of anyone who opposes Zionism and to accuse them of anti-Semitism. . . . The truth though is that Israel herself—the supposed heir of Holocaust victims everywhere—has committed in the past and still commits today crimes much worse than anything supposedly done to them by the Nazis.

Hussein was not a random commentator. At the time he wrote the article he was both a legal advisor to the Syrian government and the head of the political section of the Palestinian Liberation Organization's office in Damascus.

Similar stories run in other newspapers, like *Balsam*, published in the West Bank by the Palestinian Red Crescent, and appear regularly on Syria's state-operated radio. The thuggish rule of Saddam Hussein in Iraq used the same technique, blaming the country's woes on American imperialists and Muslim-hating Zionists.

Both the economic and political interpretations of terrorism have had their followers. Europeans have often favored the first, the United States the second. Some, however, have raised a third possibility—that Islam itself promotes violence as a way to attain martyrdom. This sentiment is found more frequently in the United States than in Europe—or at least it is given freer expression in America. Predictably, it also feeds the belief of many Muslims that the West is biased against Islam. Whatever the causes, bitter discontent and terrorism show no signs of abating.

ECONOMIC GLOBALIZATION

Protesters gathered in Seattle in 1999, in advance of the scheduled ministerial conference of the **World Trade Organization** (WTO), an intergovernmental organization seeking to liberalize trade between nations. They blocked intersections and organized large street demonstrations. Speeches and worker protest songs rang out from street corners. Some protestors set fire to dumpsters. Others broke shop windows and halted almost the entire city's commerce. Police reacted with pepper spray, tear gas, and rubber bullets in order to clear the streets. In the end, police arrested over six hundred people. The disruption of business and the task of cleaning up cost the city over $20 million.

Protesting Globalization A protestor against the World Trade Organization, one of the institutions most closely identified with economic globalization.

The "Battle of Seattle" drew attention to the intense emotions surrounding economic globalization—the development of a single, interconnected global market. A global market is much like the digital Internet, a network of networks, crossing all borders of nationality, language, culture, and class. Globalization itself was nothing new. One can think of it as an extension of long-standing regional or continental trade. The arc dates back at least to the wave of European imperialism in the 1880s and 1890s. Some historians of antiquity, fancifully enough, date the movement all the way back to the Sumerian era, when the grain-rich Mesopotamian south was linked with northernmost reaches of the Fertile Crescent, rich in iron ore. What is new today are of course modern systems of communication and transportation. Strawberries harvested one day in California can appear the next day in markets in Tokyo.

> What is new today are of course modern systems of communication and transportation. Strawberries harvested one day in California can appear the next day in markets in Tokyo.

The WTO, formed in 1995, promotes international trade by resolving disputes between nations (see Map 29.5). It also implements trade agreements between nations and, most controversially, oversees the national trade policies of individual countries. The protestors in Seattle represented labor unions, environmental groups, women's organizations, immigration activists, and others. Their

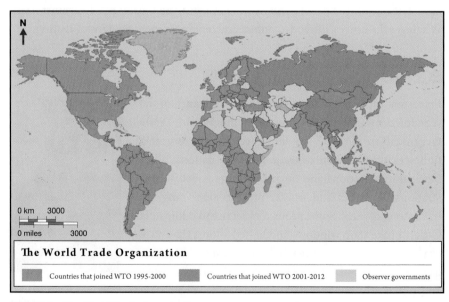

| The World Trade Organization |
| Countries that joined WTO 1995-2000   Countries that joined WTO 2001-2012   Observer governments |

MAP 29.5 **The World Trade Organization**

opposition to the WTO—indeed to globalization itself—sprang from many issues, but all ones related to the differing standards and legal protections between countries. Workers in countries like China and India do not have the same rights as American workers in regard to wages, work conditions, and employment benefits. It is therefore to any manufacturer's advantage to shift its production overseas. The savings in labor costs vastly outweigh the expense of transporting their finished goods. Some countries offer tax benefits to companies that other countries cannot afford. Still others do not require industry to observe the same environmental protection. The uneven international playing field represented a danger to the standards of living that Westerners had come to expect. Hence the trouble in Seattle.

Globalization had been opposed before, but never in such a dramatic way. More demonstrations followed, all across the United States, in opposition to the World Bank and the International Monetary Fund, two institutions viewed as the financiers of globalization. Opposition to globalization occurred in Europe too, though generally in quieter forms.

World population is rising sharply and will continue to do so until 2050 (see Figure 29.1). And that means a steady rise in the demand for everything from food and textiles to pharmaceuticals and computer components. Yet the

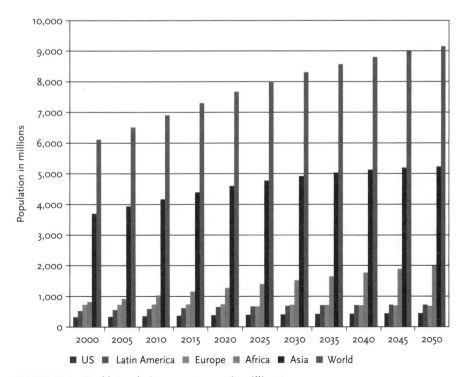

FIGURE 29.1   **World Population, 2000–2050 (in millions)**

populations of Europe and the United States are stagnating. Between 2010 and 2050 the U.S. population is projected to grow from 300 million to 400 million (a 33 percent growth, compared to the global increase of 100 percent), and the population of Europe will actually decline from 700 million to 690 million.[6] For Western corporations that want to expand their businesses, the choices are clear—either import workers (which means immigration, whether legal or illegal) or export jobs. Or both. And in their varying ways, institutions like the WTO, the IMF, and the World Bank help them do just that.

Both responses to the demographic gap between the West and the world—exporting jobs and immigrating workers—present political and social challenges. Our last chapter looks to the future.

WHO, WHAT, WHERE

al-Qaeda	Organization of Petroleum
credit default swap	Exporting Countries
European Union	Treaty of Rome
Good Friday Accord	UN Women's Conference
Irish Republican Army	World Trade Organization
Kyoto Protocol	

SUGGESTED READINGS

Primary Sources

Fukuyama, Francis. *The End of History and the Last Man.*

Irigaray, Luce. *The Ethics of Sexual Difference.*

Khomeini, Ruhollah. *Islamic Government.*

National Commission on Terrorist Attacks upon the United States. *The 9/11 Commission Report* (2004).

Rushdie, Salman. *The Satanic Verses.*

---

[6]   In 2010, the United States and Europe held 15 percent of the world's population; by 2050, they may hold as little as 8.5 percent.

Anthologies

Freedman, Estelle B., ed. *The Essential Feminist Reader* (2007).

Kamrava, Mehran, ed. *The New Voices of Islam: Rethinking Politics and Modernity—A Reader* (2007).

Oliver, Kelly, ed. *The Portable Kristeva* (2002).

Roded, Ruth, ed. *Women in Islam and the Middle East: A Reader* (2008).

Volpi, Frédéric, ed. *Political Islam: A Critical Reader* (2010).

Studies

Berman, Eli. *Radical, Religious, and Violent: The New Economics of Terrorism* (2009).

Budgeon, Shelley. *Third Wave Feminism and the Politics of Gender in Late Modernity* (2011).

Castells, Manuel. *The Information Age: Economy, Society, and Culture* (2009–2011).

Garcelon, Marc. *Revolutionary Passage: From Soviet to Post-Soviet Russia, 1985–2000* (2005).

Frieden, Jeffry A. *Global Capitalism: Its Fall and Rise in the Twentieth Century* (2007).

Gillis, Stacy, Gillian Howie, and Rebecca Munford, ed. *Third Wave Feminism: A Critical Exploration* (2007).

Hoffman, Bruce. *Inside Terrorism* (2006).

Hoogvelt, Ankie. *Globalization and the Postcolonial World: The New Political Economy of Development* (2001).

Judt, Tony. *Postwar: A History of Europe since 1945* (2005).

Keddie, Nikki R. *Modern Iran: Roots and Results of Revolution* (2006).

Kenney, Padraic. *The Burdens of Freedom: Eastern Europe since 1989* (2006).

Krueger, Alan B. *What Makes a Terrorist: Economics and the Roots of Terrorism* (2008).

Laqueur, Walter. *The Last Days of Europe: Epitaph for an Old Continent* (2009).

Malik, Kenan. *From Fatwa to Jihad: The Rushdie Affair and Its Aftermath* (2010).

Mittelman, James H. *The Globalization Syndrome: Transformation and Resistance* (2000).

Mockaitis, Thomas R. *The "New" Terrorism: Myths and Reality* (2008).

Mottahedeh, Roy. *The Mantle of the Prophet: Religion and Politics in Iran* (2008).

Post, Jerrold M. *The Mind of the Terrorist: The Psychology of Terrorism from the IRA to al-Qaeda* (2008).

Rashid, Ahmed. *Jihad: The Rise of Militant Islam in Central Asia* (2002).

Reid, T. R. *The United States of Europe: The New Superpower and the End of American Supremacy* (2005).

Roy, Sara. *Failing Peace: Gaza and the Palestinian-Israeli Conflict* (2006).

———. *Hamas and Civil Society in Gaza: Engaging the Islamist Social Sector* (2011).

Sinno, Abdulkader, ed. *Muslims in Western Politics* (2008).

Suri, Jeremi. *Power and Protest: Global Revolution and the Rise of Détente* (2005).

Westad, Odd Arne. *The Global Cold War: Third World Interventions and the Making of Our Times* (2007).

Zürcher, Christoph. *The Post-Soviet Wars: Rebellion, Ethnic Conflict, and Nationhood in the Caucasus* (2009).

For additional resources, including maps, primary sources, visuals, web links, and quizzes, please go to **www.oup.com/us/backman.**

CHAPTER 30

Hearts and Minds Going Forward

2001–Present

On September 11, 2001, long-simmering tensions between the West and the Muslim Middle East came to a full boil. And well after the "9/11" terrorist attacks on New York and Washington, DC, the violence kept coming. Hardly a week passed in 2002 without a suicide bomber maiming innocents in Israel; in 2003 the pace slowed to perhaps one massacre every other week. In March 2004 a coordinated sequence of bombs on train lines in Madrid killed 191 and wounded more than two thousand innocents. On July 7, 2005, or "7/7" in British common parlance, a team of bombers struck London's public transport system, killing fifty-two and injuring over seven hundred. Only a few months later, in September 2005, a Danish newspaper published a dozen cartoons that depicted the Prophet Muhammad in ways that Muslims around the world found offensive and blasphemous. One Danish cartoon depicted the Prophet with a black turban that was actually a lit bomb. Scores of angry demonstrations took place, and arsonists set the Danish embassies in Beirut, Damascus, and Tehran aflame. A wealthy regional politician in India offered a $10 million reward to any Muslim who beheaded the cartoonist who had drawn the most offensive of the cartoons.

DISTRIBUTION OF WEALTH IN THE GREATER WEST

A country's GDP per capita as percentage of world average ($10,500):
over 400%   100–200%   25–50%   under 10%
200–400%   50–100%   10–25%

◄ **The Cultures of the West, 2011.** This street scene from Marseilles captures some of the problems and promise of Greater Western society today. In the background stands the Église des Réformés, looking almost tangled in the utility lines that cross the sky. In the foreground a diverse group of women stroll by, chiefly involved in their cellphone conversations. Cars move past. Though a bustling scene, it evinces an odd atmosphere of isolation and disconnectedness.

- "Why Do They Hate Us?"
- War and Peace, from the Balkans to Palestine
- Israel, Palestine, and the Arab Spring
- Veiled Threats
- Debt, Taxes, and Liberty
- Free Market? What Free Market?
- What Is the Greater West Now?

CHAPTER OUTLINE

"Americans are asking," said U.S. President George W. Bush, "'Why do they hate us?'" Terrorism, though, was not by any means the whole story—perhaps not even the most important one when it comes to understanding Islam or the future of the West. The challenges include independence movements and recovery from a war in eastern Europe, hopes for strengthening of the European Union, a second Iraq war, and the status of Muslim women. The turmoil includes the glory and optimism of an "Arab Spring," a deep economic downturn, and conflict over taxation and liberty—especially between conservatives and liberals in the United States. Ultimately, adaption is underway in Europe and the Greater West.

"WHY DO THEY HATE US?"

The political resolution of the problems in Northern Ireland and in Spain largely ended the problem of domestic terrorism within Europe after 2001, except for a few fringe groups. The tensions with Europe's immigrant Muslim population became largely a matter of passionate but nonviolent demonstrations and occasional street crime. This relative quiet, though, was not so much a calming of grievances. Well-funded terrorist groups like al-Qaeda and Islamic Jihad simply had their hands full, thanks to U.S.-led wars in Afghanistan and Iraq and the spread of military activities into Pakistan. Meanwhile in Israel and the West Bank arsonists, assassins, and bombers drove the casualty counts on both sides ever higher. An Egyptian terrorist group with connections to al-Qaeda launched a bomb attack in 2005 on the popular resort city of Sharm el-Sheikh on the Red Sea, killing eighty-eight and wounding more than two hundred.

As the killings continued, non-Muslim majorities in Europe and the United States reacted in horror. That was sensible enough, but many of them also reacted less sensibly, by seeing all Muslims as terrorists, potential terrorists, or supporters of terrorism. Racism lies behind such attitudes, but so does a willing

CHAPTER TIMELINE

1994–2001
War in the Balkans; start of the first war in Chechnya

2001
United States invades Afghanistan

2004
Terrorist attack kills 191 in Madrid

1999–2009
Second war in Chechnya

2003
United States invades Iraq

2005
London suffers terrorist attack, killing 152

ignorance—and, in Europe, a greater indifference to religion. Few non-Muslim Westerners knew much about Islam prior to 9/11 and 7/7, and surprisingly few are better informed even ten years later.

Both the best and worst instincts of Western society were on display only ten days after the 9/11 attacks. In his speech to Congress, President George W. Bush was somber, dignified, and powerful. Yet his address also reflected widely held ambivalence about the Muslim world.

> The terrorists practice a fringe form of Islamic extremism that has been rejected by Muslim scholars and the vast majority of Muslim clerics. A fringe movement that perverts the peaceful teaching of Islam. The terrorists' directive commands them to kill Christians and Jews, to kill all Americans and make no distinctions among military and civilians, including women and children. This group and its leader, a person named Osama bin Laden, are linked to many other organizations in different countries, including the Egyptian Islamic Jihad and the Islamic Movement of Uzbekistan.
>
> There are thousands of these terrorists in more than sixty countries. They are recruited from their own nations and neighborhoods and brought to camps in places like Afghanistan, where they are trained in the tactics of terror. They are sent back to their homes or sent to hide in countries around the world to plot evil and destruction. The leadership of al-Qaeda has great influence in Afghanistan and supports the Taliban regime in controlling most of that country.
>
> In Afghanistan we see al-Qaeda's vision for the world. Afghanistan's people have been brutalized. Many are starving and many have fled. Women are not allowed to attend school. You can be jailed for owning a television. Religion can be practiced only as their leaders dictate. A man can be jailed in Afghanistan if his beard is not long enough.

2007
Hamas assumes
control of Gaza

2008
Israel invades
Gaza

2008–2009
Economic downturn and
financial crisis in the
Greater West

2010
Completion of withdrawl of
Western armed forces from
Iraq; beginning of Arab Spring

2011
U.S. special forces kill
Bin-Laden; Libya falls to
rebel forces, Qaddafi killed

2012
Deepening debt
crisis in Euro Zone

After stating his demand that the Taliban then in control of Afghanistan hand over the al-Qaeda terrorists or else face retribution, he then addressed a few words to peaceful Muslims everywhere:

> I also want to speak tonight directly to Muslims throughout the world. We respect your faith. It's practiced freely by many millions of Americans and by millions more in countries that America counts as friends. Its teachings are good and peaceful. And those who commit evil in the name of Allah blaspheme the name of Allah. The terrorists are traitors to their own faith, trying in effect to hijack Islam itself.
>
> The enemy of America is not our many Muslim friends. It is not our many Arab friends. Our enemy is a radical network of terrorists and every government that supports them.
>
> Our war on terror begins with al-Qaeda, but it does not end there. It will not end until every terrorist group of global reach has been found, stopped, and defeated.
>
> Americans are asking, "Why do they hate us?"
>
> They hate what they see right here in this chamber, a democratically elected government. Their leaders are self-appointed. They hate our freedoms, our freedom of religion, our freedom of speech, our freedom to vote and assemble and disagree with each other. They want to overthrow existing governments in many Muslim countries, such as Egypt, Saudi Arabia, and Jordan. They want to drive Israel out of the Middle East. They want to drive Christians and Jews out of vast regions of Asia and Africa.
>
> These terrorists kill not merely to end lives but to disrupt and end a way of life. With every atrocity they hope that America grows fearful, retreating from the world and forsaking our friends. They stand against us because we stand in their way. We're not deceived by their pretenses to piety. We have seen their kind before. They are the heirs of all the murderous ideologies of the 20th century. By sacrificing human life to serve their radical visions, by abandoning every value except the will to power, they follow in the path of fascism, Nazism and totalitarianism. And they will follow that path all the way to where it ends: in history's unmarked grave of discarded lies.

The 21st century begins with the Greater West on a new learning curve. It opens on societies that have had too little contact between them and increasingly find themselves as neighbors and colleagues.

In fact, the Muslim world in general does not hate democracy, human rights, or free speech; it hates only what it perceives as Western hypocrisy about them.

Demonstrating for Religious Freedom   Muslim women and girls demonstrate, in 2004, for the right to wear Islamic headscarves in publicly funded schools. French law requires that public schools be entirely secular, which means, among other things, a ban on religious clothing and religious symbols (Jewish skullcaps and Christian crucifixes are likewise forbidden). The protestors carry a banner that calls for "Equality" and "Fraternity"—echoes of the call-to-arms of the French Revolution of 1789. Critics of the Muslim protests point out that demonstrators have left out the first word in the call-to-arms, "Liberty."

How committed is the United States to democracy, Muslims have asked, when it overthrew the democratically elected prime minister of Iran (Mohammad Mossadegh, r. 1951–1953) and installed an autocrat like the shah, Mohammed Reza Pahlavi? How committed is it when it lavished military aid on a dictatorial regime like Hosni Mubarak's in Egypt? How dedicated to religious freedom is a country like France when it forbids Muslim schoolgirls to wear the traditional covering, the hijab? How committed to freedom of speech is Germany when it forbids, on penalty of imprisonment, the expression of doubt about the extent of the Holocaust? In the minds of many Muslims, we have been weighed in our own balance and found wanting.

The 21st century begins with the Greater West on a new learning curve. It opens on societies that have had too little contact between them and increasingly find themselves as neighbors and colleagues. The need to deal with Islamist terrorism is urgent, but a more difficult challenge awaits us all—to move from ignorance and indifference to understanding and acceptance.

WAR AND PEACE, FROM THE BALKANS TO PALESTINE

"The next great European war will begin over some damned foolish incident in the Balkans." That bit of wisdom, sometimes attributed to Otto von Bismarck, predicted the start of World War I. It also presaged opinions in much of the West about the end of the 20th century. Unfortunately, those opinions failed to understand or foresee 21st-century nationalist passion and Muslim rage beyond that region (see Map 30.1).

Nationalist passions in the Balkans had been kept in check by the heavy hand of totalitarian rulers. After the collapse of Communism, they sprang back to poisonous life. Serbs, Croats, Bosnians, and Slovenians after 1991 all wanted to secede from the political union that the Communists had forced on them, but a demographic mixing had taken place during Yugoslavia's forty years of existence. It was impossible to draw satisfying political borders when every configuration left remnants of some group as a minority among others.

Of all the peoples involved, the Serbs proved the most willing, even eager, to resort to war. Under their leader Slobodan Milosevic (1941–2006), who commanded what was left of the old Yugoslav army (the fourth largest military machine on the Continent), the Serbs began a series of wars against their neighbors. They hoped to establish a Greater Serbia that would unite all ethnic Serbs, to reclaim Balkan land claimed as their patrimony, and to purge those lands of non-Serbs. In 1994, after Serbian soldiers had massacred tens of thousands of Bosnians and driven hundreds of thousands more into exile, NATO forces finally took action with bombing raids against Serb artillery. Eventually the United Nations brought in peacekeeping forces. These wars lasted until 1995 and witnessed many scenes of horror and near-genocide. A peace deal was finally negotiated with the help of the United States, but the Serbs soon opened a new front in Kosovo and Albania, extending the violence until 2001. Milosevic himself was arrested in that year and brought to The Hague to face trial for crimes against humanity. He died in prison before the trial had run its course.

Apart from bookending the 20th century with Balkan violence, the wars here added fuel to Muslim rage against the West. The Bosnians, who were the chief victims of Serb massacre, are a predominantly Muslim people.[1] Would the European and American powers have waited two years to come to the rescue if the Bosnians had been Christians and the Serbs were Muslims? To countless Muslims around the world, the wholesale slaughter of the Bosnians took place with the silent complicity of the West. The mass murder of eight thousand Bosnian men and boys at Srebrenica in July 1995 would never have occurred, they insisted, had the religions of attackers and victims been reversed.

---

[1]   Bosnians are the largest Islamic population in Europe after the Turks.

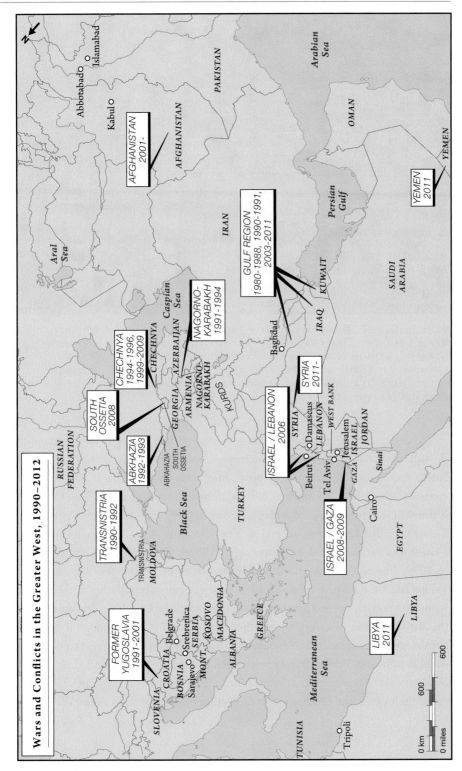

MAP 30.1   Wars and Conflicts in the Greater West, 1990–2012

Mourning the Dead   In July 1995, soldiers of the Serbian army massacred eight thousand Muslim men and boys in the Bosnian city of Srebrenica. The massacre was preceded by several days of horrendous torture of civilians, including the systematic rape of Bosnian women, even as a Dutch-staffed UN peacekeeping force looked on. Here a Srebrenica survivor, Hajra Èatiae, who lost her husband and son in the attack, helps to maintain a photo archive of the victims.

Many critics perceived a similar anti-Muslim bias in the West's reaction to the warfare between Russia and Chechnya. Chechnya is a Muslim territory in the North Caucasus, with a native population of roughly 1.5 million. As the USSR eroded in the 1980s, a Chechen independence movement arose. The Chechen National Congress achieved independence in 1991, but only three years later Russia sent in a large army to end it. The war lasted from 1994 to 1996, when a truce was declared. War broke out again shortly thereafter, lasting from 1999 to 2009. The conflicts were marked by atrocities on both sides. Russia proved unable to bring the province to heel despite enormously superior numbers and weaponry and its reckless artillery bombardment. The Chechens could not drive the Russians from the region, but they proved ruthless and adept at terrorist bombings in Moscow and elsewhere. Muslims felt a lack of interest in the West in their suffering. Europe barely responded to Russia's heavy-handedness, but it condemned the terrorism that many Chechens felt was their only option. As if to prove their point, the Chechen War drew little media attention in the West.

Two wars in the Persian Gulf, however, claimed the attention of the entire world. The first war (1990–1991) was a tense but brief affair. Iraq's ruler, Saddam Hussein, deeply in debt after his disastrous war with neighboring Iran (1980–1988), needed new oil revenues and invaded the tiny but wealthy Gulf nation of Kuwait. Kuwait was in fact one of Iraq's two principal creditors, the other being Saudi Arabia. International condemnation of Iraq came swiftly, and in seven months a U.S.-led coalition drove the Iraqis from Kuwait and established a "no-fly zone" over southern Iraq. Its goal was to protect Kuwait from fresh attack and to protect Shi'i Iraqis from retribution by Saddam Hussein's Sunni army. The coalition's forces were mostly American soldiers, with the next largest contingents from the United Kingdom and the Arab League.[2] Saudi Arabia was the staging post of the coalition's armies, and it paid the bulk of the war's cost. Both facts had dramatic consequences, since they drew the ire of Osama bin Laden, the head of al-Qaeda. They became his justification for launching the 9/11 and 7/7 terrorist attacks on the United States and United Kingdom.

The United States launched air assaults against the Taliban regime in Afghanistan in October 2001, since the Taliban had granted refuge to al-Qaeda for years. Within a matter a weeks the Taliban were crushed, although Osama bin Laden escaped into Pakistan. Rather than focusing on building up the shaky new government in Afghanistan, however, the United States under President George W. Bush turned its attention to Saddam Hussein in Iraq. He had been behind the 9/11 attacks, Bush argued, and was stockpiling advanced chemical, biological, and perhaps even nuclear weapons. In March 2003, after months of diplomatic pressure and posturing, the United States invaded Iraq—but no link between Iraq and al-Qaeda was ever found. Indeed, Hussein had long been an active hunter of groups like al-Qaeda, since their religious ideology undermined his secular Ba'athism. Nor were any of the advanced weapons systems ever found, which left the United States and its British allies open to charges of willful war making. Most Iraqis cheered the capture, trial, and execution of Hussein, but few felt that his downfall was worth the price of the invasion.

Charges of imperialism were levied against the West throughout the Arab world, charges supported by critics within the West. Accusations of oil theft, war crimes, corruption, and high-handedness swirled around the Western forces, and scandals only added to the West's public-relations difficulties with the Muslim world. American forces mistreated Iraqi prisoners at the Abu Ghraib prison

---

[2]   The Arab League consists of Egypt, Morocco, Oman, Qatar, Saudi Arabia, Syria, and the United Arab Emirates.

Public Relations Difficulties   US efforts to restore order in Iraq after the overthrow of Saddam Hussein confronted one challenge after another. One of the most infamous episodes was the public release of photos showing the torture of Iraqis held in the US-controlled prison at Abu Ghraib in 2004. This photos shows two Iraqi men resting in the shade provided by a wall—a wall bearing graffiti criticizing the US behavior. "That freedom for Bosh" castigates the president's policies.

complex, at a military facility in Guantanamo Bay in Cuba, and at secret prisons operated by the CIA. Such episodes undercut the positive image the West tried to create for its involvements in the region, which it sees as efforts to bring democracy to nations that have known only tribalism and corrupt dictatorship.

In 2007 Great Britain got a new prime minister, Gordon Brown (2007–2010), and one year later President Barack Obama was elected in the United States. Under these two leaders the West began to withdraw its troops from Iraq, bringing to a gradual end (in October 2010) a struggle that had lasted for seven years. A democratic government under a new constitution now runs Iraq, but it remains to be seen if it can withstand the separatist leanings of parts of the country and the continued attacks of Islamist splinter groups. The United States temporarily boosted its involvement in Afghanistan, in a last-ditch effort to bring down the Taliban—before effecting a transition to civilian Afghan rule under its president, Hamid Karzai.

Meanwhile, al-Qaeda's relocation to Pakistan opened a new front in the war against terrorism. Pakistan's diplomatic position had always been delicate, since its chief diplomatic and military concern has always been its troubled relations with India, to the east. The issue of Afghanistan was important to the Pakistani government chiefly as a way to coax military and economic aid out of the United States. That led the government in Islamabad to play a double game of claiming to oppose al-Qaeda and the Taliban, even while privately giving them aid and refuge. American support for Pervez Musharraf, the head of the Pakistani military and president of the country from 2001 to 2008, fueled claims about Western hypocrisy—since Musharraf had come to power in 1999 by staging a military takeover of a democratically elected government. On May 2, 2011, U.S. special forces launched a secret raid on a secure compound in Abbottabad in Pakistan, where it found and killed Osama bin Laden, who was still directing the activities of al-Qaeda after ten years on the run. His discovery at a safe house only a short distance from a Pakistani military academy prompted questions about Pakistan's role in harboring him.

ISRAEL, PALESTINE, AND THE ARAB SPRING

Meanwhile, the conflict between Israel and the Palestinians showed no sign of nearing resolution. In 2007 Palestinian leadership split between two rival factions—the Fatah party under Mahmoud Abbas, which administers the West Bank, and Hamas, which took control of the Gaza Strip. This split introduced an unexpected difficulty into the peace process, for Hamas, despite its genuine social and charitable work, is a terrorist organization, on account of which Israel steadfastly refuses to negotiate with it. Yet Hamas rose to power through open election by the Gazan Palestinians. To Israel, the way in which Hamas won power is irrelevant. Above all, what matters most is what the group has done in the past with the power it had: it has murdered and maimed thousands of innocent Israelis.

But there is more. Since 2007 Hamas has actively encouraged the radicalization of the populace. It instituted an official "Virtue Committee" whose members patrol the streets in search of anyone not observing strict rules of sexual segregation, dress, and comportment. Verbal harassment and physical coercion are common tactics. Critics have likened their actions to the excesses of the Taliban in Afghanistan.

For three weeks at the end of 2008 and the start of 2009, Israel conducted a surprise bombing campaign against Hamas called Operation Cast Lead. Inevitably, interpretations of it vary widely. Hamas and Fatah claim that the Israeli action was a callous act of aggression that killed well over a thousand Palestinian civilians and virtually destroyed Gaza's infrastructure. Israel maintains that it launched a precisely limited series of strikes against known sites of Hamas's terrorist activity and provided warnings in advance to local residents to clear each target area. A flawed UN investigation into the campaign was widely criticized, leaving the dispute alive.

Finally, a chain of spontaneous popular rebellions against corruption, oppression, and ineptitude spread through the Arab world starting in December 2010. The first eruption occurred in Tunisia, where a local street vendor, Muhammad Bouazizi, who was in despair after years of mistreatment by local officials, set himself ablaze in a busy intersection and killed himself. Crowds took to the street by the hundreds of thousands to protest the actions of the government. They saw Bouazizi as a martyr to civic freedom, and they chanted over and over their demand for vengeance. After attempting to calm the protests, the Tunisian president, who had held dictatorial authority for twenty-three years, fled to France, and a new government came to power. Only a week later the government in neighboring Algeria surrendered the emergency powers it had held for nearly twenty years.

Lebanon and Jordan came next, with crowds demanding, and receiving, new parliamentary regimes. Demonstrations in Sudan prompted its controversial president, Omar al-Bashir, to announce that he would step down from office at the end of his current term. Apart from his oppression of the people in Darfur, he is believed to have embezzled as much as $8 billion of the nation's funds.[3] Bashir is charged with crimes against humanity, including genocide, by the International Criminal Court. In Oman and Saudi Arabia, protestors won economic concessions and the right to hold elections to fill local government offices and to initiate legislation at that level.

The most spectacular revolt yet occurred in Egypt, where massive demonstrations in Cairo's Tahrir Square in 2011 brought down the forty-year dictatorship of Hosni Mubarak (in June 2012 he was sentenced to life in prison). The military took temporary control of the government, dissolved the parliament, and suspended the constitution. Subsequent mass movements arose in Morocco, Yemen, Iraq, Bahrain, and Kuwait and won at least a partial lifting of heavy-handed governments, the shifting of cabinets, release of political prisoners, and certain economic concessions. The reforms are ongoing though the prospect for the future is unclear.

The only Arab regimes to have mounted prolonged resistance to uprisings have been Libya and Syria, both nations where the government's military forces remained reliably on the regime's side. In each case, civilians withstood months of repressive measures—beatings and arrests, artillery bombardments, systematic rape, and the cutting off of food, water, and electricity. Rebels against Libya's Muammar Qaddafi finally defeated the regime after NATO airstrikes paralyzed the dictator's defenses, which allowed the rebels to stage a decisive land campaign into the capital of Tripoli. Qaddafi himself was captured and killed by a rebel mob when he fled to his home town of Sirte in October 2011.

---

[3]   The atrocities in Darfur have killed as many as four hundred thousand people and left 2.5 million homeless.

The Arab Spring   Tawakkol Karman, the leader of the organization "Women Journalists without Chains," protests against the government of Yemen in 2011. Yemen's president, Ali Abdullah Saleh, had been in power since 1978; he was forced to resign his office in early 2012.

Government intransigence has been even stronger in Syria, where the Assad regime, as of summer 2012, has not only held out but has violated UN-brokered cease-fires and intensified its resistance. The political and military situation in Syria, however, is considerably more complicated than it was in Libya. Syria's historical role as the original center of the Islamic empire and its proximity to Israel (with which it has had officially hostile yet surprisingly stable relations since the 1990s), together with international concerns to have an Arab counterweight to the regional ambitions of Iran, have disinclined groups like the UN, NATO, or the Arab League to provide direct support to the rebels.

These rebellions are known collectively as the **Arab Spring**. They are taking place in the ethnically Arab lands and represent part of the broad awakening of Arab national identity and pride (see Map 30.2). A revitalized and demo-

Islamist groups have inevitably been involved at the margins, but the Arab Spring has been overwhelmingly a civic movement, a demand of the masses for control over their own lives.

cratic belt of Arab nations across North Africa and throughout the Middle East could do much to help the people of the region prosper. As things have stood, the immense oil wealth of the area has been monopolized by either royal or dictatorial families and their cronies. Freer societies could mean not only a broader sharing of that wealth but more varied and diverse economies that

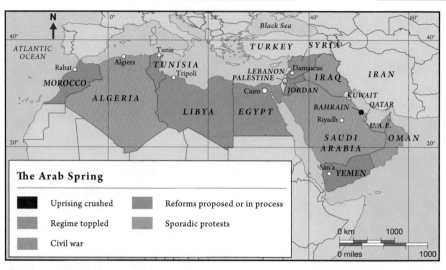

MAP 30.2   The Arab Spring

would help strong democratic traditions to take root. At the same time, the re-bellions have been secular. Islamist groups have inevitably been involved at the margins, but the Arab Spring has been overwhelmingly a civic movement, a demand of the masses for control over their own lives. If they can succeed, and in their success remove one of the chief factors behind the desperate appeal of radical Islamism, the possibility of a real, lasting, and just peace in the region could be within reach.

VEILED THREATS

The future of its women may yet determine the fate of Greater Western society in the 21st century. Despite discouraging trends in places like India and China, where gender-selective abortion thrives despite its official illegality, women still outnumber men and comprise the bulk of global society. Within the Greater West, however, a sharp divide exists in how women are treated in society.

The **World Economic Forum** (WEF) publishes an annual "Report on the Global Gender Gap," using statistics provided by the member countries them-selves, that examines the status of women worldwide. The reports examine five criteria in each country: the level of economic opportunity available to women; educational opportunity and attainment; the availability of health care, whether publicly or privately funded; levels of gender-specific crimes like rape; and the degree of political empowerment, which includes female participation in gov-ernment, the right to vote, and equal treatment under the law. The 2010 report highlights and quantifies the divide within the Greater West. Fourteen of the highest-scoring twenty nations—that is, those countries that provide the greatest equality and respect to women—are members of the European West. Fifteen of the lowest-scoring twenty nations are Muslim nations.

The WEF's criteria can be, and often are, argued to have a pro-Western bias. They represent the values of the UN Declaration of Human Rights rather than those of the Cairo Declaration. They assume that individually based gender values matter as much as family cohesion, for example, and that personal independence is superior to communal stability and cultural tradition.

The Muslim West treats women and girls profoundly differently than men and boys. In the most conservative lands women may not vote, drive a car, give testimony in court, or hold a job. Education for girls, when available at all, is often limited to the elementary level and is focused on religious schooling. In many Islamic countries the law allows women greater choice in deciding whom to marry, and it has liberalized the criteria that allow women to seek divorce. Yet domestic violence remains commonplace. It may be technically illegal, as in the case of **honor killings**—the deaths of women who are thought to have tarnished the family's reputation. Even then, however, the violence is seldom prosecuted and frequently

TABLE 30.1 **The Global Gender Gap**

20 BEST NATIONS FOR WOMEN	20 WORST NATIONS FOR WOMEN
Iceland	Nepal
Norway	Lebanon
Finland	Qatar
Sweden	Nigeria
New Zealand	Algeria
Ireland	Jordan
Denmark	Ethiopia
Lesotho	Oman
The Philippines	Iran
Switzerland	Syria
Spain	Egypt
South Africa	Turkey
Germany	Morocco
Belgium	Benin
United Kingdom	Saudi Arabia
Sri Lanka	Ivory Coast
The Netherlands	Mali
Latvia	Pakistan
United States	Chad
Canada	Yemen

goes unpunished.[4] In 2003 the government of Pakistan alone documented over twelve hundred such killings. Thanks to the Internet, the practice is far harder to overlook. Gruesome videos of women being beaten, whipped, and stoned to death are readily available to anyone with the stomach to watch them.

The phenomenon has spread to the West with the rise in Muslim immigration to Europe (see Map 30.3). Recent reports estimate that two hundred Muslim girls and women have been killed by their families in Spain in the last twenty years. Roughly a dozen honor killings occur each year in the United Kingdom. In a recent BBC poll, in fact, 10 percent of Muslim British men—which would calculate to some fifty thousand of them, nationwide—said that they would unhesitatingly kill a daughter or sister who had dishonored the family.

But 90 percent of them said they would not. Worldwide, Muslims who reject the idea of honor killing are clearly in the majority, but proponents of the practice remain a sufficiently large minority that concern for the persecution of women cannot abate. The Western media predictably but understandably focus on the most horrifying cases. They told of the 2002 gang rape of a young Pakistani woman that was ordered by a tribal court as punishment for her brother's sexual immodesty. They told of the 2004 fire at a girls' school in Saudi Arabia, where firefighters allowed only those girls who had stopped to cover themselves head-to-foot to flee the burning building. Or of the sixteen-year-old girl in Hamburg whose brother stabbed her twenty-three times in a parking lot for dishonoring the family by her refusal to wear a hijab and to marry the man (a cousin) selected for her by her father. Or of the Afghan-Canadian husband and wife who drowned all three of their teenage daughters in 2011 because they had boyfriends without their permission.

Recent studies have shown that the predominant motive behind honor killings, when they occur in Islamic countries, is some sort of real or perceived sexual impropriety. But when they occur among Muslims within Europe, the main cause—by more than a two-to-one margin—is that the women or girls were considered to have "become too Western." Even more disturbing, the honor killings committed for the supposed crime of becoming Westernized usually involve some sort of torture before the victims are actually killed. Given the virulence of such crimes, it is no wonder that Europe's Muslims have not assimilated into their surrounding cultures at a rate fast enough to please their non-Muslim neighbors. Yet the media pay little attention to the slow but steady advances made by Muslim women both

---

[4] According to the UN Population Fund, roughly five thousand honor killings take place yearly around the world, the majority in Muslim societies.

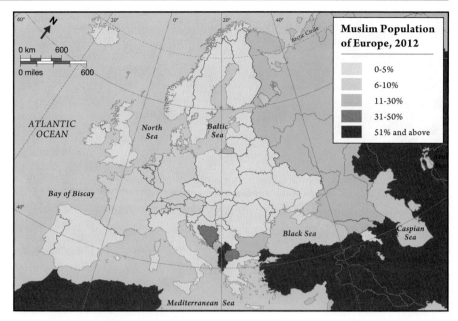

MAP 30.3   European Muslim Population, 2012

in Europe and in the Middle East.[5] Girls' schools in Egypt and Jordan are growing, albeit slowly, in number and in sophistication. Prominent women teach at some of the premier universities in Egypt, Iraq, and Turkey.

Violence against women, equal access to education and civil rights, and the right to work—all these issues are being discussed. That fact alone might have seemed impossible a generation ago. The Internet's influence here is unmistakable. Videos of the stoning of women cannot be easily ignored or dismissed; nor can the jubilant celebrations among the men who hurled the rocks. Blogs by dissidents evade censors and bring to the world news of government crackdowns on protestors. When Bill Gates (b. 1955), cofounder of Microsoft, spoke to a crowd of business leaders in Riyadh, he was asked if he thought Saudi Arabia would ever become a global leader in technology: "Not if you aren't fully utilizing half of the talent in your country," he replied. For the time being, that "half of the talent" is underappreciated.

Aside from traditional cultural conservatism, economic factors also play a role in shaping Arab attitudes toward women. Since 85 to 90 percent of Arab wealth comes from a single industry, petroleum, their nations do not have the varied

---

[5]   Women in Iran hold 10 percent of the nation's political offices, including three of its twelve vice presidencies.

Leaders of the Revolution   A group of Iranian schoolgirls listen to their president, Mahmoud Ahmadinejad, addressing the parliament in February 2011. Women have the right to vote in Iran, and currently about eight percent of parliamentary seats are held by women.

economies that would allow women to advance as they have done in Europe and in the non-Arab Muslim countries. Proven oil reserves in the Middle East, at current rates of production and consumption, will run dry by the year 2050, leaving the region economically crippled unless other sources of revenue can be found. As of 2010 plastics and petrochemicals are the two largest non-oil industries—but together they produce only enough money to cover the cost of food imports into the region.

Muslim women's growing involvement in the post-oil economy should lighten some of the social strictures under which they lived throughout the 20th century. But given the experience of women in Europe, this may take some time.

> Proven oil reserves in the Middle East, at current rates of production and consumption, will run dry by the year 2050, leaving the region economically crippled unless other sources of revenue can be found.

DEBT, TAXES, AND LIBERTY

The economic crash of 2008 highlighted painfully the problem of Western debt. Since capitalism runs on credit, debt and even long-term indebtedness are inescapable—and are not in itself harmful. People commonly purchase homes that leave them in debt to their banks or mortgage servers for thirty years. They may even refinance their loans at any point, lowering their payments but extending the indebtedness farther into the future. They also pay for college with loans that may extend into their middle age or even beyond. Cities and states issue bonds in order to provide revenues to improve infrastructure or to pay for school construction. National governments borrow domestically and internationally to fund special projects or to spur economic growth. Small companies rely on loans to expand their business, invest in new products, and modernize their equipment. Large corporations take on debt in order to acquire smaller companies—and sometimes even larger debt in order to purchase companies larger than themselves.

Problems arise, however, when too much red ink appears on the ledger. How much is too much? It depends on one's assets and their current and projected values, but also on other factors. These include the viability of the project for which the debt is assumed, the interest rate charged, and the security of the revenue stream that will repay the loan. This is all elementary finance—but the West still got itself into a mess only a few years ago. Public and private debt threatens to collapse the Euro Zone and has brought the United States close to default. Looking at public debt as a percentage of gross domestic product (GDP)—the value of all goods and services produced in a year and the best way to judge the problem—is a sobering exercise.

The problem with Greece, for example, is obvious. The nation's debt is almost one hundred times its annual GDP, and its 2010 budget added another GDP's worth of debt to the pile. At the same time, its national revenues are declining by more than 12 percent a year. Caught in so severe a bind, the nation has no way to ever pay its creditors and return to fiscal health without help. Portugal, in comparison, owes sixty-four times its GDP and slashed its 2010 budget by almost 3 percent of GDP. Its growth rate is only enough to hold steady, and it can avoid drowning only by forcing its creditors underwater. The euro, the single currency of the EU, was supposed to lessen problems like this. The easy availability of credit, though, enticed too many people, in all countries, to take on more debt. For a time it seemed that economic growth and the increase in value of what they owned would compensate.

Something similar happened in the United States. Government debt had been on the rise since the 1960s but had remained manageable, as a percentage of GDP, until the 1990s under President Clinton. At that point, a series of tax increases and cuts in social programs, combined with a decade-long rise in the stock market, created a significant budget surplus. The federal budget entered the 21st century well under control, but three events reversed the trend. First, a surge of interest in high-tech companies had driven the stock market upward in the nineties, but now the collapse of this "dot-com bubble" put many Americans

TABLE 30.2 **GDP and Government Debt Compared, 2011**

COUNTRY	GDP (by millions US)	GOVERNMENT DEBT (% of GDP)	NET VALUE OF ECONOMIC GROWTH (minus cost of debt)
Austria	379,047	40.9	0.2
Belgium	469,347	83.3	0.4
Canada	1,577,040	30.3	3.2
Czech Republic	197,674	4.8	0.6
Denmark	309,866	0.5	1.2
Finland	238,731	−57	2.4
France	2,559,850	57.2	0.3
Germany	3,280,334	52.7	0.5
Greece	301,065	97.8	−12.2
Hungary	128,629	60.1	−2.2
Ireland	206,600	39.9	−4.8
Italy	2,051,290	104.1	−1.3
Netherlands	779,310	34.4	0.4
Norway	413,056	−153.4	3
Poland	469,393	27.9	1.1
Portugal	228,859	64.3	−3
Sweden	458,725	−19.6	2.6
Switzerland	527,920	6.2	1.4
UK	2,253,552	53.5	−0.2
United States	14,447,100	66.6	2.2

out of work. Second, President George W. Bush pressed for substantial tax cuts that radically reduced federal revenues just as demand for social services began to rise dramatically. Third, the country went to war in Afghanistan and Iraq without raising taxes in order to pay for either conflict—essentially funding two wars on a credit card.

These factors combined to produce the largest budget deficits in the country's history. Soon millions of Americans took on enormous personal debt, in part because of artificially high housing values. Unscrupulous and even fraudulent loan agencies and mortgage brokers walked right in, earning specious profits by extending loans to people who could not afford them and then selling the mortgages. The sale went to the financial markets, repackaged as the hazily understood "collateralized debt obligations," that together with the credit default swaps made popular twenty years earlier by the *Exxon Valdez* settlement, helped trigger the financial crisis of 2008.

The combination of widespread debt and economic recession presents a problem—how to spur economic growth and get unemployed people back to work. To do both, governments have traditionally invested heavily in infrastructure and other projects, and they have done so by taking on debt. As more people become wage earners, their taxes pay off the public loan. But opposition to tax increases remained fervid in 2010 in the United States, especially among conservatives who prefer to balance budgets by cutting expenditures. In Europe, calls for debt financing to help out countries in critical condition (Greece, Ireland, Italy, Portugal, Spain) and to fuel job growth have been resisted by those nations (Germany especially) that would have to provide the credit.

> The Greater West has entered the 21st century engaged in full-throttle disputes over the purpose and limits of government and the responsibilities of individuals in society.

More is involved in these debates than reconciling figures in a ledger. The Greater West has entered the 21st century engaged in full-throttle disputes over the purpose and limits of government and the responsibilities of individuals in society. The disputes are not new, but they are being addressed with a fervor not seen since the middle of the 19th century.

Two related issues are at stake. The first is taxation as economic stimulus: do higher taxes help the economy or not? Remember that the story of capitalism is capital—wealth that can be used to produce more wealth. No one disputes that injecting new capital into an economy spurs investment, production, and consumption. But should that capital come from the public (that is, the government) or from private sources?

The conservative argument holds that the best way to trigger growth is to reduce taxes and spending on social programs in order to "free" capital. We should allow business owners to keep more of their wealth in order to invest in production, and we should let consumers retain more of their own wealth in order to spur the purchase of goods. That way, activity will be stimulated throughout the economy. This is the free-market view described in the mid-20th century by economists like F. A. Hayek. It was also the view of Milton Friedman, an American economist later in the 20th century (see chapter 25). An unregulated market, these economists wrote, will produce the greatest efficiency. A small but thriving portion of the economy will always produce more than a larger, intrusive portion of a halting, staggering economy. Moreover, it respects individuals' rights to control their own property.

The second issue is taxation as wealth redistribution: Taxes take from those with money and give it to those without it, in the form of social services—but should that be the goal of society? The **libertarian** argument holds that any taxation at all is evil because it is theft. By claiming a right to a portion of my income, a government is claiming a right to a portion of my labor—the labor that produces the income. But to claim someone else's capital as one's own is theft. Even worse, the ownership of someone else's labor is slavery. Once, before the American Revolution, colonists protested British taxes. No taxation, they

Campaigning against Austerity   Members of the right wing Independent Greeks party stage a rally in Thessaloniki in May 2012 against the austerity budgets put forth by the government in Athens at the behest of the European Union. The Independent Greeks currently hold twenty seats (out of three hundred) in the Greek parliament. Their most notable political plank is to call for Germany to pay reparations to Greece for the damage done to the country in World War II.

cried, without representation. Now, the argument goes, any form of taxation at all is an attack on individual liberty. Obviously, certain services are essential ones that people need not provide for themselves. National defense, most obviously, cannot be provided for without public funding. And it is unreasonable, for another example, to expect each of us to build our own roads when we wish to travel somewhere. So some compromise on principle is necessary. But libertarians hold that government ought to be as small and inexpensive as possible: it should provide only those services that citizens cannot be expected to provide for themselves.

What might those services be? Infrastructure, certainly (meaning roads, electrical grids, sewer systems, and so on), and national defense. But anything beyond that is debatable. Retirement pensions? Health care? Many conservatives would respond by asking why people shouldn't be expected to save for their own retirement. A publicly funded pension, after all, might be a disincentive to save. And if someone *has* saved but finds, on retirement, that his or her savings still fall short of what is needed, why shouldn't the individual's family help first? Why is it *everyone*'s responsibility to care for individuals who chose to spend all of their money as they were making it? For government to step in is not only contrary to an efficient economy; it actually weakens society by lessening the role of the family.

As for health care, shouldn't people be responsible for themselves? If you choose to smoke forty cigarettes a day, avoid exercise, and drink to excess, that is absolutely your right. But why is it then society's responsibility to pay for your cancer treatment, liver transplants, and physical therapy? Or consider school lunches, a fine idea for those who wish to purchase them. Why should they be publicly subsidized? Is it wrong to expect parents to feed their own children? Why is it right to subsidize a lunch provided by the school, but not the lunch a parent prepares for a child to carry to school?

The conservative argument against taxation rests on the simple principle that people are responsible for themselves and for their own families. Taxation to provide services that ought not to be the government's business in the first place is therefore unjustifiable. In the end, it does more harm than good. For the state to intrude on such matters is unprincipled, inefficient, costly, harmful to the economy, and damaging to the moral well-being of society.

FREE MARKET? WHAT FREE MARKET?

All this is willful blindness and moral idiocy, counter liberals. The blindness consists of a refusal to see that no such thing as a "free market" exists. People are not autonomous, self-owned, rational actors in a marketplace of open and equal competition. Capitalism is at root a numbers game, especially as the libertarians claim to practice it. Real human actions are not governed by and cannot be understood by numbers and formulas alone. A skilled electrician who cannot get hired because he is a member of a racial or religious minority is not subject merely to market forces. No matter how good his work or how low his rates, his struggle against prejudices—even if successful—is not played out on the same economic playing field as his white competitor. Or take a midlevel manager working for a software firm who earns only 80 percent of what her male colleagues in the same position receive. She confronts daily something more than "rational choice" in the corporate marketplace. Equal pay for equal work is a matter of fundamental justice, not of artificial manipulation of a free market. The problem with the call for small government and unregulated economies, liberals argue, is that free-market economists don't believe in sin. Or at least they talk as though they don't, whenever the subject is the economy.

The problem with the call for small government and unregulated economies, liberals argue, is that free-market economists don't believe in sin. Or at least they talk as though they don't, whenever the subject is the economy.

Not only are injustices like racism, sexism, cronyism, and class discrimination built into the system, but so are inequalities of opportunity. Large, well-stocked supermarkets provide full selections of fresh produce, artisanal breads, and shelves packed with dietary supplements. They are almost always located in suburbs, with ample parking, not in inner cities and in poorer neighborhoods. Why then is it solely the responsibility of the urban poor to maintain their own healthy diets? Even when suburban supermarkets are located near bus lines, it may take a city dweller an hour and a half to get there. A simple grocery trip can turn into an all-day affair that may get in the way of work and other responsibilities.

Moreover, even in a perfect world, capitalism has a built-in bias toward the concentration of capital. For one thing, property is inheritable but labor is not: the owner of a manufacturing plant can hand over that ownership to a son or daughter, but the factory workers cannot pass on their jobs to their heirs. Even allowing for business failures, real assets generally grow in value over time, while the long-term value of labor diminishes as workers age or as technology replaces them. Thus thriving capitalist societies do experience a degree of enrichment overall, but within that general trend lives another pattern entirely—the consolidation of wealth at the top.[6] So much for total assets, but what about annual income? In the United States more than twenty cents out of every dollar in new income is paid to the top one percent of wage and salary earners. In the United Kingdom from 1997 to 2007, the overwhelming bulk of the new jobs created were added at the very top and the very bottom of the pay scale: the executives, in other words, and their minimum-wage workers.

Economists measure wealth and income distributions using a standard called the **Gini coefficient**, named after the Italian statistician (and one-time Fascist bureaucrat) Corrado Gini (1884–1965).[7] The Gini scale ranges from a score of 0, meaning that a country has perfect equality of wealth among all citizens, to a score of 100, meaning that 100% of the wealth is owned by a single individual. According to the Gini scale, the West maintained the lowest concentrations of wealth during the decades of the welfare state. Since free-market economic policies came into effect beginning with President Reagan and Prime Minister Thatcher in 1980, however, the trend has been toward ever-greater concentrations of wealth in their two countries. From 1980 to the present, these pro-market economies have improved overall wealth, but the concentration of that wealth

---

[6]   In the United States in 2010, the four hundred richest individuals (0.000125 percent of the population) owned as much wealth (capital and assets) as the least wealthy 150 million Americans combined.

[7]   When he wasn't busy calculating his coefficients and indexing the birth rates of inferior peoples, Gini wrote a pamphlet called *The Scientific Basis of Fascism* (1927).

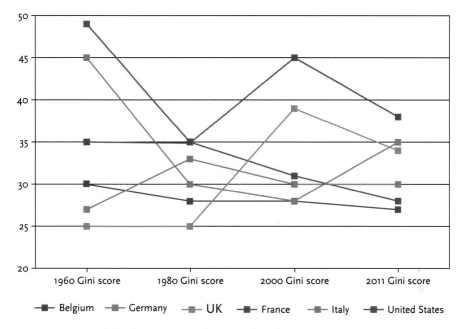

FIGURE 30.1   Wealth and Income Distribution: Selected Scores

among the richest citizens (a 50 percent increase in Britain between 1980 and 2000, a 33 percent increase in the United States) is clear (see Figure 30.1).

These trends lead to another idea: redistributive taxation—taxes intended not only to pay for essential services but to force a broader distribution of wealth as well. Liberal economists argue that these taxes *must* exist, as a matter of justice. Besides, taxes also assure continued economic growth, as a matter of practical policy. Take redistribution as justice, first. A just society gives priority to treating its people, not its material wealth, with fairness and respect, goes the argument. If there are human rights, then all people possess them, and society should see that every citizen has his or her rights recognized and protected. Does that mean that all wealth should be handed out in equal parcel to everyone? Socialists might say yes, but most liberals say no. Rather, society serves justice by seeing to it that everyone has an equal opportunity to prosper. The children of a billionaire investor and the children of a coal miner do not begin life with the same opportunities and the same chances to succeed, and hence the state has a responsibility and a right to extract, in taxes, more of the billionaire's wealth so that it can be directed to the coal miner.

Liberal thinking often follows a line of thought articulated by John Rawls, in *A Theory of Justice* (1971). Rawls imagined each of us cloaked in a "veil of ignorance." Sure, inequalities of wealth, intelligence, social class, and talents exist.

Yet none of us know where we or anyone else stands. In that case, we must all choose a future regardless of our good or bad fortune in history's lottery. An economy that lets some people begin with vastly greater means than others is unfair from the start. Fairness to all is more important than any individual's right to inherit parental wealth. In Rawls's words, "Justice is fairness," and fairness includes redistributive taxation.

> Rawls imagined each of us cloaked in a "veil of ignorance." Sure, inequalities of wealth, intelligence, social class, and talents exist. Yet none of us know where we or anyone else stands.

No one lives independently, in this view, and all our fates are connected. You can wear a seatbelt while driving a car, for example, or not—but you had better wear one. The choice is not simply a matter of personal freedom versus a paternalist state, and it is gross selfishness to think that it is. If you are without a seatbelt in an accident, your medical costs will be vastly greater than if you had worn one. Even if private insurance pays that bill, the rest of society remains affected because the demand on medical services raises the prices of medical care and insurance for all. The accident also increases the need for police officers and ambulances, as well as interrupting traffic.

Justice Is Fairness   The distribution of wealth has become increasingly a focus of political attention. Here a well-dressed figure in London's financial district walks past a homeless beggar outside the Royal Exchange (formerly a financial center, now a luxury shopping mall).

Two other major issues stand out, among many, as pressing challenges to economic growth. First is the aging of the West. The population of Europe, especially the western half of it, is getting older, since birth rates are in decline and the advantages of skilled medicine allow people to live longer lives. This problem also exists to some extent, though a lesser one, in the United States, where immigration, both legal and illegal, makes up for some of the stagnation in net population. As Britain discovered at the end of the 19th century, its aging population factored heavily in its economic and political competition with Germany, whose larger and younger population was a catalyst for its imperial growth. In parts of eastern Europe, and especially throughout the Islamic part of the Greater West, populations are growing rapidly and average ages are declining (see Map 30.4). In Iran alone, nearly two-thirds of the entire population is under the age of thirty-five; moreover, overall growth, in absolute numbers, has been dramatic: the population has nearly doubled in size since the Islamic Revolution in 1979.

An aging population means increased health costs—which forms the other major challenge to the West. The European countries provide cradle-to-grave medical care to their people, but this generosity depends on two factors to keep it going: continuing military subsidies from the United States, which frees up capital for the EU nations to dedicate to social programs, and a sizable labor force whose taxes can support the cost of medical care. Both factors are currently in doubt for the foreseeable future. In the United States, the cost of entitlement programs (Medicare for the elderly, Medicaid for the poor, and Social Security pensions for the retired) have been straining or breaking budgets for decades. The need both to address these ballooning costs and to balance that effort against the need to stimulate a sluggish recessionary economy will dominate national politics for at least another generation.

WHAT IS THE GREATER WEST NOW?

The names of historical periods and movements matter. It matters that the educated of the 18th century called themselves *the Enlightened*—even if only to expose their self-regard. In the 3rd century CE, when Germanic tribes swept into the western Roman Empire, the Romans called it an *invasion*, but the Germans later described it as a *migration* (*Völkerwanderung*). And they were both right, each from their own point of view.

The Greater West may be experiencing a similar two-faced moment now. Migration within and immigration from without is changing the entire European

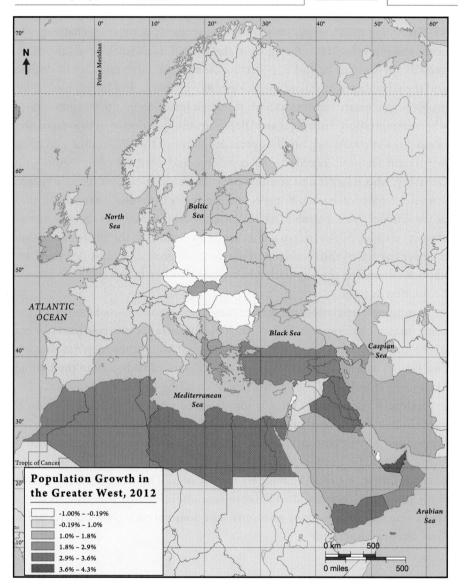

MAP 30.4   Population Growth in the Greater West, 2012

continent. New faiths are filling the spaces left by a declining Christianity. The languages heard on the streets are unfamiliar; so are the smells and tastes emanating from shops and restaurants. Nationalist passions contend with a vision of European unity that, like new clothing, seems to fit but still feels uncomfortable. Political and economic rivalries come and go, but most Europeans are cheered that no wars have broken out between any members of the EU, the EC before it, or the EEC before that. This most warlike of continents may finally have stumbled on the path to peace.

Other parts of the Greater West are undergoing almost precisely the opposite pressures and trends. The ethnic makeup of the Arab countries is becoming more, not less, homogenous. Christian populations are small and declining; the Jewish populations even more so. Israel is the most pluralistic of the Middle East nations and the most democratic, although optimists see in the Arab Spring the start of a pronounced democratic swing. Iraq may yet prove to be the first viable Arab democracy. Religious conviction runs deep, but the rifts between Sunni and Shi'i Muslims and the rivalries between clans are a continuous challenge. The likely major struggle to come within the Islamic world will be the rivalry between Arabs, Persians, and Turks; and in the working out of that contest the fate of Islam's women will be both cause and consequence. Iran's nuclear ambitions are perhaps the most pressing issue at present, but the contest will continue to heat up, especially as Arab oil wealth declines. For now, the two halves of the Greater West are confronting the challenge of understanding their own identity—as nations? Religions? Economic actors?

> Political and economic rivalries come and go, but most Europeans are cheered that no wars have broken out between any members of the EU, the EC before it, or the EEC before that. This most warlike of continents may finally have stumbled on the path to peace.

The question has already run into roadblocks. Speaking to the Council of Europe in 2005, Pope Benedict XVI (r. 2005–present) urged the European Union not to deny its own history. Christianity, for good or ill, has been a central element in the development of European culture. He insisted that the faith still has a crucial role to play in the future:

> Only a Europe with peaceful social coexistence and the exchange of cultural riches, both material and non-material, will be able to be featured as the common house of all Europeans, in which each and every one is accepted and feels at home, no one is subject to discrimination but all are required to live as responsible members of one great family of peoples. . . . Christianity has been an essential factor of unity among peoples and cultures. For two millennia, it has never ceased to promote an integral vision of the human being and human rights, and the history of the nations of the Continent as a whole attests to its extraordinary cultural fruitfulness.
>
> Eager to honour the modern requirement of a proper secularism of States, and hence of Europe with all its religious and secular elements running counter to a reductive secularism that inspires certain policies, the Holy See reaffirms its willingness and the ability of religions to help build the common European home, contributing in particular to remedy

the challenge of social disintegration and to give meaning to life and to history.

Did not European modernism, which gave the world the ideal of democracy, the meaning of the dignity of every human person and his or her inalienable rights, find in the crucible of Christianity the loftiest values in its 1,000-year-old culture, the heir to Greek thought, in the Roman institutions and in many other cultural contributions, particularly the Celtic, Anglo-Saxon, German and Slav?

In the period subsequent to the Second World War, the Fathers of Europe courageously pointed out the challenge of "justice without freedom." Today, an equally ruinous "utopia" threatens our societies with disintegration: the indifference that relativizes everything, advances nothing and, masked by its appearance of tolerance, endangers the humanity of men and women.

To confront this new challenge together at the dawn of the third millennium, to build Europe as a human community, means giving the European Cultural Convention a new impetus, to which, for its part, the Holy See fully intends to contribute.

There is an obvious difficulty here. To deny the significance of the Christian faith in shaping the Western tradition is historical nonsense, but the Western world is increasingly Muslim. To center Western identity on Christianity is just bad politics; hence the EU's refusal to acknowledge a Christian core to Western culture. But the Islamic world, too, will have to adapt to non-Muslim society. It has done so in the past, with notable success. The challenge to Islam today is the small but violent minority of Muslims who oppose any adaptation. They demand an immediate and uncompromising return to the strictest shariah. The only reform they desire is a return to a mythical pure past—a common trope of Greater Western culture, but not necessarily the most admirable or helpful one.

Efforts are underway to speed adaptation along, to improve understanding across religious lines. A controversial figure, the Swiss academic Tariq Ramadan (b. 1962), has emerged with a distinctive European version of Islam. Born and raised in Geneva, Ramadan is the grandson of the founder of the Muslim Brotherhood in Egypt, a family connection that makes many of his critics suspicious of his claims that he is not a fundamentalist. After studying philosophy and French literature at the University of Geneva, he completed a PhD in Islamic studies. He has taught at several prestigious universities and is currently on the faculty at Oxford. Ramadan argues that the Qur'an is the essential authority in Islamic life, but it must be interpreted in light of the time and place in which one lives. Muslims within Europe, he insists, have an obligation to observe the laws of the

The Face of the Greater West   A group of Berlin youths gather at the annual Holocaust Remembrance Day for an activity known as "Cleaning the Cobblestones [*Stolpersteine*]." Christian, Muslim, Jewish, and Bahai youths walk through the streets to clean and care for the roughly 3,500 commemoration-stones planted along sidewalks. Each stone bears the name of local Jewish citizens of Berlin who became victims of the Holocaust. The idea has grown in popularity, and hundreds of cities all across Europe now have *Stolpersteine*. By the end of 2011 more than thirty thousand stones had been created.

secular state. They should devise a code of Islamic life that harmonizes Qur'anic teaching and social expectation. As he expressed it in his book entitled *To Be a European Muslim* (1999):

> The European environment is a space of responsibility for Muslims. This is exactly the meaning of the notion of "space of testimony" (*dar al-shahada*) that we propose here, a notion that totally reverses perspectives: whereas Muslims have, for years, been wondering whether and how they would be accepted, the in-depth study and evaluation of the Western environment entrusts them, in light of their Islamic frame of reference, with a most important mission .... Muslims now attain, in the space of testimony, the meaning of an essential duty and of an exacting responsibility: to contribute, wherever they are, to promoting good and equity within and through human brotherhood. Muslims' outlook must now change from the reality of "protection" alone to that of an authentic "contribution."

Ramadan's outlook is not altogether new. We have often forgotten that Islam has been a Western religion from the start. The events of the Arab Spring are still recent, but the slow integration of the post-Christian European and Muslim worlds now underway in the Greater West has a chance to succeed. As it happens, one of its first test cases will occur where Western civilization began—in Iraq.

WHO, WHAT, WHERE

Arab Spring
Gini coefficient
honor killings

libertarian
World Economic Forum

SUGGESTED READINGS

Primary Sources

Ramadan, Tariq. *Islam, the West, and the Challenges of Modernity.*

———. *The Quest for Meaning: Developing a Philosophy of Pluralism.*

———. *Western Muslims and the Future of Islam.*

Anthologies

Laqueur, Walter, and Barry Rubin, eds. *The Israel-Arab Reader: A Documentary History of the Middle East Conflict* (2008).

Sandel, Michael J., ed. *Justice: A Reader* (2007).

Vallentyne, Peter, and Hillel Steiner, eds. *The Origins of Left-Libertarianism: An Anthology of Historical Writings* (2007).

Studies

Browers, Michaelle. *Political Ideology in the Arab World: Accommodation and Transformation* (2009).

Calhoun, Craig, and Georgi Derluguian, eds. *Business as Usual: The Roots of the Global Financial Meltdown* (2011).

Council on Foreign Relations. *The New Arab Revolt: What Happened, What It Means, and What Comes Next* (2011).

Holton, Robert J. *Globalization and the Nation State* (2011).

Huntington, Samuel P. *The Clash of Civilizations and the Remaking of World Order* (2011).

İnce, Başak. *Citizenship and Identity in Turkey: From Atatürk's Republic to the Present Day* (2012).

Marquand, David. *The End of the West: The Once and Future Europe* (2011).

Mearsheimer, John J. *The Tragedy of Great Power Politics* (2003).

Nussbaum, Martha C. *The New Religious Intolerance: Overcoming the Politics of Fear in an Anxious Age* (2012).

Ohana, David. *Israel and Its Mediterranean Identity* (2011).

Pope, Nicole. *Honor Killings in the Twenty-First Century* (2011).

Ruiz, Teofilo F. *The Terror of History: On the Uncertainties of Life in Western Civilization* (2011).

Sandel, Michael J. *What Money Can't Buy: The Moral Limits of Markets* (2012).

Sarotte, Mary Elise: *1989: The Struggle to Create Post-Cold War Europe* (2009).

Sen, Amartya. *The Idea of Justice* (2011).

————. *Identity and Violence: The Illusion of Destiny* (2008).

Shapiro, Daniel. *Is the Welfare State Justified?* (2007).

Stiglitz, Joseph E. *Globalization and Its Discontents* (2003).

Tavassoli, Sasan. *Christian Encounters with Iran: Engaging Muslim Thinkers after the Revolution* (2011).

Van Dam, Nikolaos. *The Struggle for Power in Syria: Politics and Society under Asad and the Ba'th Party* (2011).

Wikan, Unni. *Generous Betrayal: Politics of Culture in the New Europe* (2002).

Wilkinson, Richard, and Kate Pickett. *The Spirit Level: Why More Equal Societies Almost Always Do Better* (2009).

Young, Elise G. *Gender and Nation Building in the Middle East: The Political Economy of Health from Mandate Palestine to Refugee Camps in Jordan* (2012).

For additional resources, including maps, primary sources, visuals, web links, and quizzes, please go to **www.oup.com/us/backman.**

Reference Maps

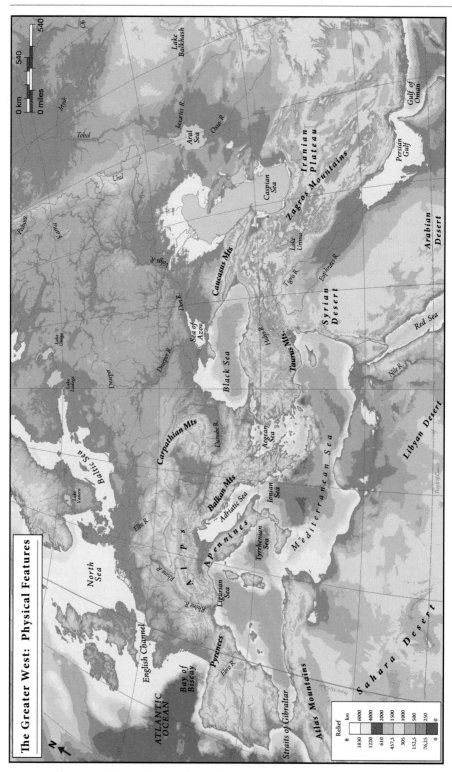

The Greater West: Physical Features

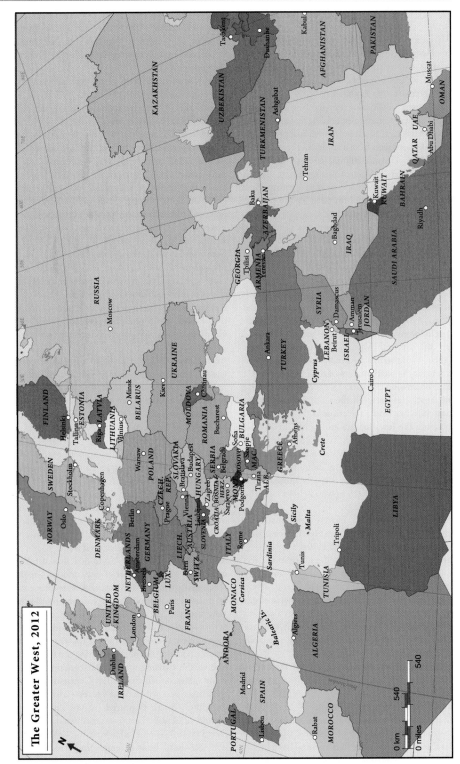

The Greater West, 2012

Glossary

A

Abbasids Dynasty of Islamic caliphs who came to power in 750 and remained titular heads of the Islamic empire until 1258, when they were unseated by the Mongols. Moved Islamic capital from Damascus to Baghdad.

absolutism Political theory granting limitless authority to a sovereign ruler, holding that a sovereign entrusted with absolute power will best protect the sovereign's subjects from disorder and chaos.

absurdity Postwar cultural concept, associated with the French-Algerian writer Albert Camus (1913–1960), that sees life as essentially meaningless.

Academy The school founded by the philosopher Plato in Athens in 385 BCE.

Act of Union Parliamentary acts (1800) that united Great Britain and Ireland.

Acts of Toleration Throughout the 17th and 18th centuries, laws promulgated to offer full or partial constitutional rights to Jews.

Afrikaners The descendants of the first Dutch settlers of South Africa; formerly known as the Boers; the language they speak is called Afrikaans.

Aggiornamento Among the issues addressed by the Second Vatican Council's meetings (1962–1965) were a reformation of the liturgy to allow for the participation of the congregation, a call for missionary work, an expression of regret for hostilities between the Catholic and Orthodox churches, and a rejection of the tradition of blaming the Jews for the killing of Christ. The word used by Pope John XXIII to describe his goal in summoning the Vatican II council—to bring the Church "up to date," literally.

Ahura Mazda The One Lord or eternal God, worshiped by Zoroastrians who believe he is the creator of all living things.

Almohads Reformist Islamic sect, made up chiefly of ethnic Berbers from North Africa, who invaded Muslim Spain in the 1170s.

amir al-umara' "Commander of commanders," a title held by those who seized civil authority from the Abbasid caliphs after 936.

Anabaptists Apocalyptic sect of Swiss exiles who rejected infant baptism, called for a second baptism in adulthood, and embraced a literal reading of Scripture and the imminent approach of Christ's Second Coming.

analytical geometry Developed by René Descartes, the application of algebra to the study of geometry.

analytic philosophy Branch of philosophy that emphasizes close and careful reasoning (as distinct from rationalist philosophy, which studies the movement of the human mind itself).

Ancien Régime The French aristocracy from 1648 to 1789, seen as a golden age (for those privileged enough to enjoy it) before the French Revolution.

anno Domini System of dating that reckons the years since the birth of Christ.

Annunaki Collective name for the gods and goddesses of the Sumerians.

Anschluss "Union," literally; the term has come to refer specifically to the political unification of Austria and Germany under the Nazi regime.

anti-Semitism Term coined in 1881 to describe the vicious hatred toward and persecution of Jews, both officially and unofficially, that emerged across Europe in the 19th century.

apartheid Official policy of racial segregation instituted in South Africa by the Afrikaner-dominated National Party in 1948.

appanage A land or estate held by a nobleman from the king of France without the requirement of performing feudal service in return.

Appeasement In the 1930s, the granting of political and territorial concessions to Hitler's Germany by many Western countries in order to preserve peace.

Arab Revolt Uprising (1916) of Middle Eastern Arab tribes against Turkish rule, which aimed to replace Ottoman imperial rule with autonomous Arab countries but instead furthered the European imperialist project by dividing the Middle East between England and France (see **Sykes-Picot Agreement**).

Arab Spring Wave of rebellions in ethnically Arab countries, beginning in Tunisia in December 2010 and rippling across Morocco, Yemen, Iraq, Bahrain, Egypt, and Kuwait. The rebellions turned violent in Libya, resulting in the eventual overthrow and death of dictator Muammar Qaddafi, and in Syria, which at the time of publication was on the brink of an all-out civil war.

Archaic period From 750 to 500 BCE, a time marked by the extension of networks of Greek colonies—primarily for peaceful, entrepreneurial purposes—around the Aegean rim, the Black Sea, and the entire perimeter of Asia Minor, across southern Italy and Sicily, and along the southern coast of France and the eastern coast of Spain, and along the northern coast of Africa.

Ark of the Covenant A chest containing the stone tables on which the Ten Commandments were inscribed, which Moses received from God on Mount Sinai. Captured by the Philistines around 1050 BCE, the ark was recovered by King David (r. 1005–965 BCE), whose son Solomon (r. 965–928 BCE) built a temple in Jerusalem to house it. The ark vanished after the Babylonians conquered Jerusalem in 586 BCE.

art nouveau   Popular style in art and design in the late 19th century, featuring flowing lines, flower-tracery, and gently erotic female forms.

Ashkenazim   Northern European Jewish cultural tradition uniquely focused on the preservation of Talmudic tradition.

askesis   Stoic term for the peace of mind acquired by the philosophical life. Later used to refer to the Christian "ascetics" who cut themselves off from society.

Assyrians   A strongly militaristic and powerful society (ca. 12th century BCE—612 BCE) of upper Mesopotamia, whose use of iron and steel for weaponry contributed to their formidable conquests.

Atheism   The rejection, or absence, of religious belief.

Augustus   Original title of the Roman emperors; given first to Octavius.

auto-da-fé   A Portuguese term meaning "act of faith." This was a public ritual of confession of sin and consequent humiliation for those deemed heretics by the Inquisition.

avant-garde   "Vanguard," literally. Term popularized by the Dada movement to describe bold artistic experimentation that questions the very idea of art.

Avesta   The holy book of the Zoroastrians.

ayatollah   Arabic, "sign from God"; the supreme clerical authority in Iran.

B

Ba'ath Party   Founded in 1947 by Arab Christian writer Michel Aflaq as the political representation of secular **Pan-Arabism**, applying socialist ideals of state-sponsored care for the masses (from the Arab word for "renaissance").

baby boom   Demographic bubble in the United States (1946–1964) when postwar prosperity and the return of soldiers from combat resulted in an elevated birthrate.

Babylonian Captivity   After the Chaldaeans destroyed Jerusalem and the Temple in 587, they took many of the surviving Jews back east as slaves, where they remained until they were released in 538 BCE by the Persian emperor Cyrus the Great (r. 576–530 BCE).

Balfour Declaration   Agreement (1917) that announced Britain's support for a national Jewish homeland in Palestine.

baptizein   Greek verb meaning "to baptize." Ritual of purification popularized by John the Baptist in 1st-century BCE Palestine. "To plunge or to dunk," literally.

barbaroi   General and pejorative term among ancient Greeks for any non-Greek peoples. English word "barbarian" derives from it.

Baroque Age   Concurrent with the **Ancien Régime**, an era in Europe of extraordinary artistic accomplishment in the service of the tremendously wealthy and privileged aristocratic class.

basileus   Title of the emperors of Byzantium.

Black Death   Successive outbreaks of bubonic plague, beginning in 1347, that killed up to a third of European and Muslim populations over the course of the 14th century.

Blitzkrieg   Nazi strategy of "lightning war" that used rapid motorized firepower to overwhelm an enemy before it could mount a defense.

Bloomsbury Group   Affiliation of writers, artists, and philosophers (including Virginia Woolf and John Maynard Keynes) who met socially in the Bloomsbury district of London in the first decades of the 20th century.

Bolsheviks   Political party led by Vladimir Lenin in the Russian Revolution that overthrew the Russian government in 1917, establishing a form of Communism that maintained power in the Soviet Union until 1991. A variation on classical Marxism, requiring the systematic use of violence, the establishment of a supposedly temporary dictatorship by Party members to effect the overthrow of prerevolutionary practices, and the violent exportation of revolution to other countries.

Book of the Dead   An anthology of prayers, poems, and similar texts collected during the Egyptian Middle Kingdom (2035 BCE–1640 BCE). Placed in the coffin, the Book of the Dead was believed to allow the deceased to enter paradise.

bourgeoisie   The prosperous and primarily urban middle class of Enlightenment Europe.

Boxer Rebellion   Violent attempt (1898–1901) by Chinese peasants, motivated by millennial Buddhist beliefs, to purge Westerners and Western influence from China.

Boyle's law   Discovered by Robert Boyle, states that the volume and pressure of a gas at constant temperature vary inversely.

Bronze Age   The period between 4000 and 1500 BCE characterized by the ability of early Near East inhabitants to smelt copper (and its alloy, bronze, which combines copper with tin) for weapons, farm implements, and tools.

Byzantine Empire   Eastern half of the Roman Empire, with its capital in Constantinople; at its height in the 4th and 5th centuries it included all of today's countries of Libya, Egypt, Israel, Jordan, Lebanon, Syria, Turkey, and most of the Balkan states.

C

caesar   Title of the vice emperors under the constitutional reforms created by Diocletian. Later evolved into German and Russian terms for emperor (*kaiser* and *tsar*, respectively).

cahiers de doléances   "Grievance notebooks," literally. Records of commoners' complaints compiled for the use of representatives to the Estates General in 1789.

Cairo Declaration on Human Rights   Adopted in 1990 by the Organization of the Islamic Conference to replace the earlier (and secular) **Universal Declaration of Human Rights** with a specifically Islamic conceptualization.

caliph   Successor to the Prophet Muhammad as political and religious leader of the Islamic world. Meaning "deputy" in the literal sense, in common usage it was roughly comparable to the English word "emperor."

capitulations   Trade agreements between the Ottoman Empire and European nations that by the 19th century overwhelmingly favored European interests.

Carolingians   Ambitious Frankish dynasty that overthrew the Merovingians, defended western Christendom against Muslim invaders, and united France.

Cathars   Christian heresy that posited the existence of two equally strong but diametrically opposed gods—one absolutely good, who created human souls, and one absolutely evil, who created the physical world. Humans are trapped in a cycle of reincarnation until they overcome materialism.

censor   A powerful office in the Roman Republic, whose duties were to maintain the census, to administer the state's finances for public works, and to preserve public morals.

census   The official list of all citizens of Rome, their property, and legal class.

Central Intelligence Agency (CIA)   American governmental agency originally created in 1947 to monitor and deter global Soviet influence. Its mission was officially limited to the gathering of intelligence but in practice the CIA has often engaged in direct political intervention.

chansons de geste   Vernacular epic poems of the 11th to 13th century about the heroic deeds of knights. "Songs of deeds."

Chartist movement   Labor movement begun by the London Working Men's Association in 1838.

chivalry   In 12th-century Europe, an ethic that embraced ideal knightly behavior: comportment, noble demeanor, learning, and piety.

Chosen People   The Hebrew Bible describes the Hebrews as God's "Chosen People," by which is meant not just the favor and protection God gives them but their obligation to obey God in all things and to live up to the high moral standards God expects of them.

Christian Democracy   Western European ideological hybrid of social conservatism and economic liberalism.

Christian humanism   Anticlerical movement of the northern Renaissance that emphasized the simple reading of Scripture (especially the New Testament), the singing of hymns, and communal prayer.

christianities   The dozens of versions of early Christianity, each with its own beliefs, liturgical traditions, and customs, that emerged in the earliest years following the death of Jesus.

Church of England   Protestant church founded by King Henry VIII of England when he broke with the Catholic Church in 1533. Also known as the Anglican Church; the monarchy is its supreme head.

Ciompi Rebellion   Popular uprising in Italy in 1378.

citizenship   As articulated by the 19th-century Egyptian reformer Rifa'a al-Tahtawi, a form of group identity that is not determined by race, creed, or ethnicity.

civil rights   The guarantee of equal access to all parts of government and society for all members of a society. In the United States, the civil rights movement refers primarily to the struggle of African Americans in the 1960s for equal access.

Classical Age   The era beginning with the defense of Greece against Persia lasting until the conquest of Persia by the Greeks under Alexander the Great (479–323 BCE), marked by vitality in civic life, economic prosperity, artistic expression, and literary achievement.

Classicism   Artistic movement that replaced the flourishes of the Baroque with a more controlled and formal sensibility.

Cold War   Term coined by American financier and presidential adviser Bernard Baruch to describe the relationship (1947–1991) between the Soviet bloc and western nations allied with the United States; each side possessed nuclear weapons, yet neither side dared to either use those weapons or disarm.

College of Cardinals   Created by Pope Nicholas II (r. 1059–1061) and given sole power to elect the next pope.

comfort women   Term used in imperial Japan for the quarter-million Chinese, Filipino, and other women captured and forced into sexual slavery in World War II.

comitatus   An assembly or council of tribal elders among the early Germanic peoples. Term coined by Roman writer Tacitus.

comites   Title of the regional governors ("counts") established under the Carolingian emperors in Europe. The term designated officeholders, not a hereditary class.

command economies   Economies that aim to provide the highest possible yield for whoever held the raw materials and captive markets

Communism   Socialist movement that advocates the destruction of capitalism and the development of a new, classless society of freedom.

The Communist Manifesto   Book by Karl Marx and Friedrich Engels (1848) that presents a Marxist view of history as class struggle.

Concordat of Worms   Established the independence of the papacy in 1122.

Conference of Berlin   International conference (1884–1885) of European nations that established the standards by which any European country could claim an African territory over another European rival, touching off the "Scramble for Africa."

Congress of Vienna   Conference of European diplomats convened from 1814 to 1815 to redraw boundaries and work toward peace after decades of conflict.

conquistadores   The 16th-century Spanish forces that subdued South and Central America.

conservatism   Political approach that values tradition and stability above the individual.

consul   In the Roman Republic, the executive office in charge of the government.

Continental System   Economic system, implemented by Napoleon, with two key aims: to create an integrated Continental economy and to bring about the collapse of Britain through the imposition of a strict trade embargo.

cottage industry   The transfer of textile production from urban industry, where it was controlled by guilds, to rural producers, particularly women. Also known as the "putting-out system."

Council of Trent   Ecumenical council convened from 1546 to 1563 to address the challenges of Protestantism by clarifying the teachings and practices of the Catholic church.

Counter-Reformation   General reform of Catholic life initiated by the Council of Trent.

covenant   The special promise God made to the Jews, symbolized by Moses's leading of the Hebrews out of bondage in Egypt and into the Promised Land; in return, the Jews agreed to live by the Torah.

credit default swap   A new kind of financial instrument invented by the J.P. Morgan investment

bank in 1994; misuse of the instrument contributed to the 2008 global economic collapse.

Crimean War   Rooted in the long-standing desire of Russia to increase its influence over the Ottoman Empire, the immediate cause of the war had to do with Russian claims to protective oversight over Orthodox Christians in the Ottoman Empire, but more strategic goals were at stake. The war (1853–1856) pitted France and Britain, who were allied with the Ottomans, against Russia. While Russia accepted unfavorable terms at a conference in Paris in 1856 that ended the conflict, both sides performed ineptly, a fact that became widely known because the war was the first conflict to be covered by journalists and photographers.

crossbow   Brutally efficient weapon, whose metal darts could pierce armor; it was the first weapon to be banned by the Catholic Church.

Cuban Missile Crisis   Standoff between the Soviet Union and the United States in 1962, when Soviet leader Nikita Khrushchev built military bases in Cuba equipped with nuclear missiles. After two weeks of intense negotiations, Khrushchev withdrew the missiles.

cuius regio   Full phrase is *Cuius regio, eius religio*, meaning "the religion of the ruler decides the religion of the realm." Compromise determined to settle the Wars of Religion in the 16th and 17th centuries. The policy guaranteed certain basic rights to the nonestablished religions.

cult of domesticity   Sentimental cultural view in the 19th century that idealized women's role in the home, discouraging them from seeking work or other opportunities outside of their domestic duties.

cuneiform   Technique of writing developed in Mesopotamia whereby wedge-shaped marks were impressed in clay tablets.

curiales   The class of urban elites in ancient Rome who, though unsalaried, were responsible for municipal government and tax collection; obliged to make up any shortfalls in civic finance from their own personal wealth, they were entitled to retain a portion of the tax revenues they collected for personal use.

D

Dark Ages   The period in Western Europe from the 4th to the 8th centuries, so named because of the chaos that reigned after the fall of the western Roman Empire and the endless depredations of various barbarian invasions.

decolonization   European withdrawal during the 20th century from its former colonies.

Deism Enlightenment-era belief in a single and possibly benevolent God who created the cosmos—but who plays no active role in it. As a result, a dual policy of religious freedom and of freedom from religious intolerance is essential to human progress.

Delian League A military alliance formed in 478 BCE (Athens assumed control a year later) among all the Greek poleis, dedicated to maintaining a strong defense—particularly against Persia.

détente A "loosening" of tensions between two nations. Used especially to describe efforts to improve diplomatic ties between the United States and the Soviet Union in the 1970s and 1980s. Ironically, *détente* is also a colloquial French term for the trigger of a gun.

dhimmi Legal status of Jewish and Christian populations living under Muslim rule; officially granted freedom of religion, Jews and Christians had to accept certain restrictions on their communal practice and pay a poll tax (jizya) in return for Islamic protection. Restrictions include bans on any public expression of faith and curtailment of the ability to build or repair synagogues and churches.

dialectical materialism In Marxist theory, the idea that history is driven forward by materialist concerns; to Lenin, this led inevitably to confrontation between the proletariat and the bourgeoisie.

Diaspora The "exile" or "scattering" of the Hebrews after the Assyrians brutally conquered the Kingdom of Israel in 721 BCE and the Chaldaeans (or Neo-Babylonians) conquered Judah in 587 BCE.

Diet The medieval German parliament.

Directory In Prussia, companies of royal commissioners and civil servants who controlled financial and judicial affairs in the provinces on behalf of the king.

Documentary Hypothesis The belief of many modern Biblical scholars that the Torah was compiled from four original sources: "J," by the Yahwist (ca. 950 BCE); "E," by the Elohist (ca. 750 BCE); "D," by the Deuteronomist (ca. 650 BCE); and "P," by the Priestly Author (ca. 550 BCE).

Dominicans Mendicant order focused on education that established schools across Europe.

E

Edict of Milan Issued by Constantine in 313 CE, legalizing Christianity and guaranteeing religious freedom for all faiths within the empire.

Edict of Nantes Decree by Henri IV in 1598 that guaranteed religious freedom, with certain restrictions, throughout France.

Edict of Toleration See **Edict of Milan**.

Elect To Calvinists, those predestined for salvation.

emir A military or naval commander, petty prince, or provincial governor.

enclosure movement Trend of aristocratic landowners toward evicting small farmers (by enclosing formerly open fields with stone walls or hedges) and instead using those fields for the more profitable grazing of livestock, especially sheep.

Enlightenment Term coined in the second half of the 18th century to describe an array of intellectual and cultural activities of the 1700s distinguished by a worldview informed by rational values and scientific inquiry.

Entente Cordiale Diplomatic agreement between England and France in 1904, whereby each country recognized the other's spheres of influence in northern Africa.

Epic of Gilgamesh One of the earliest known works of literature, originating in Sumer but first recorded by Babylonian scribes; relates the adventures of the semimythical Sumerian king Gilgamesh as he battles gods and monsters in pursuit of enlightenment.

Epicureanism Philosophy based on the work of the Greek philosopher Epicurus (341 BCE—270 BCE) that promoted a life free of pain and fear as the way to happiness.

epistemology The philosophical inquiry into the nature of knowledge (and, by extension, learning).

Essenes An ascetic and eschatological sect within Second Temple Judaism.

Estates General French parliament, established by the Capetian kings. Reestablished in 1789 (after having last met in 1614) at the behest of the French aristocracy. The three estates were the nobles, the clergy, and the common people.

Etruscans A literate and prosperous people who associated with the Latins and profoundly influenced the emerging religious and moral culture of Rome.

European Union United group of independent European nations established in 1993 to provide a process for coordinating policies formed at the level of member states.

evangelicalism Protestant style of worship developed in Protestant church that emphasizes the work of the Holy Spirit in the world and the centrality of Biblical truth while retaining more of the traditional elements of Protestant denominations.

existentialism Rationalist philosophy associated with Jean-Paul Sartre whose key tenet, "existence precedes essence," demands that we take action and make something of the world, or at least of our lives in it.

F

familia   The essential social unit of the Roman Republic, comprising an entire household.

fasces   Name of the symbol of Roman power over its citizenry—a battle-ax lashed to a bundle of birch rods. The root of the modern term **Fascism**.

Fascism   The belief that force, directly applied to achieve a specific end, is the best form of government, exemplified by the dictatorships of Adolf Hitler (r. 1934–1945) and Benito Mussolini (r. 1922–1945).

Fatimids   Dynasty of Shi'a rulers in 10th-century Egypt in parts of the Holy Land and Syria; they derived their name from Fatimah, the daughter of the Prophet Muhammad.

fatwa   An Islamic legal pronouncement.

feminist movement   A series of movements from the 19th century through the present day that aim to reform policies and practices that oppress the rights and well-being of women.

Fertile Crescent   The region of the Middle East roughly framed by the Mediterranean to the west, the Arabian Peninsula to the south, and the Tarsus and Zagros Mountains to the north and east. The Tigris and Euphrates rivers flow through the center of this region, whose rich soils and abundant water gave rise to early agriculture. The Fertile Crescent connected central Asian and eastern Mediterranean economies.

feudal bonds   The relationship between lord and vassal, whereby the lord granted dominion over property to the vassal in exchange for the vassal's pledge of service to the lord.

Final Solution   Nazi program of systematic deportation and murder of Jews throughout Germany and all German-occupied territories during World War II.

al-fitnah   "Rebellion." Used to describe an uprising against an impious ruler (not merely an unjust one).

Fourteen Points   Woodrow Wilson's proposal, presented to the Paris Peace Conference (1919), for rebuilding Europe in the aftermath of World War I; ultimately rejected because of French and British concerns.

Franciscans   Mendicant order established by Saint Francis of Assisi (1181–1226) dedicated to preaching and service to the urban poor.

Freemasonry   Secret society that claimed its origins lay in medieval trade guilds; its members, wealthy bourgeoisie and noblemen alike, met in private clubs (or "lodges") to conduct business.

Freidenkerbund   "Freethinkers' League." An early secularist group in Germany, formed in the 19th century.

Fronde   Rebellion of French aristocrats against the tax policies of Cardinal Mazarin, during the regency for the underage King Louis XIV. Began in 1648.

fundamentalism   American Protestant style of worship that insists on the presence of a fundamental Truth in every Scriptural passage and urges personal and societal reform before the approach of Armageddon; from the 1980s, fundamentalism has had considerable influence on American politics, particularly the Republican Party.

G

Gastarbeiter   The "guestworkers," chiefly from Turkey, welcomed into Germany in the postwar era to rebuild the nation. German labor shortage necessitated the importing of workers.

General Theory of Relativity   Einstein's theory (1915) describing gravity's relationship to space-time.

genocide   Term coined in 1944 by Raphael Lemkin, a lawyer and Polish Jew, to describe the extermination of a particular racial or ethnic group, such as Germany's **Final Solution**.

Ghettos   Segregated communities of Jews in European cities.

Gini coefficient   Standard for measuring wealth and income distributions, named for Italian statistician Corrado Gini (1884–1965).

Girondins   One of several factions during the French Revolution; a relatively moderate group, they championed a constitutional monarchy until they were driven from power by the more radical Jacobins.

glasnost   "Openness," literally, in Russian. Specifically, the policy in the Soviet Union under Premier Mikhail Gorbachev to relax the traditional censorship of Soviet television, radio, and print media and to permit greater freedom of speech.

Glorious Revolution   Coup in 1688 that deposed the Catholic king James II of England and replaced him with the popular Protestant ruler of Holland, William of Orange (who was married to James II's daughter Mary).

gold standard   Monetary system, initially introduced in the West by Britain in 1821 and abandoned by most countries in the aftermath of the Great Depression, that pegs a currency to the price of gold.

Good Friday Accord   Treaty signed in 1998 that ended eighty years of terrorist conflict in Northern Ireland.

Great Depression   (1929–1936) Global economic depression that began with the crash of the New York Stock Exchange on October 29, 1929, resulting in massive unemployment and economic crises worldwide.

Greater West The matrix of European and Near Eastern cultures originating in the Fertile Crescent and still resonant today through bonds of trade, intellectual cross-fertilization, cultural overlap, and religious rivalry.

Great Purge Brutal efforts, beginning with show trials in 1936, by Josef Stalin (r. 1931–1953) to eliminate anyone he considered an enemy of the Soviet Union.

guild Artisanal and commercial trade associations that set prices, quality standards, methods and volume of production, and wages paid to workers. Guilds also assigned market shares to individual artisans or merchants.

gulag Network of Soviet Russian prison camps used to incarcerate political dissidents and enemies. Begun under Lenin and greatly expanded under Stalin, the gulag accounted for the deaths of roughly a million prisoners annually from the 1930s to the 1980s.

gynaeceum Area of a private home in ancient Greece restricted to women, their children, and their servants. Greek women were strictly segregated from public life and did not enter public areas of their own homes without the permission of their husbands.

H

hadith The written record of the actions and non-Qur'anic teachings of the Prophet Muhammad. The two most significant collections are those by al-Bukhari (d. 870) and al-Muslim (d. 875).

haeresis Term for the "philosophical sects" among the Jews of ancient Palestine (Pharisees, Sadducees, Essenes). Later used to refer to the "heresies" of post-Nicean Christianity.

hajj The pilgrimage of Muslims to Mecca, held annually. All able-bodied Muslims are expected to undertake the hajj at least once in their lives.

Hamas Conservative religious-political Palestinian group (and offshoot of the **Muslim Brotherhood**) equally devoted to charitable campaigns and social work among the Palestinians and to a terrorist war upon Israel.

Haredim The so-called Ultra-Orthodox Jews of Israel; they make up somewhere between 5 and 10 percent of the population.

Hasidim Adherents to a revivalist movement in Judaism, started in the mid-18th century in the Polish-Lithuanian Commonwealth by the Ba'al Shem Tov (d. 1760). Using highly emotive language and physical expression, Hasidic Judaism challenged the rather staid formalism of synagogue worship.

Haskalah Hebrew term for "enlightenment."

Hellenistic Age The era beginning with the death of Alexander the Great (323 BCE) and concluding with the conquest of the East by the Romans (327 BCE) and marked by a broader degree of cultural cohesion than previous eras, including the development of a common dialect of Greek (**Koine**) used across the territories. Although art and literature did not flourish as they did in the Classical Age, tremendous advances were made in the sciences.

heliocentrism First articulated by Copernicus, the observation that Earth is one of several planets that orbit around a stationary sun.

helot Slave owned by the city-state of ancient Sparta. Comprising roughly 75 percent of the Spartan population, they performed virtually all the labor, leaving the Spartans themselves free to perform military and civic service.

hetaera Ancient Greek courtesan, skilled in music and witty conversation in addition to her erotic services.

hieroglyphs System of writing used in ancient Egypt, especially in official records.

higher criticism Scholarly study of the Bible that seeks to determine the origins of the Biblical texts in time and place, in the process challenging long-held beliefs about the authority of Scripture. Synonymous with **historical criticism**.

hijab The "covering" of women required in Islamic society. Varies widely from country to country, depending on ethnicity, denomination, and to some extent to class. Least extensive covering is a simple headscarf; most extensive is the full-length burqa.

Hijrah The migration, or exodus, of Prophet Muhammad and his company of the faithful from Mecca to Madina in 622 CE. Marks Year 1 in the Islamic calendar (1 AH).

historical criticism See **higher criticism**.

historical materialism In Marxist theory, the process by which economic concerns propel historical change.

Hittites Indo-European group that settled in north-central Anatolia and by 1700 BCE had united into a single kingdom whose military repeatedly challenged Mesopotamia and Egypt.

Holocaust The systematic murder of six million Jews by the Nazis.

honestiores The senatorial and equestrian classes, municipal officials, and army veterans and their status entitling them to immunity from torture, lesser criminal fines, and, in capital crimes, exemption from crucifixion.

honor killings In some Muslim countries, and among some Arab immigrant communities in the

West, the murder of Arab women thought to have tarnished the honor of their families. The murder of these women by family members is believed to restore the family's honor.

hoplites Ancient Greek infantrymen serving in a phalanx; name derives from Greek word (*hoplos*) for the smallish, circular shields they carried.

household gods Family deities who watched over the family's farmland, household, and possessions. The daily worship of the household gods was the responsibility of the paterfamilias.

hubris Arrogant self-pride, the deadliest of moral sins to the ancient Greeks; specifically, the delusional belief that one was in control of one's own fate. Frequently used as the plot device to trigger the dire events in Greek tragedy.

Huguenots The Calvinists in 16th-century France, led by Henri de Navarre.

humiliores Everyone in the Roman Empire apart from the honestiores and the slaves (the latter, in terms of the law, were counted as property rather than people). The humiliores were expected to obey the law, pay their taxes, participate in public religious rites, and hold to the ethical duties of family care and public service.

Hundred Years' War From 1337 to 1453 CE; fought between England and France, beginning when England's king Edward III (r. 1327–1377) laid claim to the French throne; France (led, at one point, by the young girl Joan of Arc) eventually won.

Hyksos ascendancy The Second Intermediate Period (1640–1570 BCE) of the Middle Kingdom, so named because of the revolt of foreign laborers against the Egyptian government.

I

Ideal Forms In Plato's philosophy, the concept of a perfect and ultimate reality, of which our own perceived reality is but a flawed and flimsy reflection. Because we have a dualistic nature composed of an eternal soul temporarily housed in a flawed and mortal body, we can apprehend and aspire to that perfection.

ijma' Arabic, "consensus"; in the Sunni tradition, a principle that embraced the use of reason to resolve a religious question among a community of scholars. Once the community's answer on any given questioned had been authoritatively expressed, the question was considered closed for all time.

The Iliad Epic composed by Homer (ca. 750 BCE) recounting the events of the Trojan War in the Mycenaean age many centuries earlier. The epic evokes a lost, heroic, semimythological, and highly romanticized version of Greek history.

illuminationism Twelfth-century Persian philosophical program that attempts to harmonize Sufism, Shi'ism, and rational philosophy.

imam In Sunni Islam, a community leader who recites Qur'anic verses during prayer services. In Shi'ite Islam, a charismatic spiritual leader, a successor and descendant of Prophet Muhammad through the line of Fatima and Ali.

imperator Title assumed by Augustus and all subsequent rulers of Rome; often translated as "emperor" but in the Republic referred to a triumphant military general.

imperialism European (and, later, American as well) dominance of non-Western cultures for the exploitation of natural resources as well as political gain.

Index of Forbidden Books A list of books proscribed by the Catholic Church, first published in 1599 and continually revised until its final suppression in 1966.

Indo-European A horde of nomadic and herding nations, loosely related by their dialects of the language family, who began to migrate from their homeland near the Black Sea toward western Europe, the Aegean, and Asia Minor from about 2000 BCE. Other groups migrated eastward.

indulgences Donations to the Catholic Church as a means of satisfying the requirements for the forgiveness of sin.

industrial revolution The burgeoning 19th-century economy driven by mechanization, factories, an investment in infrastructure, and a growing workforce

Inquisition Campaign by the Catholic Church to identify and correct heresy; heretics who would not admit their errors were punished, in some instances brutally.

intendants Officials appointed by the royal court in Versailles to oversee the administrative work of the aristocracy during the Age of Absolutism.

intifada "Uprising." Organized mass protests of Palestinians against Israeli occupation of the West Bank and Gaza (1987–1993). The Second Intifada lasted from 2000 to 2005.

Ionian League An alliance (ca. 750 BCE) of several Greek coastal cities in Asia Minor organized by the vibrant and prosperous city of Miletus.

'ird Arabic, "honor" or "purity"; in Islam, a quality that women either possessed or did not possess. If a woman lost that quality, the moral shame spread to her family; the only way to redeem the family's honor was to kill the woman who had transgressed.

Irish Republican Army Terrorist group founded in the 1910s to fight what it saw as

English tyranny and Protestant oppression of Catholics in Northern Ireland

Iron Curtain   Military and ideological barrier dividing the Soviet bloc from western Europe between 1945 and 1990.

Islam   Religion founded by the Prophet Muhammad (570–632). In Arabic, the word "islam" means "surrender" and implies the fundamental duty of mankind to submit to the absolute authority of Allah.

isonomia   Equality before the law. The term originates with the ancient Greek reformer Cleisthenes, but the notion of a single standard of behavior for all members of a community dates back to the ancient Hebrews.

Israel   One of two Hebrew kingdoms (937–721 BCE), this one in the north of Palestine with Shechem as its capital.

J

Jacobins   Radical party that seized power from the Girondists during the French Revolution. Resolutely antimonarchist, the Jacobins executed King Louis XVI and his family in 1793, outlawed Christianity, and sought to create a classless society based on radical principles.

Jacquerie   Popular uprising in France (1358).

al-Jahiliyya   Term (literally "Age of Ignorance" or "Age of Barbarism") used by Arab historians to describe the era between the death of Jesus and the birth of Muhammad.

Janissaries   Elite military caste in the Ottoman Empire, 14th–19th centuries. The ranks of Janissaries were filled with Christian children, either orphaned or kidnapped from their parents, who were then converted and given a special, highly disciplined, military upbringing.

Jesuits   Ecclesiastical order, founded by Saint Ignacio de Loyola in 1540, particularly devoted to education and missionary work.

jihad   "Struggle," literally. Refers to any conscious, intentional, and persistent effort to advance the cause of Islam in the world. The term has a broad range of meanings, from something as innocuous as a personal vow to live a more committed Islamic life to a determination to wage religious war against the perceived enemies of God.

jizya   Poll tax levied on all non-Muslims in an Islamic state.

Judah   One of two Hebrew kingdoms (937—721 BCE), this one in the south of Palestine and centered on Jerusalem. (See **Israel**.)

judges   As described in the Bible, the leaders of each of the twelve tribes of Hebrews who moved into Palestine around 1200 BCE, after being delivered from Egypt.

Junkers   Landed aristocracy in Brandenburg-Prussia in the 17th–18th centuries. In popular usage the term came in the 19th century to designate all types of conservative, wealthy elites.

justification by faith alone   Luther's understanding that one attains salvation not through the purchasing of **indulgences** or other outward acts but simply by having faith in Christ.

K

Ka'ba   The holiest shrine of Islam. Temple in Mecca housing the stone believed to mark the site of Abraham's altar to Allah. Originally a pagan shrine dedicated to all the deities of the pre-Islamic Arab tribes. Site of the **hajj**.

Kabbala   A mystical interpretation of scripture developed by rabbis that became newly popular in the 17th century in part via the influence of Sabbatai Zvi (1626–1676).

kalam   "Theology." Unsystematic effort to provide rational explanation of basic religious mysteries in early Islam on the nature of the Qur'an and the attributes of Allah.

khalifah al-rasul Allah   "Deputy of the Prophet of God," literally. Title of the ruler (caliph) of the Islamic empire.

khan   The hereditary leader of a given tribe of Mongols.

King James Bible   English translation of the Scriptures commissioned in 1604 by King James I of England.

Koine   The demotic form of Greek used throughout the Middle East during the Hellenistic Age and the early Christian era.

Kristallnacht   "Crystal Night," literally; the "Night of Broken Glass," poetically. The organized Nazi attacks on Jewish businesses, synagogues, and homes throughout Germany on November 9, 1938. Widely regarded as the turning point from Nazi anti-Semitic discrimination to blatant pursuit of genocide.

kulak   "Fist," literally. Term popularized by Lenin and Stalin to designate relatively wealthy peasant freeholders who opposed the Communist regime in early 20th-century Russia.

Kulturkampf   Otto von Bismarck's "cultural war" against Catholicism in Germany.

Kyoto Protocol   International agreement, adopted in 1997, to combat global warming by reducing greenhouse gas emissions. The United States is not among the almost two hundred nations who have since signed and ratified the protocol.

L

laissez-faire "Leave it alone," literally. Term used to identify the economic doctrine of allowing markets to self-regulate, without government interference. First articulated by Adam Smith in *The Wealth of Nations* (1776).

Lares The ancestral household gods that protected homes in the Roman world; also the statuettes that represented them in family shrines.

Late Antiquity Term ancient historians use for the Dark Ages.

Lateran Agreement Agreement (1929) between Mussolini and Pope Pius XI that recognized the Vatican as a sovereign state in exchange for the Catholic Church's support of Mussolini's Fascist regime.

latifundia Slave-worked plantations in ancient Rome, especially during the republic.

Latins Name of the original settlers of the region of Latium.

League of Augsburg Alliance forged by Holy Roman emperor Leopold I in 1686 for defense against French expansionism; members included England, the Low Countries, Sweden, and several German principalities as well as the Holy Roman Empire.

League of Nations Woodrow Wilson's proposed international body that would arbitrate disputes, oversee demilitarization, and provide for collective security.

Lebensraum "Living space," literally. The conviction that the territorial losses forced upon Germany by the Treaty of Versailles (1919) had denied the German people sufficient space in which to live and thrive. Under the Nazis, it evolved into the policy of demanding the unification of all German-inhabited lands.

legatus Commander of a legion selected by the Roman emperor from members of the Senate. In smaller provinces, the legate also served as the provincial governor.

liberalism Political view calling for civil liberties, equality under the law, the right to vote, and a free market economy.

Libertas ecclesie "Freedom for the Church!" Popular rallying cry of the Peace of God reform movement in the 10th and 11th centuries.

libertarian Political stance that supports very small and highly limited government and opposes almost all forms of taxation.

Linear A Script used by Minoan culture on ancient Crete. Underlying language has not been identified, and hence the script has not been deciphered.

Linear B Syllabic script used by ancient Mycenaeans in Crete. Underlying Language is an early dialect of Greek, and the script was deciphered by 1953.

logos "Word," literally. Neoplatonic term for the spirit of wisdom that lies at the center of creation, from which emanate the **Ideal Forms** and all the elements of the cosmos. Term adopted by early Christians (see Gospel of John) to refer to Christ as the "Word of God" made flesh.

Lollards Anticlerical heretical group that condemned Catholic corruption and worldliness, believed in the right of nonpriests to preach, and taught that to live according to the spirit of Christ was more important than to follow the many letters of the church's laws.

longbow Fourteenth-century innovation in weapons technology that, by moving bow-and-arrow weapons from cavalry to infantry, allowed for the length of the bow to be greatly increased and therefore the range of its arrows considerably expanded.

lord In the feudal system, the figure who could grant vassals dominion over manors.

lugal Old Sumerian title of city-state kings in Mesopotamia.

Lyceum School founded by the philosopher Aristotle in Athens in 335 BCE.

M

ma'at Concept of cosmic order in ancient Egypt, everything being in perfect balance; includes the notions of meaning, justice, and truth, although in a passive sense, asking people not to upset divine harmony by attempting to alter the political and religious order.

madrasa Islamic religious school attached, administratively and often physically, to a mosque. Study focused on memorization of the Qur'an, with subsequent forays into Islamic law and literature.

magi Zoroastrian priests.

Maginot Line Barricade of artillery casements, machine-gun pillboxes, tank formations, barbed wire, minefields, and concrete bunkers built by France along its border with Germany.

Magna Carta Agreement in 1215 between the king of England and English lords, establishing certain constraints on royal power.

Magna Mater The "Great Mother," Cybele. There was a passionate religious cult dedicated to this life-giving goddess. A rival for popularity with Christianity.

Mahdi Messianic figure expected by Shi'ite Muslims; believed to be the return of the "Hidden Imam" who has gone into seclusion until the end of time.

mamluk   A slave-soldier in the medieval Islamic world.

mandates   Semi-independent states created in the Middle East by the League of Nations after World War I, dividing territories of the former Ottoman Empire between Britain and France.

Manhattan Project   Secret American program to develop an atomic bomb, begun in 1939 under the scientific direction of J. Robert Oppenheimer.

manors   In a feudal system, collective farms under the authority of lords.

Mare Nostrum   To Romans, the Mediterranean ("Our Sea" in Latin).

market   Term coined by economist Adam Smith (1776) to describe commerce as a rational pattern of human behavior.

Marshall Plan   American plan to rebuild western Europe after World War II by providing cash, credit, raw materials, and technical assistance to jump-start industrial production.

al-ma'siyah   "Disobedience." Justified resistance to a ruler or government who violates religious law.

maskilim   "Enlightened Ones," literally. Jewish religious scholars in the 18th century who worked to harmonize Jewish tradition with the principles of the Enlightenment.

mawali   Non-Arab Muslim converts in the Islamic empire.

medieval   In western Europe, the period between the end of the Dark Ages and the beginning of the Renaissance.

Mehmet Ali Pasha   Pro-Western dynastic leader of Egypt (r. 1805–1848) who built a powerful Egyptian military force, professionalized the government along Western lines, and developed both industry and education.

mendicant orders   Groups (such as the Dominicans and the Franciscans) dedicated to assisting the clergy in the performance of their evangelical mission.

Mensheviks   Faction of the Russian Revolution that was generally more moderate than Lenin's **Bolshevik** faction and was ultimately defeated by the Bolsheviks in 1917.

mercantilism   The economic policy of absolutism, defining economic wealth as tangible assets and promoting protectionism with the aim of concentrating wealth among as few individuals as possible.

Merovingians   Warrior dynasty who ruled as kings of the Franks from ca. 500 to the ascent of the Carolingians (ca. 754).

messiah   In the Jewish tradition, an earthly savior who would bring justice and create a safe, unified state for the Jews.

Midrash   Rabbinic literature that explicates Biblical texts.

miles/milites   Term for the warlord(s) of the 10th and 11th centuries who emerged from the breakup of the Carolingian Empire. By 12th century the term is translated as "knight(s)."

Minoan   An ancient and wealthy commercial culture that flourished from 2000 to 1500 BCE, centered on the island of Crete and named for its legendary founder, King Minos. Later Greek culture and mythology were profoundly influenced by the Minoans, and one of the two written scripts (called Linear B) used by Minoans records an early form of Greek.

missi dominici   Itinerant representatives of the Carolingian emperor, sent out to check on the job performance of the comites in the provinces.

modernism   1. To the Catholic Church in the early 20th century, a deplorable trend toward intellectual novelty that trivialized Scriptural truth and claimed "that there is nothing divine in sacred tradition [of the Church]." 2. Highly diverse cultural movement (roughly 1860–1950) that simultaneously rejects previous attitudes about how artists should work and resists the contemporary impersonality of mass-produced culture.

monasticism   In the rapidly Christianizing world, the movement to reject normal family and social life, along with the concern for wealth, status, and power, in favor of a harsh life of solitude and spiritual discipline in communities of other monks.

Mongols   Diverse group of nomadic Asian tribes that, through a series of brutal conquests in China, Russia, and the Muslim world, covered at its height in 1279 nearly one quarter of the Earth's land surface.

monotheism   The belief in a single, supreme deity.

Morgengab   The morning gift owed by a husband to his bride after the wedding night, in compensation for her lost virginity, among early Germanic peoples.

mullah   A Persian word used primarily in non-Arabic speaking Shi'i Muslim countries (e.g., Iran, Afghanistan, Pakistan) to designate a low-level cleric. It is a term of respect rather than a designation of office. With a literal meaning of "guardian" or "caretaker," it carries a colloquial sense analogous to the English word *reverend*, stripped of any ecclesial meaning. Used primarily by Shi'i Muslims and throughout Pakistan and India by both Sunnis and Shi'a.

Mulla Sadra   The greatest Muslim philosopher of the modern era; his most important book is *The Four Journeys of the Intellect* (1638).

Muslim Brotherhood   Religious-political group founded in Egypt in 1928 that, after years of repression by Egypt's military and secular regime, assumed power following elections in 2011.

mut'a   A form of concubinage or "temporary marriage" permitted among Shi'i Muslims. Such marriages could be as short as twenty-four hours, as a means of legitimizing sexual activity.

Mu'tazilites   Dissident Muslim scholars who, counter to the tradition of **ijma'**, believed that whenever tradition and reason were in conflict, the scale tipped in reason's favor.

Mycenaean Greece   Society (1600 to 1200 BCE) marked by the dominance of mainland Hellenes in the Aegean region; named for the city of Mycenae, which according to tradition was the city ruled by the legendary King Agamemnon.

N

al-Nahda   Arabic, "awakening" or "renaissance"; nineteenth-century Islamic intellectual and cultural movement centered in Egypt that advocated the integration of Islamic and European culture.

Napoleonic Code   Systematic law code established by Napoleon that (among other principals) emphasized individuals' rights to property and standardized the legal structures for contracts, leases, and establishing stock corporations.

nationalism   A collective consciousness or awareness that the members of an individual nation-group share a depth of feelings, values, and attitudes toward the world.

naturalism   European literary movement (1850–1914) that aimed to depict the whole array of pressures, demands, irritations, and longings that shape human lives in as much specific and realistic detail as possible. Sometimes used (though inaccurately) as a synonym for Realism.

Neo-Lutheranism   German religious movement of the mid-19th century that sought to reaffirm the distinctive Lutheran heritage. However, adherents were divided among conservatives who argued for scriptural inerrancy, moderates who privileged the institutional tradition of Lutheranism, and more liberally inclined believers who believed that traditional faith and the new sciences could be harmonized.

neoorthodoxy   Protestant theology founded by Swiss Calvinist theologian Karl Barth (1886–1968) that emphasizes the absolute strangeness and "complete Otherness" of God.

Neoplatonism   Spiritual philosophy derived from Plato that influenced both late Roman paganism and early Christian theologians.

New Deal   American economic initiatives launched by Franklin Delano Roosevelt to help the nation recover from the Great Depression by increasing government spending to employ men and women, provide price supports for farmers, offer unemployment insurance and retirement benefits, and create welfare programs.

New Historians   Young Jewish scholars and journalists, mostly born in Israel, whose archival research and writing has led to a more complex and less idealistic understanding of Zionism and the founding of Israel.

New Testament   Canon of twenty-seven works written after the death of Christ by or about various apostles.

new woman   The subject of innumerable journalistic and literary works in Europe, America, and parts of the Islamic world; a woman who, thanks to tremendous economic, cultural, and political shifts, was free to travel, get an education, and have a career.

Nicene Creed   Statement of fundamental Christian beliefs issued by an ecumenical council convened by Constantine in 323–325.

nihilism   Philosophical position of extreme skepticism that holds existence to be random, even meaningless.

Ninety-Five Theses   A list, published by Martin Luther in 1517, of assertions condemning the theology of indulgences.

noble savage   The idea, popularized by Jean Jacques Rousseau (1712–1778), that non-Europeans are untainted by civilization's corrupting influences.

nome   An economic and administrative district in ancient Egypt, composed of towns and villages along defined segments of the Nile River. The chief administrator of each nome was called a *nomarch*.

North Atlantic Treaty Organization (NATO)   Defensive alliance created by the United States in 1949 to protect Western Europe.

Nuremberg Trials   Trials of Nazi leaders for war crimes before an international tribunal of judges and prosecutors from the Allied countries, held in 1945–1946 in Nuremberg, Germany.

O

Oath of Supremacy   In Britain, an oath to recognize the monarch as the supreme head of the church within the realm. The oath effectively excluded Irish Catholics from holding public office or playing any part in public life.

Olympian deities   The numerous gods, worshipped by the ancient Greeks, whose passions and exploits are recounted in Greek mythology.

On the Origin of Species by Means of Natural Selection   Book by Charles Darwin (1859) that set forth his theory of natural selection as the means by which evolution occurs.

Organization of Petroleum Exporting Countries   Group of twelve oil-exporting countries that strongly influences both the production and the pricing of oil. A 1973 boycott by OPEC drove gas prices to record levels, disrupting the American economy.

Ottoman Turks   Dynasty founded by Osman (r. 1281–1324) that established a powerful state from the Balkans to Mesopotamia to North Africa.

Oxford Movement   Mid-19th-century English movement to reinforce the traditions of Anglican Christianity.

P

pacifism   In the aftermath of World War I, a term used to describe any principled and total rejection of violence as a means of resolving disputes.

Pale of Settlement   Region of Russian Empire where Jews were allowed to live (they were generally not allowed to live anywhere else in Russia), and the site of devastating pogroms in the late 19th century.

Palestinian Liberation Organization (PLO)   Political organization of Palestinian Arabs created in 1964 in opposition to the existence of the Jewish state of Israel.

Pan-Arabism   Ideology promoting the unification of all Arabs, particularly in opposition to Western imperialism. See **Ba'ath Party**.

Pan-Slavism   Populist approach of Tsar Aleksandr III (r. 1881–1894) that resulted in vicious persecution of Russian Jews, who were portrayed as exploiters of the common Russian people.

Pantheon   A temple built by the emperor Hadrian (r. 117–138 CE) in Rome and dedicated to the whole roster of major deities within the empire.

parlements   Ancient French aristocratic-led system of legal courts reestablished during the regency of Louis XV as a way to extend aristocratic privileges; Louis XV tried to overturn the parlements when he came of age.

paterfamilias   In the Roman Republic, the head (always male) of a household. The paterfamilias had complete authority over the familia and was the sole possessor of its property.

patria potestas   "Paternal power," the authority given by Roman law and custom to the male head of a household. Patria potestas gave the man possession of everything owned by the members of his household and gave him the power of life and death over every member except his wife.

patrilinear   Describes a social system in Mesopotamia and elsewhere, a society in which only men can inherit property.

Pax Romana   The "Roman Peace," a period of general peace and prosperity in the Roman Empire from Augustus (d. 14 CE) to Marcus Aurelius (d. 180 CE).

Peace of Augsburg   Compromise settlement (1555) between Charles V and Lutheran princes that granted Lutheranism legal recognition. With this policy, the religion of the local ruler determined the state religion of the principality, with certain guarantees offered of the rights of the religious minority.

Peace of God   Tenth-century rallies, initiated by peasants, for reform of the control warlords had over the church.

Peace of Westphalia   A collection of treaties (1648) negotiated by the first general diplomatic congress in Western history. Involving over one hundred delegations, it brought a century of European conflict to a close.

Peasants' Revolt   Popular uprising in England in 1381.

Peloponnesian War   (431–404 BCE) Prolonged war between Athens, which sought to dominate all of Greece, and Sparta, one of the last holdouts against Athenian supremacy. An epidemic of typhus in 429 BCE weakened Athens, while the Spartans' alliance with Persia allowed them to challenge and defeat the Athenian navy.

Pentecostalism   American Protestant style of worship that is charismatic, even antiintellectual, in its emphasis on a mystical union with God manifested by the ability to speak in tongues and perform miraculous healings.

perestroika   Collective term for the economic policies of Mikhail Gorbachev in the Soviet Union that allowed for the limited introduction of free-market mechanisms. "Restructuring," literally.

phalanx   A fighting unit of Greek foot soldiers: eight horizontal lines of ten to twenty men each, who stood shoulder to shoulder and moved as a single unit.

Pharisees   One of three "philosophical sects" into which Judean society was divided. Unlike other Jews, they held a belief in the immortality of the soul and the resurrection of the dead; they also anticipated the arrival of a messiah.

phenomenology Philosophy associated with Edmund Husserl (1859–1938) and based on the belief that whereas the world may or may not be rationally ordered, our reactions to it are.

Philistines An urban, commercial people with origins in Mycenaean Greece who settled just south of Phoenicia and engaged in hostilities against the Hebrews.

philosophes Self-chosen term for the thinkers and writers of the Enlightenment, applied to all regardless of their ethnicity.

Phoenicians A seafaring culture that established a trade network across the islands of the Mediterranean and the northern coast of Africa; the Phoenician alphabet formed the basis of the later Greek alphabet, and their great city of Carthage (established in the 9th century BCE) later challenged Rome for domination of the entire Mediterranean.

picaresque Like *Gargantua and Pantagruel*, a literary work that is a series of loosely connected and frequently funny or scatological episodes.

plebeians The class of free landowning Roman citizens, represented in the government of the Roman Republic by the plebeian council.

plenitudo potestatis The Roman Catholic Church's "fullness of power." Describes the church's obligation to speak out on any aspect of life with a significant moral component and its right to be heard. The policy was fully enunciated in the 13th century.

pogroms Beginning in 1881, vicious attacks from 1648 on against entire Jewish communities in the **Pale of Settlement**.

polis The ancient Greek city-state (plural form *poleis*).

pontifex maximus In ancient Rome, a title ("chief priest") held by the pagan emperor; the Christian emperor Constantine used this precedent to declare himself the head of the Christian church as well.

populism As Lenin understood it, moral compromise dressed up as common sense; more generally, a political approach that pits (often cynically) the common people against an (often imaginary or exaggerated) elite. See **Pan-Slavism**.

post-structuralism Intellectual movement associated with French philosopher Jacques Derrida (1930–2004) that, by challenging the authority of language, allows feminists, ethnic minorities, and others to look for the hidden assumptions in the work of critical thinkers of the past.

Prague Spring Reforms initiated in 1968 Communist Czechoslovakia by moderate leader Alexander Dubček, who described it as "socialism with a human face"; the reforms were squashed by a Soviet military intervention in August 1968.

Princeps Epithet taken by the emperor Octavian, meaning "first in honor" (because his name appeared first on the censor's list of Roman citizens).

proletariat A term popularized by Marx to describe the working classes. A revolution of the proletariat, Marx believed, would bring about the end of capitalism and the birth of a classless society.

protectionism The blocking of imports by tariff barriers or other legal means in order to promote the interests of a domestic mercantilist economy.

Protestant Reformation Movement initiated by Martin Luther that sought to recreate what he believed to be Christian belief and practice as they had existed in the apostolic church.

psychoanalysis Technique associated with Sigmund Freud (1856–1939) that seeks to understand the unconscious mind.

Punic Wars Three wars Rome fought with Carthage between 264 and 146 BCE, resulting in Roman dominance of the entire western Mediterranean basin.

putting-out system See **cottage industry**.

Pythagoreans Group of philosophers named after Pythagoras (570–495 BCE), who had developed the famous theorem about right triangles. They sought to identify rational order and laws governing the natural world; hence their focus on mathematics.

Q

qadi Islamic religious judge.

al-Qaeda "The Base," literally. Islamic terrorist organization created in the late 1980s by former rebels against the Soviet Army in Afghanistan. Led by Usamah bin Laden until his death in 2011.

Qajar Dynasty that ruled Iran from 1796 to 1925.

Qizilbash Network of militant units who fought to defend and uphold the Safavid dynasty of Iran.

quantum theory New theory of physics proposed by Max Planck (1858–1947) suggesting that both light and matter exist as waves and as particles.

Qur'an The holy book of Islam, revealed to the Prophet Muhammad.

R

rabbi An honorific Hebrew word meaning "my master." Rabbis were originally teachers of Jewish law. During the Babylonian Captivity, far from their ruined temple, many Jews turned to their rabbis for religious guidance. Rabbis became leaders of the exiled Jews and during this time refined the laws governing Jewish life.

Rape of Nanjing   Atrocities perpetrated by invading Japanese soldiers in the Chinese capital of Nanjing in December 1937–January 1938. Hundreds of thousands of Chinese civilians were brutally murdered.

rationalism   The essential characteristic of Greek thought, from Mycenaean times to the earliest known philosophers of Miletus (Thales, Anaximander, and Anaximenes); attempts to explain the natural world through observation rather than through mythology.

rationalist philosophy   Branch of philosophy that studies the movement of the human mind itself (as distinct from analytic philosophy, which emphasizes close and careful reasoning).

realist   See **naturalist**.

Realpolitik   Politics based on strategic and tactical realities instead of idealism.

Reconquista   "Reconquest," in Spanish. Refers to the long struggle (985–1492) between Christian and Muslim warlord-princes for control of the Iberian Peninsula.

Reichstag   Name of the lower parliamentary chamber in the German imperial government, 1871–1945.

Reign of Terror   Brutal period of French Revolution (1792) during which, at the direction of Robespierre, tens of thousands of French citizens believed to be opposed in any way to the Revolution were executed.

relativity   In physics, the concept that every vantage point in the universe, whether moving or stationary, is as valid as every other vantage point; as a cultural metaphor, the new and possibly frightening idea that there are no fixed points, no absolute time, and no absolute space.

religiones licitae   The legally approved religions of ancient Rome. Christianity became one in 375.

Renaissance   Literally "rebirth" (French); an era of tremendous cultural achievement as artists, scholars, and philosophers rediscovered the works of classical Greece and Rome and applied those ideas and aesthetics to contemporary arts, humanism, and modern statecraft.

Renaissance humanism   Movement of philosophers such as Pico della Mirandola to develop human potential, to value the particular, and to assert the inherent dignity of each person.

Rerum Novarum   (Latin, "of new things.") Encyclical issued by Pope Leo XIII (1891) that recognized the intrinsic rights of private property but insisted on the equal right of workers to form labor unions.

res publica   Latin term for "republic" or "commonwealth"; a form of government based on a system of checks and balances that emerged in Rome in 509 BCE.

al-riddah   "Insubordination" or "apostasy," depending on circumstance.

Risorgimento   "Resurgence," literally. This was the name given to the 19th-century movement for Italian national reunification.

Romanticism   Cultural and artistic movement in opposition to industrialization, preferring emotion and instinct over structural order and rational thought.

Rub' al-Khali   The "Empty Quarter" of the Arabian peninsula. Area of vast and almost impenetrable desert.

Rule of Saint Benedict   A communal handbook written by Saint Benedict of Nursia (480–547) to guide the monastery he had established; its focus on the physical and intellectual as well as spiritual well-being of monks led to its being widely adopted by monastic communities across medieval Europe.

Rumi   Sufi poet (1207–1273) whose work championed Islam without disparaging other faiths.

S

Sadducees   One of three "philosophical sects" into which Judean society was divided; an aristocratic party who were reputedly strict upholders of Temple ritual, dedicated to the literal reading of Scripture and the rejection of the Oral Torah.

Saint Bartholomew's Day Massacre   Riot (August 23–29, 1572) between Catholics and Protestant Huguenots that began in Paris and spread across France, resulting in the deaths of thousands.

salons   In urban, Enlightenment-era France, regular gatherings, often hosted by wealthy or aristocratic women in their own homes, to which philosophers, artists, and other cultural figures were invited to discuss ideas.

samizdat   Secret literature of political dissidents in Soviet Russia and Communist Eastern Europe, who passed officially condemned information, literature, and uncensored documents; important especially in the 1960s and 1970s.

sans-culottes   "Those without breeches," literally. Colloquial reference to political revolutionary militants in Paris drawn from the lower orders.

satire   Literary genre, originally popular among the Romans, that flourished during the

Renaissance. Satirical writers use humor or figurative language to mock and criticize powerful people and institution.

Schlieffen Plan   Military strategy created by German chief of general staff Alfred Graf von Schlieffen in 1905 that called for German forces to circumvent French defenses by striking swiftly through Belgium and Luxembourg; this was exactly how Germany proceeded at the start of World War I nine years later.

scholasticism   Method of research and teaching in medieval universities, characterized by the application of Aristotelian logic and the attempt to harmonize all knowledge.

scientific management   Management theory that increases the productivity of labor by breaking down manufacturing into small, distinct steps.

Scientific Revolution   From 1500 to 1700, a cultural, philosophical, and intellectual shift from a view of the universe as divinely created to a concept of the natural world as a system that could be understood through study and observation.

Sea Peoples   Indo-European invaders (ca. 1200 BCE) who conquered the Hittites, ended the Egyptian dominance of Palestine, and wrought enormous destruction across southern and southeastern Europe before vanishing, possibly through assimilation into local groups.

Second Industrial Revolution   Continuation of the earlier industrial revolution but with a focus instead on producing capital goods (goods, such as steel and chemicals, used to produce other goods).

Second Vatican Council   Convened by Pope John XXIII (r. 1958–1963) as part of the effort to modernize the Church's teachings and governance.

second wave feminism   Women's movement in the 1960s and 1970s that focused on sexual health, access to abortion and contraception, equal rights in the workplace, childcare services, gender roles in society, and portrayals of women in popular culture. (The "first wave" of feminism had focused almost exclusively on women's suffrage.)

secularism   The declining power of religious beliefs and institutions and the subsequent decline in religious practice.

Sephardim   Jewish people centered around the Mediterranean, where they remained in constant contact with Arab, Greek, and Latin cultural developments.

Septuagint   A Greek translation of the Hebrew Bible created by a group of seventy-two scholars who convened in Alexandria around 260 BCE (the name is derived from the Greek word for "seventy". It includes several books later excluded from the Jewish canon.

serfs   Dependent farmers who performed labor on manors in exchange for the security and primitive justice provided by the landlord.

shah   Persian term for "emperor."

shari'ah   Islamic religious law.

She'ol   The underworld of the Hebrew Bible, to which all the dead are sent; not analogous to later Christian concepts of hell as a place of punishment.

Shi'a   Muslims who believe that political and religious legitimacy could pass only to members of the Prophet Muhammad's hereditary line.

Shoah   See **Holocaust**

simony   Paying money or presenting gifts in return for ecclesiastical office, a widespread abuse in the Roman Catholic Church in post-Carolingian era and inspiring the Gregorian Reform.

Six-Day War   Military action (June 5–June 10, 1967) initiated by Israel against Egypt, Jordan, and Syria; Israel seized the Gaza Strip, the Golan Heights along the Israeli border with Syria, the Sinai Peninsula, and the entire West Bank, including the eastern part of the then-divided city of Jerusalem. After the stunning defeat of Arab allies, much of Arab popular resentment turned toward the United States.

Social Catholicism   Nineteenth-century European Catholic movement founded on the idea that the challenge to Christian society under industrialism was structural rather than personal.

social contract   Articulated in Thomas Hobbes's *Leviathan* (1651), the theory that when people decide to live in community they enter a covenant with each other, compromising their individual free wills in return for the benefits of society. Government, which bears responsibility for preserving social stability, may therefore legitimately assert its will on the community whenever it deems it necessary to do so.

social Darwinism   Misuse of Darwin's theory of evolution by natural selection to morally justify imperialism as a healthy competition among societies.

sodalitia   Special "fellowships" within the Roman Catholic Church—that is, groups of less formal rank than religious orders, organized usually around a special theme or mission. In the debates over religious modernism, numerous sodalitia loyal to the pope were granted oversight authority of parish clergy.

sola fide   "By faith alone." Central concept in Martin Luther's theology—the notion that faith in Christ alone is sufficient to gain salvation.

sola Scriptura   "By Scripture alone." Protestant belief, also originating with Luther, that the Bible is the sole source and sufficient authority (as opposed to tradition or the church) for divine teaching.

Sol Invictus   The Unconquered Sun. Pagan cult devoted to the sun god in the Roman Empire. Identified with the emperor Constantine, who encouraged it despite his personal Christianity.

Song of Songs   Biblical book, also known as the Song of Solomon, consisting of a poetic dialogue between a bride and bridegroom. Centuries of scholars have interpreted the Song of Songs as an allegory of the covenant between God and his people.

Sophists   In Greece in the 5th century BCE, a group of thinkers who traveled from city to city teaching rhetoric and philosophy.

South Sea Bubble   Economic crash (1720) sparked when the South Sea Company, an English company formed to trade with Spanish colonies in the New World, encouraged investors to speculate wildly on its supposed ventures but then could not make good on its unrealistic promises.

space-time   Einstein's concept of time and space as elastic and therefore understood as different facets of a single dimension.

Spanish Civil War   Internal conflict (1936–1939) between conservative and liberal forces in Spain that drew anti-Fascist support from around the world. The conservatives, under the Fascist dictator Francisco Franco (r. 1936–1975), won.

special theory of relativity   Einstein's theory (1905) that maintains that all measurements of space and time are relative; the basis of the idea that nothing can go faster than the speed of light.

stadtholder   Dutch term for "Head of State" in the 17th century, usually drawn from the noble house of Orange.

Stoicism   Philosophy most famously described and taught by Seneca (4 BCE–65 CE) and Epictetus (55–135 CE) that conformed to Roman morals through an emphasis on duty, forbearance, self-discipline, and concern for others.

streltsi   Semifeudalized noble cavalrymen who made up the Russian army until it was disbanded and reorganized by Tsar Piotr I in 1698.

structuralism   Philosophy rooted in the work of Swiss linguist Ferdinand de Saussure (1857–1913) that emphasizes the structured ways in which we see, participate in, and comprehend the world.

subsidiarity   Introduced by Pope Leo XIII, the principle that sought to preserve the dignity of persons and to help them recognize their own moral responsibilities and sought to safeguard against an overreaching centralized government.

suffrage   The right to vote.

suffragettes   European activists for women's rights who, in contrast with **suffragists**, favored confrontation, aggressive action, and, whenever they thought it necessary, even violence in order to change society.

suffragists   Activists for women's rights who, in contrast with **suffragettes**, worked peaceably and within the legal system for women's rights.

Sufism   A mystical, esoteric approach to Islam that flourished in the Ottoman Empire.

sultan   "Commander," literally. Term for chief military officer in the Turkish empire. Under the Ottomans, the word came to represent the head of state.

Sultanate of Women   Period (1640s and 1650s) of the Ottoman Empire when leading members of the imperial harem effectively controlled the state, directed foreign policy, and oversaw the fiscal system.

summa   A "summary," or an encyclopedic effort to organize all thought on a given topic; a popular genre among the scholastic writers of the 13th and 14th centuries, representing the conviction that a rational order underlay all of human life.

sumptuary codes   Dress codes in the cosmopolitan, diverse mercantile cultures of the Mediterranean that regulated styles of dress in order to establish the rules of engagement among different peoples.

sunnah   The collected sayings and actions of Prophet Muhammad, used to establish Islamic legal precedents.

Sunni   Muslims who regard selection by the community as the sole legitimate means to leadership of the Islamic world.

supermen   Term used by Friedrich Nietzsche (1844–1900) to describe cultural, political, and intellectual figures with a will to power.

Sykes-Picot Agreement   Pact between England and France (1916) that took advantage of the **Arab Revolt** to divide the dominions of the Middle East between the two nations.

Syllabus of Errors   Sixty-five teachings Pope Pius X decreed irredeemably anti-Catholic in two 1907 encyclicals.

symposia   All-male drinking parties in ancient Greece where philosophical ideas were discussed.

syncretism   The union of religious doctrines.

T

taifas Petty princedoms in Muslim Spain, after the collapse of the caliphate in Cordoba in 1031.

takiyya "Concealment," literally. Practice of religious disguise permitted to Shi'i Muslims as a means to avoid persecution.

Talmud Codification of rabbinical law and commentary that became central to Jewish life starting in the Middle Ages. Two dominant forms exist: the Babylonian Talmud, compiled around 500 CE, and the Palestinian Talmud (also known as the Jerusalem Talmud), compiled around 400 CE. Reference to the "Talmud" usually means the Babylonian Talmud.

Tanakh A common name for the canonical Hebrew Bible—an acronym based on the letters T (for Torah, meaning "Instructions"), N (for Nevi'im, or "Prophets"), and K (for Ketuvim, or "Writings"). Traditionally believed to have been assembled by the "Men of the Great Assembly" around 450 BCE, modern scholars believe the compilation occurred later, between 200 BCE and 200 CE.

Tanzimat (Turkish, "reorganization"); a 19th-century movement by the Ottoman government to promote economic development and the integration of the empire's non-Muslims and non-Turks into civil society.

telos According to Aristotle, the intrinsic purpose or necessary role in the cosmic drama of every existing thing.

Tetrarchy Under Diocletian, a new system whereby the empire was formally divided into two halves with a separate emperor (**augustus**, in Latin) for each. Each half was further divided in half again, and each *augustus* therefore had a subordinate vice-emperor or *caesar*.

al-thawrah "Uprising," literally. Describes opposition to a government or ruler on account of the injustice of its rule. No directly religious overtone.

themes New system of organizing army under Byzantine emperor Heraclius in the 7th century that redistributed land to military officers and soldiers.

theory of evolution by natural selection As explained by Charles Darwin in his 1859 book *On the Origin of Species by Means of Natural Selection*, the process by which the superabundance of offspring produced by all living beings results in their competition for resources; over time, that competition favors traits in offspring that provide an advantage over their rivals.

Third Estate The branch of the French legislative body made up of elected representatives of the common people, including the bourgeoisie and wage earners. See **Estates General**.

Thirty Tyrants Committee of thirty Athenians appointed by the Spartan conquerors of Athens to rule the city.

Thirty Years' War Conflict that began in 1618 between Protestants and Catholics in Germany and gradually enveloped most of Europe, ending in 1648 after massive losses of life and property.

Tokyo Trials Trials (1946–1948) of Japanese officials for war crimes before an international tribunal of judges and prosecutors from the Allied countries.

Torah The first five books of the **Tanakh**, attributed to Moses.

totalitarianism A system of government that controls all aspects of society, using fear and intimidation to maintain power.

Treaty of Rome Treaty agreed to by Western European leaders in 1957 that established the European Economic Community to help postwar recovery and counterbalance American economic power.

Treaty of Versailles Controversial agreements that formally ended World War I on June 28, 1919, but ruinous concessions demanded from a defeated Germany were a contributing factor in the run-up to World War II.

Trinity For Christians, the doctrine in the existence of a single God in a union of three separate and divine "Persons."

trireme Ancient Greek warship with three tiers of oarsmen and a bronze-tipped battering ram on the prow.

troubadours Vernacular love poets popular in the aristocratic courts of southern France and northern Italy in the 12th and 13th centuries.

Truce of God An 11th-century decree by the reformed church banning warfare on holy days as well as the assault of religious pilgrims.

Twelve Tables The first written law code of the Roman Republic, ca. 450 BCE.

tyrant A person in a Greek polis who took power temporarily in order to bring about dramatic reform in a politically deadlocked state. In terms of social class, the tyrants were aristocrats but were allied with the masses.

U

'ulama Arab for "brotherhood" or "community," a central focus of Sunni life.

Umayyads Name of the ruling dynasty in the Islamic empire, 661–750. Governing the empire from their new capital at Damascus, the Umayyads were overthrown in 750 by the Abbasids, who transferred the capital to newly built Baghdad.

ummah   The community of Muslim believers.

uniformitarianism   Geologist James Hutton's theory that geological change consists of the slow accumulation of smaller changes—and these changes continue to happen in the present.

United Nations (UN)   Organization of member nations established in 1945, including a permanently standing International Court of Justice and International Criminal Court.

Universal Declaration of Human Rights   The first statement of global rights in history, drafted and promoted by American First Lady Eleanor Roosevelt and approved on December 10, 1948, by most members of the United Nations (Saudi Arabia, South Africa, and the Soviet Union abstained).

UN Women's Conference   International conferences sponsored by the United Nations to promote women's rights as *human* rights.

ushabti   Figures made of clay or wood, buried with well-to-do Egyptians, that represented servants who would work for one in the afterlife.

Utilitarianism   Philosopher John Stuart Mill's ethical principal that "holds that actions are right in proportion as they tend to promote happiness, wrong as they tend to produce the reverse of happiness"; based on this principle he argued that women should have the right to vote and determine their own destiny.

V

vassal   In a feudal system, a free man who pledged to serve a lord in exchange for dominion over a manor or manors bestowed by the lord.

vizier   Regional administrator under the Abbasid dynasty and later under the Ottomans. From the word meaning "burden sharer."

Volk   The German people. Related etymologically to the English word *folk* but with a different meaning. Used in a combined colloquial and mystical sense.

W

wadi   Seasonal river in Middle East.

Wahhabism   Conservative reform movement within Sunni Islam, taking its name from the 18th-century figure Muhammad ibn Abd al-Wahhab. The movement stresses returning to strict reliance on Qur'an and hadith, purging Islam of non-Arabic traditions, and restoring ethnic Arabs to leadership in international Islam.

The official sect in Saudi Arabia in the 20th and 21st centuries.

War of the Roses   English civil war for the throne (1455–1485) fought between the noble houses of York and Lancaster.

welfare states   In post–World War II Western Europe, societies in which the central government, funded by heavy taxation, provided all essential social services.

wergild   Old Germanic term—"man money," literally—for the compensation owed by an offender to his victim, according to custom.

will to power   Term used by Friedrich Nietzsche (1844–1900) to describe the passionate striving to make meaning and leave a mark on the world.

Women's International League for Peace and Freedom   Pacifist group founded in 1915 that campaigned for equal rights for all citizens, economic justice, and greater understanding and empathy between peoples.

World Economic Forum   Nonprofit foundation that encourages global political and business leaders to work together to address and resolve global business, industrial, and environmental issues.

World Trade Organization   Intergovernmental organization seeking to liberalize trade between nations.

Y

YHWH   The term for "God" used by the Yahwist author of the Torah (see **Documentary Hypothesis**), represented in English-language Bibles by the all-capitals word LORD.

Young Turks   Modernizing faction in Turkey that promoted pan-ethnic Islamic nationalism, overthrowing the sultan Abdul Hamid II in 1909 and replacing him with his half brother Mehmed V (r. 1909–1918).

Z

zakat   The giving of alms to the poor, required of Muslims.

ziggurat   Step-pyramid temples of ancient Mesopotamia, believed to be the dwelling places of the gods.

Zionism   From Hebrew *Tsiyon*, the name for the central portion of Jerusalem, but by extension referring to all of Israel/Palestine. Movement by Jews (especially from Eastern Europe) to establish a Jewish state in the Holy Land as a refuge from European persecution beginning in the 19th century.

Zollverein "Customs union." The free-trade zone established by Prussia in the early 19th century; an important early step in German unification.

Zoroastrianism Monotheistic religion founded by Zoroaster in Persia ca. 1300 BCE. In its emphasis on moral behavior, personal salvation, and the eventual victory of Good in a cosmic battle with Evil, Zoroastrianism is considered by many a precursor of Judaism (and, by extension, Christianity).

zunnar Identifying belt worn by non-Muslims in the early Islamic empire.

Credits

CHAPTER 1: pg. 2 Erich Lessing / Art Resource, NY; pg. 13 bpk, Berlin / Art Resource, NY; pg. 14 Erich Lessing / Art Resource, NY; pg. 17 © The Trustees of the British Museum / Art Resource, NY; pg. 23 Werner Forman / Art Resource, NY; pg. 28 © The Trustees of the British Museum / Art Resource, NY.

CHAPTER 2: pg. 32 Erich Lessing / Art Resource, NY; pg. 37 Réunion des Musées Nationaux / Art Resource, NY; pg. 42–43 © Trustees of the British Museum; pg. 44 Gianni Dagli Orti / The Art Archive at Art Resource, NY; pg. 47 © DeA Picture Library / Art Resource, NY; pg. 50 Erich Lessing / Art Resource, NY; pg. 51 Vanni / Art Resource, NY; pg. 54 Drawn by Boudier, from a photograph by Beato; pg. 56 Weapon heads, from Lorestan, Iran, c. 1000 BC (bronze and iron), Elamite, (4000–650 BC) / National Museum of Iran, Tehran, Iran / The Bridgeman Art Library; pg. 60 Erich Lessing / Art Resource, NY; pg. 63 Scala / Art Resource, NY; pg. 65 © Tim Page / CORBIS.

CHAPTER 3: pg. 68 Courtesy of the Library of Congress; pg. 72 © Rafael Ben-Ari / Alamy; pg. 82 © DeA Picture Library / Art Resource, NY; pg. 84 Erich Lessing / Art Resource, NY; pg. 91 bpk, Berlin / Daniel Blatt / Art Resource, NY; pg. 94 Art Resource, NY.

CHAPTER 4: pg. 96 Marie Mauzy / Art Resource, NY; pg. 98 Museum of Fine Arts, Boston; pg. 100 Gianni Dagli Orti / The Art Archive at Art Resource, NY; pg. 102 Marie Mauzy / Art Resource, NY; pg. 103 public domain; pg. 108 Erich Lessing / Art Resource, NY; pg. 113 Gianni Dagli Orti / The Art Archive at Art Resource, NY; pg. 117 Courtesy of Ralph W. Mathisen; pg. 120 © National Gallery, London / Art Resource, NY.

CHAPTER 5: pg. 130 bpk, Berlin / Antikensammlung, Staatliche Museen / Juergen Liepe / Art Resource, NY; pg. 134 Alinari / Art Resource, NY; pg. 135 Erich Lessing / Art Resource, NY; pg. 136 © The Trustees of the British Museum / Art Resource, NY; pg. 138 bpk, Berlin / Staatliche Antikensammlung / Hermann Buresch / Art Resource, NY; pg. 141 © Balage Balogh / Art Resource, NY; pg. 150 bpk, Berlin / Musei Capitolini / Alfredo Dagli Orti / Art Resource, NY; pg. 153 Vanni / Art Resource, NY; pg. 155 (left) Scala / Art Resource, NY; pg. 155 (right) Erich Lessing / Art Resource, NY; pg. 158 Erich Lessing / Art Resource, NY; pg. 162 (left) Erich Lessing / Art Resource, NY; pg. 162 (center) Alinari / Art Resource, NY; pg. 162 (right) Alinari / Art Resource, NY; pg. 164 Erich Lessing / Art Resource, NY.

CHAPTER 6: pg. 170 Erich Lessing / Art Resource, NY; pg. 175 Scala / Art Resource, NY; pg. 177 © Araldo de Luca / CORBIS; pg. 179 Scala / Art Resource, NY; pg. 184 Vanni / Art Resource, NY; pg. 190 Alinari / Art Resource, NY; pg. 193 Ancient Art and Architecture Collection Ltd.; pg. 194 public domain; pg. 197 © Roger Wood / CORBIS; pg. 201 Erich Lessing / Art Resource, NY.

CHAPTER 7: pg. 204 Erich Lessing / Art Resource, NY; pg. 213 Erich Lessing / Art Resource, NY; pg. 221 public domain; pg. 222 Erich Lessing / Art Resource, NY; pg. 225 Erich Lessing / Art Resource, NY; pg. 227 Scala / Ministero per i Beni e le Attività culturali / Art Resource, NY; pg. 228 Aegyptisches Museum, Staatliche Museen, Berlin, Germany; pg. 230 © Corbis.

CHAPTER 8: pg. 236 Giraudon; pg. 238 Scala / Art Resource, NY; pg. 240 Courtesy of the Oriental Institute of the University of Chicago; pg. 243 Courtesy of the Kekelidze Institute of Manuscripts, Tbilisi, Georgia; pg. 245 Alinari; pg. 252 (top left) Bridgeman-Giraudon / Art Resource, NY; pg. 252 (bottom left) Vanni / Art Resource, NY; pg. 252 (right) Marie Mauzy / Art Resource, NY; pg. 255 Silvija Seres; pg. 259 © Kazuyoshi Nomachi / Corbis; pg. 261 Scala / Art Resource, NY; pg. 264 Fragment from a Qu'ran with Kufic script, North African (vellum), African School, (10th century) / © The Trustees of the Chester Beatty Library, Dublin / The Bridgeman Art Library; pg. 276 © Werner Forman / Corbis; pg. 279 (left) © Patrick Ward / CORBIS; pg. 279 (right) Art Resource, NY.

CHAPTER 9: pg. 282 Bridgeman-Giraudon / Art Resource, NY; pg. 290 Réunion des Musées Nationaux / Art Resource, NY; pg. 292 Vanni / Art Resource, NY; pg. 298 SEF / Art Resource, NY; pg. 301 BN, Arabe 5847, fol 5v; pg. 309 akg-images; pg. 312 bpk, Berlin / Dietmar Katz / Art Resource, NY; pg. 315 Erich Lessing / Art Resource, NY; pg. 316 Art Resource, NY; pg. 322 Erich Lessing / Art Resource, NY.

CHAPTER 10: pg. 328 Scala / Art Resource, NY; pg. 333 Erich Lessing / Art Resource, NY; pg. 334 akg-images / Henning Bock; pg. 336 Erich Lessing / Art Resource, NY; pg. 337 Archive Timothy McCarthy / Art Resource, NY; pg. 341

Bristol Record Office BRO 04720 (folio 152); pg. 343 Gianni Dagli Orti / The Art Archive at Art Resource, NY; pg. 345 © DeA Picture Library / Art Resource, NY; pg. 348 Réunion des Musées Nationaux / Art Resource, NY; pg. 351 Snark / Art Resource, NY; pg. 354 Scala / White Images / Art Resource, NY; pg. 358 National Palace Museum, Beijing; pg. 359 Image copyright © The Metropolitan Museum of Art. Image source: Art Resource, NY; pg. 363 Image copyright © The Metropolitan Museum of Art. Image source: Art Resource, NY; pg. 368 Erich Lessing / Art Resource, NY; pg. 370 Eileen Tweedy / The Art Archive at Art Resource, NY.

CHAPTER 11: pg. 372 Erich Lessing / Art Resource, NY; pg. 376 The Bodleian Libraries, The University of Oxford; pg. 379 © National Gallery, London / Art Resource, NY; pg. 382 Scala / Art Resource, NY; pg. 385 Courtesy of the Library of Congress; pg. 386 Erich Lessing / Art Resource, NY; pg. 389 public domain; pg. 391 Scala / Art Resource, NY; pg. 393 bpk, Berlin / Kunstmuseum / Art Resource, NY; pg. 395 © DHM; pg. 399 Photo: Albertina, Vienna, from Geisberg, Der deutsche Holzschnitt in der ersten Halfte des 16. Jahrhundert, Munchen 1923–1930; 30. Lieferung, Nr. 1243; pg. 402 The Pierpont Morgan Library / Art Resource, NY; pg. 406 Snark / Art Resource, NY; pg. 409 Courtesy of the Library of Congress.

CHAPTER 12: pg. 414 The Pierpont Morgan Library / Art Resource, NY; pg. 422 Snark / Art Resource, NY; pg. 424 Library of Congress, Rare Book and Special Collections Division; pg. 425 Peter Newark American Pictures; pg. 430 National Portrait Gallery, London; pg. 433 Rijksmuseum, Amsterdam, Langdurig bruikleen van de Gemeente Amsterdam, SK-C-232; pg. 436 Kharbine-Tapabor / The Art Archive at Art Resource, NY; pg. 439 public domain; pg. 445 Scala / White Images / Art Resource, NY; pg. 448 © The Trustees of the British Museum; pg. 450 Index / The Bridgeman Art Library; pg. 452 Snark / Art Resource, NY; pg. 455 Gianni Dagli Orti / The Art Archive at Art Resource, NY; pg. 457 Erich Lessing / Art Resource, NY.

CHAPTER 13: pg. 464 Plate XX from Volume I of *The Mathematical Principles of Natural Philosophy* by Sir Isaac Newton (1642–1727) engraved by John Lodge (fl. 1782) 1777 (engraving), English School, (18th century) / Private Collection / The Bridgeman Art Library; pg. 468 public domain;

pg. 471 (left) Erich Lessing / Art Resource, NY; pg. 471 (right) Courtesy of the Library of Congress; pg. 472 Courtesy of the Library of Congress; pg. 475 (left) Scala/Ministero per i Beni e le Attività culturali / Art Resource, NY; pg. 475 (right) Réunion des Musées Nationaux / Art Resource, NY; pg. 477 Courtesy José Luís Fernández-Castañeda, S.J., parish priest of the Church of San Pedro, Lima, and Administrator of the Jesuit Order in Peru; pg. 479 (left) Erich Lessing / Art Resource, NY; pg. 479 (right) Erich Lessing / Art Resource, NY; pg. 481 to Index ; pg. 483 Museo Galileo. Florence—Photo Franca Principe; pg. 487 Erich Lessing / Art Resource, NY; pg. 489 (left) Scala / Art Resource, NY; pg. 489 (right) Bridgeman-Giraudon / Art Resource, NY; pg. 490 Royal Asiatic Society, MSS 35; pg. 492 bpk, Berlin / National Portrait Gallery / Jochen Remmer / Art Resource, NY; pg. 495 Réunion des Musées Nationaux / Art Resource, NY.

CHAPTER 14: pg. 502 National Trust Photo Library / Art Resource, NY; pg. 507 public domain; pg. 509 Réunion des Musées Nationaux / Art Resource, NY; pg. 512 HIP / Art Resource, NY; pg. 514 Gianni Dagli Orti / The Art Archive at Art Resource, NY; pg. 518 akg-images; pg. 519 Giraudon; pg. 522 © Bristol City Museum and Art Gallery, UK / The Bridgeman Art Library; pg. 525 © The Trustees of the British Museum; pg. 527 Nimatallah / Art Resource, NY; pg. 518 © Photo: Bayerisches Nationalmuseum München, Bastian Krack. Fork: Inv. No. 36/37; Knife: Inv. No. 36/38; pg. 530 © Danita Delimont / Alamy; pg. 532 public domain; pg. 535 The Pierpont Morgan Library / Art Resource, NY; pg. 542 © Roger Wood / CORBIS; pg. 548 Eileen Tweedy / The Art Archive at Art Resource, NY.

CHAPTER 15: pg. 552 Alfredo Dagli Orti / The Art Archive at Art Resource, NY; pg. 558 Gianni Dagli Orti / The Art Archive at Art Resource, NY; pg. 564 Erich Lessing / Art Resource, NY; pg. 566 (left) SSPL/Science Museum / Art Resource, NY; pg. 566 (right) Alfredo Dagli Orti / The Art Archive at Art Resource, NY; pg. 567 Erich Lessing / Art Resource, NY; pg. 569 Gianni Dagli Orti / The Art Archive at Art Resource, NY; pg. 570 Erich Lessing / Art Resource, NY; pg. 571 Eileen Tweedy / The Art Archive at Art Resource, NY; pg. 575 public domain; pg. 579 Kimbell Art Museum, Fort Worth, Texas / Art Resource, NY; pg. 584 bpk, Berlin / Art Resource, NY; pg. 585 Erich Lessing / Art Resource, NY.

An Epic Search for Truth (New York: Bloomsbury USA, 2009), pg. 260; pg. 869 © Michel Ginfray / Apis / Sygma / Corbis; pg. 870 Private Collection / The Bridgeman Art Library; pg. 873 Freud Museum, London, UK / The Bridgeman Art Library; pg. 878 Collection of Riccardo and Magda Jucker, Milan, Italy / The Bridgeman Art Library; pg. 881 (top left) Digital Image © The Museum of Modern Art/Licensed by SCALA / Art Resource, NY; pg. 881 (top right) Harper Collins Publishers / The Art Archive at Art Resource, NY; pg. 881 (bottom left) Réunion des Musées Nationaux / Art Resource, NY; pg. 881 (bottom right) Digital Image © The Museum of Modern Art/Licensed by SCALA / Art Resource, NY.

CHAPTER 24: pg. 886 akg-images; pg. 893 Courtesy of the Library of Congress; pg. 894 Courtesy of the Library of Congress; pg. 900 Trustees of the Imperial War Museum, London, neg. no. Q67814; pg. 901 The Stapleton Collection; pg. 903 US Army / Photo Researchers, Inc; pg. 904 akg-images / ullstein bild; pg. 906 US Army / Photo Researchers, Inc; pg. 910 Royal Air Force Museum; pg. 914 bpk, Berlin / Art Resource, NY; pg. 916 Keystone-Mast Collection, UCR / California Museum of Photography, University of California, Riverside; pg. 920 Culver Pictures / The Art Archive at Art Resource, NY; pg. 921 Hoover Institution Political Poster Database; pg. 922 Culver Pictures / The Art Archive at Art Resource, NY; pg. 927 © CORBIS.

CHAPTER 25: pg. 930 Getty Images / Hulton Archive; pg. 935 Image courtesy of Andy Moursund, www.postersforclassrooms.com; pg. 938 Stanford University Archives; pg. 939 public domain; pg. 940 © Hulton-Deutsch Collection/CORBIS; pg. 944 Private Collection / The Bridgeman Art Library; pg. 946 Mary Evans Picture Library / Weimar Archive; pg. 950 The Stapleton Collection; pg. 952 Rue des Archives / The Granger Collection, NYC — All rights reserved; pg. 954 The Granger Collection, NYC — All rights reserved; pg. 960 ullstein bild / The Granger Collection, NYC — All rights reserved; pg. 961 akg-images / ullstein bild; pg. 965 public domain; pg. 966 McGill University Library; pg. 970 ullstein bild / The Granger Collection, NYC — All rights reserved.

CHAPTER 26: pg. 976 public domain; pg. 981 © CORBIS; pg. 983 Adoc-photos / Art Resource, NY; pg. 988 bpk, Berlin / Joe Heydecker / Art Resource, NY; pg. 991 © DeA Picture Library / Art Resource, NY; pg. 992 © Bettmann / CORBIS; pg. 994 Courtesy of the Library of Congress; pg. 997 Library of Congress, Prints and Photographs Division, LC-DIG-ppmsca-09153; pg. 1001 Snark / Art Resource, NY; pg. 1004 public domain; pg. 1006 Art Resource, NY; pg. 1009 Art Resource, NY; pg. 1011 Courtesy of the Library of Congress; pg. 1013 Adoc-photos / Art Resource, NY.

CHAPTER 27: pg. 1016 © Werner Bischof/ Magnum Photos; pg. 1021 The Art Archive at Art Resource, NY; pg. 1023 © Bettmann / CORBIS; pg. 1025 akg-images; pg. 1028 Henri Cartier-Bresson / Magnum Photos; pg. 1030 Getty Images; pg. 1033 /akg-images; pg. 1035 Time & Life Pictures/Getty Images; pg. 1036 Bruno Barbey / Magnum Photos; pg. 1040 Jacques Pavlovsky / RAPHO; pg. 1042 © Bettmann / CORBIS; pg. 1045 ©Alinari / The Image Works; pg. 1047 © Paul Almasy / CORBIS; pg. 1053 Felix Gluck, *Modern Publicity*, 1973–74 (London: Studio Publications, 1977).

CHAPTER 28: pg. 1056 © Alinari Archives / CORBIS; pg. 1062 The Art Archive at Art Resource, NY; pg. 1064 © Hulton-Deutsch Collection / CORBIS; pg. 1067 © J. Emilio Flores / Corbis; pg. 1070 bpk, Berlin / Rotraut Forberg / Art Resource, NY; pg. 1073 © Ricardo Azoury / CORBIS; pg. 1077 Gianni Dagli Orti / The Art Archive at Art Resource, NY; pg. 1079 © David Rubinger / CORBIS; pg. 1081 Snark / Art Resource, NY; pg. 1084 Copyright Bettmann / Corbis / AP Images; pg. 1087 © Ali Ali / epa / Corbis.

CHAPTER 29: pg. 1090 © Regis Bossu / Sygma / Corbis; pg. 1096 © Zen Icknow / CORBIS; pg. 1097 © Natalie Fobes / CORBIS; pg. 1101 © Bettmann / CORBIS; pg. 1108 © Gideon Mendel / CORBIS; pg. 1112 India Today Group / Getty Images; pg. 1116 © Hubert Boesl / dpa / Corbis; pg. 1117 © Bettmann / CORBIS; pg. 1120 © Paul A. Souders / CORBIS.

CHAPTER 30: pg. 1124 © Ed Kashi / VII; pg. 1129 © Jean-Paul Pelissier / Reuters / Corbis; pg. 1132 © Manca Juvan / In Pictures / Corbis; pg. 1134 Associated Press; pg. 1137 Getty Images Europe; pg. 1142 AFP / Getty Images; pg. 1145 Associated Press; pg. 1151 © Steve Raymer / Corbis; pg. 1155 © Britta Pedersen / epa / Corbis.

Index

Page numbers followed by *t* indicate a table. Page numbers followed by *m* indicate a map. Italicized page numbers indicate a figure or photo.

A

Abbas, Mahmoud, *1087,* 1135
Abbas I (Safavid shah), 460, 540–541
Abbasid dynasty
  blooming of philosophy during, 302
  coup against the Umayyads, 297
  courting of Turks by, 316
  Damascus palace coup, 284
  ethnic egalitarianism of, 303
  fall of, 318, 352, 453
  as Islam's Golden Age, 296, 303
  length of power of, *298*
  Mamluks as bodyguards for, 318
  murder of caliph al-Musta'sim, 354
  Persianization of Islamic life by, 740
  Shi'a withdrawal of support for, 297
  state-owned estates of, 296–297
Abbas II (Safavid shah), 541
Abd al-Wahhab, Muhammad ibn, 738–739
Abdul Hamid II (Ottoman sultan), 925
Abelard, Peter, 233
Ibn Abi Talib, Ali, 265
Abortion
  access in Great Britain, 1046
  Bolshevik regime's granting access for, 965–966
  Christianity and, 206
  countries with gender-selective abortion, 1138
  Hippocratic oath opposition to, 148
  illegality/availability of, 799
  Pelletier's campaign for women's rights, 795
  RU-486 pill development, 1061t
  second wave feminism access focus, 1044–1045
  Stalin's outlawing of, 1005
  Stöcker's campaign for women's rights, 796

About Chinese Women (Kristeva), 1111
Abram/Abraham (Genesis story)
  as the father of Judaism, 71
  God's ordering of son's sacrifice, 75
  name change to Abraham, 71–72
  origin of, 70n1
  pregnancy of servant Hagar, 70
  self-/son's circumcision rite, 71
  trek to Palestine, 69–70
Absalom and Achitophel (Dryden), 573–574
Absolutism, 510–512, 678–679
  citizen passivity in the face of, 547
  comparison table, 515t
  in Europe, 526, 542–544
  French Revolution and, 599
  Hobbes/Richelieu's arguments for, 512–513
  James II and, 537
  King James Bible and, 534
  mercantilism and, 513, 521–524
  Napoleon's war against, 601–605, 722
  origins of, 508
  of the Ottoman Empire, 539–540
  Spain's defense of, 601
Absurdity, notion of, 1021–1023
Académie française (French literary society), 513
Actium, Battle of, 173, 186, 188, 987
Act of Supremacy (England), 534
Act of Union (England-Ireland), 706, 724
Acts of the Apostles (New Testament), 208t
Acts of Toleration (for the Jews), 577
Adams, Henry, 857
Addams, Jane, 1006

Address to the Christian Nobility of the German Nation (Luther), 397–398
"Address to the German Nation" (Fichte), 660–661
Adelchi (Manzoni), 717
Adenauer, Konrad, 1033–1034, 1037
Adnan, father of "Arabized Arabs" (al-Arab al-musta'ribah), 254
The Adventures of Telemachus (Fénelon), 520
The Adventurous Simpleton (Grimmelshausen), 451–452
Advice to Young Ladies on the Improvement of the Mind and Conduct of Life (Broadhurst), 698–699
Aegean Sea islands. *See also* Mycenaean age (Greece)
  Hellenes domination of, 102
  Hyksos links with, 45
  wine imports from, 137
Aelianus, Claudius, 137
Aeneas (Trojan hero), 171, 226
Aeschylus, 140, 146t
Ibn Affar, Uthman, 265
Afghanistan
  Abbas II in, 541
  al-Qaeda's influence in, 1127
  Anglo-Russian Entente and, 894
  campaigns of Alexander in, 159
  isolation of women in, 1050
  Qizilbash religious community, 540
  Reubeni's travels to, 438
  Soviet Union invasion of, 1025, 1114, 1118
  Taliban radicals in, 1114, 1127–1128, 1133–1135
  U.S. led wars in, 1126, 1133–1135, 1145
Africa. *See also* North Africa; Sub-Saharan Africa
  agricultural-based settlements, 20–21
  Catholic/Protestant missionary work, 750

Christianity's introduction to, 38
Christian missionaries in, 38
colonization of, 888
European international investment in, 891m
European trade with, 425
feminist issues in, 1112
international scramble for, 830m
luxury goods trading, 254
Mongol conquests in, 355m
1960s emigration to Britain, 1038
ongoing commercial development, 826
Portuguese ocean voyages to, 417
Protestant communities in, 1071
Punic War assault on, 183
trade routes, goods production map, 418m
trading with Phoenicians, 57
women's rights successes in, 1112
Africa poem (Petrarca), 384–385
Afrikaner Orange Free State, 894–895
Against the Grain (Huysmans), 870–871
Age of Barbarism. *See* Dark Ages in Western Europe
Age of Ignorance, 237, 253–256. *See also* Dark Ages in Western Europe
Age of Iron. *See* Iron Age
Aggiornamento, of Pope John XXIII, 1066
Agriculture
in ancient Egypt, 21, 58
in ancient Rome, 197
early sites, 5m
in England, 628–629
Europe's enclosure movement, 427–428
industrialism's influences, 941
in Mesopotamia, 4, 12
in the New World, 544–545
Philistine practices, 58
post-WW II crisis in Europe, 1019–1021
in premodern Arabia, 254
in Sumer, 3, 4–5

Ahura Mazda ("Wise Lord"), 62–65
Airplanes, development of, 821
Akhenaten (formerly known as Amenhotep IV), 49–50
Akhmatova, Anna, 205
Akkadian dynasty, 5, 6, 9, 11–12, 15–16
Aleksandr I (Russian Tsar), 515t, 616, 672
Aleksandr II (Russian tsar), 733, 913
Alexander the Great
cultural integration policy of, 193
Macedon kingdom leadership, 158
military campaigns of, 91, 124, 131, 133, 158–160, 159m, 252, 314
use of crossbow weaponry, 345–346
Alexis (Russian tsar), 515t
Al-Farabi (Islamic philosopher), 267
Alfred the Great (King of England), 233
Al-Ghazali (Islamic philosopher), 267
Ibn Ali al-Shahid, Husayn, 297
Alighieri, Dante, 205, 328.333
Al-Jahiliyyah (Age of Ignorance), 237, 254–255. *See also* Dark Ages in Western Europe
Allah. *See* Muhammad, Prophet of Allah; Qur'an
An All-Catholic France (Bayle), 561
Al-Ma'mun (caliph), 302
Al-Mar'a al-jadida (Amin), 807
Almohad dynasty, 303, 315, 324, 740
Almoravid dynasty, 303, 303m, 315, 317m, 740
Al-Nahda cultural revival (Egypt), 737–738
al-Qaeda terrorist group, 1117–1118, 1126–1128, 1133–1135
Ibn al-Qayyim al-Jawziyya, 454
Althusser, Louis, 1053–1054
Amalikites, 38, 57, 78
The Ambassadors novel (James), 883

The Ambassadors painting (Holbein), 379
Ambrose of Milan, Saint, 231n11
Amenhotep III (Egyptian pharaoh), 49
Amenhotep IV (Egyptian pharaoh), 49–50
America (pre-American Revolution). *See also* American Revolution; United States (U.S.)
break from England, 593
cattle rancher/farmer conflicts, 58n15
Columbus's discovery of, 416
declaration of independence, 560
early 20th-century farming, 4
Golden Age dreams in, 83t
Masonry in, 587
myth-making about Founding Fathers, 82
Paine's immigration to, 613–614
American Revolution, 595, 890, 935, 1147
The Americas. *See* Central America; Latin America; North America; South America
Amin, Kasim, 807–808
Ammonites, 81
Amon-Ra (patron deity, Thebes), 41, 49
Amorites (of southern Iran), 11–12, 34, 57, 78
Amos (Hebrew prophet), 87
Anabaptist apocalyptic Protestants, 403
Analytic philosophies, 860, 864–866
"An Anatomie of the World" poem (Donne), 486
Anatolia
agricultural development in, 4, 5m
Alexander's rule of, 160
cattle breeding in, 6
commercial successes, 55
Cyrus's invasion of, 61
Hittite settlements in, 11, 52, 55, 101
Mediterranean world map, 308m

Mongol invasion of, 354
Ottoman Turk invasion of, 316
railroad development
  in, 644
Selim's rule in, 453
Seljuk Turk domination of,
  364–365
Sultanate of Rum in, 318
trade activities of, 121
Anchises (Trojan hero),
  171, 172n1
Ancien Régime ("Old
  Regime") (1648–1789),
  503–549, 570. See also
  Peace of Westphalia
absolute politics,
  513–514, 515t
argument for tyranny,
  508–510
arts and literature, 526–528
banning of Jews in
  Paris, 730
birth of privacy, 531–533
civil war and restoration,
  536–538
Hobbes/the social contract,
  510–513
joint stock companies,
  543–544
limitations of Jews during, 730
Ottoman European military
  encroachments, 539
police states, 515–517
purposeful self-indulgence
  during, 518–521
putting-out system of textile
  manufacture, 547
reappearance of warfare,
  547–548
royal/national banks of
  Europe, 542–543
1648 map of Europe, 506m
slave trade/domestic
  subjugation, 544–545,
  546m, 547
social behavior norms,
  528–531
South Sea Bubble
  (1720), 544
Ancient Egypt, 20–30. See also
  Middle Kingdom era;
  New Kingdom era
agricultural settlements
  in, 21
Book of the Dead, 28, 41–43,
  44, 49

calendrical measurements of,
  752–753
centralized rule in, 26
diet in, 24–25
funeral rites of, 487
geographic highlights,
  20–21
Hatshepsut's reign, 35, 47, 48
hieroglyphic writing system,
  23–24
Hyksos's ascendancy, 41, 45
ma'at practice, 27, 28, 30,
  41–42
mythology of, 27–30
Old Kingdom Egypt, 22m
Persian conquest of, 61
pharaohs in, 25–26
Pyramid Texts, 29, 41
Ramses II, reign of, 50, 50, 51
Ramses III, reign of, 53–54
ruler worship in, 25
single ruler system, 5
social strata in, 24–27
Thutmose I, reign of, 47, 48
Thutmose II, reign of, 48
Thutmose III, reign of, 48
Valley of Kings burial
  grounds, 25, 48
wheeled vehicles in, 5
Ancient Greece. See also
  Archaic Age; Athens;
  Classical Age; Hellenistic
  Age; Miletus; Minoan
  Greece; Mycenaean age
  (Greece); Peloponnesian
  War; Polis (communities)
Aegean rim settlement,
  100–101
British Isles
  circumnavigation, 416
calendar used in, 752
colonists, hoplites, tyrants of,
  110–115, 113
cult of masculinity in,
  115–118
epic and lyric poetry, 138–139
Flaminius' role in conquest
  of, 175
Greek/Phoenician
  colonies, 111m
Hippocrates/medical
  traditions, 147–148
homosexuality in, 118
invasion by Persia, 120,
  127, 132
Ionian League, 121–123

Knossos palace complex,
  100, 100–101
Latins commercial/cultural
  contact with, 174
Linear B script, 98
military service for
  males, 112
mythology of, 97–99
Olympic games, 99, 138
panhellenic religious
  festivals, 111
phalanx unit, military
  strategies, 112–113
population losses in, 105, 109
stratified society rule,
  113–114
tyrannical rulers in,
  114–115, 144, 152
Ancus Marcius
  (Roman King), 173t
Anderson, Elizabeth Garrett
  (mother of Louisa), 786
Anderson, Louisa Garrett, 786
An Ethics of Sexual Difference
  (Irigaray), 1092, 1110
Angell, Norman, 890–891
Anglican Church, 448,
  506–507, 765–766, 1072
Anglo-French Entente
  (1904), 894
Anglo-Irish Protestants,
  723, 725
Anglo-Russian Entente
  (1907), 894
Animal husbandry, in England,
  628–629
Anna (of Russia), 515t
Anna Karenina (Tolstoy),
  748–749, 801
Annals of Islam (Caetani), 779
The Annals of the Old Testament
  (Ussher), 752
Anno Domini system of dating,
  292–293
Antigonid Kingdom (Greece),
  160–161161m
Anti-Imperialist League
  (U.S.), 850
Antioch
  Arab conquest of, 260, 262m
  in the Crusades, 317m
  early Christian communities
    in, 219, 220m
  Hellenistic world map, 161m
  Mamluk Sultanate in, 360,
    361m, 362

monasteries in, 279m
Roman Empire, 200
   CE map, 241m
   1098 siege of, 316
   Umar's defeat of, 260
Antiochus III (Seleucid
   emperor), 183
Antiochus IV Epiphanes
   (Seleucid king), 166
Anti-Semitism. See also Hitler,
   Adolf; Jewish Holocaust
   (World War II); Nazi
   Party/Nazi Germany
   in Czechoslovakia, 1079
   of Dryden, 574
   in Eastern Europe, 733–734,
      733m, 963
   of Ford, 947–948
   of Khomeini, 1096
   of Khrushchev, 1079
   literature related to, 440,
      573–574, 731–732
   of Luther, 440, 579
   of Marx, 731
   of Piasecki, 963
   in Poland, 946, 1079
   in Romania, 963
   of Stalin, 1079
   term derivation, 707, 731
   in the USSR, 1079
   of Voltaire, 579
Antiseptics, development of, 821
Antoninus Pius (Roman
   emperor), 200
Antony, Marc, 173,
   185–186, 188
Antony vs. Octavian battle
   (Rome), 185
Aphrodite (Greek deity),
   104, 171
Apologia Pro Vita Sua
   (Newman), 668n1
Appian (Greek historian), 183
Aquinas. See Thomas
   Aquinas, Saint
Ibn Arabi, 328
Arabian Nights, 328
Arab Revolt (WW I), 889, 896t,
   899–900, 911, 927
Arabs (Arab nations). See also
   individual countries,
   empires, religions and
   sultanates
   during the Age of Ignorance,
      253, 255
   Arabized Arabs, 254

Ba'athism political ideology,
   1085–1088
   call to embrace Islam, 301
   Crusades and, 314, 316
   deaths in World War I, 888
   decolonization, tribal
      rivalries, 1084
   desire for recreation of
      caliphate, 1011
   domination in India, 415
   intellectual openness of,
      266–268
   Islam embraced by, 265
   and Islamic revelation,
      256–258
   Jewish settlements in,
      939, 1075
   killing of nonvirgin
      women, 810
   mapping techniques,
      416–417
   nationalization, growing
      Zionism, 1011–1014
   1960s emigration to
      Britain, 1038
   religious, political, military
      monopolies, 296
   Second Saudi State, 739
   ulama (brotherhood/
      community), 453
   victories of, 260–261, 264
   Wahhabism movement in,
      738–740, 777, 1082, 1084
   Yemeni Arabs, 254
Arab Spring, 1126, 1127,
   1135–1138, 1138m,
   1153, 1156
Arafat, Yasser, 1117
Aramaeans, 57, 78
Archaic Age. See also Athens
   cult of masculinity during,
      115–118
   epic/lyric poetry of, 139
   expansion of Greek polis
      networks, 110, 118
   Greek sculpture popularity, 97
   importance of athletic
      games, 112
   influences in Egypt, 27
   map of Archaic Italy, 174m
   population stability in
      Greece, 111
   reemergence of Miletus, 121
   social strife during,
      113–114
   timeline of, 23, 98, 99

tyrannical rule during,
   114, 508
Archimedes of Syracuse, 163
Arendt, Hannah, 867
Aretino, Pietro, 385, 408, 477
Ariosto, Ludovico, 385
Aristophanes, 137n4, 146t, 151
Aristotle
   bust of, 155
   influence on Western
      philosophy, 150
   Metaphysics, 300
   move to Asia Minor, 158
   and the pursuit of happiness,
      155–158, 560
   studies with Plato, 151, 155
   university education
      domination, 375
Ark of the Covenant, 78, 80–81
Armenian genocide, 888, 904,
   905, 928
Armstrong, Neil, 1061t
Arnold, Thomas, 669
Arouet, François-Marie. See
   Voltaire
ARPANET established
   (1968), 1061t
Arrow/Cross Fascist Party (of
   Hungary), 963
Artaxerxes I (Persian emperor),
   91–92
Artificial nations, 707
Arts/artistic achievements. See
   also Literature/literary
   achievements; Music/
   musical achievements
   Ancien Régime, 503, 526–528
   ancient Greece, 97, 134
   Baroque era, 526
   decorative painting on
      case, 135
   epic poetry, Classical
      Greece, 138
   European modernism, 877,
      880, 948
   female modernists, 954t
   France, 513, 593
   in the Hellenistic Age, 162
   Hellenistic culture, 162
   Middle Egypt, 44
   modernism and, 880–884
   Renaissance era, 374, 379,
      382, 383, 389
   Romantic era, 656
   stage tragedies, Greece,
      139–142

Ashkenazic Judaism, 322, 436,
576, 1075
Ashurbanipal (Assyrian ruler),
35, 60
Asia
Catholic/Protestant
missionary work, 750
colonization of, 888
European international
investment in, 891m
feminist issues in, 1112
Jews in, 1075
Portuguese in, 420m
Protestant communities
in, 1071
women's rights successes
in, 1112
Asia Minor
Aristotle's residence in, 158
Byzantium's partial loss
of, 249
grain production in, 182
Greek settlements, 110
as heart of Byzantine
Empire, 248
Hellenes settlements, 99
Hittite settlements, 51
intellectualism of, 133
Ionian League alliance in, 121
Jewish communities in, 164
Miletus city location, 121
Mitanni settlements, 51
Mithras cult origination
in, 227
monasteries located
in, 279m
Muslim domination of,
365–366
Ottoman Turks in, 328, 360
place-name changes in, 365
Punic Wars and, 183
Asiatic Society, 50–51
Askesis (peace of mind)
discipline of Stoics, 231
L'Assommoir (Zola), 803
Assyrian Empire, 11
Ashurbanipal's reign, 35, 60
conquest of, 56
iron weaponry used in, 59
Israel conquered by, 71, 83,
110–111
laws/cruel punishment
practices, 59–60
map of, 59m
radical militarization of, 58

reign of Ashurbanipal, 60
second millennium
domination by, 33
Atheism/atheists
atheistic Communism, 1048
Burke and, 593
historical background, 748
Hobbes and, 512
Islam on, 1049
Knutzen's pamphlets
denying God, 473
Protestantism and, 1069
secularization and, 1063
Shelley's writing about,
746, 748
World War II saying
about, 415
Athena (Greek deity), 98
Athens
Alexander's conquest of, 124
defeat in Peloponnesian War,
119–120, 143–147
Delian League treasury
control by, 133, 146t
democracy experiment in,
124–125
festivals of, 135, 136
in the 5th century, 145t
Greek founding of, 97
leadership of Pericles, 133
leadership position of, 131
map location, 57m, 61m,
101m, 111m
military alliances of, 132
naval power of, 126
Peloponnesian War
and, 143m
social revolution
attempt, 114
Solon's leadership in, 99
theatrical culture, 133, 141
Thirty Tyrants of, 144, 152
tragedy festivals, 139–140
war with Persia, 126, 127m,
133, 143
war with Sparta, 131,
144–145, 147
Ibn Athir, Ali, 353
Atlantic slave trade, 544–545,
546m, 547
Atlee, Clement, 1046
Atomic bombing of Japan
(WW II), 979, 1000–1003
Auclert, Hubertine, 795
Auden, W. H., 327

Augsburg, Anita, 1006
Augsburg Compromise. See
Peace of Augsburg
Augustine of Hippo (Saint
Augustine), 207, 231n11,
300, 334, 406, 560
Augustus (Roman emperor),
187–190, 213, 226
Aurelius, Marcus, 200, 207,
230, 238
Aurispa, Giovanni, 384
Aurunces society, 172
Auschwitz-Birkenau concentration camp, 989–990
Austen, Jane, 699
Austo-German alliance
(1879–1918), 893m
Australia
European investments
in, 891m
Gallipoli military campaign,
896t, 898, 905, 910–911
immigration data, 841m, 892
post-WW I debt, 931
Austria
Acts of Toleration for Jewish
people, 577
alliance with Prussia, 594t
anti-Jewish sentiments, 946
church attendance
data, 1058
Congress of Vienna
attendance, 666
1848 uprising, 687
fascism in, 963
guild system in, 539, 630
Habsburg dynasty, 388, 513
Holy League
membership, 722
invasion of France, 601
Leopold I, reign of, 515t,
547–548, 557
Leopold II, reign of, 515t
Napoleon's military
campaigns, 602, 605
Ottoman Empire vs., 460,
513–514
post-1815 industrialization
failure, 636–637
Prince François-Eugène in,
515–516
railroad development, 638
Seven Weeks' War, 713
Seven Years' War, 505,
548–549

Vienna/urban
    development, 645
war with France, 595, 599
women's suffrage rights, 939
in World War I, 889–890,
    895, 896t, 897, 900, 903,
    907–908, 925
Austrian-Hungarian Empire
as an artificial nation,
    707–708
Conference of Berlin
    attendance, 828
conflicts with Prussia, 691
conflict with Boxers, 844
18th-century population
    data, 583
Franz Ferdinand's
    assassination, 892,
    896t, 900
geographic
    considerations, 637
German pacts with, 894
Ottoman disputes with,
    639, 642
restoration of royal
    families, 670
1648 Europe map, 506m
in World War I, 887–890,
    892, 894–895, 896t
Austro-German-Romanian
    alliance (1883–1916), 893m
Austro-Servian alliance
    (1881–1895), 893m
Authoritarian regimes, in the
    Middle East, 1050
Automobiles
Benz/Ford's development
    of, 821
cities transformed by, 822
gas-powered patent, 816, 821
U.S. industry subsidies, 1029
U.S. production, 827
Western Europe production,
    941, 1034
Avars, 248m, 249, 262m, 273
Ayse Hafsa (Sultana), 461t
Ayyubid Sultanate, 355m
Aztec Empire, 418m, 422,
    425, 425n3

B
Ba'al Shem Tov, 576. See also
    Eleazar, Israel ben
Ba'athism political ideology,
    1085–1088

Ba'ath Party, 1012, 1086–1088
Baby boom (post-World War
    II), 1035–1036, 1044
Babylonian Captivity, of the
    Hebrew people, 71, 83, 87,
    90, 320
Babylonian Empire. See also
    Neo-Babylonians
Assyrian fear of, 58
brutality of, 62
Chaldean peoples, 60
Code of Hammurabi, 34–38
commercial successes, 55
conquest of, 56
conquest of Judah by, 111
Cyrus's freeing of the
    Jews, 163
domestication of horses, 45
fall of Jerusalem to, 77
founding of, 34
Hammurabi's rulership, 16,
    34–38, 35m
heroics of Gilgamesh, 9
Hittite campaigns against, 52
myths/ritual prayers of,
    16, 18–19
Old Babylon, 34–40
Persian conquest of, 61–62
religious imperialism in, 38
second millennium
    domination by, 33
slavery in, 37
social stratification in, 37–38
spices for trading, 101
Bach, Johann Sebastian, 205,
    526, 657, 932
Backless bras, development
    of, 821
Bacon, Roger, 465–467, 493
Bacon, Sir Francis
four "illusions" identified by,
    493–494
Index of Forbidden Books
    condemnation of, 477
interest in scientific
    thinking, 466–467
The New Atlantis, 466, 492
The New Instrument,
    466, 485t
portrait of, 492
Baden-Powell, Robert, 870
Bagehot, Walter, 787–788
Al-Baghdadi, 489
Baha'i religion, 207, 1155
Balboa, Vasco Núñez de, 421

Balfour Declaration (1917),
    932, 938
Balkans
Bismarck on possible
    war in, 1130
Charlemagne's expansion
    into, 288–289
Dark Ages economic
    data, 270
global conflict in, 895
gold mine
    discoveries, 158
Hitler's fighting in, 980
Mongol invasion of,
    354, 362
"new soldiers" from, 539
Ottoman loss of, 620
Ottoman Turks in, 365, 367
in World War I, 897, 905
Young Turks in, 925
Banu Hashim clan, 284
Baptism tradition, 205, 214,
    221, 223
Barbarossa, Frederick, 489
Barberini, Maffeo, 478
Barca, Pedro Calderón
    de la, 526
Barnes, Djuna, 954t
Baroque Age
artistic/musical
    achievements, 526
Catholic Counter-
    Reformation and, 526
characteristics of, 504
church decorations, 518
mercantilism vs. splendors
    of, 524
Ottoman mosque style
    incorporation, 621
palaces and chateaux,
    507, 518
Barth, Karl, 205, 868, 1071
Barthes, Roland, 1018, 1053
Baruch, Bernard, 1024
Ibn Battuta, 358–360
Baudelaire, Charles, 658,
    877, 882
Bauer, Bruno, 762
Baulieu, Etienne, 1061t
Bavaria, Napoleon's conquest
    of, 605
Bayezid II (Ottoman ruler),
    437, 453
Bayle, Pierre
An All-Catholic France, 561

A Historical and Critical Dictionary, 554, 559, 561, 566
investigation of evil by, 561–562
A Philosophical Commentary, 561
Beach, Sylvia, 954t
Beatles (rock group), 1035
Beccaria, Cesare, 563–564, 584, 694
Beckett, Samuel, 1023, 1052
Beckman, Isaac, 494
Bedouin tribes, 254, 299, 830m
Beethoven, Ludwig van, 614, 655, 658
Beeton, Isabella, 696–697, 698, 870
Begin, Menachem, 1077–1078
Belfast Agreement (Good Friday Accord), 1093, 1116
Belgium
  church attendance data, 1058–1059
  Conference of Berlin attendance, 828
  EEC membership, 1106
  empire-building by, 816
  fascism in, 963
  global gender gap data, 1139t
  Green Parties in, 1098
  Léopold II, reign of, 838–840
  liberal led rebellions in, 682
  mystical experience reports, 334
  mystical experiences in, 334
  1914 German invasion of, 896t
  post-WW I reliance on colonies, 940
  railroad development, 638
Bell, William Scott, *689*
La Belle Assemblée magazine, 696
Bell's Court and Fashionable Magazine Addressed Particularly to the Ladies magazine, 696
Belzec concentration camp, 990
Benedictine monks, 278, 280, 334, 410–411

Benedict of Nursia, 238, 278, 280
Benso, Camillo (count of Cavour), 718, 720
Bentham, Jeremy, 791
Benz, Karl Friedrich, 821
Berbers
  Almoravid/Almohad movements and, 740
  Arab rule of, 264
  Islamic World map, 303m
  Muslim conquests map, 262m
Berg, Alban, 883
Bergen-Belsen concentration camp, 990
Berlin airlift, 1018, *1025*
Berlin Wall
  1961 erection of, 1070
  1989 opening of, 1025, 1091, 1092
Berners-Lee, Tim, 1061t
The Betrothed (I promessi sposi) (Manzoni), 717
Beveridge, William, 1029–1030
Beyond Good and Evil (Nietzsche), 850, 861, 1104–1105
Beyond the Pleasure Principle (Freud), 875
Biber, Heinrich Ignaz Franz, 514
Bible. *See also* Hebrew (Jewish) Bible; Jesus of Nazareth; King James (Authorized) Bible; New Testament; YHWH
  Budé's French translation, 401
  Calvin's comments about, 407, 429
  Catholic counterattack to criticism of, 769–771
  Complutensian Polyglot Bible, 402
  composition of first texts, 71
  Documentary Hypothesis of origin, 75
  Galileo's comments about, 472–473
  Higher Criticism/Historical Criticism of, 745, 759–763
  homosexuality and, 432n6
  limitations/problems with, 74
  Luther's comments about, 400, 429

Mendelssohn's German translation, 575
  1930s German bible, 69
  ongoing debate about origins, 75
  origin of Abram, 70n1
  Protestantism and, 431, 433–434, 441–442, 654, 763–768
  Saint Jerome's version, 233
  Scofield Reference Bible, 753
  Tyndale's English translation, 477
  usefulness as historical source, 71
"Biblical Legends among the Muslims" essay (Weil), 778
The Biblical Text and Its Transmission (Geiger), 747, 774–775
Biblical truth *(sola Scriptura),* 432
Bibliothèque Nationale (Paris), 401
bin Laden, Osama, 1116, 1118, 1127. *See also* al-Qaeda terrorist group; September 11, 2011 terrorist attacks
Birth control information and methods, 799–800, 1067
The Birth of the Palestinian Refugee Problem (Morris), 1059, 1080
Birth of Tragedy out of the Spirit of Music (Nietzsche), 140
Bismarck, Otto von
  Catholicism targeted by, 716
  Conference of Berlin organization, 828–829
  Franco-Prussian war engineered by, 713
  German industrial growth leadership, 826, 953
  as "Iron Chancellor" of German Empire, 658
  limited imperial interests of, 850
  Napoleon III's conflict with, 720–721
  photo of, *715*
  on possible Balkans war, 1130
  role in unification of Germany, 713, 767
  wars instigated by, 713
  Wilhelm's dismissal of, 850

Black Death (in Western
    Europe)
  arrival of, 329
  consequences of,
    351–352, 389
  coverage map, 349m
  deaths resulting from, 348,
    376, 1051
  eyewitness accounts,
    348–351
  healing efforts, 350–351
  Islamic World/European
    devastation from, 364
  Spanish flu
    comparison, 907n7
Black holes, 1061t
Black Sea, 4
Blake, William, 626–627,
    627, 659
Blank, Theodor, 1037–1038
Blitzkrieg ("lightning war")
    strategy, of
    Germany, 980
"Bloody Mary." See Mary
    (Queen of England)
Bloomsbury Group of writers,
    967–968
Bodone, Giotto di, 328
Boer Wars (1899–1902),
    829–830, 888,
    894–895, 909
Boethius (Christian
    philosopher), 231n11
La Bohème opera
    (Puccini), 871
Bohemia, Charlemagne's
    expansion into, 288
Bolshevik Party (Russia). See
    also Lenin, Vladimir
  areas controlled by, 915m
  opposition to, 914
  rise to power in Russia,
    889, 896t, 912, 919
  Romanov rule compared
    with, 921
  Stalin's Central Committee
    appointment, 964
  successes of, 935
  terrorist tactics,
    919–920, 964
  women's rights supported by,
    965–966
  Zionism and, 947
Bolshevik Revolution
    (1917), 900
Bonaparte, Joseph, 602–603

Bonaparte, Louis-Napoleon. See
    Napoleon III (of France)
Bonaparte, Napoleon. See
    Napoleon (Napoleone di
    Buonaparte)
Bonhoeffer, Dietrich, 1070
Boniface (Saint Boniface), 284,
    287, 288m
Boniface VIII (Pope), 357
Book burnings, 408–410
The Book of Advice for Viziers
    and Governors (Mehmed
    Pasha), 640–641
Book of Concord (Luther), 767
Book of Martyrs (Foxe),
    447–448
The Book of the Courtier
    (Castiglione), 528
Book of the Dead (Ancient
    Egypt), 28, 41–43, 44, 49
Books of the New Testament,
    208t, 209
Borromeo, Carlo, 478
Bosnia
  Bayezid's attack of, 367
  Charlemagne's campaign
    in, 289
  1850 Peoples of Europe
    maps, 708m
  Ottoman losses map, 640m
  Serbian massacres in,
    1130, 1132
  in World War I, 897
Boston Police Strike (1919), 935
Boucicaut, Aristide, 750
Bouhler, Philipp, 988
Boulanger, Lili, 954t
Boulanger, Nadia, 954t
Bourbon dynasty, 513, 681, 682
Bourgeoisie (middle class)
  as audience for the
    Enlightenment, 585–586
  horse-drawn train ride by, 679
  liberalism supported by, 679
Boxer Rebellion (China), 816,
    843–844
Boyle, Robert, 484–485, 554
Boyle's law, 484–485
Brack, Viktor, 988
Bradwardine, Thomas, 328
Brahe, Tycho, 468, 470–471
Brandenburg-Prussia
  Hohenzollern dynasty, 513
  rulers of, 515t
  Seven Years' War, 505,
    548–549

Brave New World (Huxley), 972
Breda battle (Thirty Years'
    War), 451
Breitenfeld battle (Thirty
    Years' War), 451
Brest-Litovsk Treaty (WWI),
    896t, 897, 903
Brethren of Common Life
    humanist school, 390,
    392–393
Britain and the Arab-Israeli
    Conflict (Pappé), 1080
British East India Company,
    543, 827, 831
British Humanist
    Association, 1063
Broadhurst, Thomas,
    698–699
Brontë, Charlotte, Emily and
    Ann, 699, 851
Bronze Age, 4
Brunner, Emil, 1071
Bruno, Giordano, 481–482
Bubonic plague, 348, 537
Bucharest, Treaty of
    (1775–1812), 640m
Buddenbrooks (Mann), 871
Buddhism, 207, 302, 843
Budé, Guillaume, 401
Buggery Act (1533 CE),
    416, 432
Bulgaria
  autonomy achieved by,
    706, 735
  EU membership, 1104
  independence declared
    by, 1091
  political rivalries of, 936
  in World War I, 895, 896t
Bultmann, Rudolph, 868
Bulwer-Lytton, Constance,
    795–796
Buonaparte, Napoleone di. See
    Napoleon
Buonarroti,
    Michelangelo, 205
Burke, Edmund, 592
  comments on Conservatism,
    674–675
  evaluation of French
    Revolution, 593, 610–613
  Hobbes's shared views
    with, 612
  Reflections on the Revolution
    in France, 610–612, 673

Bush, George W. *See also*
September 11, 2011,
terrorist attacks
invasion of Iraq, 1133
post-9/11 speech to
Congress, 1127–1128
question about terrorists
hating us, 1126
tax cuts of, 1145
Buwayhid Sultanate, 303m
Byrd, William, 448
Byron, Lord, 659, 668–669
Byzantine Empire
clashes with Persia, 255
counteroffensive vs.
Rome, 252
Justinian's leadership,
229, 248m
Muslim conquest map, 262m
as "new Rome," 248
readoption of Greek
language, 249
Seljuks defeat of, 285, 364
silkworms/manufacture of
silk, 250
wealth achieved by,
237–238, 250
Byzantium. *See also*
Constantinople
Assyrian Empire map, 59m
Charlemagne's invasion
of, 294
Corpus basis of
jurisprudence in, 249
extraordinary splendors
of, 250
Greek/Phoenician colonies
map, 111m
losses to Persia, 249
Minoan/Mycenean Greece
map, 101m
as the "New Rome," 237,
247–249
Ottoman invasion of, 384
Peloponnesian War
map, 143m
Roman Empire, 300 CE
map, 241m
Roman World, time of
Augustus map, 188m
Rome, 120 BCE map, 183m
schooling system, 250
Silk Route passage
through, 254
wars with Persia, 260

C

Caesar (junior emperor), 242
Caesar, Julius
assassination of, 189
Augustus' deification of,
189, 226
Pompey vs., 185–186, 188
sole rulership of Rome, 186
victor against Gaul, 187–188
Caesar and Cleopatra (Shaw), 850
Caetani, Leone, 779
Cahiers des doléances (grievance
notebooks), 597
Cairo Declaration on Human
Rights, 997, 1048–1050
Calendar (modern), basis
of, 210
Caligula (Roman emperor),
187, 189, 200
Callot, Jacques, 518
Calvin, Jean, 375, 400
beliefs shared with Luther,
406–407, 409
*Commentary on the
Psalms,* 405
on human nature, 429
*Institutes of Christian
Religion,* 405–406
modeling of Saint
Augustine, 406
as Protestant humanist, 401
reception of teachings
of, 407
Reformed Church
established by, 404
Reformed Church of, 404,
405–407
on Saint Paul's Epistles,
429–430
securing of legitimacy for
followers, 444
subsumation of Zwingli's
church, 403
Calvinism, 407, 443–444,
568, 1070
Cambodia, 720, 831, 832m,
1027, 1043m
Cambyses (Persian ruler),
61–62
Campion, Thomas, 448
Campo Fornio, Treaty of
(1797), 594t
Camus, Albert, 1018,
1021–1023, 1052
Canaan, land of, 77–80, 79m

Canaanites
alphabet development, 14
communication with the
Hebrews, 78
seizure of Promised Land
from, 38
trek of Abram and, 70
Canada
admittance to
NATO, 1026m
global gender gap
data, 1139t
migrations to, 727, 841, 892
national debt data, *1144*
in World War I, 898
Cancer theory
development, 1061t
Candide (Voltaire), 557,
569–570, 582
Canterbury Tales (Chaucer), 452
Canzoniere poem (Petrarca), 384
Capetian dynasty (France),
329, 340
Capitalism. *See also* Industrial
capitalism; "Signs of the
Times" essay; *The Wealth
of Nations*
Ba'athism and, 1086
Catholicism and, 1069
credit/debt as fuel for,
1035, 1143
described, 563, 630, 676
early stages of growth of, 327,
337, 474
Fascism's promotion
of, 1024
free-market capitalism, 563,
1034, 1085, 1091,
1148–1152
globalized capitalism, 1092
laissez-faire capitalism,
587–588, 676
Lenin's views on, 916,
918–919
liberal capitalism, 1071
Marx's view of, 690
Nietzsche's view of, 862
Protestantism and, 1069
rational basis of, 563
self-serving nature of, 670
unregulated capitalism,
769–770, 933, 1034
Western concerns about, 935
World Bank/IMF's
promotion of, 1025

The Capture of Miletus
    (Phrynichus), 122
Caravaggio, Michelangelo, 205
Carlists of Spain, 682
Carlos II (Spanish King), 547
Carlyle, Thomas, 658–659
Carolingian dynasty
    amalgamated society
        created by, 280
    ascent of, 285, 286–287
    Christian education
        promoted by, 310
    collapse of, 294–296
    nicknames of princelings, 295
    relocation invitation to the
        Jews, 321
    Rome's relationship
        with, 287
Carter, Jimmy, 1078
Carthage
    Byzantine Empire
        map, 248m
    control of western
        Mediterranean, 181
    Death of Augustus
        map, 188m
    location, Archaic Italy, 174m
    Muslim conquests
        map, 262m
    Philip V's support for, 183
    Phoenician founding of, 58,
        111m, 181–182
    Punic Wars with Rome, 172,
        182–183, 185
    Roman empire map, 241m
    Rome's neighbors
        map, 183m
    3rd-century location, 182m
Carthaginian Empire, 172–173
Carthusian order
    (of monks), 333
Carus (Roman
    emperor),240
Castiglione, Baldassare, 375,
    387–388, 528
Castration, popularity of, 531
Castro, Rosalía, 699
Catastrophes, beneficial effects
    of, 144–145
Catharine of Aragon, 446–447
Cathars, Crusade against, 329
Cathedrals of Christianity, 205
Cather, Willa, 801
Catherine the Great
    (of Russia), 620

Catholic Church
    (Catholicism). *See also*
    Pius X; Roman
    Catholicism; Thirty Years'
    War; Vatican
    adaptations to
        contemporary society,
        1066–1067
    age of scholasticism and,
        331–334
    artificial contraception
        debate, 1067
    Bismarck's targeting of, 716
    Charles V's defense of,
        397–398
    Christian humanist activists,
        scholars, 401–402
    church attendance data, 1059
    Corpus as model for canon
        law of, 249
    counterattack vs. Biblical
        historical criticism,
        769–771
    Edward VI's eradication
        efforts, 447
    Exsurge Domine papal bull, 396
    First Vatican Council, 771
    freemasonry condemned
        by, 587
    Gregorian Reform, 330, 395
    guild system
        complementarity, 338
    heresies of, 339–340, 339m
    Holy See of, 286, 310, 474,
        717–718, 1154
    Huguenot's peace with, 557
    Humanae vitae papal
        encyclical, 1058,
        1067–1068
    industrial capitalism
        condemned by, 769
    Irish Catholics, 723–724
    Lamentabili Sane Exitu
        decree, 772
    Latin Europe's corruption
        in, 310
    Luther's rebellion against,
        395–400
    marriage traditions, 1068
    Mary's restoration efforts, 447
    mendicant orders,
        338–340, 349
    moral indictment vs.
        industrial capitalism,
        770–771

mysticism/lay evangelism
    of, 327
Pantheon's consecration
    as, 227
Pascendi Dominici Gregis
    decree, 772
Peace of God assemblies,
    311–312
plenitudo potestatis
    principle, 330–331
Pope Honorius III, 233
Pope John Paul II, 867
Pope John XXIII, 1057
Pope Leo X, 382, 396
Pope Leo XI, 382
Pope Leo XIII, 769, 772
Pope Pius IV, 382
Pope Pius IX, 687, 718, 771
Pope Pius VII, 616
Pope Pius X, 747, 772–773
Pope Pius XII, 1064–1066
Pope Sixtus IV, 373
post-WW II reformation,
    1064–1069
Providentissimus Deus
    encyclical, 772
reinvention of, 310–313
Rerum Novarum encyclical,
    769–770, 769–771
Rubens' artistic glorification
    of, 526
Second Vatican Council,
    773, 1058, 1066, 1069
sexual morality and,
    431–434
simony abuse by, 310
social Catholicism, 770
spiritual/political leadership
    of, 718
Catholic Counter-
    Reformation, 526
Catholic Emancipation Act
    (1829), 706, 725
Catholic mysticism, 334–337
Cavafy, Constantine, 880
Ceausescu, Nicolae, 1079–1080
Çelebi, Mustafa Katip, 490–491
Celtic culture, 193, 434–435
Censor, specific duties of, 178
Central America
    Aztec Empire, 418m,
        422, 425
    European explorations
        of, 423m
    Mayan Empire, 422

Central Bureau for Nuclear
Measurements, 1062
Central Europe
ethnic minorities in, 937m
Hitler's attempted
domination of, 969–970
Jewish migrations to, 734
1942–1955 displaced
peoples, 1020m
Thirty Years' War deaths, 451
Central Intelligence Agency
(CIA), 1028–1029, 1134
Cervantes, Miguel de, 932
Chaldeans of Babylonia, 60
Chamberlain, Neville, 970, 971
Chambers, Ephraim, 566
Chaplin, Charlie, 824
Chardin, Jean-Baptiste, 503
Charitable institutions, rise
of, 683
Charlemagne (Charles the
Great)
administrative style of,
291–292
crowning as Carolingian
emperor, 284
death of, 294
European campaigns of,
288–289
imperial coronation of,
292–294
insomnia problems of, 289
power as viewed by, 291
Sword of Charlemagne, 290
Charles I (English King), 504,
536–537
Charles II (English King),
375, 537
Charles IX (French King), 444
Charles the Bald (French
King), 233, 295
Charles the Fat
(French King), 295
Charles the Simple (French
King), 295
Charles V (Holy Roman
Emperor), 396–398,
397m, 442–443
Charles X (English King), 681
Charles XII (of Sweden), 1024
Chartist Movement, 683–685
Chateau De Versailles. See
Versailles Palace
Chaucer, Geoffrey, 328,
452, 560

Chechen National
Congress, 1132
Chechnya, first/second wars in,
1126, 1132
Chekhov, Anton, 913
Chelmno concentration
camp, 990
Chemical industry
developments, 820
Child labor, 653, 803
Children of the Exile. See
Sadducees
China
Arab world trading with, 254
Boxer Rebellion, 816,
843–844
Britain's opium for silks
trade, 831
Christian missionaries
in, 416
Communist Party in,
1102–1103
conflicts with Japan, 978,
979, 984–985, 991–992
Cultural Revolution in, 1111
European trade with, 425
gender-selective abortion
in, 1138
Genghis Khan's invasion
of, 358
Mao Zedong's leadership,
869, 1036, 1111
Marco Polo's stay in, 357
mercantilism in, 523
Ming dynasty, 369
Mongol settlements in,
352–353, 356
1960s emigration to
Britain, 1038
1995 Women's Conference,
1093, 1112–1113
Pentecostal missionaries
in, 1073
Rape of Nanking in, 992
Roman Empire contacts
with, 416
Sino-Japanese War, 978n1,
985, 993
spread of farming in, 5m
support for Communist
North Vietnam, 979
Tiananmen Square student
protest, 1100–1102, 1101
trading post
establishment, 419

United Nations and, 997
"War of Resistance" against
Japan, 979
Zheng He's fleet
travels, 416n1
Chios (Aegean island), 137
Cholera epidemic, 626, 647
Cholera vaccine, 820
Chomsky, Noam, 1061t
Christian democracy, in
Western Europe, 1034
Christian humanism, 388–390,
401–402
Christianities, 218–221
Christian paganism, 275–277
Christians/Christianity. See
also Anglican Church;
Catholic Church; Church
of England; Jesus of
Nazareth; Lutheranism;
Monasticism; New
Testament; Protestantism
Africa's introduction
of, 38
baptism tradition, 205, 214,
221, 223
Book of Revelation
author, 208t
cathedrals/monasteries, 205
christianities and, 218–221
Clovis's conversion to, 285
Complutensian Polyglot
Bible, 402
Crusades, 38
Diocletian's attacks of, 224,
242–243, 277
early communities, 220m
Edict of Milan legalization
of, 238, 245
European missionaries,
833–836
1st/2nd-century spread of,
167
forced baptisms of Moors,
401–402
French criminalization
of, 601
Gospel author, 208t
influence of Peasants'
Revolt, 442
Isis-Osiris myth supplanted
by, 28
the Jesus mystery, 206–207,
209–210
Jewish basis of, 210–213

Jews seeking of peace with, 574
Latin Christianity, 292, 311,
    318, 319m
missionaries in China, 1073
Muslim persecution of,
    314–315
mysticism, 334–336
New Testament
    books, 208t
19th-century European
    decline, 749
pockets of intellectual life,
    277–278, 280
present-day population
    data, 206
problems of medieval
    warriors, 441
Protestant Renaissance,
    388–390
Roman condemnation of,
    221–225
as Rome's official
    religion, 238
secret practices of, 221–222
sexual morality and,
    431–434
Thatcher's comments
    about, 593
Trinity (Holy Trinity) of,
    224, 331, 1068
Truce of God warfare ban, 314
Churchill, John, 548
Churchill, Winston
    loss of office, 1024
    opposition to war crimes
        trials, 995–996
    speech against appeasement,
        972–973
    Sudan battle
        description, 837
Church of England, 446–449,
    506–507, 568,
    764–767, 1071
Church of Sweden (Lutheran
    Church), 507
Church of the Holy
    Sepulcher, 315
Cicero, 375
Circumcision rite of males, 71
Cisneros, Ximénez Francisco
    de, 401–402
Cistercian order
    (of monks), 333
City-states
    governing strategies, 14

individualized patron deities,
    16–17
of Italy, 380–381
of Mesopotamia, 12
of Miletus, Sparta,
    Athens, 97
of Old Babylon, 34
patron deities of, 16–17
of the Renaissance era,
    380–383
role of priesthood in, 14
of Rome, 176, 189
of Sumer, 8–9, 11, 15
Civilization and Its Discontents
    (Freud), 876
Civil rights era (U.S.), 1037
Civil War (U.S.), 827
Class, Heinrich, 889–890
Classical Age (Greece)
    achievements during, 132
    art and literature during, 162
    Athens-related events, 133
    Delian League alliance, 132,
        133, 143, 143m, 146t
    epic and lyric poetry,
        138–139
    epic poetry compositions
        during, 138
    girls/women during, 134
    Hippocrates/medical
        traditions, 147–148
    mathematics and sophistry,
        148–150
    modest lifestyles during,
        133–134
    popularity of stage tragedies,
        139–142
    slave laborers in, 135
    timeline of events, 131, 132
    women's wedding
        rituals, 135
Claudel, Camille, 954t
Clavius, Christoph, 472
Cleisthenes, 139
Clemenceau, Georges, 922,
    923–924
Clemens, Samuel (Mark
    Twain), 840, 844–845,
    849, 863
Clement V (Pope), 357
Clement VII (Pope), 382,
    410, 438
Clermont-Tonnerre, Charles-
    Henri de, 576
Climate. *See* Environment

Clinton, Bill, 1044–1045
Clinton, Hillary Rodham,
    1112–1113
Clocks (mechanical clocks),
    invention of, 327
Cloning of adult
    mammal, 1061t
The Clouds (Aristophanes), 151
Clovis (King of Salian Franks),
    239, 271, 276, 285
"Coalbrookdale by Night"
    painting
    (Loutherbourg), 627
Coalition of Labor Union
    Women (1974), 1045
Code of Hammurabi, 34–37, 37
Codreanu, Corneliu, 963
Cogito ergo sum ("I think,
    therefore I am")
    (Descartes) statement,
    495–496
Cold War. *See also* Cold War
    Berlin airlift, 1018, *1025*
    Cuban Missile Crisis,
        1025–1026
    decolonization and,
        1023–1026
    description, 1000
    ending of, 1091–1092
    erection of Berlin Wall, 1070
    Greek Civil War, 1025
    Korean War, 1025
    name derivation, 1024
    onset of, 1018
    Six-Day War,
        1040–1041, *1041*
    Soviet invasions, 1019, 1025,
        1040–1041, *1042*
    stages of, 1024–1025
    Tet Offensive in
        Vietnam, 1040
Coleridge, Samuel Taylor,
    595, 660
College of Cardinals, 312–313,
    373, 390
Colloquies (Erasmus), 391
Colombo, Cristoforo
    (Christopher Columbus)
    Caribbean landing of,
        419–420
    disappointments of, 421
    discovery of America, 416
    Haitian/Dominican
        Republic landing by, 424
    log excerpt, 420–421

Colombo (cont.)
  mistaken beliefs of, 420
  publication of first reports
    by, 422
  routes of, 418m
  sea travel innovations of, 419
  world view of, 421
Colonial Society
  (Germany), 889
Colossians
  (New Testament), 208t
Comfort women (in Japan,
  WW II), 993
Comitia curiata of Rome, 172
Commentary on the Psalms
  (Calvin), 405
Commodus, 238, 238
"Common Sense about the War"
  pamphlet (Shaw), 904
Communism
  belief in inevitability of, 692
  in the Cold War era, 1018
  collapse of, 1093, 1094m,
    1109, 1130
  in Eastern Europe, 1058
  Franco's belief in, 958
  Fukuyama's arguments
    against, 1091
  Gide's opinion of, 945–946
  Jewish people and, 946, 988
  in Russia, 960, 964–965,
    969, 1023, 1028, 1058
  unenlightened and, 581
The Communist Manifesto
  (Marx and Engels), 667,
    687–688, 692
Communist Party of Great
  Britain (CPGB), 945–946
Compasses (magnetic
  compasses), 327
The Complaint of Peace
  (Erasmus), 391–392
Complutensian Polyglot Bible
  (Cisneros), 402, 402
Compton-Burnett, Ivy, 954t
Computer networking
  developments, 1061t
Concentration camps
  in Germany, 977, 989,
    994, 1070
  non-Jewish victims of, 991t
  in Russia, 965
  in South Africa, 909
  in Spain, 960
Concert of Europe, collapse of,
  691–693

Concordat of Worms, 313
The Condition of the Working
  Class in England in 1844
  (Engels), 627–628
Condoms, use in Europe, 799
Condorcet, Marquis de,
  594t, 791
Conference of Berlin
  (1884–1885), 816, 828–829
Confessing Church
  (Germany), 1070
The Confessions of Young Törless
  (Musil), 883–884
Confucianism, 207
Congress of Vienna (1814–1815)
  "concert of Europe" collapse
    created by, 691
  efforts to return to rule of
    kings, 633, 665
  German territory
    consolidation, 636, 711
  major powers in
    attendance, 666
  redrawing European political
    map at, 633, 665, 774
  reformer's retroactive view
    of, 670
Conquistadores ("conquerors)
  armies, 422
Conservatism, 665–669
  Burke's co-founding of, 593
  Burke's comments on,
    674–675
  England's voting out of, 681
  in Germany, 711–712
  in Italy, 711
  liberalism's differences with,
    665, 667–668, 680
  loss of power in
    Britain, 667
  of the Mamluks, 363–364
  mental appeal of, 675
  Metternich's opinion of, 667
  moral component of,
    673–677
  "nation" as defined by, 711
  19th-century goals of
    government, 676
  popular opposition to, 672
  traditions valued by,
    667, 674
Conservative Judaism,
  777, 1079
The Conservative Mind: From
  Burke to Santayana (Kirk),
  1018, 1031–1032

Constantine the Great (Roman
  emperor)
  christianities and, 246
  conflicts with Pope
    Sylvester I, 247
  conversion to Christianity,
    244, 277
  Edict of Toleration of, 277
  legalization of Christianity
    in Rome, 245
  6th-Century CE map, 251m
Constantine VI of
  Constantinople, 294
Constantinople
  Black Death and, 349m
  as Byzantine Empire capital,
    237, 248, 248m
  centralized rule of, 248
  Charlemagne and, 293–294
  conquest of (painting), 368
  early Christian community
    map, 220m
  economic importance of, 250
  founding of, 238
  1415–1498 map, 418m
  Heraclitus's launching
    from, 252
  Irene's leadership of,
    293–294
  Jewish settlements in,
    289m, 320m
  Justinian's construction
    projects in, 249
  monasteries in, 279m
  Muslim conquest attempts,
    260, 262m, 362
  Napoleonic Europe
    map, 606m
  Ottoman capture of, 329,
    364, 398
  renaming as Istanbul, 367
  sacking by Crusaders, 285,
    316, 317m, 318–319,
    367–368
  1300 Europe map, 330m
  Umayyad conquest
    plans, 267
  World War I map, 899m
Constitutional monarchy. See
  also individual rulers
  in England, 503, 598–599
  in France, 598–599
  in Spain, 958
The Constitution of the
  Lacedaemonians
  (Xenophon), 119

Continental System
    aims of, 607–608
    Battle of Trafalgar and,
        593, 608
    failures of, 608–609, 615
    as replacement for
        mercantilism,
        607–610, 628
    successes of, 633, 706
    urbanism's rise from,
        609–610
Contraception debate, in
    Catholicism, 1067
Cooley, Winnifred Harper, 807
Coolidge, Calvin, 941
Copernicus, Nicolaus
    astronomical studies of,
        468–469
    Galileo's debate with,
        472–473
    heliocentric theory
        development, 469
    Index of Forbidden Books
        condemnation of, 477
    Kopernik's portrait of, 471
    Luther's condemnation of,
        469–470
    message to Pope Paul III
        by, 470
    Planck's comparison
        to, 856
    On the Revolution of Heavenly
        Spheres, 466, 469, 485t
1 Corinthians (New
    Testament), 208t
2 Corinthians (New
    Testament), 208t
Corneille, Pierre, 526
Cortés, Hernán, 416, 422,
    423m, 424, 425, 425n3
Council of Nicaea, 247, 310
Council of Trent, 466, 475–476
The Courage to Be
    (Tillich), 1060
The Courtier (Castiglione), 375,
    387–388
Crassus, Marcus, 213
Creation theory, secularism
    and, 752–755
Crémieux, Adolphe, 731
Crescas, Hasdai, 328
Crete
    Black Death map, 349m
    Byzantine Empire map, 248m
    campaigns of Alexander
        map, 159m

domains of Charles
    V map, 397m
Encyclopédie subscriptions
    map, 582m
Europe, 1648 map, 506m
First Crusade map, 317m
Hellenistic world map, 161m
Jewish settlements
    map, 289m
Knossos palace complex,
    100, 100–101
Mediterranean world
    map, 308m
Middle/New Kingdom
    Egypt map, 46m
Minoan culture in, 98,
    101m, 102
Mycenaeans takeover of
    cities, 98
Persian Empire map, 61m
Phaistos Disk
    discovery, 102
Pylos palace on, 103
Sea Peoples map, 53m
skills taught on, 102
trader culture on, 102
Crick, Francis, 1061t
Crimean War (1863–1856),
    707, 720, 850, 913
Croatia, 289, 708m, 925, 963
Croker, John W., 668
Cromwell, Oliver, 536–537
Crusades
    against the Cathars, 329
    causes of, 314–315
    church sanctioning, blessing
        of, 313–314
    East-West context of, 314
    First Crusade, 284, 316, 316
    Muslim conquests
        map, 262m
    origins of, 304–305
    sacking of Constantinople,
        285, 316, 317m, 318–319,
        367–368
    Third Crusade, 489
Cuban Missile Crisis (1962),
    1025–1026
Cult of domesticity, women
    and, 693–696
Cultural Zionism, 776
Cuneiform script, 14
Cyclopedia (Chambers), 566
Cyrus the Great (Persian ruler)
    administration strengths
        of, 296

leadership of Persia, 60–61
release of the Jews by, 71, 90,
    93, 163
timeline of reign, 35
Czechoslovakia (Czech
    Republic)
    anti-Semitism in, 1079
    Christian Democratic party
        in, 1034
    deaths in World War I, 888
    EU membership, 1109
    independence declared
        by, 1091
    political rivalries of, 936
    Soviet invasion of, 1019,
        1040–1042, 1042
    women's suffrage rights, 939

D

Dacian culture, 193
Da Gama, Vasco, 416–417
Damascus
    Assyrian Empire map, 59m
    campaigns of Alexander
        map, 159m
    Great Mosque in, 268, 284
    Israelite Kingdom map, 80m
    Land of Canaan map, 79m
    Middle/New Kingdom
        Egypt map, 46m
    Persian Empire map, 61m
    Rome, 120 BCE map, 183m
    Sea Peoples map, 53m
    Umar's defeat of, 260
Dante. See Alighieri, Dante
Daoist philosophy, 149, 207
Darius (Persian ruler),
    62, 132
Dark Ages in Western Europe
    alternate names, 237, 268
    barbarian kings,
        scholar-monks, 268–271
    calamities in, 109
    Christian religious culture
        produced by, 276, 441
    decline of, 121, 124
    decline of urban life
        during, 307
    description, 237
    ending of, 98, 105
    European economy
        during, 270m
    rulership of Clovis, 293
    timeline/start of, 98, 105
    wedding practices, 275
    writers of, 276

Darwin, Charles, 206. *See also*
  Social Darwinism
  The Descent of Man, 758
  evolution by natural
    selection theory, 753–757
  Galapagos Island prints, 756
  On the Origin of Species, 747,
    756, 758, 759, 766
  theory of creation and, 753
  The Voyage of the Beagle, 755
David (Hebrew King)
  achievements of, 80–81
  anti-Philistine campaign, 79
  Israelite kingdom
    under, 80m
  in Jewish kingship
    lineage, 211
  psalms attributed to, 88
  romanticization of, 82
  Saul's banishment of, 79–80
  sexual appetite of, 81
  timeline of reign, 70
  wives/concubines of, 81
David-Solomon era (Golden
  Age of ancient Israel), 81
Da Vinci, Leonardo, 467, *468,*
  874, 932
Dawes, Charles, 941
D-Day allied invasion of
  Normandy, 979, 983
Dead Sea Scrolls, 72, 213n3
Deborah
  (Hebrew prophetess), 84
Le Décadent (Ibsen), 870
Decembrists revolt
  (Russia), 666
Decius (Roman emperor), 224
Declaration of Independence
  (U.S.), 560, 850
Declaration of Rights
  (England), 557–558
Declaration of the Rights of
  Man and Citizen, 591,
  594t, 599
The Decline of the West
  (Spengler), 932, 933
Decolonization
  Cold War and, 1023–1026
  in Europe, 1026–1029
    1027m, 1037, 1046
  in the Middle East, 1084
Deconstruction theory
  (Derrida), 1052
Defoe, Daniel, 645, 851
Degas, Edgar, *120, 695*

Deities
  of Ancient Egypt, 27–30
  of Ancient Greece,
    97–99, 104
  of Babylon, 19, 38
  of Ethiopia, 123
  of Rome, 180, 189
  of Sumeria, 7, 13–14, 16–19
Delian League alliance,
  132–133, 143, 143m, 146t
Demeter (Greek deity), 104
Democratic Republic of
  Germany
  (East Germany), 1033
Denis of France
  (Saint Denis), 233
Denmark
  Bismarck's provocation of, 713
  Christian Democratic party
    in, 1034
  Conference of Berlin
    attendance, 828
  global gender gap data,
    1139t
  mystical experience
    reports, 334
  mystical experiences in, 334
  Peace of Westphalia and,
    505, 506m
  Thirty Years' War and,
    449–450
  universal suffrage in, 796
  in World War I, 979
Dental braces, development
  of, 821
Derrida, Jacques, 867, 1052
Descartes, René
  advances in optics,
    meteorology, physics
    by, 494n9
  Discourse on Method, 485t, 494
  Hobbes' correspondence
    with, 510
  "I think, therefore I am"
    statement, 495–496
  Locke's study of, 559
  mathematical achievements
    of, 492, 494, 496
  Newton's support for ideas
    of, 496–497
  passionate/quirky ideas of
    God, 748
  portrait of, *495*
  universal set of laws idea of,
    496, 498

The Descent of Man
  (Darwin), 758
Description of a Good Wife
  (Strathwaite), 528
Détente, during the Cold War,
  1024–1025
Deutsches Wörterbuch (Grimm
  brothers), 527
*The Development of Capitalism
  in Russia* (Lenin), 916
Dialectical materialism
  theory, 918
Dialectical materialism theory
  (Lenin), 918
Diaspora of the Hebrew
  people, 83
Dictatorships, right-
  wing, 963m
Dictionaries, 526–527
*Dictionary of the English
  Language* (Johnson),
  505, 527
*Dictionnaire de l'Académie
  française* (1698), 527
*Dictionnaire historique et
  critique. See A Historical
  and Critical Dictionary*
  (Bayle)
Diderot, Denis
  Encyclopédie, 565–567, *566,*
  583m, 584
  The Nun, 694
Dillard, Annie, 205
Al-Din Suhrawardi,
  Shahab, 456
Diocletian (Roman emperor)
  attention to fiscal crisis, 241
  background of, 240
  division of administration
    by, 242
  emperor worship promoted
    by, 242
  resignation of, 244
  Roman army support of,
    240–241
  timeline of reign, 207, 238
Diphtheria vaccine, 820
Dirac, Paul, 859
The Directory
  collapse/dissolution of, 594t
  Napoleon's protection
    of, 602
  in Prussia, 517
  summoning of Napoleon
    by, 601

Discourse on the Origins of Inequality (Rousseau), 570–571, 581
Discourses on Livy (Machiavelli), 387
"Disorder and Early Sorrow" novella (Mann), 945
Disputation Regarding the Controversies in the Christian Faith (Bellarmine), 478
Disraeli, Benjamin, 731, 828
Divination practices, in Rome, 175–176
Divine Comedy (Dante), 333
DNA molecule discovery, 1061t, 1063
Documentary Hypothesis, of Bible's origin, 75
Domat, Jean, 509
Dome of the Rock mosque (Jerusalem), 267–268, 284
Dominican mendicant order, 338–340, 349, 773
Domitian (Roman emperor), 200, 224
Don Juan, canto XI (Lord Byron), 668–669
Donne, John, 485–486
Doolittle, Hilda, 954t
Dorian peoples (Greece), 105
Doriot, Jacques, 964
Dostoevsky, Fyodor, 205, 913
Douglas, William O., 995
Drake, Sir Francis, 448
Dreiser, Theodore, 803
Dreyfus, Alfred, 890n2
Dreyfus Affair, 890
The Drinker (Fallada), 945
Droste-Hulshoff, Annette von, 699
Droysen, Johann Gustav, 712
Dryden, John, 526, 573
Ducos, Pierre-Roger, 602
Duke of Guise. *See* Navarre, Henri de (Duke of Guise)
Dunn, Matthias Dunn, *649*
Dürer, Albrecht, *389*
Dutch Reformed Church (Holland), 407
Dutch United East India Company, 543–544
Dylan, Bob, 655
Dysentery plague in France, 547

E

Early Dynastic Period, 8–9
Earth Summit conference (1992), 1099
Eastern Europe
  agricultural economy in, 629
  anti-Semitism in, 733–734, 733m
  1880–1914 Jewish emigration, 775–776, 776m
  ethnic minorities in, 937m
  fall of Communism, 1094m
  Habsburg dynasty in, 396, 620
  Hasidic Jewish communities in, 576
  1942–1955 displaced peoples, 1020m
  Orthodox Church in, 620
  Ottoman losses in, 620
  Sea Peoples annihilation of cities, 55
Easter Rebellion (Ireland), 896t
East Germany, 1003n8, 1025, 1033.1091, 1091
East India Company, 449
The Economic Consequences of the Peace (Keynes), 967
Economic globalization, 1120–1122
Economic liberalism, 1033–1035
The Economist magazine, 787–788
Economy/economics issues.
  See also Beccaria, Cesare; Capitalism; Continental System; Great Depression; Hayek, Friedrich; Industrial capitalism; Keynes, John; Long Depression; Mercantilism; Smith, Adam
Abbasid dynasty, 284
aging population health costs, 1151–1152
in ancient Greece, 132, 150
Anglo-Irish Protestants and, 724
in Athens, 144
in Austria, 514
of Babylonians, 92
Byzantine Empire, 248–250
Catholicism and, 770

early Jewish people, 94, 164
early Middle Ages, 240
England, 448, 630
Europe, Crusades-era, 313, 415
Europe, Dark Ages, 270
Europe, 1500–1700 period, 422, 426–428
Europe, late Medieval period, 329
Europe, post-World War I, 931–932, 939–941
Europe, post-World War II, 1018, 1057, 1070
Europe, pre-World War I, 888–892
Europe, 13th/14th century, 327–328
France, 520, 636
Gini coefficient standard, 1149
guild system and, 337, 630
imperialism and, 841
industrialism's influence on, 627–631, 633, 644–645, 648, 749, 803, 905
international trade and, 503–504
Islamic empire, 304
Jewish people and, 436–437
late Middle Ages, 337, 342
Lenin's New Economic Policy, 964
libertarian taxation argument, 1147
Mamluk Empire, 318
Marx and, 688–690
Mediterranean region, 307, 329, 521, 1012
nationalism and, 711, 713–714
New World gold's influence, 422
Ottoman Empire, 367, 454, 459
philosophical studies of, 151
Pope Leo XIII on, 769–770
post-Cold War, 1092–1093
Renaissance era, 379–384
Roman Empire, 173t, 177–180, 185, 193, 197–198
Sea People's influence, 55
structuralism and, 867
Sumer's declines and transitions, 7, 11, 14–15

Europe, *(cont.)*
Thirty Years' War and, 449
Turkey, 899
2008 global economic
collapse, 1098, 1143–1147
unions and, 711
wars of religion and, 452
wealth/income distribution
scores, *1150*
welfare society and,
1029–1033
women's rights and,
791–792, 796
Edgeworth, Robert and
Maria, 698
Edict of Milan, 238, 245
Edict of Nantes (1598), 417,
445–446, 554, 557, 561
Edict of Toleration, 277
Edomites, 81
Education (schooling)
in Byzantium, 250
demand for historical
knowledge, 932–936
in Egypt, for girls, 1141
in England, 803
in Finland, for women, 790
in France, 1048
in Germany, 803
in Great Britain, 803
in India, 809
in Jordan, for girls, 1141
methods of Montessori,
804–805
Muslim limitation for girls,
1139–1140
in the United States, 804
Education in the New World
(Montessori), 804–805
Education of a Christian Prince
(Erasmus), 391–392
Edward III (English King), 346
Edward VI
(King of England), 447
EEC. *See* European Economic
Community
Effi Briest (Fontane), 801
Egypt. *See also* Ancient Egypt
al-Nahda cultural revival,
737–738
British oversight of, 937
economic/political
reforms, 735
female genital mutilation
in, 811
feminist movement in, 809

global gender gap data,
1139t
intellectual life in Cairo, 456
killing of nonvirgin
women, 810
Mubarak's control of
mosques, 1114
Muslim Brotherhood of, 1086
Napoleon's military
campaign vs., 602, 621
1950s military coup d'état
in, 1082
peace treaty with Israel, 1059
railroad development in, 644
rise of Shi'a Muslims in, 266
Satanic Verses banned in,
1096n1
in World War II, 1009–1010
The Egyptian Woman feminist
journal (Sha'arawi), 809
Eighteenth Dynasty (Old
Kingdom Egypt), 45, 47
Einstein, Albert, 851,
855, 1061t
El Alamein, Battle
of (1942), 1010
Eleazar, Israel ben, 576
Electric vacuum cleaners,
development of, 821
The Elements of Geometry
(Euclid), 163
Elements of Public Economy
(Beccaria), 564
Eleventh Dynasty (Old
Kingdom Egypt), 40
Elijah (Hebrew prophet), 87
Eliot, George (Marian Evans),
699, 765, 784, 801, 851
Eliot, T. S., 884, 932, 951
Elisha (Hebrew prophet), 87
Elizabeth I (Queen of
England), 448, 524, 533
Ellul, Jacques, 1071
Ely Cathedral, 205
Emanation notion, of
Neoplatonism, 232
émile (Rousseau), 583
Emmanuel, Wilhelm, 770–771
Empedocles of Acragas, 149
Emre, Yunus, 328
Encheiridion (Handbook)
(Epictetus), 198–199
Enclosure movement, in
Europe, 427–428
*Encyclopedia Britannica, First
Edition* (1768), 566

Encyclopédie (Diderot),
565–567, 566, 583m
*The End of History and the Last
Man* (Fukuyama),
1091–1092
"Endymion" poem (Keats), 668
Engels, Friedrich
The Communist Manifesto
co-authorship, 667,
687–688, 692
*The Condition of the Working
Class in England in 1844*,
627–628
England. *See also* Hundred
Years' War
Act of Union with Ireland,
706, 724
Anglican Church, 448,
506–507, 749, 764
Antigonids trade with, 161
Bedlam Asylum founded in,
504, 532–533
beheading of Charles I, 537
Black Death, eyewitness
account, 350
bubonic plague in, 537
Celtic England, 268
Charles I, reign of, 504,
536–537
Charles II, reign of, 375, 537
Charles X, reign of, 681
Church of England,
446–449, 506–507, 568,
764–767, 1071
conservatives voted out
in, 681
constitutional monarchy in,
503, 598–599
Declaration of Rights,
557–558
dismissal of James II,
557, 559
East India Company of, 449
Edward III, reign of, 346
Enlightenment and, 584, 628
entrepreneurial culture in,
630–631
Europe's industrialization
comparison, 635
Evangelical Anglican
churches in, 764
evolving government in, 318
Felipe II's invasion of,
448–449
feudal network expansion,
307, 329

German air-raid
  in London, 896t
gin production, 545
Glorious Revolution, 505,
  538, 554
Great Fire of London, 537
guild system in, 630
Henry II, reign of, 329–330
industrial revolution in,
  626–633, 632
James I, reign of, 533–535
James II, reign of, 537, 538
Jews expelled from, 436, 573
late 16th-century rise of, 533
League of Augsburg
  membership, 557
London, Jewish
  neighborhoods, 946
Manchester/Peterloo
  Massacre, 650–652, 651
national infrastructure
  development, 632
National Secular Society, 752
Neoplatonism in, 233
nonconforming churches in,
  764–765
Oxford movement, 751
Poor Law (16th century),
  676–677
punishment for
  homosexuality in, 432–433
Puritans of England, 407,
  448, 532, 537
putting-out manufacturing
  system, 631
railroad track system
  development, 633
Romans driven from, 195
route of missionaries
  in, 288m
Scientific Revolution
  influences, 628–629
1780–1850 population
  growth, 628
terrorism in London, 1125
Thirty Years' War
  involvement, 536
trade advantages of, 422
U.S. Great Depression
  influence in, 944
War of the Roses, 446
witchcraft trials, 435
in World War I, 896t
Zionism in, 946
England's Treasure by Foreign
  Trade (Mun), 523

English East India
  Company, 523
The English Gentleman
  (Strathwaite), 528
The English Gentlewoman
  (Strathwaite), 528
Enki (god of waters), 16
Enlightenment era
  (1690–1789), 553–588.
  See also Locke, John;
  Rousseau, Jean-Jacque
  ambivalence toward the
  Jews, 576–578
  assessment of, 582–588
  Bayle/religious toleration,
  561–562
  beliefs of deists, 572
  bourgeoisie as audience for,
  585–586
  call for women's rights
  in, 791
  encyclopedias published
  during, 565–566
  free markets/irrational
  punishment, 562–565
  geographic centers of,
  562–563
  investigations of, by the
  nobility, 584
  Jewish enlightenment,
  573–574, 573m, 574
  manners/etiquette,
  importance of, 503
  origins of, 554–558
  poverty and famine
  during, 580
  reexamination of women's
  roles, 694
  scholasticism and, 333n1, 557
  term derivation, 1152
  the unenlightened and,
  578–581
  Voltaire/the limits of
  optimism, 567–570
En-Mebaragesi (Kish king), 8
Environmental
  concerns, issues
  Earth Summit
  conference, 1099
  economic development and,
  1092, 1099–1100
  Exxon Valdez oil spill, 1092,
  1096–1097, 1097, 1145
  genetics changes and, 1053
  water pollution, carbon
  monoxide, 1099

Ephesians (New
  Testament), 208t
Epic of Gilgamesh (Sumerian
  poem), 8, 38–40, 43, 60
Epictetus (Roman teacher),
  198–199
Epicureanism philosophy, 198
Epistemology, Locke's interest
  in, 563
Erasmus, Desiderius, 374,
  391, 408
  Brethren of Common Life
  alumni, 390, 393
  Colloquies, 391
  The Complaint of Peace,
  391–392
  debate with Luther, 399
  Education of a Christian
  Prince, 391–392
  Handbook of the Christian
  Soldier, 391–392
  Julius Excluded from Heaven,
  373, 391
  New Testament of, 392
  Praise of Folly, 390, 408
Erbakan, Necmettin, 1114
Erebus (Greek deity), 98
Eriugena, John Scotus, 233
Eros (Greek deity), 97
An Essay on Human
  Understanding (Locke),
  554, 559
Essay on the General Principle of
  Political Institutions
  (Maistre), 673, 675
Essay on the Inequality of the
  Human Races
  (Gobineau), 731
Essay on the Principle of
  Population (Malthus),
  1099–1100
The Essence of Christianity
  (Feuerbach), 746, 760–761
The Essence of Paris (Tahtawai),
  706, 738
Essenes (philosophical sect),
  212–214
Estates General
  (of France), 596
D'Este family (Italy), 383
Esther (Jewish heroine), 84–85
Estonia, 1091, 1104
Ethiopia
  Abyssinian peoples in,
  255–256
  deities of, 123

Ethiopia *(cont.)*
female circumcision in, 811
global gender gap data, 1139t
Italy's invasion of, 829, 958
Mussolini's invasion of, 958
Nile River origination in, 20
trade activities, 161, 254
Etruscan civilization (Italy),
111m, 172, 174–175
Euclid, 163, 266, 299, 375
Euripides, 140–141
Euro currency, 1093,
1107, 1143
Europe. *See also* Central
Europe; Eastern Europe;
Enlightenment era;
Europe, late medieval era;
European Union; Indo-
Europeans; Latin Europe;
Mediterranean Europe;
Thirty Years' War;
Welfare states in Europe;
Western Europe;
individual countries
abortion, availability
in, 799
absolutism in, 526, 542–544
advantages of seaboard
nations, 422
brutishness in the New
World, 425–426
centers of learning
map, 499m
cholera epidemic, 626, 647
collapse of concert of
Europe, 691–693
colonial unrest in, 842–845
crops introduced in, 544
decolonization era,
1026–1028
devastation from the Black
Death, 364
1800 urban population,
585–586, 586m
1830 liberal-led rebellions, 682
1848 revolutions, 685–687,
686m, 691–693, 707, 728
1850 industrialization
map, 638m
1850 People's of Europe
map, 708m
1850 urban development
map, 646m
1870, 1914 industry,
manufacturing data, 822m

1870 population data,
816, 826
1878–1914 alliances, 893m
1880–1914 immigration
data, 841m
feminist movement in,
1045–1046
1500–1800 population
growth, *426*
German nationalism,
711–716, 718–721
"gilded age" of, 836–841
industrialization in, 635–639
international investments
of, 891m
international trade networks,
542, 543m
Islamic Union of Students'
Associations, 1096
late medieval period,
329–331, 330m
map of Napoleonic
Europe, 606m
Mediterranean cities,
306–309
missionaries, 833–836
Muslim protests in, 1097
new crops introduced in,
426–427
1914 international
investments, 891m
1942–1955 displaced
peoples, 1020m
1948–1955 military
blocs, 1026m
19th-century decline in
Christianity, 749
onset of World War II, 933
openings with Ottoman
Turks, 591
Ottoman trade capitulations
with, 642–645
Protestant revival in, 1057
railroad development,
637–638
reception of Calvin's
teachings, 407
royal/national banks,
542–543
second wave feminism,
1044–1045
secularization in, 1063
Seven Years' War, 505,
548–549
1648 map, 506m

16th-17th century Wars of
Religion, 38
slave trade in, 545
suffragettes tactics in,
795–796
13th-14th century
inventions, 327
tuberculosis epidemic, 647
2010 practicing Christian
data, *1059*
U.S. Great Depression
influence in, 943–944
wealth compared to Islamic
world, 327–328
welfare states in, 1029–1033
WW I emigrations from, 888
Europe, late medieval era,
329–331, 330m
Black Death, 329, 348–352,
349m, 364, 376, 389,
907n7, 1051
chivalry, 342–346
conquest of Islamic world,
352–354, 355m
early representative
government, 340–342
guild system, 337–338
Hundred Years' War,
346–348, 347m
mendicant orders, 338–340
mysticism, 334–336
scholasticism, 331–334
European Atomic Energy
Community, 1106
European Coal and Steel
Community, 1106
European Common
Market, 1114
European Economic
Community (EEC),
1105–1107
European for Nuclear
Research, 1058
European Humanist
Federation, 1063
European Molecular Biology
Laboratory, 1062
European Organization for
Nuclear Research
(CERN), 1058, 1062
European Space Agency, 1059
European Union (EU)
description of, 1106
embargo on China
weaponry sales, 1102

global economic collapse
influence, *1144,* 1146
initial problems of,
1108–1109
Maastricht Treaty creation
of, 1092, 1106
member countries, 1104,
1106–1107, 1109
origins of, 1065, 1104–1109
Pope Benedict XVI's advice
to, 1153–1154
third wave feminism in,
1109–1111
unemployment investigation
of, 1103
Europe's Optical Illusion
(Angell), 890
Eusebius of Caesarea, 242
EU. *See* European Union
Evans, Arthur, 100–101
Evans, Marian (aka George
Eliot), 699, 765
Every Man Dies Alone
(Fallada), 945
Evolution by natural selection
theory (Darwin), 753–757
Existentialism, 867–869
Exsurge Domine ("Arise, O
Lord") papal bull
(Leo X), 396
Exxon Valdez oil spill, 1092,
1097, 1145
Eyeglasses, invention of, 327
Ezra (Hebrew prophet), 91

F

Fabian Society (socialist
organization), 791–792
Factory Act (1833), 653
Faisal ibn Ali, 938
Falkenhayn, Erich von ("Blood
Miller of Verdun"), 910
Fallada, Hans, 945
Familia (Roman social unit),
177–179, 198
Families and family life. *See
also* Women; Women,
modern; Women's rights
advice in magazines, novels,
696–697, 784
birth control information,
799–800
British birth rates, 799
brother-sister marriage,
ancient Egypt, 48

as center of Jewish life, 78
conservatism and, 677
familia (Roman social unit),
177–179, 198
German parental rights,
remarriage laws, 788
ignorance of sexual
matters, 800
industrial age influences,
645, 652–654, 784–785
monasticism's rejection
of, 277
patriarchal families,
428–431
Queen Victoria, Prince
Albert, 785
selling family members in
Sumer, 15
Stoicism and, 230
as women's duty, 783
women's restrictions,
Archaic Greece, 115–116
A Farewell to Arms
(Suttner), 699
La Farina, Giuseppe, 717
Fascism. *See also* Mussolini,
Benito
defined, 955–956
influence on women,
977–978, 1003, 1006
Inquisition comparison, 480
international appeal of,
963–964
in Italy and Spain, 955–960
Pius XII's opposition
to, 1064
tyrannical rule of, 932
"will to power" as prelude
to, 863
women in and against,
1004–1009
Woolf and, 1007
Fascist Falanga Party (of
Poland), 963
Fascist Insurrection Party (of
Croatia), 963
Fascist Party of Free Believers
(of Greece), 963
Fascist Union (of Great
Britain), 963
Fatah party, 1135
Fatherland Front (Austria
fascists), 963
Fatima (daughter of
Muhammad), 265–266

Fatimid dynasty (Egypt), 284,
303, 303m, 317m
Federal Republic of Germany
(West Germany), 1033
Felipe II (Spanish King),
448–449, 460
Female genital
mutilation, 811
Female identity, literature
of, 801
Feminist movement, 783,
791. *See also* Women;
Women, modern;
Women's rights
in Europe, 1045–1046
first wave feminism, 1044
1990s globalization of,
1111–1113
second wave feminism,
1044–1045
Sha'arawi's activism in
Egypt, 809
Stöcker's activism in
Germany, 796–798
third wave feminism,
1109–1111
Fénelon, François, 520–521
Ferdinand I (of Habsburg
Austria), 721, 896t
Ferdinando VII (of Spain),
672, 682
Fertile Crescent
connective role of, 10, 20,
33–34, 1120
French/British rule of, 1010
map of, 8m
Persia's effort at
controlling, 249
trek of Abram and, 69–70
World War II importance of,
1009–1010
Feuerbach, Ludwig Andreas,
760–761
Fichte, Johann Gottlieb,
660–661
Ficino, Marsilio, 387
Fifth Dynasty (Old Kingdom
Egypt), 40
Fifth Republic of France
(1958-present), 592
Fifth Symphony
(Beethoven), 657
Final Solution (of Hitler), 978,
988. *See also* Jewish
Holocaust (World War II)

Finland
    fascism in, 963
    global gender gap
        data, 1139t
    Lapua Party fascists in, 963
    Lutheranism in, 404
    tsarist rule in, 616
    universal suffrage in,
        796, 797m
    witchcraft trials, 435
    women's education in, 790
    in World War I, 898m, 899m
First Battle of the Marne (WW
    I), 896t, 897
First Blast of the Trumpet
    against the Monstrous
    Regiment of Women
    (Knox), 430–431
First Crusade, 284, 316, 316
First Intermediate Period
    (Ancient Egypt), 23, 26, 40
First International Zionist
    Congress, 732
First Opium War, 831
First Punic War, 172, 185
First Sino-Japanese War, 985
First Temple, 77
First Vatican Council, 771
Five Good Emperors of
    Rome, 173
Five Lectures on Psychoanalysis
    (Freud), 874
Flaminius, Titus, 175
Flaubert, Gustave, 801
Fontane, Theodor, 801
Ford, Ford Madox, 884
Ford, Henry, 821, 947
Ford Motor Company, 817,
    821, 947
Fortunata and Jacinta (Pérez
    Galdós), 801
"The Four Holy Men" painting
    (Dürer), 389
Fourteen Points (of Wilson),
    896t, 936
The Fourth Estate painting
    (Volpedo), 769
Fourth Republic of France
    (1946–1958), 592
Foxe, John, 447–448
France. See also French
    Revolution; Hundred
    Years' War; Louis XIV;
    Napoleon; National
    Assembly; Paris, France

Academie française, 513
Acts of Toleration for Jewish
    people, 577
aggression in Southeast
    Asia, 831
agricultural economy in, 629
Bibliothèque Nationale, 401
Black Death, eyewitness
    account, 350
Bourbon dynasty, 513
Burgundians in, 274
Capetian dynasty in,
    329, 340
Carolingian control of,
    286–287, 305
Carolingian princelings'
    nicknames, 295
Catholicism vs.
    Protestantism, 445
Charlemagne's Empire
    map, 289m
cholera epidemic deaths, 647
Christian Democratic party
    in, 1034
church attendance data, 1059
conditions leading to
    Revolution, 595–598
Conference of Berlin
    attendance, 828
Congress of Vienna
    attendance, 666
Continental domination
    by, 513
deaths in World War I, 888
dissolution of liberal-leaning
    parliament, 681
dissolution of National
    Convention, 594t
dysentery plague, 547
Edict of Nantes, 417,
    445–446, 557, 561
EEC membership, 1106
1848 Paris uprising, 685
empire-building by, 816
Enlightenment investigation
    by nobility, 584, 596
Estates General of, 596
European investments
    in, 891m
fascism in, 963–964
feudal network expansion,
    307, 329
financial/political
    corruption in, 592
Francis II, reign of, 444

Franco-Prussian War,
    713–714, 720–721, 890
free fall of Old Regime, 595
Fronde rebellion, 519
Greek colonies in, 110
guild system abolished
    in, 596
Henri III, reign of, 445
Henri IV, reign of, 445, 557
Hitler's occupation of
    Paris, 980
homosexuality as deathly
    offense, 432
Huguenots (French
    Calvinists), 407, 444–445,
    445, 557, 558
Jewish settlements in, 320m
Jews expelled from, 436, 573
Judaism in, 1074
League of Augsburg vs., 558
livret ("booklet") document
    for workers, 648
Louis IX, reign of, 329
Louis-Philippe, reign of,
    681–682, 685
Louis the Blind, reign of, 295
Louis the Child, reign
    of, 295
Louis the Stammerer, reign
    of, 295
Louis VII, reign of, 329
Louis VIII, reign of, 341
Louis XIII, reign of,
    509–510, 558
Louis XV, reign of, 515t,
    517, 596
Lyons/urban
    development, 646
Marseilles jewelers' guild, 309
Masonry in, 587
Mediterranean World
    map, 308m
monarchy abolished in, 594t
National Front Party, 1109
nationalization of church
    property, 594t
Neoplatonism in, 233
1968 rebellions in, 1036
pacifism declared by,
    971–972
Paris/urban
    development, 645
Philip IV, reign of, 346, 357
political periods of, 592
post-WW I reparations, 939

prostitutes in Paris, 653–654
railroad development, 638
restoration of royal
    families, 670
rise of urbanism, 609–610
Roman aqueduct in, *184*
Ruhr Valley
    occupation, 932
rulers of, 515t
Saint Bartholomew's Day
    Massacre, 417, 444–445
Sainte-Chapelle
    interior, *333*
Salian Franks in, 274
Second Empire, 592,
    802, 850
Second Republic, 592, 718
seizure of African
    territory, 829
1750, 1800 population
    growth, *633*
1789 Estate General
    lockout, 710
Seven Years' War participation,
    505, 548–549
terrorism in, 1114
Third Estate of, 596–598
Third Republic, 592, 721
trade advantages of, 422
two-chambered legislature
    in, 671
unemployment in, 1108
United Nations and, *997*
Versailles Palace,
    518–520, *519*
Vikings attack on Paris, 284
War of Devolution, 516
war with Austria,
    Prussia, 594t
women's labor and trade
    unions, 784
women's suffrage in, 939
in World War I, 887, 889,
    894–895, 897, 900,
    905–906, 910–911, 913,
    919, 921–924, 927
in World War II, 977–981,
    983, 1003, 1008–111
Franciscan mendicant order,
    338–339, 349, 357, 373.
    See also Motolinia,
    Toribio de Benavente;
    Sixtus IV (Pope)
Francis II (Austria), 515t
Francis II (French King), 444

Francis of Assisi, Saint,
    328, 338
Franco, Francisco
    Christian leadership
        compromises with, 1058
    conservative interests
        of, 959
    as inspiration for
        Guernica, 960
    leadership of Fascist
        Spain, 958
Franco-Dutch War (France vs.
    Netherlands), 517
François-Eugène of Savoy
    (French Prince), 515–516
Franco-Prussian War
    (1870–1871), 713–714,
    720–721, 890
Franco-Russian alliance
    (1894–1917), 893m
Frankfurt Assembly
    (Germany), 712–713
Franz Ferdinand (Archduke,
    Austria-Hungary), 892,
    896t, 900
Franz I (of Austria), 687
Frederick II the Great (of
    Prussia), 518n5, 568, 577
*Free Employment in a Free
    Society* (Beveridge, 1031
Freeman, Edward Augustus,
    706–707, 709
Free-market capitalism, 563,
    1034, 1085, 1091,
    1148–1152
Freemasonry, 586–587
Freethinkers' League
    (Germany), 752
French Action
    (fascist party), 964
French Empire
    (1804–1814), 592
French Popular Party, 964
French Republic
    (1792–1804), 592
French Revolution (1789), 516,
    555. *See also* Napoleon
    assessment/judgment of,
        610–615
    Austria/Prussia invasion of
        France, 591599
    as beginning of modern
        age, 591
    Burke's comments about,
        593, 610–613

criminalization of
    Christianity, 601
Declaration of the Rights of
    Man and Citizen, 591,
    594t, 599
events leading to, 592,
    595–598
execution of Louis XVI, 601
Paine's evaluation of,
    613–614
political terminology
    derived from, 591–592
Robespierre's Reign of
    Terror, 594t, 600
storming of the
    Bastille, 599
Tennis Court Oath,
    594t, 598
Thatcher's bicentennial
    comments, 592–593
timeline of, 594t
Wollstonecraft's evaluation
    of, 614
French Solidarity (fascist
    party), 964
Freud, Sigmund
    aggression theory of,
        875–876
    *Beyond the Pleasure
        Principle*, 875
    *Civilization and Its
        Discontents*, 876
    *Five Lectures on
        Psychoanalysis*, 874
    The Interpretation of Dreams,
        850, 872–873
    *Introductory Lectures on
        Psychoanalysis*, 874
    patient letter to, 875
    patterns in human life
        described by, 1053
    secularism/assimilation
        of, 776
    *Three Essays in the Theory of
        Sexuality*, 873
Friedman, Milton, 1146
Friedrich III (Brandenburg-
    Prussia), 515t
Friedrich II the Great
    (Brandenburg-
    Prussia), 515t
Friedrich Wilhelm
    (Brandenburg-
    Prussia), 515t

Friedrich Wilhelm I
(Brandenburg-
Prussia), 515t
Friedrich Wilhelm II
(Brandenburg-
Prussia), 515t
Friedrich Wilhelm III
(Brandenburg-Prussia),
515t, 766–767
Fröbel, Julius, 1104
From *Love's Redeeming Work:
The Anglican Quest for
Holiness* (Rowell,
Stevenson,
Williams), 1072
Fronde rebellion (France), 519
Fuchs, Klaus, 1003n8
Fukuyama, Francis,
1091–1092
Fundamentalism, 1073–1074

G
Gaia (Greek deity), 97
Gainesborough, Thomas, *507*
Galatians
(New Testament), 208t
Galilei, Galileo, 206
Bruno's comparison with,
481–482
conflicts with the church,
468, 472–473, 478, 482
debate with Kepler and
Copernicus, 472–473
*Dialogue on the Two Chief
World Systems,* 466,
482–483
*Discourses on Two New
Sciences,* 483
heliocentric theory
elaborations, 470, 471,
473, 478
Index of Forbidden Books
condemnation of, 477
inquisition and punishment
of, 473, 483–484
Jesuit astronomer's
acceptance of, 478
moons of Venus discovery,
471–472
The Starry Messenger, 471, 472
telescope redesign by, 471n1
Gallipoli campaign (WW I),
896t, 898, 905, 910
Gandhi, Mohandas,
842–843, *843*

Gargantua and Pantagruel
(Rabelais), 411
Garibaldi, Giuseppe, 718
Gaskell, Charles, 857
Gates, Bill, 1142
Gauguin, Paul, 880
Gautier, Theophile, 852
Gays, 1037, 1111. *See also*
Homosexuality/
homosexuals
The Gay Science (Nietzsche),
746–747
Gaza
architectural styles in, 58
Hamas control of, 1127, 1135
Hamas founded in, 1117
Israel's invasion of, 1127
Jewish population in, 437
Land of Canaan map, 79m
Middle/New Kingdom
Egypt map, 46m
Palestinian refugees in, *1081*
Six Day War and, 1040, 1041m
World War I map, 899m
Geffels, Frans, *514*
Geiger, Abraham, 747, 774–775
Gemara (Jewish legal
commentary), 320
Gender, 1138–1139. *See also*
Women, sexuality
*The General Theory of
Employment, Interest, and
Money* (Keynes), 933,
967–968
Generative grammar theory
(Chomsky), 1061t
Genghis Khan. *See also* Mongols
bubonic plague and, 348
China's pre-invasion
population, 358
death of, 354
leadership of the
Mongols, 353
lifespan of, 328
successors of, 354, 357
Taymiyyah's description
of, 1082
victories of, 353, 819, 887
Genocide
in Armenia, 888, *904,*
905, 928
in Bashir, 1136
in Serbia, 1130
George, David Lloyd, 922, *922,*
923–924

Georgia (country), 1091
German Evangelical Church
(EKD), 1069–1070
Germanic peoples
amalgamation into medieval
society, 269
Berlin/urban
development, 645
challenges in western
Europe, 271
Frankish kingdom,
271–272, 272m
inrush into Roman Empire,
239–241, 1152
mythology of, 275–276
Rome/neighbors map,
183m
Visigoth laws, 274–275
warlords, 249, 268
witchcraft beliefs of,
434–435
women's legal protections, 275
The German Ideology (Marx),
690–691
German Reichstag, 890, 895,
906–907
Germany. *See also* East
Germany; Hitler, Adolf;
Nazi Party/Nazi
Germany; Prussia; West
Germany
Adenauer's reforms in,
1033–1034
agricultural economy in, 629
Berlin airlift, 1018, *1025*
Berlin Wall in, 1025, 1070,
1091, 1092
Bible publication in, 69
Blitzkrieg strategy, 980
Cameroon, Namibia,
Tanzania seized by, 830
Charlemagne's expansion
into, 288
church attendance
data, 1059
Conference of Berlin, 816,
828–829
Congress of Vienna
influences, 636, 711
creation of dioceses in, 287
Custom's Union
establishment, 953
deaths in World War I, 888
East/West division, 1033
empire-building by, 816

Enlightenment investigation by nobility, 584
European investments in, 891m
feudal network expansion, 307, 329
feudal relations with churchmen, 307
Frankfurt Assembly, 712–713
Freethinkers' League, 752
"Germanization" of, 715–716
global gender gap data, 1139t
Hamburg/urban development, 646
Hitler's appointment as chancellor, 933
Holocaust Remembrance Day, 1155
honor killing in, 1140
hyperinflation in, 932
industrialization in, 636, 715–716
Jewish settlements in, 289m, 320m, 730
Jews expelled from, 416, 436
liberal-led rebellions in, 682
Lusitania sunk by, 888, 896t, 921
Lutheranism in, 404, 407
medical research, 16th century, 489–490
Mediterranean World map, 308m
military aid offered to Mexico, 922
missionaries in, 288m
Munich Conference, 933
nationalism in, 711–716, 718–721
1914 invasion of Belgium, 896t
1933 unemployment data, 933
1972 Olympics terrorism, 1081
occupation of Paris, 978, 980
Otto I's leadership, 329, 380
parental rights/remarriage laws, 788
Peasants' Revolt, 399, 416, 429, 442
Poland invaded by, 974, 977, 978, 981
political rivalries of, 936

Protestantism in, 396, 399–400
railroad development, 638
religious challenges in, 766–768
Roman soldier tomb in, 194
Roman World map, 188m
Russia's 1914 invasion of, 896t
Schlieffen Plan, 895
1750, 1800 population growth, 633
Seven Years' War, 505, 548–549
state-run schools, 803
Stöcker's women's rights activism, 796–798
Thirty Years War, 442
trade unions banned in, 892–893
unemployment in, 1108
unification of, 707, 711–714, 826–827
and U.S. dollar currency crisis, 941–942
U.S. Great Depression influence in, 943–944
USSR nonaggression pact, 978
witchcraft trials, 435
women's suffrage rights, 939
in World War I, 887–889, 891m, 892–897, 900, 903, 905–908, 921–925
World War II surrender of, 979
"Germany—A Winter's Tale" poem (Heine), 650
Gersonides, 328
Ghosts (Ibsen), 803, 850
Gibbon, Edward, 582
Gide, André, 945–946
Gildas (English monk), 268–269
Gilded age, in Europe, 836–841
Gilgamesh (Sumerian ruler), 9, 38. See also Epic of Gilgamesh
Gin production in England, 545
Gini coefficient standard, 1149
Ginsberg, Asher, 777
Giovanni, Archbishop of Beijing, 357

Gladiatorial games, 174–175, 175, 178, 201, 238
Glasgow Young Men's Society for Religious Improvement, 654
Global economic collapse (of 2008), 1098, 1143–1147
Global gender gap report, 1138–1139, 1139t
Globalized capitalism, 1092
Glorious Revolution (1688), 505, 538, 554, 557
Gobineau, Arthur de, 731
Godless communism, struggles against, 38
God problem (1799–1907), 745–779. See also Secularism
decline of Christianity in Europe, 749
evolution/natural selection and, 755–759
Godless universe of Nietzsche, 746–749
Knutzen's pamphlets denying God, 473
rise of secularism, 745, 749–752, 763, 775
theory of creation and, 752–755
Goebbels, Josef, 945, 961–962
Goethe, Johann Wilhelm von, 504, 582, 595, 614–615, 659
Gogol, Nikolai, 913
The Golden Bowl (James), 883
Gold standard, 933, 942, 943, 943m
Goldziher, Ignaz, 779
Goncharova, Georgia, 954t
Gonzaga family (Italy), 383
Good Friday Accord (1999), 1093, 1116
Gorbachev, Mikhail, 1025, 1091
Göring, Hermann, 994
Gospel of Matthew (New Testament), 208t
Christian's declaration as non-Jews, 223
declaration of aimed at Jewish audiences, 216–217
depiction of Jesus, 210–211
description of, 210–214
on Jesus and violence, 442

Gospel of Matthew *(cont.)*
Jesus' confusing/provocative words, 214–215
on John the Baptist, 215
on proof of Jesus' prophecy, 759
as written for Jewish audiences, 216–217, 759
Gospel of Thomas, 221
Gott, John William, 752
Gould, Stephen J., 1061t
Gozzoli, Benozzo, 382
Gracchus, Tiberius and Gaius, 185
Great Above/Great Below (Sumerian belief), 16
Great Britain
Acts of Toleration for Jewish people, 577
appeasement of Hitler, 970–972
Atlantic slave trade and, 546m
"Cat and Mouse" Act, 795
church attendance data, 1059
Communist Party (CPGB), 945–946
compulsory primary schooling, 803
Congress of Vienna attendance, 666
Conservative Party rejected by, 1032
control of Iraq by, 937
18th-century freedom from guilds, 630
empire-building by, 816
European investments in, 891m
fascism in, 963
Hitler's air raids of, 980
industrialization map, 634m
invasion of France, 601
legal rights of women recognized by, 701
limited anti-Jewish sentiments, 946
monetary system introduction, 942
munitions factory, 906
1960s emigration to, 1038
Oath of Supremacy, 723
opium for silks trade with China, 831
oversight in the Middle East, 937

oversight of Saudi Arabia, 937
post-WW I decline in religion, 1071
post-WW I reliance on colonies, 940
response to Ireland's potato blight, 727
1750, 1800 population growth, 633
Seven Years' War, 505, 548–549
Social Insurance and Allied Services report, 1029–1031
suffrage rights for women, 783, 788, 793, 932, 939
Sykes-Picot Agreement, 900
terrorism in, 1114
trade unions/Labour Party in, 892
unemployment in, 1108
Union of Muslim Organisations, 1095–1096
War of 1812 vs. America, 615
in World War I, 888, 890, 891m, 892–895, 896t, 900, 905–907, 921, 923
Great Depression (U.S., 1929)
global impact of, 942–945
Hitler/Nazis and, 961
influence on women, 977–978, 1008
international unemployment rates, 945t
military role in government during, 984
onset of, 932, 933, 942
Greater West
Benedict XVI's advice to the EU, 1153–1154
Ramadan's European version of Islam, 1155–1156
two-faced movement in, 1152–1153
Great Famine (Ireland), 726–728, 727m
Great Fire of London, 537
Great Fire of Rome, 187
Great Flood myth (of Sumer), 7–9, 74
The Great Illusion (Angell), 890
Great Mosque in Damascus, 268, 284
Great Purge (Soviet Union), 933

Great Purge, in Russia, 964–965
Great Temple of Ramses II, *51*
Greece. *See also* Ancient Greece
admittance to NATO, 1026m
anti-Jewish sentiments, 946
debt issues in, 1143, *1144*, 1146
economic collapse in, 1143–1144
fascism in, 963
independence from Ottomans, 706, 735
manufacturing/financial ventures, 1107
patriot revolt vs. Ottoman Turks, 672
unemployment in, 1108
in World War I, 892, 893m, 895, 897, 915m, 927
in World War II, 978
Greek Civil War (1946–1948), 1025
Gregorian Reform, 330, 395
Gregory IX (Pope), 330
Gregory of Tours, 269, 272, 276
Grievance notebooks *(cahiers des doléances)*, 597
Grimm brothers, 527
Grimmelshausen, Hans Jakob Christoffel von, 451–452
Grundy, Sydney, 783, 805
Guernica mural (Picasso), *960*
Guide for the Perplexed (Maimonides), 324
Guild system
abolishment of in France, 596
absence of, 18th-century Britain, 630
artisanal guilds, 330
in Austria, 539
charitability of, 338, 580
described, 337–338
in England, 630
in Germany, 505
Jewish Enlightenment era participation, 730
Marseilles jewelers' guild, 309
Napoleon's prohibition of, 603
in Renaissance Italy, 384

symbols of, 586n15
textile production in the cities, 547
Guillotine (for beheadings), 594t, 600, *600*
Guizot, François (French premier), 685
Gulags (concentration camps), in Russia, 965
Gunpowder, 364, 450
Gutenberg, Johannes, 374, 384
Guys, Constantin, 877
Gynaeceum (woman's zone), 134
Gypsies of Romania, *1108*

H
Habermas, Jürgen, 1051
Habsburg dynasty (Austria). *See also* Metternich, Klemens von
Cavour's neutralization of, 718
collapse of, 895, 936
declaration of war on Serbia, 895
1848 uprising, 687, 691
Ferdinand I, reign of, 721
formation of, 449
German unification, 714
guild commodity control in, 630
Italy's unification, 716–717
lands/reign of Charles V, 396–398, 397m, 438
Ottoman invasion of, 513–514, *514*
Ottoman losses to, 620
Ottoman uneasy relation with, 460
rulers of, 515t
secession possibilities, 691
sharing of Hungary with Ottomans, 721–723
War of Austria Succession and, 548
WW I collapse of, 723
Hadrian (Roman emperor), 200, 226
Haggai (Jewish prophet), 90
Haggard, H. Rider, 851
Hague Conventions (1899, 1907), 904–905
Hairesis (philosophical sects). *See* Essenes; Pharisees; Sadducees

Al-Hakim, Tawfiq, 808
Hamas
founding of, 1059, 1086
frustration with Ba'athists, 1088
Gaza city rally, *1087*
Gaza Strip controlled by, 1127, 1135
Israel/Muslim Brotherhood financing, 1117
Hamitic peoples, 21
Hammurabi (Babylonian ruler)
Code of Hammurabi, 16, 34–37, *37*
as first great lawgiver in Western history, 35
map of rulership area, 35m
modern history comparison, 876–877
reign of, 34
religious imperialism introduced by, 38
Handbook of the Christian Soldier (Erasmus), 391–392
Hanifa, Abu, 298
Hardenberg, Friedrich von (Novalis), 582, 660, 1104
Harding, Warren G., 939
Hardy, Thomas, 801, 803
The Harmonies of the World (Kepler), 485t
Harnack, Adolf von, 762
Harvey, William, 163, 484, 485t, 487–488
Hashemite clan, 938
Hasidic Judaism, 575–576
Haskalah movement, 575. *See also* Jewish enlightenment
Hasmonean dynasty, 166–167, 211, 213. *See also* Maccabeus, Judas; Mattathias
Hatice (Sultana), 461t
Hatshepsut (Egyptian Queen), 35, *47*, 48
Hattusilis III (Hittite chief), 52
Hawking, Stephen, 1061t
Hayek, Friedrich, 968, 1031, 1146
Heartbreak House (Shaw), 972
Heaven (in Sumerian religion), 16
"Heavenly Horse" painting (Zhou Lang), *358*

Hebrew (Jewish) Bible. *See also* Abram/Abraham; Moses; Torah; YHWH
canons, comparison of, 73t
chronology of composition of, 76t
Great Flood described in, 259
historical problems with, 74
Ishaq's Arabic translation, 299
Jewish need for Greek translation, 164–165
Luke's knowledge of, 208
maskilim (scholars), 774
Masoretic text version, 72, 73t, 74
portrayal of Solomon, 81
Psalms, 73t, 80–81, 88, 356, 729
Septuagint version, 72, 73t, 74, 133, 167
Talmudic/Rashi's commentaries, 323–324
Temple description, 81
Torah, five books of, 72, 73t, 74–75, 76t
Xenophanes comments about, 123
Hebrew people. *See also* Jewish people; Judaism; Moses
as the Chosen People, 74
division into twelve tribes, 78
ethical/religious justification for some wars, 441
move into Palestine, 77
political autonomy of, 78
priests and rabbis, 89–92
prophets and prophecy, 87–89
special covenant with God, 74
split into two kingdoms, 82–83
tribal judges, 78–79
women and the law, 83–87
Hebrew Temple, 60
Hedda Gabler (Ibsen), 801
Hegel, Georg Friedrich, 151, 748, 849
Heidegger, Martin, 867, 1054
Heine, Heinrich, 650, 659
Helen of Troy, 105–106
Helicopters, development of, 821

Heliocentric theory, 469–470, 471–473, 478, 482, 778
Hellenes culture (Greece), 99–100, 102–103
Hellenica (Xenophon), 119
Hellenistic Age
  art and literature during, 162
  commerce/manufacturing during, 160–161
  cult of Isis in, 227
  division of Egypt into dynasties, 21
  Empire map, 161m
  Epicureanism philosophy, 198
  farming/taxation struggles, 161–162
  inequitable wealth distribution, 162
  intellectual achievements, 162–163
  Jewish rebirth during, 132, 164–166, 211–213
  mathematical achievements, 163
  philosophies developed during, 198, 229–231
  Rome as natural successor, 181, 189
  scientific achievements, 162–163
  Septuagint's compilation during, 72, 167
  Stoicism philosophy, 198, 206, 229–234
  timeline of events, 131, 160
Henri III (French King), 445
Henri IV (French King), 445, 557
Henrique the Navigator, 417
Henry II (English King), 329–330
Henry VII (King of England), 446
Henry VIII (King of England), 432, 446–447, 616
Hephaistos (Greek deity), 98
Heraclitus of Ephesus, 149–150
Heraclius (Roman emperor), 249–250, 252
Heresies
  Catharism, 339, 339m

inquisition against heretics, 327, 340
  Lollardy, 339–340
Hernici society, 172
Herod Antipas, 213
Herod the Great (King of Judea), 213
Herodotus, 145
Herophilus of Chalcedon, 163
Herzl, Theodore, 707, 732, 776
Heym, Georg, 889
Heymann, Lida, 1006
Hieroglyphic writing system, 23–24
Hildegard of Bingen, 336
Hill, Geoffrey, 205
The Hill of Dreams (Machen), 871
Hinduism, 206, 207, 419
Hippocrates of Kos, 147–148, 266
Hippocratic Corpus medical texts, 147
Hippocratic oath, 147–148
Hiroshima, Japan, atomic bombing of, 979, 1000–1003
Hispaniola (present-day Haiti), 423m, 424–425
A Historical and Critical Dictionary (Bayle), 554, 559, 561
A Historical-Critical Introduction to the Qur'an (Weil), 778
Historical materialism process (Marx), 688, 689
History (La storia) (Morante), 1017–1018
History of Belgium (Pirenne), 654
History of the Church (Eusebius), 242
History of the Decline and Fall of the Roman Empire (Gibbon), 582
History of the Franks (Gregory of Tours), 269, 272
History of the Peloponnesian War (Thucydides), 145
History of the Persian Wars (Herodotus), 145
The History of Trade Unionism (Beatrice and Sidney Webb), 791

Hitler, Adolf. *See also* Germany; Nazi Party/ Nazi Germany
  air raids of Great Britain, 980
  appeasement policies toward, 969–973
  appointment as German chancellor, 933, 962, 966
  belief in Jewish annihilation, 561, 988–991
  beliefs about role of women, 1004
  Chamberlain's negotiations with, *970*
  Christian leadership compromises with, 1058
  Churchill's anti-appeasement speech, 972–973
  declaration of war against U.S., 981
  efforts at controlling central Europe, 969–970
  German recovery enabled by, 967
  inaugural speech of, 962
  increased demands made by, 971
  Jewish Holocaust engineered by, 988–991
  Mein Kampf autobiography, 932, 961, 966, 988
  Nazi party joined, controlled by, 961
  1945 suicide of, 983
  Paris occupied by, 978, 980, *981*
  Pius XII's opposition of, 1064
  Poland invaded by, 974, 977, 981
  purge of Nazi Party by, 962
  Russia invaded by, 981, 1024
  T4 Project, 987–988
  use of Damascus for staging, refueling, 1010–1011
Hittite Empire. *See also* Sea Peoples
  aggressiveness/love of war of, 52
  Asia Minor/Iranian settlements, 51–52
  Babylonian fear of, 58
  brutality of, 62
  chiefdom of Hattusilis III, 52
  commercial successes, 55

comparison of homes in, 101

David's pursuit of Hittite women, 82

destruction of, 56

invasion of Sumer, 88

Ramses II repulsion of advances of, 50

reign of, 11, 33

second millennium domination by, 33

trade route battles, 313

trade with Miletus, 121

Hobbes, Thomas

absolutism theory and, 510–512, 678–679

Burke's shared views with, 612

correspondence with Descartes, 510

Homer/Thucydides translations by, 513

interests/writings of, 513

Lenin's shared views with, 917–918

Leviathan, 504, 510, 512, 560, 917–918

life as described by, 415

Locke's disagreement with, 560

pre-*Leviathan* background, 510–511

social contract theory of, 512

views of role of government, 511–512, 612

Hobhouse, Emily, 909

Hogarth, William, *489*

Hohenheim, Philip von (Paracelsus), 467–468

Hohenstaufen dynasty, 380, 388

Hohenzollern dynasty, 513, 1007–1008

Holbein the Younger, 379

Holland

Acts of Toleration for Jewish people, 577

Brethren of Common Life, 390

Dutch Reformed Church, 407

France's war with, 595, 601

Jewish Sephardim migration to, 573

Peace of Westphalia and, 505

U.S. Great Depression influence in, 944

women's suffrage rights in, 793

Holocaust of World War II, 988–991, 1034

Holocaust Remembrance Day (Germany), *1155*

Holy League, 722

Holyoake, George Jacob, 751–752

Holy Qur'an. *See* Qur'an

Holy See (in Rome). *See also* Catholic Church; the Vatican; individual popes

arbiter role of, 286

buying and selling of, 310

1929 agreement with Italy, 718

as political football of Italian nobility, 474

Pope Benedict XVI and, 1154

Homage to Catalonia (Orwell), 959–960

Home Defense Force (Austria fascists), 963

Homer, 97, 99, 104–105, 107–109, 513

Homo erectus skeleton discovery, 1061t

Homo habilis identification (Leaky), 1061t

Homosexuality/homosexuals. *See also* Gays; Lesbians

in Ancient Greece, 118

Biblical references to, 432n6

Buggery Act and, 432–433

as deathly offense, in France, 432

discovery of possible genetic component, 1061t

Freud on, 874–875

gender wars and, 1109

Nazi murdering of, 961, 991

normality of in ancient Greece, 118

as part of Socrates' lifestyle, 151

possible genetic connection, 1061t

Protestant Christian opposition to, 432–434

Reform Jews acceptance of, 1078–1079

ritualized aristocratic homosexuality, 110, 117

Spanish Inquisition arrests for, 432

Honestiores ("the better people"), 199

Honorius III (Pope), 233

Honor killing of women, 810–811, 1111, 1140–1141

Horace (poet), 375

The Horrifying and Terrifying Words and Deeds of the Renowned Pantagruel, King of Dipsodes (Rabelais), 411

Horses, domestication of, 45

Hosea (Hebrew prophet), 87

Hügel, Friedrich von, 773

Hugo, Victor, 659

Huguenots (French Calvinists), 407, 444–445, *445*, 557, 558

Hulagu (son of Ögedai), 354

Humanae vitae ("Of Human Life") papal encyclical, 1058, 1067–1068

Humanism

Castiglione's literary representation, 388

Christian humanism, 388–389

description of, 377–378

post-WW II organizations, 1063

Protestant humanism, 401, 402–403

Renaissance-era emphasis on, 376, 388

Humanistic Judaism, 776

Hume, David, 555, 556, 578, 584

Humiliores ("the lesser people"), 199

Hundred Years' War (England and France)

battle of Crécy, 347

causes of, 346

consequences of, 346, 388

England's defeat in, 446

Joan of Arc/ending of, 348

map of, *347m*

new learning hampered by, 388

Poitiers battle, *345*

Thirty Years' War comparison, 450, *450*

Hundred Years' *(cont.)*
    timeline, 329, 340
    War of the Roses
        comparison, 446
    weaponry, 346–347
Hungarian Declaration of
    Independence, 723
Hungary
    Acts of Toleration for Jewish
        people, 577
    Budapest/urban
        development, 646
    Charlemagne's expansion
        into, 288
    Christian Democratic party
        in, 1034
    church attendance
        data, 1059
    EU membership, 1104, 1109
    fascism in, 963
    frustrated nationalism in,
        721–723
    Habsburg control of, 722
    independence declared
        by, 1091
    Lutheranism in, 404
    political rivalries of, 936–937
    USSR invasion of, 1019
Husayn, Taha, 808
Hussein, Ghazi, 1119
Hussein, Saddam, 1119, 1133
Husserl, Edmund, 850,
    866–867
Hutten, Ulrich von,
    408–410, 411
Hutton, James, 755
Huxley, Aldous, 972
Huxley, Thomas, 758, 766
Huysmans, J. K., 870–871
Hyksos ascendancy (Ancient
    Egypt), 41, 45. *See also*
    Second Intermediate
    Period

I
Ibsen, Henrik, 801, 803,
    850, 870
Ideal Forms of Plato, 154–155
Idomeneo opera
    (Mozart), 520
Ijma (consensus-seeking
    tradition), *301,* 302
Iliad (Homer), 99, 104–108, 487
Illuminationism *(al-hikmat
    al-ishraq),* 456, 458

*Illustrations of Political
    Economy* (Martineau), 791
Illyrian culture, 111m, 183m,
    193, 606m
Imams, of Shi'a Muslims, 266
Immunology, development
    of, 820
Imperialism
    aggressive vs.
        defensive, 606
    American
        imperialism, 816
    Anti-Imperialist League,
        U.S., 850
    Christian missionaries and,
        833–834
    European imperialism, 779,
        816, 841
    as a form of slavery, 836
    by Great Britain, 709,
        834–836
    by Japan, 831–832
    Kipling's poetic
        representation, 817, 818–
        819, 831
    late 19th/early
        20th century, 818
    Pearson's viewpoint on,
        816–818
    Persian light-handed
        approach, 62
    protests against, 850–853
    religious imperialism, 38
    Twain's opposition to, 844
*Imperialism, the Highest Stage
    of Capitalism* (Lenin), 918
The Importance of Being Earnest
    (Wilde), 853
Inca Empire, 416, 422
Incest themes (Greek
    mythology), 98
India
    British East India Company
        in, 831
    Christian missionaries
        in, 765
    da Gama's passage to, 416, 417
    European trade with, 425
    gender-selective abortion
        in, 1138
    Hinduism in, 206, *207,* 419
    Jesuit missions in, 476
    Mughal Empire, 491, 538–
        539, 541
    Muslim India education, 809

1960s emigration to
    Britain, 1038
    ongoing commercial
        development, 826
    third wave feminism
        in, *1112*
    unhappiness with British
        rule, 842–843
Indo-Europeans. *See also*
    Persian Empire; Sea
    Peoples
    early Greek settlements, 97
    Greater West development
        and, 33–34
    Hittite settlements, 11, 52
    languages of, 50–51, 53
    Medes settlements, 60
    migrations of, 34, 51–55
    Mitanni settlements, 11
Industrial capitalism
    abuses, inequalities of, 711
    Catholic Church
        condemnation of, 769
    conflict with traditional
        values, 658–659, 676
    criticism of, 680–685
    decline of Christianity
        and, 749
    description, 658
    Emmanuel's arguments
        against, 771
    in Germany, 953
    Leo XIII's discussion on, 1034
    Martineau's arguments
        against, 791
    Marx's views on, 690–691,
        916, 918
    Second Industrial
        Revolution and, 819–820
Industrial Democracy (Beatrice
    and Sidney Webb), 791
Industrial revolution
    (industrialization). *See
    also* Second Industrial
    Revolution
    changes brought by, 625
    demographic basis of, 628
    effects on women, children,
        652–655
    England's head start,
        626–633
    in Europe, 635–639
    Factory Act, banning of
        child labor, 653
    family life influences of, 784

first use of terminology,
626–627
in Great Britain, 632
in Ireland, 725
labor force/work condition
issues, 647–648
in the Ottoman Empire, 644,
644–645
railroads/railroad tracks,
633, 637–638, 644
religious group support,
654–655
riots and reforms, 650–652
Romanticism and, 625
slum development issues,
646–647
steam engine
development, 633
terminology origin, 627
textile manufacturing
technology, 631–632, 632
unemployment created
by, 645
urban development and,
645–650
Innocent III (Pope), 323, 328,
330, 339
The Innocents Abroad (Twain),
1012–1013
Innocent XI (Pope), 721–722
Inquisition against heretics,
327, 340
Institute for Reference
Materials and
Measurements, 1062
*In Support of the Rights of
Citizenship for Women*
(Condorcet), 791
International Humanist and
Ethical Union, 1058, 1063
International Monetary Fund
(IMF), 1025, 1104
International Space
Station, 1061t
Internet
development of, 1061t
influence on women's rights,
1141–1142
The Interpretation of Dreams
(Freud), 850, 872–873
*The Introduction to History
[Muqaddimah]* (Ibn
Khaldum), 639
Introduction to Pacifism
(Mumford), 972

*Introduction to the Principles of
Moral and Legislation*
(Bentham), 791
*Introductory Lectures on
Psychoanalysis* (Freud), 874
Ionesco, Eugène, 1023
Ionian League, 121–123
Iran
British oversight of, 937
Ethnic Persian
administration in, 369
female genital mutilation
in, 811
global gender gap
data, 1139t
Il-Khans plundering of, 366
Jewish settlements in,
1074–1075
Mongol devastation in, 364
1950s military coup d'état
in, 1082
1979 uprising, 1085
pre-Islamic revolution
liberalizing, 1047
Tamerlane's terrorism
in, 370
war with Iraq, 1096
in World War II, 1009–1010
Iranian Revolution, 1096–1097
Iraq
Basa center for liberal
studies, 302
Britain's control of, 927,
937–938, 1009, 1012
Bush/U.S. invasion of, 1133
ethnic Persian
administration in, 369
female circumcision in, 811
first Persian Gulf War, 1133
Hussein's thuggish rule
of, 1119
Il-Khans plundering of, 366
Israel's victory against, 1040
Jewish settlements in, 320,
1074–1075
Mongol devastation in,
364, 540
1950s military coup d'état
in, 1082
Ottoman control in, 735
rebuilding of holy shrines
in, 541
Sykes-Picot Agreement
and, 900
Tamerlane's terrorism in, 370

U.S. led invasion/war in,
1126, 1133, 1145
U.S. troop withdrawal
from, 1134
war with Iran, 1096
Western civilization
origins in, 3
Ireland
Act of Union with England,
706, 724
Catholic Emancipation Act,
706, 725
Christian Democratic party
in, 1034
divorce law
liberalization, 1109
Easter Rebellion, 896t
1841–1851 population
map, 727m
1848 revolution in, 728–729
Enlightenment-era indigent
labors, 580
frustrated nationalism in,
723–725
global gender gap
data, 1139t
Good Friday Accord, 1116
Great Famine (potato
blight), 726–728, 727m
industrialization in, 725
monasteries established
in, 278
19th-century intellectual
energy, 669
potato famine, 706
Irene (Roman empress),
293–294
Irigaray, Luce, 1092, 1109–1111
Irish Catholics, 723–724
The Irish Crisis pamphlet
(Trevelyan), 728
Irish Republican Army
(IRA), 1118
Iron Age, 55–60
Assyrian weaponry, 59
bronze vs. iron, 56
early weapons, 56
iron's advantages vs.
disadvantages, 55–56
Jewish persecutions, 1079
Iron Curtain
Catholic reforms and, 1058,
1065–1066
in Europe, 1023, 1037–1038
Jewish people and, 1079

Iron Gustav (Fallada), 945
The Iron Pirate
  (Pemberton), 851
Isabella II (of Spain), 682
Isaiah (Hebrew prophet), 87
Ishmael (son of Abram/
  Abraham), 70
Isis-Osiris myth, 27–30
Islamic Empire. *See also*
  Abbasid dynasty; Mamluk
  Sultanate; Muhammad,
  Prophet of Allah;
  Ottoman Empire; Qur'an;
  Safavid dynasty; Shi'a
  Muslims; Sunni Muslims
  Abbasid rebellion
    against, 284
  aggression/determination
    of, 268
  ayatollahs of, 541
  beginning of calendar,
    239, 258
  beliefs in wars of
    religion, 441
  breakup of the empire, 304
  demonization/rejection of
    modern culture, 738
  devastation from the Black
    Death, 364
  female genital
    mutilation in, 811
  growing conservativeness
    in, 503
  late 20th-century upheavals,
    1082–1085
  laws of, 265, 267
  military successes of, 264
  modern global concerns
    about, 206, 1096–1097
  Mongol invasions, defeat of,
    352–354, 355m
  mullahs (guardians), Shi'ite
    Islam, 541
  name derivation of, 257–258
  nationalism in, 735–737
  1990s militant Islamism,
    1113–1114
  1022 CE world map, 303m
  philosophers of, 267
  population data on
    practice, 206
  retreat from science by,
    490–491
  Shariah (Islamic) law, 541,
    1048, 1086, 1114, 1154

wealth compared to Europe,
  327–328
women's rights, postcolonial
  Islamic society,
  1046–1050
Islamic Government
  (Khomeini), 1085
Islamic Jihad organization,
  1097, 1126–1127
Islamic Salvation Front
  (FIS), 1114
Islamic Union of Students'
  Associations, 1096
Islam religion and teachings.
  See also Muhammad,
  Prophet of Allah; Qur'an;
  Shi'a Muslims; Sunni
  Muslims
  Abbasids/Umayyads
    embrace of, 297
  African peoples embrace
    of, 419
  Allah-Muhammad-Ali
    Trinity, 366
  Christianity and, 28, 205,
    237, 258, 262
  conversions to, 264
  growth of Wahhabism
    movement, 738–740, 777
  historical criticism of,
    778–779
  honor killing of women,
    810–811
  illuminationism and, 458
  journey (Hijrah) to Medina,
    239, 258–259
  Judaism and, 258, 262
  Ka'ba holy site, 255,
    259–260
  laws protecting Christians,
    Jews, 314
  military expansion of, 260
  new strains in Islamic
    thought, 735–736
  origins/spread of, 28, 62, 71,
    83, 237–238, 254, 258,
    260, 268, 299, 302, 369
  Ottoman pre-Islamic
    traditions, 459
  present-day population
    data, 206
  preservation of religious
    law, 735
  prohibition against men
    wearing silk, *644*

radical Islamism, 1103, 1138
Ramadan's European
  version of, 1155–1156
reformation (al-Nahda) of,
  737–742
revelations of Muhammad,
  256–258
rules for dhimmi-status
  wives, 265
science, partial embrace of,
  777–778
science, retreat from, 456,
  467, 480, 490–491,
  777–778
Shariah (Islamic) law, 541,
  1048, 1086, 1114, 1154
virtues commanded by
  Allah, 257–258
Wahhabism and, 777
women, nationalism and,
  807–809
Zoroastrianism and,
  299, 458
Israel. *See also* Judaism; Moses
  Arab Spring and, 1135–1138
  Assyria's conquest of, 71, 83,
    110–111
  Christian profile of, 1078
  conflicts with
    Lebanon, 1047
  David's expansion of borders
    of, 80
  David-Solomon era, 81
  founding of, 1018
  Jewish profile of, 1078
  Judges era, 84
  Likud political party,
    1077–1078
  myth of, 1078–1081
  as name of northern-based
    tribes, 78
  New Historians in,
    1080–1081
  Palestine's dispute with,
    1081, 1113–1114,
    1135–1138
  peace treaty with
    Egypt, 1059
  Pius XII's position on,
    1065–1066
  post-1948 Jewish
    immigration to, 1075m
  Six Day War,
    1040–1041, *1041*
  ten lost tribes of, 59–60

terrorism in, 1114
UN condemnation of, 1059,
    1076–1077
Yom Kippur War, 1059
Italy
    accessibility of, 174
    Archaic Italy map, 174m
    capture of Somalia,
        Libya, 829
    Charlemagne's expansion
        into, 288
    church attendance data, 1059
    city-states, 380
    Conference of Berlin
        attendance, 828
    Death of Augustus
        map, 188m
    divination practices,
        175–176
    divorce law
        liberalization, 1109
    EEC membership, 1106
    efforts at overthrowing
        restored regimes, 672
    1848 uprising, 686–687
    emigrations to, 365
    empire-building by, 816
    Ethiopia invaded by, 829, 958
    Etruscan civilization, 111m,
        172, 174–175
    expansion of, 957m
    fascism in, 955–960, 963m
    geography of, 173–174, 190
    Greek colonies in, 110, 111m
    Hitler's "Pact of Steel"
        with, 978
    humanism in, 389
    increasing trade with, 307
    invasion of Ethiopia, 829
    Lateran Agreement,
        933, 958
    Latium region, 171, 174,
        174m, 182m
    messianic Jews in, 437–438
    Naples/urban
        development, 645
    Napoleon's conquests in, 605
    nationalism in, 716–721
    Plato's travels to, 152
    post-1815 industrialization
        failure, 636–637
    railroad development, 638
    Renaissance era, 83t, 373,
        380, 381m, 383, 387–388,
        395–396, 397m, 403, 409

Roman Catholicism as state
    religion, 749
Roman conquests, 181
Rome's neighbors
    map, 183m
    ruins of 3rd-century wars,
        184–185
    siege of Vienna, 375
    Simplon Tunnel, 826
    3rd-century map, 182m
    tribal/ethnic groups of, 172
    unification of, 707, 716–721
    witchcraft trials, 435
    women's suffrage in, 939
    in World War I, 893m, 895,
        896t, 897, 910, 923, 927
    in World War II, 977–979,
        983, 1004, 1007–1008
Ivan V (Russia), 515t
Ivan VI (Russia), 515t
Iwo Jima, Battle of, 979, 986

J
Jackhammers, development
    of, 821
Jackson, Robert H., 995
Jacobins (French Revolution
    political club), 599,
        601–602
Jacobs, Aletta, 800, 1006
Jacobson, Israel, 575
Jacob's Room (Woolf), 954
Jain religion, global percentage
    data, *207*
James, Henry, 801, 803, 883
James I (English King),
    533–535. *See also* King
    James Bible
James II (English King), 537,
    538, 557–558, 559
Jamestown colony
    (Virginia), 536
Jami al-Tawarikh
    ("Compendium of
    Chronicles") (Rashid
    ad-Din Hamadani), 369
Janet, Pierre, 872
Janissaries (Ottoman army
    corps), 539–540,
        620–621, 642
Jankau battle (Thirty Years'
    War), 451
Japan
    abduction/enslavement of
        women, 993

attack on Pearl Harbor, 977,
    978, 983, 985
Battle of Iwo Jima, 979, 986
conflicts with China, 978,
    979, 984–985, 991–992
empire-building by, 816
increasing militarism in, 985
industrialization in,
    831–832
Jesuit missions in, 476
Meiji Restoration, 831
post-WW I debt, 931
Rape of Nanking by, 992
Russo-Japanese War,
    832–833, 983
Sino-Japanese Wars, 978n1,
    985, 993
Tokyo war crimes trial, 979,
    993–994, 996
U.S. atomic bombing of, 979,
    1000–1003
in World War I, 895
Japan-China Incident, 979
Java programming
    language, 1061t
Jefferson, Thomas, 560
Jeremiah (Hebrew prophet),
    87–88
Jerome (Saint), 334
Jerusalem, 57m, 59m, 61m
    Babylonian Captivity, 71
    Church of the Holy
        Sepulcher, 315, *315*
    Cyrus's freeing of Hebrews,
        61, 71
    Dome of the Rock mosque,
        267–268, 284
    fall to Chaldeans, 71
    Nebuchadnezzar's
        campaign in, 60
    return by the Jews to, 132
    Umar's defeat of, 260
Jerusalem Temple, 60
"Jesu, Joy of Man's Desiring"
    (Bach), 657
Jesuits (Society of Jesus). *See
    also* Barberini, Maffeo;
    Borromeo, Carlo; Tyrell,
    George
    banning of, in Germany, 716
    formation of, 475–476
    missionaries in sub-Saharan
        Africa, 476
    teaching/missionary work
        of, 477

Jesus of Nazareth. *See also* Bible; New Testament
arrest by Romans, 216
birth of, 206, 210
Christ-centered revelations, 334–335
conflicts with Jewish laws, 211, 215
confusing/provocative words of, 214–215
and the Crusades, 314
disciples of, 216–218
forgiveness of all, peace message of, 441
John the Baptist sect membership, 215
Last Supper, 209–210
as messiah (savior), 211–217
ministry and movement of, 206, 214–216
partial belief as Son of God, 217, 246
Pharisees/Sadducees criticized by, 215–216
Pilate's order for crucifixion of, 217
resurrection from the dead, 218
Strauss's critical examination of, 760
Jesus the Good Shepherd (painting), *204*
Jewish Bible. *See* Hebrew (Jewish) Bible
Jewish enlightenment, 573–574, 573m, *574*
Jewish Holocaust (World War II), 988–991, 1034
Jewish people. *See also* Abram/ Abraham; Anti-Semitism; David; Hebrew (Jewish) Bible; Hebrew people; Judaism
Acts of Toleration for, 577
Ancien Régime restrictions, 730
Babylonian Captivity of, 71, 83, 90
battle of Lachish, *60, 84*
dreams of returning to Palestine, 729
Dryden's representation of, 573–574
1880–1914 Jewish emigration from Russia, 776m

Enlightenment-era ambivalence for, 576–578
excitement over new Torah, 774
expulsion from England, France, Spain, Portugal, 436, 573
expulsion from Germany, 416
faith/morals of, 88
French settlements, 320m
genius for reinvention, 92–94
German settlements, 289m, 320m
guild system participation, 730
Hasidim (Hasidic Jews), 576
Haskalah movement, 575
of the Hellenistic era, 72
Holocaust of World War II, 988–991
late medieval hostility against, 436–441
marriage traditions, 87
migration to Palestine, 938
Muslim persecution of, 314–315
peace with Christians sought by, 574
perseverance quality of, 77
in Poland, 946
post-1948 immigration to Israel, 1075m
pre-WW II German population, 989
release from bondage by Cyrus, 71, 90, 93, 163
return to Holy Land, 734
return to Jerusalem, 132
reviling of, by Romans, 201–202
role/status of women, 83, 85
Russian pogroms against, 734, *734, 775*
segregation in ghettos, 436
story of Esther, 84–85
treatment of the Bible, 69
urbanization by, 731
Vatican's aid for, 1064
Voltaire's dislike of, 579
Jewish sciences (*Wissenschaft des Judentums*), 774–775
The Jewish State (Herzl), 707, 732

The Jews (Lessing), 577
The Jew's Beech Tree (Droste-Hulshoff), 699
The Jews—Kings of Our Time: A History of Financial Feudalism (Toussenel), 731
Joan of Arc, 348, *348*
João III (Portuguese King), 438
Joffre, Joseph, 910
1–2, 3 John (New Testament), 208t
John Bull's Other Island (Shaw), 850
John Paul II (Pope), 867
Johnson, Cornelius, *430*
Johnson, Edwin, 762
Johnson, Samuel, 505, 527, 581, 582, 656
John the Baptist, 214–215, 223, 442
John XII (Pope), 310–311
John XXIII (Pope), 1057, 1066
Joint Research Council of the European Union, 1062
Joint stock companies, 543–544
Jones, William, 50–51
Josef I (Austria), 515t
Josef II (Austria), 515t
Joseph and His Brothers (Mann), 880
Josephus (the historian), 212–213, 217
Josiah (King of Judah), 84
Journal of the Plague Year (Defoe), 645
Joyce, James, 205, 880, 884, 932, 949–951
Judah, Kingdom of (Jews)
Babylonian conquest of, 111
location of, 78, 82
Persian control of, 91
pre-exile population data, 92
status of women in, 87
strategic advantage of, 82–83
Judaism. *See also* Abram/ Abraham; Anti-Semitism; David; Hebrew (Jewish) Bible; Hebrew people; Israel; Jewish people; Moses; Solomon; Zionism; Zvi, Sabbatai

Ashkenazic Judaism, 322, 436, 576, 1075
as the basis of Christianity, 210–213
calendar used in, 752–753
centrality of home, temple, 89–90
Conservative Judaism, 777, 1079
Essene sect, 212–214
global percentage data, 207
Hasidic Judaism, 575–576
Hasmoneans disdained by, 213
international Judaism, 1078–1081
late medieval hostility against, 436–441
maskilim (biblical scholars), 774
messianic movements, 437–440
midrashic writers, 729
mixed marriages, 1078
modern-day population data, 206
modernism and, 774–777
19th-century movements, 776–777
origins of, 71
Orthodox Judaism, 775, 777, 1078
Palestinian Judaism, 206
priests and rabbis, 89–92
prophets and prophecy, 87–89
Psalms as mainstay of prayers, 729
reformation, renewal, reviling of, 319–324
Reform Judaism, 775, 1078–1079
revival and conflict, 1074–1078
Revolt of the Maccabees, 166–167
Second Temple Judaism, 163–166, 669
Sephardic Judaism, 322–324, 436, 437n9, 439, 573, 576, 1074–1076
Talmud (holy book) of, 320–324, 410, 440, 477, 729
Thatcher's comments about, 593

Ultra-Orthodox Judaism, 1078
woman and the law, 83–87
Jude (New Testament), 208t
Judea
census of, 210
claims of jurisdiction over, 164
Hasmonean rule of, 211
Herodian dynasty origins in, 206, 213
independence gained by, 164
John the Baptist's appearance in, 215
map of, 212
Pompey's defeat of, 213
religious rivalries in, 213–214
Seleucid's jurisdictional claims, 164
social tensions in, 213–214, 320
travels of Jesus through, 214
Jude the Obscure (Hardy), 803
Judges of Hebrew tribes, 78–79
Julian of Norwich, 335–336
Julius Excluded from Heaven (Erasmus), 373, 391
Julius II (Pope), 373
Jupiter (Roman deity), 180, 189
Justinian (Byzantine emperor)
building of San Vitale church, 292
Palace of Justinian (in map), 251m
reconquests of, 248m, 249

K
Ka'ba (Islam holy place), 255, 259–260
Kandinsky, Wassily, 881–883
Kant, Immanuel, 205
help for "immaturity" of mankind by, 555
passionate/quirky ideas of God, 748
personality characteristics, 556
on radical democracy, 578
Karlowitz, Treaty of (1683–1699), 640m
Karl VI (Austria), 515t
Kassites, appearance of, 57

Katerina I (Russia), 515t
Katerina II the Great (Russia), 515t
Keats, John, 659, 668
Kemal, Namik, 809
Kempe, Margery, 334–335
Kepler, Johannes, 752
confirmation of Copernicus' calculations, 468
Galileo's debate with, 472–473
The Harmonies of the World, 485t
Index of Forbidden Books condemnation of, 477
The New Astronomy of Celestial Physics, 485t
planetary motion axioms, 470–471
Keynes, John Maynard, 933, 967
Ibn Khaldun, 350, 456, 459, 639
khanqas school for creative minds (Ottoman Empire), 491
Khomeini, Ayatollah Ruhollah, 1085, 1092, 1095, 1113–1114
Khrushchev, Nikita, 1025–1026, 1042–1043, 1079
Kierkegaard, Søren, 205, 853
al-Kindi (Islamic philosopher), 267, 299–300
King, Martin Luther, Jr., 1037
Kingdom of the dead (Ancient Egypt), 1, 27–30
King George's War, 549
King James (Authorized) Bible, 448n12, 534–535, 753
King Solomon's Mines (Haggard), 850, 851
Kipling, Rudyard, 709, 817, 818–819, 831
Kirk, Russell, 1018, 1031–1032
Kish settlement (Sumer), 7
Knossos palace complex (Greece), 100, 100–101
Knox, John, 401, 430–431
Korean War (1950–1953), 1025
Kösem (Sultana), 461t
Kossuth, Lajos, 722, 723
The Kreutzer Sonata (Tolstoy), 803
Kristeva, Julia, 1111

Kronos (Greek deity), 98
Krupp Steel Works factory
  (Germany), 715
Kublai Khan (grandson of
  Genghis Khan), 356–357
Küçük-Kaynarca, Treaty of
  (1719–1774), 640m
Kuhn, Thomas, 1061t
Kulturkampf ("culture battle"),
  anti-Catholic
  campaign, 716
Kurdistan, 4
Kurdistan Workers'
  Party, 1118
Kurds (of Turkey)
  killing of nonvirgin
    women, 810
  Malmuks and, 363
  PKK's fight for
    independence, 1118
  Turks and, 937
Kyoto Protocol (1997),
  1099–1100

L

Lactantius, 243
Lagash settlement (Sumer), 7
Laissez-faire capitalism,
  587–588, 676, 679
Lamennais, Hugues de, 770
Lamentabili sane exitu decree
  (Pius X), 772
Lammens, Henri, 779
Lapua Fascist Party (of
  Finland), 963
Lares familiares (household
  gods), Rome, 180
Las Casas, Bartolomé de,
  424–425
Late Antiquity. See Dark Ages
  in Western Europe
Late Period (Ancient
  Egypt), 23
Lateran Agreement (1929),
  933, 958
Latifundia (plantations), in
  Rome, 185–186
Latin America
  emigrations to, 841
  European international
    investment in, 891m
  feminist issues in, 1112
  Protestant Christianity
    in, 1074
  women's rights successes
    in, 1112

Latin Christianity, 292, 311,
  318, 319m
Latin Europe
  Carolingians as saviors of, 280
  Catholicism's corruption
    in, 310
  Charlemagne's goal of
    uniting, 288–289
  classical traditions of, 267
  commercial networks of,
    307–308
  dissolution of unity in,
    294–295
  emigrations to Italy, 365
  1095–1291 military
    campaigns, 313
  religious unity shattered
    in, 388
  representative assemblies
    of, 340
  waves of development,
    329–331
Latini, Brunetto (writer), 379
Latins (people of Latium), 174
Latium region (Italy), 171, 174,
  174m, 182m
Latvia, 1091, 1104
Lavoisier, Antoine, 594t
Lawrence, D. H., 887
The Laws (Plato), 153, 157
League of Augsburg, 557
League of Nations, 923, 932,
  936–937
Leaky, Louis, 1061t
Leaky, Mary, 1061t
Le Brun, Charles, 526
Lefèvre d'Étaples, Jacques, 401
Leibniz, Gottlieb, 456, 458,
  559, 562
Leiden, Jan van, 403
Lemkin, Raphael, 990–991
Le Nain, Louis, 579
Lenin, Vladimir. See also
  Bolshevik party
  anti-populism arguments,
    916–918
  dialectical materialism
    theory, 918
  Marxist theory alterations
    by, 915–916
  New Economic Policy
    of, 964
  rise to power in Russia, 896t,
    897, 912
  thoughts on revolution,
    imperialism, 918–921

views on capitalism, 916,
  918–919
  zealotry of, 914–915
Lens battle (Thirty Years'
  War), 451
Leo III (Pope), 292
Leo IV (Roman Emperor), 294
Leopold I (Austria, Holy
  Roman Emperor), 515t,
  547–548, 557
Leopold II (of Austria), 515t
Léopold II (of Belgium),
  838–840
Leo X (Pope), 382, 396
  Exsurge Domine papal
    bull, 396
Leo XI (Pope), 382
Leo XIII (Pope), 769, 772
Lepanto, Battle of (1571), 460
Lermontov, Mikhail, 659, 913
Lesbians, 139, 1037, 1111. See
  also Homosexuality/
  homosexuals
Lesbos (Aegean island), 137
Lesseps, Ferdinand de, 825.
  See also Suez Canal
Lessing, Gotthold, 577
Letters of Obscure Men
  (Hutten), 409, 411
Letters on the English, 583
Letters to Atticus (Cicero), 375
Letter to Posterity (Petrarca),
  374–375
Leviathan (Hobbes), 504
Lévi-Strauss, Claude,
  1052–1053
Liberal capitalism, 1071
Liberalism
  beliefs of, 678
  bourgeoisie support for, 679
  challenges of, 677–680
  changeability of, 677–678
  differences with
    conservatism, 665,
    667–668, 680
  1830 Europe, liberal-led
    rebellions, 682
  freedom as a difficulty for,
    678–679
  on the functions of
    government, 677
  Lady Morgan's naming
    of, 668
  laissez-faire capitalism
    championed by, 679
  Locke on, 678

Marx on, 688–690
Mill on, 677–678
Newman on, 668n1
Libertarian taxation
    argument, 1147
Libya
    as Byzantine Empire
        country, 248
    culture of, 193
    independence from
        Istanbul, 925
    Italy's invasion, capture of,
        829, 958, 1114
    Jewish people in,
        1074, 1075m
    Mamluk Sultanate in,
        360, 361m
    Mussolini's invasion of, 958
    1960s uprisings in, 1082
    Qaddafi's seizure of power,
        1050, 1083
    rebel forces seizure of,
        1127, 1136
    Roman recruitments in, 193
    Six Day war and, 1040
Life magazine, 1035
Life of Cato the Elder
    (Plutarch), 178
Life of Charlemagne
    (Einhard), 293
The Life of Jesus (Revan), 747,
    761–762
The Life of Jesus, Critically
    Examined (Strauss),
    746, 760
Life of Lycurgus (Plutarch), 119
Life of Mahomet and the History
    of Islam to the Era of the
    Hegira (Muir), 779
Likud political party (Israel),
    1077–1078
Linear A/Linear B writing
    systems (Greece), 98,
    102–103
Lister, Joseph, 821
Literature/literary
    achievements
    absurdist/alienation
        themes, 1023
    Ancien Régime, 526–528
    Barque era, 526
    Bloomsbury Group of
        writers, 967–968
    book burnings, 408–410
    Christian humanist writers,
        401–402

Classical Age Greece, 162
dictionaries, 526–527
Encyclopedia Britannica, First
    Edition, 566
Encyclopédie (Diderot), 565–
    567, 566, 583m
epic/lyric poetry, Greece,
    138–139
female identity-related,
    801–802
in the Hellenistic Age, 162
modernist literature,
    948–955
monastic life and, 375
realist/naturalist schools,
    Europe, 802
related to anti-Semitism,
    440, 573–574, 731–732
Renaissance era, 384–388
in Rome, 197
in Russia, 913
satirical writings, 390–391,
    408–412
sexuality-related, 803
on social behavior norms,
    528–530
Lithuania. See also Poland-
    Lithuanian Union
    EU membership, 1104
    Germany's confiscations
        from, 716
    Holy League
        membership, 722
    independence declared
        by, 1091
    invasions in Russia, 912
    Jews in, 573, 574m
    in World War II, 978, 991
Livius, Titus (Livy), 174–175
Lizaveta (Russia), 515t
Lloyd George, David, 796
Lluís Vives i March, Joan,
    401–402
Locke, John
    An Essay on Human
        Understanding, 554, 559
    on civil rights, 560
    government functions
        defined by, 559–560
    interest in epistemology, 563
    on liberalism, 678
    patronage of by society's
        greats, 584
    on radical democracy, 578
    reading of Descartes'
        work, 559

scientific/philosophical
    background, 559
Second Treatise of Civil
    Government, 678
Two Treatises on Government,
    554, 559
Logical Investigations (Husserl),
    850, 866–867
Logos ("order and
    purpose"), 230
Loisy, Alfred, 762–763, 773
Lombards of Italy, 286
London Working Men's
    Association, 683–684
Lonergan, Bernard, 205
Long Depression
    (1873–1896), 828
Long War (1593–1600), 460
Louisiana Purchase
    (1803), 609
Louis IX (French King), 329
Louis-Napoléon (French
    King), 685–686, 850
Louis-Philippe (French King),
    681–682, 685
Louis the Blind (French
    King), 295
Louis the Child (French
    King), 295
Louis the Pious, 293, 294
Louis the Stammerer (French
    King), 295
Louis VII (French king), 329
Louis VIII (French
    king), 341
Louis XIII (French King),
    509–510, 515m, 515t, 558
Louis XIV (French King), 504,
    513, 515t
    Edict of Nantes revocation,
        554, 557
    hatred of Fénelon's
        novel, 521
    invasion of Spain, 548
    jailing of, 599
    order to build hospitals
        by, 532
    Palace of Versailles built by,
        518–520
    wars of, 516–517
Louis XV (French King), 515t,
    517, 596
Louis XVI (French King), 515t,
    594t, 601
Louis XVIII (French King),
    671, 687

Lublin/Majdanek
   concentration camp, 990
Lucas Cranach the Elder, 393
Luke, Gospel of (New
   Testament), 208t,
   209–210, 214
Lully, Jean-Baptiste de (French
   composer), 513
Luria, R. Isaac, 437
Luther, Martin. *See also*
   Lutheranism; Protestant
   Reformation
   Anabaptists denounced
      by, 403
   anti-Semitic sentiments
      of, 440
   as Augustinian monk,
      393–394
   beliefs shared with Calvin,
      406–407, 429
   Book of Concord, 767
   break with Rome by, *391*
   Brethren of Common Life
      alumni, 390, 392–393
   Copernicus condemned by,
      469–470
   debate with Erasmus, 399
   excommunication of, 375
   on human nature, 429
   *On Jesus Christ Having Been
      Born a Jew*, 440
   *On the Jews and Their
      Lives*, 440
   Leo X condemnation of, 396
   Ninety-Five Theses of,
      375, 396
   portrait of, *393*
   Protestant Reformation
      triggered by, 392–394
   rebellion against Catholic
      Church, 395–400
   On the Roman Papacy, 396
   on Saint Paul's Epistles,
      429–430
   Scriptural insights, 394
   teaching career of, 394
   *On the Thieving, Murderous
      Hordes of Peasants*, 399
   use of New Testament of
      Erasmus, 392
   *On the War against the
      Turks*, 398
   Zwingli's differences
      with, 403
Lutheranism

belief in scriptural
   authority, 767
Confessing Church
   membership, 1070
Confessional Lutherans, 767
conversions of nobles to,
   396, 400
divisiveness of, in
   Europe, 407
Dürer's support of, *389*
evangelicalism and, 1074
in Germany, 404, 407, 429
international scope of,
   400–401, 404, 407
Müntzer's interpretation of,
   428–429
National Socialist brand
   (Nazi Germany), 1069
Neo-Lutheran movement,
   751, 767
Norwegian Humanist
   Association vs., 1063
Peace of Augsburg
   compromise, 416, 442–443,
   442–445, 443, 447
Prussian Union decree
   and, 766
royalty support of, 398, 400
in the Scandinavian
   territories, 404, 507
Lutheran Reformation, 389
Lützen battle (Thirty Years'
   War), 451
Luxembourg
   Christian Democratic party
      in, 1034
   EEC membership, 1106
Lyceum school of
   Aristotle, 158
Lyell, Sir Charles,
   753–755, 857
Lyme disease vaccine, 1061t

M

Maas, Hermann, 1070
Maastricht, Treaty of (1993),
   1092, 1106
ma'at practice (Ancient Egypt),
   27, 28, 30, 41–42
Mably, Gabriel Bonnot de, 581
MacArthur, Douglas, 994
Maccabean Revolt (Revolt of
   the Maccabees),
   166–167, 211
Maccabeus, Judas, 166

Machaut, Guillaume de, 328
Machen, Arthur, 871
Machiavelli, Niccolò, 374
   Discourses on Livy, 387
   La mandragola, 385–386
   The Prince, 386–387,
      716–717
Madame Bovary
   (Flaubert), 801
Magalhães, Fernão de
   (Ferdinand Magellan),
   421–422
The Magic Mountain
   (Mann), 871
Maginot Line (at French-
   German border), 969
Magna Carta (1215 CE), 328
Magnus, Albertus, 328, 465
Magyars of Hungary
   autonomy of, 710
   battles of Mohács, 712,
      721–722
   campaigns against
      Europe, 295
   Congress of Vienna and, 723
   nationalist hopes of, 691
   Ottoman defeat of, 721
   Peoples of Europe
      map, 708m
Mahdi ("Guided One"), 297
Mahler, Alma, 954t
Mahmud II (Ottoman Empire),
   621, 642
Maier, Anna, 792
Maimonides, 285, 323–324,
   489, 575
Maistre, Joseph-Marie de, 666,
   673, 675
malawi traditions (Islamic
   Empire), 296
Male and female principles
   (Abzu and Tiamat), 16
Malthus, Thomas, 1099–1100
Mamluk Sultanate (Egypt),
   318–319, 328, 360–361,
   364, 452
La mandragola ("The
   Mandrake Root")
   (Machiavelli), 385–386
Manet, Edouard, 802
Manhattan Project, 1000
Mann, Thomas, 871, 880, 945
Manning, Henry Edward, 771
The Man of Destiny (Shaw), 850
Mansfield, Katherine, 954t

Manutius, Aldus, 384
Manzoni, Alessandro, 717
Masoretic text version
    (Hebrew Bible), 72, 73t, 74
Mao Zedong, 869, 1036, 1111
Mapping techniques,
    development of, 416–417
Marathon, Battle of, 131
Marcus Aurelius (Roman
    emperor), 200, 202, 207.
    See also Commodus
Marduk worship
    (in Babylon), 19, 38
Margaret of Provence (French
    Queen), 329
Maria Theresa (Austria), 515t
"Mario and the Magician"
    novella (Mann), 945
Marius vs. Sulla battle (Rome),
    185–186
Mark, Gospel of (New
    Testament), 208t, 209
Marlowe, Christopher, 448
Mars (Roman deity), 180
Marses society, 172
Marshall, George, 1019–1021
Marshall Plan, 1018, 1019–
    1021, 1033
Mars rover landing, 1061t
Martel, Charles, 268,
    284–287, 286
Martineau, Harriet, 791
Martyrdom in the Roman
    Empire, 242–244
Martyrologies, 243
Marx, Karl, 850
    biographical background, 687
    on capitalism/industrial
        capitalism, 690–691
    The Communist Manifesto
        co-authorship, 667, 687–
        688, 692
    dialectical materialism
        theory and, 918
    The German Ideology, 688,
        690–691
    historical materialism
        process of, 688
    laissez-faire capitalism
        viewpoint, 587–588
    on liberalism, 688–690
    patterns in human life
        described by, 1053
    publication of a Heine poem
        by, 650

role in shaping modern
    philosophy, 151
secularism/assimilation
    of, 776
writings on "Jewish
    Question," 731
Mary (Queen of England), 447
Masada (Jewish) fortress, 222
Maskilim (Jewish biblical
    scholars), 774
Masonic lodges, in
    Scotland, 586
Masoretic text version (Hebrew
    Bible), 72, 73t, 74
Massacre sites, of
    World War II, 987
Materialism and
    Empiriocriticism: Critical
    Comments on a
    Reactionary Philosophy
    (Lenin), 917–918
Mathematics
    analytical geometry
        invention, 494
    Bacon on study of, 466, 492
    Beckman's genius in, 494
    Bruno's expertise in, 481
    Classical Age Greece,
        148–150
    Clavius's expertise in, 472
    Copernicus' comments
        on, 470
    Descartes' achievements,
        492, 494, 496
    development in Sumer, 14
    Galileo's genius in, 471,
        482, 483
    heliocentrism and, 473
    Hellenistic Age
        achievements, 163
    infinite sets (Galileo), 482
    Inquisition's distrust of, 484
    Islamic world excellence
        in, 490
    Jesuit education inclusion
        of, 477
    Kepler's use of, 471
    Newton's use of, 465, 467,
        485, 497–498, 854
    Scientific Revolution and,
        466–467
    in Sumer, 14
    use of the abacus, 14
Matrimonial Causes Act
    (1857), 700

Matsui, Iwane, 992
Mattathias
    (Hasmonean ruler), 166
Mauriac, François, 205
Maurice (Roman emperor), 249
Maurras, Charles, 964
Mauthausen concentration
    camp, 990
Maximinus (Roman
    emperor), 224
Maxwell, James, 854
Mayan Empire, 422
Mazarin, Cardinal Jules,
    519–520
Measles epidemic, 424,
    424–425
Mecca city/Meccan people
    Muhammad campaigns
        against, 259
    Muhammad driven from,
        258, 261
    pagan shrine in, 255
    pilgrims' Hijrah (journey) to,
        252, 255–256, 260
Medicaid Program (U.S.),
    1029, 1152
Medical achievements
    (Ancient Greece),
    147–148, 163
Medical advances, 826
Medicare Program (U.S.),
    1029, 1152
Medici, Cosimo de', 374, 382
Medici, Lorenzo de', 382, 386
Medici, Piero de', 382
Medieval era. See also Dark
    Ages in Western Europe
    comments on Plutarch's
        essays, 232
    conquests of Muslims
        during, 38
    convents/monasteries
        established during,
        278, 279m
    defined, 269
    disdain for Islamic
        philosophers, 267
    Gregory of Tours
        chronicling of, 269–270
    late medieval Europe,
        329–331, 330m
    monasteries, 278
    university map, 331m
Medieval society
    (defined), 269

Medina city, 258

Mediterranean Europe, 306–309, 308m, 320m

Mediterranean Sea ("Our Sea") (Mare nostrum), 190–193, 195

Mehmed II (Ottoman leader), 364, 367

Mehmed IV (Ottoman ruler), 439

Mehmed Pasha, Sari, 640–641

Mehmed V (Ottoman sultan), 925

Mehmet Ali Pashi (Egyptian ruler), 706, 736–737, 737, 739

Meiji Restoration (Japan), 831

Mein Kampf (Hitler), 932, 961, 966, 988

Meléndez Valdés, Juan, 582

"Melian Dialogue" (Thucydides), 146

Memoirs (Metternich), 666–667

Memoirs (Saint-Simon), 520

Mendelssohn, Moses, 575, 730, 774

Mendicant orders. *See* Dominican mendicant order; Franciscan mendicant order

Men of the Great Council, 72

Mentuhotep II (Egyptian pharaoh), 40–41

Mercantilism
absolutism and, 513, 521–524
Continental System replacement of, 607–610, 615, 628
description, 521–522
devastation caused by, 513
James I belief in, 535–536
modern opinions of, 523–524
Mun's defense of, 523
poverty and, 524–525
protectionism championed by, 522–523
reign of, 521
Smith's critique of, 563

Merovingian dynasty, 285

Mesopotamia
agricultural developments, 4
ancient Egypt comparison, 27

cities of, 12–13
commercial successes, 55
cuneiform script development, 14
deep thoughts of people of, 19–20
elaborate funeral rites of, 487
invasions of, 11
patrilinear inheritance practices, 12
religious practices, 13, 16–20
sewage issues, 13
slavery in Sumer, 15
solar studies, 14–15
Sumerian dominance in, 6, 8–9
Sumerian mathematics, 14

Messianic Judaism, 437–440

Metaphysics (Aristotle), 300

Metaxis, Ioannis, 963

Metternich, Klemens von, 666–667, 687, 691

Mexico. *See also* Tenochtitlan (Mexico City)
Cinco de Mayo holiday in, 720n6
conquest of, by Cortés, 416, 422, 424, 425n3
German offer of military aid, 922
Napoleon III's campaign vs., 720
women's conferences in, 1112

Micah (Hebrew prophet), 87

Michelangelo, 205, 395, 874, 932

Microsoft Corporation, 1061t

Middle Ages, 237–280. *See also* Byzantine Empire; Byzantium; Constantine the Great; Constantinople; Dark Ages in Western Europe; Diocletian (Roman emperor); Mecca/Meccan people; Medina city; Muhammad, Prophet of Allah; Qur'an; Rome/ Roman Republic; Shi'a Muslims; Sunni Muslims
"Age of Ignorance" period, 253–256
barbarian kings/scholar-monks, 268–271

body as money, women as property, 273–275
Christian paganism, 275–277
classical traditions, western expansion, 266–268
divided estates and kingdoms, 271–273
Edict of Milan, 238, 245
imperial crisis, 238–239
intellectual life, pockets of, 277–280
the Islamic revelation, 256–258
map of Muslim conquests, 262m
Muslim defeat of Persian Empire, 260
Nicene Creed, 246, 768
overreach of Rome, 239–242
rise of "New Rome," 247–249
Roman Empire map, 241m
waterwheel/windmill inventions, 625

The Middle Class Gentleman (Molière), 504, 528

Middle East. *See also* Arabs (Arab nations); Arab Spring; Islamic Empire; individual countries, dynasties, empires, religions and sultanates
agricultural settlements, 4
Arab nationalism in, 1044
attitudes towards women, 1141–1143
authoritarian regimes in, 1050
Cairo Declaration on Human Rights, 997, 1048–1050
iron weapons proliferation, 35
martyrdom and empire, 242–244
1990s Islamic issues, 1113
Six Day War, 1040–1041
wars of religion in, 452–454
in World War II, 1009–1011

Middle Kingdom era (Ancient Egypt), 40–45
architectural/sculptural arts, 44
donkey travel in, 44–45
instructions left by pharaohs, 44

map, ca. 1000 BCE, 57m
privilege of salvation to
  nobles in, 30
public building programs, 41
reign of Mentuhotep II,
  40–41
revolt of Semitic-speaking
  foreigners, 45
second millennium
  domination by, 33
timeline of, 23, 34
writings produced during,
  42–43
Middlemarch (Eliot), 784, 801
Midhat, Ahmed, 809
Midrashic writers, 729
Midway, Battle of (1942), 986
Mikhail I (Russia), 515t
Milan Cathedral, 205
Miletus
  appreciation for
    rationalism, 122
  as birthplace of philosophy,
    122–123
  geographic location, 57m,
    101m, 111m, 121
  Greek founding of, 97
  Ionian League membership,
    121–122
  merchant oligarchy
    government, 121–122
  Persian control of,
    124–126, 127m
  tyrannical rule of, 115
Milhemet mitzvah ("war of
  religious obligation"), 38
Mill, John Stuart, 666
  on liberalism, 677–678
  The Subjection of Women,
    784, 786–787
  women's suffrage rights
    advocacy, 788
Milosevic, Slobodan, 1130, 1132
Milosz, Czeslaw, 205
Milton, John, 205, 526
Milvian Bridge Battle,
  238, 244
Ming dynasty (China), 369
Minoan Greece
  Knossos palace complex,
    100, 100–101
  Linear A/Linear B writing
    system, 98, 102
  maps, 57m, 101m
  origins on Crete, 98

Phaistos palace, *102*
  timeline of, 101
  trade networks, 101
Minor Hebrew Prophets, 87
Minos (Minoan King), 101
Miriam (sister of Moses), 84
Mishnah (Jewish rabbinical
  laws), 320
Mishneh Torah
  (Maimonides), 324
Miss Julie (Strindberg), 803
Mitchel, John, 727
Moabites, 57, 81
Mobius, Paul Julius, 871
Modernism
  art and, 880–884
  experiment, trauma and,
    948–955
  irony and, 877–880
  leading artists of, 879t
  musical achievements, 883
  Pius X's rejection of, 747,
    772–773
  secularism, the Jews and,
    774–777
  women and, 954t
Modern politics, birth of,
  683–685
"Modern Times" movie, *824*
"A Modest Proposal" essay
  (Swift), 580–581
Mohács, battles of, 712, 722
Molcho, Solomon, 437–438
Moldavia, 720
Molière (Jean-Baptiste
  Poquelin), 513, 528–529
Mommsen, Theodor, 851
Monasticism, 205, 251m, 269
  Benedictine monks, 278,
    280, 334, 410–411
  Carolingian dynasty
    monasteries, 286–287
  defined, 277
  5th-9th century
    popularity, 278
  literature/classical learning
    and, 375
  medieval era monasteries, 278
  reforms of, 333–334
Monet, Claude, 882
Mongols
  Ali ibn Athir's description of,
    353–354
  annihilation of Baghdad,
    285, *298*, 329, *354*, 540

caliphate destruction
  by, 328
Chinese as favored
  targets, 353
destruction of Kiev,
  358–359
engraved passport, *359*
extent of empire, 355m, 358
Genghis Khan leadership of,
  348, 353
Hulagu's leadership, 354
in-fighting of, 356
lineage/historical
  background, 352–353
Muslim Byzantine World
  map, 319m
Ögedai's leadership, 354
Seljuk Turks defeated by, 364
Temüjin's leadership, 353
trade interests of, 359–360
world domination desired
  by, 318
Monnier, Adrienne, 954t
Montessori, Maria, *804*,
  804–805
Mont Saint-Michel
  monastery, 205
Moody, Elizabeth, 528
Moon landing (U.S.), 1061t
Moore, Marianne, 954t
Moral component of
  Conservatism, 673–677
Moralia ("Ethical Matters")
  (Plutarch), 232
Morante, Elsa, 1017–1018
Moravian theologians, 1070
More, Thomas, 375,
  408–409, 428
Morgenthau, Henry, Jr.,
  995–996
Morrill Act (1862), 827
Morris, Benny, 1059, 1080
Mosaddegh, Muhammad, 1029
Moses
  commandments given to,
    85, 334
  death of, 77
  Ezra as "second Moses," 91
  five Biblical books
    attributed to, 72
  leadership of Hebrews,
    50, 74
  march of liberation
    leadership, 77–78
  role in line of prophets, 258

Mosley, Oswald, 963

Motolinia, Toribio de Benavente, 425

Mount Sinai burning bush, 74, 85, 334

Mouvement de Libération des Femmes (MLF), 1046

Mozart, Wolfgang, 857, 932
  The Abduction from the Seraglio opera, 621
  Idomeneo opera, 520

Mrs. Beeton's Book of Household Management (Beeton), 696–697, 698, 870

Mrs. Dalloway (Woolf), 801, 932, 954–955

MS-DOS operating system, 1061t

Mu'awiya (Syrian governor), 265

Mubarak, Hosni, 1114

Mughal Empire (India), 491, 538–539, 541

Muhammad, Prophet of Allah, 252
  birth of, 239, 255
  campaigns against Meccans, 259
  death of, 260
  exile from Mecca, 258, 261
  Hashim clam/Quraysh tribe heritage, 255
  Islamic revelations of, 256–258
  Islam leader, 252
  Jewish population defeated by, 255, 258–259
  journey to Medina, 239
  military ventures of, 259
  preaching successes of, 258–259
  purification of the Ka'ba, 259–260
  Quraysh leaders conflicts with, 258

Muhammad Khan Qajar (Qajar dynasty), 541

Muir, Sir William, 779

Mullahs (guardians), Shi'ite Islam, 541

Mulla Sadra, 456, 458

Mumford, P. S., 972

Mun, Thomas, 523

Munich Conference (1938), 933

Munich Olympics terrorism (1972), 1081

Müntzer, Thomas, 428–429

Muqaddimah ("Introduction to History") (Ibn Khaldun), 456, 459

"Musée des Beaux Arts" poem (Auden), 327

Musharraf, Pervez, 1135

Music/musical achievements. *See also* Bach, Johann Sebastian; Beethoven, Ludwig van; Mozart, Wolfgang; Schubert, Franz; Wagner, Richard
  Ancient Greece, 116–117, 120, 134, 138
  Baroque Age, 504, 514, 526
  castrati in operatic male roles, 531
  female modernist composers, 954t
  Hildegard of Bingen, 336
  influences of Christianity, 205, 280
  modernism, 883
  Sufis/Ottoman Empire, 491

Musil, Robert, 883–884

Muslim Brotherhood, 1086, 1117

Muslims. *See also* Ottoman Empire; Ottoman Turks
  Ba'athism political ideology, 1085–1088
  belief in wars of religion, 4441
  Charles Martel's defeat of, 284
  defeat of Persian Empire, 260
  global percentage data, 207
  historical criticism beliefs of, 778–779
  jihad-stoked medieval conquests of, 38
  map of conquests, 262m
  prayer routine of, 259–260

Muslim Studies (Goldziher), 779

Mussolini, Benito
  boasts of an Italian Fascist utopia, 1005
  Christian leadership compromises with, 1058
  countries invaded by, 958
  imprisonment of, 983
  March on Rome by, 956–957, 961
  Pius XII's opposition of, 1064
  political opposition crushed by, 957–958

Mustafa IV (Ottoman Empire), 621

Mut'a form of marriage, 299

Mu'tazilites ("the Dissenters") scholars, 302

Mycenaean age (Greece)
  appearance of, 98
  as backdrop for Homer's *Iliad,* 104–106
  competition for raw materials, 103–104
  deities affiliated with, 104
  destruction of, 98, 105
  Dorians invasion/conquest of, 105
  heroes and kings of, 99–104
  map of, 101m
  as origins of Philistines, 58
  population losses in, 105, 109
  presence of rationalism, 123
  Pylos palace, 103
  rivalries of, 53
  Sea Peoples upheaval in, 105
  seizure of Knossos, 98
  Trojan War, 104, *108,* 109
  warrior vase finding, *103*
  wealth of the kings, 109

Mycenaean Greece

The Myth of Sisyphus, 1022–1023

Mythologies (Barthes), 1018, 1053

Mythology
  of Ancient Egypt, 27–30
  of Germany, 275–276
  of Sumer, 7–9, 17–18

"Mytilenian Debate" (Thucydides), 146

N

Nagasaki, Japan, atomic bombing of, 979, 1000–1003

Naoroji, Dadabhai, 817, 842

Napoleon (Napoleone di Buonaparte)
  annulment of marriage, 616

background of, 601

Beethoven's admiration for, 614

Continental System of, 607–610, 615, 628, 633, 706

coronation of, 604–605

crowning as emperor, 593

death of, 593

Directory dissolved by, 594t

divisive legacy of, 617–618

downfall of, 615–619

educational system created by, 603, 618

empire-building by, 605–607

fair taxation system created by, 618

Goethe's meeting with, 614–615

individuals' rights emphasis of, 602–603

invasion of Egypt, 602, 621

invasion of France, 593

invasion of Russia, 617

invasion of Syria, 621

Jacobin cause supported by, 601–602

map of Napoleonic Europe, 606m

marriage to Marie-Louise, 616

military campaign successes, 602

nullification of liberal constitution of, 672

overthrow of Spain's Ferdinand VII, 602–603

plotting of return by, 666

position as consul, 593, 602n3

predictability of failures of, 675

return to France, 594t

rights/freedoms restricted by, 604

rise of, in France, 591

war against absolutism of, 601–605

Napoleonic Code, 602–603, 607

Napoleon III (of France), 686, 720–721

Narodnaya Volya ("Will of the People") Party, 733–734

Nasser, Gamal Abdul, 1074–1075

Nathan the Wise (Lessing), 555, 577

National Abortion Rights Action League (1968), 1045

National Assembly (France)

Clermont-Tonnerre's debate at, 576

dissolution of, 594t

feudalism abolished by, 594t

Paine's election to, 613

storming of the Bastille by, 599

National Convention (France), 594t, 601

National Front Party (France), 1109

Nationalism

of Arab groups, 622

defined, 709–710

Freeman's theory on, 706–707, 709

in Germany, 711–716, 718–721

Islam, women and, 807–809

in the Islamic world, 735–737

in Italy, 716–721

19th-century spread of, 709–711

Orwell's definition of, 709n1

Romanticism compared with, 709

romantic nationalism, 731

royalism and, 669–673

Treaty of Vienna and, 660

Nationalism and identity (1801–1903), 705–742

"National Life from the Standpoint of Science" essay (Pearson), 816–818

National Organization for Women (NOW), 1019, 1045

National Secular Society (England), 752

National Socialist Lutheranism (Nazi Germany), 1069

National Society for Woman's Suffrage (Great Britain), 793

National Union Fascist Party (of Norway), 963

A National Vision (Erbakan), 1114

Native Americans

forced baptisms of, 205

smallpox epidemic decimation, 425

Natural History (Pliny), 376

Naturalist school of literature, 802

Nausea (Sartre), 868–869

Navarre, Henri de (Duke of Guise), 444–445

Nazi Party/Nazi Germany. See also Hitler, Adolf

anti-Semitic racism in, 946

Basque town bombed by, 960

Blitzkrieg strategy, 980–981

Hitler's purge of, 962

influence of U.S. Great Depression, 961–962

Jewish Holocaust, 988–991, 1034

National Socialist Lutheranism in, 1069

occupation in France, 592

onset/rise of, 713, 877, 960–964

role of Goebbels, 945, 961–962

T4 Project, 987–988

WW II military strategies of, 980–981

Nazi-Soviet Pact, 978, 980

Nazi Women's League, 1004

Nebuchadnezzar II (neo-Babylonian king), 60, 83

The Necessity of Atheism (Shelley), 748

Neo-Babylonians, 60, 83

Neolithic Age, 99, 124, 625

Neo-Lutheran movement, 751

Neo-Nazi skinheads, 1109

Neoorthodoxy (dialectical theology), of Protestantism, 1071

Neoplatonic philosophy, 229–234, 387. See also Pico della Mirandola, Giovanni

Nero (Roman emperor), 187, 198, 200, 206, 224

Nerva (Roman emperor), 200

Netherlands
    Conference of Berlin
        attendance, 828
    Dutch Golden Age, 433
    East India Company of, 449
    EEC membership, 1106
    England's aid of, 449
    global gender gap
        data, 1139t
    liberal-led rebellions in, 682
    Napoleon's conquering
        of, 605
    post-1815 industrialization
        failure, 636–637
    power shifts in, 416
    role in Habsburg dynasty
        formation, 449
    settlement in
        Manhattan, 449
    William of Orange, 538
    witchcraft trials, 435
The New Astronomy of Celestial
    Physics (Kepler), 485t
New Deal program (U.S.), 967
New Kingdom era (Ancient
        Egypt), 45–50
    commercial successes, 55
    as Egypt's golden age, 45
    extension of salvation to
        nobles, 30
    map of, 46m
    military might of, 46, 47
    monotheism
        introduction, 49
    priests vs. pharaohs, power
        struggles, 25, 45
    reign of Amenhotep III, 49
    reign of Amenhotep IV,
        49–50
    second millennium
        domination by, 33
    timeline, 23, 34
    Valley of the Kings, 48
    wheeled vehicles in, 25,
        44–45
Newman, John Henry, 668n1
New Rome, rise of, 247–249
New Testament. See also Bible;
        Gospel of Matthew; Jesus
        of Nazareth
    books of, 208t, 209, 214, 230,
        759–760
    chronological flaws of,
        209–210
    composition of last
        books, 207

Erasmus's comments,
    391–392
Greek language of, 160
passion narratives,
    217, 219
Saint Jerome's version, 233
Newton, Sir Isaac
    gravity idea development,
        498, 858
    natural law idea promoted
        by, 554–555, 918
    Philosophiae Naturalis
        Principia Mathematica,
        465, 467, 485,
        497–498, 854
    religious convictions of, 748
    support for Descartes
        by, 496
    Voltaire's study of, 568
The New Woman (Prus), 801,
    807–808
The New Womanhood
    (Cooley), 807
The New Woman play
    (Grundy), 783, 805
New World, 415. See also
        Central America; Latin
        America; North America;
        South America
    agricultural trade, 544–545
    Balboa's voyages, 421
    brutishness of Europeans in,
        425–426
    Colombo's voyages to,
        419–420
    conquistadores armies, of
        Cortés, 422
    Cortés' expeditions, 422,
        423m, 425
    epidemics, 416, 424–425
    European explorations of
        Americas, 423m
    export of slaves to, 545
    French territories in, 548
    gold/silver discoveries, trade,
        422, 426, 523
    Magalhães' global
        circumnavigation,
        421–422
    missionary challenges
        in, 474
    new crops/enclosure
        movement, 426–428
    post-discovery agonies of
        Europe, 511
    slave trade, 544–545

Society of Jesus girl's
    schools, 476
South Sea Bubble and, 544
taming of "Godless heathen"
    in, 38
trade with sub-Saharan
    Africa, 419
Nicaea
    Council of Nicaea,
        247, 310
    name change to Iznik, 365
    Roman Empire map, 241m
Nicene Creed, 246
Nicholas V (Pope), 373
Niebuhr, Reinhold, 868, 1071
Nietzsche, Friedrich
    Beyond Good and Evil, 850,
        861, 1104–1105
    Birth of Tragedy out of the
        Spirit of Music, 140
    The Gay Science, 746–747
    "God is dead" quote of, 745
    nihilism philosophy,
        860–863
    photograph of, 748
    "supermen" as envisioned
        by, 863
    The Twilight of the
        Idols, 862
    "will to power" of, 863
Nightingale, Florence,
    788–789
Nihilism philosophy
    (Nietzsche), 860–863
Nikolai I (Russian tsar), 720
Nikolai II (Russian tsar), 913
Nile River, 5m, 8m, 20, 22m,
    26, 28–30
Nin-Khursaga
    (Earth goddess), 16
Nippur settlement (Sumer), 7
Nordenflycht, Hedvig, 791
Nördlingen battle (Thirty
    Years' War), 450
North Africa. See also
        Carthage
    Arab conquests in, 260–261
    Dark Age economy, 270m
    Greek colonies in, 110–111
    Hitler's fighting in, 980
    increasing trade with, 307
    Jews in, 1075
    localized rule in, 188
    Muslim conquests in,
        260–261, 314
    1990s Islamic issues, 1113

Ottoman control in, 364–365
Punic War in, 183
rise of Shi'a Muslims in, 266
Septuagint Bible used in, 167
spread of Islam to, 299
Wahhabism in, 1082
in World War II, 979, 980–981
North America. *See also* Canada; Mexico; United States
adventurer landings in, 421
Atlantic slave trade and, 546m
crop introductions to Europe, 426
Dutch settlement in Manhattan, 449
England's Virginia settlement, 449
European emigration to, 841m
European explorations of, 423m
European international investment in, 891m
introduction of crops to Europe, 426–427
Jamestown/Plymouth colonies, 536
Jesuit missions in, 476
Jewish emigration to, 776m
South Sea Company trading in, 544
Viking raiders in, 416
Virginia settlement in, 449
North Atlantic Treaty Organization (NATO)
airstrikes in Libya, 1136
airstrikes in Serbia, 1130
founding of, 1018, 1025
West Germany's admittance to, 1033–1034
Norton, Caroline, 700
Norway
fascism in, 963
global gender gap data, 1139t
universal suffrage in, 796
Norwegian Humanist Association, 1063
Nosferatu (Stoker), 952–953
Notre Dame de Paris Cathedral, 205

Novalis (Friedrich von Hardenberg), 582, 660, 1104
Nubians, 45, 47
Numa Pompilius (Roman King), 173t
Numerianus (Roman emperor), 240
The Nun (Diderot), 694
Nur-Banu (Sultana), 461t
Nuremberg war crimes trials, 979, 988, 990–991, 993–994, 996

O

Oath of Supremacy, 723
Öcalan, Abdullah, 1118
O'Connor, Flannery, 205
Octavian, 173, 185–186, 188
Odyssey (Homer), 99, 105, *108*, 109, 950
Oedipus at Colunnus (Sophocles), 142
Of Crimes and Punishment (Becaria), 555, 564–565
Ögedai's (son of Genghis Khan), 354
O'Keefe, Georgia, 954t
Old Babylon, 34–40
Old Kingdom Egypt, 22m, 23, 26, 40
Oliveira de Salazar, António, 963
Olympian deities, 98
Olympic games (Ancient Greece), 99, 138
Omdurman, Battle of (Sudan), 816
"On Denoting" essay (Russell), 866
1 Thessalonians (New Testament), 208t
"On Isis and Osiris" poem (Plutarch), 229
On Jesus Christ Having Been Born a Jew (Luther), 440
On Platonic Theology (Ficino), 387
On the Deaths of Those Persecuted for Christ (Lactantius), 243
On the Destruction of England excerpt (Gildas), 268–269
On the Jews and Their Lives (Luther), 440
On the Motion of the Heart and Blood (Harvey), 485t

On the Origin of Species by Means of Natural Selection (Darwin), 747, 756, 758, 759, 766
On the Roman Papacy: An Institution of the Devil (Luther), 396
On the Spiritual Element in Art (Kandinsky), 882
On the War against the Turks (Luther), 398
"Open Christmas Letter" (British suffragettes, WW I), 907–909
Operation Barbarosso, 981
Operation Cast Lead (Hamas), 1135
Oppenheimer, J. Robert, 1000
Opus Maius ("Large Study") (Bacon), 466
Oracle of Apollo at Delphi, 231
Oral Torah, 90, 211–212, 1051
"Oration on the Dignity of Man" (Mirandola), 377
Order of the Preachers. *See* Dominican mendicant order
Oresme, Nicole, 328
Organization of the Islamic Conference (OIC), 1019, 1048, 1096
Origin and Nature of Secularism (Holyoake), 751–752
Orlando, Vittorio, 922
Orlando Furioso mock-epic (Ariosto), 385
Orthodox Church (Eastern Europe), 620
alliances with governments, 749
Bolshevik abolishment of, 920
Calvin and, 407
Catholic Church and, 319, 1066
Pseudo-Dionysius as saint in, 233
Orthodox Judaism, 775, 777, 1078
Orwell, George, 709n1, 959–960, 1024
Ostrogoths (from Germany), 239
Otto I (German emperor), 3 29, 380

Ottoman Empire. *See also*
    Ottoman Turks
abolishment of, 889
absolutism of, 539–540
artificial nation examples,
    707, 709
Bayezid II's leadership, 437
Bulgaria's achievement of
    autonomy, 706
Byzantium invaded by, 384
capture of Constantinople,
    329, 364, 398
collapse of, 936
Conference of Berlin
    attendance, 828
consolidation, transition to
    Turkey, 809
domination of Islamic
    world, 452
emergence of, 328, 360
European military
    encroachments, 539
Greece's independence from,
    706, 735
industrialization in, *644,*
    644–645
Janissaries army corps,
    539–540, 620–621, 642
Jewish escape from, 775
Jewish Sephardim migration
    to, 573
khanqas school for creative
    minds, 491
limited control left by
    1878, 735
Long War vs. Austria, 460
Magyars of Hungary
    defeated by, 721
Mehmed II, reign of,
    364, 367
Mehmed IV's
    leadership, 439
parceling out, by League of
    Nations, 937
periodic separatist
    movements in, 624
Romania's achievement of
    autonomy, 707
Selim I, reign of, 437,
    453–454, 461t
Selim II, reign of, 461t
Selim III, reign of, 461t, 542,
    620–621, 642, 735, 1024
17th-century
    decentralization of,
    620–622, 620m

siege of Vienna, 505
1683–1812 losses,
    640m–641m
16th/17th century
    consolidation, 729
slow railroad
    development, 644
steamship investments, 644
Suleiman, reign of, 83t, *368,*
    398, 416, 454, 461
Sultanate of Women,
    461, 461t
Tanzimat in, 706, 740–742
as "the sick man of Europe,"
    642–645
trade capitulations with
    Europe, 642–645
uneasy relations with
    Habsburgs, 460
waning of the
    sultanate, 455
war with Persians, 459–460
welcoming of Jews, 437
in World War I, 895, 896t
World War I surrender
    of, 896t
Zvi's messianic Judaism in,
    417, 438–440, 729
Ottoman Turks, 364–368
defeat of Byzantine
    Empire, 319
1821 Greek patriot
    revolt, 672
emergence of, 328
14th/15th century
    leadership by, 1084
gunpowder, cannons used
    by, 364
invasion of Austria, 513–514
Mehmed II's leadership,
    364, 367
openings with Europe, 591
relation to Mongols, Tartars,
    Seljuk Turks, 360
siege of Vienna, 375
The Outline of History (Wells),
    934–935
Owenson, Sydney (Lady
    Morgan), 668
Oxford Association for the
    Advancement of
    Science, 758
Oxford English Dictionary
    (1928), 527
Oxford movement
    (England), 751

P
Pacifism, 971–972
Pact of Umar, 262
Padova, Marsiglio di, 328,
    379, 388
Pagans/paganism
    Bishop Gregory on, 269
    Byzantine purge of, 248
    Christian paganism,
        275–277
    community emphasis of, 228
    forgiveness of relapsed
        Christians, 224
    Imperial Age pagans, 230
    Jesus and, 207
    Ka'ba shrine in Mecca, 255,
        259–260
    legality of, 246
    objections to Qur'an, 258
    Platonic tradition and, 231
    Plutarch's support for, 232
    purification of Ka'ba
        against, 259
    Qur'an objections to,
        257–258
    Qur'ranic authority
        conversions of, 263
    religious basis of, 233
    revitalization in Rome,
        227–228
    strength/vitality of pagan
        cults, 225–229
    Temple altars, 166
Pahlavi, Reza Shah, 1010,
    1047, 1129
Paine, Thomas, 592, 611,
    613–614
Pakistan
    global gender gap
        data, 1139t
    military activities in, 1126
    1950s military coup d'état in,
        1082
    1960s emigration to
        Britain, 1038
    rape of women as
        punishment, 1140
Palatine Chapel, 292
Palestine. *See also* Hamas
    alphabet development, 14
    Arab Spring and, 1135–1138
    Balfour Declaration
        and, 938
    British control of, 927,
        937–938, 1012
    Byzantium loss of, 249

Christianity's beginnings
in, 206
early human
settlements in, 21
Essene sect in, 213
Hamas' opinion of,
1086–1088
Hittite military efforts in, 52
Hyksos' links with, 45–46
Israel's dispute with, 1081,
1113–1114, 1135–1138
Jewish settlement in, 69–70,
76–78, 92, 734, 776m, 777,
938, 1013, 1078
Mamluk rule in, 328, 361m
Morris on refugee problem
in, 1059, 1080
Muslim Brotherhood view
of, 1086–1088
Muslim conquest map, 262
New Kingdom victory
against, 45
Ottoman control of,
735–736
Persian campaign
against, 251
railroad development
in, 644
Septuagint Bible used in, 167
terrorism in, 1114
Thutmose III extension
into, 48
Twain's visit to, 1012–1013
wars of religion and, 441
West Bank/Gaza Strip
occupancy, 1078
in World War I, 911
Palestinian Judaism, 206
Palestinian Liberation
Organization (PLO),
1040, 1117, 1119
Palestinian Mandate,
938–939, 1013
Palestrina, Giovanni Pierluigi
da, 205
Pamela, or Virtue Rewarded
(Richardson), 580
Pan-Arabism, 1012
Pan-German League, 889
Pan-Slavism, 913
Pantheon Rome/Roman
Republic, 207
Pantheon temple, 226
Papal States, 286, 331m, 380,
506m, 543m, 582m,
687, 771

Paper mills, 327
Pappé, Ilan, 1080
Papyrus, 24
Paracelsus. See Hohenheim,
Philip von
Parallel Lives (Plutarch),
231–232
Paris, France
Bibliothèque Nationale
in, 401
Black Death in,
349m, 350
Capetian dynasty in, 329
centers of learning in,
331m, 499m
charities in, 652
cholera epidemic, 647
Collège de France in, 401
domains of Charles V
map, 397m
in the Enlightenment,
562–563, 586m
Erasmus' studies in, 390
exile of Isabella of Spain
in, 682
food riots (French
Revolution), 594t
grievance notebooks of
common people, 597–598
Hitler's occupation of, 978,
980, 981
Hundred Years' War
map, 347m
industrial age
population, 645
land area, Charlemagne's
era, 311
Masons in, 587
1968 rebellions in, 1036
Notre Dame cathedral, 205
prostitution/sexual
exploitation in, 653–654
Protestant Reformation
map, 404m
Saint Bartholomew's Day
Massacre, 444
suffrage issues, 795
Vikings attack in, 284, 295
women's rights conference,
784, 793
Paris food riots (1792), 594
Paris Peace Conference (1919),
889, 896t, 922, 923, 927,
936, 967, 969
Parlements, reintroduction by
Louis XV, 596

Parsi. See Zoroastrianism
religion
Pärt, Arvo, 205
Parthenon, completion of, 133
Party of God organization,
1097
Party of Islam organization,
1097
Party of Liberation
organization, 1097
Pascendi Dominici Gregis
decree (Pius X), 772
Passarowitz, Treaty of
(1700–1718), 640m
Passion narratives, New
Testament, 217, 219
Pasteur, Louis, 820
Pasteurization process, 820
Pater familias (male head of
household), 177, 177–178,
180, 189
Patria familias ("paternal
power"), 177
Patria potestas (paternal
power), 177
Patriarchal family,
428–431, 430
Patricide themes (Greek
mythology), 98
Patrilinear inheritance
practices, 12
Patton, George, 1023–1024
Paul III (Pope), 470
Paul the Deacon, 276
Paul VI (Pope),
1066–1067, 1069
Pavel (Russia), 515t
Pax Romana (Roman Peace),
195, 198, 200–201, 223,
225–226, 230, 308
Peace of Augsburg (1555 CE),
416, 442–445, 447
Peace of God assemblies,
311–312
Peace of Westphalia (1648)
conditions for monarchy
established by, 509
Congress of Vienna
and, 633
defined, 505
influence on map of Europe,
505–506, 506m
influence on Ottoman
Turks, 513–514
international law ideas
and, 993

Peace of Westphalia (cont.)
 lasting influence in
  Europe, 528
 power shifts caused by,
  507–508, 513, 548
 religious principle
  establishment by,
  506–507
 royal absolutism established
  by, 508
 success in maintaining
  peace, 516–517
 Wars of Religion ended
  by, 752
Pearson, Karl, 816–818
Peasants' Revolt
 (England), 343
Peasants' Revolt (Germany),
 399, 416, 429, 442
Pelletier, Madeleine, 795
Peloponnesian War
 beneficial effects of
  catastrophes in, 144–145
 collapse of Greece during,
  143–147
 map of countries
  involved, 143m
 optimism of Sophists
  crushed by, 150
 Thucydides view of, 145
 timeline of, 131, 132, 133,
  146t, 152
 Xenophon's observation of,
  119–120
Pemberton, Max, 851
Pennsylvania Steelworker's
 Strike (1919), 935
Penrose, Robert, 1061t
Pentecostalism, 1072–1073
People of the Book, 257,
 262–263, 1083. See also
 Christians/Christianity;
 Judaism
People of the Land. See
 Pharisees
"People's Charter" petition
 (London Working Men's
 Association), 683–684
Pepin of Heristal, 285–286
Pepin the Short, 285–288
Pérez Galdós, Benito, 801
Periander of Corinth, 115
Pericles (Athenian leader), 133
"Pericles' Funeral Oration"
 (Thucydides), 146

Persian Empire. See also Cyrus
 the Great; Safavid
 dynasty
 Alexander's conquest of, 133,
  158, 252
 Arab rulership, 264
 Artaxerxes I's leadership,
  91–92
 Athenian attack in
  Sardis, 126
 attacks against, 239
 Baghdad recaptured by,
  540–541
 belief in inferiority of other
  cultures, 818
 Byzantium's war with, 249,
  256, 260
 calendrical measurements of,
  752–753
 Cambyses' reign, 61–62
 campaign against Lydia, 124
 campaign against
  Scythians, 121
 challenges of governing, 61
 conquering of Egypt, 61
 control of Miletus, 121, 126
 creation of new mode of
  statecraft, 62
 Cyrus's reign, 60–61
 Darius' reign, 62
 defeat at Gaugamela, 133
 design of temples, 64
 eating and drinking habits,
  136–137
 empire maps, 61m, 127m
 freeing of the Jews, 132
 geographic location, 46m
 Holy Land campaign of,
  250–251
 Il-Khans leadership,
  368–370
 illuminationism in, 458
 intellectual life in, 456
 invasion of Greece, 120,
  127, 132
 Ionian cities revolt
  against, 99
 Ionian League break
  with, 122
 Pericles' peace treaty
  with, 144
 political/social successes
  of, 62
 Qajar dynasty, 541
 Rome's clashes with, 255

Silk Road's passage
  through, 254
 single currency of, 61–62
 surrender to the
  Muslims, 260
 unknown origins of, 55, 60
 Valerian captured by,
  239–240
 writing acquired by, 63
 Zoroastrianism beliefs, 55,
  60, 62–65, 83, 263
Persian Gulf wars, 1133
Persian Wars, 125–127,
 127m, 132
Persian Zoroastrians, 83
Peter II (Russia), 515t
Peter III (Russia), 515t
Peter I the Great (Russia),
 505, 515t
Peterloo Massacre (England),
 650–652, 651
Peter the Deacon (of Pisa), 290
Peter the Great
 (Russian Czar), 505
Petrarca, Francesco, 374–375,
 384–385
Phalanx units, military
 strategies (Greece),
 112–113
Pharaohs in Ancient Egypt,
 25–26
Pharisees (philosophical sect),
 212–214, 216, 223
Phenomenology, 866–867
Philemon (New
 Testament), 208t
Philip IV (French King),
 346, 357
Philip IV (Spanish King), 329
Philippians (New
 Testament), 208t
Philip V (Macedonian
 King), 183
Philistines, 38, 58
Philo of Alexandria, 166, 217
Philosophiae Naturalis Principia
 Mathematica (Newton),
 465, 467, 485, 485t,
 497–498, 854
A Philosophical Commentary
 (Bayle), 561
Philosophical Dictionary
 (Voltaire), 572–573, 583
Philosophical Letters on the
 English (Voltaire), 568

Philosophical sects (hairesis).
  See Essenes; Pharisees;
  Sadducees
Philosophy. *See also* Aristotle;
  Nietzsche, Friedrich;
  Plato; Sartre, Jean-Paul;
  Socrates
  analytic philosophies, 860,
    864–866
  in Ancient Greece, 122–123,
    148–149, 148–150, 152,
    198, 221, 229–231, 267
  Athenian contributions, 143
  Bacon's interest in, 466, 492
  in the Byzantine
    Empire, 249
  cosmological component
    of, 468
  Descartes' interest in, 492
  Diderot's contributions
    to, 565
  distinction from
    religion, 229
  Epictetus' interest in,
    198–199
  existentialism, 867–869
  Hegel's contributions to, 151,
    748, 849
  Hobbes' interest in, 510–511
  illuminationism, 456
  Islamic Empire and, 296,
    300–301
  logic and language, 864–866
  Marx's studies in, 687
  Miletus as birthplace of, 122
  Muslim scholars encounters
    with, 302
  Neoplatonic philosophy,
    229–234, 387
  Newton's interest in, 465,
    467, 485, 492,
    497–498, 854
  nihilism, 860
  phenomenology, 866–867
  rationalist philosophy, 860
  Rousseau's studies of, 570
  Sadra's comments
    about, 456
  structuralism, 867
  Umayyad objections to, 267
Phocas (Roman emperor), 249
Phoenicians
  alphabet development, 14, 58
  appearance of, 57
  Atlantic Ocean journeys, 416

colony map, 111m
communication with the
  Hebrews, 78
as Roman ancestors, 173
successes of, 57–58
Phonograph, development
  of, 821
*The Physical Life of Woman:
  Advice to the Maiden, Wife,
  and Mother*
  (Napheys), 798
Physics. *See also* Einstein,
  Albert; Planck, Max
  Bacon's study of, 466
  Boyle's discoveries, 485
  Descartes' advances
    in, 494n9
  Dirac's comments on
    Einstein, Planck, 859
  early foundations of, 122
  Galileo's studies of, 471,
    478, 482
  Hellenistic era, 162
  Hobbes' interest in, 510, 513
  Islamic world excellence
    in, 490
  Madame Curie's work in,
    821, 854
  radioactive elements,
    854–855
  relativity and space-time,
    856–859
  special theory of
    relativity, 851
  uncertainty principle, 856
  Voltaire's interest in, 568
  wave/particle theory,
    854–856
  X-rays, 854
Piasecki, Boleslaw, 963
Picasso, Pablo, 851, 880, *960*
Pico della Mirandola,
  Giovanni, 374, 377–378,
  387, 560
The Picture of Dorian Gray
  (Wilde), 851,
  852–853, 871
Piedmont-Sardinia Kingdom,
  666, 718
Pierson, Allard, 762
Pieter Bruegel the Elder, 326
Pilate, Pontius, 217–218, 768
Pilgrimages. *See also* Mecca/
  Meccan people; Medina
  by Christians, 315, 394

to Jerusalem, 334
  by Muslims, 260, 315,
    541, 735
Pindar, 138, 146t
Pirenne, Henri, 654
Pisistratos (Greek tyrant),
  114, 124
Pius IV (Pope), 382
Pius IX (Pope), 687, 718, 771
Pius VII (Pope), 616
Pius X (Pope)
  excommunications by,
    763, 773
  Lamentabili sane exitu
    decree, 772
  modernism rejected by, 747,
    772–773
  papal decrees issued by, 772
  Pascendi Dominici Gregis
    decree, 772
  Syllabus of Errors, 772–773
Pius XII (Pope), 1064–1066
Pivati, Gianfrancesco, 566
Pizarro, Francisco, 422
Plagues. *See* Black Death;
  Bubonic plague; Measles
  epidemic; Smallpox
  epidemic
Planck, Max, 855–856
Plataea, Battle of, 127, 146t
Plato
  Academy school founded
    by, 152
  birth of, 146t
  bust of, *155*
  Ideal Forms of, 154–155
  influence on Western
    philosophy, 150
  passionate/quirky ideas of
    God, 748
  The Republic, 152
  The Symposium, 137–138
Plebian Council of Rome, 172,
  180–181
Plenitudo potestatis principle,
  of papal authority,
  330–331
Plessis, Armand-Jean du
  (Cardinal de
  Richelieu), 509
Plutarch
  Life of Cato the Elder, 178
  Life of Lycurgus, 119
  Moralia ("Ethical Matters")
    of, 232

Plutarch (cont.)
  narrative of Athenian
    campaign, 232
  "On Isis and Osiris" poem, 229
  Parallel Lives, 231–232
  self-dedication as a
    priest, 231
Pneumatic braking systems,
  development of, 821
"The Poem of the Righteous
  Sufferer," 18
Poetry
  Iliad, 99, 104–108, 487
  Odyssey, 99, 105, 108,
    109, 950
  Renaissance era, 375
  of Rumi, 366
  of Sa'di (Sufi poet), 369
Pogroms against Jewish people
  (Russia), 734, 734, 775
Poland
  anti-Semitism in, 946, 1079
  Christian Democratic party
    in, 1034
  deaths in World War I, 888
  Enlightenment-era indigent
    labors, 580
  EU membership, 1104, 1109
  fascism in, 963
  Hitler's invasion of, 974, 977,
    978, 981
  Holy League
    membership, 722
  independence declared
    by, 1091
  liberal-led rebellions in, 682
  Lutheranism in, 404
  Masonry in, 587
  monasteries established
    in, 278
  mystical experience
    reports, 334
  Napoleon's conquests
    in, 605
  "Pact of Steel" with Italy, 978
  political rivalries of, 936
  post-1815 industrialization
    failure, 636–637
  Sudetenland captured
    by, 978
  women's suffrage rights, 939
  in World War I, 892, 896t,
    897, 910, 912,
    915m, 926m
  in World War II, 977–981,
    988–991

Poland-Lithuanian Union, 505,
  514, 573, 574m, 583–584,
  722, 1024
Polio vaccine, 1061t
Polis (communities)
  Athens leadership of, 128
  citizenship
    requirements, 116
  described, 109
  dietary patterns, 136–138
  entrepreneurial pursuits
    in, 110
  interdependence of, 113
  leadership positions, 119
  male military service in, 112
  religion/religious
    celebrations in, 135–136
  strengths of Sparta
    polis, 125
  symposia all-male drinking
    parties, 137–138
Polish-Swedish War
  (1600–1629), 573
Politics
  Arab political
    monopoly, 296
  Augustus' political
    system, 187
  Congress of Vienna political
    map, 633, 665, 774
  French political periods, 592
  Persian Empire successes, 62
  Renaissance era, 380–384
Politics (modern), birth of
  (1815–1848), 665–701.
    See also Conservatism;
    Liberalism
  bourgeoisie support for
    liberalism, 679
  1830 liberal-led
    rebellions, 682
  1848 revolution,
    685–687, 686m
  France/two-chambered
    legislature, 671
  industrial capitalism and its
    critics, 680–685
  novels/popular magazines,
    696–701
  proletariat class, 683
  restoration of royal
    families, 670
  rise of charitable
    institutions, 683
  royalism and nationalism,
    669–673

suffrage rights, 681
  women and the cult of
    domesticity, 693–696
Polybius (Greek historian), 181
Pompey the Great
  conservative Senate support
    of, 186
  defeat at Pharsalus, 232
  Julius Caesar vs., 185,
    186, 188
  victory at Judea, 213
Pontifex maximus ("chief
  priest"), 246
Poor Laws and Paupers
  Illustrated
  (Martineau), 791
Pope, Alexander, 582
Poquelin, Jean-Baptiste (aka
  Molière), 513, 528–529
Pornocracy period (Catholic
  Church), 310
Portolan charts, invention
  of, 327
The Portrait of a Lady
  (James), 801
Portugal
  Angola/Mozambique seized
    by, 830
  in Asia (1536–1580), 420m
  Christian Democratic party
    in, 1034
  Conference of Berlin
    attendance, 828
  fascism in, 963
  Jewish synagogue
    painting, 575
  Jews expelled from, 436, 573
  Lisbon earthquake, 569, 569
  mystical experiences in, 334
  19th-century intellectual
    energy, 669
  ocean voyages of, 417
  Peace of Westphalia
    and, 505
  post-1815 industrialization
    failure, 636–637
  trade advantages of, 422
  in World War I, 895
Poseidon (Greek deity), 104
Post-structuralism, 1051–1052
Potato blight (Phytophthora
  infestans), in Ireland,
  726–728, 727m
Pound, Ezra, 877
Poussin, Nicolas (French
  painter), 513, 526

Poverty and Un-British Rule in India (Naoroji), 817, 842

Powell, Enoch, 1038–1039

Practical Education (Robert and Maria Edgeworth), 698

Prague Spring, 1019, 1041

The Praise of Folly (Erasmus), 390, 408

Prankhurst, Adela (daughter of Emmeline), 793–795

Prankhurst, Christabel (daughter of Emmeline), 793–795

Prankhurst, Emmeline, 793, 793–795

Prankhurst, Sylvia (daughter of Emmeline), 793–795

Presbyterianism, 407, 430, 568, 749, 764

Presidential Commission on the Status of Women (1961), 1045

Priests and rabbis (ancient Israel), 89–92

Primordial Chaos (Greek mythology), 97

The Prince (Machiavelli), 386–387, 512, 716–717

Princeps Augustus. *See* Augustus (Roman emperor)

Principia Mathematica (Russell and Whitehead), 851, 866

Principles of Geology (Lyell), 754, 755

The Principles of Scientific Management (Taylor), 817, 823–825

Printing press, 374, 384

Prisons and Prisoners (Bulwer-Lytton), 795–796

De Profundis ("Out of the Depths") Wilde, 853

Prolegomena to the Historical Origins of Islam (Wellhausen), 779

Proletariat
bourgeois' relationship with, 114
defined/meaning of, 683
Marx's viewpoint of, 690–691
tyrants as dictatorships of, 114

Promised Land, Hebrews seizure of, 38

The Prophet Muhammed: His Life and Teaching (Weil), 747, 778

Prophets and prophecy (Hebrew kingdom), 89–92

Prostitution
Archaic period, 116
Baudelaire's description of, 877
in Europe, 610, 646, 653–654
forced prostitution, in Japan, 993
in Hellenic-era Greece, 134
Picasso's painting of, 880
Protestant efforts at curbing, 431
in Rome, 179, 187
Schnitzler's description of, 870
Zola's description of, 802

Protestant Anglo-Irish, 724

Protestantism. *See also* Calvin, Jean; Luther, Martin; Thirty Years' War
Anabaptist apocalyptic sect, 403
Anglo-Irish Protestants, 723, 725
atheism and, 1069
belief in wars of religion, 441–442
Christian humanism and, 401
church attendance data, 1059
comments of Cardinal de Richelieu, 509–510
Council of Trent and, 475
efforts at curbing prostitution, 431
emphasis on Biblical truth, 432
England's adoption of, 442, 447, 538
European revival, 1057
Fr. Bellarmine's confrontation of, 478
fundamentals of, 1071–1074
historical criticism of the Bible and, 763–768
industrial-era Bible-reading societies, 654
missionary work, 750
neoorthodoxy, 1071

the patriarchal family and, 428–431
post-WW II, 1069–1071
sexual morality and, 431–434
surprise at Jewish refusal of conversion, 440
Sweden's defense of, 450
as theology, 405–407
Third World growth, 1069

Protestant Reformation, 392–394. *See also* Luther, Martin
Hobbes and, 511
influence of the church, 506
international scope of, 400–410
liquor distillation and, 545
map of, 404m
Protestantism without Luther, 402–403
Prussian Union decree and, 766–767

Protestant Renaissance, 388–390

The Protocols of the Elders of Zion, 707, 731

Proto-Indo-Europeans, 51

Proverbs (Hebrew Bible), 81

Providentissimus Deus encyclical (Leo XIII), 772

Prus, Boleslaw, 807–808

Prussia. *See also* Brandenburg-Prussia
alliance with Austria, 594t
conflicts with Austria-Hungary, 691
Congress of Vienna attendance, 666
the Directory in, 517
economy of, 543m
Franco-Prussian War, 713–714, 720–721, 890
industrialization in, 636
invasion of France, 601
linen weavers riots, 650
Napoleon's conquests in, 605
palace of Frederick II, 518n5
Protestant Reformation and, 404m
restoration of royal families, 670
revering of Kant in, 584
Thirty Years' War and, 516
war with Denmark, 713

Prussia. *(cont.)*
war with France, 595, 599
Wilhelm III, reign of,
671–672, 895
Wilhelm IV, reign of,
691, 712
Prussian Union decree (1817),
766–767
Psalms (Hebrew Bible), 73t,
80–81, 88, 356, 729
Pseudo-Dionysius the
Areopagite, 233
Psychoanalysis, sexuality and,
872–875. *See also* Freud,
Sigmund
Ptolemaic Kingdom, 161m
Puccini, Giacomo, 871
Punic Wars, 172, 182–183, 185
Purcell, Henry, 205
The Pure Theory of Capital
(Hayek), 968
Puritans of England, 407, 448,
532, 537
Pushkin, Aleksandr, 659,
913, 932
Putnam, Hilary, 1051–1052
Putting-out system of textile
manufacture, 547, 641
Pyramids of Egypt, 25
Pyramid Texts (Ancient
Egypt), 29, 41
Pythagoras, 148–149

Q
Al-Qaddafi, Muammar, 1050,
1083, 1137
Qadesh battle, 52
Qahtan, progenitor of "pure
Arab" people (al-Arab
al-aribah), 254
Qajar dynasty (Iran), 541
Qizilbash militant units, 540
Quakers/Quakerism, 568
Quantum theory, 850,
855–856
Quarterly Review article
(Croker), 668
Quintius, Lucius, 178, 210
Quisling, Vidkun, 963
Qur'an
on the Arabs, 1083–1084
belief in wars of religion, 441
Çelebi's comments on, 491
denunciation of
metaphysics, 453

essence/core message of,
255–257, 298
on Jews and Christians,
257–258, 262
Khomeini's comments
about, 1085
Meccan revelations,
258–259
Muslim Brotherhood
and, 1086
pagan conversions and, 263
philosophical vs. Qur'anic
studies, 267, 298–302
Ramadan's comments
about, 1155
Rumi's reference to, 366
The Satanic Verses and, 1095
science and, 778
sexual modesty
teachings, 298
Society of Jesus vs., 477
on taking up arms for the
faith, 441
Taymiyyah's focus on, 363,
453, 490
Weil's writings about, 778
Quraysh tribe, 255, 258, 265

R
Rabbis and priests, 89–92
Rabelais, François, 408,
410–412, 560
"Race and Language" essay
(Freeman), 706–707
Racine, Jean, 526
Radical democracy, 578
Radical Islamism, 1103, 1138
Radiology, developments
in, 821
Radios, development of,
821, 826
Railroads
England's track system
development, 633
European development of,
637–638
Ottoman Empire's slow
development, 644
Second Industrial
Revolution and, 820
Transcontinental Railroad,
U.S., 826
Raleigh, Sir Walter, 448
Ramadan, Tariq, 1154–1155,
1154–1156

Ramses II (Egyptian
pharaoh), 50, *51*
Ramses III (Egyptian
pharaoh), 53–54
Rashi, 323–324
Rashid ad-Din
Hamadani, 369
Rationalist philosophies, 860
Rational punishments,
563–565
Rational self-interest
investigations, of
Beccaria, 564
Rawls, John, 1150
Realist literature, 802
Rebellion themes (Greek
mythology), 98
Red Menace fears
(in the U.S.), 935
*Reflections on the Revolution in
France* (Burke),
610–612, 673
Reformed Church (of Calvin),
404, 405–407
Reform Judaism, 775, 777,
1078–1079
*Regarding the Faith and Its
Relations with the Civil and
Political Order*
(Lamennais), 770
Reign of Terror (French
Revolution), 594t, 600
Reinsurance Treaty
(1887–1890), 893m
Relativity theory (physics),
856–857
Religion/religious practices.
See also Bible; Catholic
Church (Catholicism);
Christians/Christianity;
Crusades; Hebrew
(Jewish) Bible; Islam
religion; Jesus of
Nazareth; Jewish people;
Judaism; Lutheranism;
New Testament;
Orthodox Church
(Eastern Europe);
Protestantism; Sufism
Anglican Church, 448,
506–507, 765–766, 1072
Church of the Holy
Sepulcher, 315, *315*
conversions of religion,
207–208

divination, in Rome, 175–176
Dutch Reformed Church, 407
Evangelical Anglican church, 764
evangelicalism, 1074
fundamentalism, 1073–1074
Galileo's conflicts with, 468, 472–473, 478, 482
German Confessing Church, 1070
German Evangelical Church, 1069–1070
Greek panhellenic religious festivals, 112
Hinduism, 206, 207, 419
household gods, Rome, 180
Lutheran Reformation, 389
Pentecostalism, 1072–1073
Protestant Reformation, 392–394
Protestant Renaissance, 388–390
in Sumer, 13, 16–20
wars of, 441–442
World Council of Churches, 1074
World Religion graph, 207
Religious imperialism, 38
Rembrandt (Rembrandt van Rijn), 489, 589, 932
Renaissance era
artistic achievements, 374, 379, 382, 383
city-states, 380–383
classical learning during, 375–376
economic/political matrix, 380–384
Hohenstaufen dynasty, 380, 388
humanism element of, 376–378
in Italy, 373, 380, 381m, 383, 387–388, 395–396, 397m, 403, 409
lack of scientific interests in, 467
literary achievements, 375–376, 384–388, 390–392
self-naming of, 373
statecraft element of, 378–380
Renaud, Jean, 964

Report on the Principles of Public Morality (Robespierre), 600
Representative government, late-medieval era, 340–342
The Republic (Plato), 152, 157
Rerum Novarum ("Of New Things") encyclical (Leo XIII), 769–771
The Resourceful Earth (Simon), 1100
Res publica (commonwealth) of Rome, 176
Reubeni, David, 437–438
Revan, Ernest, 709, 747, 761–762
Revelation (New Testament), 208t
Revelations of Divine Love (Hadewijch of Flanders), 336
Revolution of 1848 (Europe), 685–687, 686m, 691–693
Rexist Party (Belgium's fascists), 963
Rhea (Greek deity), 97
Rhineland Confederation, 605
Rhodes, Cecil, 829
Rhythm method, of birth control, 799
Richardson, Samuel, 580
Richelieu, Cardinal de (Armand-Jean du Plessis), 509–510, 519–520
Richter, Richard, 800
Riesser, Gabriel, 731
Rifah (Welfare) Party (Turkey), 1114
The Rights of Man (Paine), 613
Right-wing dictatorships, 963m
Rijn, Rembrandt van, 489
Rijswijk, Treaty of (1697), 558
Rilke, Rainer Maria, 880, 883
"River of Blood" speech (Powell), 1039
The Road to Serfdom (Hayek), 968
Roberts, David, 737
Robespierre, Maximillian, 592
beheading of, 594t, 600
leadership of the Jacobins, 599
Reign of Terror instigated by, 594t, 600

Rocque, François de la, 963–964
Roman Catholicism
Charles II and, 537
as replacement for Orthodox Church, 319
as state religion of United Italy, 749
Romania
autonomy achieved by, 707, 735
Christian Democratic party in, 1034
deaths in World War I, 888
EU membership, 1104
Gypsies of, 1108
independence declared by, 1091
political rivalries of, 937
in World War I, 895
in World War II, 978, 991
Romanov, Mikhail I, 514
Romanov Empire (Russia), 513–514, 620, 913, 921, 936
Roman Peace (Pax Romana), 195, 198, 200–201, 223, 225–226, 230, 308
Romans (New Testament), 208t
Romanticism cultural movement, 625, 655–661
nationalism compared with, 709
writers associated with, 659–660
Rome, Treaty of (1957), 1105–1106
Rome/Roman Republic. See also Constantine the Great; Senate of Rome
administration of, 172
adoption of Greek achievements, 198
ancestry of, 173
anti-corruption efforts, 184
Battle of Actium, 186
building of Pantheon, 207
Caesar's sole rulership of, 186
calendar used in, 752
Carolingian's relationship with, 287
Carus' leadership, 240
Christianity as official religion, 238

Rome *(cont.)*
  clothing, diet, houses of,
    179–180
  condemnation of
    Christianity by, 221–225
  conquest of the East, 131
  constitution of, 181
  contacts with China, 416
  Decius' leadership, 224
  Diocletian's leadership, 207,
    224, 238, 240–244, 277
  Domitian's leadership,
    200, 224
  election of plebian
    consul, 172
  establishment of res
    publica, 176
  expansion of, 180–185
  extension of citizenship, 173
  familia (social unit),
    177–179, 198
  First Punic War, 172
  "Five Good Emperors" of,
    173, 200–202
  fondness for Asian
    luxury, 197
  foundation myths of,
    171, 172
  geographic considerations,
    173–174
  gladiatorial games, 174–175,
    175, 178, 201, 238
  Great Persecution of
    Christians, 242, 243–244
  Hadrian's leadership,
    200, 226
  Hellenic roots of, 172–173
  Heraclius' leadership,
    249–250, 252
  household gods of, 180
  imperial crisis/decline of,
    238–242
  internal wars and struggles
    of, 185–187
  kings of, 173t
  legalization of
    Christianity, 245
  legendary kings of, 173t
  Leo IV's leadership, 294
  links to Homeric heroes,
    172–176
  lives and values of, 195–200
  luxury disdained by, 175
  map of neighbors, 183m
  Marcus Aurelius' leadership,
    200, 207, 230, 238

  martyrdom and empire,
    242–244
  Maurice's leadership, 249
  Maximinus' leadership, 224
  Mediterranean-based links,
    191, 192m
  Nero's leadership, 187, 198,
    200, 206, 224
  Numerianus'
    leadership, 240
  origins, 173
  pater familias, 177, 177–178,
    180, 189
  Phocas' leadership, 249
  plantations in Rome,
    185–186
  plebian consul of, 180–181
  Polybius' championing
    of, 181
  religious influences,
    175–176
  as republic of virtue,
    178–180
  rise of New Rome, 247–249
  self-beliefs about
    origin, 171
  slavery in, 197
  smallpox virus in, 239
  tax collection methods, 241
  Tetrarchy system division
    of, 242
  themes of Roman army, 250
  Theodosius' leadership, 246
  300 CE map, 241m
  Twelve Tables (law code),
    172, 176–178, 177t
  Valerian's leadership, 239
Romulus (Roman King), 173t
La Ronde ("A Circle Dance")
  (Schnitzler), 870
Röntgen, Wilhelm, 854
Roosevelt, Eleanor, 997
Roosevelt,
  Franklin Delano, 967
Roosevelt, Theodore, 800
Rotavirus vaccine, 1061t
Rousseau, Jean-Jacque, 554,
  555, 567
  belief in human goodness,
    571–572
  Confessions, 570
  *Discourse on the Origins of
    Inequality*, 570–571, 581
  Emile, 583
  influence on Western
    culture, 569

  noble savage popularized
    by, 571
  opinion of Voltaire, 569,
    570, 588
  on the point of
    Enlightenment, 571
  Voltaire's opinion of,
    569, 570
Rovere, Giuliano della, 373.
  See also Julius II (Pope)
RU-486 abortion pill, 1061t
Rubens, Peter Paul, 526
Rule of Saint Benedict, 278
Rumi (Jalal ad-Din
  Muhammad Balkhi),
  328, 366
Ibn Rushd (Islamic
  philosopher), 267
Rushdie, Salman, 1095–1096
Ruskin, John, 374
Russell, Bertrand, 864–866
Russia. *See also* Bolshevik
  Party; Soviet Union;
  USSR (Union of Soviet
  Socialist Republics)
  agricultural economy in, 629
  anti-Semitism in, 731–734
  Bloody Sunday, 914
  Conference of Berlin
    attendance, 828
  Congress of Vienna
    attendance, 666
  deaths in World War I, 888
  Decembrists revolt, 666
  educational rights for
    women, 790
  1880–1914 Jewish
    emigration from, 776m
  failed revolution in, 888
  Great Purge in, 964–965
  Gulag (concentration
    camps) in, 965
  Holy League
    membership, 722
  invasions of, 912–913
  Lenin's rise to power, 896t
  liberal-led rebellions in, 682
  literary artists of, 913
  Masonry in, 587
  Mongol destruction of Kiev,
    358–359
  Napoleon's invasion of, 617
  Narodnaya Volya Party,
    733–734
  New Economic Policy
    in, 964

Nikolai I, reign of, 720
Nikolai II, reign of, 913
1914 invasion of
    Germany, 896t
19th-century intellectual
    energy, 669, 735
oppression and terror in,
    964–966
Orthodox Church in, 620
Pan-Slavism in, 913
Peter II, reign of, 515t
Peter III, reign of, 515t
Peter I the Great , reign of,
    505, 515t
pogroms against Jewish
    people, 734, 734, 775
political rivalries of, 936
post-1815 industrialization
    failure, 636–637
as the "Red Menace," 935
reign of Peter the Great, 505
restoration of royal
    families, 670
Romanov Empire, 513–514,
    620, 913, 921, 936
rulers of, 515t
Russo-Japanese War, 832–
    833, 983
serfdom abolished in, 707
Seven Years' War
    participation, 505,
    548–549
Stalin and, 918, 960
streltsi (noble cavalrymen)
    of, 516
Swedish Vikings invasion of,
    912, 1024
totalitarianism rule in, 964
wars with Chechnya,
    1126, 1132
witchcraft trials, 435
in World War I, 896t
Russian Confederation, 1091
Russian Orthodox
    Church, 920
Russian Revolution, 897, 915m
Russo-Japanese War,
    832–833, 983

S
Sabines society, 172
The Sacred Fount (James), 803
Sadat, Anwar, 1078
Sadducees ("philosophical
    sect"), 211–212, 214,
    216, 223

Sa'di (Sufi poet), 369
Safavid dynasty (Iran),
    456, 459
    domination of Islamic
        world, 452
    fall of, 505
    Isfahan as capital of, 542
    origins of, 540
    Qizilbash militant units, 540
    shahs of, 540–541
Safety razors, development
    of, 821
Safiye (Sultana), 461t
Saint Bartholomew's Day
    Massacre (France), 417,
    444–445
Saint Jerome, 233
Saint John, Gospel of, 230
Saint-Just, Louis
    Antoine, 560
Saint-Simon, Duc de, 520
Salamis naval battle, 127
Salk, Jonas, 1061t
Sallust (historian), 375
Salvation Army, 747
Sand, George, 699
Sappho (Greek poet), 138–139
Sarai/Sarah (wife of Abram/
    Abraham), 69–71, 84
Sargon I (Akkadian King), 5,
    9–11, 10m
Sartre, Jean-Paul, 867–869,
    869, 1023
Sassanid dynasty,
    239–240, 240
Sassoon, Siegfried, 911–912
The Satanic Verses (Rushdie),
    1092–1096, 1095
Satires
    of Erasmus, 390–391, 408
    of Menippus, 408
    of More, 408–409
    of Rabelais, 408, 410–412
    of von Hutten, 408–410
Ibn Saud, Muhammad,
    739, 938
Saudi Arabia
    British oversight of, 937
    coalition staging during
        Persian Gulf war, 1133
    democratic elections
        in, 1136
    global gender gap data,
        1139t
    honor killing of young girls
        in, 1140

Israeli victory against,
    1040–1041
Muslim Brotherhood
    financing, 1117
oil-rich/poverty disparity in,
    1050n9
persecution of women in,
    1140
Satanic Verses banned in,
    1096n1
Saud's leadership, 938
Wahhabism in, 454n14
Saussure, Ferdinand de, 1052
Saxony
    Napoleon's conquests
        in, 605
    Seven Years' War
        participation, 505,
        548–549
Scarlatti, Alessandro, 526
Scarlatti, Domenico, 526
Schelling, Friedrich, 659
Schleiermacher, Friedrich, 760
Schlieffen, Alfred Graf
    von, 895
Schlieffen Plan, 895
Schmidt-Phiseldek, Justus
    Friedrich von, 1104
Schnitzler, Arthur, 870
Schoenberg, Arnold, 883
Scholasticism, age of,
    331–334, 331m
Scholem, Betty, 940
Scholem, Gershom, 940
School of Good Manners
    (Moody), 528
Schubert, Franz, 650
Schumann, Robert, 650
Science/scientific
    achievements. See also
        Einstein, Albert; Galilei,
        Galileo; Newton, Sir
        Isaac; Physics; Planck,
        Max; Scientific
        Revolution (16th and 17th
        centuries); Sklodowska-
        Curie, Marie
    in the 13th and 14th
        centuries, 327–328
    of the Abbasids, 302
    in ancient Greece, 133n1,
        145, 148m150, 299,
        385, 386
    Bacon's assault on, 465–466
    in the Byzantine
        Empire, 249

Science/scientific (cont.)
early Christianity, 233
of the Egyptians, 25
electron discovery, 854
energy/electricity, 854
eschewing of, by Sunni
Islam, 458–459
ethical costs of, 487–490
heliocentric theory, 469–470,
471–473, 478, 482, 778
Hellenistic Age, 162–163
Islamic retreat from,
490–491
in Islam's medieval
period, 456
1950–2000 breakthroughs,
1061t
of the Persians, 62, 301
quantum theory, 850,
855–856
radioactive elements,
854–855
relativity and space-time,
856–859
Renaissance era lack of
interest, 467
of the scientific
philosophers, 122
secularism and, 1060–1064
special theory of
relativity, 851
of the Sumerians, 25
taboos against bodily
desecration, 487–488
uncertainty principle, 856
X-rays, 821, 854
Scientific management,
823–825
Scientific Revolution (16th
and 17th centuries). See
also Bacon, Roger; Bacon,
Sir Francis; Copernicus,
Nicolaus; Descartes,
René; Galilei, Galileo;
Kepler, Johannes; Newton,
Sir Isaac
Boyle's work in chemistry,
484–485
broadening of, 484–487
choices for westerns society,
498–499
description, 467
during the
Enlightenment, 553
ethical costs of science,
487–490

Harvey's identification of
blood circulation, 163,
484, 485t, 487–488
human anatomical
dissection, 488–490, 489
inquisition and inquiry,
479–484
Islamic retreat from science,
490–491
Scofield Reference Bible, 753
Scotland
Masonic lodges in, 586
mystical experience
reports, 334
Presbyterian Church,
407, 749
U.S. Great Depression
influence in, 944
witchcraft trials, 435
Scouting for Boys: A Handbook
for Instruction in Good
Citizenship (Baden-
Powell), 870
Sea Peoples
destruction/disruptions
caused by, 55, 58, 105, 124
limited knowledge of,
53–54, 57
map of territory, 53m
mysterious disappearance
of, 55
timeline of appearance, 35
wall engraving of defeat
of, 54
weaponry advantages of, 56
weapons used by, 52
Seattle General Strike
(1919), 935
Second Battle of the Marne
(WW I), 897
Second Empire of France
(1852–1870), 592,
802, 850
Second Industrial Revolution
described, 819–820
key inventions/
developments, 820–826
medical advances, reduced
mortality, 826
overproduction issues,
825–826
scientific management,
823–825
workplace changes
during, 783

Second Intermediate Period
(Ancient Egypt), 41
Second Punic War, 183
Second Republic of France
(1848–1852), 592, 718
Second Saudi State, 739
Second Temple, 90
Second Temple Judaism,
163–166, 669
Second Treatise of Civil
Government (Locke), 678
Second Vatican Council
(Vatican II), 475, 773,
1058, 1066–1069
Second wave feminism,
1044–1045
Secularism
Anglican Church and,
765–766
Arab Nationalism and, 1011
Ataturk's commitment
to, 928
concerns about the rise
of, 1034
Holyoake's campaign for,
751–752
involuntary
secularism, 770
Jewish wariness about, 732
modernism and, 774–777
modern medicine's
contribution to, 750
rise of, 745, 749–752,
763, 775
science and, 1060–1064
Tanzimat promotion of, 741
term derivation, 748
theory of creation and, 752
toleration's contribution
to, 751
Secular Judaism, 776
Secular Zionism, 776
Segev, Tom, 1080
Seleucid Empire
Antiochus III, reign of, 183
Antiochus IV Epiphanes,
reign of, 166
extensions into India, 161
Jewish Hellenization in, 165
Jewish rebellion against, 166
jurisdictional claims of
Judea, 164
Maccabean revolt
against, 211
Selim I (Ottoman sultan), 437,
453–454, 461t

Selim II (Ottoman sultan), 461t
Selim III (Ottoman sultan), 461t, 542, 592, 620–621, 642, 735, 1024
Seljuk Turks
  Byzantine Empire defeated by, 285, 364
  as early Crusades enemy, 316
  11th-century arrival, 369
  Mongol defeat of, 364
  relation to Ottoman Turks, 360
  victorious campaigns of, 365
Semiautomatic rifles, development of, 821
Senate of Rome
  admittance of other tribes, 172
  Augustus and, 187
  Caesar and, 186
  constitution, 181
  Domitian and, 200
  Gracchi brothers vs., 185
  patrician lineage in, 177
  Pompey's appointment as sole consul, 186
  relationship with emperors, 200–201
  res publica establishment, 176
Seneca (Roman statesman), 198
Sephardic Judaism, 322–324, 436, 437n9, 439, 573, 576, 1074–1076
September 11, 2011, terrorist attacks (U.S.), 1093, 1114, 1116, 1117, 1125
Septuagint version (Hebrew Bible), 72, 73t, 74, 165, 167
Serao, Matilde, 699
Serbia
  deaths in World War I, 888
  massacre of Bosnians, 1130, 1132, 1132
  wars of Milosevic, 1130
Servius Tullius (Roman King), 173t
The Seventh Million: The Israelis and the Holocaust (Segev), 1080
Seven Weeks' War (1866), 713
Seven Years' War (1756–1763), 505, 548–549

Seville Cathedral, 205
Sexuality
  literature of, 803
  psychoanalysis and, 872–875
  realist/naturalist depictions of, 802–803
  societal beliefs about women, 800–801
Sexual morality
  Freud on, 877
  Protestantism and, 431–434
Sforza family (Italy), 382–383
al-Shabbi, Abu al-Qasim, 808
Shakespeare, William, 231n12, 384n2, 448, 527, 660, 932
Shamash (sun god), 16, 18
Shariah (Islamic) law, 541, 1048, 1086, 1114, 1154
Shaw, George Bernard, 850, 904, 972
She (Haggard), 851
Shelley, Mary, 659
Shelley, Percy Bysshe, 659, 746, 748
She'ol (Biblical underworld), 88
Shi'a Muslims
  customs of, 297–298
  holy shrines in Iraq, 541
  as Islam standard-bearer, 453
  rebellion by, 297
  schism with the Sunni Muslims, 265–266, 283
  Turkey's understanding of, 937
Shintoism, 207
Shlaim, Avi, 1080
Sickle cell anemia treatment, 1061t
Siege of Antioch, 316
Sieyès, Abbé de, 602
"Signs of the Times" essay (Carlyle), 658–659
Sikh religion, 207
"The Silesian Weavers" poem (Heine), 650, 660
Silk route (trading route), 254, 369
Simon, Julian, 1100
Simony abuse, by Catholic Church, 310
Simplon Tunnel (Swiss-Italian border), 826

Ibn Sina (Islamic philosopher), 267
Sister Carrie (Dreiser), 803
Sistine Chapel, 373
Six-Day War (Israel), 1040–1041, 1041
Sixtus IV (Pope), 373
Sklodowska-Curie, Marie, 821, 854
Slavery
  in Ancient Egypt, 24
  Atlantic slave trade, 544–545, 546m, 547
  in Babylonian Empire, 37
  in Classical Greece, 135
  in Europe, 545
  revolt in Sparta, 118
  in Rome, 197
  in Sumer, 15
Slavs, 249
Slovakia, deaths in World War I, 888
Smallpox epidemic
  in Aztec Empire, 425n3
  in Hispaniola, 424–425, 425
  in Rome, 239
  vaccine development, 628n1, 750
Smith, Adam, 555, 563
Smith, William, 753
Sobibor concentration camp, 990
Social behavior norms, 528–531
Social Catholicism, 770
Social contract theory (Hobbes), 512
Social Darwinism, 818, 849, 888
Social Insurance and Allied Services report (Beveridge), 1029–1031
Social Security program (U.S.), 1029
Society for the Diffusion of Useful Knowledge, 652
Society for the Prevention of Cruelty to Animals, 683
Society for Women's Legal Rights (Holland), 793
Society in America (Martineau), 791
Society of Saint Vincent de Paul, 652

Socrates, 131
annoying personality of, 152
birth/death of, 146t
influences on Western
philosophy, 151
methods vs. ideas of, 151–152
reputation for drinking
wine, 138
Sophist tradition training,
150–151
Södergran, Edith, 954t
Sola Scriptura (Biblical
truth), 432
Solomon (Hebrew King,
David's son), 81–82
Solon (Greek tyrant), 124
Somalia, female circumcision
in, 811
Somme, Battle of (WW I),
896t, 912
Song of Songs (in Hebrew
Bible), 81, 86
Son of God. See Jesus of
Nazareth
Sophists/sophistry (Greece),
150, 152
Sophocles, 140
South Africa
diamond/gold mining, 894
Satanic Verses banned in,
1096n1
South America
adventurer landings in, 421
Atlantic slave trade
and, 546m
1815–1914 immigration
data, 892
European explorations
of, 423m
international plundering
in, 449
introduction of crops to
Europe, 426–427
Jesuit missions in, 476
Protestant communities
in, 1071
Southeast Asia, 1038. See also
Vietnam War
South Sea Bubble (1720), 544
South Sea Company, 544
Soviet Union. See also Cold
War; Russia; USSR
(Union of Soviet Socialist
Republics)
Afghanistan invaded by,
1025, 1114, 1118

Battle of Stalingrad, 979
collapse of, 1069, 1091, 1092,
1094m, 1103
Czechoslovakia invaded by,
1019, 1040–1042, 1042
decolonization issue, 1028
fall of Communism, 1094m
Gorbachev's
leadership, 1091
land blockade in
Berlin, 1025
nuclear program of,
1003, 1024
onset of Great Purge, 933
origin of, 888
properties seized by, 1058
Russian Revolution
map, 915m
socialist labor propaganda
poster, 921
Spanish Civil War and, 959
Stalin's nuclear program,
1003, 1024
support for Communist
North Vietnam, 979
U.S. European military
shield and, 1036
in World War II, 977, 978,
980–981, 999,
1002–1003, 1010
Space-time theory, 856–859
Spain
absolutism defended by, 601
Acts of Toleration for Jewish
people, 577
admittance to
NATO, 1026m
agricultural economy in, 629
Balboa's voyages to New
World, 421
Barcelona/urban
development, 646
battles with Netherland, 449
Black Death, eyewitness
account, 350
Charlemagne's expansion
into, 288
church attendance
data, 1059
Conference of Berlin
attendance, 828
conservative vs. liberal
rebellions, 682
fascism in, 955–960
forced baptisms of Moors,
401–402

France's war with, 595
global gender gap
data, 1139t
Habsburg dynasty, 513
honor killing of women
in, 1140
increasing trade with, 307
invasion of England,
448–449
invasion of France, 601
Jews expelled from, 436, 573
Louis XIV's invasion
of, 548
monasteries established
in, 278
mystical experiences in, 334
Napoleon's conquests
in, 605
nullification of liberal
constitution, 672
Philip IV, reign of, 329
post-1815 industrialization
failure, 636–637
restoration of royal
families, 670
rulers of, 515t
Second Punic War and, 183
terrorism in, 1116, 1125
trade advantages of, 422
War of Devolution, 516
weakened constitutional
monarchy in, 958
witchcraft trials, 435
Spanish-American War, 831
Spanish Civil War
(1936–1939), 933, 959
Spanish flu epidemic, 907n7
Spanish Inquisition, 373
Sparta
dietary restrictions,
118–119
geographic location, 61m,
101m, 111m
Greek founding of, 97
helots (slave) revolt, 118
militarization of citizenry in,
118–120
youth culture of, 120
Special theory of relativity
(Einstein), 851, 857
Speculum of the Other Woman
(Irigaray), 1110
"Speech to the Frankfurt
Assembly" (Droysen), 712
Spengler, Oswald, 932,
933, 934

Spinning machine, water-
    powered, 631–632, 632
Spinoza, Baruch, 417, 456, 457,
    458, 575, 577, 748
Spiritual anxiety, religious
    observance and, 1057,
    1058–1060
Spurgeon, Charles
    Haddon, 815
Stage tragedies (Classical
    Greece), 139–142
Stalin, Josef
    abortion outlawed by, 1005
    anti-Semitism of, 1079
    blockade of West
        Berlin, 1025
    Britain/U.S. fears of, 972
    brutal control by, 960, 1041
    Eastern Europe domination,
        1019, 1021
    Five Year Plans of, 964
    Great Purges of, 964–966
    Gulags created by, 965
    humanitarian crimes of, 969
    industrial production focus
        of, 1003, 1005
    negotiations with
        Hitler, 978
    offer of U.S.-Japan
        mediation, 1002
    Poland possessed by,
        980–981
    show trials of, 986
    Soviet nuclear program of,
        1003, 1024
    world domination desired
        by, 970
Stalingrad, Battle of, 979
Stanley, Henry Morton, 839
Starry Night painting (Van
    Gogh), 850, 880
Steam engine, development
    of, 633
Steel industry, 824, 1010
Steen, Jan Havickszoon, 433
Stein, Edith (Saint Teresa
    Benedicta of
    the Cross), 867
Stendahl (Marie-Henri
    Beyle), 659
Stephen II (Pope), 286
Stimson, Henry, 1002
Stöcker, Harriet, 796–798
Stoics/Stoicism, 198, 206,
    229–234
Stoker, Bram, 952

The Stones of Venice
    (Ruskin), 374
The Story of Civilization
    (Durant), 935
The Stranger (Camus), 1018,
    1021–1023
Strathwaite, Richard, 528
Strauss, David Friedrich, 760
Stravinsky, Igor, 883
Strindberg, August, 803
Stringfellow, William, 1071
Strozzi, Filippo, 376
Structuralism, 867, 1051, 1054
The Structure of Scientific
    Revolutions (Kuhn), 1061t
Stuart dynasty (England), 533
A Study of History
    (Toynbee), 935
Sturluson, Snori, 296
Stuttgart Confession of Guilt
    (1945), 1058, 1070
The Subjection of Women (Mill),
    784, 786–787
Sub-Saharan Africa
    gold trading with
        Mediterranean
        World, 308m
    Jesuit missionaries in, 476
    kidnapping/export of slaves
        to New World, 545
    luxury goods trading
        with, 254
    Muslim conquests in, 328
    Nile River origination in, 20
    prized commodities of, 419
Sudan
    Battle of Omdurman, 816
    female genital mutilation
        in, 811
    Israel's victory against, 1040
Suetonius (historian), 280, 375
Suez Canal, 816, 825,
    826, 1012
Suffrage rights
    in Austria, 939
    in Czechoslovakia, 939
    in England, 650, 681,
        682, 684
    in Finland, 785
    in France, 602, 795
    in Germany, 939
    in Great Britain, 783–784,
        788, 793, 932, 939
    in the greater West, 797m
    Guizot's opposition to, 685
    in Holland, 793

Mill's advocacy for, 788
    opposition to female
        suffrage, 784, 788, 793
    Prankhurst's reform tactics,
        793, 793–795
    suffragists and suffragettes,
        793–796
    in the United States,
        788, 939
Sufism, 458, 491
    Islamic society challenged
        by, 328
    khanqas school emphasis
        on, 491
    Mamluks enthusiasm
        for, 363
    origins of, 453
    Ottomans enthusiasm
        for, 366
    popularity with the
        Turks, 367
    Turkish affinity for, 453
Suicide bombings, 1114,
    1116, 1125
Suleiman the Magnificent
    (Ottoman Emperor), 83t,
    368, 398, 416, 454, 461
Sultanate of Rum
    (in Anatolia), 318
Sultanate of Women, 461, 461t
Sultanates
    Ayyubid Sultanate, 355m
    Buwayhid Sultanate, 303m
    Mamluk Sultanate, 318–319,
        328, 360–361, 364, 452
    Selim I, 437, 453–454, 461t
    Selim II, 461t
    Selim III, 461t, 542,
        620–621, 735, 1024
    waning of, 454–456
Sumer
    Akkadian domination of, 9,
        15–16
    cities and settlements
        of, 6–8
    development of writing, 5
    Early Dynastic Period, 8–9
    economic specialization in, 7
    Epic of Gilgamesh depiction
        of, 40
    farming in, 4
    geographic location of, 3–4
    Great Flood myth, 7–9, 74
    kings, warriors, priests,
        scribes, 6–9
    map of, 8m

Sumer (cont.)
    mythological tales of, 17–18
    oral custom/written law
        in, 15
    as origin of Western
        civilization, 3, 4
    religious practices, 13
    role of scribes, 14
    slavery in, 15
    trade development, 6
Sumerian mathematics, 14
Summa contra Gentiles 2.79
    (Aquinas), 332
Sunni Muslims
    Almohad reformist sect, 324
    customs of, 297–298
    ijma consensus-seeking
        tradition, 301, 302
    as Islam standard-
        bearer, 453
    mut'a form of marriage, 299
    name derivation of, 266
    rigidity of, 458–459
    schism with the Shi'a
        Muslims, 265–266, 283
    takiyya's importance to,
        298–299
    Turkey's understanding
        of, 937
Suttner, Bertha von, 699
Sweden
    Christian Democratic party
        in, 1034
    Conference of Berlin
        attendance, 828
    defense of
        Protestantism, 450
    global gender gap data,
        1139t
    League of Augsburg
        membership, 557
    Lutheran Church
        established in, 507
    monasteries established
        in, 278
    royal/national banks,
        542–543
    Seven Years' War
        participation, 505,
        548–549
    Stockholm/urban
        development, 646
Swift, Jonathan, 580–581, 851
Switzerland
    as an artificial nation, 707

global gender gap
    data, 1139t
Peace of Westphalia
    and, 505
Reformed Church of
    Calvin, 404
Simplon Tunnel, 826
witchcraft trials, 435
women's suffrage in, 939
Sword of Charlemagne, 290
Sykes-Picot Agreement
    (1916), 900
Syllabus of Errors (Pius X),
    772–773
Sylvester I (Pope), 247
Symposia, all male-drinking
    parties, 137–138
The Symposium (Plato),
    137–138
Syncretism (defined), 165
Syria, 4
    Ba'athism in, 1085–1088
    conflicts with
        Lebanon, 1047
    female genital mutilation
        in, 811
    global gender gap
        data, 1139t
    Hitler's use of Damascus in
        WW II, 1010–1011
    Hittite military efforts
        in, 52
    Hyksos links with, 45
    Napoleon's invasion of, 621
    New Kingdom victory
        against, 45, 47
    newspaper attack on
        Jews, 1119
    Ottoman Turks in, 328
    trek of Abram and, 70
Syrian Jews, 166
Szálasi, Ferenc, 963
Széchenyi, István, 723

T
T4 Project (Nazi Germany),
    987–988
al-Tahtawai, Rifa'a, 706, 738
Tailleferre, Germaine, 954t
Taittinger, Pierre, 964
Takiyya, of Shi'i Muslims,
    298–299
Taliban (Afghan radicals),
    1114, 1127–1128,
    1133–1135

Tallyrand-Périgord, Charles
    de, 503
Talmud (Jewish holy book),
    320–324, 410, 440,
    477, 729
Tamerlane Empire, 116n6, 329,
    357, 370, 818
Tanakh (Hebrew Bible), 72,
    73t. See also Hebrew
    (Jewish) Bible
Tanzimat (reforms) in the
    Ottoman Empire, 706,
    740–742, 808
Tarquinius Priscus (Roman
    King), 173t
Tarquinius Superbus (Roman
    King), 173t
Tartarus (Greek deity), 97
Tatars, 329, 352, 369–370
Taurus Mountains, 4
Taylor, Frederick Winslow,
    823–825
Ibn Taymiyyah, 363, 453–454,
    490, 1082
Taymiyya-Wahhabi sect,
    739–740
Taymur, Mahmud, 808
TCP/IP development, 1061t
Tectonic plate theory, 1061t
Telegraph, development of,
    820, 826
Telephone, development of,
    820, 826
Television development, 1061t
Temple of Solomon, 82
Temporary Discharge of
    Prisoners for Ill Health
    Act (Great Britain), 795
Temüjin. See Genghis Khan
Temür Khan (son of Kublai
    Khan), 357
Ten Lost Tribes of Israel,
    59–60, 83, 84
Tennis Court Oath (French
    Revolution), 594t, 598
Tenochtitlan (Mexico City),
    423m, 425
Terrorism/terrorist groups. See
    also Hamas
    al-Qaeda, 1117–1118,
        1126–1128, 1133–1135
    domestic vs. foreign
        attacks, 1114
    in Ireland/North Ireland,
        1116, 1118

Islamic Jihad organization, 1097, 1126–1127
in London, 1125
9/11 terrorist attacks, 1093, 1114, *1116*, 1117, 1125
1972 Munich Olympics, 1081
1998–2001, Greater West, 1115m
in Spain, 1116, 1125
suicide bombings, 1114, 1116, 1125
in Syria, 1118–1119
Taliban, 1114, 1127–1128, 1133–1135
Tess of the d'Urbervilles (Hardy), 801
Tet Offensive (Vietnam), 1040, 1042
Tetrarchy system of empire division, 242
Textile manufacturing technology, 547, 631–632, *632*, 641
Thales, 121–123
Thasos (Aegean island), 137
Thatcher, Margaret, 592–593
Themes of Roman army, 250
Theodore II (Russia), 515t
Theodosius (Roman emperor), 246
Theological-Political Treatise (Spinoza), 577
Theophanes (Byzantine chronicler), 251
The Theory of Communicative Action (Habermas), 1051
A Theory of Justice (Rawls), 1150
Thermopylae, Battle of, 127, 146t, 183, 987
Thionville battle (Thirty Years' War), 451
Third Crusade, 489
Third Dynasty of Ur, 12
Third Estate (of France), 596–598
Third Intermediate Period (Ancient Egypt), 23, 56
Third Punic War, 183
Third Republic of France (1870–1940), 592, 721
Third wave feminism, 1109–1111, *1112*
Third World countries

growth of Protestantism, 1069, 1071–1072
overcoming poverty in, 1099
post-WW II spiritual energy in, 1057
Thirty Tyrants of Athens, 144, 146t, 152
Thirty Years' War (Europe)
battles fought during, 450–451
devastating effects of, 449–450
England's involvement in, 536
Grimmelshausen's description of horrors, 451–452
Prussian Army composition, 516
significance of, 450–451
weaponry used in, 450
Thomas Aquinas, Saint, 205, 328, 332–333
A Thousand and One Nights (al-Hakim), 808
Thrasyboulos of Miletus, 115
Three Emperors' alliance, 893m
Three Essays in the Theory of Sexuality (Freud), 873
The Threefold Cord: Mind, Body and World (Putnam), 1051–1052
Three Guineas (Woolf), 978, 1006–1007
Thucydides, 145–147
Thutmose I (Egyptian pharaoh), 47, 48
Thutmose II (Egyptian pharaoh), 48
Thutmose III (Egyptian pharaoh), 48
Tiananmen Square student protest (China), 1100–1102, *1101*
Tiberius, 189
Tigris and Euphrates Rivers, 3–6
Tillich, Paul, 868, 1060
Times of Troubles (1601–1613), 514
To Be a European Muslim (Ramadan), 1155–1156
Tokyo war crimes trial, 979, 993–994, 996

Tolstoy, Leo, 913, 932
Anna Karenina, 748–749, 801
The Kreutzer Sonata, 803
War and Peace, 587, 616n6
Tombstone of Roman soldier, *194*
Torah (of Hebrew Bible)
authorship issues, 761–762
avoidance of mention of celibacy, 87
canon comparison, 73t
centrality to daily observances, 78
challenges of daily life and, 320
chronology of composition, 76t
Deuteronomist's influence on, 76–77
first appearance of five books of, 75
Jesus and, 211, 215
Jewish life defined by, 90
Moses' receiving of, 74
new edition publication, 774
observance variations, 89
Oral Torah, 90, 211–212, 1051
Priestley Author's influence on, 77
rabbinical reforms promoted by, 91
Russian discovery of scroll remnants, 734
and the Tanakh, 72
women's roles established by, 85
Totalitarianism, 572n9, 932, 964, 968–969.1031, 1128
To the Lighthouse (Woolf), 954
Toussenel, Alphonse, 731
Toynbee, Arnold, 935
Trafalgar, Battle of, 593, 608
Tragedy art form, 138–142
Trajan (Roman emperor), 200, 208
Transcendental Wisdom (Mulla Sadra), 456
Transcontinental Railroad (U.S.), 826
Transjordan, 937–938
Trans-Siberian Railroad, 1012
A Treatise on Painting (da Vinci), *468*

A Treatise on the Winning and Working of Collieries engraving (Dunn), *649*

Treatise on Toleration (Voltaire), 578–579

Treblinka concentration camp, 990

Trench warfare, in World War I, 896t, 901–905

Trevelyan, Sir Charles, 728

Tribal religions, global percentage data, *207*

Trinity (Holy Trinity) of Christianity, 224, 331, 1068

Trinity of Islam, 366

Triple alliance (1882–1915), 893m

Tristan (Mann), 871

"Triumph of Death" painting (Pieter Bruegel the Elder), *326*

Trojan Horse, *108*

Trojan War (Greece), 104, *108*, 109, 171

Truce of God (of reformed church) warfare ban, 314

The True Law of Free Monarchies (Stuart), 533

Truman, Harry S., 1000–1003

Tuberculosis (consumption) epidemic, 647, 871

Tudor dynasty (England), 533

Tullius Hostilius (Roman King), 173t

Tunisia
economic/political reforms, 735
Israel's victory against, 1040

Turgenev, Ivan, 913

Turhan Hatice (Sultana), 461t

Turkey. *See also* Mamluk Sultanate; Ottoman Turks
admittance to NATO, 1026m
as Byzantine Empire component, 248
constitutional reform in, 888
deaths in World War I, 888
female circumcision in, 811
global gender gap data, 1139t
"guest workers" in Germany, 1037
19th-century intellectual energy, 669

Ottoman consolidation, transition to, 809

Rifah (Welfare) Party in, 1114

silk weaving mill, late 19th century, *644*

Tulip Period, *622*
in World War II, 978, 1009–1010

Twain, Mark (Samuel Clemens), 840, 844–845, 849, 863, 1012–1013

Twelve Tables (Roman law code), 172, 176, 177–178, 177t

The Twilight of the Idols (Nietzsche), 862

Two Treatises on Government (Locke), 554, 559

Typhus vaccine, 820

Tyrants/tyranny
in ancient Greece, 114–115
in the Archaic period, 110, 111m, 508
argument in favor of, 508–510
in Asia Minor, 121–122
of the Carolingians, 310
in Classical Greece, 114–115, 508
defined, 114
in Miletus, 121–122, 124, 126
of Renaissance Italy, 382
Thirty Tyrants, in Athens, 144, 152
viciousness of Periander of Corinth, 115

Tyrell, George, 773

U

Ukraine, independence declared by, 1091

Ulama (brotherhood/community), 453

The Ultimate Resource (Simon), 1100

Ultra-Orthodox Judaism, 1078

Ulyanov, Vladimir Ilyich, 914–916

Ulysses (Joyce), 880, 932, 949–951

Umayyad dynasty
Abbasids rebellion against, 284, 297
Islamic World, 1022 CE map, 303m

move from Mecca to Damascus, 267
secession from the empire, 303
Shi'ite's battle against, 297
timeline of, 239, 267
use of jihad for personal gain, 268

UN Atomic Energy Commission, 1024

Uncertainty principle, 856

UN Conference on Environment and Development (1992), 1099

The Unenlightened, 578–581

Uniformitarianism theory (Lyell), 754–755

Union of Egyptian Women-Intellectuals, 809

Union of Muslim Organisations, 1095–1096

United East India Company, *1028*

United Kingdom
bin Laden's attacks in, 1133
global gender gap data, 1139t
honor killing of women in, 1140
Jewish mixed marriages in, 1078n8
1997–2007 employment data, 1149
Northern Ireland separatists in, 1114
in World War I, 900

United Mineworker's Strike (1919), 935

United Nations (UN)
Camus' human rights campaigns, 1023
condemnation of Israel, 1059, 1076–1077
establishment of, 979
Universal Declaration of Human Rights, 979, 996–999
Women's Conference, 1093

United States (U.S.). *See also* America (pre-American Revolution); Great Depression
admittance to NATO, 1026m

Anti-Imperialist
  League, 850
appeasement policies of, 969
Atlantic Slave trade in, 546m
atomic bombing of
  Japan, 979
belief in manifest destiny
  of, 710
CIA agency developed by,
  1028–1029
civil rights era, 1037
college education
  grants, 1029
currency crisis (1924),
  941–942
dead body policies, 488
education reforms, 788,
  790, 805
1815–1914 immigration
  data, 892
embargo on China
  weaponry sales, 1102
empire-building by, 816
European investments
  in, 891m
FHA program, 1029
German emigration
  to, 767
global gender gap
  data, 1139t
gold standard abandoned by,
  933, 943
Great Depression, 932, 933,
  941–945
Iraq invaded by, 1133
Japan's Pearl Harbor
  attack, 978
Jewish emigration to, 776
labor strikes, 932
libertarian taxation
  argument, 1147
Louisiana Purchase, 609
Medicare/Medicaid
  programs, 1029, 1152
Medicare Program,
  1029, 1152
Morrill Act (1862), 827
9/11 terrorist attacks, 1093,
  1114, *1116*, 1117, 1125
northern industrialization
  in, 655
Philippines peace treaty, 831
post-Civil War
  reconstruction, 827
post-WW I economics,
  931–932

reasons for entering
  WW I, 921
"Red Menace" fears of, 935
Roosevelt on family
  limitation, 800
Scofield Reference
  Bible, 753
second wave feminism,
  1044–1045
September, 2011 terrorist
  attacks, 1093, 1117
Social Security
  program, 1029
spiritual renewal in, 1057
suffrage reforms, 788
technological developments
  in, 821–826
third wave feminism
  in, 1109
2001 terrorist attacks
  in, 1093
2008 economic collapse,
  1098, 1143–1147
Vietnam War and, 484,
  1042–1043, 1043m
war with Afghanistan,
  1126, 1133–1135, 1145
welfare spending in,
  1035–1036
women's rights in, 790, 804
women's suffrage rights, 939
in World War I, 887–888,
  892, 895, 896t, 900, 905,
  921–924
in World War II, 977, 978,
  981, 984–986, 1000–1003
Universal Declaration of
  Human Rights, 979,
  996–1000
Universal History (ibn Athir),
  353–354
Universal-Lexicon
  (Zedler), 566
UN Women's Conference,
  1111–1112
Uranus (Greek deity), 97
Uruk (Sumerian ruler), 9
Uruk settlement (Sumer), 7
U.S. Bureau of the Budget, 941
Ushabti figures (Ancient
  Egypt), 44
Ussher, James, 752–753
USSR (Union of Soviet
  Socialist Republics). *See
  also* Russia; Soviet Union
anti-Semitism in, 1079

collapse of, 1132
détente with the West,
  1024–1025
establishment of Polish
  boundary, 915m
invasion of Hungary,
  1019, 1041
nonaggression pact with
  Germany, 978
post-WW II tensions with
  the West, 1003
United Nations and, 997
Utopia (More), 375,
  408–409, 428
Utu (sun god), 16, 18

V

Vaccine developments,
  820, 1061t
Valerian (Roman
  emperor), 239
Valéry, Paul, 931, 949
Valley of the Kings (Egypt),
  25, 47, 48
Valois, Marguerite de, 444
Van Gogh, Vincent, 850,
  880–881
The Vanity of Human Wishes
  (Johnson), 656
Vasari, Giorgio, 373–374
Vatican
  Academy of Vatican
    Nights, 478
  Bismarck's break
    with, 716
  Catholic Reformation and,
    1064–1069
  First Vatican Council, 771
  Lateran Agreement with
    Italy, 933, 958
  Napoleon III and, 720
  Pius IX as "prisoner of,"
    718, 771
  Second Vatican Council,
    475, 773, 1066–1069
Vatican Council, 771
Velázquez, Diego, 796
Venetian Empire, 308m, 453,
  461t, 506m, 722
Venus (Roman deity), 180, 189
Verdun, Battle of (WW I), 896t
Vergerio, Pier Paolo, 374, 376
Versailles, Treaty of (1919),
  889, 896t, 900, 923, 933
Versailles Palace (France),
  518–520, *519*

Vichy/Nazi-occupied France (1940–1945), 592
Vico, Giambattista, 934
Victoria (British Queen), 828
Vienna, Treaty of (1815), 660, 667, 676, 682, 717, 888
Vietnam War
    anti-Americanism attitudes and, 1077
    location map, 1043M
    Tet Offensive, 1040, 1042
Vikings
    attack on Paris, 284, 295
    attacks/campaigns of, 295, 304
    expansive raids by, 416
    invasion of Russia, 912, 1024
    reaches of, 416
    Sturluson's description of, 296
A Vindication of the Rights of Man (Wollstonecraft), 592, 614
A Vindication of the Rights of Woman (Wollstonecraft), 614, 791
Virgil (poet), 375
Virginia, Jamestown colony, 536
Visconti family (Italy), 382–383
Visigoths (from Germany), 239, 248m, 262m, 264, 274–275
Vital, R. Hayyim, 437
Vittorio Emmanuele II (Piedmont-Sardinia king), 718, 720, 771
Vivaldi, Antonio, 526
Viziers (defined), 296
Viziers (Islamic Empire), 296
Vocabolario degli Accademici della Crusca (1612), 527
Volpedo, Giuseppe Pellizza da, 769
Voltaire (François-Marie Arouet), 554, 555, 563, 932
    biographical background, 567–568
    Candide, 557, 569–570, 582
    doubts of goodness of mankind, 567

fallout with Frederick the Great, 568
Jews despised by, 579
Leibniz praised by, 562
Letters on the English, 583
Philosophical Dictionary, 572–573, 583
Philosophical Letters on the English, 568, 583
Rousseau's opinion of, 569, 570, 588
Treatise on Toleration, 578–579
Vosici society, 172
The Voyage of the Beagle (Darwin), 755

W
Wagner, Richard, 709
Wahhabism movement, 738–740, 777, 1082
Wallachia, 720
War and Peace (Tolstoy), 587, 616n6
Ward, Mary, 788, 789–790
War of Devolution (France vs. Spain), 516
War of the Austrian Succession, 548
War of the League of Augsburg, 517
War of the Roses (England), 446
War of the Spanish Succession, 517, 547, 549
Wars of Religion, 38.
    See also Crusades; Thirty Years' War
    in the Middle East, 452–454
    Peace of Westphalia and, 752
    reaction of Christians to, 441–442
    reaction of Muslims to, 441
"The Waste Land" (Eliot), 932, 951
Waterloo, Battle of, 593
Watson, James, 1061t
Wave-particle duality, 856
The Wealth of Nations (Smith), 555, 563
Weaver, Thomas, 629
Webb, Beatrice, 791–792
Webb, Sidney, 791
Weil, Gustav, 747, 778

Weinberger, Moses, 776
Welfare states in Europe, 713, 1029–1033
    Adenauer's endorsement of, 1034
    British endorsement of, 1033
    Cold War influence, 1043
    country-to-country variation, 1029
    creation of programs, 967, 1021
    decline of religious observance in, 1058, 1063
    feminism and, 1045–1046
    Gini coefficient wealth data, 1149
    Kirk's dissent from, 1031–1032
    Powell's warnings about costs of, 1038
    taxation for funding, 1035
Wellhausen, Julius, 779
Wells, David Ames, 821
Wells, H. G., 934–935
West, Rebecca, 954t
Western Europe. See also Black Death; Clovis; Dark Ages in Western Europe
    challenges of living in, 271
    Christian Democracy in, 1034
    Christian identity of, 1058
    cultural composition of, 268
    disposable income in, 1034–1035
    farming in, 5, 269
    feudal bonds in, 306
    generation of rebellion in, 1035–1039
    Indo-European cultures in, 51
    libraries of, 280
    manors, serfs, lords, vassals and, 305–306, 306
    missionary strategies in, 276
    monasticism movement, 278, 286
    reinvention of, 304–307
    Second Industrial Revolution in, 819–820
    urbanization of, 188
    welfare spending in, 1035–1036
    women shortage in, 275
West Germany

admittance to NATO, 1018,
1026m, 1033–1034
Cold War role of, 1025
EEC membership, 1106
Green Parties in, 1098
Marshall Plan
influence, 1033
wealth patterns in, 1037
women's issues in,
1044, 1046
Westphalia Kingdom, 605
Westphalia Treaty. *See* Peace of
Westphalia (1648)
Wharton, Edith, 801
What Is to Be Done?
(Lenin), 917
Whitehead, Alfred North, 866
"The White Man's Burden"
poem (Kipling), 817,
818–819, 831
Wilberforce, Samuel, 758,
765–766
Wilde, Oscar
*The Importance of Being
Earnest,* 853
The Picture of Dorian Gray,
851, 852–853, 871
De Profundis ("Out of the
Depths"), 853
Wilhelm III (of Prussia),
671–672, 895
Wilhelm IV (of Prussia),
691, 712
William III of Orange, 558
William of Ockham, 328, 388
William of Orange (Prince of
Orange), 538
Wilson, Harold, 1046
Wilson, Woodrow
Fourteen Points of,
896t, 936
Paris Peace Conference
attendance, 922, 923, 936
Wissenschaft des Judentums
("Jewish sciences"),
774–775
Witches and witchcraft
execution of a witch, 436
in Greek mythology, 109n5
roots of belief in, 434
sexuality concerns and, 435
threats attributed to, 428
trials (1450–1759) for, 435
"war of all against all"
and, 416

Witte, Emanuel de, 575
Wittgenstein, Ludwig,
864–866
*Wives' and Widows' Gazette of
Fashions* magazine, 696
Wojtyla, Karol (Pope John
Paul II), 867
A Wolf among Wolves
(Fallada), 945
Wolfe Tone, Theobald, 724–725
Wollstonecraft, Mary, 614, 791
"The Woman Courtier" comedy
(Aretino), 385
Women. *See also* Suffrage
rights; Women, modern;
Women's rights
Britain's recognition of legal
rights of, 701
Catholic mysticism
experiences, 336
conferences of, in
Mexico, 1112
cult of domesticity and,
693–696
disgrace of remaining single,
785–786
domestic violence
against, 1140
fascism's influence on,
977–978, 1003, 1006
female genital mutilation
of, 811
French labor and trade
unions, 784
Germanic peoples legal
protections, 275
Great Depression's
influences on,
977–978, 1008
Hebrew laws related to,
83–87
honor killings of, 810–811,
1111, 1140–1141
hunger for reforms for,
783–788
in/against fascism,
1004–1009
industrial age influences,
645, 652–655
Islam, nationalism and,
807–809
Japan's abduction,
enslavement of, 993
literature of female
identity, 801

male vs. female brain size,
798–799
Matrimonial Causes Act
(1857), 700
in modernist cultural
life, 954t
mysticism experiences, 336
Napheys/Adler on sexual
appetite of, 798
nonvirgins killed in Arab
nations, 810
Ottoman Sultanate of
Women, 461, 461t
pacifist campaign
participation, 1005–1006
postcolonial Islamic society
status, 1046–1050
as property, in Middle Ages,
273–275
restrictions in Hellenic era,
134, 137
rights in Babylonian
Empire, 37
role of, in Jewish society,
83–87
The Saturday Review's slur
of, 784
Saudi Arabia's persecution
of, 1140
segregation in Classical Age
Greece, 134
shortage of in Western
Europe, 275
societal beliefs about
sexuality of, 800–801
status of in Judaism, 83, 85
wedding rituals, Greece, 135
Women, modern (1860–1914).
See also Suffrage rights;
Women's rights
desire for reforms, 783–786
focus on the "new woman,"
805–807
love and, 796–803
male vs. female rights,
788–792
school, work and, 803–807
Women's Conference (Beijing),
1093, 1112–1113
Women's Congress against
War and Fascism
(WCWF), 1006
Women's International League
for Peace and Freedom
(WILPF), 1006

Womens March on Versailles
(French Revolution), 594t
Women's National Press Club
(U.S.), 1008
Women's rights. *See also*
Feminist movement; *The
Subjection of Women;*
Suffrage rights
in 5th/6th century
France, 274
arranged marriages banned
in Sweden, 790–791
beliefs about sexuality of
women, 800–801
best nations for
women, 1139t
Bolshevik Party support for,
965–966
Clinton's speech about,
1112–1113
education in Russia,
Sweden, 790
Enlightenment-era call
for, 791
global gender gap and,
1138–1140
Hitler's Nazi Women's
League speech, 1004
industrial-age influences,
645, 652–654, 784–785
Internet's influence on,
1141–1142
labor/trade unions in
France, 791
men's rights vs., 788–792
Muslim girls, women
demonstrations, *1129*
1878 first international
congress, 784
in postcolonial Islamic
society, 1046–1050
post-WW II era, 1044–1046
Stöcker's activism in
Germany, 796–798
The Subjection of Women and,
784, 786–787
in West Germany,
1044, 1046
worst nations for
women, 1139t
Women's Social and Political
Union (WSPU),
793–794, 796
Woolf, Virginia, 801, 802–803,
884, 932, 953–955, 954t,
978, 1006–1007

Wordsworth, William, 595,
656, 657, 660
World Council of
Churches, 1074
World Economic Forum
(WEF), 1138–1139
World in Conflict video
game, 1093
World Trade Center attack,
1093, 1117
World Trade
Organization (WTO)
"Battle of Seattle" against,
1093, 1120
founding of, 1093
global role of, 1120–1121
World War I (1914–1918),
898m, 899m
Anglo-French Entente, 894
Anglo-Russian Entente, 894
Arab Revolt, 889, 896t,
899–900, 911, 927
Austria in, 889–890, 895,
896t, 897, 900, 903,
907–908, 925
Austrian-Hungarian Empire
in, 887–890, 892,
894–895, 896t
Axis powers vs. Allied
forces, 895
balance of power in,
892–896
Battle of the Somme,
896t, 912
Bloody Sunday in
Russia, *914*
Bosnia in, 897
Brest-Litovsk Treaty, 896t,
897, 903
Britain in, 890, 891m,
892–895, 900, 905–907,
921, 923
collapse of Habsburg
Empire, 723
death data, 888
Denmark in, 979
end of war armistice signing,
887, 900, 922
entry of U.S., 753
European alliances, 893m
European population
data, 826
events leading to, 888–892
fall of Ottoman Empire, 364
fight for "God and country"
in, 38

Finland in, 898m, 899m
France in, 887, 889,
894–895, 897, 900,
905–906, 910–911, 913,
919, 921–924, *927*
Gallipoli campaign, 896t,
898, 905, 910
Germany in, 887–890, 891m,
892–897, 900, 903,
905–908, 921–925
Greece in, 892, 893m, 895,
897, 915m, 927
home-front mobilization,
905–909
issuance of patents and, 821
Italy in, 893m, 895, 896t,
897, 910, 923, 927
Lawrence on ending of, 887
Marne, First and Second
battles, 897
1914–1918 table
of events, 896t
onset of, 888, 896t
"Open Christmas Letter,"
907–909
Poland in, 892, 896t, 897,
910, 912, 915m, 926m
postwar actions of
Japan, 833
suffragettes and, 796
Sykes-Picot Agreement, 900
Treaty of Versailles, 889,
896t, 900, 923, 933
trench warfare in, 896t,
901–905
United States in, 887–888,
892, 895, 896t, 900, 905,
921–924
weapons innovations,
909–911
Zetkin's opposition to, 795
Zimmerman telegram, 922
World War II (1937–1945),
977–1014. *See also* Hitler,
Adolf; Nazi Party/Nazi
Germany
amends-making process,
993–996
atrocities and holocaust,
987–993
Battle of El Alamein, 1010
Battle of Iwo Jima, 979, 986
Battle of Midway, 986
Battle of Stalingrad, 979
D-Day, allied Normandy
invasion, 979, 983

deaths in, *980*
ending of, 1018
France in, 977–981, 983,
1003, 1008–1011
German concentration
camps, 977, 989,
994, 1070
German surrender, 979
Germany's invasion of
Poland, 974, 977, 978, 981
Italy in, 977–979, 983, 1004,
1007–1008
Japan's invasion of
China, 978
Japan's Pearl Harbor attack,
977, 978, 983, 985
Japan's surrender, 979
Jewish Holocaust, 988–991
Lithuania in, 978, 991
massacre sites of, 987
Middle East in, 1009–1011
Nazi military strategies,
980–981
1939 onset in Europe, 933
North Africa in, 979,
980–981
Nuremberg war crimes trials,
979, 988, 990–991,
993–994, 996
Operation Barbarossa, 981
in the Pacific, 983–987
Poland in, 974, 977–981,
988–991
postwar agricultural,
refugee crises, 1019–1021
Rape of Nanking,
in China, 992
Romania in, 978, 991
Soviet Union in, 977, 978,
980–981, 999,
1002–1003, 1010

Tokyo war crimes trial, 979,
993–994, 996
Turkey in, 978, 1009–1010
United States in, 977, 978,
981, 983–986, 1000–1003
Writing developments
alphabet development,
14, 58
cuneiform script, 14
hieroglyphic writing system,
23–24
Linear A/Linear B, Greece,
98, 102–103
Linear B script, 98
in the Persian Empire, 63

X

Xenophanes of Colophon, 123
Xenophon, 119–120, 146t,
151, 299
Xerxes, 126, 127, 127m, 131,
143, 158
X-rays, developments in,
821, 854

Y

Yassin, Shaikh Ahmed, 1117
Yeats, William Butler, 883
Yemeni tribes, 254–255, 299
YHWH (term for God), 75,
78–79, 81, 87–89, 92–94,
123, 165, 213, 215, 217,
439, 441
Yiddish language, 575, 946
YMCA, 683
Yom Kippur War (1973), 1059
Young Patriots fascist
party, 964
Young Turks, 888,
925–928, 1085

Z

Zechariah (Jewish
prophet), 90
Zedler, Johann Heinrich, 566
Zeno of Elea, *149*, 149–150
Zetkin, Clara, 795
Zeus (Greek deity), 97,
104, 189
Zheng He (Chinese
Admiral), 416n1
Zidonians, 81
Ziggurats (religious pyramid-
like mounds), 13
Zimmerman telegram, 922
Zionism
Arab nationalism and, 978,
1011–1014
Arabs and, 939
assimilation and, 729–734
Bolshevism and, 947
Britain's policy debates
over, 946
Cultural Zionism
movement, 776
defined, 732
Eastern European Jewish
support for, 732–733
in England, 946
establishment of
Palestine, 777
Maas' beliefs in, 1070
Secular Zionism
movement, 776
Zola, Émile, 802, 803
Zoroastrianism religion, 55, 60,
62–65, *207*, 299
Zvi, Sabbatai, 417,
438–440, 729
Zwingli, Ulrich, 401,
402–403